CARDIGANSHIRE
COUNTY HISTORY

VOLUME 3

Interior of Seion Congregational Chapel, Aberystwyth, showing the arcading by Richard Owen of Liverpool, 1878.

CARDIGANSHIRE COUNTY HISTORY

General Editor: Ieuan Gwynedd Jones

VOLUME 3

Cardiganshire in Modern Times

Edited by

Geraint H. Jenkins and Ieuan Gwynedd Jones

Published on behalf of the Cardiganshire Antiquarian Society

in association with the

Royal Commission on the Ancient and Historical Monuments of Wales

by the University of Wales Press

CARDIFF

1998

© Cardiganshire Antiquarian Society, 1998

British Library Cataloguing-in-Publication Data.
A catalogue record for this book is available from the British Library.

ISBN 0–7083–1489–9

Jacket design by the Royal Commission on the Ancient and Historical Monuments of Wales
Typeset at University of Wales Press
Printed in Wales by Gwasg Gomer, Llandysul

PREFACE

When the first volume of the Cardiganshire County History was published in 1994 the Editorial Board agreed that the next volume in the sequence of three would be the third volume, and that it should be published within three or four years following the publication of the first. The structure and contents of the volume had already been determined, and a number of authors had accepted our invitation to contribute to it and had submitted their chapters. With the launch of Volume 1 the remaining chapters were allocated, and it is greatly to the credit of all the contributors that this volume has appeared within the timescale originally envisaged. We thank the contributors most warmly and sincerely for giving so much of their time, for responding so readily to our insistent demands, and for their patience and support while the volume took shape. It is with great pleasure and no little pride, therefore, that we present this volume to the Antiquarian Society, to the people of Ceredigion, and to the public at large.

This final volume covers the period from the beginning of the eighteenth century to the present day, a period when the county experienced greater changes in its economic, social and intellectual life than it had ever experienced in its long history. In this deeply rural county, remote from great centres of population and lacking good communications, changes in the structure of society came with remarkable slowness for the best part of a century. The age of Victoria had dawned before fundamental social changes gained a momentum which would eventually transform the whole of county society. Even then the transformation was gradual and subtle rather than revolutionary. There was no industrial revolution on a scale to match what was happening in other parts of Wales; the promise of mineral riches blazed only intermittently, and never for long periods of time. Yet, the industrialization experienced elsewhere in Wales and England profoundly affected social developments in the county throughout the period covered by this volume. The insatiable demands of labour in the iron and coal districts of south Wales attracted migrants from all parts of the county, and thousands of farmers and agricultural workers joined their compatriots from Carmarthenshire and Pembrokeshire in the coal mines of Glamorgan and Carmarthenshire. No social change is more fundamental than population change, and one of the major concerns of this volume is to understand and to evaluate the social effects of out-migration on the county as a whole. At the same time, it is salutory to remember that the county's loss was Wales's gain, for what the migrants took with them was their language and culture, thus immeasurably enriching the communities where they settled.

The volume gives due weight to the political and cultural life of the county, and especially to the religious developments for which it was greatly admired for much of the period in question. Chapters are devoted to various aspects of intellectual life, the educational institutions, especially the two Universities, the National Library of Wales, the grammar schools and the old academies which were its pride and for which it was famous. Uniquely in a county history, the volume contains an exhaustive inventory by Mr David Percival of the Royal Commission on Ancient and Historical Monuments of Wales of all the chapels of the county. Based on a list prepared by the National Library of Wales and research conducted by Mr John Wyn Pritchard for the Board of Celtic Studies of the University of Wales, this is the first-fruit of the Commission's plan to prepare an inventory for the whole of Wales. We are proud that this County History is the first to publish such an important source.

Once again it is a pleasure to put on record our gratitude to the old Dyfed County Council, the old Ceredigion District Council, and the present Ceredigion County Council for their generous and unfailing support for the County History. Without their financial support a large enterprise such as this could never have succeeded, and we wish to thank them most sincerely. In the preparation of this volume we have benefited greatly from the advice and practical help of many persons. We are particularly indebted to Mr Peter White, Secretary of the RCAHMW, and Emeritus Professor J. Beverley Smith, Chairman of the RCAHMW, for their constant encouragement and support. The staff of the RCAHMW have been a tower of strength, and we owe a special debt to Mr John Johnston for the design of the volume and in particular for the layout of the illustrations in the chapter by Dr Peter Smith. Thanks are due to Mr Charles W. Green for preparing the cartographic material, and Ms Rosemary Jones and Ms Hilary Malaws also deserve mention for their courtesy in dealing with matters of copyright. We also owe sincere thanks to the staff of the National Library of Wales for helping us gain access to a rich corpus of books, maps and illustrations. We wish to thank the officers of the Society and members of the Editorial Committee for their constant support and encouragement, and especially to the Honorary Secretary, Mrs Mary Burdett-Jones, for her ready co-operation. Ms G. M. Parry cheerfully undertook the typing and re-typing of the whole work, and we offer our deepest thanks to her and also to Mrs Mary Madden for preparing the Index. Invaluable secretarial assistance was provided by Mrs Aeres Bowen Davies and Ms Siân L. Evans of the University of Wales Centre for Advanced Welsh and Celtic Studies. Last but not least, we thank the staff of the University of Wales Press, especially Susan Jenkins and Ceinwen Jones, for their sustained interest in this major enterprise and for seeing the volume through the press with great efficiency.

Geraint H. Jenkins
Ieuan Gwynedd Jones

April 1998

CONTENTS

FIGURES

TABLES

THE CONTRIBUTORS

J. W. Aitchison, MA, Ph.D.
Gregynog Professor of Human Geography, University of Wales, Aberystwyth

D. I. Bateman, MA, F.R.Ag.S.
Formerly Professor of Agricultural Economics, University of Wales, Aberystwyth

Harold Carter, MA, D.Litt., FRGS
Emeritus Professor, University of Wales

Alun Eirug Davies, MA, Dip. Lib.
Formerly Senior Sub-Librarian, University of Wales, Aberystwyth

Margaret M. Escott, BA, M.Sc., DIC, Ph.D.
Senior Research Officer, History of Parliament

W. Gareth Evans, M.Ed., MA, Ph.D., F.R.Hist.S.
Reader, Department of Education, University of Wales, Aberystwyth

Rhidian Griffiths, MA, M.Litt., Ph.D., Dip. Lib., ALA
Keeper of Printed Books, National Library of Wales, Aberystwyth

J. Kendal Harris, BA
Formerly Chief Executive, Ceredigion District Council

David Jenkins, M.Sc.
Formerly Senior Tutor, Department of Extra Mural Studies, University of Wales, Aberystwyth

David Jenkins, BA, Ph.D.
Welsh Industrial and Maritime Museum, Cardiff

Geraint H. Jenkins, BA, Ph.D., D.Litt.
Professor and Director, University of Wales Centre for Advanced Welsh and Celtic Studies

Gwyn Jenkins, MA
Keeper of Manuscripts and Records, National Library of Wales, Aberystwyth

J. Geraint Jenkins, MA, D.Sc. Econ.
Formerly Curator, Welsh Folk Museum and the Welsh Industrial and Maritime Museum, Cardiff

Ieuan Gwynedd Jones, MA, D.Litt., F.R.Hist.S.
Emeritus Professor, University of Wales

J. Graham Jones, MA, DAA, Dip. Lib., ALA
Assistant Archivist, The Welsh Political Archive, National Library of Wales

Ann Kelly Knowles, BA, M.Sc., Ph.D.
Mellon Fellow in Geography, Wellesley College, Wellesley, Massachusetts

C. Roy Lewis, BA, Ph.D.
Senior Lecturer in Geography, University of Wales, Aberystwyth

W. J. Lewis, M.Sc. Econ.
Formerly Senior Lecturer in Education, University of Wales, Aberystwyth

R. J. Moore-Colyer, B.Sc., Ph.D., F.R.Hist.S., FSA
Professor of Agrarian History, University of Wales, Aberystwyth

David Percival
Royal Commission on the Ancient and Historical Monuments of Wales

Peter Smith, BA, D.Litt., FSA
Formerly Secretary of the Royal Commission on the Ancient and Historical Monuments of Wales

P. D. G. Thomas, MA, Ph.D., F.R.Hist.S.
Emeritus Professor, University of Wales

Roland G. Thorne, MA
Formerly Deputy Editor, History of Parliament

R. F. Walker, MA, D.Phil.
Formerly Senior Lecturer in History, University of Wales, Aberystwyth

Sandra E. Wheatley, B.Sc., Ph.D., FRGS
Map Curator, University of Wales, Aberystwyth

Peter White, BA
Secretary, Royal Commission on the Ancient and Historical Monuments of Wales

Moelwyn I. Williams, MA, Ph.D.
Formerly Keeper of Printed Books, National Library of Wales

ABBREVIATIONS

AC	*Archaeologia Cambrensis*
AGHR	*Agricultural History Review*
BBCS	*Bulletin of the Board of Celtic Studies*
BL	The British Library
Ceredigion	*Journal of the Ceredigion Antiquarian Society*
CA	*The Carmarthenshire Antiquary*
CCHMC	*Cylchgrawn Cymdeithas Hanes y Methodistiaid Calfinaidd*
CH	*The Carmarthenshire Historian*
DWB	*The Dictionary of Welsh Biography down to 1940* (London, 1959)
ECHR	*Economic History Review*
JAE	*Journal of Agricultural Economics*
JEH	*Journal of Economic History*
JHSCW	*Journal of the Historical Society of the Church in Wales*
JMHRS	*Journal of the Merioneth Historical and Record Society*
JRASE	*Journal of the Royal Agricultural Society of England*
JRSS	*Journal of the Royal Statistical Society*
JWBS	*Journal of the Welsh Bibliographical Society*
MC	*Montgomeryshire Collections*
NLW	Manuscript at the National Library of Wales
NLWJ	*National Library of Wales Journal*
PH	*Pembrokeshire Historian*
PP	Parliamentary Papers
PRO	Public Record Office
TCAS	*Transactions of the Cardiganshire Antiquarian Society*
TCHS	*Transactions of the Caernarvonshire Historical Society*
TDHS	*Transactions of the Denbighshire Historical Society*
THSC	*Transactions of the Honourable Society of Cymmrodorion*
TIBG	*Transactions of the Institute of British Geographers*
TRHS	*Transactions of the Royal Historical Society*
WHR	*Welsh History Review*
WJA	*Welsh Journal of Agriculture*
WWHR	*West Wales Historical Records*

CHAPTER 1

THE POPULATION OF CARDIGANSHIRE

J. W. Aitchison and Harold Carter

THE analysis of population change is seldom straightforward, largely because of two crucial problems. The first is that the areas of reference do not remain constant. Thus, for example, the census returns switched in 1891 from what had been called the 'ancient' county of Cardiganshire to the new administrative county established after the local government legislation of 1888. Earlier, the first census was based on the 'registration' county, which was considerably larger than the ancient county. More recently, the administrative county disappeared in 1974 to become the District of Ceredigion within Dyfed. In April 1996 Ceredigion once again emerged as a unitary county authority. At a finer level the boundaries of parishes have been frequently changed, especially by the Divided Parishes Acts of 1876 and 1879 and by the Local Government Act of 1929. More recently, after the administrative reforms of 1974, communities have replaced the old civil parishes with such major modifications that they are not easily compared.

The second problem is that there has been a series of changes relating to the census enumeration itself. The first censuses at the beginning of the nineteenth century were certainly unreliable, and effective household data is not available until 1851. More recently the latest censuses have seen modification of the basis of enumeration. In 1981 the usual place of residence became the basis in place of location on census night, and in 1991 those households wholly absent on census night were added either by means of late forms or by imputation; they had been simply omitted in 1981. Thus it is possible to present three different totals for the population of Cardiganshire/Ceredigion in 1991: 63,940 on the 1971 basis, which included visitors, that is, it counted all those present on census night; 61,109 on the 1981 basis, which excluded visitors, that is, it included those resident but only in households wholly or partly present; 63,094 on the 1991 basis, which included those resident, excluded visitors but included households wholly absent either by means of late enumeration or by imputation. Yet again, the date of the census can affect the results. In 1921 the census was held on 19, 20 June, later than usual and within the summer holiday season so that returns were greatly distorted by the location of holidaymakers, thereby making the whole run of figures 1911, 1921 and 1931 difficult to compare.

It is not always easy to make adjustments for these changes; in some cases it is impossible. Census data, therefore, always need to be treated with some discrimination. The alternative, the Registrar General's estimates, are simply what they are termed – estimates.

Taking these reservations into account, some initial conclusions can be drawn from the run of figures in Figure 1 which graphs the population of Cardiganshire/Ceredigion from 1801 to 1991.

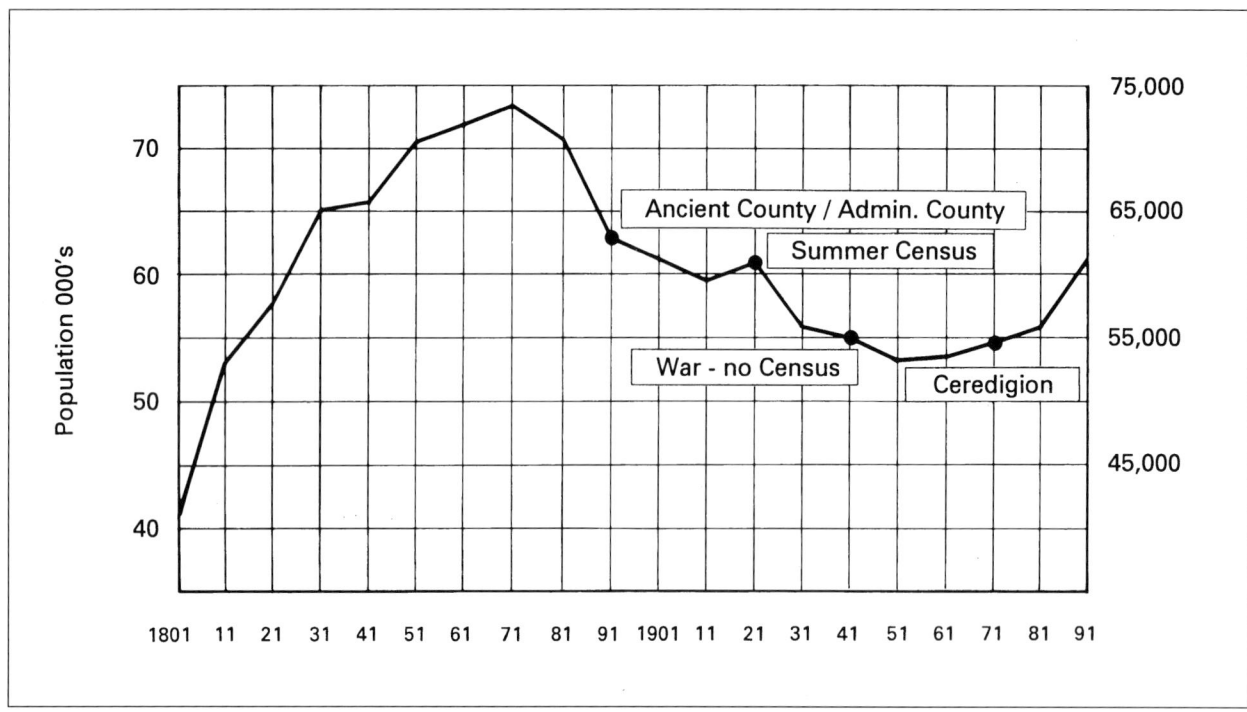

Fig. 1: The population of Cardiganshire, 180 1991.

Four phases in the population evolution can be identified. From 1801 to 1841 there was a rapid increase; decennial increases of over 10 per cent were recorded, with a maximum between 1811 and 1821 of 14.97 per cent. This was a continuation of a period of growth which characterized the latter half of the eighteenth century. The population of Cardiganshire has been estimated at 32,000 in 1750, giving an increase of 34.2 per cent to the 42,956 of the first census of 1801. After 1841 the pattern of increase was maintained, but the rate of growth was much lower, falling below 10 per cent per decade and characteristically being nearer 2 per cent; it was 2.95 per cent between 1841 and 1851 and only 1.66 per cent between 1861 and 1871. The peak population of 73,441 was reached in 1871 and there followed a third phase of rapid decline, by as much as 10.87 per cent between 1881 and 1891. That was modified to a much lower rate of decline. The one outstanding figure of a 9.36 per cent loss between 1921 and 1931, as well as the small gain of 1.67 per cent between 1911 and 1921, were probably caused by the anomalous date of the 1921 census. The lowest population figure of 53,278 was reached in 1951. The slightly increased population figure for 1961 is possibly anomalous because of the presence of construction workers on the Rheidol hydro-electric scheme. But after that date a new inflexion, constituting the fourth phase, took place and population increased at a growing rate to 1991, by as much as 10.4 per cent between 1981 and 1991, to reach 61,109 on the 1981 basis, or 63,094 on the 1991 basis.

The general explanation for these phases of population development is not difficult to determine. After 1750 there was a general country-wide increase in farm prices, followed by a rising demand generated by the Napoleonic Wars. This period of agricultural prosperity also coincided with the high point of lead mining in Cardiganshire. Settlement by the process of enclosure of the upland moors reached its highest point during the first part of the nineteenth century. The 1851 census noted that the increase of population in Llanfyrnach between 1821 and 1841 was 'ascribed to the inclosure and cultivation of the waste'.[1] It would be a mistake to give an impression of unhindered prosperity for the agricultural labourer and the small farmer. Even so, John Davies ascribes the growth to increased fertility based on perceived advantages rather than on any improvements in health or sanitation. There was a new 'confidence of young couples that there would be a livelihood for them if they married and had a family. The factors underlying that confidence are the primary key to the growth in the population. It could stem from the knowledge that adequate sustenance would be available from a hectare or two of potatoes, or from a holding carved from the common land . . . and by the assumption that poor relief would ensure that a family would not starve.'[2]

Given the basic environmental limitations on agriculture and the necessary short-term character of mineral exploitation, there were manifest restrictions on population growth. Moreover, the extension of population produced its own Malthusian checks. After 1875 the increasing importation of food from distant sources undermined agriculture, whilst lead production, also influenced by foreign imports, plummeted. In his book *Lead Mining in Wales*, W. J. Lewis included a graph of the output of lead ore in Cardiganshire.[3] The graph of the population of Cardiganshire mirrors that of lead ore production. Moreover, the developing iron and coal mining areas of south Wales provided a relatively accessible source of employment, and the census consistently associated a fall in population with emigration: 'The decrease of population in the parishes of Brongwyn, Troedyraur, Bettwsevan and Penbryn is attributed to migration into Glamorgan and emigration to America.'[4] The latter was a notable alternative, but the nearness of the coalfields in Wales meant that overseas emigration was always limited. Even so, there was a steady stream of movement to the United States throughout the century. In the census returns of 1831 and 1841 'several parishes stated exactly how many persons had emigrated. The entire county of Cardiganshire lost 145 males and 128 females between January and 7 June 1841 – more than any other county in Wales.'[5] Again, Cardiganshire had long-standing links with London, both via the drovers and the seasonal employment of women in horticulture. Ravenstein in 1885 had developed his 'laws of migration' largely as a response to the massive population movements of the nineteenth century.[6] Most change, he maintained, was the result of a series of short distance movements, but the exception was the attraction of the metropolis. Certainly London became a significant target for Cardiganshire emigrants, some of whom built up businesses far beyond any scale they could have achieved at home. There were, therefore, strong underlying tendencies towards decline which eventually led to a phase of rapid retreat from the peak population reached in 1871.

This decline was continued after the First World War, even though depression restricted the source of employment in the industrial areas. As early as 1871 the census had recorded loss due to 'the migration of agricultural labourers to the mineral districts in search of employment, manual labour having been considerably dispensed with since the introduction of machinery'.[7] There was

[1] Census of England and Wales, 1851. Vol.2, p.449.
[2] J. Davies, *A History of Wales* (London, 1993), p.321.
[3] W. J. Lewis, *Lead Mining in Wales* (Cardiff, 1967), p.179.
[4] Census of England and Wales, 1871, Vol.2, p.545.
[5] A. E. Davies, 'Wages, prices, and social improvements in Cardiganshire, 1750–1850', *Ceredigion*, X, no.1 (1984), 50.
[6] E. G. Ravenstein, 'The laws of migration', *Journal of the Royal Statistical Society*, 48 (1885), 167–235.
[7] Census of England and Wales, 1871. Vol.2, p.545.

an underlying and continuing rural depopulation owing to the depression in agriculture and above all because of increased mechanization and capitalization in farming. The report *Depopulation in Mid-Wales* estimated that the region (of which Cardiganshire was a part) lost 23.2 per cent of its agricultural workers between 1951 and 1960. And since many of those engaged in agriculture were not farm workers but holders of small farms which were amalgamated or simply abandoned, the total loss was nearer 29 per cent.[8] There is little point in a specific study of Cardiganshire rehearsing the general causes of depopulation and their circular and cumulative character. All that needs to be noted is that during the first half of the twentieth century Cardiganshire became a classic example of the whole gamut of causes and consequences associated with rural depopulation, and indeed the process continued after the Second World War and is still operative. Employment opportunities are necessarily limited in a peripheral and largely thinly peopled rural area where agriculture is greatly constricted in the life chances it can offer.

There has, however, been one major change in population movement which initiated the fourth phase noted earlier. It is epitomized in the description sometimes given of 'rural retreating', or by the more conventional term, 'counterurbanization'. The period following the erosion of long-established conventions during the 1960s generated in many distaste for the materialism of the metropolitan lifestyle, a 'bonfire of the vanities', and led some to seek a different physical and social environment in the countryside. Throughout the western world the cities began to lose population and the small towns and countryside to register increases. Rural mid-Wales became a clear target primarily for those from the midland counties of England and from the south-east, and immigration became a characteristic feature of its population pattern. Underneath, the old pattern of depopulation proceeded, but it was masked by a dominant inward flow. Thus the 1991 Census County Report for Dyfed presents a summary table (Summary table C) which uses the 1981 base to examine change. The District of Ceredigion grew from 55,353 to 61,109, a percentage increase of 10.4 per cent. But the District showed a natural decrease of population with an excess of deaths over births giving a loss of 2.3 per cent. An increase of 12.7 per cent by migration was the basis of the increase registered. All this has given a new character to population change, with a most recent period of growth contrasting with a long preceding phase of decline.

These changes are epitomized in the sex ratios, that is, the proportion of males to females expressed as a percentage. At the first census of 1801 the figure stood at 90.5 per cent and was 93.3 per cent in 1821. Thereafter it showed a steady decline, reaching the quite remarkable level of 78.5 per cent in 1891. If at that census the ratios are calculated for the age groups which are crucial to marriage and family formation, then whereas the figure for the 15–19 group is the same as that for the county as a whole the percentages for the succeeding groups are as follows: 20–24: 73.4; 25–29: 63.9; 30–34: 67.5; 35–39: 68.4. These are quite astonishing ratios and mark the substantial loss of young males to employment offered in the industrial south. Even in 1851 Merthyr Tydfil returned some 2,292 of its inhabitants as born in Cardiganshire. All this is a direct contradiction of one of Ravenstein's 'laws of migration', namely that females are more migratory than males.[9] Some strange interpretations appeared as a result. Kenneth O. Morgan has observed:

> On all sides, therefore, Cardiganshire manifested the grim symbols of a depressed area – the loss of young males . . . and a truly staggering surplus of unmarried females. The proportion of females

[8] *Depopulation in Mid-Wales* (HMSO,1964), p.6.
[9] Ravenstein, 'Laws of migration', 167–235.

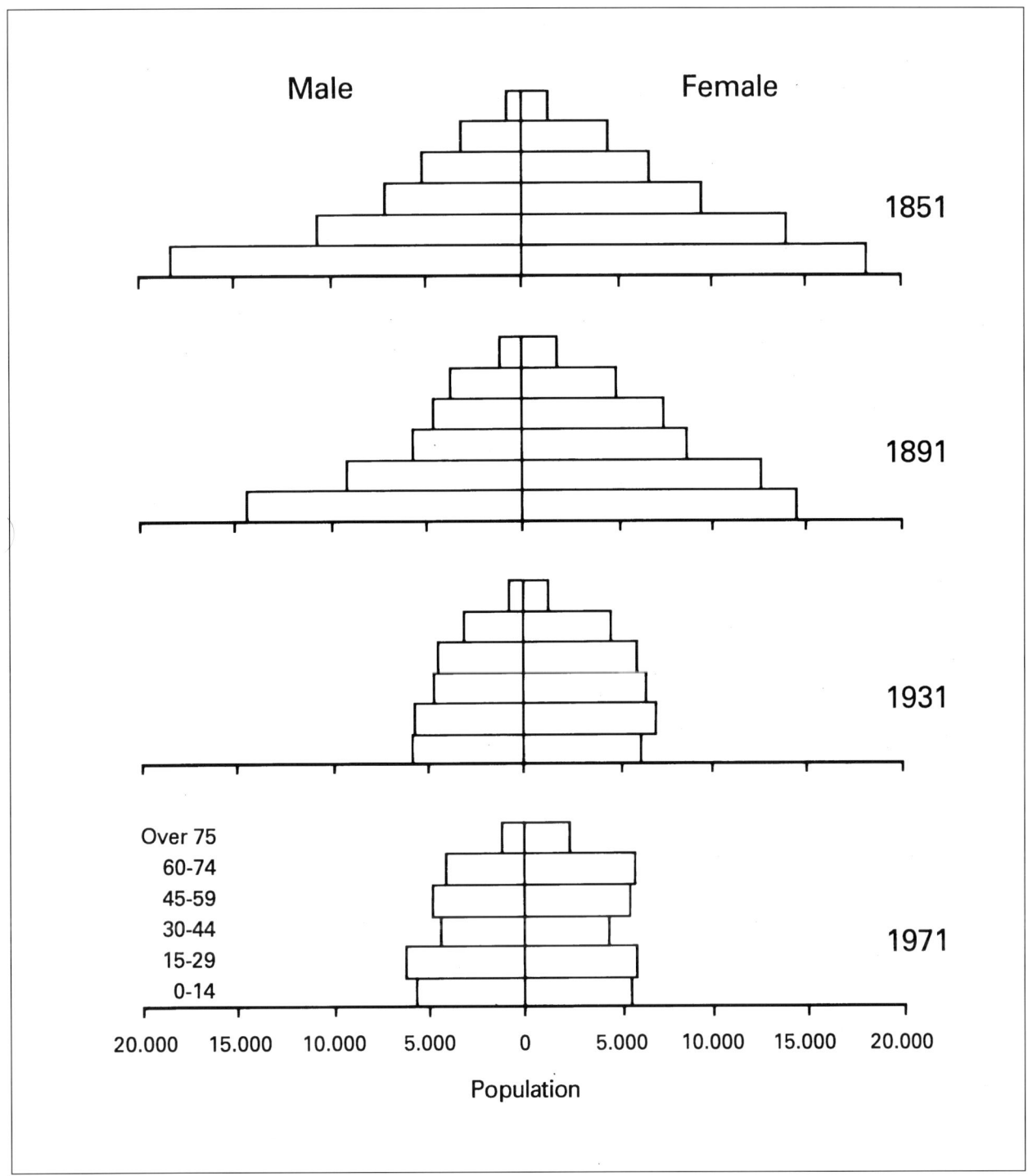

Fig. 2: Population pyramids for Cardiganshire: 1851, 1891, 1931, 1971.

Note: Those for 1851 and 1891 are for the Registration County. Those for 1931 and 1971 are for the Administrative County.

to males was the highest for England and Wales recorded in six successive censuses: in 1891, there were 1,274 females for every 1,000 males [the sex ratio of 78.5 noted above; 1000/1274 × 1001]. The census commissioners quaintly attributed this phenomenon to the difficulty that monoglot Welsh women from Cardiganshire found in gaining employment in domestic service outside the county. It is clear, however, that this, like so much else in the demographic structure of Cardiganshire, really rested in the long-term pressures of economic decline.[10]

The huge surplus of young women had a disastrous impact on the marriage rate and hence on the birth rate. These ratios have recovered to a near standard situation by the end of the twentieth century. By 1951 the ratio was 88.5 and by the succeeding census it had reached 94.1. It has remained about that level subsequently, and stood at 94.3 at the 1991 census.

The decline during the nineteenth century, and its consequences, are revealed also in the age-structure of the population, which is displayed as standard age pyramids for four dates in Figure 2. The dates selected were determined by the availability of reliable data by 1851, and the avoidance of 1921 for reasons already given and for 1941 when there was no census. The 1851 shape is that of the classic pyramid, with its sloping sides partly the result of a high death rate among the young. For the youngest group, 0–14, males exceed females as is to be expected from the tendency for male births to be slightly greater in number than female. In detail, the male numbers are clearly greater in the under-5 group (6,247 to 6,068) but are virtually equal in the 5–9 and 10–14 groups. But the dominance of male emigration which gives the female excesses, already commented upon, are clearly visible and females are more numerous in all the other age groups. By 1891 these trends have been exacerbated. There is still the classic pyramid shape, but the falling numbers of children being born, and a greater survival rate, have shortened the base and the sides of the pyramid are tangibly steeper. However, the imbalance between males and females gives a marked skew to the pyramid. The under-15 group is still balanced, but the succeeding group, 15–29, is seriously distorted by the presence of 9,154 males but of 12,194 females. By 1931 the trends apparent in 1891 have completely altered the shape of the diagram. The consequences of migration and the loss of a young family-rearing population have become visible. The total has substantially shrunk, although it must be added that the decline in numbers is largely due to the change from the registration county to the administrative county. But the pyramid has been replaced by a barrel shape as a consequence of the substantial diminution of the youngest groups and the expansion of the oldest as more survive to an older age. In 1971 there were greater numbers, both male and female, over 75 than at any other date. That, of course, to a degree is a reflection of the universal western demographic transition as birth rates and death rates declined, the former with the greater lag contributing to the population expansion of the first part of the century, while falling death rates have engendered a subsequent ageing population.[11] But superimposed in Cardiganshire was the process of outmigration which has already been noted.

The population history which has been summarized can best be examined by considering in greater detail different parts of the county. A selection of four parishes from five parts of the county was made. These parts include a northern area which is essentially the Aberystwyth hinterland

[10]K. O. Morgan, 'Cardiganshire politics: the Liberal ascendancy, 1885–1923', *Ceredigion*, V, no.4 (1967), 316.
[11]C. Thomas, 'Rural settlements in the modern period', in D. Huw Owen (ed.), *Settlement and Society in Wales* (Cardiff, 1989), pp.250–3.

Fig. 3: The population of four parishes on Mynydd Bach, 1801–1991.

Note: Following the Divided Parishes Act Llangeitho received 137 persons from Llanbadarn Odwyn, 1871–1881.

extending east to the upland marches with Montgomeryshire; the central coastal area around Aberaeron and the Aeron valley; the southern coastal area around Cardigan; Mynydd Bach, constituting a central outlier of the high plateau of central Wales; and part of the upper Teifi valley including the mountain border with Radnorshire and Breconshire. In all these cases the shapes of the parishes mean that seldom are simple geographical areas properly represented.

The most crucial area is Mynydd Bach (Figure 3), which is centrally located in the county and is an appropriate base against which to review the other areas. The population graphs of the four parishes – Lledrod Isaf, Llangeitho, Blaenpennal and Nancwnlle – are very similar in outline. The only major divergence which occurs was due to a boundary change (Llangeitho 1871–81). The graphs follow the more general pattern which has been outlined for the county, with a quite rapid growth in the early part of the nineteenth century to a peak population in the period 1851–81, followed by a steady, inexorable decline until 1971. There follows a distinct 'kick-up' which reflects the counterurbanization process and the immigration which was its consequence.

Morgan Davies analysed this area of Mynydd Bach in 1968. He identified 170 dwellings above the 900-foot contour and suggested a threefold grouping of them. Eighty-eight were permanently occupied and were predominantly associated with small farms run as family units. Even so, he identified among them what he called 'hobby farmers', who derived their main income from other activities carried on elsewhere. Six of the total were vacated farms which had been converted to holiday cottages and represented the forerunners of the later occupation by incomers, the precursors of a more permanent rural-retreating. A further seventy-six formed a third category of vacant or derelict dwellings. Davies concluded: 'this is the direct result of depopulation caused by the movement of people out of the area and a break in the family-farming tradition, for today few young persons wish to stay on the land. Hence, with the passing of a generation which is not being replaced, the hearth becomes cold and yet another farmhouse begins to decay and the land once

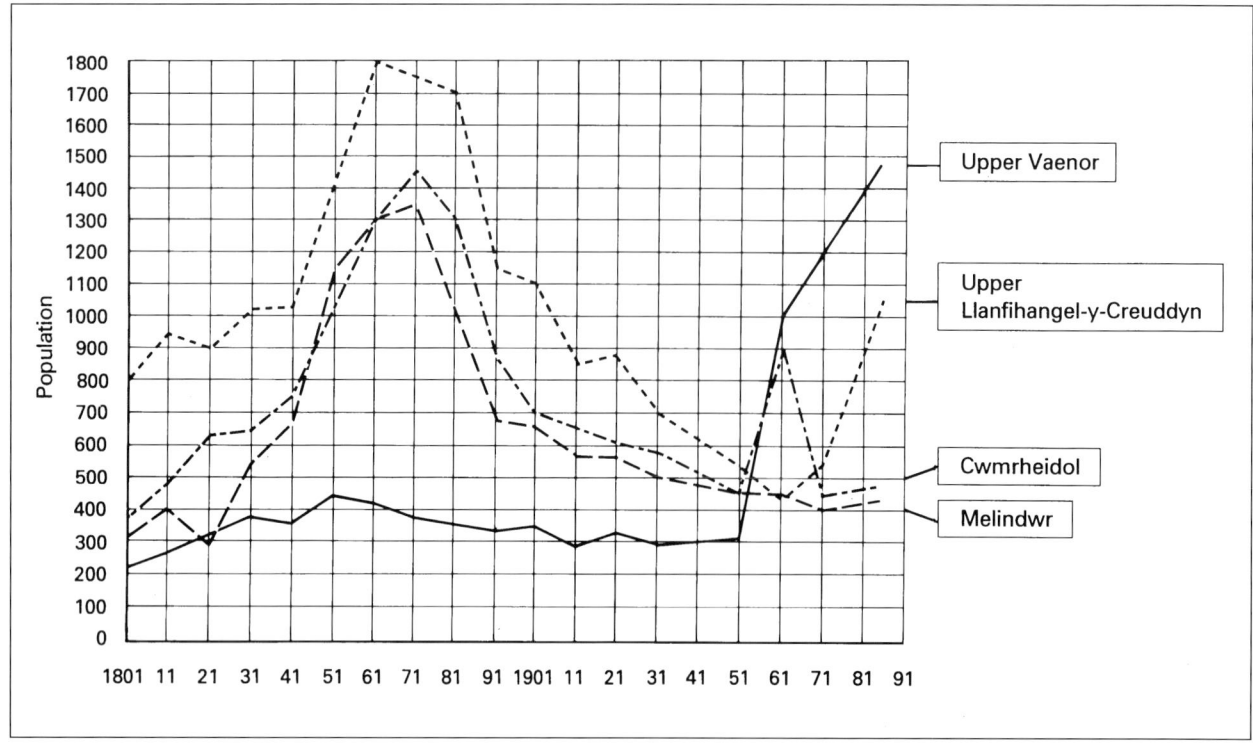

Fig. 4: The population of four parishes in north Cardiganshire, 1801–1991.

Note: Following the Divided Parishes Act Melindwr gained nineteen persons from Parcel Canol, 1871–1881. Following the Local Government Act of 1929 part of Upper Llanbadarn-y-Creuddyn was added to Upper Llanfihangel-y-Creuddyn, which enabled the latter to gain 52 persons between 1931 and 1935.

tilled with such care and devotion quickly reverts to nature.'[12] Such dwellings, located at nearly 1,000 feet, have been more attractive as summer holiday cottages, for the severity of winter occupation has made them unsuitable as permanent homes for the rural-retreater. Even so, the most recent censuses show the characteristic increase which has been brought about by in-migration, for all these parishes show losses by an adverse birth/death ratio.

The examination of the northern area (Figure 4), the parishes of Cwmrheidol, Melindwr, Upper Llanfihangel-y-Creuddyn and Upper Vaenor, reveals both similarities and contrasts with Mynydd Bach. The general trends visible in the graphs are very similar to those of the Mynydd Bach parishes, but the actual movements are greatly exaggerated. This has occurred as a result of the superimposition on the underlying trend of three other activities, lead mining, urbanization and capital works. The rapid increase in three of the parishes in the latter part of the nineteenth century was the direct product of lead mining. As in so many mineral enterprises, boom was followed by collapse as lodes were exhausted and supplies from vastly greater overseas sources became available. Population tracked mineral output and numbers fell as rapidly as they had risen. Moreover, the development of coal mining, especially in south Wales, provided a ready alternative for displaced lead miners. But in more recent times these parishes, too, provided dwellings built for lead miners

[12]M. L. Davies, 'The rural community in central Wales: a study in social geography', in E. G. Bowen,
  H. Carter and J. A. Taylor (eds.), *Geography at Aberystwyth* (Cardiff, 1968), p.207.

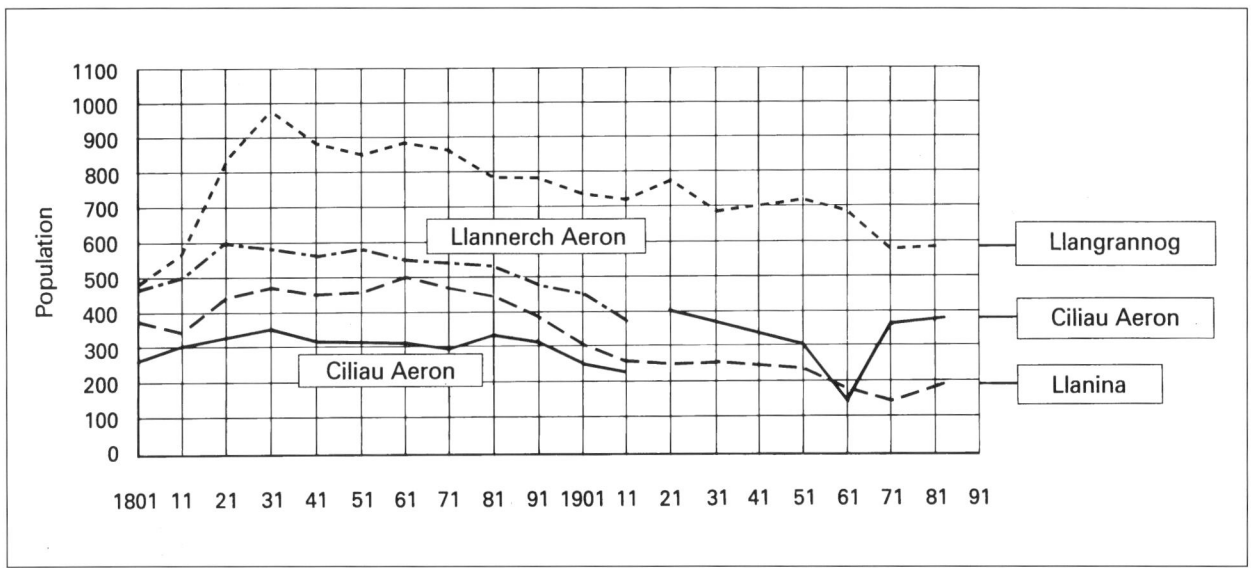

Fig. 5: The population of four parishes in central coastal Cardiganshire, 1801–1991.

Note: Llannerch Aeron was joined to Ciliau Aeron, and the name Ciliau Aeron was adopted in 1934. Llanina included Cydplwyf.

which could be readily converted into holiday homes or more permanent rural retreats. Again they were partly in small villages which provided a more congenial environment than the isolated single farmhouse. Here, too, is the kickback of the recent censuses as a consequence of in-migration.

But the more spectacular rises are due to other reasons, primarily the growth of Aberystwyth. The populations of the towns will be considered later, but a process of suburbanization has characterized the towns of Cardiganshire as of every other county. The very rapid increase of the population of Upper Vaenor is a direct consequence of the development of commuter estates of private housing outside the boundary of the town. This is also true, although to a lesser extent, of Upper Llanfihangel-y-Creuddyn. The third influence is that of capital works and that can be seen in the spectacular peaking of the population of Cwmrheidol between 1951 and 1961. The construction of the hydro-electric scheme on the river Rheidol greatly inflated numbers at a time when the basis of the census was not usual place of residence but location on census night. The rapid decline marked the completion of the scheme and there is the now familiar kick-up in the most recent decades.

The group of central coastal parishes (Figure 5) – Llannerch Aeron, Ciliau Aeron, Llangrannog and Llanina – again shows a parallel with those of Mynydd Bach, but the more favourable environmental conditions, together with the advantage of a seaside location, mean that the trends are much less exaggerated and the rise and fall of population modified. Although this area has been a target of inward migration due to its coastal character, this does not emerge with any clarity from the data for these parishes.

The southern group (Figure 6) again shows what is now identified as the universal trend, but with considerable modification. Unfortunately, the extent of boundary changes makes analysis difficult. The dominant feature is the growth of Aber-porth during and after the Second World War. This is another example of the impact of capital investment, this time in the form of the Royal Aircraft

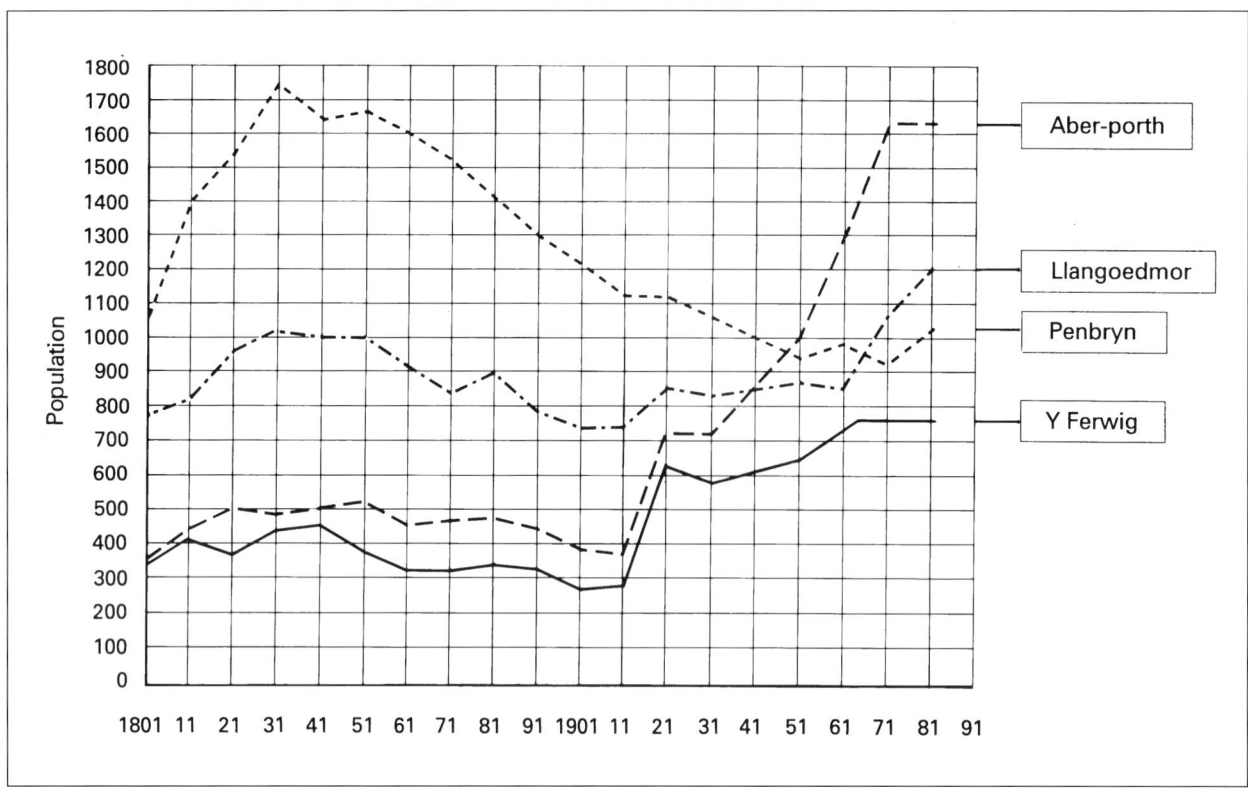

Fig. 6: The population of four parishes in south Cardiganshire, 1801–1991.

Note: Following the Local Government Act of 1929 Blaen-porth was combined with Aber-porth, Llangoedmor was extended to include Llechryd and part of Tre-main, but lost part of Y Ferwig. Y Ferwig was extended to include the whole of Mwnt and part of Tre-main.

Establishment. That, together with suburban growth associated with Cardigan town, has produced a very much clearer recovery of population than in the central coastal area just to the north. Llangoedmor and Y Ferwig in particular return significant increases.

Finally, the parishes of the upper Teifi valley and its upland fringes (Figure 7) show much the same pattern as Mynydd Bach, which is no more than an outlier of this inner section. But the even greater altitude and isolation meant that the impact of rural depopulation was even more severe. The population of all these parishes, with the exception of Caron-is-clawdd, which includes the town of Tregaron, has halved from the maxima recorded around 1861–71 to the minima around 1971. Even here increases between 1971 and 1981 are evident.

The well-nigh universal increases in the period 1971–81 deserve some attention. Figure 8 plots all those parishes which showed an increase of population between the two dates of more than 20 per cent, while Figure 9 plots the same increase between 1981 and 1991 and adds those communities where the population increased by over 10 per cent by migration, that is, those people with a different address a year before the census. This latter figure includes local as well as long-distance moves and by itself is not an indicator of immigration. There are three areas which stand out. The first is Aberystwyth and its immediate hinterland, where suburban extension was the main cause,

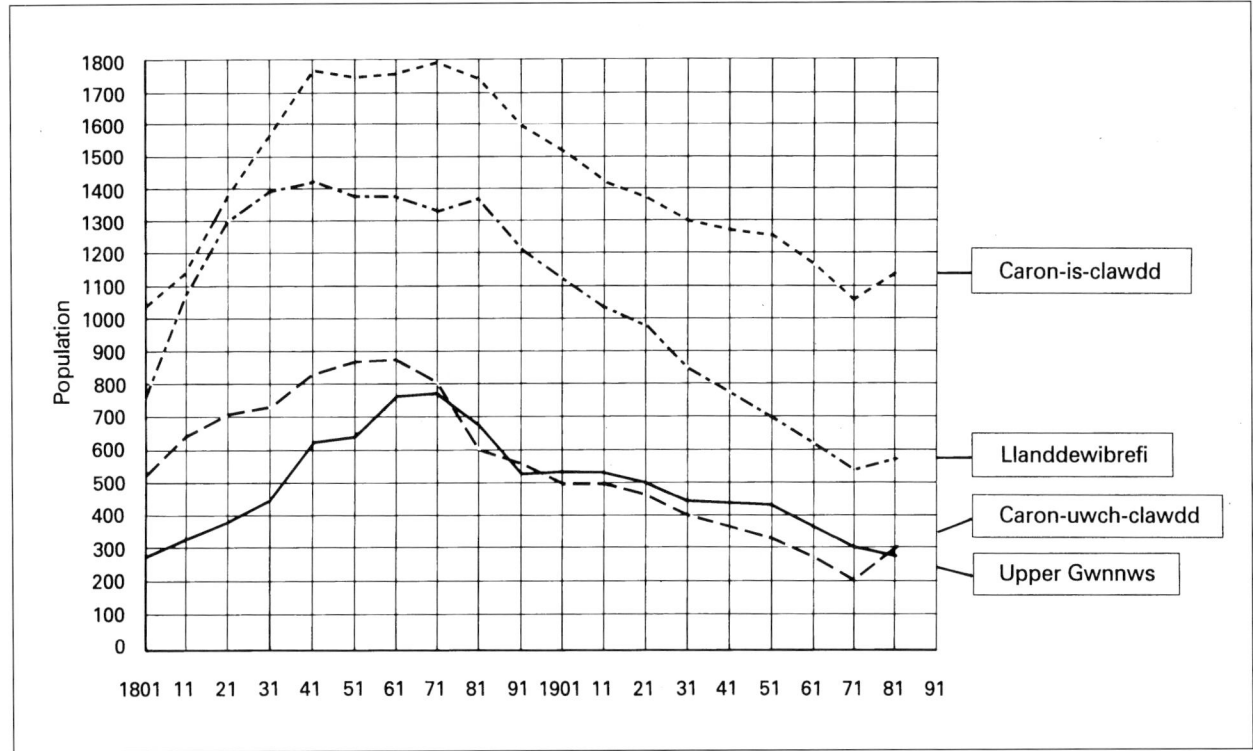

Fig. 7: The population of four parishes in the Upper Teifi Valley, 1801–1991.

Note: Following the Local Government Act of 1929 part of Upper Gwnnws was transferred to Caron-uwch-clawdd, and Llanddewibrefi was created out of the former parishes of Doethie Camddwr, Doethie Pysgotwr, Garth and Ystrad, Gogoyan, Gorwydd, Llanio, Prysg and Carfan. These parishes have been combined to give population totals before 1921.

accompanied by a significant inward movement of people. The second is the central block covering Mynydd Bach which appears on both maps. The third area is the central and southern coastal group from Aberaeron and through New Quay. These latter two have been the main receptors of in-migration. The only other area is in the middle Teifi valley, while Caron-uwch-clawdd, Pontarfynach and Ysbyty Ystwyth are representative of the inner upland areas where in-migration has also been apparent.

There is one remaining element of the population which has been partly drawn into the discussion in the comments on suburbanization, that is the towns (Figure 10). In treating them, however, a host of problems arise. In the first instance a town can be either underbound, that is, its built-up area is less than its administrative boundary, or it can be overbound, that is, the built-up area is greater than and overlaps the administrative limits. Populations vary according to those situations, especially when adjustments are made to bring built-up area and administrative area into line with each other. Although allowance can be made for the decade in which change occurs, it is virtually impossible to take it back to earlier decades. Commuter populations beyond the administrative boundary are not included and any decision to draw a realistic limit is necessarily arbitrary. Again, until the decision to register usually resident population in 1981, numbers could be inflated by the presence of summer visitors; the June census of 1921 has already been mentioned as creating problems, and the same is true of the presence or absence of students in small university

Fig. 8: Parishes showing population increase of over 20 per cent, 1971–1981.

towns at the time of a particular census. All this means that it is impossible to establish a consistent line of population change. The graphs in Figure 10 stress especially the rapid growth of Aberystwyth as a market, tourist and university town and as the dominant centre in Cardiganshire. In terms of its urban rank it measures alongside towns such as Carmarthen, Haverfordwest and Caernarfon as significant centres for rural hinterlands, forming a crucial layer in the urban hierarchy of Wales. The recent decreases in population are of course related to a universal situation where people have moved out of urban centres and into the surrounding suburbs. It is difficult to give a realistic figure for the population of the town but, together with the immediately adjacent parishes, it was 13,371 in 1981 or, if one takes a more liberal interpretation of a 'metropolitan area', it was 17,318. By 1991 a figure of some 20,245 can be suggested by taking a relatively liberal view of what constitute commuter suburbs. The main feature of the other towns is that they do not replicate the rural parishes but reveal slow growth, and where recent decrease is apparent the reason is again suburbanization.

    The changes which have been described have of necessity influenced the structure of the population. Indeed, those changes and that structure are necessarily interlinked. Population change

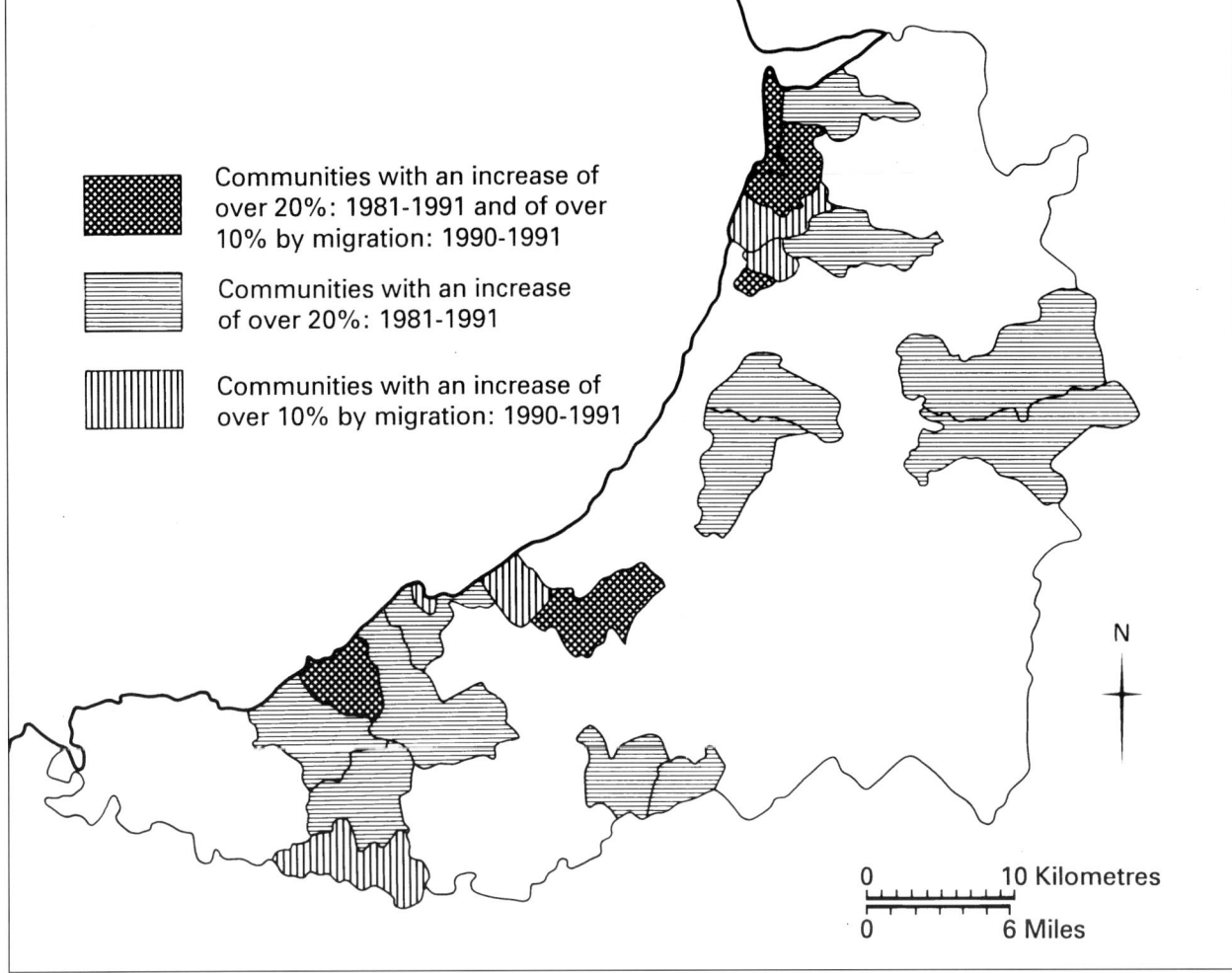

Communities with an increase of over 20%: 1981-1991 and of over 10% by migration: 1990-1991

Communities with an increase of over 20%: 1981-1991

Communities with an increase of over 10% by migration: 1990-1991

N

0   10 Kilometres

0   6 Miles

Fig. 9: Communities showing population increase of over 20 per cent, 1981–1991, and with migration of more than 10 per cent at the 1991 census.

can only take place as a result of natural processes, births and deaths, and of inward or outward movement, and these have already been invoked in the explanation of change offered. Both have a crucial impact upon age structure.

It has been suggested that, at the beginning of the nineteenth century, population increase, which was well-nigh universal in the county, was a product of increased fertility. These trends are best identified by a more detailed study than the published census provides and an analysis of north Cardiganshire between 1851 and 1871 has been provided by G. J. Lewis. Lewis surveyed the enumerators' returns for eleven parishes which lay north of Aberystwyth, but excluding Llangynfelyn and the anomalous parish of Ysgubor-y-coed, which was regarded for administrative purposes as part of Montgomeryshire. He concluded:

> the population of the study area increased steadily during the first half of the nineteenth century. The period from 1801 to 1811 was one of prosperity for these rural parishes, as war demands stimulated agricultural production and, by 1851, the local lead-mining industry was expanding

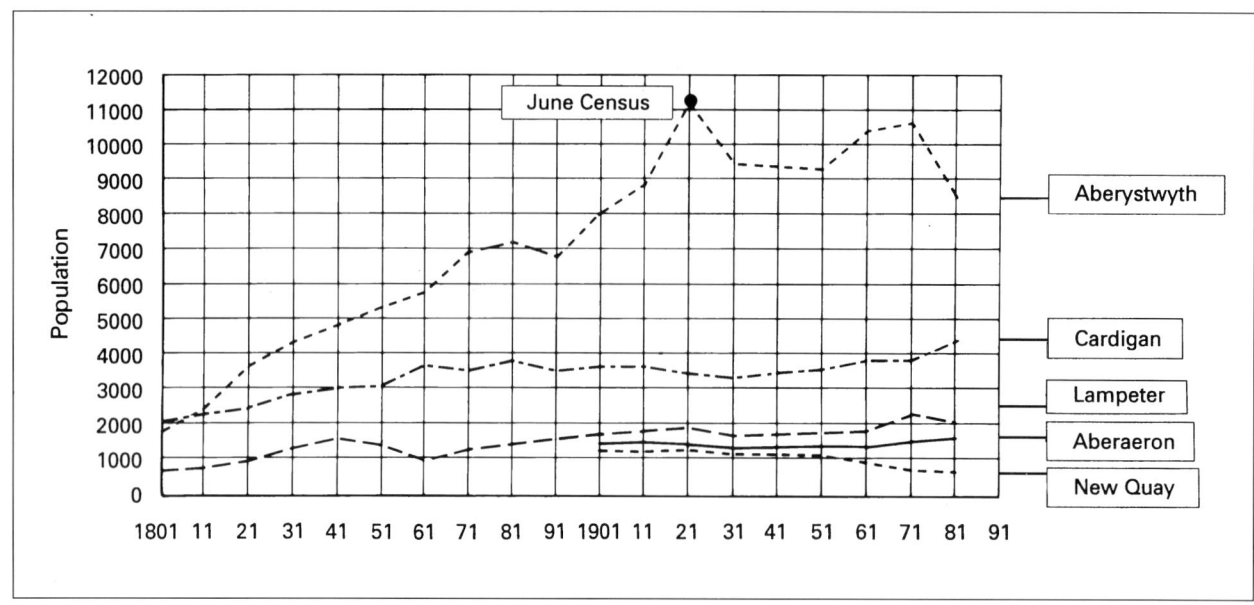

Fig. 10: The population of towns in Cardiganshire, 1801–1991.

rapidly. The resultant age structure was typical of rural areas which had experienced fairly rapid growth up to the middle of the nineteenth century. 38 per cent of the population were children below nine years of age; and over half were below twenty, thus indicating a fairly high birth rate; on the other hand, only 12 per cent were over fifty years of age. There was a slight predominance of females in virtually all age groups, but only in the 10–19 group were the females particularly predominant, indicating a certain degree of male out-migration.[13]

This is a picture of an area with a young demographic structure producing the classic age pyramid with steeply sloping sides.

By 1871 significant changes had taken place which are evident from the age pyramid (Figure 11). Agricultural depression had led to the fall in the rural population which has already been identified in all the graphs presented. By 1871, Lewis observes, 'some of the agricultural parishes were beginning to suffer from an acute loss of population by migrations. Among the agricultural parishes there was a net out-migration of 3 per cent to adjoining parishes and of nearly 7 per cent over distances. Among the latter group, nearly 68 per cent were below 35 years.'[14] The lead mining areas were to follow a similar route a little later. The consequences were a loss of the younger population, especially of women of childbearing age, evidenced in Figure 11 by the decline of those in the 20–50 age groups, and a subsequent entrenched pattern of an ageing population with a declining birth rate and an increasing death rate. All this was accompanied by a continued loss of young people by net out-migration.

It is interesting to note that even where there was not the same massive population loss, a similar restructuring took place. In his study of Aber-porth, David Jenkins observes that, unlike its inland neighbours, the parish had more people living there in 1931 than in the first census of 1801. 'The

[13]G. J. Lewis, 'Mobility, locality and demographic change: the case of north Cardiganshire, 1851–71', *WHR*, 9, no.3 (1979), 350–1.
[14]Ibid., 358.

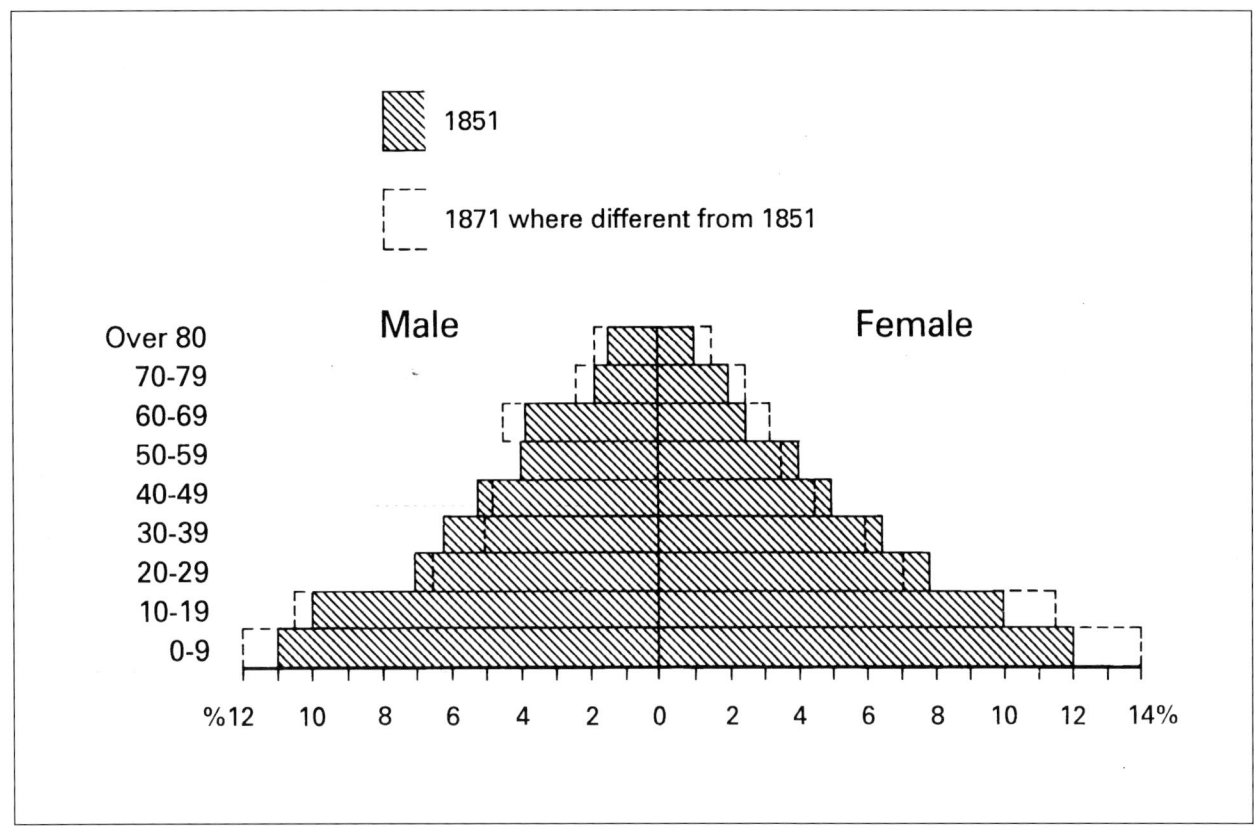

Fig. 11: The age structure of parishes in north Cardiganshire, 1851 and 1871.

sea had provided work and kept together the nucleus of the present population.'[15] But he notes: 'while for the whole of England and Wales those below the age of 40 make up 61.7 per cent of the total population, in Aber-porth this group is proportionately smaller – 47.1 per cent of the total. There is a greater percentage than the national average in each of the older age groups.'[16] The reasons lie in the emigration of the young, partly because local farming could not sustain the increase, as his examination of the farming and land system demonstrates, and partly because the mobile young seek new domains to experience.

The universality of the consequences can be seen in Tables 1, 2 and 3. Table 1 demonstrates the massive emigration which characterized Cardiganshire during the second half of the nineteenth century, when every decade recorded a net migration loss. The repercussion on natural change is seen in the progressive lowering of the rate of natural increase in a county losing its young people of reproductive age. The figure fell from over 10 per cent in the third quarter of the century to only 2 per cent at the end of the century. The same process continued to the First World War, following which the whole situation was quite spectacularly reversed. A clear loss by natural processes set in caused by an excess of deaths over births, accompanied by a gradual increase by net migration.

[15]D. Jenkins, 'Aber-porth. A study of a coastal village in south Cardiganshire', in E. Davies and A. D. Rees (eds.), *Welsh Rural Communities* (Cardiff, 1960), p.8.
[16]Ibid.

TABLE 1: Population change in Cardiganshire by natural increase and migration, 1841–1991

Date	Total change		Natural increase		Net migration	
	Amount	Per cent	Amount	Per cent	Amount	Per cent
1841–51	+1612	+1.68	+11040	+11.50	−9428	−9.82
1851–61	−213	−0.22	+9100	+9.32	−9313	−9.54
1861–71	+468	+0.48	+10628	+10.91	−10160	−10.43
1871–81	−2732	−2.79	+8528	+8.77	−11314	−11.56
1881–91	−8754	−9.20	+6968	+7.32	−15722	−16.53
1891–01	−3676	−4.26	+3592	+4.16	−7268	−8.41
1901–11	−1938	−2.34	+1089	+2.19	−3747	−5.53
1911–21	+1002	+1.67	−582	−0.97	+1584	+2.65
1921–31	−5697	−9.36	−962	−1.58	−4735	−7.78
1931–51	−1906	−3.45	−3164	−5.73	+1258	+2.28
1951–61	+370	+0.69	−1020	−1.19	+1390	+2.61
1961–71	+1234	+2.30	−828	−1.54	+2062	+3.84
1971–81	+2577	+4.70	−1831	−3.34	+4412	+8.03
1981–91	+5758	+10.40	−1273	−2.30	+7031	+12.70

Notes:
1. From 1841 to 1911 the figures relate to the registration county since data are only available for that basis. From 1921 they refer to the administrative county.
2. Owing to the June date of the 1921 census, the changes for 1911–21 and 1921–31 are distorted by the presence of summer visitors.
3. Source: John Williams, *Digest of Welsh Historical Statistics* (2 vols., The Welsh Office, 1985), and the 1981 and 1991 Censuses.

TABLE 2: Changes in the population of Cardiganshire, percentage change, 1921–1931

Area	Natural change	Migration change	Total change
Aberaeron UD	−6.7	−5.2	−13.3
Aberystwyth MB	−2.2	−13.3	−15.5
Cardigan MB	−2.6	−1.7	−4.3
Lampeter MB	−4.8	0.9	−3.9
New Quay UD	−6.8	−4.5	−11.3
Aberaeron RD	−1.2	−7.0	−8.2
Aberystwyth RD	−2.1	−7.4	−9.5
Cardigan RD	−1.5	0.2	−1.3
Lampeter RD	0.1	−9.0	−8.9
Llandysul RD	−0.8	−5.5	−6.3
Tregaron RD	−1.5	−10.1	−11.6

TABLE 3: Changes in the population of Cardiganshire, percentage change, 1931–1951

Area	Natural change	Migration change	Total change
Aberaeron UD	−20.7	27.1	6.4
Aberystwyth MD	−6.6	4.9	−1.7
Cardigan MB	−4.4	10.0	5.6
Lampeter MB	−10.0	13.3	3.3
New Quay UD	−18.9	17.2	−1.7
Aberaeron RD	−2.9	−3.5	−6.4
Aberystwyth RD	−7.0	2.4	−4.0
Teifiside RD	−2.2	1.2	−1.0
Tregaron RD	−5.1	−7.2	−12.3

Thus, by the decade 1981–91, a natural loss by 2.3 per cent is offset by a substantial gain of 12.7 per cent by net migration.

The crucial period of change can be seen in an analysis of the period 1921–51 in the smaller administrative areas. The continued ageing of the population meant that every one of these administrative areas over a period of some thirty years, with one very minor exception, showed a loss of population by an excess of deaths over births. In all the Rural Districts there was also a loss by net out-migration. The consequences are demonstrated in the 1961 census, when 6.6 per cent of the population of Cardiganshire was in the 0–4 age group compared with 7.9 for England and Wales, while the figures for the 5–9 age group were 6.4 and 7.0 respectively. If the proportion under nine is taken, then the resulting figure of 13 per cent can be set alongside the figure of 38 per cent for the northern parishes of Lewis's study of 1851. Cardiganshire had lower proportions in all the age groups below 45, apart from 15–24, and higher proportions in all the groups over 54. Here, then, were the consequences of a century of population decline – an elderly population, with all the social and economic consequences which followed.

By 1991 the net in-migration which has been noted had done much to turn the demographic situation around, or at least to bring it more in line with the national situation. The 1981 census had shown that 5,598 of those recorded had changed their addresses in the previous twelve months. Of these, 639 had a former address in England. The equivalent figures for 1991 were 6,365 movers and 1,342 previous English or Scottish addresses. There were a further 342 from outside Great Britain. This was reflected in the birthplace data, with 19,581 having been born in England as against 40,040 in Wales. The total non-Welsh born represented 35.6 per cent of the population of Cardiganshire.

The age structure pyramid for 1991 (Figure 12) displays what is sometimes called the beehive shape of mature populations. The extremes of the nineteenth century and the inter-war period no longer dominate. Even so, the basic problem, now universal in the West, of an ageing population remains. There is a declining youthful base to support an ever increasing number of elderly people. Between 1981 and 1991, as has been indicated earlier, there was a decrease by natural processes of some 2.3 per cent which was offset by a migratory gain of 12.7 per cent to give an overall gain of 10.4 per cent. The problems implicit in that situation are highlighted by the diminishing number of the young and active and the increasing numbers in the older groups. Thus, in 1991, females over

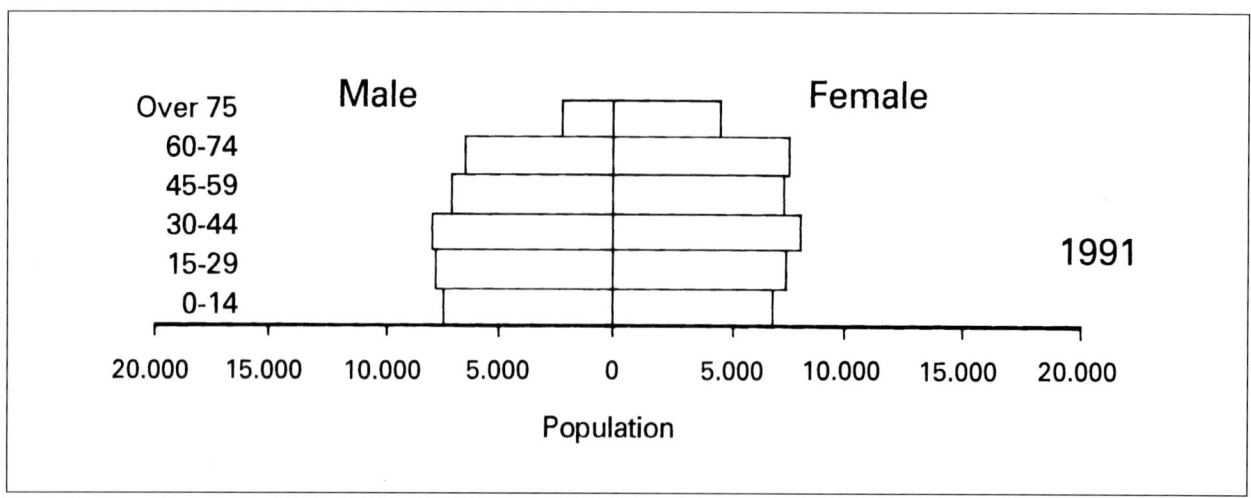

Fig. 12: Population pyramid for Cardiganshire: 1991.

75 numbered 3,507, two and a half times the number in 1851, three times the number in 1931. In contrast, those between 0 and 15 in 1991 were only a third of those in 1851. Even so, it must be noted that the comparison using 1851 data is of the later administrative county with the former registration county. But even in the administrative county of 1911, the number in the 0 to 4 group was 4,848 compared with 3,625 in 1991. The demographic situation is now once more in line with rural areas in the West, but a wide range of current concerns, such as social policy, care in the community and the well-being of the Welsh language, have their origins in the nature of the population.

CHAPTER 2

AGRICULTURE AND LAND OCCUPATION IN EIGHTEENTH- AND NINETEENTH-CENTURY CARDIGANSHIRE

R. J. Moore-Colyer

'WE HAVE not progressed beyond the observation that enclosures occurred at a very early stage in some places and remarkably late elsewhere', observed Matthew Griffiths in *Settlement and Society in Wales* (1989). Given the expanding corpus of physically weighty and expensive volumes concerned with the historical geography of Wales, his assertion is all the more remarkable. While we now know that some of the field systems of north-west Wales, with their associated scatters of round huts, are of Early Bronze Age provenance, and that the uniform and rectilinear fields of many upland areas are linked to parliamentary enclosure of the late eighteenth and early nineteenth centuries, we remain substantially ignorant of the temporal pattern of enclosure between these extremes. Thus, although we can talk of 'early' enclosure of the Cardiganshire lowlands with some confidence, a miasma of uncertainty descends when we attempt to pin down the origins of field enclosure with more precision, and of the numerous areas of research demanding the attention of future landscape historians in this county, this is among the more pressing.[1]

Most of the county's pre-Conquest forest had been cleared by the late sixteenth century, and a modern traveller in the lowland parishes would have recognized the basic layout of today's farms and landscape features. The frequent mention by name of many of these farms in medieval and early modern documents lends strength to the argument that present-day holdings whose architecture bespeaks a Victorian origin may, in some cases, represent the culmination of at least a millennium of more-or-less continuous husbandry. Excavation, documentary search and fieldwork will help to prove the point. Our traveller may also have noted, perhaps with some regret, that incursions were already being made into the two remaining great tracts of forest, the Fforest yr Esgob in the south-western part of Llanddewibrefi parish and the wooded area straddling the Teifi between the latter parish and Llanwnnen. These were to disappear almost entirely in the

---

[1]For details, see S. Thomas, 'Land occupation, ownership, and utilisation in the parish of Llansantffraid', *Ceredigion*, III, no.2 (1957), 125; C. Thomas, 'Place-name studies and agrarian colonization in North Wales', *WHR*, 10, no.2 (1980), 162; B. Howells, 'Open fields and farmsteads in Pembrokeshire', *PH*, 31 (1971), 10–11; M. I. Williams, *The Making of the South Wales Landscape* (London, 1975), pp.139–42; B. Howells, 'Social and agrarian change in early modern Cardiganshire', *Ceredigion*, VII, nos.3–4 (1974–5), 256; D. Huw Owen (ed.), *Settlement and Society in Wales* (Cardiff, 1989); R. J. Moore-Colyer, 'Farms and fields in nineteenth-century Wales: the case of Llanrhystud, Cardiganshire', *NLWJ*, XXI, no.1 (1989), 32–57.

seventeenth century due to the inexorable expansion of agriculture and the growth of the lead mining industry.[2]

Two centuries later most of the remaining open lowlands of Cardiganshire had been enclosed either by way of mutual agreement between landholders or by private Act of Parliament. The uplands, after growing cereals for Bronze Age farmers and providing summer grazings under the *hafod/hendre* system, had long since sunk into a state of dereliction and, apart from small enclosures associated with *hafodydd* or squatters' dwellings, they remained for the most part open and unimproved. Great blocks of intractable peat covered the higher hills, while the wetter uplands were the preserve of rushes, and large expanses of the drier slopes played host to thousands of acres of pernicious, inedible bracken. Such was the 'waste', the land beyond the limits of cultivation, which was soon to receive the attention of the enclosure surveyor. The potential value of the 'waste', comprising over 20 per cent of England and Wales in 1801, was brought sharply into focus during the Napoleonic Wars as both Parliament and people came to realize the fundamental importance of food security.[3] So great was public concern that, to many, the conquest of the 'waste' became almost synonymous with the conquest of France and, with the passing of the General Inclosure Act of 1801, an intensified assault on the waste was launched.[4] Piecemeal attempts had already been made to 'improve' hill land and to drain lowland marshes on various estates throughout the kingdom, with Cardiganshire's major contributor being Thomas Johnes of Hafod, whose efforts to enhance the productivity of the hills above Devil's Bridge had been widely acclaimed.[5] The value of agricultural products in the years preceding the price inflation brought about by the wars with France had not, however, been sufficiently high to justify the heavy capital sums required for wasteland renovation, and landlords with cash to spare had preferred to invest in Government funds or industrial projects which usually yielded a higher return than investment in land improvement. But dramatic improvements in the fortunes of wartime agriculture and thus increased estate rental income effected a complete change of attitude. Money deposited in Government securities now yielded a mere 6 per cent return compared to a return of 20 per cent on capital investment in enclosure and consequently the move to enclose was greatly accelerated.[6]

In Wales further impetus to enclosure and reclamation both of upland and lowland 'wastes' came from growing population pressure. Regardless of short-term fluctuations, the population of the county had steadily increased from around 17,000 in the mid-sixteenth century to some 43,000 in 1801.[7] Since there were at this time few alternatives to farming as a means of earning a living, people clamoured for the creation of more farm units, while growing family sizes imposed pressure

[2]See W. Linnard, *Welsh Woods and Forests; History and Utilisation* (Cardiff, 1989), passim.

[3]M. I. Williams, 'The enclosure and reclamation of waste land: England and Wales in the eighteenth and nineteenth centuries', *TIBG*, 51 (1970), 57–64; J. Chapman, *A Guide to Parliamentary Enclosures in Wales* (Cardiff, 1992), pp.49–57.

[4]The smooth passage of the General Inclosure Act through Parliament was aided by the report of a select committee sponsored by the first Board of Agriculture. Subsequently, the 1845 Inclosure Act gave rise to the appointment of the Inclosure Commissioners who, in 1851, were incorporated with the Tithe and Copyhold Commissioners. This body had become the Land Commission by 1882.

[5]R. J. Colyer, 'The Hafod Estate under Thomas Johnes and Henry Pelham, Fourth Duke of Newcastle', *WHR*, 8, no.4 (1977), 257–84.

[6]J. D. Chambers and G. Mingay, *The Agricultural Revolution* (London, 1967), p.84.

[7]Howells, 'Social and agrarian change', 258–9; A. J. Parkinson, 'Wheat, peat and lead: settlement patterns in west Wales, 1500–1800', *Ceredigion*, X, no.2 (1985), 111–19.

on the incomes of existing holdings. To some extent this potentially explosive 'land hunger' situation was defused by permanent migration to the industrial south or emigration to America or the Imperial dominions. But the chronic problem remained and the only feasible solution seemed to be to enclose the upland and lowland commons and so provide an opportunity for carving out more individual farm holdings. The occupiers of these holdings, it was believed, would bring an increased acreage into cultivation, improve the quality of pasture land, and eventually benefit from the rapidly growing urban markets of south Wales and the English Midlands.

For generations 'squatting' on common or waste land had been for many people an alternative to destitution. The offspring of large families, lead miners, craftsmen, wool workers and many others, saw the occupation of a few acres of common land as a means of securing a supply of food, which would be extremely valuable during periods of escalating prices. Although illegal and officially frowned upon, squatting was actively encouraged by some landlords keen to extend the limits of their own property. Indeed, in Cardiganshire, where almost two-thirds of the uplands comprised Crown land, owners of several of the larger estates, including Hafod and Nanteos, were quite prepared to encroach – often on a large scale – by unlawfully extending their boundary fences. But, so far as commons enclosure was concerned, the small squatters with their *tŷ-unnos* dwellings and encroachments along the edge of the waste created the biggest problem.[8] If manorial courts were often prepared to admit encroachments where proper application to the court had been made, illegal squatting was generally resisted on the grounds of violation of farmers' common rights. The latter were equivocal in their attitude towards squatters. Concerned though they were with the infringement of their grazing rights, many took the view that squatter holdings, by providing a living of sorts for poor families, would reduce the burden of poor rates, a substantial proportion of which came from farmers' pockets. Others were afraid to take action against the squatters, whom they saw as an unruly and violent element in the community, for fear that to do so would jeopardize both their own physical safety and that of the sheep and cattle grazing the commons.

Landowners unsympathetic to the cause of the squatters entertained no such fears, and by legal, quasi-legal and coercive measures strove actively (often in concert with their tenants in whom common rights were vested) to remove the intruders.[9] Commoners themselves deeply resented any attempt to deprive them of rights held 'since time out of mind' and efforts to promote local enclosure created an undercurrent of bitterness and discontent which often erupted into rioting and physical abuse of the perpetrators of the enclosure. Subsequent to the enclosure of common lands near Nanteos in 1819, William Powell, owner of the estate, built a farm on one of his allotments, thereby incurring the wrath of the ex-commoners. 'The man who inhabited it received intimation that if he did not quit they would burn it about his ears; they were as good as their word for during his absence they threw out all his furniture and burn't the house.'[10] John Hughes, the surveyor appointed by the commissioners who proposed to enclose the uplands around Llanrhystud, was so

[8]C. Thomas, 'Colonisation, enclosure and the rural landscape', *NLWJ*, XIX, no.2 (1935), 135–7; R. U. Sayce, 'Popular enclosures and the one-night house', *MC*, XLVII (1941–2), 112–14; *Select Committee on Commons Inclosure*, 1844, BPP, VII, pp.441–2; D. Williams, 'Rhyfel y Sais Bach; an enclosure riot on Mynydd Bach', *Ceredigion*, II, no.1 (1952), 39–52.
[9]Strategies adopted by the Trawsgoed estate office are exemplified in the agent John Beynon's struggles with squatters in the Llanfihangel-y-Creuddyn district (NLW Crosswood Deeds and Documents I, 1182, 1184, 1185; II, 663).
[10]NLW Llidiardau MSS (unnumbered), Elizabeth to George Parry.

Fig. 13: Gogerddan and its Park, 1822. (*Copyright National Library of Wales*).

terrified by the threats of the commoners' womenfolk who attacked him, ' . . . in half Squadrons, well-equipped, strongly organised and defended as to the breast by a dripping pan which acted as a cuirass and armed with missile weapons of all description', that he was disinclined to proceed with the work.[11]

The struggle to resist enclosure, catalysed by poverty, population pressure and a suspicion that the end result would be an inequitable redistribution of the enclosed territory, represents a fine example of the determination of the peasantry to defend its traditional rights. Yet, throughout the course of the nineteenth century, enclosure went ahead and resistance steadily declined as increasing numbers of people found employment in the industrial south and others came to realize the pointlessness of opposing what could not be avoided. Allocation of enclosed land may, in many cases, have been inequitable, payment of tithe on enclosures may have been unpalatable to a predominantly Nonconformist community, and illiterate squatters may have been unable to substantiate rightful claims. But enclosure was virtually inevitable and, indeed, was welcomed by

[11]NLW Nanteos Letter Books. The long and violent resistance of the Cardiganshire peasantry to the enclosure of common and 'waste' land is highlighted by the celebrated case of Augustus Brackenbury, the Lincolnshire man who purchased land from the commissioners of the Llanrhystud Mefenydd Enclosure in 1819. See W. J. Lewis, 'A disturbance on Llanrhystud Mountain', *Ceredigion*, IV, no.3 (1962), 312–13; D. J. V. Jones, 'More light on "Rhyfel y Sais Bach" ', ibid., V, no.1 (1964), 84–93.

many, including smaller occupiers who readily seized the opportunity to increase the size of their holdings. This applied equally to those squatters able to prove or purchase legal title and thereby join the growing band of small owner-occupiers.[12]

In other localities, however sympathetic commissioners may have been, the allotment of enclosed commons received by tenant farmers and cottagers alike often failed to compensate for the forfeiture of grazing rights, a matter of major significance within a predominantly pastoral agricultural situation. By limiting the scope of summer grazing available to the individual farmer, enclosure cut back his stock-carrying capacity, causing many contemporaries to argue that the creation of new upland farms considerably reduced the value of adjacent lower-lying holdings. Furthermore, many of these, close to the margin of the *ffridd*, tended to be absorbed into the new farms as the long stone walls and rectilinear enclosures were etched upon the face of the common land.

Throughout Britain as a whole, consolidation by enclosure is generally assumed to have acted as a stimulant to agrarian change, particularly where the enclosed land was occupied by forward-looking entrepreneurial farmers.[13] It is highly improbable, in view of the primitive state of upland farming in nineteenth-century Cardiganshire, that the mere division of hill or common with stone walls or quickset hedges effected any widespread improvement in productivity. The creation by landlords of more compact holdings by means of sale and exchange might be argued to have enhanced overall management efficiency, and enclosure *per se* may have enabled some measure of grazing control, but any general improvement was probably limited by technical factors. Put simply, the carving out of enclosed farms in the uplands was accompanied neither by advances in methods of pasture and arable land improvement nor, to any great extent, by improvements in the genetics of livestock. In fact, despite the work of Thomas Johnes of Hafod, it was only with the scientific and technological developments of the first half of the twentieth century that the hill farms created by upland enclosure were enabled to become truly productive.[14]

Yet this is not to deny that enclosure of the upland and lower-lying 'wastes' may have benefited some farmers, more particularly those who supplied the market with specialist outputs, including wool and dairy products. However *environmentally* marginal 'waste' might have been, a well-enclosed holding would have created an opportunity for the enterprising farmer to improve his husbandry standards and thereby enhance his income. This would have been especially the case where a by-employment enabled him to earn cash, of which a proportion would be available, if he wished it, for investment in his farm. Such a farmer might well have been in a position to overcome a situation of environmental marginality in much the same way as many farmers in the 1970s and 1980s, perceiving the high profits accruing to corn growing, expanded their cereal acreages onto land enjoying a low comparative advantage for the growth of cereal crops. It is perhaps worth making the general point that, in the context of agricultural practices in the past, we should be careful to question the conventional wisdom which tends to place too much emphasis on environmental and demographic determinism at the expense of 'economic' considerations in the broadest sense of that word.

[12]I. Bowen, *The Great Enclosures of Wales* (London, 1814), pp.14–37; A. E. Davies, 'Enclosures in Cardiganshire, 1750–1850', *Ceredigion*, VIII, no.1 (1976), 116.

[13]Chambers and Mingay, *Agricultural Revolution*, pp.95–6; for a full review of this subject and an outline of revisionist arguments, see J. M. Neeson, *Commoners: Common Rights, Enclosure and Social Change in England, 1700–1820* (Cambridge, 1993).

[14]R. J. Colyer, *Man's Proper Study; A History of Agricultural Science Education at Aberystwyth* (Llandysul, 1982), chapter 4.

Farmers and farms

Richard Jefferies, that astute and elegant commentator on the English countryside, frequently wrote of the changelessness of nature which was mirrored in the attitudes of men who lived and worked on the land. 'Go out among them', he advised, 'and collect from the majority their views and sentiments and in this age of progress they will be found to correspond almost exactly with those of their forefathers as recorded by history.'[15] This conservatism and concern with the preservation of traditional lore, cultural attitudes and farming methods is central to the cohesion of most peasant communities wherein physical and psychological security is considered essential for survival. Suspicious of outsiders and distrustful of change, such societies view the entrepreneur and the model farmer as disruptive forces whose activities, however beneficial they may be to the individual concerned, constitute a threat to the majority whose daily lives are dictated by the old order, old methods and old customs. Moreover, where a considerable amount of the agricultural work is carried out by community self-help, individuality might be viewed as a negation of traditional obligations towards society.[16] As in medieval England, where the communal organization of agriculture restricted individual initiative and thus the flow of investment, community involvement within several sectors of farming may have been one of the factors responsible for the persistence of so-called 'hereditary prejudices' in the Welsh countryside in the eighteenth and nineteenth centuries. After all, though a society based upon mutual dependence cemented by genetic relationships provides security against most disasters, and a bulwark against the adverse flow of fate, it rarely allows full rein to the innovator.

Contemporary observers in the eighteenth and nineteenth centuries almost universally condemned the conservative attitude prevailing among Welsh farmers and expended a great deal of effort criticizing the agricultural community.[17] While resistance to change may be ascribed in part to so-called 'peasant mentality', this argument must not be pushed so far as to deny the existence of other considerations, of which shortage of capital was one of the more important. Among the smaller farmers, whose income derived primarily from the sale of livestock and livestock products, relatively little remained to build up capital reserves after living expenses, rent and restocking charges (and occasionally ex-farm investment payments) had been met. This, combined with climatic conditions, was a significant factor limiting the spread of the turnip crop in the county, the annual growing costs of which amounted to £6 4s. 0d. per acre in the mid-nineteenth century.[18] A farmer contemplating the adoption of such a crop or, indeed any new technique or technology with

---

[15] R. Jefferies, *The Toilers of the Field* (London, 1892), p.46.

[16] See, for example, G. Hunter in A. H. Bunting (ed.), *Change in Agriculture* (London, 1970), pp.26–8; M. M. Postan, *The Medieval Economy and Society* (London, 1975), pp.46–8.

[17] Typified in J. Evans, *Letters written through . . . South Wales* (London, 1804), p.322 and in the frustrations of the Hafod agent, Hall W. Keary (University of Nottingham MSS Nec 8684). More recently, Daniel Parry-Jones has neatly summarized the problem of 'hereditary prejudice' in his anecdote of the enraged Cardiganshire farmer who found that his sons had defied tradition by borrowing a cart to shift a pile of manure instead of using the venerable time-honoured sledge. 'The notion of time saving threw his mind into a state of confusion', observed Parry-Jones, 'it meant the replanning of the whole year's work and he was not equal to it' (*My Own Folk*, Llandysul, 1972, p.80).

[18] T. Morgan, *An Essay on the Systems of Agriculture . . . in Carmarthenshire* (Carmarthen, 1852, pp.17–18.

high capital and recurrent costs, would need to be convinced that the investment would be justified by a high return. In the eastern and southern counties of Wales, where soil conditions and climate were suited to the crop and where a generally higher level of agrarian prosperity prevailed, the turnip culture was widely adopted by 1800. In Cardiganshire, however, the wet, acid soils were on the whole unfavourable both to the growth of the plant and to folding the crop with sheep, and farmers were understandably reluctant to commit money to the system. Besides, many were wedded to the concept of on-farm self-sufficiency so that even though they may have been *aware* of the value of a turnip crop within the farm rotation, the planting of turnips would have necessitated a reduction in cereal acreage and thus of the subsistence base.

Terrain and climate apart, a further reason for the widespread adherence to outdated agricultural methods was the fear that any attempt to improve productivity would be swiftly followed by demands from landlords for an increase in rent. If this was the case, there is little evidence for it in the historical record and where it is possible to identify an 'improving' farmer and follow his rent payments through estate records, there is no evidence to sustain the argument that rent increases followed farmer initiative *unless* the landlord himself had been party to the improvement. In cases where a landlord invested in farm infrastructure he would quite reasonably expect a return on his capital in the form of increased rent since this investment created conditions whereby potential farm productivity, and hence farm income, would rise. The Welsh Land Commissioners, in the closing years of the nineteenth century, found little justification for the complaints that landlords penalized enterprising tenants by advancing their rents, a conclusion supported by evidence from the rentals and accounts of a whole range of estates in the county.

The historiography of west Wales in the eighteenth and nineteenth centuries places heavy, and perhaps undue, emphasis upon the opposition of practical farmers to technical change and technological 'improvements'. Yet this was a common theme throughout the kingdom wherein, by the later years of the eighteenth century, there were so many ideas abroad that it was extremely difficult to differentiate between those based on sound common sense and others which were little more than the hare-brained schemes of wealthy gentlemen with more money than practical wisdom. As the wild theories of Justus von Liebig and other equally absurd notions became widely propounded (with little experimental justification), the growing body of agricultural chemists and their associates came to be viewed with contempt by practical farmers whose accumulated wisdom they had chosen to ignore. The working farmer whose capital, as Edmund Burke had pointed out, 'is more feeble than commonly imagined', had too much to lose to bother himself with the unproven experiments of so-called scientists and gentlemen amateurs. The latter, pronounced the farmer and scientist John Bennett Lawes in 1846, 'have endeavoured to account for, and sometimes to pronounce as erroneous, the knowledge which ages of experience have established; and they have attempted to generalise without the practical data necessary to accomplish their end with success'.[19]

[19]J. Caird, *The Landed Interest and the Supply of Food* (5th edn., London, 1967), p.57. Besides, many tenants chose to keep their money to themselves, or to contribute to the economic development of the county by investing in coastal trading, fishing, or other sectors of rural industry. In any event, the fact that some farmers died in possession of quite substantial wealth gives lie to the quite erroneous belief that they were, as a class, universally poor and constantly on the brink of penury. See, for details, R. J. Colyer, *The Welsh Cattle Drovers* (Cardiff, 1976); R. J. Moore-Colyer, 'Of lime and men: aspects of the coastal trade in lime in south-west Wales in the eighteenth and nineteenth centuries', *WHR*, 14, no.1 (1988), 54–77.

By the mid-nineteenth century, there were rather more than half a million farms in England and Wales, of which 70 per cent were under 50 acres in size, and many of these were located in Wales.[20] In this county, in the late eighteenth and early nineteenth centuries, farm size probably averaged around 100 acres, with the smaller, more compact estates in lower-lying areas having a higher proportion of smaller holdings. Thus at Cilgwyn, Llanllŷr and Noyadd, 60 per cent of farms occupied fewer than 100 acres compared with 37 per cent at Nanteos, Gogerddan and Trawsgoed, estates which embraced a large acreage of hill land.[21] By the closing years of the nineteenth century, the smallest unit in south-west Cardiganshire capable of supporting a man and his wife without a regular source of supplementary income was reckoned to be 30 to 35 acres. Such holdings, with their own sets of cultivation and hauling equipment, could be effectively worked with a single pair of horses. Below these was a large substratum of smaller farms occupied by people with by-employment who, more often than not, owed harvest obligations to larger farms in return for cultivation or carrying services. Finally there was the *lle buwch* smallholding, the first rung on the farming ladder, usually under the tenancy of a craftsman or casual labourer, who would also turn to the larger farms for various services which he would repay by contributing his labour to the harvesting team on that farm.[22]

In 1843 it was estimated that the gross annual output of a moderately large Welsh farm of £60 per year rental amounted to approximately £180, of which £1 weekly remained for general maintenance and the support of the farmer's family after necessary costs had been met.[23] A relatively modest sum which, it must be remembered, was supplemented by home-produced food, this surplus allowed for the accumulation of some savings which, potentially at least, were available for investment in improved farming techniques. The position of the smaller farmer was less satisfactory. Obliged to own and maintain a full set of basic equipment to cultivate his farm, he realized that this was often under-utilized and, despite his limited capital, he was keen to expand so as to spread the fixed costs of his limited acreage. By increasing the scale of operations he could respond to adverse market conditions by farming an increased acreage with a small increase in recurrent costs and he was thus keen to secure the tenancy of an adjacent or nearby unit when such became available. This almost obsessive concern to accumulate more acres, together with the deeply ingrained sense of identity with the land characteristic of west Wales in general, combined to fuel the problem of land hunger which persisted for much of the nineteenth century. Moreover, it had the effect of creating friction in the community as men competed for scarce tenancies and bid rents both beyond their pockets and out of proportion to the productive potential of the land. If the acquisition of further acres by multiple occupation promoted security (and, incidentally, reduced the pressure on family members to emigrate), it also further reduced the total number of holdings available to farmers' sons and others keen to begin farming. The Tithe Apportionment for the parish of Llanrhystud, for example, provides numerous illustrations of multiple occupations of both

---

[20]C. Thomas, 'Estate surveys as sources of historical geography', *NLWJ*, XIV, no.4 (1966), 433; A. Griffiths, 'Agricultural development in south Wales, 1830–1875: the case of some Glamorgan parishes', *Morgannwg*, XVII (1973), 29–30.

[21]R. J. Colyer, 'The size of farms in late eighteenth and early nineteenth-century Cardiganshire', *BBCS*, XXVII, no.1 (1976), 119–26.

[22]D. Jenkins, *The Agricultural Community in South-West Wales at the Turn of the Twentieth Century* (Cardiff, 1971).

[23]*The Welshman*, 22 December 1843.

small and larger farms. Thus in 1839 Richard Evans rented both Blaenperis (32 acres) and Gwarolchfa (56 acres) from Elizabeth Gibbs; Lewis Davies held Blaenyresgair (32 acres) in addition to Esgair Fawr (47 acres), while David Jones of Gilfachafel (182 acres) tenanted adjoining Fachwen (58 acres) and John Jones of Llettygrugiau Uchaf (53 acres) also occupied the adjacent farm of Ffynnonwen (74 acres).

While farming increased acres may, in some cases, have constituted a recipe for survival, it may equally have acted as a disincentive to land improvement. While landlords did not, in most cases, consciously attempt to exploit the phenomenon of land hunger, they were nevertheless tempted to accept the tender of the highest bidder, even though his capital reserves may have been quite inadequate to manage an additional, or larger, farm. Had they been more careful to equate a tenant's capital availability and farming skills with the size and type of holding which he was permitted to occupy, there would have been some likelihood of the latter improving his farm. Instead, he struggled to farm on a larger scale with inadequate capital and was consequently unable to adopt improved methods even if he had wished to do so.

An important effect of multiple occupation of farms was to reduce the total number of holdings available for farmers' sons or others wishing to gain a foothold on the farming ladder. In the southern and eastern districts of Wales, higher wages and the potential for alternative employment eased the pressure on farms, but in early nineteenth-century Cardiganshire there were few realistic alternatives to the land as a means of making a living. True, the lead, woollen and craft industries offered some opportunities, but to a man in search of the security which occupation of a farm provided, these were poor substitutes. Even seasonal migration to Herefordshire to work at the harvest, or the unhappy few months spent each year in the mines and factories of Glamorgan, would be palatable if he knew that his own holding awaited him in his home county. Since the land was the home of the people who had, as the Welsh Land Commission put it, '. . . a kind of moral right to have a means of obtaining thereon their livelihood through life', any threat to traditional links with this land was viewed as a threat to the stability of society itself.[24]

Because labour requirements generally increased by one man for each 50-acre increase in farm size, demand for the smaller farm that could be worked with the minimum of hired help was especially intense. Also, by the 1850s, the comparative advantage of dairy and livestock farming helped to maintain rents on all categories of farms in western Britain at higher levels than those obtaining elsewhere.[25] The overall situation in the county is summarized in Table 4 with reference to the Nanteos and Trawsgoed estates, where rents on the smaller farm tended to remain higher than those of larger units both during the boom years of the Napoleonic Wars and the subsequent period of agrarian depression.

A source of major concern to the rural community was the growing prospect of permanent farm amalgamation on many of the larger estates. In the earlier years of the eighteenth century farms had been let on long leases, often for three lives, during which the burden of building maintenance fell wholly upon the tenant. As the life leases began to terminate towards the end of that century and the beginning of the next, shorter-term leases, wherein the landlord undertook the cost of maintaining

---

[24] *Royal Commission on Land in Wales and Monmouthshire*, Report, 1897, p.332; Moore-Colyer, 'Farms and fields', passim.
[25] J. Caird, *English Agriculture, 1850–51* (London, 1851), p.481.

TABLE 4: Rents per acre

| | Rents per acre of farms on Nanteos Estate | |
Farm size class	1815	1819
0–49 acres	14s. 9d.	11s. 0d.
50–99 acres	12s. 0d.	8s. 9d.
100–49 acres	12s. 3d.	8s. 9d.
150–99 acres	13s. 0d.	8s. 0d.
200–49 acres	7s. 0d.	5s. 0d.
250–99 acres	4s. 0d.	3s. 4d.
300–49 acres	1s. 6d.	1s. 2d.
350–99 acres	1s. 6d.	1s. 0d.

| | Rents per acre on the Trawsgoed Estate | | |
Farm size class	1798	1814	1816
0–49 acres	4s. 6d.	12s. 7d.	9s. 0d.
50–99 acres	3s. 6d.	11s. 0d.	8s.10d.
100–49 acres	2s. 7d.	8s. 2d.	6s. 9d.
150–99 acres	2s. 5d.	9s.11d.	7s. 4d.
200–49 acres	2s. 4d.	10s. 0d.	7s. 5d.
250–99 acres	3s. 3d.	12s. 0d.	7s. 2d.
300–49 acres	2s. 6d.	9s. 2d.	5s. 9d.
Over 350 acres	1s. 7d.	5s. 9d.	4s. 0d.

farm buildings, were introduced and, in view of generations of neglect, landlords found themselves faced with heavy capital expenditure necessary to retrieve these buildings from a state of dereliction. Accordingly there was an inevitable temptation when a lease expired, a farmer quit his holding or a tenant died, for the landlord to amalgamate that farm with an adjacent one, thereby saving on the maintenance costs of several groups of buildings. This attempt to reduce the costs of estate management was a cumulative process by which, over a period of time, a number of farms would be amalgamated, one good set of buildings erected and the new package let to a deserving, financially sound tenant. As the century progressed, some landlords came to regard amalgamation as a means of stimulating more efficient methods of farming, especially in arable areas where the new farm machinery could only be justified on extensive acreages. Moreover, as cottage industries went into decline and changing agricultural technology in England limited the potential for migrant harvest labour, opportunities for part-time employment steadily decreased. Under these circumstances the farmer was increasingly obliged to rely upon his farm as his sole source of income and many landlords rightly realized that the small, ill-equipped farm was no longer able to provide a satisfactory level of income. Hence amalgamation was the first stage in the progress towards larger farms, much in demand in the mid-century following the change from mixed to predominantly grassland farming.

To many smaller tenants, permanent amalgamation was anathema since, as the number of larger farms increased, so the total number of homesteads decreased and many young married couples were compelled to leave the county or even to emigrate. There was widespread sympathy with the view that those brought up on the land had an inalienable right to remain at their own hearths, yet the plain fact was that times were changing and rural society had no alternative but to change accordingly. Deprived of the fruits of his migratory labour, the small tenant could no longer expect to survive on the income from his farm, particularly during periods of depression, and even had no amalgamation occurred, many would have been driven to seek alternative occupations either at home or abroad. The cynical view that amalgamation represented a heartless dereliction of duty on the part of landed proprietors cannot be sustained in the context of the changing conditions of the mid to late nineteenth century wherein the financial position of landlords dictated retrenchment and economy, and socio-political circumstances altered the nature of the traditional relationships between landlord and tenant.

Leases and land tenure

During the first three-quarters of the eighteenth century, farm leases granted by landlords almost invariably spanned a period of three lives, the majority of agreements being in manuscript form or effected by word of mouth. As these were replaced by printed, and often bilingual documents, estate offices sought to use the lease as a means of persuading farmers to pursue good husbandry by adopting rotational farming and other beneficial measures. As time went by, husbandry clauses became more sophisticated, and leases granted both for a series of lives and a term of years imposed limitations as to the acreage of certain crops to be grown, a complete prohibition of the deleterious practice of 'paring and burning', and, in many cases, specific instructions regarding the use of turnips or leys as breaks in continuous cereal cultivation. In addition, agreements frequently aimed to ensure that farmers did not cultivate more land within a given year than they could effectively manure. Such was the case at Trawsgoed, Cilgwyn, Allt-lwyd, Derry Ormond, Castle Hill and Hafod, all of which estates had adopted the printed agreement by the 1850s.

The printed agreement, with its husbandry clauses and stipulations as to the division of responsibility between landlord and tenant with regard to building repair and general improvements, had many theoretical advantages. Yet there remained formidable difficulties in persuading tenants to keep to their agreements, in particular where the adoption of rotational farming was concerned.[26] Equally difficult was the enforcement of the ancient food and service rents which remained a particular feature of tenancy agreements on many estates until late into the nineteenth century. These were, of course, extremely useful in the maintenance of a gentleman's household and, between 1876 and 1878, the owners of Gogerddan benefited from their tenants to the extent of 21 days 'carriage' duty, 12 turkeys, 56 geese, 12 ducks, 628 fowls, 2 tongues and no fewer than 2,570 eggs.[27] The continued insistence by landlords upon part-payment of rent by way of antiquated food or service dues must have done little to improve landlord/tenant relations. Indeed, it is evident that tenants resented the servility and dependence implied by this system, especially by the late

[26]As the Nanteos agents reported to their masters with almost tedious frequency; see, for example, NLW Nanteos Letter Books, Hugh Hughes to W. E. Powell, 9 May 1812; John Hughes to W. E. Powell, 14 May 1812.
[27]NLW Gogerddan MSS Box O. For other examples, see NLW MSS 36–45 and NLW Crosswood Deeds and Documents, passim.

nineteenth century when many of them had come to disregard notions of paternalism and to insist that relations with their landlords were of a strictly business nature.

As the eighteenth-century leases for lives began to fall in, there was a tendency throughout Wales to replace them by leases of seven, fourteen or twenty-one years, and, eventually, to substitute for the lease the simple annual tenancy. Cardiganshire mirrored the overall situation so that although the Trawsgoed and Noyadd Trefawr estates were still granting some life leases as late as 1850, most estates had progressed through the lease of a term of years to the annual tenancy.[28] The life lease system, wherein farms were let at the low rents prevailing a century earlier, was all very well in a situation where prices and profits varied little from year to year, but it did not enable landlords to share in the rich profits enjoyed by many farmers in the Napoleonic War years. Accordingly landowners eagerly awaited the termination of long leases in order to impose annual tenancies at a more realistic level of rent, notwithstanding that the profitability of Cardiganshire pastoral farming by no means approached that of the arable regions of England or the southern and eastern regions of Wales.

Yet the trend towards annual tenancies did not negate family succession, which tended to become the rule rather than the exception, with most landowners in the county permitting the succession of a hard-working and dedicated son or widow. In 1800 Lletyllwyd on the Gogerddan estate was occupied by Richard James at a yearly rent of £60. In 1808 he was succeeded by his wife Anne, the rent being increased to £85 in 1811 and subsequently reduced to £75 in 1813, when Thomas James assumed the management of the holding. Twelve years later his brother Richard took over and was himself succeeded by a maiden sister, who continued to run the farm until 1871 at an annual rent of £72.[29]

Mainly for sentimental reasons, some contemporaries deplored the termination of the long lease system, but landlords were only too happy to greet the end of an arrangement which gave tenants their farms at a more-or-less nominal rent, thereby providing very little stimulus towards better farm management. 'Although the cry is for leases', wrote Robert Gardiner, the Trawsgoed agent in 1869, 'proprietors are justified in wishing the tenants to give some evidence of their desire and intention to do more than they have hitherto done before granting leases. This is all the more necessary when one has so many poor, lazy and indifferent tenants so thickly sown over the country.'[30] Agricultural considerations apart, the replacement of the lease by the yearly tenancy helped to strengthen the political control of landlords over their tenants. The passing of the Reform Act of 1832 extended the franchise, previously only enjoyed by the lessee, to the annual tenant paying rent in excess of £50. Thus it was clearly in the landlord's interest to adjust to an annually renewable tenancy agreement so to secure a degree of political control over his tenants which he could exert if he felt moved to do so. There is evidence, too, that by the 1840s the tenants themselves usually expressed a distinct preference for the annual tenancy which relieved them of the need to carry out farm repairs at their own cost. This apart, the long lease arrangements had committed tenants to long-term rent

[28]By 1839 only two of the fifty-two Tŷ-glyn tenants held leases for lives, while at Nanteos 90 per cent of tenants held short-term leases in 1815, with most of those being converted to annual tenancies over the next decade (NLW Tyglyn MS 28).

[29]Numerous other examples of family succession upon death or retirement of farmers are given in Moore-Colyer, 'Farms and fields', passim.

[30]NLW Nanteos MSS, R. Gardiner to Captain Phelp, 14 December 1869.

agreements during periods of financial uncertainty, besides affording them less opportunity of obtaining rent abatements in hard times than was the case with the annual tenancy.

Nevertheless, as radical writers tirelessly complained, farmers enjoyed neither legal security of tenure nor provision for tenant right before the passing of the Agricultural Holdings Acts of 1875 and 1883. For centuries the medieval concept of *quidquid solo plantatur solo cedit* had implied that whatever improvements a tenant might make would automatically pass to his landlord upon the former's quitting his holding, and that the landlord had no strict legal obligation to compensate his outgoing tenant for these improvements. In reality, local custom and common sense provided some relief. In Glamorgan, for example, a customary arrangement geared to a complex system of compensation to the outgoing tenant for crops in the ground and unexhausted manurial value had long been in operation.[31] The 'Glamorgan Custom', or at least a modified form of it, was in operation on many estates in Cardiganshire throughout the first three-quarters of the nineteenth century, stimulated, perhaps, by Thomas Johnes's practice of compensating tenants for unexhausted manurial residues when they relinquished their tenancies on the Hafod estate. By 1850 Gogerddan tenants enjoyed compensation for manures applied throughout the last five years of their occupation, a procedure followed at Trawsgoed, Nanteos, Tan-y-bwlch and Castle Hill by the seventies. On the latter estate the landlord undertook to pay an outgoing tenant the *actual* cost of clover and ryegrass sown the previous spring, along with two-thirds of the value of existing crops of corn, hay and turnips. At the same time, the Cilgwyn estate paid both full compensation for unexhausted manures and half the cost of lime applied during the final two years of the tenancy, together with one-third of the value of any oilcake fed to cattle and sheep over the previous twelve months. It appears, then, that while many landlords contracted out of the provisions of the 1875 Act, and, in some cases, did not widely apply the 1883 Act (as their tenancy agreements bear witness), they did effect their own arrangements for compensating outgoing tenants. Having agreed to compensate tenants in this way, landlords attempted, by contributing both towards capital and recurrent expenses, to stimulate improved farm management. On the Mynachdy estate in the 1830s, the landlord bore the full cost of drainage works and half the cost of lime purchase, while at Castle Hill and Derry Ormond building works were undertaken with estate capital and tenants' labour. This was so at Gogerddan in the 1850s, although by the 1880s the estate provided both materials *and* labour for the construction of new farm buildings and the maintenance of existing structures. A somewhat different arrangement operated at Trawsgoed whereby tenants erecting their own buildings were granted allowances against their annual rents.

Yet tenants enjoyed no *legal* security of tenure and despite a tendency for family succession on the older and larger estates, the annual tenancy system still implied lack of security. This was particularly acute among tenants holding land on estates bought in the 1870s and 1880s by rich *arrivistes*, many of whom attempted to run their estates along commercial lines and to insist upon a reasonable return, in terms of rent, upon capital invested.[32]

---

[31] A. W. Jones, 'Glamorgan custom and tenant right', *AGHR*, 31, no.1 (1983), 1–13; J. R. Fisher, 'Landowner and tenant right, 1845–52', ibid., 31, no.1 (1983), 15–24.
[32] D. Howell, *Land and People in Nineteenth-Century Wales* (London, 1978).

Rents

The passing of the old life-lease system and its replacement by shorter-term tenancy arrangements, combined with the inbuilt phenomenon of land hunger, caused agricultural rents in the county to remain higher on a per acre basis than those obtaining in many other parts of England and Wales. By taking on a farm at a high level of rent, a farmer was, in theory at least, obliged to manage his land in as intensive a manner as possible if he were effectively to meet rent demands and provide for the needs of himself and his family. However, given the run-down state of farms on many estates at the beginning of the nineteenth century, 'high' farming – if technically feasible on the particular soil type – was only possible where extensive improvements to basic farm infrastructure were undertaken. While this was possible in situations where tenants were prepared to match a landlord's capital investment with resources of their own, few were willing to do so, with the result that income remained at relatively low levels and farmers complained with monotonous regularity of their inability to meet rent demands. Protestations of poverty were often merely contrivances to delay rent payments, yet the letters of estate agents frequently refer to the need to postpone the rent audit until after the local fair, when farmers would have the opportunity to sell livestock as a means of raising cash to pay the rent. Thus, on the August Rent Day of 1831, the Nanteos agent wrote that he was 'ashamed what little I received and gave them until another Rhos Fair to see what that would do for them'. A year later, he wrote: 'Your tenants have, I am inclined to think, presumed too much of my dread of distraining as I can only get promises from them. The Rent Day being so near at hand . . . I am disposed to give them the opportunity of disposing of their pigs at the fair about this time and not employing the men of law to proceed.'[33]

The fortunes of arable farming reached an unprecedented peak in the inflationary years of the Napoleonic Wars. Most farmers grew a little corn, primarily for consumption on the farm, but they were not really in a position to take advantage of the opportunities offered by high wartime prices since they lacked both the technical ability to grow cereal crops efficiently and, in most cases, enough suitable land to do so on a large scale. Those who persisted with traditional stock-rearing gained some advantage from increased livestock prices, although the price advance in this quarter was less dramatic than that in the arable sector. But as far as estate administrators were concerned, farming in the county was booming and rents of both small and large estates advanced on the crest of this boom. Rent rolls at Cilgwyn, Mynachdy and Abermeurig grew substantially during the war years, while on the northern parts of the Nanteos and Gogerddan estates rents reached their wartime peaks of £7,331 and £7,119 respectively in 1815 and 1811. At Trawsgoed, the largest estate in the county, income from rents almost trebled, from a mere £4,032 in 1798 to a massive £11,286 in 1814.

The inflationary bubble eventually burst with the peace following Waterloo. The inevitable agrarian depression followed, with falling cereal and livestock prices being catalysed by declining demand for food consequent upon the unemployment ushered in by the arrival of 400,000 ex-servicemen onto an already shrinking labour market.[34] Although there were noticeably fewer

---

[33]NLW Nanteos Letter Books. For further details, see R. J. Colyer, 'Some aspects of land occupation in nineteenth-century Cardiganshire', *THSC* (1981), 79–97.
[34]E. L. Jones, *The Development of English Agriculture, 1815–1873* (London, 1968), pp.11–13.

Fig. 14: Nanteos and its Park, 1854. (*Copyright National Library of Wales*).

complaints of 'depression' from the livestock areas of Britain than from those whose fortunes were based on arable crops, Cardiganshire farmers were eventually exposed to generally unfavourable livestock prices throughout most of the 1820s and 1830s, more especially when demand for lean cattle in the grazing regions of England was in decline.[35]

If landlords were to avoid the embarrassment of having farms thrown 'into hand' during periods of depression, they were forced to assist their tenants in maintaining solvency, and various methods were adopted to achieve this objective. At Nanteos, arrears of rent were often allowed to accumulate during times of hardship; these were frequently written off by the estate when it became clear that it was useless to insist upon payment if this meant the farms being abandoned by their tenants. Temporary abatements were also granted, so that by 1826 the Nanteos rental had declined to 83 per cent of its 1808 level and continued to remain below the 1808 level over the next decade. Conversely, at Gogerddan, notwithstanding abatements and the accumulation of arrears, the total rental in 1818 still exceeded the 1800 figure by 50 per cent. This was due principally to the obsessive concern of tenants to maintain a hold upon their 'ancestral' farms as the three-life leases fell in, albeit at a substantially advanced rent, which, for the first time in generations, was set at a realistic

[35]For further details, see Colyer, *Welsh Cattle Drovers*, chapter 2.

level. During the immediate post-war years, abatements were widespread, being granted in some cases voluntarily and in others as a direct result of pressure from tenants, so that when the Derry Ormond tenants threatened to quit their farms *en masse* in 1816, they succeeded in securing a substantial abatement.[36] Adam Murray, reporting to the Lord Chancellor on the moribund condition of the lunatic Earl of Lisburne's Trawsgoed estate, observed that the tenants could not meet the prevailing level of rent and unless an abatement were given there was a distinct possibility that many would quit their holdings. This directly resulted in a reduction in the rental of the estate from £11,286 to £9,044.[37] On the small Abermeurig estate, where an overall cash allowance of five shillings in the pound was returned to tenants between 1816 and 1820, the owner was careful to maintain some flexibility in tenancy agreements to allow for adjustments in the event of improved agrarian conditions. On 12 August 1816, the rent for Dyffryn was set at £160, '. . . if the corn and cattle and butter sell at greater prices on the 12 of May next, then £170'.[38] The return of a proportion of the rent to the tenants during times of depression, or the 'allowance' as it is often termed in estate rentals, was, of course, similar to the abatement. It was essentially a temporary affair which could be withdrawn when agrarian conditions improved or, less often, when the landlord could no longer afford to lose this proportion of his income. For reasons of self-interest or a genuine concern for the well-being of their tenants, most landlords were aware of the importance of periodic assistance of this kind.

Despite the depressed agrarian conditions of the early years and the temporary abatements granted, the period between the mid-1830s and the mid-1870s witnessed a general upward trend in estate rental income, due to the transfer from leasehold to annual tenancy, and a general revaluation of farm rents in the light of improved agricultural profitability after 1850. Rents at Trawsgoed had reached £10,084 by 1850, and increased by a further £3,000 over the next thirty years, while at Gogerddan rents advanced from £6,446 to £11,810 between 1852 and 1880.[39] A rather less dramatic increase occurred at Nanteos, from a trough in 1826 when rental income was a mere £4,866, to £6,093 in 1850 and a peak of £7,192 in 1873, the year in which extensive sales of land reduced annual income for subsequent years by rather more than £2,500. It is significant that, on this particular estate, the highest post-Napoleonic War rental income was actually less than the annual rent collected in 1815. As in the early post-war years, the intermittent agrarian crises of the remainder of the century prompted frequent abatements of rent, so that Cilgwyn tenants enjoyed a 'considerable abatement' in 1822, while their counterparts at Hafod, who paid annual rents in excess of £5, were granted a 10 per cent allowance in 1844.[40] In the same year, John Lloyd Davies of Alltyrodyn actually lowered his rents in the order of 30, 25 and 15 per cent, according to the situation and state of husbandry of the farm. 'Upon a low farm', he remarked, 'I have thought five per cent sufficient or no reduction at all; but on a high farm affected by bad seasons I have given much more.'[41] By arranging to reduce rents on a selective basis, a procedure adopted on certain English estates, he was able to encourage those tenants who had attempted to manage their farms

[36]NLW Derry Ormond MS 206.
[37]Crosswood Deeds and Documents, 6578.
[38]NLW, J. E. Rogers Lewis Deposit, 1971.
[39]NLW Crosswood and Gogerddan rentals.
[40]University of Nottingham MSS, Nec 8574.
[41]Commission of Enquiry in South Wales, *BPP*, XVI, 1844, p.5.

according to the tenets of good husbandry. Rent reductions, as opposed to temporary abatements or allowances, were relatively rare. The problem was that, however willing a landlord may have been to make a permanent reduction in his rents, his own financial burdens in the form of mortgage interest payments and annuities usually prevented this, unless, like Lloyd Davies, he enjoyed a comfortable non-landed income. In the early 1840s, when the Nanteos agent proposed a 12 per cent reduction in rents as opposed to an annual allowance, which he believed 'would give them confidence and induce them to do justice to their lands and cultivate them with greater spirit', his employer, whose estates were teetering on the verge of financial collapse, was unable to afford a rent reduction, preferring instead to give a 10 per cent annual allowance and to bear the expense of the property tax and highway rates.[42]

The combination of climatic, mercantile and economic factors which culminated in the 'Great Depression' of the early 1880s had little initial effect in the livestock-rearing areas of Wales. Imports of foreign grain had precipitated the collapse of cereal prices and the ruin of many arable farmers, but imports of meat had had, as yet, little effect upon domestic prices. By the mid-1880s, however, the development of refrigerated ships facilitated the cheap and rapid transport of carcass meat from America and elsewhere, so that imports gained a growing share of the market and became increasingly influential in the determination of domestic prices. The growing availability of cheap, albeit poor quality, imported meat soon began to influence the prices of store cattle and sheep by bringing about a reduction in the demand for lean animals from graziers and fatteners. To the Cardiganshire farmer, this inevitably meant a decline in income and, as livestock prices fell during the mid-1880s, tenants began to clamour for rent abatements. To the landowner, the depression could hardly have occurred at a worse time, with mortgage capital sums being due for payment on many estates, and local and national taxes steadily increasing. Nevertheless, it was desirable to maintain tenants on their farms and the majority of estates offered the usual palliative of temporary abatements. In 1883, before the price slump had begun to take effect, Sir Pryse Pryse of Gogerddan had permitted his tenants, 'who had paid up their rents in full on the proper days', a rent abatement of 10 per cent by way of celebrating the coming of age of his second son. Five years later he granted a 15 per cent abatement, which was originally intended to operate for three years, although it was reduced to 7fi per cent in 1891 on account of a temporary improvement in livestock prices. The year 1892 brought with it a further collapse in prices which induced Sir Pryse to write to his agent from his retreat in St Raphael, permitting a further 10 per cent abatement to tenants whose rents exceeded £20. This was increased to 15 per cent the following year and remained at the same level until the outbreak of the Great War.[43] Nanteos tenants were less generously favoured, being given a 10 per cent allowance in 1880–2 and 1885–9, the same allowance being reintroduced in 1892, reduced to 5 per cent in 1897, and withdrawn in 1899. Continual rent abatements, of course, inevitably led to reduced incomes on both large and small estates. Not only did gross income decline (in the case of Gogerddan from £11,810 in 1880 to £8,466 in 1890), but many years of accumulated rent arrears were written off in despair. Moreover, an increasing volume of land sales,

---

[42]NLW Nanteos Letter Books.
[43]NLW Gogerddan Rentals. For an admirable summary and full bibliography of farming during the 'Great Depression', see R. Perren, *Agriculture in Depression, 1870–1940* (Cambridge, 1995). A. W. Ashby and I. L. Evans, *The Agriculture of Wales and Monmouthshire* (Cardiff, 1944) contains statistical details.

enforced upon a landowner whose reduced rental left insufficient cash to meet annual encumbrances, had the effect of further reducing rents and landed income.

It was argued by the Nonconformist and Liberal lobbies that Welsh landlords failed to respond to the realities of agrarian depression by granting *permanent* reductions in rents along the lines adopted in the arable areas of England. Here rent reductions were designed to encourage tenants to remain on their holdings, thereby ensuring that farms would remain tenantable for the future. On the small Cardiganshire farms, devoted mainly to livestock, relatively little capital in the form of drainage, land improvement and farm buildings had been invested by either party to the tenancy agreement, so that desertion by a tenant would have had less disastrous consequences than would have been the case on the larger arable farm where heavy investment in improvements had been going on for a period of years. Besides, in the few instances where tenants quit their farms, the omnipresent land hunger usually yielded another tenant in due course. Under these conditions, landlords were under less pressure to make permanent rent reductions than their brethren in arable England and, despite the accusation that they exploited the situation by 'screwing up' the rents, they were, by and large, exonerated from this charge by the Welsh Land Commission. Indeed, on the major estates of Cardiganshire there is no substantial evidence that landowners 'squeezed' their tenants for rents any more than was consistent with good estate management.

Farming practice: crop husbandry

Present-day Cardiganshire is first and foremost a pastoral county, the hills and uplands of the north and east being dominated by sheep and cattle rearing and the vales of the south by the dairy farm. The gradual shift from the mixed farming pattern characteristic of the county in early modern times was given impetus by the suppression of border disorder following the Acts of Union (1536–43) and later by the passing of the Irish Cattle Act (1666). Subsequent to the Acts of Union the cattle-droving trade was greatly facilitated and, with the prohibition of livestock imports from Ireland, demand for Welsh cattle by English graziers increased dramatically to the considerable advantage of livestock producers in the county. Even so, corn-growing was by no means abandoned and although livestock sales comprised the mainstay of the agricultural economy, most farmers in both hill and lowland continued to grow a small acreage of cereals until the early years of the twentieth century. Thus, some 50 per cent of land on the Nanteos estate in 1819 was under arable cultivation. Local grain production was vital to the economy of the farm and its household and to the well-being of the local community in general, and, because carry-over stocks were usually only modest, a harvest shortfall was a cause of real concern. Low yields might bring about dramatic local increases in prices, serious nutritional suffering among the poor and, worst of all, a temptation to consume next year's seedcorn which, of course, would reduce subsequent harvest yield. Under these circumstances rioting was commonplace, prayers were offered for better times, and the gentry felt obliged to buy in corn for free distribution to the poor, or, at least, for sale to them at subsidized prices.

Unseasonal weather, in the form of a long dry spring or a wet harvest, could seriously affect cereal yields even on farms where the standard of husbandry was sufficiently high for the establishment of a promising crop at sowing time. But most farmers in the county appear to have been far from exemplary corn growers and, ignoring the basic principles of rotation, were wedded to the idea of growing cereal crops in continued succession until the exhausted soil failed to produce enough grain to repay production costs. As one observer bluntly put it, this practice yielded little more than 'weeds and disappointment'.[44]

By the late eighteenth century forward-looking farmers in the eastern parts of Wales and the Vale of Glamorgan had followed the example of their landlords by introducing the Norfolk Four Course rotation, or one of its many variants, to their farming system. The Norfolk system, in principle, involved the introduction of clover, a legume supplying nitrogen to the soil, and the turnip crop, which provided both a break from cereals and a supply of winter forage for sheep and cattle whose manure would, in turn, nourish subsequent cereal crops. On light, relatively alkaline and well-drained land, the Norfolk system proved an admirable means of integrating livestock and arable enterprises and of ensuring the maintenance of soil fertility. The wet, acidic conditions of the soils of Cardiganshire constituted a major stumbling-block to the successful cultivation of the turnip crop and this, combined with high growing costs and the conservatism of the tenantry, tended to frustrate the attempts of local gentry to introduce crop rotation. Despite offers of premia by the county's Agricultural Society and the persuasive efforts of men like Benjamin Hall of Cilgwyn, who instructed his agent to give a silver cup to 'the tenant who cultivates ye largest part of his farm in ye rotatory system without taking 2 successive crops', farmers continued to resist growing the turnip crop. Although by the 1830s and 1840s some of the more progressive among their numbers had adopted the cultivation of the turnip, and, to a lesser extent, the swede and mangold where soil conditions were favourable, in the main these crops were rejected by the smaller tenant farmer. Indeed, as late as the 1880s, when the profitability of livestock farming had increased relative to that of arable, many tenants in the western parts of Wales still regarded root crop feeding as a fad suited only to 'fancy farmers'.

The type and acreage of cereal crops grown on farms in the eighteenth and nineteenth centuries depended upon local soil conditions, the local topography, the quality of drainage and the extent of the croppable area. Growing cereals was never easy, given the predominance of moist summers, yet most farmers attempted to grow a small acreage of grain crops, predominantly for their own use. It was even considered shameful if a man could not produce his own wheaten or barley bread from his own resources.[45] Wheat occupied in the order of half the arable acreage of Glamorgan and 20 per cent of that of Breconshire in 1800, yet it was relatively uncommon in west Wales, where barley and rye bread was a fundamentally important component of local diet.[46]

The prevalence and distribution of barley was substantially linked to the requirements of the many small brewing concerns around the county, together with those of the farmhouses themselves, the larger of which brewed beer and ale throughout the autumn and winter months. Demand for barley, both for direct consumption in the form of bread or livestock feed and for brewing meant

[44]C. Hassall, *General View of the Agriculture of Pembrokeshire* (London, 1794), p.16.
[45]NLW Glyneiddan MS 91.
[46]D. Thomas, *Agriculture in Wales during the Napoleonic Wars* (Cardiff, 1963), pp.61–7. Due to the limitations of space no consideration has been given to the detailed husbandry of the various crops mentioned in this chapter. I have, however, written at length on this subject in 'Crop husbandry in Wales before the onset of mechanisation', *Folk Life*, 21 (1983), 49–70. Meanwhile, statistical data of both crops and livestock are set out in John Williams, *Digest of Welsh Historical Statistics* (2 vols., The Welsh Office, 1985), vol.I.

that prices in the county were generally maintained at higher levels than the average for Wales as a whole, so that in the event of a bad harvest the poor suffered considerably as prices escalated.

Apart from oats and rye, both widely cultivated in the county in the eighteenth and nineteenth centuries, cereal crops rarely thrive under acidic soil conditions. Accordingly an essential prerequisite of successful corn-growing was the application of appropriate dressings of lime in order to reduce acidity, improve soil structure and facilitate the uptake of nutrients by plant roots. For centuries lime had been widely used throughout the county, either on its own or as a compost with farmyard manure, seaweed and sea-sand. Since lime was seen by many farmers as a kind of universal panacea, there was a tendency towards excessive application, a practice which, under certain circumstances, could induce deficiencies of plant nutrients. The traveller Richard Warner, among others, was well aware of this when he observed that the farmer, ' . . . by his indiscriminate use of it on every sort of soil, . . . misapplies its properties and frequently rather injures than benefits his farm by the mistaken donation'.[47] At the other extreme, inadequate capital, ignorance and burdensome tollgate costs meant that in some areas liming was 'scantily and slovenly done'.[48]

Unlike neighbouring Montgomeryshire, which enjoyed a plentiful supply of limestone from the quarries of Llanymynech, Cardiganshire had no such natural sources and the bulk of the limestone used in the county arrived by sea from Caldey Island, the Gower or south Pembrokeshire. The production of quicklime (calcium oxide) from limestone (calcium carbonate) necessitated burning the raw material with coal or culm in kilns, of which there were a number along the coastline, owned either by merchants or groups of farmers.[49]

Farmers from the southern parishes could, if they so wished, buy ready-prepared slaked lime from Llandybïe in Carmarthenshire or from Cardigan town, but besides being expensive, loads of slaked lime incurred heavy tollgate costs in the cross-country journey back to the farm. Toll payments on lime were a major cause of annoyance and in addition to contributing significantly to the discontent which eventually erupted in the Rebecca Riots, the levying of toll on lime reduced the amount of the material used and, in effect, limited agricultural productivity. The more enlightened local gentry were well aware of this, as exemplified by the correspondence in 1797 between W. P. Lloyd of Glansefin and John Phillips, Cwmgwili, wherein the former argued that if lime, coal and culm were not soon exempted from toll, the agriculture of the country would soon be in ruins.[50]

Lime was by no means the sole 'manure' applied to the fields; it was frequently complemented by dressings of seaweed, sea-sand and farmyard waste, either in fresh or composted form. In the southern coastal parishes, composting of seaweed with lime was a widespread practice and such were believed to be the virtues of sea-sand as a manure for barley that farmers thought nothing of carrying it many miles inland.[51] Seaweed in particular, with its high concentration of nitrogen and trace elements, was used extensively in the much-renowned barley land along the coast – so much so that when Thomas Johnes of Hafod tried to cajole his tenants into adopting more rational farming practices, he was moved to draw their attention to the 'constant Produce' of continuous

[47]R. Warner, *A Second Walk through Wales* (London, 1810), p.58.
[48]Ibid., p.151.
[49]The economic, social, agricultural and technical aspects of the lime trade and lime-burning at the coastal kiln are considered in R. J. Moore-Colyer, 'Of lime and men', passim; idem, 'Coastal limekilns in south-west Wales', *Folk Life*, 28 (1989–90), 19–30.
[50]Carmarthen RO, Cwmgwili MS 450.
[51]W. Davies, *General View of the Agriculture of South Wales* (2 vols., London, 1815), II, p.151.

barley crops in the parishes of Llansanffraid and Llan-non, where seaweed alone had been used as a manure.[52] In slight contradiction to Johnes, Walter Davies (Gwallter Mechain) found sea-sand to be the chief manure of the Llan-non barley tract, in 'perpetual alternation' with seaweed.[53]

Throughout the United Kingdom as a whole, there was a substantial increase in the importance of organic fertilizers and livestock feeds between 1800 and 1850. Guano, bones and, in particular, oilcakes, found their way to farms the length and breadth of Britain, the latter being fed to livestock in order to improve the manurial quality of the dung so essential for cereal crops. With the discrediting of Liebig's belief that sufficient nitrogen was washed from the atmosphere to preclude its need as a fertilizer, interest developed in discovering inorganic sources of nitrogen, phosphate and potash. By the middle of the century, superphosphates had been developed, and the emphasis shifted from the importation of organic to inorganic sources of nutrients, especially in the form of German potash and Chilean nitrate.[54]

On the whole, the gentry of Cardiganshire tended to follow current trends, being readily prepared to use new sources of fertilizer as these became available. Against such a background of a *general* increase in the use of these materials, one might postulate that in fact fertilizer use fluctuated according to the changing prosperity of farming over time, in much the same way as chemical inputs into agriculture in the late 1980s declined after some thirty years of unprecedented expansion. The land agent Adam Murray, who had optimistically taken on the tenancy of one of the Trawsgoed farms during the prosperous years of the Napoleonic Wars, explained to the Select Committee on Agriculture of 1833 that he had attempted to farm 'very high' by purchasing ground bones from Liverpool and applying to his arable acreage no fewer than 6,000 loads of seaweed and dung each year. Whatever the benefits of so doing in terms of high yields of both cereal and root crops, he had been forced to conclude that after the post 1815 slump artificial manuring in any shape or form was no longer a viable proposition. Tenants in a more modest way of business would doubtless have agreed.

The adoption of new agricultural technology by the nineteenth-century farmer depended upon several factors, including capital availability, farm size and the relative abundance and cost of labour. Important, too, was the degree of literacy in the local society, the extent to which landlords used the institutional framework of estate management to encourage innovation, and the vigour and persuasiveness of opinion-leaders, whether tenants or freeholders. In the eastern borderlands of Wales, the vales of Glamorgan and Clwyd and parts of Pembrokeshire, where arable farming provided the bulk of farm income and where industrial concerns competed for labour, farmers were keenly aware of the benefits of intensifying their farms and responded by adopting the principles of rotation and by investing in new plant and machinery. The position in Cardiganshire was rather different. Isolation (both physical and cultural), appalling roads, and the innate conservatism of the

[52]T. Johnes, *A Landlord's Advice to his Tenants* (Hafod, 1800), p.5. Among Johnes's more bizarre notions was that of transporting burnt lime from Glamorgan to the Cardiganshire coast in copper-lined vessels, a subject which he discussed in his correspondence with Edward Williams (Iolo Morganwg) (NLW MS 21281, f.215).
[53]Davies, *General View*, p.163.
[54]L. J. Peel, 'Science, energy and agriculture since 1800', *Acta Museorum Agriculturae*, XII (1977), 60–3. For details of the use of lime, guano, oilcake dust and phosphatic fertilizers on farms in Cardiganshire, see NLW Lucas MSS 631 and 643; NLW MS 11539B; NLW MS 6642A; J. Ll. Davies, 'A Cardiganshire farmer's diary', *WJA*, X (1934), 16–17.

pastoral farmer combined with the nature of the predominantly upland terrain to ensure the persistence of 'antiquated' forms of farm transport such as the packhorse, the home-made slide car and sled.[55] It seems likely that agents for the manufacture of the new farm machinery viewed upland Wales rather despairingly as a lost cause and thus did little to promote the sale of their products in these remoter regions.[56] As a result, most of the farming community continued until late in the nineteenth century to depend upon a wide range of simple hand tools and one or two sizeable implements, often co-operatively owned by a number of neighbouring farmers.[57] Such implements were made by the local wheelwright or carpenter or, in the case of very isolated farms, by the farmer himself.

Drawn by oxen and horses, with the latter becoming increasingly used in the eighteenth century, locally produced harrows, rollers and ploughs cultivated the unrewarding soils of the country.[58] The traditional wooden Welsh plough, usually manufactured by local blacksmiths, necessitated the use of three or four horses or oxen in single file and was almost universally decried by early nineteenth-century observers. The lighter Rotherham Plough, patented in the 1730s, was a wheel-less implement fitted with an iron share and mould-board and was capable of being pulled by two horses or oxen. Adopted by the more progressive farmers and landlords, this efficient implement was vigorously resisted by many tenants who preferred to use the ancient wooden plough (which failed to turn a true furrow slice) or its cumbersome wheeled counterpart. One Cardiganshire gentleman, incensed at the unwillingness of his men to use the Rotherham plough, ordered all the old ploughs to be burnt, only to discover the Rotherham ploughs in the ditch several days later and his men happily ploughing with traditional implements borrowed from a neighbour. Testily he remarked: 'I have seen various kinds of human beings in different parts of the globe, from latitude 10 to latitude 54, but none so obstinately bent on old practices as the Welsh.' Gradually, however, the advantages of speed and effective inversion of the sod dawned upon farmers, and local ploughwrights were quick to seize upon the idea of producing adaptations of the Rotherham plough and its derivatives suited to local conditions. Iron from foundries in Aberystwyth and Cardigan was available for local machinery manufacture by the 1840s, and the iron-framed plough, complete with a mould-board designed for use on sloping fields, became the rule rather than the exception.[59]

Throughout the winter months, farm staff spent a good deal of their time threshing and winnowing the sheaves of corn gathered during the previous harvest. Since medieval times threshing had involved the use of the flail, a tool which continued to be used on many farms long after the

---

[55] J. G. Jenkins, *Agricultural Transport in Wales* (Cardiff, 1962), p.13.

[56] J. Gibson, *Agriculture in Wales* (Aberystwyth, 1879), p.98.

[57] J. G. Jenkins, *Life and Tradition in Rural Wales* (London, 1976), p.131.

[58] For the relative efficiency of oxen and horses, see J. Wilson (ed.), *Rural Cyclopedia*, III (Edinburgh, 1882); J. A. Clarke, 'Practical agriculture', *JRASE*, XIV (1878), 628–31. For the use of horses in the economy of eighteenth- and nineteenth-century Wales, see R. J. Moore-Colyer, 'Horses and equine improvement in the economy of modern Wales', *AGHR*, 39, no.2 (1991), 126–42; idem, 'Blacksmiths, farriers and horses in Wales', *Folk Life*, 29 (1990–1), 76–80.

[59] E. Scourfield, 'The interpretation of the history and development of farming techniques in Wales as illustrated by the collection at the Welsh Folk Museum', *Acta Museorum Agriculturae* (1978), 115–31. The iron-framed harrow only gradually replaced the wooden-framed implement which had remained virtually unchanged since the tenth century. The fact that harrows were generally re-sharpened by local blacksmiths in return for a small quantity of corn or perhaps the loan of the farmer's plough-team for hauling a load of coal to the smithy from the nearest coal port is indicative of the degree of interdependence between the craftsman and the farm.

arrival of horse, water and steam threshers. This was as much the case in England as in Wales and may be explained in terms of the concern of parish authorities to reduce seasonal unemployment by persuading farmers to employ men in threshing rather than throwing them on the parish during the winter.[60] Despite the introduction and diffusion of static and portable drum threshers from the 1780s, and of locally produced winnowing equipment, the flail was by no means totally eclipsed in the course of the next century, so that in the 1870s the occupier of one 260-acre farm in the south of the county employed two men solely for the purpose of flail threshing in the autumn months.[61]

A tedious and soul-destroying business, carried out in the dismal months of winter, flailing and winnowing were jobs rarely welcomed by farm staff. Harvest, however, with its prospect of extra wages, was another matter, and the months of July and August were times of eager anticipation as everyone awaited the ripening of the corn. Supplementary labour required for harvesting came either from itinerant workers or villagers under some obligation to the farmer. Smallholders and landholding craftsmen, for example, for whom the farmer might have ploughed or carted hay or manure, would return this obligation by working for an agreed period in the harvest fields of the larger farmers. Similarly, non-landholding cottagers who grew their potatoes in a farmer's field accumulated a work debt, normally discharged at hay or harvest time. As a family required between two and five 100-yard rows of potatoes each year, and the work debt amounted to one day's work per row, many farms were able to gather most of their harvest with either paid or unpaid work-debt labour.[62] Each farm was linked to a work group of cottagers with a debt to discharge at the corn and potato harvest, so that this system placed mutual obligations upon each party. The cottagers realized that a specific amount of labour would be required of them each year in return for the privilege of planting out potatoes on the farm, while the farmer in turn knew that to renege upon his duties to the work group might bring about difficulties at harvest time.

Dependence upon one's neighbours for periodic help was a salient feature of the community and, although less formally organized than the haymaking groups, co-operative harvest work-groups were characteristic of the agricultural economy in the days before mechanization. Until the mid-nineteenth century work-groups would often include farmers recently returned from their annual migration to the west Midlands, where they had reaped early wheat crops on a contract basis. These and other farmers would combine to form a reaping party (*Y Fedel Wenith*), and agree to organize the harvest on their respective farms in such a manner as to enable mutual co-operation. The decision when to commence the harvest in the area, 'guided by such sayings . . . which embodied the experience and garnered wisdom of many generations', would be followed by a special supper to steel the group for the task ahead.[63] As they feasted and caroused, farmers and villagers would remember that harvesting was an occasion of considerable stress, tension and fatigue. The presence of women in the fields, the continual tempo of the work, and family rivalries sometimes led to

---

[60]Thus, the flail was called 'the poverty stick' in Cardiganshire. See G. E. Evans, *The Farm and the Village* (London, 1967), p.85.

[61]Gibson, *Agriculture in Wales*, p.104. See also C. S. Read, 'On the agriculture of south Wales', *JRASE*, X (1849), 34; Jenkins, *Agricultural Community*, p.253; R. Trow-Smith, *English Husbandry* (London, 1951), p.207; S. McDonald, 'The progress of the early threshing machine', *AGHR*, 23, no.1 (1875), 70–2. For introductions of threshing machines by Cardiganshire gentry, see inter alia, NLW Lucas MSS 641–2, and for winnowing see H. Evans, *The Gorse Glen* (Liverpool, 1947), pp.33–7.

[62]Jenkins, *Agricultural Community*, pp.52–4.

[63]D. Parry-Jones, *Welsh Country Upbringing* (Liverpool, 1944), p.63.

fighting and quite often to accidents. Older men, who may have found employment difficult to secure at other times of the year, were usually engaged in the hazardous operation of unloading wagons and building ricks, and their names frequently occur in reports of harvesting accidents.[64]

Throughout the eighteenth and nineteenth centuries, harvest techniques varied according to the specific cereal crop and, to some extent, according to weather conditions. During the earlier period, the serrated-edged sickle and the smoothly ground reaping hook were used for wheat, barley and oats, with methods of harvesting and binding varying widely with locality. By 1800, however, the oat and barley crops were generally harvested with the scythe, with or without a wooden cradle (*cadair*) attached, and this implement also became increasingly popular for mowing stands of wheat.[65] The growing use throughout Britain of the Hainault scythe and its local variants had an important effect on the sexual distribution of harvest labour in that it tended to reduce the involvement of women in the highly paid task of corn-cutting as opposed to merely binding and stacking. Women could handle the reaping hook or sickle without too much difficulty, whereas the heavy scythe proved a match for all but the strongest. This did not, however, reduce the total work available since the scythe cut more corn per sweep than the reaping hook and, by leaving it in greater disarray, necessitated more effort in the binding process. In other words, the adoption of the scythe for the corn harvest meant that there were, in fact, more opportunities for women, albeit in the less well-paid areas of the operation.[66]

Bell's Mechanical Reaper, operated by a single horse pushing from behind, had been patented in 1828. It was widespread in England by the mid-1850s and, in a somewhat modified form, also became popular in parts of Wales over the next decades. Even if some Welsh commentators believed that the reaper would never supersede the scythe, since by delivering the corn in a tight bundle rather than a thin swath its use would result in more ear-sprouting, there was no escaping the fact that the machine's work output was far higher than that achieved by hand labour. Whereas a man with a scythe could cut as much corn in a day as two or three men with reaping hooks or sickles, a reaper, operated by one man and a horse, disposed of the same amount of standing corn as six men with scythes.[67] Besides increasing the work output per man on the farm, the reaper and other increasingly sophisticated agricultural machines necessitated such an increase in horse power that between 1871 and 1921, a period when the arable acreage of Wales was in decline, the number of working horses per 100 acres of cultivated land advanced from 2.6 to 3.2.[68]

The arrival of the reaper heralded the end of the lucrative harvest mowing work, often the prerogative of migrant harvesting groups on larger farms in some parts of the country. Even so, plenty of work remained for binders and carters, and as these tasks were normally carried out by the farm's permanent labourers and their families, they enjoyed the extra harvest wages previously paid to the mowing gangs. In the 1880s, as the fortunes of arable farming began to plummet drastically in parallel with a steady increase in the real value of wages, the newly developed reaper-binder was widely adopted. Indeed, such was the effect of increasing labour costs that by 1898 the owner of the Highmead estate, reckoning the cost of mowing by hand at 10*s.* per acre and reaper-binding at

[64]R. Samuel (ed.), *Village Life and Labour* (London, 1975), pp.33–7.
[65]Techniques and methods are described in detail in Moore-Colyer, 'Crop husbandry', passim.
[66]M. Roberts, 'Sickles and scythes: women's work and men's work at harvest time', *History Workshop*, 7 (1979), 7–20.
[67]Evans, *Gorse Glen*, p.111.
[68]J. Davies, 'Horse labour on Welsh farms 1571–1927', *WJA*, VI (1930), 44.

2s. 6d., considered that capital investment in a reaper-binder could be amply justified on a hundred acres of arable land.[69] Inevitably, the advent of the reaper-binder rendered redundant the tradition of family work in the fields and hammered firmly the final nail into the coffin of the itinerant harvest gang. Also, by leaving less waste than the reaper, it reduced dramatically the potential for gleaning, thereby severing a centuries-old bond between farm and village.

Farming practice: animal husbandry

Until the middle years of the eighteenth century pastoral farming in the county had been dominated by the *hafod/hendre* system of transhumance, an arrangement of medieval, if not earlier, origins. In essence, the system involved the occupation of two holdings, the lowland *hendre*, comprising a group of farm buildings and dwelling houses, and the upland *hafod* (or *lluest*), a cottage with associated enclosures where, by tradition, cattle were tended between 1 May (*Calan Mai*) and All Souls Day (*Calan Gaeaf*). On the *hendre*, usually a permanent site with fertile, well-drained soil, arable crops were grown in the appropriate season and were enabled to flourish undisturbed after cattle had been moved to the *hafod* in the summer months. Since the predominant hill grass, *Molinea caerulea*, provided palatable pasture of reasonable digestibility when intensely stocked in order to forestall rank summer growth, the upland holdings could support substantial numbers of cattle, thereby relieving pressure on the *hendre*.[70] Built of posts, wattle and turf, the earlier *hafodydd* and *lluestydd* were probably insubstantial structures, and the element *rhisgl* (bark) incorporated in some contemporary farm names (e.g. *Hafod-y-rhisg*) suggests that roughly hewn or unstripped timber might have been used. *Las*, *wen*, *goch* and other suffixes relating to colour, either of the daubed walls or surrounding vegetation, are common, as are those referring to birds, animals and trees like *Hafodgelyn* (holly), *Hafod-wernos* (alder) and *Lluestcornicyll* (plover).[71] If daily life in these draughty shacks was less than comfortable, things were little better in the stone-built *hafodydd* of Snowdonia, which Thomas Pennant visited in the late eighteenth century: 'These houses consist of a long, low room with a hole at one end to let out the smoke from the fire which is made beneath. Their furniture is very simple; stones are the substitution of stools and the beds are of hay, ranged along the side . . .'[72]

From these insalubrious habitations the occupier emerged each morning to attend to the needs of his animals, milk his cows and cultivate the small enclosed plots of land usually associated with the *hafod*. Although there were local variations in the organization of the *hafod*, depending upon its distance from the *hendre*, the normal procedure was for the older men and some of the womenfolk to migrate to the hills, leaving the more robust members of the family on the *hendre* to look after the arable crops and any remaining livestock. Tradition dictated departure from the *hendre* on 1 May

[69]NLW Highmead MSS, Box Y. For the effects of other aspects of technological change on Welsh agriculture, see R. J. Moore-Colyer, *Farming in Depression, Wales, 1919–1939*, Welsh Institute of Rural Studies Working Paper No.6 (1996).

[70]E. Davies, '*Hendre* and *Hafod* in Caernarvonshire', *TCHS*, 40 (1979), 19–20; idem, '*Hafod, Hafoty* and *Lluest*': their distribution, features and purpose', *Ceredigion*, IX, no.1 (1980), 1–41; C. B. Crampton, 'Hafotai platforms on the north front of Carmarthen Fan', *AC*, 117 (1968), 125.

[71]M. Richards, '*Hafod* and *Hafoty* in Welsh place-names', *MC*, LVI (1959), 16–17; idem, '*Meifod, lluest, cynaeafdy* and *hendre* in Welsh place-names', ibid., 56 (1960), 177–8.

[72]T. Pennant, *Tours* (London, 1810), pp.334–5.

Fig. 15: A cattle fair at Tal-y-bont, photographed by John Thomas. (*Copyright National Library of Wales*).

but, in fact, migration was always delayed until spring sowing of cereals and potatoes had been completed and sufficient spring grass was available on the hills.[73]

In the late seventeenth and early eighteenth centuries, sheep came to replace cattle as the mainstay of the upland economy and while sheep continued to be milked for butter and cheese production, the *hafod* remained as a 'summer dairy'. However, with the waning of this practice and the trend towards keeping sheep merely for meat and wool, the upkeep of a summer *hafod* was no longer absolutely necessary since the animals did not require constant supervision and could be taken from the hill for such periodic tasks as shearing and washing. Nevertheless, in some cases, the *hafod* maintained its connection with the *hendre* for many years. After all, it provided a convenient sheltering-place for men visiting the hills to look over their flocks. Moreover, given the insanitary conditions of many lowland farms, people may well have relished the idea of escaping to the bracing air of the mountain *hafod* with its well-dunged enclosure capable of producing summer vegetables. But gradually the ancient system of transhumance came to an end and there arose a tendency towards the separation of the *hendre* from the *hafod* by which the latter often evolved into a self-contained upland farm.[74] In fact, in areas where population increase and large family size had imposed pressure on land resources, this process had probably been in motion from as early as the sixteenth century, new *hafodydd* having been created by sons of occupiers of an existing *hafod* who, no

[73]R. J. Colyer, 'Aspects of the pastoral economy in pre-industrial Wales', *JRASE*, CXLIV (1983), 45–6.
[74]E. Davies, 'Sheep farming in upland Wales', *Geography*, 20 (1935), 109.

longer able to be supported by the family holding, moved further upslope to carve out farms which had little connection with the lowland *hendre*.[75]

Evidence for the regular cultivation of clover, sainfoin and 'artificial grasses' in the remote reaches of west Wales is difficult to unearth.[76] Walter Davies, writing around 1800, maintained that the rye grasses were rarely cultivated before 1740 and that 'until recently' the seeds of few cultivated types were available, with the exception of Rye Grass (*Lolium perenne*), Yorkshire Grass (*Holcus lanatus*) and Suffolk Grass (*Poa Annua*).[77] On the other hand, the availability or otherwise of seeds may have been a matter of indifference to many smaller farmers both on the upland and lowland, whose regular practice continued to be that of allowing arable land to 'tumble down' to grass rather than adopt any conscious reseeding policy. Even where 'artificial' grasses and clovers were planted, their chances of becoming effectively established within the sward were not helped by the practice of mixing seeds imported from England with those of local rye grasses which, more often than not, were contaminated with the vigorous couch grass (*Agropyron repens*).[78]

Although few attempts seem to have been made to rationalize the grazing of livestock on lowland pastures, it was a prime objective among farmers to obtain adequate quantities of winter forage, since the overwintering capacity of their farms determined the number of stock summered on the upland pastures. Before the widespread use of root crops in the later years of the nineteenth century considerable reliance was placed upon 'foggage' (autumn-saved pasture), gorse, hay (occasionally from flooded water meadows) and even tree-browse for the purpose.[79]

The hay harvest was, of course, of vital importance to the farmer and on most small farms the safe gathering of the hay depended upon mutual co-operation between individual farmers and other members of the community. This mutual dependence, often maintained and reinforced by genetic relationships, normally transcended political, religious and cultural differences in the interest of harvesting the all-important hay crop. Neighbouring farmers and their relatives, and villagers having a harvest debt resulting from the 'potato-setting' arrangement so admirably described by David Jenkins, would join with other labourers, and each man or woman would be given a task which was very largely determined by his neighbours' estimate of his speed, trustworthiness and capacity for work. A highly complex co-operative arrangement existed at mowing time, whereby each farm contributed scythemen, either from its own labour force or from villagers owing a 'harvest debt'. Once assembled, the mowing crop would either move from farm to farm according to the conditions of the crop on individual holdings or, in certain circumstances, would visit farms in a fixed sequence determined by custom over many years.

The business of deciding when the hay was ready to be carried was an occasion for lengthy debate when everyone proceeded to some point in the middle of the field and assessed the state of the crop. This was a moment, as Parry-Jones has pointed out, when ' . . . all the treasured wisdom of the past, accumulated in the course of hundreds of years, would pass from mouth to mouth as each

[75]E. Davies, '*Hendre* and *Hafod* in Denbighshire', *TDHS*, 26 (1977), 70–1.

[76]For which, see A. R. Mitchell, 'Sir Richard Weston and the spread of clover cultivation', *AGHR*, XXII, no.2 (1974), 160–1; C. Lane, 'The development of pastures and meadows during the sixteenth and seventeenth centuries', ibid., XXVIII, no.1 (1980), 18.

[77]Davies, *General View*, p.588.

[78]T. Lloyd and D. Turnor, *A General View of the Agriculture of Cardiganshire* (London, 1794), p.21.

[79]For details, see Moore-Colyer, 'Pastoral economy', passim, and idem, 'The horse in British prehistory; some speculations', *Archaeological Journal*, 151 (1995), 1–15.

made his contribution . . . it was something quite impressive to behold, as becomes any rite, solemn, unhurried, deliberate and punctuated by deep and prolonged silence.'[80] Rain at any time during the hay harvest was worrying: at the final stage of the haymaking process, the culmination of several hundred hours of work, heavy summer storms could prove catastrophic. On the last day of July 1839, a year which farmers in south Wales would have had good cause to remember, the rain ceased to fall after almost three weeks of daily storms which had carried away most of the meadow hay and ruined the remainder. So great was the extent of the damage and the fear of the consequences for livestock over the following winter that prayers for more clement weather were regularly offered in chapels and meeting-houses during the deluge.

While the most arduous (and well-paid) task in the hayfield, that of mowing, was generally the prerogative of the menfolk, the role of women in the hay harvest was vital. Judging from Lipscomb's remark on his journey through Wales in 1802, many women were perfectly capable of carrying out heavy work in addition to the relatively light tasks of turning, cocking and carting. As he rode through Pen-y-bont in Radnorshire, he noted with pleasure that the women 'share with the stronger sex the most arduous exertions and business of husbandry and they are very commonly seen either driving the horse affixed to the plough or leading those which draw the harrow'.[81]

Tedders, swath turners, hayloaders and other machines, although common in England and south and east Wales in the mid-nineteenth century, made little headway in this county against the pitchfork and rake until the 1890s. Even the horse-drawn reciprocating mowing machine was little-used until the early 1900s, due largely to the cheapness of labour relative to the cost of the machine and the specialist skills required for its maintenance.[82]

Since little attempt was usually made to provide a dietary regime capable of fattening cattle or producing milk during the winter months, the bulk of the hay crop was used as a maintenance diet for ruminant livestock and horses. Production, both of live weight gain and milk, normally coincided with the onset of grass growth in the spring and thus calving was timed accordingly. Since butter-making was the principal objective of the cow keeper, he was anxious to wean his calves as early as possible so as to maximize butter yield from the six- to seven-month lactation, so that calves were rapidly transferred to diets of skim-milk and hay, and on the more prosperous farms, a linseed gruel.[83]

The whole gamut of butter-making techniques involving settling, separation and churning, passed down from farmer's wife to daughter over the generations, have been fully described elsewhere and will not be repeated here save to observe that, despite the gradual changeover from wooden to metal utensils – a factor partially responsible for the decay of the cooper's craft – nineteenth-century milking equipment and butter-making methods had altered little since medieval times.[84] Before the

---

[80] D. Parry-Jones, *Welsh Country Characters* (London, 1952), pp.100–3.

[81] R. Lipscomb, *Journey into South Wales* (London, 1802), pp.111–12. Even so, the wages received by women for field work were invariably less than those of the men and frequently only exceeded a boy's wages by a narrow margin. NLW Cwmgwili MS 639 gives details of haymakers' wages at Cwmgwili in 1789.

[82] Trow-Smith, *English Husbandry*, p.206; W. B. Hall, 'On the agriculture of Pembrokeshire', *JRASE*, 23 (1887), 89–90.

[83] C. B. Jones, 'Welsh Black cattle', *JRASE*, 77 (1916), 45–6.

[84] See, for example, J. Lewis, 'Some aspects of the history and development of dairying in Carmarthenshire' (unpublished University of Wales MSc thesis, 1948); R. U. Sayce, 'Milking and dairying', *MC*, LII (1952), 120–54; Jenkins, *Agricultural Community*, passim; Evans, *Gorse Glen*, pp.131–5.

expansion of the market for fresh butter in the last quarter of the century, the bulk of the butter produced on the farm was preserved with salt and casked during the summer months or, where the farm was within easy reach of a town, sold as 'rolls' in the local market. Markets like Aberystwyth, Llandysul and Tregaron provided outlets for the majority, any surpluses remaining being sold to dealers for disposal in the growing towns of the valleys of south Wales. While it brought the county into contact with a wider market for its butter, the railway system also ushered in competition in the form of a flow of imports of Irish, Danish and New Zealand butter. So intense indeed was the competition from imports and so rapid the development of taste for foreign butter, that the butter markets in south Cardiganshire were saved only by the preference among some Glamorgan miners for the highly salted Welsh product.[85] Many farmers responded by abandoning the process of salting and casking in favour of selling fresh, unsalted 'pound butter' on the local market, but others stubbornly refused to yield to the realities of changed demand and continued to rely upon sales of preserved butter to the Valleys. A dumbfounded John Gibson, realizing that rail transport could rapidly convey fresh produce to markets the length and breadth of the kingdom, could not understand why farmers doggedly persisted in salting their butter: 'There is not reason in these days of railways for salting butter and keeping it until it is worth 2d. or 3d. a pound less than if it had been sold fresh.'[86] Skim milk, the principal by-product of butter-making, was generally fed to calves in the spring months, but once these animals had been weaned in the early summer it was available for conversion into cheese. This was a highly labour-intensive process involving heating the milk, squeezing and milling the curd and, once the cheeses had been made, turning and polishing them daily so as to maintain quality and texture. At the Highmead dairy, cheese-selling normally started the following January when, despite shrinkage losses of up to 10 per cent of cheese weight during the storage period, prices were up to 1d. per pound higher than those in the summer markets.[87]

Pigs, either for home consumption or for sale, played a small though important role in the farm economy. Even though the pig market tended to fluctuate widely, feeding pigs on whey and 'chat' potatoes yielded such profits that in some years farmers claimed to have sows yielding double the return of a milch cow. Relatively little attention was paid to the genetic improvement of the native pig, which, though described by most critics in disparaging terms, had the considerable virtues of large mature size and a high ratio of lean to fat. This was ideal from the point of view of bacon production but, unfortunately, the animals took a great deal of time to mature, a problem which could have been resolved by careful selection for early maturing among the native type. However, few efforts were made in this direction, preference being given to mating the long-bodied, flop-eared Cardiganshire pig with early-maturing English breeds from Berkshire, Leicestershire, Hampshire and Suffolk. Such was the rate of introduction of these animals that by the mid-nineteenth century pure-bred natives were becoming rare on both the farms of the gentry and tenant occupiers. 'There is still an occasional lot of pigs of the old fashioned kind exhibited in our fairs', wrote Thomas Morgan in 1852, 'but they no longer command the prejudiced preference given them in the olden time.'[88] A general appreciation of the importance of early maturity led to a progressive increase in

[85]D. Howell, 'Rural society in nineteenth century Carmarthenshire', *CA*, XIII (1977), 73–4.
[86]Gibson, *Agriculture in Wales*, p.25.
[87]B.G. Charles, 'The Highmead Dairy, 1778–97', *Ceredigion*, V, no.1 (1964), 80.
[88]Morgan, *An Essay*, p.137.

cross-breeding, although farmers appear to have been careful to preserve both the large mature size and foraging characteristics of the traditional type.

The eclipse of the native pig by constant crossing to 'exotic' breeds was paralleled by the gradual disappearance of many local varieties of Welsh sheep and cattle during the eighteenth and nineteenth centuries. By the 1790s sheep breeds like the Ryeland, Dorset, Cotswold, Southdown and even the ill-fated Merino were regularly to be seen on pastures elsewhere in south-west Wales.[89] Regardless of Lloyd and Turnor's observation that the introduction of sheep scab in the county could be attributed to the use of English breeds, and the justifiable assertion that many of these were ill-suited to the damp climate of Wales, the 'exotic' animals commanded substantially higher prices than native stock.[90] Added to this was the problem of restraining the native sheep from its natural penchant to 'range', which caused many landowners, concerned by damage to plantations and sown pastures, actively to discourage their tenants from rearing these animals, and it is not difficult to see that the days of the old native breeds were numbered. On the hills, however, cross-breeding was less frequently practised and, by all accounts, the hardy hill sheep, acclimatized through centuries of natural and unconscious human selection, exhibited a considerable degree of compensatory growth when taken as store animals to the lush pasturelands of England.[91]

In the light of present-day knowledge of population genetics it is easy to criticize the Welsh farmer for failing to improve native breed types of cattle and sheep prior to importing 'exotic' stock. In mitigation, however, any attempt to develop breed improvement plans was fraught with problems and difficulties, especially on the unfenced hills where age-old feuds over sheepwalk boundaries continued over the generations. Because the sheepwalk associated with a given farm was rarely in proportion to the overwintering capacity of the enclosed lowland acreage, farmers were often tempted to overstock their sheepwalks, with the inevitable result that sheep strayed onto neighbouring grazing. Irate neighbours, equally anxious to graze their stock on someone else's stint, then proceeded to drive away the offending sheep to remote areas of the hills, leading to a state of less than neighbourly coexistence.

'Sheep systems', as such, were virtually non-existent on the mountain sheepwalks, the animals merely being run on the hills from the late spring through to the autumn, when weaned lambs were brought down to lowland stubble. Although some ewes were wintered on the lowland, many of the smaller farms had insufficient land for this purpose and ewes were left on the hills to fend for themselves over the winter months. As the majority of farmers believed the winter feeding of ewes to be unremunerative, lamb birth weights tended to be low and milk yields poor, so that mortality could often reach catastrophic levels. Where root crops and good hay were not available for winter maintenance, both breeding animals and lambs would have become more susceptible to the

[89]C. Hassall, *General View of the Agriculture of Carmarthenshire* (London, 1794), p.36; Davies, *General View*, p.249. For the attempt to introduce the Merino, see F. Bladon (ed.), *Diaries of Col. R. F. Greville* (London, 1930); A. Aspinall (ed.), *The Later Correspondence of George III* (Reading, 1970); H. B. Carter, *His Majesty's Sheep Flock* (London, 1964).

[90]Lloyd and Turnor, *General View*, p.23.

[91]Changes in the nature of Welsh sheep breeds in the eighteenth and nineteenth centuries are paralleled in the cattle population, to which detailed consideration is given in R. J. Colyer, 'Some Welsh breeds of cattle in the nineteenth century', *AGHR*, 22, no.1 (1974), 1–17; idem, 'Sheep and cattle, 1750–1850', in G. E. Mingay (ed.), *The Agrarian History of England and Wales VI* (Cambridge, 1989), pp.313–50. The latter, along with Colyer, 'Pastoral economy', provides details of cattle and sheep husbandry.

Fig. 16: Sheep-shearers at Pumlumon, photographed by John Thomas. (*Copyright National Library of Wales*).

debilitating effects of liver fluke and intestinal worms, while wool quality was frequently spoiled by tick infestation. Liver fluke in particular could devastate sheep flocks grazing the poorly-drained hills, and where farmers failed to eliminate fluke-bearing snails by fencing off wet areas, losses from this source must have been considerable.

Lowland farmers with land capable of growing turnips could purchase yearling lambs or wethers to fatten for the spring market, but local poverty and the lack of urban markets during the first three-quarters of the nineteenth century meant that there was little demand for fattened lamb and the animals were usually driven away, together with lean cattle, to be fattened on the grazing lands of the English Midlands. Subsequently, the growth of tourism and the increase in the real value of wages stimulated demand for fat lamb, thereby encouraging farmers to keep a growing proportion of their flocks on the lowland and to reduce the extent of range hill grazing. Thus, in Cardiganshire, stocking density of sheep in summer on the lowlands increased from 90 to 437 animals per thousand acres between 1867 and 1900, while the corresponding stocking on the hills declined from 397 to 195 animals over the same period.

Wool production, of course, was fundamentally important both to the economy of the farm and the cottage. To the poorer cottagers, the sale of knitted gloves and stockings crafted from shed wool gathered from the hedgerows and walls was a significant supplement to household income and the regular arrival of the itinerant stocking dealer was eagerly awaited.[92] In cottages and on farms,

[92]'Ap Adda', 'The stocking dealer', *The Red Dragon*, II (1882), 41–3.

handloom weavers continued to thrive in the southern parishes of this county until the 1820s, with farmers employing servants as much for their ability to weave as for their skill in the field. But this was all to end with the development of the power loom in the mid-nineteenth century and soon virtually every district in the south and many parts of the north had their own woollen factories to supply the local market.[93]

The fleeces carried by farmers to the factory to be turned into cloth or blankets varied enormously in quality, depending upon their area of origin and the care taken in shearing and storage. The short, thick fleeces generally found south of the Aeron valley were ideally suited to the hat trade around Llangwyryfon and Lledrod, with the long-staple coarse wool of the north usually being spun into flannel and blankets for household use. As a rule, sheep were sheared annually. Nevertheless, some flockmasters in the north of the county favoured shearing twice yearly on the grounds that December shearings yielded wool of ideal felting quality, while wool taken in June absorbed dye more effectively than a full year's growth. Unfortunately, fleece value was often reduced by the presence of kemp, dirt and other foreign matter, and shearing itself and the subsequent storage of the wool was sometimes carried out in a slovenly manner. By the 1870s, however, when Welsh fleeces were obliged to compete with a steadily increasing flow of Australian imports, more attention was being paid to the shearing process and specialist shearing teams were employed.

The development of specialist labour needs across a whole range of farm activities, consequent upon the expansion of mechanization and the growing market for quality food products, brought with it profound changes in the association between the farm and the local community towards the end of the nineteenth century. As the reaper-binder and other mechanical contrivances rendered farmers independent of the village work groups for assistance at harvest time, so did cottagers become increasingly unfamiliar with the farm and there followed a steady waning in mutual interest in each other's affairs. This apart, a general increase in farm mechanization in the early years of the twentieth century tended also towards a change in the relationship between the farmer and his labourers. As emigration maintained wages at a relatively high level, the labourer's need for perquisites was reduced and thus to his recently gained political independence he was able to add a sense of freedom from the implicit subservience required in a system whereby payment of wages, especially to the living-in servant, was often partially in kind. The aftermath of the Great War, with its profound social and economic consequences, ensured that henceforth the farmer and worker would tend to view their relationship from a no-nonsense customer/contractor standpoint. And yet, in an industry where master and man usually worked closely together and son followed father in the same business over the generations, the relationship could never be entirely free from an element of sentiment. Farming, especially in closely knit communities, involved the sort of teamwork which industry never managed to achieve, and contributed to the persistence of at least some sense of mutual identity of purpose between employer and employed.[94]

[93]J. G. Jenkins, *The Welsh Woollen Industry* (Cardiff, 1969), pp.247–87; idem, 'Rural industry in Cardiganshire', *Ceredigion*, VI, no.1 (1968), 90–127.

[94]Yet the notion of farmer and labourer comfortably coexisting in a sort of shared alliance against the gentry which was argued by some historians of an earlier generation has more recently been debunked as a groundless myth. D. A. Pretty, *The Rural Revolt that Failed: Farm Workers' Trade Unions in Wales, 1889–1950* (Cardiff, 1989). The argument that there was no real or perceived social and economic difference between smaller Welsh farmers and their labourers can probably no longer be sustained. However, for a contrary view, see D. W. Howell, 'Labour organisation among agricultural workers in Wales, 1872–1921', *WHR*, 16, no.1 (1992), 63–92.

CHAPTER 3

THE LANDED GENTRY OF CARDIGANSHIRE

R. J. Moore-Colyer

N THE the late summer of 1770 a weary English traveller was entertained by Mr William Wynn of Maesyneuadd in Merioneth, where he enjoyed to the full the ample pleasures of cellar and table for which the Welsh country mansion was widely celebrated. As he sat in the smoking room, 'as clouded with fume as Fleet Street on a foggy day before Christmas', he ruminated on the qualities of his host, a fluent Welsh speaker, indefatigable sportsman and local magnate of semi-princely powers. Acting as his own agent and thereby spending many hours of the day out of doors, Wynn enjoyed robust health to counteract the fact that 'He eats like a hunter, drinks like a fish and smokes like a Dutchman'.[1] This notion of the bucolic, hard-drinking sporting squire ruling with the proverbial rod of iron over his petty kingdom has tended to become an *idée fixe* among historians of eighteenth- and nineteenth-century Wales, and even the apologist for the gentry can scarcely deny that for every Sir Roger de Coverley there were several Sir Pitt Crawleys. Yet, as in all other social groups, the gentry comprised a broad church. If there were men like John Pugh Vaughan Pryse of Bwlch-bychan (1818–1903), third son of Pryse Pryse of Gogerddan, who reckoned a week ill-spent if four days of it had not been passed in the hunting field, or Richard Humphrey Edmund Pryse (1867–1929), for whom the pleasures of the bottle ultimately led to destitution, or the psychopathic and thoroughly objectionable Roderick Richardes of Penglais (d.1846), there were others who pursued a more contemplative and temperate lifestyle.[2] The houses of Hafod and Alltyrodyn, for example, were *lacunae* of culture and civilization where a warm welcome was afforded to scholars and antiquaries working in well-stocked libraries accumulated by several generations of owners. If Nanteos was hardly noted as a haven for the muses under the life tenancies of William E. Powell (1788–1854) and his unpopular son, the arch-Tory W. T. R. Powell (1815–78), who justifiably earned the opprobrium of his tenants in the 1868 election, the succession of George Ernest John Powell in 1878 heralded a sea change. A graduate of Brasenose College, Oxford, and one who had devoted himself to literary and dilettante pursuits, Powell was intimately associated with Swinburne and Longfellow and was among the earliest translators of the Icelandic sagas. Yet, in common with

[1] J. Jackson, 'Letters from and relating to north Wales', *JMHRS*, IV, no.4 (1962), 166–7.
[2] References in this chapter relating to the Gogerddan family are cited in R. J. Colyer, 'The Pryse family of Gogerddan and the decline of a great estate, 1800–1960', *WHR*, 9, no.4 (1979), 407–31. See also idem, 'Roderick Eardley Richardes and Plas Penglais, Aberystwyth', *Ceredigion*, X, no.1 (1984), 97–103. For George Powell, see 'George Powell, Swinburne's "Friend of many seasons"', *Anglo-Welsh Review*, 19 (1970–2), 75–85; R. Brinkley, 'George Powell of Nanteos: a further appreciation', ibid., 21 (1972), 130–4.

Thomas Johnes (1748–1816), whose celebrated translations of the Chronicles of Froissart, Monstrelet and Joinville were printed on his own press at Hafod, Powell's cultural horizons stretched far beyond the confines of Cardiganshire, and in this respect the two men stand apart from the generality of the Cardiganshire gentry, whose interests, both cultural and otherwise, tended to be focused on strictly local matters.

While there were singular exceptions, as in the case of the Evans family of Highmead, self-indulgence and hedonism characterized the lifestyles of many gentlemen in Georgian and Victorian Cardiganshire, and the hunt, the bottle, the bedchamber and the card table probably held more attractions than the morocco-bound volumes accumulating dust in the library. Custom dictated that a gentleman occasionally spent time 'looking over prints', or listening to the painful efforts of the ladies of the household as they wrestled with piano and harpsichord, but few would do so with anything akin to enthusiasm. After all, they were primarily outdoor men, the more prosperous among them having the money and leisure to enjoy the many sporting and equestrian pleasures which possession of an ample estate afforded. To a man like William E. Powell of Nanteos, whose attitudes typify those of the county magnate, there was little purpose in owning an estate of upwards of 25,000 acres if its amenities could not be enjoyed to the full. Lord Lieutenant, *Custos Rotulorum* and MP for the county, Powell spent money on a princely scale to sustain an elegant lifestyle, maintain his string of racehorses in training at Newmarket, and support his ever-spreading pack of foxhounds. A partial absentee, like many of his fellows he blithely disregarded the fact that his aspirations outstretched his financial resources, and either from ignorance or indifference, he seemed oblivious to the systematic embezzlement of his property by his many employees. Bailiffs and sub-agents pocketed rents, mining agents appropriated mineral royalties, forestry workers stole timber, and the Nanteos butler dispensed good cheer to all and sundry in his master's absence.

According to his grandfather, Edward Corbet of Ynysymaengwyn, Powell was 'subject to every imposition', while his lawyer, in appealing for retrenchment against a rapidly approaching financial crisis, observed in 1812 that 'you are involving yourself in every quarter and *selling your estate* to pay a set of servants and others who seem to be living upon you in all directions'.[3] To Powell and others of his class, these tedious remonstrations cut little ice. Good housekeeping, thrift and economy were vulgar considerations, all very well for tradesmen perhaps, but not the sort of matters to concern a gentleman. When all was said and done, a gentleman *spent* money and relied on his salaried agents to ensure that money was available, and to extricate him from periodic financial embarrassment.[4]

Gogerddan, Nanteos, Trawsgoed and Hafod, and the lesser properties of Castle Hill, Llidiardau and Mabws apart, there were relatively few landed estates in the north of the county. Not so, however, in the southern parishes, more especially in the vale of the Teifi, where fifty or more were closely linked by a complex web of social, marital and sporting ties. Here, in this balmy countryside, dominated by Coedmor and Bronwydd, the local gentry trod a carefully orchestrated social round in which family liaisons were nurtured, convenient marriages arranged and class bonds fostered in the pursuit of mutual interests. By the mid-nineteenth century Coedmor had become the acknowledged focal point for local society and the mansion and its spacious grounds witnessed innumerable hunt meetings, croquet afternoons, *soirées* and other kindred diversions.

[3]NLW, Nanteos MSS, Box I.
[4]R. J. Colyer, 'Nanteos: a landed estate in decline 1800–1930', *Ceredigion*, IX, no.1 (1980), 58–78.

Fig. 17: Sir Pryse Pryse of Gogerddan (1838–1906), seated centre, with his servants at Ynys-hir, Eglwys-fach. (*Copyright National Library of Wales*).

A regular host at these social events was the scholarly Thomas Lloyd of Coedmor, who defeated E. M. Richards in the celebrated 1874 election, and became the last Tory MP for the county, holding his seat until 1880. In strict contrast to his son, Lloyd's father (another Thomas) was imbued with social and moral qualities more generally associated with the eighteenth than the nineteenth century. A staunch Whig and Lord Lieutenant of the county, Lloyd's dedication to his official pursuits was parallelled only by his enthusiasm for the bottle and his performance in the bedchamber. He sired numerous illegitimate children, who were generally put to work as servants in the mansion, their mothers being compensated with farms or smallholdings on the estate at nominal rents. Nor did Lloyd's legitimate sons receive many favours from their father. Although he succumbed to family pressure and educated the eldest boy (the above-mentioned Thomas) at Rugby, he doggedly refused to go to the expense of educating his remaining male offspring. Instead, they were sent out to labour on local farms. A similar sort of callous disregard for the future of younger sons was demonstrated by Sir Pryse Pryse of Gogerddan (1838–1906), a Welsh-speaking Unionist and churchman who, as a young man, had been educated at Eton and had travelled widely in Europe and Australia. For all his excellent qualities as a sympathetic and caring landlord, Sir Pryse firmly believed in keeping his younger sons short of money and, according to one of their acquaintances, they were only enabled to survive by selling fruit to the patrons of the Aberystwyth theatre.[5] Of Sir

[5]This anecdote was related to me by the late Major Herbert Lloyd-Johnes of Dolaucothi and Cirencester. For a lovingly nostalgic evocation of county life in the late nineteenth century, see H. M. Vaughan, *The South Wales Squires* (London, 1926).

Pryse Pryse's six sons, two succeeded him in the baronetcy, one became his hunting manager, and another died of septicaemia as a result of a fox bite. The two remaining sons had rather sad histories. After being declared bankrupt in 1898, Herbert William Pryse (1872–1946) worked at various menial tasks in the Daimler factory in Coventry before returning to die in Cwmsymlog. His brother, Richard Humphrey Edmund Pryse (1867–1929), spent his early manhood in India, earning a living as a starter at race meetings. Eccentric, unstable and alcoholic, Pryse passed his middle years in a variety of nursing homes before taking to the road as a vagrant. Having been found utterly destitute in a barn near Aberystwyth, he was taken in by his kinsmen at Tŷ Mawr, Ciliau Aeron, and finally died at the dining table in that house.

Interesting and entertaining as these introductory anecdotes of the eccentricities and peculiarities of the Cardiganshire landed gentry may be, they do less than justice to a social group whose activities and attitudes profoundly influenced the lives of those around them. Warts there may have been, and prominent warts at that; yet, as the remainder of this chapter will reveal, social, commercial, religious and agricultural developments in this county were inextricably linked to the attitudes, aspirations and economic status of the occupiers of the *plas*.

The accumulation of land

Among an earlier generation of economists it was frequently alleged that men assembled landed property by one, or all, of three methods: patrimony, matrimony and parsimony. To this generalization the Cardiganshire gentry were no exception, and whereas families like the Vaughans of Trawsgoed could claim unbroken connection with their estates, either in the male or female line, since medieval times, others accumulated their property by way of freehold purchase, or the rather disreputable method of advancing money on mortgage to neighbouring freeholders and subsequently foreclosing on that mortgage. If other families formed the nucleus of estates during the squabble for monastic lands after the dissolution of the monasteries, or during the redistribution of landed property after the civil wars, to others again a convenient marriage was viewed as the most felicitous means of rising in the landed world. In this respect the abundance of local lines terminating with heiresses in the seventeenth and eighteenth centuries served as a powerful magnet to fortune-seekers both from the landed and professional classes. Thus, James Loxdale, a Shrewsbury lawyer, married the Williams heiress of Castle Hill, while Edward Loveden Loveden, a cantankerous and gout-stricken Oxfordshire landowner, enjoyed a windfall of more than 30,000 acres when his wife Margaret, daughter of Lewis Pryse of Gogerddan, came into her father's property in 1779.

Besides enabling the accumulation of land and status, marriage facilitated the development of powerful political and social groupings. Thomas Lloyd, the first of that name to live at Cilgwyn, was a minor gentleman, who managed to win the hand of the Cilgwyn heiress while practising as a lawyer in the courts of the Council of Wales and the Marches. His son eventually married into the wealthy Vaughan family of Golden Grove, while *his* son espoused the widow of Thomas Lloyd of Coedmor in 1672, thereby gaining a further 5,800 acres and establishing a base for the subsequent fortunes of the house of Coedmor.[6] Like most Welsh landed gentry, the Johnes family of Dolaucothi

---

[6]F. Jones, 'Lloyd of Gilfachwen, Cilgwyn and Coedmor', *Ceredigion*, VIII, no.1 (1976), 81–7.

laid claim to a lineage of great antiquity. The Dolaucothi estate came into the Johnes family by way of the marriage of James Johnes of Llanbadarn Fawr to the widow of James Lewis, sheriff of Cardiganshire, and heiress to Dolaucothi. Their son extended the family properties by marrying the heiress of Thomas Lloyd of Llanfair Clydogau, while a grandson, yet another Thomas, secured a further heiress in the form of Jane, daughter of William Herbert of Hafod Uchtryd. Following the death of this Thomas in 1733, the various properties devolved upon his cousin, Thomas Johnes of Pen-y-bont, near Tregaron, father of Thomas and John Johnes, respectively of Llanfair Clydogau and Dolaucothi. The subsequent marriage of Thomas Johnes into the wealthy Knight family of Croft Castle in Herefordshire provided the financial platform from which Thomas Johnes of Hafod (1748–1816) could launch himself on his exciting, if ultimately ruinous, adventures at Hafod.[7]

The Hafod romance, of course, was only made possible by extensive mortgaging of the Hafod estate and the sale of unsettled properties elsewhere, and if Thomas Johnes was able by various means to sustain his mortgage commitments, this was not the case with other landowners. For example, the Llanllŷr estate, near Tal-sarn, came into the ownership of the Lloyd family by way of Hugh Llewellyn Lloyd in 1553. For one reason or another Llanllŷr was subject to mortgage charges which, by 1720, had become so burdensome that the Lloyd mortgagee was obliged to sell to a member of the Lewes family of Llysnewydd, whose descendants occupy the property today.[8]

Marriage, even if it carried with it the agreeable prospect of an extension to a man's landed territory, was not without its concomitant expenses for an outsider marrying into a gentry family. Indeed, the business of quartering one's name and arms with those of one's wife required a private Act of Parliament and could well entail almost as much expenditure as a petition for divorce. This, however, did not deter men like Edward Loveden, whose name, following his marriage to Margaret Pryse, appeared regularly in subsequent Pryse pedigrees, nor, for that matter, his descendant Edward Pryse, whose coupling with the Noyadd Trefawr heiress necessitated further quarterings so that he eventually became Sir Edward Webley-Parry-Pryse.

A useful, if strictly illegal, means of extending the bounds of an estate was that of encroaching on unenclosed land. This procedure, coupled with strenuous efforts to establish legal title to encroachments, was practised with alacrity by landowners of the late eighteenth and nineteenth centuries. In the rolling upland country of mid and east Cardiganshire there were few clearly marked boundary lines, and in many cases only custom and word-of-mouth dictated the points at which private property ended and Crown land began. Landowners fished happily in these murky waters to the discomfiture of the Crown's agents, who fought at length to maintain the Crown's rights against such notorious encroachers as Thomas Johnes of Hafod, and successive representatives of the house of Vaughan of Trawsgoed. In a county like Cardiganshire, where some two-thirds of the land area nominally belonged to the Crown, it is hardly surprising that the latter expressed growing concern at the extent of private encroachment, more especially where this involved the potential loss of manor lordship rights and manorial revenues. The *Fourth Report on the Land Revenues*, published in 1809, complained of the Crown being 'deprived of its just Rights by too much forbearance', but none the less cautioned against over-involvement in expensive legislation,

[7]NLW, Dolaucothi, vol.25. For details, see R. J. Moore-Colyer, *A Land of Pure Delight: Selections from the Correspondence of Thomas Johnes of Hafod (1748–1816)* (Llandysul, 1992).

[8]T. I. Davies, 'The Vale of Aeron in the making', *Ceredigion*, III, no.3 (1958), 202–3. Davies also chronicles the progress of the Stedmans of Strata Florida and their association with the Vaughan family of Trawsgoed.

thereby 'exciting great dissatisfaction' among landowners. There seemed to be two workable solutions: either the Crown could sell its rights by auction or it could accept the encroachments as a fact and allow the encroacher to hold on to his ill-gotten gains *provided* he recognized the Crown's rights by the payment of a peppercorn rent.[9]

To many Cardiganshire landowners who had encroached on Crown lands, this was anathema, and they fought tooth and nail to deter Crown interference. James Loxdale of Castle Hill is a typical case in point. Claiming that the Crown's action against him was '. . . a proceeding worthy only of the darkest age of feudalism and tyranny', he engaged in a costly law suit, only to be eventually forced to part with £24 1s. 6d. to buy out the Crown's interest in his encroachments.[10]

As happened so often when landlords engaged in expensive and usually fruitless litigation against the Crown and official bodies, Loxdale's legal costs far outstripped the final settlement. Yet in the dozens of cases involving enclosures, encroachments and boundary disputes recorded in estate documents, landowners were prepared to go to the very brink before reaching an agreement. Going to law seems to have held the same *frisson* as the uncertainties of the hunting field; the thrill of the chase, the anticipation of danger, and the prospect of a kill. Moreover, land equated with status and power, and it seems almost to have been a matter of honour to stand up against anyone, official or otherwise, who questioned the rights and privileges of the class exercising that status and power.

Charity, patronage and culture

If some landed families viewed charity and patronage as the reasonable expectations of a society which permitted them to enjoy wide-ranging rights and privileges, others saw them as a means of promoting social stability or even of advancing their own status in rural society. When the Bowens of Llwyn-gwair or the Evanses of Highmead devoted substantial proportions of estate income to various causes, they did so out of a genuine conviction that their efforts would help to alleviate the condition of the 'deserving poor'.[11] Similar notions lay behind the efforts of Lady Bonsall of Fronfraith to found the Aberystwyth Dispensary for the Relief of the Sick Poor, an institution which continued to function with the support of the houses of Nanteos and Gogerddan after her death in 1817.[12]

Thomas Johnes of Hafod, whose obituary in *The Cambrian* applauded his 'general philanthropy and amiable disposition', claimed always to have employed any poor man who troubled to apply for work. Perhaps, like James Hamlyn Williams of Edwinsford, who firmly believed that the distribution of mutton to the poor would ensure the salvation of his soul, Johnes looked to a blissful reward beyond the grave.[13] A more realistic indication of his motives lay in a single sentence of one of his numerous letters to the Liverpool antiquary William Roscoe, in which he observed that in 1812 he

---

[9]*Fourth Report on the Land Revenues of the Crown, by John Fordyce, Surveyor General to the Lords Commissioners of His Majesty's Treasury*, Appendix II (London, 1809), pp.80–1.
[10]NLW, Castle Hill MSS 2533, 2536–7, 2544, 2546, 2550.
[11]NLW, Llwyngwair MS 8; NLW, Highmead MSS (unnumbered).
[12]R. J. Colyer, 'The gentry and the county in nineteenth-century Cardiganshire', *WHR*, 10, no.4 (1981), 500.
[13]Ibid., 501.

employed far more labourers than required in order 'if possible to prevent mischief'.[14] To a society still recovering from the shock of events in France after 1789, and holding its breath in fear of similar calamities at home, it was highly desirable 'to prevent mischief' if the *status quo* was to be preserved. Small wonder, then, that benches of magistrates and individual gentlemen strove frenetically to pre-empt destabilizing occurrences like food riots in times of scarcity by arranging for shiploads of grain to be made available at the ports of Aberystwyth, Cardigan and Aberaeron for free distribution or for sale at reduced prices to the clamouring poor.[15] However much they comforted themselves with the thought that charity was a Christian obligation, there remains the overwhelming impression that charitable acts and donations on the part of the Cardiganshire gentry (and their fellows elsewhere) were either consciously or unconsciously used as a convenient excuse for neglecting the root causes of poverty: inadequate wages, poor housing and an inequitable and inhuman system of poor relief. Rather than come to grips with these stark realities, they resorted to temporary palliatives and 'doles' which, as David Williams of Bronmeurig astutely observed to William Powell of Nanteos in 1817, 'neither bless the giver nor the receiver'.[16] Reduction of the poor rates, to the benefit of their farming tenants (and also indirectly to themselves), was of prime consideration to most landowners and may have underpinned their attempts to encourage 'prudent habits' among the labouring poor. The Pryses of Gogerddan, for example, backed the foundation of various local Friendly Societies, and other gentry families actively supported the establishment of a savings bank at Aberystwyth following the passing of the Savings Bank Act in 1817.[17]

Education, too, received the attention (sometimes not wholly welcome) of the gentry. In the early years of the nineteenth century few parishes in the county were provided with schools, education in the main being the province of Nonconformist ministers who attempted to instil the rudiments of learning in chapel lofts, farmhouses or even stables. Alarmed at the propaganda advantages which this might yield to the Nonconformist cause, the gentry, despite the protestations of the former, who lobbied for the provision of School Boards, took action to establish schools under their own patronage. Thus, in 1812, Pryse Pryse of Gogerddan, Matthew Davies of Cwmcynfelin and George Bonsall of Glanrheidol became trustees of a charitable institution for the education of children 'according to the established principles of the Church of England'.[18] Four years later Pryse subscribed £200 and William Powell of Nanteos £50 towards the National School at Aberystwyth, while Pryse provided generously for a similar institution at Lampeter.[19] But these were trivial affairs alongside the lavish patronage of John Scandrett Harford. A Bristol-domiciled banker, author and art collector, Harford came into possession of the Peterwell and Millfield estates by marriage to the daughter of Richard Hart Davies in 1821. Absentee landlord he may have been, yet Harford spent hugely on the improvement of his estate and the provision of a pure water supply to Lampeter,

---

[14]R. J. Colyer, 'The Hafod Estate under Thomas Johnes and Henry Pelham, Fourth Duke of Newcastle', *WHR*, 8, no.4 (1977), 258.

[15]D. J. V. Jones, 'The Corn Riots in Wales, 1793–1801', *WHR*, 2, no.4 (1965), 325–7; NLW, Owen and Colby MS 2150.

[16]NLW, Nanteos MSS, Box 32.

[17]57 Geo. III, c.130. See A. E. Davies, 'Wages, prices and social conditions in Cardiganshire, 1750–1850', *Ceredigion*, X, no.1 (1984), 46–9.

[18]A. L. Trott, 'Church day schools in Aberystwyth during the nineteenth century', *Ceredigion*, II, no.2 (1953), 68.

[19]T. Richards to E. L. Loveden, December 1819; J. Hughes to Pryse Pryse, January 1825, (unnumbered) NLW, Gogerddan MSS.

besides more homely projects, including making cottage allotments available for denizens of the town. In the hope that Bishop Burgess's projected College at Lampeter 'would tend to civilise and improve the vicinity', Harford donated Castle Field for the College building and subsequently became one of its most generous benefactors.[20] In this particular enterprise he was joined by John Jones of Derry Ormond, subsequently Treasurer to the College, and John Johnes of Dolaucothi, the unfortunate County Court judge who died at the hands of his deranged butler in 1876.[21]

Since the Toleration Act of 1689 the Welsh gentry in the main had shown little hesitation in certifying the meeting places of most Protestant Dissenters. Methodists, however, with their concern to avoid official severance from the Church and their unwillingness to register meeting houses, were subject to distrust, if not intolerance in some quarters. The likes of Edward Corbet of Ynysymaengwyn and John Pugh Pryse, two fiercely anti-Methodist Merioneth landowners, who viewed alienation from the established Church as tantamount to treason, were fortunately rare in Cardiganshire where, as a whole, the landed classes were tolerant of religious Dissent in its various manifestations.[22] If, with a few notable exceptions, the gentry held firm patrician convictions as to the nature of society, and stood four-square in support of Empire, Crown and established Church, common sense and political expediency tended to temper their views of Nonconformity. However much they might disapprove of Dissenting theology and social attitudes, they could not ignore the fact that many Nonconformists held freehold land with associated voting rights and whereas a landowner exercised a considerable degree of control over the voting behaviour of his *tenants* prior to the Ballot Act of 1872, the freeholders remained their own men and could, of course, readily influence the outcome of an election contest. It was, then, politic to treat local Nonconformists with great care. When a group of Nonconformists sought leave to build a meeting house in the parish of Penbryn on land belonging to the Gogerddan estate, the proprietor was advised by his agent, 'I am of opinion it is of your interest to grant them a lease as there are many freeholders belonging to that congregation and will be affronted if you will refuse it.'[23]

It was clear by the early nineteenth century that honours in the battle for the hearts and minds of the people were moving in one direction: away from the church and towards the chapel. Most gentry probably cared little for theological niceties and nuances, but the liberal social ideals embodied in Nonconformity were a matter of concern, if not alarm, in some quarters. If erosion of allegiance to the Church implied a threat to the old order, something had to be done, and as new chapels were built, often on land which they themselves had granted, and with financial help from estate sources, landowners rallied to the cause of restoring decaying churches and building new ones according to the style of Butterworth and his school. Isaac Williams of Cwmcynfelyn, a Tractarian

[20]D. T. W. Price, *A History of Saint David's University College, Lampeter* (vol.1, Cardiff, 1977), passim.

[21]H. Lloyd-Johnes, 'John Jones (1800–1876)', *Ceredigion*, III, no.1 (1956), passim. See also E. Inglis Jones, 'Derry-Ormond', ibid., II, no.3 (1954), 127–37. The contribution of Alban Thomas Jones Glynne to the development of Aberaeron is chronicled in R. Owen, 'My Dear Reverend Cousin', *Ceredigion*, VIII, no.2 (1977), 223–5.

[22]H. Thomas, 'Edward Corbet, Ynysmaengwyn: an eccentric country squire', *JMHRS*, IV, no.2 (1962), 140–5; P. R. Roberts, 'The social history of the Merioneth gentry, *c.*1660–1840', ibid., IV, no.3 (1963), 219.

[23]NLW, Gogerddan MSS (unnumbered). Good Churchmen though they may have been, the Pryses were foremost in opposing the rapacious demands of the absentee Sir John Chichester who drew £6,000 in tithes from Cardiganshire in 1843. See J. Barber, ' "A fair and just demand?" Tithe unrest in Cardiganshire, 1796–1823', *WHR*, 16, no.2 (1992), 177–206.

Fig. 18: A painted ceiling at Trawsgoed, one of the most beautiful and elaborate of its kind in west Wales. (*Crown copyright RCAHMW-NMR*).

and a close friend of Newton and Keble, built Llangorwen church in the Clarach valley; T. J. Waddingham of Hafod restored Thomas Johnes's Eglwys Newydd, besides building a new church at Devil's Bridge, while the Gogerddan family's activity in the field of ecclesiastical building was especially remarkable. Pryse Pryse provided a gallery for St Mary's, Cardigan, at 'his sole expense' in the 1820s, and later on other members of the family followed his example by building new churches at Borth, Penrhyn-coch and Tal-y-bont, and restoring the ancient edifices at Llangynfelyn and Llanbadarn Fawr.[24]

From the middle years of the eighteenth century the Cardiganshire gentry, in common with others of their class in the rest of Wales, were becoming increasingly Anglicized and in many cases indifferent to their native cultural traditions. The Englishmen and Anglicized Welshmen marrying

[24]NLW, Aberglasney MS 28; I. G. Jones, 'The rebuilding of Llanrhystud Church', *Ceredigion*, VII, no.2 (1973), 99–116.

into Cardiganshire families may well have subscribed to Welsh-language publications and sponsored eisteddfodau, but they probably did so as a matter of form rather than out of any genuine concern for fostering the ancient tongue. Frequently educated at the great English public schools, and subsequently exposed to the wider world by way of the Grand Tour, their cultural horizons were extended such that many came to view their own cultural roots as homely or even banal. With the notable exception of Thomas Johnes, whose Hafod library before its destruction by fire in 1807 housed the remarkable collection of manuscripts by Edward Lhuyd, few local families bothered themselves with archaic Welsh literature or the preservation of manuscript material, the net result being that henceforth native cultural conservation would be inextricably linked with Nonconformity and the artisan classes rather than with the *plas*.[25] Even among those gentlemen who rarely left Wales, contact with the growing number of tourists in pursuit of the 'picturesque', stimulated interest in the allegedly 'sophisticated' culture of the salons of Bath and London, so that harpsichords and pianos found their way into drawing rooms where walls were adorned with family portraits by Reynolds, Ramsay, Lawrence and Gainsborough.[26] Meanwhile, the wealthy filled their libraries with books and folios of manuscripts. David Lloyd of Alltyrodyn collected extensively, while Thomas Johnes spent hugely on library acquisitions, scouring the continent for Froissart manuscripts and examples of volumes from the early European presses. Like Johnes, who spent £2,000 on the collection of Paris de Meyzieux alone, George Powell of Nanteos assembled a fine library from which he was able to donate some 900 volumes to the Aberystwyth Literary Institute in the 1860s.[27] But these were rare birds among the flock. The majority of gentlemen who bothered to collect books contented themselves with strictly practical works concerned with agriculture or legal matters, among which were scattered the odd novel, historical work or theological tome. The inventory of the goods of John Lloyd, a younger son of the Bronwydd family who died in 1827, values his books at £28 6s. 0d., these being principally agricultural works along with an English bible (£3 15s. 0d.) and a single volume of 'Humphrey Clinker' (3s.).[28] As with the Peterwell library, a collection typical of a family with few academic or cultural pretensions, there were virtually no items of Welsh interest among Lloyd's books. Conspicuously absent, too, from the Peterwell collection at the time of its sale in 1781 were books on agriculture and estate management; the library comprised the usual volumes of the classics, together with a handful of major titles by Shakespeare, Johnson, Gibbon and Bolingbroke.[29] Not so, however, the library of the Bowens of Llwyn-gwair, of which the catalogue records numerous agrarian tomes, a variety of Greek, Latin, French and English dictionaries and a copy of Burke's *Essay on the Sublime*. Again, no Welsh-language material is recorded although books reflecting Welsh and Nonconformist interest are widespread throughout the

[25]See J. P. Jenkins, 'The demographic decline of the landed gentry in the eighteenth century; a south Wales study', *WHR*, 11, no.1 (1982), 45. The view that the landed gentry reneged upon their traditional paternalistic duties and abandoned their role as guardians of the cultural tradition has been challenged by, among others, Prys Morgan and Matthew Cragoe. See, in particular, M. Cragoe, *An Anglican Aristocracy: The Moral Economy of the Landed Estate in Carmarthenshire, 1832–1895* (Oxford, 1996). A somewhat less sympathetic judgement is delivered by M. Humphreys in *The Crisis of Community: Montgomeryshire, 1680–1815* (Cardiff, 1996).

[26]D. Bell, *The Artist in Wales* (London, 1957), passim.

[27]E. Rees, 'An introductory survey of eighteenth-century Welsh libraries', *JWBS*, X, no.4 (1971), 197–258.

[28]NLW, Bronwydd MS 3907.

[29]H. Lloyd-Johnes, 'A Cardiganshire library', *NLWJ*, IX, no.3 (1956), 304–5.

collection, as might be expected in the library of one of the few county families with strong Methodist connections. Of the 439 books owned by the Bowens, all but 112 were of a religious or quasi-religious character, several 'Lives' of Howel Harris and the works of Vicar Prichard nestling alongside such edifying tracts as Brooke's *Satan's Devices* and *Cordial for a Fainting Soul*.[30]

Agents, lawyers, and estate management

Whereas most of the lesser Cardiganshire gentlemen lived on their estates and managed their own affairs, with the assistance perhaps of a bailiff or the family lawyer, larger landowners relied upon a complex managerial hierarchy orchestrated by a resident agent. In cases where the owner was a partial absentee, it was the agent's duty not only to manage the estate but also to keep a careful eye on his employer's social and political interests in the county. He was, in effect, 'the man on the ground', with an enormous variety of physically and mentally demanding duties which would have taxed the endurance of all but the strongest of men. The agent supervised and co-ordinated the various departments of the estate, fixed and collected rents and fees, settled boundary disputes, put into effect arrangements for enclosure and consolidation, oversaw the bailiff of the home farm, looked after the mansion in the absence of its master, settled the latter's debts when he was hemmed in by creditors, besides a bewildering brief of other tasks.[31] At the end of each year it was the agent who drew up the estate accounts for submission to his employer, or, in the case of the major estates of Trawsgoed, Gogerddan, Nanteos and Hafod, to the owner's London lawyer for checking and auditing.

With some notable exceptions, estate management in this county was largely the preserve of attorneys, solicitors and even clergymen, some of whom were not above using the estate's resources for their own social and financial benefit. For example, Herbert Lloyd of Carmarthen, nephew of the notorious Sir Herbert Lloyd of Peterwell, was a lawyer in whom, it was said, 'a reckless streak had blurred the distinction between the pursuit of reputation and notoriety'. For many years agent to the Johneses of Dolaucothi and Hafod, Lloyd was closely engaged in local political intrigue, concurrently managing, by various devious means, to exploit the local gentry's penchant for litigation in order to feather his own nest. By prudent investment of his gains in banks, turnpikes and trading vessels, together with a lucrative sideline in mortgage foreclosures, he secured an ample fortune which he subsequently managed to dissipate.[32]

The fatal tendency of the Cardiganshire landowner to go to law over the most trivial issues frequently led to prodigious legal complexities from which the lawyers more often than not emerged as the ultimate winners. Difficulties over succession to estate titles provided a particularly fruitful source of revenue to the lawyer and lawyer/agent. When Alban Thomas Jones Gwynne of Mynachdy and Tŷ-glyn died in 1819, he left no legitimate children and the several claimants to his property engaged in a disastrous lawsuit which drained the estate of its resources. So much so that when Gwynne's eventual successor, Captain Alban Thomas Davies, returned from Indian Army

[30]For references, see R. J. Colyer, 'The gentry and the county', 506–7.
[31]See R. J. Colyer, 'The land agent in nineteenth-century Wales', *WHR*, 8, no.4 (1977), 401–25.
[32]R. G. Thomas, 'Herbert Lloyd of Carmarthen', *THSC* (1977), 109–19.

service in the 1840s to take up his inheritance, he found Tŷ-glyn to have been virtually stripped of furnishings, fittings and family silver at the instigation of the Aberystwyth lawyer, James Attwood.[33]

Walter Davies (Gwallter Mechain) probably had the lawyer/agent in mind when he emphasized the division between 'professed land stewards, well-versed in several departments of land economy' and those who 'aspire no higher than receiving rents and fees and drawing up cumbersome leases and contracts, little calculated to benefit either landlord or tenant'.[34] Such men, often Anglicized and frequently ignorant of the *mores* of the Welsh tenant farmer or villager, were the subjects of abuse and vilification both from chapel pulpit and radical press. Samuel Roberts, and later Thomas Gee and Henry Richard, pulled no punches in their withering criticism of the agents whom they viewed as avaricious and overbearing, if not downright malicious in their treatment of those less fortunate than themselves.[35] By the mid-nineteenth century many of the agents on the larger estates were ignorant of Welsh, and if proprietors like E. C. L. Fitzwilliams of Cilgwyn insisted that his agents be at least capable of *speaking* the language, they were generally in the minority.[36] Unlike his father William, the unpopular W. T. R. Powell (d.1878) of Nanteos had no Welsh. Nor, indeed, did his agent W. E. Phelp, so that in negotiations with the tenants a go-between, one Davy Edwards, was employed, the results of such an arrangement placing little strain upon the imagination![37] The language problem on those larger estates employing English, Scots or Anglicized Welsh agents was highlighted in the report of the Welsh Land Commissioners in 1897. Exonerating most land-owners from hiring unscrupulous agents, and dismissing the radicals' charge that as a class they were rapacious and unfeeling, the Commission nevertheless felt moved to emphasize the point that ability to speak the language should be a prime consideration in the choice of an agent for a Welsh estate.[38]

This difficulty did not, as a rule, apply on the smaller estates where proprietors tended to use Welsh-speaking agents/stewards, frequently employing substantial tenants for the purpose. Drawing up a reference for one David Davies, an applicant for the Castle Hill agency in 1818, John Lloyd of Mabws wrote that '. . . he knows how to deal with our countrymen in this part of the world and will obey any instructions you may think proper to give him, being a down-right sober countryman, not over-gifted in the English language, but passable'. Moreover, in a reference to the practice whereby agents were required to pledge security for the rents collected, Lloyd was able to confirm that being 'a moneyed man his security is unquestionable'. In all probability David Davies and men of his ilk, accustomed as they were to the ways of their fellow farmers, would have taken a more tolerant view of the anachronistic farming methods and reactionary outlook of the tenantry than their brethren on the larger estates. The latter, more especially those recruited from Scotland, complained almost unceasingly of the inefficiency and obscurantism of the tenants in their charge and their voluminous letterbooks echo with frustration.[39]

The zeal with which an agent undertook his duties could depend to a large extent upon the whims of his employer. A perpetual absentee landlord, content with receiving his rents and having

[33]NLW, Tyglyn MS 76.
[34]W. Davies, *General View of the Agriculture of South Wales* (2 vols., London 1815), I, p.120.
[35]See, for example, H. Richard, *Letters and Essays on Wales* (London, 1883), p.122.
[36]NLW, Cilgwyn MS 43.
[37]Colyer, 'Nanteos: a landed estate', 70.
[38]*Royal Commission on Land in Wales and Monmouthshire*, Report 1897, p.260.
[39]NLW Llidiardau MSS (unnumbered).

little interest in their source, would impose few pressures on the agent and allow him a free rein in managing the property. On the other hand, in the majority of cases where owners were personally involved in their estates and the protection of their political, sporting and social interests, estate letterbooks abound with instructions and advice from owner to agent. While most of this advice was well-intentioned and even occasionally useful, persistent badgering of agent by employer, particularly where this involved the former in a lengthy correspondence over trivial matters, often led to a straining in mutual relations. Never was this more the case than when it came to the matter of money, as John Hughes, agent and solicitor to the Nanteos estate, discovered.

The personal profligacy of William Edward Powell of Nanteos had plunged the estate into acute crisis for much of the first decade of the nineteenth century, and early in 1811 Hughes had begged his master to adopt 'the assistance of a little stoicism (which) may hold you up from sinking under the many difficulties that I am afraid now surround you'. But the creditors continued to clamour and as pressure from the banks to settle estate debts mounted, Hughes's letters to the seemingly indifferent Powell took on a note of desperation. 'Unless you help me', he wrote bluntly later in the year, 'they will most assuredly send me to gaol.' Somehow the crisis was averted and Hughes struggled on for a few years until in June 1814 he received an extraordinary and apparently unprovoked missive from Powell in which he was accused of fiddling the estate accounts and threatened with instant dismissal. Hughes was baffled. He rapidly penned a series of letters itemizing the improvements to the estate under his management, notwithstanding 'the negligence of former agents', expressing his resentment of the constant insults which he had had to bear from Powell's servants, and voicing his belief that the principles of justice and ingenuousness 'which have ever characterised your house are in you extinguished'. This being so, 'it cannot surely be wondered that I now feel loath to comply with any request of yours and that I wholly divest myself of those feelings of devotion and regard which I once entertained'.[40] Remarkably enough these differences seem to have been settled, and twenty years later the tenacious Hughes was still wrestling with the thankless task of maintaining the solvency of the Nanteos estate.

Farming and forestry

Among the embattled agent's many tasks was the supervision of the estate home farm. By the beginning of the nineteenth century, farming had become a 'fashionable' occupation for gentlemen. Sir John Sinclair had described it as being 'not only a healthy but a useful employment', while the antiquary Malkin held that 'the farming of gentlemen must be beneficial to the public whatever it may be to themselves'.[41] In theory, the home farm was a showcase; a model unit wherein novel methods of husbandry and management could be practised for the emulation of the tenantry, although this role was probably of doubtful benefit in this county. Compared to the counties of Carmarthen and Pembroke, where landowners such as John Mirehouse of Brownslade, John Campbell of Stackpole and John Vaughan of Golden Grove were in the forefront of agricultural

[40]NLW, Nanteos Letter Books (unnumbered), J. Hughes to W. E. Powell.
[41]T. Bowick, 'On the management of a home farm', *JRASE*, XXXII (1862), 25. B. H. Malkin, *The Scenery, Biography, and Antiquities of South Wales* (2 vols., London, 1807), II, p.416.

improvement, Cardiganshire had few agricultural innovators.[42] The agrarian experiments of Thomas Johnes of Hafod were of little local relevance, however eccentrically innovative they may have been, besides which Johnes's farming was dictated as much by aesthetic as husbandry considerations. As a whole, the home farms of the gentry in this county were practical units, whose owners preferred to follow than to lead, and while they actively attempted to improve their husbandry operations for the benefit of their tenants, they only seem to have introduced novelties when these had been well-tried elsewhere. In practical terms, to a farmer hoping to realize a cash surplus at the end of the year, this was by no means a bad principle.

But if profit was a useful bonus, it was of secondary concern on most home farms where far greater significance was attached to the ability of the holding to produce consumables for the *plas* and general estate establishment. Bailiffs would be expected to deliver barley for brewing, milk for butter and cheese-making, and meat for household consumption, besides ensuring supplies of food for the kennels and stables. Moreover, where the owners maintained other residential establishments in London, Bath or elsewhere in Wales, deliveries of fresh food and game would be regularly despatched from the home farm. Like James Hamlyn Williams of Edwinsford, who maintained houses in Berkeley Square and Clovelly in Devon, the Harfords of Falcondale, domiciled for most of the year at Blaise Castle near Bristol, expected their Welsh farms to keep their larder well-supplied with produce.[43] By their very nature as 'models', most home farms carried abnormally high overhead costs so that it is unrealistic to compare their performance with that of tenanted farms of similar size, where husbandry methods and management aspirations were rather less ambitious. Few tenants' holdings, for example, would have been stocked with the Channel Island, Hereford and Ayrshire cows or, for that matter, with the Southdown sheep, which grazed the Gogerddan home farm in the 1820s. The latter, embracing 336 acres and a further 171 acres of woodland, typifies the home farm of the larger estate, where, between 1818 and 1822, a wide range of crops and livestock were produced, with almost a third of the total output being consumed by the house and establishment. Over the same period the farm returned a net profit in three years out of five, although this would have been substantially greater had not significant quantities of meat and cereals been given as charitable donations to the poor or sold at subsidized rates to estate workers. In this respect the home farm probably played an important function in local food supplies in times of scarcity when cheap meat would have helped sustain landless labourers and low cost cereals allowed the cottager to feed his pig without necessarily depriving himself.[44]

Besides being overall supervisor of the home farm, the estate's agent was also involved with forestry management, an important activity on many properties. For generations Welsh timber had been decimated; for shipbuilding in the sixteenth century, charcoal for lead and iron smelting in the seventeenth and eighteenth, and increasingly in the latter century for bark to service the tanning industry. So rapidly was timber being felled, stimulated in part by a quadrupling in the price of bark between 1800 and 1813, that few travellers in Wales failed to bemoan the fact. The dyspeptic John Byng, for example, noted that the woods around Dolgellau were 'wasting every hour', the

[42]F. Jones, 'The Vaughans of Golden Grove', *THSC* (1966), 188; idem, 'Some farmers of bygone Pembrokeshire', ibid. (1943–4), 133–51; D. Howell, 'The economy of the landed estates of Pembrokeshire', *WHR*, 3, no.3 (1967), 267.
[43]NLW, Falcondale MS 165.
[44]R. J. Colyer, 'The Gogerddan Demesne Farm, 1818–1822', *Ceredigion*, VII, no.2 (1973), 172–85.

surrounding air being 'quite impregnated with the smell of the charcoal fire'.[45] Realizing that timber was a renewable source of wealth and that relatively low-cost investment in forestry would be likely, in the long term, to yield a greater return than a comparable investment in agriculture, late eighteenth- and nineteenth-century landowners sought to replant and manage their woodlands in an efficient manner. In Cardiganshire, of course, Thomas Johnes was paramount among the 'spirited planters'.[46]

On a rather less dramatic scale, Johnes's example was followed on the smaller estates of Mabws, Castle Hill and Tŷ-glyn. Elsewhere the estate yards of Gogerddan, Nanteos and Trawsgoed mounted substantial planting ventures, with larch and spruce dominating the outlying parts of the estate, and decorative hardwoods adorning areas closer to the mansion, At Lodge Park, the Gogerddan outpost standing magnificently above the Dyfi estuary, 36,500 oak, 7,000 ash and 2,500 Scots pine were put down in 1793, while 3,700 oak, 900 ash and 800 firs were concurrently planted close to Gogerddan mansion itself.[47] Tree planting as such was relatively inexpensive, especially where seedlings and transplants had been raised in the estate's own nursery. Planting, though, was only the beginning of a long production cycle during which walls and fences needed to be constantly maintained if the young trees were to survive the ravages of sheep, weeding needed to be carefully carried out and thinnings regularly effected. As a labour-intensive activity, estate forestry accordingly provided a valuable source of local employment.[48]

Field sports and game preservation

Of the many privileges conferred by the ownership of land, the right to pursue game for the purpose of sport and the delectation of the table was among the most closely guarded. By 1800 long-established property qualifications had ensured that the taking of winged game remained firmly the preserve of the squirearchy, and since privilege invariably promoted discontent, the question of game rights developed into a major *cause célèbre* as the nineteenth century wore on. The passing of the 1831 Ground Game Act, by which tenant farmers were denied the right to destroy rabbits and hares, was greeted with dismay by those who relied on the unimpeded growth of arable and forage crops for a living. Indeed, in Cardiganshire, as in other parts of Wales where seasonal malnutrition all too commonly affected working people, resentment of this contemptible piece of legislation widened further the growing rift between landlord and tenant.

As a class, the Cardiganshire gentry were indefatigable sportsmen, and much of their leisure time was taken up with hunting, coursing and shooting. These group activities were regarded as both useful (in the sense that they helped stock the larder and reduce the predator population) and as a means of cementing social, political and dynastic liaisons.

Fortunately for the inhabitants of the county, landowners resisted any temptation to follow the example of Baron Charles Frederick de Rutzen, who introduced wild boar to the woods near

---

[45]C. Andrews (ed.), *The Torrington Diaries* (4 vols., London, 1935–8), I, p.149.
[46]J. T. Barber, *A Tour Through South Wales and Monmouthshire* (London, 1803), p.118.
[47]NLW, Gogerddan MSS (unnumbered).
[48]For further details, see J. M. Lindsey, 'Forestry and agriculture in the Scottish Highlands 1700–1880: a problem of estate management', *AGHR*, 25, no.1 (1977), 23–36.

Slebech in Pembrokeshire and was only narrowly dissuaded from the bizarre notion of releasing wolves in the same area.[49] Nevertheless they went to great lengths to conserve their game and the despised keepers, many of them 'imported' from England and Scotland, joined battle with a growing army of poachers, who roamed the countryside with net and snare. Poor men, too, mounted nocturnal forays on the game coverts, their hunger pangs overcoming any terror they may have felt for the keeper and his henchmen. Despite the prohibition of the appalling spring gun and mantrap and the relaxation of some of the more severe penalties for poaching in 1827 and 1828, the man unfortunate enough to be caught in the illegal pursuit of game could anticipate little sympathy. At best he could expect a savage beating from the keeper and at worst a lengthy period of imprisonment. Quarter Sessions Order Books bear witness to the way in which 'bad blood' between families could lead to a poacher being betrayed by his neighbours, while estate diaries and letterbooks vividly detail the bloody affrays between keeper and poaching gangs and underline the assiduous devotion of keepers to their task.[50]

Game protection and the resultant damage to growing crops was deeply resented by farmers, many of whom aided and abetted the poacher at his trade, and if the scope of game damage as a whole was deliberately exaggerated by radical politicians, there can be little doubting the widespread destruction wrought by the rabbit in mid-nineteenth-century Cardiganshire. By this time these voracious and prolific creatures had reached pestilential numbers throughout Wales. Initially introduced in the thirteenth century, the rabbit had so increased its numbers (especially in coastal parishes, where it was less subject to natural predators) that it had become a serious menace to crop production by 1800. The legislation of 1831 permitted an inexorable rise in population to the extent that, in 1885, a modest-sized shooting party on a Merioneth estate was able to kill no fewer than 5,086 rabbits in a single day.[51]

The Nanteos letterbooks, among other documents, highlight time and again the desperate concern of tenant farmers over the devastation of their crops by the insatiable rabbit. In 1845, for example, Edward Richard of Gwarfelin complained to the Nanteos agent that rabbit damage was costing him £126 annually, while the same agent maintained in 1863 that unless dramatic action was taken against these animals, tenants in the Tregaron area would no longer be able to pay their rents.[52] Apart from covert activity, there was little the farmer could do, given the restrictions imposed by the 1831 Act, while the attitudes of estate officers towards the problem varied widely. Some took a liberal view, perhaps prompted in this direction out of fear that farmers might combine together to refuse the tenancies of farms overrun by rabbits.[53]

The rabbit was regarded by most sportsmen as a rather contemptible creature of little sporting value and the principal objection to its destruction by tenants and others lay in the fact that they might equally be tempted to take pheasants, partridges and other more desirable game. Pheasants were relatively rare in early nineteenth-century Cardiganshire, yet the countryside teemed with other sporting species. Partridges and hares lurked in the cornfields, woodcock haunted the woodlands, and riverside meadows and estuarine waters were host to abundant snipe, duck, teal and water-rail.

[49]F. Jones, 'Some further Slebech notes', *NLWJ*, 14, no.3 (1966), 335–50.
[50]See, for example, NLW, Nanteos Letter Books, 1860–3.
[51]C. Matherson, 'The rabbit and the hare in Wales', *Antiquity*, 15 (1941), 372–8.
[52]NLW, Nanteos Letter Books, 1845 and 1863.
[53]As happened from time to time in Merioneth. See D. Howell, 'Merioneth agriculture and the farming community a century ago', *JMHRS*, VIII, no.1 (1977), 72.

The shooting fraternity of the eighteenth and nineteenth centuries was not without its critics. Yet the most savage comments were reserved for the foxhunting community, epitomized in William Shenstone's curt observation that ' . . . the world may be divided into people that read, people that write, people that think, and foxhunters'. Shenstone's view may have been echoed by those whose social and economic position debarred them from the field, yet foxhunting (and the mounted chase of other species) was seen by most landed gentlemen as a valuable, if not essential, rural institution. Before the railways brought the newly rich to the Welsh countryside, thereby expanding the size of the hunting field and increasing the potential for crop damage, the hunt was essentially a local affair. It provided, or at least was alleged to provide, a cohesive force in the locality, bringing together the common interests of landlord and tenant, so that the former enjoyed his sport and the latter some protection from the predations of foxes. Besides, the hunt indirectly supported the local community by purchases of food for horse and hound and by contributions (often substantial) to charities of one description or another. Again, each hunt required extensive support services, drawing upon the community for huntsmen, grooms, kennel-keepers, earth-stoppers and all manner of other minor posts essential to the success of the pack. To a degree, then, there was a unanimity of interest between the hunting field and other country sports regarded by many as an essential counterbalance to the forces of radicalism threatening rural stability.[54]

Estate finances

The lengthy process of estate accumulation, often extending over several centuries, was accompanied by strenuous efforts to ensure that the assembled property remained firmly under the control of the family. This was achieved by means of the legal device known as the 'family settlement'. Originally conceived in the seventeenth century as a means of reducing damage to an estate resulting from fines imposed on an owner committing a felony or treason, the settlement gradually evolved into a mechanism for preventing a profligate heir from dissipating his inheritance. By custom the settlement was effected on the marriage of the eldest son and heir, whereupon he was declared tenant-for-life with the right to enjoy revenue from the property, but without the right to dispose of capital or real estate. Following his death, that real estate was normally entailed to his eldest son. Concurrently, the settlement made provision for the bride's jointure, together with portions or annuities for daughters and younger sons of the marriage, money for this purpose usually being raised by means of the long-term mortgage.[55]

A significant, and often tragic, side effect of the family settlement was the right granted an eldest son to borrow against his future expectations, which could be a recipe for disaster where the heir had a tendency towards extravagance, as occurred, for example, in the Trawsgoed estate. By the late seventeenth century the Vaughans of Trawsgoed held some 30,000 acres in the county, besides substantial properties in Montgomeryshire, west Somerset and north-east England. A great deal of

[54]D. Itzkowitz, *Peculiar Privilege: A Social History of English Foxhunting, 1753–1855* (Harvester Press, 1977), p.176. The subject of field sports in Wales in the eighteenth and nineteenth centuries is explored by R. J. Moore-Colyer, 'Gentlemen, horses and the turf in nineteenth-century Wales', *WHR*, 16, no.1 (1992), 47–62; idem, 'Field sports, conservation and the countryside in Georgian and Victorian Wales', *WHR*, 16, no.3 (1993), 308–26.

[55]B. W. Harvey, *Settlement of Land* (London, 1973), pp.11–34.

the English property, conveniently lying outside the family settlement, had to be sold by John Vaughan (1670–1721), 1st Viscount Lisburne, to discharge his eldest son's gambling and drinking debts, while the latter's subsequent profligacy as life tenant of the estate between 1721 and 1741 laid up an ample store of financial problems for future generations. The second Viscount, besides supporting numerous mistresses and entertaining on a princely scale as an MP, neglected the management of the estate and set into motion the first of a series of mortgages which were to bedevil the estate for most of the nineteenth century. Subsequent efforts at retrenchment were to no avail and estate debt, standing at £41,000 in 1833, had risen alarmingly to £67,875 by 1849. Despite increasing rental income, and a ready inflow of money from mineral royalties and sales of land to railway companies (all of which allowed the Vaughans to purchase parts of the Hafod and Abermarlais estates in the 1830s), most of this land had to be sold in the 1850s, together with the remainder of the family properties in the north of England.

The family settlement usually required the appointment of trustees, whose function was to see that the estate was satisfactorily managed, that rents were appropriated according to the settlement, and that the life-tenant behaved responsibly in the discharge of his duties. A particular function involved protecting the interests of family members enjoying jointures, allowances and annuities, all of which absorbed a substantial proportion of estate income. A succession of long-lived annuitants, like a large number of younger brothers or marriageable sisters, could prove a thorn in the side even of the best of family men. One can only imagine the relief of the first Earl of Lisburne at the death of the surviving dowager in 1791, after a widowhood of some 51 years at an annual cost to the estate of £400, or, for that matter, the thoughts of the heir to Derry Ormond, in the mid-nineteenth century, who was obliged to furnish £1,000 yearly to his widowed mother from an estate income of £3,580.[56] Inheriting widows, too, were not without their problems, so that when Alban Thomas Jones Gwynne of Mynachdy died childless in 1819, his wife found the estate so encumbered with various jointures that she secured a Chancery decree permitting her to dispose of the unentailed Tŷ-glyn Aeron property.[57]

These unavoidable fixed outgoings could have a crippling effect on the overall economy of an estate. 'Extricate me from these Horrible Annuities', wrote the naval officer Captain Webley-Parry of Noyadd Trefawr to his lawyer in 1824 prior to the coming of age of his son, 'and you secure my firmest friendship; reflect only on these ruinous annuities.'[58] The situation at Gogerddan, where, by the late nineteenth century £5,000 annually was required for the growing army of dowagers and annuitants, was a typical example of the problem. Having secured by mortgage in 1786 £1,000 per year by way of a marriage settlement for one of his daughters, Edward Loveden subsequently mortgaged his Buscot property in Oxfordshire to provide an income for his unmarried daughter, Jane. Sir Pryse Pryse sold off the Buscot estate in 1858, whereupon the total mortgage debt on Gogerddan declined from £38,750 to £25,800. Nevertheless, by 1860, when gross estate revenue stood at £15,000, a mere £1,117 remained after payment of outgoings to meet interest charges and to provide an income for the life tenant.

---

[56]NLW, Derry Ormond MS 500. See also G. Morgan, *A Welsh House and its Family: The Vaughans of Trawsgoed* (Llandysul, 1997).

[57]NLW, Mynachty MS 13.

[58]NLW, Noyadd Trefawr MS 1381.

TABLE 5: Mortgage debts chargeable against some Cardiganshire estates

Estate	Date	Rental	Total Debt
Aber-mad	1761	-	£4,500
Mabws	1825	£1,600	£21,494
Noyadd Trefawr	1828	£2,000	£18,214
Mynachdy	1830	£4,000	£10,000
Derry Ormond	1873	£2,800	£28,000
Derry Ormond	1895	£3,580	£26,000
Bronwydd	1877	£5,300	£94,000

Whether applied as a capital sum to discharge encumbrances, or used as an income generating device for annuitants, interest accruing to a mortgage could make heavy inroads into estate income. The Cardiganshire estates of Ernest Augustus, Earl of Lisburne, supported yearly mortgage and annuity charges of £5,896 in the mid-1840s, so that from a rental of slightly less than £10,000 only a modest balance remained for personal expenditure, household costs and estate maintenance.[59]

Further examples of the level of mortgage debt chargeable against some Cardiganshire estates are set out in Table 5.[60] Debt creation was a very simple matter for families whose aspirations outgrew their pockets or others who wished consciously to demonstrate their wealth and power to the world around them. And what more effective symbol of wealth, influence and social pretension than a fine new house to dominate the estate and the surrounding countryside? The first three-quarters of the eighteenth century had witnessed the replacement or redevelopment of many of the older manor houses as tastes changed and *amour propre* superseded comfort and convenience. Nanteos, Gogerddan, Trawsgoed, Llanllŷr, Coedmor, Llanina, Alltyrodyn and others emerged from the foundations of older buildings, their quasi-classical façades closing in the ballrooms and reception rooms demanded by an increasingly sophisticated gentry class. The return of John Nash to Wales in 1784 excited considerable interest, and gentlemen looking over Ffynonau, built for James Colby in 1793, or the delicate Dolaucothi façade of the following year, clamoured to secure the architect's services or, at the very least, those of his followers.[61] Palladian Llysnewydd, created for the Lewes family in 1795 (and dynamited by one of their descendants in the early 1970s), Llannerch Aeron, Mynachdy, and several other Cardiganshire houses exhibit the direct or indirect influence of Nash, while the Mynachdy family's creations in Aberaeron probably owe much to his precepts.[62]

[59]Crosswood Deeds and Documents, I, 1504.
[60]NLW, Noyadd Trefawr MSS 1431, 1436; Tyglyn MS 22; Derry Ormond MSS 314, 408; Mynachty MSS 103–5; Ceredigion RO, D/LL/3/70; D/LP/2/18. Mortgage and bond debts on most of these estates pale into insignificance alongside the Stackpole estate in Pembrokeshire, which had accumulated debts of £123,274 in 1793, their discharge necessitating the sale of 10,000 acres of land in 1802. D. Howell, 'Pembrokeshire gentry', in T. Barnes and N. Yates (eds.), *Carmarthenshire Studies* (Carmarthen, 1974), pp.170–1.
[61]See T. Davies, *John Nash, The Prince Regent's Architect* (Newton Abbott, 1973); Nash's career in Wales has been admirably described in Richard Suggett, *John Nash, Architect in Wales: Pensaer yng Nghymru* (Aberystwyth, 1995).
[62]R. J. Moore-Colyer, *The Teifi: Scenery and Antiquities of a Welsh River* (Llandysul, 1987), passim.

Enthusiasm for house building persisted into the nineteenth century, notwithstanding the financial burdens carried by many estates. Alban Thomas Jones Gwynne grafted a private chapel onto Tŷ-glyn in 1809, while a few years later Captain William Webley-Parry was desperately trying to sell off property in St Dogmael's to help finance his remodelling of the Noyadd Trefawr house.[63] In 1843 a new wing and a portico were added to Nanteos under the supervision of the Shrewsbury architect Edward Haycock, most of the stone and timber for the project coming from the estate. For this reason, perhaps, the building works cost William Powell the modest sum of £2,880. Sometime afterwards Sir Thomas Lloyd of Bronwydd, a man of antiquarian bent, built the splendidly eclectic Gothic Bronwydd onto the framework of the original eighteenth-century house. Lloyd's architect, Richard Kyrke Penson (1815–85), whose achievements at Bronwydd were to lead to his appointment as county surveyor for the counties of Cardigan and Carmarthen, completed the work at a total cost of £7,085 14s. 9d. The fact that this far exceeded the original estimate of £3,280 suggests that various extra works were carried out during the course of construction, and even then the house was without a water supply and plumbing system, which were fitted (at a cost of £600) towards the end of the century.[64]

If the occupants of Castle Hill, Bronwydd, Gogerddan, Nanteos and elsewhere were well-placed to enjoy the amenities both of their houses and their lands, they were none the less continually aware of the heavy recurrent costs involved in the management of landed property. Houses required almost constant maintenance, forestry plantations necessitated day-to-day attention, and general estate repairs and the maintenance of tenanted farms absorbed money at an alarming rate. Taking Nanteos as a typical example, overall estate expenditure for the early and late nineteenth century, *net* of fixed outgoings in the form of annuities and mortgage interest charges, breaks down according to the following table:

TABLE 6: Overall estate expenditure at Nanteos

Date	General estate repairs and improvements	Household, stables and kennels	Home farm	Rates and taxes	Gardens and timber	Miscellaneous and landlord's personal drawings
1815–1819 [Mean Expenditure £6,753]	47%	20%	14%	1%	7%	11%
1899–1909 [Mean Expenditure £4,861]	44%	30%	3%	7%	6%	10%

On the assumption that the increased proportion of expenditure in the household, stables and kennel arose from the fact that the home farm was in the occupancy of a tenant from the 1850s onwards, and that administrative changes necessitated higher payments of rates and taxes, the

[63]NLW, Tyglyn MS 76; NLW, Noyadd Trefawr MS 1405.
[64]NLW, Bronwydd MSS 4242–3, 5880–1, 3508. Details of the contents of both larger and smaller gentry houses in the country are typified in inventories for Bronwydd, Tŷ-glyn and Castle Hill in the following NLW MSS: Bronwydd 534 and 3807, Tyglyn 97 and 26, and Castle Hill 890.

overall pattern of expenditure was much the same for the two periods, with estate repairs and improvements swelling up the bulk of the outlay. By 1800 tenanted farms in the county were in a sad state of neglect, due largely to the eighteenth-century policy of letting out holdings on long leases under which tenants bore the cost of building repairs. Dereliction in many cases was so advanced by the Napoleonic Wars that landlords, fully realizing the importance of conveniently laid-out and well-maintained buildings as an element in efficient farm management, themselves undertook the burden of building and repair costs, even where long leases still remained in force. This was a largely pragmatic decision enforced upon them by the unpleasant prospect of having numerous untenantable farms on their hands. At Nanteos, £2,000 of gross rental was being spent annually on building improvements between the end of the Napoleonic Wars and the mid-1860s, with over 80 per cent of the total estate labour bill being in the form of payments to labourers, carpenters, plumbers, sawyers and masons. In like manner, the Gogerddan estate office spent between £2,500 and £3,500 per year in the 1850s, sums which represented 45 per cent and 55 per cent respectively of the total expenditure exclusive of mortgage and annuity payments.

Unfortunately, however vigorous the attempts of estate offices to maintain and improve tenanted farms and cottages in the mid-century, the neglect of previous generations was all too evident in the poor condition of those properties by the 1880s and 1890s. As early as 1811, a return of the Peterwell estate had attributed the very slow increase in the growth of the local population to dilapidated housing conditions.[65] J. S. Harford, with his ample non-agricultural funds, was eventually to rectify the situation. Other landowners, entirely reliant on their landed income, were in a less favoured position, and however much they might have *wanted* to upgrade their estates, financial limitations were compelling. A combination of mortgage commitments, payments to annuitants under family settlement, and debts accumulated by predecessors, created such heavy interest charges that what little remained of rental income was often barely enough to allow for the maintenance of existing structures, let alone to finance the wholesale remodelling of farm buildings. Besides, the problem was one of sheer scale. In the 1830s, Nanteos (21,900 acres), Trawsgoed (42,000 acres) and Gogerddan (28,600 acres) encompassed 133, 168 and 142 farms in addition to hundreds of cottages and urban properties. With contemporary rentals standing at £5,900, £9,800 and £5,800 respectively, surplus income after the deduction of fixed annual outgoings was simply not sufficient for a 'holding operation' to prevent further deterioration. Given that a farmhouse with a dairy, living room, parlour/kitchen and service room, cost around £130 to build in 1825, while the replacement of a 20′ × 40′ stable and a 20′ × 30′ barn absorbed £38 and £40, the refurbishing of a whole estate could be enormously expensive.[66] Whereas building costs tended to decline as the century advanced, the fact remained that when spread across the large number of farms on the average estate, even a relatively high proportion of net income devoted to building improvement would only have a modest impact. This, of course, was one compelling argument in favour of the amalgamation of farms, a subject discussed elsewhere in the present volume.

That *some* improvement was undertaken in the middle and later years of the century cannot be denied, as witness the wholesale replacement of thatch with slate, and the many farmhouses and buildings on estates throughout the county which carry inscribed dates of the period above their

[65]NLW, Falcondale MS 8.
[66]Crosswood Deeds and Documents, II, 823, 863; NLW MS 9871C.

portals. Nevertheless, the general pattern seems to have been one of progressive deterioration, to the extent that on some estates insufficient cash was available even to maintain the buildings erected in the prosperous days of the Napoleonic Wars. The problem was further compounded as landlords began sell off property in the 1880s and 1890s. These sales, forced upon them by a combination of economic and social factors, led to a contraction in the size of a given estate, thereby increasing the proportion of fixed charges carried by each acre and accordingly reducing the proportion of income available for building purposes.

There may be some strength in the argument that the buildings erected by landlords throughout this period were of questionable relevance to the needs of a predominantly pastoral economy. Equally, there can be no doubting the generally poor condition of dwelling houses on many estates in the late nineteenth century, which led one witness to the 1870 Commission on the Employment of Women and Children in Agriculture to complain that few of the Cardiganshire gentry were 'duly alive to their moral responsibilities and true interests in providing improved accommodation for the class upon whose comfort and welfare so much of their own prosperity depends'.[67] But this remark, in common with the standard radical allegation that landlords doggedly *refused* to improve the farming conditions of their tenants or the housing of the working poor, must be viewed within the political context of the time and probably dismissed as a piece of polemical propaganda. A landlord possessed even of the slenderest intellectual resources would have realized that inattention to farms on his property would eventually result in those farms becoming untenantable and thus a burden to the estate. As a class the gentry, with generations of stewardship experience behind them, undoubtedly recognized the duties they bore towards their tenants, and the trust they held for future generations. The simple fact was that in many, if not the majority of cases, the economic doldrums into which they had sunk by the 1870s and 1880s largely precluded them from discharging these duties and trusts.

Decline

The changing social and political scenario of the final decades of the nineteenth century created shock waves among the Welsh landowning classes. The county and parish council elections had exposed the age-old notion of unswerving tenant loyalty as the myth, which it had probably always been, and the paternalistic order was clearly doomed. If the socio-political benefits of landownership were rapidly declining – to the delight of the radical polemicists – so too were the economic benefits, and as rental incomes declined and taxation increased throughout the depressed years of the eighties and nineties, many questioned the worth of retaining possession of ancestral lands. Since income tax, land tax, succession duty, highway, police and education rates fell heavily on the landed interest, while the growing number of villa dwellers whose incomes derived from non-landed sources were relatively immune, why struggle on with a moribund estate? There were, after all, alternative areas of investment in the form of joint-stock companies which yielded returns far in excess of landed rents.[68] Thus was the die cast and landowners countrywide sought means of disposing of their estates.

[67] *Royal Commission on the Employment of Women and Children in Agriculture*, Report 1870, p.33.
[68] H. Craigie, 'Taxation and the landed interest', *JRASE*, XIV (1878), 385–415.

But in legal terms this was impossible since the provision of various family settlements denied a life-tenant the opportunity to alienate his property, and it was only with the passing of the Settled Land Act of 1882 that he was at last allowed to do so.[69] This Act enabled a life-tenant, with the approval of his trustees, to dispose of real estate and to invest the capital so realized for the purpose *either* of effecting improvements to remaining property and paying off encumbrances and mortgages, *or* purchasing stocks to yield income for annuitants. Cardiganshire landowners were quick to see the advantages of the Act, particularly where it gave them an opportunity to rid themselves of outlying areas of land whose distance from the core of the estate made them difficult and expensive to administer. Accordingly, the Gogerddan estate disposed of 3,000 acres in the parishes of Troed-yr-aur and Betws Ifan in 1882 and more than 200 acres in north Cardiganshire between 1886 and 1895.[70]

Disregarding the decline in livestock prices, which had decimated farm incomes in the eighties, land-hungry tenant farmers were keen to buy their holdings so that demand for real estate remained buoyant. When the Moelifor estate near Llanrhystud came onto the market in 1884, tenants purchased almost half the land, while Trawsgoed tenants paid over £16,000 for 1,161 acres of outlying farms sold by that estate in 1900.[71] The almost desperate concern of farmers to secure the freehold of their holdings arose from an obsessive fear that if they failed to do so such holdings might fall into the hands of speculators from the professions or industry, who would then adjust rentals upwards in order to exact a return on their capital outlay. With this in mind, they thought little of taking on their own mortgage commitments to ensure future security, a procedure made the more necessary by the entry of affluent London-Welshmen into the land market. Time and again tenants found themselves bidding against outsiders whose enthusiasm for the possession of a few acres of their native soil caused them to force up prices, often to quite unrealistic levels.[72] By today's standards, levels of mortgage on freehold purchase appear modest indeed, but to a farming population already suffering a widespread and profound economic depression, interest, let alone capital repayments, could impose serious stresses. In 1888 a farmer in Rhydlewis bought the freehold of his 146 acres for £825, and was unable to repay even a proportion of his £600 loan before 1895. Four years earlier a neighbour had borrowed £2,000 at 4 per cent interest to finance the purchase of his farm, yet within the passing of a decade not only was the capital debt unpaid, but he had been forced to borrow a further £500.[73]

Although the fiscal legislation of 1894 and the spectre of estate duty had worried many landowners, it had a relatively unimportant effect on land sales over the next decade. Lloyd George's 1909 budget, however, with its revolutionary proposals for Incremental Value Duty and

[69]45 & 46 Vic., cap.38.

[70]NLW, Sale Catalogues.

[71]Ibid.

[72]*Welsh Gazette*, 8 August 1918. In some cases where sitting tenants were given first refusal to purchase and offered the opportunity to reach a private agreement with the estate office, sales proceeded without acrimony. But where a landowner failed to come to terms with his tenant and opted for auction, local rivalries and tensions could lead to threats and even acts of violence. This was particularly so when local individuals affronted the community by bidding at auction against a sitting tenant. See R. Phillips, *Tredegar: The History of an Agricultural Estate, 1300–1956* (Newport, 1990), p.222; W. R. Morgan, *A Pembrokeshire Countryman Looks Back* (Tenby, 1988).

[73]D. Jenkins, 'The community and the land in south Cardiganshire at the close of the nineteenth century', *Folk Life*, 8 (1970), 7.

Undeveloped Land Duty, precipitated a knee-jerk reaction among a nervous squirearchy, who responded by offering further large acreages for sale.[74] Many were gravely concerned about the future and viewed the prospect of progressive fiscal erosion of their properties and the 'rights' associated with those properties with little short of horror. Sir Edward Webley-Parry-Pryse of Gogerddan and Noyadd Trefawr echoed the general gloom when he addressed his tenants on the subject of the 1908 budget proposals which, he averred, would compel him 'to go and find a new home somewhere else'. Significantly, his remarks were written off by the liberal *Welsh Gazette* as 'arrant nonsense'.[75]

Whatever Pryse and others may have felt, nothing could stem the tide. As sons and heirs were mown down with depressing regularity in the Great War, and landowners were forced to come to terms with the dramatic social changes and increased cost of living following in the wake of peace, there seemed little purpose in going on.[76] Since there were buyers in plenty, both among their own tenants and among outsiders, they released increasing acreages for sale.[77]

Although Hafod was sold *en bloc* to the Waddingham family in 1872, the early phases of the dispersal of the Cardiganshire estates were characterized by sales of outlying property. Eventually, however, economic and fiscal pressure enforced sales closer to the nucleus of the estate so that the early years of the present century witnessed the disappearance of many old families from the smaller properties and the wholesale contraction of the great estates. For generations the Thomas family had occupied Llanfair, lying alongside the Teifi close to Llandysul, and yielding an annual rent of £815 from its 1,521 acres. Following the sale of ten farms and various peripheral fields and cottages in 1884, further properties came under the hammer in 1899 until finally, in 1908, the auctioneer John Francis was able to offer for sale the Llanfair house and its demesne lands, which by this time were unoccupied.[78] The rate and extent of the decline of the major estates was extremely dramatic. Trawsgoed and Gogerddan had been scaled down by 17,000 and 19,500 acres between 1870 and 1930, while Nanteos encompassed a mere 4,336 acres on the death of the last male heir in 1930. Nanteos has had a somewhat chequered history since its alienation from the Powell family, yet other seats such as Mabws, Mynachdy, Llanllŷr and Castle Hill remain as family homes, with Penglais serving as the residence of the Vice-Chancellor of the University of Wales, Aberystwyth. Other mansions became farmhouses, pigsties and poultry-sheds, or were simply abandoned to the forces of decay. The plight of Mount Gernos was typical of the syndrome of decline experienced by smaller houses. By 1907 mortgage commitments had enforced land sales to the extent that only the home farm, the mansion and 192 acres remained. These were eventually sold in 1916, whereupon the mansion was extensively renovated by the new owner. When he was compelled to sell in 1922, the property came into the ownership of a farmer-cum-livestock dealer, who unceremoniously stripped

[74] Estate duty was levied at the rate of 8 per cent in 1894, and was increased to 20 per cent in 1914 and 40 per cent in 1925.

[75] *Welsh Gazette*, 9 September 1909.

[76] For the situation in Wales as a whole, see J. Davies, 'The end of the great estates and the rise of freehold farming in Wales', *WHR*, 7, no.2 (1974), 188–99.

[77] NLW, Sale Catalogues; NLW MS 9871C; NLW, Bronwydd MSS 7281–7282; NLW, Amphlett Lewes deposit; NLW, Morgan Richardson MS 973; NLW, Tyglyn MS 17; NLW, Crosswood Deeds and Documents, I, 1476; *Welsh Gazette*, 28 December 1938.

[78] NLW, Morgan Richardson MSS 1311, 1316, 1426, 1436.

the mansion of its fittings and converted the shell into a piggery, in which form it survived until 1960.[79] Thomas Johnes's extraordinary folly at Hafod suffered similar indignities following the death of its last occupier in 1938. Having quietly mouldered into dereliction, it was destroyed by dynamite in 1958 to leave an unsightly pile of rubble as monument to the achievements of one of the county's more remarkable landlords.[80]

In the space of little more than a century, changing social and economic conditions had brought about the eclipse of a class whose influence in Cardiganshire had been enormous. If there remain few official testimonies to their works beyond the marble slabs embellishing the walls of parish churches, the landscape itself bears mute testament to their activities. The great oaks at Mabws, the miles of upland stonewalling enclosing Johnes's improved pastures at Hafod, the elegant design of the Trawsgoed gardens, the moulding of the farms in the Teifi and Aeron valleys, and the azaleas, rhododendrons and monkey puzzles county-wide are monuments in themselves. And if we are tempted to dismiss them as trivial monuments to a leisured, and even parasitic class, we should ponder upon the quality of landscape which their successors in the countryside are likely to bequeath to future generations.[81]

[79]Jenkins, *Agricultural Community*, pp.24–5.
[80]For the later owners of Hafod, see J. R. E. Borron, 'The Waddinghams of Hafod', *Ceredigion*, XI, no.4 (1992), 385–404; J. Macve, 'W. G. Tarrant: last squire of Hafod', ibid., XI, no.1 (1989), 59–73; E. D. Evans, 'Hafod in the time of the Duke of Newcastle (1785–1851)', ibid., XII, no.3 (1995), 44–61.
[81]For the sad saga of abandonment and dereliction, see T. Lloyd, *The Lost Houses of Wales* (London, 1986).

CHAPTER 4

THE STRUCTURE OF RURAL SOCIETY IN NORTH CARDIGANSHIRE, 1800–1850

Anne Kelly Knowles

THE main theme of this chapter is that the people of rural north Cardiganshire responded to the physical and social constraints which inhibited their region's economic development with a variety of flexible strategies for family survival. These strategies included localized solutions such as the development of squatter settlements on common and Crown lands and cottage textile production, as well as seasonal and short-term migration to more prosperous regions outside their native district. As was the case in some other regions in Britain, the combination of livestock agriculture, proto-industry, and the full exploitation of available land helped sustain local population growth while limiting the loss of population to permanent out-migration. At the same time, the very strategies devised to maintain a traditional, agricultural way of life and family attachments to land became part of the process of change by involving rural people more deeply in the larger capitalist economy of Britain.

Physical and social constraints

Any study of the structure of a rural society and its economy must consider the physical endowments of the region in question, for the qualities of topography, soil, climate, and underlying geology fundamentally affect the kinds of agriculture and other economic activities that residents of a given region can profitably pursue. The economy of upland Wales was historically limited to livestock-based agriculture, largely because of the physical limitations of the natural environment. The mudstones and grits of highland Wales weather rapidly, and tend to form podzolized, acidic soils that are leached of the organic matter and nutrients essential to crop growth. Topography and climate exacerbate these deficiencies in upland areas. Rainfall increases and average temperature falls with elevation, and greater cloud cover reduces the solar radiation that reaches the soil. These conditions intensify the leaching action of moisture percolating through well-drained soils and the waterlogging of soils that are poorly drained. Lower temperatures in particular reduce biological activity and slow decomposition, so that plant litter accumulates at the surface, gradually forming a peaty topsoil and subsurface peat. Extensive deforestation of the uplands during the Middle Ages aggravated these conditions and did much to create the barren landscape and sheep-based economy now considered characteristic of Wales.[1]

---

[1] C. A. Lewis (ed.), *The Glaciation of Wales and Adjoining Regions* (London, 1970), p.139; L. F. Curtis, F. M. Courtney, and S. T. Trudgill, *Soils in the British Isles* (London, 1976), pp.11–13, 22, 67; B. W. Avery, *Soil Classification for England and Wales* (Harpenden, 1980).

In north Cardiganshire, these conditions are most acute – and impose the most severe limits upon agriculture – where the land rises above 700 to 800 feet and where mean annual precipitation exceeds 50 inches. This includes most of the region that lies east of a line running from Tal-y-bont to Tregaron, and the isolated upland of Mynydd Bach. Low fertility of the soils in these areas stems chiefly from constant leaching, which farmers traditionally tried to counteract through the application of lime and other fertilizers. Lowland soils elsewhere in the region include much more fertile alluvial gley soils along river floodplains and brown earths and cambic stagnogley soils on gentle slopes.[2] The basic division between upland and lowland became embedded in the structure and geography of rural Welsh society, both in the distinction between winter and summer dwellings (*pentre* or *hendre* and *hafod* or *lluest*) and in the concentration of population and the development of villages and market towns in lowland areas. While the line separating upland from lowland in terms of land use and social formation was fluid, changing with periodic alterations in climate and population, it generally respected the fundamental physical differences between the two kinds of regions until unprecedented growth of the rural population in the early nineteenth century compelled families to colonize marginal upland areas, with, as we shall see, important consequences for rural society and the strategies families developed to survive.

Another kind of physical constraint was the degree to which the region's topography inhibited the development of transportation, which, in turn, created structural disincentives to the development of commercial agriculture. Cardiganshire as a whole had few paved roads until the late nineteenth century, and the unpaved tracks and narrow footpaths that connected farms and villages did not easily accommodate wheeled traffic. Although small amounts of wheat and other grains from lowland farms were exported from Aberystwyth, most ships leaving the port during the middle of the century carried lead ore, oak bark, or ballast.[3] Most produce was consumed locally, and the chief agricultural export remained livestock on the hoof. Generally speaking, farms in north Cardiganshire were too remote to benefit significantly from, or to change much in response to, the rapid growth of urban markets during the heyday of the industrial revolution in Britain.

There were also important social constraints upon economic activity in north Cardiganshire, some of which were directly related to the physical difficulties posed by the land itself. Farmers were generally averse to taking risks with new crops or innovations in livestock breeding because of their long, hard experience with poor soils and the potential for loss due to bad weather. Oats and barley produced more reliable crops than wheat and other more marketable grains, and Welsh mountain sheep were hardy enough to survive all but the worst winters. If farmers experimented with the new crops and lowland breeds of sheep and cattle recommended by eighteenth- and early nineteenth-century improvers such as Thomas Johnes of Hafod, they risked failure and destitution, particularly if they had little or no capital reserves to invest in purchasing new inputs and improving their land sufficiently to yield successful results. Perhaps the most important constraint upon enterprise among the farming population, however, was the fact that the great majority of Welsh farmers rented their

[2]'Soils of Wales', Soil Survey of England and Wales (1983) (scale 1:250,000). On the use of lime, see R. J. Moore-Colyer, 'Of lime and men: aspects of the coastal trade in lime in south-west Wales in the eighteenth and nineteenth centuries', *WHR*, 14, no.1 (1988), 54–77.
[3]D. W. Howell, 'The impact of railways on agricultural development in nineteenth-century Wales', *WHR*, 7, no.1 (1974), 45; W. J. Lewis, *Ceredigion: Atlas Hanesyddol* (Aberystwyth, 1955), p.44; Lewis Lloyd, 'The port of Aberystwyth in the 1840s', *Maritime Wales*, 5 (1980), 43–61.

land. Scholars and other social observers have long debated whether the condition of tenancy itself caused, let alone justified, the often exteme conservatism of farmers in Cardiganshire and other parts of west Wales.[4] There is little doubt, however, that tenants and small freeholders had few incentives to invest their meagre savings in improving the land they farmed when they faced so many obstacles to finding markets for surplus produce. Given this catalogue of physical and social constraints, why did the population of rural north Cardiganshire continue to grow up to 1851? Part of the answer awaits more detailed analysis of the county's demographic history, for we do not yet know whether natural increase was primarily due to lower rates of mortality, a higher birth rate, improved nutritional status, or some combination of these and other factors. My question is really why so many people stayed in the region during a period when their compatriots in south Cardiganshire and the rest of south Wales were flocking to work in the iron furnaces, coal mines, and growing industrial towns of the Blaenau.[5] Why did even fewer of the hard-pressed people of north Cardiganshire choose to emigrate to the United States, as did thousands of Welsh people from north-western counties between the end of the eighteenth and the middle of the nineteenth centuries? And lastly, what were the social consequences of the population growth resulting from their persistence? A thesis developed by the agricultural historian Joan Thirsk offers at least a partial answer to these questions.[6] Decades ago, Thirsk introduced the notion that rural handicrafts (what would later be called proto-industry) developed in regions of precarious agriculture not because those regions possessed abundant supplies of the natural resources required to produce certain handicrafts or because they had ready access to markets in which to sell them, but rather because those regions had a characteristic mix of cultural conditions and access to land. The key factors in communities that developed a semi-agricultural, semi-industrial patchwork of subsistence, while at the same time sustaining a relatively dense population were: a populous community of small farmers, either freeholders or tenants whose tenure was so secure that it amounted to freehold; a pastoral economy based on dairying or on breeding and rearing livestock for sale, which left people enough time to seek by-employment off the farm; and adequate resources to support a tradition of partible inheritance and/or continued access to unenclosed commons for grazing livestock.

The next section of this chapter will consider the extent to which the features of north Cardiganshire society during the period 1800–1850 mirrored those of Westmorland (which provided the basis for Thirsk's study), notably the supplementation of farm income with part-time work in knitting stockings, producing textiles, and mining. North Cardiganshire will also be compared with certain aspects of life in western Ireland, drawing on Lynn Hollen Lees' thesis that

[4]This question is a recurring theme in the work of R. J. Moore-Colyer, including his edition of the letters of Thomas Johnes, *A Land of Pure Delight: Selections from the Letters of Thomas Johnes of Hafod, Cardiganshire (1748–1816)* (Llandysul, 1992), and in D. W. Howell, *Land and People in Nineteenth-Century Wales* (London, 1978) and *Patriarchs and Parasites: The Gentry of South-West Wales in the Eighteenth Century* (Cardiff, 1986). It also appears in public and governmental debates on the condition of agriculture in Wales, notably in the parliamentary proceedings on land reform reported upon in the Royal Commission on Land and Wales and Monmouthshire, 1894–6, NLW, Lleufer Thomas MS 3601E; and the anti-landlord diatribe by Samuel Roberts, 'Ffarmwr Careful, Cilhaul-Uchaf', in *Gweithiau Samuel Roberts* (Dolgellau, 1856), pp.73–106.

[5]For a discussion of the relative uninvolvement of north Cardiganshire people in migration to the iron district of south Wales, see A. K. Knowles, *Calvinists Incorporated: Welsh Immigrants on Ohio's Industrial Frontier* (Chicago, 1997), chapter 2.

[6]J. Thirsk, 'Industries in the countryside', in F. J. Fisher (ed.), *Essays in the Economic and Social History of Tudor and Stuart England* (Cambridge, 1961), pp.70–88.

emigration was significantly delayed from the most backward and densely populated regions of the west of Ireland because of a paradoxical combination of geographical remoteness from capitalistic economic change and the use by residents of internal migration as a strategy for sustaining traditional attachments to family land.[7] The principal focus will be on two interior districts located north of the river Aeron, namely the upland farming communities of Mynydd Bach and two parishes along the south-eastern edge of the lead mining district.

Population growth during a period of rural crisis, 1821–1851

Population growth during the demographic transition was quite variable within Cardiganshire. Peak periods of population increase were registered in the 1821 or 1831 census for much of the county, including many southern parishes in the lower Teifi valley. The lead district in north-east Cardiganshire experienced its most dramatic growth between about 1835 and 1870, when investment in modernizing and expanding the mines created many new jobs. Population in agricultural districts located in north-central Cardiganshire crested between 1831 and 1851. In each of these areas, growing population meant greater competition for land, especially among young couples looking for small farms to support their growing families.

Table 7 shows the decadal changes in population for parishes on or near Mynydd Bach, the ridge of upland that curves south-west from Lledrod to Tal-sarn. In every parish, the acres of land per person declined significantly between 1801 and the year of peak population later in the century, although the percentage decline ranged from a low of 24 per cent (Cilcennin) to a high of 44 per cent (Llanbadarn Odwyn).

Increasing population sent ripple effects through local society. Heightened competition for tenancies meant that some young couples had to wait many years before being able to set up their own households. Thomas J. Jones and his wife Elizabeth Morgan offer a typical example. Thomas was born at Fron Felin, a tenant farm near the village of Llangeitho, in 1810. He spent much of his childhood working on the next farm his parents rented, an eleven-acre tenancy called Brynamlwg, near Pen-uwch. As a young man he went out to work as an agricultural labourer and carpenter on farms in the valley around Llangeitho. In 1836 he and Elizabeth married and moved to her family's farm, Pontbrencarreg, near Llwynpiod. Sometime between 1841 and 1843, the couple (now with a young son) finally obtained their own eight-acre tenancy at Cerrigllwydion, on the moors of Pen-uwch.[8]

The geography of Thomas Jones's life was also typical of rural people in his part of Cardiganshire. Raised on small upland farms, he found employment at larger, more prosperous lowland farms along the Aeron valley. The tenancy he and Elizabeth eventually occupied was smaller than their parents' farms and was located on rougher ground, higher up the slopes of Mynydd Bach. One of the characteristic responses to land scarcity in north Cardiganshire during the mid-nineteenth century was encroachment upon the commons. That common land still existed in sufficient quantity

[7]L. H. Lees, *Exiles of Erin: Irish Migrants in Victorian London* (Manchester, 1979), pp.23–4, 40–1.

[8]D. T. Davis, *Us Davises* (Oak Hill, Ohio, 1950), pp.6, 8; W. R. Evans, *Sefydliadau Cymreig Jackson a Gallia, Ohio* (Utica, N.Y., 1896), p.69; obituary of Thomas J. Jones, *Y Cyfaill o'r Hen Wlad* (1870), 259; Census for the parish of Llangeitho, 1841.

TABLE 7: Population increase on Mynydd Bach and in Cardiganshire

Parish	1801	1811	1821	1831	1841	1851	Acres per person 1801 / peak year
Blaenpennal[1]	331	403	473	543	503	505	12.40 / 7.56
Cilcennin	530	546	551	695	647	640	6.42 / 4.90
Llanbadarn Odwyn	312	401	467	558	504	492	14.18 / 7.93
Llanbadarn Trefeglwys	756	879	920	982	1045	965	8.31 / 6.01
Llanddeiniol	215	250	219	254	273	251	9.66 / 7.61
Llangeitho	250	279	332	377	431	442	8.60 / 4.86
Llangwyryfon	430	539	601	533	642	595	8.94 / 5.99
Llanrhystud	1148	1230	1375	1525	1608	1516	7.64 / 5.45
Llansanffraid	777	1016	1172	1206	1222	1286	7.01 / 4.23
Llanychaearn	497	538	630	688	666	538	8.41 / 6.08
Nancwnlle	457	569	635	686	774	783	10.07 / 5.88
Trefilan	226	214	278	313	317	308	9.74 / 6.94
Upper Lledrod	308	149[2]	485	481	501	534	10.91 / 7.77[3]
All parish totals:	6237	7013	8138	8841	9133	8855	
Cardiganshire:	61290	70067	81765	90690	96002	97614	

Notes:
[1]Chapelry of Blaenpennal.
[2]This low figure may be a typographical error in the original source.
[3]Combined average for Upper and Lower Lledrod.
Source: Census of Great Britain, 1851, Population Tables, part II, vol. 2 (London, 1854), 'Birth-Places of the People, Division 11, Monmouthshire and Wales', pp. 36–9.

to be encroached upon is in itself significant, and stems from the relative abundance of Crown lands in Cardiganshire and local resistance to enclosure of the commons in the early part of the century, most famously by violent means during *Rhyfel y Sais Bach* (the War of the Little Englishman, 1820–6) on Mynydd Bach.[9] Llangwyryfon parish still had 230 acres of common land in 1842. The parishes of Llanbadarn Odwyn and Nancwnlle (which includes Pen-uwch) had 574 and 521 acres of common land, respectively, at about the same time. These and other upland parishes on Mynydd Bach acquired squatter settlements such as Trefenter, Pen-uwch, and Blaenpennal, which in time developed into communities with exceptionally high proportions of freeholders. In 1830 land tax records showed freeholds accounting for 19 per cent of all holdings in Nancwnlle and 17 per cent of those in Llangwyryfon. When those parishes were surveyed for reapportionment of tithes around 1840, freeholds had risen to 27 per cent of Nancwnlle holdings and 32 per cent of those in Llangwyryfon.[10]

Thus one of the basic strategies employed by rural people to continue their involvement in agriculture and to remain in their native *bro* was to settle on marginal land, either as an interim

[9]D. Williams, *The Rebecca Riots* (Cardiff, 1955), p.62; idem, ' "Rhyfel y Sais Bach": an enclosure riot on Mynydd Bach', *Ceredigion*, II, no.1 (1952), 39–52; Richard Phillips, 'Amgáu tir ar Fynydd Bach', ibid., VI, no.4 (1971), 350–63.
[10]NLW tithe apportionment schedules for Llangwyryfon (1842), Llanbadarn Odwyn (1845), and Nancwnlle (1839); Roberts and Evans Collection / Cardiganshire Land Tax Assessments, 1830, Nancwnlle no.62/61/1–15; Llangwyryfon no.60/44/1–32.

residence while waiting for a larger farm to become available, or as a long-term residence that would provide basic subsistence from garden produce, potatoes, and a few animals, which the family would necessarily supplement with agricultural labour and/or craft employment, as Thomas Jones did in his capacity as labourer and carpenter. Today, the ruins of two-room stone cottages in Trefenter stand as reminders of this phase of upland colonization, as do names of holdings first officially noted on tithe apportionment schedules and maps, such as Blaen-y-gors, Caermynydd, Lluest-y-pwdel, and Tan-y-llethr, all in Nancwnlle parish.[11] Such colonization and persistence helped to increase the proportion of freeholders in Cardiganshire, particularly in the north, to among the highest rates in Wales. In contrast to many continental European countries and some parts of England, most farmland throughout Wales was rented under tenancy agreements. In north Wales, as little as 5 per cent of farms in a given parish belonged to freeholders at mid-century. According to the Tithe Commission surveys, from 20 to 35 per cent of farms in north Cardiganshire were freehold properties.[12] In seven Mynydd Bach parishes, freeholds accounted for an average of 30 per cent of all farms, with Llangeitho leading at over 40 per cent (see Table 8).

TABLE 8: Land tenure on Mynydd Bach, c.1840

| Parish | Freehold | | Tenancy | |
	No. / per cent	Mean acres	No. / per cent	Mean acres
Cilcennin	17 (21.0%)	52.9	64 (79.0%)	37.2
Llanbadarn Odwyn	32 (34.4%)	23.2	61 (65.6%)	49.4
Llanbadarn Trefeglwys	37 (22.8%)	29.3	125 (77.2%)	37.0
Llangeitho	27 (40.3%)	27.1	40 (59.7%)	35.4
Llangwyryfon	38 (32.2%)	9.7	80 (67.8%)	39.7
Nancwnlle	38 (27.1%)	13.3	102 (72.9%)	34.8
Trefilan	4 (8.0%)	24.9	46 (92.0%)	43.9
Total	193 (27.1%)	23.0	518 (72.9%)	39.0

Sources: Tithe apportionment schedules for Cilcennin (1840), Llanbadarn Odwyn (1845), Llanbadarn Trefeglwys (1839), Llangeitho (1839), Llangwyryfon (1842), Nancwnlle (1839), Trefilan (1838).

Here, as elsewhere in Wales, freeholds were typically smaller than tenant farms, and many freehold farmers lived a precarious existence trying to scratch a living from twenty or fewer acres, often stony or boggy acres at that. Still, the relative prevalence of freehold farming in north Cardiganshire may have been an important element in a distinctive local *mentalité*.[13] *Mentalité* encompasses cultural

[11]Tithe apportionment and map of Nancwnlle parish (1839). These holdings do not appear in the tax assessment rolls up to 1830 and so were probably built during the 1830s; Roberts and Evans Collection, Nancwnlle no.62/61/1–15.

[12]J. Davies, 'The end of the great estates and the rise of freehold farming in Wales', *WHR*, 7, no.2 (1974), 212; R. J. Moore-Colyer, 'Farmers and fields in nineteenth-century Wales: the case of Llanrhystud, Cardiganshire', *NLWJ*, XXVI, no.1 (1989), 36–7; D. Jenkins, *The Agricultural Community in South-West Wales at the Turn of the Twentieth Century* (Cardiff, 1971), pp.145–56. I am grateful to Lloyd G. Owens for permission to use the Trefdraeth Poor Rate Book.

[13]One of the best English-language summaries and explorations of *mentalité* is James A. Henretta, 'Families and farms: *Mentalité* in pre-industrial America', *William and Mary Quarterly*, 35 (1978), 3–32.

predilections of all kinds, including economic attitudes and behaviour and personal expectations. It is possible that the relative availability of land and something of a tradition of small-scale freeholding in this region may have made people all the more tenacious in holding onto, or claiming, what land was within their grasp. In this respect, residents of north Cardiganshire resembled impoverished agriculturalists in the west of Ireland, who annually migrated hundreds of miles to work as labourers on English farms in order to pay ever-increasing rents for their subsistence holdings in Ireland.[14] And like those determined Irish workers, who migrated in order to remain rooted in their home soil, the people of Mynydd Bach and other rural districts sought out alternative sources of income to keep their homes anchored in north Cardiganshire. The immediate incentive to migrate was the acute distress caused by widespread economic depression following the cessation of the Napoleonic Wars in 1815. The wars had spurred agricultural production by inflating prices for farm produce (and farm rents), while also temporarily relieving population pressure in rural areas by enlisting young men in the war effort. After the wars, rural population increased even more swiftly, and the alternating curses of low agricultural prices throughout the post-war years and periodic severe crop failure created an urgent need for cash income in rural areas.

Non-farm occupations

One of the most readily available means of earning a little cash in north Cardiganshire *c.*1830–50 was to knit stockings. Rapid industrialization and urbanization in the iron and coal districts of north-east and south-east Wales, as well as in industrial districts in England, created a growing demand for durable, affordable garments to clothe workers and their families. Stockings made from the coarse wool of Welsh mountain sheep found ready buyers, and a stocking trade developed in which travelling agents circulated between rural marketing centres and industrial towns. Although Cardiganshire did not have a stocking market comparable to the weekly market in Bala, a significant stocking trade did emerge in parishes along the edge of the Cambrian Mountains, where mountain passes gave access to the lead districts to the north, Merthyr Tydfil and other iron towns to the south, and the English Midlands to the east. Knitting stockings became a leading employment for women and girls throughout the upper Teifi district, bringing in valuable cash earnings that contributed towards the payment of rent and other expenses. In the 1841 census of Gwnnws Uchaf and Caron parishes, the occupation of 'knitting stockings' ranked second among all female employments, accounting for 16 per cent of working women and girls, compared with 48 per cent who worked as farm or domestic servants and the nearly 15 per cent listed as paupers (Table 9). For the poorest rural people, knitting stockings for sale to itinerant tradesmen could mean the difference between abject poverty and some kind of independence.[15] Participation in this cottage industry continued to grow. By 1851 the town of Tregaron had 176 hosiers, most of them women.[16]

Knitting stockings held a number of advantages for rural people. It was work that required no capital and very little skill. It could be performed by women and children as well as men (although

[14]J. Lucassen, *Migrant Labour in Europe 1600–1900: The Drift to the North Sea*, trans. D. A. Bloch (London, 1987), p.113.

[15]Census for Gwnnws Uchaf and Caron parishes, 1841; Howell, *Land and People*, p.103.

[16]E. Jones, 'Tregaron: the sociology of a market town in central Cardiganshire', in E. Davies and A. D. Rees (eds.), *Welsh Rural Communities* (Cardiff, 1960), p.74.

TABLE 9: Female occupations in Gwnnws Uchaf and Caron Parishes, 1841

	Percentage	Number
Servant	48.4	78
Stocking knitter	16.1	26
Pauper	14.9	24
Farm wife	8.1	13
Wood picker	5.6	9
Grocer, innkeeper, merchant, shopkeeper	3.1	5
Labourer	2.5	4
Milliner	0.6	1
Smithy's assistant	0.6	1
Total	99.9*	161

* Sum does not equal 100% due to rounding error.
Source: Enumerators' returns for Gwnnws Uchaf and Caron parishes, 1841.

no men were listed as knitters in the Gwnnws or Caron census in 1841) and could fill time when other work was not possible, during evening visits to friends or even while walking to London, if one is to believe the tales told of *merched y gerddi*, the 'garden girls' who migrated to work in the capital city's market gardens. Families with no sheep of their own could glean wool from roadside hedges and the commons where sheep grazed in the summer months. Cottagers from as far away as the coast of Cardigan Bay were still known to glean wool from the wild terrain around the Teifi Pools at the turn of the twentieth century, doubtless continuing a tradition established long before.[17]

Spinning and weaving were also important by-employments which provided full-time work for some families. Weaving villages such as Tal-y-bont developed to meet the needs of growing mining communities in the lead mining district. Isolated fulling mills *(pandai)* and small woollen factories more typically served rural farming areas, such as the facilities located at Llanrhystud, Swyddffynnon, and Ystradmeurig, where local farmers could exchange wool, spun thread, or farm produce for finished cloth.[18] North Cardiganshire as a whole did not develop anything like the scale or degree of mechanization that emerged in mill villages such as Dre-fach and Llandysul along the lower Teifi valley. As with the region's agriculture, the northern part of the county was generally too remote and inaccessible from urban-industrial markets to make investment in mechanized textile production seem worthwhile; nor did a significant putting-out system develop comparable to that in Montgomeryshire and Merioneth. Industrialization did little to alter the dispersed, local production of textiles in north Cardiganshire until a railway line was completed to Aberystwyth in 1864, bringing cheap factory-made cloth and garments within the physical and financial reach of rural consumers.

[17] J. G. Jenkins, *The Welsh Woollen Industry* (Cardiff, 1969), p.251; J. Williams-Davies, ' "Merched y gerddi" – mudwyr tymhorol o Geredigion', *Ceredigion*, VIII, no.3 (1978), 291–9; E. Edwards, *Byr Hanes am Blwyf Nantcwnlle* (privately published, 1930), pp.15–16; W. Jones-Edwards, *Ar Lethrau Ffair Rhos* (Aberystwyth, 1963), p.17; J. R. Jones, *Sôn am y Bont*, ed. E. D. Evans (Llandysul, 1974), pp.69–71.
[18] 'Pandy (fulling mill) at Llanrhystud', watercolour by E. P. Owen (1835), in NLW Drawing Vol. 317, p.74; 'The millstream at Swyddffynnon', watercolour by anonymous (dubbed 'a Welsh Primitive'), in Drawing, Vol. 56, p.6; Jenkins, *Welsh Woollen Industry*, pp.302–3.

Fig. 19: 'Pottling': *merched y gerddi* placing strawberries in small baskets in London in the 1840s. (*Copyright National Library of Wales*).

Mining provided another source of non-farm income for people in north Cardiganshire. Since the importance of the lead mining industry is discussed elsewhere in this volume,[19] the focus here is on the geography of the industry, particularly the rather limited geographical range of the industry's appeal to part-time and full-time labour during the first half of the nineteenth century, and the role it played as an adjunct to the agricultural economy of the region. There is no question that the growth of Cardiganshire's lead mines in the mid-nineteenth century attracted thousands of in-migrants to the hills around Pumlumon. Between 1801 and 1851 the population of the parish of Gwnnws Uchaf grew from 270 to 642, an increase of 138 per cent. This compares with a county-wide

[19]See chapter 8.

population increase of 59 per cent during the same period. The enumerators' returns for mining districts clearly shows that the increase was caused by industrial expansion rather than natural increase or agricultural development. For example, in 1851 Melindwr parish had 311 lead miners, mine labourers and ore dressers compared with just 101 farmers and farm labourers.[20]

The chief attraction of lead mining to residents of the region was the unskilled and semi-skilled work it offered at roughly double the prevailing wage for agricultural labour, although the two or three shillings a day earned by casual labourers was less than the industry standard elsewhere in Britain. The poverty of the surrounding countryside created a sufficient economic gradient to attract 'plenty of labour . . . at low wages'.[21] The scarcity of high-paying positions, which typically went to skilled Cornish miners and engineers, and the industry's limited scale of operations in north Cardiganshire meant that the lead mines attracted little unskilled labour from outside their immediate hinterland. The *Mining Journal* of 1843 mentions mine employees coming from an area with a radius of about fifteen miles, approximately the distance from Cwmystwyth to Aberystwyth and Llanychaearn, places where the census enumerator noted 'the removal of families to the adjacent [lead] mining district' in 1851.[22] This distance is intriguingly similar to the 'labourshed' of another Welsh industry during this period. In his recent study of workers in Caernarfonshire slate mines before the advent of rail transport, Peter Ellis Jones determined that most of them lived no more than fifteen miles from the quarry where they worked, although in that case most of the workers migrated weekly from their farms or cottages and returned home to stay with their families one night a week. Research by the American local historian and genealogist Edward T. Porter further shows that children employed in Cardiganshire mines at mid-century rarely lived more than 2.5 miles from the mine where they worked and that most mine workers under the age of fifteen lived within 1.5 miles of their place of employment.[23]

Thus, in several regards, the lead mines of north-east Cardiganshire were a localized industry. With the exception of Cornish miners, who were recruited for their special skills, the mines chiefly attracted workers from a restricted hinterland. And even in parishes such as Gwnnws Uchaf, where the relatively large Esgair-mwyn mine was located, work in the mines was often a seasonal or part-time occupation. 'To many of the men', noted W. J. Lewis, 'mining was merely a means of earning enough to enable them to pay the rents and so to keep possession of their farms.' His conclusion is supported by a comparison of individuals' occupations, as listed in the census, and their status as land owners, for many freeholders in Gwnnws Uchaf and Caron gave their occupations as miners, craftsmen or merchants.[24]

[20]Census for Melindwr parish, 1851, quoted in A. E. Benjamin, 'Melindwr, Cardiganshire: a study of the censuses 1841–71', *Ceredigion*, IX, no.4 (1983), 331.
[21]A. E. Davies, 'Wages, prices, and social improvements in Cardiganshire, 1750–1850', *Ceredigion*, X, no.1 (1984), 35, table 1; W. J. Lewis, *Lead Mining in Wales* (Cardiff, 1967), pp.269, 286–8, 265–73, quotation on p.288.
[22]Ibid., p.269 and note 85; Census of Great Britain, 1851, *Population Tables*, part II, vol. 2, 'Birth-places of the people', p.39.
[23]P. E. Jones, 'Migration and the slate belt of Caernarfonshire in the nineteenth century', *WHR*, 14, no.4 (1989), 621–6; Censuses for Llanfihangel-y-Creuddyn, Ysbyty Ystwyth, and Gwnnws Uchaf, 1851, 1861, 1871. I am grateful to Ed Porter for providing this data and for estimating distances to work, based on tithe map information.
[24]A. J. Parkinson, 'Wheat, peat and lead: settlement patterns in west Wales, 1500–1800', *Ceredigion*, X, no.2 (1985), 125; Lewis, *Lead Mining in Wales*, p.276.

TABLE 10: Male occupations in Mynydd Bach parishes, 1841

	Percentage	Number
Agricultural or unspecified labourer	46.4	372
Farmer	15.7	126
Skilled craft (butcher, carpenter, cooper, glazier, joiner, mason, miller, smith, tanner, tinman or craft apprentice)	13.1	105
Clothing manufacturer or trader (clothier, hatter, spinner, tailor, weaver, wool carder)	10.4	83
Servant	7.7	62
Professional (clergy, clerk, schoolmaster, surgeon)	1.5	12
Pauper	0.7	6
Grocer, merchant, shopkeeper	0.6	5
Other (carrier, collier, independent, pensioner, publican, scholar, tinker)	3.7	30
Total	99.8*	801

* Sum does not equal 100 per cent due to rounding error.
Source: Enumerators' returns for parishes of Cilcennin, Llanbadarn Trefeglwys, Llanddeiniol, Llangeitho, Llangwyryfon, Nancwnlle and Trefilan, 1841.

TABLE 11: Male occupations in Gwnnws Uchaf and Caron parishes, 1841

	Percentage	Number
Servant	22.9	82
Miner	18.4	66
Labourer (unspecified)	18.4	66
Farmer	17.0	61
Skilled craft (butcher, cabinetmaker, carpenter, cooper, manufacturer, mason, miller, saddler, smith, tiler or craft apprentice)	8.1	29
Clothing manufacture or trader (clothier, hosier, shoemaker, tailor, weaver)	6.1	22
Shepherd	2.8	10
Merchant (shopkeeper, egg merchant, livestock dealer)	2.2	8
Pauper	1.7	6
Professional (officer, clergy, surgeon, surveyor)	1.1	4
Other (mole catcher, wood picker, gamekeeper)	1.1	4
Total	99.8*	358

* Sum does not equal 100 per cent due to rounding error.
Source: Enumerators' returns for parishes of Gwnnws Uchaf and Caron, 1841.

The lead mines were also local in the sense of having a geographically limited economic impact. In addition to providing jobs for male miners and women and girls who worked in the crushing sheds, the lead mines gave a boost to the local agricultural economy by creating demand for draft animals and for provisions to feed the animals and adult male workers, many of whom lived in barracks near the works. Mine owners also paid farmers to haul partially processed ore down the winding roads to Aberystwyth. But the mines of Cardiganshire and south Montgomeryshire had nothing like the transforming impact of the early coal mines in Denbigh and Flintshire or the iron works in Glamorgan and Monmouthshire. They did not give rise to towns, let alone major urban-industrial conurbations. The mining villages which grew up around them, such as Cwmystwyth and Ystumtuen, always had the air of frontier settlements, with their rough-built barracks, scattered stone cottages, and predominantly male populations. In short, up to the middle of the century, the lead mines of north Cardiganshire contributed peripherally rather than centrally to the region's primarily agricultural economy.

The 1841 census figures for male occupations in parishes on Mynydd Bach and in Gwnnws Uchaf and Caron reflect the geographic and economic divide that distinguished the lead district from more purely agricultural districts. Only one man in the seven Mynydd Bach parishes examined here had an industrial occupation (a solitary collier), while over 18 per cent of males working in Gwnnws Uchaf and Caron parishes were employed in mining (Tables 10 and 11). Of the nearly 23 per cent of males in the latter two parishes who were listed as labourers, an unknown proportion may have also worked occasionally, if not full-time, as labourers in the mines. The occupational figures also suggest that the structure of society in the lead district was somewhat simplified in comparison to non-industrial areas. Mynydd Bach supported a considerably higher proportion of skilled craftsmen, for example, as well as more men employed as tailors, weavers, and hatters. These individuals served the needs of a community with more families and a denser population. The differences between the craft occupations in the two areas may also be significant, particularly the manufacturer (perhaps of metalwork or engine parts) and tiler whose skills filled a need in the lead district, as compared to the glazier and joiner who may well have found work building chapels on Mynydd Bach. The much higher proportion of servants relative to agricultural labourers in Gwnnws Uchaf and Caron is difficult to interpret and may simply reflect a differing preference for the two terms among census enumerators in the two districts.

Female occupations also differed markedly in the two areas. Knitting stockings was apparently unknown on Mynydd Bach, or at least was not recognized as such (Table 12). In addition, a much smaller proportion of the female population on Mynydd Bach was identified as belonging to the impoverished class of pauper, although a few women listed as 'poor spinster' may have been paupers by another name. Both categories indicate a state of dependence more than occupation. If women and girls on Mynydd Bach did not suffer from the same extremes of poverty as their sisters in the lead district, their choices of work seem to have been more confined. Servants accounted for almost 58 per cent of working females on Mynydd Bach, compared with 48 per cent in Gwnnws and Caron. Labourers and farmers (perhaps including what are called 'farm wives' in the other parishes) raised the total percentage of women engaged in agricultural callings to almost three-quarters of the female working population. Just what the large class of 'independent' women did is difficult to say, although they probably included young women with dowries who had not yet married, farm widows, and wives and relatives of small landlords and substantial tenant farmers who could afford to hire servants to take care of many household tasks.

With the broad economic and occupational structure of rural north Cardiganshire in mind, we can now attempt a fuller assessment of the applicability of Thirsk's paradigm. The region generally matches the three main points of her description, although certain aspects more closely fit the situation on Mynydd Bach or in the lead district. The Mynydd Bach region was undoubtedly a populous community of small farmers, both freehold and tenant. If the tenure of tenants during

TABLE 12: Female occupations in Mynydd Bach parishes, 1841

	Percentage	Number
Servant	57.7	255
Independent	20.8	92
Labourer	9.3	41
Pauper	5.2	23
Farmer	5.0	22
'Poor spinster'	1.1	5
Other (egg merchant, scholar, schoolmaster, shopkeeper)	0.9	4
Total	100	442

Source: Enumerators' returns for parishes of Cilcennin, Llanbadarn Trefeglwys, Llanddeiniol, Llangeitho, Llangwyryfon, Nancwnlle and Trefilan, 1841.

decades of rising population and competition for land was not always so secure that it amounted to freehold, many families did enjoy tenancy of the same holding over several generations.[25] Some of those who were not fortunate enough to inherit the title or right to a smallholding or tenancy encroached upon common land to create their own base for family subsistence, a key part of the third element in Thirsk's paradigm. The occupational information in the enumerators' returns, paired with information about land tenure in land tax records and tithe schedules, suggests that the pastoral economy of Mynydd Bach and the mixed pastoral and industrial economy of Gwnnws Uchaf and Caron parishes left people enough time to seek by-employment off the farm, whether in rural crafts, clothing manufacture, or mining. The consequences during the period from 1800 to 1850 were somewhat different for the two regions. The lead mining district developed a semi-agricultural, semi-industrial patchwork of subsistence in which the poorest people became reliant upon knitting stockings and part-time work in the mines, much as had happened two hundred years earlier in Westmorland. On Mynydd Bach neither small-scale industry nor a significant handicrafts trade developed, but the population grew more rapidly. By adding a fourth element to Thirsk's paradigm, namely seasonal and temporary migration in support of subsistence, we can gain a fuller understanding of the continued population growth and the eventual crisis it caused on Mynydd Bach.

The economic role of migration and emigration

Studies of rural districts in Wales have often made passing mention of emigration to the United States, Canada, Australia or Patagonia. Emigration was usually sporadic from rural Wales, unlike the more sustained streams of emigrants who left the industrial districts of south Wales throughout the late nineteenth century. Any mass departure from the countryside was a dramatic event which

[25]Research into the family histories of emigrants from Mynydd Bach revealed many families where a son remained on the family's tenant farm after the rest of his siblings left, as well as evidence of the same family holding the property during the emigrants' grandparents' generation, confirming the point made in R. J. Colyer, *The Welsh Cattle Drovers* (Cardiff, 1976), pp.2–3.

made a vivid impression upon local memory, and was duly – sometimes ritualistically – recorded in the annals of local history.[26] Many professional Welsh historians have also written about emigration, either at a general level or with great attention to biographical detail.[27] Rarely, however, have scholars closely considered either the geography or the local social and economic context of emigration within a particular Welsh region, both of which can shed light on the nature of that region's society as well as the causes of the emigration itself.

One way that families could surmount physical and social obstacles in order to secure subsistence was to diversify their employments within their locality, often by taking advantage of economic development elsewhere, such as the industrialization of south-east Wales, or by home production of woollen goods for export. Another way was to export their labour by migrating seasonally or temporarily to locations offering wage employment. Migration for the purpose of earning cash income to support the family at home was a long-established tradition in many parts of Europe by the early nineteenth century. Jan Lucassen, among others, has documented centuries-old migration traditions connecting particular rural districts to destinations which offered seasonal employment to casual and semi-skilled labourers, such as German workers migrating annually to brickworks in the Netherlands, and construction workers leaving rural communities in the Auvergne for up to nine months a year to work in Paris and other French cities and towns.[28] The migrant worker was typically 'a small or tenant farmer able to maintain his farm and meet the basic needs of his household only thanks to extra income earned away from home'. His or her migration would be timed according to the seasonal demands of the industry or the seasonal freedom allowed by the home economy. On upland Cardiganshire farms, female labour could most easily be spared during the summer months when livestock grazed on summer pasture, while men were more free from responsibilities immediately before or after the summer harvest or during the winter months. Migration was also tied to life cycle, with the largest proportion of migrants of both sexes either in their late teens, when young people needed to save towards a future marriage, or middle age, when parents could leave children in the care of others and particularly husbands could leave their wives with children old enough to help on the farm.

Two well-known migration traditions in north Cardiganshire followed these patterns, namely the summer migrations of young women to south-east England to work in London's market gardens and the hop fields of Kent, and the migration of male work crews to harvest grain in Herefordshire and the Vale of Glamorgan.[29] Although migration from north Cardiganshire to the iron districts was relatively rare during the early nineteenth century, men from the region did participate in the

[26]The most striking example of ritualistic folk memory of a single emigration event is the telling and retelling of the 1795 emigration from Llanbryn-mair, from the letter George Roberts wrote to his nephew Samuel Roberts more than fifty years after the event (published in S. R.'s periodical, *Y Cronicl*, vol. 8, in 1850), to the fictionalized account of the emigration by W. A. Bebb, *Dial y Tir* (Llandybïe, 1945).

[27]D. Williams, *Cymru ac America / Wales and America* (Cardiff, 1975); G. A. Williams, *The Search for Beulah Land* (London, 1980); H. M. Davies, *Transatlantic Brethren* (Lehigh, PA, 1995).

[28]Lucassen, *Migrant Labour in Europe*, pp.76–86, 196–7; A. C. Meyering, 'Did capitalism lead to the decline of the peasantry? The case of the French Combraille', *JEH*, 43 (1983), 121–8.

[29]Lucassen, *Migrant Labour in Europe*, pp.3, 96–9, 215; Williams-Davies, 'Merched y gerddi', 291–9; W. Linnard, 'Merched y gerddi yn Llundain ac yng Nghymru', *Ceredigion*, IX, no.3 (1982), 260–3; A. Redford, *Labour Migration in England, 1800–1850* (2nd edn., Manchester, 1964), p.133; M. I. Williams, 'Seasonal migrations of Cardiganshire harvest-gangs to the Vale of Glamorgan in the nineteenth century', *Ceredigion*, III, no.2 (1957), 156–9.

general trend which G. S. Kenrick of the Varteg Iron Works in Monmouthshire observed in 1840: 'there are many who come from Cardiganshire to the ironworks, for five to seven months in the winter season, live economically while here, and take home from £15 to £20 to their families, which pays the rent of their little farm, and purchases for them clothing and a few luxuries'.[30]

Thus migration not only removed surplus population from the countryside, but also played a vital role in maintaining marginal agriculture and in sustaining the growth of rural population up to the middle of the nineteenth century, particularly in regions where increasing numbers of households could not live by farming or craft production alone. In this respect migration went hand in hand with the adoption of the potato as a staple in the family diet: both provided sustenance to people in regions where the size of land holdings was progressively shrinking, although neither the potato nor scarcity of land were ever such dominant forces in rural Cardiganshire as they were in the west of Ireland.[31]

As yet no one has published a detailed, conclusive study of migration from Cardiganshire to any of the destinations known to have been important in the early nineteenth century. The lack of systematic sources of data on internal migration frustrates any such effort in much of Wales, as Arthur Redford noted seventy years ago.[32] My own evaluation of Cardiganshire migration traditions concludes that north Cardiganshire was considerably less involved in migration to the iron districts around Merthyr Tydfil, although perhaps more involved in migration to London than were southern parts of the county (Fig. 20).[33] The 1851 census information on the birthplace of residents of Merthyr Tydfil shows a far greater proportion and number of migrants from south Cardiganshire than from parishes north and east of the river Aeron, while later data drawn from membership lists of the Cardiganshire Society of London suggest particularly strong links between the capital city and east-central parishes. Additional evidence from the obituaries of Welsh emigrants marks the region around Mynydd Bach as an epicentre of emigration.[34] The obituary data also indicate that Mynydd Bach was the last region in Wales to experience a significant period of emigration to the United States during the early nineteenth century, with few people leaving the region until 1835–1850, more than three decades after emigration traditions were well established in the counties of Caernarfon, Merioneth and Montgomery, and even post-dating the first major industrial emigrations from Glamorgan and Monmouthshire to Pennsylvania.[35] If indeed this was the case, what might the relatively late departures of emigrants tell us about the structure of rural society in north Cardiganshire?

[30]G. S. Kenrick, 'Statistics of the population of the Parish of Trevethin (Pontypool) . . . and inhabiting part of the district recently disturbed', *Journal of the Royal Statistical Society*, 3 (1841), 370.
[31]Lucassen, *Migrant Labour in Europe*, pp.113, 165, 169; R. N. Salaman, *The History and Social Influence of the Potato* (Cambridge, 1949), pp.417–19. On the role of the potato in the labour system of south Cardiganshire, see Jenkins, *Agricultural Community*, pp.51–3.
[32]Redford, *Labour Migration in England*, p.10.
[33]Knowles, *Calvinists Incorporated*, chapter 2.
[34]Census for Merthyr Tydfil, 1851; 'Rhestr o'r Aelodau', *Cylchgrawn Cymdeithas Ceredigion Llundain*, 1 (1934–5), 42–55; immigrant obituaries compiled from *Y Cyfaill o'r Hen Wlad*, *Y Cenhadwr Americanaidd*, and other Welsh-American journals, supplemented with biographical and genealogical information on emigrants from Mynydd Bach. For a full discussion of the immigrant obituary database and a list of sources, see Knowles, *Calvinists Incorporated*, chapter 1 and bibliography.
[35]Knowles, *Calvinists Incorporated*, chapters 1, 2; eadem, 'Immigrant trajectories through the rural-industrial transition in Wales and the United States, 1795–1850', *Annals of the Association of American Geographers*, 85, no.2 (1995), 246–66.

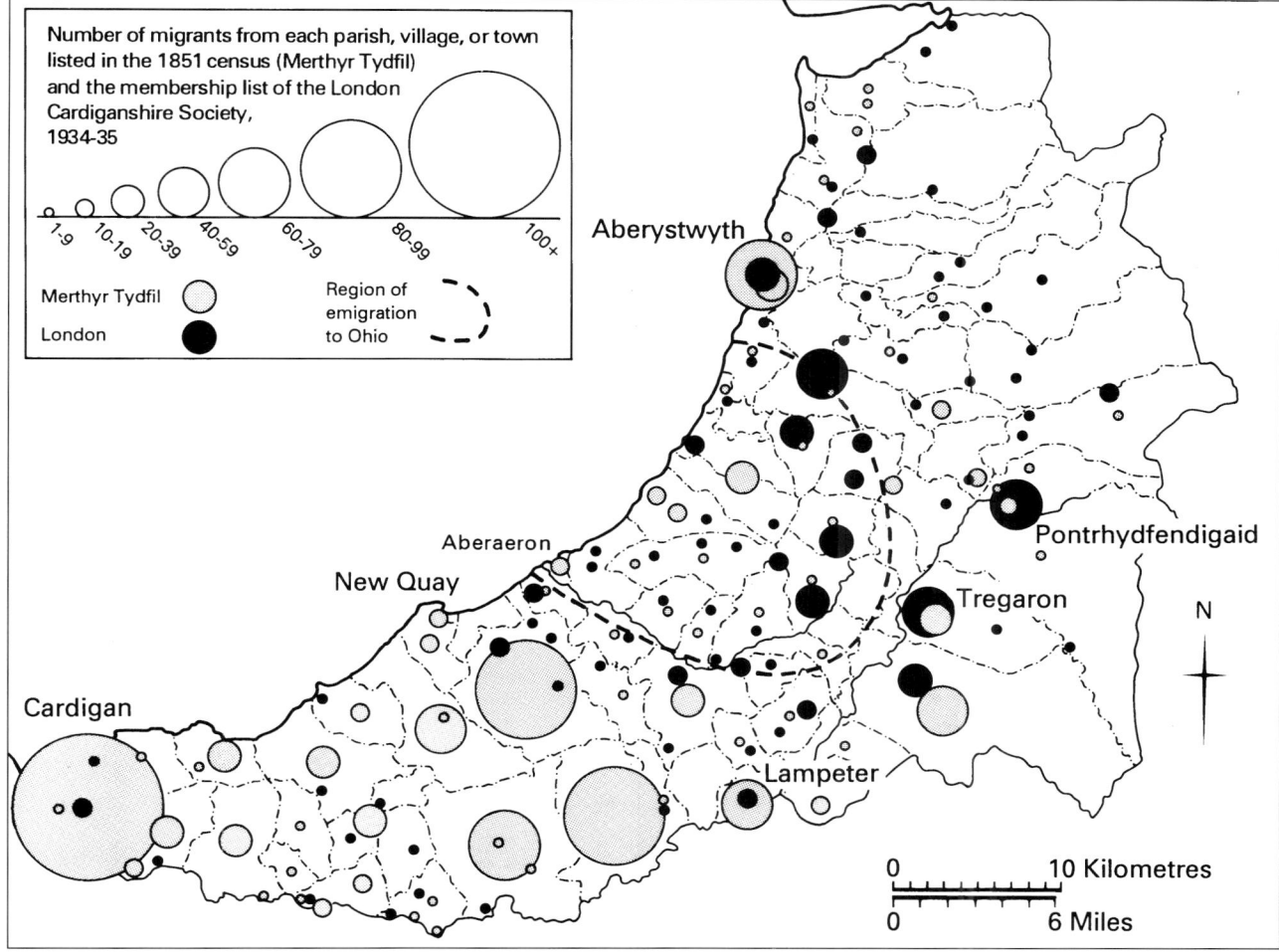

Fig. 20: Migration regions in mid-nineteenth-century Cardiganshire.

First, the postponement of emigration from Mynydd Bach reinforces the importance of continued access to land to the social fabric of this region. So long as land was available for colonization, the region could continue to retain population, even though encroachment resulted in small, poor farms which were incapable of supporting families on their own. The evident hesitancy of Mynydd Bach residents to emigrate thus lends support to the notion that the *mentalité* of local society included the hope and, for some, the expectation of owning land. Local people may also have taken a special pride in the resistance their parents and grandparents had shown during *Rhyfel y Sais Bach*, as well as benefiting from the lack of parliamentary enclosure in general in the region.[36] As local supplies of

[36]In *The Great Enclosures of Common Lands in Wales* (London, 1914), pp.47–56, Ivor Bowen notes the following enclosures in the Mynydd Bach region after *Rhyfel y Sais Bach*: Nancwnlle (1850), Blaenpennal (1851), Llangeitho Common (1856) and Llanddewibrefi (1863). The National Library of Wales possesses three original enclosure awards for the area, which are identified and dated as the Pen-uwch area in 1857 (probably Bowen's Nancwnlle); the Llangeitho Common in 1860; and Blaenpennal in 1864 (probably Llanddewibrefi).

land became more seriously depleted, however, emigration emerged as a more attractive alternative. It is also significant that the first people to leave Mynydd Bach for the United States during the peak period of emigration were mostly substantial tenants and their adult or late-teenaged children – people who probably harboured the highest expectations for achieving self-sufficiency in agriculture and who were least tolerant of land scarcity and encroachment upon the commons that they customarily used for summer pasture.

Second, the slowness of Mynydd Bach's people to embrace emigration may indicate a deep-seated conservatism that went beyond farmers' wariness about experimenting with new crops. Emigration overseas was a difficult step for most rural people, for it meant severing deep emotional attachments to family, friends and land, as well as facing the frightening dangers of sailing across the Atlantic and trying to make a new start in unfamiliar territory. Yet farming families from Penrhyn Llŷn to Llanbryn-mair had chosen to emigrate while those on Mynydd Bach stayed at home. One cultural factor that may partially account for the regional discrepancy in the timing of emigration is the influence of Calvinistic Methodism in north Cardiganshire, particularly the region around Mynydd Bach. This dated from Daniel Rowland's emergence as the leading evangelist of his generation in the mid-eighteenth century and continued through to the days of Ebenezer Richard. Richard died in March 1837, a few months before the first large party of Mynydd Bach emigrants set sail from Aberystwyth, bound for Ohio.[37] One cannot be sure how many people in the region embraced Calvinistic Methodism, let alone how many actually tried to live according to the strict tenets laid down in the denomination's *Rules of Discipline* (authored by Richard, among others).[38] Nevertheless, the biographies of those who emigrated during the peak period strongly suggest that they were religious people for whom Calvinistic Methodism provided a template for many aspects of life, including morality and the proper conduct of business affairs. It is not surprising that such people resisted the idea of emigrating until a Calvinistic Methodist minister from their own neighbourhood had persuaded them that they could establish fruitful farms as well as the means of grace in a part of the United States that he personally considered 'the best place for the Welsh'.[39]

Conclusion

Wherever rural Europeans became involved in migration traditions, whether overseas or within their native country, the experiences they encountered and the increased circulation of ideas and material goods changed the home society. Declining population in the countryside stabilized rural society even as the concepts of individual freedom, consumerism, and what Marx called the destruction of space with time revolutionized the way people in rural communities thought about themselves, their families, and the outside world. At the beginning of this chapter it was suggested that the strategies families in Cardiganshire used to maintain their traditional way of life

[37] Personal communication with genealogist Lucille McFee, Madison, Wisconsin, based on the ship's manifest of *The American*, arriving at New York City on 25 July 1837.
[38] *The History, Constitution, Rules of Discipline, and Confession of Faith, of the Calvinistic Methodists, in Wales* (3rd edn., Mold, 1840).
[39] E. Jones, *Y Teithiwr Americanaidd: Neu Gyfarwyddyd i Symudwyr o Gymru i'r America* (Aberystwyth, 1837), p.15. For a full discussion of emigration from Mynydd Bach, see Knowles, *Calvinists Incorporated*, chapter 3.

paradoxically involved them more deeply in the industrial and consumer capitalism that rapidly emerged in British cities and indeed throughout the British empire. Cottagers in Tregaron knitting coarse woollen stockings for sale to workers in Merthyr Tydfil provide one example of how major economic developments outside Cardiganshire penetrated the countryside and influenced the occupations and decisions of rural people. As Christopher Clark discovered in his study of early nineteenth-century Massachusetts, apparently small, scattered decisions by farmers and their children to engage in wage labour, even on a part-time basis, had a powerful cumulative effect over time. Participation brought the capitalist system into people's homes, changing their concepts of work and worth, and particularly changing the range of occupations and places that the younger generation would consider when they reached the age of choosing their means of independence.[40] The creative solutions developed by people in north Cardiganshire to piece together family subsistence during a period of substantial increase in the rural population helped to sustain their involvement in agriculture and their native society. At the same time, they helped bring population pressure to the point where more drastic solutions became necessary.

[40]C. Clark, *The Roots of Rural Capitalism: Western Massachusetts, 1780–1860* (Ithaca, NY, 1990).

CHAPTER 5

LAND AND COMMUNITY AROUND THE CLOSE OF THE NINETEENTH CENTURY

David Jenkins

Observers and participants

IN SUCH works as *The Agriculture of Wales and Monmouthshire*, the country's agricultural holdings are classified according to size in the following way: holdings 'From 1 to 5 Acres', 'From 5 to 20 Acres', 'From 20 to 25 Acres', 'From 50 to 100 Acres', 'From 100 to 150 Acres', 'From 150 to 300 Acres', 'From 300 to 500 Acres', and 'Over 500 Acres'. This is in no way surprising.[1] But if instead one had listened to the talk of farmers and farm workers and persons connected with farms and farming, one would have heard rather of *lle buwch* (cow place), *lle ceffyl* (horse place), *lle bach* (petty place), *lle jogel* (considerable place) and *lle mawr* (large place). These expressions of idiomatic speech would have enabled one to recognize the 'native' classifications employed by those people whose holdings were classified by Ashby and Evans in their somewhat different and formal way. In fact, one could have seen that in the communities in which they lived people identified and classified holdings of land in two parallel ways:

i. 'Cow place'; 'two cow place'; 'three cow place'; i.e. sufficient land to maintain one, two, three cows.[2]
    'horse place'; sufficient land to maintain a horse.
    'A place of a pair of horses'; land on which the work of tillage could be done with one pair of horses so that the sowing could be completed in proper time.
    'A place of two (or three) pairs of horses'; land which required the work of two (or three) pairs of horses in order that tillage and sowing were accomplished in due time.

ii. 'Petty place', 'considerable place', 'large place'.

It is not to the details of these classifications that one directs attention but to the fact that they are classifications of quite different kinds. That of Ashby and Evans is a classification properly devised by themselves as researchers to suit their own purpose, namely to enable them to discourse on the subject of their choosing. It is an 'observer's classification' and it is based upon their own judgement

---

[1]A. W. Ashby and I. L. Evans, *The Agriculture of Wales and Monmouthshire* (Cardiff, 1944), p.281.
[2]The originals are in Welsh but are given here in translation.

of what is of consequence and upon their own criteria of what is relevant to their ends; it proceeds from their own analytical concepts.

In contradistinction, the other two classifications are 'participant's classifications'. They express the considerations which were of consequence to local communities, assessed according to their own lights. A 'cow place' was of consequence because it provided its holder with 'milk and butter sustenance', whereas those people who lacked cow places were often obliged to make do with the skimmed milk and butter milk which were available at farms after churning. A 'horse place' was important because it provided the person who farmed it with the opportunity to accumulate the very modest capital he needed before he could hope to get a farm of his own: he acquired the capital by employing the horse for haulage work such as the carting of building materials, the removal of furniture, the moving of loads of fuel, and especially the haulage of goods from the railway stations before the days of deliveries by lorry, all of which he undertook while his wife looked after the holding. Since there were two sources of income, there was an opportunity to save. A 'place of a pair (two, three pairs) of horses' required not only the horses but a ploughman to work each pair of horses: thus the expression indicated the general character of the holding as well as its overall size.

In the second 'participant's classification' which was mentioned, a 'petty place' was one which was likely to lack some part of the whole complement of stock and equipment to be found on 'considerable places' and 'large places': a 'petty place' would not, for instance, keep a bull, though a bull's services were essential until artificial insemination came soon after the end of the Second World War. Thus a farm was a 'petty place' in that it was dependent on a larger farm: at the same time, many occupiers of petty places provided the ancillary services which were needed by all and sundry occupiers of land, such as dealing in butter and eggs, slaughtering pigs, and more recently investing in stock lorries and hiring out specialist farm machinery.

In all these cases, which are revealed by and through the terminology of colloquial speech, the criteria of relevance depend on what counted locally: the classifications and their details are 'participants' classifications' involving the participants' concepts, in contradistinction to the 'observers' concepts' of Ashby and Evans. Moreover, it is these participants' concepts which were mutually meaningful to people, part and parcel of their common stock of ideas, and available to them to enable them to refer to, and discuss, matters pertaining to holdings of land in a mutually intelligible way.

Three things need saying about the distinction which has been drawn between 'participants' concepts' on the one hand and 'observers' concepts' (including classifications) on the other. First, the one set of concepts does not invalidate the other; they are not alternatives, such that if one set is right the other is wrong. In fact, they are both necessary, as can be gathered from the use made of them below. Second, one would not think of attributing the one set of concepts to the enunciators of the other, for they belong to different categories of thought. Third, the distinction between participants' concepts and observers' concepts is applicable to multifarious ideas and activities, not solely to a discussion of holdings of land. To this it may be added that the three considerations newly presented are relevant wherever the distinction between the two sets of concepts can be made.

Local idiom

During the 1950s and 1960s, while enquiring about the society which had once been known to those who were by then elderly, one was repeatedly struck by the wealth of idiomatic expression which characterized their speech. Today there still exists in Cardiganshire the remnant of an earlier society whose survivors live among incomers (*dynion dî*oad*) and among natives who are estranged in whole or in part from the language and modes of thought and conduct which were once widespread. And there remains a wealth of colloquial expressions, of idioms which were current at the time when agriculture was the chief single source of employment and when most people shared the same cultural heritage. A suggestion of this common background is to be seen in the following statistics which are taken from the census reports of 1901,[3] and which provide information about the language spoken by those aged three years and upwards (Table 13):

TABLE 13: Language spoken by those aged three and upwards

Rural District	Total Population	Population 3 years and upwards	English only	Welsh only	Both English and Welsh
Aberaeron	8170	7222	109	5394	2199
Aberystwyth	13457	12617	694	6703	5163
Cardigan	3400	3222	161	1535	1513
Lampeter	3783	3518	82	2262	1172
Llandysul	8175	7720	182	5201	2333
Tregaron	7947	7494	123	5537	1824

Note: Since various replies were defective, the number of speakers does not correspond exactly to the total population aged three and upwards.

In 1901 again, 80 per cent of the population of the county had been born within its boundaries, and another 10 per cent in adjacent counties. What concerns us here is that the expressions which were common currency and which were mutually meaningful to the people who once constituted the agricultural community can help whoever wishes to see the society in question through the eyes of its members, in terms of the concepts which were the stock in trade, the mental furniture of the people involved. It is worth noting that all the expressions which follow are still in current usage at the present time. They are generally to be heard in the speech of men and women who did not receive a secondary education, and since English expressions are often employed instead of Welsh ones the casual listener may not hear the idioms or realize that they are known and spoken.

When I was in the garden of a neighbour I had known for many years she pointed to one of the flowers that grew there and named it *swch y mochyn* (the pig's snout). I had never previously heard her

[3]HMSO, *Census of England and Wales*, 1901; County of Cardigan, p.40.

so refer to a snapdragon. But for that one occasion, I would not have stumbled on its colloquial name. A mechanic friend of mine said, when a corpulent man drove to his garage, 'He is like a calf sucking two cows' (*fel llo yn sugno dwy fuwch*), while, according to the same friend, a mutual acquaintance of ours was 'like a bee in an urn' (*fel cachgi mewn stên*), noisy but insubstantial. Another acquaintance, a retiring and unremarkable man, was said to be 'like an acorn in a sow's belly' (*fel mesen ym mola hwch*). In common speech people are not said to recover from tiredness, rather they 'cast tiredness' from them (*bwrw blinder*); when one recuperates from illness, one is 'on the mend' (*ar iachâd*), and the sick have a chance of recovery when 'the face of the year' (*wmed y flwyddyn*) arrives, when the shortest day is past. When an old sailor whom I knew well referred to a man who had died suddenly, he remarked that the deceased 'had gone between hand and sleeve' (*fe ath rhwng llaw a llawes*), indicating how sharply his life had been cut off. Meanwhile a 'funeral for men and servants' or perhaps 'for men and juniors' (*angladd gwŷr a gweision*) indicated a funeral 'for gentlemen only'. One has heard a woman foreseeing modern psychoanalytic ideas when referring to hysteria as 'escaping fits' (*pwle dihangol*). It may be noted that, on first hearing such sayings, one does not necessarily know whether they are idioms of common speech or an individual's way of putting words together. Casual observations will not decide the issue, but the issue counts for the words express notions. Figures of speech are figures of thought.

I have frequently heard it said of a man of healthy appearance, 'It's a sermon to see him' (*Mae'n bregeth i weld e*), while a matter to ponder over is expressed with the words, '*mae'n bregeth meddwl*' (it's a sermon to think). 'Come to the deacon's pew' (*dewch i'r côr mawr*) is an invitation to the fireside, to the place of prominence. Those who are overly concerned with propriety in speech are said to be *santageg*, which is not readily translatable, while those who retail undesirable gossip are said to be 'raking stories' (*rhacanu storïe*), which reminds one strongly of 'raking up muck'. He who crosses his bridges before he reaches them 'goes ahead of worry' (*mynd o flaen gofid*), while the idle man is 'nursing hands' (*magu dwylo*). He does his work 'like today and tomorrow' (*fel heddi a fory*), while the diligent works 'like a fulling mill', whose hammers fall regularly and consistently (*fel melin ban; pannu arni*). One is familiar enough with the expression 'lead horse' (*ceffyl blaen*) for the man who requires the limelight: less familiar is the 'wooden deacon' (*diacon pren*), to wit the man who seeks a prominent place but who lacks the qualities of leadership.

Many of these expressions are names of things: 'the ox's drivel' (*drifil yr ych*) is gossamer, a 'bull's path' (*llwybr tarw*) is a direct line, 'preacher's bread and butter' (*bara menyn pregethwr*) is thinly sliced bread and butter. Sailors differentiated between *ochor tywy* (weather side) and *cysgod gwynt* (wind shelter or wind shadow), the lee side, and I have heard of farmers distinguishing between *oil treulio* and *oil tresi*, lubricating oil and harness oil, while dwellers in upland Cardiganshire spoke of *toriad y dŵr* (the breaking of the water) to denote the topographer's 'watershed'.

There are other expressions which are names for types of people, that is types of people who are differentiated and identified, not by a researcher but by members of the society, from among their fellows. A 'horned sheep' (*dafad gornog*) is a man who readily differs from and disagrees with other people, and is ready to be at odds with them. He may not be a 'good neighbour' (*cymydog da*) nor contribute to the maintenance of 'good neighbourhood' (*cymdogaeth dda*). While the imagery of these sayings is often colourful, it is more to the point that they are the products of a people who were members of a particular type of society and in consequence they are a lead to the nature of that society. One does not doubt that each expression was coined by an individual, but one who lived among his fellow men: only the common perception of the relevance and meaningfulness of an expression rendered it common currency.

When, for instance, farmers were members of co-operating groups, and when there was an inescapable interdependence on others in order to secure the hay and corn harvests, the maintenance of 'good neighbourhood' was linked to the doing of necessary labour and to securing one's livelihood. It hardly helped the work of a co-operating group if its members were at loggerheads. But if one maintained 'good neighbourhood' by avoiding all contentious and divisive issues there was another price to pay, namely, slowness to modify one's ways when circumstances changed. When that happened there was an opportunity for the 'horned sheep' to act and to 'bring to buckle' (*dwyn i fwcwl*) those things which others were unready to do. It can be seen that the idioms pertain to a social and cultural context and can be perused as expressions of that context.

It has been remarked above that these expressions were coined in a particular type of society: they obviously reflect a society in which the work of agriculture was extremely prominent; they also reflect a society in which people knew who their fellows were, and in which other people's opinions counted. These things are characteristic of rural agricultural communities in many lands and one is struck repeatedly by similarities between rural Cardiganshire and what inquirers have observed in other countries.

When, for instance, one asked about the annual round of work on farms at the end of the nineteenth century, the replies received were not in terms of normal calendar dates but according to the calendar of the fairs of that period, and of ecclesiastical feastdays. Such and such was done *sha ffair Fedi* (at the time of September fair), or *sha ffair Glame, Glangaea, Gynon, Dydd Sadwrn Barlys* (at the time of May fair, November fair, Cynon's fair, Barley Saturday), or *sha gŵyl Ddyrchaf(a)el, gŵyl Fathla, gŵyl Fihangel* (at the time of the feast of the Ascension, the feast of Bartholomew, Michaelmas). Candle light was available at suppertime on farms until *gŵyl Ddewi*, the feast of St David. One then did without a light until *Ffair Fedi*, September fair.

When one inquired about seasonal matters not connected with agriculture, the replies nevertheless were commonly in terms of the characteristic work of the farming year: this or that was done 'at the time of the hay harvest' or 'at the time of potato planting', and so on. It is all strikingly similar to what George Ewart Evans has said of rural Suffolk. He coined the phrase 'the prior culture' to refer without bias to the life which once was lived in the area which occupied his attention, and of the language of the inhabitants of that region he remarks '. . . in the old prior culture the language of the ordinary unlettered people of East Anglia was singularly concrete, free of most abstractions. They would, for instance, rarely talk of early summer but of beet-singling time or haysel; and autumn would be Michaelmas-time, or sowing of winter corn. Just as an old lady once remarked to me when I showed her some healthy-looking apples: "Those apples will keep till apples come again." She avoided the abstract phrase *till next season* as though by instinct. The old dialect speakers relate all states or qualities to objects or persons, and this concreteness gives the dialect a poetic quality that is full of images which capture and hold the interest of the listener.'[4] A similar tendency in the speech of those who grew up in 'the prior culture' of Cardiganshire can be noted: the parallelism indicates the link between the character of the society and the linguistic usages of its members.

[4]G. E. Evans, *Where Beards Wag All* (London, 1977), pp.177–8.

In the 'prior culture' of Cardiganshire people differentiated between *y gwŷr mawr* (the great people) or *y gwŷr byddigion* (the gentry) or *y blue bloods*, on the one hand, and *pobol gyffredin* (ordinary people) on the other. Of some it was further said that they were *tipyn o* (somewhat of) *gounty blood*, descendants of gentry children who had neither inherited nor emigrated from the area. It was also said of some that they were *rhywbeth gwell n'ai gily'* (something better than others), or in parts of mid-Cardiganshire *rhywbeth gwell na pheido*. Until recent years there were some yet alive who remembered such families at the turn of the century, whom they named to me and categorized according to the expressions now under consideration, families who from documentary sources can be traced to people who owned land during the seventeenth and eighteenth centuries, for instance, those who owned and occupied Cwmcoednerth, Rhydlewis, *c*.1900, whose family history can be ascertained from documents in the Morgan Richardson Deeds and Documents Collection in the National Library of Wales.[5]

One may further instance the family of Theophilus Jones (d.1908) of Pengelli in Troed-yr-aur parish, the descendant of his namesake (d.1758) of Blaenplwyf Ystrad in the parish of Llanfihangel Ystrad, to whom William Williams of Pantycelyn sang the least informative of elegies: the details may be found in the Pengelli Collection of Deeds and Documents, again in the National Library of Wales. *Tipyn o gounty blood* and *rhywbeth gwell na'i gily'* are secondary or sub-categories in that it is the priority of other categories which renders them meaningful. One should add that they were not mutually exclusive categories.

Among 'ordinary people', further differentiation was recognized between 'farmers' (some of whom might be *rhywbeth gwell na'i gily'*) and *pobol tai bach*, 'the people of the little houses', namely people without land, or at the most sufficient land to keep a cow, for *tŷ bach* (a little house) denoted a house without land. One finds the category referred to in the colloquial proverb *Unwaith y flwyddyn mae pobol tai bach yn lladd mochyn*, 'It is once a year that the people of the little houses kill a pig'. (This reference to the slender means of such people was a metaphor for spending money.) 'A little house' may still be heard used in the sense here indicated, for I recently heard it said of a substantial farmer who had retired to a large cedar wood bungalow that he now lived in a 'little house', which clearly referred not to the size of the house but to the fact that there was no land attached to it.

These expressions are or were part and parcel of colloquial speech. They denote categories of people, categories which were identified by and were meaningful to the members of the local society, according to criteria which pertained to them, not to a researcher. They are not technical terms (it would be vain to interpret the composition of industrial communities in terms of such categories). They make the society manifest 'from within'; they indicate the way that those who constituted the society understood it. They do not comprise a ready-made description of the society, and the expressions that have been considered here refer primarily to the society according to its relationship to the ownership and occupation of land. This was clearly of great importance, but it was not all important. While people were 'farmers' and 'people of the little houses', they were also 'the people of the chapel' and 'the people of the world'. They were also Davieses, Thomases, Joneses, Williamses, i.e. sets of kinsmen, and the various categories did not always coincide. Thus the expressions are a key rather than the individual items of a final description.

[5]NLW, Morgan Richardson Deeds and Documents, nos. 766–7, 791, 814, 820, 821, 822, 823, 857, 859, among others.

One may elaborate further on their significance by quoting the words of P. A. Winch: 'the nature of the unity of a human society . . . is that it is a unity essentially involving *concepts* . . . the interaction of human beings in society . . . involves communication, speech, and mutual understanding (or of course, *mis*understanding.) . . . It follows . . . that one cannot give a full account of the nature of a human society without giving an account of the way in which concepts enter into the relations which men have to each other in such a society.'[6] The significance of the idioms which have been mentioned above is this: they expressed concepts concerning the society; they contributed to people's mutual comprehension of their relations with their fellows; they provided the vocabulary whereby people communicated with one another day in day out; without communication there would be neither community nor society.

The society and the land

By 'society' one means people as they stand interrelated: by 'social structure' one means the relatively stable patterns of those interrelationships. When land was worked by people rather than by machines, the way in which people were 'organized', in order to do the work of the land, entered prominently into the ways in which they were interrelated, within the social structure. Before the coming of equipment such as the mowing machine and the corn self-binder in the late nineteenth century and early twentieth century, there were three main ways in which people were ordered to work the land, namely the farm household, the group of farms which co-operated with one another for certain tasks in the course of the year, and *y fedel*. This was the work group of cottagers who were connected with each farm, each cottager paying a 'labour debt' (*dyled gwaith*) for rows of potatoes planted on the farm's land, thus providing the extra labour required at the harvests. An account of each follows below.

The farm household

The two heads of each farm household were the *mishtir* (master) and the *mishtres* (mistress), who were known as such to all who worked at the farm, whatever the occasion. The master looked after the farm's financial affairs and managed it (as well as much other work besides), while the mistress was responsible for running the farmhouse, the dairy, the poultry, and the maids who were employed for general work rather than as house servants as such. It need hardly be remarked that where the farm was occupied by a family, the husband and wife would be 'master' and 'mistress'.

'The highest work of the farm' (*gwaith uwcha'r ffarm*) was by common acknowledgement work with the horses, which included much of the work of cultivation. It was undertaken by the sons if they were of suitable age; in default, servants were employed, being in the normal way unmarried men living in. The colloquial term for 'farm servant' is *gwas ffarm*: the word *gwas* means both 'servant' and a junior, unmarried man, as can be seen in the words which a father might use when bidding his young son to accompany him, *Dere mla(e)n was*, 'come on (g)was'.[7] Sons and servants were equivalents in respect of the way in which farm work was organized: they were unmarried (for sons remained

[6]For further discussion, see P. A. Winch, *The Idea of a Social Science* (London, 1958).
[7]*Geiriadur Prifysgol Cymru*, s.v. *gwas*.

unmarried while living at home, marrying as and when they could secure holdings of their own, whereupon each became 'master'). Sons and servants did the same work with horses; they frequently shared the same sleeping accommodation in the stable – or storehouse – loft; they ate together in the *rwm ford*, literally the 'board (or table) room', in those farms which featured such a room. It is noteworthy that at meal times servants took precedence over labourers: when, for instance, food was placed on the table in a pot the chief servant helped himself first, followed by the other servants and then by the labourers, a practice which is readily intelligible if it is borne in mind that servants correspond to sons in the way in which a farm's staff was ordered. Meanwhile, the master ate in the kitchen, which was the living room. Characteristic of the *rwm ford* was that it had no fireplace, was entered from within the house rather than directly from outside, and on occasion had a window in the internal wall which separated it from the kitchen. It was not a room to linger in. The farm's children, male and female, ate in the 'board room', as did servants and labourers from other farms who were present at meal times; in contradistinction a neighbouring farmer would be invited into the kitchen, as would a farmer's son. Farm house practices distinguished clearly between seniors and juniors, between those in authority and those under authority, as they did between farmers and all others who worked on farms.

All the work of the farm would be undertaken by the members of the family if that was practicable; if it was impracticable, then just as servants were employed for working with horses, so full-time labourers would be employed for general labouring work; these were men who lived in their own homes and were clearly distinguished from servants. All were known by the name of the farm where they were employed, for instance *gwas y Dyffryn* (the servant of Dyffryn), *gweithwr Penrallt* (the labourer of Penrallt), as the case might be. When farms employed labourers it was they who cared for the store cattle: a servant would not be engaged to care for cattle except as a last resort, for the work was considered lowly. Casual workers who were often highly skilled were known as 'hired men' (*dynion hur*); they were not known by a farm's name.

Farm servants were engaged by the year formally from one November hiring fair to the next: they drew their earnings as occasion required rather than receiving regular payment. Similarly farmers' sons received money on such occasions as fairs and weddings but did not receive a regular wage. Farm servants collected the balance due to them at the end of the period for which they had been engaged and it was then that they paid off outstanding debts they had incurred in the course of the year to the cobbler and the tailor. Full-time farm labourers were similarly engaged from one November fair to the next but, unlike the servants, they were paid a regular wage.

The census data of 1901 show that in Cardiganshire there were 20,952 males aged ten and over. Of these 16,775 were in employment, 7,283 of whom were engaged in agriculture, including 2,905 'farmers and graziers': it was much the largest single category of male employment. In comparison the total number of craftsmen engaged in the building trade was 1,817, chiefly carpenters and masons. It is difficult to be certain about the details of female employment in agriculture. The maids who were engaged on farms were enumerated among the employed females, whose total number is given as 1,487 (i.e. in agriculture).[8] This figure cannot include farm wives, for in 1913 there were more than 6,000 holdings of land in Cardiganshire; 3,055 of them were larger than 20 acres, including 1,817 which were larger than 50 acres.[9] Where these were occupied by married couples,

---

[8] Census of England and Wales, 1901, Vol.2, pp.30–2.
[9] Ashby and Evans, *Agriculture of Wales*, p.281.

the wives were certainly engaged in agriculture. One concludes that many more women were engaged in agriculture than the census indicates. In consequence it is abundantly clear that farm work was overwhelmingly the largest single category of general employment and it is no wonder, therefore, that other occupations were often patterned in the manner that farm work was patterned, where that was practicable. Just as farm servants were engaged from one November fair to the next, so woollen workers who were employed in small factories which stood on many a farmyard were engaged in the same way and shared the same sleeping accommodation as farm servants. One man I knew mentioned being one of fourteen who slept in the storehouse loft of a farm some two miles from Llandysul: he and two others were farm servants, while the remaining eleven were woollen workers who lived in and were fed at the farm. (The cloth was taken from that factory by horse and cart, for sale at Llangyfelach fair.) One also notes that the owners of certain small woollen mills which stood on farmyards in the Teifi valley arranged to set out potatoes in farm fields, the workers paying the labour debt to secure the potatoes wherewith their employers fed them. And it is noteworthy that the colloquial for 'shop assistant' was *gwas shop*, which is the parallel of *gwas ffarm*, 'farm servant'.

Reverting to farm households as such, it has been mentioned that farm servants were distinguished from labourers; the servants lived in and were the equivalent of sons in the way the farm's work was ordered. It is sometimes said that this practice, which ensured close contact between employer and employee, was characteristic of Wales, for in England farm staff lived out. But if one returns to the seventeenth century one finds the distinction between 'servants in husbandry' living in and 'labourers in husbandry' who lived out, even in south-east England, a distinction which was to survive in Cardiganshire long after it had disappeared in southern England. In fact, what is sometimes called 'pre-industrial organization' survived in south-west Wales almost into living memory, and was nowhere more prominent than in the organization of the household. Linguistic usage indicates that the farm household was patterned on the family in the way that was common in various occupations before the coming of modern industrial modes of organization.[10]

Nowadays it is normal to distinguish between 'family' (of parents and children) and 'household' (of all who dwell in one house, regardless of kin connections), but in the past in south-west Wales and elsewhere in the country the words which commonly denoted 'household' were *tylwyth* (kin), *teulu* (family) and *pobol* ('people', which is still frequently used to denote kin, as in the phrases *yr un pobol* and *dy bobol di*, i.e., 'the same people', 'your people'). These usages are to be seen in the verse of Rees Prichard (1579?–1644), which is telling because he composed for people at large, following in a long tradition whereby the learned wrote for the unlearned and the literate for those who were illiterate. For that reason, he employed words and idioms in the senses in which they were commonly understood by his hearers, and in this he is a guide not only to the vocabulary of those whom he addressed but to their cast of mind, to their shared understandings. One stanza of his shall suffice; in it he advises the head of the household how to treat its members:

> *Bid mor brudd dy garc a'th chwant*
> *Roi dysg i'th was, fel dysg i'th blant,*
> *Felly dysgai Abram ffyddlon*
> *Ey dŷ a'i dylwyth fel ei feibion.*[11]

[10]P. Laslett, *The World we have Lost* (London, 1965), chapter 1.
[11]Rees Prichard, *Y Seren Foreu, neu Ganwyll y Cymru* (Llandovery, 1841), p.574.

(Be as serious in your concern and your desire to teach your servant as your children, so the faithful Abraham taught his house and '*tylwyth*' [household] as he did his sons.)

Over two hundred years after Rees Prichard's day, *tylwyth* was the collective name for a farm's staff in the vale of Tywi in the vicinity of Llangynnwr.[12]

The case was similar in north Cardiganshire. Writing from his home therein in 1760 Lewis Morris described the order of his *tylwyth*, man and beast, *Fy nhylwyth i yn ddyn ac yn anifail*. He enumerated its members thus: himself, his wife, his daughter, his shepherd, his cowherd, '*Sian y Gwartheg (nid cowmon sydd yn y wlad yma)*', i.e. 'Jane the Cattle (it is not a cowman in this country)', Will y Grifft, Arthur the ploughman, the petty maid, the horses, cattle, and sheep. By *tylwyth* Lewis Morris denoted his household, man and beast, as he put it.[13]

Similarly, in a late eighteenth-century work, the Denbighshire-born John Jones (Jac Glan-y-gors) contrasted farmers' practices in good and bad times. When food was cheap and taxes low, they engaged the children of the labourers in their employ, as well as their fathers, but when taxes were high and food dear, then *Ni cheidw neb ond cyn lleied o deulu ag y medrant*,[14] 'no-one keeps anything but the smallest family that he can'. Clearly what the author meant by 'family' is what would now be considered a farm's staff, which is unsurprising where and when the farm staff was patterned on the family.

Consistent with this is what Hugh Evans noted in the same area of Denbighshire in the early nineteenth century, namely that servants addressed the farmer and the farm wife of the holding where they were engaged as *Ewythr* (Uncle) and *Modryb* (Aunt).[15] In view of what has just been said, it should be borne in mind that within families and kin groups relationships might well be strained; what has been noted refers in the first place to the way in which relationships were patterned rather than to their quality, which must have varied in particular cases.

By the end of the nineteenth century, those familiar with the society sensed the change that was occurring. Hugh Evans remarked that *Ewythr* and *Modryb* had by then been displaced by *Mishtir* and *Mishtres*,[16] while W. Llewelyn Williams reflected on the state of things in south-west Wales when he told the commissioners who enquired into farming in Wales during 1894–6: 'I remember when servants had a kind of domestic competition on the hearth as to who could make the best wooden spoon or basket, or string onions. There is now nothing of this kind. The servants are gradually losing their character as members of the family, and do not remain as much in the farm kitchen.'[17] The pre-industrial order was passing.

Perhaps the case concerning family and farm staff at the end of the nineteenth century may best be conveyed by noting that there was both a separation between them and also a linkage or overlap, namely, the equivalence of sons and servants in the organization of farm work. Separation and linkage alike had parallels in the layout of the farmhouse and in the names of the rooms of the house. A living room in which food was prepared was generally known as *cegin* (kitchen), which derives from the Latin *cucina*; but if a room other than the living room was provided for the

---

[12]G. Evans, 'On the farm a century ago', *CH*, VIII (1971), 72.

[13]J. H. Davies (ed.), *The Letters of Lewis, Richard, William, and John Morris* (2 vols., Aberystwyth, 1907–9), II, p.178. But note that 'deiriman' is to be seen in the Hearth Tax details of 1670.

[14]J. Jones, *Seren Tan Gwmwl* (Wrexham, n.d.), p.33.

[15]H. Evans, *Cwm Eithin* (Liverpool, 1950), p.38.

[16]Ibid.

[17]*Royal Commission on Land in Wales and Monmouth, Evidence* (5 vols., London, 1895), III, p.65.

preparation of food, a distinction was then made between *cegin* (or *cegin ore*, best kitchen) and *cegin gefn* (or *cegin fach*, *cegin mas*, *cegin fas*), the back kitchen (petty kitchen, out kitchen). Meanwhile the *rwm ford* was the mess room of farm children and farm staff alike.

Regarding the provision and use of rooms, students of vernacular architecture have noted a change from an earlier time when a whole household of people of unequal rank shared one room to a later time when separate provision was made for members of the family (in the restricted sense of the word). It is unclear when this came about in south-west Wales, but Fox and Raglan have shown that in the lowlands of Gwent it can be dated to the second half of the sixteenth century among those who were well-to-do. They mention cases where heavy oak doors provided with drawbars separated the room reserved for the family (namely the parlour) from the 'hall', which was accessible to farm staff.[18] In substantial farms in the Tywi valley *nouadd* (hall) was used in the nineteenth century for the living room, in contradistinction to *cegin* (kitchen), where the cooking was done;[19] to my knowledge the same usage prevailed until recently in some Cardiganshire farms which were once the home of the well-to-do. One notes that in south-west Wales in the late nineteenth and early twentieth centuries, it was taken entirely for granted as being in the order of things that while the staff had access to the *cegin gefn*, the *cegin ore* was exclusively for the family.

Co-operation between farms

Cardiganshire is not the richest of counties and most of its farms are relatively small. In the local terminology of the greater part of the county, a farm of 150 acres was a 'large place'. Ashby and Evans inform us that there were 6,474 holdings in the county in 1913; of these, 4,657 were under 50 acres, while 249 exceeded 150 acres and only 9 exceeded 300 acres.[20] Moreover, it is clear that many of the larger holdings enumerated by Ashby and Evans were upland farms where the returns per acre were low. Those things being so, farms could only be staffed to perform the routine work of the year, securing by other arrangements the labour needed for occasions when work was most pressing, namely the hay and corn harvests, virtually everywhere, and the sheep shearing on the country's upland farms. Some of these requirements were met by co-operation between farms, as for the hay harvest and the sheep shearing, while it was the cottager work group which provided the labour for the corn harvest.

Farms generally had at least two hay harvests, that of seed hay (*gwair hade*) and that of hay which grew in a field reserved as grassland (*gwair gwndwn*). This field was usually near to the farmyard, where it was fertilized by drainage or seepage from farmyard manure. Large farms might have a third harvest of naturally propagated hay which grew on slopes which could not be otherwise utilized, while upland farms harvested 'moorland hay' (*gwair rhos*) or 'short moorland hay' (*gwair rhos gota*), naturally propagated hay which needed cutting while still unripe and which was harvested from the same patch of moorland each year. Every harvest involved two chief occasions, first the mowing and, some days later, the carting. Thus a farm's hay season might be prolonged and last for six or seven weeks on occasion, as diaries show. The harvest was of particular consequence before artificial feeding stuffs became readily available: the normal practice was to feed seed hay to the

---

[18]C. Fox and Lord Raglan, *Monmouthshire Houses* (3 vols., Cardiff, 1951–4), II, pp.28–31, 70–2.
[19]See, e.g., W. Ll. Williams, *Gwilym a Benni Bach* (Wrexham, n.d.).
[20]Ashby and Evans, *Agriculture of Wales*, p.281.

horses and naturally propagated hay to the cattle. It is an indicator of the importance of the hay harvest that at that season farmers were proverbially touchy; it certainly provided Dafydd Jones (Isfoel) (1881–1968) with the subject of his skit 'Y Dwymyn Wair' (Hay Fever).[21]

In communities where virtually everyone knew everyone else, i.e. knew their family background and their kin relationships, where the limitations on the range of daily contacts kept the people of any locality in close and unavoidable contact with one another, in a period when individuals were in considerable measure dependent on the help of others in time of hardship, the circumstances were such that the maintenance of good or tolerable relationships was of no little importance. Nothing exemplifies this better than the customary arrangements for the hay harvest of farms which co-operated for that occasion. In some such groups it was the practice for the farmers to contact one another and discuss informally the state of the crop on each farm and to decide in which order the hay should be mown. But in other groups farms mowed in the same order every year, whatever the state of the crop, a practice which would be unintelligible if farm work were considered in isolation from the other requirements of daily life. While discussion within each group about the state of each year's crops was technically more efficient in that it allowed for varying the order of the mowing to suit the condition of each farmer's crop, such annual discussion also allowed room for disagreement, discontent and bad feeling among neighbours who remained interdependent even when there was ill-feeling between them. On the other hand, mowing in a fixed order was technically less efficient, but it left no room for disagreement. It gave priority to being good neighbours rather than to mowing hay in optimum condition; technical agricultural considerations yielded to more general ones.

Generally it was adjacent farms that co-operated for the hay harvest, but such farms did not constitute exclusive groups like a number of separate cells. Instead each farm was the focus of its own group and farms that co-operated with it were not necessarily obliged also to work with one another. In consequence groups of co-operating farms overlapped with one another over the whole countryside, the same farms co-operating year after year. New machinery which came during the late nineteenth century and the early years of the twentieth century extended this pattern rather than the contrary. When threshing machines arrived, farms which had co-operated for the hay harvest came to co-operate to provide sufficient workers to satisfy the requirements of working the threshing machinery. Until then farms had threshed with a flail, independently of one another. Similarly, farms which co-operated for the hay harvest and the threshing came to co-operate with one another when potato digging machines were introduced, for a considerable number of workers was required to keep up with the machine, in contrast to the earlier conditions when potatoes were harvested with the hoe. It was the coming of balers and combined harvesters after the Second World War which allowed of independence instead of the earlier interdependence.

Regarding co-operation at sheep shearing, reference will be confined to the upland farms of what is now the 'green desert' of the north and east of the county, *y mynydd mawr* (the great mountain) in contradistinction to *y mynydd bach* (the little mountain), which is at a lower elevation.[22] It comes as a

[21]D. Jones (Isfoel), *Cerddi Isfoel* (Aberystwyth, 1956), pp.42–3.

[22]The proper name 'Y Mynydd Bach' is well known: less well known is 'y mynydd mawr'. It can be found, for instance, in B. T. Hopkins's song to a native of the area (Miss Cassie Davies), wherein he refers to her thus: 'Mynnodd merch y mynydd mawr / Loywaf yrfa lafurfawr.' (The daughter of the great mountain sought the most bright and diligent career.) See D. J. G. Evans (ed.), *Deri o'n Daear Ni* (Llandysul, 1984), p.52.

surprise to realize that those who once reared and tended sheep in that most rural area were not 'country people' (*pobl y wlad*). Rather were they 'mountain people' (*pobl y mynydd*). The expressions indicate that the contradistinction which dwellers in the uplands found meaningful was not that between *gwlad a thref* (country and town) but between *gwlad a mynydd* (country and mountain). Their farms were 'mountain farms' (*ffermydd mynydd*) in contradistinction to 'country farms' (*ffermydd gwlad*): they have been described in a most revealing way by Evan Jones in *Cymdogaeth Soar-y-mynydd* and in *Balchder Crefft*.[23] One notes that in no connection is it clearer than in the one now under discussion that certain local idioms, while they distinguish classes of people, also exemplify the traits of thought of the people concerned. Each 'mountain farm' was reckoned in terms not of fields but of *esgeirydd*, the ridges which separated one stream from another of those which drain into the rivers Teifi and Tywi. When shearing time came, the 'unit' according to which the sheep were collected was the ridge, each in its turn. Adjacent farms co-operated for the shearing, working according to familiar rules of procedure. These procedures were clearly defined, were of a customary nature, and were conducted as established before anyone at the turn of the century could recall, for there was no account of how or when they were evolved or instituted. In accordance with these 'rules', shearing began on the last Friday in June of each year; farms sheared in the same order every year; each farm had its set number of days for shearing; any farm(s) that failed to shear in the proper place in the order moved to the end of the rota, the common cause of such failure being wet weather, for sheep can only be sheared when they are dry. Shearing lasted two or three weeks, according to conditions. Masters and men from each farm assisted at those farms with which they co-operated, as did certain others. Commonly a 'mountain farm' was linked with a 'country farm' in order to provide it with seed corn (oats), while many a 'country farm' sent sheep to graze the land of farms on higher ground during the summer. The shearing season came before haymaking began on 'country farms', and it was therefore practicable for 'country men' who were connected with mountain farms to spend the whole of the shearing season on the mountain, moving from one farm to another as the shearing proceeded. Until the Second World War many teenage boys from among 'country people' of the Tregaron area spent several weeks on 'the mountain' in summer, moving from farm to farm while they helped the shearers, their exact whereabouts unbeknown to their parents. It is known that 110 people assisted at the shearing at the largest of the mountain farms at the beginning of the twentieth century, namely Nantstalwyn, which had a flock of 4,000 sheep. A photograph taken in 1912 shows that there were forty-nine present that year at the shearing at Nant-yr-ast. Undoubtedly life would have been impossible on the mountain but for the practices which enabled farms to accomplish in co-operation what they could not have managed separately.

Y Fedel, 'the work group'

Land is of limited value to either landowner or tenant without labour to work it. Some Cardiganshire estates secured labour for their home farms by requiring their tenants to pay rents partly in the form of labour debts until the third quarter of the eighteenth century and later: for instance, the rental of the Noyadd Trefawr estate as revised in 1743–4.[24] There follows a selection of examples from that rental. The tenant of Trefaes Fawr was required to provide six reapers, two

---

[23]E. Jones, *Cymdogaeth Soar-y-mynydd* (Swansea, 1979); idem, *Balchder Crefft* (Llandybïe, 1976).
[24]NLW, Noyadd Trefawr MS 742.

Fig. 21: The labour force for the hay harvest at Rhydlewis, 1924–1925. (*Copyright Museum of Welsh Life, St Fagans*).

horses to carry corn, two horses to carry hay, two other horses on occasion (with, one must assume, a man to lead the horses whenever they were required) in addition to paying his cash rent, as well as performing other duties. The same tenant held Penlan (in Blaen-porth parish), providing the estate with an additional three days' reaping, other duties, and his cash rent. For Trefaes Fach another tenant provided one plough and harrow (among other things); the rent of Esger Wilym included the provision of three reapers, as did the rent of Tre-wen; the rent of Rhos included the providing of six reapers, Nantyderrin two reapers, Penlan (in Aber-porth parish) four reapers, Llethr Gwared two reapers, while Cnwcygigfran in Clydau parish was required to provide three reapers, three haymakers and horses on occasion. All the above owed other duties besides. It is very much as George Owen described things in north Pembrokeshire in Elizabethan times. The corresponding Noyadd Trefawr rental of 1778 shows substantially increased rents, no labour debts, and on occasion a nominal sum as of one shilling in lieu of 'duties'.[25] Other cases where tenant farmers were required to provide labour when the landlord so demanded can be cited until the middle years of the nineteenth century.[26]

Cottager tenants of estates might similarly be required to pay their rents partly in labour, for instance on the Gwernant estate. In 1795 one John Lloyd Williams MD, who had spent his working life in India, purchased the remnant of the medieval estate of Gwernan' 'yn Nhrefdreyr' (in Troed-yr-aur), as Lewys Glyn Cothi put it. He built a Georgian mansion, decorated its approaches with trees planted according to the disposition of the armies at Waterloo, acquired further farms, became

[25]NLW, Noyadd Trefawr MS 738.
[26]NLW MS 9956B.

a 'prominent agriculturalist', and kept estate papers which included a 'Harvest Account' of 1829. This shows that thirty-four people (including women) from nineteen dwellings owed him a total of 200 days' labour debt, which was presumably instituted after he acquired the estate. It is reasonably clear that the people involved were cottagers, including a carpenter, and that the labour required from them was part of the rent paid for their cottages. Should the landowner require more than 200 days' labour the cottagers must needs provide it, and were paid for it: should the landowner require fewer than 200 days, those cottagers of whom less than their due labour was required were expected to reimburse their landlord at a rate of around 6½d. per day.[27]

It remained the case that farms seasonally required more labour than their staff could provide until the coming of machinery (which first reached the area in the closing decade of the nineteenth century), notably the hay-mowing machine and the corn self-binder. Until then it was not possible to run any holding of whatever size as a self-contained and independent unit. While upland farmers received their cash income partly from the sale of sheep and wool, others profited chiefly from the sale of store cattle and of salt butter offered for sale to the butter dealers at the area's market towns. Cows do not give milk for butter making nor give birth to calves to rear for sale as store cattle without the services of a bull. Bulls, however, are expensive animals to keep and it was impractical to keep them on farms of less than sixty to seventy acres. We know from Ashby and Evans's data that 72 per cent of holdings were less than fifty acres,[28] and we can conclude that no more than a quarter of all holdings could keep bulls, which means that three-quarters of all holdings, or thereabouts, were dependent on the other quarter. Each summer saw a procession of cows being taken along country lanes to be served at farms which kept bulls, and payment was generally in the form not of cash but of a labour due payable at the hay harvest.

Thus the smaller holdings could not be run as independent units. The other reason why farms could not be run as independent units has been mentioned above, namely labour needs at certain times of the year, especially at the corn harvest, a consideration applicable even more to the larger holdings than the smaller ones. This is best explained by taking one large farm as an example. This was a farm of 220 acres which had forty to fifty acres under corn annually. When scythes were used for the harvest, it was one day's work for each scythesman to cut an acre of corn. Thus forty to fifty working days were required to cut the corn. Corn cut by scythe lies on the ground in swathes and must be bound into sheaves by hand. Wheat was bound 'at the tail' (*wrth gwt*) of the scythesman by a woman following the scythesman and making the 'bindings' for securing each sheaf out of the straw as she went along. Thus as many working days were required to bind the wheat into sheaves as were required to cut it. The position was different in respect of barley and oats. Oats were cut when of 'dove hue' (*lliw'r glomen*) and barley when less ripe than wheat was when the latter crop was cut, *yn grin aeddfed*. Oats and barley were then allowed to lie 'to acquire a tan', for a period ideally of nine days; I was told that this loosened the grain in the ear and thus facilitated threshing when that task was undertaken with a flail.

If one asks people with experience of binding these crops how long the work took, the answers vary. Some experienced people claim that it took just as long to bind the corn as to cut it. Others, equally experienced, claim that the binding could be done in half the time required for the cutting.

---

[27]NLW, Ticehurst Wyatt Collection, uncatalogued.
[28]Ashby and Evans, *Agriculture of Wales*, p.281.

This variation is to be expected, for binding corn was affected by one consideration that did not affect its cutting, namely the presence or absence of thistles in the crop. Thistles would make one's hands bleed in no time, though some old men had hands so hard that thistles would not penetrate them. If we assume that binding the crop called for something like three-quarters the time required to cut it, we shall not err seriously. This means that cutting and binding the crop of a 220-acre farm required some seventy to seventy-five working days. This done, the sheaves were then placed four or six together in stook, and carried when dry from the stooks to the spot where they would be built into a stack. It remained to thatch the stack, and to that end it was necessary to thresh with a flail in order to provide the thatching straw. By the 1890s some of the ropes used for thatching were of coconut fibre and were purchased in the local shops, but the others were straw rope made in the stack yard and known as 'finger tip rope' (*rheffyn pen bys*). It was given this name because it was made by twisting lengths of straw around one's finger to produce sufficient straw rope for the thatching. Thus, in sum, about a hundred working days were needed to complete the farm's harvest work.

This, however, assumes favourable weather conditions in an area characterized by variability of rainfall, wind, and hours of sunshine. Under good harvest conditions a cradle was fitted to each scythe when cutting corn. This was a light frame and the cut corn fell on to this frame; this allowed the scythesman to tip the corn on to the ground in quantities and in a manner convenient for binding into sheaves. But when the wind and rain had laid the corn the cradle could not be used and it was then necessary to use either a 'bare scythe' (*pladur foel*) or to bring out the reaping hook. The hook was still – to my knowledge – used in the county during the harvest of 1951. On such occasions binding was difficult work, requiring more time than was needed when the corn was harvested under more favourable circumstances.

But the worst conditions were those which followed prolonged drought during the growing season. The growth of straw was then so short that the harvesters had to 'hand reap' (*dwrn fedi*) the crop, seizing the whole crop, one handful at a time and cutting each handful with a sickle or reaping hook held in the other hand. Moreover, the straw was then too short to allow the binder to use it in order to bind the sheaves. It was therefore necessary to go to the stack yard and make enough 'finger tip rope' of straw, using either one's hands or a small tool like a brace, in order to make the rope which was to be used to bind the sheaves. This was considered the mark of a difficult harvest, and it is hardly necessary to note that under such conditions many more working days were required. But worse conditions were remembered. In some very dry years (1887 and 1893 were mentioned to me) the growth was so short that it could not be cut at all and there was nothing to be done but pull out the whole crop by the roots, the crop then being known as *llafur cito*, which may perhaps be rendered 'stunted corn'. When this was necessary, each harvester struck the roots against his boot when he pulled each handful. This got rid of some of the dust adhering to the roots but the rest made threshing painful work, for clouds of dust made it impossible for the threshers to work for periods of more than twenty minutes. While this occurred generally only in exceptional years, it might well be necessary to harvest the crop on a dry bank in this way even when it was unnecessary over the greater part of the cultivated area. I know of some cases after the First World War, as late as 1921.

Thus, to harvest the crop of a 220-acre farm, something like 100 working days were required under good conditions, and rather more under adverse conditions. But the farm's staff consisted of only eight people, including the farmer (whose time was taken up in management), his wife, and two maids. There were six working days in the week and a number of duties that could not be set aside for the duration of the harvest: the care of horses and cattle, milking, butter making, collecting the eggs, the care of pigs and poultry, the preparation of food and much other work besides. Under the changeable weather conditions of the area, it is clear that the harvest could not be safely secured year in year out without the services of others than those who were regular members of the farm's staff.

In this area and during the period within the memory of those I questioned, although farms co-operated at the hay harvest they did not co-operate at the corn harvest. Each farm secured its own corn crop and extra labour did not come by co-operative work. Yet the corn crop was too important to leave to chance the provision of the extra labour required. Wheat was grown 'for the use of the house', that is, to provide bread, which was a major staple. Barley and oats provided winter feed for the animals. The extra labour needed to harvest these crops was provided by the practice of the first importance both to the work of agriculture and to the social structure of the community.

This was the practice of 'setting out potatoes', whereby 'the people of the little houses' set out rows of potatoes in a farmer's field, for which they owed a labour debt of one day's work at the corn harvest for each row of potatoes that they 'set out'. The labour debt was definite and was referred to in the expressions 'labour debt' (*dyled gwaith*), 'harvest debt' (*dyled cynhaeaf*), 'potato debt' (*dyled tato*) and 'potato duty' (duty *tatw*). People spoke not of individuals setting out potatoes but of households, and households might have rows of potatoes in the fields of more than one farm to a total of eight rows or so on occasion. The potato rows were of a standard length of 120 yards and the farmer provided a load of farm manure for each row of potatoes. To be strictly accurate, the labour debt was not so much for the potato ground but for the loads of manure supplied by the farmer, one for each row, so that if a cottager could provide a load of manure he would not owe a labour debt for that row of potatoes.

People did not ask one another 'How many rows of potatoes have you?', but rather 'How many loads of manure have you?' Where the central ridge of south Cardiganshire rises to moorland, people burnt turves and the ash was kept to fertilize a row of potatoes. Along the coast people burnt culm made of a mixture of small coal (imported by coastal sailing craft) and clay. The ash was again kept for delivery to the 'potato field'. At the potato setting cottagers came to set first the farm's potatoes and then their own, each cottager household providing its own seed potatoes. At the potato harvest cottagers harvested first the farm's potatoes and then their own. Thus, even when a cottager provided manure for a row of potatoes, he still contributed labour towards setting and harvesting the farm's potatoes, and a harvest labour debt (payable at the corn harvest only) for those potato rows for which farm manure had been provided. Virtually all cottagers set out potatoes and there were many cottager families in which the husbands worked in the mining valleys of south Wales and took their holidays in August and September so that they could return home and pay the 'harvest debt' that was due. In some areas of mid-Cardiganshire there was a sufficiency of labour available to enable some farms to continue to reap wheat with a reaping hook until 1908–10. (As wheat straw grows taller than that of barley or oats, less advantage is gained by cutting it with a scythe with a cradle attached; thus people continued to harvest wheat with a hook while the scythe was used for barley and oats.) In the case of the 220-acre farm which has been noted, around a hundred working days were required to secure the crop. Twenty-four cottager families set out potatoes; on average each had four rows of potatoes apiece. Ninety-six working days were thus secured for the farm.

Attached to each farm, therefore, was a work group of cottagers; these were such important functional groups that in their absence the society would have been different in many other respects.

Their social significance was twofold. First, they were operative throughout the year and not only at harvest time. Cottagers were required to attend at the farms to set potatoes and to weed the potato rows; the cottagers' wives were expected at the hay harvest, for which they received a measure of butter known as 'debt butter' (*menyn dyled*). Attendance at the hay harvest was a protracted business since the full hay harvest might well last six weeks or so, as has been noted, and work at the hay harvest did not contribute towards paying the 'potato debt', which was paid at the corn harvest. Shortly afterwards cottagers would again attend the farm for the potato harvest. (One notes that the labour debt was paid at the harvest at which farms did not co-operate.) Moreover, while the practice of setting out potatoes provided the farmer with harvest labour, it provided the cottager with essentials to his subsistence. He gained not only potato ground but also straw for bedding for the pig or pigs the cottager kept in the sty in his garden. His wife received buttermilk at the farm when butter was made and oatmeal when the corn had been ground. If the cottager required the use of a horse and cart to move a load or to collect coal from the railway station, he borrowed the farm's horse and cart – for an extra day of labour debt. If the farm required extra labour, for instance, help in the dwelling house when there was illness, the farmer turned to members of his own work group for help.

Potato setting and the associated work group thus bound cottagers and farmers into a group operative throughout the year, year in year out. This being so, the second social consequence of this way of arranging the work of the land becomes clear. Status was closely connected with the ordering of these groups, for in all their operations the farmer occupied a superior position. He decided when the various operations were to be performed; normally, he sent a petty servant to inform cottagers when potatoes were to be set, when the corn harvest was to begin, and when the potatoes were to be harvested. It fell to the cottagers to respond as the custom required them to do. On the other hand, this same ordering of work put shackles on extremes of behaviour, for a farmer would be in serious difficulties with his harvesting operations should people seek to move to other farms to set out their potatoes.

The ordering of the work of the land in this way was at the same time an ordering of people in a customary way. It had further consequences than those mentioned above. Everyone was familiar with farm work, and farmers and cottagers alike were brought into personal contact. They knew one another's affairs and kin relationships; they knew the good and the bad, the happy and the sad, toward and untoward events in each other's daily lives. Agricultural operations were inescapably linked with life in the community, for good or ill.

It will be appreciated that the exact details of the rural order outlined above could not have preceded the introduction of the potato, which became commonly established in the course of the eighteenth century. It may therefore be that the whole order was devised in that period, but what evidence there is suggests otherwise. It appears that in earlier times cottagers paid with labour at the corn harvest for the right of gleaning. One notes that *medel* is related to *medi*, to reap. In that case, it was a long-established order which disappeared during the early years of the twentieth century.

Conclusion

Regarding the relationship between farm practice and social structure, one further matter deserves mention. Local idiom, which is clearly related to the work of the land, indicates that people distinguished three main elements in the society, *gwŷr mawr* (gentry), farmers, and *pobol tai bach* (cottagers). Here we shall mention two notions as to how these expressions relate to the structure of the society. With respect to the first notion, in all likelihood one's immediate reaction to the expressions under consideration is that they indicate the three main divisions of the society which, if put together like building blocks, would constitute the whole.

But the expressions can be considered in another and a different way, indicating the manner and method wherein and whereby people stood interrelated. It is the individual who 'sees' himself, and is 'seen' by others, to be one of the 'great people', or a 'farmer', or one of 'the people of the little houses', and in daily life it is in contradistinction to his fellows that a man 'sees' himself in one or other of these capacities, and is so seen by others. But in contradistinction to what fellows? For one's fellows are very varied. One cannot answer without reference to context: someone is 'husband' in contradistinction to 'wife', 'parent' in contradistinction to 'child', 'son' or 'daughter' in contra-distinction to 'father' or 'mother'; someone is 'one of the Thomases' (or Davieses, etc.) in contradis-tinction to the Joneses, etc. One is a 'man of the little houses' in contradistinction to 'farmer' or to *gwŷr mawr*.

Those who stand in contradistinction in one context may stand differently in another context. Those who stand in contradistinction as 'nephew' and 'uncle', for example, are yet 'the same people' in contradistinction to a different set of kinsmen. And though 'a man of the little houses' and a 'farmer' are contradistinguished on the harvest field, yet they are both *pobol gyffredin*, 'ordinary people' in contradistinction to 'the great people'. The expressions constitute a set of contra-distinctions which, in turn, entails and exemplifies habits of thought; the idioms were meaningful only because, and as long as, people perceived them to be so. With the changes that came around the close of the nineteenth century, the practices of agriculture altered and the expressions were emptied of their older significance.

CHAPTER 6

CARDIGANSHIRE AGRICULTURE IN THE TWENTIETH CENTURY: AN ECONOMIC PERSPECTIVE

D. I. Bateman

Introduction

AT THE time of writing – the mid-1990s – agriculture is in a state of crisis. The immediate and highly publicized symptoms of that crisis include not just the reductions in farming incomes which occurred during the 1980s but also the pressures suggesting that even greater cuts may be expected in the future. The causes of these pressures go deep and are comparable in their significance with the reasons that led, for instance, to the repeal of the Corn Laws in 1846 or to the permanent introduction of agricultural support in Britain in 1947. In a word, the cause is that existing policies have simply become outmoded. The goals of agricultural policy as previously understood have either been achieved and surpassed, or have failed to be met at all, or have come to be seen as inappropriate. High levels of support for farming have produced levels of food output beyond what is necessary domestically; they have disrupted international trade in agricultural products to an extent which has become threatening to trade in other products too; they have cost consumers and taxpayers more than they are willing to continue paying; they have failed to achieve the desired income objectives for the agricultural community; and they have, to a large extent, ignored the environmental consequences of agricultural activity. The significance of this for the historical interpretation of agriculture in Cardiganshire is the highly interventionist stance of government that has been the hallmark of twentieth-century agriculture. In the twentieth century, the history of Cardiganshire agriculture must be seen, as never before, as a history of agricultural *policy*.

The external pressures

The policies which have influenced Cardiganshire agriculture have rested, not always explicitly, on five main objectives. These are: efficiency, food supplies, farm incomes, rural population and society, and the natural environment. In addition, there have been other influences that might

This chapter has benefited from the advice and comments of Mr Peter Garbett Edwards, Dr D. J. Griffiths, Professor J. D. Hayes, Mrs Dot Jones, Professor Peter Midmore and Professor John Williams. Mr Michael Freeman of the Ceredigion Museum helped with the selection and identification of the illustrations.

perhaps be better recognized as constraints rather than objectives: budgetary cost, concern for the third world, and animal welfare. The relative influence of the various objectives has changed over time, with periods of stability in terms of what governments are trying to achieve interspersed with periods of rapid adjustment.

At all times it is likely to be an objective of policy that agriculture (or any other industry) should be *efficient*. In this context, efficiency is defined in economic rather than technical terms, that is, it refers to the efficiency of resource allocation that is the supposed consequence of free markets. From 1846 this objective was dominant – with its corollaries of cheap food supplies to consumers but generally low prices for farmers.

The First World War brought a different objective to the forefront of policy: the issue of *food supplies*. The original steps to introduce support were, however, both hesitant and short-lived. It was only towards the end of the war that the government began serious efforts to increase output, and even that concern was abandoned soon after the war finished as farmers were subjected to 'the Great Betrayal'. Nevertheless, the period of intervention, however short, set a precedent: over the whole of the period under review, it was the need (perceived or genuine) to expand domestic food supplies that turned out to be the major reason for agricultural support policies – the most influential objective in terms of shielding Cardiganshire agriculture from the worst pressures of the free market.

In the meantime, the return, in the 1920s, to free markets drew attention to yet another objective, for, in the circumstances of the time, free markets placed a degree of pressure on *farm incomes* that was considered unacceptable. It is important in understanding the changes which took place in Cardiganshire agriculture to be clear how the farm income problem arises. The process of economic development is, by definition, one in which agriculture becomes a diminishing sector of the economy. In a free market, this effect can only be achieved through the pressures imposed by falling real prices for agricultural products and also by a fall, at least in relative terms, in agricultural incomes. Given, then, falling prices and falling relative incomes, what is the mechanism of adjustment? It is farmers themselves whose incomes suffer in the first instance, and it is they who take action to try and maintain their position. This action may take several forms, all of which are apparent in the changes which occurred (sometimes despite support) in Cardiganshire agriculture. First, farmers may, by taking advantage of new technology, be able to manage with a smaller labour force, permitting them to maintain their own incomes by reducing the level of employed labour or (perhaps as a second choice) of family labour. As part of the change they will often find it profitable to increase their degree of specialization of production (a process that will be reinforced if government support mechanisms offer some assurance of price stability). Second, especially if the farm is a small one with no work-force but the farmer and spouse, it may be that the only way they can keep themselves fully employed, given the existence of labour-saving technologies, is by increasing the area of their farm, thus reducing the number of other commercial farmers in the region. Third, since an increase in farm size will often not be practicable, an alternative is for some members of the farm family (possibly the farmer himself) to seek off-farm employment, either full-time or part-time. Fourth, if none of these opportunities exist, and if the farmer is a tenant, he may seek to maintain his own income by asking for a rent reduction, thereby shifting the problem of adjustment to the landlord with the likelihood that the landlord/tenant system of land tenure may give way to owner-occupation. Fifth, if the worst comes to the worst, the farmer may be forced to give up. Whichever of these occurs, the outcome is that the economic pressures lead to changes both in the structure of agriculture and in the size of the population able to obtain a direct living from the land.

If the agricultural sector only were affected by these income pressures, all this would be of little interest to the rest of the community. It would be comparable to the changes which have seen the demise of blacksmiths, village bakers and the like. The importance of agriculture arises from the fact that the decline of agricultural incomes and hence of agricultural employment has been a cause of changes in *rural population and society* – a fourth objective of policy which also began to assume importance in the inter-war years.

The extent to which agriculture matters in terms of rural society obviously depends partly on its varying importance in the economies of different regions. In Cardiganshire especially, the consequences of agricultural decline have been more obvious than elsewhere because, locationally disadvantaged as it is and lacking any large town where a reserve labour force can attract employers, there is less chance of an offsetting growth in other sectors of the economy. Agriculture in Cardiganshire, therefore, has the capacity to act – and for most of the twentieth century has acted – as the engine of rural decline. The consequences have been social as well as economic. The decline in employment opportunities has weakened the local infrastructure (the viability of local schools, railway lines, hospitals, etc.), thereby making the area still less attractive as a place either to take or to offer jobs. Thus, a process which began simply as one of economic change in a single industry became one of social change in a whole community – with agriculture as the causal factor. In the particular case of Cardiganshire, the effect was reinforced by the decline in lead mining.[1] There are cultural consequences too: the distinctiveness of a region's culture and language requires some degree of stability in its population, and there is evidence to suggest that the farming sector, as one of the most stable elements, is the custodian of traditional culture.[2]

The Second World War reintroduced the objective of food production. The support which this entailed meant that farm incomes automatically benefited, so that the problems of rural society seemed less evident. Furthermore, at the end of the war, the case was recognized for a continuance of the support to agriculture. The objectives were stated explicitly in the 1947 Agriculture Act: 'a stable and efficient agricultural industry capable of producing such part of the nation's food and other agricultural produce as in the national interest it is desirable to produce in the United Kingdom, and of producing it at minimum prices consistently with proper remuneration and living conditions for farmers and workers in agriculture and an adequate return on capital invested in the industry.' If recognition of the malaise of rural society generally was only implicit, this did not seem to matter at the time.

The main policy-tool chosen to achieve the objective was support for agricultural prices through deficiency payments to farmers, a method which raised farm receipts without raising consumer prices. Price support, combined with rent control, ensured that farmers (both tenants and owner-occupiers) prospered. For a time, economic concepts of efficiency were almost forgotten, as both government and farmers' unions held up agriculture as a model in terms of such technical measures of efficiency as growth of output per hectare or per man. With such targets, the concomitant decline in numbers employed (mostly a decline in employees rather than farmers) was seen as an advantage rather than a problem.

[1] *Depopulation in Mid Wales* (HMSO, London, 1964).
[2] E. Jones, 'The linguistic implications of agricultural change in Wales' (unpublished University of Wales M.Sc. thesis, 1989).

Over time, the inevitable conflict between the high support levels necessary to maintain farm incomes and the need to maintain the competitiveness of British agriculture by ensuring that prices did not diverge too much from those on the world market became more and more apparent. In other words, economic efficiency was beginning to come to the fore again when, in 1973, entry to the European Community (EC) reversed, if only for a time, the pressures for restraint. With the new agricultural policy consequent upon entry, there was a significant increase not only in the level of support but also a change in method, causing higher food prices as support costs were shifted from the taxpayer to the consumer. These higher consumer prices combined with a concern, already evident, about food consumption and health to intensify a move away from consumption of animal products on which the agriculture of Cardiganshire depends almost exclusively.

But static (in some cases, falling) consumption and rising output were clearly not compatible on a permanent basis. The incompatibility evidenced itself in several ways: an increasing burden of support cost which was politically unacceptable; growing stores of unwanted produce which, in the context of food shortages in the Third World, were seen to be morally unacceptable; and the disruption of the agricultural trade of 'First World' countries as the EC disposed of its unwanted surpluses at bargain prices. Furthermore, there was an increasing recognition that agricultural policy was not, after all, achieving all that might be hoped for: much of the support was going to richer farmers and richer regions rather than to poorer ones such as Cardiganshire; much of it was going into land prices; and much was going outside the agricultural sector altogether.

By the 1980s these reasons were causing the level of food production to receive much lower priority in terms of governmental objectives. At the same time, there developed a new emphasis on quality rather than quantity, a growing public perception that some agricultural practices might be producing food that was itself positively harmful or conflicted with an increasing concern for animal welfare, and a much strengthened interest in the natural environment and the effect that agriculture was having on it. Protection of the natural environment in particular became yet another objective of agricultural policy. Increasingly intensive farming practices were making it more and more apparent that land is not just a resource for producing agricultural output. It also contributes to social needs in other ways – the quality of landscape, water supplies, wildlife and archaeological features, and access – all 'non-market benefits' for which the market works inefficiently because property rights are ill-defined or are seen to be inadequate. Legislation such as the National Parks and Access to the Countryside Act of 1949 had gone some way towards addressing these problems, but for most people (including farmers) the issue remained a peripheral one. By the 1980s, however, it was emerging as a major issue, of particular concern in an area as naturally attractive as Cardiganshire – a concern which offers opportunities and threats both to farmers and to the local economy.

At the time of writing, then, *food supplies* no longer constitute a major objective of agricultural policy, and even the issue of *farm incomes* no longer has the priority it once did. Instead, there is a renewed drive for *efficiency* with an expectation of further reductions in agricultural employment. While concern for the *natural environment* is of growing significance, the objective that is of greatest current concern throughout the European Union is *rural population and society*. It is this perspective which will predominate in the selection of material in the account of Cardiganshire agriculture which will be presented in the next section. The history itself, however, has been determined by the changing pattern of importance of all five of the objectives that have been major influences on the way agriculture has developed in Cardiganshire.

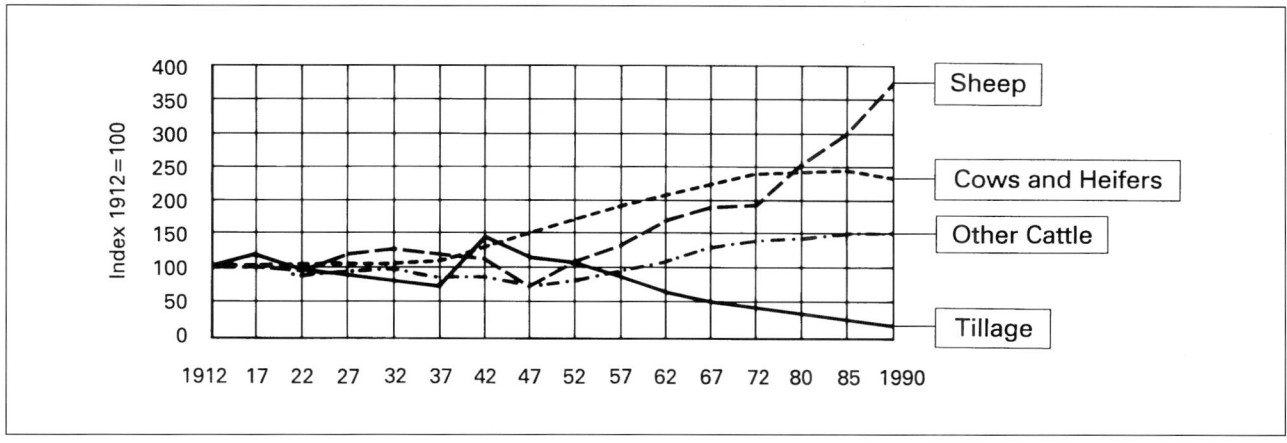

Fig. 22: Index of livestock numbers and tillage area in Cardiganshire, 1912–1990.

The development of agriculture in Cardiganshire, 1914–1990

The most obvious link between the agricultural industry and the rural economy is via output. The larger the physical output, the greater will be the opportunities for local processing industries to develop; and the larger the value of output, the greater will be the amount of money coming into the local area, creating jobs as it is spent either on agricultural inputs or on goods and services required by farm households.

Changes in the output of agriculture in the twentieth century – in Cardiganshire, as elsewhere – can be summarized in three words: growth, specialization and fluctuation, all of them responses to the opportunities and incentives provided by technological development and economic support. The specialization is represented, above all, by the decline in tillage (mainly cereals) area – in percentage terms from 15 per cent to 3 per cent over the period, with a peak of 21 per cent during the Second World War (Fig. 22). The main crop grown (almost half the total) was oats and it is only since the 1960s that oats have been overtaken by barley. Wheat, always the least attractive cereal, nevertheless accounted for 10 per cent of the tillage at the beginning of the period (Fig. 23), but was in decline from the end of the First World War and was negligible by soon after the Second World War. The other crops, potatoes, turnips and swedes, have also been in decline throughout the period. Livestock enterprises, however, were naturally always the most important and there was specialization here too, as evidenced by the description, now sounding almost archaic, of a sample of small Welsh pastoral farms as late as the 1930s: 'On all the holdings a few dairy cows are kept . . . ; sheep and pigs are present on most of the farms, together with some poultry. Horses are always kept as they are needed for the farm work.'[3]

The growth is indicated by two things. First, the rate at which the number of livestock expanded far exceeds what would have been possible simply by substitution for cropping. Over the period, the

[3]W. H. Jones, 'A statistical analysis of farm accounts', *Journal of Farm Economics*, 16, no.4 (1934), 613–23.

reduction in the already small cropping area coincided with increases of 133 per cent, 49 per cent and 275 per cent in the numbers, respectively, of dairy cows and heifers, of other cattle, and of sheep. Second, these increases in numbers were bolstered by increases in yields. Unfortunately, milk yields, the most relevant figure for Cardiganshire, are only available on a reliable basis from just before the Second World War, but between then and 1986 they exactly doubled.[4] But the changes were not always steady. The fluctuations included a peaking of the tillage area during both world wars; a long period of stability in the size of the dairy herd from the end of the First World War to the 1930s, with all the increase in this sector concentrated in the period from then to the mid-1970s; a decline in other cattle numbers until beyond the end of the Second World War, with the increase again concentrated – this time in the period from the 1950s; and, most strikingly of all, a decline in sheep numbers which did not return to their 1917 level until the early fifties since when the numbers have more than tripled.

These increases are made even more remarkable by the fact that they coincided with a loss both of land (mainly to forestry) and, as will be seen, labour. They were made possible by technological change of many different kinds – improved grasses, better methods of conservation, better breeds (for instance, the displacement of Shorthorns by Friesians), bought-in fertilizers and other inputs (especially the replacement of the home-fed horse by the diesel-fed tractor), milking machines and bulk collection. The turn of the nineteenth century, indeed, has been identified from contemporary quotations as the time at which 'farming methods which for centuries had existed in a state of almost mediaeval simplicity' in Cardiganshire began a period of readjustment.[5] The changes had consequences, not only for the nature and quantity of labour required, but also for the social relationships within the rural community.[6]

But technological change is only permissive. Farmers will not adopt it unless economic circumstances either encourage, or force, them to do so. In the early years of the First World War, prices rose only in response to market pressures, but from 1916 farmers were offered various incentives to increase production. Prices of the main agricultural products reached their peak in 1920 (two to three times the pre-war level for cereals, but with generally smaller increases for other products).[7] By 1923 prices had returned to the 1916 level and the period to the mid-1930s was one of continuous price fall for agricultural products. Most spectacularly, wheat prices fell to 'the lowest price recorded by the Corn Returns (started in 1771), and probably the lowest since the sixteenth century'.[8] For the products of most importance to Cardiganshire, the falls were less drastic, but still serious enough. Fat cattle prices by 1935 were at their lowest level since 1911, and the All Products index, at its nadir in 1933, was lower than at any time since 1914. Since the peak year of 1920, the index had dropped by 62 per cent.

There is no doubt of the hardship that the changes brought in the inter-war period. Out of a sample of Welsh farms, the number making actual losses reached a peak (30 out of 68) in 1932–3 when even the *average* farm in the Cattle and Sheep (Poor Land) group had a total annual income of

---

[4]H. F. Marks, *A Hundred Years of British Food and Farming*, ed. D. K. Britton (London, 1989).

[5]G. W. Williams, 'The disenchantment of the world: innovation, crisis and change in Cardiganshire, *c*.1880–1910', *Ceredigion*, IX, no.4 (1983), 303–21.

[6]D. Jenkins, *The Agricultural Community in South-West Wales at the Turn of the Twentieth Century* (Cardiff, 1971).

[7]*A Century of Agricultural Statistics* (HMSO, London, 1968).

[8]Ibid.

Fig. 23: The wheat harvest at Llanrhystud in 1903. The men are sharpening reaping hooks and the women preparing corn stalks for binding the sheaves. (*Copyright Museum of Welsh Life, St Fagans*).

only 15*s.* 4*d.* for each of the 1.74 members of the family working on the farm – a figure which compares with £110 9*s.* 8*d.* only three years earlier.[9] Of course, farm families could, and did, live off their own farm produce but, significantly, the extent to which they were able to do this also fell in Wales during this same period: 'own' milk consumption fell by 16 per cent, butter the same, cheese 62 per cent, poultry 12 per cent, and potatoes 28 per cent, though there were offsetting rises for sheep and eggs.[10] Although farmworkers' wages were to an extent protected after 1924 by the Agricultural Wages Act, even they suffered a fall of 10 per cent or so, as well as a significant increase in unemployment;[11] a Welsh study of some Lincolnshire data on agricultural workers' budgets concluded laconically: 'it is very difficult to see how the diet of these households may be brought up to physiological requirements during the present war conditions when there was inability, and apparently no urgent desire to give them an adequate diet in peace time.'[12]

Although the cereal-producing areas were hit hardest in terms of the extent of price fall, they were at least protected by the relatively small importance of agriculture to their economies. In

[9]*Report on Research and Advisory Work in Agricultural Economics, 1934–35* (Aberystwyth, 1935).

[10]J. P. Howell, 'Quantities and value of food products consumed in the farm house', *WJA*, 11 (1935), 48–61.

[11]A. W. Ashby and J. H. Smith, 'Agricultural labour in Wales under statutory regulation of wages, 1924–1937', *WJA*, 14 (1938), 5–30.

[12]J. R. E. Phillips, 'Agricultural workers' budgets', *WJA*, 16 (1940), 60–9.

Cardiganshire there was little else, and that little else was also in decline. Thus, rural deprivation and farm incomes came increasingly to the forefront, first as a problem and then as an objective of specific policies. In Cardiganshire the most important elements of the new policies were the setting up of the Milk Marketing Board (MMB) in 1933 and the introduction of fat cattle subsidies from 1934. The significance of the MMB stems from the fact that while British milk producers could not compete with prices that were adequate for overseas producers of butter and cheese, they had, because of transport costs, natural protection in the market for milk for liquid consumption. For instance, in 1934–5, the average liquid price in England and Wales was about 15d. per gallon and the manufacturing price about 4d.[13] Until the coming of the MMB, however, Cardiganshire, with its small population and poor transport system, had little access to this lucrative liquid market. The MMB altered all that by introducing a system of 'pooled prices': all farmers in England and Wales now received approximately the same price for their milk (12d. per gallon in 1934–5) irrespective of whether it was sold for the liquid or the manufacturing markets. Cardiganshire milk producers effectively began to receive a cross-subsidy from those in south-east England and elsewhere. A rough estimate suggests that milk producers' returns in Cardiganshire could have risen by as much as 20 per cent or more – a significant boost to the economy of the county, and one that continued up to, and even beyond, entry to the European Community in 1973. The immediate consequence was that between 1932 and 1942 dairy cattle numbers in Cardiganshire rose from 17.1 per cent to 22.1 per cent of all livestock units, the increase being concentrated in the south of the county.

These policies to revive rural areas through the medium of agricultural policy were overtaken when, from 1939, food output became once again the policy objective. The new policies provided guaranteed prices for most agricultural products (including all those of major significance for Cardiganshire), as well as other forms of financial assistance ranging from subsidies on various inputs to supports directed specifically to hill and upland farmers. In addition, County War Agricultural Executive Committees were set up to encourage, exhort and, if necessary, force farmers to expand. As far as prices were concerned, the magnitude of change was similar to that in the First World War. Between 1939 and 1947, the All Prices Index rose by 133 per cent, and those of fat cattle and milk by 105 per cent and 160 per cent respectively. Again, cereals received the greatest emphasis with a price rise of 235 per cent, explaining the observed rise in Cardiganshire of the tillage area (mostly oats) to levels not previously seen since the beginning of the Agricultural Census in the 1860s.

This time Cardiganshire's new-found agricultural prosperity did not disappear with the end of the war. Successive governments maintained a quite remarkable degree of consistency in this policy of unprecedented peacetime interventionism. Even in real terms, prices remained nearly stable until 1955[14] – an enormous incentive to output given that technological improvements were simultaneously reducing costs of production. After the mid-fifties, farm prices began to fall at a significant rate in real terms, and continued to do so until the early seventies, but technological change afforded some protection to most. Entry to the EC in 1973 not only reversed for a time the price falls, but also had another effect of particular importance to Cardiganshire. Support directed specifically to farmers in disadvantaged areas had been introduced in Britain with the Hill Farming

[13]A. W. Ashby and I. L. Evans, *The Agriculture of Wales and Monmouthshire* (Cardiff, 1944), pp.63–4.
[14]Calculated from C. H. Feinstein, *Statistical Tables of National Income, Expenditure and Output of the UK* (Cambridge, 1972) and *A Century of Agricultural Statistics*.

Act of 1946. Within the EC, this took on a new life under the Less Favoured Area policy, which provided for the payment of Hill Livestock Compensatory Allowances (HLCAs). These allowances were significant from two points of view. First, they were important in principle because, in their small print, they recognized explicitly the non-agricultural case for intervention – both the regional case (i.e., as a means of reducing depopulation) and the environmental one. Second, they soon became of enormous importance in value terms, representing a major source of farm income in Cardiganshire.

Thus, output continued to expand – in Cardiganshire, in Britain, and in the EC as a whole. Eventually, for the reasons given earlier, the policy proved impossible to maintain. By the late seventies, prices of the main agricultural products were falling again in real terms. In addition, milk output was constrained by quotas after 1984. In the face of the changed situation, milk and beef production in Cardiganshire became relatively stable but, with HLCAs remaining a major source of support to agriculture, farmers now saw sheep production as the way to maintain their incomes: by 1990 the number of sheep in Cardiganshire was more than five times what it had been at the end of the war. As this expansion seemed to be drawing to a close, there was a new shift in policy when much of the county was designated an Environmentally Sensitive Area – a designation offering some benefit to farm incomes if little to the environment.[15]

The critical feature of the agricultural industry, it has been argued earlier, is its contribution to the economy of the county. What are the implications of the changes which have been described? Superficially, it appears that they should have strengthened the rural economy. The increases in physical output provided an enormously greater volume of resources available for local processing at the end of the period compared with the beginning. Furthermore, as far as the prosperity of agriculture itself is concerned, the increases in output were probably at least enough to offset the decline in real price of agricultural produce so that the value of output of Cardiganshire farmers – the sum available to provide incomes for those employed in or supplying inputs to farming – was at least as high at the end of the period as at the beginning.

Yet the economic and social role of the industry declined beyond recognition, and this is reflected in the number of agriculture-related jobs. Despite some limitations, the most consistent indicator of trends in total employment in agriculture is the Population Census. It is important to note, though, that the Population Census categorizes people according to their main employment, thereby omitting the considerable number (and increasing proportion) of part-timers. The census reveals that the increases in output were accompanied by a reduction in agricultural employment over the period from 10,663 in 1911 to 3,240 in 1991 – a decline of 69.6 per cent. The reason, of course, is the technological improvements which resulted primarily from the need for increased food output and which were directed too often by the belief that efficiency could be measured by output per man. A comparison with figures for Wales as a whole is instructive. The percentage change in agricultural employment was almost the same – just marginally less in Cardiganshire than in Wales as a whole. What differentiated Cardiganshire from the rest of Wales were two things: first, even at the beginning of the period agriculture was more than three times as important in Cardiganshire as in Wales (39.0 per cent of employment compared with 12.0 per cent); second, and more

---

[15]G. Hughes, 'ESAs in the context of a "culturally sensitive area": the case of the Cambrian Mountains', in M. Whitby (ed.), *Incentives for Countryside Management: The Case of Environmentally Sensitive Areas* (Wallingford, 1994), pp.135–52.

significantly, as agricultural employment declined there was no offsetting increase in other employment in Cardiganshire. By 1971, indeed, other employment had risen by 23.8 per cent in Wales, but had fallen by 11.7 per cent in Cardiganshire.[16] Since that time, the activities of the Development Board for Rural Wales have helped to achieve significant increases in employment outside agriculture, but, even so, the industry still represented at the end of the period as much as 13.3 per cent of total employment compared with only 3.2 per cent in Wales.

The numbers of farmers and farmworkers have not moved in parallel. For earlier years, farmers are not covered in the agricultural census although numbers of farm holdings can be used as a proxy – probably a poor indicator of absolute numbers but perhaps acceptable as an indicator of change. On this basis, the number fell from 6,530 in 1912 to 3,213 in 1988, having declined more or less continuously throughout the period 1912 to about 1980 and having remained stable (or even slightly increased) since then. Only since the 1980s has the actual number of farmers been recorded reliably in the agricultural census. The pattern that had emerged by then was as follows: the total number of farmers, partners, directors and working spouses in Cardiganshire was in the range 4,300 to 4,800 (just over 70 per cent of the total agricultural labour force); the numbers increased continuously within this band from 1980 to 1986, and fell continuously afterwards; the proportion of farmers etc. who are classified as full-time has decreased continuously throughout the eighties – from over 59 per cent at the beginning to 53 per cent at the end – giving a number of whole-timers that accords reasonably well with the 1991 Census of Population figure of self-employed agriculturalists of 2,581. In brief, the number of farmers in the area roughly halved over the whole period under review; it had stabilized by the early eighties; by the latter part of the eighties a new downward trend was reasserting itself; and, if trends continue, part-time farmers will soon be the majority.

Turning to farmworkers, there were, in total, over 5,800 in the early 1920s – only slightly fewer than the number of farmers. Apart from an unexplained rise in the early 1930s, the trend was steadily downwards (even during the war). The number had fallen to a little over 3,000 by the late 1950s and by 1990 it had been reduced to 1,611 – by then only about half the number of farmers.

There is a possible distinction between the significance of whole-time workers as compared with that of part-time and seasonal workers. The groups can only be distinguished clearly from 1957. From that time the number of whole-time workers has declined almost continuously, falling to as few as 510 by 1990 – the biggest fall in any part of the farm labour force. On the other hand, the combined numbers of part-time and seasonal workers – clearly less important in economic terms, and perhaps different in social terms too – showed considerable stability in the 1960s and early 1970s and, in the 1980s, actually increased. As recently as 1957, whole-timers had outnumbered seasonal and casual workers by nearly four to one, but by 1990 the total number of workers had declined to 1,600, and less than one-third of these were whole-time.

The position on total direct employment – farmers and farmworkers together – can be summarized as follows. At the beginning of the period some 10,000–11,000 people had their main employment directly in agriculture, probably 40 per cent of these as farmworkers; at the end, the number had declined to 3,240, and the percentage of farmworkers to 18.7 per cent. The rate of decline was not significantly different from that in other parts of Wales, but what was different about

[16]John Williams, *Digest of Welsh Historical Statistics* (2 vols., The Welsh Office, 1985).

Cardiganshire, for most of the period at least, was its failure to generate new jobs to replace those lost in agriculture. The importance of agriculture in the economy had declined from 39 per cent of all jobs to 13.3 per cent. There are, however, two reasons for regarding this as an underestimate of the economic importance of the industry. First, there is a large number of part-timers and seasonal workers for whom agriculture is not the main employment – thus the Agricultural Census records not 3,240 but 6,132 people working in agriculture. Second, we have not yet discussed the indirect employment associated with agriculture.

When considering the economic importance of the agricultural industry, it is important to take account of indirect employment. There are three types. These are, first, employment in industries processing agricultural products (downstream effects), second, employment in industries supplying agricultural inputs (upstream effects), and, third, employment – in local shops, post offices and garages – created by the expenditure of farmers, farmworkers and those in related industries (expenditure effects). The potential significance is considerable. For example, for the year 1988, the net product of agriculture in Cardiganshire (the amount available for providing incomes to farmers and farmworkers to create direct employment) has been estimated to have been £21.4 million,[17] but the total value of sales was almost four times as large as this (£76.8 million) and it is this that provides an indicator of the opportunities for employment in processing industries. The difference between these two figures (£44.0 million) is the amount spent on inputs – an indicator of the opportunities in supplying industries. In practice, however, most agricultural outputs are processed outside Cardiganshire, most inputs are supplied from outside, and the bulk of farm household expenditure goes on products from outside. Most of the potential, therefore, is lost through these 'leakages'. Despite this, it has been estimated that for Wales as a whole, in the late 1980s every 100 direct jobs in agriculture in effect produced a further significant contribution to employment equivalent to sixty to ninety indirect jobs elsewhere in Wales.[18] For a smaller area, such as Cardiganshire, the proportionate leakage would be larger, and the knock-on effect within the county smaller, but still by no means insignificant. The interesting question is whether and how it changed during the twentieth century.

Taking the downstream effects first, the increasing output and growing specialization might have been expected to provide significant and growing opportunities in slaughtering and dairy processing – though store stock, almost by definition, do and always have moved out of the area for fattening. In practice, it seems certain that the employment in local processing was in fact greater at the beginning of the period – there were, for instance, still seventy-two corn mills and seventy-seven woollen mills in the early part of the century.[19] Stock would have been slaughtered behind butchers' shops or on farms, and milk processed locally either on the farm or later in dairies such as Tivyside Creameries and Felin-fach. During the century the combination of lower transport costs and economies of scale in processing have combined with legislative and administrative pressures (for hygiene, and for slaughtering in consuming rather than producing regions) to move processing not only off the farm but out of the county.

[17]Author's estimates.
[18]P. Midmore, 'The impact of agricultural policy on income and employment in Wales – an input-output approach' (unpublished University of Wales Ph.D. thesis, 1987).
[19]J. G. Jenkins, 'Rural industries in Cardiganshire', *Ceredigion*, VI, no.1 (1968), 90–127.

Turning to upstream effects, a similar pattern emerges. At the beginning of the century, agriculture in Cardiganshire was 'largely self-sufficient' and even later in the century the county still had 114 blacksmiths' shops as well as saddlers, lime-burners, maltsters and 'lip-workers'.[20] Feeding-stuffs were largely home-grown, machinery locally produced, fuel grown on the farm as oats and grass rather than bought-in as diesel, horses taking the place of imported machinery, locally built walls replacing imported barbed wire, and so on. Again, although formal quantification remains to be undertaken, there can be little doubt that employment in supplying industries has fallen significantly.

Expenditure effects have been subject to contrary influences over the period. First, incomes of farm families and farmworkers have risen very significantly in absolute terms, if not in relative ones. Second, the number of such families has fallen dramatically. Third, the extent to which they spend their household incomes on locally produced goods has also plummeted: basic requirements such as food, clothing, furniture and housing are now much more likely to come from outside the area, while the increase in incomes which has occurred is even more likely to be spent on goods from outside, such as washing machines and televisions. The net effect on local opportunities has almost certainly been a reduction. In summary, one of the biggest changes in Cardiganshire agriculture over the period has been the erosion of local self-sufficiency – a technical change with the most severe economic and social consequences.

Hitherto, this section of the chapter has tried to trace the major observable changes in agriculture in Cardiganshire in the twentieth century. Because the study of knock-on effects is a new one, precise quantitative evidence on indirect employment in earlier periods is lacking. Nevertheless, two things can be said with reasonable confidence about the combined direct and indirect role of agriculture in the economy of Cardiganshire. First, and most obviously (and despite the growth in output), its relative importance has diminished beyond recognition during the period – agriculture is no longer, with lead mining, the sole economic life-force of the county. But, second, even at the end of the period, agriculture still remains a major element of the local economy, accounting directly for 13.3 per cent of main forms of employment, and having knock-on effects that are generally thought to be larger than those of other industries.[21] The argument that agriculture is the 'backbone of the Cardiganshire economy' is one that has some justification even in the 1990s, and so, therefore, is the corollary that it has the potential to act in the future as it has in the past as the powerhouse of rural decline.

Characters and culs-de-sac

This history of agriculture in Cardiganshire has been approached by asking the question: 'How did we get where we are?' This gives an apparent inevitability to what has happened, but it is reasonable to ask: 'Could it all have been different?' Although events in Cardiganshire seem to have been shaped primarily by happenings in the United Kingdom or in the world, nevertheless it is possible to identify some turning points, some movements that started, faltered and disappeared, and some

---

[20]Ibid.

[21]P. Midmore, *Input-Output Models in the Agricultural Sector* (Aldershot, 1991).

personalities (some of them in Cardiganshire itself) who had a vision that never materialized. It is also true that Cardiganshire was not merely the passive recipient of external pressures: in some respects events within the county influenced the world outside.

The central theme to be identified as a might-have-been is land tenure. Related to tenure are a series of subsidiary themes – co-operation, farm size, farm research and advice, and rural resource management. The personalities include, above all, Sir George Stapledon, but there are also many others, only some of whom can be mentioned here.

Land tenure is fundamental. At the beginning of the century the great landed estates were still in existence and the majority of farmers were tenants rather than owner-occupiers. Some of the weaknesses of the system were apparent even at the beginning of the period.[22] It gave power to feckless and oppressive landlords to exploit their tenants; the inherent lack of security left tenants with little incentive to farm efficiently or to improve the land; and there was little incentive for landlords to take account of wider social considerations such as access to the countryside or the maintenance of archaeological remains – 'non-market benefits'. Later in the century two further weaknesses became apparent: in the thirties, agricultural development was inhibited by the fact that landlords no longer had the resources to foster it; and when, in the two world wars and since, government support was made available, the improved incomes inevitably accrued, not to the tenants to whom help was ostensibly directed, but (through higher rents and land prices) to landlords.

At the beginning of the period there occurred, in consequence of the land tenure problems as they then appeared, a growing movement for a restructuring of landownership – including the proposal of the Welsh-born Alfred Russel Wallace (more famous for his contribution to the theory of evolution) 'to restore the Land to the People and the People to the Land'. He proposed to make the state the ground landlord, thus creating communal ownership over the residual rights in land.[23] His ideas received considerable local support, notably from Dr Evan Pan Jones, 'the forgotten man of Welsh radicalism', who founded Cymdeithas y Ddaear i'r Bobl (Society of the Land for the People).[24] In the event, however, a completely different restructuring of landownership, already under way, was intensified by the outbreak of the First World War. Most of the old estates were broken up and tenants replaced by owner-occupiers, complemented by institutional landowners such as the Forestry Commission and the water authorities. It was not only the estates that disappeared, but also the radical proposals for reform of land tenure. Motivated 'not by economics but by history', the Welsh farmer, according to one rosy view, entered 'at last into his inheritance'. Cardiganshire became the leading county of owner-occupiers in the whole of Britain, with owner-occupation accounting by 1970 for 69.6 per cent of the land, compared with 15.9 per cent in 1909.[25]

Certainly the changes solved some of the problems of the landed estates, but they created new ones, some of which might indeed have been better handled either under the more radical systems

[22]D. I. Bateman, 'Heroes for present purposes? A look at the changing idea of communal land ownership in Britain', *JAE*, 40, no.3 (1989), 269–80.

[23]A. R. Wallace, *Land Nationalisation: Its Necessity and its Aims* (London, 1892).

[24]P. Jones-Evans, 'Evan Pan Jones – land reformer', *WHR*, 4, no.2 (1968), 143–59.

[25]J. Davies, 'The end of the great estates and the rise of freehold farming in Wales', *WHR*, 7, no.2 (1974), 186–211.

of reform or even under the best of the old landlords. The problems associated with the new system soon became apparent: the farming ladder which had allowed the labourer an entry to independence was now less readily available; those who did farm had less access to economies of scale in production or marketing or the purchase of inputs than might have been available through a large landlord; they had less opportunity to familiarize themselves with the latest scientific techniques than a progressive landlord could have provided; and, if non-market benefits were a problem with the great landlords whose range of interest was constrained by the size of their estates, then the owner-occupiers of Cardiganshire had an even narrower focus. To quote one source: 'Welsh agriculture was in danger of disintegrating into an excessive number of small units with no guiding principle and no leading personalities to hold it together and help it over the gulf which separates the quasi-mediaeval from the modern.'[26]

Co-operation provides one way of overcoming the diseconomies of scale inherent in small farms, and one that above all springs from local initiatives. At its best it not only overcomes the problems it was set up to deal with but also encourages all those who participate to look beyond the farm-gate and to engage themselves in the wider community. Welsh farmers were particularly active in this field, the movement being most widespread where the Welsh language was in common use.[27] In 1903 Cardiganshire already had more requisite societies and a greater combined turnover than any other county. Its thirteen societies accounted for nearly one-fifth of the total number and over one-quarter of the total turnover in the whole of Great Britain.[28]

The importance of local personalities in ensuring these developments is well identified,[29] with Augustus Brigstocke (of an old Cardiganshire family) the main leader:

> The first registered co-operative society in Wales was the Vale of Tivy Agricultural Society Ltd., which began its legal existence on 17 February 1902, followed in a matter of days by Llandyssul Agricultural Society Ltd., Emlyn Agricultural Society Ltd. and Llanarth and New Quay Agricultural Society Ltd., and the beginning of the story of agricultural organisation is easily traced to Augustus Brigstocke. If there are laurels for the Number One Co-operator, I would be prepared to support his claim.[30]

Brigstocke also founded a University Scholarship in agricultural co-operation at Aberystwyth, which ensured that co-operation became part of the teaching curriculum at an early stage, playing 'a not inconsiderable part in furthering the development of the movement'.[31] Most of the early societies supplied requisites (some specially imported by ship into Cardigan), but others handled the sale of dairy products.

The Welsh Agricultural Organisation Society (WAOS) – as the central organization for co-operatives – was set up in Aberystwyth in 1922, replacing the former separate AOSs for north and

[26]Ashby and Evans, *Agriculture of Wales*, p.93.
[27]Ibid., pp.121–2.
[28]*Fourth Annual Report of the Agricultural Organisation Society* (London, 1904).
[29]Jenkins, *Agricultural Community*, pp.266–8; S. Howell, 'They began it all', in E. R. Thomas (ed.), *Farmers Together: Golden Jubilee Volume of the Welsh Agricultural Organisation Society* (Aberystwyth, 1972), pp.32–6.
[30]Howell, 'They began it all'.
[31]J. R. E. Phillips, 'Historical retrospect', in Thomas (ed.), *Farmers Together*, p.56.

south Wales. When the English AOS disappeared in response to financial pressures in 1924, it is likely that the WAOS would have gone the same way but for the efforts of another of the personalities identified by Howell, namely A. W. Ashby.[32] He it was who initiated the unique 'Joint Scheme' in 1926, under which his department within the university effectively kept the WAOS in existence. Ashby's importance to agriculture was worldwide, but Cardiganshire was his base during his most productive years from 1924 to 1946, and Aberystwyth was the centre where for most of that period he held the first and, at that time, the only Chair in Agricultural Economics in Britain. Furthermore, much of his effort was directed to and inspired by the problems of Wales – in agriculture and, more significantly, in the rural community generally; indeed, it was said of him that 'rural Wales was his parish, the country folk of Wales his parishioners'.[33]

To those who spoke of farming as a way of life, Ashby would say 'farming is a rotten way of life'. This realistic view underlay his own clearly defined objectives:

> Merely to make agriculture productive or its employees prosperous . . . would scarcely be worth striving for unless accompanied by spiritual growth of the people . . . From associational life in its many forms – the schools and churches, the friendly society and trade unions . . . the co-operative societies, women's institutes and village clubs – will develop habits of thought, judgement and action which will place the civilisation of rural areas on the plane which is desired.[34]

Victorian in tone this may be, but it represented a composite view of rurality and community that was to give way almost entirely in official circles to one that was narrowly agricultural and financial. Ashby saw his role as combining in a complementary way farm-level advice, research and university teaching. At the farm end he initiated an enormous body of research focusing on the role of farming in the rural economy; he taught or appointed a considerable body of (mostly) Welsh young men and women (among them John Morgan Jones, J. Llefelys Davies, Pryse Howell), who made significant contributions to the agricultural industry; and he played a major part in a range of government commissions and committees, especially those concerned with the Agricultural Marketing Acts and the creation of the Milk Marketing Board. Ironically, it is likely that Ashby's work in helping to develop Marketing Boards (effectively compulsory co-operatives) undermined his contemporaneous efforts to encourage voluntary co-operatives, and it may explain in part the failure of voluntary co-operatives to thrive in Britain as they have elsewhere. The Second World War strengthened the need for centralization and, with notable exceptions, co-operatives remained as much a promise as an actuality, continuing generally as a rather narrow, commodity-based means of raising incomes rather than as a communal approach to the improvement of the rural economy and society. The 'weak and delicate plant'[35] of 1922 was (in a different metaphor) still only 'jogging along' in 1936.[36]

[32]D. I. Bateman, 'A. W. Ashby: an assessment', *JAE*, 31, no.1 (1980), 1–14.

[33]'Tributes to A. W. Ashby C.B.E.', *Journal of the Proceedings of the Agricultural Economics Society*, X, no.4 (1954), 274–6.

[34]A. W. Ashby, 'A collection of the writings of A. W. Ashby, 1912–1953'. Paper 42. A private collection in four volumes available in the libraries of the University of Wales, Aberystwyth, and the Agricultural Economics Research Institute, Oxford.

[35]Thomas (ed.), *Farmers Together*, p.10.

[36]H. E. Roberts, 'The present position of the Co-operative Movement in Wales', *Cambrian News*, 26 June 1936.

It has never developed into the oak that its founders envisaged, but rather into a well-established perennial, alternately blossoming and withering according to the changing seasons.

By their nature, national Marketing Boards have less of a basis in the community and less potential for grass roots involvement. Nevertheless, the MMB in its early days did not ignore such concerns. J. Llefelys Davies, from a Cardiganshire farm, was involved with the Board from its outset until his retirement as General Manager in 1963 (when he returned to Cardiganshire), and he was not indifferent to the social needs of the area from which he sprang. He was instrumental in establishing the MMB creamery at Felin-fach, which not only took milk from the local farms but also provided jobs in a depressed area for farm families – jobs which remained until a later group of MMB managers, with the narrower objective of profitability rather than farm family welfare, thought fit to close the creamery on 'efficiency' grounds. In the 1990s the MMB itself was wound up and replaced by a national (England and Wales) co-operative.

Farm research and advice is another area where much of the responsibility traditionally resided with the landlord. In the twentieth century, however, technology has moved so fast that no Thomas Johnes or any other landlord, however well-intentioned, could have kept pace with it (Fig. 24). Here, above all, it was recognized from early in the century that there was a major role for the state. Cardiganshire, especially through the Welsh Plant Breeding Station (later the Institute of Grassland and Environmental Research), has been at the forefront of the research. The Station, directed at the outset by Sir George Stapledon, led the world in grassland research from the 1920s, and it was even said by a former Minister of Agriculture that without him there could have been no military victories in the Second World War.[37] His own interests were much wider than food production, however, and there is still much that is relevant in his visionary ideas. He shared Ashby's enthusiasm for rural society rather than agriculture alone, and as early as the 1930s he developed detailed proposals for a National Park, mostly in Cardiganshire, as a kind of ecological experimental station for the integration of nature and man – urban as well as rural:

> I am concerned primarily with the proper utilization of the land surface of Great Britain, and it seems to me that the first thing to be decided is the priority of the innumerable claims that a modern state makes on its land surface . . . I think that more weight should be given to its use relative to health, pleasure and mental balance than even for food production, although in a subsequent chapter I shall argue in favour of growing all the food that is possible . . . The most valuable product of the land, I am endeavouring to argue, is the human being.[38]

He wanted traditional demonstration farms replaced by 'experimental farms, research farms, mad farms'. He had, furthermore, a profound suspicion of the narrow science that was ultimately to dominate much agricultural research:

> Every man who has done anything in this world, and who has made a success of his life, knows perfectly well that his success has owed little or nothing to the necessarily small body of facts that were pumped into him at school, or even at a university . . . The whole trend of education has been to glorify book learning and proficiency in the various subjects – subjects! there are no

---

[37] R. Waller, *Prophet of the New Age: The Life and Thought of Sir George Stapledon, F.R.S.* (London, 1962), p.3.

[38] R. G. Stapledon, *The Land Now and Tomorrow* (London, 1935), pp.7–8, 226.

Fig. 24: Ceredig Jones ridging potatoes at Pwllpeiran, Cwmystwyth, in the late 1940s. (*Copyright Museum of Welsh Life, St Fagans*).

subjects. It is only the true countryman who appreciates the fact that . . . all divisions into subjects are artificial . . . Solitude, silence and contemplation, for these the country still provides and these are the woof and warp of wisdom. Yet modern education will have nothing to do with them. In so far as agricultural research is concerned, I am convinced that a serious mistake has been made in the endeavour to organize such research in terms of subjects – chemistry, physiology, genetics, economics – rather than in terms of the basal problems of agriculture itself . . . There are very few problems in agriculture the solution of which lies in the power of any one narrow specialist . . .[39]

Despite the views of Ashby and Stapledon, scientists not only became increasingly specialized, but they focused on narrow objectives such as maximizing output per man or per acre without regard or thought for the effects this would have on the number of farmers and farmworkers, the natural environment, the social environment and language, or even on farm incomes which generally fall rather than rise as the result of agricultural 'improvements'.

[39]Ibid., pp.300–3.

Agricultural research is of no use if it does not reach the farmer. In the nineteenth century, the efforts of landlords in farm advice had been complemented by agricultural societies,[40] but, as was the case with research, the need for state intervention was recognized early in the twentieth century. Both Ashby and Stapledon came to the University as 'Advisory Scientists' (joining there Sir Bryner Jones, Professor of Agriculture, and another notable leader in the agricultural development of the county). They worked closely with local farmers, who provided both an inspiration and a test-bed for ideas. The most notable was perhaps Captain Bennett-Evans, described admiringly by Stapledon as a man 'who single-handed and of his own inititative was waging war against the elements and the Forestry Commission'.[41]

The advisory work included the Aberystwyth Short Courses for farmers and their sons (and sometimes daughters), courses which provided some of them with their first foot on an academic career.[42] After the Second World War, the advisory functions were taken from the universities and handed over to the new National Agricultural Advisory Service (later ADAS, the Agricultural Development and Advisory Service). Nevertheless, it was Cardiganshire again that provided the home for the Welsh headquarters of ADAS. Ironically, ADAS and WPBS not only acquired the estate-owners' research and advisory functions but also their properties – at Trawsgoed and Gogerddan respectively. They also, again like the former estate owners, became major employers in the area – an indirect knock-on benefit of agriculture for the rural economy and one which remains to be quantified.

For farmers, the staff of these bodies, many of them locally born, have included some of the personalities of the area. And yet, the indigenous (and unsubsidized) home-bred developments also catch the imagination. Despite all the state aid, agricultural shows, many of them small and localized, continued to be major events of the area – arenas where farmers could learn from each other, where non-farmers could still meet farmers, and where the social and the agricultural converged. Again, Cardiganshire can claim a special contribution, for the first Welsh National Show (the predecessor of the Royal Welsh Agricultural Show) was held at Aberystwyth in 1904 and annually thereafter until 1909, when it became for many years peripatetic. The prime movers in establishing the show included two local men, Mr (later Sir) Lewes Loveden Pryse of Gogerddan and Mr D. D. Williams, a farmer's son from Tregaron and a member of the staff of the Agricultural Department of the University.[43]

Change in farm size is another requirement that had to be handled differently under a system of owner-occupation. As technology changes, there are bound to be alterations in what constitutes an efficiently sized farm – changes which have occurred more rapidly in the twentieth century than ever before. The market can bring about a restructuring of holdings (and indeed it has done so), but it is likely to be slow and inefficient compared with what could be planned and (perhaps painfully) implemented by a single landowner, whether private or communal. When realization of this finally dawned on the authorities, they created (under the Agriculture Act of 1967) the idea of Rural

[40]R. J. Colyer, 'Early agricultural societies in south Wales', *WHR*, 12, no.4 (1985), 567–81.
[41]Waller, *Prophet of the New Age*, p.168.
[42]R. J. Colyer, *Man's Proper Study* (Llandysul, 1982), pp.57–8.
[43]D. J. Griffiths, 'Agriculture in Ceredigion: amaethyddiaeth yng Ngheredigion', *Blwyddlyfr y Royal Welsh Journal*, 52 (1983), 14–22.

Development Boards (RDBs), with powers which included authority to amalgamate small farms into 'commercial' units – using compulsion if necessary. The first two such Boards proposed were for the Pennines and for mid-Wales. While Pennines farmers accepted and welcomed the development, the farmers of mid-Wales responded angrily: 'Farmer-owners have sweated long hours, often for more than one generation to buy their farms. Now it is proposed to eliminate the word "free" from the term freehold . . . [It is] an effrontery, a gratuitous insult and a travesty of human rights.'[44] After an often acrimonious public inquiry held in Aberystwyth the proposal was abandoned.

A full history of the RDB issue remains to be written, but two aspects are obviously significant. First, it was one of the few examples in twentieth-century agricultural history where a small localized group of farmers was able to prevail over Whitehall wisdom. Second, this abortive effort seems to have had an unforeseen consequence when, a few years later, the Development Board for Rural Wales (DBRW) was created. Although this body had a confusingly similar name to the former RDB, it had a very different function – to strengthen the economic and social fabric of the whole of mid-Wales in order to offset the debilitating effects of the decline in employment in traditional industries. But, supposedly to reassure those who might regard this as a new name for the old concept, it was made clear that the new DBRW (and its grants) would be kept well away from the most rural industry of all, agriculture. Thus were farmers punished! In retrospect, it is possible to sympathize with both sides in the RDB debate. A procedure to facilitate the difficult process of restructuring was (and is) desirable, though not one based on a misguided Whitehall belief that the only good farmer is a full-time one. By the 1990s, part-time farms had become respectable, with 'pluriactivity' representing the policy-makers' jargon for their new-found solution to the problem of maintaining rural societies.[45]

The final theme to be discussed in this section is rural resource management. In the 1990s such problems as wildlife, landscape, water supplies and access to the countryside are on everyone's lips. But as well as issues of conservation, there is the equally important one of development. When, and under what circumstances should a theme park, a craft centre or a long-distance footpath be created to bring local employment and prosperity? How can it be ensured that such developments are integrated and complementary rather than jarring and competitive? Such issues impinge on the interests of society as a whole, but the consequences are not priced. The market cannot help.

Again, this is linked to the tenure system because the best of the old-fashioned landlords could see their estates as whole and could use their authority to develop and implement an integrated estate-wide strategy which could be adjusted to changing circumstances of technology and demand. They may not have had the interests of society at heart, but they had, however inadequately, a wider interest than that of a few hundred acres. A wider communal ownership might have been better still. But how was this role in rural resource management to be met under a system of owner-occupation?

Co-operative community effort might have provided a way but, as we have seen, co-operation did not develop in this direction. Where voluntary co-operative bodies have developed, they have appeared to represent only particular interest groups – the farmers' unions, the wildlife trusts, the Council (later Campaign) for the Protection of Rural Wales, the Ramblers' Association – never the whole local

[44]Anne-Marie Sherwood, personal communication.
[45]D. I. Bateman and C. Ray, 'Pluriactivity and the family farm in Wales', *Journal of Rural Studies*, 10, no.1 (1994), 1–13.

community interest. In the event, the job of rural resource management fell to a plethora of quangos and conservation bodies and schemes: the Countryside Commission, the Nature Conservancy Council, the National Parks, the Countryside Council for Wales, Environmentally Sensitive Areas, Tir Cymen, and the requirements of the Town and Country Planning Acts. If these bodies and schemes have roots, they are not to be found in Cardiganshire. For farmers, and for the rural community generally, they are top-down structures, to be mildly (or strongly) resented, and their proposals resisted even when they offer long-term benefits to the area (as the aborted Cambrian Mountains National Park could have done had farmers not opposed it). Could it all have been different?

Where non-market benefits were important, government intervention seemed to be the only way of protecting them under a system of fragmented landholding. Yet, rural areas like Cardiganshire have a strong sense of community, of permanence, of concern for the local environment that might have made a less centralized approach both possible and more effective. Only in the two or three years preceding the time of writing has it begun to be apparent to policy-makers that there was an opportunity to marshall local talent and enthusiasm, and, curiously, the recognition has generally come from Brussels rather than London or Cardiff. EC initiatives such as the LEADER schemes[46] have created opportunities for community-led developments directed towards integrated rural development. In effect, a strategy for a new kind of co-operative is developing, a co-operative with a rural and community focus rather than an agricultural and financial one.

What, then, emerges from this review of personalities and possibilities? Perhaps only the point that, even in state-run twentieth-century agriculture, there is still just a little room for the individualist, the local, the idiosyncratic. On occasions Cardiganshire has broken away from the herd and has even led it. Things could have been different, perhaps better. In any event, in one respect at least Cardiganshire has had at Aberystwyth what can legitimately be regarded as the agricultural centre of Wales. In this small town have been concentrated most of the agriculture-related institutions that have been created in Wales during the course of the century – the Institute of Grassland and Environmental Research, the Welsh headquarters of ADAS, the Forestry Commission, the Meat and Livestock Commission, one of the farmers' unions, the Welsh Agricultural Organization Society, the Welsh Agricultural College and the University's agricultural departments. What other county in Britain can match this record?

Conclusion

In conclusion, there are three questions which might be asked. To what extent has the county contributed to the achievement of the objectives identified at the outset? To what extent were the changes observed in Cardiganshire agriculture the result of the policies adopted? In what ways should the original objectives now be changed to meet the needs of the future?

As far as the objective of food supplies is concerned, for most of the twentieth century the emphasis in national policies has been on quantity rather than quality. If, at the end of the period, there is an increasing concern with 'healthy eating', this is a perspective which depends on hindsight. Given that

---

[46]P. Midmore, C. Ray and A. Tregear, 'The South Pembrokeshire Leader Project: an evaluation' (unpublished report, Department of Agricultural Sciences, University of Wales, Aberystwyth, 1994).

sheer output was the objective, it is obvious that this could only be achieved through policies pursued at a national level. There is no possibility that scientific techniques and policy institutions would have developed without government support for agricultural research; nor would the new techniques have been disseminated without government-financed educational and advisory services, or adopted without the financial incentives provided by government. But Cardiganshire can claim to have participated fully and enthusiastically in this massive increase in food production that has been one of the most striking national endeavours of the twentieth century, and to have contributed substantially at every level – science, policy-making, education and advice, and (the ultimate target) production itself. The achievement has been spectacular – to such an extent, indeed, that, at the time of writing, increased production has ceased to be an objective and, short of some natural or man-made disaster, is unlikely to become so in the foreseeable future. This should not lead to a false sense of security – the unforeseeable usually happens! But nor should it lead anyone to undervalue the achievement which, if output had been the only objective, would have been one of unqualified success.

The diminished importance of production has led to a re-emphasis on efficiency as an objective. Achievement in this respect is a matter about which there must be serious doubt. In the usual technical terms – output per man, or per cow or per hectare – the increase in efficiency in Cardiganshire as elsewhere has been unprecedented. An alternative approach to measuring economic efficiency is to use market forces as an indicator. On this basis, agriculture in Britain, dependent as it is on a high degree of protection and support, is highly inefficient. In Cardiganshire especially, agriculture is exceptionally exposed because of the special assistance given to the Less Favoured Areas. In terms of the market, it must be accepted that agriculture in the county is not only (in these terms) inefficient, but – more important for those dependent on it – highly vulnerable.

As regards the objective of farm income support, the achievement nationally is again doubtful. Policy-makers with too little understanding of economics have not appreciated that neither support mechanisms nor technological change raise incomes in the way that intuition suggests. Techno-logical change benefits the individual farm, but if all farmers adopt the improvement (as, sooner or later, they are forced to do) the effect is a fall in price – there is benefit to the consumer but little or none to farm incomes. Support mechanisms tend to be reflected in the prices of inputs, especially land, rather than in farm incomes; furthermore, once introduced, they are hard to remove. For the future, farm incomes are likely to continue to be a problem in the sense that they are under pressure, but the political strength of the farming lobby is reduced and the question is being asked why low farm income should constitute a case for support any more than low incomes of building entrepreneurs or small shopkeepers. Many would argue that the problem of farm incomes is not so much how, or how much, to support them, but rather how to escape from the support treadmill created by the institutionalization (e.g., in high land prices) of the high support levels of the past.

The farm income problem has, in effect, merged into what previously seemed a separate, but also unfulfilled objective – the maintenance of the rural population and society. The continuing importance of agriculture in Cardiganshire has not been caused by agricultural employment itself holding its own in the county better than elsewhere, but rather by the failure of other industries to come to the area (at least until the activities of the DBRW from 1977). As a result, the view that agriculture is the backbone of the rural economy is one which can still be upheld. But, in the twentieth century, agriculture has been the powerhouse of rural decline, and while in most other parts of Britain it has now lost that power, in Cardiganshire its dominance is still such that it retains it – an impending danger at at time when we are nearing the end of the twentieth century's flirtation with the most highly-interventionist agricultural policy ever seen in Britain.

Even as late as 1942 farmers were seen as 'the unpaid landscape gardeners of the countryside'[47] and it was only from the 1980s (beginning perhaps with the Wildlife and Countryside Act of 1981) that agriculture began to be perceived as having a negative rather than a positive influence on the remaining objective – the environment. Fortunately, Cardiganshire had in any case escaped almost unscathed from the landscape and wildlife depredations associated with agricultural expansion in less well-blessed counties. Such despoliation as had occurred in Cardiganshire had come from forestry rather than from agriculture, though there had also been concern about the hill land 'improvement' and overgrazing encouraged by such policies as HLCAs. The introduction of the Cambrian Mountains ESA could well be the forerunner of a succession of such policies. In this respect, there is room for some optimism concerning the future of Cardiganshire agriculture if landowners are willing to exploit the opportunities by acting co-operatively in a way which will benefit the economy without harming the environment. There remains, as in the past, a continuing role for scientists, advisors and educationalists who now need to develop farming techniques which are compatible with environmental sustainability, not in competition with it.

Finally, it is probably time to recognize that a new objective is coming into being: animal welfare. Legislation to protect animals has existed at least since before the Prevention of Cruelty to Animals Act of 1849. By implication society has long accepted the concept of animal rights. Up to now, however, the cost that such legislation imposed on farmers was probably negligible. What gives the issue new importance is that the increasing strength of feeling on this issue could have significant implications for the Cardiganshire economy in the future. Concern about conditions of animal transport could mean a return of slaughtering from consumption areas, where it has largely moved, back to the production areas, a shift which farmers have long supported because it would improve both their incomes and their contact with buyers. Failing that, a continuing growth of vegetarianism would weaken still further the animal-based farming of the area.

In summary, at the end of the period under study the time has come to recognize that we no longer need an agricultural policy as such, but a new regional policy, one which can be directed to the problems of areas where traditional industries are declining, whether the area is Merseyside or mid-Wales, whether the industry is car manufacturing or agriculture. The regions in which agriculture is the focus industry are diminishing and will continue to diminish, but this is not a reason for ignoring it for in Cardiganshire it remains of central importance to the economy, society and culture. This need is already recognized in the European Union,[48] but less so in Britain – despite the fact that farm pluriactivity, diversification and part-time employment are growing and thereby linking agriculture's prosperity ever more closely to the rest of the economy in a reciprocal rather than a one-way embrace. But we still lack an integrated approach to the development of the county, one which recognizes that agriculture, tourism, the environment and the development of new industries are all interlinked in determining its economic and social structure. There is hope as well as danger here, but it requires a willingness – on the part of farmers as well as policy-makers – to adapt in the future, just as they have in the past.

---

[47] *Report of the Committee on Land Utilisation in Rural Areas* (HMSO, London, 1942).
[48] *The Future of Rural Society* (EC Commission, 1988), COM (88), 501.

CHAPTER 7

RURAL INDUSTRIES IN CARDIGANSHIRE

J. Geraint Jenkins

CARDIGANSHIRE is a county of considerable cultural and scenic variety and that variety is also reflected in the nature of its rural industries. For instance, the industrial activity which characterized the coastal towns and villages was quite different from that of the upland core of the county and from the rural craft activity which dominated the valleys of the main rivers that flow into Cardigan Bay. In the lush valleys of the Teifi, Aeron, Rheidol and Ystwyth, for instance, life was never as hard as it was in the upland core of Cardiganshire; nature was kinder, the soils were better and there was shelter for man and beast. Dwellings were far more comfortable and the valley villages supported numerous craftsmen who supplied most of the needs of communities. In addition, a plentiful water supply provided power for a variety of small industries such as wood turning, leather and textile production which brought a certain degree of wealth to the specialized artisans of those valley communities.[1]

In upland Cardiganshire conditions were rather different. To many of the inhabitants of the hill country, life was almost a scavenging existence which involved gathering from the mountains and fields and processing those harvests to provide essentials for survival. Local raw materials were fully utilized to produce food and shelter, medicines and clothes, tillage tools and fuel, and ingenious skills were evolved to ensure survival. The life of many hill farming families was a constant battle against natural elements and few could afford to employ the services of full-time craftsmen to produce essentials. To till his land and fence his fields, the upland smallholder was forced by circumstances to depend on his own ingenuity in making the best possible use of the resources available to him. A great deal of the equipment used by hill farmers was made by farmers themselves and many of them displayed considerable craftsmanship in making the essentials for survival. Hand rakes, tool handles, feeding baskets, field gates and transport vehicles were all made by farmers from the raw materials available to them. The large number of professional full-time craftsmen who lived in the valley communities of Cardiganshire were rarer in the hills.

In every rural community, however, there were always some people who, although not trained as craftsmen, were more competent that others in producing the necessities of life. One smallholder might earn a local reputation as a carver of shepherd's crooks or hand rakes, while another might

[1]For the background, see I. C. Peate, *Y Crefftwr yng Nghymru* (Aberystwyth, 1933); idem, *Welsh Folk Crafts and Industries* (Cardiff, 1945); idem, *Tradition and Folk Life* (London, 1972); J.G. Jenkins, *Crefftwyr Gwlad* (Llandysul, 1971); idem, *The Craft Industries* (London, 1972); idem, *Traditional Country Craftsmen* (London, 1979).

have a reputation for making horse-drawn sledges or lip-work seed baskets, and neighbours would go to them for the supply of those essentials. These were the part-time, amateur craftsmen with dextrous hands (*y dynion dethe*), who were an important element in most rural communities.[2]

Cardiganshire, with its long coastline and villages which seem to cling to the edge of the land, witnessed a craft activity which was completely different from that of the agricultural sections of the county. These were the highly specialized craftsmen who fulfilled the needs of those whose livelihood was based on the sea and its harvest. Boatbuilders and ropemakers, copper workers and anchor smiths, sailmakers, netmakers and pulley-block makers were all of considerable importance in the sea-orientated villages and towns of the county. With the demise of coastal trading activity and the spectacular decline in inshore fishing, most of those skills have long disappeared.

The market towns of the county supported a large number of craftsmen who supplied the needs of a town's hinterland by those people who regarded Cardigan or Lampeter or Aberystwyth as their own market town. Some indication of the importance of country towns as a supplier of goods is provided by the following examples from early nineteenth-century trade directories: in 1830 Cardigan had three bakers, thirteen bootmakers, two coopers, five dressmakers and milliners, two straw-hat makers, two weavers, four blacksmiths, three curriers, three saddlers, six tailors, two whitesmiths (tinsmiths), one corn miller, seven carpenters, four glaziers, five maltsters, two printers, two tanners and one stonemason. In addition, since it was an important port it also supported an anchor smith, two shipbuilders, two pulley-block makers and three sailmakers, together with a number of foundry workers employed in one of the two foundries concerned with agricultural as well as maritime essentials.

In the same year, although the town had not fully developed as a port, Aberaeron had one woollen manufacturer, one bootmaker, one baker, one carpenter, one corn miller, one hat-maker, one blacksmith and two shipwrights. For its part, Aberystwyth had eight bakers, eleven carpenters and joiners, two dressmakers, seven tailors, twenty bootmakers, three curriers, six maltsters, four saddlers, two straw-hat makers, one brewer, four lime-burners, three shipwrights, two tinsmiths, two hat-makers, four tanners, one cooper, five cabinetmakers, eight stonemasons, two corn millers, two skinners, three wheelwrights, one nailmaker, one ropemaker and one sailmaker.

It was not only the market towns which supplied the day-to-day requirements of the population, for every village and rural neighbourhood had its contingent of craftsmen who supplied essentials and made tools, utensils and a whole range of goods the community required. In the production of hand tools for agriculture – and much of the craft activity was connected with this work – each craftsman was concerned with producing equipment that was well suited to the needs of a locality. Local conditions of topography, soil and vegetation were all factors which affected the design of tools. For example, the Aberaeron billhook, whose design was limited to Cardiganshire, was a tool specifically designed to deal with the heavy thorn growth of hedges. The long-handled triangular-bladed Aberaeron shovel was well suited for use on steep slopes, while horse-drawn ploughs built at such places as Llanfihangel-y-Creuddyn, Sarnau, Ffostrasol and Betws Ifan were well suited to dealing with the soil of the locality in which they were used. One further example will suffice to

[2]I. C. Peate, 'Rhai o grefftau Ceredigion', *TCAS*, 7 (1930), 50–5; J. G. Jenkins, 'Rhai o grefftau Ceredigion', *Ceredigion*, IV, no.3 (1962), 213–30; idem, 'Rural industry in Cardiganshire', ibid., VI, no.1 (1968), 90–127.

illustrate the importance of the craftsman in village life. In 1890 the small south Cardiganshire village of Rhydlewis had two carpenters, one stonemason, one leather currier, one baker, five tailors, one tanner, two corn millers, three clogmakers, one basket-maker, one pinmaker, six boot-makers, one blacksmith, eight weavers and two saddlers.

Types of rural industry

It is obvious that an isolated county like Cardiganshire had a great variety of industry within it and it is only during the twentieth century that the age-old pattern of life, where the craftsman was an important element of the population, has been eroded. The craft industries of the county may be divided into the following broad categories:

1. *Extractive industries*, such as lead and silver extraction, which employed specialized craftsmen within the industry. Blacksmiths, woodworkers, pattern-makers and brass founders were all essential for the smooth running of an extractive venture and many of the mines of north Cardiganshire were self-sufficient for equipment and structures. In this category, too, lie the self-sufficing activities of peat cutting that was especially important in the hill districts and on the low-lying marshes of Cors Fochno and Cors Caron. There were also short-lived ventures like the extraction of salt at Ynys-las.

2. *Processing industries*, where raw materials produced within the area were converted for use by the people or for working by other craftsmen. Thus the many tanneries of the county produced leather which could be made into a finished product by saddlers and bootmakers. Of the processing crafts, the most important were corn milling, tanning, woollen manufacturing, limestone-burning and malting barley. Most of these trades had to be carried out in purpose-built or converted buildings and required a wide range of immovable equipment. In the majority of cases water-power was required to operate machinery and consequently most of these industries occupied valley locations.

3. *Creative crafts*, usually carried out by individual craftsmen in workshops whereby the needs of the community were supplied. In some cases, such as tailoring, saddlery and dressmaking, where the tools of operation were few and light, itinerant craftsmen who were able to visit the remotest farmsteads were commonplace. Creative crafts fall into three distinct groups:

   (a) Those concerned with supplying the day-to-day needs of a local community. These were the crafts essential to every self-sufficing group and included blacksmithing, carpentry, undertaking, stonemasonry, tailoring, bootmaking and basket-making. Some of the maritime trades of the past were also in this category.

   (b) Crafts which came into existence because of the presence of a particular raw material. These included bowl turning, wood carving and tool-handle making, all of which utilized the heavy timber products of the Teifi valley. It included the production of clog soles for the clogmaking factories of the north of England by itinerant woodworkers, who utilized the alder trees of the county, and hat-making, especially in the Tre'r-ddôl, Gors-goch and Pen-uwch districts, where there were ample supplies of wool. Fishing may also be regarded as a craft which came into existence in order to take advantage of the variety of fish in rivers and off the coast.

(c) Home crafts, such as butter and cheesemaking, breadmaking and beer brewing, and amateur activities such as embroidery and needlework, straw-lip work and spoon carving, were often carried out as a spare-time leisure activity by country people.

Corn milling

One of the most widespread of all the rural industries in the county was that of corn milling, and a water-driven mill was to be found on the banks of most streams. In the 1920s the following were in operation in the county:

Clarach (Ruel)
Llandysul (Dôl Ifor)
Troed-yr-aur (Cwmhyar)
Llandre (Cynnull Mawr)
Llangeitho (Felin Fawr)
Tre'r-ddôl
Brongwyn (Trewen)
Nancwnlle (Felin-goed)
Betws Leucu (Felin Fawr)
Tal-y-bont
Llanrhystud (Felin-gwm)
Rhydowen
Llanio
Blaenpennal
Ponthirwaun
Cardigan (Felin Newydd)
Lledrod (Ty'n-y-porth)
Tal-y-bont (Elerch)
Llanllwchaearn (Pont-bren)
Pontrhydfendigaid
Tregaron (Fullbrook)
Llanafan (Wenallt)
Capel Bangor (Rhiw Arthen)
Llanfair Orllwyn
Rhydlewis (Brithdir)
Blaenannerch (Blaenpistyll)
Brongest

Llechryd (Penrallt)
Llangunllo (Gernos)
Llandysul (Cletwr)
Ciliau Aeron (Rhiwbren)
Llanddewibrefi (Gorwydd)
Llangeitho (Rhydypandy)
Y Ferwig (Felin Bedr)
Penbryn (Llan-borth)
Aberaeron
Llanrhystud (Rhiw-bwys)
Aber-porth
Llanbadarn (Coedgwgan)
Llangrannog (Felin Isaf)
Lampeter
Cardigan (Felin Ganol)
Llannarth (Llyfannog)
Llandyfrïog (Cwrrws)
Llanllwchaearn (Nant y pelau)
Penparc (Felin fach)
Rhyd-y-felin (New Mill)
Tŷ'r Graig (Gwnnws)
Llanbadarn (Melin y Person)
Capel Madog (Felin Hen)
Aberystwyth (Mill Street)
Rhydlewis (Felin Cwm)
Maes-llyn

Gilfachreda (Wern)
Llandysul (2) – Pontweli
Ciliau Aeron (Tŷ Gwyn)
Llanddewibrefi (Gogoyan)
Llangeitho (Felin-fach)
Llwyndafydd
Aber-arth
Nancwnlle (Felin fach)
Llanrhystud (Felin Fawr)
Llangwyryfon (Pont-faen)
Llanbadarn (Trelowlgoed)
Llangrannog (Felin Uchaf)
Llanddeiniol (Carrog)
Llanfair Clydogau
Cribyn (Hafod Wen)
Talgarreg
Llandysiliogogo (Synod)
Cwmtydu (Felin Huw)
Llannerch Aeron (Pandy)
Felin-fach
Llanilar (Dyffryn)
Aberystwyth (Melin y Môr)
Llandre (Felin Gyffin)
Aberystwyth (Morfa Mill)
Mydroilyn
Swyddffynnon

Melin Pont-bren, now at the Museum of Welsh Life but originally located on the banks of the River Soden in the parish of Llanllwchaearn, is typical of the small corn mills which once dotted the Cardiganshire landscape. Like most other Cardiganshire mills, it is a stone-built, hip-roofed building of three floors, with a lower building containing a kiln for corn drying attached. The mill is built on a slope, so that at the back only two floors appear above the ground, while at the front it has three floors. A narrow doorway at the back leads to the first floor, or 'stone floor', of the mill, while at the front another door, located on the pine end of the building, is wide enough to admit a cart to the ground floor. The all-iron, over-shot water wheel was made by S. F. Kelly of Cardigan, and a wooden trough, whose angle may be controlled by a lever on the first floor, leads from the mill race *pinfarch* and pond. The flow of water along the mill race is controlled by a wooden trap door. Not

Fig. 25: Melin Pont-bren, originally located in the parish of Llanllwchaearn but now at the Museum of Welsh Life, St Fagans. (*Copyright Museum of Welsh Life, St Fagans*).

only does the wheel drive the machinery, but it also provides power for the chain hoist, by which sacks of grain were lifted from the ground floor through two pairs of hinged trap doors in the other floors to the top of the building or 'bin floor'.

The top floor was used for storing grain and it contains the entrances to four shutes leading to the milling machinery on the first or 'stone' floor. The first of these pieces of milling machinery is a pair of French burr mill stones, usually preferred for milling barley, a cereal crop which was especially important in south Cardiganshire before 1914. Millstone grit stones were preferred for wheat and oat milling and Melin Pont-bren has a pair of well-used stones of this type. The quality of a mill stone is of vital importance to the miller and both the fixed bed stones and the revolving runner stone had to be dressed (*cyfogi*) at regular intervals with a special hammer known as a 'mill bill'. Deep grooves of a regular pattern had to be cut into the stones to ensure that they ground the corn efficiently and distributed the flour at the periphery of the stone. A home-made gauge consisting of a piece of wood with a feather marker for testing the true running of the stones was also an essential piece of equipment in stone dressing. Both pairs of stones are enclosed in a wooden casing with hoppers for feeding the grain above. On the first floor of the building, too, is the grain cleaner, for when seed was brought into the mill for grinding it was hauled from the ground floor of the building to the top floor by means of the chain hoist. Before it could be milled, impurities had to be removed and the grain had to be passed through the cleaner, with its series of oscillating sieves, to remove all the materials which could not be milled. The cleaned grain came out of the seed cleaner through a shute to the ground floor of the building, where it was sacked and hoisted again to the top floor. The other piece of equipment on the first floor is a flour bolter (*mashîn fflowro*), which, with its series of revolving brushes, was used for refining flour and ensuring that the best and finest grained flour was separated from the bran and inferior flour (*blawd coch*). On the first floor, too, the mill's main driving gear with apple-wood cogs on the cast iron wheels is located, together with the revolving shaft, connected to the water wheel.

On the ground floor are found the shutes and troughs for the milled flour and husks, together with a winnower (*mashîn nithio*), mainly used for winnowing oats. In this, oats were sieved to separate the husks from the flour. The room adjoining the mill is the kiln where oats were gently heated for some hours before milling. A fire was lit in the grate underneath a metal-bottomed, perforated grain container, the walls of the device being of stone. The oats were placed on the metal, a fire of culm lit underneath and the oats gently heated, the grain being gently mixed every twenty minutes or so with a long-handled wooden rake known as a *corloc*. Usually oats were roasted for three hours and, after cooling for twelve hours or more, the grain was milled. It was then winnowed and the oat kernels were again milled. Occasionally the husks, too, were milled. Oatmeal was, of course, a staple diet in south Cardiganshire, essential for making such foods as *sucan*, *bwdran*, *cawl dŵr* and *cawl llaeth* as well as *bara ceirch*.

Blacksmithing

The great changes that have taken place in rural life have affected the blacksmith more than any other rural craftsman. Until 1914, perhaps until 1939, the smith was an essential member of every rural community and even in the early thirties there were at least 104 blacksmiths' shops in constant work in the county. These were located at:

Llan-non	Llanwenog (2)	Capel Seion
Swyddffynnon	Abermagwr	Tre'r-ddôl
Cilcennin	Betws Ifan	Capel Bangor
Penparc	Tre-groes	Llangwyryfon (2)
Lampeter (Peterwell Crescent and Drovers Road)	Sarnau	Llandygwydd
	Cenarth	Penparcau
Dre-fach	Ciliau Aeron	Llangoedmor
Llanychaearn	Llanilar	Mydroilyn (Capel Ficer)
Llanfair Clydogau	Cardigan (Strand)	Tal-sarn
Cross Inn (New Quay)	Lledrod	Cwm-cou
Caerwedros	Llandysul	Maes-llyn (Pant-teg)
Llannarth	Bwlch-y-groes	Llwyn-y-groes
Felin-fach	New Cross	Ystradmeurig
Cardigan	Maes-llyn	Aber-banc
Mydroilyn	Penrhiw-llan	Aberaeron (2)
Cross Inn (Llan-non)	Capel Wig	Blaenannerch
Llangeitho (2)	Oakford	Beulah
Llangybi	Pentregât	Tregaron (4)
Cilcennin	Pont-rhyd-y-groes	Bronnant
Llanddewibrefi	Prengwyn	Tyn'reithin

Bangor Teifi	Blaen-porth	Blaencelyn
Llanio	Llanfair Orllwyn	Blaenpennal
Llanrhystud (4)	Rhydlewis (Bryn Dulais)	Ffynnon Geitho
Bow Street	Llangrannog	Brongest
Aber-arth	Tre-main	Aberystwyth
Neuaddlwyd	Abermeurig	Eglwys-fach
Pontrhydfendigaid (2)	Llanfihangel-y-Creuddyn	Tal-y-bont
Blaen-porth	Nancwnlle	New Quay
Borth (Dôl-y-bont)	Rhydlewis (Salamanca)	Dihewyd
Pennant	Ponthirwaun	Cwrtnewydd
Cardigan	Cribyn (2)	Synod Inn

For as long as the horse remained the main motive power on farms and the equipment of the farmer remained simple, the blacksmith was essential in every locality. Not only was he concerned with shoeing horses, but he was also responsible for making and repairing a wide range of agricultural and domestic equipment.[3]

Like other craftsmen, blacksmiths were concerned with supplying a distinctly local market and the tools and implements which they manufactured were well-suited to local needs of soil, vegetation, and topography. The well-known Aberaeron billhook, which until quite recently was still being manufactured by a large Midland edge-tool manufacturer, was originally designed and manufactured at the Aberaeron forge. It is interesting to note that, as locally made farm tools disappeared from the scene, their manufacture, very often to a traditional pattern, was taken over by large-scale manufacturers in English cities and they continued to be produced to old local patterns of tool-making long after they had ceased to be manufactured in their district of origin. The Aberaeron shovel, with its long, curved handle and triangular blade, was especially designed to suit the needs of a hilly country. The Aberaeron shovel was still made in Cardiganshire in 1990 by Griff Jenkins of Cwrtnewydd and the tradition of the Aberaeron shovel works, established in 1850, was still being continued in the county.[4] In addition to the Aberaeron forge, which attained some national fame for making shovels, billhooks and sickles, most other country blacksmiths were capable of producing them.

Harvesting hooks, twelve inches in diameter for women and thirteen inches in diameter for men, were manufactured in considerable quantities, but no Cardiganshire blacksmith was capable of producing totally satisfactory scythes. Ploughshares, mould-boards, coulters, and indeed complete ploughs were made in the county and the smithies at Llanfihangel-y-Creuddyn, Sarnau, Maes-llyn, Ffostrasol and Betws Ifan (Y Lion) gained considerable fame for the quality of their ploughs in the nineteenth century. The mould-boards of these ploughs were well designed for ploughing sloping fields. In some cases mould-boards were designed by farmers and made by local blacksmiths. For example, in the 1880s David Evans of Rhydlewis designed a mould-board for turning a sod in one piece and this was made by John Owens of Aber-porth with mould-boards manufactured at the Bridgend Foundry, Cardigan.

Harrows, often wooden-framed implements with metal tines, were also manufactured locally, and in west Wales re-tining harrows or sharpening them was a task undertaken by blacksmiths for payment in kind rather than in money. A small stack of corn, known as *llafur golym*, was often given

[3]R. Phillips, 'Oes aur y ceffylau', *Ceredigion*, V, no.2 (1965), 125–42.
[4]D. M. Rees, 'Industrial archaeology in Cardiganshire', ibid., V, no.2 (1965), 121–2.

to the blacksmith in lieu of cash for this task. Payment, too, could be made by the haulage of coal or culm to the smithy from the nearest coastal village.

One of the most important tasks of all undertaken by smiths was that of completing the iron work for carts. In binding tyres and making hub bands, body struts and axle irons, most Cardiganshire blacksmiths worked in conjunction with nearby wheelwrights. But in all cases the wheels brought to the forge for tyreing belonged to the wheelwright, who paid the blacksmith in cash for his services. The price of tyreing varied, but in the 1850s John Williams of Cellan charged six shillings a pair for banding a cart wheel; for making iron arms for attaching to wooden axles, he also charged six shillings. A set of shaft irons cost four shillings, cart body irons three shillings, and hub bands two shillings.

Tyreing a wheel was an extremely complex process and many a tale is told of how country blacksmiths and wheelwrights, with tempers frayed, argued about the respective merits of construction techniques.[5] To tyre a cart wheel, an open fire of wood shavings was made in the corner of the blacksmith's yard and wheel bands, cut to size, scarfed, bent and welded, were heated until they were almost white hot. Alternatively, if the forge hearth was wide enough, tyres were heated inside the smithy, while occasionally tall furnaces, where four or more tyres were heated simultaneously, were used. The wooden wheel was bolted down on the metal tyreing plate – a circular platform which may still be seen outside most smithies – and the wooden wheel screwed down onto it. The tyre, grasped with tongs, was dropped on the wheel, so that the wooden rim burst into flames. Before the fire could do any damage, water was poured on to it and as it cooled it contracted and the tyre became firmly fixed in place.

Not all blacksmiths were proficient shoeing smiths and farriers, but a large proportion of the time of most blacksmiths was concerned with making horse shoes and with shoeing. In one week in 1873, for example, John Williams of Cellan shoed twenty-eight horses. Farriery demanded not only dexterity in shaping metal but considerable knowledge of the anatomy of the horse's foot, its diseases, and methods of curing those diseases. When a horse was brought to the smithy for shoeing, the old shoes were removed and the hooves filed and carefully measured across. A rod of iron was then taken and a length equal to 3/ times the diameter of the hoof was cut off with a cold chisel and sledge. Each rod was then heated in the fire, bent in the middle, and shaped. With a punch, nail holes were cut in the iron and the actual shoeing began. Occasionally a horse had to be felled for shoeing.

Special nails for fastening shoes were also made in the smithy. A rod of iron (*gwialen hoelion*), some eighteen inches long, was heated and cut to the required size on the cutting edge of the *hardy*, which was inserted in the anvil orifice. It was then inserted in the nail heading tool, which consisted of a flat metal bar fitted at each end with a perforated knob. The perforation complied with the size and shape of the nail shank and was also countersunk to correspond to the nail head. After inserting the red-hot piece of metal in the nail hole, the tool was placed over the anvil orifice and the head hammered into shape. All that remained was to point the nail either with a rasp or on a pointing horse (*ceffyl pwyntio*). After several reheatings, fittings and hammerings the farrier made sure that the shoe fitted the hoof. It was then nailed firmly into place. Great care had to be taken that the nails pointed outwards so as not to damage the sensitive flesh of the foot. With a light shoeing hammer, the nails were knocked in and their points clenched as they emanated through the side of the hoof.

[5] J. G. Jenkins, *Agricultural Transport in Wales* (London, 1963), pp.63–81.

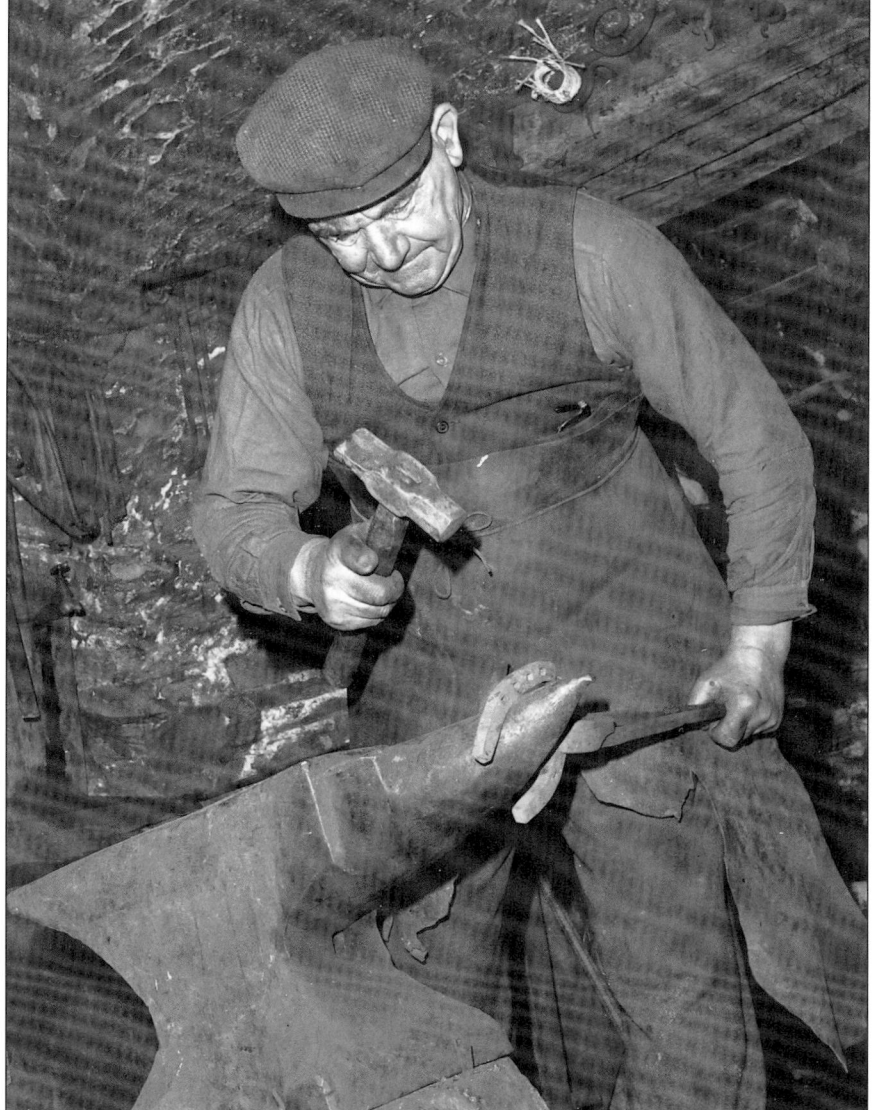

Fig. 26: Elias Owens, blacksmith at Abermagwr in 1968. (*Copyright Museum of Welsh Life, St Fagans*).

The blacksmith's trade has changed considerably, for the present-day craftsmen of Cardiganshire are more akin to agricultural engineers than creative craftsman; their main concern is repairing a wide range of agricultural tools and implements. In the 1920s the late Elias Owens, who operated his blacksmith's shop in the north Cardiganshire hamlet of Abermagwr, completed a two-year apprenticeship with Evan Williams of Beulah. Elias Owens was twenty-two years old when he began this apprenticeship; he was not paid at all except for his board and lodging. A £12 bond was paid to the blacksmith. For the first few months the apprentice began with the simpler tasks, like removing nails from horses' hooves, filing hooves and dismantling implements, before gradually graduating to other more complex tasks, so that within two years Owens was competent to deal with most of the tasks of the country blacksmith. After a further period of training as an improver at Beulah and as a journeyman with Ben Jones of Tre-groes, Elias Owens moved to Abermagwr to work with Mr Jenkins in the Trawsgoed estate smithy. In 1930 he took over as a master blacksmith at Llanfihangel-y-Creuddyn and in 1934 he also took over the Abermagwr smithy, working three days at Llanfihangel and two at Abermagwr. By 1937 the Llanfihangel smithy had closed and Elias Owens spent all his time at Abermagwr. The thirties were difficult times for country blacksmiths and many of them were forced to close, but the war brought new prosperity, although the nature of the work had changed considerably by then. Most of the work now was devoted to the repair and renovation of agricultural implements rather than true creative craftsmanship. In the twenties and thirties blacksmiths were concerned with such tasks as building gates, ploughs and harrows, with shoeing horses and tyreing wheels, as well as with decorative wrought iron work. All these tasks were done with the minimum of machinery: the forge fire had to be blown by hand; iron had to be drilled, welded and filed by hand; and the craftsman had to work long hours to make ends meet. At Beulah, for example, the working day was from 8 a.m. to 8 p.m.

Since 1935 conditions have changed, for although the blacksmiths of Cardiganshire draw their customers from a much wider area they complete their work at a much faster rate. Electric power has replaced hand work: the craftsman has electric drills, electric grinders, and screw-making machines; he has electric fans instead of the old hand-operated bellows; he has oxyacetylene welding equipment and a great deal of other machinery that has helped to make his life less strenuous than in the past.

The woollen industry

Cardiganshire lay well outside the sphere of influence of the Guild of Weavers and the Guild of Fullers in Carmarthen, which, in the sixteenth century, influenced the development of cloth manufacturing in the countryside around Carmarthen. The industry in Cardiganshire was one of scattered homesteads, simple, unfettered, and independent. It continued as such until the early part of the nineteenth century, although there is evidence to suggest that textile workers became increasingly more important after the sixteenth century. In the eighteenth century, for example, one writer noted that: 'The wool is manufactured into all forms and colours, supplying the inhabitants with every vestment even to his shirt.'[6] Another described how flannel was used for covering coracles, as being 'of more durable substance, may be more easily prepared and keeps out the water much longer than canvas'.[7] By the end of the seventeenth century, ecclesiastical records show that weaving had become a distinct occupation and both men and women were concerned with producing cloth as a full-time occupation. Most of this was to supply a local market, but a small proportion was sold at country fairs.

[6]B. L. Maudet Penouet, *Letters describing a Tour of South Wales* (London, 1797), p.86.
[7]E. Donovan, *Descriptive Excursion through South Wales and Monmouthshire* (2 vols., London, 1805), II, p.228.

By the early seventeenth century, too, fulling mills had appeared in the county and during the next hundred and fifty years they became more and more common. Some indication of the distribution of the woollen industry in pre-nineteenth-century Cardiganshire is provided by the distribution of the place-names *pandy* or *felin ban* (fulling mills) and the word *deuntur* or *dintir* (tenter). They occur at the following places:

Llanwnnen	Tal-y-bont	Cenarth
Henllan	Tre'r-ddôl (1662)	Llangoedmor (1774)
Llanwenog (1843)	Llanfair Clydogau	Llanwnnen
Llan-non	Eglwys-fach	Penbryn (Melin Llwyn Eos 1610–1722)
Cardigan	Llanbadarn-y-Creuddyn	St Dogmaels
Llandysiliogogo (1616)	Lledrod	Aberystwyth (1657)
Llangeitho	Troed-yr-aur	Llanbadarn Fawr (Pandy Maes-bangor 1810)
Cellan (1722)		

In some districts the place-name *deuntur*, signifying the position of tenter frames for drying fulled cloth, occurs in close proximity to the place-name *pandy*. At Cardigan, for example, *Cnwc-y-dintir* on the north side of the town is located on a bank above *Y Felin Ban* in the valley below.

The process of fulling consists of 'the closing together of the threads of woven woollen fabrics by pressing and kneading with the assistance of soap or acid liquor'.[8] The *pandai* of Cardiganshire, in common with those of the remainder of Wales, contained heavy water-driven wooden hammers, measuring anything up to ten feet in length, under which cloth was placed for finishing. Human urine, soap, and fuller's earth were added to the cloth and the hammers would fall on the cloth for some hours until it had shrunk considerably and the threads fully closed together. The water-driven fulling mill was important in that it marked the first stage in the transition of woollen manufacturing from a fully domestic craft to a factory industry. Until the late eighteenth century, and even the late nineteenth century in some districts, the other processes of textile manufacture – carding, spinning and weaving – remained principally domestic industries, carried out in farmhouses and cottages. Finishing, however, was carried out at a fulling mill from the late sixteenth century onwards. Quite often, as in the case of Melin Llwyn Eos, Penbryn, the craft of fulling was combined with that of corn milling; the same head of water and wheel was used to drive the fulling stocks and the mill stones.

By the first decade of the nineteenth century, machinery for carding had appeared in Wales and was adopted by a number of textile manufacturers in north Cardiganshire. By 1809 a water-driven carding engine was in use at Tal-y-bont, where Thomas Morgan from the Caersŵs district of Montgomeryshire established the Leri Mills. The carding machine, with its complex of revolving rollers, not only required considerable space but also water-power. For this reason most of the early engines were accommodated in existing fulling mills. By 1840 carding engines as well as spinning jennies, jacks and hand mules were known throughout the county and the processes of preparing yarn for weaving as well as finishing cloth rapidly became the domain of factory workers rather than domestic craftsmen. Nevertheless, a certain amount of domestic carding and spinning continued in Cardiganshire until the end of the nineteenth century.

[8] E. K. Scott, 'Early cloth fulling and its machinery', *Trans. Newcomen Soc.*, XII (1931–2), 1.

Although by 1820 a number of carding and spinning mills accommodated hand looms, weaving was primarily a domestic industry, carried out by specialized weavers in their cottage homes. Their monopoly was more or less unchallenged until the widespread adoption of the power loom around 1860, first in the Teifi valley at Llandysul, Henllan and Lampeter and then in the remainder of the county. By 1880 weaving, too, had become overwhelmingly a factory industry despite the persistence of a number of isolated weaving shops in all parts of the county.

The nineteenth century therefore saw the emergence of Cardiganshire as one of the most important textile manufacturing regions in Wales.[9] It witnessed the decline of domestic manufacture and the concentration of the industry in factory buildings, containing power-driven machinery evolved by eighteenth- and nineteenth-century engineers. It was the age of factory building in the county. These factories fall into three distinct categories:

1. Factories that were established primarily to supply the needs of lead mines in north Cardiganshire. The principal ones were:

Tal-y-bont	Lower Mill: Cwm Mill, Leri Mills (1809); Ceulan Mills (1860), Pandy
Borth	Dôl-y-bont (enumerated in 1895)
Devil's Bridge	(c.1849–1934)
Llandre	Glanffrêd or Forge Mill (1830–1930)
Llanfihangel-y-Creuddyn	(closed c.1928)
Pontrhydfendigaid	(enumerated 1875, 1895)
Pont-rhyd-y-groes	Gwarfelin (c.1860–1923)
Ystradmeurig	Gwnnws (c.1820–1927)

2. Factories in the Teifi valley and its tributaries that were part of the important west Wales textile-manufacturing district. This region was the most important textile-producing district in Wales between 1860 and 1930. In the heyday of the industry the village of Dre-fach Felindre alone had forty-five mills, Cwm Morgan had five, Llanybydder five and Pencader four. The region extended into east Cardiganshire, where the following mills were operating:

Aber-banc	Dolfelin (enumerated 1875), Aber-banc Mill (1875–1926), Tower Hill (1855–1925)
Cardigan	Trewindsor (1844–1963), Another mill enumerated 1875, 1895
Capel Dewi	Broneinon (1870–1969), Rock Mills (1865–1969)
Cellan	(1885–1952)
Cribyn	Waun Penbryn (1880–c.1900), Pen-wern (1840–1953)
Henllan	Trebedw (1885–1958), Cwerchyr (1890–1932)
Lampeter	Dolwen (1860–1927), Pencarreg (enumerated 1875), Glanduar (enumerated 1875)
Llandysul	(some in Carmarthenshire) Ffrwd-wen (c.1870–1928), Abercerdin (1870–1946), Teifi Mills (1880–1922), Chestnut Mills (1925), Gelli Aur (c.1895–1928), Pantolwen (c.1895–1962), Twelly Mills (c.1870–c.1925)
Llanfair Clydogau	Pandy (c.1923), Ffatri Llanfair (–c.1927)
Llanwenog	Maes-y-felin (1870–1932)
Llanwnnen	Pandy (1870–c.1901)
Maes-llyn	(1880–1969)

[9] J. G. Jenkins, *The Welsh Woollen Industry* (Cardiff, 1969), chapter 6.

Newcastle Emlyn	5 factories (all but one on the Carmarthenshire side of the Teifi)
St Dogmaels	(1870–1922)
Llanybydder	5 factories (all on the Carmarthenshire side)
Pentre-cwrt	4 factories (all on the Carmarthenshire side)
Dre-fach	Maesyfelin (c.1870–1923)
(Llanybydder)	

3. Rural factories mainly concerned with supplying a local market

Aberaeron	Aeron (1829–1950)
Aber-arth	Glynarth (c.1850–1957)
Blaen-pennal	Bontgoy (c. 1929)
Bronnant	(–c.1930)
Brongwyn	Craigyrhuad (c.1870–1923)
Cilcennin	(1798–c.1948)
Llanddewibrefi	Foelallt (1907), mainly concerned with London House (–1900) with stocking knitting; Ffatri Jerry (–c.1900)
Llangeitho	Rhydypandy (enumerated 1875)
Llangrannog	(c.1855–1912)
Llanina	(enumerated 1875)
Llangybi	(enumerated 1925)
Llannerch Aeron	Felin-gwm (enumerated 1925)
Llanrhystud	(c.1800–1926). Contents of the mill at the Museum of Welsh Life, St Fagans, Pandy (–1919) Fulling only
Llan-non	(enumerated 1875)
Llechryd	(enumerated 1875)
Lledrod	Crognant (–c.1902)
Mydroilyn	(enumerated 1875)
New Quay	(enumerated 1875)
Penbryn	Ffatri Troed-y-rhiw (–c.1860); Llwyn Eos (c.1610–1630) Fulling only
Pont-siân	(enumerated 1875, 1925)
Rhydlewis	Dolwen (–1898), Moelon (–c.1903)
Swyddffynnon	
Talgarreg	Ffatri (1840–1924), Crugyreryr (c.1856–1945), Lower Factory (c.1860–1940)
Tal-sarn	Cwmcafan (1815–1922)
Tregaron	3 mills enumerated 1875 mainly concerned with producing knitting yarn for domestic hand knitters
Troed-yr-aur	Glan-rhyd (enumerated 1875), Curlew Weavers (1965–)

i. North Cardiganshire

The organization of the woollen industry in north Cardiganshire in the early nineteenth century was somewhat similar to that in the adjacent counties of Merioneth and Montgomery. Small carding and fulling mills were established on the banks of swiftly flowing streams, providing a large number of domestic spinners and weavers with raw materials and finishing woven cloth for domestic weavers. Nevertheless, with the addition of spinning machines in the period 1820–40 and the installation of hand looms in many of the mills at the same time, all the processes of textile manufacturing could be found in the same building. By 1835 the Leri Mills at Tal-y-bont had carding machines, fulling stocks, a hand mule for spinning, together with a number of hand looms.

Fig. 27: The Llanrhystud Woollen Mill, *c.*1932. (*Copyright Museum of Welsh Life, St Fagans*).

Some of these looms were available for hire to outside weavers for a few days or a few weeks a year. In addition to weavers who carried out their work at the Leri Mills, Thomas Morgan, the owner, employed a number of outworkers who wove yarn, spun at the mill, on hand looms in their homes. The flannel was sold back to the mill at a fixed price of seventeen shillings per piece of 25 yards in the 1840s. This was then sold on the open market by Thomas Morgan, the price of a piece usually being in the region of £2. The weavers, both male and female, lived in an extensive area stretching from Penrhyn-coch in the south to Corris in the north.

Most of the flannel was sold locally, both to farmers and lead miners, or at fairs in Aberystwyth, Machynlleth, and Tal-y-bont. Thomas Morgan also paid regular visits to the Newtown Flannel Exchange, where goods manufactured in north Cardiganshire were sold to drapers from London, Shrewsbury and other English towns and cities. Some of the spinners employed at the Leri Mills in the 1830s and 1840s, using the same hand mule still being used in 1975, were paid a piece-rate wage, the average earnings being ten shillings a week. Others were paid a fixed wage. Part-time spinners were also employed, many of them farm labourers who undertook work at the mill when farm work was slack. They were paid a piece-rate wage, averaging threepence a pound for spun wool. In addition to spinners and weavers, Thomas Morgan also employed carders, who were usually paid at the rate of threepence per pound for carded wool. In 1845 the staff of the mills consisted of thirty-five weavers (all but three of them outworkers), nine spinners (all but two part-time workers), two carders, one warper, and three general textile workers.

During the nineteenth century the Leri Mills flourished; Cwm Mill, a hundred yards below the Leri Mills, was built in the 1860s to cope with the spinning. By the end of the nineteenth century thirty people were employed full-time at the mill which produced tweed, flannels, knitting yarn, blankets and shirt and underwear flannel for a wide area of north Cardiganshire. With the exception of the Leri and Ceulan mills at Tal-y-bont, which were able to take advantage of the popularity of north Cardiganshire as a tourist centre, none of the others in the area was able to survive the depression of the 1920s. This, combined with the contraction of the local market, led to the closure of the majority of the mills in the twenties. The Ceulan Mills, established in 1860, survived until the late 1950s. It was a well-equipped mill on two floors with water-driven machinery. In 1955 it had the following equipment:

> Willey for disentangling wood
> 60-inch carding set consisting of two-part scribbler, Scotch intermediate feed, and two-part carder with single rubber
> > condenser giving twenty-five good threads
> Hand mule of 300 spindles
> Twisting frame of 45 spindles
> Warping mill and creel
> Weft winder of 10 spindles
> Two power looms (1 × 110 inch, 1 × 40 inch)
> Hank-making machine
> Dye vat and fulling machine.

In the early 1950s it employed six people and was concerned with making knitting yarns, blankets and tweeds of very high quality, most of which were sold locally.

ii. Teifi Valley Mills

The mills of the Teifi valley and its eastward flowing tributaries were generally larger than those of north Cardiganshire, and were part of an industrial complex which attained considerable prosperity between 1860 and 1920. It was a short-lived prosperity, for most of the productive capacity of the mills in south-east Cardiganshire was aimed at producing flannel for the industrial regions of south Wales. The mills thrived mightily after power looms were introduced into the industry around 1860, and the introduction of power-driven machinery for carding, spinning, weaving and finishing brought a sudden expansion in the industry, with new mills established in all parts of south-east Cardiganshire. 'There is hardly a spot on the banks of any stream', said Daniel Jones, the historian of Llangeler and Pen-boyr, 'where it would be convenient to build another factory or mill.'[10] After 1860 mills were built along the banks of most eastward flowing streams in the county. In the heyday of the industry, two distinct types of mill could be distinguished.

First, there were rural mills which still worked in the tradition of the old self-sufficing economy. More often than not they were run by the mill-owner and his family, often in conjunction with a

Fig. 28: Dan Lewis of the Maes-llyn Mill using a willey for disentangling and oiling raw wool, 1947. (*Copyright Museum of Welsh Life, St Fagans*).

smallholding. Pen-wern Mills, Cribyn, for example, was run in conjunction with a six-acre holding, Trebedw, Henllan, with a three-acre holding, and Rock Mills at Capel Dewi with a six-acre holding. Many of these mills were inaccessible, for they were located near adequate water-power supply rather than easy marketing facilities. Many were located along rutted cart tracks and waterlogged footpaths, several miles from the nearest roadway or railway station. Trewindsor Mills, near Cardigan, which closed in 1963, was located at the bottom of a gorge and was approached by numerous footpaths and a very steep, mile-long, rutted cart track.

For as long as these rural mills were operating, and many were still in production in the 1950s, they used machinery and water power which had in most cases been installed at the mill when it was first built. There were exceptions, of course: Pen-wern Mills, Cribyn, was rebuilt and re-equipped in 1912, but on the whole machinery at these mills dated from the last quarter of the nineteenth century. The mills produced a wide range of products ranging from blankets to *carthenni* (blankets), from shirt flannel (*gwlanen crysau*) to underwear flannel (*gwlanen dronsus*), and from rough suitings (*brethyn cartre*) to knitting yarn. Many of the mills also installed stocking-knitting machines. Some of the mills, too, were concerned with processing wool brought in by farmers in the locality for making up into cloth, yarn and blankets.

[10]D. E. Jones, *Hanes Plwyfi Llangeler a Phenboyr* (Llandyssul, 1899), p.357.

In addition to selling products directly to the public from the mills, owners of the smaller mills in east Cardiganshire attended local markets and fairs. The owner of Trewindsor Mills, for example, always had a stall at Cardigan market, while the owner of Penwern Mills had a stall at Tregaron market. Some of the mills were more adventurous, for although a proportion of their products was sold locally, supply exceeded demand by a considerable amount. Mill-owners looked towards industrial south Wales for their markets and many attended fairs and markets in that area. Again most of the products were sold directly to the public. For example, in June 1908, Mr Price, the owner of Pen-wern Mills, Cribyn, sold goods to customers at Clydach, Ammanford, Swansea, Cross Hands, Tumble, Llanelli, Neath, Cydweli, Pontardawe, Morriston and Brynaman, as well as to a large number of local customers.

Second, the more mechanized 'urban' type mill was more concerned with supplying a national wholesale market. During the last quarter of the nineteenth century a number of mills employing up to a hundred people became common in west Wales. They were few in Cardiganshire, although a number were established in villages on the border with Carmarthenshire, such as Pentre-cwrt, Llandysul, Dre-fach Felindre, Newcastle Emlyn and Llanybydder. Most were completely new ventures although some were extensions of old mills, as was the case with Dolwion Mill, Dre-fach, which began as a fulling mill in the early nineteenth century.

The larger mills were not necessarily located near the source of water power, but their location depended entirely on adequate road and rail facilities to take their products to a wholesale market. Those at Newcastle Emlyn, Llandysul and Llanybydder were established in close proximity to the railway. The railway brought coal for driving the gas engines or steam plant; it brought raw wool, not usually Welsh wool; and it took away fine shirtings, flannel, tweed and blankets produced by the mills. These products were not aimed at the retail trade but rather at wholesalers in south Wales, London and elsewhere. In order to sell their goods, mill-owners paid frequent visits to wholesalers. Between 1912 and 1920, for example, the largest mill in Cardiganshire – Maes-llyn Mills – sold products to drapers and wholesalers in Birmingham, Aberdare, Hirwaun, Newport Pagnell, Wolverhampton, Maesteg, Cheltenham, Newport, Neath, Pontyberem, Ystalyfera, Abersychan, Port Talbot, Llansamlet, Middlesborough, Swansea, Caerphilly, Clydach, Treherbert, Pontardawe, Stafford, Presteigne, Glasgow, Bletchley, Brecon, Llanelli, Bridgend and Y Gilfach-goch. The main products sold were dress flannel, shirt flannel, drawers, aprons and shawls. The records of the mill show that a few local tailors, such as John Jones of Gwynnant, Rhydlewis, were supplied with tweed, but there are no references to farmers bringing wool to the mill for processing nor to the attendance of mill-owners at local markets or fairs.

In many cases the larger mills were run by non-working owners and for driving mill machinery they installed gas engines and, later, electric power to run the most modern machinery available at the time. The equipment of Maes-llyn Mills, for example, consisted of:

A large willey
2 hopper-fed 60-inch carding machines, one of 5 parts, the other of 4, each producing 72 good threads
Two self-acting mules, each of 300 spindles
Twisting frame – 40 spindles
Hank-making machine
90-inch warping mill and creel
20 spindled weft winder
8 looms

Teazel gig
Fulling machine
Scouring machine
Dye plant.

Pantolwen Mills, Llandysul, which operated on a slightly smaller scale, were completely re-equipped in the 1920s. They had:

A large willey
A hopper-fed, 66-inch, five-part carding machine
Two self-acting mules, one of 325 spindles, the other of 300 spindles
82-inch warping mill and creel
Weft winder, 20 spindles
Fulling machine
Hydro extractor
Dye plant
4 looms.

The mill, which closed in 1962, was mainly concerned with producing *carthenni* for a large wholesale market.

iii. Rural factories

Outside the two main areas of concentration a large number of truly rural mills supplied the needs of the local population. Almost every river valley had its mill, to which local farmers brought wool for processing; in many cases they paid the mill-owner in goods rather than in cash. Lower Factory, Talgarreg, for example, which closed in 1940, was exclusively concerned with producing a wide range of products for local farmers. Its modest, water-driven equipment comprised:

A small willey
3-part carding set producing 20 good threads
Semi-automatic mule of 120 spindles
42 spindle hand twisting machine
2 looms.

It seems surprising that such a widespread industry as the woollen industry in Cardiganshire should have declined to such an extent that only one mill (Rock Mills with Broneinon, Capel Dewi), together with one weaving shop at Troed-yr-aur, was in full production in 1991. The decline of the industry, already apparent in the early 1920s, continued unabated from then on. The end of the First World War spelt disaster for the industry, particularly in the Teifi valley: the price of wool fell from 4s. 6d. a pound to 9d. a pound within the space of a few months, a catastrophic fall which forced many small mills to close down.

During the First World War, however, the woollen industry of west Wales had flourished as never before. Mills were reorganized, new pieces of equipment were bought and extra staff were engaged in an effort to increase production and meet the overwhelming demand for flannel, blankets and uniform material. The villages of the middle Teifi valley in particular flourished on government contracts, and anyone who could spin, card or weave took full advantage of the situation. Much of the flannel produced during the war was 'angola', an inferior mixture of wool and cotton, widely used for making shirts. This was very cheap to produce, but the demand for it was so heavy that its

Fig. 29: Benjamin Evans, of Brynllin, Bwlch-llan, preparing bramble ties to make a lip-work basket. (*Copyright Museum of Welsh Life, St Fagans*).

sale brought considerable wealth to the textile manufacturers of west Wales. In 1915, for example, one mill alone – the Maes-llyn Mill – fulfilled a War Office contract for seven hundred dozen shirts. While War Office contracts continued, profits were high and the industry flourished. But the mills of west Wales were not geared to meet conditions in the highly competitive conditions of the post-war era. Had more factories been re-equipped with the proceeds of war and had the standard of workmanship been improved, the industry would have been in a much stronger position to withstand the depressed conditions of the inter-war period.

By 1920 the seeds of depression were already bearing fruit, and the period 1920–5 in particular was one of considerable difficulty in the county. Government surplus stocks of flannel and blankets were thrown on the open market at ludicrously low prices, so that the woollen manufacturers were forced to meet unfair competition by cutting their costs and prices. Flannel shirts, for example, which were sold at 52s. 6d. a dozen, wholesale, in 1916 were sold at 38s. a dozen in 1923. The golden age was over; the price of wool fell from an all-time high of 54d. in 1918 to as little as 9d. per pound in 1921. The wages of textile workers were cut and hundreds were dismissed.

In addition to all the other difficulties, the miners of south Wales went on strike in April 1921, and since south Wales was still the main market for the textiles of west Wales the consequences were extremely serious. Once the strike ended in June, wages were slashed, price lists were cut, privileges were taken away, and victimization was rife. No longer could south Wales provide the assured market for the products of rural woollen mills.

The woollen manufacturers of west Wales failed in their attempt to meet changing conditions; many still produced inferior angola as they had done in wartime, but they failed to sell it. Most of them still concentrated on the production of flannel for shirts, vests and 'drawers', but the demand for flannel underwear fell rapidly in the early 1920s. The introduction of knitted underwear produced by the hosiery manufacturers of the east Midlands, Scotland and the north of England had an adverse effect on the demand for woven woollen goods generally. In the post-war era, knitwear became readily available in the shops of south Wales. Yet the mills of west Wales continued to produce thousands of yards of flannel which they could not sell. Fewer people required the striped shirting flannel, the linsey skirts, the hersey drawers and the fringed nursing shawls which were still being produced by the textile manufacturers of Cardiganshire. A change in fashion also meant that the hard, thick tweed suitings provided by the factories were no longer in demand, and as a result many village tailors went out of business.

In many of the mills of west Wales in the 1920s, neither men nor machinery were employed in the most economical manner. Most of the weavers were middle-aged, for the industry was failing to attract young people, and many of them were not prepared to undergo a period of training. Many had been trained on hand looms and when power looms were widely introduced into the industry they could not imagine the possibility of one man being able to look after more than one loom. It was not uncommon to encounter a fully trained weaver looking after a single width loom, running at a very moderate speed, whereas in Yorkshire and the other textile manufacturing districts it was common practice for one person, often a woman, to look after a pair of double-width power looms. In many cases, too, machinery was liable to break down at frequent intervals, and there were no competent textile engineers capable of repairing the machines in the region. Thus, in the mills of Cardiganshire, there was not only obsolete machinery but also much that had been roughly repaired and liable to break down again. Often the breakage of a piece of machinery meant weeks of waiting before a local blacksmith, carpenter or handyman could undertake repair work. Woollen manufacturers were also prone to buy second-hand machinery in Yorkshire rather than spend a little more on the newest type of machinery. Although some of the larger factories were re-equipped with new machinery between 1910 and 1922, far too many were content to use the machinery that had been installed when the mills were built, possibly some sixty years earlier.

Although the market for Welsh textiles has been extended considerably, particularly with the introduction of double weave ('tapestry') bedcovers, furnishing fabrics and light tweeds, the number of mills supplying that market has declined alarmingly. One of the main reasons for the decline was the difficulty experienced by mill-owners in recruiting labour. Wages in the woollen industry compared unfavourably with those of other occupations. At the other end of the scale, when factory owners wished to retire, they experienced great difficulty in selling their mills, and consequently production ceased.

Fishing

Not surprisingly, given its long coastline and numerous rivers and streams well blessed with fish, the county's fishing industry had been well established for many centuries. From the Middle Ages until at least the end of the nineteenth century, off-shore sea fishing in particular made a substantial contribution to the economy of Cardiganshire.[11] Salted herrings were an important item of export in the Middle Ages and Aberystwyth, in particular, was an important fishing port. Until the end of the eighteenth century Aberystwyth reigned supreme as a centre of the fishing industry. 'What it is chiefly resorted to for, and contributes to its Wealth', claimed one eighteenth-century writer, 'is its Fishing Trade for Cod, Whitings, but principally Herrings . . . The Herring Fishery here is in most so exceedingly abundant that a thousand barrels have been taken in one night . . . In addition to herrings, they have such an abundance of Cod, Pollack, Whiting, Common Whiting, Ray and other fish that they set but little value upon them. Bottlenoses and porpoises sometimes run on shore in shoals and blue sharks are frequently caught upon the coast, from all of which they make considerable quantities of Oil.'[12] The Aberystwyth herring industry declined in the late eighteenth century: 'for the herring industry flourished here about thirty years since', claimed H. P. Wyndham, 'but that fish is now a stranger to the coast'.[13] By 1830 fishing at Aberystwyth was relatively unimportant, though herrings and cod were still caught occasionally.

In spite of its decline in Aberystwyth, offshore herring fishing flourished in other coastal settlements throughout the nineteenth century. Aberaeron, for example, had 'a lucrative herring fishery, in which about thirty boats, with seven men to each, are engaged'. At Aber-porth, 'the herring fishery in the bay gives occupation to a great number of hands and imparts during the season an appearance of activity and bustle to Aber-porth and its vicinity, but the fishing for turbot, cod and mackerel is scarcely worth pursuing'. If Aber-porth in the nineteenth century was famous for its *sgadan* (herring), New Quay had 'Fish of very superior quality . . . soles, oysters and turbot being taken in great numbers'. Llangrannog had a large herring fishery, while Cardigan and the Teifi estuary had its fleet of offshore herring boats. St Dogmaels was regarded as 'one of the principal stations for the herring fishery . . . where the boats engaged in it are commonly of from eight to twenty tons burthen, with masts and sails, but mostly open, without decks and manned by six or eight men; the herring generally make their first appearance on the neighbouring coast between the middle and the end of September, which is considered the best period of the season, as they will then bear carriage to distant markets, and the harvest being commonly over, the fisherman can be better spared from agricultural labours'.[14]

In 1884 a contemporary writer offered some detail of the fishing industry in Cardiganshire. Borth was well known for its shrimps – the fishing being carried out by 'sailors' wives and widows and superannuated sailors'. About twenty boats were engaged in fishing at Borth. The Aberystwyth

[11] J. G. Jenkins, *Maritime Heritage. The Ships and Seamen of Southern Ceredigion* (Llandysul, 1982); idem, *The Inshore Fishermen of Wales* (Cardiff, 1991).

[12] H. Moll, *A New Description of England and Wales* (London, 1724), p.265.

[13] H. P. Wyndham, *A Tour through Monmouthshire and Wales in 1774 and 1777* (London, 1781), p.183.

[14] S. Lewis, *Topographical Dictionary of Wales* (2 vols., London, 1833), I, pp.3, 20, 24; II, p.300.

Fig. 30: Coracle fishermen at Cenarth in 1936. (*Copyright Museum of Welsh Life, St Fagans*).

fishery, too, had revived by the mid-nineteenth century and the town was 'the most considerable fishing station in Cardigan Bay. Many trawlers come here from a distance, chiefly from Fleetwood, Liverpool and Hoylake; and from fifteen to twenty of their boats may often be seen at one time anchored opposite the Marine Terrace'. The boats were from thirty to forty tons each, with 'the beams of the tracks from twenty five feet to forty five feet long, and the usual mesh from two and a half to three inches'. At Aberystwyth in 1884 about three hundred persons were engaged in catching turbot, brill, mackerel, sole, herring, cod, ray, mullet, together with salmon off the mouths of the rivers.[15]

The First World War hastened the decline of the offshore fishing industry in Cardiganshire, and only in recent years has there been a revival of activity, with lobster fishing in particular making a substantial contribution to the economy of the county. With its ever-growing popularity as a tourist centre, amateur sea-fishing has increased considerably, but the extent of the industry is much less than it was a hundred years ago. At that time, each village on the Cardiganshire coast had its complement of full-time fishermen and farm workers, who spent a part of every year catching herring and other fish. A variety of equipment was used for offshore fishing in Cardiganshire, including drift nets of various types, seine nets and hooked lines. At Llanddewi Aber-arth the

[15]D. C. Davies, 'The fisheries of Wales', *Trans. Liverpool National Eisteddfod* (Liverpool, 1894), p.307.

Fig. 31: Seine netsmen from St Dogmaels at work in the Teifi estuary in 1971. (*Copyright Museum of Welsh Life, St Fagans*).

remains of what was once a fish weir may be seen. Weirs were usually built between tide marks, so that at high tide they were covered and at the ebb completely uncovered by water; this meant that any fish which entered the trap could be caught when the sea receded. Weirs were usually built of wooden stakes with stone or wattled walls, and were invariably located wherever there was a large expanse of ground left uncovered at low water.

Inland, too, fish traps could be found on the Ystwyth and the Teifi, as well as on other rivers, and the place-name *Pysgodlyn* indicates where fish were artificially bred for the table. Coracles had been used on the Teifi at least from the Middle Ages and Malkin described how 'The Salmon on the Tivy is esteemed the most excellent in Wales; the principal fishery and a very abundant one is between Kilgerran and Llechryd . . . There is scarcely a cottage in the neighbourhood of the Tivy or the other rivers in these parts abounding with fish, without its coracle hanging by the door.'[16] The number of coracles operating on the Teifi has declined alarmingly, and there are only two licences on the river above Llechryd Bridge. No further licences are to be issued to fishermen on that stretch of the river, so that the present generation of coracle fishermen on the Teifi is likely to be the last. There is, however, no limitation on the number of coracle licences below Llechryd Bridge, where the river is regarded as tidal.[17]

[16]B. H. Malkin, *The Scenery, Antiquities, and Biography, of South Wales* (London, 1807), p.206.
[17]J. G. Jenkins, *Nets and Coracles* (Newton Abbot, 1974); idem, *The Coracle* (Golden Grove edn., 1988).

Among the most unusual methods of fishing which has persisted to this day in Cardiganshire is that of using seine nets in the Teifi estuary below St Dogmaels. This is an industry which has declined, for in 1937 there were thirteen boats engaged in this trade, whereas today only a handful of boats operate in the estuary. Currently the seine net fishermen operate in one of four pools – Pwll Castell, Pwll Nawpis, Pwll y Perch and Pwll Sama – although the silting up of the river and its change of course has meant that a number of pools have disappeared. Early in the twentieth century at least sixteen teams could be seen at work in the estuary and there were few regulations regarding fishing hours, meshes and seasons. To decide which team should go to which pool, lots were drawn at the St Dogmaels Netpool and the teams proceeded down river to their allotted pools. At the end of the tide the boat was steered to the centre of the pool, the net being paid out to a half-moon shape from the shore of the river. One man was employed as a shore-man holding the head rope of the net, another steered the boat, while the other two paid out the net from the stern of the boat. One was concerned with paying out the headrope with its cork floats, another with the bottom rope and its lead weights. Slowly the boat drifted downstream and after the whole net had been paid out it was steered towards the shore. The boat was then anchored and the three fishermen, together with the shoreman, pulled in the rope and net. If a salmon or a sewin was caught in the net it was knocked on the head with the wooden *cnocer* or *priest*.

Epilogue

The pattern of life which meant that the inhabitants of Cardiganshire looked no further than the boundaries of their own neighbourhood or an adjacent market town for all the necessities of life has changed considerably during the twentieth century. The First World War was certainly a watershed between the ancient, unchanging way of life and the destruction of the rural neighbourhood as an economic and social entity. After the Second World War that change was completed as the natural resources of the countryside were less effectively exploited. The products of modern, international industry became increasingly available, even in the remotest corners of the country. Raw materials, once regarded as essential for the survival of a community, were neglected and skills that once were considered a vital qualification for many countrymen were forgotten. Mass production, mass transportation and mass advertising played their part in the break-up of the ageless pattern of life and in the obliteration of many rural skills. New ideas and technologies which ignored all national and regional boundaries led inexorably to the destruction of the rural neighbourhood as a social and economic unit.

Nevertheless, in Cardiganshire in the 1990s, craft work of all kinds has become the flagship of a flourishing and developing tourist industry and the hand craftsman has become the cornerstone of many facilities concerned with the interpretation of the more recent traditions of the people of Wales. But whether more than a handful of these artisans represent the authentic traditions of the county is questionable. Many of the products which emanate from workshops have precious little to do with the traditional craftsmanship of the countryside, where utilitarian needs were inevitably married to beauty of form and good design. Only a few of the age-old crafts of Cardiganshire have survived into the late twentieth century, for the majority of craftsmen of our times produce goods which appeal very largely to a tourist market.

Even so, a few skilled men have been able to meet the challenge of changing circumstances. One or two blacksmiths, for example, produce wrought iron work of high quality and others have taken advantage of the vogue for horse-riding to act as farriers; but, in general, the traditional craftsmanship of Cardiganshire has changed beyond all recognition. Local raw materials are hardly ever used today and skills which were once commonplace in the countryside have disappeared completely from contemporary workshops. Yet, the revival of forgotten skills could have a relevance for the future, for in a post-industrial era when oil resources begin to run dry or in the face of a catastrophic collapse of our economic system, the skills of the past may, at least, provide a basis for survival. The remembering of forgotten skills, the revival of obsolete techniques and the utilization of long-forgotten raw materials may yet offer the basis for a new but different future.

CHAPTER 8

LEAD MINING IN CARDIGANSHIRE

W. J. Lewis

IN THE late seventeenth century the lead mining industry in Cardiganshire embarked on a period of striking development. In 1690 a valuable vein of silver-lead ore was discovered by a shepherd at Esgair-hir on the Gogerddan estate.[1] Anxious to profit from the discovery, Sir Carbery Pryse of Gogerddan began to work the mine himself. Since the ore was argentiferous, the mine was claimed by the Mines Royal Society, but Pryse refused to hand it over.[2] As a result, the dispute was brought before the House of Lords. The first hearing went in Pryse's favour but, because it was proved that the sample of ore shown at the hearing was not from Esgair-hir, there was a retrial.[3] The Lords, composed almost entirely of landowners, sided with the squire of Gogerddan. As a result, Parliament passed an Act which deprived the Mines Royal Society of its monopoly and gave to landowners the right to work and profit from all mines on their land, provided they sold any argentiferous ore to the Crown at £9 a ton.[4] Delighted with this, Sir Carbery is said to have ridden on horseback from London to Gogerddan in forty-eight hours to spread the glad tidings.[5] Insofar as this Act opened the mines to far more people, it increased the supply of capital available. It also increased the supply of labour, for incoming mine promoters often brought in skilled miners. Sir Carbery began to work Esgair-hir with vigour, but was prevented from raising much ore by drainage problems. He then formed a company, but before it could become fully operational he died, and work at the mine ceased.[6] His successor, Edward Pryse, showed no aptitude for mining.

In 1697 Sir Humphrey Mackworth, the Neath coalowner, called at a tavern in Llanbadarn Fawr and heard of the company's predicament. He made inquiries and was informed that, if managed properly, Esgair-hir would provide work for 600 men and yield an annual profit of over £70,000.[7] Mackworth then took a lease on the mines and soon realized that more capital would be required. To obtain this he devised a scheme whereby partners in Carbery Pryse's company could either sell their shares to Mackworth or exchange them for tickets in a lottery. His plan was immediately accepted and

[1]R. Hunt, 'Notices of the history of the lead mines of Cardiganshire', *Memoirs of the Geological Survey of Great Britain*, II, Part 2 (London, 1848), p.645; W. R. Scott, *The Constitution and Finance of English, Scottish and Irish Joint-Stock Companies to 1720* (3 vols., Cambridge, 1910–12), II, p.443.
[2]M. Stringer, *Opera Mineralia Explicata* (London, 1713), p.258.
[3]Scott, *Joint Stock Companies*, II, p.443; *Calendar Treasury Books, 1689–92*, p.1460.
[4]*Journal of the House of Lords*, XV, pp.355–6, 363; Hunt, 'Notices', II, Part 2, p.646.
[5]Hunt, 'Notices', II, Part 2, p.646.
[6]NLW, Nanteos MSS, 1 July 1693. Agreement between Sir Carbery Pryse and others.
[7]W. Waller, *An Essay on the Value of the Mines, late of Sir Carbery Pryse* (London, 1698), pp.8–9; Swansea Public Library, Mackworth Papers B721.

the Company of Mine Adventurers was formed in 1695. One of its aims was the granting of 'several Charities' out of the profits 'to the Poor of every county in England and Wales'. The sale of tickets for the lottery was opened to the general public in October 1698; over £25,000 was subscribed on the first day. In five months enough tickets had been sold to enable the prize draw to be held. Those who held the first 700 tickets to be drawn were also to share in the management of the company.[8]

One of the men behind the scheme was William Waller, a former employee of the Mines Royal Society in Westmorland, where he had been dismissed for some misdemeanour. He then made a practice of invading the rights of the Society until he was forced to leave the area. He settled in Cardiganshire and attached himself to Sir Carbery Pryse, whom he persuaded to defy the Mines Royal Society. It was Waller, too, who persuaded Mackworth to take over the mines. The company's prospectus, written by Waller, contained many exaggerations, such as the statement that Esgair-hir had 'eight large veins of silver, lead and copper . . . which can't be parallelled in the whole of the Christian World'. He called the mine 'the Welsh Potosi' to emphasize its similarity to the great silver mines of Bolivia. Thousands of pamphlets describing the mine and its prospects in glowing terms were distributed throughout Britain in order to attract investors.

In practice, the much-publicized treasures of the Welsh Potosi proved difficult to unearth and it was not long before shareholders became restive. Statements, most of them misleading and prepared by Waller, were sent out in an attempt to restore confidence. The main difficulty was ridding the mine of water and Waller 'was not skilled in engines' which could do this work. Eventually committees of inspection visited the mine and found much to condemn in Waller's management. He was dismissed and forced to leave his house at Ynys-hir. He then went to London where he conducted a campaign of vilification against the Company of Mine Adventurers.[9]

For the first ten years of working the mines of Cardiganshire, the company had little to show. Although it leased twenty-eight mines, fifteen of them did not produce any ore worth recording. A total of 3,658 tons of ore was produced up to August 1708, but at a very high cost. Only 1,123 tons were raised at 'the Great Mine of Esgair hire' and what Waller called 'the Glorious Work of Goginan' yielded only twenty tons, which cost £627 to raise.[10] Mackworth was accused of misleading the public; he was brought before the House of Commons and found 'guilty of many notorious and Scandalous Frauds'. There is little or no evidence to suggest that he gained financially by his actions.[11] As for Waller, the question was asked: 'How a certain person that was so poor in 1698 as to want Money to buy bread for his Family came to be so Rich in a few Years as to abound both in Money and Plate.'[12]

This period saw the introduction of two important improvements in mining and smelting practice – the use of gunpowder for blasting the rock and the use of coal for smelting the ore. Gunpowder made mining much less 'slavish' and less costly. It was first used in 1705 at Cwmsymlog, where Thomas Bushell is said to have spent £11,000 on driving the main adit to find the lost silver-lead vein. According to Lewis Morris, had he used gunpowder this could have been done for £1,000.[13]

[8] *Journal of the House of Lords*, XV1, p.358; Hunt, 'Notices', II, Part 2, p.647.
[9] W. J. Lewis, *Lead Mining in Wales* (Cardiff, 1967), pp.80–90.
[10] S. Evans, 'An examination of Sir Humphrey Mackworth's industrial activities' (unpublished University of Wales MA thesis, 1950), p.101.
[11] Ibid., pp.198, 202.
[12] Stringer, *Opera*, p.273.
[13] NLW MS 603E, f.34.

The other change was only to be expected from a coalowner like Mackworth. Towards the end of the seventeenth century the reverberatory furnace was used successfully to smelt ore with coal.[14] In 1700 Mackworth instructed Waller to build such furnaces at Garreg and men were sent to Melincryddan, near Neath, to learn the new process.[15] But smelting at Garreg was not a success and it soon became clear that it would be cheaper to send the ore to be smelted at Neath. As a result, smelting in north Cardiganshire almost ceased.

Another change, probably initiated by Waller, was the setting of 'bargains' in the mines. Until this began miners were paid day wages which ranged during the seventeenth century from 6d. to 9d. a day. Waller believed that piecework would be more profitable to the company. The miners were offered bargains, the prices of which were estimated beforehand by 'setting a Lusty Willing Fellow', fortified by an occasional 'pipe and dram', to work under supervision in the parts of the work concerned. These parts were then openly auctioned to the miners, the bargain going to the lowest bidder, care being taken to ensure that the bid was not higher than the estimated cost. While the bargain was being worked the men were paid subsistence wages of 1s. a week.[16] When the bargain finished, the men received what was owing to them. Sometimes the subsistence paid amounted to more than the value of the ore which they had raised and they had to work without pay until they had paid off their debt. Miners on piecework had to pay for the tools, candles and gunpowder which they used.[17] Since skilled miners were scarce, Mackworth brought in workers from Yorkshire, probably on Waller's advice.

The withdrawal of Sir Humphrey Mackworth from the Company of Mine Adventurers did not put an end to its activities in Cardiganshire, but there was little life in its efforts following his departure. In 1715 only two of the company's mines – Cwmsymlog and Ceninog – were being worked and in 1722 it began to dispose of all its mines except those on the Gogerddan estate.[18] Although the price of ore in the first quarter of the century was reasonable – £7 to £8 a ton – there was little activity in the industry after 1710. The Mine Adventurers' fiasco and the South Sea Bubble failure were not conducive to investment in mining.

Thomas Pryse of Gogerddan sought to revive interest in the industry and he himself worked the Pencraig-ddu mine, which was reported to be yielding ore containing 44 oz of silver to the ton of lead. There were also works at Ystumtuen, Goginan, Cwmystwyth and at Strata Florida, where Lady Campbell and the Stedmans owned mines.[19] But the amounts raised were small. They were shipped to be smelted at the Llangyfelach Smelting Works near Swansea. Other mines were being worked by unemployed miners trying to make a living at Nant-goch, Nantycagle, Blaenceulan, Ynyscynfelyn and Allt-y-crib. All such miners agreed to sell their ore, dressed for the market, to the landowner at £4 a ton, about half the market price. Other miners were granted permission to rework the waste dumps at Cwmsymlog and Henfwlch on the same terms.[20]

[14]J. Percy, *The Metallurgy of Lead* (London, 1870), pp.216–17.

[15]Evans, 'Sir Humphrey Mackworth', pp.76, 80.

[16]William Shiers, *A Familiar Discourse or Dialogue concerning the Mine-Adventure* (London, 1700).

[17]NLW, Powis Castle Deeds and Documents, MS 3522.

[18]NLW Gogerddan MSS, List of Papers sent to Boys and Co. regarding Caeneiniog Law Suit, 1856; 28 November 1722, William Bird to Thomas Pryse.

[19]Ibid., 11 December 1725, Articles of Co-partnership; J. Woodward, *An Attempt towards a Natural History of the Fossils of England* (London, 1729), Part 2, p.84.

[20]Gogerddan MSS. Agreements and notes dated 22 May 1733, 26 April 1733, 6 June 1733, 12 July 1734.

Another revival began when, in the 1730s, a rich discovery was made at the Old Darren mine, which had been idle since the mid-seventeenth century. The new vein was rich in silver – 60 oz to the ton of lead – and yielded ore worth about £20 a ton. But such was the ignorance of mine promoters that it was sold for only £11 a ton.[21] As usual, such a discovery attracted both capital and mine promoters into the area. Some brought with them their own force of skilled miners. Among them was the Flintshire Mining Company, which arrived in 1740 and took leases of the Darren and other Gogerddan mines.[22] Among the partners were Thomas and George Parry of Llidiardau, near Aberystwyth. They did well at the Darren mine but there was little profit in their other mines, partly because they lacked the capital to work the mines properly. These 'Fflintshire Gentlemen' were not popular 'for they act(ed) but indifferent as to their payments'.[23] Other companies which entered the county at this time were Scott Bowdler & Co. of Shrewsbury and two Flintshire smelting concerns, Messrs Smedley and Richardson, and J. Totty and Sons of Holywell. All seem to have been successful and considerable quantities of ore were shipped to the smelteries on Deeside.[24]

One of the most unexpected and unwelcome results of the Old Darren discovery was a marked increase in the interest taken by the Treasury in Crown lands in the mining area. Claiming that part of the Old Darren discovery was on Crown land, the Treasury leased part of the mine to Edmund Moore, who brought with him a number of Cornish miners. He was also granted a lease by the Treasury of other mines within the Crown Manor of Cwmwd y Perfedd.[25] Among other mines claimed by the Treasury was Bwlch-gwyn, which had long been worked by the Powells of Nanteos. It is clear that the latter's claim was doubtful for he agreed to pay a life pension of 40s. per annum to each of three old Ystumtuen miners on condition that they swore that the mine had always been part of the Nanteos estate.

Welsh landowners had always been bitterly opposed to the claims of the Crown to the wastes and unenclosed lands of upland areas. They maintained that such lands, though open, were part of their freehold and essential to the native way of life. When the Treasury began to claim royalties from mines on these lands, feelings ran high. It was this disagreement which brought Lewis Morris into prominence in the area.[26] An experienced miner, Welsh-speaking and highly intelligent, Morris was difficult to fool. It is likely that it was he who first alerted the Treasury to the Crown's loss of royalties in Cardiganshire. A most conscientious Deputy Steward of the Crown Mines of Cardiganshire, he made it clear to landowners that he would always uphold the claims of the Treasury. This made him very unpopular and led to some violent scenes, especially when he claimed for the Crown and brought to good profit the old mine of Esgair-mwyn. This so excited the envy of the landowners concerned, mainly Lord Lisburne and the Revd Dr William Powell of Nanteos, that they decided to take possession of the mine by force. In February 1753 a small army made up of landowners, Grogwynion miners and Nanteos tenants marched to the mine and took possession. Morris was threatened with a pistol by the notorious Herbert Lloyd of Peterwell, Lampeter, and thrown into

---

[21]Ibid., Lewis Morris to William Vaughan, Nannau, 12 February 1742.
[22]NLW Llidiardau MSS 1743–5, The Flintshire Company's Mines in Cardiganshire and Merioneth-shire.
[23]Gogerddan MSS 1741; William Thomas to Thomas Pryse,
[24]Lewis, *Lead Mining*, p.96.
[25]Llidiardau MSS, 8 January 1741; Gogerddan MSS, 30 January 1741, William Thomas to Thomas Pryce.
[26]D. Ll. Thomas, 'Lewis Morris in Cardiganshire', *Y Cymmrodor*, XV (1901), 1–87.

gaol in Cardigan. While he was there, the Revd Dr Powell of Nanteos ordered his men to carry away £2,000 worth of ore lying unsold on the bank at Esgair-mwyn.[27]

At first Morris was strongly supported by the Treasury, which not only had him released from prison but also sent a detachment of soldiers to repossess the mine. But such was the power and influence of landowners that Treasury officials began to change their attitudes and Lewis Morris was forced to yield Esgair-mwyn mine to his opponents. The mine was then worked by John Paynter of Hafod, a Derbyshire miner, for Lord Lisburne, who had to pay a royalty of 50 per cent to secure the lease.[28] It proved an expensive mine to work at first and the royalty was twice reduced, but after 1765 a great deal of ore was raised there.

North of the Rheidol, in the early 1740s, the Darren discovery led to another attempt by the moribund Mine Adventurers to work Cwmsymlog and Grogwynion mines, but with so little success that they surrendered their leases. In 1748 Cwmsymlog was leased to William Corbett, whose manager, John Paynter, reopened an old shaft and discovered new veins of ore, one of which was an extension of that which had yielded so much silver to Sir Hugh Myddelton in early Stuart times. This ore yielded 13 cwt of lead to the ton of ore and 74 oz of silver to the ton of lead. Although worth £19 a ton at that time, it was sold by Corbett to Flintshire smelters for only eleven guineas, but he still made a profit which averaged £500 a year during the period 1751–76.[29] It is worth noting that almost two-thirds of this ore was raised within Crown lands, but the whole royalty was paid to Gogerddan.

The Nanteos mines were in poor shape at this time and Thomas Powell was extremely jealous of Thomas Pryse's success at Cwmsymlog. Claiming to be Lord of the Manor of Aberystwyth, Powell tried to levy a toll on all ore entering the town. As a result Corbett was briefly unable to fulfil his commitments to some Swansea smelters. But a threat to consult 'Eminent Counsell' regarding the rights claimed by Powell put an end to the obstruction. During the blockade an attempt was made to ship the Gogerddan duty ore from Clarach, but it proved too difficult.[30]

During the second half of the eighteenth century smelters from Swansea worked mines in the area. Chauncey Townsend was involved in the Esgair-mwyn battle, and he later took up the leases of Grogwynion and Logau-las. When Corbett's lease of Cwmsymlog expired, the mine was taken by James, son of Chauncey, who entrusted the working of the mine to a certain John Smith, who, in turn, brought Thomas Bonsall of Bakewell, Derbyshire, into the area. Within a few years Bonsall had become a leading figure in the industry; by 1785 he was working fifteen mines in Cardiganshire on his own account, producing more than £25,000 worth of ore in that year alone.[31]

Apart from Cwmsymlog, there was little life in the mines north of the Rheidol in the second half of the century. The total duty from all the other Gogerddan mines in the parish of Llanfihangel Genau'r-glyn was less than £5 in 1774. In an effort to make some money, John Pugh Pryse of Gogerddan worked the Island mine himself in 1768, but with scant success. His successor, Edward Loveden, did the same at Esgair-fraith in the 1790s, but achieved little.[32] There was much more

[27]Powis Castle Deeds and Documents, MSS 21937; Tegwyn Jones, *Y Llew a'i Deulu* (Talybont, 1982), pp.23–6.
[28]Powis Castle Deeds and Documents, MS 1216, 11910.
[29]NLW MS 604D, f.55; Gogerddan MSS, 12 December 1754, William Tilsley to Thomas Lloyd.
[30]Gogerddan MSS, 5, 15 November, 12 December 1751, William Tilsley to Thomas Lloyd.
[31]NLW MS 3113C; G. Eyre Evans, *Aberystwyth and its Court Leet* (Aberystwyth, 1902), p.119.
[32]Gogerddan MSS, 17 November 1768, D. Morgan to John Pugh Pryse; Esgair-fraith disbursements to December 1797.

activity in the southern part of the mining area, where most of Bonsall's mines were situated. His most rewarding ventures were the eight Nanteos mines, especially Cwmystwyth, which yielded profits of between £2,000 and £3,000 per annum for a number of years. Even when prices were low during the French Wars, the annual gains were a clear £1,000. Bonsall is reputed to have made a fortune of over £40,000 out of mining in north Cardiganshire. He was knighted in 1796.[33]

Another prominent man in the industry during the last quarter of the century was John Probert, one-time steward to Lord Powis. In association with the latter, Thomas Johnes of Hafod and others, he began mining in 1769 at Fairchance near Ffair-rhos, a rich mine but subject to frequent flooding.[34] Probert then took over other mines and by 1790 every mine of importance, except Cwmystwyth, in the southern part of the mining area was in his hands, including Grogwynion, Logau-las and Esgair-mwyn. Even when trade was poor in the 1790s, he continued to open new mines, two of which were at Llwynwnwch and Fron-goch. Unfortunately, the price of ore was then so low that a rich find at the former could not be developed. This was the period when Probert tried hard – but unsuccessfully – to get a footing first in the East India Company lead trade and then in the Mediterranean trade.[35]

There was also some lead mining in other parts of the county. Ore was raised on the lands of the Bishop of St David's in the Llanddewibrefi area in the Middle Ages. Small amounts from the same area were exported from Aberaeron in the late eighteenth and early nineteenth centuries. Another mine which used this port to export its ore was at Llanfair Clydogau. This work began in 1760 when Chauncey Townsend discovered a valuable vein of silver-lead ore in the bed of the Clydogau River. It yielded the best part of 80 oz of silver to the ton of lead and was worth £24 a ton in the 1760s.[36] Lead ore was also being raised in 1747 at New Quay in a work which resembled a quarry. Work continued there on a small scale into the nineteenth century when the concern was called the Wheal Neptune Mining Company, but very little ore was raised.

The French Wars at the turn of the century had a depressing effect on the lead mining industry. Napoleon's activities in Europe caused markets to disappear almost overnight and trade was handicapped by a marked feeling of insecurity. Chester and Bristol, the main outlets for Welsh lead, were badly placed for such European trade as did exist and, because of the war at sea, the cost of shipping was high. There was still a home demand for lead but it suffered from pronounced fluctuations which were reflected in prices. During the first decade of the nineteenth century the price per ton of lead ore varied from just over £10 in 1800 to £20 in 1813. There was also a considerable increase in the costs of production. As a result, the state of the industry in 1815 was described as follows: 'No mines flourish at present.'[37]

But a few mines were in profit, notably some of those owned by the wealthy and efficient John Probert and Thomas Bonsall. Much of the credit for the former's success lay with Job Sheldon, who took over the management of the Probert Company in 1800 and kept it profitable throughout a difficult period. He began to work his own mines while still employed by Probert. At a time when many unemployed lead miners were leaving the area, Sheldon maintained an adequate labour force

[33]Evans, *Aberystwyth and its Court Leet*, p.119.
[34]Powis Castle Deeds and Documents, MS 3708; NLW, Calendar of Crosswood Deeds, p.240.
[35]Powis Castle Deeds and Documents, MSS 3795, 3822, 4024, 4062.
[36]Gogerddan MSS, 19 November 1768, Chauncey Townsend to Lewis Pryse.
[37]NLW MS 1762Bii, f.121; D. E. Bick, 'Remnants of mining in Ceredigion before the nineteenth century', *Ceredigion*, VIII, no.3 (1978), 355–9.

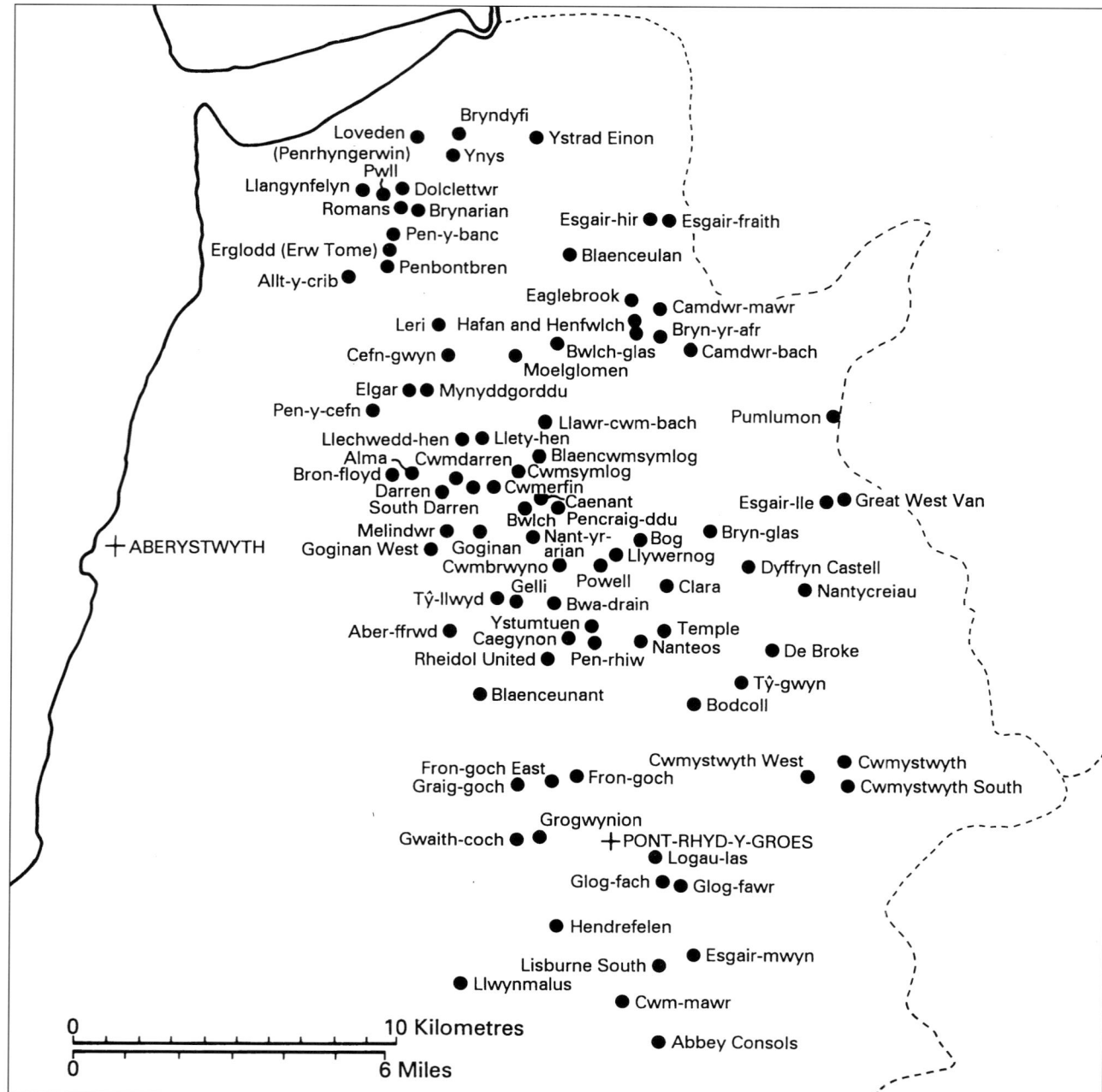

Fig. 32: The lead mines of north Cardiganshire.

by keeping the mines working when prices were low and by supplying his miners with corn when it was very scarce.[38] When the demand for lead was low he put his men on to raising blackjack (zinc ore) which, though it sold at a very low price, helped to maintain the works. He was always careful to sell all his ore in the best market. Although Somerset potters paid £5 a ton more for local ore than that paid by the smelters, no Cardiganshire mineowner took advantage of this, and it was left to the ore merchants of Bristol to supply the needs of the potteries of Barnstaple and Bideford. Sheldon, however, sent ore directly to these ports. One of his most successful mines was Cwmsymlog, where he had 300 men at work in 1813. He also played a leading part in Aberystwyth life, serving as mayor twelve times until 1833, when he was accused of using his office as mayor to become the owner of some valuable town property at a very low price.[39]

The most productive mine of the period was the ancient work of Cwmystwyth. In 1811 there was a notable discovery at the Copper Hill section of the mine where ore could be raised at a cost of £8 a ton; it yielded on average a profit of at least £5 a ton even at a high royalty of one-seventh.[40] In 1822 Cwmystwyth and other Nanteos mines were leased to two Yorkshiremen, Sir George Alderson, an alderman of London, and his brother Thomas, who brought with them skilled miners and smelters. Within a few months they had discovered a vein at Cwmystwyth which was said to be capable of yielding 5,000 tons of ore a year. In the event it proved to be even richer than this; between November 1826 and March 1827 they raised 13,235 tons of ore. To save on the high cost of transport and to increase even further their share of the profit, the Aldersons built a smeltery at Devil's Bridge. This was the last attempt to smelt lead ore in Cardiganshire and was unique also in its use of peat as the source of heat. Unfortunately, the Aldersons' business affairs elsewhere were so parlous that in 1834 they were declared bankrupt.[41] They were obliged to surrender the Nanteos lease and smelting ceased at Devil's Bridge.

The unexpired lease was taken over by Lewis Pugh of Aberystwyth, a snapper-up of unconsidered trifles. Lying unsold at Cwmystwyth was a large quantity of ore, which he bought at £5 a ton. Within a few weeks the price of ore had almost doubled and Pugh made a huge profit. During the remaining ten years of his lease, Cwmystwyth yielded about 11,000 tons of ore, which Pugh could afford to sell only when the price was favourable. He paid the Powells of Nanteos almost £20,000 in royalties.[42]

By then, the Cornish invasion had begun. In 1824 the Williams family of Gwennap brought with them to Cardiganshire a considerable number of key men and working miners.[43] From 1824 until 1833 they worked mines on both the Trawsgoed and Gogerddan estates. But the times were against them; the price of pig lead dropped from £25 a ton in 1825 to £11 10s. seven years later and, despite their efficiency, the Williamses lost over £20,000 and surrendered their lease.[44] They were succeeded in 1834 by John Taylor, a Cornish mining engineer who probably did more for the industry in Cardiganshire than any other man.

[38]Powis Castle Deeds and Documents, MSS 3735, 3757, 4196.

[39]Evans, *Aberystwyth and its Court Leet*, p.16.

[40]Nanteos MSS, 4 May 1813, J. Edwards to W. E. Powell.

[41]A. Francis, *History of the Cardiganshire Mines* (Aberystwyth, 1874), p.99; R. Hunt, *British Mining* (London, 1887), p.903.

[42]Nanteos MSS, Mine Accounts 1834–45.

[43]J. Rowe, *Cornwall in the Age of the Industrial Revolution* (Liverpool, 1953), pp.60, 121, 123.

[44]Gogerddan MSS, 2 December 1851, Matthew Francis to P. Pryse.

On taking over a mine, Taylor would first explore it thoroughly and, if it proved promising, would spare no expense on the preparation of the ground and the installation of the necessary machinery. At the Lisburne Mines he drove long levels to drain the workings and to open new ground, built new reservoirs to supply his machinery with water power, and cut fresh watercourses to take the water to the water wheels. Instead of setting up ore-dressing floors at each mine, as was done elsewhere, he built up-to-date floors at strategic points to serve a number of mines. He also built good 'barracks' where his miners could live comfortably when away from home. Taylor spent £15,000 on such work at the Lisburne mines alone, the first example of rational planning in mid-Wales. As a result, these mines were worked regularly from 1834 to 1893 and produced a total of 107,174 tons of lead ore and over 50,000 tons of zinc ore, which together were worth £1,138,783.[45] In the meantime a similar policy at the Gogerddan mines held by Taylor was not so successful, except at the Goginan mine, which proved profitable. John Taylor and sons were also good to their workers; unlike most other employers, they paid them regularly and tried to provide regular employment during lean times.

When Pugh's lease of Cwmystwyth and other Nanteos mines had expired, these works became unpopular with mining promoters, largely because Powell demanded a royalty of one-seventh of the value of the ore, the highest in the county. As a result, the mines were idle over long periods, much to the distress of miners and their families, especially in the village of Cwmystwyth. Eventually, in 1845, once the royalty was reduced, the mines were leased to Abel Gower and Company, who appointed Matthew Francis, an experienced Cornish mining engineer, as manager. He set about sinking shafts and opening new ground which laid bare a rich vein.[46] But this operation was so expensive that it used up almost all the company's reserves and they were forced to surrender the lease. The mines were then taken over by John Taylor, who once again profited considerably from the work of his predecessors. Under this new management, Cwmystwyth again proved profitable.

The success of the Taylors attracted more prospectors and capital into the area, but some of the newcomers had more money than sense and were easily duped by unscrupulous, self-styled mining engineers. On the advice of one of the latter, two Salford men spent over £7,000 on machinery and other equipment at a Llangynfelyn mine before proving the mine itself, and subsequently lost all their money. Others were more successful: in 1843 John Horridge made a rich discovery at the Cwmsebon mine, which yielded £197 in royalties from only one pipe of ore.[47]

By the mid-1840s the growth of the manufacturing industry in Britain and abroad had so increased the demand for lead that almost every mine in mid-Wales was active. Money and miners poured into the area and it was reported in the *Mining Journal* of 1850 that at no time over the previous hundred years had the Cardiganshire mines been so prosperous. Of the seventy-three listed mines, forty were officially at work and many others were being worked by small groups of men working on tribute. The Lisburne mines yielded a profit of £7,378 in 1848 and were valued in the stock market at £45,000. The Taylors were also doing well at Cwmystwyth and Goginan. The £5 shares of the latter were selling at £250 each in 1850, while the Lisburne Mines shares, originally

[45] O. T. Jones, 'Lead and zinc. The mining district of north Cardiganshire and west Montgomery-shire', *Memoirs of the Geological Survey*, XX (London, 1922), p.195. See also S. J. S. Hughes, 'The decline of mining at Cwmystwyth', *Ceredigion*, VIII, no.4 (1979), 422–4.

[46] Francis, *Cardiganshire Mines*, p.100.

[47] Gogerddan MSS, 7 March 1846. Llangynfelyn Mine; 1842, Cwmsebon Royalty Returns.

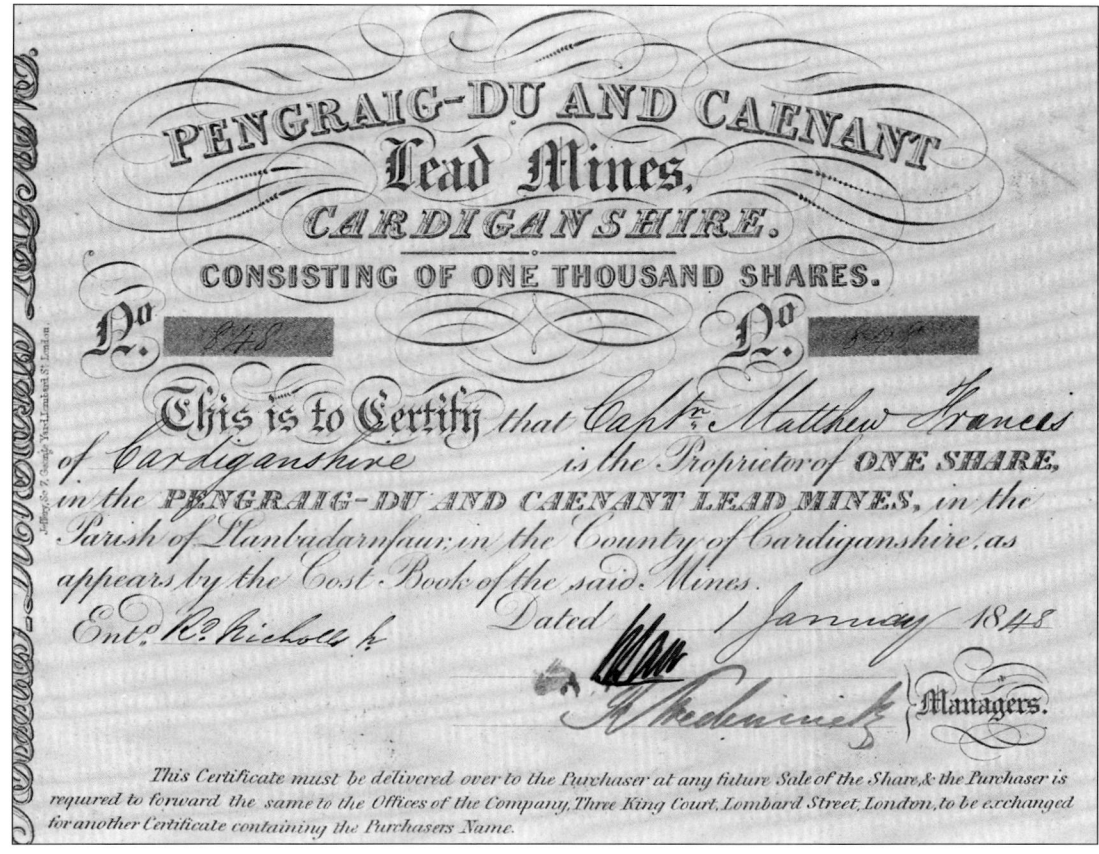

Fig. 33: A share certificate of the Pencraig-ddu and Caenant lead mines, 1848. (*Copyright National Library of Wales*).

priced at £75, had a market value of £600 each.[48] The Lisburne Mines Company paid between £60,000 and £70,000 a year in wages alone and another £30,000 to £40,000 to tradesmen and other interested parties in the Aberystwyth area.[49]

But the success of the Taylors and a few others concealed the fact that mining in Cardiganshire was, in general, far from healthy. Even in 1857, at the height of the boom, when there were sixty mines officially at work and many more being worked unofficially, only ten produced more than 200 tons of ore each. Of the 7,573 tons produced in that year, over 7,000 tons came from only five mines; 4,749 was produced at the three Lisburne mines of Fron-goch, Glog-fach and Logau-las. Cwmystwyth produced 1,281 tons and Cwmsymlog, then called East Darren, yielded 1,050 tons.[50]

Production began to fall in Cardiganshire in the 1870s while there was still a strong demand for lead ore. The main reason for the decline was the reluctance of many mining companies to set aside funds to tide them over in difficult times. The majority of mining promoters were interested only in quick returns and easily gained profits. Little or no provision was made for exploring and opening

[48]*Mining Journal* (1850), 282, 525, 570.
[49]*Report of the Commissioners on the Salmon Fisheries* (London, 1861), p.164.
[50]*Mineral Statistics* (1857).

up new ore ground when existing deposits were exhausted. Since high returns raised the price of shares, many mine promoters paid all the profits in dividends and when production showed signs of falling they sold their holdings at substantial profits. The company working Cwmerfin made handsome profits in the 1860s, but none of these were used to search for new deposits. As a result, a fall in the price of lead when existing deposits were approaching exhaustion soon made the company bankrupt. On the other hand, a few concerns like the Lisburne and East Darren Companies ensured that new ore deposits were continually being sought and that there was sufficient capital set aside to enable them to survive periods of depression. The general opinion in the lead mining world in the 1870s and early 1880s was that the decline in the industry was largely due to mismanagement and financial malpractice. These factors, together with growing competition from abroad, had a depressing effect on the industry.

At the beginning of the nineteenth century Britain was the leading producer of lead in the world. Its supremacy was first challenged after 1825 when the price of lead was so high that Spain began to develop its own rich silver-lead deposits. Soon it was producing 42,000 tons of ore a year and competing with British ore to such an extent in European markets that the price of ore dropped from £25 a ton in 1825 to less than £13 in 1831. As a result there was a sharp drop in British exports. A reduction in the duty on imported ore led to the much cheaper Spanish ore being imported by British smelters. Later, an increase in the import duty resulted in the establishment of a thriving smelting industry in Spain which adversely affected the smelting industry of south Wales.

In the 1840s another serious competitor – North America – appeared. By 1844 it was underselling the British product all over the world. What saved the British industry from further decline was a marked deterioration in the quality of Spanish ore and a rapidly increasing home demand for lead, especially by local authorities forced to make improvements in sanitary arrangements by the enormous increase in urban populations. The latter demand was such that imports of lead ore increased and import duties were abolished. Britain then became an importer rather than an exporter of lead. Import duties in the United State further reduced the overseas market for British lead. In 1884 Australian ore began to invade British markets; then came Mexican ore, all of which was cheaper than the British product. Faced with such competition the home mining industry went into a steep decline and investors lost interest in British mines.

The effect of the above was first felt keenly in Cardiganshire in 1878, when a sharp drop occurred in the price of ore and a number of mines were closed. The John Taylor family began to withdraw from the area when they gave up the lease of the Goginan mine in 1878.[51] This was followed by the surrender of all their Gogerddan mines. At Cwmystwyth an output of 600 tons in 1848 increased to well over 1,000 tons a year from 1850 to 1868. However, because of the exhaustion of existing deposits, the high royalty and a reluctance to develop new ground, production dropped to less than 350 tons per annum. A reduction in the royalty to one-fourteenth persuaded the Taylors to form a new company in 1875, but a fall in the price of ore to £8 a ton in 1878 made the mine unprofitable. A further reduction in the royalty to one-eighteenth made little difference, for ore was by that time worth only £6 a ton and in 1885 the Taylors went into liquidation and sold the mine machinery.[52] Their example was followed by a number of other mine promoters and the output of ore from the

[51]*Mining Journal* (1879), 48.
[52]Nanteos MSS, 9 October 1885, John Taylor to S. Lewis.

county fell from an average of about 6,000 tons a year in the 1870s to just over 2,000 tons in 1885.[53] Only the Lisburne Mines were still in profit.

Unemployed miners reacted by seeking to work mines on their own. In 1872 seventeen agreements to let mines to working miners were issued on the Gogerddan estate. The same happened elsewhere in the county. Local tradesmen, faced with a decline in the demand for their goods, combined with others to take leases of idle mines or financed working miners to raise ore. Landowners lowered royalties and stopped demanding rents for non-productive mines in order to keep the industry alive, but to no avail. As early as 1879 the only Cardiganshire mines on the dividend list were the Grogwynion and Lisburne Mines. The situation continued to deteriorate; in the 1890s ore was on average only £6 a ton, and for a short time not even the Lisburne Mines could make a profit.[54] In 1893 the Taylors, the industry's most famous mining family, withdrew completely from the county. Their first and main concern had been the Lisburne Mines – Frongoch, Logau-las, Glog-fach, East Glog-fach and Glog-fawr. During the period from 1839 to 1893, the only year in which the works did not yield a profit was 1841. The shareholders received a total of £247,285 in dividends.[55]

Lead mining in Cardiganshire would probably have ceased by the end of the nineteenth century had there not been an increase in the demand for blende, i.e. zinc ore. This mineral, known to the miners as 'Black Jack' or just 'Black', had been raised in small quantities in Cardiganshire since about 1780. But its price was so low, rarely above £3 a ton, that it was never more than a supplementary product. There were times when it could not be sold at all. When the price reached £4 a ton for a while in 1785, Bonsall raised significant quantities at the Nanteos mines of Dyffryn Castell, Tyn-y-fron, Ffrwd-ddu and Nantrhiwrugos, works which were rich in blende. Sheldon, too, produced fair amounts when the price was right, but the total amount of zinc ore raised in the county remained very small until the late 1850s.

In 1837 H. W. Crauford patented galvanized iron. Spelter works were erected in Swansea and Deeside, but the price of ore remained so low that only three mines in Cardiganshire produced it.[56] As a result of the growth of settlements in the colonies, however, the demand for galvanized iron sheeting increased enormously and to compensate for the decline in the demand for lead ore more blende was produced. By the 1870s it had become a major product in some mines despite its low price of less than £4 a ton. The most important source was the Fron-goch mine, where the Taylors raised over 50,000 tons in a few years. When the Cornishmen surrendered the mine it was taken over by John Kitto of Llanidloes, who worked it almost entirely for blende until 1895, yielding £8,000 in royalties to Lord Lisburne.[57] It was then taken over, first by a Belgian firm and then by the Lisburne Development Company, both primarily concerned with raising blende. The same thing happened at Cwmystwyth where, after 1916, Henry Gammon set out to raise both lead ore and blende. He spent large sums of money on new machinery, equipped the mines with new mechanical rock drills and erected an up-to-date zinc concentration plant. But, even after spending

[53]*Mining Journal* (1880), 216.
[54]*Mining Statistics* (1888).
[55]Crosswood MSS, Mining Records 1839–93.
[56]D. T. Williams, *The Economic Development of Swansea and of the Swansea District to 1921* (Cardiff, 1940), p.88.
[57]J. M. Howells, 'The Crosswood Estate; its growth and economic development, 1683–1899' (unpublished University of Wales MA thesis, 1956), p.393.

£17,000 on such work, he still had not made a profit. The mine was then taken over by Brunner Mond and Company but they, too, failed to make it pay.[58]

As the industry continued to decline after 1880, such actions as those taken by the Belgians, Gammon and others were taken in several other mines, but with little or no success. By 1914 mining was in such a poor state that even the high price of lead and zinc during the First World War failed to revive it. Although zinc ore fetched over £10 a ton, the annual output of blende was rarely more than 400 tons. The output of lead ore did increase to just over 1,800 tons in 1916, but subsequently it declined markedly. In 1921 the county produced only fourteen tons of lead ore and sixty-three tons of blende.[59] Largely because of the enterprise of a Cornish mining engineer named Nancarrow, there was a short revival in the Pont-rhyd-y-groes district in 1927, when 247 tons of lead ore and 464 tons of blende were raised. But this soon finished and thereafter Cardiganshire did not figure as a producer of ore in the Government's annual reports. Work continued at a few mines, but very little ore was produced. The last mine to yield ore was probably Penrhyngerwin, near Tre'r-ddôl, but the results were not even listed. Because of an outbreak of fire underground, caused by an electrical fault, the mine was closed in 1939 and lead mining in Cardiganshire came to an end.

Mining techniques

As in all industries with a long history, the methods of mining and smelting changed considerably over the years, but not in all branches. Techniques used in German mines and described by Agricola in *De Re Metallica* in the sixteenth century were still in use in Cardiganshire three centuries later. When Robert Hunt visited mines in Saxony in 1848, he found the methods used almost identical with those in mid-Wales.

Some valuable deposits were found as a result of the uprooting of a tree, the washing away of the soil-cover in a rainstorm, landslides, or during ploughing. Miners also associated ore deposits with poor plant growth or with areas where flowers were paler in colour than normal. Barren mountain slopes were 'said to be a sign of metalls, the Vapours that come from them destroying the Plants and Grass'. It was also considered to be 'a good sign to meet with dry Earth if it be yellow, red, black or green or any other extraordinary Colour'. Fossils, too, were carefully examined for signs of the mineral, and some miners would not harm moles because their burrowings so often revealed the existence of lead ore.[60] Yet another way was to observe grass on a frosty morning, though it had to be a 'Calm and Sunshiney Morning' with a moderate white hoar frost. If a vein of ore lay near the surface, the grass would appear to be less frozen or 'less covered with Hoary Dew'.[61] Sometimes 'orey' pebbles were found in streams, and the distance from the source of the mineral was judged by the degree of wear shown by the pebble.[62]

[58]Nanteos MSS, 25 March 1909, 16 August 1911, Henry Gammon to Lord Lisburne.

[59]*Annual Report of H M Chief Inspector of Mines* (London, 1921), p.84; see also G. Hall, 'A note on the decline of mining in Cardiganshire', *Ceredigion*, VII, no.1 (1972), 85–8.

[60]T. Heton, *Some Account of Mines* (London, 1707), pp.91–5; J. Pettus, *Fodinae Regales* (London, 1670), p.3.

[61]W. Hooson, *The Miners Dictionary* (Wrexham, 1747), Appendix 4.

[62]Georgius Agricola, *De Re Metallica* (1556), trans. by H. C. and L. C. Hoover (London, 1912), p.37.

Superstitious people were convinced that ore could be discovered by relying on dreams, watching for lines of fire, seeking the guidance of underground spirits, or using a divining rod. It was believed that the sulphurous vapours given off by the ore would sometimes reveal themselves at night as lines of fire. At least one mine in Cardiganshire was supposed to have been discovered in this way by a farm servant who reported having seen such a phenomenon late at night. According to Lewis Morris, the line indicated by the fire proved to be the outcrop of a valuable vein of ore.[63] People of all classes engaged in mining fervently believed that there was 'some Being that Inhabits in the Concaves and the Hollows of the Earth'. These beings or spirits were 'kind to some Men of Suitable Tempers' and would direct them to the ore by their knocking.[64] Known to the miners as 'knockers', they were credited with the ability to lead certain miners to new or lost veins by signalling with knocks underground. This belief was widespread until the late nineteenth century. Lewis Morris believed firmly in the existence of knockers and maintained that they had been heard at Esgair-mwyn until the lode was discovered, after which the noises ceased. He stated also that at Llwyn-llwyd nearby, underground spirits had been heard pumping and wheeling a barrow in the mine, though there were no pumps at work.[65] This was regarded by the miners as a sign that it would be worth investigating a part of the work that would need pumping, and the manager acted upon this.

Attempts were also made to discover ore by 'Divinatory Rod or Wand'. Many used the forked twig, but there were different opinions regarding the best wood for the purpose. Some would use only hazel, but others liked a different wood for each metal, hazel for silver, pitch pine for lead and tin, ash for copper, but iron or steel for gold. The rod used by other diviners, however, was quite different. It had to 'be a Hazel cut before the Sun rise, especially the Moon increasing, and above all, about the day of the Annunciation of the Virgin Mary, it must be a Yard long, of one Springs growth. Then you must tie it in the middle to your Staff with a Thread, and carry it thus up and down (in a calm Morning) where you suppose there may be Mines; and when you come over where any be, the Rod will bow down its Root-end towards the Earth'. This was not believed to be entirely reliable because there were 'Certain Unlucky Hours governed by particular Planets and Constellations, during which the Rod will not Work', even for those who could use it.[66]

Following the discovery of ore came the problem of extraction. Until late in the Tudor period, this was usually done by digging a trench along the vein and following the lode down into the bowels of the earth, a practice known as the Roman method of mining. According to Lewis Morris, 'in Esgair y Mwyn the Ancient Britons (or as some say the Romans) dug an Open Cast or Trench along the vein after their manner for about a hundred Yards in Length about Twenty Yards Broad and in Depth about Eighteen Yards'.[67] Once these early mines were in operation, the greatest problem was often drainage. Where possible, the trenches were dug so that water could drain away through one or both ends of the cut, as at Darren, but it was rarely possible to do this. Most of the mines were just large holes in the ground where dead water could easily accumulate. In some workings the excess water was hauled up in buckets on ropes. In others it was customary to build a series of dams across

[63] Powis Castle Deeds and Documents, MS 21900. Lewis Morris, 'A history of the Crown manor of Mevenyth', chapter 17.

[64] Hooson, *Miners Dictionary*, s.v. 'knockers'.

[65] Hugh Owen (ed.), *Additional Letters of the Morrises of Anglesey (1735–1786)*, Part 2 (London, 1949), pp.312, 321.

[66] Heton, *Some Account*, pp.95–6, 99.

[67] Powis Castle Deeds and Documents, MS 21900, chapter 13.

the floor of the trench so that water from the section to be worked could be thrown by means of hollow wooden shovels into other sections and the process repeated until as much ore as possible had been raised. There was obviously a limit to the use that could be made of such a process and, unless the natural drainage in such works was good, many had to be abandoned while still very shallow. Sometimes the trenches were filled in after mining had ceased because of the belief that ore was a living substance which would grow again and replenish the stock of mineral in that part.

The digging and extraction of the ore was carried out with the aid of mattocks and picks except when the vein was so hard that hammers and wedges had to be used, one miner holding a little *pique* or punch of iron having a long handle of wood which they called a *gad*, another with a great iron hammer or sledge driving the punch or wedge into the vein. When confronted with very hard rock which would not yield even to iron wedges, the miners resorted to *fire-setting*. Specially prepared wood and shavings were piled against the rock surface or, better still, packed into cracks and hollows, and set alight by means of the flame from the miner's candle. Larger pieces of wood were then piled on to the fire and, finally, cordwood. When cordwood was scarce it was mixed with charcoal, or horse bones, which were excellent for the purpose and made a very fierce fire. These fires were left to burn for periods of from three to fourteen hours and then, while the rock was still hot, cold water was thrown on to it, causing it to crack and crumble. It was believed by some that better results were achieved by using vinegar instead of water. Wedges were then driven into the cracks to complete the loosening. Evidence of the use of this fire and cold douche method was still clearly to be seen at Cwm Darren in Cardiganshire early in the twentieth century.[68]

Once digging began, loosened ore was collected carefully into baskets, and the waste thrown out. Once the trench had reached a certain depth, the miners built a square frame across the top, mounted a *stowse* or windlass upon it and hauled up the ore and waste in baskets or small tubs. Mines were therefore deep trenches or systems of trenches lined on the surface with heaps of waste material. As the mines increased in depth, the work of raising the waste became very heavy and so, just above their heads, the miners constructed floors or stages of wood called *bunnings* onto which they threw the rubbish. These stages stretched for the whole length of the mine and became covered over, except just under the stowse, where they sank six or eight feet more and, after clearing some ground, began other *bunnings* under the former onto which the refuse was thrown as before. As the number of *bunnings* increased, the clear space under the stowse became like a shaft and had to be lined with timber or stone to strengthen it, a process known as *ginging*. There was obviously a limit to the use of these stages and some of the waste had to be hauled to the surface by means of the windlass. In time, the disposal of the waste would prove so difficult and expensive that the mine would be abandoned.

Ore was removed from the mines in baskets, which were carried by men and women on their heads or strapped to their backs. Many of the trenches had steps at one end with wooden facings behind which was packed waste material. Where the trench was narrow, pieces of wood called *stemples* were wedged between their vertical sides, serving as steps for the labourers and shoring up the sides. When the workings were deep and wide, wooden ladders were used. After shafts came into use, large baskets were hauled up by means of ropes and windlasses. Later, rectangular boxes known as *corffes* were filled with ore and raised in the same way; in time these gave way to tubs and *kibbles*

[68]K. Carpenter, 'Notes on the history of Cardiganshire lead mines', *Aberystwyth Studies*, IV (1923), 99.

which were sometimes hauled up on rails fastened to the sides of the shafts. Where it was possible to use day levels, the ore was at first carried out in a rectangular box with handles at each end. This yielded first to legless wheel barrows, and then to the conventional type, and certain levels were designated wheel-barrow levels because they were fitted with a plank to take the wheel.

The adits of the seventeenth century were rectangular in section, about six feet high and three to four feet wide. They were driven into the hillside by men using picks, sledges and iron wedges, and fires. The loosened rock was broken into small fragments and then cleared. The sinking of a shaft demanded a similar technique, but in hard rock, as at Esgair-hir *c.*1700, sharp chisels screwed to iron rods of various lengths were used to pound the rock into small pieces.[69] As the scale of mining increased, more thought had to be given to methods of drainage. Whenever possible, drainage levels were used but, as mines became deeper, means had to be found to raise water to the drainage level or to the surface. This was done by sinking sump shafts, i.e. shafts having excavations at their bottoms into which water would drain from the mine workings. This water was raised to the mine surface in a number of ways. At Ystumtuen in the 1740s it was done by means of a horse whim, consisting of a large horizontal drum which, by means of a pulley and rope, raised water (or ore) in kibbles. The drum was turned by one or two horses.[70]

Another method was the chain pump used at Esgair-mwyn in the 1750s. Two men turning a toothed wheel raised water by drawing up an endless chain to which were attached knobs of cloth and leather. The ascending knobs forced the water to the surface through a wooden pump cylinder. Turning the wheel was very hard work indeed; no man could work at it for more than six hours and there were thirty-seven pumpers at Esgair-mwyn.[71] Another, more effective, and widely used method was to make the sump shaft wide enough to accommodate not only the winding gear but also a vertical line of pumps from the sump to the surface. Each pump was operated by man whose work it was to raise water to the man above. There were eleven such pumps placed one above the other in the sump shaft of the Darren mine in 1748, raising water from a depth of 380 feet to the channel in the Great Level, which carried it out of the mine. In time the pumps came to be operated by a water-wheel via a line of linked iron rods, a method adopted at almost every mine.[72]

In 1785 an attempt was made to drain the extremely wet Fairchance mine by means of a water pillar engine operated by a water-wheel. Its arrival at the port of Aberystwyth posed a serious problem, for it weighed 15fi tons and was too heavy for local teams of underfed horses. It eventually reached the mine, but the engineer assigned to look after the pump found life in Ffair-rhos so unbearable that he absconded. Francis Thompson, a noted mining engineer, then intervened and the pump worked fairly well until the mine was closed in 1791.[73]

Thomas Bushell's method of using bellows to blow fresh air into the workings remained in use until well into the nineteenth century, but the bellows and air pumps became bigger and were worked by water power. When dynamite came into use for blasting in the 1850s, more powerful means of ventilation had to be introduced and water-driven fans were used.

[69]Shiers, *Familiar Discourse*, p.52.
[70]NLW MS 603E, f.44.
[71]W. Pryse, *Mineralogica Cornubensis* (London, 1778), pp.150–1.
[72]NLW MS 603E, f.3.
[73]R. Jenkins, 'Francis Thompson's visit to the Cardiganshire mines in 1788', *Trans. Newcomen Soc.*, XI (1930–1), 158–9.

In the early days of mining the ore was smelted just as it came from the mine except for some breaking up of the larger lumps. By the sixteenth century ore-dressing had become common. This was a treatment which involved two processes: the reduction of the pieces of ore into a small size and the separation of the ore from the waste. First of all, women and children undertook a preliminary sorting by hand, on a stationary or rotating picking table, to eliminate as much waste as possible. The remainder was placed on a large stone slab and broken into very small pieces by means of a flat-faced iron mallet known as a *bucker*. This was also the work of women and children; the bucking of two hundred weight of ore per person was a good day's work. Lastly, to separate the ore from what refuse was still left, the broken stuff was placed in a sieve and jerked up and down in a tub of water. The waste tended to come to the surface, while the much heavier ore sank to the bottom of the sieve. The latter was then ready for smelting. In time the sieve was replaced by the much more efficient *jigger*, a strong rectangular sieve, which could be raised and lowered with a jerky action by lever. After each jigging the good ore was removed and the remainder rejigged several times.[74]

This method remained in principle part of ore-dressing until the late nineteenth century, but various refinements were introduced and in the larger mines the process became much more mechanized. The first ore-crushing machine was installed at Cwmystwyth by Thomas Bonsall in 1788. It consisted of ore stamps driven by a water wheel and attended by only one man and a boy; it could do as much work as had formerly been done by twenty women.[75] The more effective ore-crushing machines did not appear until the 1840s.

During the nineteenth century, ore-dressing was undertaken to a greater degree of nicety than anywhere else in Britain. In the 1840s the Goginan mine had the most up-to-date ore-dressing floor in Britain. There were at least seven water-wheels driving crushers, revolving sieves, *jiggers*, revolving conical surfaces known as *buddles*, on which the separation was done by flowing water, and other processes, all of which produced an excellent lead ore, weighing only one twenty-fourth of the ore stuff brought out of the mine. As the century progressed, methods of ore-dressing became increasingly refined. By 1900 the ore stuff went through nineteen processes to ensure the extraction of the maximum amount of lead ore.

In Tudor times the smelting of the ore was carried out near the mine itself in a hearth which consisted of a raised circle of stones enclosing a fire onto which was thrown more and more fuel mixed with ore. Provision was made for the melted lead to run out into hollows in the ground where it was allowed to harden. These hearths were followed by more elaborate ones, called *boles*, built on western facing slopes to take advantage of the prevailing winds. Later, bellows were installed to make the fires fiercer. The fuel used was always a mixture of 'black and white coal', i.e. charcoal and wood.[76]

Despite improvements in smelting, there developed a severe shortage of timber near mines and when mining began to increase smelters were forced to move to areas where wood was more plentiful. As a result, smelteries large enough to deal with the output of several mines were built at Garreg, Ynys-hir and Tal-y-bont. These larger works were equipped with water-driven ore stamps and bellows. The Ynys-hir works also contained a refinery to extract the silver from the lead ore. This had been neglected in the past because it was believed that refining spoilt the lead.

[74]Agricola, *De Re Metallica*, pp.267, 283, 292–3, 310; *Mining Journal* (1857), 470.
[75]Jenkins, 'Francis Thompson's visit', 160.
[76]Agricola, *De Re Metallica*, p.393.

Smelting and refining continued in the county until the early eighteenth century when the coal-fired reverberatory furnace was introduced into the area by Sir Humphrey Mackworth; it was not a success. Apart from some sporadic attempts to use the Garreg furnaces for smelting in the 1750s and late 1760s, no more smelting was carried out in Cardiganshire until 1786 when John Probert built a smeltery at Penyrangor in Aberystwyth. Here, too, the high costs of importing coal and other necessities, combined with the inefficiency of the manager of the works, proved too much for Probert and Company and the enterprise ended in 1791.[77] The only other attempt to smelt lead ore in the area was that made by the Aldersons at Devil's Bridge in the 1820s.

Transport

The transport of ore from the mine to the port was always difficult, for most mines were in remote upland areas almost destitute of roads of any kind. In such places the only possible means of transport was the packhorse, fitted with two panniers, often of basketwork, into each of which was loaded a hundredweight of ore. In the 1740s Lewis Morris used sixty-three packhorses to carry ore from Esgair-mwyn to Aberystwyth harbour.[78] A few years later the ore from Chauncey Townsend's mines was carried by packhorses brought at the height of the mining season from Pembrokeshire by men who lived near the mines while there was work available and until the weather deteriorated. Such transport continued to be used well into the nineteenth century.

Wheeled vehicles did not make their appearance until late in the eighteenth century. In 1764 upland Cardiganshire was described by a mine owner as a place 'where a wheeled carriage was never seen'.[79] Lewis Morris actually built a road and made some use of wagons,[80] but the gradual improvements in the road system wrought by the turnpike trusts were, in general, of little benefit to mine operators, for most works were in remote hilly areas. Few country parishes in Cardiganshire took proper care of their roads. In 1800 John Probert, who very much wanted to use wagons for ore transport, brought an action against the township of Tregaron for neglecting its roads.[81] He lost the case but there was no doubt that roads were poor. Nor was there much improvement during the nineteenth century. In the 1870s John Taylor gave the heavy cost of road maintenance as one of his reasons for withdrawing from mining in one part of Cardiganshire.

The cheapest form of transport was by sea. During the seventeenth and early eighteenth centuries, almost all the ore and lead was shipped from the Dyfi port of Garreg. By the mid-eighteenth century, however, the bulk left the port of Aberystwyth, which was ranked as only a creek within the port of Aberdyfi, wherein lay the office of the collector of customs. The difficulty of communicating with the customs officer ten miles away was a serious hindrance to the trade of Aberystwyth and there was much rejoicing in the town when the Customs House was moved from Aberdyfi to Aberystwyth in 1759. Thereafter the port grew rapidly. Only one ship was registered in

[77]Powis Castle Deeds and Documents, MSS 18634–18967.
[78]Powis Castle Deeds and Documents, MSS 21928–21934.
[79]NLW MS 1759B, Book IV, f.22; Powis Castle Deeds and Documents, MS 2894.
[80]Powis Castle Deeds and Documents, MSS 21928–21934.
[81]Powis Castle Deeds and Documents, MS 4065.

Aberystwyth in 1701, but by 1815 there were as many as 157.[82] Lead ore dominated the exports; of the 13,000 tons shipped from the port in 1851, 10,490 were of lead ore.[83] The trade was greatly helped after 1834 by improvements to the harbour, which helped to clear away much of the sand bar which had previously troubled shipping.

The railways connecting Aberystwyth with Shrewsbury and Swansea were built in 1864 and 1867 respectively, but their effect on lead mining was limited. At first some Cardiganshire ore was sent by rail via Carmarthen, but this was found to be expensive and was used only by a few mine owners with small works near the Carmarthen line. The great bulk of the ore was produced by the Lisburne Mines Company, which owned the steamships *Countess of Lisburne* and *H. E. Taylor* and therefore preferred to send their mineral by sea.[84] This kept the port of Aberystwyth busy long after there was rail communication with south Wales. The port benefited from the railways insofar as a number of Montgomeryshire mine owners stopped using the Dyfi estuary ports and sent their ore by rail to be shipped from Aberystwyth.

Use was made of narrow gauge mineral lines to the east of Aberystwyth. The first to be laid was the short-lived Plynlimon and Hafan Tramway, built in 1897 to carry stone from the Hafan Quarry to connect with the Shrewsbury line at Llandre. It may also have carried a little ore from the mines of Esgair-hir and Bryn-yr-afr to Aberystwyth. A more lasting venture was the Vale of Rheidol Railway. Because of the large numbers of mines in the upper part of the Rheidol and Ystwyth Valleys, it had long been argued that a mineral line should be built to serve this area. The first suggestion, made in 1880, was that a line be built from Trawsgoed railway station past the Grogwynion and Lisburne Mines to Pont-rhyd-y-groes before turning towards Devil's Bridge and mines in that area.[85] But this proved too expensive a plan and, instead, the present Vale of Rheidol line was built and opened in 1902. It ran to the Aberystwyth railway station and, via a narrow track line built by the Taylors, to the harbour.

Labour

Until well into the eighteenth century, there was always a shortage of labour for the mines of Cardiganshire. At the end of the seventeenth century, it was proposed that some of the money spent on the poor and on prisoners be saved by employing paupers, debtors and selected criminals to work in the mines on the moorlands and wastelands of Wales.[86] Later, the Company of Mine Adventurers sought to use condemned criminals, and twenty-seven such men were sent to north Cardiganshire.[87]

Apart from the time when Lewis Morris managed mines in the mid-eighteenth century, the industry was controlled by Englishmen, men like William Waller from northern England, John Paynter, Thomas Bonsall and Job Sheldon from Derbyshire and Edmund Moore from Cornwall. The following century saw the coming of the Aldersons, the Williamses and the Taylors. Until the

---

[82] *The Cambrian Register*, III (1818), 340.
[83] NLW, E. A. Lewis Papers, Aberystwyth Harbour Returns, 1851.
[84] NLW MSS, Aberystwyth Port Books, 1875–1910.
[85] *Mining Journal* (1880), 668, 761.
[86] M. Stringer, *English and Welsh Mines* (London, 1699), p.16.
[87] Shiers, *Familiar Discourse*, pp.142, 146.

Fig. 34: A group of Cardiganshire lead miners. Note the candle on some of the hats, the only means of illumination normally used underground. (*Copyright Dr W. M. Ashton*).

late 1730s, even skilled miners had to be brought from England, though shortly afterwards Cardiganshire mines began to profit from the reserve of skill being built up in Flintshire. Darren and some other mines were worked by Flintshire men. Soon afterwards came some Cornishmen, but the main influx from Cornwall did not begin until the 1820s.

Mining was never a well-paid occupation and low wages in mid-Wales were among the factors which attracted mine operators. In the early days of the industry, day wages were paid, but by the seventeenth century piecework rates were also common, with employers supplying candles, ropes and other equipment. Earnings in Cardiganshire ranged from an average of about 6*d.* a day in the early seventeenth century to 9*d.* in the 1690s. As stated earlier, it was the Company of Mine Adventurers which first started the practice of selling bargains to the miners. Both the employer and the taker of the bargain had the right to raise or lower the price if it proved disadvantageous. At Esgair-hir in 1700 a bargain set to Andrew Slack at 25*s.* a ton was cancelled because he was earning too much.[88] At Fron-goch in 1793 the bargain set to one miner proved so poor that the price was raised by 13*s.* a ton.[89] The best-paid workman around 1752 was the top pumper, who earned 9*s.* a

[88]Ibid., Appendix, p.2.
[89]Powis Castle Deeds and Documents, MS 21940.

Fig. 35: The remains of the productive Esgair-hir lead mine, 1960. (*Copyright W. J. Lewis*).

week. Masons, carpenters and blacksmiths earned 13*d.* to 14*d.* a day. At Esgair-mwyn around 1750 miners were paid from 1*s.* to 14*d.* a day, while labourers received from 8*d.* to 11*d.*[90] But this was short-lived; by the end of the century wages in Cardiganshire mines had fallen to 10*d.* for miners and 1*s.* for blasters. Piecework yielded an average of 7*s.* a week.[91] During the depression which accompanied the French Wars wages dropped to an average of 5*s.* to 6*s.* a week.[92]

Surface and open cast workers worked for twelve hours a day. Underground the shift (known as the 'stem') was of eight hours' duration, with from one to three stems being worked in every twenty-four hours. Time was measured by candle; in the 1740s candles numbered fifteen to eighteen to the pound; two and a half candles took eight hours to burn. The candle set to burn in a sheltered spot to measure time was known as the 'Watch Candle'.[93]

The rise in the price of food during the early nineteenth century forced mine operators to increase wages from the 12*d.* to 18*d.* a day in the first decade to 2*s.* a day in 1826. But after this there was little improvement; earnings averaged 15*s.* a week for miners and 11*s.* for labourers in the 1870s

---

[90]Powis Castle Deeds and Documents, MSS 21928–21934.
[91]Powis Castle Deeds and Documents, MS 2522.
[92]R. Warner, A *Walk through Wales, in August 1785* (2nd edn., Bath, 1799), p.65.

and, because of the decline in the industry, remained at that level until the end of the century. As a result of the inflation caused by the First World War those few miners still working in the county in 1929 received as little as 5s. 6d. to 6s. a day.[94]

Wages were often paid at irregular intervals and real earnings were also reduced by the 'truck' system – the selling of goods to the miners by the mine owners. It began as an honest attempt to supply the needs of those compelled to live in barracks away from home or living in small cottages near mines in remote areas. The practice began to be abused seriously around 1750 when John Ball became mining agent to the Mine Adventurers and others. Not only did he overcharge the men for tools, candles and gunpowder, but he also refused to pay subsistence wages except in the form of corn, cheese and other goods at inflated prices at his shop in the mine buildings. Of the £30 15s. 9d. owed in wages to a group of Grogwynion men, only 3s. was received in cash. To acquire more cash, miners often had to sell goods back to Ball at low prices.[95] It was said in 1764 that this was 'the accustomed way of satisfying ye Miners' for it yielded a certain profit of fifty per cent.[96] John Paynter and even the wealthy Sir Thomas Bonsall saw nothing wrong in the institution of truck. It persisted until the 1790s when a serious shortage of labour forced mine owners not only to pay their workers in cash but also to sell them goods at market prices.

The low level of men's wages meant that their wives and children also worked in the mines. In the 1830s children could earn 2s. a week at the age of ten years and 3s. at the age of twelve.[97] Women earned 6d. a day in 1800 and were supposed to get 10d. a century later, but they often received less. Many of the miners were also smallholders. This was of advantage to the mine operators because it kept wages low. But it had its drawbacks; during potato planting and at the peat, corn and potato harvests, mining often had to give way to farming at a time when the weather favoured the raising of ore. Such absenteeism did not survive the depression caused by the French Wars, but the miner-farmer remained a feature of lead mining until the industry came to an end.[98]

Mining was clearly harmful both to people and animals. Water which drained out of mine workings and waste heaps poisoned the land and rivers and killed many fish and animals. In 1919 it was reckoned that some 3,000 acres of land were affected. The inhaling of silica-laden dust in mines also proved harmful to miners, many of whom suffered from what they called *Y Belen*, a feeling akin to a hard lump in the lungs. This, together with poor living conditions, was responsible for the high incidence of tuberculosis among miners and their families in Cardiganshire.[99]

The closure of the mines in the inter-war years led to a marked depopulation of the mining area. Many of the miners moved to the coal mines of south Wales, leaving behind them scores of abandoned mines and cottages, the remains of which bear silent witness to an industry which once played a prominent role in the socio-economic history of the county.

[93]BL MS 14951, f.38.
[94]NLW MS 7873F, Welsh Mines Corporation Ltd, Wages Book 1920–9.
[95]Powis Castle Deeds and Documents, MSS 9095, 1315, 3318, 3330.
[96]Powis Castle Deeds and Documents, MS 3215.
[97]A. H. Dodd, *The Industrial Revolution in North Wales* (Cardiff, 1933), p.364.
[98]*Mining Journal* (1877), 501.
[99]*County Medical Officer of Health Report* (Cardiganshire), 1930, p.3.

CHAPTER 9

SHIPPING AND SHIPBUILDING

David Jenkins

Iɴ 1561 the coastline of Cardiganshire was described as having 'no trade of merchandise, but all full of rocks and dangers'.[1] Three centuries later, in 1861, maritime activity in the county was enjoying a remarkable heyday, with hundreds of sailing vessels engaged in the local coasting trades, larger ships venturing further afield, and a considerable number of skilled craftsmen ashore employed in shipbuilding and its ancillary trades. At the end of the twentieth century, however, there are few signs left of this great era of maritime activity in the county, save for a few ruined lime-kilns and the harbours, intended to promote local commerce, which now provide shelter for vessels that go to sea for pleasure rather than profit. A tradition of merchant seafaring that developed gradually from the late seventeenth century onwards is all but dead and Cardiganshire, once one of the greatest nurseries of seamen in the British Isles, has turned its back on the sea. It is these themes that this chapter will address.

In 1565 Elizabeth I, fearful of Catholic Europe and eager to suppress the piratical tendencies of some of her subjects, appointed a Royal Commission to survey the ports and creeks of Wales and the vessels using those ports. A year later the Cardiganshire commissioners were able to report, 'no ships, barks or vessels . . . [but] fisher boats of the burden of 4 or 5 tons for . . . the exercise of fishing'.[2] It was noted that fishing activity was particularly intense from Michaelmas onwards, suggesting that it was centred on the harvesting of the vast shoals of herring which congregated in Cardigan Bay each autumn. Indeed, it was the existence of this herring fishery that provided one of the earliest stimuli for maritime commercial activity in the area. Salt, vital for the preservation of the often large catches of herring, was imported from France and Ireland as well as from Liverpool, though most of the vessels involved in this trade were not locally owned. Return cargoes for these vessels consisted of casks of salted herring, small cargoes of grain and oak bark for tanning purposes. By the late seventeenth century, however, locally owned vessels engaged in these trades began to appear in the Welsh Port Books, and in 1685 the Cardigan vessel *The Good Behaviour* took a cargo of oats from the Teifi to London.[3]

The pace of maritime activity quickened considerably during the eighteenth century. In the north of the county the exploitation of the lead reserves in the Rheidol and Ystwyth valleys led to demands for improvements to the harbour at Aberystwyth, which had been described in 1561 as 'a barred

---

[1] Quoted in W. J. Lewis, *Born on a Perilous Rock: Aberystwyth Past and Present* (Aberystwyth, 1980), p.75.

[2] E. A. Lewis, *The Welsh Port Books (1550–1603)* (London, 1927), p.xxxviii.

[3] W. J. Lewis, *The Gateway to Wales: A History of Cardigan* (Dyfed County Council, 1990), p.46.

haven of no value'. After some petitioning, the Customs House was transferred to Aberystwyth from Aberdyfi in 1763, but it was not until 1780 that the town secured an Act of Parliament which enabled it to establish a body of Harbour Trustees with the aim of improving the harbour facilities. Hopelessly disorganized and unwilling to spend money on anything but their own occasional entertainment, the Trustees achieved little of lasting value over the ensuing years. By 1799, however, the port of Aberystwyth could boast ninety-nine vessels with a total tonnage of 3,537 net tons, and it was the most important port in Wales for the export of lead ore.

Throughout the county in general, moreover, there were changes conducive to increased maritime activity in the late eighteenth century. Between 1750 and 1801 it has been estimated that the population of the county increased by almost a fifth. The growing use of lime to 'sweeten' the acidic soils of the county provided a considerable impetus for shipping, for much of the lime was brought by sea from the Gower and numerous locations in south Pembrokeshire, such as Caldey Island, Lydstep and West Williamston. Before the lime could be used on the land it had to be burnt in kilns, many of which were established at various coastal locations in the late eighteenth century: the first lime-kilns at Aber-porth, for instance, were in operation as early as 1773.[4] The fuel used to burn the lime was culm – anthracite dust – which also had to be imported to Cardiganshire from Llanelli, Pen-bre, Saundersfoot, Hook and Nolton. It also came to be adopted (rolled with clay) as a domestic fuel throughout the coastal areas of the county.

Burgeoning trade naturally led to an increased demand for shipping, though it is difficult to estimate the number and type of vessels built locally prior to the introduction of compulsory registration of merchant vessels in 1786. The shipping registers of the port of Cardigan, however, indicate that during the last quarter of the eighteenth century twenty-eight smacks and sloops were built for local owners at ports between Cardigan and Aberaeron, chiefly at Cardigan and New Quay, but with as many as eight of them built at Llangrannog or Aber-porth.[5] These vessels were quite small, with an average tonnage of some 25 to 30 net tons, but they nevertheless reflect the increased demand for shipping to serve the expanding coastal trade in lime and culm. The general increase in local commercial activity was also reflected in other developments, such as the founding in 1785 of the Cardigan Mercantile Company by the brothers Thomas and John Davies of Newport. They bought the large warehouse built on the south bank of the Teifi in 1745 by David Parry of Noyadd Trefawr and were to become heavily involved in the general trade of the port, particularly the importing of timber.

These commercial developments were complemented by improvements to harbour facilities at a number of locations along the county's coastline in the early nineteenth century. Although Cardiganshire would never be able to boast an enclosed floating dock, substantial works were undertaken at Aberaeron, New Quay and Aberystwyth between 1800 and 1840. The harbour at Aberaeron was the first to be improved: by the turn of the century the crude pier that had protected the landing place at the mouth of the Aeron was ruined and periods of stormy weather often resulted in great banks of shingle forming a bar which blocked all navigation. On 28 July 1807, however, a private bill providing for the construction of harbour walls and the levying of tolls and dues to maintain them was presented before the House of Lords. This bill was the brainchild of the

[4] I am indebted to Mr David Jenkins, Aberystwyth, for this information.
[5] J. G. Jenkins, *Maritime Heritage: The Ships and Seamen of Southern Ceredigion* (Llandysul, 1982), pp.99–125.

Revd Alban Thomas Jones Gwynne, lord of the manor of Llyswen which comprised Aberaeron. By 1811 the works had been completed under the supervision of William Green of Aberystwyth. The improved harbour soon became the commercial focus of a considerable hinterland which stretched as far inland as Lampeter and the upper Aeron Valley.[6]

The Revd Jones Gwynne was also the instigator in 1820 of a scheme to provide a substantial pier to protect the harbour at New Quay. The initial proposals proved too costly and the scheme eventually embodied in the New Quay Harbour Act of 1835 was based upon plans drawn up by a young engineer called Daniel Beynon.[7] The 1830s also saw positive steps taken to eradicate the problems of the bar which so often blocked the harbour entrance at Aberystwyth. In 1836 the Trustees eventually secured an Act of Parliament which enabled them to finance works which included the diversion of the river Ystwyth so that it scoured the harbour mouth, and the construction of a breakwater that protected the new works from the prevailing south-westerlies. Thereafter it was possible for larger vessels to enter Aberystwyth without fear of being stranded for some weeks.

The vessels which carried the coastal trade of Cardiganshire from the late eighteenth century onwards were built chiefly within the county. Most of them were single-masted smacks and sloops, built to suit local trading requirements. Of paramount importance was the fact that these vessels often had to discharge their cargoes on an open beach; even in locations where there were harbours, it was not uncommon for them to dry out at low tide. It was vital, therefore, that ships could stand upright on the sands where they settled at low tide, and they also needed to be strongly built to withstand the considerable strain imposed on the hull of the vessel when not supported by water. Their size was limited by the fact that they were often required to sail in narrow channels or along rivers where there was little draught. Thus the smacks and sloops built in the county were practical and simple bulk carriers, capable of carrying cargoes of up to fifty tons and ideally suited to the trades in which they were engaged.

Many of these vessels were built at locations where it is very difficult today to imagine any kind of shipbuilding activity. The requirements and preparations were few: any piece of level land convenient to the sea or a navigable river would suffice to lay down the keelblocks, although in 1777 the sloop *Blessing* was built in a field half a mile from the beach at Penbryn and had to be hauled on rollers to the shore to be launched![8] A sawpit needed to be dug and a supply of timber secured. Oak, the staple shipbuilding timber, does not grow well in areas exposed to salty sea breezes and much of the timber was initially obtained from inland estates such as Bronwydd or Coedmor, for whom the shipbuilding industry provided a convenient market. The vessels were built very occasionally according to detailed plans, but more usually from wooden half-hull models of the ship carved beforehand by the shipwright to the requirements of the owner. The construction of a vessel from such a model, using only the simplest tools, required great skill, with the initial sawing of the timber the most critical part of the process. Once the hull was complete, it was caulked by using a special mallet and chisel to drive oakum (a mixture of rope fibre and tar) in between the hull and deck planking; the entire hull was then given a thick coating of tar or pitch.

Once the basic construction of the hull was complete, the vessel was 'fitted out', and during the early decades of the nineteenth century the major shipbuilding ports – Cardigan, New Quay,

---

[6]D. L. Jones, 'Aberaeron: The community and seafaring, 1800–1900', *Ceredigion*, VI, no.2 (1969), 201–42.

[7]S. Campbell-Jones, 'Shipbuilding at New Quay, Cardiganshire, 1798–1878', ibid., VII, nos.3–4 (1974–5), 274.

[8]Jenkins, *Maritime Heritage*, p.97.

Aberaeron and Aberystwyth – all saw the establishment of ancillary industries essential to the completion of locally built ships. Foundries specializing in the production of anchors and chains were established at both Cardigan and Aberystwyth by the 1830s, while local blacksmiths produced the smaller metal fittings required on board. Blockmaking – the manufacture of wooden pulleys vital to the running rigging of a sailing vessel – became important, as did ropemaking and sailmaking. Names such as Ropeyard Hill in Cardigan and *Cae Ropos* at Trefechan, Aberystwyth, mark the locations of once-busy ropewalks where the laborious process of spinning hemp yarn to make rope was undertaken. Sailmaking was undertaken in large, well-lit lofts where there was plenty of room to lay out the sails. There were four sailmakers at Cardigan in 1844, while New Quay had six sail-lofts at various times during the nineteenth century. So great was the number of apprentices at the sail loft owned by John Jones of New Quay in the 1860s that it was possible to form a brass band![9]

New Quay was the most important shipbuilding centre in Cardiganshire in the nineteenth century. Some 240 vessels were built at New Quay itself and Cei Bach between 1800 and 1882 by at least nine different builders, the most prominent of whom was David Davies of Pen-y-wig, who was in business between 1833 and 1866. Aberystwyth came a close second, with 224 vessels built between 1800 and 1880, many of them constructed by three generations of the Evans family, who were the port's most prominent builders. At Aberaeron, where ninety-three vessels were built in the nineteenth century, the major shipbuilders were the Harries family – John Harries and his sons John and David – who built twenty-three vessels between 1838 and 1844. At nearby Aber-arth twenty-five vessels were built in the early nineteenth century, but a great flood in 1846 ruined the little port's suitability as a shipbuilding centre, forcing the local builder Evan Jones to move his business to Aberaeron. At Cardigan 124 vessels were built in the yards located at the confluence of the Mwldan brook and the Teifi. The foremost shipbuilder here was John Williams, who built his first ship in 1845 and remained in business until the 1870s.

During the first half of the nineteenth century the majority of vessels built by these yards were small smacks and sloops intended for the coastal trade. Once completed, these vessels would be handed over to their new owners, though they were very rarely owned by one person only. They were rather the property of consortia made up of farmers, merchants and seamen, those people most concerned with the trade of the vessels. According to the practice enshrined in successive Merchant Shipping Acts, each ship was divided into sixty-four shares, but the more normal unit of shareholding was four sixty-fourths or one-sixteenth of a ship, generally known in Cardiganshire as an ounce – *owns o'r llong*. The following, for instance, were the joint owners of the 34-gross-ton Aber-porth sloop *Mary Ann*, built in 1825.

John James, master mariner	16	shares
Evan Griffiths, farmer	4	shares
John Davies, farmer	4	shares
David Davies, farmer	4	shares
Michael Evans, farmer	8	shares
Abel Walters, gentleman	4	shares
Samuel Davies, farmer	8	shares
Daniel Davies, farmer	8	shares
David Griffiths, farmer	8	shares
Total	64	shares

[9]Campbell-Jones, 'Shipbuilding at New Quay', 291.

The liability of shareholders holding sixty-fourth shares was unlimited and each year they took a cut of the profit made by the vessel that was in proportion to their shareholding.

The trading pattern of these vessels during the first three-quarters of the nineteenth century is well illustrated in the various voyage books and accounts that have survived for the 28-gross-ton sloop *Fanny* for the years 1835–40.[10] Built in 1828, she was owned by a consortium of farmers and mariners from Aber-porth and managed by David Morgan of Treferebella, Aber-porth. This little vessel was engaged almost exclusively in the import of culm and lime to ports in the south of the county. As was the normal practice with coasting sloops and smacks, the *Fanny* was laid up on the Teifi from late autumn until early spring each year, thereby avoiding the worst of the winter weather and enabling repair work to be undertaken at the Cardigan shipyards. The trading season normally commenced in March; in 1835 the *Fanny* was ready to begin her trading for that year on 2 March. Depending on the weather, such vessels were able to undertake about twenty return voyages before they were laid up again in late October or early November.

It is unfortunate that the voyage and account books which have survived for the *Fanny* for the years 1835–40 are not concurrent. Nevertheless, it can be deduced that in 1839 she made nineteen return voyages which brought a gross income of £46 19s. 0d., and the same number again in 1840 which brought a gross income of £47 17s. 6d. Running expenses – repairs, wages and provisioning – over the two years amounted to £51 3s. 4d., which left a clear profit of £45 3s. 2d. over two years to be divided amongst the shareholders. Of the voyages undertaken in 1840, sixteen entailed carrying limestone, chiefly from Lydstep and Pembroke to Cardigan and Aber-porth, though one cargo was discharged at Mwnt beach. The cargoes of culm, presumably from the westernmost pit in the South Wales Coalfield at Tre-frân, were all loaded at Nolton and discharged at Aber-porth. The accounts seem to suggest that the ship's master was responsible for the actual purchase of the cargo on behalf of the consignees when limestone was loaded, whereas the more usual practice of charging a freight rate was maintained with cargoes of culm. The process of discharging these cargoes – *arllwys y llong* – was quite an occasion in coastal villages such as Aber-porth or Llangrannog. Farmers' carts were hired to remove the culm and lime from the beaches between tides with the help of casual labourers, usually described as 'porters' in the accounts of the *Fanny*.

Industrial conditions aboard these vessels were both primitive and dangerous, though life on board the coasting smacks, manned usually by master, mate and boy, often from the same village and sometimes related, was not as hard as that on board deep-sea sailing vessels. The voyages were quite short and the accounts of the *Fanny* show that fresh food and provisions – tea, coffee, salt herrings and beef, potatoes, leeks and bread – were taken on at most ports of call. It is also clear that the temperance movement of the 1830s had not made much headway among the crew of the *Fanny*; a 'welcome home drink' was often enjoyed and invariably charged to the vessel's account! Nevertheless, the living conditions in the tiny fo'c'sle of these vessels were very basic. In rough weather the clothes of the crew might be wet through for many days, and if the stove could not be lit they had no means of drying them, nor of preparing warm food and drinks. Moreover, these little vessels, trading regularly along a lee shore, were very much at the mercy of storms. At least forty-five locally owned smacks and sloops were driven ashore and wrecked along the Cardiganshire coast in the nineteenth century.[11]

[10]Documents loaned to the author by the late Mr Frank Chagnon, Aber-porth.
[11]T. Bennett, *Welsh Shipwrecks: Vol.1, Aberdyfi to St. David's Head* (Haverfordwest, 1981), pp.6–10.

Fig. 36: Four coastal trading smacks beached on Traeth y Llongau, Aber-porth, *c.*1890. Note the lime kiln above the beach. (*Copyright Welsh Industrial and Maritime Museum*).

The *Fanny* was engaged almost entirely in the import of various commodities essential to the county's economy, but there was some export trade as well. A few miles up the Teifi from Cardigan, substantial slate quarries had been developed at Cilgerran by 1800. Although not of such high quality as that produced in north Wales, local slate was widely used in slab form and was exported coastwise and to Ireland. Barges were used to carry the slate down the Teifi to Cardigan where it was loaded onto sea-going vessels. The quarries were owned by the Lloyd family of Coedmor, who owned four vessels which were chiefly engaged in the export of slate in the early nineteenth century. The Stephens family of Llechryd, who established themselves as slate merchants in Cardigan, also owned a number of vessels. Lead ore from the numerous mines in the Aberystwyth area was exported from the port to Deeside, Llanelli, Swansea and Bristol. The arrival in the area in 1834 of John Taylor from Flintshire led to a considerable boost in the seaborne transport of ore to Deeside, but the output of the local mines peaked in 1856 and thereafter competition from cheaper foreign ores led to a gradual decline in the lead mining industry. Much ore was sent to south Wales by rail after the opening of the Manchester and Milford route in 1867, although even as late as 1900 half the production of ore from mines in the Aberystwyth area was still exported by sea.

Britain was moving towards its pinnacle of world-wide economic power in the mid-nineteenth century. Future industrial competitors such as Germany or the United States had not begun to pose serious competition and Britain's merchant fleet dominated world trade. These developments were soon felt in the little shipyards of Cardiganshire which, by the 1840s, were building vessels designed to trade further afield than the coasting smacks and sloops. As early as the 1810s the Cardigan Mercantile Company owned the snow-rigged vessels *Active* and *Albion*, both of about 150 gross tons, which imported timber from North America and which also took emigrants from Cardigan to the New World. By modern standards, these vessels were tiny, but there were good reasons for their small size. The amount of cargo usually available for loading at any one time in one port was small and cargo was hand-worked at most ports. Many ports were small and shallow, and unable to accommodate large vessels. Long ocean voyages in vessels of about 100 gross tons, often less than a hundred feet in length, were therefore commonplace despite the apparent economic absurdity of such voyages by present-day standards.[12]

The relatively small size of these deep-sea traders meant that the shipyards of Cardiganshire were able to participate in their construction. During the first half of the nineteenth century many of the larger vessels were two-masted square riggers – either brigs or snows – but by the mid-nineteenth century the more economical fore and aft schooner rig, which could be handled by smaller crews, was becoming popular. Of the forty-six vessels built at Aberaeron between 1840 and 1860, thirty were schooners; similarly, schooners accounted for fifty-seven of the eighty-three vessels built at various shipyards in New Quay during the same period. Most of these vessels were of about 80–120 gross tons and required a crew of no more than seven men.

Vessels such as these, engaged on a variety of home and foreign trades, often did not return to their home port unless it was for maintenance and repairs. The expanding coal trade from the ports of south Wales provided outward cargoes for many vessels and they returned with cargoes of grain from the Black Sea, sugar from the West Indies, coffee from Brazil, and hides from the River Plate. Many Cardiganshire schooners also participated in the slate trade from ports in Caernarfonshire. Considerable numbers of ship portraits have survived showing schooners from Aberystwyth and New Quay sailing into the Bay of Naples, with Vesuvius smoking in the background, at the end of a long voyage from Newfoundland with cargoes of salted fish. The brig *Hetty Ellen* of Aberystwyth achieved a brief moment of fame when, in 1861, she was chartered to sail from Glasgow to the estuary of the Zambezi with a miscellaneous cargo of supplies for the renowned African explorer and missionary David Livingstone![13] But not all the locally owned vessels sailed so far. Many were regularly employed during the 1860s and 1870s carrying cargoes of steam coal from Cardiff to Liverpool or Barrow, and returning with iron ore from Duddon destined for the ironworks of south Wales.

Since local vessels were now sailing much further afield than had formerly been the case, effective insurance arrangements became vital. Most towns and villages along the Cardiganshire coast saw the establishment of mutual insurance societies during the latter half of the nineteenth century. The Aberaeron Mutual Ship Insurance Society, for instance, was established on 13 December 1864, and New Quay acquired its first such society two years later. Other ship insurance societies at New Quay were the Gomer Ship Insurance Society and the Prince of Wales Ship Insurance Society.

[12]B. Greenhill, *The Ship: The Life and Death of the Merchant Sailing Ship* (HMSO, London, 1980), p.14.
[13]Robin Craig, '*Hetty Ellen* of Aberystwyth and Doctor Livingstone', *Maritime Wales*, 2 (1977), 33–47.

Fig. 37: A typical Neapolitan ship portrait depicting the schooner *Edith Eleanor*, built at Aberystwyth in 1881, in the Bay of Naples. (*Copyright Welsh Industrial and Maritime Museum*).

Even small villages such as Aber-porth could boast their own insurance societies. The Aber-porth Mutual Ship Insurance Society was set up in 1877 by nineteen local men, who were either master mariners or shareholders in locally owned vessels. However, the society's reserves were clearly limited; any ports or beaches at which vessels insured by the society encountered problems were placed 'out of bounds', and vessels were no longer permitted to use such ports![14] Sailing further afield also demanded improved standards of navigation. Cardigan's 'Navigations and Mathematical School' was opened in 1830, though the county's most celebrated teacher of navigation was the redoubtable 'Cranogwen', Sarah Jane Rees of Llangrannog. Born the daughter of a master mariner in 1839, she often sailed with her father and eventually acquired a master mariner's certificate. For many years a teacher at the village school, she also coached generations of local boys in the art of deep-sea navigation. She died in 1916.

Life on board vessels sailing deep-sea – *hwylio ar led*, as it was known in Welsh – was very different from that experienced on the local sailing coasters. Voyages were much longer – anything up to two years away from home in some cases – and the availability of fresh food and water was much

[14]PRO, B.T.31/2397/11955.

reduced on long ocean passages. Seamen had a working week of over eighty hours, and four hours on and four hours off. The main deck of sailing vessels was frequently awash when the vessel was laden with cargo, so that at best a sailor was almost continually wet and, at worst, he might be washed overboard with little chance of rescue. Working aloft in the rigging was even more perilous. Considerable strength and a steady nerve were required to work up to a hundred feet above the heaving deck of a ship in a storm. In such circumstances, attempts by sailors to furl a heavy, sodden sail might lead to physical injury. A leading authority on the history of merchant sailing vessels has stated that they were 'probably the most dangerous vehicles ever regularly used by man'.[15] Despite the hardships, however, the coastal communities of the county by the mid-nineteenth century regarded seafaring not merely as an occupation but as a way of life.

Such bustling maritime activity began to wane, however, from the 1860s onwards following the arrival of the railway in Cardiganshire. By 1864 both Aberystwyth and Llandysul were served by rail, and in 1886 the *Cardi bach* made its first run from Whitland to Cardigan. By 1895 the branch to Llandysul had been extended to Newcastle Emlyn. The railway soon proved to be a more convenient method of transporting goods to many parts of the county. The growing use of guano in place of lime as an agricultural fertilizer further undermined the once lively coastal trade. Many locally owned coastal traders rarely visited their home ports with cargoes of culm and lime. For instance, the ketch *Florrie*, owned by the author's great-grandfather Captain David Jenkins of Aberporth, only visited a port in the county once during the three years he owned her from 1897 onwards. The vessel was mainly employed carrying coal from Cardiff and Swansea or slates from Porthmadog to a variety of destinations around Britain, Ireland and the Channel Islands. The 1880s saw the end of shipbuilding in Cardiganshire; in 1882, the smack *Three Sisters* was the last vessel built at the once busy shipyards of New Quay, while the ketch *Cadwgan*, completed a year later at Aberaeron, was destined to be the last wooden sailing vessel built in the county. Ships continued to be repaired in local yards for some decades thereafter, but ancillary industries such as sailmaking, ropemaking and blockmaking gradually went out of business. The New Quay sailmaker Jenkin Jones transferred his business to Cardiff in 1837, where he turned his hand to the production of hatch cloths and awnings for the port's growing fleet of steamers.

Nevertheless, the coastal trade did not collapse entirely with the advent of the railway to Cardiganshire. Some enterprising individuals in the county's coastal towns realized that steamships could compete with the railway, and as early as 1856 the Cambrian Steam Packet Co. Ltd. was established at Aberystwyth to provide a regular passenger and cargo service from Aberystwyth to Liverpool and Bristol on the steamer *Plynlymon*. In 1863 the Aberayron Steam Navigation Co. Ltd. was founded to connect the port with Bristol. This firm was wound up following the loss of its only steamer, the *Prince Cadwgan*, in 1876, but a year later the Aberaeron Steam Packet Co. Ltd. was established to maintain the service, using the Clyde-built *Ianthe*. Not to be outdone, local tradesmen at Cardigan set up the Cardigan Steam Navigation Co. Ltd. in 1869, operating a service to Bristol with the delightful little steamer *Tivyside*. Within seven years she faced local competition when the steamer *Seaflower* was acquired by the rival Cardigan Commercial Steam Packet Co. Ltd. Many of these companies survived until the First World War, carrying both passengers and general cargo from Liverpool and Bristol to Cardigan, Aberaeron and Aberystwyth.

[15]Greenhill, *The Ship*, p.28.

During the inter-war years other local owners operated a number of steam coasters. Captain James George of Tre-fin in Pembrokeshire ran the coasters *Thomond* and *Ben Rein* between 1911 and 1936, while Captain James Davies of Cardigan owned the steamer *Teifi* between 1926 and 1930. These little steamers, carrying cargoes of coal, fertilizer and flour, were regular visitors to Cardigan and Aberaeron. In 1925 the company which eventually became known as British Isles Coasters Ltd. was set up at Cardigan by Captain W. G. James. By 1934 it had a fleet of five coasters, most of which only rarely came to Cardigan, being engaged instead on coastal tramping around the British Isles. One of their smaller vessels, the *Drumlough*, was often to be seen at Cardigan, however, and she had the dubious honour of being the last merchant vessel to visit Aberaeron with a cargo of flour from Cardiff in 1934. In 1938 British Isles Coasters took delivery of a Dutch-built motor vessel, the *West Coaster*, designed specifically to trade up to Cardigan without coming to grief on the notorious Teifi Bar, but she rarely visited the port, and was more regularly employed on the fruit trade from the Channel Islands to Southampton and London. The firm was wound up in 1946 when Captain James saw little commercial future for the once busy port of Cardigan. A few vessels visited Aberystwyth with cargoes of roadstone from north Wales in the early 1950s, but thereafter the county's local maritime trade virtually came to an end.[16]

The few coasters that continued to trade to Cardiganshire ports from the 1860s onwards could not offer employment to all the county's many seamen, and during the second half of the nineteenth century many mariners from the area took berths aboard vessels sailing from Britain's major ports. One of the most successful in the era of the sailing ship was Captain Lewis Davies, born in Cardigan in 1833. He first went to sea on the local schooner *Anna Letitia* in 1847; ten years later he gained his master's certificate at the age of twenty-four. By 1864 he was a master with the famed 'Black Ball Line' of Liverpool, commanding the emigrant clipper ship *Royal Dane*, a regular trader to Australia. Having retired from active seafaring in 1882, he established himself as a shipowner at Liverpool with the purchase of the aptly named iron ship *Cardigan Castle*, of which he had been master since 1870. He went on to acquire four further iron ships and barques, which he operated in the Australian trades until 1905, and eventually he emigrated to Sydney, where he died in 1919. He would appear to have been the only Cardiganshire man to establish himself as a shipowner at the great Merseyside port, whose substantial Welsh shipowning community was dominated by natives of Llŷn and Anglesey.[17]

In the 1860s and 1870s Swansea was the copper-smelting capital of the world. Much of the copper ore smelted at Swansea came originally from Anglesey and Cornwall, but as these home reserves were exhausted, new sources had to be discovered further afield. Important reserves were discovered in Chile in the early nineteenth century and by the 1870s Swansea shipowners had built up a considerable fleet of sailing vessels involved in the arduous trade around Cape Horn. The 'Swansea copper ore barques', as they were known, came to be renowned the world over. Sailing outwards, heavily laden with cargoes of coal, they returned to Swansea equally heavily laden with dense copper ore, having passed through some of the most dangerous oceans of the world. The demand for experienced seamen to man these ships brought many Cardiganshire mariners to

[16]For more information on these various companies, see R. S. Fenton, *Cambrian Coasters* (Kendal, 1989).

[17]Information on the career of Captain Lewis Davies has been obtained from the Lloyd's Captains' Registers and Mr George Hawkes of Ormskirk.

Swansea and they were prominent among the crews of the copper ore barques. The example of Captain William Williams of St Dogmaels is typical. In 1869, at the age of thirteen, he went to sea on the Cardigan smack *Hopewell*, but by 1875 he was an AB on the copper ore barque *Lord Clyde*, owned by Tullochs of Swansea. He later served as bosun on two other Tulloch vessels, the *Acacia* and the *Talca*, both of which had crew members from St Dogmaels and Cardigan. By the 1880s, however, the copper ore trade had begun to decline and, having obtained his first mate's certificate in 1885, William Williams joined the Cardiff-based firm of John Cory and Sons.[18]

During the latter half of the nineteenth century Cardiff was transformed from a modest borough town on the bank of the river Taff into the 'Coal Metropolis of the World'. At its commercial peak in 1913, some 10fi million tons of coal were exported from the port to destinations all over the globe. The provision of ships to handle these exports attracted to Cardiff seamen and shipowners from all parts of the British Isles and further afield; many of them were Welsh and a significant number came from Cardiganshire. The county's contribution to Cardiff's success as a port was extremely significant. At least seven shipping companies established at the great coal port between 1881 and 1916 were founded by Cardiganshire seamen and many of the ships which they owned were manned to a considerable degree by natives of coastal communities such as Aber-porth, Llangrannog and New Quay.[19]

As maritime activity along the Cardiganshire coast declined during the last quarter of the nineteenth century the county's seamen increasingly turned to Cardiff and its shipping for employment. Ironically, the railway, whose advent was chiefly responsible for the decline of local shipping, also provided a convenient means whereby seamen could travel to Cardiff to join ships. Between 1870 and 1950 they were to form a significant element in the great mixture of seamen that made up Cardiff's celebrated 'Tiger Bay'. Among the many mariners from Cardiganshire who joined Cardiff-owned ships was Captain Evan Thomas, the elder son of Hezekiah Thomas of 'Dolwen', Aber-porth, a family which had long been involved in the maritime trade around the coast of south-west Wales with their 47-gross-ton ketch, *Pheasant*. By the late 1870s Thomas was master of the steamer *Henry Anning*, owned by a Cardiff company of south Devon origins. Also employed by Anning's at that time was an astute young clerk from Merthyr Tydfil named Henry Radcliffe, and early in 1881 Thomas and Radcliffe came together to establish their own shipping venture.

This was an era of expansion for Britain's merchant marine; between 1850 and 1900 Britain's foreign trade doubled in both bulk and value and the vast majority of this trade was handled in vessels which flew the Red Ensign. South Wales fulfilled a world-wide demand for steam coal, while Britain's growing population and expanding manufacturing industries necessitated the import of a wide range of foodstuffs and raw materials. Of particular significance to Cardiff shipowners was the iron ore trade with Spain, and later the import of cereals from the Black Sea and the River Plate. These trades were dominated by Britain's expanding fleet of tramp steamers, destined to be joined in 1882 by Thomas and Radcliffe's first vessel, *Gwenllian Thomas*, built by the famous Palmer yard at Jarrow.

[18]I am indebted to the late Mr Peter Jones of Barry for information relating to Captain William Williams.

[19]For a more detailed discussion of the remaining section of this chapter, see D. Jenkins, 'Cardiff tramps, Cardi crews: Cardiganshire shipowners and seamen in Cardiff, *c.*1878–1950', *Ceredigion*, X, no.4 (1987), 405–30.

Fig. 38: The tramp steamer *Clarissa Radcliffe*, built by Ropner's of Stockton on Tees in 1904 to the order of Evan Thomas, Radcliffe & Co. of Cardiff, and manned by large numbers of seamen from Cardiganshire. (*Copyright Welsh Industrial and Maritime Museum*).

Both partners risked very little of their own money in the venture. They took one share between them in the *Gwenllian Thomas* and were successful in raising the bulk of the capital by selling shares to a wide range of people, chiefly within Wales. As they acquired further vessels in the 1880s (they had sixteen by 1890), each new ship was vested in the ownership of a single-ship company, with its own group of shareholders, and managed by Thomas and Radcliffe as directors. It was therefore continually necessary to solicit new shareholders to invest fresh capital and a particularly bizarre episode in the history of Cardiff shipowning occurred during the 1880s when the Cardiganshire-born minister, the Revd John Cynddylan Jones, began to act almost as a stockbroker for the companies' shares. In return for peddling Radcliffe stocks during his preaching engagements around Wales, Jones received 2½ per cent of the profits of the various single-ship companies, and Henry Radcliffe also loaned him substantial sums of money on various occasions. This 'unholy alliance' soon became a lively topic of conversation in maritime circles, with one London shipping journal unkindly dubbing Jones as 'chaplain to the fleet'. Jones demanded a larger percentage of the profits and when Captain Thomas died suddenly in 1891, aged forty-nine, he sought to prevent Henry Radcliffe from taking his younger brother Daniel into partnership. His attempted *coup* failed ignominiously, however, and the reverend gentleman's interest in things maritime came to an abrupt end![20]

[20]J. G. Jenkins, 'Y Parch John Cynddylan Jones', *Maritime Wales*, 8 (1984), 69–75.

Another well-known Cardiganshire minister, the Revd Thomas Levi, also came to play a prominent role in shipowning circles in the early 1880s. One of Levi's members at the Tabernacl Calvinistic Methodist chapel in Aberystwyth was a local grocer, John Mathias, born in Penparcau in 1837. Mathias also had investments in shipping and by 1875 he was managing owner of two local sailing vessels, the schooner *Miss Evans* and the brig *Solway*. On 5 October 1883, however, Mathias and a number of associates established the Glanrheidol Steamship Co. Ltd. in order to acquire and operate the newly built 1,005-gross-ton steamship of that name. Far too big to enter the harbour at Aberystwyth, the *Glanrheidol* was intended for the coal trade out of Cardiff, and she was followed by further larger steamers – the *Glanystwyth, Glanhafren, Glantivy* and *Glanayron* – between 1888 and 1894. A prominent shareholder in each of the single-ship companies which owned these vessels was Thomas Charles Edwards, first principal of the College at Aberystwyth, while Levi, also a substantial shareholder, was recorded as a director of a number of these firms by 1901. By 1896 Mathias's younger son Richard had opened an office in Cardiff, where much of the daily management of the fleet was undertaken, but the company's registered office remained at Aberystwyth.

As these two fleets expanded during the late Victorian era, it was only natural that their founders should look to their native county for seamen to crew them. Many masters and mariners from Aberystwyth and Borth served on the Mathias vessels, popularly known as *llongau Aberystwyth* (the ships of Aberystwyth), while Radcliffe's fleet drew upon the coastal villages in the south of the county, a tradition which continued notwithstanding the death of Captain Evan Thomas. It was a natural for some of the more ambitious master mariners who served on Cardiff's steamers to devote the skill and experience gained at sea and ashore to the establishment of their own shipping ventures. In July 1896 Captain James Jenkins of Aber-porth, a master with Evan Thomas, Radcliffe & Co. since 1890, took this step. Within a year he took W. J. Williams, a former clerk from Radcliffe's office, into partnership, and in 1899 they were joined by James Jenkins's cousin, Captain David Jenkins, who had also served with Radcliffe's since 1884. Williams left the partnership in 1904, by which time James and David Jenkins, trading as Jenkins Brothers, were operating six substantial steamers, again registered in the name of single-ship companies, from offices at the Merchants' Exchange, Cardiff.[21]

It is axiomatic that there are 'right' and 'wrong' times to enter into shipping; James Jenkins and his partners were fortunate in that the years around the turn of the century were characterized by good freight rates (enhanced by the Boer War) that gave their venture a good financial foundation. By 1903, however, freight rates were declining once more and by 1908–9 they were less than half those prevailing in 1900. During these years two other master mariners from Aber-porth entered into shipowning and discovered, to their cost, how difficult running ships could be at a time of relative slump. The first was Captain Daniel Jenkins of Aber-porth, younger brother of David Jenkins of Jenkins Brothers, who in 1903 set up the Aberporth Steamship Co. Ltd. in order to acquire an 1886-built steamer, which he named after his native village. Also in that year Captain Thomas Owen of 'Glanhowny', Aber-porth, went into partnership with Henry Bartlett of Cardiff in order to establish the Glanhowny Steamship Co. Ltd., for which they bought an even older vessel, built in 1884. Both ships were former Radcliffe vessels, sold off in order to make way for larger, more modern vessels.

---

[21]D. Jenkins, *Jenkins Brothers of Cardiff: A Ceredigion Family's Shipping Ventures* (Cardiff, 1985).

Fig. 39: Captain Simon Thomas of Aber-porth with crew members aboard the steamer *Gathorne* at Seville in 1897. This was the first vessel acquired by the shipping firm established in Cardiff in that year by Captain James Jenkins of Aber-porth. (*Copyright Welsh Industrial and Maritime Museum*).

Both ventures proved lamentable financial failures and the scandal which surrounded their eventual demise was widely discussed. With freight rates low and repair bills on the twenty-year-old steamers proving very costly, both companies were soon in considerable difficulties, especially since new vessels acquired by Cardiff owners at that time could carry as much cargo in one voyage as the *Aberporth* or the *Glanhowny* could manage in three. In June 1905 the *Aberporth* foundered and sank in the Black Sea, and at the subsequent inquiry it was revealed that the old steamer was insured at some £5,000 in excess of her true value! Two years later, in May 1907, the *Glanhowny* was lost on passage to Antwerp. Before his sudden death in 1906, Captain Owen had been trying to persuade Henry Bartlett to sell the vessel, and the scandal deepened when it was revealed that this ship, too, had been over-insured to the tune of some £4,500 at the time of her loss. A month later the Jenkins Brothers vessel, *Powis*, sank in calm sea off Seriphos in the Aegean, the last of a trio of highly dubious losses. Although the Jenkins Brothers weathered both the economic storm and the barrage of criticism, the two companies established in 1903 had both been forced into liquidation by their creditors by the summer of 1910.

On the eve of the First World War, therefore, there were three major companies of Cardiganshire origins at Cardiff: Evan Thomas, Radcliffe & Co., John Mathias and Sons, and Jenkins Brothers. This formidable trio operated forty steamers with an aggregate deadweight capacity in excess of a quarter of a million tons. Cardiganshire men figured prominently among the crews of these vessels, both as deck officers and engineers; many of the latter had received their initial training at foundries in Aberystwyth and Cardigan. It should be emphasized, however, that seafarers from the county were also to be found serving on board ships other than those owned by their kinsmen at Cardiff, and also in the tramp fleets of the Clyde, north-east England and London. Large numbers of seamen from coastal communities in west Wales became dependent on the tramp steamers of Cardiff and elsewhere for their livelihood and there was often a closely related nucleus of Welsh-speakers among the crews.

Life was hard at sea. Seamen often worked for up to ninety hours each week, four hours on and four hours off, regardless of the weather. Living conditions aboard were often abysmal, with crowded verminous accommodation, primitive sanitary facilities, and food which was generally tedious and sometimes inedible. There was no formal leave at that time and women living in coastal villages were well-used to bringing up their families single-handed in the absence of their husbands. Deprived of the solace of family life, seamen looked elsewhere for spiritual comfort. Many Cardiganshire seamen were deeply devout Christians, who held services on their vessels in distant ports on Sunday evenings. Other seamen, meanwhile, found 'alternative' attractions and several who might not have tippled in their native villages were only too familiar with the bars of 'Tiger Bay' and other sailortowns all over the world. Despite its hardships, however, going to sea offered far greater opportunities to young men from the coastal communities, especially when compared with their country cousins. Diligent and able youths might, with good fortune, find themselves commanding vessels at the age of thirty, and the more enterprising in their midst, such as Evan Thomas or James Jenkins, could become shipowners in their own right.

The First World War marked a turning point in many aspects of the social and economic history of Wales. At Cardiff, most shipping companies suffered considerable losses, with Radcliffe losing twenty-five vessels to enemy action. Nevertheless, the war brought inflated freight rates in its wake, a factor which tempted some investors to enter into shipowning, among them two brothers from Blaencelyn near Llangrannog. In 1915 Captain Evan Owen, an experienced master who had served with a number of Cardiff firms, set up a company in partnership with E. L. Williams of Penarth, while in 1916 his elder brother David (who had been a master with Radcliffe's since 1887) also established himself as a shipowner at Cardiff. By 1919 Owen's somewhat incongruously named Anglo-Belgique Shipping Co. Ltd. operated six steamers, while his brother's County Shipping Co. Ltd. had two vessels.

Late in 1920, however, Cardiff's brief yet spectacular post-war shipping boom collapsed and the port's coal trade stagnated as a result of the advent of oil maritime fuel and the flooding of the market by reparation coal from Germany. During the 1920s many Cardiff shipping companies either abandoned, or were forced out of business. David Owen was forced to sell up in 1924; John Mathias and Sons wound up their shipping interests in the same year, and James Jenkins sold his two remaining ships in 1927. Evan Owen struggled on until Barclays Bank foreclosed on him in September 1933. Of the Cardiganshire-founded firms, this left only Radcliffe's in existence, but the difficulties prevalent at that time are reflected in the fact that eleven of their sixteen ships were laid up in June 1933.

Radcliffe's continued to recruit crew members from Cardiganshire at this time, largely because the firm's marine superintendent was Captain B. T. Morris of Bryngwyn, near Newcastle Emlyn. Many seamen from the area, however, found employment with tramping firms on the north-east coast, particularly Walter Runciman's Newcastle-based 'Moor Line', and others found their way to some of the great liner companies; Captain David Francis James of New Quay was commodore of the British India Line in the 1930s, while Captain John Treasure Jones of Cardigan became the well-known master of some of Cunard's passenger liners, such as the *Queen Mary*. Most mariners from Cardiganshire, however, were manning the tramp fleets of Cardiff and the north-east coast when the Second World War broke out in September 1939. For them there was no 'phoney war'; the first Cardiff ship was lost to enemy action within five days of 3 September, and Radcliffe's lost eleven vessels during the war, several of them among the north Atlantic convoys which were vital to Britain's survival. By 1945, 30,000 merchant seamen had lost their lives, with many Cardiganshire men in their midst.

Cardiff emerged into an uncertain post-war world in which the demand for south Wales steam coal had all but disappeared; coal exports from the port in the late 1940s averaged only around a million tons per annum. The decline in the city's status as a major port and shipowning centre during the 1950s meant that it was no longer the Mecca for seamen from Cardiganshire that it had been at the turn of the century. The economically buoyant 1950s witnessed the emergence of a far wider range of occupations, which removed the economic necessity of going to sea to earn a living. Some young men from the county still went to sea, but they served with companies based in London or even overseas, manning oil tankers and bulk carriers. Since the late 1950s, moreover, a revolution has taken place in merchant shipping world-wide. Ships have generally become much larger, there are fewer of them, and they can be operated by smaller crews. The merchant fleets of third-world countries have expanded enormously in recent years, to the detriment of the British merchant marine, while the low wage costs of seamen from countries such as Russia or the Philippines have resulted in a further contraction of employment opportunities at sea. The combined effect of all these factors is that by today hardly anyone from Cardiganshire goes to sea to earn a living.

Maritime activity, however, has not totally disappeared from the county. As recently as 1987, Captain Roger Meredith of Aberystwyth made a brave but short-lived attempt to revive trade at the port by establishing Ystwyth Shipping Ltd.. The little motor coaster *Sara M*, of which he was master owner, arrived at Aberystwyth on 23 October 1987 with a cargo of timber from Sweden for a local building firm. By March 1988, however, he was forced to sell the vessel, and the much hoped-for revival of maritime trade at the port never materialized. More successful was the shipbuilding firm, F. L. Steelcraft, based on the mouth of the River Leri, near Ynys-las. In December 1983 this company launched a 106-foot steel schooner which is still in service in the West Indies, while in the spring of 1991 it completed an unusual floating fire station to be moored on the Thames at Lambeth.

In the maritime history of Cardiganshire, therefore, the wheel has come full circle. Just as fishing was the main maritime activity in the county in the sixteenth century, so it is today. During the intervening centuries, the county's maritime activity developed from fishing to coastal trading, and achieved its zenith in the nineteenth century when ships from Cardiganshire sailed to all parts of the globe. The county's seamen went on to man the tramp steamers which distributed the 'black diamonds' of south Wales all over the world. Within the last forty years, a tradition of seafaring that had evolved gradually over many centuries has disappeared, and it is unlikely ever to be fully revived.[22]

[22]I am indebted to Mr David Jenkins, formerly of the Department of Continuing Studies, University of Wales, Aberystwyth, for his advice and comments. This chapter is dedicated to the memory of the author's father, Mr Samuel Jenkins, who died on 10 April 1993. A native of Aber-porth and a descendant of a long line of seafarers, he had a deep and abiding interest in the maritime history of his native county.

CHAPTER 10

COMMERCIAL RELATIONS

Moelwyn I. Williams

Introduction

BEFORE the coming of the railways to Cardiganshire in the second half of the nineteenth century, the cheapest and most reliable means of transport was water.[1] In this land-locked region of west Wales, traffic along the pre-turnpike roads and mountain tracks was extremely difficult and often hazardous, though not impossible.[2] Even at the beginning of the nineteenth century, Benjamin H. Malkin knew of 'no district so confined within itself' and found that a letter 'is two complete days in going from Havod to Cardigan a distance of only forty miles within the county'.[3]

In view of the unsatisfactory state of the roads and primitive trackways, full advantage was taken, wherever convenient, of the facilities afforded by the numerous creeks, inlets, and landing places which dotted the coastline between the Dyfi estuary and the Teifi. The general dependency on water transport in the eighteenth century may be gauged by the fact that in 1768 there were in England and Wales some 580 places from and to which goods could be sent by water.[4] Of that total, fifty-three ports and creeks were located along the Welsh coast between Chepstow and Chester and no fewer than twelve such places were to be found along the coast of Cardiganshire between Cardigan and Aberleri. In addition, there were small landing-places along the two navigable rivers – the Dyfi and the Teifi. The Teifi was navigable from Cardigan to the village of Llechryd where slates, tin, and the agricultural produce of the rich Vale of Teifi had once been transported by barge and small boats to the port of Cardigan for shipment coastwise and to Ireland. The Teifi itself was at one time 'full of coracle men' engaged in the profitable fishing of its famous salmon, 'the best and largest in Britain'. The beaver was also present there 'as nowhere in Britain', providing quantities of pelts (skins) for the hatting industry far beyond the shores of Cardigan Bay.[5] Even in the Middle Ages both Cardigan and Aberystwyth were important centres of a not inconsiderable fishing industry, but there was a difference between the two centres insofar as Cardigan fishermen confined

---

[1] In 1763 land carriage of lead-ore from Esgair-mwyn to the port of Aberystwyth was 14s. per ton, whereas its carriage by sea from Aberystwyth to Swansea was only 1s. per ton.
[2] R. R. Davies, *Conquest, Co-existence and Change: Wales 1063–1415* (Oxford, 1987), pp.144–5.
[3] B. H. Malkin, *The Scenery, Antiquities, and Biography of South Wales* (2nd edn., 2 vols., London, 1807), II, p.25.
[4] Baldwin's *London Directory* (11th edn., London, 1768).
[5] D. Defoe, *A Tour through England and Wales* (2 vols., London, 1927), II, p.59.

themselves mainly to salmon-fishing on the Teifi. It would appear, therefore, that the port of Cardigan was for some time much busier than Aberystwyth, for besides being the centre of the trade along the Teifi valley it also had a long-standing maritime connection with Irish ports.[6]

The Dyfi was navigable as far inland as the village of Derwen-las which, though situated within Montgomeryshire, was accessible to the north Cardiganshire villages of Glandyfi, Eglwys-fach, Furnace, Tre'r-ddôl and Taliesin for the exchange of local produce for goods and commodities brought up the Dyfi from the port of Aberdyfi.[7] But more significant was the 'creek' at Garreg, a mile or so down river from Derwen-las, where once there were smelting-houses and silver mills, and where the lead trade was made possible by access downriver to Aberdyfi.[8] Consequently, Aberdyfi was once the place where most of the lead ore of Cardiganshire was 'shipped off'.

Attention should also be directed to the ferry that once operated between Aberleri and Aberdyfi, which facilitated the conveyance of commodities and 'passengers and their horses from north Cardiganshire to Merionethshire and *vice versa*'.[9] Similarly, the ferry which once linked Cardiganshire and Pembrokeshire from a point adjacent to the port of Cardigan[10] also afforded trading facilities and passenger conveyance by water between those two counties and beyond.

It is evident, therefore, that the several ports, creeks, landing-places, navigable rivers and ferries combined to form a network of centres which were exploited for the promotion of the maritime and commercial interests of Cardiganshire from the Middle Ages onwards.

Maritime trade

Maritime activities along the Cardiganshire coastline in the eighteenth century were centred mainly on the herring fishing industry and its ancillary occupations. One of the commodities essential to the fishing trade was salt, and by the end of the seventeenth century the demand for it had increased both in trade and domestic use, for the local population depended heavily on salted fish and salted flesh of all kinds, including beef, pork and bacon. Salt had been imported from early times to meet the requirements of the castles of Cardiganshire and the neighbouring communities, especially after slaughtering oxen and cows and then 'preparing them for the larder after salting them'.[11] Continuity in the commercial connections arising out of the demand for salt is worthy of note, for salt had to be imported to Cardiganshire initially from La Rochelle (in French boats) and from Ireland (in Irish boats). Legislation accompanying the Salt Laws allowed unlimited exports of rock salt from Liverpool to Ireland, where it could be sold more cheaply than in England. This anomaly led to a considerable degree of smuggling along certain stretches of Cardigan Bay. In August 1704 New Quay was the centre of serious disorders when a number of customs officers from Aberdyfi were confronted with a situation in which they found 'three boats laden with salt very near the shore with a multitude of ye

---

[6]I. J. Sanders, 'Trade and industry in some Cardiganshire towns in the Middle Ages', *Ceredigion*, III, no.4 (1959), 327 et seq.

[7]M. I. Williams, 'The port of Aberdyfi in the eighteenth century', *NLWJ*, XVIII, no.1 (1973), 97–8.

[8]L. Morris, *Plans of Harbours, Bars, Bays and Roads in St George's Channel* (London, 1748), p.9.

[9]J. E. Lloyd, *The Story of Ceredigion* (Cardiff, 1937), p.60.

[10]E. M. Pritchard, *Cardigan Priory in the Olden Days* (London, 1904), p.35.

[11]R. A. Griffiths, 'Gentlemen and rebels in later mediaeval Cardiganshire', *Ceredigion*, V, no.2 (1965), 148–9.

country people to the [number] of above 150 men and 200 horses in order to the conveying of it away without payments of the Queen Dutyes'. With the subsequent relaxation of the Salt Laws, salt became more easily available from the English counties of Cheshire, Lancashire and Gloucestershire, and from Liverpool whence there was a 'considerable trade in Salt with Aberystwyth'.[12] Aberaeron, too, imported substantial quantities of salt from Ireland and Chester to meet the demands of its own fishing industry. Here salted herrings were in great demand among the poor people in the agricultural hinterland. It is also on record that people came from as far afield as Hereford 'to purchase baskets of the fish which were transported in panniers slung across packhorses'.[13]

The flourishing state of the Cardiganshire fisheries in the early decades of the eighteenth century is highlighted by Lewis Morris who, in 1745, was engaged to survey the harbours, bars and bays of St George's Channel.[14] On 5 October of that year Morris was in Aberystwyth and there he witnessed '47 fishing boats of about 12 ton each (being as many as could get out on that tide because of rough seas on the bar) took among them 2,160 maces of herrings which at 126 to the hundred and five of these hundreds to the mace come to 1,360,800 fish . . . all in one night'; he was of the opinion that this would often happen if Aberystwyth 'had a convenient harbour'. He further observed that Aberystwyth supplied the very middle of England with fresh herrings equal to, if not better, than those which were cured. Morris further noted that from the month of September to October 1745 there were fifty-nine sloops from Aberystwyth alone, and between Aberdyfi, Borth, Aberaeron and New Quay another fifty-eight made a total of ninety-seven fishing boats.[15] By the end of the century Aberystwyth was considered the largest fishing station in Cardigan Bay, providing employment for over 300 people operating seventy-five boats.

Besides the fishing industry, Lewis Morris observed that Cardiganshire was a county abounding with veins of lead and silver ore which, later on, were exported in goodly quantities, along with the products of local arboriculture and agriculture – oak bark, oak poles, corn and some manufactured goods.

By the early years of the eighteenth century, the volume and variety of foreign imports to Cardiganshire was impressive. In addition to wine and salt from France and Brittany, deals and brick-stones were imported from Norway, and rye from Amsterdam and Rotterdam. There were also various goods imported from the Iberian ports of Oporto, Bilbao and Lisbon. In 1704, for instance, a shipment of 930 oranges from Lisbon was saved from a wreck off Cardigan, and another of 17,300 oranges and lemons, destined for Lord Lisburne at Trawsgoed, 'got itself stranded at Llansantffraid'.[16] Tobacco, and sometimes tobacco pipes, were among other exotic goods which figure in the lists of cargoes carried coastwise to Cardiganshire. During the seventeenth century the north American trade with the great port of London was almost dominated by imports of tobacco and industrial raw material.[17] In consequence, the 'taking of' tobacco became fashionable and its

[12]G. Eyre Evans, *Aberystwyth and its Court Leet* (Aberystwyth, 1902), p.87.

[13]S. Campbell-Jones, 'Shipbuilding at New Quay, 1779–1878', *Ceredigion*, VII, nos.3–4 (1974–5), 273.

[14]Morris, *Plans of Harbours*, p.10.

[15]In October 1808 fishermen from Aberaeron and New Quay together caught nine million herrings in a single night. See W. J. Lewis, 'The condition of labour in mid-Cardiganshire in the early nineteenth century', *Ceredigion*, IV, no.4 (1963), 324.

[16]E. A. Lewis, 'The port books of the port of Cardigan in Elizabethan and Stuart times', *TCAS*, 7 (1930), 24.

[17]N. Zahedieh, 'London and the colonial consumer in the late seventeenth century', *ECHR*, XLVII, no.2 (1994), 239–61.

properties were advocated by many medical men. In the course of time, tobacco found its way to the Cardiganshire countryside as it did in even greater quantities to other parts of south Wales. Regular supplies were kept up by importation from the entrepôt ports of Bristol, London and Liverpool. Extant records indicate that as early as 1660 onwards imports of tobacco had been steadily increasing. On 14 July 1698, for example, an exceptional quantity of some 3,300 lbs of Virginia tobacco from Liverpool was unloaded from the *Providence* of Liverpool at the port of Cardigan.

In 1718 a tobacco addict composed *Cân o Senn iw hên Feistr Tobacco*[18] (A Song of Rebuke to his old Master Tobacco), the first publication of the first printing press set up on Welsh soil at Trerhedyn in the parish of Llandyfrïog, in 1718. Throughout the eighteenth century, tobacco and snuff were imported into Cardiganshire from Bristol and Liverpool. For instance, on 29 June 1785, '448 lbs of manufactured tobacco and 85 lbs of snuff' were unloaded from the *True Briton* from Liverpool on the quayside in Aberystwyth.[19]

During the eighteenth century Bristol developed into the 'Metropolis of the West' and its status influenced greatly the activities and commercial relations of several ports in south and west Wales, including the ports of Cardigan Bay. The other entrepôt ports – London, Exeter, Plymouth, Chester and Liverpool – were also centres frequented by west Wales shipping whence a wide range of merchandise was transported coastwise. But throughout the second half of the century national maritime trade was interrupted in no small measure by successive wars – the Seven Years War (1756–63), the American War of Independence (1776–83) and the Napoleonic Wars (1793–1815). Because of the uncertainty of the Mediterranean trade, the southern entrepôt trade was seriously affected and as a result Bristol attracted most of the trade of the south and west Wales ports. The Napoleonic Wars in particular affected the coastal trading between Wales and Ireland. Cardigan, for example, previous to that struggle had enjoyed 'a considerable export trade in lead and corn with Ireland'.[20] Oats, butter and other dairy products from Cardiganshire were sent in goodly quantities to Bristol, and even pigs were reared in Cardigan for Bristol drovers.[21] It is also most significant that some Bristol capitalists were engaged in the activities of the Cardiganshire lead mines.[22]

Commercial expansion

The second half of the eighteenth century witnessed two major developments which affected the nature and volume of maritime trade of all Cardiganshire ports and creeks. First, from *c*.1750 onwards, large areas of south Wales were becoming industrialized and consequently the distribution of the population between rural and industrial regions changed rapidly. The subsequent increase in the population of the non-agricultural regions created a corresponding increase in demand for the produce of the agricultural areas to feed the growing industrial work-force. Consequently, the agricultural regions of Cardiganshire (as of other Welsh counties) gradually responded. Local

[18]Written by Alban Thomas (d.1740?), cleric, poet, and translator, a native of Rhos, Blaen-porth.
[19]NLW MS 7980A.
[20]Revd John Evans, *Letters Written during a Tour of South Wales* (London, 1804), p.317.
[21]W. E. Minchinton, 'Bristol – metropolis of the west in the eighteenth century', *TRHS*, IV (1954), 74.
[22]F. Green, *Calendar of Crosswood Deeds* (Aberystwyth, 1927), p.143.

farmers were encouraged to adopt more enlightened methods of husbandry and to that end Thomas Johnes of Hafod, along with other local 'improvers', founded the Cardiganshire Agricultural Society in 1784, and later, in 1800, he himself published (from his own press) *A Cardiganshire Landlord's Advice to his Tenants*.

The Agricultural Society offered *inter alia* a number of premiums to those farmers who achieved certain specified standards in production, land reclamation and the planting of trees. Between 1786 and 1796 a million forest trees were planted in response to the premiums offered by the Society. It is believed that Thomas Johnes himself planted upwards of 5,000,000 trees within approximately 1,500 acres of his estate at Hafod Uchtryd. In this context it is worth nothing that, between 1794 and 1799, cargoes of oak, bark, cordwood and oak-poles were regularly shipped from Aberystwyth to Newry, Belfast, Strangford, Dublin, Waterford, Castleton, Dundalk and Drogheda in Ireland and to Douglas in the Isle of Man. During the same period 1,200 tons of oak-bark alone were exported to Ireland and the Isle of Man. Hazelnuts, too, were exported from Aberystwyth, as on 8 January 1796 when '35 bags of hazel nuts [containing] 229 bushels' were exported to Dublin. On 12 March following '5 tons of oak-bark and 2 tons of holly trees' were exported to Belfast.[23]

It is important to bear in mind that the highland region of Cardiganshire was said to be so full of cattle that it was described as 'the the nursery, the breeding place for the whole kingdom of England south of the Trent', but that these conditions were not due to the fertility of the region, for although the feeding of cattle required a rich soil, 'the breeding of them does not, the mountains and moors being as proper for that purpose as richer land'.[24] However, although there was a flourishing cattle trade, it had little bearing on the maritime trade of the county, for the cattle were driven on the hoof by the native drovers along the age-old trackways that cobwebbed the mid-Cardiganshire landscape.[25] Pigs were also driven in their thousands to south Wales and Bristol. Indeed, as late as 1880 a new trade in pigs began, and between August 1881 and August 1882, '25,000 pigs . . . were shipped by the Aberaeron Steam Packet Company to Bristol'.[26]

In order to facilitate the application of more efficient methods of husbandry in extensive areas of rural Cardiganshire, it was necessary to enrich the native soil which was high in acid content but deficient in alkali. Consequently there was an increased demand for lime. But it was first necessary to import the basic limestone in greater quantities from outside the county, mainly from Hook in south Pembrokeshire, Caldey Island, Gower, and occasionally from Aberthaw in the Vale of Glamorgan. When Richard Pococke visited Aberystwyth in *c.*1730, he noted that 'the town has a good harbour for small boats of which they have several employed chiefly in the herring-fishing [industry] and in bringing limestone from Milford Haven to make lime for manuring the land'. But having brought the lime to the ports and creeks it was then necessary to burn it to produce the required lime. Therefore coal, and more frequently culm,[27] had in turn to be brought coastwise

[23]For further details, see Ceredigion RO, ADX 119/53.
[24]Defoe, *A Tour through England and Wales*, II, p.59.
[25]H. Carter (ed.), *Atlas Cenedlaethol Cymru. National Atlas of Wales* (Cardiff, 1989). Section 4.4, Map 4.4c.
[26]D. L. Jones, 'Aberaeron: the community and seafaring, 1800–1900', *Ceredigion*, VI, no.2 (1969), 210.
[27]Culm (basically the waste dust from anthracite mining areas) was used generally since it was cheaper than coal and could be made to last longer by mixing it with clay; it was also sometimes made into briquettes for domestic use.

from the coal-producing areas such as Saundersfoot, Pen-bre and Swansea, whence came the best quality but most expensive coal. By 1840 limestone was also being imported from Red Wharf (Anglesey), Drogheda, Dundalk, Cork and the Skerries, and coal came from Flint, Neath, Newport, Llanelli and Porthcawl.[28] The limestone was processed in kilns which were often built by local merchants and the more enterprising farmers. Eventually lime-kilns proliferated along the coastline adjacent to the ports and creeks where the lime and fuel were brought. Many of the kilns are still visible, albeit in a decayed state, and perhaps providing the only landscape evidence that remains to remind the observer of the importance of lime, coal and culm in the economic life of Cardiganshire in the eighteenth and nineteenth centuries.

The second development which modified but also enhanced the commercial activities of Cardiganshire was centred on the lead mining industry south of the Rheidol, together with the increasing output of the Cwmsymlog, Darren, and Esgair-mwyn mines (especially after 1740), which exerted additional pressure on the port of Aberystwyth in particular.[29] By 1759 there were 'thirty to forty vessels of from fifteen to sixty tons burden constantly employed particularly in exporting lead-ore and black-jack, of which there were from three to four thousand tons annually shipped coastwise to South Wales, Flint and Chester'.[30] Similarly, at Llechryd, high above the port of Cardigan on the Teifi, the abundance of wood for the making of charcoal encouraged Benjamin Hammet to set up a tin-works in 1760. But here again the basic raw materials such as pig-iron, slab-iron and chemicals had to imported, mainly from Bristol, and brought up the River Teifi from Cardigan. The finished products were later brought down river and then exported from the port of Cardigan. Although situated on the Pembrokeshire side of the Teifi, the once important slate quarries at Cilgerran depended entirely on the maritime facilities afforded by the port of Cardigan and added to its importance. By 1840 there were as many as six quarries at work in the area, employing upwards of 120 persons.

These developments combined to create a real demand for more and perhaps bigger boats in which to carry the heavier cargoes of limestone, coal, culm, lead-ore and copper-ore. The volume of trade in the port of Aberystwyth had already increased to such an extent that in 1759 the so-called 'Big Fourteen of Aberystwyth' resolved to present a petition to Parliament requesting the relocation of the Customs Office from Aberdyfi to Aberystwyth. The petition was successful and in 1763 the Customs House was set up at Heol y Wig, Aberystwyth. William Mavor, an English tourist who visited Aberystwyth in *c*.1770, noted that the trade there 'was brisk and expanding' and that the exports from the harbour included 'oak-bark, birch-bark, oak-timber, lead-ore, black-jack, copper-ore, corn, butter, poultry and Welsh ale'. The imports included 'baulk-timber, deals, hemp, pitch, tar, rosin, Russian iron (items destined for use in the expanding ship-building industry), groceries, flax, porter, cider, wines, brandy, rum, Geneva etc'.

At the end of the eighteenth century the port of Cardigan was still a centre of vigorous trading activities. Indeed, during the period 1775–80 it was ranked ninth among the ten leading ports in the coastal trade of England and Wales (London excepted), measured in tonnage of their coastal shipping belonging to each port[31] and the proportion of their coastal shipping tonnage (fishing

[28]NLW, Aberystwyth Borough Records, F11; Ceredigion RO, ADX 119/53.
[29]W. J. Lewis, *Lead Mining in Wales* (Cardiff, 1967), p.108.
[30]NLW, Powis Castle Deeds and Documents.
[31]D. H. Aldcroft and M. Freeman, *Transport in the Industrial Revolution* (Manchester, 1983), p.151.

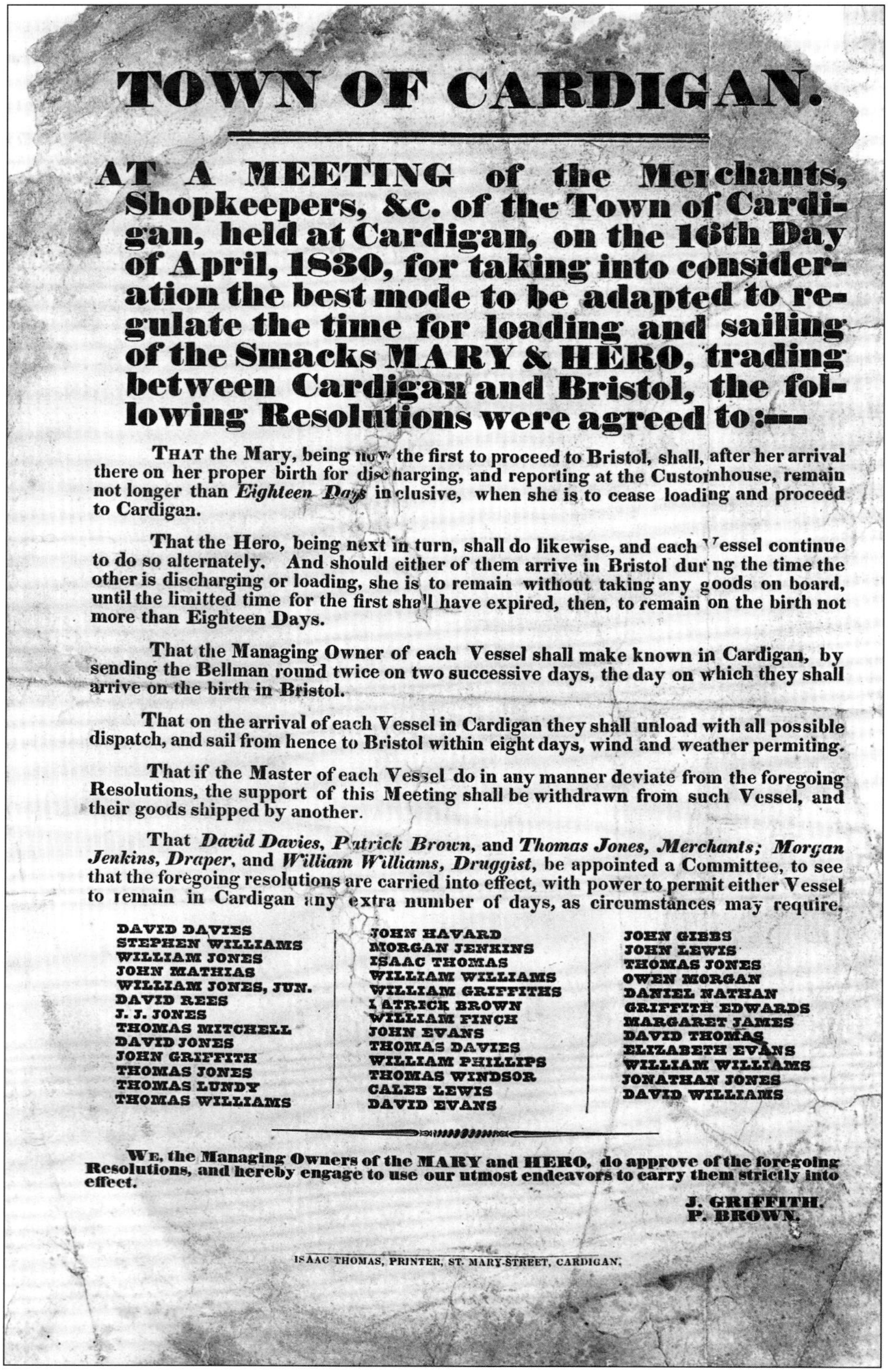

TOWN OF CARDIGAN.

AT A MEETING of the Merchants, Shopkeepers, &c. of the Town of Cardigan, held at Cardigan, on the 16th Day of April, 1830, for taking into consideration the best mode to be adapted to regulate the time for loading and sailing of the Smacks MARY & HERO, trading between Cardigan and Bristol, the following Resolutions were agreed to:—

THAT the Mary, being now the first to proceed to Bristol, shall, after her arrival there on her proper birth for discharging, and reporting at the Customhouse, remain not longer than *Eighteen Days* inclusive, when she is to cease loading and proceed to Cardigan.

That the Hero, being next in turn, shall do likewise, and each Vessel continue to do so alternately. And should either of them arrive in Bristol during the time the other is discharging or loading, she is to remain without taking any goods on board, until the limitted time for the first shall have expired, then, to remain on the birth not more than Eighteen Days.

That the Managing Owner of each Vessel shall make known in Cardigan, by sending the Bellman round twice on two successive days, the day on which they shall arrive on the birth in Bristol.

That on the arrival of each Vessel in Cardigan they shall unload with all possible dispatch, and sail from hence to Bristol within eight days, wind and weather permiting.

That if the Master of each Vessel do in any manner deviate from the foregoing Resolutions, the support of this Meeting shall be withdrawn from such Vessel, and their goods shipped by another.

That *David Davies, Patrick Brown*, and *Thomas Jones, Merchants; Morgan Jenkins, Draper*, and *William Williams, Druggist*, be appointed a Committee, to see that the foregoing resolutions are carried into effect, with power to permit either Vessel to remain in Cardigan any extra number of days, as circumstances may require.

DAVID DAVIES	JOHN HAVARD	JOHN GIBBS
STEPHEN WILLIAMS	MORGAN JENKINS	JOHN LEWIS
WILLIAM JONES	ISAAC THOMAS	THOMAS JONES
JOHN MATHIAS	WILLIAM WILLIAMS	OWEN MORGAN
WILLIAM JONES, JUN.	WILLIAM GRIFFITHS	DANIEL NATHAN
DAVID REES	PATRICK BROWN	GRIFFITH EDWARDS
J. J. JONES	WILLIAM FINCH	MARGARET JAMES
THOMAS MITCHELL	JOHN EVANS	DAVID THOMAS
DAVID JONES	THOMAS DAVIES	ELIZABETH EVANS
JOHN GRIFFITH	WILLIAM PHILLIPS	WILLIAM WILLIAMS
THOMAS JONES	THOMAS WINDSOR	JONATHAN JONES
THOMAS LUNDY	CALEB LEWIS	DAVID WILLIAMS
THOMAS WILLIAMS	DAVID EVANS	

WE, the Managing Owners of the MARY and HERO, do approve of the foregoing Resolutions, and hereby engage to use our utmost endeavors to carry them strictly into effect.

J. GRIFFITH.
P. BROWN.

ISAAC THOMAS, PRINTER, ST. MARY-STREET, CARDIGAN.

Fig. 40: Regulations regarding the loading and sailing of the smacks *Mary* and *Hero* at Cardigan, 1830. (*Copyright National Library of Wales*).

vessels excluded). That is to say, the smaller ports tended to have a much bigger coastal than foreign trade, so that the average tonnage entering coastwise into some Welsh ports was greater than the total entering from foreign ports. It follows, therefore, that in common with other ports the coastal trade in the Cardigan Bay region represented the exchange of goods between places whose limited hinterland was not easily or readily connected by internal or overland transport.[32] In 1835 the total number of ships belonging to the port of Cardigan is given as 291, with an aggregate tonnage of 15,195. In the year ending 5 January 1830, four foreign and 582 coasting vessels were cleared outwards. The chief imports in that year included timber from Norway and North America, coal from Liverpool and south Wales, culm from Swansea and Pembrokeshire and manufactured goods from Bristol which found their way to several shops in the town of Cardigan and the adjacent rural areas. In 1836, for instance, a trade list of freight from Bristol to Cardigan included 350 items of various household goods and utensils, implements, fruit, coffee (in casks in 25 lb bags), brandy, cider at 1fi*d.* per gallon, rum, spirits of all kinds, tea, tobacco, and spices. Freight sent outwards from Cardigan to Bristol included butter, barley, wheat, oats, rolls of leather, basil kips, calf skins, and eggs in boxes.

The extent to which the port of Cardigan served the surrounding countryside was illustrated in a public notice that appeared on the Welsh Back in Bristol in 1826 stating: 'For Cardigan / the smack *Phoenix* / John James, master / A Regular Trader / Now lying at the Back and ready to take goods for the undermentioned places, and will sail in ten days after commencing – Aberaeron, Aberporth, Boncath, Dinas, Eglwyswrw, . . . Kilgerran, Kenarth, Llanfyrnach, Llanarth, Llanddewi Brefi, Llanrhystud, Llechryd, New Quay, . . . Penbryn etc.' Similarly, on 23 January 1852, the following advertisement appeared in Cardigan: 'Just arrived a quantity of superior French white potatoes from the lower Seine Valley, imported expressly for early seed and on sale at Warehouses on the quay . . .'

The port of Cardigan gradually lost its importance as a centre for maritime trade, for here as elsewhere in Cardiganshire the advent of the railway heralded the demise of the port. The extension of the railway from Whitland in 1880, the later silting up of the Teifi estuary and finally the adverse economic consequences of the Great War combined 'to terminate the maritime trade of this one-time hive of industry'.[33]

At the beginning of the nineteenth century Aberystwyth, apart from its general commercial activities, was deemed the largest fishing station in Cardigan Bay. It provided employment for some 300 persons operating 'nine second class and sixty eight third class boats', but it was largely dependent on boats from Hoylake, Fleetwood and Liverpool. Aberaeron also had its own fleet of sixty-eight boats, in addition to a large number that came from elsewhere, but here too the industry was in decline.[34] The dearth of herrings off the coast of Aberystwyth in the 1840s was so acute that they were imported from the Skerries, Caernarfon, Port Murray, Dublin, the Isle of Man and even from Cardigan! Between 29 August and 20 October 1860 some 144 tons of herring[35] were exported from those centres to Aberystwyth. Lobsters were also imported from Pwllheli. Throughout the second half of the nineteenth century the fishing industry continued to decline. Following the First

[32]Ibid., p.180.
[33]J. G. Jenkins, 'The port of Cardigan', *Maritime Wales*, no.8 (1984), 26–93.
[34]C. Matheson, *Wales and the Sea Fisheries* (Cardiff, 1929), p.38.
[35]Approximately 322,560 herrings.

World War, the inshore fisheries of Cardigan Bay were in a 'parlous condition', and by the late 1920s Aberystwyth had only nine small boats employed in fishing for herrings, whiting and mackerel.[36] It is sometimes claimed that, as a result of the general commercial developments which occurred in Cardiganshire in the second half of the nineteenth century, the fishing industry suffered a 'sudden demise'. However, it should be remembered that fishing in Cardiganshire had been mainly herring-fishing which generally occurred between September and late December each year, and that it was a part-time occupation pursued mainly by 'fishermen-peasants' who tended to combine agricultural, or related work, with fishing. Later in the nineteenth century, and in the twentieth century, even townsmen are known to have combined fishing with another occupation.[37]

The changing social scene

In the closing decades of the eighteenth century, but more especially during the early decades of the nineteenth century, the flurry of commercial activity in and around the several ports of Cardiganshire reflected in many ways contemporary changes in the economic and social scene. The emergence of new social classes created new patterns of material requirements which were reflected in the variety of cargoes imported into· the county. The increasing number of shopkeepers – apothecaries, grocers, drapers, milliners and other retailers – formed a 'shopocracy',[38] the new bourgeoisie who eventually exercised a dominant role in local financial, political, and religious affairs. They were among the richest members of society and some, like the landed gentry, were able to build new houses or renovate or rebuild existing houses. Moreover, the gradual increase in population generally created new demands for building materials – stone (Bath and Portland), bricks, cement, tiles, slates, laths and timber – which in turn created further demands on shipping capacity which was reflected in the transportation coastwise of wrought iron, anchors, sails and masts from Swansea, Bristol, London and elsewhere. On 22 March 1786, *The Grace and Peggy* arrived in Aberystwyth from London with a cargo which included '3 masts, 3 bowsprits, 1 gaff, 2 masts two booms, 2 gaffs (ten yards), for two sloops; 8 bundles of sails for ships and 2 sloops'.[39] Again, on 28 March, the *Anne and Peggy* arrived in Aberystwyth from Swansea with '3 tons of wrought iron, 10 anchors, and a suit of sails for a sloop'.

The local building industry in and around the main ports was also dependent on the import of some essential materials. For instance, on 11 July 1785, 20,000 slates were unloaded at Aberystwyth from *The Nancy* of Beaumaris, and the following day a further 14,000 slates were unloaded from the *Hannah*, also from Beaumaris. In short, between 31 May and 29 December 1785, some 75,000 slates were imported to Aberystwyth from Caernarfon and Beaumaris. Again, between 3 May 1785 and 3 May 1786, upwards of 20,000 bricks and tiles were brought by sea to Aberystwyth from Bridgwater and Liverpool.

Household furniture and apparel were also frequently imported from London, Bristol, Liverpool and Barmouth (probably to be re-exported); 'earthenware' too was included in cargoes imported

---

[36]Matheson, *Wales and the Sea Fisheries*, p.41.
[37]Jones, 'Aberaeron: the community and seafaring, 1800–1900', 215.
[38]I. G. Jones (ed.), *Aberystwyth: 1277–1977* (Llandysul, 1977), pp.96–112.
[39]NLW MS 7980A.

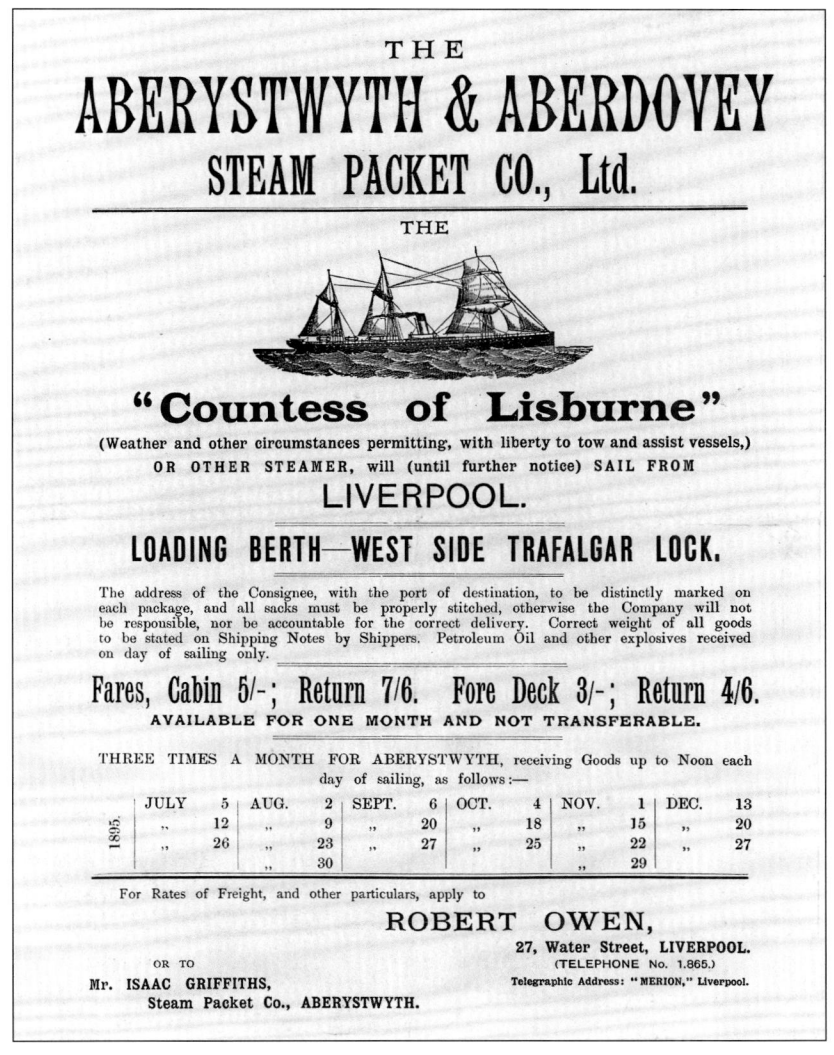

Fig. 41: A poster depicting the sailing times of the steamer *Countess of Lisburne* from Liverpool to Aberystwyth, *c.*1900. (*Copyright National Library of Wales*).

from Bideford, Liverpool and Chester. On 27 October 1785 '12 chains, iron ware, 2 dozen iron pots and kettles' were imported from Liverpool. A more 'usual' cargo, imported from Bristol, arrived at Aberystwyth on board *The Fame* on 21 September 1785, consisting of '1 h'hd treacle; 5 h'hds and 12 k'kns Muscovado sugar; 4 tierces and 10 hampers of refined sugar; 10 sides of glass; . . . 2 trusses linen drapery; 4 bags logwood; 2 boxes ginger bread; . . . 3 chests, 5 boxes English hard soap containing 16 cwts 20lbs; 3 boxes English tallow candles containing 17 dozen; 2 boxes 2 baskets of tobacco [cont.] 3 cwts and 30 lbs; 2 baskets of snuff qty 200 lbs'.[40]

It also appears from the list of goods imported that there was a significant demand for more exotic goods such as tobacco, snuff, spirits and wines which, perhaps, reflected a growing affluence among

[40]Ibid.

the new social classes which were emerging in late eighteenth- and early nineteenth-century Cardiganshire. The following items arrived at Aberystwyth on board the *Fanny* from Liverpool on 6 April 1786: '1 h'hd containing 699 lbs of manufactured tobacco; 3 casks [cont.] 20 cwts refined sugar; 1 pipe, 1 hamper containing 143 galls red wine; 2 casks cont. 36 galls of white Spanish wine; 1 cask cont. 6 galls of rum; 1 cask [cont.] 6 galls brandy; 1 cask cont. 34 galls of sweets;[41] 6 barrels of porter; 3 bags of dyewood; 3 casks of groceries; 1 box of apothecary ware; 1 chest cont. 60 lbs manufactured tobacco'. Again, on 21 July 1786, the *Nancy* sailed into Aberystwyth harbour with the following cargo from Liverpool: '1 h'hd cont. 6 cwt refined sugar; 1 cask containing 2 cwts ground sugar; 6 pieces of balk qts two loads [of] fir timber; 3 parcels cont. 57 lbs manufactured tobacco; 8 casks cont. 84 galls rum; 1 cask cont. 12 galls brandy; 2 casks cont. 22 galls Geneva; 2 casks cont. 40 galls sweets; 2 casks 1 hamper cont. 51 galls white Spanish wine (sound); 2 casks 2 hampers cont. 84 galls red Port-Wine; 2 casks 2 hampers cont. 36 galls red port-wine; 5 cwt flax; 5 crates earthenware; 235 bushels white-salt'.[42]

It is interesting to observe that cargoes of coal, culm and lime were frequently conveyed along the coast to neighbouring creeks. Such cargoes were conveyed from Aberystwyth to Clarach, Wallog and Borth. Occasionally Llansanffraid, Aberaeron and New Quay were served in that way. There were also numerous instances of passengers (some of them emigrants to America) taking advantage of the 'water-conveyance' from Aberystwyth to Barmouth, Porthmadog, Caernarfon and Liverpool and *vice versa*.

Throughout the first half of the nineteenth century, the pattern of trade along the Cardiganshire coast continued unchanged even though the volume varied from port to port. The economic demands of local agricultural communities were nevertheless gradually changing. For example, whereas limestone had been imported in large quantities for use on the land, during the latter part of the nineteenth century there were increasing demands for basic slag and superphosphates as well as guano – the latter especially after the First World War. The new fertilizers were imported mainly from Europe.

From *c*.1894 to 1913 the foreign trade of Aberystwyth was mainly with the following ports, whence an impressive array of cargoes came: Antwerp – timber, cement, railway rails, iron pipes, drainpipes, clay bricks; Alderney – dynamite; Fredrikstad – timber, herring-boards, laths, poles and 'wood goods'; Gefla – deals and boards; Ghent – cement, basic slag, superphosphates; Gothenburg – timber; Halifax (Nova Scotia) – timber; Landerneau – basic slag, superphosphates; Mobile Bay (Gulf of Mexico) – timber; Calais – timber; Norville (Canada) – timber; Piteå (Sweden) – deals, timber; Riga – timber; Rouen – superphosphates; Roscoff – onions; Sheet Harbour (Nova Scotia) – timber; Spry Bay (Nova Scotia) – 'wood goods'; Trondheim – 'woodgoods'; Uleaborg (Finland) – timber.[43]

Between 8 July 1913 and 24 November 1922 no foreign vessel (apart from one inward shipment in 1915) entered the port of Aberystwyth, and during the next seventeen years (1922–39) there were apparently only forty inward sailings from foreign countries. Imports then comprised in the main cement and drainpipes from Antwerp; cement 'in bags' from Brussels; superphosphates 'in bags' from Vlaardingen, Rouen and Ghent; basic slag from Ghent and Antwerp; deals and boards from

[41] Wine that is not dry.
[42] NLW MS 7980A.
[43] Ceredigion RO, CE/abm/2/3–4.

Fig. 42: Old sailors from Borth photographed by John Thomas. (*Copyright National Library of Wales*).

Kötka (Finland) and Sundsvall; herring-boards and lath poles from Fredrikstad; and onions from Roscoff. Basic slag and superphosphates generally arrived in bags for the Farmers' Co-operative stores and local merchants, as well as for individual farmers in the neighbouring villages. The inter-war years therefore witnessed the gradual demise of the port of Aberystwyth.

Likewise the coastal trade of Cardiganshire gradually declined partly because of the improved state of inland traffic, but mainly as a result of the extension of the railways to the county. First came the railway from Shrewsbury to Aberystwyth in 1864, to be followed in 1867 by the Milford Junction line that ran from Carmarthen via Lampeter and Strata Florida to Aberystwyth.[44] Nevertheless, goods and commodities of all kinds continued to be imported by sea and distributed to several inland and coastal villages. In 1867 cargoes of different varieties were landed in Aberystwyth destined for Abermagwr, Borth, Capel Bangor, Cwmystwyth, Cnwch-coch, Devil's Bridge, Goginan (oil for the lead mines), Llangwyryfon, Llanrhystud, Pont-rhyd-y-groes, Rhosgellan,

[44]These were later followed by lines from Carmarthen to Llandysul 1867; Whitland to Cardigan 1880; Lampeter to Aberaeron 1911.

Tregaron and Ystumtuen. Coal came from Chester, Flint, Neath, Newport, Porthcawl and Llanelli; grain from Gloucester, Poole, Plymouth and Yarmouth; flour and oatmeal from Drogheda; lime from Red Wharf Bay, Caernarfon, Milford and Tenby; earthenware from Bideford; slates from Caernarfon, Aberdyfi and Cardigan; potatoes from Belfast, Newry and the Isle of Man; wheat from St David's; general cargoes from Bristol and Liverpool and, less frequently, from London.[45] Many imported items were assigned to individual local traders: in June 1869 Thomas Powell, grocer of Aberystwyth, received 'two tierces of sugar and 2 lumps of cheese' from Bristol; H. Davies, ironmonger of Aberystwyth, in turn received '1 bundle [of] whisks, 2 hampers of brushes; 4 bars of iron, 4 casks of greese [sic]; 1 cask of whiting, 1 cask ockre [sic]' also from Bristol; Richard James, a local tanner, received a delivery of 'salted hides, sewing machines, shoes, and candles' from Bristol. Local gentry such as Lord Lisburne at Ffosrhydgaled also depended on supplies transported by sea to Aberystwyth. Large quantities of liquor, wines and ales were regularly imported to replenish the stocks of twenty-eight local hotels and inns. Some indication of the astonishingly wide variety of goods shipped to various consignees in Aberystwyth and the surrounding district is given in the cargo carried in the *Countess of Lisburne* from Liverpool on 24 January 1908, which included: 'bags of potatoes, sugar, rice, lard, cheese, salt, bacon, oranges, dates, apples, nuts, tomatoes, onions, grapes, peas, butter, soda, cases of salmon, plums, tabioca [sic], crystals, sardines, ham, tea, starch and mahogany boards'. The more melancholy side of life was also, at times, catered for, as in 1909 when the *SS Dora* carried as part of her cargo from Liverpool '72 coffin boards'.[46]

Exports from Aberystwyth and district were still made up of lead ore, black-jack, timber, kips, sheepskins, porter, ale and rags. On 27 March 1860 lead ore was exported from the Lisburne mine, Cwmerfin and Goginan mines, Cwmystwyth, Allt-y-crib, south Darren, east Darren, Cefnbrwyno and other mines. Bark was also exported to Newry, Derry and Glasgow. The export of zinc ore advanced appreciably between 1860 and 1888 but subsequently there was an irreversible decline in that trade. In short, by the end of the first decade of the twentieth century the whole of the export trade from Aberystwyth had become moribund. The declining coastal trade was confined mainly to general merchandise imported from Liverpool, Bristol and sometimes London. At the outbreak of the Great War the inward coastal trade also languished and from 1914 until 1926 there were no commercial activities *per se* in and around the port of Aberystwyth. There were subsequently intermittent sailings into the port between 1926 and 1939, but thereafter came a period of decline and eventual commercial desuetude. On the basis of surviving records, it would appear that the last cargo exported from Aberystwyth consisted of 'stone dust' sent to Liverpool on board the *SS Oak Villa* on 16 May 1935;[47] the last substantial cargo imported into Aberystwyth appears to have been in 1954 when the *Lady Sophia* arrived from Pwllheli with 'chippings' for the County Council.

A similar sequence of declining fortunes befell other Cardiganshire ports and creeks. By the beginning of the First World War the handful of ketches which still remained in New Quay 'carrying cargoes of coal and culm' had nearly all vanished.[48] Aberaeron, in turn, declined

[45]NLW, Aberystwyth Harbour Records F11.

[46]Aberystwyth Borough Records, Manifest Books F12.

[47]Aberystwyth Borough Records, Manifest Books F12. See also T. H. Merchant, 'Aberystwyth harbour since 1925', *Ceredigion*, IV, no.3 (1962), 281–9; D. Jenkins, *The Passing of a Port 1860–1939* (Aberystwyth, 1980).

[48]Campbell-Jones, 'Shipbuilding at New Quay', 63.

appreciably, especially after the railway connecting it with Lampeter was completed in 1911. By 1942 the last commercial vessel had sailed out of the port of Cardigan. By the end of the twentieth century most, if not all, of the old centres of commercial activity which dotted the Cardiganshire coastline had been transformed, mainly into anchorages for pleasure boats. Unfortunately, these developments have either blurred or removed visual evidence of the use made of these centres and the original purposes for which they were constructed and maintained over several centuries.

CHAPTER 11

THE TOWNS OF CARDIGANSHIRE, 1800–1995

C. Roy Lewis and Sandra E. Wheatley

Introduction

THE last two centuries have witnessed major changes in the urban structure of Britain; these have included increases in the number, size and function of towns, internal redevelopment, decentralization, suburbanization and the progressive spread of urban influences into the countryside. While these changes have been most pronounced in and around the main metropolitan centres, the same general processes have been at work throughout Britain and have left their mark on all towns, albeit less strongly and on a more limited scale in small places. It is the aim of this chapter to explore the proposition that the towns of rural Cardiganshire, which, in terms of size and status lie towards the bottom of the urban hierarchy, have been shaped by many of the same trends and processes which have been widespread in their operation and impact. Despite this, there are some features which derive from their location in a peripheral rural area with a low and scattered population. In such an area of limited opportunities, small towns play a vital role as both service and employment centres. In specific terms, this study will examine the inherited form of towns at the beginning of the nineteenth century; the impact of new functions on that legacy since 1800 and the expansion of the urban system through the creation of new towns; the processes of suburbanization and decentralization which commenced in the nineteenth century and accelerated in the twentieth; and the characteristics of the contemporary urban system.

Before addressing these matters, it is necessary to specify what constitutes a town for the purposes of this study. In the absence of a standard definition which enjoys universal support, it is appropriate to focus on those places which meet some or all of a number of criteria or indicators of urban standing in rural Wales – a minimum population of around 1,000 housed in a compact built-up area, an agricultural market, the supply of shops, services and professional facilities for the local area, the presence of special functions (such as maritime, tourist, industrial or educational activities), which help to sustain an urban economy. On the basis of this mix of criteria, there are seven settlements in Cardiganshire which warrant consideration as towns: Aberystwyth, Cardigan, Lampeter, Aberaeron, Llandysul, Tregaron and New Quay. Ranging in population size in 1991 from 11,576 in Aberystwyth (but nearly 19,000 if its student population and all of its peripheral

[1]Present-day population figures are based on 1991 Census data and have been taken from *Ceredigion Local Plan: Consultation Draft. Volume 1: Written Statement* (Aberaeron, 1995).

extensions are included) to 915 in New Quay,[1] these places certainly act as service centres for their immediate localities and contain (or have in the past) a variety of special economic activities which enhance their status. In passing, it should be noted that three other towns are also closely tied to the county: Machynlleth in the north, and Newcastle Emlyn and Llanybydder in the Teifi valley.[2] However, since they fall under the administrative jurisdiction of neighbouring counties, they will not be considered here.

Continuity of urban form

At the beginning of the nineteenth century the inherited urban legacy comprised the Anglo-Norman market towns of Aberystwyth, Cardigan and Lampeter (although the borough itself was a Welsh foundation in 1285),[3] and Tregaron and Llandysul, which had emerged as indigenous focal points for their local catchments. Each was small and had a relatively simple layout.[4] One of the biggest – Aberystwyth – with a population of 1,758 in 1801, was still largely contained within the curtilage of its town walls, though there was a small suburb at Trefechan. The street pattern was the plan carried forward from Edward I's bastide of 1277, and was dominated by the cross roads formed by the meeting of the main axes of Bridge Street – Pier Street and Church Street (Upper Great Darkgate Street) – Great Darkgate Street. The only other street of note was Little Darkgate (Eastgate), which lay parallel to Great Darkgate. The town bore all the hallmarks of its medieval structure: a crumbling castle and a decayed perimeter wall, a central market place, burgage plots, intra-mural open spaces and a small harbour. Cardigan's nucleus, housing a population of 1,911 in 1801, was even more basic; it was dictated by one major thoroughfare (High Street), which ran northwards along the ridge from the castle overlooking the crossing point of the River Teifi. This linear axis was intersected by a number of smaller streets, most notably Market Lane, St Mary Street and a lane to the quay (now Quay Street). By the late eighteenth century extensions had been built, outside this formerly walled medieval core, eastwards towards St Mary's Church, westwards towards the quay and the River Mwldan, and northwards beyond High Street into Pendre. Figure 43 reveals the layout in 1834.

Lower down the settlement hierarchy, Lampeter comprised little more than the High Street and St Peter's Church, its small extent reflecting both its insignificance as a market and its very limited employment base. Expansion into Market Street, College Street and Bridge Street occurred later, largely in the second half of the nineteenth century, when it took on a much more developed urban appearance. Likewise, Tregaron and Llandysul had simple structures. Tregaron had a rather loose layout around its central triangular-shaped 'Square'.[5] Two features underpinned its form – the convergence of roads on the bridging point of the River Brenig and the church dedicated to St Caron. However, apart from the Square itself and perhaps a secondary cluster in Pentref to the

[2] A description of the wider urban system is given in C. R. Lewis, 'Retail trade and spheres of influence', in H. Carter (ed.), *Atlas Cenedlaethol Cymru. National Atlas of Wales* (Cardiff, 1989), Section 8.7.
[3] I. Soulsby, *The Towns of Medieval Wales* (Chichester, 1983).
[4] Valuable descriptions of the internal structure of castle towns are included in H. Carter, *The Towns of Wales* (Cardiff, 1965).
[5] E. Jones, 'Tregaron: the sociology of a market town in central Cardiganshire', in E. Davies and A. D. Rees (eds.), *Welsh Rural Communities* (Cardiff, 1960), pp.67–117.

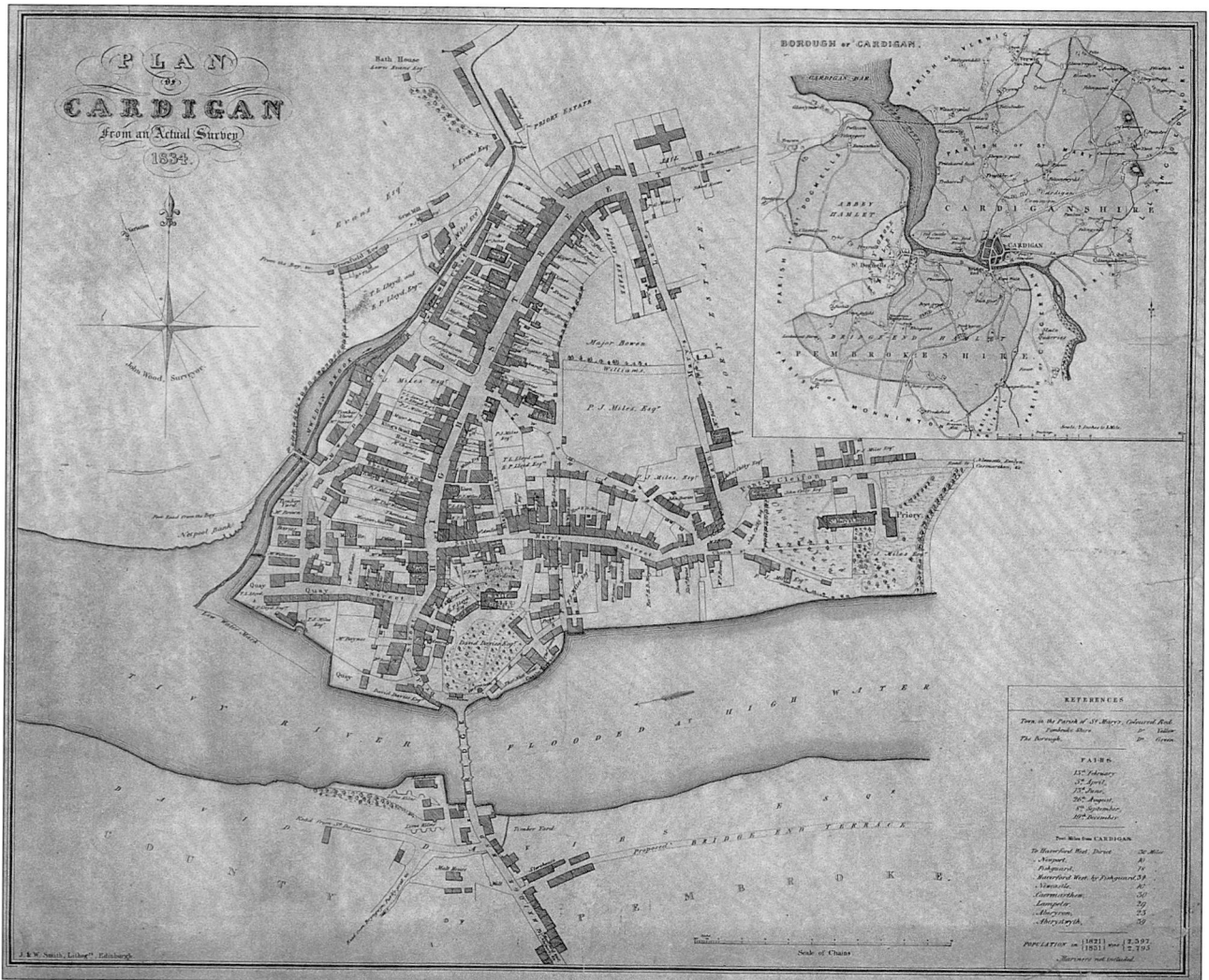

Fig. 43: John Wood's plan of Cardigan, 1834. (*Copyright National Library of Wales*).

north-east, the settlement was inchoate, with properties scattered along the roads on both sides of the river. Llandysul's form can, at best, be described as embryonic urban at the beginning of the century; it was made up of houses clustered near the bridge across the Teifi (including the small community of Pont-tyweli in Carmarthenshire) and along what was to become its one main thoroughfare, the Bridge Street–High Street axis.

New functions and new towns

All five places have shown remarkable continuity in both their form and function over the last two centuries insofar as the street layout of their cores has remained largely unchanged and their traditional role as service centres for their local rural catchments has been retained. However, they have progressively drawn apart in terms of their relative commercial status: while Aberystwyth and Lampeter have gained in standing as new activities have been added to their profiles and Cardigan has consolidated its hold on the trade of the lower Teifi valley, Tregaron and Llandysul have languished at the bottom of the urban hierarchy, squeezed by the competition from other larger centres and the low demand from the sparse populations of their immediate hinterlands. This is not to say that Tregaron and Llandysul were totally bypassed by the stimuli which encouraged urban expansion in other parts of rural Wales, for both were linked to the railway network (Llandysul in 1864 and Tregaron in 1866), and Llandysul benefited from woollen manufacturing in its vicinity in the late nineteenth and early twentieth centuries,[6] but at these settlements these new activities simply enhanced their service role rather than attracting new functions and fostering long-term growth. However, it must be stressed that these places had considerable local standing until the combined effects of continued rural depopulation and the widespread use of motor transport gradually undermined their prospects. Examination of the commercial structure of Tregaron in the nineteenth century, for instance, shows that it had a large cattle-droving trade and that it contained a range of inns, shopkeepers, banks and craftsmen, who serviced the scattered farms and villages of the Teifi uplands. Most were located in and around the Square, but the settlement as a whole was peppered with activities which testified to its role as an important local service centre. This basic function has continued and underpins the economic life of the town today.[7]

In contrast to the picture in Tregaron and Llandysul, the nineteenth century brought a variety of activities to the other places which enhanced their standing and which partly determined their character in the twentieth century. These activities may appear insignificant in comparison with the massive industrialization which occurred elsewhere in the country, but they were of considerable importance when viewed in the context of rural west Wales, where they led to increases in both the size and number of towns. Improved facilities or new functions were added to Cardigan, Aberystwyth and Lampeter, and new towns were created at Aberaeron and New Quay.

i. New functions in old towns

Cardigan's domination in the south of the county was reflected in the rise of its busy port, where merchants, mariners and shipbuilders profited from its growing trade. A measure of the activity in its shipyards, most notably those at Netpool, is the number of vessels built between c.1775 and 1875: comprising mainly sloops, smacks, schooners and brigs, and ranging in size from under twenty tons to about sixty tons, the total was 196, of which the majority was launched in the first half of the nineteenth century.[8] Shipbuilding itself spawned a profusion of associated businesses, including

[6]J. G. Jenkins, *The Welsh Woollen Industry* (Cardiff, 1969), chapter 6. See also G. W. Williams, 'The disenchantment of the world: innovation, crisis and change in Cardiganshire c.1880–1910', *Ceredigion*, IX, no.4 (1983), 310.

[7]An historical survey of some of Tregaron's functions is given in *Tregaron: The W.I. looks around its Town and Country* (Pontrhydfendigaid, 1984). Background information is also given in I. G. Jones, 'The Tregaron of Henry Richard', *Ceredigion*, II, no.2 (1990), 147–69.

[8]W. J. Lewis, *The Gateway to Wales: A History of Cardigan* (Dyfed County Council, 1990). This provides much useful local information on the town, especially for the nineteenth century, and has been used as a source of material. See also J. G. Jenkins, 'The port of Cardigan', *Maritime Wales*, 8 (1984), 76–93 and L. Lloyd, 'The ports and shipping of Cardigan Bay', ibid., 4 (1979), 3–61.

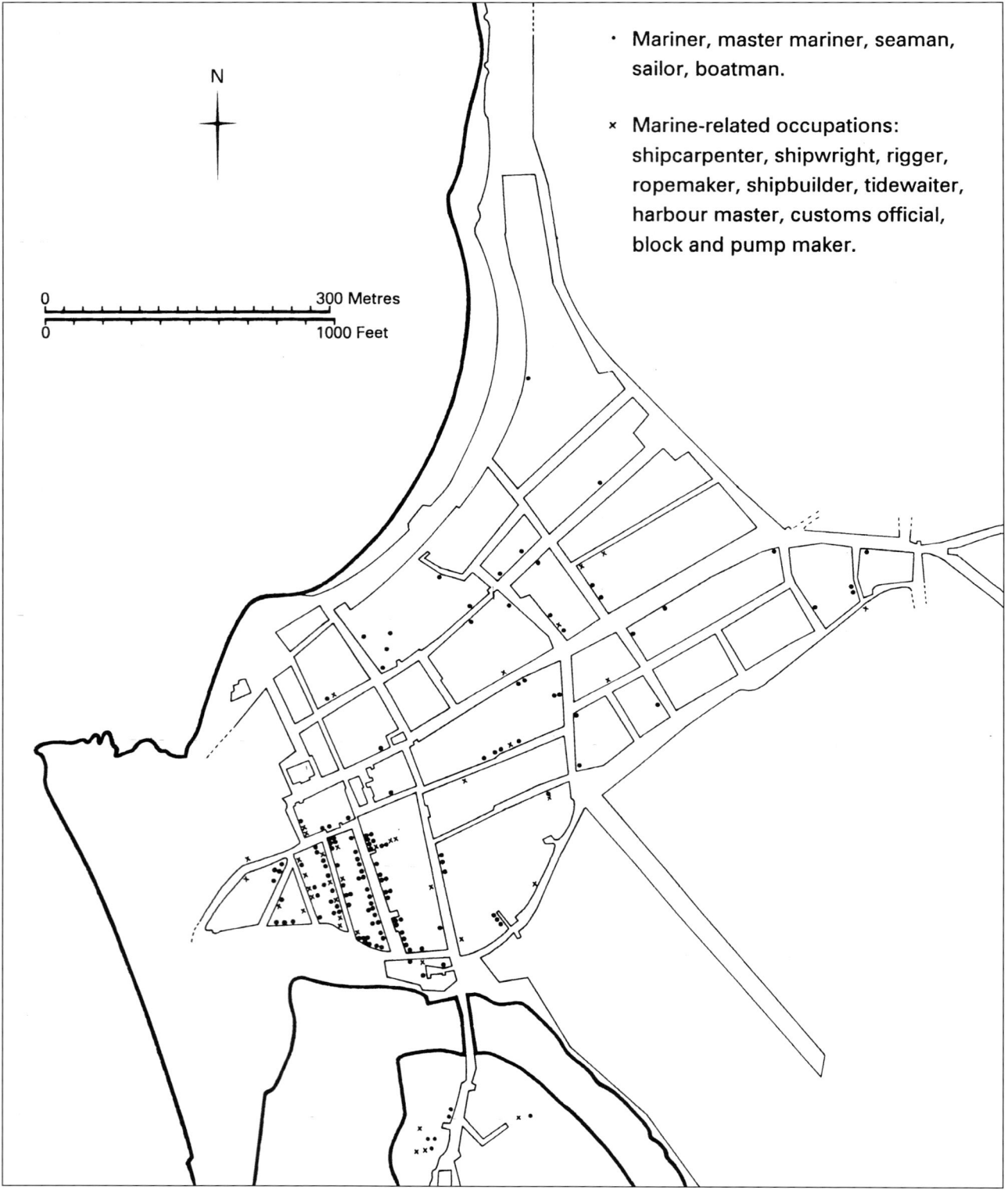

N

• Mariner, master mariner, seaman,
  sailor, boatman.

× Marine-related occupations:
  shipcarpenter, shipwright, rigger,
  ropemaker, shipbuilder, tidewaiter,
  harbour master, customs official,
  block and pump maker.

0   300 Metres
0   1000 Feet

Fig. 44: The distribution of household heads in marine and marine-related occupations in Aberystwyth in 1851.
(*Copyright Harold Carter and Sandra E. Wheatley*).

foundries, ropeworks, smithies and sail lofts, which further expanded the occupational structure of the town. These businesses not only supplied the shipyards but also responded to the varied demands of a wide agricultural hinterland, making, for example, ploughs, grinding and crushing mills, threshing machines and rickcloths. Typical was the Bridge End Foundry, which made anchors, chains and other iron fittings for ships but which over the years diversified into water wheels, farm machinery and marine engines, and eventually in the twentieth century into motor cars. Running alongside the expansion of the port was the growth of commerce in the town centre; the one reinforced the other, for many of the wares on sale in the shops were shipped in to order, from Bristol and Liverpool in particular. At the same time the nineteenth century saw the continued success of the traditional market and fair function, perhaps best symbolized in the erection in the late 1850s of new buildings which included a market hall, a grammar school, a guild hall and a slaughterhouse. Thus, the port and its associated activities served to consolidate Cardigan's role as the principal centre for the lower Teifi region. While the arrival of the railway in 1885 hastened the decline of shipping, by then Cardigan's status was firmly based. The railway station at Bridge End became the new link to the wider world, until it finally succumbed in 1963 to the widespread adoption of motor transport.

The expansion of the port in Cardigan was mirrored in Aberystwyth where, until the coming of the railway in 1864, the landing facilities of the harbour at the mouth of the river Rheidol provided the town and its hinterland with their dominant means of trade.[9] Likewise, ships were built on both sides of the river, but mainly along the northern arc from Trefechan Bridge to Ro-fawr, adjacent to Shipbuilders Row (now South Road). As late as the 1870s quite large vessels were being constructed, including the largest ever built, the *Caroline Spooner* of 1,100 tons, which was launched in 1877. As elsewhere, shipbuilding created a demand for fixtures and fittings of all kinds which was met by the establishment of specialized works making items such as ropes, blocks, sails, chains and anchors. By the middle of the nineteenth century the streets near the harbour could be legitimately described as a 'maritime quarter' (Fig. 44).[10] While a large part of the port's trade was directly concerned with handling general merchandise for the town and its agricultural catchment, it was overlain by the requirements of the mining industry of north Cardiganshire. Sporadic shipments of lead ore provided cargoes for its wharfs until the collapse of the lead mining industry in the early twentieth century – indeed, the narrow-gauge Vale of Rheidol Railway was extended to the north quay in 1902, but by then mining was in its death throes. Important for the occupational structure of Aberystwyth was the demand for machinery in the mines, for this helped to sustain a number of iron foundries. The biggest was Green's Foundry in Alexandra Road which, from the mid-nineteenth century until its closure in 1908, manufactured mining equipment and steam engines for home and overseas markets.

Thus, like Cardigan in the nineteenth century, Aberystwyth benefited from the expansion of its port and allied activities and strengthened its hold over the trade of the locality. Moreover, it

[9] W. J. Lewis, *Born on a Perilous Rock: Aberystwyth Past and Present* (Aberystwyth, 1980). This has been used as a source for local detail on Aberystwyth. See also L. Lloyd, 'The port of Aberystwyth in the 1840s', *Maritime Wales*, 5 (1980), 43–96.
[10] H. Carter and S. E. Wheatley, 'Residential patterns in mid-Victorian Aberystwyth', in I. G. Jones (ed.), *Aberystwyth, 1277–1977* (Llandysul, 1977), pp.46–84.

Fig. 45: John Wood's plan of Aberystwyth, 1834. (*Copyright National Library of Wales*).

acquired two other functions which were both to enhance its standing and influence its character and layout in the twentieth century: it developed as a resort and it became the home of the first University College of Wales. Like many of Britain's seaside resorts, Aberystwyth experienced two phases of development. Its first phase was in the late eighteenth and early nineteenth centuries, when it gained in popularity as a watering place for well-to-do visitors, particularly the gentry of mid-Wales and the borderland. Some changes occurred in parts of the old town with the building of impressive late Georgian town houses for local landed families, including the Pughs of Henblas, the Powells of Nanteos and the Pryses of Gogerddan, the opening of Assembly Rooms in 1820, which offered a variety of social activities in the summer season, and the laying out of the fashionable Laura Gardens and Laura Place between Sir Uvedale Price's Castle House and the new Assembly Rooms. However, there was also expansion beyond the medieval wall on two main axes, northwards along the seafront towards the Marine Baths and eastwards on North Parade across the Morfa Swnd. Wood's map of 1834 shows the impact of this first phase on the form of the town (Fig. 45). The second spur to the resort's development was the construction of railways from mid-Wales and beyond in 1864 and from south Wales in 1867. Aberystwyth began to attract a much larger middle- and working-class clientele and, as the numbers of visitors increased, further infilling and expansion of the town occurred. The station and railway yards formed a distinctive quarter at the landward end of Terrace Road; working-class terraces were built within and outside the medieval limits; the promenade was extended northwards to Constitution Hill, which itself was laid out with walks which could be reached by a cliff railway built in 1896; and more hotels, boarding houses and places of entertainment appeared. During the transformation from a small market town into a resort, its population increased from 1,758 in 1801 to 8,014 in 1901.

The other important ingredient in the urban economy which was to have a very marked impact on its employment structure, facilities and physical layout in the twentieth century was the founding of the University College of Wales in 1872. From its first home in the insolvent Castle Hotel on the seafront (now the Old College), for the first eight decades or so of its life it gradually built or acquired various premises in the town for academic departments and halls of residence. A legacy of this process is its residential accommodation on the promenade, including the former Alexandra Hall at the foot of Constitution Hill. Following the Second World War, however, the University decided to proceed with the extensive development of a site on the hillside overlooking Cardigan Bay, and since the 1950s the Penglais campus has taken shape, providing academic, leisure and residential facilities for its growing numbers of staff and students. With its student population of around 6,000 by 1996, the University has become an increasingly important element in the economic profile of the town.

Like Aberystwyth, Lampeter is also the home of one of the Colleges of the University of Wales and it, too, has seen diversification beyond its traditional market and service function. From its opening in 1827 until recent times, however, St David's College remained a very small institution with a limited curriculum; for most of this century its annual intake of students was usually under sixty, and before 1963 it failed to exceed a hundred. Its main purpose was the training of ordinands for the Church, especially the Church in Wales. Despite successive crises over low numbers and finance, it managed to survive until, eventually, it was placed on a firmer footing in 1971 when, after many overtures, it was admitted as a constituent College of the University of Wales.[11] Since the mid-1960s St David's has increased its student intake, expanded the range of degree courses, and built new academic, residential and leisure facilities around the original nineteenth-century nucleus. By 1995 the total complement of students was around 1,500. Thus, while Lampeter has continued its established market and service role for the upper Teifi region, its size, status and occupational structure have been expanded by the presence of the University.

[11]D. T. W. Price, *A History of St David's University College, Vol.2: 1898–1971* (Cardiff, 1990).

ii. *New urban communities*

Whereas in Cardigan and Aberystwyth the expanded port activities of the nineteenth century were simply added onto pre-existing towns which had long maritime traditions, in Aberaeron and New Quay the urban communities were created *de novo* in association with harbour facilities. Although the coastline between Aberystwyth and Cardigan had numerous small inlets and landing places where vessels were both built and beached with their cargoes of coal, lime and other general supplies, there was a long stretch of Cardigan Bay which was devoid of a purpose-made harbour. This was remedied when Aberaeron and New Quay were established as ports to serve the middle part of the county.

Like so many creeks in west Wales, by the end of the eighteenth century the mouth of the river Aeron was used for the import of commodities such as coal, salt, limestone and slate, and the export of local produce, including grain, lead and herring. At this stage, however, the settlement itself was an undistinguished seafaring village, comprising a cluster of houses and inns near the river bridge, some small warehouses which had been built to cater for the growing trade, and a few farms. This became the nucleus for the subsequent development of Aberaeron in the nineteenth century.[12] Until his death in 1805, the site was owned by the landowner Lewis Gwynne of Mynachdy; it then passed to his mother's family, the Joneses of Tŷ-glyn, and specifically to the Revd Alban Thomas Jones, who took the name of Gwynne. It was the new owner who set about improving the harbour under the powers of 'An Act [of 1807] to enable the Reverend Alban Thomas Jones Gwynne, his heirs and assigns, to repair and enlarge or rebuild the quay or pier within the harbour or port of Aberayron, in the County of Cardigan; and to improve the said harbour, and to regulate the moorings of ships and vessels therein'.[13] The initial achievement was fairly modest, namely the construction of two piers at the mouth of the harbour, but later in the century other improvements were made to the river basin, including the building of stone walls. While this investment may not have led to any great increase in trade, it did provide enhanced facilities for the continuation of the traditional import and export of goods for the locality. An appreciable part of the business involved the coastal shipment of agricultural merchandise, but there were also occasional voyages to distant parts in search of particular cargoes, such as timber from Canada and the Baltic. The port also offered residents a means of travel to the wider world, as was shown in an advertisement of 1858: 'The Plynlymon steam ship, Capt. Wm. Wright Master. Steam communication between Liverpool, Aberystwyth and Bristol. Taking in goods or Passengers for Holyhead, Portmadoc, Aberystwyth, Aberdovey, Cardigan, New Quay. Cabin 12/-, Storage 7/-.'[14] In addition to providing employment for mariners and fishermen, shipping supported a variety of craft occupations, particularly in the building and repair of vessels. One study has revealed a steady increase in the number of ships built at Aberaeron up to the middle of the century, with a trend towards larger vessels (Table 14),[15] and this was reflected in the employment structure of the town and its immediate

[12]D. L. Jones, 'Aberaeron before the Harbour Act of 1807', *Ceredigion*, IX, no.4 (1983), 363–87.
[13]Idem, 'Aberaeron: the community and seafaring, 1800–1900', ibid., VI, no.2 (1969), 201–42.
[14]Ibid., 210.
[15]Ibid., 217. This is based on data in M. Hughes, 'Historical geography of the sea-faring industry of the coast of Cardigan Bay during the eighteenth and nineteenth centuries' (unpublished University of Wales MA thesis, 1952).

vicinity (Table 15).[16] Thus, although on a much smaller scale in comparison with Cardigan and Aberystwyth, the various activities of the port helped to establish an urban community. Significantly, too, Aberaeron emerged as the local retail and service centre for the Aeron district.

TABLE 14: Number of ships built at Aberaeron, 1780–1870

	Number	Total Tonnage
1780–90	2	52
1790–1800	1	30
1800–10	6	151
1810–20	8	146
1820–30	8	289
1830–40	9	416
1840–50	19	1362
1850–60	22	2181
1860–70	15	1600

TABLE 15: Numbers employed in shipbuilding and seafaring in Aberaeron and the immediate vicinity, 1841–1861

	1841	1851	1861
Shipwrights	2	7	7
Shipbuilders	-	5	4
Sawyers	2	5	5
Blacksmiths	4	6	6
Sailmakers	-	-	1
Seamen	24	56	61
Master mariners	-	18	21
Ship carpenters	7	3	17
Fishermen	1	-	-
Pilots	-	-	3
Tidewaiters	-	-	1
Total	40	100	126

The steady but unspectacular increase in trade stimulated modest urban growth, but it was slow. From the outset, Gwynne was keen to encourage development and announced in 1811 that he would 'give liberal encouragement to such persons as might be disposed to take building leases near the harbour'.[17] Building plots were laid out around a simple grid of streets on the north bank of the river, broken by two quite striking features – a large Town Hall, erected in about 1840 on Market Street, and an open square, Alban Square, adjacent to North Road. While the latter was distinctive

[16]Ibid., p.222. These data are compiled from the decennial census returns.
[17]W. J. Lewis, *Aberaeron* (Aberystwyth, 1984), p.9. Some information on the growth of the town is also given in G. M. Jones, 'Notes on Aberaeron', *Ceredigion*, VI, no.3 (1970), 285–94 and H. V. Phythian-Adams, 'The planning of Aberaeron – some new evidence', ibid., VIII, no.4 (1970), 404–7.

in Aberaeron, it was a poor relation of the earlier fashionable squares of Europe, as has been noted by Harold Carter:

> Alban Square is directly in the line of the 'Piazza' which characterised the cities of Renaissance Italy and developed into the 'Place Royale' in France, which, in turn, was copied and imitated, with minor national variations, all over Europe. But in this setting, remote from the immediate sources of derivation, in an area without the capital to sustain urban architecture at any level, and in a country where the true civic tradition of Europe never flourished, the square fails completely. The surrounding buildings are out of scale, for they are far too small for the large central area. This area, in turn, is not paved and embellished but is a hedged field, now used as a football pitch. Nothing more sadly epitomises the fact that urban living was not really of Wales than this extremely interesting, but remote and forlorn imitation of the Piazzas and Grandes Places of Europe.[18]

Until the middle of the century development was largely concentrated on the northern edge of the inlet, but the second half of the century witnessed its spread along North Road (including the completion of Alban Square) and further building across the river to the south, for example, in Bellevue Terrace and Greenland Terrace. Within this layout, the axes of Market Street and North Road became (and have remained) the favoured locations for the majority of commercial premises, with some overspill into Alban Square and adjacent streets. This commercial growth stemmed from its role as a service centre for the farms and villages of the locality; indeed, it has been reported that in the 1890s the inhabitants of Gilfachreda regarded Aberaeron, four miles away, as 'a major city'![19] The twentieth century has seen peripheral development of both private and municipal housing, particularly to the south and south-east. Whereas the visual appearance of most of the modern expansion is quite ordinary, the nineteenth-century core remains impressive, comprising attractive terraces with brightly decorated Georgian-style façades.

While maritime trading remained a feature of the harbour into the twentieth century, it progressively declined from the 1870s onwards in the face of competition from the railway and later road transport, and from the inability of the port to cope with larger ships. Decline started with the opening of the Carmarthen–Lampeter–Aberystwyth railway in the 1860s which made inroads into the trade from the town's hinterland; eventually in 1911 a connecting branch line was built to Aberaeron. During the twentieth century it continued to function as a small retail, service and administrative centre and, as some compensation for the loss of its traditional shipping activities, it has benefited from its popularity as a holiday and retirement town. Although it has a resident population of only about 1,500, it is greatly expanded in the summer months by visitors.

At the end of the eighteenth century New Quay was a little fishing village overlooking the bay between Llanina Point to the east and New Quay Head to the west, which gave shelter to its fleet.[20] The population of the entire parish was only 678 in 1801. In addition to its primary function of fishing, there was some trade in limestone and coal for its lime kilns and in small shipments of general merchandise for local farms and villages. Shortly after the start of the new century, however,

---

[18]Carter, *Towns of Wales*, pp.295–7.
[19]Quoted from Hettie Glyn Davies in G. W. Williams, 'The disenchantment', 306.
[20]W. J. Lewis, *New Quay and Llanarth* (Aberystwyth, 1987). This has been used as a source of local detail on New Quay. Another useful source is S. C. Passmore, *Farmers and Figureheads. The Port of New Quay and its Hinterland* (Dyfed County Council, 1992).

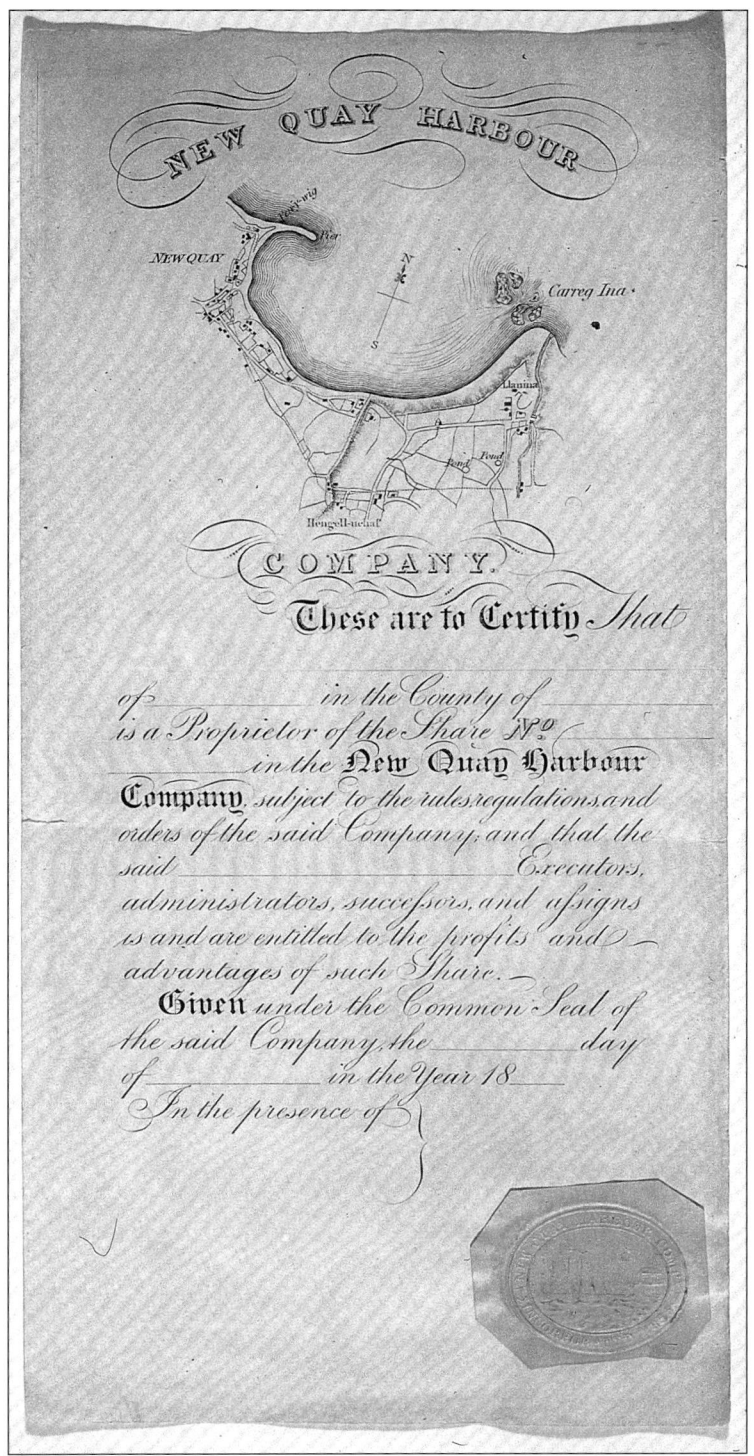

Fig. 46: Shareholder's certificate for the New Quay Harbour Company, early nineteenth century. (*Copyright National Library of Wales*).

various improvements were suggested for the harbour, including its development as a packet station for Ireland. Provision was made for better landing facilities to encourage trade, and a stone pier was built to give further protection in the bay. One of the earliest schemes was that promoted by Alban Thomas Jones Gwynne (the founder of Aberaeron) in 1820, but the construction estimates for the pier designed for him by the engineer John Rennie were too expensive. Improvements did not occur until over a decade later when, under the auspices of the Harbour Company formed in 1833 (Fig. 46), a pier and storehouse were built. This investment was accompanied by an increase in trade and the growth of the settlement. On the shipping front:

> the pier soon proved its worth; in the second half of the 1830s there were 5,000 people living in the port's hinterland who were entirely dependent on New Quay for provisions and materials which could not be produced locally. At this time some 3,000 tons of coal, culm and limestone were imported annually. There were 13 lime kilns on the beaches at Dolau, Traethgwyn and Cei Bach, all in constant use for supplying lime to farmers whose carts entered and left the village in a steady stream at certain times of the year.[21]

The village itself began to expand beyond the nucleus of the Dolau, Wellington Place, Church Street, and the houses in Pengeulan and Glyngoleu; most notably, work started on rows of terraced houses on the adjacent slopes (for example, Rock Street), which were gradually completed over the course of the century. By 1900 the settlement had a simple layout, comprising a number of streets (some fairly steep) leading up the cliff from the harbour to a series of terraces on the hills beyond. What was built ranged from quite ordinary working-class houses to substantial properties with Georgian-style façades.

As in the other ports, shipbuilding was also a feature of the local economy, and likewise supported a variety of associated crafts such as smithies, foundries and rope and sailmaking. Thus, in the nineteenth century, New Quay was transformed from a village into a small town which, through its harbour and a network of carriers' carts, helped to service the demands of part of the interior of the county. Although a railway was not built to New Quay itself, the presence of accessible stations elsewhere in west Wales undermined its maritime trade. However, this loss was cushioned by a new activity: by the late nineteenth century, the town began to grow in popularity as a seaside resort, and this function increasingly dictated its character in the twentieth century when the use of its harbour for leisure craft, the conversion of residential property into hotels, guest houses and holiday homes, and the development of large caravan parks nearby were major changes. During the twentieth century New Quay's permanent population remained at around a lowly 1,000, but holidaymakers in the summer often swelled the number of residents to well over 5,000.

Suburbanization and decentralization

Having discussed the special stimuli which encouraged urban growth – most notably port, resort and educational functions – attention will now be given to the changes which occurred in the

---

[21]Ibid., p.9.

internal structure of settlements. Whereas for the first half of the nineteenth century the towns of Cardiganshire remained relatively compact and retained some remnants of their pre-industrial (or pre-modern) character, as the century wore on a new trend took hold which was to have far-reaching consequences for their layout in the following century: this was the increasing popularity of living at lower density in the suburbs. At first this was expressed through the building, for relatively well-to-do families, of large detached and semi-detached Victorian and Edwardian villas set in their own grounds towards the edge of town. Later in the twentieth century, however, this fashion gradually filtered down the social hierarchy and revealed itself first as early ribbon development along the main roads into settlements and then in peripheral estates of both private and local authority houses. Accordingly, towns were gradually transformed by the addition of clusters of detached and semi-detached houses and bungalows; this process is still continuing and, indeed, through commuting, is increasingly affecting surrounding villages as well.

Whereas this trend was under way in the large cities of England in the early nineteenth century, as seen, for example, in the residential development of Victoria Park in Manchester and Edgbaston in Birmingham, in west Wales it began late in the century. At the outset it seems that retailers, professionals and those of private means began to forsake the traditional town house and the practice of working and living in their premises at the centre. In contrast to the rather mixed land-use arrangement of the compact pre-industrial town, the emerging modern town saw the place of work separated from the place of residence, with the former becoming the lock-up shop or office and the latter a house on or near the edge. One consequence was that the town core became more clearly defined as a central business district. This was not a sudden transformation, however, nor was it dramatic in small places. Well into the twentieth century the two patterns existed side by side. In both Cardigan and Aberystwyth in the middle of the nineteenth century there is clear evidence of the continuity of pre-industrial features, for many of the business leaders lived on their premises and the local gentry still resided in the old nuclei. Bridge Street and Pier Street in Aberystwyth retained their late Georgian town houses, and St Mary Street in Cardigan accommodated Oliver Lloyd of Coedmor, Abel Anthony Gower of Castell Maelgwyn, Thomas Amlot, Major Thomas Bowen and a number of business families.[22]

Before extensive suburbanization occurred, there was an infilling of the original nuclei of the largest towns to accommodate those employed in both the skilled and unskilled tasks associated with their new activities. It can be argued that this infilling, sometimes of very poor quality houses at high density, made the town centres less attractive to wealthier residents and acted as a 'push' towards later suburban spread. By the 1850s parts of Cardigan, for instance, were characterized by small houses, inadequate sanitation and overcrowding, typified by cottages in the immediate vicinity of the castle in Bridge Parade and Green Street, and near the quays in Mwldan. The situation in these areas was further aggravated by the keeping of livestock, and the presence of noxious workshops, such as the slaughterhouse, which drained directly into the river Mwldan. In passing, it can be noted that these unwholesome conditions did not go unnoticed by the Town Council: spurred on by the fear of infectious disease, and conforming with the national trend, it obtained powers to tackle the worst excesses of uncontrolled growth. Infilling was perhaps even more marked in Aberystwyth. Within the old town, terraces of houses were built to accommodate those engaged in the various

---

[22]Lewis, *The Gateway*, p.84.

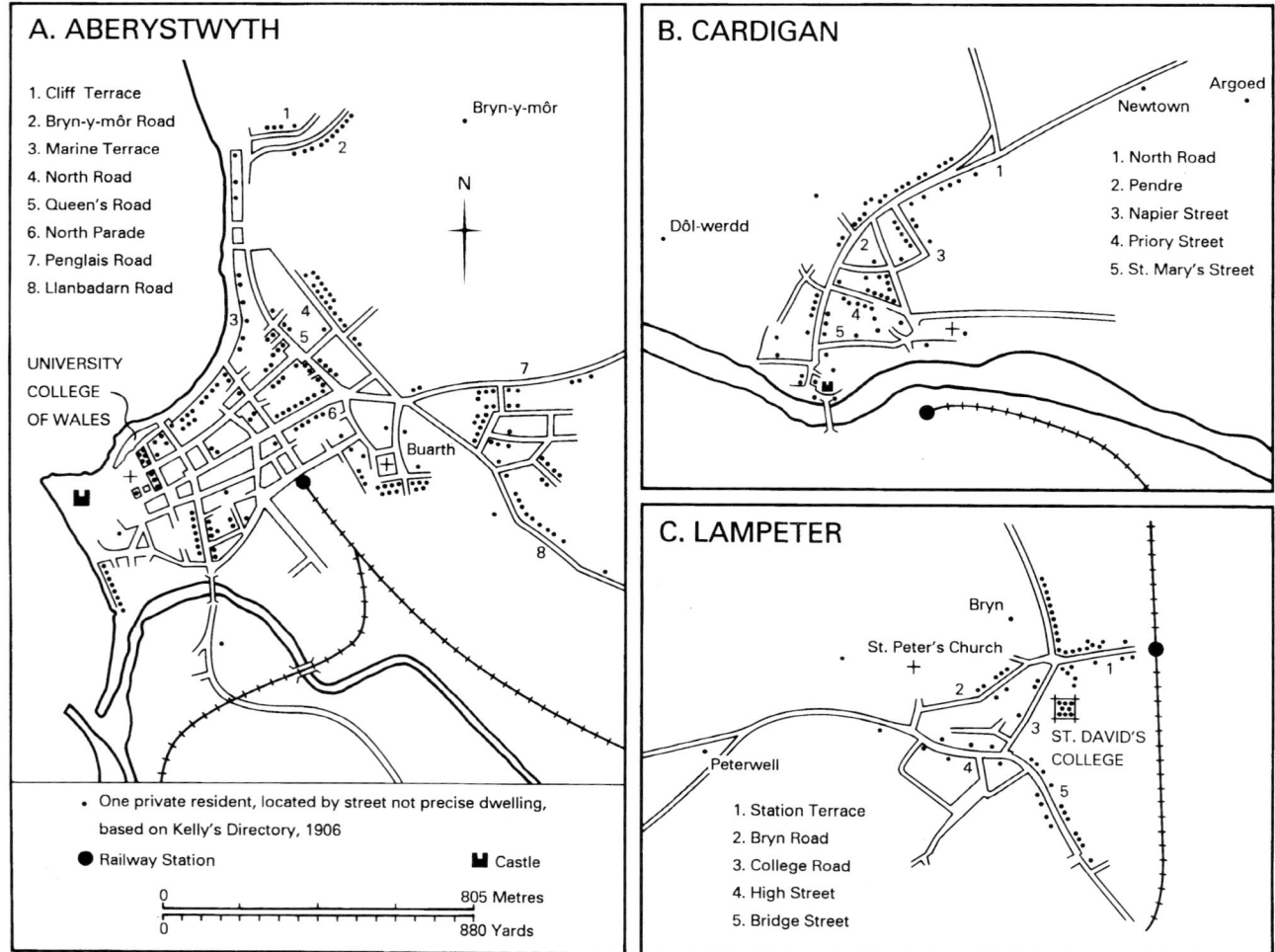

Fig. 47: The distribution of 'private residents' in Aberystwyth, Cardigan and Lampeter in 1906, based on Kelly's Directory.

trades in and around the harbour, and this continued after the coming of the railway, for example with the completion of Powell Street, William Street and George Street on the vacant land owned by the Powells of Nanteos between Bridge Street and Mill Lane (now Mill Street). Particularly distinctive was the development of courts for poorer residents on the burgage plots behind the main thoroughfares of the medieval town. For example, short rows of cottages approached by narrow alleys were pushed in behind both Great Darkgate Street and Eastgate Street; these included Eagle Court, White Horse Court, Britannia Court and Chalybeate Court between the former and Queen Street, and Laurel Place, Gateway Buildings, Albert Court and Windmill Court leading off the latter. They also appeared elsewhere as the town spread beyond the wall. Again, local health reports and contemporary descriptions reveal that efforts were made to improve standards, especially in the most congested parts.[23]

[23]Carter and Wheatley, 'Residential patterns', pp.46–84.

One of the inevitable consequences of continued building was that the old cores became more congested and less desirable as places of residence. Those who could afford to do so began to look to the urban fringe. Initially, in Aberystwyth the move to the edge was in the form of terraced town houses outside the wall, along North Parade and into Queen's Road,[24] but by the end of the nineteenth century villas had become the norm. By 1905 they had spread across the north-eastern quadrant of the town into Bryn-y-môr, North Road, Penglais Road, the Buarth and Llanbadarn Road and its adjacent streets, such as Caradog Road and St David's Road. This is well illustrated in Figure 47A, which shows the distribution of those described as 'private residents' (the well-to-do and local dignitaries) in Kelly's Directory of 1906. The die was cast for what was to occur in the twentieth century. The period 1905 to 1950 saw the consolidation of this part of Aberystwyth as a zone of largely private suburban residences, with further building near Llanbadarn Road (as in Iorwerth Avenue), and on the lower slopes of Penglais, most notably in Elysian Grove and Caemelyn.[25] The outward march has continued since 1950 with the completion of Dan-y-coed and Pen-y-graig and a whole series of modern housing estates at Waunfawr beyond the University campus, the largest being Maeshendre, Rhoshendre, Maesceinion, Heol Alun and Erw Goch. In addition, building has proceeded eastwards along the northern side of the Rheidol Valley towards Llanbadarn and on the plateau and upper slopes above at Cefn Esgair and Cefn Llan. In contrast, most of the other side of the valley has been used for the suburban municipal housing estates of Penparcau; these occupy the flanks of Pen Dinas to Southgate and beyond into Tyn-y-fron. More recently, private housing further out in this direction at Crugiau has almost formed a continuous link with the neighbouring village of Rhydyfelin. Thus the process which began in the late nineteenth century has had a dramatic impact on the form of the town in the twentieth century. Moreover, the main streets of the core have progressively lost their residential function and status. The primary thoroughfares of the old town, together with streets immediately beyond the line of the wall (most notably Terrace Road, Chalybeate Street and part of North Parade) make up the central business district. While these streets contain some new premises, more generally modern shop fronts have been inserted into nineteenth-century buildings.

For most of the nineteenth century the development of Cardigan involved the consolidation of the original nucleus and the adjacent areas of Mwldan, Pendre and the St Mary Street axis. Apart from sporadic building across the river at Bridge End, the main zone of expansion was northwards along North Road and into Priory Street, William Street, St Mary's Lane and Napier Street, which were erected to the east of Pendre. This suburban sector was largely of terraced properties, but the laying out of Victoria Gardens in 1897 and building at what became known as Newtown further out on North Road were forerunners of the more open suburban spread which was to follow. Figure 47B, which shows the distribution of 'private residents' in 1906, identifies this northern suburban expansion. During the twentieth century this northern sector was destined to accommodate most growth, with ribbon development of detached and semi-detached properties occurring along the Aberystwyth and Verwig roads and estates of private and council houses. The pattern has been repeated on a much smaller scale to the south beyond Castle Street and on St Dogmael's Road.

[24]H. Carter and S. Wheatley, 'Fixation lines and fringe belts, land uses and social areas: nineteenth-century change in the small town', *TIBG*, 4 (1979), 214–38.
[25]H. Carter, 'Aberystwyth: the modern development of a medieval castle town in Wales', ibid., 25 (1958), 239–53.

Little expansion has occurred to the east, where the modern bypass effectively serves as the boundary of the built-up area. Within this overall structure, the central business district mirrors the dominantly northward growth: High Street and Pendre form its elongated core, but it also includes Priory Street as a secondary spur and some overspill into side streets.

The most striking feature of the larger towns in the late nineteenth and twentieth centuries, therefore, has been suburbanization. As this has occurred, so their cores have been given over to lock-up commercial premises and some of their older infill sites have experienced clearance and redevelopment. The process of spread has been equally characteristic of the smaller towns, with the main roads leading into them being gradually lined with houses and bungalows and the interstices between them occupied by private and council estates. In Lampeter, for example, as can be seen from Figure 47C, by the early twentieth century suburban extensions had been built beyond the nucleus, especially to the north. In turn, these have been overtaken by later peripheral growth. What differences there are between settlements derive from the scale rather than the type of development.

Having identified suburbanization as the primary process which has shaped Cardiganshire's towns during the twentieth century, attention must also be drawn to another trend which has had some impact on the larger centres of rural Wales, namely the decentralization of retailing. Perhaps the most notable feature of shopping in Britain since the 1960s has been the steady growth in edge-of-town stores, and indeed, entire shopping centres. These have emerged in response to a wide variety of factors, such as inner urban congestion, the increased use of the motor car for one-stop bulk shopping, the willingness to travel greater distances, the availability of land for car parks and the rise of the national supermarket chains. At first it might be thought that towns in the more peripheral parts of Britain would be immune to such changes and that the established shopping centres at their hearts would continue to be the foci for all trade, as they have been for centuries. In large part this may be the case, but they are certainly not untouched. The most visible impact has been colonization by the grocery supermarket chains and their quest for edge-of-centre sites with parking facilities. In Cardiganshire this can be seen at the three largest towns: in Lampeter, the main supermarket is located off-centre in Bridge Street; at Cardigan, a large store has been built on the northern edge near the junction of Aberystwyth Road with the bypass; in Aberystwyth, the process began with the building of a supermarket at Waunfawr, to be followed by other stores in Park Avenue and at Parc-y-llyn on the new eastern approach road. Individually they are not major developments in national terms, but they do have important local consequences, including the restructuring of established shopping centres and increased competition for existing businesses within the towns and the wider locality. What is evident from patterns of patronage is that consumers welcome the choice, convenience and ease of shopping by car.

The contemporary urban system

The contemporary urban system comprises two bands of towns which function to varying extents as the retail, service, administrative and market centres for the county. One band is located along the coastal fringe, and extends from Machynlleth (in Montgomeryshire) in the north of the county, through Aberystwyth, Aberaeron and New Quay, to Cardigan in the south; the other set is spaced

Fig. 48: Pony-trekkers at the Square in Tregaron. This addition to the economy is a reminder of the importance of leisure activities in the modern history of the county. (*Copyright D. Caronian Jones, Tregaron*).

along the Teifi valley, from Tregaron furthest inland, through Lampeter, Llanybydder (in Carmarthenshire), Llandysul and Newcastle Emlyn (also in Carmarthenshire) to Cardigan at the estuary. Of these, the seven which lie within Cardiganshire form a loose hierarchy: Aberystwyth, with a population (including students and residents in its outer fringe) approaching 19,000, is at the top; Cardigan and Lampeter are of intermediate status, though the former, with a population of 4,350 and a greater range of facilities, overshadows the latter, with its lower population (including students) of about 3,500; the four places at the bottom have populations of under 1,500 – in the 1991 census, Aberaeron, Llandysul, Tregaron and New Quay recorded figures of 1,493, 1,300, 1,177 and 915 respectively. Overlying their service function, the status of many places is enhanced by the economic benefits derived from other activities, most notably the universities in Aberystwyth and Lampeter, and catering for holidaymakers, especially, but not exclusively, on the coastal fringe (Fig. 48). There is also evidence that some places are viewed as attractive retirement centres; both Aberaeron and New Quay, for instance, have high proportions of their populations over sixty years of age.

Most of the day-to-day and weekly shopping needs in the county are met by the facilities in these seven towns (together with towns near the county boundary) or in the smaller villages. To that

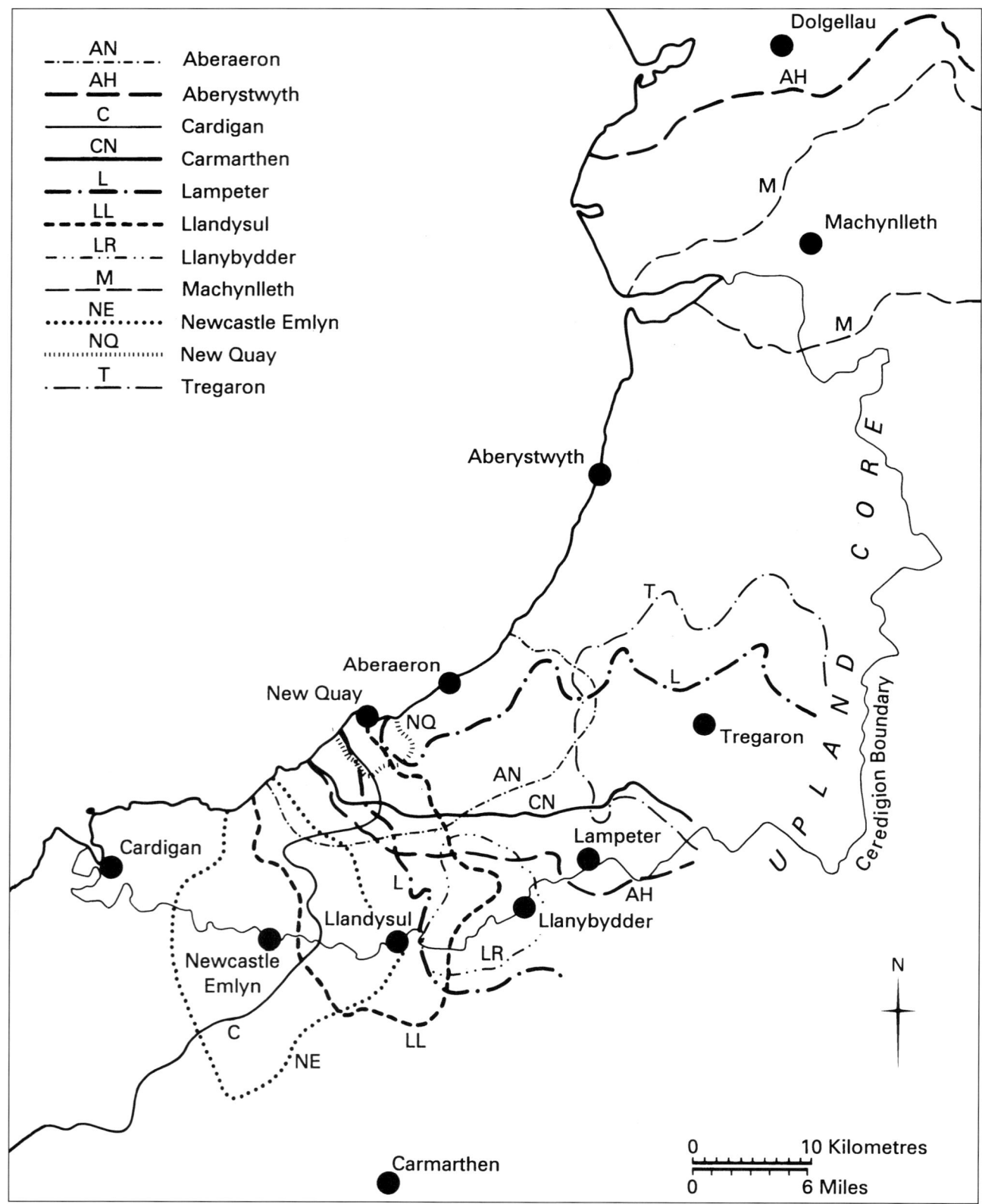

Fig. 49: The spheres of influence of shopping centres in Cardiganshire. (*Copyright G. Rowley*).

extent, there is a continuation of the pattern described by Rowley in his detailed studies of the late 1960s and early 1970s in which he asked consumers to indicate those centres at which they usually obtained a variety of goods and services, such as clothes, household items, professions and entertainment.[26] Figure 49, compiled from his work, summarizes the maximum spheres of influence in Cardiganshire; the catchment boundary of each centre is identified by the alphabetical notation in the key. It can be seen that Aberystwyth dominates the north, with a sphere of influence which extends from the lower Dyfi valley to beyond Aberaeron in the south. Along the southern edge, its catchment overlaps with the outer limit of that of Carmarthen, which draws in the communities of the Teifi valley. Lying within these extensive spheres of influence are the intermediate towns of Cardigan and Lampeter, with the former attracting trade from the lower Teifi, the coastal fringe and north-east Pembrokeshire, and the latter from the middle and upper Teifi. Nestling within these catchments are the towns of lower status: Newcastle Emlyn, Llandysul, Llanbydder and Tregaron meet the local needs of the middle and upper Teifi; New Quay and Aberaeron serve part of the coastal fringe between Cardigan and Aberystwyth; and Machynlleth has a catchment in the lower Dyfi.

However, this is only part of the picture, for the county is by no means self-contained. There is a considerable flow of consumers to more distant places for more specialized shopping. Undoubtedly one of the main attractions which offsets the deterrent of distance is greater choice, especially in the large national chain stores. Also, a distant place may contain a particular business (such as a furniture store in Llanidloes, or a department store at Cross Hands), which attract people from a very wide area. The more usual destinations for shopping trips are Shrewsbury and Swansea, but consumer surveys have shown that many other places are patronized; these include Chester and Liverpool to the north-east, Telford, Birmingham and Hereford in the west Midlands, and Cardiff and Llanelli in south Wales. This is not a complete list, but it is sufficient to reinforce the point that the towns of Cardiganshire are in the lower half of the wider shopping hierarchy and that consumers look elsewhere for some of their requirements. Put simply, the low scattered population is insufficient to support a wide choice of specialized shops and services in the immediate locality.

In addition to their role as service centres, these towns are the main sources of employment. Retailing, professions, administration and education provide the livelihoods both for their own populations and, with agriculture, for those in their rural hinterlands who live within daily commuting distance. To that extent, towns help to sustain communities in the countryside. In common with mid-Wales as a whole, however, the employment structure of the county shows little diversity outside the established service sector. For a long period the area experienced steady depopulation as large numbers, especially the young, left in search of work elsewhere. The reasons are not hard to find. Agriculture has consistently shed jobs, and other indigenous activities such as lead mining and the woollen industry were relatively localized and short-lived. Between 1871 and 1951 the total population of the county fell from 73,441 to 53,278.

Against this background, the small towns of rural Wales have an important part to play in trying to stabilize population and employment. While the increase in the permanent residents of the county from the 1950s to 63,094 (excluding students) in 1991 in part reflects inward retirement migration and a general drift to the countryside, it can be shown that new jobs have been created in

[26]G. Rowley, 'Central places in rural Wales', *Annals of the Association of American Geographers*, 61 (1971), 537–50.

some towns, for example, in the expansion of the universities at Aberystwyth and Lampeter, and in the growth of tourism. Furthermore, over recent decades deliberate planning policy has sought to stimulate a wider range of opportunities for work at selected growth centres. This approach has been favoured at a variety of scales and by various agencies, including the Development Board for Rural Wales, Dyfed County Council and Ceredigion District Council. The accepted strategy has been to develop small industrial estates with factory premises across the county, with most investment in the towns of Aberystwyth, Cardigan and Lampeter. This strategy is reinforced in the *Ceredigion Local Plan* (1995): 'The urban centres of Aberystwyth, Cardigan and Lampeter are defined as major employment centres. The plan allocates 28.6 hectares of land . . . for the development of industrial warehousing, storage or other appropriate employment undertakings.'[27] In Aberystwyth, it envisages expansion at the Glanyrafon industrial estate and the development of Parc-y-llyn and the marina in the harbour; at Cardigan, it includes relocating the livestock market in Parc Teifi and consolidating factory employment at Pentood and near the abattoir; and in Lampeter, three additional blocks of land are allocated for employment. The District Plan recognizes that the smaller places of New Quay and Tregaron, and perhaps Aberaeron and Llandysul, may also be able to attract new businesses and thereby spread jobs more widely. Thus, in addition to performing its traditional task of servicing the needs of the community, the contemporary urban system plays a key role in providing work for the relatively small and scattered population in this rural area.

[27] *Ceredigion Local Plan*, p.43.

CHAPTER 12

THE DOMESTIC ARCHITECTURE OF THE COUNTY

I. *The Rural Domestic Architecture*

Ffermdy, Plas a Bwthyn

Peter Smith

SINCE Cardiganshire has not so far been covered by an intensive RCAHM inventory survey, any description of its historic architecture can only be tentative.* However, the county gives the *impression* of having relatively few buildings of any great age. Most of the parish churches were rebuilt or very heavily restored during the nineteenth century, leaving only a handful retaining significant pre-Reformation features and details. The two stone castles, Aberystwyth and Cardigan, are major fortresses, but they have suffered far more than many of their peers in both north and south Wales from the ravages of the civil wars as well as from later depredations. The only two important historic urban centres, Aberystwyth and Cardigan, were very largely rebuilt in the

*This chapter is based on the archives of the Royal Commission on Ancient and Historic Monuments in Wales as conserved in the National Monuments Record for Wales and was assembled with the help of its staff. Except where shown, all illustrations are Crown Copyright. Figure 91 is the copyright of Mr Arthur Chater. A number of maps (updated) and perspective drawings have been taken from my book, *Houses of the Welsh Countryside*, first published for the Commission in 1975. I am indebted for the layout work and pages of illustration to Mr John Johnston and Mr Charles W. Green, under the direction of Mr D. J. Roberts, and for the typing to Mrs L. M. Jones and Ms S. L. Evans. I should like to express my thanks for assistance in the field by Mr Richard Suggett and for photography by Mr I. N. Wright. I must thank the Chairman, Secretary and Commissioners for releasing all these members of their staff to assist me in a work which should be regarded as a collective Commission undertaking. I must also thank Mr E. R. Heaton for permission to use his plans of Berllan-deg (Fig.81c) and for help with the survey of Aberdwynant (Fig.94b). I must also thank Mr Gerald Nash for permission to copy his distribution map of earth-walled structures, a most important feature which I had neglected to itemize myself. I must thank the owners of houses who have allowed me to disturb their privacy while making my surveys. On one occasion only have I been refused entry to a private house. Without such indulgence and generosity this chapter would not have been possible. It should be emphasized that this chapter is intended only as a historical outline. For detailed accounts of individual buildings, not only the major houses, but churches, chapels and also public buildings, it should soon be possible to consult the survey of Cardiganshire now being prepared by Mr Thomas Lloyd and Mr Julian Orbach for the *Buildings of Wales* series.

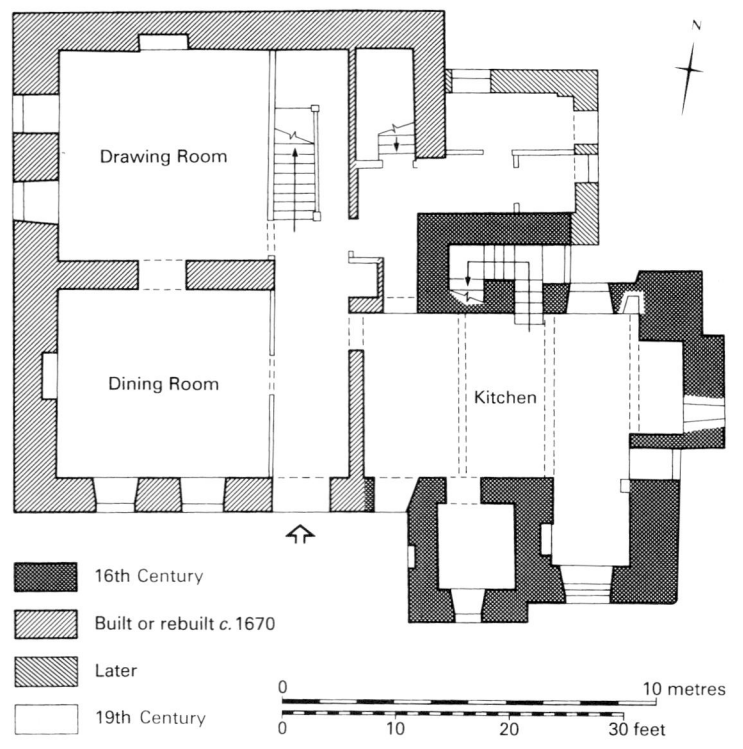

Drawing Room

Dining Room

Kitchen

16th Century

Built or rebuilt c.1670

Later

19th Century

0 ____ 10 metres
0   10   20   30 feet

nineteenth century, leaving both with a negligible heritage of earlier domestic architecture, less than Machynlleth or even Barmouth and certainly less than Presteigne, Ruthin, Llanidloes, and Denbigh. Not only is there nothing comparable to the wealth of pre-Reformation farmhouses to be found in the borderland counties, but there is also less surviving early rural building than in the other counties of west Wales (Figs. 51–3). Some of this dearth may be attributable to the prolonged retention of primitive and not very durable forms of construction until comparatively late, when most of it was swept away in a wave of late eighteenth- and nineteenth-century rebuilding. Throughout the rural parts of the county two types of dwelling predominate: the single or one-and-a-half storeyed cottage of the labouring poor and smallholders and the small storeyed house of the tenant farmers. Each normally has its fireplaces and chimneys on the end walls and its front doorway more or less midway between them flanked by vertically-proportioned windows. Very few such dwellings appear to date from before the eighteenth century, while the majority are almost certainly later. Among the houses of the squires the story is much the same – hardly anything survives from before the Reformation and very little from before the eighteenth century. There is a singular dearth of early date-inscriptions, which do not become common until the middle of the nineteenth century. There are several of post-1850 date around Llandysul, reflecting the belated industrialization of the lower Teifi valley (Fig.52).

In terms of historic building construction, Cardiganshire is evidently a region where the exterior walls were of a mass material, stone or earth. There is no historic half-timbered, black-and-white tradition in the county, such as is to be found in neighbouring Montgomeryshire, although the most westerly examples of such framed buildings are to be found almost within sight of the Cardiganshire/Montgomeryshire county boundary. Earth-wall building is still to be found extensively, extending over the south and middle parts of the county as far north as Bow Street which, until the twentieth century, was a village of earth-walled, mainly single-storey cottages (Fig. 54).

The earth wall is most characteristic of such cottages, but it occurs in places in storeyed farmhouses, as instanced by Pen-wern (Llanfihangel Ystrad). The earth wall was noted a century ago by Sir O. M. Edwards as a feature of the county. In the course of a railway journey through Cardiganshire, the thatched roofs filled him with homesickness for the land of slates: 'Peth rhyfedd i mi oedd y tŷ pridd cyntaf a welsom. O bridd y gwneir y tai – fel y bobl – ac y mae golwg hyfryd arnynt pan wedi eu gwyngalchu.' (It was strange for me to see the first earth house we saw. The houses – like the people – are made of earth, and they look pleasant when whitewashed.)[1] It is possible that the recent prevalence of the earth wall may account for the rarity of surviving sixteenth- and seventeenth-century architectural wall features. Early stone windows, doorways, and chimneys are far fewer, apparently, than in the adjacent county of Merioneth, where good quality

[1] O. M. Edwards, *Tro Trwy'r Gogledd. Tro i'r De*, ed. Thomas Jones (Wrecsam, 1958), p.184.

Fig. 50: (opposite) Plas-y-wern (Llannarth) has more early detail than any mansion in Cardiganshire. The older part (to the east) has a massive end fireplace and lateral outshots (both characteristic of Pembrokeshire) and a projecting rear stairway built round a stone pillar (a stair known in Glamorgan). The stair leads to a first-floor chamber and loft in the roof. The parlour block (to the west) built *c.*1677, incorporates a dogleg stair. Other features are a broken pediment front doorway, ovolo-moulded wooden windows, bolection-moulded panelling and highly original plaster ceilings.

building stone was perhaps more easily available, or was at least much more generally used. Associated with the earth-walled tradition, however, are two characteristic structural features, the scarfed-cruck frame (Fig. 57) and the wickerwork fireplace hood and partition (Fig. 55), also common in Carmarthenshire, a county which Cardiganshire much resembles. The scarfed-cruck occurs in two major British concentrations – in Carmarthenshire and Cardiganshire – as well as in Devon, Somerset and Dorset. However, there are important structural differences between the two groups. The Welsh scarfed-crucks are nearly all face-pegged without a mortice (Fig. 57), while the west of England examples are mainly side-pegged through a mortice. However, both are associated with areas where earth wall is common, and seem to have evolved as a means of supporting the point-load of a roof truss when the earth wall was deemed insufficiently strong. The alternative form of full (unjointed) cruck construction seems in contrast mainly associated with areas of half-timbered or stone building (Fig. 56). There are, however, a handful of full crucks in the county, and the assumption is that they are older than the scarfed variety, some of the latest of which appear to date from as late as the early nineteenth century. The alternative to some form of cruck was an A-frame truss resting on the wall tops or with curved feet which reached the beams carrying the first floor (Fig. 71). No ornamental forms of roof are known in domestic architecture (in marked contrast with Merioneth but in line with Pembrokeshire), although Cardiganshire churches include four historic cusped arch-braced roofs.[2] There are no examples of aisled construction or of hammerbeam roofs, though this is a deficiency which Cardiganshire shares with the rest of south-west Wales as well as with the counties of Glamorgan and Brecon.

Another common characteristic of the county's vernacular architecture is the wickerwork partition and wickerwork fireplace hood (Figs. 55, 58–9), the most recent of which the late E. D. Jones thought he could remember still being built around Llangeitho in his childhood in the early twentieth century.[3] The construction itself consists of an interwoven web of hazel rods or later riven laths stiffened with poles and covered with clay daub. It is not to be confused with the half-timbered, black-and-white fireplace hoods noted in neighbouring Montgomeryshire, where the wattle panels are embedded in a properly wrought and visible timber framework creating the black-and-white pattern. The wickerwork construction is most easily detectable as a fireplace hood. The earlier hoods so constructed continued through the roof into the open air (Figs. 59, 67, 95), but latterly most were fitted into a stone chimney corbelled out from the face of the stone wall close to the ridge (Fig. 94d). The former existence of a wickerwork hood can often be deduced from such corbelled stone chimneys which stand above a chase on the inside of the gable wall and which long survive the ruin of the less durable parts of many an abandoned Cardiganshire cottage. Alternatively, the presence of a recent red-brick shaft rising above the roof of an otherwise traditional cottage would suggest the replacement of an older wickerwork chimney.

It is possible that this extensive use of wickerwork, mainly for internal features, is derived from an earlier and long vanished use of wickerwork for external walls. This conjecture may receive some support from the occasional survival of the external round corner in both stone and earth-walled

[2] See also R. F. Suggett, 'Tŷ John Morgan and its roof: the medieval king-post in Cardiganshire', *Ceredigion*, XI, no.4 (1992), 425–32. Suggett suggests that this cusped roof found in a Cenarth cottage must have been taken from a nearby church.
[3] Information in conversation with the author.

building (Figs. 96, 97). It might be argued that in pure wickerwork construction corners would have been rounded and that some later mass-walled buildings might well have followed this rounded model.

Another impermanent building material, once extensively if not universally employed in Cardiganshire, is thatch for the roof covering. A century ago the county was noted for its picturesque thatch roofs which contributed much to the charm of the rural scene. In his description of south Wales as it was at the beginning of the twentieth century, A. G. Bradley noted:

> . . . since dropping down into Carmarthenshire we have passed from a land of slate and stone roofs into a land of thatch. And not only that but Carmarthenshire and still more Cardigan boasts the quaintest and most picturesque thatched cottages in the world . . . the roof is a thing of joy and a work of art that throws the thatched cottages of Devon and Northamptonshire, the best of their kind known to me in England, hopelessly in the shade . . . the artistic concealment of the chimneys in their braided sheaf of thatch, the billowy nature of the roof comb, and the neat roping of the fringes of gables, eave and comb, gives the south Welsh type a distinction unapproached elsewhere. Fifty years hence there will probably be none left. Today there are thousands scattered over Carmarthen, Cardigan, and Pembroke and in the course of our tour we shall go through whole villages mainly composed of these delightful and primitive habitations.[4]

Alas, the gloomy prophecy at the end has been all too completely fulfilled. Only the restored Bryngolau (Llanfihangel Ystrad), now a restaurant, preserves the ancient outward appearance of the traditional Cardiganshire thatched farmstead (Fig. 74). Possibly Wordsworth was thinking of the same thatched roofs when, a century before Bradley, he wrote of the 'sweet shire of Cardigan' in his singularly unmemorable poem 'Simon Lee the old Huntsman'. Thatching must have ceased early in the twentieth century and almost all the little thatch that now survives is under corrugated iron (Fig. 96). Like some other non-durable forms of construction, thatch was primarily used for economic reasons, and when it ceased to be economic it ceased in Cardiganshire to be employed, unlike richer areas such as the Vale of Glamorgan and parts of south-west and eastern England, where building owners are able to pay for the most beautiful, if no longer the most economical roof covering, ever devised by man.

Although none of these early types of house and cottage now exist in anything like their complete and original condition, we are fortunate in having a profusely illustrated record of one (no longer standing) which existed more than a hundred years ago, a record which in itself does much to explain why so few early buildings appear to survive, and why the later rebuilding in the county has been so extensive. Stephen Williams's account, 'An Ancient Welsh Farm-House', published in *Archaeologia Cambrensis* in 1899, but based on a survey made in 1888, was perhaps the earliest serious foray ever made into the study of Welsh vernacular architecture (Figs. 58, 59).[5] It describes a single-storeyed, open-roofed cottage incorporating most of those features we have come to regard as once characteristic of the county – a thatched roof (albeit of turfs), a wall-frame of crude, face-pegged,

---

[4]A. G. Bradley, *Highways and Byways in South Wales* (London, 1903), pp.150–1.
[5]S. W. Williams, 'An ancient Welsh farm-house', *AC*, XVI (1899), 320–5. Mr G. A. G. Griffiths has argued that the house is evidence of early aisled building in south Wales. See 'Some aspects of medieval peasant building in the Vale of Glamorgan during the later Middle Ages' (unpublished University of Wales M.Phil. thesis, 1995).

scarfed crucks, a fireplace hood and partitions of wickerwork. All that is missing are earth-containing walls. These, in fact, were of stone but possibly replacing a cob or clom wall. The house has indeed one unusual feature, that is two upright posts supporting the roof. These have been interpreted as relics of a tradition of aisled building. In the opinion of the present writer, they are props later inserted to hold up a collapsing structure. More supporting props can be seen in the Worthington Smith drawing illustrating the fireplace and the exterior wall. Williams believed the house might be early, coeval perhaps with Strata Florida Abbey, the ruins of which were not far distant. However, if the quality of the carpentry is compared with Welsh carpentry tree-ring dated to the early fifteenth century, doubts must arise whether, if constructed in this fashion, it could have endured from pre-Reformation times, and whether it was in fact any older than the eighteenth century, but illustrative of a stage in the evolution of the dwellings of the rural poor from short-lived shanties built of impermanent materials to the durable home.

Our historic dwellings should, of course, be considered not only in terms of construction and design, but also in terms of the social classes which had them built, namely the landowners, the substantial tenant farmers generally holding their farms by long leases from the landowners, and the poor, smallholders and labourers. Generally the higher the social class, the older are likely to be the earliest surviving dwellings.

Any historical narrative describing the development of domestic architecture in Wales as a whole should begin with the quasi-military first-floor halls and tower-houses associated with the age of the castles, and follow with the primarily single-storeyed open-halls surviving from the century or so before the Reformation. The story should continue with the sub-medieval storeyed houses which first appeared in the sixteenth century, and which gradually superseded the open-hall house as the dwelling of both the landowners and the substantial tenant farmers, although most of the labouring poor of Cardiganshire continued to live in primarily single-storeyed cottages until recent times, as was the case in the rest of west Wales, Ireland and Scotland. The sub-medieval storeyed house developed out of the hall-house, but long retained many of the salient features of its progenitor, especially the hall, the large dominant room (although no longer open to the roof but carrying a chamber above), entered at the lower end and retaining the seat of honour at the higher. Such houses tended to be symmetrical about their long axes but asymmetrical about their short axes, and sited down the slope (Figs. 60–74). These sub-medieval storeyed houses were in turn slowly superseded by centrally planned houses, ultimately inspired by the aesthetics of the Renaissance which, from about 1650, began to form the basis of the landowners' houses and then, in the course of the eighteenth century, those of their richer tenants (Figs. 62, 75–89). Such houses tended to symmetry about their short axis, and to be sited across the slope so that the main entry faced downhill. Sometimes, however, the main entry might be on the uphill side in order to secure a basement fitted into the falling ground at the rear.

However, both the first and second phase of this development cannot be studied in Cardiganshire because no certain examples of the first and little of the second have so far been discovered. Here, in conspicuous contrast with neighbouring Pembrokeshire, no tower-houses and seemingly no first-floor halls have been identified, while in contrast with neighbouring Montgomeryshire and Radnorshire, remains of the medieval open-hall phase so far discovered are very slight, indicated only by structural fragments insufficient for detailed reconstructions (Figs. 56, 94a). It is only with the third phase, the sub-medieval storeyed house, that our story can begin to take on flesh and bone.

It is true that we have a handful of cruck-trusses (compared with over two hundred identified in Radnorshire) to indicate the former existence of substantial yeoman hall-houses. At Preswylfa (Llanfihangel-y-Creuddyn) we have a two-bay hall framed by two complete and substantial cruck-trusses (Figs. 56, 94a), but not enough to provide us with a complete plan which we have to imagine from virtually complete examples still surviving in the borderland counties (Fig. 62a). Out of such halls, however, there emerged the sub-medieval storeyed house whose varying plan-forms were the result of grafting enclosed fireplaces, overall upper floors and substantial stairs onto an architectural tradition which had previously been without any of these features. Out of this process emerged a number of characteristic plans which can best be arranged in a typological sequence (Figs. 60, 61).

The most archaic was the lateral fireplace plan, having the fireplace on the long wall of the hall, thus interfering with neither of those fundamental medieval features, the cross-passage at one end and the High Table at the other. Next in the progression is the 'hearth-passage' plan, where the fireplace is sited internally so that it backed on to the passage and faced the High Table. Out of the 'hearth-passage' plan developed the 'lobby-entry' plan where the fireplace does not back on to the passage, but is built in it, so that the entry to the house is not by the medieval passage but by a small lobby. Finally there is the end-fireplace, direct-entry, plan where the main fireplace stands on the site of the 'High Table', eliminating it altogether, but allowing the passage to be retained, which it often was in early houses of this type. The replacement of the medieval open-hall house by the sub-medieval storeyed house as the dwelling of the squire and of the substantial farmer extended over a long period of time, beginning in richer regions just before the Reformation but still incomplete in the poorer districts at the time of the industrial revolution. It appears that the change took place late in Cardiganshire (as in the north of England), probably only making significant progress by the second half of the seventeenth century (although we have in Caernarfonshire and Merioneth evidence that the process had began more than a hundred years before this). Although the sub-medieval farmhouse seems to have arrived late in the county, one striking fact is how it continued to be built long after more fashionable 'Renaissance' forms of plan had become general. Several seemingly nineteenth-century Cardiganshire farmhouses have sub-medieval forms of plan (Figs. 65, 69).

Not only does the time-scale of the sub-medieval house show great regional variation but so also does the geographical incidence of the various different plan-types (Fig. 61). It would appear that there are in Cardiganshire (in contrast with Pembrokeshire and Somerset) few lateral chimney sub-medieval houses at the *farmhouse* level. It is clear that there were fair numbers of the 'hearth-passage' (chimney-backing-on-the-entry) type, as in Carmarthenshire, Breconshire, Monmouthshire and Glamorgan, and also in Devon, Dorset, the Cotswolds, the northern Pennines, and the North York Moors. But what is striking about the Cardiganshire examples is how late most of them are. We are reasonably confident that our third sub-medieval family, the lobby-entry family, has only a modest following in the county, in striking contrast with neighbouring Montgomeryshire which is covered with examples. Most of the Cardiganshire instances are cottages of the end-fireplace, lobby-entry type (Figs. 58, 59, 94), but a few longer house examples are known (Figs. 71, 72). The extent of our fourth class, the direct-entry, cross-passage, end-chimney type, is uncertain because of the difficulty of distinguishing, on the basis of outward appearance alone, sub-medieval direct-entry, end-chimney houses from the typologically later, symmetry-seeking, Renaissance-inspired, end-chimney, central stair-passage houses. All that can be said for certain is that the early, end-chimney, sub-medieval house is well known in Caernarfonshire and Merioneth, appears to be well represented in Pembrokeshire, and ought to be common in Cardiganshire. For this reason, our Cardiganshire hatching of the sub-medieval house distribution map (Fig. 61) must remain very tentative. Each group will now be considered in turn.

Ynyscreigiog (Ysgubor-y-coed) is a rare example of an early lateral-chimney house (Fig. 63). However, examples of the hearth-passage family are quite numerous. The earliest known representative appears to be the now ruined Cefn-gwyn (Ceulan-y-maes-mawr), rebuilt in 1682 (according to the date-inscription over the porch) in the form of a *pen uchaf* (the part above the entry containing the hall and originally an inner room), and a very long *pen isaf* which now contains a small fireplace in its end-gable. In its present state it is impossible to say whether Cefn-gwyn was the rebuilding of a long-house (i.e. a house where the dwelling and adjoining byre share an entrance in such a way that in its developed form the house was entered through a cross-passage feeding-walk in the byre) (Fig. 68).

The hearth-passage family can be divided into those which were fairly certainly long-houses, as built, and those where the *pen isaf*, or 'down-house' in northern English parlance, was clearly domestic from the start. Finally, we should remember the existence of a subset where there was no down-house at all (Fig. 67). As our map shows (Fig. 61), the hearth-passage plan was to be found in strength across much of south Wales. Among the certain Cardiganshire long-houses we should mention Rhiwson-uchaf (Llanwenog), Allt-ddu (Llanddewibrefi), and Sychnant in the same parish (Fig. 68). Besides these there are also a number of substantial farmhouses whose plan form strongly suggests they may have been built as long-houses of the hearth-passage type, although since much altered. For example, Penrhyngerwin (Ysgubor-y-coed) and Maesnewydd (Ceulan-y-maes-mawr) have their main entry beyond the hall fireplace and extending beyond a very extensive but now domestic down-house (Figs. 64, 65).

However, in contrast with these hearth-passage houses of the long-house type we have to place others which are either ambiguous or clearly not long-houses. Penwalken (Llandysul) is a little low hearth-passage house with rounded corners and wickerwork fireplace hood. The room at the entry-end is too small to have been a byre and was probably a dairy. The 'inner-room' (the room reached through the hall) is clearly a parlour (Fig. 93).

Other houses illustrate the classic pattern of an inner-room parlour and an outer-room dairy common in parts of England but not very common in Wales. A good example is Blaen-llain (Llanwenog), which has the byre added to the parlour end, and is therefore as different from the traditional developed long-house, i.e. the house part entered through the feeding walk, as can be imagined, a very long house, perhaps, but not a long-house in the technical sense. Further long houses (but not long-houses) are illustrated by Ffos-y-ffin and Tŷ-llwyd, both in Llangeitho parish (Fig. 69). In each the byre was added at the parlour end, but without any internal access between byre and parlour.

A feature of many hearth-passage houses is the structural break where the *pen isaf* (the 'down-house') joins the *pen uchaf*, the main part of the dwelling containing the hall, or as it would now be known, the 'living-room'. In a few cases it can be demonstrated that the addition of the *pen isaf* was clearly anticipated when the *pen uchaf* was built, as keyed masonry was incorporated in the quoins to lock in the expected extension when funds became available to build it. There is clear evidence for this at Tŷ-llwyd (Llangeitho) illustrated in Fig. 69.

These structural breaks, more widespread among the hearth-passage group of sub-medieval houses than any other, have been variously interpreted. According to one view, they are no more than what they appear, that is the progressive *enlargement* of a dwelling from a small nucleus. According to another, they are more the progressive *reconstruction* of an older house that had once occupied the same site, a reconstruction which may have involved a change in room use. In the nature of the evidence neither interpretation is capable of proof or disproof, nor is the significance of a handful of 'hearth passage' houses without a downhouse, and therefore entered directly through the gable-end wall, beyond ambiguity, for many may be interpreted either as houses whose *pen isaf* has been removed, or where the building programme was never completed or were always envisaged as complete entities (Figs. 66, 67).

The end-entry, hearth-passage type may be the source of one very odd type of plan which has been discovered in small numbers in mid-Cardiganshire, and that is a house entered through a doorway in the end wall of a lean-to so that one reaches the main living room through a lean-to dairy as instanced by Tycerrig (Blaenpennal) and Carnau (Nancwnlle), both probably early nineteenth century.

Compared with the hearth-passage type, the lobby-entry type is comparatively poorly represented in Cardiganshire in spite of its immense popularity in neighbouring Montgomeryshire, where it constitutes the predominant sub-medieval house-type. In Cardiganshire only one example has so far been discovered of the mature and fully developed form of the internal fireplace, lobby-entry plan, where the fireplaces are arranged back to back so that one fireplace heats the middle room and the other the outer-room in a three-unit sub-medieval house, although this form of the plan is again very common in neighbouring Montgomeryshire. Although we have hypothesized that the lobby-entry plan follows the hearth-passage plan, our one sub-medieval example with back-to-back fireplaces, Gwastadgwrda (Betws Leucu) must be exceptionally early, built or rebuilt as it was, within a cruck framework (Fig. 72a). However, examples of single-internal-fireplace houses do occur. A good instance is the long ruinous Neuadd-lwyd (Ysgubor-y-coed) in the north of the county, not far from the Montgomeryshire border. It is a three-unit house incorporating a hall standing between a small inner room·and a large outer room of uncertain purpose (Fig. 70). A lateral outshut incorporating a porch opening onto a small lobby flanked by the single fireplace gives access to the hall on the right and the large outer room on the left. The fireplace, sited to provide a small lobby between it and the porch, appears structurally an insertion into what may have been originally an open-hall house. The lobby-entry form of long-house is strikingly illustrated by Ynyseidiol (Ysgubor-y-coed). Although rebuilt as a central-stairway house in the nineteenth century, the original doorway opening on to a lobby between house and adjoining byre is still clearly visible (Fig. 71). A few miles deeper into Cardiganshire stands an entirely domestic three-unit lobby-entry house of manifestly later, probably nineteenth-century date. At Wenffrwd (Ysgubor-y-coed) the three-unit plan consisted of a middle living-room, a downhill parlour at the entry end, and an uphill dairy away from the entry, a sequence of rooms common in Montgomeryshire (Fig. 72b).

Our final group of sub-medieval houses may be classified as the end-chimney, direct-entry type. It is characterized by having the main fireplace on the end wall and the entrance more or less midway along the long wall. There is thus no close association between fireplace and entry as there is with the other previously discussed families of sub-medieval houses. However, this group is often outwardly similar to the later Renaissance-inspired symmetrical houses built around a central staircase, for these also have the chimneys on the gable-end walls and their entries more or less midway between them, and it is often impossible without a careful interior examination to decide to which group a house actually belongs.

We know that the end-chimney sub-medieval house was the norm in Caernarfonshire and west Merioneth, and that examples there are known which date from before the middle of the sixteenth century (Fig. 73b). Good instances are Garreg-fawr (Waunfawr, Caernarfonshire), now re-erected in the Museum of Welsh Life at St Fagans, Plas-du (Llanarmon), also from Caernarfonshire, and Brynyrodyn (Ffestiniog, Merioneth). These houses are characterized by a cross-passage entry giving onto a hall on one side, and two secondary rooms (cold parlour and store-room) on the other. In many the first floor is reached by a winding stair alongside the hall fireplace. It is at present difficult to know if many of the very large numbers of end-chimney houses to be seen in the Cardiganshire countryside have this early pattern of plan until an exhaustive house-to-house search has been made. A possible candidate is Plas Dolcletwr (Llangynfelyn), sadly recently damaged by fire (Fig. 73a). In spite of its early nineteenth-century reconstruction, this house still preserves a number of unmistakably early features, roof-trusses with curved feet, early beams, and a pre-glazing wooden window – the only instance so far known in the county. Although the site of the original doorways is not certain, it is likely they were on the long walls. Another seemingly early end-chimney direct-entry house stands at the opposite end of the county, namely Crugbychan (Y Ferwig). Here the central stairway is a later modification (Fig. 73c). The nineteenth-century Einion Cottage in the village of Furnace retains all the essential features of the early, direct-entry, end-chimney plan (Fig. 73d).

Both Dolcletwr and Crugbychan have general proportions similar to the classic Snowdonian model. But other Cardiganshire examples have more elongated proportions such as the now lost Porthangel (Llangorwen), which had a massive projecting end fireplace, rather reminiscent of Pembrokeshire, heating an exceptionally long hall. Another unusually long end-chimney house with a massive projecting end fireplace is Cnwc-y-gneuen (Gwynfil). The root form of their plan is difficult to conjecture.

Sometimes a house of exceptional length can be explained by the existence of unheated store-rooms placed midway between the large hall-kitchen heated by a massive projecting end fireplace at one end and a small parlour heated by a much smaller fireplace on the opposite end wall, as instanced by Pen-y-graig (Llanychaearn). Here the middle room is combined with a dog-leg stair, so it is possible that this house is as late as the 1789 date inscribed over a window, but from outside it looks an asymmetrical sub-medieval rather than a symmetrical late eighteenth-century dwelling (Fig. 74a). A house with a remarkably similar plan, internal store-rooms combined with stair, is to be found at Cwmllechwedd-isaf (Lower Lledrod). Here again a large end hall (living-room kitchen) is heated by a massive projecting end fireplace, while the parlour at the opposite end is heated by a shallow and diminutive fireplace.

It is unfortunate that the interior partitions at Glynyrhelyg (Llanwnnen) have been lost. Early surviving features of this direct-entry house include a series of scarfed-cruck roof trusses carrying rafters of roughly trimmed branches, and a thatched roof now preserved under corrugated iron, as well as clear evidence for a wickerwork hood to the hall fireplace. A surviving glazed mullioned window suggests this now gutted dwelling might date from the seventeenth century. The house and the adjoining byre are structurally continuous (the byre repeating the scarfed crucks of the house), but there is no sign of any intercommunicating doorway, and it is evident that main doorway was midway along the long wall, later greatly widened when the house was converted into an agricultural building after the construction of the nearby Victorian farmhouse. The site of the stairs is not known. At Garn-lwyd (Llanddewibrefi) another end-fireplace, direct-entry house, the winding stairway survived, alongside the wickerwork fireplace hood. The entry is by opposed doorways, the rear door giving onto a rear lean-to dairy.

This random collection of sub-medieval, end-chimney, direct-entry houses, discovered and recorded more or less by chance, suggests that a systematic search would uncover many more. They merged imperceptibly into the Renaissance-inspired central-stairway house which had first appeared in landowners' houses during the seventeenth century. The earlier examples had the stair in a projecting rear turret. An instance, although much altered, is Tŷ-glyn (Llanddewi Aber-arth Upper), possibly dating from as early as 1624 if a date-inscription, now reset on a farm building, is to be believed (Fig. 78a). The much altered Abbey Farmhouse (Strata Florida) has a projecting rear turret which probably once contained the stair (Fig. 77), while the stair turret at Plas-y-wern (Llannarth), shown on Fig. 50, enclosing a column stair is an early anticipation of this idea. The emergence of the squire's house, consisting of hall and parlour built on each side of a central entrance-passage leading to a stair in a rear turret, is well illustrated by Gelli (Trefilan), whose surviving mullion-and-high-transom windows suggest a late seventeenth-century date (Figs. 75, 76). The exterior of Gelli illustrates the difficulty of achieving a symmetrical elevation, given that the hall fireplace is much larger than the parlour fireplace. The placing of the dairy and store-rooms to the rear under a catslide roof at Gelli was to be imitated in countless farmhouses. Later houses incorporating a rear projecting turret containing a central stairway are Hafod (Nancwnlle), illustrated in Fig. 78b, and Penywennallt (Llandygwydd).

It was eventually appreciated that there was no need to place the stairway in a rear projection and that it could equally well, and with less expense, be placed in the main body of the house. The earliest instance of this plan in Wales appears to be Tyfaenor (Abbey Cwm-hir, Rads.) as shown on Fig. 79, built c.1650, and it occurs not long afterwards in the rebuilding of Plas-y-wern in 1677 (Fig. 50). It is strange how long this form of access, known in collegiate building since the Middle Ages, took to be adopted for other types of domestic architecture. The form appears in small Cardiganshire houses in the eighteenth century, as at Henblas (Llanbadarn Fawr), probably dating from the mid-eighteenth century, or Neuadd (Llanddewibrefi), dated by an inscription over the main door to 1758 (Fig. 80).

Thus the stone-walled farmhouse consisting of a central stairway flanked on one side by a kitchen-living-room and on the other by a parlour, each room heated by a gable chimney, had gained widespread acceptance by the mid-eighteenth century, and appears to have largely superseded all earlier types of house. However, it is possible that some conceal older but rebuilt sub-medieval, end-chimney, cross-passage houses, though how many only an inventory-type door-to-door search will reveal. Certainly the giant end fireplace which characterized the sub-medieval house seems to survive, and clearly continued to frustrate the quest for absolute frontal symmetry. Two alternative solutions to the problem are seen endlessly repeated. Granted that the large hall fireplace would result in a front door off-centre between the gable walls, the builder had a choice of placing the windows equidistant from the front door, leaving unequal distances between the hall-kitchen window and the parlour window and their respective outside corners or placing each window equidistant between the door and the quoin, which meant that the panels of wall on each side of the doorway were unequal (Figs. 80, 81). This problem seems not to have arisen to such an extent in the brick-built English lowlands, where absolute symmetry was more usually achieved. In Cardiganshire complete symmetry is rare before the late nineteenth century.

In spite of this failure to achieve true symmetry, these little villa-type farmhouses are an agreeable aspect of the rural scene. The proportion of window to wall is excellent, unlike that found in the freely planned modern farmhouses which have been slowly replacing them. The vertical proportions of the windows, giving a view of both field and sky, are pleasing both from within and without, while the sliding sashes provide a very precise control of ventilation, both at ceiling and floor level. And even if the placing of the fireplaces on the end walls is not conducive to effective heat insulation, it allowed an unobstructed central stair, and the best possible circulation, making it possible to avoid the passage-room, especially upstairs. It is possible the growing popularity of the plan in the eighteenth century is connected with the growth of literacy, for it was easy to find in such houses a room in which to read undisturbed. It is not surprising that they remained in favour with the farming class from their first general adoption sometime in the eighteenth century virtually until the outbreak of the Second World War.

Many were built with ranges of farm buildings attached at the gable ends, but even when so arranged the builders thought of the house as if it were a separate entity. There is no suggestion of the sub-medieval long-house plan where the house appears to be entered through a doorway in the byre unless this feature survives from the earlier house as at Pen-yr-allt (Llanychaearn). In the new houses the front doorway stands between the living-room window and parlour window, and the house unit is quite distinct and easily identifiable, even when it has a barn and byre built as part of the same range. Many of the larger farmhouses, however, were built completely detached from their farm building and this from an early date, an instance being Lluest (Llanbadarn Fawr), which probably dates from the early eighteenth century. The form of the plan is double-pile, but the rear has a series of roofs at right-angles to the main roof, instead of the more common arrangement of rear range built parallel to the front, the two divided by a central valley (Fig. 82b). It is unfortunate that successive renovations have deprived this house of most early fittings and features, apart from a surviving roof-truss, while the exact site of the original stair is a matter for conjecture. Standing apart from the house, however, is a range of farm buildings, a corn-barn flanked by granary on one side and an attached byre on the other, all recently converted into dwellings. It is a good instance of the larger Cardiganshire farmhouse approaching the scale of landowners' dwellings. Another good example of the double-pile is Lisburne House (Llanfihangel-y-Creuddyn), where the fireplaces are arranged on the spine wall, and both front and rear are under the same roof (Fig.82a).

Socially, below the two-storeyed farmhouses of the substantial tenant farmers are cottages of the smallholders and labourers. These may be classified as entirely single-storeyed, partially single-storeyed, that is *croglofft* cottages with the living-room (hall) open to the roof but alongside a parlour, or parlour and store-room side by side with loft over, and finally cottages with an overall loft lit either by gable-windows, or low windows under the eaves, or dormers. At this stage they become virtually indistinguishable from the poorer storeyed farmhouses.

The same patterns of plan as are found among the farmhouses occur also among the cottages. Needless to say, no lateral-chimney cottages have been discovered. There are, however, a few 'hearth-passage' cottages, many of the minimal end-entry type (Figs. 92, 93). There are also a handful of the end-chimney lobby-entry type (Fig. 94). But these are all greatly outnumbered by the direct-entry midway between the end-chimneys type, which still survive in numbers too numerous to compute (Figs. 95, 96). One can only cite a few characteristic examples of each class.[6] The common end-chimney type exhibits a number of variants, mostly dependent on whether it has its living-room open to the roof, or ceiled, providing an overall loft floor. In their ground-floor plan most of these cottages are basically similar to the sub-medieval direct-entry, end-chimney house (Fig. 73), that is they consist of a hall/living room one side of the entry, and usually a small parlour and store-room on the other (Fig. 73). If there is a small farm building attached there is normally no internal access. However, there are hints here and there of another arrangement altogether, where the secondary unit is not a parlour, but a byre, giving a long-house, defined as a house with internal access between living-room and cowshed. A rare instance of such a plan is Wig-wen-fach (Llanddewi Aber-arth), though even here the entry for the cattle is separate from the entry for the human occupants (Fig. 97).

The end-entry type of cottage (related to the 'hearth-passage', group of larger houses) is well represented by the little dwelling just to the north of the bridge over the river Clarach at Llangorwen, and appropriately named Pen-y-bont (Figs. 92, 93). It consists of living-room and parlour on the ground floor, the living-room heated by a substantial stone fireplace, and the parlour by a much smaller fireplace. There is no sign of there ever having been a *pen isaf* and indeed this seems to be precluded by a window in the gable wall over the doorway and the proximity of the Clarach brook running not far away from the front door. A similar cottage, rather more modest in scale, is Pen-lôn (Llanfihangel Ystrad), consisting of a living-room heated by a wickerwork fireplace and entered by a doorway alongside in the end wall (Fig. 93d). An inner-room parlour provides the only additional domestic accommodation, but a byre added to the parlour end of the cottage suggests that this was a smallholding whose occupants' income from farming was supplemented by other work. But the remains of dwellings smaller even than these, now long since deserted, may be found in large numbers on the hills to the east of Tregaron, cottages consisting of a single room open to the roof, once heated by a wickerwork hooded fireplace (Fig. 93b). Alternatively, rather longer than average cottages are to be found in three main units, consisting of a hall between the inner parlour and outer dairy, small versions of the classic 'hearth passage' house (Fig. 93a).

The other type of cottage having the entrance and main fireplace in close proximity is the end-chimney lobby-entry type. To such a classification belonged 'The Old House at Strata Florida', so painstakingly illustrated and described by Stephen Williams and Worthington Smith, to which we have referred earlier, chiefly for its structural features (Figs. 58, 59). It clearly was of the end-fireplace lobby-entry type, the entrance lobby giving onto an open hall at the far end of which were attached rooms whose original purpose is unclear. The presence of animals may well date from its abandonment as a dwelling and is not necessarily proof that it originally functioned as a long-house with animals and humans under the same roof. Certainly there was no common entry, or entry by feeding walk, for the human entry was at the other end of the house alongside the fireplace. A later end-chimney, lobby-entry cottage, probably mid-nineteenth century, is Spite (Llanddeiniol), built on what looks like an encroachment alongside the main road from Aberystwyth to Aberaeron (Fig. 94d). While the hall is open to the roof, the secondary rooms, parlour and pantry side by side

[6]See also Mark McDermott, 'Two examples of vernacular architecture in the parishes of Llan-santffraid and Aberarth', *Ceredigion*, VIII, no.3 (1978), 323–8.

are sited under a small loft room reached by a ladder-stair in the *croglofft* tradition. The well-built walls and vertical sliding sash windows are characteristic of good nineteenth-century building construction, but the plan-form is completely archaic. Other instances of the same plan-form are to be found at Tynewydd (Llanychaearn), and Tyn-rhyd (Llanrhystud Haminiog).

However, these two groups of cottages planned with the entrance and the fireplace in close proximity appear to be greatly outnumbered by those with the entrance more or less midway between the end fireplaces as in Figs. 95, 96. This pattern, very similar to the end-chimney sub-medieval house, may have been preferred because at the time most of them were built a symmetrical 'double-fronted' villa was the height of fashion. The question which arises from the alternative types, where the fireplace and entry were closely associated, is why a handful of householders continued to prefer them and build them, even when vastly outnumbered by the fashionable symmetrical central-doorway type. Since our vernacular builders never left a written record of why they chose a particular plan, we shall never know.

At the opposite end of the social spectrum were the mansions of the great landowners. We know of none illustrating the great halls of the late Middle Ages. There appears to be no Cochwillan or Gloddaeth, no Althrey Hall or Plasnewydd (Ruabon) or Tretower Court to illustrate the lifestyle of the pre-Reformation Cardiganshire magnate. Of houses illustrating the sub-medieval phase, the outstanding example is Plas-y-wern (Llannarth). It originated as a large single-range, end-fireplace, storeyed house, its main room possibly on the first floor, probably dating from the sixteenth century to which later additions, including a notable seventeenth-century dog-leg stair, were made. Both the sub-medieval phase and the central-stairway phase are illustrated in a single mansion which contains more good early detail than any other house in the county (Fig. 50).

The early-Renaissance phase among the major Cardiganshire landowners would have been well represented by Trawsgoed, home of the Vaughan earls of Lisburne, had the multi-gabled mansion depicted by Thomas Dinely survived in the condition he found it at the time of the Duke of Beaufort's visit in 1684 (Fig. 83). As it is, no easily identifiable features attributable to the seventeenth century have survived the extensive later rebuilding of what is probably the largest dwelling in the county and the residence of its only noble family.

Nanteos was built or rebuilt by the Powells in 1739–57 (as recorded by date-inscriptions on quoin stone and rainwater head). It replaced an earlier house of which little visible now remains which stood on the other side of the stream which forms a central feature of the landscaped park. Although modified in the nineteenth century, much of the original plan (Fig. 85) and building features survive, and some are of outstanding quality (Fig. 89). The plan, consisting of a series of rooms arranged each side of a wide entrance hall and staircase, is typical of the axial planning of the period, while the entrance hall, stairs and spacious long gallery, which form the main circulation on the first floor, is a notable illustration of the 'Palladian' taste of the early Hanoverian squires.

The architect of the original house is unknown, but it is likely that the well-known Shrewsbury country-house architect, Edward Haycock, was responsible for much of the later work, including the Doric portico. The handsome detached stable-block to the rear with the Doric gateway have been attributed to different hands, of which the most probable is the obscure Aberystwyth architect W. R. Coulthart. The famous Rococo music room has no known designer or certain date. Certainly the plasterwork in many of the reception rooms and bedrooms is much later than 1739.

A further major country house is Alltyrodyn (Llandysul) which, although built about a century after Nanteos, has a basically similar ground-floor plan (Fig. 87). Here again the entrance hall and stairway are in separate compartments. A feature of Alltyrodyn is the service courtyard attached to the rear of the house. An attached service courtyard is also a feature of Llannerch Aeron (Ciliau Aeron), built to the designs of John Nash in 1794 before his return to London to achieve fame and fortune (Fig.86). It embodies many of the internal and external features of what has come to be known as the 'Regency Style', low-pitched roofs ending in widely projecting eaves supported on curved brackets. Instead of the formal axial plan centred on the entrance hall with a stairway behind directly in line (as at Nanteos and Alltyrodyn), Nash surprises the visitor by placing a top-lit stair at right-angles to the entrance-hall. Other innovative features include a segmental interior wall to the drawing-room, blind-windows concealing asymmetry (a subterfuge deplored by Nash's Victorian purist critics), and the arrangement of the main windows so that they do not focus on the drive, but rather on the surrounding parkland. The concealment of the service block from the visitor approaching by the main drive by judicious planting is characteristic of the architect's ingenuity. Early nineteenth-century architecture owes much to Nash, so much so that work by other hands is often attributed to him. Some credit is due to Edward Haycock, the Shrewsbury architect who undertook much work for the Welsh squires in a competent, late classical style, such as at Plas Llangoedmor near Cardigan and probably Mynachdy for Colonel Alban Thomas Jones Gwynne (Fig. 88). It is more than likely that Haycock was also responsible for the layout and very pretty façades of Aberaeron, developed as a planned town under Gwynne's ownership.[7]

The abandonment of axial planning and classical symmetry and formality among the gardens and houses of the landowners is most famously characterized by Hafod, first built for Thomas Johnes, rebuilt again after a disastrous fire, and finally rebuilt for Johnes's successor, the Duke of Newcastle. Alas, nothing now survives of this house, once a monument to the pursuit of the picturesque and the sublime. While the tenant farmers built their new villa-type farmhouses as close to the conventions of classical architecture as they could, the richer proprietors increasingly experimented with houses in a picturesque style derived successively from Medieval, Tudor, or Jacobean architecture, as instanced by Glandyfi Castle, Bronwydd (Llangynllo), rebuilt in 1853 (Fig. 90), or Lluest Gwilym (Llanbadarn Fawr), built in 1889.

The nineteenth century saw the appearance of major village settlements, in the south as a result of the belated emergence of a textile industry supplying industrial south Wales with flannel, and in the north as a result of an expansion in lead mining. The growth of such street villages as Tal-y-bont, Taliesin and Eglwys-fach should be noted. It is revealing to compare their solidly built stone-walled terraces, all of two storeys, with the little that now remains of the single-storey, earth-walled terraces of Bow Street, a monument to an earlier, and more agricultural age. Several different patterns of plan can be discerned in Cardiganshire terraces. Perhaps because the county never became very densely populated, the 'double fronted' cottage, with two rooms each side of the door, effectively two main rooms in length, but only one main room in depth, remained remarkably common, giving

---

[7]Henry V. Phythian-Adams, 'The planning of Aberaeron – some new evidence', *Ceredigion*, VIII, no.4 (1979), 404–7. See also Richard Suggett, *John Nash. Architect in Wales: Pensaer yng Nghymru* (Aberystwyth, 1995), for a full discussion of the works attributed to Nash in Wales.

a street pattern of window-door-window, window-door-window as at Llanfihangel-y-Creuddyn (Fig. 80). However, the alternative single-fronted plan, one main room in length but two in depth (which achieved a considerable saving in frontage), tended to gain ground and may easily be recognized from the pattern of window-door, window-door, along the length of the terrace. A final pattern runs door-window, window-door – door-window, window-door, a pattern which enabled adjacent living-rooms to share a chimney stack – a considerable saving, leading to its almost universal adoption for streets of semis which became common after the First World War.[8]

The twentieth century was to see major changes in the economic, social and political structure of the county which had repercussions for architecture. The faltering industrialization embodied in mining in the north and weaving in the south went into decline and finally expired. Coastwise shipping and the shipbuilding which was its by-product likewise came to an end as first rail, and then decisively, road connections replaced seaborne trade. The result was that in addition to its long and enduring dependence on agriculture, the county had to look to the well-established tourist trade, centres of learning and the provision of higher education, particularly for undergraduates who wish to study as far from home as possible, agricultural institutes, forestry, and defence establishments to fill the gap left by industrial decline.

Other changes reflecting developments in the structure of society became manifest. The late burst of enlarging houses already too large, particularly evident at Trawsgoed and Nanteos, showed how reluctant landowners were to realize that their long ascendancy was about to end, and the *raison d'être* of their stately homes about to disappear. The aristocracy paid dearly for the First World War in both treasure and in blood, as instanced by the death of the last of the Powells of Nanteos in the final days of that calamitous conflict. To judge from the names of fallen officers on village war memorials, by 1918 almost every *plas* in the county must have been in mourning. After the war ended, death duties and agricultural depression added to the squires' woes, while the supply of cheap servants to service their spacious homes and extensive gardens began to dry up. As the landed families departed, their mansions were turned, if they were fortunate, into institutions, government offices, old peoples' homes or hotels, or, failing such adaptations, were demolished as in the case of Hafod Uchtryd and Derry Ormond, or left to slow decay as at Bronwydd (Llangynllo). Within little more than a generation a class which had risen out of the ruins of Glyndŵr's rebellion, which had been placed securely in the saddle by the Tudors, and which had dominated Wales ever since, quietly faded away.[9]

The fate of their erstwhile tenants was rather happier. Often able to purchase on favourable terms the farms their ancestors had rented from the great estates, they emerged as a class of prosperous yeomen, in some ways a newly emerging minor local aristocracy intermarrying with their own kind, their economic position assured after the Second (and for the United Kingdom the less calamitous) World War, by government subsidies or guaranteed prices for their products. They were also fortunate in inheriting comparatively modern and mostly well-built houses which largely

---

[8]See also J. B. Lowe, *Welsh Industrial Workers Housing 1775–1875* (Cardiff, 1977); idem, *Welsh Country Workers Housing 1775–1875* (Cardiff, 1985); Eurwyn Wiliam, *Home-made Homes* (Cardiff, 1993).
[9]For the sad decline of so many of the houses of the gentry, see Thomas Lloyd, *The Lost Houses of Wales* (London, 1986), revealing losses, particularly of the larger and the later mansions on an alarming scale.

dated from the previous century, symmetrical stone boxes which, supplied with electricity and plumbing, continue to dominate the rural scene. Thus while Suffolk, Essex, Kent and Sussex illustrate the 'Great Rebuilding' of the fifteenth century, while the Cotswolds and Montgomeryshire illustrate the 'Great Rebuilding' of the seventeenth century, the Cardiganshire farmscape is essentially that of the eighteenth and nineteenth century. Were Wordsworth to return to the 'sweet-shire' he would recognize much that was emerging in his day. Its hedgerows and woodlands still largely surviving, its beauty might still move him to verse, better, we hope, than 'Simon Lee'.

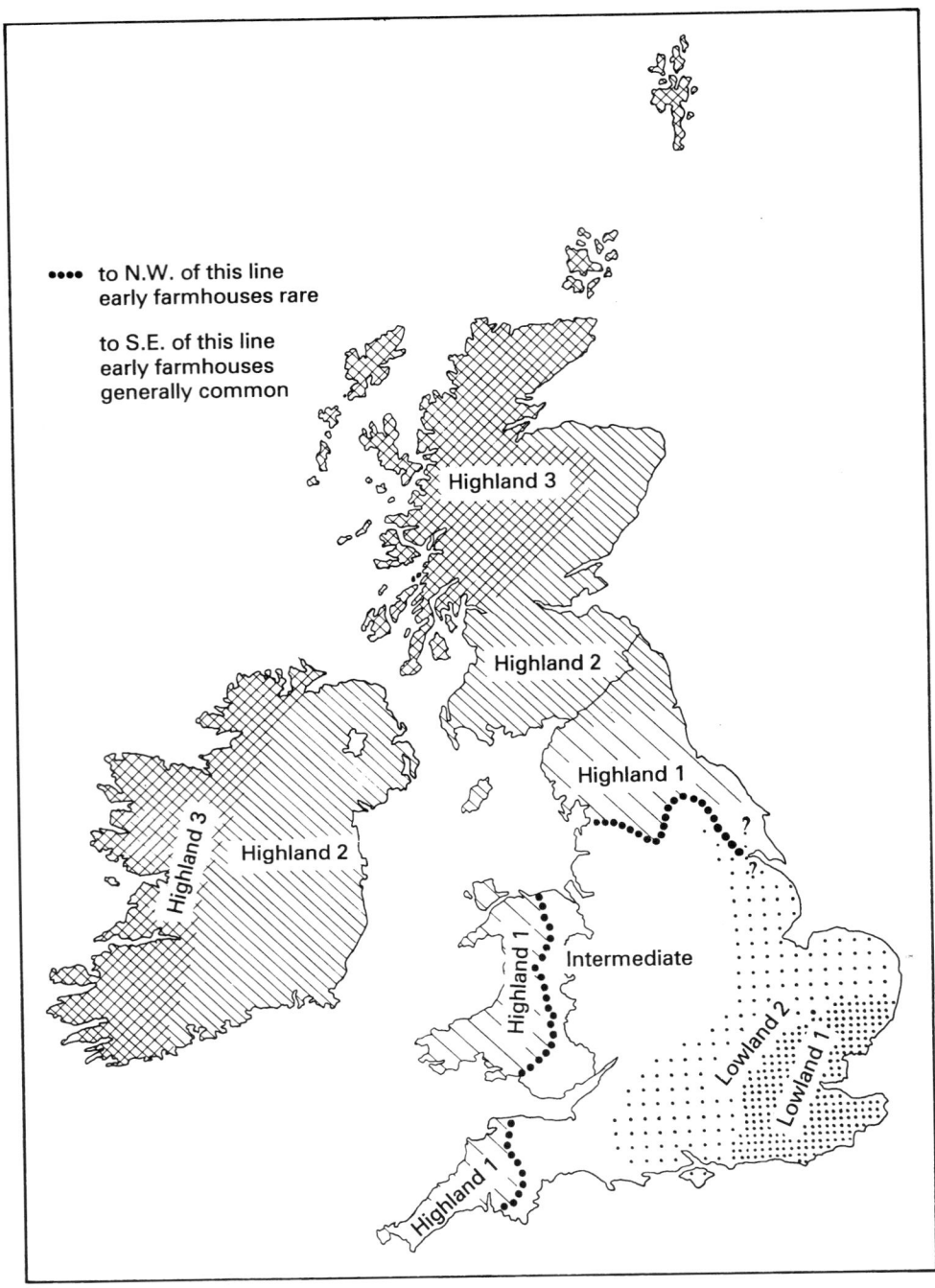

Fig. 51: Building Regions of the British Isles. This map is the first to show the architecture of Cardiganshire in context. It suggests the character of local architecture is dependent on its distance from London and the terrain, lowland or highland. It proposes a series of regions extending from an 'inner lowland' zone enclosing London and marked by a great wealth of early houses to an 'outer highland' zone where early farmhouses rarely survive. It suggests that while eastern Wales falls into an intermediate zone characterized by a great wealth of early houses and by a mixture of lowland and highland features, west Wales has much fewer early houses and the architecture is predominantly highland in spite of extensive tracts of low-lying terrain.

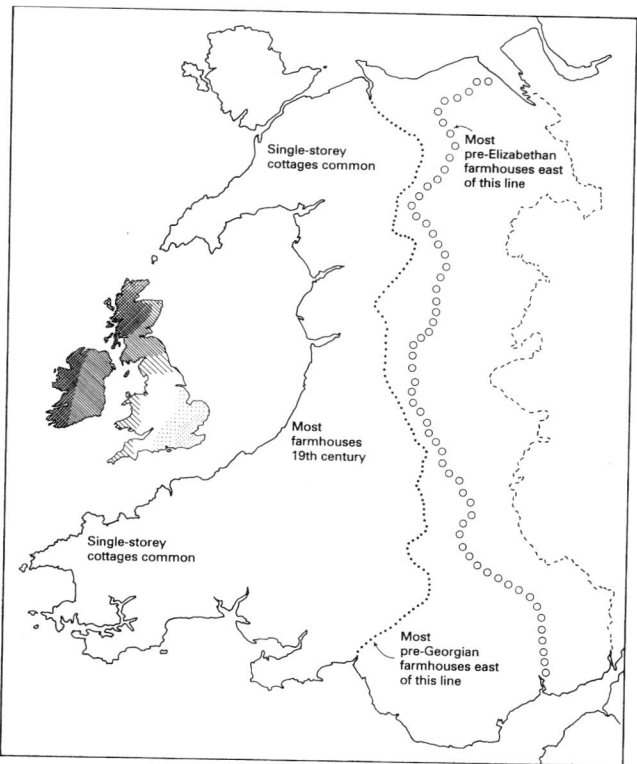

Dolcletwr Villa (Pont-siân) 1877

Fig. 52: Welsh Building Regions. In contrast with the borderland there are few houses in Cardiganshire dating from before the eighteenth century, while many (*as above*) are Victorian. Nineteenth-century date-inscriptions are common around Llandysul, reflecting the late prosperity of the textile industry.

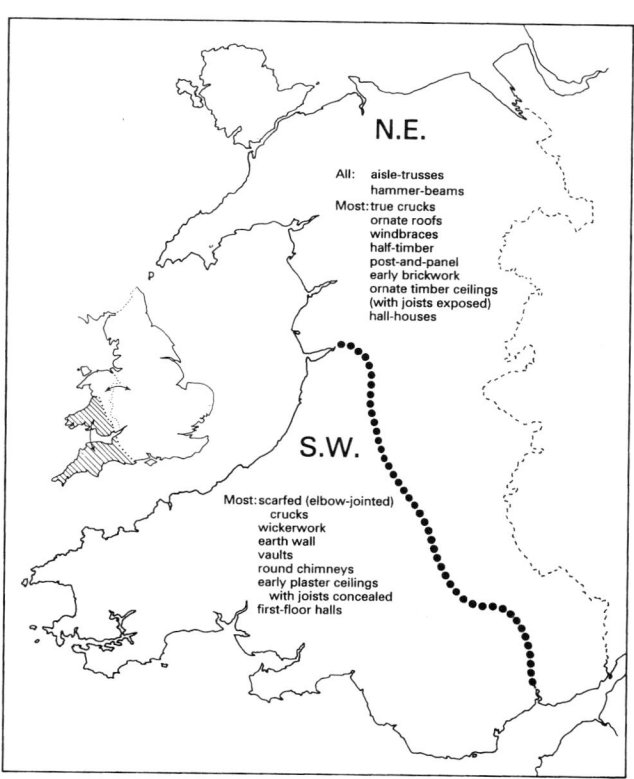

Wig-wen-fach (Llanddewi Aber-arth)

Fig. 53: Welsh Building Regions (cont.) shows the contrast between NE and SW. Cardiganshire qualifies positively for a place in the SW by the abundance of wickerwork (*above*), earth wall (clom), as well as scarfed-cruck construction, and negatively by the absence of the ornate roof and half-timbered wall or partition.

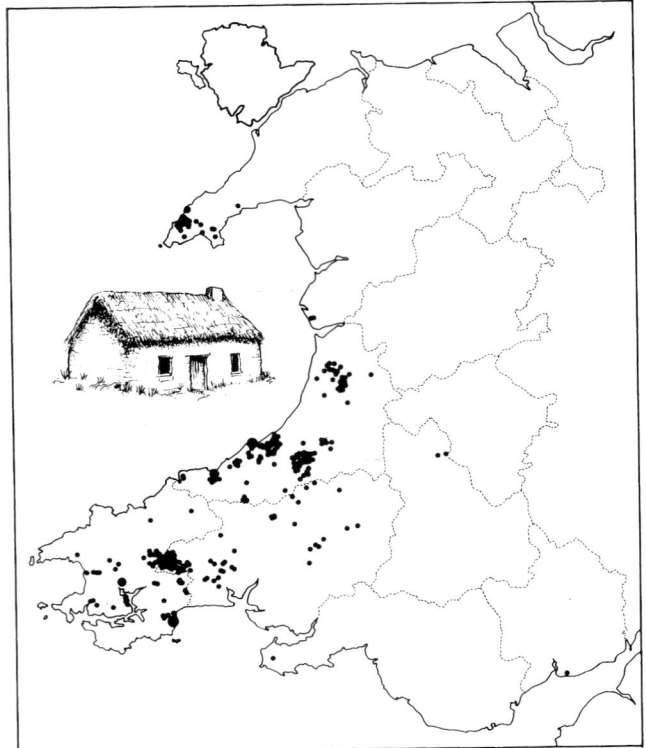

Corn-barn, Pen-wern (Llanfihangel Ystrad)

Fig. 54: Earth wall. This map (traced from one first prepared by Gerallt Nash) shows the strength of the earth wall (clom, pisé de terre, cob) tradition in SW Wales. At Pen-wern (*above*) the storeyed farmhouse and most of the buildings are also of this material.

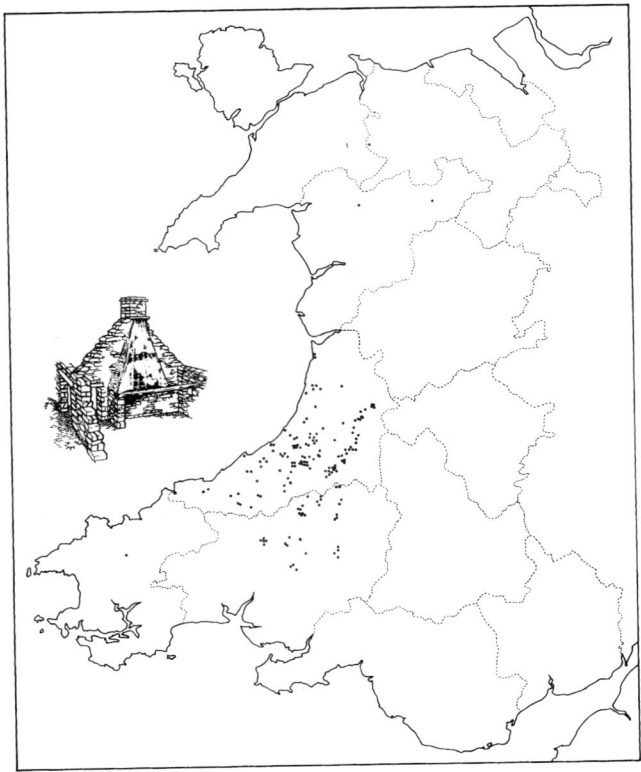

Wig-wen-fach (Llanddewi Aber-arth)

Fig. 55 Wickerwork firehoods, another characteristic of the Cardiganshire vernacular building tradition, still survive in quantity both here and in Carmarthenshire.

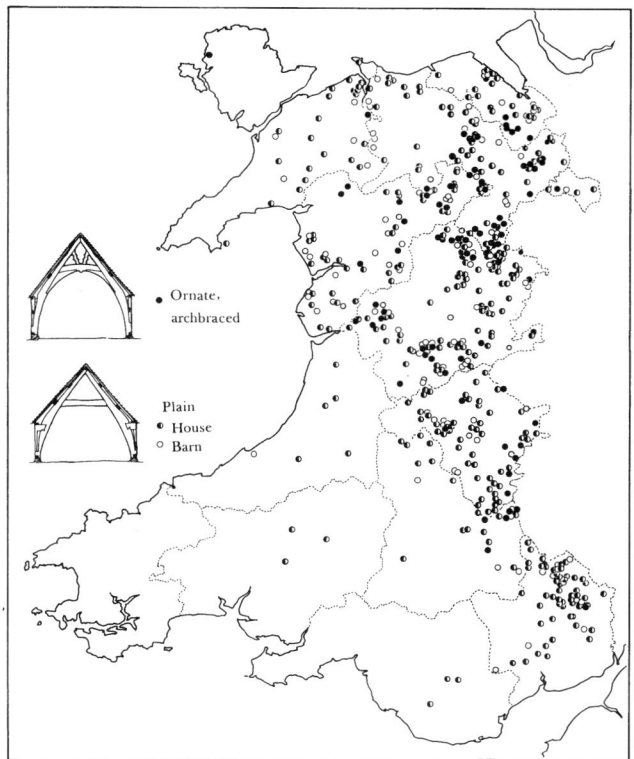

Preswylfa (Llanfihangel-y-Creuddyn)

Fig. 56: Crucks. Although common in the Welsh borderland and much of north Wales, few crucks have been found to the west of the Newport/Machynlleth line. A Cardiganshire example is, however, illustrated above, giving a good impression of an open hall interior.

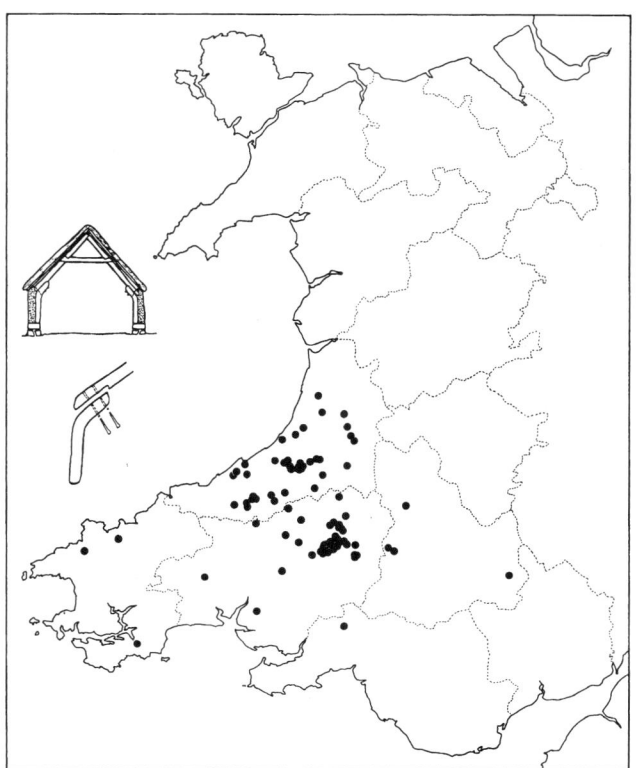

Wig-wen-fach (Llanddewi Aber-arth)

Fig. 57: Scarfed crucks. Far more widespread in Cardiganshire than the cruck is the derivative scarfed-cruck (also common in SW England). In Wales it is usually face-pegged.

Fig. 58: An Old House near Strata Florida. These well-known drawings made in 1888 by the artist, Worthington Smith, for the antiquary, Stephen Williams, illustrate many of the features noted on the previous maps, the wickerwork fireplace hood, wickerwork partitions, and scarfed crucks. However, the posts supporting the roof are unique. Are these evidence of an ancient local tradition of aisled construction, as suggested by Mr G. A. G. Griffiths, or a repair made to a collapsing building? Evidence for repair is clear in the forked trunk propping the principal and the strut supporting the purlin (Fig. 59 *top opposite*).

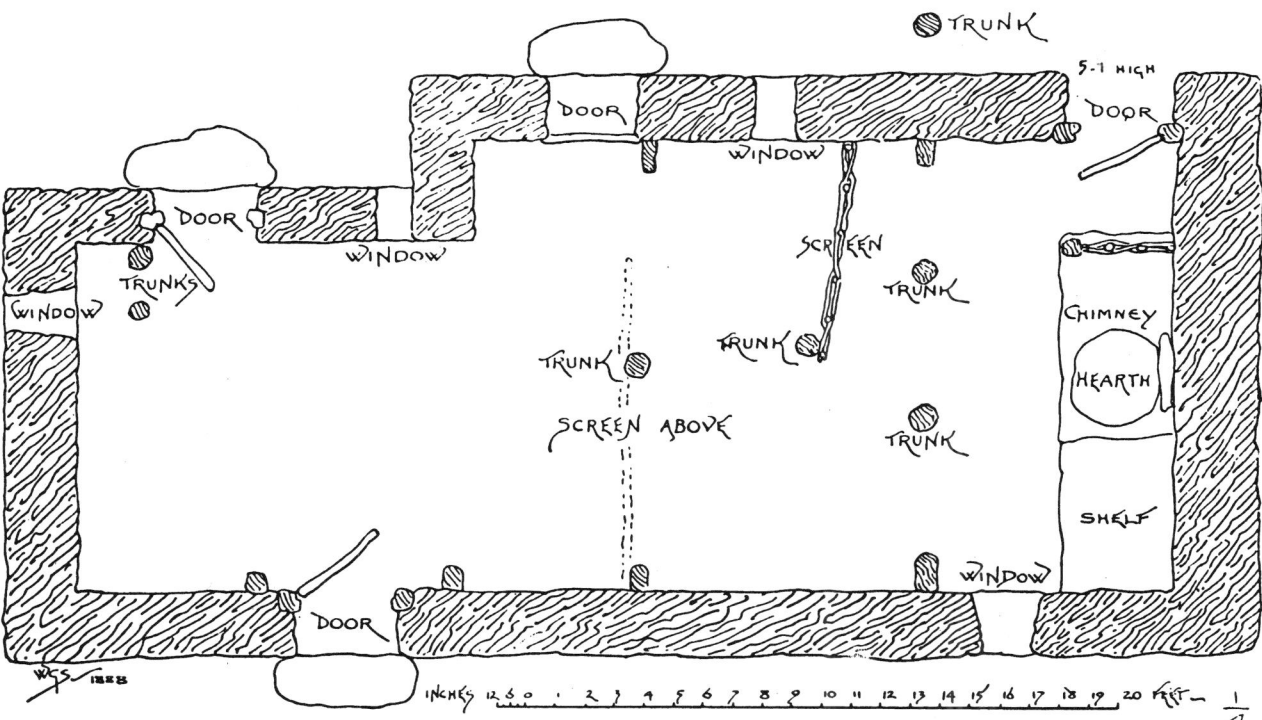

Fig. 59: An Old House near Strata Florida (cont.) The plan, lobby-entry by end-fireplace, occurs elsewhere in the county. The 'trunks' suggest a repair made perhaps when stone replaced earth, a common modification to our vernacular buildings. The small annexe at the end away from the fireplace may be of a later date and built when the dwelling was converted to agricultural use. Although we have echoes here of the dwelling of 'twisted branches of trees sufficient to last the year' of Giraldus Cambrensis, it may be doubted if there is anything older than the eighteenth century, built during the change from the impermanent to the durable farmstead.

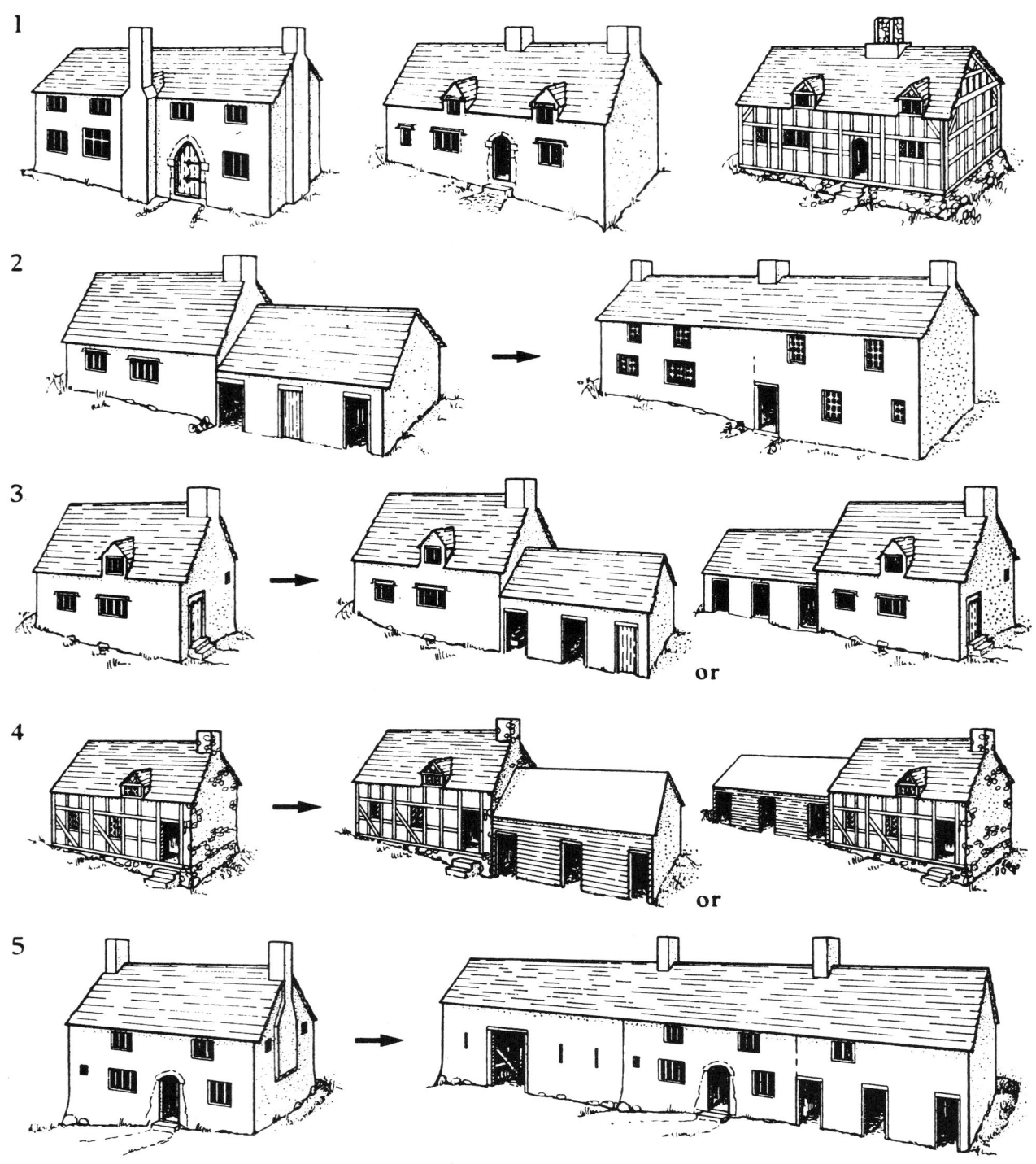

Fig. 60: Sub-medieval house-types, showing the houses that emerged in Wales (and in England too) as the medieval hall gave way to the storeyed house fitted with fireplaces. Examples of most can be found in Cardiganshire, though not in the half-timbered versions, but all are greatly outnumbered by the fully developed 'Renaissance-Victorian' farmhouse (Fig. 62 *bottom right*).

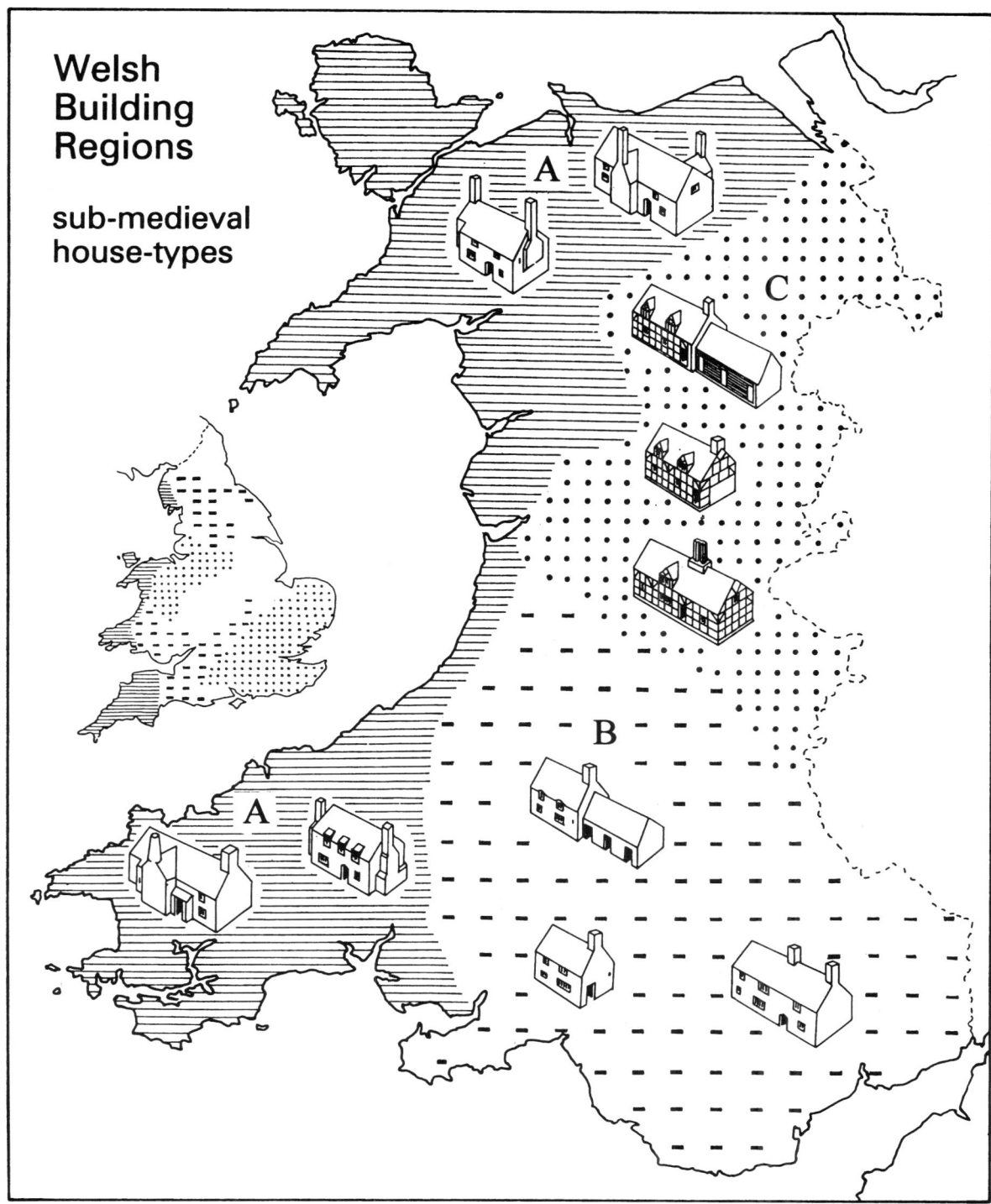

Welsh Building Regions

sub-medieval house-types

Fig. 61: Sub-medieval house-types (cont.) showing the main locations. Sketching-in Cardiganshire proved difficult because of the lack of many surviving examples other than end-chimney cottages. These and a small number of 'hearth-passage' houses are the basis of our estimate. A preference for a house with a fireplace on the outer wall is evident in the western coastlands (as also in western France), an indication of a mild climate.

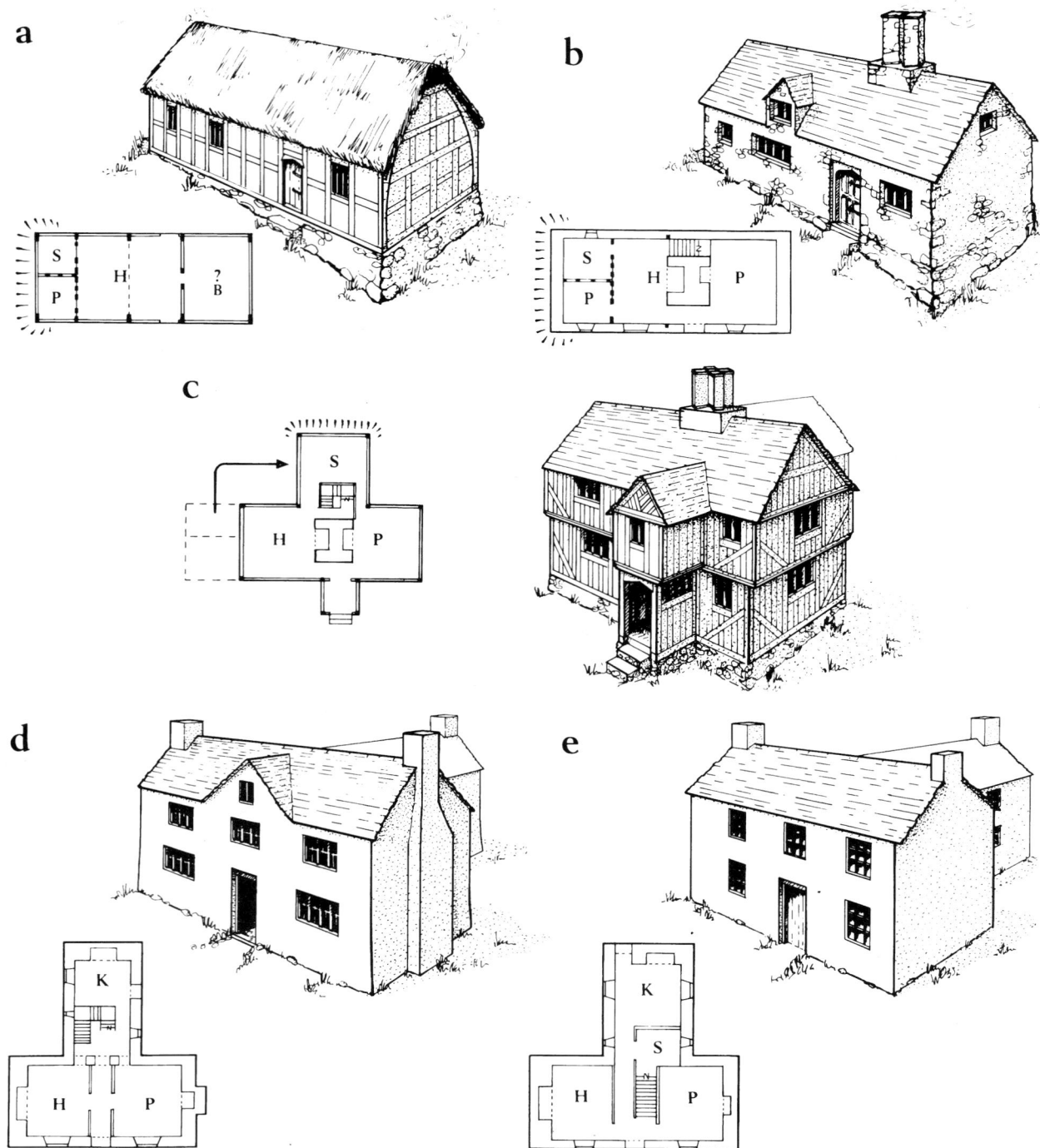

Fig. 62: The development of the farmhouse from the late Middle Ages to the nineteenth century. Only fragments (none with half-timbered walls) of **a** the cruck-framed open hall (e.g. Preswylfa, Fig. 56) have been found in Cardiganshire. Of **b** the sub-medieval house with fireplace (possibly converted from an open hall as Fig. 72**a**) there are some instances, but the great majority of Cardiganshire farmhouses are variants of **e**, the Georgian-Victorian central-stairway house (Figs. 80, 81).

Fig. 63: Ynyscreigiog (Ysgubor-y-coed), a lateral-chimney house, probably the earliest in the sub-medieval series, but rare in Cardiganshire. The notable tall tapering chimney suggests high social status which the house's links with the Pryse family of Gogerddan confirm. The siting of the house on a stone outcrop overlooking the marshes of the Dyfi is memorable. Note the windows in the gable-end wall.

Fig. 64: Penrhyngerwin (Ysgubor-y-coed), a hearth-passage house, the next in the sub-medieval series which occurs extensively in Cardiganshire. The main fireplace backs onto the entrance. Although rebuilt *c.*1880 the original plan is still discernible. Such plans appear to have had as their object the preservation of the dignity of the high table, placing the fireplace close to the entrance and away from the table. They are peculiar to England and Wales.

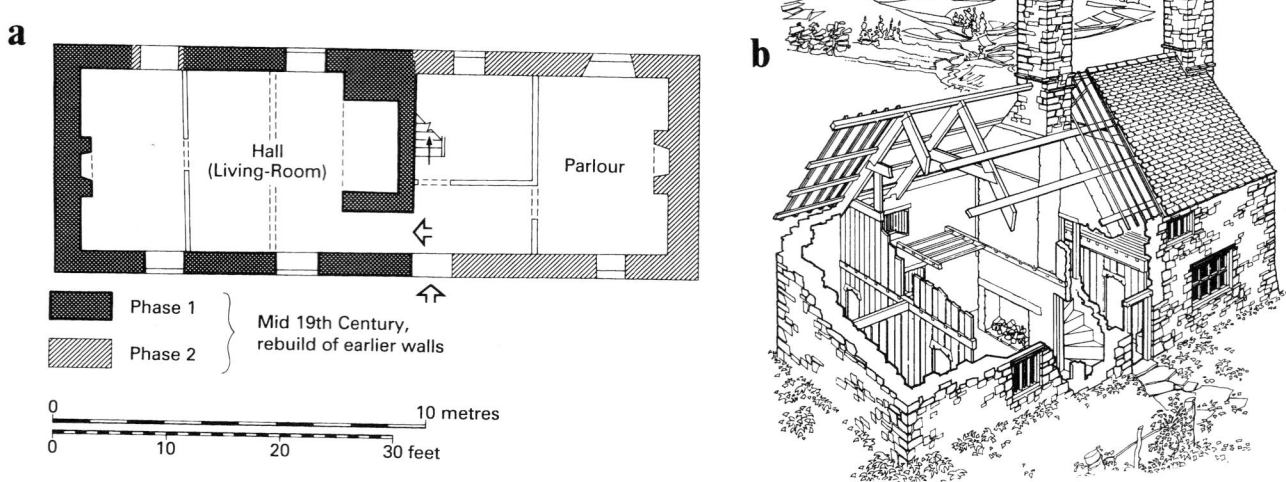

Fig. 65: Further illustrations of the hearth-passage house, **a** Penrhyngerwin (Ysgubor-y-coed), and **c** Maesnewydd (Ceulan-y-maes-mawr), were largely rebuilt in the nineteenth century. However, **b** Trewalter (Llan-gors, Brecs.), dated 1653, preserved more of its original appearance where a clearly defined passage between opposed doorways divided house and down-house (*pen isaf*), in this case a parlour. In neither Cardiganshire house is there any indication of the original function of the *pen isaf*.

Fig. 66: Talwrn (Caron-uwch-clawdd) is an instance of the mini 'hearth-passage' house. There is no *pen isaf* (down-house), so the entry is through the end wall. The little 'lean-to' alongside is surely an afterthought. The details and general proportions suggest the house is nineteenth century, or a nineteenth-century rebuild.

Fig. 67: This unidentified house from the Cardiganshire collection of photographs at St Fagans is another 'mini' hearth-passage house. Were a byre added we would have a long-house. However, the window over the front door makes it improbable that a byre has been taken away. Note the braided thatch chimneys peeping through the corrugated iron cladding, showing that not only the fireplace hood, but the chimney shaft itself, was of wickerwork, and built before the last phase of the wickerwork fireplace, when the hood was fitted into a corbelled stone chimney which carried the flue into the open air (*Museum of Welsh Life, St Fagans*).

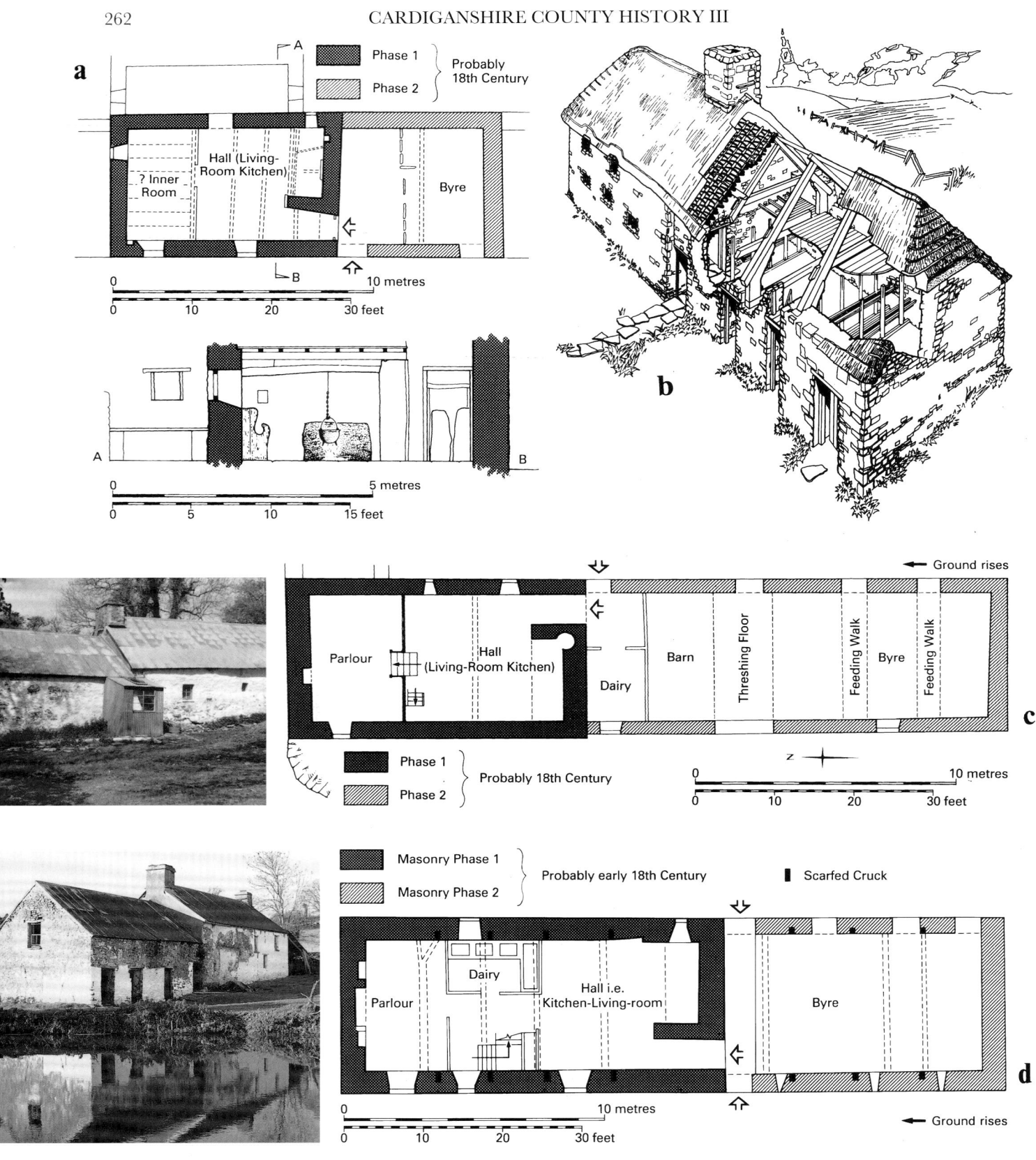

a

A

Phase 1 ⎱ Probably
Phase 2 ⎰ 18th Century

? Inner Room

Hall (Living-Room Kitchen)

Byre

B

0   10 metres
0   10   20   30 feet

A   B

0   5 metres
0   5   10   15 feet

b

Ground rises →

Parlour

Hall (Living-Room Kitchen)

Dairy

Barn

Threshing Floor

Feeding Walk

Byre

Feeding Walk

Phase 1 ⎱ Probably 18th Century
Phase 2 ⎰

z

0   10 metres
0   10   20   30 feet

c

Masonry Phase 1 ⎱ Probably early 18th Century
Masonry Phase 2 ⎰

▮ Scarfed Cruck

Parlour

Dairy

Hall i.e. Kitchen-Living-room

Byre

0   10 metres
0   10   20   30 feet

Ground rises →

d

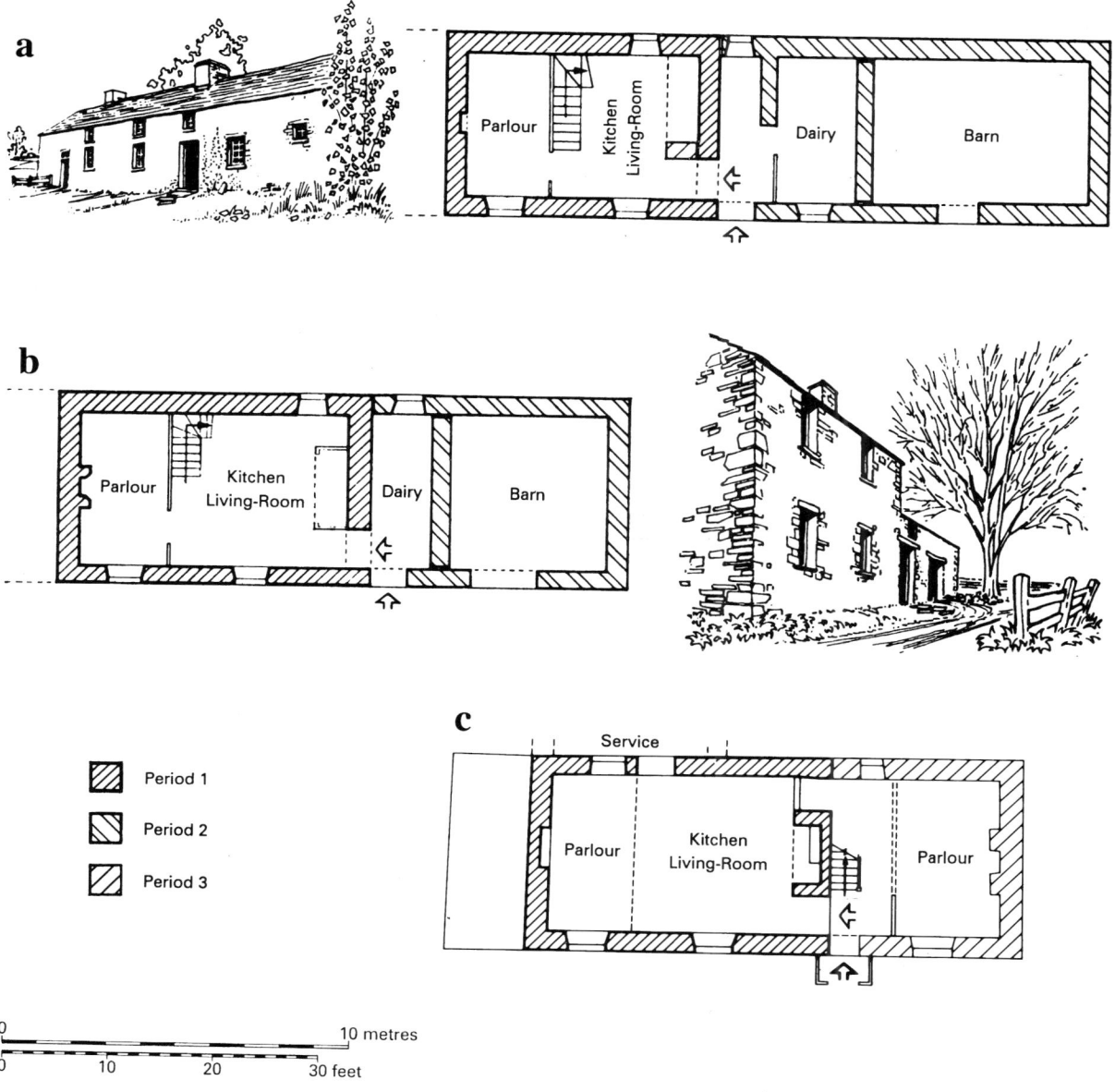

Fig. 68: (opposite) Of all hearth-passage variants the best known is the long-house where the house is entered by a feeding walk in the adjacent byre which constitutes the *pen isaf*, or down-house, as at **a** Sychnant (Llanddewibrefi), **c** Allt-ddu (Llanddewibrefi) and **d** Rhiwson-isaf (Llanwnnen), happily to be restored. Similar to these Cardiganshire examples is **b** Tŷ'r celyn (Llandeilo) showing the characteristic scarfed-cruck construction, and structural joint between house and byre, the byre built against the house, indicative of the successive building (or rebuilding) of house and byre.

Fig. 69: Other hearth-passage houses are illustrated by **a** Ffos-y-ffin, and **b** Tŷ-llwyd,both in Llangeitho parish, as well as **c** Plas-bach (Pentre-bach). None seems older than the nineteenth century, though reproducing this ancient form of plan. At **a** and **b** the house is entered through a dairy, while at **c** the *pen isaf* is evidently a parlour. In each there is a clear structural break between house and down-house, the latter built against the former.

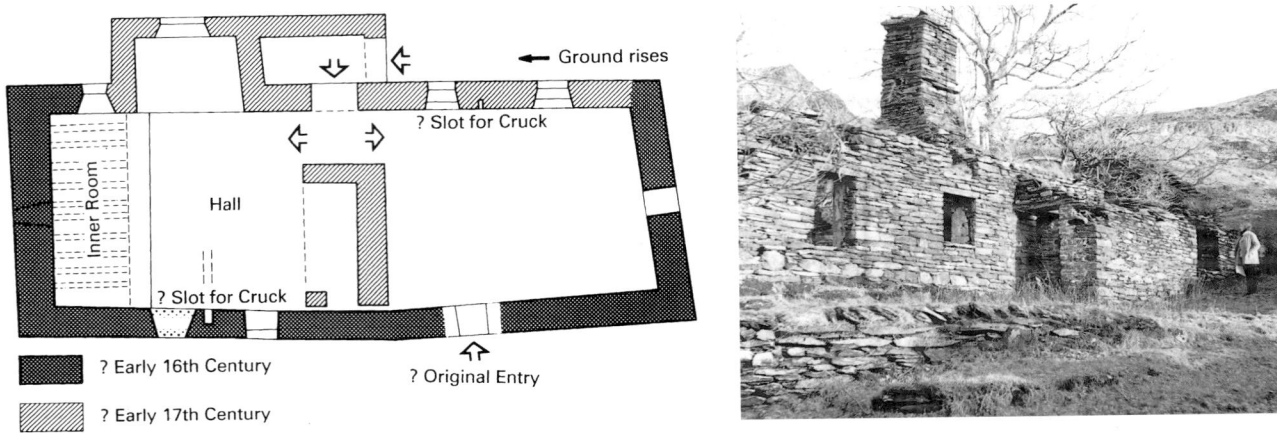

Fig. 70: Neuadd-lwyd (Ysgubor-y-coed) had eventually a sub-medieval, internal-fireplace, lobby-entry plan, typologically later than the internal fireplace, hearth-passage plan, and less common than the hearth-passage group in Cardiganshire. In this case the fireplace seems to have been inserted into what had been an open hall heated by an open hearth. Possibly it had been placed backing on the entry in the hearth-passage tradition. The main entry (through the porch) creating a lobby is probably a modification made when the *pen isaf* acquired domestic type windows. Possibly the *pen isaf* was originally a byre. The purpose of the outshot alongside the porch is unclear.

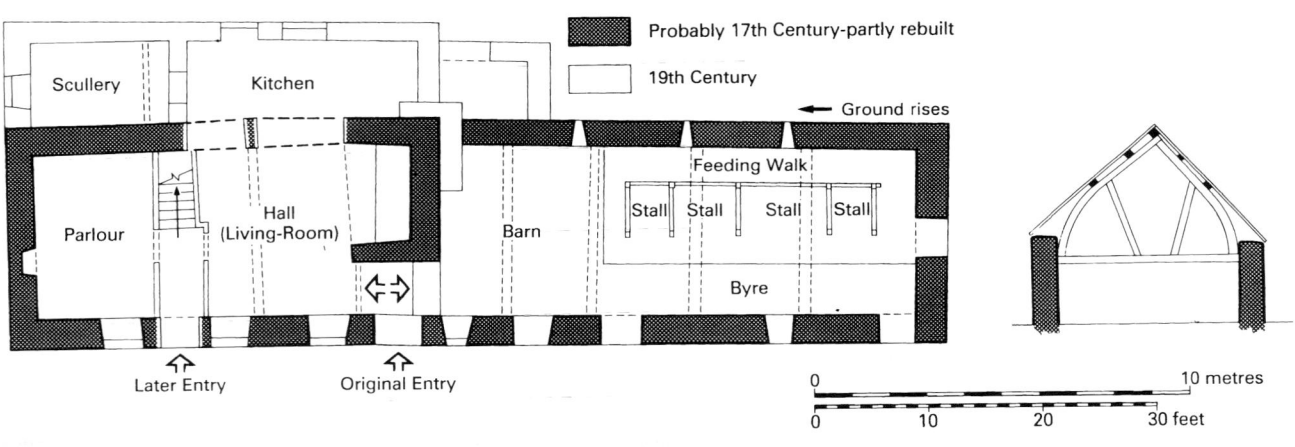

Fig. 71: Ynyseidiol (Ysgubor-y-coed) was, before its Victorian reconstruction, a good example of an internal-fireplace, lobby-entry, long-house, where instead of being entered through a feeding-walk in the byre (in the hearth-passage tradition) the building was entered through a lobby giving on to the house in one direction and the byre in the other.

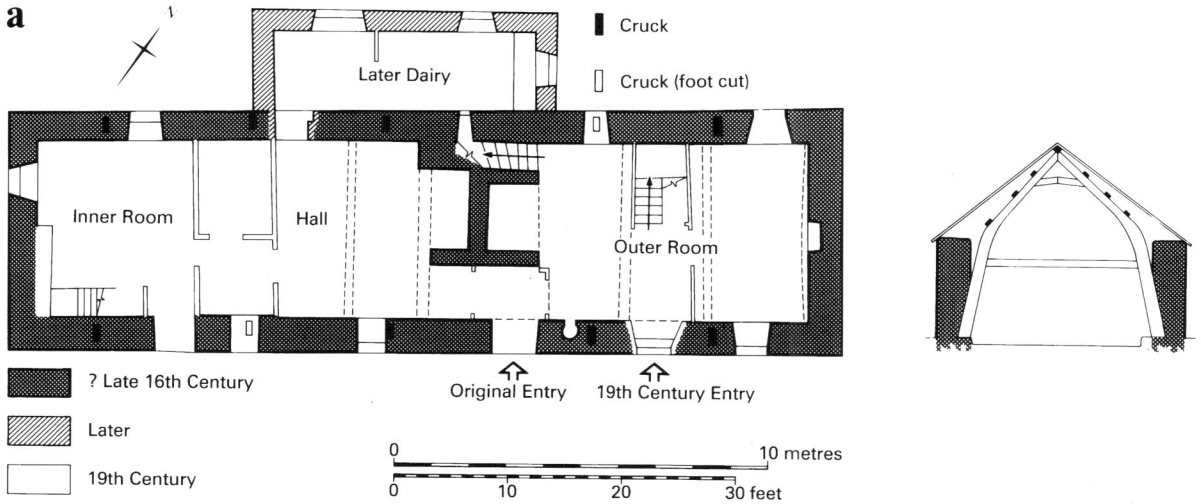

a

Cruck

Cruck (foot cut)

Later Dairy

Inner Room

Hall

Outer Room

? Late 16th Century

Later

19th Century

Original Entry

19th Century Entry

0   10 metres

0   10   20   30 feet

b

Fig. 72: **a** Gwastadgwrda (Betws Leucu) is a very rare example in Cardiganshire of a lobby-entry house incorporating back-to-back fireplaces. The crucks may be contemporary with the storeyed house. At **b** Wenffrwd (Ysgubor-y-coed) we have much later, probably nineteenth-century version, of the lobby-entry plan, the rooms arranged in the form (standard in neighbouring Montgomeryshire) of hall between outer room parlour and inner service-rooms.

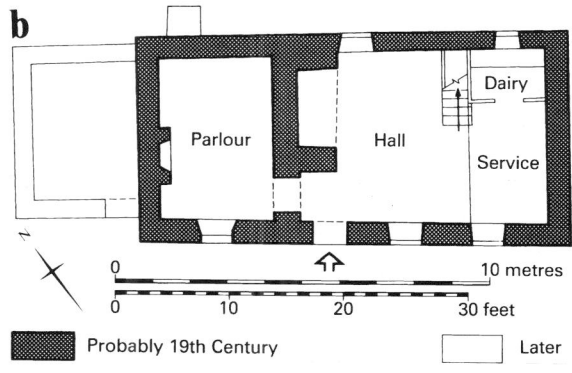

b

Parlour

Hall

Dairy

Service

0   10 metres

0   10   20   30 feet

Probably 19th Century

Later

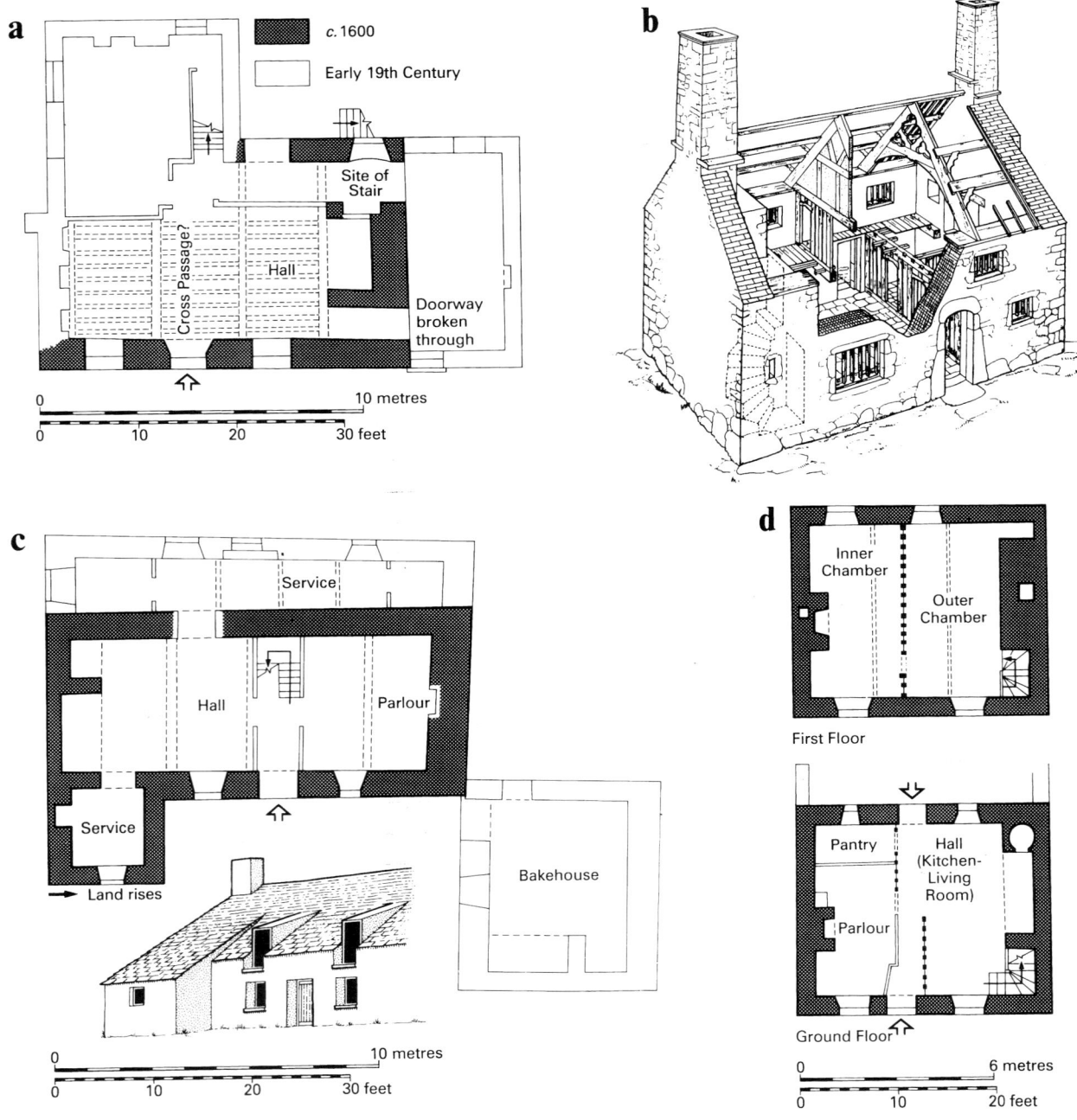

Fig. 73: Our final sub-medieval house is the end-chimney, direct-entry type dominant in Gwynedd as illustrated by **b**. Though single-storey cottages closely related to this plan are common in Cardiganshire (*see* Figs. 95,96) it has been difficult to find *houses*, partly perhaps because of their outward similarity to the later central-entry, central-stairway group (*see* Figs. 80, 81). However, Plas Dolcletwr (Llangynfelyn) **a** is a possible instance, as is **c** Crugbychan (Y Ferwig) assuming the central stair is a later insertion. Although nineteenth-century, **d** Einion Cottage (Furnace) reproduces the essential plan features, the opposed doorways dividing living-room/hall from small parlour and pantry, the fireplace-stair giving access to outer and inner chamber. The lack of independent access to each chamber no doubt led to the later adoption of the central stairway (Figs. 79, 81).

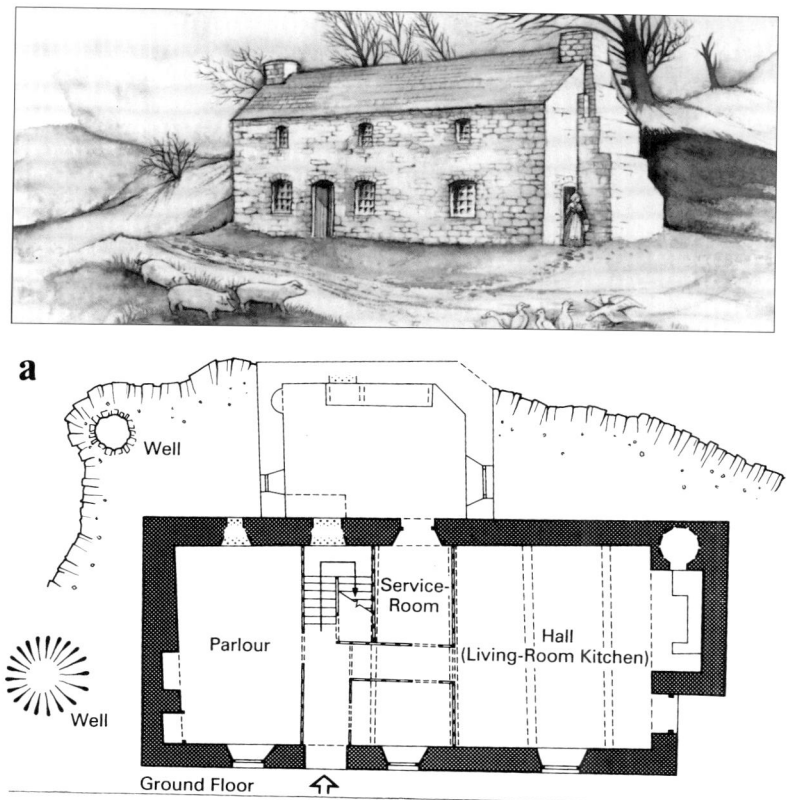

Fig. 74: Other end-chimney houses are **a** Pen-y-graig (Llanychaearn) and **b** Bryngolau (Llanfihangel Ystrad).
Bryngolau, with its restored thatched roof, is a reminder how rural Cardiganshire would have looked only a hundred
years ago. Pen-y-graig shows how the direct-entry plan was being taken over by the central stairway. The massive hall
fireplace (reminiscent of Pembrokeshire) looks old but an inscription suggests the house was built as late as 1789.
Water-colour by Jane Durrant.

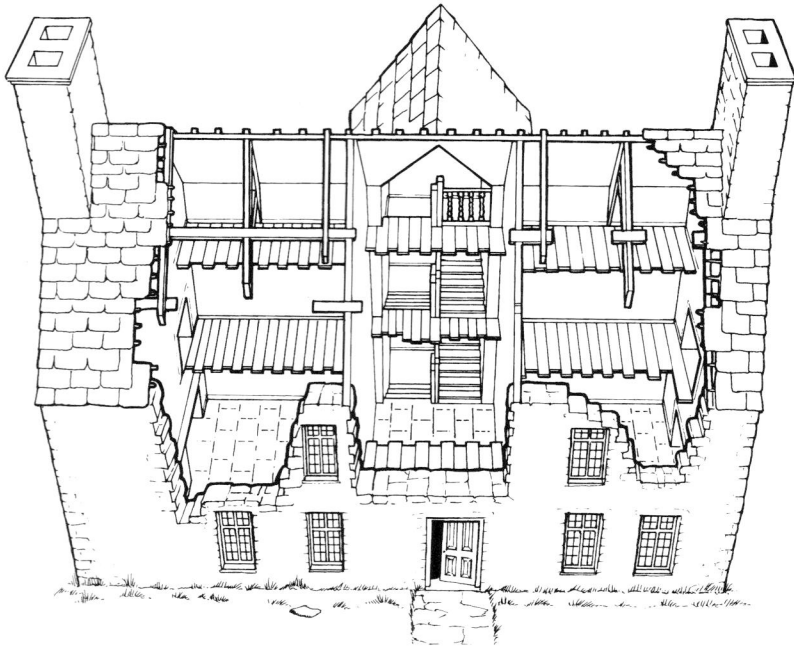

Fig. 75: Gelli (Trefilan) has a Renaissance-inspired, more-or-less symmetrical, centralized plan of a type which began gradually to supersede the earlier, sub-medieval patterns. The new plan appears first among the houses of the squires. The central stairway in a turret has a direct link to the front door. The plan thus comes close to satisfying the fashion for a symmetrical front and providing circulation giving independent access to most rooms, particularly the chambers on the upper floors. The projecting stair turret, dating in Wales from the sixteenth century, was later discarded for a stair in the body of the house, a cheaper alternative, as in the cross-wing (on the right) added in the early nineteenth century.

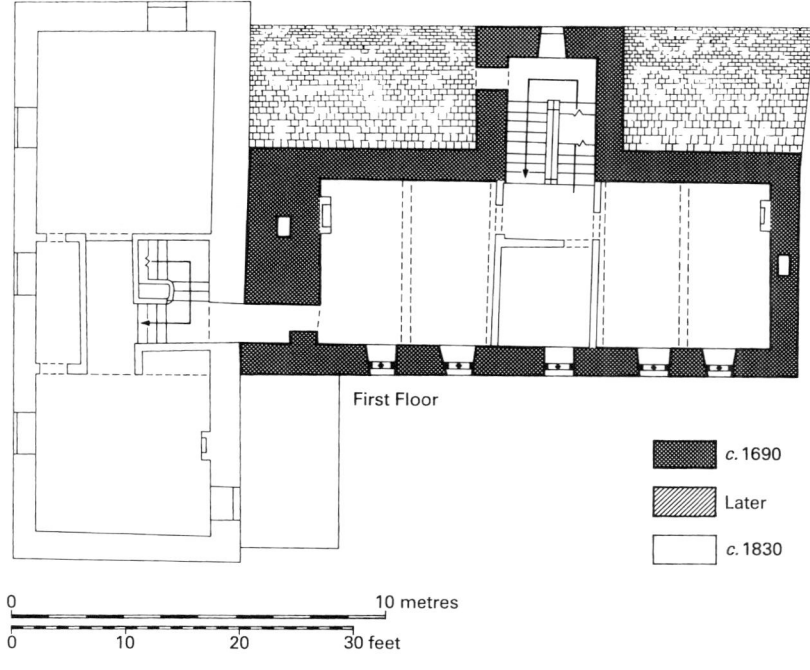

First Floor

c.1690

Later

c.1830

0   10 metres

0   10   20   30 feet

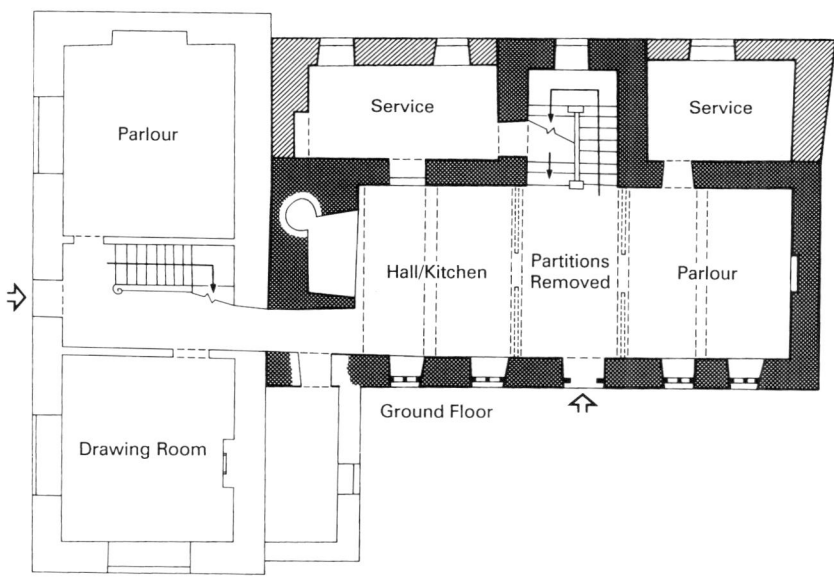

Parlour

Service

Service

Hall/Kitchen

Partitions
Removed

Parlour

Drawing Room

Ground Floor

Fig. 76: Gelli (Trefilan) showing the improved circulation provided by the centralized plan. The advantage of having several rooms, where it was possible to read without being interrupted by through traffic, must have weighed with an increasingly literate population. Another feature, later adopted by countless farmsteads, was placing the service-rooms, dairy and pantry, to the rear of the main block, under a catslide roof, rather than in line with it. This further emphasized the prestige of the front, even though absolute symmetry was rarely achieved because of the unbalancing effect of having the kitchen-living-room fireplace much larger than the parlour fireplace. Note: parlour windows have been restored on both drawings.

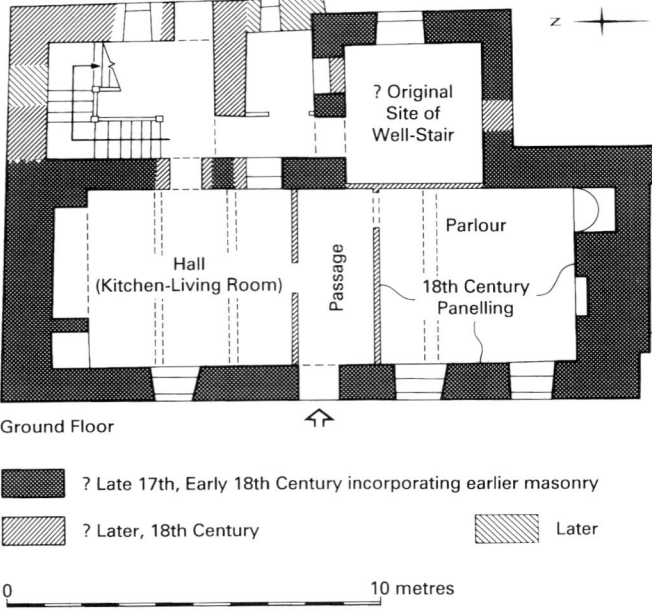

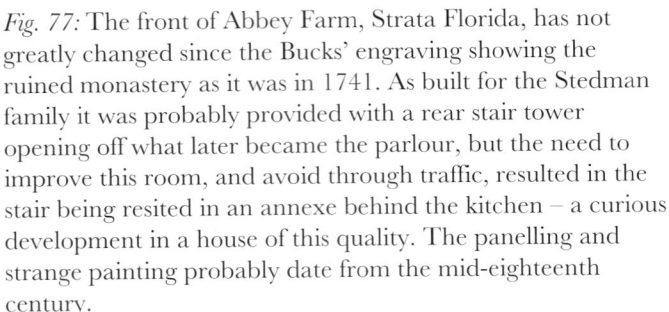

Fig. 77: The front of Abbey Farm, Strata Florida, has not greatly changed since the Bucks' engraving showing the ruined monastery as it was in 1741. As built for the Stedman family it was probably provided with a rear stair tower opening off what later became the parlour, but the need to improve this room, and avoid through traffic, resulted in the stair being resited in an annexe behind the kitchen – a curious development in a house of this quality. The panelling and strange painting probably date from the mid-eighteenth century.

This is not an easy house to understand.

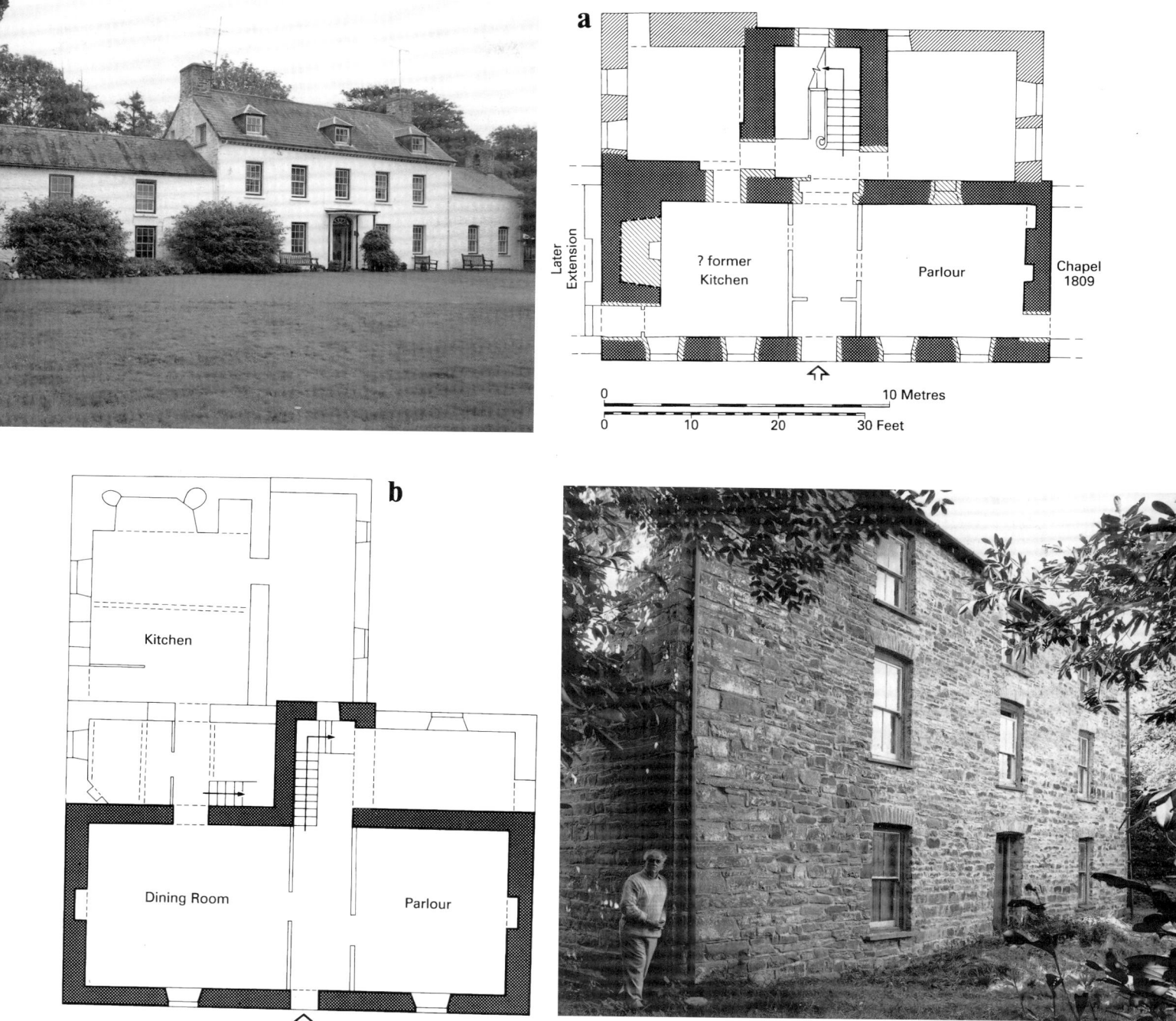

Fig. 78: Other gentry houses with stair turrets are **a** Tŷ-glyn (Llanddewi Aber-arth Upper) and **b** Hafod (Nancwnlle). Tŷ-glyn is probably a mid-eighteenth century reconstruction of a seventeenth-century house involving complete refenestration and refitting. No detail of the earlier house survives save a sundial dated 1624 reset on a farm building in 1767. The units on each side of the turret are probably mid-eighteenth century. The private chapel on the right dates from 1809, built by the squarson, the Revd Alban Gwynne, the founder of Aberaeron. The front of Hafod, in the form of a parlour block added to an older house, although early nineteenth century, retains the by then archaic stair turret.

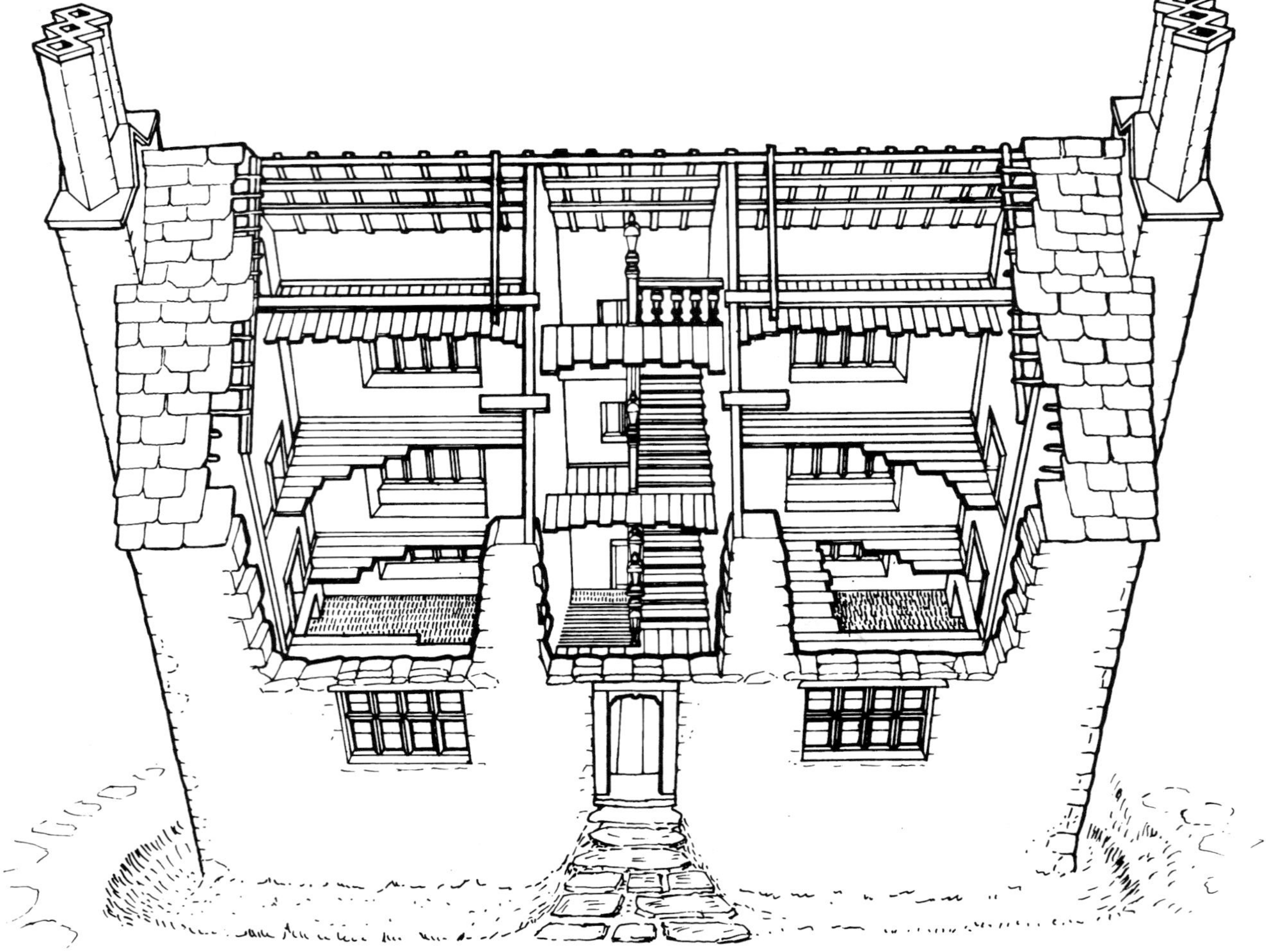

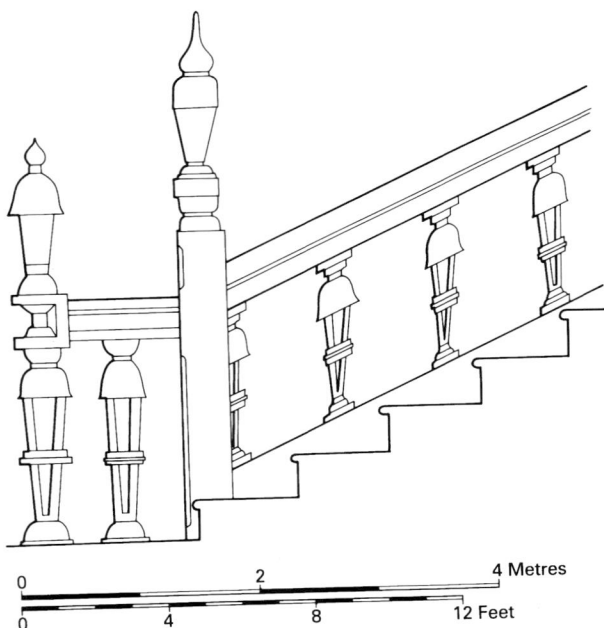

0   2   4 Metres

0   4   8   12 Feet

Fig. 79: Tyfaenor (Abbey Cwm-hir, Rads.) probably built *c.*1650 for Richard Fowler, then high sheriff of Radnorshire, is the earliest house in Wales to be built around a central stairway immediately opposite the front door, without a stair tower, and giving independent access to each room in the house, completely obviating the passage-room, but requiring fireplaces on the external walls. Such houses, built in the eighteenth and nineteenth centuries, still at the end of the twentieth century dominate the landscape of Cardiganshire and the rest of west Wales (*see* Fig. 80 *opposite*).

Neuadd (Llanddewibrefi), 1758

Bryngwin-canol (Ceulan-y-maes-mawr)

Tyn-y-berllan (Llanilar), *c.*1900

Row of cottages (Llanfihangel-y-Creuddyn)

Tir-bach (Nancwnlle)

Castellhywel (Pont-siân)

Fig. 80: Central-stairway houses, 18th–19th century. Note the variations in window spacing. Castellhywel is a rebuild of an older house.

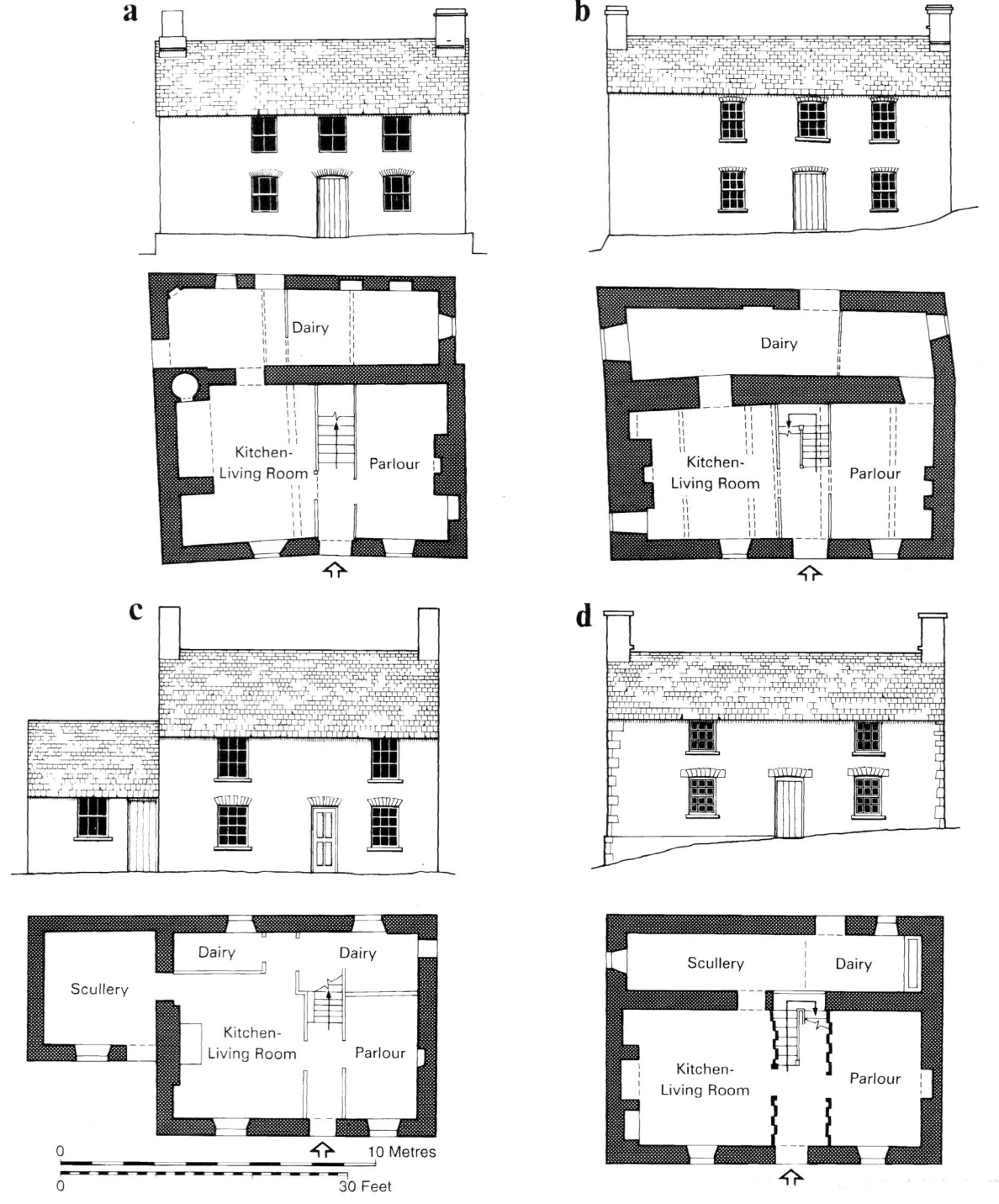

Fig. 81: Central-stairway houses (18th–19th century) still dominate the Cardiganshire countryside as at **a** Gwar-cwm-isaf (Llangynfelyn), **b** Pant-swllt (Talgarreg), **c** Berllan-deg (Abermagwr) and **d** Pwll-ffein (Pont-siân), selected among hundreds to illustrate variable window arrangements, set either equidistant from the door (*above*) or equidistant between door and outer quoin (*below*).

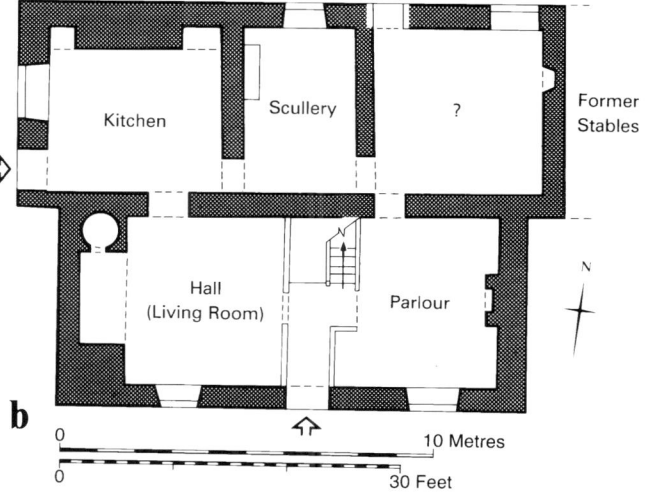

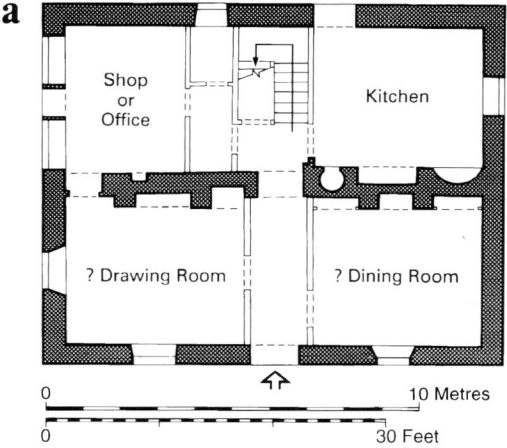

Fig. 82: Substantial double-pile houses, with large rear rooms, either under a wide overall roof as at **a** Lisburne House (Llanfihangel-y-Creuddyn), separate gabled roofs at right-angles to the main house as at **b** Lluest Farm (Llanbadarn Fawr), or the full 'double-pile' under a second parallel roof and central valley as at **c** Pwll-glas (Ceulan-y-maes-mawr). All have the central stairway.

Fig. 83: It is appropriate to introduce the section on the houses of the magnates with Thomas Dinely's drawing of Trawsgoed (Llanafan) illustrating the *'Progress of the Duke of Beaufort'*. It shows the house as it was in 1684 with a wealth of details of Stuart and possibly earlier date. Clearly several building periods are to be seen, the right wing with its lateral chimney probably the oldest. The left with its steep gables would be worthy of a Cotswold manor. The centre seems to reflect the naive classical details of the early seventeenth century. Alas, all this was swept away, or totally hidden in successive rebuildings. As Dinely can usually be relied upon, Cardiganshire has clearly lost a remarkable seventeenth-century house.

Fig. 84: Nanteos (Lower Llanbadarn-y-Creuddyn) was built (or rebuilt) 1739–1757 according to inscriptions. Additions, porch and dining room, were made in the nineteenth century by different architects including Edward Haycock and W. R. Coulthart. The interior contains work of various periods of which the finest is the Palladian long gallery, and the best known the Rococo music room, probably a late-Victorian confection.

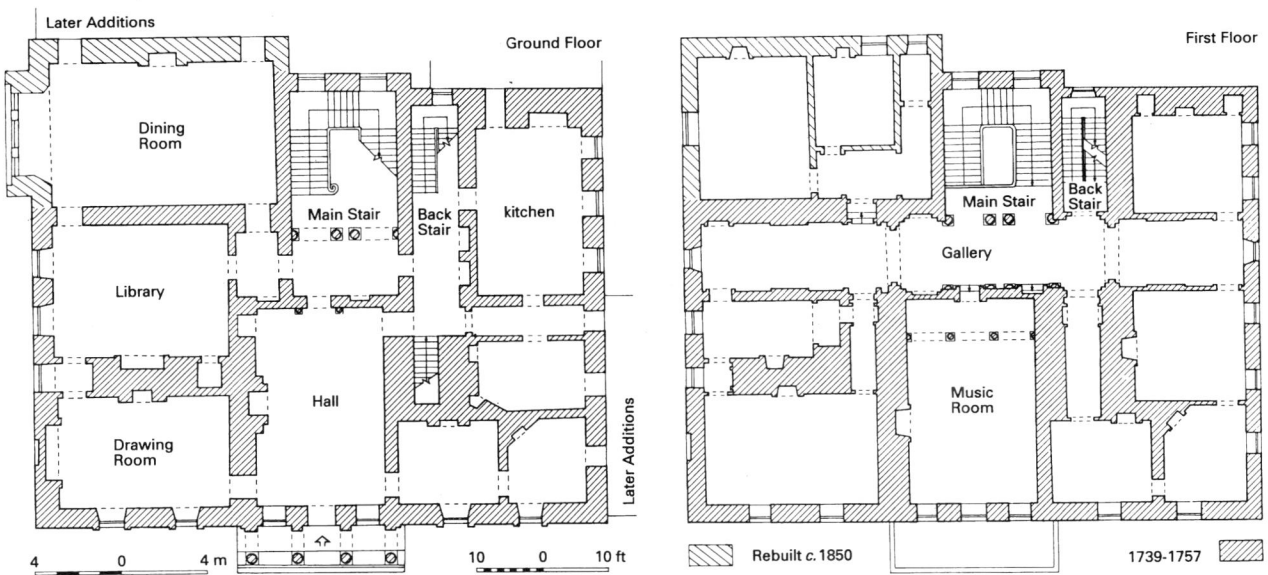

Fig. 85: Nanteos. The plan, a square-proportioned 'double-pile' layout with two 'prestige' fronts facing the approach and the park, is typical of the eighteenth century. The rooms are arranged about an axis of central hall and stairway on the ground floor and about a long gallery at right-angles on the first floor. This is a non-standard reduction drawing.

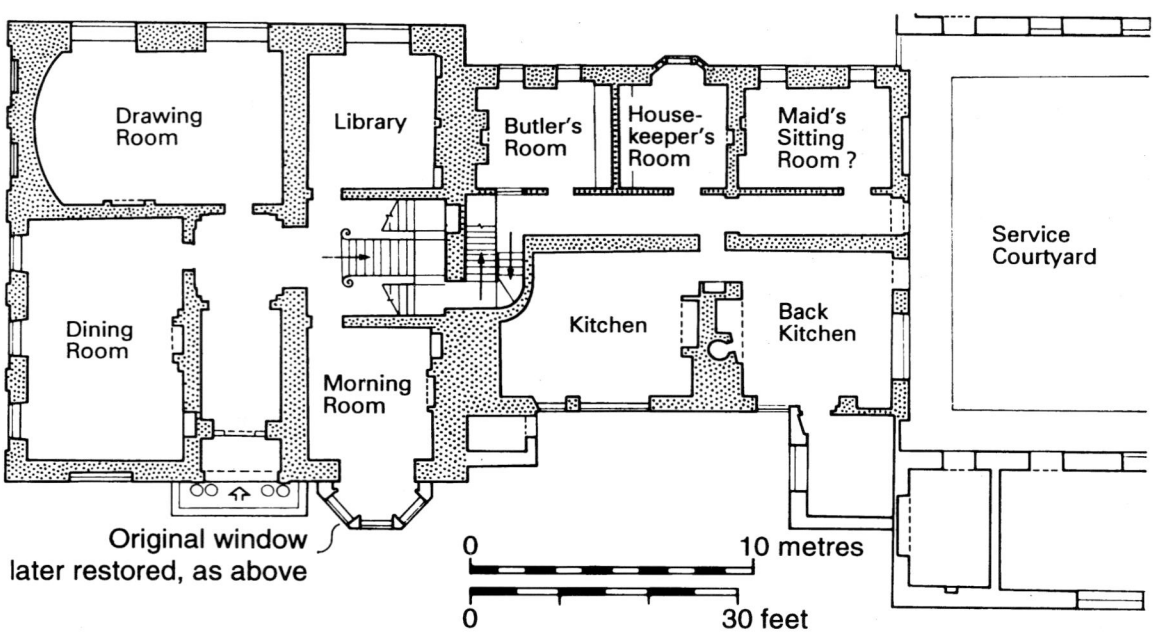

Drawing Room   **Library**   **Butler's Room**   **House-keeper's Room**   **Maid's Sitting Room ?**

Service Courtyard

Dining Room   **Kitchen**   **Back Kitchen**

Morning Room

Original window later restored, as above

0   10 metres

0   30 feet

Fig. 86: Llannerch Aeron (Ciliau Aeron), built in 1794 to the designs of John Nash, incorporates many features popularized by the architect, the venetian window under tympanum, the blind window, smooth stucco walls, and broad eaves. The plan makes an interesting contrast with Nanteos. The main rooms look away from the drive towards the park; instead of being aligned on the entrance, the stairs are reached through a right-angled turn, and come as a surprise, top-lighting adding to the drama. The servants quarters are segregated in the rear away from the reception rooms, their quarters screened by judicious planting and left unrendered. This is a non-standard reduction drawing.

Fig. 87: (opposite) Alltyrodyn (Llandysul), *c.*1827 embodies many of the features popularized by Nash, smooth stucco and broad eaves. However, the layout is a good illustration of axial planning, each room made to appear as symmetrical as possible. The service courtyard is one storey lower than the main house. The view from the entrance hall through to the stairs is impressive, as is the view from the principal rooms to the Teifi valley. This is a non-standard reduction drawing.

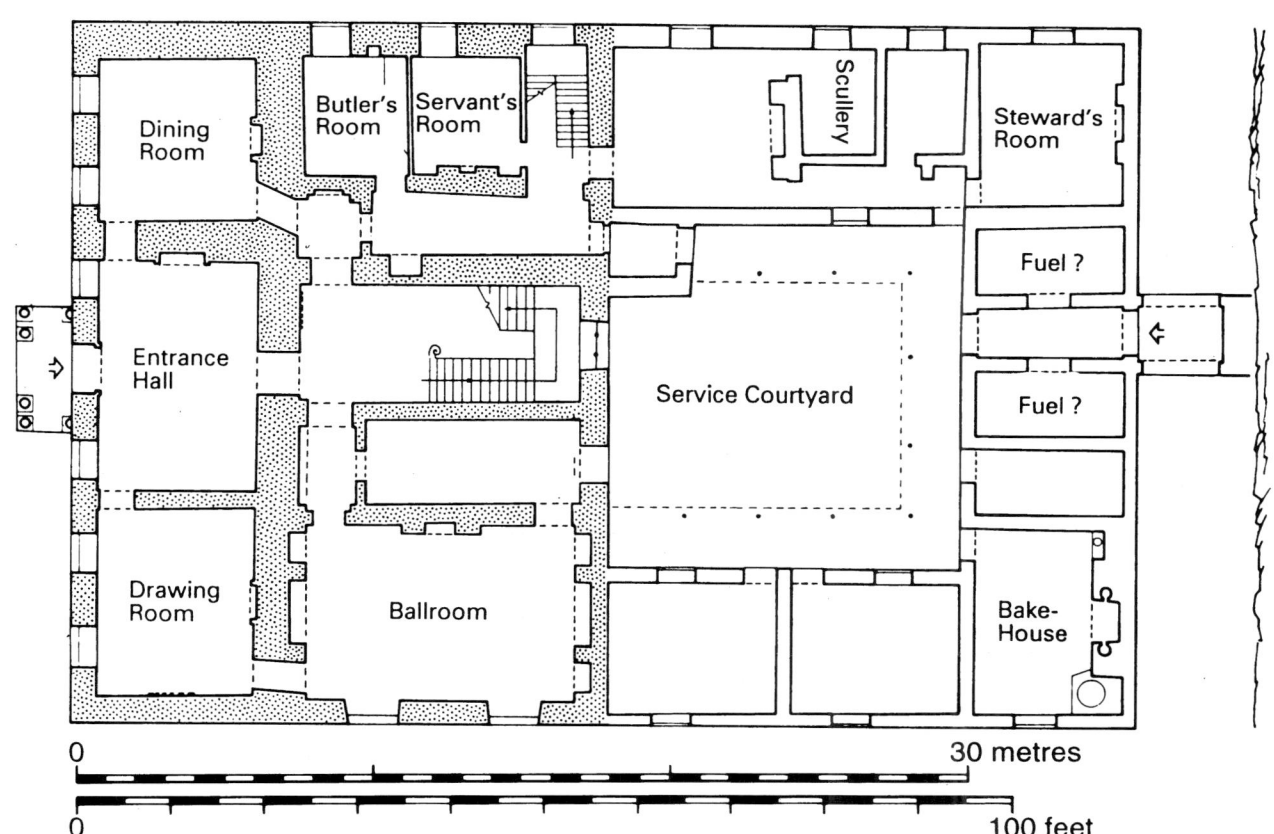

Dining Room	Butler's Room	Servant's Room		Scullery		Steward's Room
						Fuel ?
Entrance Hall			Service Courtyard			Fuel ?
Drawing Room	Ballroom					Bake-House

0   30 metres

0   100 feet

Fig. 88: Mynachdy (Llanbadarn Trefeglwys), general view and stair, probably designed by Edward Haycock, exemplifies the lightness and elegance of early nineteenth-century classical architecture.

Fig. 89: In contrast with Mynachdy (*opposite*) is the stair and gallery of Nanteos (Lower Llanbadarn-y-Creuddyn) illustrating mid-eighteenth century Palladian at its finest, the work of an unknown architect.

Fig. 90: The Sir Walter Scott Gothic of Glandyfi Castle, built *c.*1810, makes an interesting contrast with the previously illustrated late classical, then also at the peak of its popularity. The site was chosen by the Jeffreys family for its incomparable vistas, but the architect is unknown.

Fig. 91: Bronwydd (Llangynllo) is a later expression of Gothic romanticism. Although containing earlier fabric, the visible structure and detail here are mid-Victorian, the work of R. Kyrke Penson, built 1853–6 for Sir Thomas Davies Lloyd, high sheriff of Cardiganshire in 1851. The round towers are probably inspired by Cashel. Had the architect or client visited Ireland?

Fig. 92: In contrast with the mansions of the magnates are these cottages, Pen-y-gaer (Nancwnlle) and (*below*) Pen-y-bont (Llangorwen). Each is related to the 'hearth-passage' group of sub-medieval houses, the entry behind the fireplace or in the end wall. Pen-y-gaer is of clom, Pen-y-bont of stone.

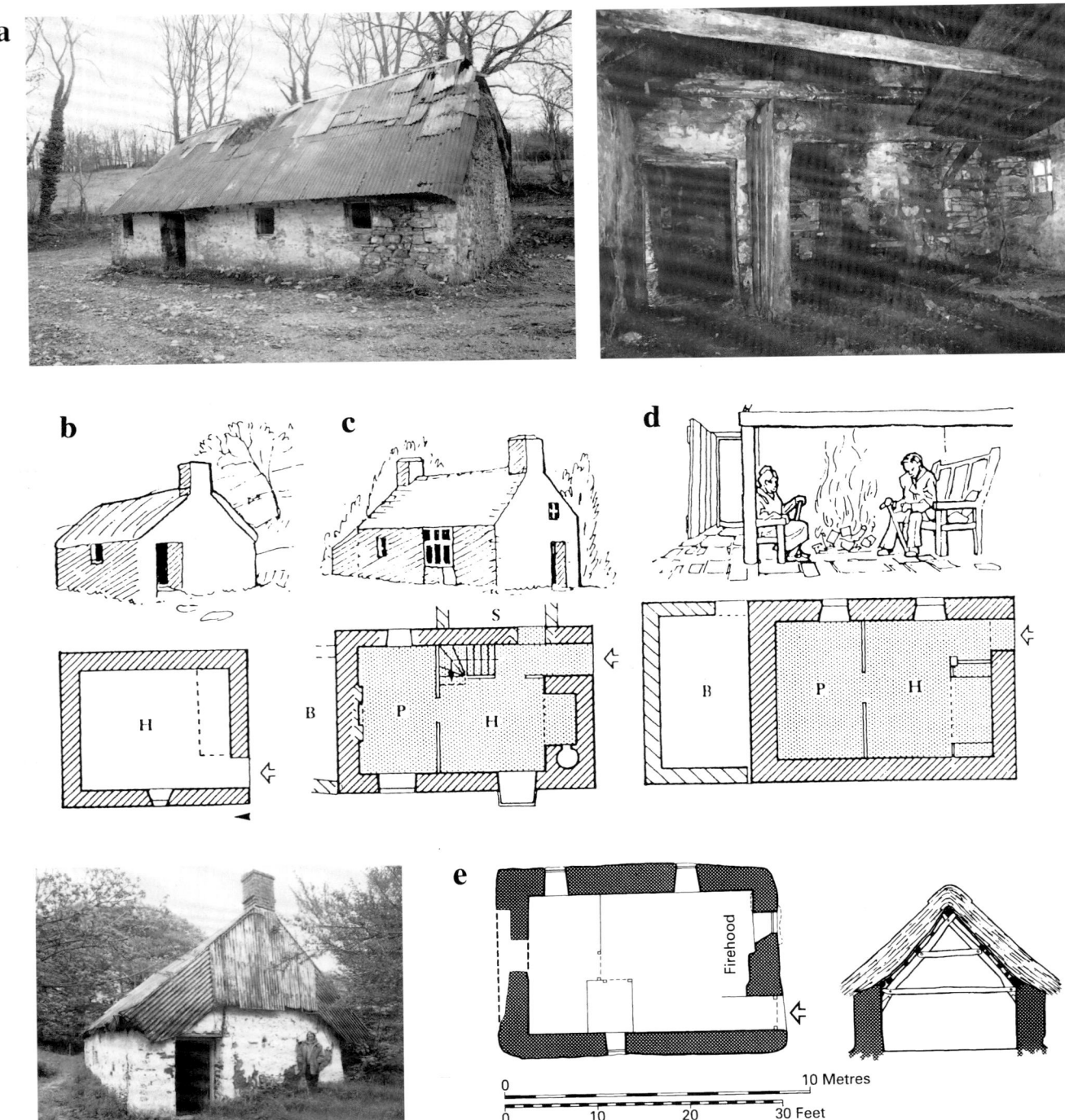

Fig. 93: Further cottages of the sub-medieval, hearth-passage group: **a** Penwalken (Llandysul), showing the entry behind the fireplace, and the view from the living-room towards the fireplace and outer room, **b** cottage near Waun-groes (Caron-is-clawdd), **c** Pen-y-bont (Llangorwen), **d** Pen-lôn (Llanfihangel Ystrad), **e** Pontbrenmydr (Henfynyw Upper). Note the scarfed-cruck frame and clom walls (partly rebuilt in stone) and round quoins at **e**. All save **c** have wickerwork fireplace hoods. Plan of **e** was prepared by V. M. Evans for the National Trust.

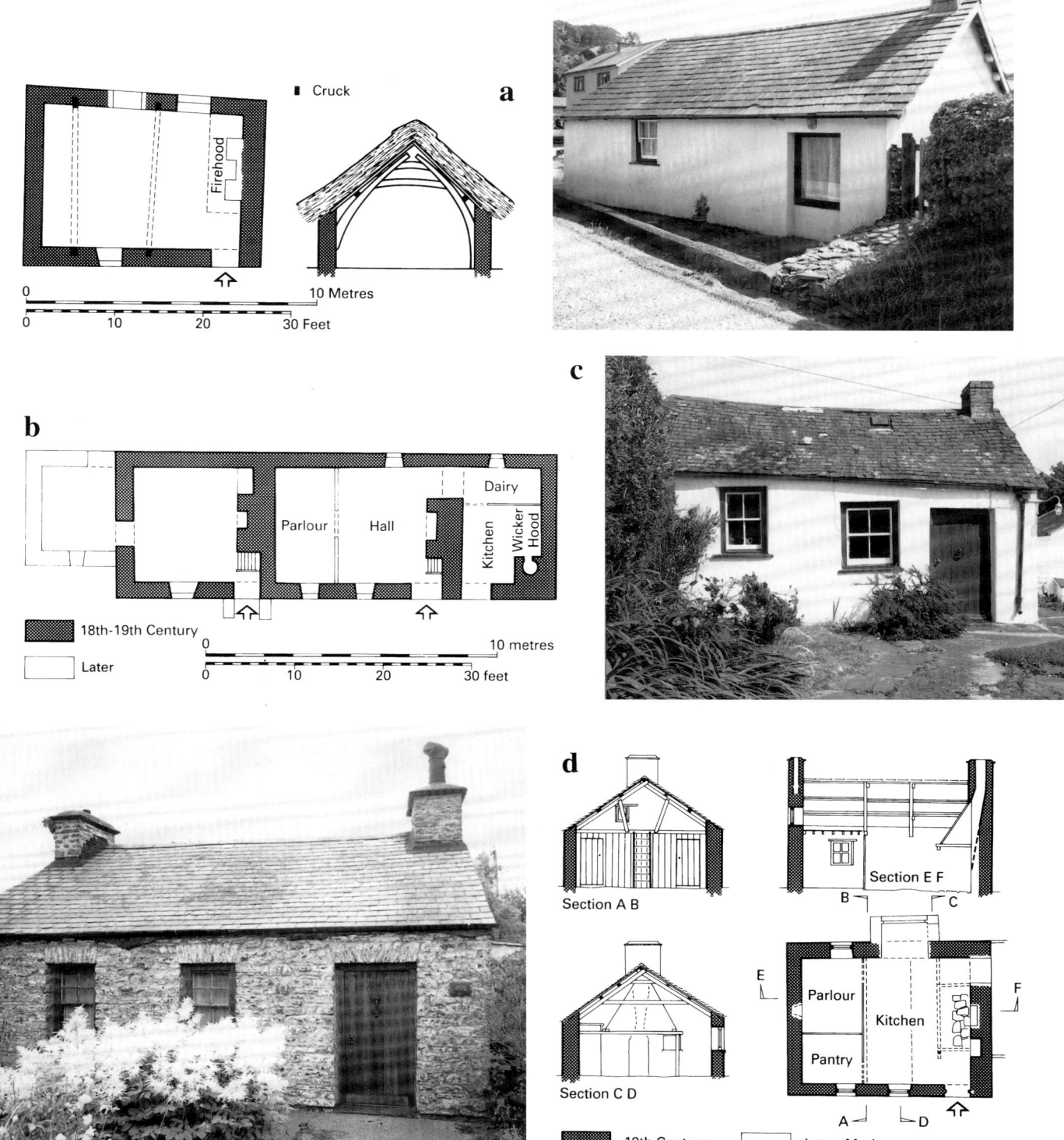

Fig. 94: End-chimney, lobby-entry cottages: **a** Preswylfa (Llanfihangel-y-Creuddyn), **b** a terrace at Aberdwynant (Llanafan), **c** Llwyncelyn, Cnwch-coch (Lower Llanfihangel-y-Creuddyn) and, **d** Spite (Llanddeiniol). Somewhat less common than the hearth-passage, this group has a wide date range from cruck-framed Preswylfa (*see also* Fig. 56) to Spite, which seems entirely nineteenth century, its classic *croglofft* layout notwithstanding.

Fig. 95: The direct-entry, end-chimney cottage, however, far outnumbers all other cottage groups as instanced by **a** Brynamlwg (Llangwyryfon) consisting of hall (living-room) open to the roof, and alongside pantry and parlour under small chamber in the loft, **b** Pen-rhiw (Llansanffraid) with farm unit added alongside, and c an unidentified cottage from the region of Ponterwyd in the collection at St Fagans. Note the roof of thatch enclosing a wickerwork fireplace. How was the only heated room lighted? (*Museum of Welsh Life, St Fagans.*)

Fig. 96: Other end-fireplace, direct-entry cottages **a** Glan-rhyd (Llanfihangel-y-Creuddyn), **b** cottage at Rhydybeillen (Llannarth) and, **c** Yr Efail (Pont-siân) internally much altered. Some of these cottages have secondary farm buildings attached, but without original internal access between house and byre. Although these primarily single-storey cottages are a familiar feature of the Cardiganshire scene, they do not appear in either the quantity or in the concentrations familiar in Caernarfonshire or Anglesey, while in construction, as instanced by the thatch, earth wall and round corners, they are often more archaic than those of Gwynedd.

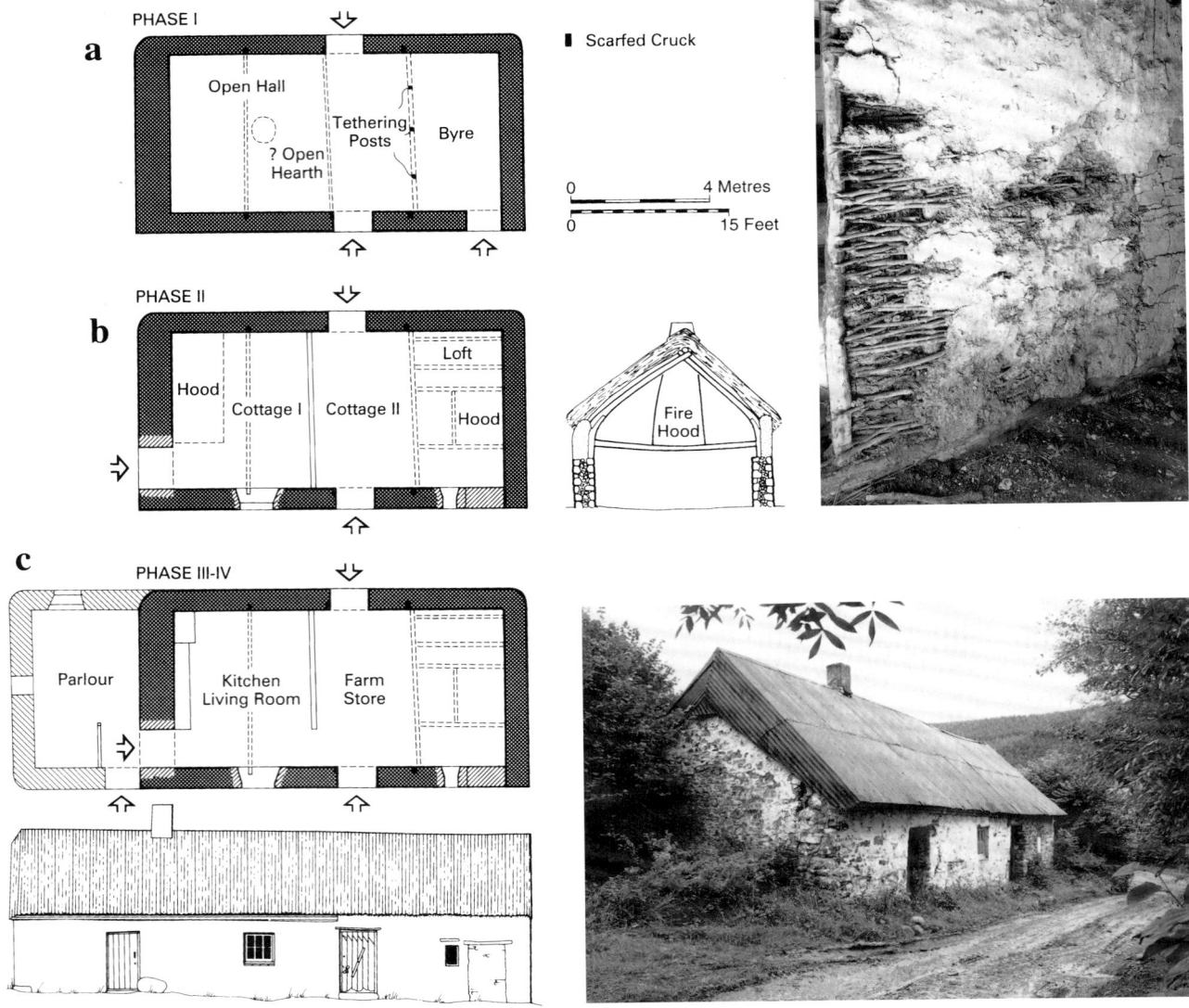

Fig. 97: Wig-wen-fach (Llanddewi Aber-arth), recently surveyed for the National Trust by V. M. Evans, makes an interesting contrast with the cottages on the previous page. The abundance of doorways can only be explained by assuming fundamental changes of plan in the lifetime of the house which probably began as **a** a long-house with a separate entry (*on the right*) for the cattle seemingly tethered in view of the family, who would have entered by the opposite doorways of the cross-passage. How many such houses are yet to be discovered in the county? The drawings show **a** the long-house as built, probably with open hearth, **b** byre abandoned and house converted into two single-room cottages, each with a hooded fire place, **c** byre end converted into farm store, hall end modernized and enlarged. Did Simon Lee live in such a cottage?

> Beside their moss-grown hut of clay,
> Not twenty paces from the door,
> A scrap of land they have, but they
> Are the poorest of the poor.

II. *The Secular Urban Architecture in Context*

Peter White

At the end of the twentieth century Cardiganshire remains essentially a rural county; its five towns are all small, and three of them have relied heavily upon their maritime location for the growth they have enjoyed. Two of them, namely Cardigan and Tregaron, have developed organically, at a pace and in a form largely dictated by the circumstances of such a deeply rural county. But the other three, Aberaeron, Aberystwyth and Lampeter, have strong visual characteristics derived from architecture heavily influenced by patronage. Indeed, this group of three towns is sufficiently distinguished architecturally to be capable of appreciation in a perspective which stretches far beyond Wales and certainly into England.[1]

It is appropriate to begin with Cardigan and Tregaron. Neither their architecture nor their planning are distinctive, with two exceptions, namely the erstwhile county gaol, and the Guildhall, both in Cardigan. The former building, designed by John Nash, provides an immediate introduction not only to his work in the county, for he was one of the best-known architects of his day, but also to the web of personal relationships of which he was a part.[2] But the towns themselves are entirely what they seem, settlements which have developed to facilitate the economic exploitation of the interior using the Teifi valley as an artery.

The appearance of Cardigan, a town of medieval foundation, focused on a twelfth-century castle, expresses the nature and prosperity of a late eighteenth- and early nineteenth-century county town which was also a seaport, and the majority of its buildings can be dated to this period. Public buildings include the Shirehall, fragments of the county gaol, and the former Customs House. By way of domestic architecture there are gentry houses, particularly in Bridge Street and St Mary's Street, merchants' houses in High Street and Quay Street, as well as banks and inns, and some fine warehouses, a necessity for perishable commodities at a time when shipping was dependent upon wind and tide rather than steam, and particularly so in Cardigan given the difficulty of navigating the estuary. The extent of the town was reliably mapped by John Wood in 1834.

Of the public buildings, one fragmentary, one intact, two are of particular note. The gaol was designed between 1791 and 1796 by John Nash, who had moved to Carmarthen in 1785. Fragments of the original fabric survive in buildings in North Road.[3] His other work in the town was a private commission, Prior House, a villa for Elizabeth Johnes (of Croft Castle and, significantly, a relative of the Johnes of Hafod), which now forms part of the Memorial Hospital.[4] These were early fruits of the connection which Nash had quickly made in Carmarthen with the local magistrates and which brought him work, particularly in the Aberystwyth area, over about twenty years.

The Guildhall in Cardigan is of quite another generation. It was designed in 1858–60 by R. J. Withers and is reputedly the first Ruskinian Gothic civic building in Britain. Its scope and planning are

---

[1] H. V. Morton, *In Search of Wales* (5th edn., London, 1933), pp.178–85.
[2] R. Suggett, *John Nash, Architect in Wales: Pensaer yng Nghymru* (Aberystwyth, 1995), pp.13–18.
[3] Ibid., pp.25–30.
[4] Ibid., pp.37ff.

Fig. 98: The Guildhall, Cardigan (undated). *(Copyright RCAHMW-NMR (Thomas Lloyd Collection)).*

certainly remarkable: a council room, corn-exchange, news room, grammar school and markets were all housed here.[5] Otherwise, the buildings of the later nineteenth century in the town are recognizable by the use of Cardigan red brick; a fine example of this material in use is provided by Priory Terrace, a row of houses of the 1870s probably designed by William Woodward, the owner of the brickworks.

Tregaron is the furthest town from the mouth of the Teifi and it is on the margin in respect of size, status and architectural quality.[6] Its most prominent buildings are the inn on the market square, the church, and the former Union workhouse, now a hospital. It is a singularly functional settlement of little architectural but of some vernacular interest.

In almost total contrast is the small planned seaport of Aberaeron. Any discussion of its development is a forceful reminder of the influence of patronage. The place owes its very existence to the Revd Alban Thomas Jones Gwynne, who became its proprietor by inheritance.[7] In its development, which is so formal in its nature, he was almost certainly influenced by the Shrewsbury architect Edward Haycock. The town is remarkable not so much because it is a planned settlement – they occur in Wales at a similar period, for example, in Swansea (Morriston) and at Milford Haven (Neyland, Pembroke Dock, and indeed Milford itself);[8] nor because it was a seaport planted on a relatively inhospitable stretch of the coastline, but rather for its imaginative plan and the consistency deployed

[5]R. Dixon and S. Muthesius, *Victorian Architecture* (London, 1978), pp.169–70.
[6]H. Carter, *The Towns of Wales* (Cardiff, 1966), pp.350–1.
[7]S. Lewis, *A Topographical Dictionary of Wales* (2 vols., London, 1833), I.
[8]Carter, *Towns of Wales*, chapter 14.

over the long period of its development. The social stratification implied by the architecture is transparent; the double-fronted houses facing the harbour and the square are clearly for those of some substance in this seafaring community, and they contrast with the terraced houses in the back streets.

Its success resulted from its strong links with Bristol, and the demands of the hinterland accessible from the Aeron valley and Lampeter, although the emphasis on fishing and shipbuilding is readily apparent, as commodity trading tended to lead to a demand for extensive warehouse space which is lacking at Aberaeron. Lampeter's own self-generated prosperity must also have had an effect.

Aberystwyth is the largest and by far the most important town in the county. It has been variously described as 'The Brighton of Wales' and 'The St Andrews of Wales'.[9] Both are appropriate; Aberystwyth is nothing if not eclectic both in function and architecture. H. V. Morton pithily summed matters up in the 1930s: 'Aberystwyth is leading a double life. It is not the simple seaside town praised on the railway posters. Behind its hotels and boarding houses, its pretty hills, its inadequate pier and its half-moon of blue-grey shingle is something even more important than holidays: it is the oldest University town in Wales.'[10] The town was certainly among the score or so of the earliest British seaside resorts in the pre-railway age, and it hosted the foundation college of the University of Wales half a century later. Like Cardigan, it is a settlement of medieval origin, although the castle within the town was founded later, by Edward I, and is consequently much larger; the centre of the town still follows the medieval street plan. By the eighteenth century the town had become heavily dependent on the export of lead and the import of commodities to enable the upland and otherwise agricultural hinterland to function. The harbour, which was in active use until well into the twentieth century, still retains functional architecture in the form of warehouses and kilns, although the hoppers for ore storage and the hard-won Customs House, built in 1828, have gone. The narrow, terraced streets of artisan housing originally for the sailors and shipwrights, though 'improved' throughout the nineteenth century, still form a recognizable quarter. Immediately to the north of this area the late eighteenth century witnessed important developments.

The unique architectural character of Aberystwyth, for such it is, derives from the dual nature of developments which took off during the late eighteenth century, and the diversification which added a new dimension during the middle of the nineteenth century. The small settlement economically dependent on the harbour, perhaps paradoxically fortunate in its remote location, hemmed in by mountains, and with a tolerable bathing beach, became a resort. As at Aberaeron, patronage was critical. At Aberystwyth it was a group of local gentry families, among them the Powells of Nanteos, the Vaughans of Trawsgoed, the Johneses of Hafod and the Pryses of Gogerddan, who were instrumental in taking matters forward. Between twenty and thirty of the numerous seaside resorts which were eventually to develop around the coast of Wales and England originated in the late eighteenth century; the earliest and most substantial of them were Scarborough and Weymouth, which enjoyed the patronage of the gentry of York and George III respectively. Towards the end of the century it was Brighton, with its proximity to London and the patronage of the Prince Regent, which had risen to prominence, largely as a result of Dr Russell's efforts in extolling the virtues of sea bathing.[11] In Wales, Swansea was the largest town at this time[12] and was the most frequented resort

---

[9]W. J. Lewis, *Born on a Perilous Rock* (Aberystwyth, 1980), pp.194.
[10]Morton, *In Search of Wales*, p.179.
[11]J. A. R. Pimlott, *The Englishman's Holiday: A Social History* (Hassocks, 1976), pp.52ff.
[12]Ibid., p.78.

of the Welsh coast; on 14 August 1786 the *Gloucester Journal* reported: 'Swansea, in point of spirit, fashion, and politeness, has now become the Brighton of Wales.' But by 1797, this accolade was claimed for Aberystwyth also. Brighton, although one of the fastest growing towns of the whole country, was still small in size; it had six streets in 1760, and fifteen by 1800, with a population which had doubled to 7,000 since 1780. It was said, between 1788 and 1823, to be 'no doubt the gayest, most fashionable place not only in England, but in all Europe'.

It is important to remember that these perceived affinities were attributed qualitatively, and related as much to patronage, fashion and style as to amenity and architecture. It is equally important to note the relative scale of Aberystwyth; it received 1,500 visitors, among them its share of people of quality including politicians and aristocrats, at a time when Brighton received 20,000.[13]

But Aberystwyth did have the added attraction of its surroundings, a landscape reminiscent of the Grand Tour: 'It is pleasantly situated at the lower extremity of the valley of the Rheidol, amid lofty hills and on a bold eminence overlooking the bay of Cardigan.' Lewis's description, published in 1833, goes on to note 'it consists principally of two long streets, from which others, branching off nearly at right angles, lead down to the sea shore. The houses are in general well-built, and of respectable appearance, several of them being large and handsome, especially as are of modern (*sic*) erection, which are principally of stone.' A map published by John Wood in 1834 shows exactly the extent of the town at this time; and it should be noted, with hindsight, that Lewis meant that there were two *fashionable* streets.[14]

Many buildings survive from this important period in the town's history as a fashionable resort. It was a time when visitors were as likely to take a house, or apartments in one, as to stay in a hotel. Lewis noted the lodging houses of Marine Terrace; the Belle Vue, 'a spacious and commodious hotel'; other hotels were the Gogerddan Arms, whose building is still to be seen on the corner of Bridge Street and Great Darkgate Street, and the then newly rebuilt and surviving Talbot Hotel. A number of noteworthy 'large and handsome houses' which are shown on an earlier map, of *c.*1790, and which survive, are to be found in Bridge Street, particularly noteworthy among them number 26 ('Ceredigion') the former Pryse family town house, and number 35 ('Westminster'), the former town house of the Pughs of Henblas. Much of the 'show' of such houses was in the plasterwork and detailing to the ground floor rooms, and the staircase, and much of this survives. That part of Marine Terrace at the foot of Pier Street was constructed by 1809, while the northward sweep of the terrace as far as the Marine Hotel was in being by 1834. Much of the fabric of Pier Street is of the late eighteenth century, as a glance above the shopfronts will show, and near the junction with King Street are some rare surviving examples of the bow-fronted façades, subsequently banned under a local bye-law, which were an architectural characteristic of contemporary Weymouth and Brighton. In North Parade, where the houses numbered 26 and 28 abut, the contrast between the stone-built eighteenth-century town house and its brick-built Victorian successor is clearly to be seen; the former has a fine doorcase, but only high ceilings to the ground and first floors, while the latter has polychromatic brickwork and generous ceiling heights throughout.

At the heart of the eighteenth-century resort was Laura Place; completed by 1809, here are some of the 'best' houses, including the town house of the one of the resort's principal patrons, William

[13]Ibid., p.76.
[14]Lewis, *Topographical Dictionary* (1833), I.

Powell, magistrate and MP, of Nanteos. The terrace is named after his wife, Laura Phelps, and was probably designed for him by G. S. Repton, the youngest son of Humphrey Repton, the landscape gardener, and friend of John Nash. G. S. Repton worked in Nash's office from 1801 until 1820.[15]

During the 1790s Nash was responsible for the design of the grandest house in the town, Castle House, located just to the north of Laura Place, on the site now occupied by the Old College. It was built for Sir Uvedale Price of Foxley Hall, Herefordshire, a leading personality in the picturesque movement, an interest which was so strongly represented locally among other patrons of the town, among them the Johnes of Hafod, where Nash also worked.[16]

When visiting a place of resort, polite society expected three attributes: appropriate lodging, a place to promenade, and, above all, a building where assemblies could be held. The provision and character of the first survives to be seen; the second was provided by the development of Marine Terrace, and by Castle Hill – 'crowned with the venerable ruins of that ancient fortress, and forming another favourite promenade, affording, from different points, various extensive, romantic, and interesting views of the sea, the neighbouring hills, and the surrounding country'.[17]

The importance of the third – assembly rooms – cannot be overstated. 'At assemblies, visitors to resorts could get to know each other, new arrivals to the town could meet local society, and local society could learn about the new arrivals.'[18] In 1797 Jane Austen's cousin, Eliza de la Feuillade, wrote from Lowestoft: 'This place still contains a good many families, but as there are no Rooms, there is no opportunity of getting acquainted with them.' The conduct of assemblies had been laid down as early as 1707 by Richard 'Beau' Nash, a native of Swansea, who was Master of the Ceremonies at Bath from 1705 until 1758.[19] So, in July 1820, on land given by Powell immediately adjoining Laura Place, an Assembly Room, paid for by subscription, was opened. The design is attributed to G. S. Repton:[20] 'handsomely built in the Grecian style of architecture (it) consists of a very handsome assembly and promenade room, forty-five feet long, and twenty five feet broad; a card room, twenty five feet long, and eighteen feet wide, opening into the assembly room by folding doors; and a billiard room of the same dimensions as the card room'. It still survives, although altered.

According to 'Beau' Nash, assemblies were open to 'people of every degree, condition and occupation of life, if well dressed and well behaved', but in fact social and political distinctions were often strictly adhered to.[21] So, with its assembly rooms, promenades, a theatre, bathing facilities, with machines available, hot sea-water baths (in Lower Portland Street) and even a chalybeate well (roughly on the site of the modern railway station), Aberystwyth in the 1830s could be considered a resort with every facility. By way of comparison, Swansea, after a long struggle, had completed its assembly rooms in 1821.[22]

But even with turnpike roads 'among the best in the principality', Aberystwyth was still remote: a whole day's travel from Shrewsbury and over forty-eight hours from London; and expensive – 22

[15]H. M. Colvin, *A Biographical Dictionary of British Architects, 1600–1840* (3rd edn., Yale, 1995), pp.800–1.

[16]S. Lewis, *A Topographical Dictionary of Wales* (2nd edn., 2 vols., London, 1840), I; Suggett, *John Nash*, pp.65–71.

[17]S. Lewis, *Topographical Dictionary* (1833), I.

[18]M. Girouard, *The English Town* (Yale, 1990), p.132.

[19]Pimlott, *The Englishman's Holiday*, pp.46–8.

[20]Colvin, *Biographical Dictionary*, p.801.

[21]Girouard, *The English Town*, chapter 7.

[22]D. Boorman, *The Brighton of Wales: Swansea as a Fashionable Seaside Resort c.1780–c.1830* (Swansea, 1986), chapter 4.

shillings inside – and 16 shillings outside – for a journey, in 1816, as far as Kington on the English border.[23]

Railways brought a new meaning to the term resort; they made it possible, physically, if not always economically, for the many rather than the few to travel. Among the architectural consequences, as the possibility of those among the mercantile classes being away from work became possible, were the appearance luxurious or 'grand' hotels, and the development of estates of substantial houses in seaside towns. Interestingly, both tendencies had started in Brighton before Stephenson's railway line was built, because the town was so close to London. These new classes of visitor and resident would include retired people, and those who were being liberated from constant attendance at their business by the almost concurrent extension of limited liability legislation. In extreme cases, like Hove, on the south coast, or Lytham, on the north-west coast, the residential development of a substantial part of the town (or in these cases, conurbation) can be seen in this way. At the other end of the scale, and indeed the country, a place like Ilfracombe came to boast two or three streets of fine detached houses as an almost immediate consequence of the arrival of the railway. And the railway-led development of exclusive seaside hotels continued for the best part of a century, as Oliver Hill's striking Midland Hotel in Morecambe, of the 1930s, demonstrates.

Thomas Savin believed that his railway company's link would stimulate the further growth of Aberystwyth in this way. In fact, the coming of the railway in 1864 began an era which continues today, and which took the town along a superficially similar, but in reality the quite different path identified by H. V. Morton. Savin engaged the architect John Pollard Seddon to convert Price's Castle House into the grand hotel, considered appropriate for a rail-served resort. By the summer of 1865, although incomplete, the new hotel was open for business; within a year the enterprise had crashed.[24] Yet, other large hotels were built to take advantage of the railway link. Of them, the former Queen's Hotel (1866), latterly the County Hall, survives to give an outward impression of the scale of Aberystwyth's version of this type of building of the new tourism. Located right on the promenade, it is integral with the remainder of the terraced façade fronting the bay. Within its peer group it must rank as a modest affair, for elsewhere the grand hotel, very large, often in its own grounds, or at least set back from the promenade and architecturally very distinctive, became the building type to set the quality and 'tone' of the burgeoning resort in places like Scarborough, Blackpool, Folkestone, Eastbourne, Bournemouth, Torquay, and even as far afield as Falmouth.

In this context the scale of development at Aberystwyth was of a lower order altogether. Here the small hotel and boarding house thrived, with buildings right on, and entirely suited to, its uniform seafront. The architect who made the most significant contribution was none other than J. P. Seddon, whose grand plans were outlined in *Building News* in November 1865: 'Mr Seddon, not satisfied with the erection of a splendid hotel, appears ambitious to remodel Aberystwyth. Seeing that the town is likely to become the favourite watering place of Wales . . . he suggests the erection of a new crescent of modern and noble houses, and another half-crescent of villas . . . to be of a superior character to attract permanent residents . . . another plan was to rebuild the Belle Vue Hotel.' In fact, all that was built was Victoria Terrace, which runs northwards from the Queen's Hotel, designed 'to meet the peculiar requirements of a sea-side place, by making each floor contain a sitting room, bed and dressing rooms,

[23]Lewis, *Born on a Perilous Rock*, p.122.
[24]J. R. Webster, *Old College, Aberystwyth: The Evolution of a High Victorian Building* (Cardiff, 1995), passim.

Fig. 99: The Queen's Hotel, Aberystwyth, built in 1866. *(Copyright RCAHMW-NMR).*

and to be as complete in itself as possible. It is intended to diversify the houses, and to introduce among them several larger ones, with rooms on each side of the entrance.'[25] What Seddon intended as apartments seemed to have functioned over time as boarding houses or small hotels, and the whole ensemble is outwardly strongly reminiscent of Douglas, Isle of Man, where the design of this type of building has been studied in some depth. Here also, one of the biggest hotels, the Villiers, was located at the end of a terrace, just as the Queen's Hotel was in Aberystwyth.[26]

The need for more modest accommodation was probably an expression both of the distance from and the social structure of the nearest centres of population, the industrialized south of Wales and the Black Country. Neither had large populations of rich rentiers necessary to sustain luxury hotels, but they were home to a relatively large number of skilled and semi-skilled workers who enjoyed considerable social and physical mobility.[27] As the nineteenth century wore on, the development of new resorts, among them particularly Llandudno with its grand hotels, on the north Wales coast, exploited at Aberystwyth's expense the potential of the Merseyside and Manchester conurbations.[28]

But it is strongly arguable that the substance of Aberystwyth's development, and therefore of its more distinctive buildings, was not brought about by the evolution of the resort, which had occurred

[25]M. Darby, *John Pollard Seddon* (London, 1983), pp.31–4.
[26]T. A. Bawden and L. S. Garrad et al., *The Industrial Archaeology of the Isle of Man* (Newton Abbot, 1972), 101–11; Marcus Binney, 'Demolition man', *The Times Magazine*, 12 August 1995.
[27]H. Perkin, *The Age of the Railway* (London, 1971), chapter 8; A. Briggs, 'The background of the Parliamentary Reform Movement in three English cities (1830–2)', *Cambridge Historical Journal*, X, no.3 (1952), 293–317.
[28]Perkin, *Age of the Railway*, p.219.

so early. The decision by Hugh Owen and his associates, anxious to found a University for Wales, to buy the defunct Castle Hotel for £10,000 in March 1867 was the critical factor. Barely five years later the first students were enrolled. After a number of reverses, Seddon was re-engaged, and by 1890 the most prominent building on the seafront, now the Old College, was largely completed. The impact of the University on the townscape of the seaside resort has been, and remains, considerable. Alexandra Hall, another prominent seafront building to house women students was completed and opened in 1896; the striking Chemical Laboratories, on rising ground above the town, were built in 1907; and the brave but rather brutal campus on Penglais Hill was developed post-war to an overall design by Percy Thomas and Dale Owen.[29] The existence of the College went on to inspire the establishment of the National Library of Wales, which was granted its charter in 1907; its building, designed by Greenslade and Blomfield and looking out over the bay from high above the town, was in occupation from 1916. The effect of these institutions has been profound, and unparalleled in their day in any other seaside town. From the latter part of the nineteenth century, substantial houses were developed, particularly in the Llanbadarn Road area, not solely for the 'traditional' seaside resort needs of total or relative retirement, but also to serve the singular indigenous needs of a growing centre of culture and scholarship. Other effects are less noticeable, but no less important for the fabric of the town, for the useful life of many more modest buildings has been prolonged, not least on the seafront itself, to house increasing numbers of students and staff. It is, by way of a postscript, salutary to note that Brighton did not achieve Aberystwyth's duality of function until a century later, in the 1960s.

Finally, there is Lampeter. At the beginning of the nineteenth century this town must have been much like Tregaron, and in a modest way it owes even more to patronage and education than Aberystwyth. Described in the first edition of Lewis's *Dictionary* as 'small and straggling, consisting for the most part of low houses indifferently built',[30] by the mid-1840s, perceptions had changed sufficiently for the second edition to record: 'The town, which is small, has been of late years much improved by the erection of many good houses on leases granted by J. S. Harford Esq.'[31] The catalyst was the foundation of St David's College, the foundation stone of which was laid on 12 August 1822. This institution, the first university foundation outside Oxford or Cambridge in England and Wales, came about through the coincidence of the interests of Bishop Thomas Burgess of St David's and J. S. Harford, lord of the manor and banker from Bristol, a city which, as late as 1801, was still the fourth largest in the kingdom. Its economic sphere of influence, if nothing else, certainly encompassed Lampeter.[32] This small town had seen already the foundation, in 1805, of one of a group of grammar schools to improve the educational provision of the area (its building of 1823 survives in Church Street), but Harford's gift of land and funds were critical to the foundation of the College.

There is continuing discussion about the design of the College buildings themselves, whether they are derived from an Oxford college model, or from an almshouse model,[33] but there are other matters which are worthy of note. The design was the work of Charles Cockerell, who was put

[29]D. Chablo, 'University architecture in Britain, 1950–75' (unpublished University of Oxford D.Phil. thesis, 1987), chapter 2.
[30]Lewis, *Topographical Dictionary* (1833), II.
[31]Lewis, *Topographical Dictionary* (1840), I.
[32]Lewis, *Topographical Dictionary* (1833), II.
[33]W. H. Harris, 'St David's College Lampeter', *Ceredigion*, I, no.1 (1950), 43–52.

Fig. 100: A line engraving of St David's College, Lampeter, by C. J. Smith after F. Mackenzie, 1827–1830. *(Copyright National Library of Wales).*

forward by Harford as the architect. Cockerell, whose father had been a fellow pupil of Sir Robert Taylor with Nash, knew Blaise Castle, Bristol, which Harford owned, and much admired Nash's work on the Hamlet, a model village there for estate workers. So here is another link of the Nash connection.[34]

The second matter is the effect of the College on the town. Lewis quickly noted the increased prosperity, which seems in fact to have been partly due to the economic effects of the College itself, not least in attracting some visitors, and partly due to Harford's own direct attempts to 'improve' the place. As it is, the town of today is almost entirely of the nineteenth century, mostly of stuccoed terraces, some with canted bays for the better off, and many without, together with a few substantial houses on the road towards Aberaeron.

By way of conclusion, there are two points which can be drawn from this account of the urban architecture of the county. The first is that through their connections (or because of Nash's

[34]D. Watkin, *The Life and Work of C. R. Cockerell* (London, 1974), pp.80–1; J. Thomas, 'Saint David's College, Lampeter: tradition and innovation in the design of its first building', *Ceredigion*, X, no.1 (1984), 57–81.

fortuitous sojourn in Carmarthen), the local gentry involved architects of national standing in the design of public buildings. Secondly, and despite its remote location, the county attracted two significant educational institutions, which not only provided economic substance to the favoured towns, but also provided them with an architectural texture of some considerable quality.

CHAPTER 13

TOURISM IN CARDIGANSHIRE, 1774–1974

R. F. Walker

THE late eighteenth century saw the birth and slow growth of what would develop in the course of two centuries into one of the county's major industries. Several powerful influences brought about the establishment of tourism. One was the growing appreciation of the health-giving qualities of sea bathing, which produced the rise of seaside resorts, led by Scarborough, as rivals to the inland spas.[1] Another potent factor was the Romantic revival, with its cult of the picturesque: scorning the tame scenery of southern England, travellers resorted to the wilds of Scotland, the Lake District and Wales, there to shudder pleasurably while contemplating towering crags, foaming torrents and 'stupendous gulphs'. Although Cardiganshire could not rival the awful grandeur of Snowdonia, it did have scenery that was striking enough. From 1793 a third force came into play: the Revolutionary and Napoleonic Wars closed the continent to British travellers for some twenty years, so they turned to the discovery of their own country.[2]

In 1774 H. P. Wyndham toured through Wales.[3] He found Aberystwyth agreeably situated and on its beach sea bathing had begun in the summer season. He saw little to commend in Cardigan but enjoyed a walk up the Teifi to Llechryd and was ferried over the river below Cilgerran by coracle. The upper Teifi valley he found 'insipid and unpleasant'. With a taste for antiquities he viewed what little was visible of Strata Florida abbey, found *Bedd Taliesin* disappointingly plundered and rightly concluded that the defences of Aberystwyth castle had included a barbican. The turnpike road from Llanidloes through Devil's Bridge to Aberystwyth was good, as were roads on lower ground; mountain roads were 'as good as the nature of the country will admit of'. He deemed it wise to plan routes in advance, particularly as guides were frequently ignorant.[4] Cardigan, Aberaeron, Aberystwyth and Lampeter all had good inns, but that at Ffair-rhos was execrable. Tourists were still rare, for in six weeks in Wales Wyndham did not meet 'a single party of pleasure'.[5]

In August 1798 the Revd Richard Warner of Bath and his indefatigable companions travelled on foot from Rhayader up the Elan valley and down the Ystwyth,[6] spending the night in an

---

[1]Sheridan placed *The Rivals* in fashionable Bath, but called his adaptation of *The Relapse* by Vanburgh *A Trip to Scarborough*.

[2]Sir Richard Colt Hoare travelled in Europe up to 1791, but in 1793 turned to Wales: M. W. Thompson (ed.), *The Journeys of Sir Richard Colt Hoare, 1793–1810* (Gloucester, 1983), p.14.

[3]H. P. Wyndham, *A Tour through Monmouthshire and Wales, 1774 and 1781* (2nd edn., Salisbury, 1781), pp.85–100.

[4]Ibid., pp.118–20.

[5]Ibid., Preface, p.i.

[6]Revd Richard Warner, *A Second Walk through Wales* (London, 1799), pp.141–72.

uncomfortable inn at Pentre.[7] Fortunately the party had been invited to breakfast at Hafod by Thomas Johnes. There they duly admired his house, especially the octagonal library, explored the woodland and riverside walks and the rock cut passage leading to an unexpected waterfall. They noted of course Johnes's extensive tree planting and his improving agriculture. After staying the night the party made its way to the inn at Devil's Bridge. Here Warner, sketchbook under arm, climbed down the eastern side of the Mynach falls to find a suitable stance. He slipped and would have fallen into the abyss but for a borrowed alpenstock with which he checked his fall and was able to scramble back up to the inn, badly shaken. Leaving the turnpike road, the party descended to the floor of the Rheidol valley, admiring successive waterfalls, and reached Aberystwyth by way of Llanbadarn. Aberystwyth they found 'a very neat market town'. 'Being a bathing place much company resorts to it in the summer season, where they find good lodgings and convenient bathing machines.' Setting off on the main road to Machynlleth, the party diverged in search of a non-existent castle and got hopelessly lost. They failed to find Tal-y-bont, where they knew there was an inn, tried orienteering across country with a compass and a small map, and were eventually fortunate to meet a miller's boy, who directed them safely to Machynlleth, having covered at least twenty-five miles instead of eighteen. In September they returned to Aberystwyth by boat from Aberdyfi, stayed a night at Aberaeron and walked on to Aber-porth and then down to the Teifi at Llechryd.[8] After visiting Sir Benjamin Hammet's works at Castell Maelgwyn, they proceeded to Cardigan for a pleasant boat trip up river to view Cilgerran castle.

Warner's travels show that in north Cardiganshire the principal objectives of the tourist were Hafod, Devil's Bridge and Aberystwyth and in the south the lower Teifi valley. Exploration could be dangerous, as at the Mynach falls, and away from the main roads it was easy to get lost without a guide. In 1798 strangers travelling on foot aroused suspicion: in Cardigan, while being escorted by a militiaman, Warner and his friends were taken for prisoners, either French invaders or Irish rebels. Obtaining reliable directions or a knowledgeable guide long remained necessary. In 1854 George Borrow decided to make for Ponterwyd cross-country from Machynlleth, even though he was warned at the Wynnstay Arms that it was 'an awful road, or no road at all'. As far probably as Glasbwll there was a good road, but thereafter the way was hard to find and people encountered were far from helpful. Eighteenth-century maps do optimistically show a road all the way to Ponterwyd,[9] but Borrow was decidedly lucky to discover 'the Welch Potosi', the mines of Esgair-hir. Here a mine official insisted on finding him a guide, a miner returning home to Ponterwyd. The route they took was probably by various mine tracks by way of Dôl Rhuddlan and Bwlch Ystyllen and down the right bank of the Rheidol to Ponterwyd.[10]

As long as public transport in Cardiganshire remained rare, walking remained one of the principal ways of exploring the country, and even when transport became available walking remained popular and guide books gave special advice to walkers. Nicholson's guide of 1813,

[7]Described in 1803 as 'one of the most wretched and detestable imaginable': B. H. Malkin, *The Scenery, Antiquities, and Biography of South Wales* (2nd edn., 2 vols., London, 1807), II, p.53.
[8]Warner, *Second Walk*, pp.329–35.
[9]E.g. Thomas Kitchen, *Map of Cardiganshire* (London, 1756). Traces of the road are still to be seen south of Cefn-coch.
[10]George Borrow, *Wild Wales* (Everyman edn., 1906), pp.442–56, 466. The inn where he stayed does seem from his description to have been on the site of the present hotel which bears his name.

however, warned walkers that at hotels they might not receive the same consideration as carriage company. Much good advice was given as to what to wear and what to carry – including a compass, a telescope, a pocket Flora and a portable plant-press – on choice of footwear and care of the feet.[11] The edition of 1840 limited the weight of luggage to be carried in a calf-skin case to four or five pounds, and recommended that, instead of an umbrella, the walker should carry a cloak of oiled silk which could be folded up small.[12] Before main stage-coach routes were established, the principal alternatives to walking were riding one's own or a hired horse or travelling by post-chaises where they were available. Nicholson advised the traveller to buy a sure-footed Welsh pony on entering Wales: the best horse for a country is a horse of that country. Luggage could be carried in saddlebags, though he noted that B. H. Malkin had ridden one horse while his servant carried the luggage on another.[13] Sir Richard Colt Hoare rode his own horse or used his own or a hired post-chaise.[14] In Aberystwyth in 1796 four or five post-horses were for hire but there was no post-chaise in 1798. Chaises soon became available at Aberystwyth and Devil's Bridge and Lampeter had one by 1803.[15] Therefore, when families visited Aberystwyth in the late eighteenth century, they must have used their own carriages. The different modes of transport are well illustrated by the diary of Frederick Jones recording his holidays in Aberystwyth between 1798 and 1823.[16] On his earlier visits he rode to Aberystwyth, but in 1811 he used the coach service opened from Kington in 1809. In 1815 and 1816 he hired post-chaises for the journey to Aberystwyth and for local visits, but returned by coach. In 1820 he bought his own laundalette and drove it to Aberystwyth in 1822. For his final visit in 1823 he used this carriage and two saddle horses.

It is hardly an exaggeration to say that for much of the nineteenth century the history of tourism in Cardiganshire was the history of Aberystwyth, the main resort and the base for exploration inland. The publication of the earliest Aberystwyth guide in 1816 was prompted by 'a great influx of strangers', who came every year for their health or pleasure.[17] Reaching Aberystwyth was now easier because of recent improvements to the turnpike roads and the opening of the new road from Dyffryn Castell through Ponterwyd.[18] From the town's three principal inns, the Gogerddan Arms, the Old Black Lion and the Talbot, there were now frequent coaches to Shrewsbury and Worcester and thence to London.[19] Besides the main inns there were at least twenty-five others and eleven lodging houses.[20] Frederick Jones tended to spend his first night at the Old Black Lion or the Talbot and then to take lodgings on Marine Terrace, North Parade or Bridge Street. On the beach there were bathing machines and the sea was said to be free from impurities.[21] Warm sea water baths could be taken in the bath house built on the Terrace by Dr Rice Williams in 1810 and the town had some claim to be a spa after the discovery in the 1770s of a chalybeate spring 'by no means

[11][G. Nicholson], *The Cambrian Traveller's Guide* (2nd edn., Stourport, 1813), pp.v–viii.
[12]Revd E. Nicholson, *The Cambrian Traveller's Guide* (3rd edn., London, 1840), pp.vii–viii.
[13]Nicholson, *Cambrian Traveller's Guide* (1813), pp.v–vii.
[14]Thompson, *Journeys of Colt Hoare*, p.17.
[15]Ibid., 63, 227; R. C. B. Oliver, 'Holidays at Aberystwyth, 1798–1823', *Ceredigion*, X, no.3 (1986), 272; Malkin, *Scenery*, II, p.25.
[16]Oliver, 'Holidays', pp.269–86.
[17]*The Aberystwyth Guide* (Aberystwyth, 1816).
[18]W. J. Lewis, *Born on a Perilous Rock* (Aberystwyth, 1980), pp.121–2.
[19]*Guide* (1816), pp.81–2.
[20]Ibid., pp.91–101.
[21]Ibid., pp.82–4.

unpalatable'.[22] The castle was 'a picturesque heap of ruins' amid which John Probert of Shrewsbury had laid out pleasant walks with a splendid view.[23] In the season there were regular assemblies and plays, though there was no proper theatre.[24] In the wake of fashionable visitors, the English theatre had arrived. From about 1780 professional companies performed under the patronage of local gentry, particularly at the time of the autumn race meetings.[25] The upper floor of the Guildhall was used as a theatre until about 1820, and between 1813 and 1826 companies also performed in a warehouse near Trefechan bridge. The need for a purpose-built theatre eventually led to the erection of one in 1831 at the end of North Parade, giving Thespian Street its name.[26] Aberystwyth had its critics: in 1808 its prices were said to be as high as those of Weymouth,[27] while Sir Richard Colt Hoare thought it an indifferent place for bathing and compared it very unfavourably with Tenby.[28]

In 1819 Frederick Jones found Aberystwyth 'quite crowded with genteel company' and during his visits he could count on meeting friends and relations from among the gentry of the border counties.[29] In 1820 the Assembly Rooms, designed by George Repton, were opened in Laura Place. In this elegant building visiting nobility and gentry attended balls and assemblies, properly regulated by a Master of Ceremonies. There was a bar and rooms for cards and billiards and for reading the London newspapers.[30] Frederick Jones attended plays and balls and subscribed to the Assembly Rooms when they opened.[31] From the mid-1830s the Improvement Commissioners and the reformed Corporation provided the town with good paving and lighting, a water supply and a small police force.[32] By the mid-1820s the Belle Vue had joined the ranks of the principal hotels and by 1840 there were some fifty houses on Marine Terrace, many of them providing accommodation. The number of permanent residents had increased and the population had risen from 1,758 in 1801 to 4,916 in 1841.[33] The Assembly Rooms season was from July to October; on the beach there was 'every luxury connected with sea bathing' and a new bridge over the Ystwyth had given access to Tan-y-bwlch beach. For sportsmen there were races at Gogerddan, sea and river angling, archery and cricket clubs and in winter the Gogerddan foxhounds and harriers.[34]

In the decade before the railways came,[35] Aberystwyth's connections with the outside world were comparatively good. The Belle Vue and the Gogerddan Arms were now the principal coaching

[22]Ibid., pp.56–7.
[23]Ibid., pp.24–7.
[24]Ibid., p.57.
[25]The earliest playbill dates from 1789.
[26]R. F. Walker, 'Entertainment in Aberystwyth, 1780–1977', in I. G. Jones (ed.), *Aberystwyth, 1277–1977* (Llandysul, 1977), pp.114–15. See also C. Price, *The English Theatre in Wales* (Cardiff, 1948) and idem, *The Professional Theatre in Wales* (U.C. Swansea, 1984).
[27]*Cambrian Traveller's Guide* (Stourport, 1808), p.13.
[28]Thompson, *Journeys of Colt Hoare*, p.230.
[29]Oliver, 'Holidays', 269–86.
[30]Lewis, *Born on a Perilous Rock*, p.197.
[31]Oliver, 'Holidays', 276–7, 281, 284.
[32]H. C. Jones, *Aberystwyth Borough, 1277–1974* (Aberystwyth, 1974), pp.17–20.
[33]Nicholson, *Cambrian Traveller's Guide* (1840), pp.23, 25–6; E. A. Benjamin, *Footprints in the Sands of Time: Aberystwyth, 1800–1860* (Carmarthen, 1986), pp.12, 17.
[34]Nicholson, *Cambrian Traveller's Guide* (1840), pp.23, 25–7.
[35]A period well recorded in the guides by T. O. Morgan: his *New Guide to Aberystwyth and its Environs* (2nd edn. Aberystwyth,1858), pp.13–38, is the principal source used.

Fig. 101: The Falls of Mynach, Devil's Bridge. An engraving published by H. Humphreys, Aberystwyth. (*Copyright National Library of Wales*).

inns, with frequent services to Shrewsbury and Kington and in summer through Snowdonia to Caernarfon, while the Talbot had coaches to Oswestry. The journey to London, however, still took two days. The steamer *Plynlymon* provided a weekly service to Liverpool and Bristol, and in July 1858 a day trip to Dublin.[36] The theatre had now lost popularity with the upper classes and had closed in Aberystwyth in 1845.[37] There were promenades in the Assembly Rooms twice a week in the season, with balls in August and during the autumn race week. The ladies' bathing machines, moved by horses and provided with female attendants, were ranged in front of Marine Terrace, separated from the men's machines by the Bath Rocks. For 'delicate constitutions' there were

[36]Benjamin, *Footprints*, facing p.36.
[37]Walker, 'Entertainments', p.115.

showers in Dr Rice Williams's baths, and warm, tepid and cold shower baths were also available at No.14 Marine Terrace. The discovery of a 'dungeon' and a sixty-foot-deep well in 1845 had added to the interest of the castle. There were many good walks, over Constitution Hill to Clarach and Wallog and along Tan-y-bwlch beach, for example, while the twelfth-century Aberystwyth castle south of the Ystwyth now merited a mention.

Inland from Aberystwyth, there is no doubt that the dramatic Mynach falls at Devil's Bridge were the greatest attraction, and were particularly impressive when in full spate.[38] Visitors viewed the falls and the cauldron above the bridge with wonder mixed with terror, their eyes 'confused by the awfulness of the scene'.[39] Thomas Johnes's inn, rebuilt in 'Swiss Cottage' style by the duke of Newcastle, was much appreciated.[40] Rather slippery steps had been placed on the east side of the falls when George Borrow visited them in 1854.[41] In 1858 both the Belle Vue and the Talbot provided omnibuses to Devil's Bridge in summer.[42] In the early nineteenth century the celebrity of the Mynach falls was rivalled by Thomas Johnes's mansion and grounds at Hafod.[43] Many distinguished visitors were loud in their praises, but Sir Richard Colt Hoare thought the house was badly situated and 'a singular and not an elegant specimen of Gothic'. He even criticized the celebrated library and, though he admired the woodland walks, he thought George Cumberland's fulsome description greatly exaggerated.[44] Malkin duly described the grounds and was so impressed by the waterfall in the cave that he used an engraving of it as the frontispiece to his book.[45] Though rebuilt after the disastrous fire of 1807, Hafod tended to slip out of prominence after Johnes's death, when the estate was in Chancery from 1816 to 1831. Local guides continued to quote at length accounts by earlier visitors and to give details of Johnes's tree planting and sowings of hopeful acorns.[46] During the repairs made by the Duke of Newcastle, owner from 1832 to 1845, visitors were not admitted to the house.[47] By the time George Borrow visited Hafod, Henry Hoghton had set his architect Anthony Salvin to work, remodelling the house in an Italianate style, though it was still incomplete in 1854.[48] Borrow found it 'beautiful but fantastic' and was puzzled by its mixture of styles.[49] It was said in 1858 that the walks in the grounds were still much frequented.[50]

Pumlumon, the highest point in a region of exceedingly wet and desolate moorland, attracted visitors for two reasons: it was high and it was the source of the rivers Rheidol, Severn and Wye. Tourists were warned that it was the most dangerous mountain in Wales because of its many bogs, and it was essential to hire a guide if one could could be found.[51] The summit might be reached

[38]Colt Hoare had preferred the Rheidol falls until he saw the Mynach falls after heavy rain: Thompson, *Journeys of Colt Hoare*, pp.63, 230.

[39]*The Cambrian Tourist or Post-Chaise Companion* (8th edn., London, 1834), p.108.

[40]Nicholson, *Traveller's Guide* (1840), p.271.

[41]Borrow, *Wild Wales*, p.475.

[42]Benjamin, *Footprints*, facing p.36; Morgan, *New Guide* (1858), advert at end.

[43]E. Inglis-Jones, *Peacocks in Paradise* (London,1950) is the classic account of Johnes and Hafod.

[44]Thompson, *Journeys of Colt Hoare*, p.63.

[45]Malkin, *Scenery*, pp.60–7 and frontispiece.

[46]Nicholson, *Cambrian Traveller's Guide* (1813), p.567; *Aberystwyth Guide* (1816), p.121 et seq.; *Cambrian Tourist* (1834), p.112.

[47]Nicholson, *Cambrian Traveller's Guide* (1840), p.509.

[48]J. A. Thomas, 'The architectural development of Hafod, 1807–82', *Ceredigion*, VII, no.3 (1974–5), 223–5.

[49]Borrow, *Wild Wales*, p.502.

[50]Morgan, *New Guide* (1858), p.119.

[51]Nicholson, *Cambrian Traveller's Guide* (1813), p.1071; idem, *Traveller's Guide* (1840), p.510.

from Eisteddfa Gurig, and a descent made by the ridge to above Dyffryn Castell.[52] George Borrow hired a guide at Dyffryn Castell and followed the ridge route to the summit. Not content with viewing Llyn Llygad Rheidol from above, the tireless Borrow made the difficult descent to the lake and then climbed over the northern spur of the mountain to visit the sources of Severn and Wye.[53] The gorge of the Rheidol at Parson's Bridge was 'a chasm scarcely less repulsive in its aspect' than that at Devil's Bridge, and visitors to it passed Ysbyty Cynfyn church with its 'druidical circle' of standing stones in the churchyard wall.[54] Those with a taste for antiquities visited Llanbadarn Fawr and Llanddewibrefi churches with their ancient crosses and inscribed stones. Even after the excavation of 1847 there were few remains above ground at Strata Florida,[55] but with its rich historical associations and as the burial place of Dafydd ap Gwilym it naturally attracted visitors like George Borrow.[56] The beauty of the Rheidol valley below Devil's Bridge was much appreciated and a new road from Llanafan bridge to Pont-rhyd-y-groes opened up a fine stretch of the middle Ystwyth valley, but as yet there was no road up the Llyfnant valley.[57]

Most visitors to the Teifi valley came for the fishing from the Teifi Pools downwards. The Teifiside towns attracted little comment, though from the 1820s St David's College, a little piece of Oxbridge deposited in Lampeter, received some attention. On the coast from 1807 onwards Aberaeron was transformed from a straggling hamlet into a most attractive little town, thanks to the adherence of its founder, Revd Alban Thomas Jones Gwynne, and his successor, Colonel Alban Gwynne, to an excellent plan.[58] By 1840 it was forecast that this gateway to the beautiful vale of Aeron would become 'a place of considerable resort'.[59] The same could not be said of Cardigan. In 1803 Malkin had decided that the town was 'handsome from a distance' but not on close acquaintance.[60] The 'inconsiderable fragments' of the castle did not detain travellers, who paid more attention to the Guildhall (1764) and John Nash's gaol (1797).[61] Cardigan grew in the first half of the nineteenth century but its amenities did not keep pace with its growth. By 1853 it was in a deplorably insanitary condition.[62] A traveller might be comfortably accommodated at the Black Lion but the medieval squalor of the town would not incline him to stay long. Early in the century the wooded gorge of the Teifi above Cardigan had been its greatest attraction, but slate quarrying had destroyed this asset. By mid-century quarry waste had reduced the width of the river channel by two-thirds and its depth by three-quarters, 'the wilful destruction of a fine navigable river'.[63]

Finding the way and asking the way posed many problems to the early nineteenth-century traveller. Good, large-scale maps of Cardiganshire had been made but could not conveniently be

[52]Morgan, *New Guide* (1858), pp.155–88.
[53]Borrow, *Wild Wales*, pp.491–8.
[54]Nicholson, *Cambrian Traveller's Guide* (1813), p.1096; Morgan, *New Guide* (1858), p.113.
[55]The earliest fieldwork undertaken by the Cambrian Archaeological Association: S. Williams, *The Cistercian Abbey of Strata Florida* (London, 1889), pp.182–4.
[56]Borrow, *Wild Wales*, pp.508–10.
[57]Morgan, *New Guide* (1858), pp.58–62.
[58]J. M. Howell, 'The birth and growth of Aberaeron', *TCAS*, 4 (1926), 7–11; H. V. Phythian-Adams, 'The planning of Aberaeron – some new evidence', *Ceredigion*, VIII, no.4 (1979), 404–7.
[59]Nicholson, *Traveller's Guide* (1840), p.5.
[60]Malkin, *Scenery*, p.118.
[61]Nicholson, *Cambrian Traveller's Guide* (1813), pp.327–8.
[62]W. J. Lewis, *Gateway to Wales: A History of Cardigan* (Dyfed County Council, 1990), pp.85–6 for the repulsive details.
[63]Ibid., p.49.

carried. The small-scale maps in some guide books were most untrustworthy off the main roads.[64] From the 1830s, however, one-inch-to-the-mile Ordnance Survey maps appeared and were regularly revised. Communication with local people could be difficult since few English travellers knew Welsh and few people in rural Cardiganshire knew English. Guide books might have sections on Welsh pronunciation and Welsh place-name elements, which might help a little.[65] The landlord of an inn might know English, be able to give directions and possibly teach the traveller useful Welsh phrases. George Borrow had learned Welsh from a stable groom in his native Norfolk and north of the Dyfi his Welsh served him well enough. But on his way from Hafod through Pont-rhyd-y-groes, he asked a group of young people gathered for a wedding what was going on. The girls answered but started giggling, '*Dyn oddi tir y gogledd! he-he-he!*'. The men joined in deriding an apparent northerner and Borrow hastened on his way to Ysbyty Ystwyth pursued by the advice to go home to his goats in Anglesey.[66]

In the mid-1860s the railways came to Cardiganshire. In 1863 the Aberystwyth and Welsh Coast Railway reached Borth from Machynlleth and in 1864 was completed through to Aberystwyth. The following year the A & WCR merged with four other lines to become the Cambrian Railways. The Manchester and Milford Railway came north from Pencader to Lampeter and Tregaron. When it reached the neighbourhood of Ystradmeurig, the plan to plunge expensively through *terra incognita* to Llanidloes via Llangurig was abandoned and instead the line came down the Ystwyth valley, reaching Aberystwyth in 1867. These lines in conjunction with the LNWR and the GWR linked Cardiganshire with all parts of the kingdom and in particular with London.[67] With the coming of the railway, Borth began to develop as a holiday resort. In 1813 it had been singularly described as 'a miserable fishing cottage'.[68] In 1858 Lower Borth was a row of cottages whose menfolk fished or cut peat from Cors Fochno. Tourists were already coming from Aberystwyth to ride or drive on the four miles of magnificent sands and the village children had developed their own little trade, collecting pretty shells to sell to them.[69] By 1878 Borth was listed as 'a small watering place,[70] and by 1883 it was attracting more visitors and had a large hotel, the Cambria.[71] The railway encouraged schemes for grand hotels in Aberystwyth. The large Queen's Hotel (1866) was a success but its intended rival, the Castle Hotel, failed. Thomas Savin, a prominent railway entrepreneur, had ambitious schemes for a chain of coastal hotels.[72] His Castle Hotel, built by J. P. Seddon in 1865, incorporated the eccentric Castle House of 1792, and he offered package holidays, one payment covering rail travel and hotel accommodation. Savin went bankrupt in 1866. In the long term this proved advantageous for Aberystwyth, for the unfinished hotel was bought for a song and became the home of the University College of Wales in 1872.[73]

[64]E.g. the map in *Cambrian Tourist or Post-Chaise Companion* (London, 1834).

[65]E.g. Nicholson, *Cambrian Traveller's Guide* (1813), pp.viii, xi.

[66]Borrow, *Wild Wales*, p.503. This was not the only occasion when Borrow encountered hostility by south Walians toward their northern compatriots.

[67]R. W. Kidner, *The Cambrian Railways* (2nd enlarged edn., Headington, 1992), pp.17, 21, 23, 25, 31.

[68]Nicholson, *Cambrian Traveller's Guide* (1813), p.47.

[69]Morgan, *New Guide* (1858), pp.122–4.

[70]*Wales Register and Guide* (London, 1878), p.9.

[71]*Blackie's Picturesque Guide to Wales* (8th edn., Edinburgh, 1883), p.235.

[72]Kidner, *Cambrian Railways*, p.15.

[73]E. L. Ellis, *The University College of Wales, 1872–1972* (Cardiff, 1972), pp.22–4; J. R. Webster, *Old College, Aberystwyth: The Evolution of a High Victorian Building* (Cardiff, 1995), chapters 1, 3 and 4.

Fig. 102: Marine Terrace, Aberystwyth, *c*.1930. (*Copyright National Library of Wales*).

By 1875 Aberystwyth had grown considerably;[74] its population according to the 1871 census was 6,720. The Queen's was now the principal hotel, its new Assembly Rooms replacing those in Laura Place. Next in esteem were the Belle Vue, the Gogerddan Arms (or Lion) and the Talbot, and there were fifty-six inns. Lodging houses numbered 163, fifty-seven of them on Marine Terrace.[75] Buses from the principal hotels met all trains, and both the Queen's and the Belle Vue provided coaches daily to Devil's Bridge in summer. By 1878 Morris's temperance hotel ran daily brakes to Devil's Bridge and a Wednesday wagonette to Pumlumon with 'a safe guide in attendance'.[76] *Blackie's Guide* of 1883 provided a map of the way to the summit from Eisteddfa Gurig. By then Devil's Bridge was receiving 4,000 visitors a year. A new descent to the falls was provided by the flight of 118 steps called Jacob's Ladder and in 1867 an iron bridge had spanned the foot of the falls. The hotel fitted out lady visitors with 'an elegant and appropriate Garibaldian or Turkish costume' in flannel in which to essay the descent and a refreshment pavilion had been added to the hotel. Extensive plantations still survived at Hafod and the walks in the grounds and to Eglwys Newydd to see Chantrey's monument to Mariamne Johnes were much frequented.[77]

Many improvements were made in Aberystwyth, notably to the water supply and the sewerage system, while tree planting relieved the greyness of the streets.[78] On the Pier, built in 1865 and

[74]*Worrall's Directory of South Wales* (Oldham, 1875), pp.23–5.
[75]The number may be compared with the 127 of Tenby, the most popular resort in Pembrokeshire.
[76]*Wales Register and Guide*, pp.76–8, 117.
[77]*Blackie's Guide* (1883), pp.240–5, 246–7.
[78]Jones, *Aberystwyth Borough*, pp.18, 23, 25.

rebuilt in 1872, there were daily band concerts in summer. The promoters of the Queen's Hotel had built a new length of promenade in front of it and its proprietor persuaded the Corporation to build Victoria Terrace northwards to the foot of Constitution Hill.[79] Bathing continued to be strictly regulated, which may explain the comment in 1861 that Aberystwyth was 'free from the dissipations of some watering places'.[80] For other outdoor exercises there were archery and cricket clubs and many good walks, for example, to Clarach, a valley then noted for its early harvests and good crops.[81] Provision for indoor entertainment gradually increased. The Temperance Hall of 1864 was mainly used by local people,[82] but in the 1880s, when drama was regaining favour, the Laura Place Assembly Rooms became a theatre in the summer. Concerts were also held there or in James's Hall behind Terrace Road or in the large first-floor room of the Corn Market, Market Street, rebuilt in 1870.[83]

In the Teifi valley, Lampeter, 'an ill-built, straggling town', was still noted in 1875 mainly for its fishing and the college.[84] Tregaron remained a quiet market town with one good inn, the Talbot, fourteen others, a temperance coffee house but only one lodging house. Coaches met trains at Strata Florida station for Pontrhydfendigaid,[85] and in the 1880s for Strata Florida abbey. In 1887–8 Stephen Williams carried out excavations which revealed a fairly complete plan of the abbey church and uncovered the eastern chapels with their splendid tiles.[86] The abbey was now firmly back on the tourist map and the Manchester and Milford Railway ran excursions from Aberystwyth for visitors to view the excavations.[87] The Carmarthen and Cardigan Railway company had been formed in 1854. It never reached Cardigan but by 1864 it had reached Llandysul – and gone bankrupt.[88] Llandysul thus became a railhead, linked by coach to Newcastle Emlyn and Cardigan. It had two hotels and nineteen inns in 1875 and visitors came to fish or to admire the scenery of the Teifi valley.[89] Although the importance of Aberaeron as a seaport was declining after the 1870s, as a small seaside resort it was increasing in popularity. Its principal hotel, the Feathers, built in the 1840s and extended to meet demand, maintained a high reputation.[90] Like that of Aberaeron, New Quay's seaborne commerce declined but it increased in favour as a resort. The new terraces of houses built in mid-century added to the village's natural attractions and gave it a most picturesque appearance. It established its annual regatta in 1874[91] and in 1875 was said to be 'rising in importance as a bathing place'. It had a modest three lodging houses as well as twenty-five inns.[92] New Quay may have been the more popular because it had mixed bathing and no bathing machines,

[79] Blackie's Guide (1883), p.227.
[80] T. J. Tillotson, Picturesque Scenery in Wales (1861; reprint Barry, 1972).
[81] Blackie's Guide (1883), pp.232–3.
[82] Wales Register and Guide (1878), p.75.
[83] Walker, 'Entertainments', pp.116–17.
[84] Worrall's Directory, pp.187–8.
[85] Ibid., pp.403–4.
[86] Williams, Strata Florida, pp.190–204.
[87] D. M. Robinson and C. Platt, Strata Florida Abbey and Talley Abbey (CADW, 1992), p.21: illustration of railway poster.
[88] Lewis, Gateway to Wales, p.94; D. Davies, Those were the Days, Cardigan, II (Cardigan, 1992), p.94.
[89] Worrall's Directory, pp.126, 213; Wales Register and Guide, p.10.
[90] Blackie's Picturesque Guide to Wales (Edinburgh, 1872), p.63; Blackie's Guide (1883), p.235; Wales Register and Guide, p.9; Howell, 'Birth and growth of Aberaeron', 16.
[91] W. J. Lewis, New Quay and Llanarth (Aberystwyth, 1978), pp.7–8, 36.
[92] Worrall's Directory, pp.7–9.

and, like Aberaeron, it particularly attracted south Wales miners on holiday.[93] In the second half of the century Cardigan was setting its house in order, perhaps helped by a decline in population.[94] By the late 1880s it had gas lighting, decent pavements, a better water supply and a sewerage system. The completion of the new Guildhall in 1860 gave the town a new focal point.[95] Leased to the GWR, the Carmarthen and Cardigan Railway reached Newcastle Emlyn in 1885, and there it stopped, ten miles short of Cardigan. The Whitland and Taf Vale Railway, opened mainly as a mineral line, reached Crymych in 1875, nine miles short.[96] Cardigan was linked, however, by regular coach and horse-bus services to Crymych, Narberth Road station (Clunderwen) on the main GWR line, to Llandysul, New Quay, Aberaeron and Aberystwyth and to north Pembrokeshire.[97] The town had two good hotels, the Black Lion and the White Hart, and about three dozen inns.[98] No doubt the temperance movement had had some effect, for there had been sixty-eight inns in 1844 : by 1881 Cardigan had a Temperance Hotel.[99] Visitors did not as yet find Cardigan attractive with its steep and narrow streets and poor shops.[100] There was little to see of the castle and even less when the keep was incorporated into a new house, Castle Green.[101]

A touring theatre company first visited Cardigan in 1825, probably playing in the old Shire Hall. The 1840s saw regular visits, particularly during Hunt Week under the patronage of local gentry. The Shire Hall, the Angel Inn, a 'New Theatre' near the Shire Hall and a warehouse in Quay Street all served as temporary theatres. There was then a break until the 1880s when companies returned, now to the new Guildhall.[102] Cardigan's future was not to be linked to the English theatre but rather to the Welsh eisteddfod. Two-day provincial eisteddfodau were held in 1866 and 1868. One in 1878 was called the Semi-National and in the 1880s there was the Dyfed Annual Eisteddfod.[103] Eventually the railway arrived, from the south. The GWR completed the W & TVR from Crymych to its Cardigan terminus in 1885.[104] The coming of the railway encouraged an important new venture, for a syndicate was formed to develop Gwbert as Cardigan's own seaside resort. The old Gwbert Inn became the Cliff Hotel, and visitors were carried there by bus from Cardigan station. It was soon discovered that there were other good beaches within easy reach, including Poppit, Tresaith, Llangrannog and Aber-porth.[105] It was a pity that Cardigan did not continue with the Water Concerts held on the Teifi from time to time in the late nineteenth century.[106]

[93]Lewis, *New Quay*, p.34.

[94]*Worrall's Directory*, p.111.

[95]Lewis, *Gateway to Wales*, pp.19–21, 27–8, 65–6, 87, 99; Davies, *Cardigan*, I (Cardigan, 1991), pp.9–10, 23.

[96]Lewis, *Gateway to Wales*, p.94; Davies, *Cardigan*, I, pp.9–10, 23.

[97]*Worrall's Directory*, pp.110, 113; Lewis, *Gateway to Wales*, p.93.

[98]*Worrall's Directory*, p.115.

[99]Davies, *Cardigan*, I, pp.5, 17.

[100]*Blackie's Guide* (1872), p.67.

[101]Ibid. (1883), p.257; *Wales Register and Guide*, 1878, p.115. The builder, John Bowen, is said to have used the dungeons as his wine cellar.

[102]Lewis, *Gateway to Wales*, pp.137–8.

[103]Ibid., 140; Davies, *Cardigan*, I, pp.50–3.

[104]Davies, *Cardigan*, II, pp.88–90. The bankrupt W & TVR was bought by the GWR in 1888: ibid., p.91.

[105]Davies, *Cardigan*, I, pp.40–1.

[106]W. E. James, *Guidebook to Cardigan and District* (Cardigan, 1899), p.62 for a full account of these enchanting evenings.

The late nineteenth and early twentieth centuries saw two developments in transport which were to be of particular importance to tourism. The earlier was the development from the 1870s of the 'safety' bicycle, which, with pneumatic tyres from 1888, completely superseded the 'ordinary' or 'penny-farthing'. The bicycle was not only a quick and cheap way of getting to and from work; for town dwellers it provided a way of getting out into the countryside. Cycle clubs were soon formed: by 1892 Cardigan had a flourishing club, based on the Black Lion, which organized sightseeing expeditions into north Pembrokeshire.[107] There were evidently clubs at Aberaeron and Tal-y-bont and an Aberystwyth club had its headquarters at the Lion Royal, as the Gogerddan Arms was now called.[108] English clubs and individual cyclists undertook tours in Wales, often using trains to reach a base for touring. Visitors might hire cycles almost anywhere. The Cyclists' Touring Club[109] provided its members with maps, road books, repair kits and lists of hotels and lodging houses offering discounts to cyclists and distinguished by the sign of the winged bicycle wheel.

The first motor car appeared in Cardigan in 1901, and in that year, too, Aberystwyth had its first motor taxi.[110] The first places where motorists could obtain 'motor spirit' and accessories and have their batteries recharged in Aberystwyth were cycle shops.[111] As long as private cars were few, motor buses were of greater importance to tourists, since they often acted as feeders to and distributors from the railway stations. In Aberystwyth Jones Bros. pioneered local bus services and charabanc trips to places of interest from 1905, while in Cardigan T. M. Daniel started a bus service to Newcastle Emlyn in 1904.[112] Many local services were started by the GWR, Aberaeron to Lampeter and Aberaeron to Aberystwyth in 1906, New Quay to Llandysul and a charabanc trip from Aberystwyth to Aberaeron and New Quay in 1907.[113] It was also in the early years of the twentieth century that the last extensions to the railways of Cardiganshire were made. The Vale of Rheidol narrow-gauge railway opened its line from a terminus in Park Avenue, Aberystwyth, to Devil's Bridge in 1902. Originally intended to carry lead ore from the Rheidol valley mines to a wharf on Aberystwyth harbour, it speedily became a major tourist attraction with its magnificent views of the upper Rheidol valley.[114] By 1904 there were eight trains a day to Devil's Bridge.[115] From the 1860s there had been plans for a rail link to Aberaeron, but it was not until 1906 that the Lampeter, Aberaeron and New Quay Light Railway Order was obtained. The standard-gauge line with a speed limit of 25 mph, worked by the GWR, opened from Lampeter to Aberaeron in 1911, but the extension to New Quay was never built. The line markedly improved the accessibility of Aberaeron to visitors.[116]

---

[107]Davies, *Cardigan*, I, p.37; ibid., II, p.32.

[108]W. J. Lewis, *Aberaeron* (Aberystwyth, n.d.), p.36; photograph in White Lion Hotel, Tal-y-bont.

[109]Founded as the Bicycle Touring Club in 1878.

[110]Davies, *Cardigan*, I, p.39; Lewis, *Born on a Perilous Rock*, p.129.

[111]*Aberystwyth: The Official Guide of the Corporation*, ed. G.W. May (London, 1903), adverts for E. G. Piears, Terrace Road, and J. M. Michell, Queen Street.

[112]Lewis, *Born on a Perilous Rock*, p.129; Davies, *Cardigan*, I, p.39.

[113]L. Cozens, *Aberayron Transport* (London, 1957), pp.73–4.

[114]Lewis, *Born on a Perilous Rock*, p.126; Kidner, *Cambrian Railways*, p.42. For the detailed history of the line, see L. Cozens, *The Vale of Rheidol Railway* (Sutton, 1950) and W. J. K. Davies, *The Vale of Rheidol Light Railway* (London, 1964).

[115]Kidner, *Cambrian Railways*, pp.42, 77, 159. The line was taken over by the Cambrian Railways in 1913.

[116]Cozens, *Aberayron Transport*, pp.4, 15, 18, 23.

Fig. 103: Uncle Tommy's Minstrels, Aberystwyth, *c.*1939. (*Copyright National Library of Wales*).

Between about 1890 and 1914 Aberystwyth was at the peak of its popularity and prosperity, a well-being which was reflected in the confident and exuberant architecture of that period. The principal hotels had been joined by the Waterloo, a temperance hotel larger than the Queen's, and until 1906, when it became a theological college, by the Cambria. On the promenade, adjoining houses had been thrown together to form large boarding establishments, of which Plynlymon was the largest. The number of visitors was increasing, largely thanks to the railways' continued provision of cheap tickets and through coaches from London, south Wales and the principal English cities. The Cambrian Railways, always short of freight, consistently strove to build up their passenger traffic. The train journey from London now took about seven hours.[117] The New Promenade, a splendid municipal enterprise completed in 1903, ran round the Castle Point to link Marine Terrace to South Marine Terrace and the harbour. Perhaps the most striking development of the period was the great increase in the provision of indoor and outdoor entertainment. In 1891 James' Hall was replaced by David Phillips' Hall, built over his livery stables in Terrace Road. This rather ramshackle building provided a wide range of entertainment in the 1890s, including plays, comic operas, 'nigger' minstrels and a host of miscellaneous shows. In 1896 a superior rival appeared, the Pier Pavilion, built at the landward end of the pier and seating some 2,000 people. In summer it provided a varied programme of choirs, light comedies, musical comedies, concert parties

[117]*Aberystwyth Guide* (Aberystwyth, 1903).

The Market Street Cinema

"THE HOUSE OF DISTINCTION"

The FIRST Picture House in Aberystwyth (Established 1910)
Altered, Re-seated and Re-organised in 1923

The Last Word in Comfort and Beauty : Perfect Ventilation,
Faultless Projection, Brilliant Music, High-Class Programmes

DISTINCTIVE IN EVERY SENSE OF THE WORD

For Times of Showing, etc., see Daybills

Fig. 104: The Market Street Cinema, Aberystwyth. (*Copyright National Library of Wales*).

and on Sundays sacred concerts. In 1896 also the new Cliff Railway enabled a leisurely ascent of Constitution Hill to be made. The Market Hall of 1870, demolished in 1895, was rebuilt as the New Market Hall in 1898 and its large first-floor room served as both theatre and concert hall. Late in 1902 Phillips' Hall was burned down, to be replaced by Phillips' Arcade on the ground floor, with the extravagant Coliseum, seating over 1,000 in its stalls and two galleries on the upper floors, opened in 1905.[118] Its summer programme duplicated that of the Pier Pavilion. The cinematograph in various forms had appeared in Aberystwyth in the 1890s. From 1900 to 1910 the New Market Hall alternated silent films with live entertainments, but in 1910 Arthur Cheetham's 'Picture Palace and Electric Theatre' was permanently established. It was soon copied, for by 1913 the Rink Picture Theatre had taken over an indoor skating rink in Portland Street. Out of doors, on top of Constitution Hill, walks, terraces, gardens, kiosks, a camera obscura, a bandstand, refreshment rooms and the wooden Victoria Hall had transformed the scene. In 1913 this 'Luna Park' provided dances, concerts and many other amusements. By the seaside pierrots and concert parties performed on the pier, on a promenade bandstand and in the castle grounds. They also used an open-air stage in the Elysian Grove on Penglais Hill, whence a lamplit Lovers' Walk extended downhill to the Sylvan Palace, used for shows in inclement weather.[119] On the aptly named Aqua Terra beside the Rheidol, pleasure grounds included a seven-acre lake where an incredible variety of craft – including steam gondolas – could be hired.[120]

At Borth the Cambria Hotel had tennis and croquet, with an excellent golf links close at hand. The Vale of Rheidol railway, the Llyfnant valley, Strata Florida, Lampeter College, the gardens of Nanteos and Trawsgoed and, suprisingly, boating at Llanilar, were all favourably mentioned in the Guide of 1903. For the historian, the naturalist and the earth scientist, quite the best guide to the Aberystwyth district was that prepared for the NUT conference of 1911.[121] The infant National Library of Wales was temporarily housed in the Old Assembly Rooms, but George V was to lay the foundation stone of its fine new building that year. 'Motor tourists' were now flocking to Devil's Bridge; at Hafod the walks and Mariamne Johnes's garden were still open to tourists; combined rail and bus tickets were available for visitors to the Llyfnant and Artist's Valleys.[122] With the outbreak of war in 1914, however, tourism came to an abrupt end for five years.

Another war, that of 1939 to 1945, forms a great divide across the half-century between the 1920s and the 1970s. The most obvious developments in tourism, the rise of motor transport and the growing popularity of different kinds of holidays in different types of accommodation were common to both sides of the divide, but after it they accelerated and were accompanied by significant new changes. The inter-war years were by no means ones of continued prosperity, for the tourist trade had its booms and slumps following those in the national economy. While 1930 was a moderately good year for holiday resorts, 1931 was a disaster. Recovery was apparent by 1936 and by 1938–9 prosperity had returned.[123] The GWR took over all railways in Cardiganshire in 1922 and it continued to be a constant and valuable ally with its advertisements, holiday guides, cheap tickets

[118]Michael Freeman, The Coliseum (Aberystwyth, 1994).
[119]Walker, 'Entertainment', pp.117–20.
[120]Aberystwyth Guide (Aberystwyth, 1903), advert.
[121]J. Ballinger (ed.), Aberystwyth and District (Aberystwyth, 1911) was mainly the work of members of staff of the university college.
[122]Ibid., pp.190, 261, 274, 275, 286 and many adverts.
[123]The experience of the writer's family, closely involved in tourism in Pembrokeshire, bears this out.

and excursion trains, while for Aberystwyth it built a fine new station in 1924. The late 1930s were the most profitable years ever for the former Cambrian Railways lines.[124]

By 1920 the number of motor garages in Cardiganshire had increased significantly: Aberystwyth and Cardigan had three each, Lampeter two and Aberaeron, New Quay and Borth one each.[125] Early garages tended to be in town centres, often in former livery stables, and hotels might well turn their stables into garages: in the early 1920s the Lion Royal, Aberystwyth, boasted a garage for a hundred cars.[126] While many guide-books continued to be essentially railway based, others paid particular attention to the needs of motorists. *Moorhead's Wales* in 1926 reminded them that the speed limit outside towns was 20 mph, but also assured them that police traps were rare in Wales. Petrol, then only 1s. 7d. a gallon, was available in almost every village, though for some years it was prudent to carry a spare can strapped to the running board. RAC and AA patrols helped motorists in difficulty but as yet there was only the occasional red triangle to warn them of hazards. The road from Rhayader up the Elan valley and down the Ystwyth was to be avoided as 'a derelict altogether unsuitable for either cars or cycles'. The coast road from Aberystwyth to Cardigan 'being mostly a succession of steep pitches, with none too good a surface . . . is an unusually trying road'.[127] Roads were improving, however: all main roads and many minor ones were at least tarred, keeping down the clouds of dust that had plagued early motorists. Signposting was greatly extended and improved, notably by the AA with its black and yellow signposts and round village name plates.[128] County councils followed suit and introduced lower signposts, car height rather than carriage height. The motoring organizations provided their members with maps and guides and lists of recommended hotels and garages. 'AA and RAC recommended' became a common feature of hotel advertisements. It should be remembered that the lower-paid man was more likely to own a motor cycle than a car. The married man would take his wife on holiday riding pillion, and when they had a child they would invest in a bike and sidecar.

Another development of the inter-war years had been anticipated by the formation in 1907 of the Caravan Club of Great Britain. Early caravans were of the horse-drawn, gypsy type, briefly favoured by Mr Toad. With the development of more powerful and reliable cars the trailer caravan appeared, at first comparatively small and light. Lists of authorized camping sites were provided for members of the Caravan Club. A notable social phenomenon of the twentieth century, common to western Europe, was the desire of town dwellers to get out into the countryside. Caravanning was one way of doing this and camping, fostered by youth clubs, the Boy Scouts and the Boys' Brigade, was another. An Association of Cycle Campers had been formed in 1911 and by 1919 the Camping Club of Great Britain and Ireland had been set up. Campers might travel by car, by bicycle or on foot and their club gave them lists of farms and other sites where they might camp. Cycling and walking, 'hiking' as it was called in the 1930s, enjoyed increasing popularity. In 1930 the Youth Hostels Association of England and Wales was formed and at their hostels extraordinarily cheap, though spartan, accommodation was available for cyclists and walkers who were members. The earliest hostels in Cardiganshire were at Ponterwyd (1934) and Llanilar (1936–8).[129]

[124] Kidner, *Cambrian Railways*, p.7.
[125] *Kelly's Directory of South Wales* (1920), pp.49, 78, 110, 345, 445, 689.
[126] E. J. Burrow, *Motoring in Wales* (RAC Guide, n.d.), p.74.
[127] The Blue Guides, *Moorhead's Wales* (1926 edn.), pp.xlviii, l, li.
[128] These disappeared in 1940 and few returned, but Llanddewibrefi still had one in the early 1970s.
[129] Information from YHA headquarters, St Albans.

In the early 1920s many new bus routes were opened by small local companies. Between 1925 and 1933 many of them were absorbed by larger companies or the GWR. In 1930 the GWR abandoned the bus side of its enterprises and by 1939 most bus routes in Cardiganshire were run by Crosville, Western Welsh or James of Ammanford.[130] Few villages in Cardiganshire were not within reach of a bus service. Perhaps of more importance to tourists were the charabanc and motor coach tours, pioneered in Aberystwyth by Jones Bros. and Primrose Motors, at first with small fourteen-seaters but then with increasingly large coaches. Tours were not confined to Cardiganshire beauty spots, for in 1931 Primrose Motors offered visits to Betws-y-coed, Llandrindod Wells and Tenby.[131] One unusual trip about 1930 was by a six-wheeled vehicle from Aberystwyth to a proclaimed destination of 'Plynlymon Summit'.[132] The Aberystwyth Guide of 1931, however, notes a GWR bus from Devil's Bridge to the foot of Pumlumon.[133] Many day trippers came to Cardiganshire by coach from the Midlands and south Wales. A typical chapel outing from south Wales might go to Cardigan and on to Gwbert for the afternoon, with tea at the Cliff Hotel, followed by a return journey by way of Cenarth Falls and Newcastle Emlyn. More popular was a morning drive to Aberystwyth, then on to Devil's Bridge after lunch, an exploration of the falls and then tea at the refreshment rooms.[134] But despite the increase in road transport, the majority of visitors to the resorts of Cardigan Bay still came by rail, though those going to New Quay had to complete their journey by bus.

To judge by the corporation's official list of accommodation, by 1924 Aberystwyth had regained its pre-war popularity. There were seven licensed hotels, twenty-six private hotels and boarding houses, nine recommended inns, seven furnished houses and no fewer than 319 apartment houses. One grand hotel, the Waterloo, burned down in 1911, had been lost. More groups of promenade houses had been thrown together to form hotels, the origin of the Avondale, the Deva, the Marine, the Stafford and others. While there were fewer inns, there were eleven refreshment rooms in 1920,[135] which gradually came to call themselves cafés. In 1931 the promenade was extended further southwards to the harbour's wooden jetty.[136] On the promenade there were the traditional entertainments, in a new bandstand from 1935, and children's shows in Castle Corner. But 'Luna Park' had not revived and the Elysian Grove closed in 1926, though the Sylvan Palace still stood. In a pavilion in a quarry in northern Queen's Road the Quarryettes concert party performed and held dances, but again only until 1926.[137] There was, however, increased provision for outdoor games. The 18-hole golf course above Bryn-y-môr had opened in 1911; hard tennis courts opened in 1923 and there were soon two bowling greens and two putting greens.[138] A popular alternative to coach

[130]L. Cozens, *Aberayron Transport*, pp.75–6; Kidner, *Cambrian Railways*, p.163; Lewis, *Aberystwyth*, pp.128–9.

[131]Lewis, *Born on a Perilous Rock*, p.129; *Aberystwyth Official Guide* (1924), adverts; *Aberystwyth, the Biarritz of Wales* (Aberystwyth, 1931), adverts. *Moorhead's Wales* (1926) thought coach tours 'rather a superficial way of seeing the country'.

[132]Kidner, *Cambrian Railways*, p.163; H. C. Jones, *Aberystwyth Yesterday* (Barry, 1980), plates 50, 51.

[133]*The Biarritz of Wales* (1931).

[134]Outings by Tenby Methodist Chapel in 1931 and 1935.

[135]*Kelly's Directory* (1920), pp.78–84.

[136]Jones, *Aberystwyth Borough*, p.24.

[137]Walker, 'Entertainment', p.121.

[138]*Aberystwyth Guide* (1924); *Moorhead's Wales* (1926), p.142.

tours was a trip in the bay or to Aberdyfi in the large motor launches that competed for custom on the north beach.[139] Indoor entertainment was now dominated by the cinema. The original marine baths on the promenade had been demolished in 1892, having been superseded in 1880 by two indoor swimming baths in Bath Street. In 1919 one of these closed and became the Majestic cinema, successor to the Rink. The other bath survived for mixed bathing, but by 1939 it had been floored over to make a concert hall. Cheetham's cinema was largely rebuilt in 1923 as the Palladium and by 1924 the Pier Pavilion was showing films. In the late 1920s these cinemas hastily installed sound systems and in 1931 the Coliseum changed from a theatre to become the town's fourth cinema.[140] In 1935 the burning down of the Palladium reduced the number to three.

From 1922 Aberystwyth possessed a superb concert hall, the College Hall in Queen's Road, seating 2,000. While Sir Walford Davies was Professor of Music (1919–26), there were festivals of classical music under famous conductors. The hall also served as a conference centre, where the NUT met in 1933.[141] In the hot August of that year the wooden hall caught fire and was completely destroyed. Fortunately, the same year saw the erection by the corporation of a new hall, called King's Hall from 1935, on the Waterloo Hotel site. This ambitious municipal enterprise provided a range of entertainments under one roof. In the basement was an amusement arcade; the ground floor was a very good ballroom which, since it had a large stage, also served as a theatre and concert hall; on the first floor was a large gallery and refreshment rooms; on the roof was a roof garden and the whole was topped off by a clock tower. For many years it was to play an important part in the life of the town and of the college. In summer an excellent municipal orchestra played in the daytime and in the evening the hall often provided repertory theatre. On 4 September 1939 King's Hall had the distinction of being the only theatre in Great Britain to open.[142] In the 1930s there was also live theatre in the Quarry pavilion, where the Rogues and Vagabonds, a professional company largely funded by Marguerite Evans, wife of the notorious Caradoc Evans, performed.[143] Her company also toured extensively in Cardiganshire towns and villages.[144] In the 1930s there was much to see and do in Aberystwyth, including the May Queen and Music Festivals, sports tournaments, the Cardiganshire Eisteddfod, the agricultural show, sheepdog trials, the annual Carnival and much else.[145] In 1931 that perceptive observer H. V. Morton came to Wales preparing *In Search of Wales*. At Tal-y-bont he visited the Leri mill and watched its ancient machinery still working perfectly.[146] Here he anticipated future tourists' interest in water mills. In Aberystwyth he found the National Library of Wales with its priceless collection of manuscripts, and the University College. The architecture of the latter he found amusing, (he called it 'Early Marzipan'), but he appreciated the importance of its work, especially in agriculture. He might well have concluded that

[139]Jones, *Aberystwyth Yesterday*, plate 25: the *Worcester Castle* receiving passengers, *c.*1937.

[140]Freeman, *Coliseum*. For some years it interspersed live entertainment with films.

[141]*The N.U.T. Conference: Aberystwyth Souvenir* (Aberystwyth, 1933) does not compare as a local guide with that of 1911, but there were interesting sections by E. G. Bowen (Human Geography), pp.10–22, and Professor Lily Newton, who suggested good botanical walks, pp.33–41.

[142]Walker, 'Entertainment', pp.122–3.

[143]*Alias* Oliver Sandys, *alias* Countess Barcynska. *Moorhead's Wales* (1926), p.xl, warned that *My People* and *Capel Sion* by Caradoc Evans gave 'an unflattering view of the more unpleasant side of life in Wales'.

[144]R. F. Walker, 'The Little Theatre, Aberystwyth 1946–1961', *Ceredigion*, XI, no.3 (1991), 290; 'Oliver Sandys', *Caradoc Evans* (London, 1946), pp.112–15.

[145]Listed in *The Biarritz of Wales* (1931).

[146]H. V. Morton, *In Search of Wales* (London, 1936), p.176.

with its great library Aberystwyth was a New Hafod, with Professor R. G. Stapledon as the true heir of Thomas Johnes in his role as improving agriculturalist.[147]

Before 1914 'Breezy Borth' had insisted that it was a quiet resort with no day trippers or noisy amusements.[148] Between the wars Borth guides stressed that it was essentially a place where visitors might enjoy 'nature unadorned'.[149] But Borth was growing: in the nineteenth century terraces had extended the village northwards and there were new houses in Upper Borth. Growth continued between the wars with bungalows appearing towards Ynys-las, but Borth was still quiet.[150] The Cambria, now called the Grand Hotel, had 120 bedrooms, an assembly room and a refreshment room. Twenty-nine apartment houses were listed in 1920 but the number grew to 136 in the 1930s.[151] By 1920 Aberaeron had twelve inns besides the Feathers Hotel, seventeen apartment houses and two refreshment rooms.[152] The town remained small but it retained its popularity, particularly with visitors from south Wales.[153] One special attraction was lost in 1931 when the aerial ropeway across the harbour became disused.[154] New Quay in the 1920s had two good hotels, the Black Lion and the Queen's, seventeen inns, a refreshment room and a few apartment houses.[155] Undoubtedly attractive, and often compared to the fishing villages of Cornwall or Brittany, New Quay became increasingly popular and by 1933 its amenities had been improved by electric lighting and new water supply and sewerage systems. There were tennis courts and a bowling green and the annual regatta, revived in the 1890s, attracted many visiting yachtsmen.[156] In 1920 Cardigan had sixteen hotels and inns: the Black Lion was now AA and RAC recommended and the Commercial provided transport to nearby beaches. There was a Temperance Hotel and a Temperance Bar, but few apartment houses. The Pavilion, built in 1912 as a concert hall, had inevitably become a cinema and there were boating and golf clubs.[157] Gwbert won praise for its fine sands, its golf course and its cliff scenery.[158] Cardigan's main claim to distinction was the annual provincial eisteddfod, and the experience gained with these was to enable Cardigan, in difficult wartime circumstances, to stage the National Eisteddfod of 1942.[159]

During the Second World War only a trickle of tourists came to Cardiganshire, but very many soldiers, airmen and evacuated children were introduced to the county, and many would return on holiday. The return to normal after 1945 was slow. There were few private cars on the road, new ones were almost impossible to buy and continued petrol rationing restricted the use of old ones. The railways carried the bulk of tourist traffic but motor coach companies swiftly resumed business. By the late 1940s Associated Motorways advertised that practically every town in the Midlands and southern England was linked to Aberystwyth via the great hub of Cheltenham.[160] Once again young

---

[147]Ibid., pp.178–85.
[148]*Breezy Borth* (Aberystwyth, 1907).
[149]H. Ll. Roberts, *Borth Guide Book* (n.d. but 1920s).
[150]*Moorhead's Wales* (1926), p.138.
[151]*Kelly's Directory* (1920), pp.109–10; *Borth, Cardiganshire. Official Guide* (n.d.).
[152]*Kelly's Directory* (1920), pp.48–9.
[153]The population was only 1,313 in 1921: *Moorhead's Wales* (1926), p.225.
[154]Cozens, *Aberayron Transport*, p.5.
[155]*Kelly's Directory* (1920), pp.687–9; *Moorhead's Wales* (1926), p.224.
[156]E. B. Davies, *New Quay* (Aberystwyth, 1933), pp.5, 43, 46; Lewis, *New Quay*, p.35.
[157]*Kelly's Directory* (1920), pp.342, 344–5.
[158]*Moorhead's Wales* (1926), p.229.
[159]Davies, *Cardigan*, I, p.57.
[160]*Welcome to Aberystwyth, where Sunshine Awaits You* (n.d., *c*.1948), adverts.

people in particular responded to the call of the open road and in 1945 the YHA doubled its pre-war membership. A series of new hostels opened in Cardiganshire. While Ponterwyd closed in 1946 and Llwyndafydd was only open for a year (1949–50), Pentre-cwrt, Llandysul, was open from 1940 to 1969 and Poppit Sands (1950), Blaencaron, Tregaron (1950), Borth (1952), Ystumtuen (1960), Llanddewibrefi (1962), and New Quay (1971) were all still open in 1974.[161]

As late as the mid-1950s local guides were still railway based,[162] but the decline of the railways, nationalized in 1948, had already begun despite vigorous advertising, cheap tourist tickets and special trains.[163] The chief competitor of the railway was now the private car rather than the motor coach. Passenger services on the uneconomical Lampeter–Aberaeron and Pencader–Newcastle Emlyn lines had been suspended soon after the return of peace and the Whitland–Cardigan line finally closed in 1963.[164] Then, in 1964, the Ystwyth washed away the track near Trawsgoed and this convenient act of God led to the closing of the Aberystwyth–Carmarthen line.[165] Amazingly, instead of promoting the Vale of Rheidol line, especially after it became the only steam line on the system, British Rail economized by stripping it of much that was of interest to railway enthusiasts and might well have closed or sold the line but for the work of a voluntary Supporters' Association formed in 1970.[166]

In 1946 Aberystwyth prepared for business as usual, with its promenade hotels and boarding houses now de-requisitioned and the usual host of apartment houses. Many regular annual events were revived. The Municipal Orchestra played on the promenade bandstand in the mornings, early evenings and Sunday afternoons. On most evenings there were dances in King's Hall, with Old Time evenings on Thursdays. Every Sunday evening in summer there were celebrity concerts in King's Hall with well-known soloists and the orchestra.[167] On weekdays the Sea Breezes concert party performed on the bandstand in the afternoons and the Eight O'Clock Follies in the Forum Concert Hall in the evenings. The Castle Follies entertained children in the Castle Corner. Significantly, on Aqua Terra, the Aberystwyth Holiday Camp had been set up, with chalets, caravans and pitches for touring caravans and tents.[168] Late in 1946 the Forum Concert Hall became the Little Theatre and in 1947–8 it was shared by a concert party and a repertory company.[169] Three cinemas still prospered, the Coliseum, the Pier and the Forum, formerly the Majestic and now renamed the Celtic. The August Test Concerts, started in 1945, attracted large audiences, but King's Hall entertainments came to feature radio stars rather than those of eisteddfod or oratorio. By 1948 the Holiday Camp had its own entertainments centre.[170] In fact, business was not as usual but had declined markedly. Accommodation on the promenade was

---

[161]Information from Miss Sue Tunnicliffe, YHA headquarters, St Albans.

[162]E.g. *Gossiping Guide to Wales* (Cardiff, 1954), a much better guide than its name suggests.

[163]Kidner, *Cambrian Railways*, p.151: the Cambrian Coast Express, averaging 30 mph west of Shrewsbury, hardly deserved that title.

[164]Lewis, *Gateway to Wales*, p.95.

[165]Kidner, *Cambrian Railways*, p.178.

[166]Ibid., pp.191, 205.

[167]Aberystwyth was fortunate in having the services of two accomplished local musicians, Evered Davies, who conducted the orchestra and the dance band, and Charles Clement, a superb accompanist.

[168]*Aberystwyth Official List* (1946–7), pp.3–5, 42. Aqua Terra was subject to periodic flooding, sometimes serious, as in 1973.

[169]Walker, 'Little Theatre', 289–93.

[170]*Welcome to Aberystwyth* (n.d., c.1948), passim.

reduced when the College took over Plynlymon and the Stafford Hotel as student hostels and other properties as hostel annexes or academic departments. In 1951 the day of the grand hotel may be said to have passed with the closing of the Queen's Hotel and its conversion into council offices. The Belle Vue, the Talbot and many smaller hotels survived but in 1960 the Lion Royal became another college hostel. By 1950 the King's Hall orchestra and the concert parties were running at a loss.[171] Of particular relevance to the decline of Aberystwyth were developments at Borth and Clarach: an Aberystwyth guide of about 1951 carried advertisements for Brynowen Caravan Park, Borth, and for Clarach Bay Caravan Park.[172] In Borth the Grand Hotel, renamed Pantyfedwen, served as an emergency college hostel in the immediate post-war years. It resumed its role as a hotel but failed. No satisfactory alternative use was found for it and it was ultimately demolished, leaving a smaller rival nearby as the Grand Hotel. About 1948 Borth offered accommodation in boarding houses, apartment houses, furnished houses, flats and bungalows.[173] By the early 1960s the scene was dominated by six caravan parks, Glanlerry, Brynowen, Y Fron, Pen-y-graig, Golden Sands and Aberleri Farm. Static caravans were available at Aberleri and most of Brynowen's caravans were static. Brynowen now advertised on-site entertainments, fashion shows and bingo and it had television. Borth was no longer quiet: it had an amusement arcade called Funland.[174] In the early 1950s Clarach Bay had static caravans with toilets and showers.[175] By 1964 it was offering commodious chalets, sleeping up to six, with sitting rooms and kitchens, water and electricity laid on, and television.[176] As the larger sites like the 50-acre Brynowen developed, they added to their facilities shops, laundrettes, amusement arcades, clubs with licensed bars and halls for dances, films and live entertainment. Their patrons had little need to go into Aberystwyth.

From the 1950s onwards it became increasingly difficult for live entertainment in Aberystwyth to pay its way. By 1950 the Regency Players in the Little Theatre had found that the town could not support a professional company in winter.[177] A series of repertory companies took the Little Theatre from 1950 to 1959 and all found it hard to make ends meet. Charles Denville's company was particularly unlucky, for they opened a month after the Blaen-plwyf television transmitter had come into operation. Jack Bradley, who had been fairly successful in 1952–4, attempted a season in 1958 which ended in financial ruin. A last repertory company attempted a season in the fine summer of 1959 but it collapsed after three weeks. A concert party season was tried in 1960, but in 1961 the theatre was converted into the Conway Cinema, replacing the Pier, which had closed as a cinema after a fire.[178] By 1953 the Test Concerts and the associated drama festivals were losing money and in 1957 were abandoned, causing Aberystwyth to be compared unfavourably with much smaller Cardigan, which was successfully maintaining its semi-national eisteddfod.[179] In the 1960s live entertainment continued on the promenade and in King's Hall, and the celebrities who appeared were now those of television. Famous bands came to play for dances, including Victor Sylvester, Eric Winstone and Cyril Stapledon, but their popularity was rivalled by groups like the Bachelors,

[171]Walker, 'Little Theatre', 298.
[172]*Aberystwyth, where Holiday Fun Begins* (n.d., but *c*.1951).
[173]*Guide to Borth* (n.d., c.1948).
[174]*Borth, Cardiganshire* (n.d., probably 1960).
[175]*Aberystwyth, where Holiday Fun Begins*, p.58.
[176]*Aberystwyth for the Perfect Holiday* (Aberystwyth, 1964), pp.46–7.
[177]Walker, 'Little Theatre', 291–9 for the seasons 1947–50.
[178]Ibid., 301–18.
[179]Ibid., 320.

the Dakotas and the Rolling Stones. Showjumping was a comparative novelty and crowds gathered on the promenade to await the finish of a section of the Milk Race. In general live entertainment had moved decidedly downmarket since 1946, with bingo at the Pier and an eight o'clock show in King's Hall called Zip-a-Hoy.[180] In winter, it is fair to add, King's Hall was the venue for first-class orchestral concerts, plays and operas. Astonishingly, when cinemas elsewhere like the Pavilion in Cardigan were closing, Aberystwyth's three cinemas were still open in 1974.

Though Aberaeron was flanked by caravan sites, they did not intrude seriously on its quiet charm. The story of post-war New Quay was very different and resembled that of Borth and Ynys-las. Always popular with yachtsmen and sea anglers, New Quay profited from its association with Dylan Thomas and from the visits of stars of stage and screen.[181] By the mid-1950s it was difficult to find accommodation,[182] and the problem was aggravated by incomers buying second homes, as many as 150 by the 1970s. While the winter population was only about 800, in summer there were as many as 6,000 visitors.[183] These were accommodated in a growing number of caravan sites. In 1978 it was recorded that at New Quay there were six sites on the coast, nine within a mile of the coast and another four further out, with a total of 1,400 pitches. Along the coast of Cardiganshire there were seventy-four sites, forty-one of them on the coast itself.[184] Some sites like Morfa Bychan south of Aberystwyth were a serious intrusion on the coastal scenery. South of New Quay, with the exception of Aber-porth, the smaller resorts down to Gwbert had comparatively few caravans. In 1969 the county council prohibited the establishment of any new sites or the extension of any existing ones within a mile of the coast. A New Quay saturation area was decreed, stretching back from the coast to A487: here no new sites were allowed.[185] It was calculated in 1972 that the Aberystwyth district might receive 20,000 tourists in a year. Hotels, guest houses and boarding houses provided some 2,000 bed spaces, while there were 2,800 caravans and chalets and up to 400 pitches for tents.[186]

From the 1960s onwards the main roads, especially A487 and A44, the main link eastwards were steadily improved, though it was increasingly recognized that road communications from the middle and south of the county to Carmarthen and south Wales, and ultimately to the motorway, were woefully inadequate. On the railway to Shrewsbury diesel power replaced steam in 1965 and journeys were made speedier by the closing of small stations and halts.[187] In the mid-1950s it was still easy to park a car in Aberystwyth, in the large municipal car park in Park Avenue, on the promenade or in the wider streets.[188] But with the great increase in road traffic the problem of parking in all Cardiganshire towns became acute and seemingly insoluble. One-way systems had to be introduced in Cardigan and Aberystwyth and even in Llandysul. The need for bypasses was realized but many years were to pass before they were built. Although traffic built up, the number of visitors did not, largely due, as elsewhere, to the growing attraction of cheap package holidays,

[180]*Aberystwyth for the Perfect Holiday* (1964); *Aberystwyth, What to See and How to See it* (Aberystwyth, 1969), an excellent publication by the *Cambrian News*.
[181]Lewis, *New Quay*, p.24.
[182]*Gossiping Guide* (1954), pp.58–9.
[183]Lewis, *New Quay*, p.39.
[184]*Cardiganshire Coast, a Management Initiative* (n.d., c.1978), p.8.
[185]*Aberaeron and New Quay Area Draft Local Plan* (Ceredigion District Council, 1988), p.33 and map.
[186]*Aberystwyth Area District Plan* (1972), p.83.
[187]Kidner, *Cambrian Railways*, pp.110, 183.
[188]W. Locke, *Aberystwyth and North Wales* (n.d., c.1950), p.44; *Gossiping Guide* (1954), p.42.

notably to the shores of the Mediterranean, where sunshine awaited the visitor more surely than in Aberystwyth.

Many developments in post-war tourism were depressing, but there were others that augured well for the future. Fewer families came to Aberystwyth for a week or a fortnight in a hotel or boarding house, but many came for shorter stays, using the town as a touring centre. Day trippers still came by coach and others stayed overnight on long-distance tours. The number of foreign visitors gradually increased. Many caravanners came to see what the town had to offer, and not only when it rained. The Great Hall, opened in 1970 on the Penglais campus of the College, soon displaced King's Hall as a concert hall and conference centre. People attending conferences were identified as an important group of visitors.[189] These might be accommodated on the campus, but like visitors who stayed in the self-catering halls developed by the College from 1966 onwards they spent money in the town. In 1972 Theatr y Werin opened alongside the Great Hall and provided an excellent playhouse for professional touring companies in winter and matinees and evening shows for visitors in summer. The founding of a drama department in the college in 1973 led to a series of excellent summer shows for children.

Inland, the completion of the Rheidol hydro-electric scheme in 1964 diversified the rather barren landscape of Pumlumon with the lakes of Nant-y-moch and Dinas, while lower down the Cwm Rheidol reservoir with its dam and waterfall added to the beauty of the valley.[190] A scenic route was opened up from Ponterwyd, over the Nant-y-moch dam and by a series of old mine roads to Tal-y-bont. Another, from Ponterwyd by the lakes of Blaen Melindwr and Pendam to Penrhyn-coch became a favourite afternoon drive. In the east motorists tackled the improved but still difficult roads from Tregaron to Abergwesyn and from Llanddewibrefi to Farmers, no longer the preserve of the rally driver.[191] In the woodlands they had planted over wide areas of north Cardiganshire, the Forestry Commission opened up attractive walks and picnic sites. Their publications instructed visitors in the nature and the use of the forests,[192] and local guides described the forest walks in detail.[193] Much of Thomas Johnes's plantations had been felled during the two wars and afterwards. The Forestry Commission had leased part of the Hafod estate in 1929, but it was not until it bought most of the estate in 1950 that replanting, not always sympathetically, really began. By the Second World War only part of the mansion was habitable. Thereafter its condition deteriorated so seriously that in 1958 it had to be completely demolished.[194] In 1974 the Caravan Club had a site near the ruins. It was to be many years before a sustained local effort was made to ensure that something of Thomas Johnes's lost paradise might be regained.

Judging by the disappearance from Aberystwyth beach of the motor launches, the call of the sea had waned, but there came a call of the mountains with the new activity of pony-trekking, first apparently at Tregaron but soon at centres all over the county.[195] By the 1960s there was growing interest in industrial archaeology and especially in the remains of the lead mining industry. A

[189]*Aberystwyth Area District Plan* (1972), p.83.

[190]*Aberystwyth, What to See* (Aberystwyth, 1969), p.31; V. Rees, *Shell Guide, Mid-Western Wales* (London, 1971), p.9.

[191]Rees, *Mid-Western Wales*, p.10; *Aberystwyth, What to See*, pp.109–10.

[192]E.g. *The Cambrian Forests* (HMSO, London, 1959).

[193]*Aberystwyth and the Coast and Countryside of Ceredigion* (n.d., *c*.1980) has a good list.

[194]J. R. E. Barron, 'The Waddinghams of Hafod', *Ceredigion*, XI, no.4 (1992), 398–9; J. Macve, 'W. G. Tarrant: last squire of Hafod', ibid., XI, no.1 (1988–9), 59, 64–5, 70–1.

[195]*Aberystwyth, Coast and Countryside*.

particularly successful venture was the formation in 1973–4 of the lead mining museum at Llywernog near Ponterwyd. In the 1960s, too, surviving or revived water mills, especially woollen mills, with their attractive products, grew in popularity. Many of the mills were in the south of the county and it was appropriate that in 1976 a Museum of the Woollen Industry was located at Drefach-Felindre.[196] A wider interest in rural crafts resulted in craft shops and potteries springing up everywhere. But the tourist did not have to leave his town base to find things of interest. Accompanied by the splendidly illustrated pamphlets prepared by Aylwin Sampson in the early 1970s, the discerning tourist strolling through the streets of Aberystwyth, Aberaeron or Cardigan could discover many architectural delights.[197] The listing of ancient and historic buildings by CADW and the establishment and extension of Conservation Areas should ensure that these shall remain for the pleasure of future visitors.

[196]*Blue Guide: Wales and the Marches* (1979 edn.), p.350. It is a branch of the Museum of Welsh Life.
[197]A. Sampson, *Aberaeron* (Aberystwyth, 1971); idem, *Cardigan (*Aberystwyth, 1972); idem, *About Aberystwyth* (2nd edn., Wellington, 1975).

CHAPTER 14

POOR LAW ADMINISTRATION IN CARDIGANSHIRE, 1750–1948

Alun Eirug Davies

THE basis of poor law administration in eighteenth- and early nineteenth-century Cardiganshire, as elsewhere in England and Wales, was the parish.* Some seventy-six separate parishes and divisions of parishes were involved. No incorporations had occurred in the county and the provisions of Gilbert's Act of 1782 (22 George III, c.83), which enabled parishes to unite for purposes of an improved method of administration, had not been adopted anywhere. The two Acts of Parliament passed in the reign of Elizabeth I still formed the basis of poor law administration until 1834. The Act of 1597–8 (39 Elizabeth, c.3) ordered the appointment of overseers of the poor and empowered them to provide relief for all destitute persons, while the temporary Act of 1601 (43 and 44 Elizabeth, c.2), made permanent in 1640, ordered 'the churchwardens of every parish, and four, three or two or more justices of the peace . . . (as) overseers of the poor of the same parish' to maintain the impotent poor and set the unemployed able-bodied to work. Thus the vestry originally constituted a parish meeting which met annually under the auspices of the church in vestry. The vicar, churchwardens, overseer of the poor, vestry clerk, together with the occupiers of land or property above a certain value, normally constituted the membership of a vestry.

Towards the end of the eighteenth century some parish vestries tried to limit the number of persons attending each meeting. This foreshadowed the Sturges Bourne Act of 1819, 'An Act to amend the Laws for the Relief of the Poor' (59 George III, c.12). The Select Vestry Act, as it was called, was adopted by several vestries in Cardiganshire. The number of select vestries in the county in 1822, 1823, 1825, 1826 and 1834 was eleven, seventeen, twenty-four, eleven, and seven respectively.

Vestries met when occasions demanded it, and not more than three or four times a year in the mountainous and more rural parishes. The intention was not to meet too frequently in order to discourage the poor from applying for relief. The Select Vestry Act of 1819 required the vestry to

*Vestry minutes, overseers account books, Quarter Sessions order books, Parliamentary papers and reports, Royal Commission reports, reports of the Poor Law Commissioners, reports of the Poor Law Board, Ministry of Health reports, as well as newspapers such as *The Cambrian* and *The Welshman*, all constitute unrivalled sources of evidence for the operation of the Poor Law and have been consulted in the preparation of this chapter. See also my thesis 'Poverty and its treatment in Cardiganshire, 1750–1850' (unpublished University of Wales MA thesis 1968) and my articles in *Ceredigion*, 1968, 1976, 1978 and 1984.

meet once a fortnight, or more often if necessary. The fortnightly meetings proved unpopular in many parishes that had adopted the Act because they were considered to be too frequent and involved the parishes in extra expense.

By the year 1750 overseers of the poor were to all intents and purposes merely servants of parish vestries, and did very little on their own apart from providing relief between vestry meetings. They were appointed by the vestry for a period of one year. The parish of Llanilar, in 1829, drew up a list of all 'Fit Persons to Serve the Office of Overseer'. Tregaron vestry from 1814 appointed annually occupiers of the 'oldest Tenements in the parish to serve the office'. Often the appointment of an overseer would be quashed by justices of the peace in Quarter Sessions after an appeal by the person chosen to serve as overseer. In rural districts farmers were usually overseers, while shopkeepers held the office in towns and villages. By the year 1834 overseers were considered by Poor Law officials to be totally incompetent. Their inexperience and the interference of their private occupations were given as reasons for their inefficiency. 'Their object', wrote one assistant Poor Law Commissioner, 'is to get through the year with as little unpopularity and trouble as possible; their successors therefore have frequently to complain of demands left unsettled, and rates uncollected, either from carelessness or a desire to gain the trifling popularity of having called for fewer assessments than usual.'[1] That overseers were not always honest in their dealings is evident from occasional entries in vestry books.

The Select Vestry Act of 1819 allowed open vestries 'to elect any discreet person or persons to be assistant overseer or overseers of the poor', and to specify their duties and fix their salaries. Their duties were basically the same as those of the overseers. Few Cardiganshire parishes took advantage of the Act to appoint assistant overseers. The number in the county in 1822, 1823, 1825, 1826 and 1834 was ten, eleven, twenty, ten, and eighteen respectively.

Both open and select vestries in Cardiganshire, as elsewhere, had clerks to assist the ratepayers in their work. As early as 1766 a clerk was appointed to serve the parish of Llanrhystud at an annual salary of ten shillings. Only the more educated members of the community could undertake the duties of vestry clerk as defined by a member of Aberystwyth select vestry in 1834 – 'to assist the Overseers, and to look into all Parish Accounts, and attend to all instructions of the Select Vestry'. Schoolmasters and curates often held the office.

In order to carry out the functions of relieving the poor in time of need, vestries needed funds. This was provided by the Act of 1601 (43 Elizabeth, c.2), which ordered churchwardens and overseers of the poor of each parish 'to raise weekly or otherwise, by taxation' for maintaining the poor. The assessment was done by the vestry and rarely by the churchwarden or overseer as laid down by the Act. 'Interference on the part of the Overseers on the Select Vestry has never in one instance taken place, because every body has only to pay his exact and just quota',[2] retorted an Aberystwyth official in 1834. 'But when we rate new houses, or raise or lower the rate of others, as they may rise or be depreciated in value, if we differ in opinion about what the premises ought to be rated at, we always put it to the vote before the whole vestry.' The occupier of a house rated at £20 knew that he had 20s. to pay; the occupier paid 5s. for a house rated at £5. The tithe and other

---

[1] *Report from His Majesty's Commissioners for Inquiry into the Administration and Practical Operation of the Poor Laws*. Appendix A. Reports of Assistant Commissioners. Pt.II, No.27. Report of Stephen Walcott, HC 44 (1834), XXIX, p.184a.
[2] HC 44 (1834), XXXII, p.637c.

properties were valued as being worth a certain amount in each parish assessment. The rate was spoken of as one of so much in the pound. In the parish of Llanrhystud in 1750 the rate of fourpence in the pound was assessed on the parish by the vestry towards the relief of the poor. By 1800 it had risen to four shillings in the pound. Contemporary observers were aware of loopholes in the system. Alfred Ollivant, clerk to the Lampeter vestry, claimed that the process was deficient in many parishes. Assessments were very old, 'made when the cultivation of the different parts of the Parish was different to what it is now, and consequently properties are very unequally assessed. In my own Parish till last year several Freeholds were not assessed at all, in consequence probably of their having been waste land when the assessment was made.'[3] The local enclosure act forced Llanrhystud vestry in 1817 to assess those occupiers of lands and houses who had not hitherto been assessed to the poor rate. In any event, if an occupier thought the rate levied on him was unfair, he could always appeal to the Quarter Sessions for redress, which had the authority either to quash the rate and order the vestry to make another one, or to amend the rate. Cardiganshire Quarter Sessions Order Books testify to this.

Supervising the work of the vestry and the officials were the justices of the peace. From Petty and Quarter Sessions they carried out a number of duties affecting the poor laws. Justices could commit to houses of correction anyone refusing to pay the rates. They were also called upon to examine the legal settlement of strangers before deciding to commit them to the house of correction or pass them on to some other parish. The examination of parish accounts until 1819 was another duty undertaken by justices of the peace.

That there was an enormous increase in the amount of money spent on poor relief, particularly after 1780, is evident. For the three years 1748, 1749 and 1750, the sums £293, £306 and £307 respectively were spent on relief in Cardiganshire. In 1776 poor relief cost the county £1,085 and then there was a steady rise to £20,418 in 1819. This was the peak year for poor relief expenditure and thenceforward the annual amount disbursed on poor relief fell to £14,577 in 1824. From that year a further upward trend began, with expenditure reaching its maximum in 1833 with a total of £19,566. On the eve of the Act of 1834 the county was spending £19,311 on poor relief, or the sum of 5s. 9d. per head of the population.

There were no workhouses in the county in 1834. Cardigan vestry drew up a plan of a workhouse for the poor of the borough and formulated a set of rules for its operation in 1785.[4] Otherwise the house of correction and the poorhouse were the nearest to the workhouse system in eighteenth-century Cardiganshire. The house of correction for the county was erected at the top of High Street in Cardigan. It appears that the house of correction and the gaol were housed in the same building. Here poor prisoners were housed and set to work. When James Neild visited Cardigan in 1803, the new gaol built by John Nash in 1797 still served as a house of correction. A treadmill had been installed. Debtors were said to be sleeping on straw in rooms 'with fire-places, but no fuel'.[5] Both lunatics and felons were confined to the same rooms. Poor prisoners were not granted allowances

[3] Ibid., p.638c.
[4] Quoted in W. J. Lewis, *The Gateway to Wales: A History of Cardigan* (Dyfed County Council, 1990), p.107. For accounts of the poor in eighteenth-century Lampeter, see B. Phillips, *Peterwell: The History of a Mansion and its Infamous Squire* (Llandysul, 1983), pp.97–112 and G. Morgan, *Cyfoeth y Cardi* (Aberystwyth, 1995), pp.131–43.
[5] J. Neild, *An Account of the Rise, Progress, and Present State of the Society for the Discharge and Relief of Persons Imprisoned for Small Debts throughout England and Wales* (London, 1808), pp.130–1.

and in times of need they were told to apply to their respective parishes for relief. In 1817 poor prisoners received 'one shilling each in the Week out of the allowance of three shillings and sixpence for Bread and that in future the allowance for bread shall amount only to the sum of two shillings and sixpence'.[6]

Relief by means of the poorhouse was practised by several parishes. Dihewyd vestry in 1784, for instance, decided 'to build a house in the church yard wall, for the poor; of 8 yards in length, and twelve feet wide' with the proviso that 'whosoever that will not carry stones must, in lieu of it, pay 8d. each'.[7] There is some evidence to suggest that vestries agreed to build a poorhouse for the parish near Mydroilyn, where the poor were to be 'admitted and maintained and properly employed'.

The principal methods of relieving the poor in Cardiganshire were by payments of rents out of the rates; by exempting cottages from rate assessments; by regular periodical relief; and by casual or occasional assistance in money or in kind.

The paying of the rents of pauper cottages was widespread in the county. Parishes spent £16 7s. on the payment of rents for the poor in 1776. The overseer and churchwarden of the parish of Llanrhystud noted in 1834 that the parish rented out to the poor twenty-three cottages ranging from 30s. to £5, bringing the total rent paid yearly to £50 1s. 6d. Twenty-four persons occupied rent-free cottages. One of these cottages was situated in Aberystwyth. During the period of distress after the Napoleonic Wars the authorities tried to impose economies, and in some cases they refused to pay house rent and confiscated items of furniture to pay the rent. In 1821 Llanrhystud vestry ordered the overseers 'to fetch the Clock and other unnecessary Articles from the house of Richard Morris and sell the same by Auction in order to pay arrears of Rent to Mr John Evans'. About a year later they wanted to herd two families into one rent-paid cottage, exclaiming that the parish paid 'more Rent for Houses for the Poor than is reasonable or necessary – That there are several Houses rented by the Parishes large enough to contain two families and that in future two families be plac'd in such houses'. This parochial interference with rents made paupers 'a very desirable class of tenants'. Paupers were preferred as tenants over the independent labourer, and the miserable cottages of the poor often became a source of profitable investment. Re-letting was also practised. Such methods of relief tended to obliterate the distinction between pauper and the independent labourer.

A second method of relieving the poor in Cardiganshire was to exempt pauper cottages from the rates or, if the properties were assessed, the rates were paid by the parish authorities. Cottages were frequently exempted from the rates at Aberystwyth and Lampeter in 1834; they were not generally assessed in the parish of Llansanffraid. In the township of Llanrhystud Mefenydd, occupiers of property assessed to the value of £6 10s. 8d. were exempted from payment of rates on account of poverty.

The granting of regular relief or allowances was confined in the main to the aged, the married, and widows with families. A list of paupers to be thus relieved, with the amount for each, was generally made out by the vestries at the beginning of each parochial year. A vestry would be called by the overseers, or temporary relief would be granted if the list were to be amended. The township of Llanrhystud Mefenydd granted allowances of 2s. a week in general. But they were not received by the paupers until the end of the year. Paupers living outside the parish were paid every quarter.

[6]Cardiganshire Quarter Sessions Order Books, 28 July 1817.
[7]Quoted by G. Eyre Evans, *Cardiganshire* (Aberystwyth, 1903), p.220, from Dihewyd Vestry Minutes, 19 January 1784.

Llanddewibrefi vestry granted relief to paupers living as far away as Merthyr Tydfil. Before 1810 regular recipients of relief were often ordered to wear a badge.

Occasional or casual relief was given to paupers in money or in kind – fuel, clothing, barley, potatoes, medical attendance. The clerk of the Lampeter vestry claimed that relief 'given in kind, instead of money, advantageous, as the Poor are bad economists, and, therefore, lay out their money improvidently; besides which, it has the effect of preventing the heads of the Family from spending it on drink'. The sick paupers of the town and neighbourhood of Aberystwyth had the benefit of the services of a local dispensary.[8] It was founded on 18 February 1821 by Richard Williams. Rich benefactors, including Dame Winifred Bonsall, Colonel William Powell, MP, of Nanteos, and Pryse Pryse, MP, of Gogerddan, were prominent subscribers. Overseers of the poor were invited to become subscribers on payment of two guineas. The aim of the institution was to relieve the sick poor and in 1838 it became the Aberystwyth Infirmary and Cardiganshire General Hospital. Pauper lunatics or idiots were not so fortunate. There was no lunatic asylum in Cardiganshire in 1834. Such cases were boarded with parishioners. The more violent were committed to the house of correction. In 1830 Cardiganshire vestries spent £10 9s. 4d. in maintaining insane paupers. In July 1836 there were ninety-six pauper lunatics in the county.

The problem of finding work for the unemployed labourers in Cardiganshire was common to the whole country. The establishment of a 'parish farm' for the employment of the able-bodied was not adopted in Cardiganshire. In the absence of employment, labourers were forced to apply to the parish for relief. The policy of Aberystwyth Select vestry was to relieve unemployed labourers until they eventually found work. Temporary work was granted to single able-bodied labourers when they were unemployed or sick. Able-bodied labourers with families were granted allowances in times of need in the parishes of Llansanffraid and Lampeter, while at Aberystwyth, wherever there was a large family and the parents had little money, the children would be maintained. In answer to the question 'Can you state the Particulars of any attempt . . . to discontinue the system (after it has once prevailed) of giving to able-bodied Labourers in the Employment of Individuals Parish Allowance on their own Account, or on that of their Families?', both Aberystwyth and Llansanffraid officials denied that the 'attempt' had ever been made by their vestries. The effect of placing the married and unmarried labourer on a different footing was alleged to be to force the labourer into early and improvident marriage and then to encourage him to produce a large family. The census returns of 1821 for the parish of Llanfihangel Ystrad referred to the 'frequent early marriages which take place in order to enable the parties to have a better claim to Parochial relief'. Two parish officials denied the existence of any difference in the wages paid by the employer to the married and the single able-bodied labourer as a result of parish allowance. Even if the pernicious Speenhamland system, whereby labourers in employment were granted allowances according to a scale, based on the size of the family and the price of bread, was not adopted by Cardiganshire vestries, there is no evidence either of the older, and equally pernicious, Roundsman system. Paupers were often sent round the parish to work for their board and lodging, in return for clothing provided by the vestry, but they did not earn money.

While the very aged were often placed with their relatives, older children were placed with farmers, tradesmen, craftsmen, or artisans as apprentices. Apprenticeship was one way of relieving

[8]G. Eyre Evans, *Aberystwyth and its Court Leet* (Aberystwyth, 1902), p.119; see also D. I. Evans, 'Hospital services in Aberystwyth before 1848', *Ceredigion*, V, no.2 (1965), 168–208.

the parish vestry of its burden of orphan and deserted children. Small premiums were paid to the masters at intervals. Llannarth vestry gave 46s. with an apprentice in 1768 for a two-year apprenticeship; the same parish gave 70s. in 1802. Children were apprenticed to the following employers at the turn of the century: blacksmiths, carpenters, curriers, farmers, feltmakers, hatters, joiners, plasterers, shoemakers, surgeons, saddlers, shopwrights and tanners.

It was the 'lax administration of the law, and . . . unjustifiable application of money raised for the relief of poor'[9] that convinced the Poor Law Commissioners of the need to change the method of administering the Poor Laws after 1834 in Wales. It might be implied from this that the Old Poor Law was not harshly executed. Examples of kindly treatment to individual paupers have frequently been found in the vestry books. But the concern of local authorities to keep down the rates was reflected in the callous attitude of parish vestries towards pregnant women – remove them lest the children should become a charge on the parish. So at Tregaron in 1797 – 'the Overseers shall, at the expense of the Parish bring Orders of Removal against pregnant Women now residing within this parish'. Similarly it is seen in their attitude towards cottage building on the common – stop the practice lest the squatters gain a settlement by residence. Again at Tregaron in 1816 – 'We shall not suffer any fence to be erected on the Common or Mountain opposite the Parish of Caron . . . in order to inclose into field or fields any part thereof – and we do hereby unite in determination that we shall march in a body and demolish any such inclosure which may be made'. Poor law administration, with its lack of central direction and trained officials, its variety of methods of relieving the poor, and its rising costs, became totally inadequate in the eyes of the central government. Hence the Poor Law Amendment Act of 1834.

'An Act for the Amendment and better Administration of the Laws relating to the Poor in England and Wales' (4 and 5 William IV, c.76) was passed on 14 August 1834. A central board was set up consisting of three Commissioners known as the 'Poor Law Commissioners for England and Wales' to execute the Act. Their terms of reference were 'to make and issue all such Rules, Orders, and Regulations for the Management of the Poor, for the Government of Workhouses and the Education of the Children therein, and for the Guidance and Control of all Guardians, Vestries, and Parish Officers, so far as relates to the Management or Relief of the Poor, and the keeping, examining, auditing, and allowing of Accounts, and making and entering into Contracts in all Matters relating to such Management or Relief . . .' To assist them in their work, the Commissioners were empowered to appoint Assistant Commissioners, not to be confused with the inspectors with the same title who had conducted the Poor Law enquiry of 1832–4. The whole of Wales, except Monmouthshire, became the responsibility of William Day from January 1836. By 1840 he had made 655 visits to Wales. He was assisted by Sir Edmund Head from March 1836, and by 1840 he had made 602 visits. Cardiganshire became the sole responsibility of Sir Edmund Head in July 1838 and Sir Richard Digby Neave from April 1839. Their 'accepted pattern of action consisted of inspection, report, and advice'.[10]

The first duties of the Commissioners were directed to the formation of unions. 'The limits of unions which we found most convenient', wrote the Commissioners, 'are those of a circle, taking a market town as a centre, and comprehending those surrounding parishes whose inhabitants are

[9] *Third Annual Report of the Poor Law Commissioners* (1837), p.32.
[10] T. H. Marshall, *Social Policy in the Twentieth Century* (2nd edn., London, 1967), p.19.

accustomed to resort to the same market.'[11] According to Harold Carter, this method of division was based on the principle of the 'association of "town" and "country" into one town or city region', a 'revolutionary' method which 'if it had been followed through, would have produced a very different system from that which eventually emerged'.[12] Doubts had been expressed by various ratepayers as to the need for a union at Tregaron in view of the existence of one at Lampeter. Poverty, a small population of 9,558, a low rateable value, and an extensive area of sixteen or eighteen miles by fourteen or fifteen miles were used as arguments against its formation. It was doubted that economies would be achieved where the average rate amounted to £1,884. A union was formed at Tregaron, however, because of its importance as a market town to the inhabitants of the hundred of Pennardd. Sir Edmund Head wrote to the Poor Law Commissioners in 1837 'that if we had fixed the centre for this district 12 miles off at Lampeter not one of the guardians of all the hamlets of Llanddewibrefi, or of Caron parish could ever have dreamt of attending there – some parishes too such as Ysbyty Ystrad Meurig, Ysbyty Ystwyth, Uwch-clawdd would necessarily have been attached to Aberystwyth at a distance of from 14 to 20 miles from that town'.[13] Similarly, Aberystwyth was said to be, like most towns of the county, 'placed at one extremity of the union, but its growing importance and the goodness of its market make it peculiarly fit for a centre'.[14]

Cardiganshire was thus divided into five unions. The Aberystwyth Union was formed on 5 May 1837, Aberaeron followed on 8 May, Cardigan on the following day, and Lampeter and Tregaron Unions on 15 May. The union boundaries did not coincide with the administrative county boundary. The Cardigan Union comprised seventeen Pembrokeshire parishes in its total of twenty-six. The Aberystwyth Union, consisting of thirty parishes and townships, extended northwards to the limits of the county boundary, leaving out the township of Ysgubor-y-coed, which William Day annexed to the Machynlleth Union, and southward to include Llanrhystud. Twelve parishes in south Cardiganshire were annexed to the union of Newcastle Emlyn.

After the formation of the unions, Boards of Guardians, consisting of elected ratepayers and ex-officio Guardians, were set up in each union to administer poor relief and govern the workhouse. Guardians were elected by ratepayers and property-owners. Voting took place in private; the ballot papers were left at each elector's residence and were collected the following day when signed. In Cardiganshire most Boards were dominated by farmers or clergymen. Justices of the Peace residing in any parish in the union and acting for the county qualified as ex-officio Guardians. Labourers had no opportunity of becoming a Guardian because of the property qualification, namely, the occupation of property above a certain value in annual rent. The Commissioners also determined the number of Guardians per union, the number being in proportion to the rateable value of each parish. Thus, after consulting the principal inhabitants, Sir Edmund Head in 1837 recommended an annual rent of £20 as a qualification for the office of Guardian in the Aberystwyth union and one Guardian was assigned to each parish, except Aberystwyth, which was granted four. The Commissioners recommended a total of thirty-four Guardians for the Cardigan union and an annual rent of £25 as the qualification. The qualification for the office in the poorer unions of

[11] *First Annual Report of the Poor Law Commissioners* (London, 1835), p.19.
[12] H. Carter, 'Local Government and Administration in Wales, 1536–1939' in J. A. Andrews (ed.), *Welsh Studies in Public Law* (Cardiff, 1970), p.41.
[13] PRO, MH12/15858, 27 March 1837, Sir Edmund Head to PLC.
[14] PRO, MH12/15796, 27 March 1837.

Lampeter and Tregaron was an annual rent of £15. These amounts were often too high, and for the next twenty years or so it was difficult, particularly in the poorer unions, to find persons of property to serve as Guardians. The ordinary administration of relief was the duty of the relieving officer under the direction of the Board of Guardians. Auditors to examine and audit the accounts of each union were also appointed by the Boards.

Following the formation of unions and the appointment of Boards of Guardians, Assistant Commissioners sought to persuade the Guardians to approve the building of workhouses. Aberaeron Union was the first to build a workhouse in Cardiganshire in 1839 (where the Cottage Hospital is housed today). The Guardians realized that without a workhouse the union would derive little benefit from the Poor Law Amendment Act and the Board of Guardians would be 'continually exposed to the necessitous demands of able bodied Labourers'[15] unable to obtain wages sufficient to maintain their families. The prospect of being forced to enter the workhouse would persuade many paupers now in receipt of relief to do without it. The placing of every mother applying for parish relief in the workhouse would reduce the number of chargeable bastards. The workhouse would result in a reduction of expenditure on pauper rents and force the Guardians to provide work for the able-bodied poor. By the end of 1839 the workhouse was ready to receive its first paupers. It was built by William Green and the original contract was estimated at £1,200. The entire cost of the building, architect's services, added walls and furnishing came to £1,793. The union borrowed the sum of £1,800 at 4 per cent interest from the Exchequer Loan Commissioners.

The Cardigan Union workhouse was also erected in 1839 and was ready for the reception of paupers in 1840. The intention was to house 120 inmates. The total cost of the building came to £3,250. This amount was also borrowed from the Exchequer Loan Commissioners, initially at 5 per cent, but subsequently at 4 per cent. On 28 December 1839 Thomas Lundy and his wife were appointed master and matron at a salary of £35 and £25 respectively, subject to the approval of the Poor Law Commissioners. There were sixty-five inmates on 1 January 1844 – eleven males, twenty females, thirty-one children and three vagrants. A shed and a piggery were erected in the workhouse yard. Able-bodied paupers worked in the shed and during board meetings the horses of the Guardians were stabled there. Visitors were allowed between the hours of nine and twelve in the morning and between two and six in the afternoon by permission of the governor. Paupers were permitted to attend divine service every Sunday morning; between May and September they were allowed to attend afternoon and evening service. Able-bodied paupers and mothers of illegitimate children, however, were to attend service at the workhouse.

The Aberystwyth Union workhouse was ready for the reception of inmates in 1841. The sum of £3,000 was borrowed from the Exchequer Loan Commissioners at 4 per cent interest. A full description of the new building appeared in the columns of *The Welshman*.[16] 'So much has been said of late against the new Poor Law Act . . . that it becomes the duty of every well-wisher of the poor to make strict enquiry, whether these laws are really of that cruel and tyrannical nature which the ultra Tories represent them to be . . .', wrote the correspondent. The site was declared to be ideal, the bread offered to inmates was said to be wholesome – more so than any bread obtainable outside. Work in the form of stone-breaking was available to able-bodied paupers who refused to work and had thrown themselves on the parish. 'In other words', continued the correspondent, 'when they

[15]Aberaeron Union Board of Guardians, Minute Book, 9 May 1837, 17 February 1841.
[16]*The Welshman*, 19 August 1842.

find that the workhouse is no bed of roses for them, and that the question is whether they are to work hard in the workhouse or at their own homes, they always prefer the latter alternative upon the principle of preferring the least of two evils.' The workhouse, however, never housed many inmates at any time; there were only six paupers in August 1843. When Aneurin Owen, Assistant Poor Law Commissioner, visited the workhouse early in 1847, he reported that the building was generally adequate for the needs of the union in size and internal arrangements. The workhouse, though intended to hold 200 inmates, housed only twenty-six inmates and two vagrants in March 1847. There were no separate wards for sick and infectious cases. The old women's day room was used as the vagrant's ward. Work was available for vagrants, though the Guardians preferred to allow them to leave without breakfast rather than set them to work. County magistrates seldom committed vagrants for refusal to work. Since March 1847 a schoolmistress had been appointed to teach the five boys and eight girls in the workhouse at an annual salary of £30.

The Tregaron and the Lampeter Boards of Guardians used delaying tactics over the workhouse question. As early as 1838 the Poor Law Commissioners noted with approval that the Tregaron Union had agreed to build a workhouse. By 1841, when William Day visited the union, the Guardians had refused 'with a population of about 10,000 and expenditure of £2,000 it is useless to persuade them', he wrote.[17] By 1847 it was the failure of the potato crop, and the 'bad yield, scarcity and high price of grain and provisions' that persuaded the Guardians not to comply.

There was a general belief in Wales that the 'evils arising from the Poor Laws were entirely unknown within its limits, and that any change in the mode of administering these laws was altogether unnecessary'.[18] Sir Edmund Head, however, claimed that in Cardiganshire 'most erroneous views exist as to the object of the poor rates and their legal application' and 'that there is no reason to believe that the unassisted efforts of the present authorities can in any way remedy these or any other existing evils, and therefore that some new organization is absolutely necessary'.[19] The 'new organization' was embodied in the principles of the New Poor Law. The Commissioners were convinced that the introduction of the two essential elements involved in the New Poor Law system, the constitution of an elected Board of Guardians to provide relief and the establishment of workhouses to test the genuineness of destitution, would raise the character of Welsh farmers by enabling them to take an active part in parish affairs, and lead to the abolition of the system of payment of rents and to provide accommodation for the large numbers of illegitimate children and their mothers.

Cardiganshire people were by nature conservative in their ways and on the whole reluctant to change over from 'a state of uncontrolled license in the administration of relief to the stringent provisions of the New Poor Law'.[20] 'The law', wrote William Day in 1838, 'has come by surprise upon them, finding them in many indeed in most instances with long arrears of debts and liabilities. Where these have not been liquidated it has created a prejudice against the new order of things, where they have, it has necessarily thrown an increased burthen upon the rates of the current year, which has been unfairly attributed to the same source. I think myself therefore bound to state that

---

[17]PRO, MH12/15858, 1841, William Day to PLC.
[18]*Third Annual Report of the Poor Law Commissioners* (London, 1837), p.32.
[19]PRO, MH/15817, Edmund Head to PLC.
[20]W. Day, *Correspondence with the Poor Law Commissioners, with Observations on the Working of Certain Points of the Poor Law and on Sir James Graham's proposed Alteration of the Law of Settlement* (London, 1844), p.27.

though these prejudices are daily abating the present state of the public feeling in North Wales is still far from friendly to the New Poor Law.'[21] When he visited the twenty-six unions of south Wales in 1840, he found less direct opposition, but little difference otherwise. The same abuses prevailed and the same prejudices were displayed by both Guardians and ratepayers – ignorance and indifferent enmity. The ratepayers and Guardians of the three more prosperous unions – Aberystwyth, Aberaeron and Cardigan – did not complain of the changes as much as the ratepayers and Guardians of the two poorer unions of Lampeter and Tregaron. They were not prepared for the change and some of the changes were not popular.

What form did this opposition take? It is doubtful whether there were any persons in the county who posed as leaders of what came to be described by the Poor Law Commissioners as the 'popular manifestation against the law'. Aggrieved individuals often wrote to the Poor Law Commissioners in London asking them to intercede on their behalf at Board of Guardians meetings, but the Commissioners were 'expressly restrained by law from interfering for the purpose of ordering relief in any individual case'.[22] In 1837 twelve Welsh Unitarian ministers signed a 'Protest' addressed to the Poor Law Commission describing the new law as oppressive and cruel. Letters were sent to each by the Poor Law Commission asking for specific cases but none was ever received. In 1838 Lampeter petitioned Parliament for a total repeal of the law. Another petition was presented by Llandysul ratepayers in 1842 'praying that the Poor Law Amendment Bill may not pass into a law'. In 1846 an extraordinary meeting of the Cardigan Board of Guardians was held at Cardigan Town Hall in order to draft a petition to both Houses of Parliament condemning the new poor laws. The vice-chairman, R. D. Jenkins, contended 'that the poor of this country ought to be supported by the nation at large'.[23]

It seems that some measure of opposition to the new law emerged from the irritation felt by parish officers and ex-officio Guardians at their loss of influence under the new system and some jealousy of elected bodies such as the new Board of Guardians. 'In the hill Unions', wrote Nassau Senior, 'isolated as they are both by position and with the misfortune of a distinct language without the advantage of a middle class the magistrates dislike the change . . . The farmers regret the days of pauper rents and certain convenient peculations.'[24] In the adjoining counties of Pembroke and Carmarthen, hostility erupted into violent attacks on workhouses. This did not occur in Cardiganshire, although the threat to destroy them always existed. The authorities were aware of this and asked local officials for permission to use the workhouse as barracks. During the Rebecca Riots, Colonel Thomas Love had requested that a detachment of infantry should be housed in the Aberystwyth workhouse in order to replace the troop of horse already stationed in the town and to guard against similar outrages – 'considerable apprehension being entertained that an early attack would be made upon the Gates leading into the Town'. By 1844 particular features of the New Poor Law were the subject of general complaint. The grievances, as the evidence submitted to the Commissioners of Inquiry for South Wales shows, centred on the excessive expenditure of the new administration, principally (though not exclusively) on account of the high salaries of the officers, and the operation of the bastardy clauses.

[21]PRO, HO73/54, PLC to the Right Honourable Lord John Russell, Report on the state of Public Opinion respecting the Poor Law, 28 December 1838.
[22]PRO, MH12/15858, PLC to Clerk of the Tregaron Board of Guardians, 30 September 1837.
[23]*The Welshman*, 5 February 1846.
[24]PRO HO73/54.

The provision of relief after the declaration of the unions was under the direct control of the Guardians. In 1838 it was reported that no order to discontinue outdoor relief had been issued to the unions even where workhouses were about to be built. Boards of Guardians carefully inspected and revised their lists of paupers. On 2 March 1839 the Cardigan Guardians requested the relieving officer to bring all new applicants for relief before the Board provided they were healthy and did not live far from the town. A week later they refused relief to all dog-owners. In 1841 the Aberystwyth Guardians decided to reduce the weekly relief granted to several aged paupers from 3s. 6d. to 2s. with the alternative of entering the workhouse where they would be better fed, clothed and lodged. Relief, however, continued to be predominantly outdoor and this was often given partly in money and in kind. In Cardiganshire it was the general practice for farmers to give paupers small allotments for settling two, four or six bushels of potatoes, according to the size of the family. In May 1839 Aberystwyth Guardians granted assistance to able-bodied paupers with families to purchase seed potatoes because of the high price of food. In 1843 a great deal of relief was granted to able-bodied persons, although by that year the number receiving relief had fallen because employment was available in the lead mines of the locality. The number of adult able-bodied paupers relieved in the union county of Cardiganshire, according to the Poor Law Commission, in the quarter ending 25 March 1840, was 1,430. Of this total thirteen were relieved in the workhouses. Similarly, in the Lady Day quarter of 1846, 6,292 paupers (204 indoor, 6,088 outdoor) were relieved in the union county.

Although the structure of poor law administration was radically altered by the Poor Law Amendment Act of 1834, the structure of poor relief remained very much the same. The erection of three workhouses seems to have made very little difference. The number of inmates – children, vagrants and the chronic sick in the main – was small. Where employment was often not available, the workhouse test was meaningless. The Poor Law Commissioners had no answer to the problem of providing work for those willing to take it. Workhouses could have accommodated many able-bodied labourers who required relief, yet Guardians preferred to grant outdoor relief rather than fill these 'Bastilles'. The real problem confronting the New as well as the Old Poor Law systems was not pauperism but poverty and, as William Day so pointedly remarked, 'that is an evil which no Assistant Commissioner can remedy'.[25]

In 1847 the Poor Law Commission gave way to the Poor Law Board which, in turn, lasted until 1871. Despite the additional burdens imposed upon the rates, such as the erection of workhouses and the payment of union officers' salaries, the Board claimed that the amount annually spent on poor relief had decreased absolutely since 1834. Law charges as well as the expenses of the removal of paupers had also declined substantially since 1834. Money expended on the poor of seven Welsh unions, including Aberystwyth, which had erected workhouses, was less by £16 6s. in every £100 in 1849–50 than the average annual amount expended in the same unions before their formation. For every £100 they spent before 1837, £83 4s. was spent in 1849–50. In the two unions of Lampeter and Tregaron, which were without workhouses, the sum spent in 1849–50 was more by £4 12s. than the average annual amount spent in the same unions before their formation. For every £100 they spent before 1837, the sum of £104 12s. was spent in 1849–50. In the workhouses inmates were lodged, clothed and fed. Attempts were made to provide help according to needs. Pauper

[25]Day, *Correspondence*, p.32.

schools were set up for the young. In 1852 seven boys and girls attended the Aberystwyth Union workhouse; twenty-nine boys and girls attended the Cardigan Union workhouse school. There was a general feeling of repugnance against sending children to the workhouse. The chairman of the Aberystwyth Board of Guardians wished to remove this feeling. In the workhouse the children 'avoided the contagion of vicious example . . . ; well trained in habits of order and cleanliness, and now that they had engaged a schoolmistress at a liberal salary, the children were to receive a good education'.[26]

Lampeter and Tregaron Boards of Guardians were still not convinced. The order for the erection of the workhouse for the union had been entered in the Tregaron Minute Book as early as March 1846, but the actual decision was postponed from time to time by adjournment and occasional obstruction. The presence of Edward Hurst and Hugh Owen as a deputation of the Poor Law Board at one of the meetings failed to persuade them. Hurst intimated that unless the building commenced, measures would be taken to force the Guardians to carry out their resolution. The affairs of the union were said to be 'in a most unsatisfactory state'. In 1851 'the misconduct of the Clerk, which led the Board to call on him to resign, his want of power, his embarrassed circumstances, and his low social position' operated 'very detrimentally to the interests of the union'.[27] Even as late as 2 January 1855 the Poor Law Inspectors were still serious in their intention to dissolve the Tregaron Union.

Even where workhouses had been built, Poor Law administration was less uniform than the Board intended. Guardians still preferred outdoor relief to workhouse internment. By January 1850 there were 6,656 paupers in receipt of relief in Cardiganshire – the population in 1841 was 75,136. During the half-years ending 25 March 1853 and 1854 indoor relief cost the union county £284 and £417 respectively; outdoor relief cost £8,604 and £8,860. The workhouses were filled in the main with sick, aged, orphaned and mentally defective people. According to the 1851 census, the Aberystwyth Union workhouse had nineteen inmates, including seven children listed as 'bastards', three widowers, two widows born in Ireland and described as 'deserted'. There were times when Guardians were discouraged from sending too many paupers to the workhouses. They received a circular, dated 21 August 1854, stressing 'the importance of guarding against any over-crowding in the workhouse, and of revising the workhouse dietary, should such revision be deemed necessary by the Medical Officer'. The circular was the consequence of the recurrence of cholera in several parts of the country. The poorer classes, however, still feared and hated the workhouses because of the stigma attached. It was argued that the spread of Benefit Societies in the country was largely the result of the salutary horror of 'coming upon the parish'.

The assistance afforded to the outdoor pauper was generally in money or kind, and was frequently of a temporary character. The outdoor pauper might also occupy a house and pay a rent for it. The five Boards of Guardians provided relief with the available resources as best they could under the circumstances. The chairman of the Aberystwyth Board of Guardians boasted that there had not been a single division upon one single point at Board meetings while he had been chairman. His aim had been 'to take great care of the poor and aged, and to prevent imposition'. But the rise in the poor rates was alarming to the Guardians. The Aberystwyth Board of Guardians petitioned Parliament in May 1849 to adopt some measures for checking the rapid rise in the county rate. The

[26] *The Welshman*, 9 April 1847.
[27] PRO, MH12/15860.

Fig. 105: Stone-breaking workshop and hoppers in Bronglais Workhouse, Aberystwyth, *c.*1880. *(Crown Copyright RCAHMW-NMR).*

non-payment of poor rates worried the local authorities. The Petty Sessions for the lower division of the Tregaron Union summoned several people for non-payment in August 1850. In January 1851 the magistrates for the lower division of Troed-yr-aur heard complaints against the overseers of numerous parishes in that part of the county who had been summoned by the clerk to the Cardigan Union for non-payment of union calls. In almost every case the inhabitants were unable to pay their poor rates regularly.[28]

There were factors beyond the control of the Poor Law Board and Boards of Guardians. In 1855 the increase in poor expenditure was attributable mainly to the increase in the price of provisions, especially bread and cheese. This was particularly the case where relief was given in kind. In the same year the potato crop failed in the counties of Cardigan, Carmarthen and Radnor. Vagrancy would often swell the numbers of paupers receiving assistance. The authorities were particularly concerned in the late forties and fifties. The county had its core of habitual vagrants, but whether the vagrancy problem was as serious as the local press or poor law authorities suggested is doubtful. From 1848 it

[28] *The Welshman,* 17 January 1851.

was laid down that relief would not be granted to habitual vagrants on mere application. Their circumstances would be investigated and their needs ascertained before relief was to be granted. Boards of Guardians were urged to discriminate between real and simulated destitution. Yet the tramp nuisance was said to be as 'rife' as ever in north Cardiganshire in 1849. There was remarkable variety in the treatment of vagrants, although attempts were made to diminish the differences. Poor Law Inspectors either spoke at board meetings or made suggestions in the visitors' book in favour of the erection of vagrant wards, the allowance of food, the regular imposition of taskwork, and the assistance of the police. Guardians were determined to keep costs down.

In 1871 the Poor Law Board was replaced by the Local Government Board as a result of an administrative merger of Poor Law, Public Health and Local Government. There was no change in policy. The Local Government Board was determined to adhere to 'sound principles which the authors of the Poor Law Amendment of 1834 desired to make of universal application'. There was still a desire to control and diminish the amount of out-relief by providing more workhouses. Great exertions were made by inspectors during 1872–3 to persuade the Lampeter and Tregaron Boards of Guardians to build workhouses in the unions: 'We are of opinion that no Union should be allowed to remain without a workhouse adequate to its necessities, as a test of destitution of able-bodied applicants for relief and as a place of refuge for the aged, the sick, and for the orphan children.' The Union of Lampeter had 723 outdoor paupers in 1872 out of a population of 9,973; Tregaron had 699 out of 10,677. Francis Bircham, the Poor Law Inspector for Wales, referred to the Union of Aberystwyth as an example of the 'improved and enlightened administration of the poor law'. Pauperism, according to Bircham, had been considerably reduced since 1871. When urging the Cardigan Union Guardians to restrict outdoor relief, he wrote:

> The only Union in the county (Cardiganshire) where pauperism at all approaches the average condition of things throughout England and Wales is that of Aberystwith, where, with a population of 27,439, the per-centage of paupers is 3.9. It is but a very few years since this and the Cardigan Union were much on an equality in this respect, for I find that during the half year ended Lady-day 1871, 33 in-door and 1,755 out-door paupers were relieved in Aberystwith, forming a total of 1,788 or 7 per cent of the population, which was but little lower than Cardigan at that time. During the corresponding half year 1875, however, the accounts from Aberystwith tell a different tale. The in-door paupers were then 59, the out-door 1,098 – total 1,157, or about 4 per cent of the population; and the saving in money being at the rate of £2,200 per annum, whereas in the Cardigan Union, during this half year of 1875, 1,389 paupers received out-door relief alone, or nearly 300 more than in Aberystwith, the population of which exceeds that of Cardigan by 10,000.[29]

The building of new workhouses in Lampeter and Tregaron in 1876 was expected to reduce pauperism and check rising expenditure in the unions. The Lampeter workhouse was a building of brick and stone with accommodation for fifty paupers. Evan Jones was the first master, Abel Evans, the medical officer, Mrs Hannah Jones, the matron. The Tregaron workhouse was built on the Llanddewibrefi road to accommodate thirty paupers. James Roberts, Merthyr Tydfil, was the first master, and was succeeded by Morgan Morgan in 1878; the first matron was Tabitha Biddle

[29]*Sixth Annual Report of the Local Government Board* (1876–7), p.xxi-xxii. For an account of the Aberystwyth Poor Law Union, see D. Jones, 'Pauperism in the Aberystwyth Poor Law Union 1870–1914', *Ceredigion*, IX, no.1 (1980), 78–101.

Roberts. When the workhouse first opened its doors there were seven paupers. Outdoor relief predominated throughout the county and was itself an indication of the prevalence of low wages and surplus labour.

The second half of the nineteenth century was a period of great charitable activity and voluntary organizations for the relief of poverty developed. The Charity Organisation Society (COS), founded in 1869, existed in Cardiff and Swansea, but was short of money. A period of distress, such as the severe winter of 1878–9, called into play considerable charitable activity, particularly from churches and chapels. The Cardigan branch of the Soup Kitchen Movement operated between 1888 and 1895. The aim of the Aberystwyth, Llanbadarn and District Nursing Association was to nurse the sick poor in their homes, free of charge. During the year ending 30 September 1905, the number of cases attended by the nurses was 235, and the number of visits paid was 6,662. The charities succeeded in keeping deserving people from applying to Boards of Guardians for relief, but in any event the church and chapel charities were not endowed. In addition, there was little cooperation between Guardians and their relieving officers on the one hand and charitable societies on the other. A relieving officer was expected to make further investigation if an applicant for relief was receiving money from a local charity.

Changes came with the Local Government Act of 1894 within the limitations of the 1884 franchise. A considerable number of working men and a smaller number of women could now vote and become councillors. The composition of Boards of Guardians changed. In the fifty-three unions in Wales, eighty-eight women were elected. Aberystwyth union had one lady Guardian in 1906. In addition to democratization, the Act contributed to the use of more Welsh in the administration of the poor law. The Act saw the election of more Welsh-speaking Guardians. 'These gentlemen who never spoke a word before have found their tongues and they are ready to speak in their Welsh, and they do. But when they pay their own rates, and they feel that out of every half-crown that old Mrs Evans gets they are paying 1s. 5d., and they are very careful.'[30] The minutes of the Tregaron Board of Guardians were first written in Welsh on 20 August 1907. They were repeated in English. The Local Government Board, however, insisted that the minutes of the proceedings of Boards of Guardian be written in English. A duplicate set in Welsh could be made. Tregaron Board of Guardians decided to record the minutes 'for the future in the English only'. The next set of minutes in the Welsh language appeared on 15 April 1924. The Minister of Health agreed to the minutes being recorded in Welsh but insisted that financial matters should be minuted in both languages.

By the end of the nineteenth century the Local Government Board was being forced to produce circulars that were contrary to the principles of the 1834 Act. In 1900 the Board issued a circular impressing on Boards of Guardians the need for the removal of children, as far as possible, from workhouses; that adequate relief should be given to aged and deserving outdoor paupers; that a special class of aged and deserving inmates of the workhouse should be created, to whom special privileges should be given. There were very few children in the union workhouses of Cardiganshire. Aberaeron had two children, Aberystwyth one, Cardigan eighteen, Lampeter three, and Tregaron six. Aberystwyth boarded its children out and there was no prospect in Cardigan of any special provision being made for the workhouse children unless boarding out could be adopted.

---

[30]*Royal Commission on the Poor Laws and Relief of Distress* (1909). Appendix. Vol.I. Minutes of evidence. Answer to question 5328, p.273.

With regard to adequate outdoor relief to deserving outdoor paupers and the aged, outdoor relief had been the practice in Cardiganshire; whether it was adequate is another matter. Outdoor relief was given to all who could look after themselves. The return showing the number of persons over sixty years of age in receipt of relief from Cardiganshire Guardians on 1 September 1903 showed that the ratio per cent of paupers over sixty years to total number of paupers over sixteen years of age was 73 per cent, whereas the average throughout England and Wales (excluding London) was 69 per cent. The Union County of Cardiganshire consisted of six unions – Aberaeron, Aberystwyth, Cardigan, Lampeter, Newcastle Emlyn and Tregaron. There were 1,329 paupers over sixty, and those over sixteen totalled 1,800. When the Old Age Pensions Act 1908 conferred a right to an old age pension on every man or woman, whether married or single, having attained the age of seventy, it was claimed that the new pension system had 'already been to a great extent anticipated by outdoor relief, which was rarely refused to old people' in Wales.

Cardiganshire workhouses were too small in size to give serious consideration to the formation of a special class of aged and deserving inmates. In Wales there were eight workhouses where the number of inmates exceeded 800, thirteen where the number exceeded 50 and was under 100, and seventeen where the number of inmates was less than 50. Aberystwyth and Cardigan union workhouses belonged to the second category, Aberaeron, Lampeter and Tregaron to the third. There was no call for any special treatment or formation of a separate class at Aberaeron, Lampeter and Tregaron. The workhouses had become receptions for sick and infirm persons rather than able-bodied paupers.

Differences of opinion over what to do with the able-bodied poor led to the appointment in 1905 of the Royal Commission on the Poor Laws and Relief of Distress. The report, published in 1909, gives some interesting figures for Cardiganshire. There were 2,331 paupers in the county, of whom 205 were relieved in the workhouse, and 2,126 relieved outside. Of the 205, 41 were able-bodied adults, 69 not able-bodied, 21 were adult casual paupers, 43 were lunatics and idiots, and 31 were children. Of the 2,126, 169 were able-bodied, 1,385 were not able-bodied, 95 were lunatics and idiots, and 454 were children. The occupations or former occupations of male paupers aged sixteen years and upwards were shepherds, agricultural labourers, ·and farm servants in the main. Pauperism was highest in the unions of Aberystwyth, Newcastle Emlyn and Cardigan. More women than men received outdoor relief but men predominated in the workhouses. The 454 children receiving outdoor relief were boarded out or maintained in voluntary, preventative or training homes. In the workhouses there was no attempt at classifying the inmates; the numbers would have been too few. Bircham, the Poor Law Inspector for Wales, ascribed the increase in out-relief in Wales to the inexperience of the newly elected Welsh-speaking Guardians, although he detected a reduction in the rate of pauperism in Wales since 25 March 1895. He ascribed the reduction in the rates from nearly 6 per cent to a little over 3 per cent in the Cardigan Union to a reduction in the population. The population was also declining in the Aberystwyth Union with the closure of the lead mines, and emigration to the south Wales coal mines. Bircham insisted that Guardians ought to be stricter with the undeserving, which meant, in effect, more for the deserving.

Nothing was done about the recommendations of the Royal Commission on the Poor Laws and Relief of Distress before 1914. The Liberal Party, through its own programme of social reforms, including free school meals and regular medical inspections, unemployment insurance and labour exchanges for the unemployed, contributed to the campaign for the break-up of the Poor Laws. In

Fig. 106: Some of the residents of Bronglais Workhouse, Aberystwyth, in the early twentieth century. (*Copyright National Library of Wales*).

Cardiganshire the Aberaeron workhouse closed its doors in July 1914 and the inmates were removed to Lampeter. The Guardians remained in office in order to look after the outdoor paupers (about 200), the majority of whom were members of the tramping fraternity. The workhouse was converted into a Cottage Hospital for the Union. The sanitary arrangements at the workhouse were defective and there was no water. It would have cost between £500 and £1,000 to upgrade the building. The sick paupers were removed to neighbouring union workhouses, but no provision was made for tramps. The Local Government Board had long urged the desirability of classifying the inmates, but the numbers were too small. The Tregaron workhouse was closed in 1915 and the twenty inmates were accommodated in the Aberystwyth workhouse. The building was to be used as a hospital. There had been on occasions as many as forty inmates in the Tregaron workhouse. But outdoor relief was cheap and continued for the able-bodied. In 1884, 450 persons were in receipt of outdoor relief in the union. Since 1884 agricultural conditions had deteriorated so that a large proportion of the male population migrated to the South Wales Coalfield and other industrial areas. The number of persons in receipt of relief on 1 September 1903 was 153; by 1915 it had declined to 120. The Cardigan workhouse was to be managed by a committee of twelve, six from Cardiganshire and six from Pembrokeshire. The Lampeter workhouse was taken over by Cardiganshire County Council. Carmarthenshire County Council was compensated for its interest. Newcastle Emlyn workhouse closed its doors in 1915.

Between the wars the movement for the abolition of the Poor Law continued. The dole was introduced as a protection for the unemployed against destitution. The responsibilities of the Poor Law authorities were transferred to other agencies such as health, education, welfare and employment. It was recognized that the strategy of poor law administrators to reduce pauperism had failed. The inter-war period witnessed an attempt to resolve the issue and decide the future shape of welfare. It was now believed that government had a duty to promote the material well-being of society. Obviously, the voluntary movement, so active in the second half of the nineteenth century, could not maintain essential services such as relieving the unemployed,

The Local Government Act 1929 (19 and 20 George V, cap.17) removed the responsibility for poor relief to the Public Assistance Committees. Boards of Guardians ceased to exist and their powers were handed over to the County Councils, who appointed Public Assistance Committees. The final meeting of the Tregaron Board of Governors took place on 18 March 1930. Fifteen Guardians were present. The minutes confirmed the Charity officials' books; an honorarium of £20 each was granted to the Clerk, B. Idris Evans, and the Relieving Officer, J. H. Davies, for extra work in connection with the transfer of functions. Other matters discussed included the appointment of a District Medical Officer and a Public Vaccinator, a vaccination contract, and tenders for coal and stone for the casual wards. The final meeting of the Cardigan Board of Guardians was held at Albro Castle on 31 March 1930. The union had a bank balance of £3,474 2s. 3d.; out-relief had cost £179 3s. 10d.; 241 outdoor paupers and seventy-seven vagrants had been relieved. A farewell luncheon was organized by the clerk, E. B. Evans, who declared 'that it was with very great regret that he came to the end of his term as clerk to the Board'.

The first meeting of the Public Assistance Committee for the county of Cardigan under the Local Government Act was held at the Lampeter Town Hall on 19 February 1930. The meeting was held in order to arrange preliminaries for the transfer of the duties of Boards of Guardians to the County Council on 1 April 1930. With the passing of the Local Government Act 1929, it was hoped that the Poor Law would be administered more efficiently and economically by the County Councils than by the Board of Guardians. The task of Public Assistance was 'to provide such relief as may be necessary to the lame, impotent, old, blind and such other persons as are poor and unable to work'. The duties were threefold: institutional treatment, outdoor relief and vagrancy. The Poor Law was not abolished and the mixed workhouse survived. Aberystwyth (Bronglais), Cardigan and Lampeter Union workhouses became public assistance institutions. Cardigan Union workhouse was placed under the joint management and ownership of Cardiganshire and Pembrokeshire County Councils. Lampeter workhouse was taken over by Cardiganshire Council, with Carmarthenshire County Council being compensated. The strict means testing enforced often provoked resentment and humiliation. The 1930 Poor Law Act abolished the workhouse test and the term 'pauper'. In each institution there were to be found maternity and mental cases, the aged and infirm, other sick persons who were the responsibility of the Guardians, and those who were homeless. Children had been removed from the workhouse and were boarded out. The number of persons in receipt of relief on 31 March 1934 and 28 September 1935 in the county of Cardigan was 105 and 98 (institutional) and 1,312 and 1,269 (domiciliary). With unemployment reaching high levels, particularly in Glamorgan, the Unemployment Assistance Board was set up and charged with the task of helping the able-bodied unemployed. The vagrant and the homeless were also the concern of the National Assistance Boards and they took over the casual wards as state institutions, to be known as

Reception Centres. The Tregaron Casual Ward on the Pontrhydfendigaid road (Bryntirion) was opened in 1930. But whereas the casual wards had taken in any wayfarer, the Reception Centres were charged with taking in persons of 'an unsettled way of life' – habitual tramps only. Vagrants could now claim welfare payments. The Vagrancy Act of 1930 abolished the offence of 'sleeping out'; the defendant was only liable if he 'persistently wandered about, or refused to go, after being directed, to a reasonably accessible place of shelter'.

In 1942 the Beveridge Report proposed the introduction of a system of social welfare – state care 'from the cradle to the grave'. The responsibility of the state for the material well-being of its citizens was recognized more explicitly than ever before and the term Welfare State was coined. The Poor Law was abolished with the passing of the National Assistance Act in 1948. The Bronglais, Cardigan and Lampeter workhouses ceased to exist. The old Bronglais workhouse and its occupants were taken over by the Mid-Wales Hospital Board as a geriatric unit until the new hospital in Caradog Road was completed in 1966. The geriatric unit was moved to the North Road Hospital and Bronglais was demolished. The old Lampeter workhouse became an old people's home. The workhouse, the intimidating symbol of the Poor Law, had been removed for ever.

CHAPTER 15

PARLIAMENTARY REPRESENTATION: FROM THE GLORIOUS REVOLUTION TO THE FRENCH REVOLUTION, 1688–1789

P. D. G. Thomas

By THE late seventeenth century Parliament was becoming the centre of the British political stage, and membership of the House of Commons increasingly coveted by the ruling landed class. It conveyed not merely prestige but local power. MPs, unless inveterate in their hostility to the royal government, had the ear of ministers in matters of patronage. In Wales the absence of an established aristocracy meant that they themselves could aspire to the posts of Lord Lieutenant, the official representative of the sovereign in each county and commander of its militia, and of *Custos Rotulorum*, head of the county bench of magistrates, which was in the eighteenth century the effective body of local government in matters social and economic as well as legal. MPs normally had a decisive voice in such official appointments as to their county bench, church livings, customs posts and other offices in the gift of the Crown, while army commissions and civil service posts might be obtained for relatives and friends. A political 'interest' could thereby be created which might serve a family for generations of goodwill. There were high stakes to play for at parliamentary elections, and whereas Welsh representation at Westminster had hitherto been shared quite widely among the gentry, now it was a matter of contention between a few leading squires in each county. In Cardiganshire the most influential family from Tudor times had been the Pryses of Gogerddan, whose extensive estates had early enabled them to establish a predominance in the shire constituency, where there was an electorate of between 700 and 1,000 forty-shilling freeholders.

Cardiganshire had another MP for its boroughs, of which Aberystwyth, Atpar, Lampeter and, more dubiously, Tregaron claimed to share as out-boroughs with the county town of Cardigan. Control of Cardigan itself was of especial importance to aspiring borough MPs, for the burgesses (or freemen) of all boroughs had to vote there, and its mayor acted as returning officer, with power to decide on votes of doubtful validity. He was chosen each Michaelmas by the burgesses from among the Common Council. It was in this body, a co-opting oligarchy of thirteen members, that effective power lay, and command of it was a perquisite of the Cardigan Priory estate, whose owner Hector Phillips sat as borough MP from 1679 until his death in 1693. But there existed much potential for conflict within the constituency, for each borough had the right to create voters. Aberystwyth was ruled by the Pryse family. Lampeter was a manorial borough within the estate of nearby Peterwell, and in about 1713 control passed to Walter Lloyd of Voelallt on his marriage to the heiress daughter of the deceased Daniel Evans. Tregaron was also a manorial borough, on the Nanteos estate, which changed ownership when William Powell, son of judge Sir Thomas Powell of Llechwedd Dyry, married the heiress of Cornelius Le Brun in 1696 and presumably acquired possession on the death of his father-in-law in 1703. Only the fifth borough, Atpar, the part of Newcastle Emlyn on the Cardiganshire side of the river Teifi, was not to become the scene of political manipulation. Its burgesses voted until the later eighteenth century, but in declining numbers after the mysterious collapse of its municipal structure in 1741 made future creations impossible.[1]

The political pre-eminence of Gogerddan had suffered a temporary eclipse after the restoration of Charles II to the throne in 1660. One reason was the rise of the Vaughans of Trawsgoed (then called Crosswood) to the rank of second family in Cardiganshire. The able lawyer and politician Sir John Vaughan and his son Edward held the county seat from 1661 until the latter's death in 1683. At Westminster both were prominent members of the country or Whig party opposing the influence of the Stuart court, whose supporters, dubbed Tory, included the Pryse family. This national political conflict was to influence electoral contests in Cardiganshire, but was never the overriding consideration. Local family rivalries both preceded and transcended party labels.

At the 1685 general election, the only one held in the reign of James II, the new owner of Trawsgoed, John Vaughan, was under age, and Sir Carbery Pryse of Gogerddan took the opportunity to arrange the election of John Lewis of Coed-mawr, a local squire by now resident in Berkshire. But young Vaughan was a keen Whig supporter of the Glorious Revolution that deposed James II in 1688, and at the ensuing 1689 election he challenged Lewis, who won narrowly by 385 votes to 363. Lewis had been supported not only by Pryse but also by his own relative Sir Thomas Powell, who so strongly disapproved of the Revolution that he resigned his judgeship.[2] The contest was therefore a Tory triumph over the Whigs, but it may have been because the margin of victory was so narrow that Pryse himself stood next year, at the general election of 1690, when he defeated Vaughan in highly suspicious circumstances. The poll began at Aberystwyth but was adjourned to Cardigan when Pryse was leading by 148 votes to 91. Vaughan refused to go to Cardigan, where Pryse polled a further thirty-seven votes and was then declared elected. When Vaughan's petition of complaint was heard by the Committee of Elections of the House of Commons, he produced witnesses to support his assertion that he had some 400 voters ready at Aberystwyth. Pryse countered with the claim that he had had 300 more unpolled at Cardigan. The merits of Pryse's return were evidently dubious, for only by a majority of one did the House of Commons confirm his election.[3]

These stormy contests were followed by a brief period of quiescence, perhaps the result of a compromise, tacit or otherwise, between the Gogerddan and Trawsgoed interests. Both were strengthened during the next few years. The Pryse family achieved a notable coup by the acquisition of the Cardigan Priory estate on the death of Hector Phillips in 1693, and their ally, John Lewis, was returned for the borough constituency at both the subsequent by-election and the general election of 1695. In 1690, too, there came the discovery of extensive deposits of silver and lead ore at Esgair-hir

[1] P. D. G. Thomas, 'Eighteenth-century elections in the Cardigan Boroughs Constituency', *Ceredigion*, V, no.4 (1967), 402–23. Parts of that article have been incorporated in this chapter.
[2] NLW, Nanteos MSS, L 45, 50. *Commons Journals*, X, 188–9.
[3] *Commons Journals*, X, 371, 426, 486–7.

on the Gogerddan estate. Sir Carbery Pryse, in order to work this mine, entered into a partnership with such Tories as his uncle and designated heir Edward Pryse of Glanffrêd, William Powell, and William III's first minister, the Earl of Danby: but he died in 1694 while the venture was still crippled by lawsuits against the monopolistic Society of Mines Royal. Trawsgoed influence in Cardiganshire had meanwhile been strengthened by the deployment of official patronage by John Vaughan's kinsman Lord Carbery, in his role of *Custos Rotulorum*. Vaughan now seized the chance to take the shire seat at the 1694 by-election. High in royal favour himself, he was raised to an Irish peerage as Viscount Lisburne in June 1695 and was returned again at the general election of that year.

Three years later the Gogerddan interest compelled him to vacate the seat without a fight. There had arrived in Cardiganshire the disruptive personality of Sir Humphrey Mackworth from Glamorgan. An inveterate speculator in mining projects, in 1698 he bought out the Gogerddan share in the Esgair-hir mine for £16,440, and reconstructed the partnership as the Company of Mine Adventurers, with the Duke of Leeds, the former Earl of Danby, as governor and Mackworth in effective control as his deputy. Mackworth money helped to restore Gogerddan's political fortunes. At the general election of 1698 John Lewis moved to the county seat, being replaced as borough member by Gogerddan nominee Sir Charles Lloyd of Maesyfelin. But Sir Humphrey soon developed his own political ambitions in Cardiganshire. In April 1700 he instructed his mine manager to allow both Lord Lisburne and William Powell coal at their own price. 'And amongst other things, I pray make an interest to establish a fishery in that country, set up a woollen manufacture, maintain the poor, etc. These thoughts being well spread beforehand, will prepare the way better than if they suspect there was any design in it.'[4] Six months later Mackworth's candidature was out in the open, for on 15 October the Duke of Leeds wrote to William Powell:

> I know you are a considerable partner in the lead mines, and therefore I doubt not but you will be ready to concur in anything which may tend to their advantage. I find several of the partners to be of opinion (as I am myself) that it might be useful to our Company, if Sir Humphrey Mackworth could be the member in the ensuing Parliament.

Mackworth, the Duke urged, should therefore be supported by the Powell family and by Lewis Pryse, who, in 1699, had succeeded his father Edward in the Gogerddan estate at the age of sixteen. Powell accepted the argument, but held out little hope for the county, where 'a great many [are] nearly related to our present representative', John Lewis.[5] Mackworth's campaign nevertheless compelled Lewis to move back to the borough constituency, while he himself took the county seat in the general election of January–February 1701. Gogerddan power, however, was underlined when, at the second election of that year, in December, Lewis Pryse took the county seat although under age: but both he and William Powell warmly supported Mackworth in 1702 at the election held on the accession of Queen Anne.[6] Henry Lloyd, a friend of both Mackworth and Pryse and a London lawyer of Carmarthenshire antecedents, was returned for the borough constituency at both these

---

[4] Quoted by M. Ransome, 'The parliamentary career of Sir Humphrey Mackworth', *Birmingham Historical Journal*, I (1948), 232–54. Quotation is at p.236.

[5] Nanteos MSS, L 41.

[6] Ibid., L 53; NLW MS 14362E, pp.115–18 (diary of Sir Humphrey Mackworth).

elections, defeating in December 1701 an interloping Shropshire barrister, Sir Thomas Powys, in circumstances that remain obscure.

Lewis Pryse was one of many Tories who looked to a golden political future under Anne, anticipating that the official favour engrossed by Trawsgoed under William III would henceforth be deployed on his behalf. He wrote to William Powell on 21 April 1702. 'I am now in great hopes of putting my Lord Lisburne's nose out of joint in his arbitrary government in the county . . . We shall take all care imaginable in settling the officials of our county in order to improve our interest, and I dont question but we shall meet with such a favourable compliance from the government as shall answer our expectation.'[7] His hopes were disappointed. Lord Carbery remained as *Custos* of Cardiganshire until his death in 1713, even though in 1710 Pryse made a vigorous protest to Robert Harley, head of an incoming Tory ministry, that Carbery had been perverting Crown influence to assist Lord Lisburne and his Whig friends.[8]

Two years earlier, following a decade of electoral eclipse, Lord Lisburne had renewed the Trawsgoed challenge to Gogerddan at the general election of 1708, doubtless encouraged by a national Whig revival as the successful war party and locally by this deployment of patronage. Three years earlier, in 1705, Lewis Pryse had taken the borough seat and had displaced Mackworth as county member by his crony John Pugh of Mathafarn in Montgomeryshire, leaving a disgruntled Sir Humphrey to find a seat at Totnes. In 1708 Pryse was returned without a contest in the borough constituency on 20 May, but in the county Pugh faced a formidable challenge from a new Whig ally of Lisburne, Thomas Johnes of Llanfair Clydogau, who had also acquired the Hafod estate in 1704. So threatening was this attack that Pugh withdrew to the safe borough seat of Montgomery, perhaps by arrangement with Pryse, who stood himself as the only candidate who could avert defeat. At a three-day poll early in June, Pryse won by 383 votes to 347. Johnes petitioned, mainly about a temporary adjournment of the poll that had, he claimed, deceived many of his voters into leaving: but even a Whig-dominated House of Commons confirmed Pryse's election when the case was eventually decided in January 1710.[9]

Lewis Pryse thereupon opted to sit for the county, vacating the borough seat. Pryse's intention was to offer it to a Tory neighbour, John Meyrick of Bush in Pembrokeshire, but more important party men were seeking a safe seat after the Tory losses of 1708. The idea was soon floated that Sir Thomas Mansel of Glamorgan, a close associate of the leading Tory Robert Harley, should press Pryse to offer it to the able young Henry St John, the future Lord Bolingbroke, then out of Parliament. Nothing more was heard of that idea, but as early as June 1708 rumour was afoot that Sir Humphrey Mackworth, also without a seat, would approach Pryse.[10] The Company of Mine Adventurers had collapsed, and Mackworth was anxious to become an MP to avoid legal prosecution. During 1709 he campaigned vigorously among the local squires, extravagantly promising Cardiganshire the transfer of Shrewsbury's cloth trade, Aberystwyth a quay, and Cardigan a new church spire. Lewis Pryse did not welcome Sir Humphrey's return to Cardiganshire politics, and in the autumn of 1709 was still attempting to ensure that Meyrick did not succumb to Mackworth's blandishments and withdraw.[11] Failing in this, he negotiated an arrangement whereby Sir

[7]Ibid., L 53.
[8]British Library (BL), Additional MS 70205 (unfoliated).
[9]*Commons Journals*, XVI, 267–9.
[10]NLW, Penrice and Margam MSS, L 612.
[11]Ibid., L 651.

Humphrey agreed not to contest the by-election on promise of a seat at the next general election. Pryse, at the request of Robert Harley, nominated the eminent Tory lawyer Sir Simon Harcourt, recently unseated by a partisan Whig vote of the Commons. Mackworth, notorious for his enmity towards Harley, then reneged on his promise and enlisted the ready support of Lord Lisburne against Gogerddan. But the poll was abandoned when Harcourt was leading by 169 votes to 69.[12]

This Gogerddan success was deceptive, for Lewis Pryse had mismanaged what was undoubtedly the dominant interest in Cardiganshire; in December 1709 Lisburne had sought to exploit the situation by informing William Powell that he was 'very ready to contribute towards the establishment of a good correspondence between families so absolutely necessary for the good of this poor and now shattered country'.[13] Pryse's seemingly high-handed behaviour had offended former Gogerddan allies like Powell and John Lewis, and there is some inferential evidence that he neglected the patronage requests of his supporters.[14] Moreover, his resolute refusal to ally with local Whigs proved an electoral disadvantage when other men were less inflexible. Pryse, indeed, was not merely a Tory but an avowed Jacobite. In 1710 the Whig Secretary of State, Lord Sunderland, was informed that Pryse, John Pugh, William Powell and other squires 'at a gentleman's house at Aberystwyth drank to the Pretender's health and return upon their knees': a prosecution would have resulted but for the change of ministry that year.[15]

What was remarkable was that it should have been Mackworth who engineered the downfall of Gogerddan. By early 1710 contemporaries must have written him off as a spent force. While Sir Humphrey was at Cardigan, a petition to Parliament from creditors and proprietors of the bankrupt Company of Mine Adventurers demonstrated that he had resorted to dubious expedients to maintain its credit; silver had been secretly purchased elsewhere and then sold in London at a loss as being the product of the Cardiganshire mines. On 21 March the House of Commons voted Mackworth guilty of fraud.[16] Although Sir Humphrey escaped punishment because of the dissolution of Parliament, the case had made him notorious. Yet he was elected for Cardiganshire at the general election of 1710.

Lewis Pryse put forward John Meyrick for the borough constituency, and stood himself again for the county. But Mackworth contrived to build a formidable coalition against him by arranging an electoral agreement to cover nine years, or three general elections. To his new Whig allies he now added John Lewis and William Powell. Pryse had thought it impossible for anyone to unite the Whig lord of Trawsgoed and the Tory squire of Nanteos, 'the two most distant persons on earth in opinion', so Meyrick commented to Sir Thomas Mansel. It was an open secret that Sir Humphrey had 'disposed of £500 to make them easy'. Pryse, by contrast, had rejected the idea of an alliance with Walter Lloyd of Voelallt because of 'the objection of his being a Whig, which goes further with him than any man on earth', and Mackworth had bought off Lloyd's pretensions with £200. Meyrick, safely returned as borough member, was writing while the county poll was actually in progress, to explain Pryse's impending defeat:

[12]BL Additional MS 61367, f.111: Mackworth to Marlborough, 19 January 1710; *The Post-Boy*, 4 March 1710; *Commons Journals*, XVI, 395.
[13]Nanteos MSS, L 46.
[14]Ibid., L 44.
[15]Penrice and Margam MSS, L 695.
[16]*Commons Journals*, XVI, 353, 355–69, 391, 395.

Lewis Pryse thought himself safe in this position, that my Lord Lisburne would never be for Sir Humphrey, nor William Powell for Walter Lloyd for his principle . . . , but powerful gold has wonderfully operated in this affair. When I left the poll Mr Pryse was foremost by about 30 but he had not above 30 more to poll, and Sir Humphrey had about a 100, 50 that he expected to lose it by forty, which will be no shameful defeat, since there was so strong a union of both parties against him.[17]

The Gogerddan interest had indeed nearly matched the combined strength of the other leading squires in Cardiganshire. But Pryse did not challenge the opposing coalition at the next general election, in 1713, when it was presumably in consequence of the nine-year agreement that the Whig Thomas Johnes replaced Mackworth as county MP. Even the defection of Nanteos, with its control of Tregaron, did not threaten the Gogerddan hold on the borough constituency, where Lewis Pryse nominated a Carmarthenshire relative, Owen Brigstocke, to succeed Meyrick on his appointment as a judge in 1712, and a Pembrokeshire Tory Sir George Barlow in 1713.

The Hanoverian Succession in 1714 marked a return to normality in Cardiganshire politics. The new Whig supremacy at Court and Westminster ended the national two-party contest for power, and put local patronage in the hands of Trawsgoed. Lord Lisburne became Lord Lieutenant and *Custos*, being succeeded in those posts on his death in 1721 by his eldest son, the second viscount. This new situation impelled the Cardiganshire Tories, already confronted with a Whig as sitting county member, to put their house in order. Lewis Pryse, laid up at Bath with gout, by 'the request of his friends all over England, is desirous of having an honest gentleman to represent your county and indeed there was never more need'. So wrote Sir George Barlow's brother John to William Powell on 13 September, when he passed on Pryse's suggestion 'that you will please to stand yourself for member for the county and he will appear for you with his interest before any one. If you decline he begs you will join with him either to stand himself or join in setting up some honest gentleman.'[18] This approach was evidently rebuffed, for Pryse himself wrote to Powell, suggesting that they should compose their differences: 'This is not a time for honest people to be quarrelling about straws.' He then mentioned the possibility of Brigstocke as candidate, but was uncertain whether he would be either acceptable or willing.[19] In the end Pryse himself was obliged to stand, although remaining in Bath. He defeated Thomas Johnes when put forward for election, 'which I was so far from seeking, that I never asked a vote for it, and was chose even against my inclinations. I know not how far a man is obliged to stand to the choice a county makes of him.' So he wrote to the Speaker on 18 February 1716 in response to a summons to attend the House of Commons, pleading continued ill-health as the reason. Messengers sent to bring Pryse to Westminster failed to find him at Gogerddan or elsewhere, Pryse claiming in a letter delivered to them by his doctor that a journey to London would be fatal. He was expelled from the Commons for contempt on 23 March 1716, but a new writ was not issued until 6 December 1717, after a petition from Thomas Johnes had lapsed.[20]

Pryse's ill-health was genuine, but his enemies saw it as an excuse for not swearing allegiance to the new dynasty. Lord Lisburne, writing as Lord Lieutenant to Secretary of State Paul Methuen on 4 January 1717, portrayed the county as a hotbed of disaffection in the wake of the Jacobite

[17]Penrice and Margam MSS, L 695.
[18]Nanteos MSS, L 32.
[19]Ibid., L 55.
[20]*Commons Journals*, XVIII, 40, 260, 367, 391, 411,493, 654.

Rebellion of 1715. The blame he put squarely on Lewis Pryse and William Powell: 'The one was expelled the House of Commons for refusing the oaths, the other never took them since the Revolution, and for their zeal against the government no men so famous in that part of his Majesty's dominions. They are the managers of the correspondence between the malcontents of North and South Wales.' They had aided and abetted 'the harbouring of rebels . . . who had escaped out of Chester gaol, a party of which threatened to burn my house, . . . and the horrid and abominable language in all public places given the King and his family and not taken notice of, so terrified the people in general, that neither the commissions issued out by me, nor even the order of the Privy Council could either in the time of the rebellion or since be put into execution, and had I gone down without the grant of some regular forces, I had nothing to expect but to have been murdered'.[21] The exiled Stuarts certainly counted on Pryse as a supporter, for he was the recipient of a letter of 7 April 1717 from the Earl of Mar, leader of the 1715 rebellion and now Secretary of State to 'James III', informing him that a landing was intended during October in Pembrokeshire, one of many Jacobite plots that never got beyond the planning stage.[22]

One professed motive behind Lisburne's report had been the hope that energetic government action 'would recover the honest party out of their dejection and enable us to choose a loyal gentleman to serve in Parliament'.[23] The strength of the combined Gogerddan–Nanteos interest obviated that possibility. Owen Brigstocke was returned unopposed as its candidate at the by-election consequent on Pryse's expulsion.[24] For the next election Pryse had, by 1720, offered the county seat to another suspected Jacobite, Carmarthenshire squire Francis Cornwallis of Abermarlais. With the support also of William Powell and John Meyrick, he was returned unopposed at the general election of 1722.[25]

Before that took place the death of Lewis Pryse in August 1720, at the age of thirty-seven, threw Cardiganshire politics into confusion. The Gogerddan estate passed to his next male heir Thomas Pryse, a boy of about four, son of his father's second cousin John Pryse. During his long minority various members of the Pryse family sought to make use of the Gogerddan interest for their own purposes, and other Cardiganshire families, Whig and Tory alike, attempted to capture the borough seat in this period of Gogerddan weakness.

Lewis Pryse had there returned Cardiganshire squire Stephen Parry of Noyadd Trefawr in 1715, and he was re-elected in 1722: but his death on 15 December 1724 was followed by three borough contests within a decade. William Powell's son Thomas was persuaded to stand at the by-election, although his father disclaimed responsibility. Thomas Powell wrote to the mother of young Thomas Pryse, suggesting an alliance of Gogerddan and Nanteos that would later be of advantage to her son, but her approval was overruled by her second husband, who resorted to the creation of new non-resident burgesses at Aberystwyth. He would seem to have been the Thomas Pryse of Dôl who stood against Powell at the by-election of April 1725, when Powell won in a contest for which the poll figures are not known. This renewed clash of Gogerddan and Nanteos was deplored by local Tories.[26] A reconciliation between them at the general election of 1727 is indicated by the

---

[21]PRO State Papers Domestic, 35/8. f.68.
[22]P. D. G. Thomas, 'Jacobitism in Wales', *WHR*, I, no.3 (1962), 285.
[23]State Papers Domestic, 35/8, f.68.
[24]Nanteos MSS, L 34.
[25]Ibid., L 39 (a) and 2(b), NLW, Edwinsford MSS, no.2908.
[26]Nanteos MSS, L 52.

unopposed return for the borough of the retiring county member, Francis Cornwallis, while Thomas Powell stood as Tory candidate for the county against the second Lord Lisburne, who won by 404 votes to 340.

Powell soon had another opportunity to satisfy his political ambition, for Francis Cornwallis died in August 1728. His determination to take advantage of Nanteos control of Tregaron had already been indicated by the creation there in 1725 of a hundred additional burgesses, after his return at the by-election. A further 800 were enrolled on 23 October 1728. But Thomas Pryse of Dôl had no intention of tamely surrendering Gogerddan control of the borough constituency. At Michaelmas 1728 he became Mayor of Cardigan, and thus the returning officer; the county town alone would supply over 500 voters at the by-election for the Gogerddan candidate, Richard Lloyd of Mabws.[27] Lloyd was a kinsman of the Pryse family, and the fact that he was a Whig who supported Sir Robert Walpole's ministry illustrates the divorce of local rivalries from national politics.

The by-election poll began on 1 May 1729 and continued for several days. Proceedings were violent and disorderly. Each side accused the other of drawing swords, and Thomas Pryse was threatened with pistols by Powell's supporters when he announced his intention of conducting a scrutiny of the poll, which had given Powell a majority of 1224 votes to 924. The mayor compromised by a double return of both candidates as elected, passing the problem to the House of Commons. The return of Lloyd was described as by a majority of the burgesses of Cardigan, Aberystwyth, Lampeter and Atpar, that of Powell as by a minority of the burgesses of these towns and a majority of those of Tregaron, 'being another reputed out-borough'. Thus was foreshadowed the aim of Lloyd and his allies not merely to win the seat, but also to strike a mortal blow at Nanteos influence in the constituency by securing the complete disfranchisement of Tregaron. After both candidates had petitioned, the Committee of Elections examined the case and reported to the House of Commons on 7 May 1730.[28]

Counsel for Lloyd had claimed that the right of election was in 'the burgesses in general of the Town of Cardigan, and the out-boroughs of Aberystwyth, Lampeter and Atpar only: and the claim of Tregaron as an out-borough, was but a pretence, that place being but a lordship, belonging to the petitioner, Mr Powell'. Even the evidence produced by Powell's counsel showed that the consistent parliamentary pretensions of Tregaron dated merely from 1701: only one earlier precedent was proffered, a dubious one for 1663, and the statement by one witness that Tregaron burgesses had not been prevented from voting 'of late years' was a double-edged weapon. A further weakness of Powell's case was Tregaron's lack of status as an 'ancient borough' as specified in Henry VIII's enfranchising legislation: evidence of a mayor in the reign of Charles II was countered by a statement that the office had been discontinued in 1683. Such extraneous factors as evidence of the small size of Tregaron and of the recent mass creations of voters there may also have swayed the Committee; but ministerial support of Lloyd was doubtless a key factor in the Committee's resolution that burgesses of Tregaron did not have a right to vote in the Cardigan boroughs constituency.

Despite this disaster Powell fought the case to the end. He next claimed that only 'the resident burgesses' of the remaining four boroughs could vote, and his witnesses said that he had asked in

[27] NLW, Gogerddan MSS. List of Cardigan Burgesses, 8 February 1730.
[28] *Commons Journals*, XXI, 387–8, 407, 571–4. I have examined the case more fully in *Ceredigion*, V, no.4 (1967), 405–8.

vain for the distinction of residence to be made at the poll. But evidence was produced that a similar objection had been overruled in 1725, and that all burgesses had voted then and in 1729. Powell's hope of a majority on a resident franchise was ended by a resolution of the Committee that the right of election lay in 'the burgesses at large of the boroughs of Cardigan, Aberystwyth, Lampeter and Adpar, only'. The poll, when amended in accordance with this franchise, gave Lloyd a majority of 918 votes to 465. Powell's only chance now lay in making good his claim of irregularities during the poll, but the evidence of malpractice he submitted was insufficient to explain the large majority for Lloyd, who was declared duly elected. Powell had evidently anticipated a majority from either of the two probable electorates, all the burgesses of all the boroughs, or the resident burgesses only: presumably many Nanteos nominees had been admitted in Aberystwyth and Cardigan in the days of the Powell–Pryse alliance. But if the disfranchisement of Tregaron appears an act of political partisanship, it should be remembered that it was not reinstated in the borough constituency a century later by the Reform Act of 1832. The resolution of 1730 that defined the constituency also removed any doubt over the franchise: even if non-resident burgesses had not voted before 1725, they were now entitled to do so. The full implications of this ruling were soon to be exploited by various borough patrons.

The Gogerddan interest had taken advantage of Richard Lloyd's ministerial support in Parliament to maintain control of the borough constituency, but he proved to be a Whig Trojan Horse. During the 1730s Lloyd created a formidable 'Whig interest' in Cardiganshire, based on alliances with Walter Lloyd of Voelallt and now also of Peterwell, and with Thomas Johnes of Llanfair and Hafod, who had succeeded his namesake cousin, the MP of 1713, in those estates in 1733. He took advantage of the temporary weakness not only of Gogerddan but also of Trawsgoed, where the second Lord Lisburne was a spendthrift who plunged the estate into debt. At the general election of 1734 Richard Lloyd replaced Lisburne as county member by Walter Lloyd. Lisburne did not contest the seat, but showed his resentment by allying with the local Tories against Richard Lloyd in the borough constituency. There Lloyd defeated Walter Pryse of Painswick in Gloucestershire, who owned Abernantbychan in Cardiganshire and had earlier been hand in glove with Thomas Pryse of Dôl. The circumstances of this contest are entirely unknown, apart from a triumphant letter sent by Lloyd to Sir Robert Walpole on 12 June. 'I have been ever since I came into the country much harried in elections, and have succeeded both in town and county, the latter without opposition, and the former I got by a majority of no less than 300, where we have not more than 1000 voters had they been all polled.'[29]

The electoral wheel was soon to turn full circle, with the return of two Tories at the next general election in 1741. Both candidates in the borough contest of 1734 had claims on the Gogerddan interest, and it may well have been divided between them. But three years later Thomas Pryse at last came of age, and his intention to claim the seat was soon made manifest by the mass creation of voters. The number of votes that had given Richard Lloyd a majority in 1734 was now swamped by new burgesses at Cardigan and Aberystwyth. The poll began on 29 May 1741 and continued until 6 June, when Pryse had a majority of 1034 votes to 697. Analysis of a surviving poll-book reveals the basis of his victory:[30]

[29]Cambridge University Library, Cholmondeley Houghton MSS no.2212. By permission of the Syndics of the Library.
[30]NLW, Brigstocke MSS. I have analysed this more fully in *Ceredigion*, VI, no.1 (1968), 128–9.

TABLE 16: Results of the 1741 election in the Cardigan Boroughs constituency

	Pryse	Lloyd	Total
Cardigan	559	135	694
Aberystwyth	317	152	469
Atpar	146	152	298
Lampeter	12	258	270
	1034	697	1731

Lloyd evidently retained a residual share of the Gogerddan interest at Cardigan and Aberystwyth, derived from his earlier connection with the Pryse family; and his overwhelming majority from Lampeter is confirmatory evidence of his electoral alliance with Walter Lloyd of Peterwell. In the political context of the time the result represented a defeat of a ministerial supporter by an opposition candidate, for Pryse was faithful to the Tory tradition of his family, and it was hailed as such by the opposition newspaper, the *London Evening Post*, which claimed: 'All the free and uninfluenced voters showed their regard to the country interest in espousing the worthy gentleman chose in opposition to ministerial influence' – hardly an accurate portrayal of events.[31]

Walter Lloyd lost the county seat at the same election. According to a 1755 recapitulation of events by Wilmot Vaughan, the future fourth Lord Lisburne, the cause of this setback was the behaviour of young Thomas Johnes of Dolaucothi, Carmarthenshire, son of Johnes of Llanfair, who 'broke the Whig interest of this county' by opposing Lloyd.[32] But that was a simple and biased version of events by one who had been a boy of about twelve at the time. The Trawsgoed family itself was in disarray, for on the death of John, second Viscount Lisburne, in January 1741, his brother Wilmot claimed the title and estate by successfully establishing that an apparent son of John by his second wife was illegitimate. The new third Lord Lisburne succeeded his brother as Lord Lieutenant, but to Vaughan's chagrin lost the post of *Custos* to young Johnes, though he was barely of age. It may be surmised that this was the price for Johnes to withdraw his candidature, and one arranged by that friend to his family, Henry Arthur Herbert, later first Earl of Powis, a man much consulted by government in Welsh matters. Thomas Johnes the *Custos* was to play a leading role in Cardiganshire politics for the next four decades, even though in 1748 he moved from Dolaucothi to Croft Castle in Herefordshire, having married its heiress in 1746.[33]

The withdrawal of Johnes was of no avail. The weakness and dissension among the local Whigs opened the way for Thomas Powell of Nanteos to launch a successful campaign. A four-day poll began at Cardigan on 9 June, conducted with undisguised partiality by the ministry-appointed sheriff in favour of Walter Lloyd. At the close Powell was nevertheless ahead by 352 votes to 346, whereupon the sheriff made a private scrutiny of the poll, struck off 12 votes for Powell and 2 for

[31] *London Evening Post*, 11 June 1741.
[32] BL Additional MS 32856, ff.52–3. This, and other letters to the Duke of Newcastle, were published by David Williams, 'Cardiganshire politics in the mid-eighteenth century', *Ceredigion*, III, no.4 (1959), 303–18.
[33] NLW, Dolaucothi MSS, I/40. For his appointment as *Custos* in 1741, see the *Gentleman's Magazine*, XI (1741), 164.

Lloyd, and then returned the latter as elected by 344 votes to 340.[34] Powell petitioned the House of Commons, and this was one of many dubious returns reversed after the fall of Walpole's ministry in February 1742. Lloyd had intended to fight the case, in the obvious hope of support from the administration. In December he was busy preparing lists of freeholders and their qualifications on both sides. Anticipating a possible void election, he wrote to young Johnes, now evidently reconciled, that 'not knowing the event a friendly sheriff must be had in case of a new election'.[35] But after Walpole's resignation Lloyd made no attempt to dispute the case, and Powell was awarded the seat on 22 March.[36] Richard Lloyd was more pertinacious in protesting about Pryse's borough election. For five successive years he submitted a petition complaining of the mayor's partiality and of intimidation of his voters; but when the case was ordered to be heard on 23 January 1746 he requested postponement; the petition was thereupon dismissed, and a new writ issued for the borough constituency, since Thomas Pryse had meanwhile died on 21 May 1745, leaving a seven-year-old heir in John Pugh Pryse.[37]

Mindful of the events during his own minority, Thomas Pryse by his will had established a trust for the Gogerddan estate; those named as trustees included the two leading Welsh Tories, Sir Watkin Williams Wynn of Wynnstay in Denbighshire and Sir John Philipps of Picton Castle in Pembrokeshire. Their political brief was to return Tory MPs and preserve intact the Gogerddan interest. At the borough by-election of 1746 they therefore arranged for the return of Philipps's Tory neighbour, John Symmons of Llanstinan. He was unsuccessfully opposed by Walter Lloyd of Peterwell in a contest for which no poll figures are known, but the prospect of another challenge for the control of the borough constituency during a Gogerddan minority, based this time on mastery of Lampeter instead of Tregaron, led the Tory trustees to agree on a compromise with the Cardiganshire Whigs at the general election of 1747. The Gogerddan nominee was to have the borough if no challenge was made to a Whig in the county, but in both constituencies wrangles developed as to who should obtain the respective nominations.

For the county the sole evidence comes from a letter written on 10 July 1755 by the indignant Wilmot Vaughan of Trawsgoed to the then Prime Minister, the Duke of Newcastle. Thomas Johnes was at first again a candidate, but then resigned his claim in favour of John Lloyd of Peterwell, who had succeeded his father Walter earlier in the year. He did so without informing Lord Lisburne or 'any of the principal gentlemen' of the Whig interest. Vaughan's anger stemmed from the usurpation by Johnes of the role traditionally adopted by the Trawsgoed family.[38] His alliance with John Lloyd cut out Trawsgoed from electoral influence and allowed the new master of Peterwell to take the county seat in 1747.

Representation of the borough constituency was in doubt because of disagreement among the Gogerddan trustees. The claim of Thomas Powell of Nanteos, now deprived of the county seat, was favoured by Sir Watkin Williams Wynn and by young John Pugh Pryse's mother and stepfather, the Revd John Lloyd. It was Lloyd, writing on 20 June 1747 from his wife's estate of Rug in Merioneth, who announced their joint decision to Thomas Lloyd of Abertrisant, the only Cardiganshire trustee

---

[34]NLW, Wynnstay MSS, L 1219. *London Evening Post*, 25 June 1741.
[35]Dolaucothi MSS, VI/36.
[36]*Commons Journals*, XXIV, 24, 144.
[37]Ibid., XXIV, 31–2, 348, 492, 697; XXV, 13, 39.
[38]BL Add MS 332856, f.612.

Fig. 107: Sir Herbert Lloyd, Peterwell (1719–1769), MP for Cardigan Boroughs 1761–1768. *(Copyright National Library of Wales).*

of Gogerddan. 'We have consulted togeather, and are come to the following Resolution. That if Mr Powell for our future Justification will under his Hand fully promise you to promote & preserve the Gogerthan Interest, till Master Pryse comes of Age, & then be ready to resign the Burroughs to him, that he has our Consent to represent it, & we hope will meet with no Opposition from the rest of the Trustees.'[39] It evidently did, however, for John Symmons retained the Cardigan Boroughs seat.

Sir John Philipps was clearly resolved that his Pembrokeshire neighbour should keep the seat until John Pugh Pryse came of age, and was pressing the other Gogerddan trustees to this effect before the end of 1752.[40] For news had come of a Peterwell canvass in the borough constituency. John Lloyd's younger brother Herbert also had parliamentary ambitions, and he had recently married Anne, sister both of Thomas Powell, who died on 16 November 1752, and of the Revd Doctor William Powell, who succeeded to Nanteos on his brother's death. On 16 March 1753 the Revd John Lloyd told his fellow trustee Thomas Lloyd that he had received a messenger from Herbert Lloyd. 'The purport was to beg Gogerddan interest at the next general election for the town, and assurances of the friendship of Nanteos and Peterwell when John Pugh Pryse shall have occasion for their interest.' John Lloyd at first refused to commit himself either to John Symmons or Herbert Lloyd.[41] His concern was to avoid a contest: 'as my wife has suffered so much by electioneering already, I'll be at no expense for anyone'.[42] This left the way open for Philipps to negotiate another compromise with Peterwell when the Lloyd brothers realized that they had been over-ambitious. Dr William Powell had promptly declared that Nanteos would not support Peterwell unless Herbert Lloyd obtained the Gogerddan interest.[43] The final outcome was foreshadowed in the following letter by Sir John Philipps to Powell on 19 April 1753:

> I have lately received a letter from Mr John Lloyd of Peterwell acquainting me that either he or Mr Johnes intend to offer their service next election of a member for Cardiganshire, and proposing that all opposition to Mr Symmons should drop, provided there is no opposition to them in the county.

Philipps commented that, following the death of Thomas Powell, there was no Tory to put up for the county and that there could be no intention of jeopardizing Symmons' borough seat by supporting one Whig against another.[44] This was a clear hint to William Powell not to support his Whig neighbour and friend Wilmot Vaughan, son of the third Lord Lisburne, with whom he may already have been forming what was to be an enduring and remarkable alliance. The 1754 election accordingly saw the unopposed re-election of both John Lloyd and John Symmons. But Wilmot Vaughan was not willing to accept the exclusion of the Trawsgoed interest from electoral influence resulting from the Gogerddan–Peterwell bargain, and an opportunity arose for him to redress the situation. It must soon have become apparent that John Lloyd's state of health was precarious, for by early 1755 Vaughan had already secured the promise of Powell's support in the event of a vacancy.[45] By March rumours reached Vaughan in London that Lloyd was dead and Thomas

---

[39] D. Jenkins, 'The Pryse family of Gogerddan II', *NLWJ*, VIII, no.1 (1953), 178–9.
[40] Gogerddan MSS, Thomas Lloyd to John Simmons [*sic*], 16 December 1752.
[41] Berkshire County Record Office, Pryse MSS, J. Lloyd to T. Lloyd, 16 March 1753.
[42] Ibid., J. Lloyd to T. Lloyd, 23 March 1753.
[43] Ibid., J. Lloyd to T. Lloyd, 30 March 1753.
[44] Nanteos MSS, L 114.
[45] Ibid., L 133.

Fig. 108: A portrait by Sir Joshua Reynolds of Wilmot Vaughan (d.1800), first Earl of Lisburne. *(Copyright National Library of Wales (private collection)).*

Johnes a candidate. Although Lloyd was not to die until 23 June, a premature by-election campaign began, with Vaughan writing to the Gogerddan trustees.[46] The Revd John Lloyd of Rug had no hesitation in supporting Powell's endorsement of Vaughan: 'May the families of Nanteos and Gogerddan be ever friends.'[47] But Sir John Philipps refused to commit himself, informing Powell that he would prefer 'an honest man if it is practicable to bring such a one in', and continued:

> It is my desire to preserve your family interest, and that of Gogerddan (for which you know I am a trustee) and to keep every body out that would undermine either. This well deserves consideration, and you know when a man is once possessed of a seat, it is no very easy matter to remove him, especially if he is a time server, as most men are now.[48]

All this was clearly directed against Wilmot Vaughan as an adherent of the Whig ministry of the Duke of Newcastle, and with good grounds, as both Vaughan's immediate behaviour and future career were to demonstrate. Playing his role as scion of Cardiganshire's leading Whig family, Vaughan had promptly applied to Newcastle for support.[49] But his alliance with Nanteos gave a pretext for obstruction to Thomas Johnes, who told Vaughan 'that neither he or his friends approved of my having Mr Powell's countenance, that it was strengthening the Tory Party and putting the reins into their hands'. Aware that Newcastle would be given the same story, Vaughan therefore penned an explanation that was passed on to the Duke, that 'if this affair had been rested solely on the Whig Interest and Mr Powell had not offered so generously his assistance, the Tories would have carried the county for one of their own friends, and the utmost that can be expected from the state of parties here is to have a Whig chosen without too nice an inquiry into the principles of those who espouse him'. By his alliance with William Powell, he had broken the Tory interest. Vaughan professed to be puzzled at the behaviour of Thomas Johnes: 'As he has no prospect of succeeding himself and is not desirous to be in Parliament I do not understand what good purpose it serves to perplex me.'[50]

Rivalry for the Whig leadership in Cardiganshire was the underlying motive. Johnes portrayed Vaughan's behaviour 'to Lord Powis in a very invidious light', so Vaughan complained to Newcastle on 10 July. 'Besides I know not by what authority Mr Johnes places himself at the head of the Whig Party . . . I have above an equal share of the Whig interest in my favour.'[51] One charge made by Johnes was that Vaughan had promised the Tories support at a future election. On being assured in July that that was not so, Lord Powis promised to 'write to Mr Johnes and recommend to him not to carry matters to extremity'. Johnes was then rumoured to be sponsoring Herbert Lloyd as a rival candidate, but by the end of the month he had agreed to support Vaughan.[52]

Wilmot Vaughan was returned at the by-election in December, but before the next general election the political scene in Cardiganshire had been transformed by the coming-of-age of John Pugh Pryse of Gogerddan. By 1759 both Vaughan and Johnes had offered him the county seat, Vaughan apparently without making any stipulation about the borough. He was outbid by Johnes,

[46]Ibid., L 134.
[47]Ibid., L 106.
[48]Ibid., L 115.
[49]BL Add MS 32855, f.346.
[50]BL Add MS 32856, ff.52–3.
[51]BL Add MS 32856, ff.612.
[52]BL Add MS 32857, ff.115–16, 431.

as he indignantly reported to Newcastle, again Prime Minister, in July 1759. Sir John Philipps, 'upon a proposal made to him by Mr Johnes of Llanfair and Mr Lloyd of Peterwell', would recommend young Pryse as county member. Pryse was also to stand for the borough seat, and, if successful in both, cede it to current MP John Symmons.[53] Pryse officially declared his candidature on 25 July.[54] Vaughan was portraying his Whig rivals as having sold out to the local Tories. After consulting George II himself, Newcastle therefore promised him full support.[55] But this did not amount to much. Vaughan failed in a request to have Johnes removed as *Custos* as a mark of ministerial disapproval.[56] And in January 1760 Johnes countered by explaining to the Duke that Vaughan had misrepresented the electoral situation in Cardiganshire:

> Mr Pryse, the present candidate for the County of Cardigan, has the absolute command for the town, and nothing but an immoderate expense can even give him the least uneasiness for the borough; by our present connections with him, we have a certainty of one Whig for the town, and a good chance of his becoming another himself for the county.[57]

Sir John Philipps and the other Gogerddan trustees had been tricked. Although the original proposal by Thomas Johnes and Herbert Lloyd had been as Vaughan described it, once the purpose of dividing Gogerddan from Trawsgoed had been achieved Herbert Lloyd announced he would challenge Pryse in the county unless he was given the borough seat; and, with Vaughan also a candidate, this threat sufficed. Even the hostile Vaughan later admitted that Lloyd had 'defeated the original intention with some dexterity and address'.[58]

Newcastle remained firm in support of Vaughan despite this account by Johnes, and when a general election was occasioned in 1761 by the accession of George III, he asked Lord Keeper Henley to appoint Vaughan's nominee as sheriff: 'Mr Vaughan and his family have always been true friends of the government, which engages me so strongly in his favour.'[59] But the Duke's influence was waning in the new reign. Vaughan's opponents obtained the shrievalty for their man, and Vaughan, unfairly and obliquely blaming the Duke, announced to Newcastle the withdrawal of his candidature, 'it having been my original resolution never to stand a contested election in opposition to government'. He made this bitter comment:

> It is not however a little mortifying that the interest of a family who from the Exclusion Bill to this day have constantly and warmly supported the true principles of this constitution should be sacrificed by administration to an unknown young man whose ancestors till within these few years never took the oaths or aided and approved any one measure of government.

To signify the family discontent, his father Lord Lisburne would resign as Lord Lieutenant, a post held by the Vaughans since the Hanoverian Succession.[60] The political climate was changing, and

[53] BL Add MS 32893, f.300.
[54] Dolaucothi MSS, 12/1.
[55] BL Add MS 32893, ff.432, 471.
[56] BL Add MS 32894, ff.513–14.
[57] BL Add MS 332901, f.359.
[58] NLW MS 14215C, ff.1–2, Letters to James Lloyd of Mabws.
[59] BL Add MS 32916, ff.92–3.
[60] BL Add MS 32918, f.248. This was a short-lived gesture. Vaughan himself became Lord Lieutenant in 1762.

with it the rules of the political game by which the Trawsgoed family had benefited from support of Whig ministers for so long. To be deemed a Tory under George III was no longer to incur automatic official ostracism. But in any case Thomas Johnes himself had powerful connections within the traditional Whig establishment, and could justifiably claim that the bargain with Gogerddan had secured the borough seat for Herbert Lloyd. There must have been a contest in the constituency, for on 20 April Lloyd published an address of thanks to the borough electorate: 'Your steady and spirited behaviour on this occasion, in resenting and defeating an opposition, raised and maintained from personal pique, and private motives only, I have the deepest sense of, and can never forget.'[61]

This opposition to Herbert Lloyd was probably instigated by Wilmot Vaughan and William Powell, even though neither had direct influence in any borough; for the Trawsgoed–Nanteos alliance was once again excluded from the electoral arrangements. But Lloyd is one of the most notorious characters in Cardiganshire history, and it may well be that his tyrannical behaviour towards tenants, dependants and neighbours already lay behind such animosity towards him.[62] Certainly it is clear that during the next few years opinion in the county swung overwhelmingly against him. Long before the next election it was apparent that the great majority of Cardiganshire squires did not want such a man as one of their parliamentary representatives, and their leaders responded to this opinion. By the end of 1766 John Pugh Pryse had created a thousand new burgesses at Cardigan and Aberystwyth. Moreover, a subscription by the local gentry raised £500 towards a legal attack on the claims of Lampeter to be a parliamentary borough; for, like the now disfranchised Tregaron, it had no charter.[63]

Lloyd had no intention of yielding his seat without a struggle, for he had tasted the sweets of politics: although his various attempts to obtain offices of profit from different ministers were all unsuccessful, he secured a baronetcy in 1763, for no obvious reason save the presentation of congratulatory addresses to George III.[64] Always prone to exaggerate his influence, Sir Herbert, on 2 January 1766, assured the Duke of Newcastle, now Lord Privy Seal in the first Rockingham ministry, that 'my interest for a member to succeed at Cardigan . . . cannot fail of success, as one of the contributory boroughs is my own and are the majority of the electors of the town of Cardigan'.[65] A year later that was certainly not true, and, to counter the Gogerddan creations, Lloyd arranged for the admission of over 1200 more burgesses in Lampeter between 19 January and 14 March 1767.[66]

The political temperature in Cardiganshire remained high throughout 1767. On 22 January Lloyd informed his Carmarthenshire ally Griffith Philipps of Cwmgwili that 'the county at present is much inflamed, and a general meeting must soon be held before we are quieted, and if my friends

[61] *London Evening Post*, 28 April 1761. The existence of a 1767 list of Lampeter burgesses 'that polled at the last general election' is confirmatory evidence of a contest in 1761. NLW, Falcondale MSS, no.10.

[62] On this, see Bethan Phillips, *Peterwell: The History of a Mansion and its Infamous Squire* (Llandysul, 1983).

[63] Carmarthen Record Office, Cwmgwili MSS, no.109. A total of 303 new burgesses was admitted in Aberystwyth alone at Michaelmas 1766. G. Eyre Evans, *Aberystwyth and its Court Leet* (Aberystwyth, 1902), p.13. Nothing came of the attack on Lampeter.

[64] Phillips, *Peterwell*, pp.140-1.

[65] BL Add MS 32973, f.21.

[66] Falcondale MSS, nos. 5–7, 11.

do not deceive me, I shall at that meeting make no small appearance for this county'.[67] Sir Herbert had declared himself candidate for the county, 'merely to intimidate Mr Pryse, hoping it may have the same effect as upon the last occasion. If Mr Pryse avoids the snare, which I think he ought to do, for his own credit and interest, the *Comet* will blaze no more.' Such was the opinion of Wilmot Vaughan, now fourth Lord Lisburne since the death of his father in 1766, to his ally James Lloyd of Mabws, son-in-law and heir of Richard Lloyd. Sir Herbert had even approached his old foe Lisburne with the offer of an electoral alliance against Pryse, only to meet a predictable snub.[68]

John Pugh Pryse deemed that it was incumbent on him, as county MP and leading landowner, to resolve the crisis. On 7 August he informed William Powell that 'finding how uneasy the gentlemen of the county are I have wrote by this morning's post to advertise a public meeting at Cardigan for 22 August'.[69] There Pryse announced that he would respond to the popular resentment against Sir Herbert by standing against Lloyd in the borough constituency. Thomas Johnes reflected the general astonishment in a letter to his brother John:

Pryse's behaviour is most extraordinary, . . . to give up the county without opposition which he himself might have had upon the same terms as long as he pleased . . . and to endeavour to represent the town at a very certain large expense and upon very precarious terms . . . I could not have thought that Pryse would have been brought to have sacrificed his interest to the resentment and passions of others. I heartily hope he may lose his borough, and if the Bart can but act with any degree of steadiness Pryse stands very fair to be out of Parliament.

Pryse's tactic had failed in its immediate purpose, that of dividing Johnes from Lloyd by an offer of the shire seat. Johnes resisted all blandishments and remained loyal to Sir Herbert. 'I had great difficulty to withstand the offers made me. Pryse wished to support me, he said. Lord Lisburne's friends and Dr Powell desired nothing more than that I should represent the county. James Lloyd offered me every assistance . . . I kept them in suspense to the very last and those that wished me to stand out of compliment only suffered a great deal by their countenances, for fear I should take them at their words.'[70] His private scepticism to his brother as to the sincerity of some assurances were well founded; for Lisburne, although back in Parliament since 1765 as MP for Berwick, where he had succeeded his uncle Thomas Watson, had made little secret of his intention to contest the county even 'to a poll'.[71] He was now unanimously adopted at the meeting, even though barely on speaking terms with Pryse.[72] Some thought Johnes had declined only because he believed he could not defeat Lisburne, and that he might have been wrong in this assessment.[73] Johnes may indeed have had second thoughts, for he tried to obtain a sheriff of his own choice for the election year.[74] No opposition was made to the return of Lisburne at the general election when it came in 1768. He deemed it politic to thank William Powell as 'the principal instrument' in his success.[75]

[67]Cwmgwili MSS, no.109.
[68]NLW MS 14215C, f.1.
[69]Nanteos MSS, L116. For a copy of the advertisement, see the *Gloucester Journal*, 17 August 1767.
[70]Dolaucothi MSS, 10/40.
[71]NLW, MS 14215C, f.2.
[72]*Gloucester Journal*, 31 August 1767.
[73]NLW, Powis Castle MSS, no.3485.
[74]Nanteos MSS, L 148.
[75]Ibid., L 147.

Political interest centred on the borough constituency, where Sir Herbert Lloyd spared no effort to retain his seat. The election of the mayor of Cardigan at Michaelmas 1767 was bitterly contested, since he would be the returning officer for the Parliamentary election. Pryse's candidate John Lewis was chosen by a large majority, but Lloyd nevertheless had his candidate Ben Davies also sworn in. The town had two mayors for some months, and the dispute was taken to the Court of King's Bench. There, early in 1768, the verdict was given in favour of Lewis; but Lisburne, conveying this good news from Pryse to Powell, warned that 'there is nothing his opponent will not attempt'.[76]

John Pugh Pryse had meanwhile changed his mind about challenging Lloyd himself. He took the opportunity to move to the Merionethshire seat now falling vacant, and then produced in Pryse Campbell a candidate ideally suited to counter Lloyd. Son of Lewis Pryse's daughter Mary, heiress of Glanffrêd, and John Campbell of Stackpole Court in Pembrokeshire, Campbell had been an MP for Scottish constituencies since 1754 and was a rising young star of the ministry, a Lord of the Treasury since 1766. His Gogerddan pedigree and the prospect of ministerial support over any election petition submitted to the House of Commons made Campbell a formidable candidate. On 26 January he informed William Powell that Pryse had that day 'offered me the Borough of Cardigan in a very kind and handsome manner which I accepted. . . . He told me he should this post write to you and his other friends to acquaint them with the resolutions he had come to . . . He told me that it would be necessary that I should send an agent to Cardigan. I said I should be entirely directed by you. I was told that Sir Herbert Lloyd was afraid of my being the candidate. He asked me sometime ago if I was, and that if I was he desired to talk with me, but I think we may bid him defiance.'[77]

Lloyd persisted with his campaign, since his evident offer of a negotiated compromise had been spurned. He ordered his Lampeter burgesses, reputed to be over 2,000 in number, to attend at Cardigan on election day, 24 March 1768, with the intention of coercing Ben Davies into acting as mayor. His hope of thereby obtaining a double return was finally dashed by the refusal of Davies to play such a role. Davies met Lloyd on the road to Cardigan, and the latter immediately returned home, abandoning his prospective voters. His reason for a prompt return was fear of being arrested for debt: membership of Parliament conferred immunity from such a fate.[78] Sir Herbert's social and political ambitions were expensive, and the financial strain of his extravagant mode of life had in recent years been intensified by gambling losses.

Chance afforded Lloyd one more opportunity to re-enter Parliament. Pryse Campbell died on 4 December 1768, at the age of forty-one, and John Pugh Pryse, now MP for Merioneth, had no obvious candidate to fill the vacancy. He consulted in London with Lord Lisburne, and they left the decision to Dr William Powell, who was to discuss the matter with the local gentry. 'Your son, Mr Thomas Powell, if he should be inclined to stand, was our first object', wrote Lisburne to Powell. 'Our measures have extended no further than to have a candidate ready supported by government, to oppose any attempt from the baronet.'[79] John Symmons, son of the former borough member, promptly asked Pryse and Powell for their support,[80] but nothing more was heard of his candidature.

[76]Ibid., L 148.

[77]Ibid., L 93. Powell approved. Ibid. L 94. Thomas Johnes acknowledged to his brother John, 'Pryse Campbell is a much more formidable opponent than Pugh Pryse, as he is very sure to have every influence that government can give.' Quoted by Phillips, *Peterwell*, p.188.

[78]Phillips, *Peterwell*, pp.189–91.

[79]Nanteos MSS, L 149.

[80]Ibid., L 129.

Sir Herbert Lloyd was supported again by *Custos* Thomas Johnes, but on condition that if 'another candidate would appear that was more likely to succeed than himself, he was ready to decline'. What occurred was an upsurge of support for his own namesake son, later famous as the master of Hafod, even though he was currently abroad on the Grand Tour and would not be of age until 20 August.[81] But Lloyd then reneged on his promise. 'Both sides have unanimously named my son, and he only objects to it . . . This breaks through every engagement', Thomas Johnes wrote to his brother John on 2 January 1769, instructing him to 'make every burgess you can for Mr Pryse, with whom Lord Lisburne and . . . I am determined to act for the future.' He was careful to explain, however, that 'I am by no means angry he has refused my son, as I am upon no account desirous he should come into Parliament, but it was a sacrifice I was willing to make for the peace of the county.'[82]

Evidently neither young Johnes nor Powell was deemed a suitable adversary for Sir Herbert Lloyd. Instead his opponents drafted in a complete stranger to Cardiganshire, Ralph Congreve of Aldermaston in Berkshire, whose only qualification appeared to be sufficient wealth to stand the contest. The poll began on 5 January and continued until 13 January, when Congreve was returned with a majority over Lloyd of 1,950 votes to 1,704. He did not even attend the election, a circumstance Lloyd mocked by producing a tinker boy to impersonate him.[83] Lloyd petitioned against the return, his main charge being the partiality of the Mayor of Cardigan, who had admitted illegal votes for Congreve and then refused to hold a scrutiny.[84] The parliamentary session ended before his complaint was heard, and the merits of the case were never to be examined, for Sir Herbert died on about 19 August.[85]

It seems likely that the transfer of some two hundred voters for Johnes, enrolled ironically as Lampeter burgesses, had tipped the balance against Lloyd.[86] Certainly Thomas Johnes believed that as a result of the negotiations prior to this by-election his son was assured of a Cardiganshire seat at the next general election, for he told Lord Powis so in 1770.[87] Events were to show that Lisburne, Pryse and Powell did not consider themselves bound by any such undertaking, even when a vacancy was obviously likely to occur for the borough constituency. By December 1773 Congreve was so failing in health that John Adams, nephew and successor to Sir Herbert Lloyd in the Peterwell estate, wrote to ask William Powell for support in filling the probable vacancy for the 'remainder of the present Parliament only, as this will not interfere with anyone who may succeed at the general election'.[88] Adams was doubtless already assured of the Carmarthen borough seat that he was to hold in the next Parliament. Congreve survived another two years, but the expectation of a vacancy in the borough constituency led to a flurry of activity.

[81]E. Inglis-Jones, *Peacocks in Paradise* (London, 1950), pp.54–5.
[82]Dolaucothi MSS, 10/47.
[83]For a full and lively account of this by-election, see Phillips, *Peterwell*, pp.192–202.
[84]*Commons Journals*, XXXII, 177–8.
[85]The legend of his suicide has been convincingly demolished by Phillips, *Peterwell*, pp.205–10.
[86]An incomplete copy of the poll, with 1,049 votes for Lloyd and 1,028 for Congreve, listed 190 Congreve voters from Lampeter. Only 5 per cent of these 2,077 voters lived in the relevant borough, but 70 per cent did reside in Cardiganshire. NLW, Abermeurig MSS, 8/14/2.
[87]Powis Castle MSS, uncatalogued. Thomas Johnes to Lord Powis, 20 February 1770.
[88]Nanteos MSS, L 92.

Thomas Johnes now claimed fulfilment of the promises he understood had been made in 1769; writing to William Powell on 11 December 1773, he claimed: 'I had flattered myself that harmony and unanimity would have reigned . . . I thought it was tacitly understood at the last contest that the town and county for the next general election were then settled. In consequence of which when Lord Lisburne spoke to me at the last Cardigan Assize about the county, I never hesitated to promise him any assistance in my power.'[89] His indignation stemmed from a precipitate move by John Pugh Pryse, which Cardiganshire speculation later attributed to fear of an alliance made between Johnes and Lord Lisburne at that very meeting to obtain control of both constituencies.[90]

Pryse was abroad at the time, and from Paris, without consulting any of the Cardiganshire gentry, he offered the borough seat at the next general election to a distant relative, Sir Robert Smyth, who lived in Essex but claimed to be a son of Cardiganshire.[91] Pryse wrote to inform Cardigan Council of his decision early in November, giving instructions concerning Smyth's nomination. But not until 28 November, when he had learnt of opposition to his candidate, did he write to ask Lord Lisburne and William Powell to support Smyth.[92] Sir Robert Smyth himself had already written to Powell in optimistic vein on 16 November: 'I flatter myself that I have many friends in the neighbourhood, and I hope the same influence that the last election supported an entire stranger, will not be less strenuously exerted in favour of one who glories in being a native of the county.'[93]

Many Cardiganshire squires deplored 'Mr Pryse's conduct in setting the whole county in a flame so great a length of time previous to the general election'.[94] *Custos* Thomas Johnes sought to take advantage of this reaction by breaking the Gogerddan alliance with Nanteos and Trawsgoed. He wrote to William Powell on 11 December, urging that 'for a person totally unknown in Cardiganshire to declare himself at this distance a candidate without any other introduction than a mandate from Mr Pryse to the Council of Cardigan arrogates such a superiority in the latter that the last contest for that town by no means justifies, and I think is unpardonable in the former'.[95] To his brother John he more frankly condemned Pryse's behaviour as 'duplicity . . . I thought him incapable of', obviously as a breach of promises he believed had been made in 1769. Young Johnes was evidently the rival candidate by the end of 1773 and he reaped the reward of his father's long support of Peterwell by obtaining the backing of John Adams, who had at his command the numerous voters created by Sir Herbert Lloyd: 'He promises my son every support and assistance in his power, for which reason I am determined he shall stand and I make no doubt of being able to succeed.'[96]

But there was no prospect of dividing Nanteos and Trawsgoed from Gogerddan. William Powell hoped to preserve 'the peace of the county', and that would not be achieved by opposition to Gogerddan. Lord Lisburne was annoyed at the action taken by Pryse, whom he had previously advised to consult 'the gentlemen of the county' before any decision; but he accepted Powell's advice, informing him on 27 December that 'I have wrote to Mr Pryse . . . and have assured him,

[89]Ibid., L 102.
[90]Ibid., L 107.
[91]Ibid., L 154, 155.
[92]Ibid., L 117, 155.
[93]Ibid., L 126.
[94]Ibid., L 117.
[95]Ibid., L 102.
[96]Dolaucothi MSS, 14/1.

what I ever intended, that I shall act in concert with him and you and support his nomination with my best services'.[97] Not even the unexpected death of John Pugh Pryse on 13 January 1774 altered Lord Lisburne's resolution. Gogerddan again passed to a distant branch of the Pryse family, in the person of Lewis Pryse of Woodstock, Oxfordshire, who remained faithful to the electoral plans of John Pugh Pryse.

A few weeks later Lisburne was approached by Thomas Johnes with the suggestion of an electoral alliance that would include an equal share of the total cost. Lisburne informed Powell on 9 March that he had rejected the proposal, which he attributed to fear of the cost of the borough contest, but he expected Johnes to retaliate by canvassing the county: 'It is intended to put me both to trouble and expense.'[98] Johnes did indeed seek support there from March until at least May,[99] and as late as September a press advertisement informed Cardiganshire freeholders that there would be a contest.[100] But at the end of August the senior Johnes opted to fight Radnorshire, and Lisburne was able to boast of an unopposed election on 26 October.[101] The same day Johnes conceded defeat in Radnorshire, and set off to assist his son at Cardigan.[102]

In the borough constituency both sides had found the polling of new burgesses impossible under the so-called Durham Act of 1763, which prohibited burgesses from voting until a year after their admission. The Gogerddan family had overlooked this law, for the Leet Courts of both Cardigan and Aberystwyth were closed until May, and the next general election was due by March 1775.[103] Over 4,000 new burgesses were to be admitted in Cardigan between May and October 1774, but this was too late: their votes were not valid at the election.[104] John Adams had displayed more foresight. The Lampeter Court had merely been adjourned, and Thomas Johnes took advantage of this to admit hundreds of new burgesses there between January and April 1774: but the decision of the North ministry to hold a snap general election in October 1774 invalidated these votes as well.

The Cardigan Boroughs election began on 20 October, and the poll continued until 31 October. The mayor of Cardigan, Thomas Colby, was a Gogerddan nominee, determined to ensure Smyth's success. He announced his intention of admitting any burgesses who had voted in any former election, despite demands by the managers for Johnes for evidence of their admission, and he asked only to see the stamped admissions of those who had never polled before. The admissions of all voters for Johnes were produced, and often examined by both the mayor and Smyth's managers. An announcement was made that to shorten the poll, and so avoid a scarcity of food in Cardigan, a scrutiny of the votes would later be conducted; but, as in 1769, no scrutiny took place, and Smyth was returned with a majority of 1,488 to 980.[105] In a letter of 30 October to his brother John the elder Thomas Johnes reported that on Friday, 28 October, 'we finished polling our men, which amount to about one thousand. They continued the poll all day yesterday and do not propose closing it till tomorrow. They are now upwards of four hundred men before us, and I suppose mean

[97]Nanteos MSS, L 155, 156.
[98]NLW, Crosswood MSS, Series III, no.24.
[99]Dolaucothi MSS, 14/3, 7.
[100]*London Evening Post*, 3 and 6 September 1774.
[101]*London Evening Post*, 5 November 1774.
[102]NLW, Harpton MSS, C 131.
[103]Nanteos MSS, L 107.
[104]S. Douglas, *The History of the Cases of Controverted Elections*, III (London, 1777), pp.181–2.
[105]Ibid., III, pp.182–6.

to have one hundred more at least. It is impossible more violence or virulence can be exerted, but I hope I shall be able to disappoint them, though it will be a dear bought victory.'[106]

What Johnes had in mind was an appeal to the House of Commons, where, under an Election Act of 1770 intended to ensure impartial decisions, cases were now examined by a small Election Committee of fifteen MPs selected by lot. The Cardigan petitions, one from Johnes and another from various burgesses, were only submitted on the last possible day, however, and the hearing was postponed until the following session.[107] On 31 October 1775 it was fixed for 28 November, although Smyth had wanted a delay until 26 January. 'Finding administration did not support him in his decision, he went immediately into opposition, which at this time can do him no good', so *Custos* Thomas Johnes told his brother John a week later. This comment, and his request for gifts of salmon to be sent to two prominent ministerial MPs, Richard Rigby and Hans Stanley, places a question mark against the reputed impartiality of such Election Committees.[108] Neither was on the Cardigan Election Committee, but thirteen of the fifteen members were ministerial supporters. The elder Johnes made careful preparations for the hearing, allowing a fortnight for witnesses to travel from Cardiganshire. It was 'a complicated, confused business', he told his brother after a consultation on 4 November with his lawyers, 'They advise bringing up a great many people, which must be complied with.'[109]

The Cardigan Election Committee sat for nine days, until it made a report on 7 December. Its attention first centred on the poll for Sir Robert Smyth, and this was divided into seven classes. Those not found at all in the corporation books were given up by Smyth's counsel. Secondly, there were a number whose names were there, but whose descriptions differed. Smyth contended that Johnes should reveal any discrepancies, Johnes that Smyth should prove each identity: 'That the names being the same could never be taken as evidence of the identity of the person, in Wales, where it is well known there are always great numbers of persons of the same name, even in the same parish, and that there are not, perhaps, above a dozen of different names in a whole county.' The Committee resolved that individual objections should be made and answered. Thirdly, the validity of some sixty or seventy of Smyth's voters depended on a list of 1,289 Cardigan burgesses compiled in 1741. Counsel for Johnes argued that identities were impossible to establish; there were, for example, nineteen men called David Thomas. The Committee resolved that the list was not admissible as evidence, and, on the next two categories of voters, allowed the votes of burgesses whose admissions had been stamped during the election, but not of those who had polled before obtaining a stamped admission. Next, votes of burgesses admitted within a year of the election were disallowed under the 1763 Act. Finally, the Committee resolved that the onus of disproving the identity of voters whose names and description in the corporation books agreed with those on the poll lay with the petitioner.

New lists proposed on the basis of these resolutions must have shown a reduction of 566 on Smyth's poll, for his counsel admitted that there was then a majority of fifty-eight for Johnes.

---

[106]Dolaucothi MSS, 14/12.
[107]Dolaucothi MSS, 14/15; *Commons Journals*, XXXV, 30, 301. Only burgesses from Cardigan, Aberystwyth and Lampeter petitioned. In 1774 two from Atpar tried to vote, but could produce no evidence of admission. Douglas, *Elections*, III, p.81.
[108]Dolaucothi MSS, 14/26.
[109]Ibid., 14/25–6.

Attention now turned to the validity of his voters, most of whom were from Lampeter. Some suspicious circumstances came to light, notably that John Adams and the candidate Thomas Johnes had closeted themselves at Peterwell with the Lampeter borough records. The Committee, however, resolved that the identity of Johnes's voters had been scrutinized at the poll. The conclusion of the Committee was therefore that Johnes had been duly elected, and this was accepted by the House of Commons on 7 December 1775.[110] His father wrote triumphantly that day to his brother John: 'The business is all over. The contest after ten days' attendance finished this afternoon. Their number of 1488 is reduced to 690 . . . Our poll amounting to 980 was thoroughly established, so that we had a most complete victory.'[111] It is not clear how far the success of Johnes was due to Gogerddan negligence and mismanagement, and how far to malpractices at Lampeter undetected by the Election Committee. Sir Robert Smyth was clearly concerned lest he might be held responsible for the defeat of Gogerddan, for on 11 December he wrote to assure Dr William Powell that he had neglected nothing: 'Although the contest has been tedious and expensive to myself, I shall be very glad to enter the lists the first opportunity, if my old friends will support me in the same handsome manner. . . . I have not the least doubt but the gentlemen of the county will exert themselves to prevent a paltry contributory borough from imposing a representative upon them, against the general sense of the county.'[112]

Before the next election what seemed to many a temporary Johnes triumph was converted into more permanent control by the politically inexplicable decision of the Gogerddan family to sell the Cardigan Priory estate to *Custos* Thomas Johnes. As early as November 1768 John Pugh Pryse had intended to sell it, giving the first refusal to Lord Lisburne, who, however, thought little of its political significance. In a private comment to James Lloyd of Mabws he said: 'The Priory estate is to be valued only at present from its annual produce, as it must be a very distant expectation to entertain of drawing any advantage from the borough.'[113] The political evidence of the 1774 election suggests that the estate was then still in Gogerddan hands, and an indenture of 1803 implies that the Johnes family acquired it directly from Gogerddan.[114] By the time of the next general election, in the autumn of 1780, control of the constituency seems to have been in the hands of the younger Thomas Johnes.

His father, although defeated in Radnorshire in 1774, had been returned there at a 1777 by-election, but died on 12 May 1780. His son thereupon decide to vacate his Cardigan seat and opt for the prestige of that county constituency. John Adams, who was about to lose his Carmarthen seat, already intended to stand for Cardigan Boroughs at the general election.[115] He now came forward at the by-election, for Lord Lisburne wrote to William Powell on 22 May that 'the field seems open to Mr Adams, who tells me he is a candidate and is applying for the several interests. Had Mr Powell[116] inclined to offer his service an universal concurrence would have attended him . . . As matters stand now . . . it seems as if Adams would have no competition, and in that respect he is fortunate, having

[110]*Commons Journals*, XXXV, 408, 463, 478. For the Committee's report, see Douglas, *Elections*, III, pp.171–229. For another analysis of this evidence, see H. J. Lloyd-Johnes, 'The Cardigan Boroughs election, 1774', *Ceredigion*, VII, no.1 (1972), 50–5.

[111]Dolaucothi MSS, 14/28.

[112]Nanteos MSS, L 128. Smyth, however, became MP for Colchester from 1780 to 1790.

[113]NLW MS 314215C, f.11.

[114]*NLW Calendar of Crosswood Deeds* (Aberystwyth, 1927), p.298.

[115]NLW MS 14215C, f.11.

[116]William Powell's son Thomas.

so keen an appetite for Parliament.'[117] Lisburne was doubtless assuming that Johnes would now return the electoral help he had received from Adams, who may well have commenced his canvass on that assumption. But Johnes had other ideas. The candidate he favoured was John Campbell, son of Pryse Campbell, whose family link with Gogerddan was less significant than the support of Thomas Johnes. For on the death of Lewis Pryse in 1779, control of the main Gogerddan estate had passed to his son-in-law Edward Loveden of Berkshire, who had not intervened much in Cardiganshire politics. Loveden was merely one of several squires Campbell wrote to for support after he had already announced his candidature:[118] among them also was William Powell, if his son Thomas had no intention of standing, 'to whom I should instantly give up my pretensions'.[119] Thomas Powell did not stand, and John Adams publicly withdrew his by-election candidature on 5 June, since a general election was imminent.[120] Campbell was returned a week later.

Adams did then genuinely intend to fight Campbell at the general election:[121] and he maintained a threat to do so until the end. As late as the week before the election was due on 14 September, Campbell was concerned about the possibility of such a challenge, instructing an attorney to 'bring all papers with you, particularly those that relate to Lampeter', presumably fearing that Adams might deploy what remained of Sir Herbert Lloyd's mass burgess creations.[122] There was no poll, for Campbell subsequently claimed that he did not have 'the disagreeable reflection of having occasioned dissensions'.[123]

In 1780 Lord Lisburne retained the shire seat without a contest,[124] having confided to his ally James Lloyd as early as 16 May that 'as to the county, I have already received so many assurances that I trust all will be quiet there'.[125] Lisburne was a junior member of Lord North's ministry, serving at the Admiralty Board from 1770 to 1782, and had become first Earl of Lisburne in 1776. He accordingly profited from the death of the elder Thomas Johnes that year to regain for his family the post of *Custos*, having first ascertained that the younger Johnes did not desire it.[126]

During the next few years the configuration of British politics was redrawn. By December 1783 Lord Lisburne, a loyal Northite, was an adherent of the Fox–North coalition opposed to the ministry of the Younger Pitt. For once the Trawsgoed interest was threatened by government hostility, and with the death of William Powell on 21 December 1780 Lisburne had lost his chief prop of the Nanteos interest. A request to Thomas Powell for support in the county, made as early as 20 December 1783, evidently fell on deaf ears.[127] What substance lay behind Lisburne's subsequent fears for his seat is impossible to assess. In January 1784 he anticipated that Loveden, now a Pittite MP for Abingdon, would form a coalition with Thomas Powell 'to give me all the trouble in their power'. But neither would oppose him in person, 'and if not, I am at a loss where they were to look for a candidate'; and he was assured, he then thought, of the support of Thomas

---

[117]Nanteos MSS, L 157.
[118]NLW MS 14215C, ff.53–4.
[119]Nanteos MSS, L 95–7.
[120]*Gloucester Journal*, 3 July 1780.
[121]NLW MS 14215C, ff.57–8.
[122]Abermeurig MSS, no.3.
[123]*Gloucester Journal*, 2 October 1780.
[124]*Gloucester Journal*, 9 October 1780.
[125]NLW MS 14215C, ff.51–2.
[126]NLW MS 14215C, ff.51–2, 57–8, 62.
[127]Nanteos MSS, L 158.

Johnes and John Adams.[128] But, by 9 March, he was among the opposition MPs targeted by the Pitt ministry. 'I have not escaped notice', he wrote to James Lloyd, 'and from the best authority I learn that, setting aside his solemn promise in writing and every verbal assurance, Mr Johnes will be prevailed upon to raise an opposition in the county and do everything in his power to prevent my re-election.' The danger now lay in an alliance between Johnes and Powell, who had been consulting together in London, for Loveden had recently assured Lisburne in the House of Commons itself that 'he had no desire to give me trouble'.[129] The next day, 10 March, Johnes effectively put Lisburne's fears to rest by a renewed assurance of support, and his agents duly engaged his freeholders for Lisburne. The Treasury efforts to 'kindle a flame' in Cardiganshire came to nothing, although Powell remained hostile, convening a meeting of his friends on 5 April.[130] Lisburne's election address announced that 'an opposition is commenced against me',[131] but there is no evidence of a poll when he was returned on 28 April.

The election of John Campbell, also a Northite but more of a trimmer, passed without incident. The only evidence comes from two newspaper advertisements, and merely serves to emphasize Campbell's role as the nominee of Thomas Johnes. He was abroad at the time, and it was Johnes who issued an address to the burgesses of Cardigan, Aberystwyth and Lampeter, 'in the name of my absent friend'.[132] It was also Johnes who a few weeks later thanked the burgesses for unanimously re-electing Campbell in his absence.[133]

This peace was deceptive. It was not to be expected that any master of Gogerddan would tamely surrender control of the borough constituency which had so long remained with his family interest. Over 1,100 new burgesses were created in Aberystwyth at Michaelmas 1788.[134] Edward Loveden was simultaneously endeavouring to revive Gogerddan power in the county, with Thomas Powell his intended nominee. 'Look at Lisburne. Hath his seat cost him much expense and trouble', Loveden commented to Powell in January 1787, when making this proposal. 'When you give me assurances to move in your behalf, I will grant leases enough to secure a large majority.'[135] Before the end of 1788 Powell and Loveden had begun 'a public canvass for county and borough' to overthrow the control of Lisburne and Johnes.[136] But no challenge was to be made in either constituency at the next general election, and thirty years were to pass before Gogerddan and Nanteos regained control of the parliamentary representation of Cardiganshire. Although different families were temporarily in the ascendant, it is apparent that by the age of the French Revolution little had changed in Cardiganshire politics in the century since the Glorious Revolution. Not only were parliamentary elections still a matter of concern only for the gentry, but within that political system Gogerddan and Nanteos were again united against Trawsgoed and its allies, after all the fluctuations of the intervening period. Such underlying rivalries were more enduring than the transitory party labels which gave them political colour.

[128] NLW MS 14215C, ff.77–8.
[129] NLW MS 14215C, ff.81–3.
[130] NLW MS 14215C, ff.86, 91–2.
[131] *Hereford Journal*, 8 April 1784.
[132] *Hereford Journal*, 1 April 1784.
[133] *Hereford Journal*, 29 April 1784.
[134] Evans, *Aberystwyth and its Court Leet*, p.143.
[135] Nanteos MSS, L 67.
[136] Crosswood MSS, Series III, no.62.

CHAPTER 16

PARLIAMENTARY REPRESENTATION: FROM THE FRENCH REVOLUTION TO THE PASSAGE OF THE REFORM BILL, 1790–1832*

Margaret M. Escott

CARDIGANSHIRE expected its representatives at Westminster to be men of distinguished Welsh ancestry with large estates in the county, who would foster the interests of the squirearchy, grace their social functions, and display largesse. Between 1790 and 1832 it was a privilege guarded by four families with estates of over 30,000 acres: Thomas Johnes of Hafod and the Vaughans of Trawsgoed, Earls of Lisburne, retained control until Johnes's death in 1816, when the Powells of Nanteos and the Pryses of Gogerddan resumed their former pre-eminence. Lesser squires could not, however, be overlooked, for many boasted ancient Welsh pedigrees and connection with a past Member which generated an automatic right to consultation and political weight beyond their incomes. Furthermore, their support at county and borough meetings could prove crucial in an era which saw organized petitioning and reporting of Parliament and political meetings increase, and when Members were urged openly to make contractual pledges and bow to the dictates of their constituents on matters of policy.[1] There was only one contested election, that in 1812 for the less prestigious and secure Cardigan Boroughs seat, but there is ample evidence in other years of pre-election manoeuvring by candidates and others whose estates, rivalries, dynastic and party affiliations crossed county boundaries, especially into neighbouring Carmarthenshire and Pembrokeshire.[2]

*I wish to thank the History of Parliament Trust, particularly Mr Roland Thorne and Dr David Fisher, for access to transcripts in the Trust's archive. Division and party lists used throughout are those held by the Trust and have not been cited individually.

[1] R. D. Rees, 'Election ideals current in south Wales, 1790–1832', *WHR*, 2, no.3 (1965), 233–50; idem, 'South Wales and Monmouthshire newspapers under the Stamp Acts', ibid., 1, no.3 (1962), 301–24; F. Jones, 'The old families of south-west Wales', *Ceredigion*, IV, no.1 (1960), 1–18; R. J. Colyer, 'The gentry and the county in nineteenth-century Cardiganshire', *WHR*, 10, no.4 (1981), 497–535; *Greal y Bedyddwyr*, V (1831), 192; *The Cambrian*, 22 January 1820, 3 September 1825, 22 September 1827, 1 March, 21 June 1828, 14 February 1829, 8 January 1830; Carmarthen RO, Aberglasney MSS 30, G. Bonsall to P. Pryse, 28 January 1821; History of Parliament Trust, Aspinall Transcripts, H. Evans to P. Pryse, 19 October 1829.

[2] Prominent among this group were the Bowens of Llwyn-gwair, the Brigstockes of Blaen-pant and Gellidywyll, Saunders Davies of Pentre, Davis and subsequently Harford of Peterwell (Falcondale), Herbert Evans of Highmead, the Gwynnes of Mynachdy, John Jones of Derry Ormond, the Leweses of Llanaeron, Llanllŷr and Llysnewydd, James Richard Lewes Lloyd of Dôl-haidd, the Lloyds of Alltyrodyn, Bronwydd, Coedmor, and Kilrhue (Cilrhiw), Lloyd, later Lloyd Philipps, of Mabws and Dale Castle, the Webley Parrys of Noyadd Trefawr and the Williamses of Gwernant.

Lists of county voters drawn up from land tax returns in 1799 and 1823 show that there were proportionally more 'independent' freeholders in the south-west of the county, that copyhold was rare, and that tenant farmers were more likely to be enfranchised in the boroughs than the county constituency, whose estimated electorate had declined to 636 in 1823. Furthermore, by 1823, over 17 per cent of county voters held their freeholds in Cardigan and its contributory boroughs, Aberystwyth and Lampeter, which polled 725, 219 and 152 burgesses respectively in 1812.[3] Borough politics were essentially parochial and oligarchic. Each corporation had long been managed by partisan mayors and portreeves to represent particular gentry interests, albeit not to the complete exclusion of trades and professional men and wealthy newcomers.[4] Gogerddan gradually eclipsed Hafod and Nanteos at Aberystwyth;[5] Peterwell remained dominant at Lampeter;[6] while at Cardigan, which remained strategically the most important and potentially the most open of the boroughs, great store was set on controlling the mayoralty, and thereby the election writ, through the Priory estate. Even so, the influence of the Bowens of Llwyn-gwair and Troed-yr-aur, the Brigstockes of Blaen-pant, who owned Cardigan Island, the Vaughans of Trawsgoed at Blaen-porth, and the Pryses of Gogerddan, whose Abernantbychan estate extended into the borough, could not be overlooked. Presentment fees levied in addition to the £3 stamp duty paid on burgess admissions varied from 2s. 6d. at Lampeter to 10s. 6d. at Aberystwyth, and 13s. 6d. at Cardigan.

The alliance forged in 1774 between Thomas Johnes of Hafod and Wilmot Vaughan, Earl of Lisburne, held firm at the general election in June 1790, when neither boroughs nor county was contested despite an early show of opposition from Thomas Powell of Nanteos and Edward Loveden Loveden of Buscot Park in Berkshire, who managed the Gogerddan interest during his son Pryse's minority.[7] The threat, nevertheless, proved sufficient to persuade the sitting Member, John Campbell of Stackpole Court, who had been elected in 1780 on Thomas Johnes's interest, to embark on an early canvass of his Cardigan Boroughs constituents in March 1789.[8] Campbell's main interests lay in Nairnshire, Pembrokeshire and Carmarthenshire, where he was to inherit his friend John Vaughan's Golden Grove estate in 1804 and assume control of the 'Blues' and the borough of Carmarthen

---

[3]NLW, Gogerddan MSS, Cardiganshire freeholders books, 1799 and 1823. The figures per hundred in 1823 were: 24 in Upper and 70 in Lower Genau'r-glyn; 67 in Upper and 60 in Lower Ilar; 22 in Upper and 40 in Lower Pennarth; 78 in Upper and 65 in Lower Moyddyn; 60 in Upper and 150 in Lower Troed-yr-aur. Forty-five, fifty-nine and seven freeholders lived in Aberystwyth, Cardigan and Lampeter respectively. The fourth contributory borough, Atpar, ceased to function as a corporate borough after 1741. It was not formally disfranchised, but had no freemen in this period. D. A. Wager, 'Welsh politics and parliamentary reform, 1780–1835' (unpublished University of Wales Ph.D. thesis, 1972), pp.367, 370, estimated the pre-1832 county electorate at 750 and the borough electorate at 2,300. This last figure and that of 4,000 cited in F. O'Gorman, *Voters, Patrons and Parties, The Unreformed Electoral System of Hanoverian England, 1734–1832* (Oxford, 1989), p.54, cannot be verified. Gogerddan MSS RB55; NLW Crosswood MSS ser.IV, no.15; *PP* (1831–2), XLI, 34–9; XXVI,510; P. D. G. Thomas, 'Eighteenth century elections in the Cardigan boroughs', *Ceredigion*, VI, no.4 (1967), 402–23; D. Williams, *The Rebecca Riots* (Cardiff, 1971), p.21.
[4]*PP* (1835), XIII,197–8, 307–12, 419–22; NLW, Aberystwyth Borough Records A4; Ceredigion RO, CDM/3–46.
[5]G. Eyre Evans, *Aberystwyth and its Court Leet* (Aberystwyth, 1902), pp.14–16; *Carmarthen Journal*, 23 November, 6 December 1833.
[6]G. Eyre Evans, *Lampeter* (Aberystwyth, 1905), pp.44–5.
[7]NLW, Crosswood MSS ser.III, no.62.
[8]Carmarthen RO, Cwmgwili MSS 280; NLW, Dolaucothi MSS V7/43.

despite being resented as a foreigner.[9] In national politics he had aligned with the Whigs during the 1788–9 regency crisis which threatened William Pitt the Younger's ministry – an event which coincided with his courtship of and marriage to Lady Caroline Howard, daughter of the fifth Earl of Carlisle, whose political circle he now joined.[10] Campbell's diaries show that during the 1790–6 Parliament he was a keen observer, albeit a nervous contributor to wartime defence debates; he advocated the abolition of the slave trade, for which the county, Atpar, Cardigan and Newcastle Emlyn petitioned in March 1792.[11] On 12 April 1791 he had voted for Grey's resolutions criticizing the Pitt Ministry's decision to compel Russia to evacuate the Black Sea port of Oczakov, but he supported Pitt in February 1794 over the use of Hessian troops and was counted among the Whig supporters of Pitt's Ministry after the Duke of Portland joined it in July 1794.[12] He now applied to Pitt for an English peerage, which he was granted at the dissolution in 1796, when similar requests forwarded by the Duke of Portland on Lisburne's behalf were rejected.[13]

As befitted a county MP, Lisburne steered the 1791 Cardiganshire roads bill successfully through Parliament. This was a typical piece of corrective local legislation, which sought to make Cardiganshire's floundering turnpike trusts profitable.[14] Lisburne, like Johnes, had voted against the government on the Oczakov question, but, dogged by ill-health and worsening family finances, he paid little attention to his parliamentary duties after 1792.[15]

Pryse Loveden of Gogerddan was of age at the next general election in 1796, the year of *y lecsiwn fawr* in Carmarthenshire; and his father, who boasted ministerial backing and Powell's support, suggested putting him forward for the county.[16] As he informed Loveden, Lisburne was

. . . not a little mortified by the offers you mention to have been made to your son Mr Pryse Loveden to support his pretensions as a candidate for the County of Cardigan at the general election, however, to be as candid and explicit with you as possible, I cannot relinquish the distinguished honour myself and family have for such a series of years enjoyed without taking the sense of the county and offering them the services of my son, Lt. Col. [John] Vaughan. It was certainly not my intention to have disturbed the peace of the county at so early a period, I therefore the more lament the sentiments that have been avowed as they infallibly lead to consequences which are very obvious. After this explanation you are well aware I can have few

---

[9]See also M. Cragoe, 'The Golden Grove interest in Carmarthenshire politics, 1804–21', *WHR*, 16, no.4 (1993), 467–93.

[10]R. Thorne (ed.), *The House of Commons, 1790–1820* (hereafter cited as Thorne), III, p.446; D. Howell, *Patriarchs and Parasites: The Gentry of South-West Wales in the Eighteenth Century* (Cardiff, 1986), pp.14–15.

[11]Carmarthen RO, Cawdor MSS 1/225, 244; A. Aspinall (ed.), *The Later Correspondence of George III* (Cambridge, 1962–70), II, p.185 (no.1033); BL Add MS 48222, f.79; *Commons Journals*, XLVII, 589, 601.

[12]Thorne, III, p.446.

[13]Cawdor MSS 1/224; PRO, 30/8/120, ff.98–100; 30/8/121, f.29; 30/8/148, f.170; BL Egerton MSS 2137, ff.87, 142; Crosswood MSS, ser.III, nos.54–67; R. D. Rees, 'Parliamentary representation of south Wales, 1790–1830' (unpublished University of Reading Ph.D. thesis, 1962), p.542.

[14]*Commons Journals*, XLVI, 10, 158, 166, 177, 217, 223, 316, 340.

[15]J. M. Howells, 'The Crosswood estate, 1547–1947', *Ceredigion*, III, no.1 (1956), 70–88.

[16]Dolaucothi MSS V11/33.

observations to make except that it would have afforded me sensible gratification if our interests and views had not interfered.[17]

Vaughan's party was 'very active', but Lisburne could not afford a contest and it fell to Thomas Johnes, who feared opposition in Radnorshire, to defend their interest in the county and offer Vaughan his support in the boroughs, where Campbell was standing down. John Vaughan had already been recommended to Portland as a likely government supporter, capable of returning a nominee for Berwick on Tweed.[18] The parties did not proceed to a poll, partly because the gentry chose to support Johnes rather than an unknown young man. Pryse was in any case so reluctant a candidate that the Whig James Greene, husband of Ann Brigstocke of Blaen-pant, was considered, but he opted for an unopposed return for Arundel in the Duke of Norfolk's interest. Loveden's attempt to bargain for the boroughs seat to compensate for his likely defeat at Abingdon was resented.[19] Indeed, Johnes had predicted from the outset that the Gogerddan canvass was 'too impatient and ridiculous',[20] and he gave the following description of its outcome:

> He [Loveden] was indifferent who came in for this county and town provided Mr Vaughan and myself were excluded. No county ever behaved more handsomely nor has anyone ever received more personal marks of attachment, which as long as I retain, he may vent his malice but can never carry it into effect . . . Nor has any election cost so little, considering there was a sort of contest; a few hundreds will pay for all. My opponent does not come off so cheap.[21]

Lisburne remained disgruntled, and for a period in the autumn of 1797, when his father's latest application for a peerage was rejected, John Vaughan cast a number of opposition votes in protest. He soon tired of this tactic, however, and, to the annoyance of his constituents, he neglected their interests and concentrated on his military career. As his elder brother, Wilmot, was insane, he inherited the 40,000-acre Trawsgoed estate on his father's death in 1800;[22] but it was Johnes who succeeded to the offices of Lord Lieutenant and *Custos* which then fell vacant.[23]

Johnes's prediction that Loveden would choose to 'vent his malice' again before the 1802 election proved correct, but he could achieve little in either the county or boroughs. Pryse Loveden, who had changed his name to Pryse on succeeding his mother to Gogerddan in 1798, was as reluctant as ever to stand, and William Edward Powell of Nanteos was still a minor.[24]

As the parties realigned nationally between 1801 and 1812, greater emphasis was placed on factional loyalties and the independence and allegiance of individual Members to particular

[17]Gogerddan MSS, Lord Lisburne to E.L. Loveden, 14 April 1796, printed in D. Jenkins, 'The Pryse family of Gogerddan', *NLWJ*, VIII, no.2 (1953), 117.

[18]Thorne, III, p.486; Cawdor MSS 1/129; Crosswood MSS, ser.III, no.71; Dolaucothi MSS V3/38; V7/66, 74; V16/51, 78.

[19]Berks. RO D/EP11, Loveden to Sellwood, 9 May 1796; Cawdor MSS 1/129; NLW, W. Evans George MSS 1575.

[20]Dolaucothi MSS V16/51.

[21]H. M. Vaughan, 'Some letters of Thomas Johnes of Hafod', *Y Cymmrodor*, XXXV (1925), 204, also cited in Thorne, III, p.486.

[22]BL Egerton MSS 2137, ff.121, 161; PRO 30/8/152, ff.131, 133; 20/8/195, f.176; *Gentleman's Magazine* (1800), I, 89; Cwmgwili MSS 504; Thorne, II, p.446.

[23]PRO 30/8/148, f.170.

[24]Berks. RO D/EP11, Loveden to Sellwood, 1 November 1801; Cwmgwili MSS 504; Thorne, II, pp.486–7.

ministries than on the old Whig and Tory labels, although these continued in use. In March 1801 Pitt was forced to resign because he supported Catholic emancipation, the King replacing him with the 'Tory' Addington, who, in turn, had to make way for Pitt again in 1804. Lord Grenville's predominantly 'Whig' administration, appointed after Pitt died in 1806 and known as the 'ministry of all talents', proved short-lived and was succeeded by 'Tory' coalitions headed by the Duke of Portland, from March 1807 until September 1809, and Spencer Perceval, from October 1809 until May 1812, when Lord Liverpool became Prime Minister – an office he retained until he suffered a stroke in 1827. According to lists of the various 'Parties' in the House of Commons, Johnes supported both Pitt, 1804–6, and Grenville's administrations, and remained in opposition with the latter group during Portland's ministry. By 1810 the 'Whigs' considered him one of their 'thick and thin' supporters – a claim belied by the few parliamentary votes he subsequently cast.[25] Vaughan's name, like that of Lisburne, featured on Whig Club lists in the 1790s but by 1812 he was regarded as an inactive independent Member, inclined to support the Whig opposition.[26]

Johnes, too, attended the House of Commons sparingly and rarely spoke in debate, but he was usually at Westminster when local legislation was considered and for great occasions like the budget.[27] While his health permitted, he made a virtue of holding his 'parliament' at Hafod, which had to be rebuilt after the 1807 fire. His constituents took pride in his connections and reputation as an innovative farmer and forester, improving landlord, enlightened employer, scholar and patron of the arts. Although tradesmen in Aberystwyth waited overlong for their bills to be paid, the tenure of the county seat of the ailing, heirless and impoverished squire of Hafod was not seriously threatened.[28]

While Johnes lived, the likely opening lay in the boroughs, where, at the 1806 election, Gogerddan enlisted the help of the infamous Carmarthen attorney Herbert Lloyd – recently dismissed as Johnes's agent. Rumours circulated of a threat to Johnes and that Colonel John Lloyd of Mabws would oppose Vaughan, but they proved to be little more than abortive ploys by Herbert Lloyd to rally support for himself in Carmarthen.[29] Vaughan had more to fear when Portland forced another general election in June 1807, and Admiral George Bowen, who had strong Cardigan and government connections, and Admiral Edward Hamilton, campaigned against him. He lost no time in applying to Johnes's cousin, John Johnes of Dolaucothi and others for support.[30] Trawsgoed agents and the corporation of Cardigan refused to grant the challengers access to past pollbooks and burgess admission lists to prepare their canvass; thus discouraged, both backed down.[31] Since Aberystwyth burgess presentment records for the period 1786 to 1807 do not survive, political activity is difficult to monitor. The only important local bill enacted in the first decade of

[25] Thorne, IV, p.311.

[26] Annotated lists in History of Parliament Archive, Boxes L24 and L25.

[27] Dolaucothi MSS V7/58.

[28] R. J. Moore-Colyer, 'Thomas Johnes of Hafod (1748–1816), translator and bibliophile', *WHR*, 15, no.3 (1991), 399–415; W. Linnard, 'Thomas Johnes of Hafod, pioneer of upland afforestation in Wales', *Ceredigion*, VI, no.3 (1970), 309–19; D. Jenkins, *Thomas Johnes o'r Hafod* (Cardiff, 1948), and E. Inglis Jones, *Peacocks in Paradise* (London, 1950), passim; Thorne, IV, pp.310–11; Dolaucothi MSS V7/58.

[29] Cawdor MSS 1/133.

[30] Dolaucothi MSS V11/36.

[31] *The Cambrian*, 9 May, 13, 27 June 1807; Thorne, II, pp.487–8.

Fig. 109: Thomas Johnes of Hafod (1748–1816), MP for the county, 1796–1816. (*Copyright National Library of Wales*).

Fig. 110: William Edward Powell of Nanteos (1788–1854), MP for the county, 1816–1854. (*Copyright National Library of Wales*).

the nineteenth century was that sought by the Revd Alban Thomas Jones Gwynne of Mynachdy in 1807 to develop Aberaeron; the only other petitions were for the relief of debtors in Cardigan gaol.[32]

Change, however, was at hand. In 1807 the Bristol banker and Member for Colchester, Richard Hart Davis, bought the Peterwell estate and thereby control of Lampeter. Shortly afterwards he and his partner William Miles, East India Company agent Albany Wallis, and John Bowen purchased what had been Johnes's property in Cardigan from his mortgagee, the Marquess of Lansdowne.[33] Predictably, Davis was soon seeking 'any political information respecting Cardigan', and 'a list of the gentlemen it would be necessary to write to in Cardiganshire preparatory to an election for Cardigan'.[34] He enfranchised his tenants, but the allegiance of non-resident burgesses created for Johnes at Lampeter remained a potential problem. Aware of the difficulties he faced as an outsider, Davis, for whom Griffith Jenkins of Cilbronnau acted as steward, determined 'to go on temperately and ultimately to conquer prejudice by good offices *if possible*'. Prior to the 1812 election, he sought unsuccessfully to secure the election of a partisan mayor/returning officer at Cardigan, to engineer a

[32]*Commons Journals*, LVII, 45, 91; LVIII, 653; LIX, 47; LXI, 12; LXII, 157, 212, 262, 312, 601, 633, 650, 804; LXVI,135.

[33]W. J. Lewis, *The Gateway to Wales: A History of Cardigan* (Dyfed County Council, 1990), p.8; NLW, Peterwell MSS 135–6, 142; N. Carlisle, *A Topographical Dictionary of the Dominion of Wales* (London, 1811).

[34]NLW, Highmead MSS, R. H. Davis to H. Evans, 16 May 1810, 2 February 1811.

split between Johnes and Vaughan, and to persuade William Owen Brigstocke, who could rely on the support of Lord Cawdor, to stand for the boroughs. Davis, however, made much of his 'influence' with Lord Liverpool and played successfully on Pryse's new-found ambition to succeed Johnes in the County to discourage him from standing for the boroughs and persuade him to back Major Herbert Evans of Highmead against Vaughan. Evans, a stalwart of the 'Blue' or Whig party in Carmarthenshire and a prominent Teifi valley magistrate, was a kinsman through his first marriage of the Lloyds of Alltyrodyn, and by his second, of Sir Robert Seymour, Member for Carmarthenshire and brother of the second Marquess of Hertford. Herbert Lloyd, 'a host in himself', was on their side.[35]

Hopes that Vaughan would retire through lack of funds, or that he could be ousted for under £2,000, proved misplaced.[36] He remained in control at Cardigan, whose mayor, George Price, more than matched the burgess-making activities of Gogerddan at Aberystwyth and Peterwell at Lampeter. Vaughan retained Johnes's support, and to Evans's dismay, won that of William Edward Powell, the young heir to Nanteos and Pryse's rival in waiting for the county seat. With Powell, who had been advised to support Vaughan rather than risk being 'placed as the representative of Boroughs *half rotten*', came his kinsman William Lewes of Llysaeron and the Lloyds of Bronwydd, Dôl-haidd and Mabws, who had ever mistrusted Thomas Powell's alliance with Gogerddan.[37] The Vaughan party, who met at the Salutation Arms inn at Atpar and sported Orange, started late but topped the poll throughout, and on 29 October, after a gruelling fifteen-day contest, Vaughan was declared the victor by 588 votes to 508. Lloyd of Mabws nominated him, and Pryse proposed Evans, whose followers wore the old Tory Blue favours of Gogerddan and the west Wales Whigs. George Price reputedly rejected eighty of Evans's voters, and corporation officials at Aberystwyth and Lampeter made it impossible for Vaughan's agents to gain access to their books by dispatching them to Buscot.[38]

The number of seats contested in Britain had fallen from seventy-one in 1807 to fifty-seven in 1812, but in the counties of Cardigan, Carmarthen and Pembroke gentry support was bargained for and dynastic alliances and party strength tested at the poll in five of the seven seats,[39] thereby encouraging candidates and their supporters to negotiate inter-constituency pacts.[40] Three of these returns, including Cardigan Boroughs, were petitioned against.[41] With financial support from Gogerddan and from Richard Hart Davis, who also faced a costly petition against his own return for Bristol, Evans's friends prepared case studies to support their petition alleging partiality and corruption by George Price.[42] It was presented to the Commons on 14 December 1812 and heard

---

[35]Highmead MSS, P. Pryse to H. Evans, 21 July 1812, R. H. Davies to same, 30, 31 October, 1, 14 November 1811, 14, 21, 30 April, 20, 26 June, 9, 15, 19, 21 July, 2 September 1812; Cawdor MSS 1/133.

[36]Highmead MSS, R. H. Davis to H. Evans, 19 July 1812.

[37]Thorne, II, p.486; Nanteos MSS, L204–6, 726, 787–91, 830–37, 1209–12.

[38]NLW, Powis Castle MSS 4163–5, 4218; Gogerddan MSS, Selwood to Loveden, 14 September, William Williams to P. Pryse, 4 October, letters to Mrs P. Pryse, 17, 19 October 1812; Handbills re 1812 election; NLW, Falcondale MSS III/43–4, 126–7; *Gloucester Journal*, 19, 26 October, 2 November 1812.

[39]Rees, 'Parliamentary representation', pp.190–1, 287–91, 300, 310–13. For Pembrokeshire, see R. Thorne, 'The Pembrokeshire elections of 1807 and 1812', *PH*, VI (1979), 5–24.

[40]Highmead MSS, John Jones to H. Evans, 12 June, Herbert Lloyd to same, 4 October 1812.

[41]The others being Carmarthen, Pembroke Boroughs and Pembrokeshire.

[42]Highmead MSS, R. H. Davis to H. Evans, 17 October 1812; Falcondale MSS III/44; IV/124–133; *The Cambrian*, 5, 19 December 1812; Dolaucothi MSS V17/21; Nanteos MSS L838.

by a parliamentary committee of fifteen appointed on 16 March 1813.[43] Davis's attempt to pack the committee with supporters failed, and it reported in Vaughan's favour on 2 April. Powell of Nanteos was among the witnesses summoned before it.[44] Lloyd of Mabws organized a subscription to finance counter-petitioning and legal action against corporation officers at Aberystwyth and Lampeter.[45] Aberystwyth Court Leet was repeatedly adjourned for swearing in burgesses at short notice in the event of a second election, but mass admissions ceased as the threat waned, and from 1813 only burgesses who paid their own stamp duty were admitted. Burgess-making also continued at Cardigan, where George Bowen of Llwyn-gwair and Lloyd of Mabws refused to admit Evans's supporters. Davis obtained a new charter for Lampeter by Act of Parliament in 1814 and, with the next election in mind, made 600 of his own men burgesses.[46]

In Cardiganshire, as elsewhere, an increase in local legislation, which was invariably costly and appealed to vested interests, cannot be dismissed as a factor in parliamentary elections, although there is little evidence that it produced strict party splits or featured in lampoons. In 1812 the latter poured scorn on Evans as an 'upstart' and 'the tool of a Bristol Monopolizer' and partisanly hailed Vaughan as the champion of independence, or condemned him for voting to keep duties on seaborne coal and refusing to vote on Catholic emancipation.[47] However, the entrepreneur and 'perpetual mayor' of Aberystwyth, Job Sheldon, believed Pryse had come out against Vaughan 'for opposing the road over Ponterwyd bridge to Llanidloes'. Before the election the 1811 Llanddewibrefi enclosure bill was withdrawn, and that for Llanrhystud, which contributed to later unrest at Mynydd Bach, proceeded slowly through Parliament before becoming law on 20 May 1812.[48] After the election Parliament passed Acts to enclose Llangynfelyn and Llanfihangel Genau'r-glyn (1813), and Gwnnws and Lledrod (1815), and a second Llanddewibrefi enclosure bill failed.[49] Organized petitioning increased. In 1813 the clergy of the archdeaconry and the inhabitants of Aberystwyth and Cardigan petitioned against Catholic emancipation, and when the bill came before the Commons on 24 May Vaughan voted against it, and Johnes, though expected to support it as hitherto, did not vote.[50] Further anti-slavery petitions from Aberystwyth and Cardigan followed in June 1814 and the boroughs also petitioned for the promulgation of the Christian religion in India.[51] Aberaeron was chosen as the venue for a county meeting on 11 March 1816, which petitioned for government action to alleviate the effects of post-war depression after the 1815 disturbances at Mynydd Bach.[52]

[43]*Commons Journals*, LXVIII, 58, 314.

[44]Highmead MSS, R. H. Davis to H. Evans, 13, 17 February 1813; *Commons Journals*, LXVIII, 340, 372.

[45]Falcondale MSS III/128, 130.

[46]Aberystwyth Borough Records A4; Evans, *Aberystwyth and its Court Leet*, pp.154–6; W. Evans George MSS 1629; Highmead MSS, Griffith Jenkins to H. Evans, 5 August, David Lloyd to same, 8 August 1813; Evans, *Lampeter*, pp.42–9.

[47]Gogerddan and Highmead MSS, Handbills re 1812 election.

[48]*Commons Journals*, LXVI, 49, 62, 143, 159, 198; LXVII, 38, 140, 329, 384; Powis Castle MSS 4128.

[49]*Commons Journals*, LXVIII, 47, 284, 421, 466–7, 537, 580, 583, 587; LXX, 43, 141.

[50]*Commons Journals*, LXVIII, 143, 203, 477; Thorne, IV, p.311.

[51]*Commons Journals*, LXVIII, 530, 533, 551; LXIX, 441, 500, 515.

[52]Highmead MSS, W. to H. Evans, Wednesday [?] September, 15 September, 4 October 1815; D. J. V. Jones, *Before Rebecca. Popular Protests in Wales, 1793–1835* (London, 1973), pp.35–6, 41–3, 48–50; idem, 'Distress and discontent in Cardiganshire, 1814–19', *Ceredigion*, V, no.1 (1966), 280–9.

It was alleged that

> . . . agriculture is at a stand, and those supported by and connected with it are in the utmost misery: rents are unpaid, and the poor rates are daily becoming heavier; the commercial world, the tradesmen, the artificers and the manufacturer participate in the general difficulties; the immense reduction of issues by the Bank of England has affected credit, destroyed many and closed more Provincial Banks and produced a great scarcity of circulating medium:

The petition was presented on 10 May 1816, the day the writ was moved for the by-election caused by Johnes's death on 23 April.[53] His estate remained in Chancery until September 1832.[54]

Speculation that Vaughan might try to regain the county seat for Trawsgoed, that Lewes of Llysnewydd or Lloyd of Mabws, whose grandfather had represented the boroughs, would build on their local and magisterial strength to seek election, and that Davis would 'try his powers', was soon overshadowed by a dynastic struggle with political overtones between Gogerddan and Nanteos, both of which had heirs of age. Vaughan lacked money and had confirmed his almost habitual inattention to county matters during the recent depression and rioting. There was support for Lloyd of Mabws, but, mindful of his grandfather's experience in the boroughs, he announced he would not risk inflicting the ruinous expense of a contest on his family.[55]

Since 1812, when Powell, who acted solely through his kinsmen and agents, was thought to have displayed the better judgement, both he and Pryse had made a point of socializing with squires at race meetings, dinners, balls and assemblies, but they had shied from magisterial duties and county meetings which, Pryse claimed, from 'their vicinity to the scene of action [Cardigan]', gave Vaughan's friends, 'the Teifi confederates', every advantage.[56] On learning of Johnes's death, Powell lost no time. He retained the Atpar attorney and clerk of the peace, John Beynon, who had laboured successfully for Vaughan in 1812, applied for the vacant county lieutenancy, obtained copies of the freeholders' lists, and enlisted help in Carmarthen, Haverfordwest and Tenby. He canvassed furiously in Cardiganshire and beyond, heeding warnings not to enter into a pact to assist Davis in the boroughs, making sure of the Leweses, and securing the support of the Bishop of St David's and Lord Cawdor's interest.[57] Pryse neither expected nor wanted the campaign to begin in earnest until after the county meeting on 14 May, when Vaughan was expected to make his views known, and he proceeded with less urgency despite Herbert Evans's warnings and Powell's printed letters 'fly[ing] about in all directions . . . no freeholder in the county is without one'.[58]

Lewes of Llysnewydd and Brigstocke of Blaen-pant nominated Powell on 14 May – an indication that he was supported by Dynevor and Stackpole Court, west Wales's leading Tory and Whig

---

[53] *Commons Journals*, LXXI, 356, 358.

[54] Howells, 'The Crosswood estate, 1547–1947', *Ceredigion*, III, no.1 (1956), 78–80; H. Lloyd Johnes, 'John Johnes (1800–76) of Dolaucothi', ibid., III, no.1 (1956), 4; R. J. Colyer, 'The Hafod estate under Thomas Johnes and Henry Pelham, fourth Duke of Newcastle', *WHR*, 8, no.3 (1977), 265, 270–6.

[55] Nanteos MSS L721, 1247, 1257; Aberglasney MSS 30; *The Cambrian*, 4 May 1816; *Carmarthen Journal*, 10 May 1816.

[56] Highmead MSS, P. Pryse to H. Evans, 19 May 1813, W. Evans to same, 24 August, 16, 18 September 1815; Nanteos MSS L669, 680, 699–714, 830; Dolaucothi MSS V17/21; *Carmarthen Journal*, 10 May 1816.

[57] Nanteos MSS L484–5, 508, 510, 530, 720, 721, 727–8, 892, 999, 1018–9, 1173, 1246–7, 1457, 5299(ii).

[58] Aberglasney MSS 30.

houses. James Richard Lewes Lloyd of Dôl-haidd proposed Pryse and Herbert Evans seconded. Powell won the show of hands, but many north Cardiganshire voters, who could be relied upon to support Pryse at a poll, were absent; and Lloyd of Mabws, who was probably also representing Vaughan, and Gwynne of Mynachdy, had yet to declare and had misgivings about both nominees. The result, which Job Sheldon claimed was arrived at 'by the toss of a coin', was an agreement which excluded Trawsgoed and Peterwell and gave Powell the county seat on the understanding that he would support Pryse in the boroughs at the next election. Gwynne, who publicly declared his neutrality and spoke of the need for a strong local Member to lobby for repeal of the duty on seaborne coal, insisted that Powell would be 'on trial' until the next election. Lloyd of Mabws agreed with him.[59] With their concurrence, Powell was returned unopposed on 27 June, proposed by Lewes of Llysnewydd and seconded by Lloyd of Dôl-haidd.[60]

Powell also obtained the county lieutenancy, but in November 1816 his request for a baronetcy was rejected, and in February 1817, soon after Vaughan's insolvency was made public, he learnt of a plot by Pryse's friends to oust him.[61] He urged the government to act to alleviate local currency shortages,[62] and hurried to Cardigan to chair a county meeting which petitioned against distress and the duties on coal and culm, on which a three-year reduction was secured that autumn.[63] The sheriff, Davies of Maesycrugiau, reminded him: 'it is for your future to put your wits to work in the Commons House of Parliament to relieve the distressed as much as lay [sic] in your power'.[64] No action was taken to restore Cardigan's coinage privilege, but the Chancellor of the Exchequer, Nicholas Vansittart, agreed to 'bring the Cardiganshire memorial before government and see if there are any articles in store which can be applied to the relief of the petitioners'.[65] On 29 April landholders and tenants from Powell and Vaughan's strongholds in Caron, Gwnnws, Llanddewi-brefi, Ysbyty Ystwyth and Ystradmeurig, 'entirely loyal to the government and faithful to the constitution as by law established', petitioned for a road-building programme to relieve distress.[66] Soldiers had been stationed at Aberystwyth since the 1816 riots, and popular unrest remained localized, endemic and compounded by difficulties in funding the militia.[67] Powell had cast two anti-government votes in February 1817, but he voted with ministers to suspend *habeas corpus*, and supported Charles Watkin Williams Wynn, the Grenvillite Member for Montgomeryshire, in the June 1817 speakership election.[68] Possibly mindful of events in 1816, his address at the June 1818 general election focused on local issues.[69]

Nanteos co-operated uneasily with Gogerddan over endowments at Aberystwyth and Davis gave Lampeter a new town hall and market.[70] He offered Evans, who was still interested, his Lampeter

[59] *Carmarthen Journal*, 17, 24 May 1816; *The Cambrian*, 18, 25 May 1816; Powis Castle MSS 4151; *The Spectator*, 1 January 1831. According to Nanteos MSS L486(i), Powell and Pryse signed a written agreement.
[60] *The Cambrian*, 1 June 1816.
[61] Nanteos MSS L486(i) & (ii), 487; *Carmarthen Journal*, 12 January 1817.
[62] BL Add MSS 38425, ff.38–42.
[63] *The Cambrian*, 11 January, 27 February, 20 September 1817.
[64] Nanteos MSS L676.
[65] Nanteos MSS L1201.
[66] *Commons Journals*, LXXII, 218.
[67] Nanteos MSS L950.
[68] Thorne, IV, pp.875–6, 901–2.
[69] *Carmarthen Journal*, 12 June 1818.
[70] Highmead MSS, P. Pryse to H. Evans, 31 December 1817, 15 January 1818.

votes[71] but Evans had already agreed to support Pryse, who wrote to him on hearing a false report of Vaughan's death in February 1818:

> The agreement entered into at Cardigan I feel I could not with any propriety swerve from, and under this impression certainly intend to offer myself as its representative and request your kind support.[72]

Pryse had joined Brooks's Club on 3 June 1816, and as a professed Whig with Liberal sympathies he promised:

> you will ever find me firmly attached to our excellent constitution, a strenuous friend to the strictest economy in the public expenditure, and a warm supporter of every good measure which may appear to me conducive to the good of my country.[73]

Vaughan, though aggrieved, made no show of opposition and Pryse succeeded him without a contest. Unusually, and possibly to prevent a late challenge by Pryse for the county, both elections took place on the same day, 25 June 1818. Pryse's nomination by the Tories, Lewes of Llysnewydd and Lloyd of Mabws, and Powell's by the Whigs, Bonsall of Fronfraith Hall and Gwynne, put the stamp of political consensus on proceedings.[74]

After the election, Cardiganshire, like every Welsh county except Merioneth and Pembroke, petitioned for protective duties on agricultural imports. The petition was presented on 19 February 1819, and four days later Powell and Pryse voted against the government's plan to spend public money on the Windsor Castle establishment.[75] Pryse's opposition vote was expected, but Powell's was a protest vote, for he generally expressed his 'independence' in support of Lord Liverpool's Tory government. Neither made major speeches in Parliament. On strongly partisan issues such as Tierney's censure motion, which was defeated on 18 May 1819, and the renewal of the Foreign Enlistment Act, Powell and Pryse's votes cancelled each other, and they usually did so for the remainder of their long parliamentary careers. However, since neither was an assiduous attender of the Commons, it is hard to judge whether absences such as that of Powell from divisions on repeal of the coal and malt duties on 22 May and 9 June, or that of Pryse in December 1819, when the Seditious Acts were passed, were for personal or political reasons.

A county meeting at Aberaeron adopted a loyal address to the Prince Regent in 1819,[76] and the towns marked the end of the long reign of George III in February 1820 with the usual addresses of condolence and congratulations to the new monarch as they prepared for a general election.[77] Reports that Pryse had 'determined to have the county', throwing Powell *'on the boroughs, if you are not opposed there'*,[78] gained credence amid growing evidence that Nanteos, which faced problems in the

[71]Highmead MSS, R. H. Davis to H. Evans, 27 February 1817, 7 February 1818; Nanteos MSS L1209.

[72]Highmead MSS, P. Pryse to H. Evans, 3 February 1818.

[73]Ceredigion RO, ADX/78/7.

[74]*Carmarthen Journal*, 12, 19, 26 June, 3 July; *The Cambrian*, 13, 20, 27 June 1818.

[75]*Commons Journals*, LXXIV, 129.

[76]*North Wales Gazette*, 11 November 1819.

[77]*Carmarthen Journal*, 18 February 1820; *The Cambrian*, 26 February 1820.

[78]Nanteos MSS L930.

Cwmystwyth lead mines and at Aberystwyth, was on the verge of financial collapse. Powell, who customarily divided his time between Bath, London and Newmarket, was urged to hasten to Nanteos, but the 1816 agreement held firm. Access to government patronage and his readiness to co-operate with potentially difficult squires like Gwynne, made him hard to challenge, and, having overcome the 'general exposure which the county is too over fond of', he was returned unopposed on 16 March.[79] Pryse had been elected on the tenth, proposed by Lewes of Llysnewydd and seconded by John Lloyd Williams of Gwernant. The returning officer was Captain William Henry Webley-Parry of Noyadd Trefawr, who leased the Priory estate from Davis. The latter, though financially embarrassed after over-speculating during the 1819 currency crisis, again offered Evans his support in vain. Mabws and Alltyrodyn were now in trust for minors and Vaughan's friends were conspicuously absent, but leading dignitaries from all three towns signed Pryse's indenture, and there is no evidence of an attempted dual return or pre-election burgess creations.[80]

Following the election, Davis sold out in Cardigan to the banker Philip John Miles. His son-in-law and partner John Scandrett Harford of Blaise Castle and his brother bought Peterwell, and Harford, who was himself prepared to sell much of it by 1828, built a new mansion at Falcondale.[81] Pryse paid for a gallery to be built at St Mary's Church in Cardigan, and Aberystwyth and Cardigan furnished him with petitions to present against the duties on seaborne coal. At Aberystwyth, Powell and Pryse contributed handsomely towards the Crynfryn dispensary and the town hall, which was opened in 1823.[82]

The health of George IV's estranged wife Queen Caroline had been drunk at the Proclamation at Aberystwyth, and there was great interest in her trial. Aberystwyth and Lampeter were illuminated after the Lords threw out the bill of pains and penalties in November 1820, but at Cardigan 'the inhabitants were not all of one mind' and 'some pains were taken to repress the popular feeling'.[83] Pryse faithfully supported the Queen's cause in Parliament, whereas Powell only voted against the omission of her name from the liturgy, on 20 January 1821, and divided with government on 6 February 1821 when a censure motion was brought, criticizing their handling of the affair. Bonsall feared lest his fellow magistrates at the Quarter Sessions should approve an address congratulating ministers, and he was ready to amend it, 'but nothing was proposed'. He informed Pryse on 28 January: 'We are not strong enough here to propose an original address without you, but with you we should beat them on the subject ten to one.'[84] There were greater celebrations in the Cardigan area when the popular Tory barrister, John Jones of Ystrad, defeated Cawdor's nominee, the nabob Sir William Paxton, at the Carmarthen by-election in July 1821.[85]

At Westminster Powell continued to oppose Catholic relief and parliamentary reform, and he voted in support of the government's economic and fiscal policy despite continued manifestations of

[79]Nanteos MSS L368–73, 378, 394–5, 662, 675, 741–3, 929–30, 949–52; R. J. Colyer, 'Nanteos: a landed estate in decline, 1800–1930', *Ceredigion*, IX, no.1 (1980), 60–8; *Carmarthen Journal*, 17, 24 March 1820; *The Cambrian*, 25 March 1820.

[80]*The Cambrian*, 26 February, 18, 25 March 1820; Ceredigion RO, CDM/34–40; Falcondale MSS III/3–4; Aberystwyth Borough Records A4.

[81]A. Harford, *Annals of the Harford Family* (London, 1909), pp.85–6; NLW, Edwinsford MSS 3083.

[82]D. Samuel, *Old Aberystwyth* (Aberystwyth, 1890), pp.4–10; *Aberystwyth Guide* (1816), pp.3–87; Evans, *Aberystwyth and its Court Leet*, pp.47–8, 119, 190; *Carmarthen Journal*, 23 February 1821. For Powell's disputes with the Corporation, see Nanteos MSS L371, 373, 394, 395, 502.

[83]Nanteos MSS L1434; NLW, Glanpaith MSS C330; *Carmarthen Journal*, 24 November, 1, 8 December 1820.

[84]Aberglasney MSS 30.

[85]*Carmarthen Journal*, 13 July 1821.

distress in Cardiganshire. His attendance was as ever sporadic. It was a time of grave concern about the health of his wife (who died in September 1822) and of mounting family debts and encumbrances which forced sales and remortgages amid accusations of treachery by agents who regarded him as an absentee who 'neither understands nor takes the least interest in farming'.[86] Pryse remained with the opposition, choosing not to vote on Catholic relief, which he privately supported, but which Aberystwyth and north Cardiganshire petitioned against in 1825. He won local acclaim by leading resistance to Lord Chichester's tithe extortion schemes, and for his parliamentary vote for Brougham's motion of 11 June 1824 condemning the trial and execution of the Methodist missionary John Smith, who had been indicted for encouraging slaves to riot at Demerara.[87] In 1823, however, he moved from Gogerddan to Buscot, where his father's death heralded a period of financial instability; thereafter he lost interest in the tithe campaign and Cardiganshire legislation other than the bill to amend the Genau'r-glyn Enclosure Act, in which he had a vested interest.[88] On 9 April 1824 Pryse voted against making a £500,000 government grant for the construction of new churches but, when the corporation's campaign for a new church at Aberystwyth (which drew £1,298, to be repaid from church rates, from the fund) gained momentum in 1825, he, like Powell, contributed £250 towards the new St Michael's Church.[89] Neither Member assisted in the passage of the bill to establish St David's College, Lampeter, which was introduced to the Lords on 17 June, rushed through the Commons on the following day, and granted royal assent on 21 June 1824.[90] Locally, its instigators, Harford and Bishop Burgess, had turned to Evans of Highmead, Gwynne, Jones of Derry Ormond and Archdeacon John Williams for advice and support, and the new College was soon represented on the Corporation of Lampeter.[91] Herbert Evans had observed:

> The County of Cardigan complained marvellously when Johnes and Vaughan were the representatives, I think the present Members no better – Powell treads too closely in Johnes's step as to distress and in course cannot be independent in his parliamentary conduct. Pryse like Colonel Vaughan has something else to do than attend to his duty . . . If I had been returned I am sure one session of St. Stephens's campaign would have put me safe enough six feet under the ground.[92]

Aberystwyth and Cardigan had become important centres for Methodist and Baptist assemblies, and branches of Y Cymreigyddion flourished in both towns. Aberystwyth petitioned against slavery both before and after Thomas Clarkson brought the anti-slavery society's campaign to the town in

[86]R. J. Colyer, 'Nanteos', 65–6; Nanteos MSS L368–71, 373, 376–9, 395, 545, 581–627, 926; J. Barber, 'A fair and just demand? Tithe unrest in Cardiganshire, 1796–1823', *WHR*, 16, no.2 (1992), 190.

[87]Barber, 'A fair and just demand', 181–201; *Seren Gomer*, VII (1824), 189–90, 224–5.

[88]PRO, Prob. 11/1657/265; PRO, IR26/916/433; R. J. Colyer, 'The Pryse family of Gogerddan and the decline of a great estate, 1880–1960', *WHR*, 9, no.4 (1979), 410–12; idem, 'The enclosure and drainage of Cors Fochno, 1813–37', *Ceredigion*, VIII, no.2 (1977), 181–92; NLW MS 19001C; *Commons Journals*, LXXVIII, 54, 159; LXXXIX, 63, 191, 364, 435, 468, 504; Gogerddan MSS, Pryse–Morris correspondence, 17 March 1823 to 4 July 1829.

[89]I. G. Jones, 'Religion and politics: the rebuilding of St Michael's Church Aberystwyth and its political consequences', *Ceredigion*, VII, no.2 (1973), 117–23.

[90]*Commons Journals*, LXXIX, 510–11, 521, 525.

[91]Harford, *Annals of the Harford Family*, pp.85–8; *The Cambrian*, 24 February, 10 March 1827, 28 November 1829.

[92]NLW, Lucas MSS 625.

July 1824, and in 1826 the upper half of the county and Cardigan also petitioned.[93] However, as Clarkson, who stayed at Coedmor, recalled:

> Major Bowen at last seemed to consent to a petition against drawbacks and bounties, if necessary, but to no other, or at least, to no Petition which should imply that Government had not done their duty to the utmost.[94]

Powell and his brother Richard became freemen of Cardigan in October 1824 during the mayoralty of William Owen Brigstocke, Junior, and he kept a higher profile at the races and sessions.[95] Alltyrodyn and Mabws were no longer in minority and Lewes of Llanaeron warned:

> though *high in popular favour* it is better by personal courtesy to 'nip in the bud' any political coalition in persons who *would be great men*.[96]

Amphlett had taken the lease of the Priory, which he retained until 1827, and Thomas Bowen, on being re-elected mayor, made new appointments on the Common Council and admitted fifty-nine freemen at special courts in Cardigan on 13 and 27 December 1824.[97] The court leet at Aberystwyth was adjourned repeatedly between October 1825 and the general election, but only eight burgesses were created.[98] The June 1826 general election, fought nationally on emancipation, was one of 'unusual quiet' in south Wales, pre-empted in Cardiganshire by an election for county coroner at which the late coroner's son, John Howell Thomas of Lampeter, backed by Lloyd Williams of Gwernant and Price of Pigeonsford, defeated Lloyd of Dôl-haidd and Philipps of Aberglasney's nominee, David Lewis of Newcastle Emlyn.[99] There were complaints against the Salmon Fisheries Act and Game Laws and mob protests at Mefenydd, but consensus prevailed among the gentry for repeal of the Test Acts, against Catholic emancipation, and against amending the Corn Laws – government legislation which Powell and Pryse had wisely voted against on 11 and 18 May 1826.[100] Pryse was returned unopposed at a cost of £158 4s. on 13 June, proposed by Lloyd of Dôl-haidd and seconded by Thomas Lloyd of Cilrhiw, who also nominated Powell on the

[93]*The Times*, 15 April 1824; *The Cambrian*, 19 June, 18 December 1824, 22 January, 26 March, 10 December 1825; 21 January, 11 February 1826; *Commons Journals*, LXXIX, 297; LXXXI, 60, 372.
[94]NLW MS 14898A, Thomas Clarkson's diary, pp.12–13.
[95]Ceredigion RO, CDM/44; *The Cambrian*, 20 August, 3, 10 September, 1 October 1825.
[96]*The Cambrian*, 17 July 1824; Nanteos MSS L936.
[97]Nanteos MSS L1176; *Carmarthen Journal*, 20 April 1827; Ceredigion RO, CDM/14, 45–46; Gogerddan MSS RB55; *PP* (1831–2), XXVI, 510, specifies only nine admissions in 1824 and fourteen in 1825.
[98]Aberystwyth Borough Records A4.
[99]*Carmarthen Journal*, 19 May; *The Cambrian*, 27 May, 10 June 1826.
[100]Carmarthen RO, Coedmor MSS D/DL/850–66; Gogerddan MSS, Notice of Lewis Davies and Morgan Richard of Llanychaearn, 19 December 1825; Nanteos MSS L1050–8; D. Williams, ' "Rhyfel y Sais Bach", an enclosure riot on Mynydd Bach', *Ceredigion*, II, no.1 (1952), 39–52; D. Jenkins, 'Rhyfel y Sais Bach', ibid., I, no.2 (1951), 199–200; D. J. V. Jones, 'More light on Rhyfel y Sais Bach', ibid., V, no.1 (1964), 84–93; R. Phillips, 'Ychwaneg am "Ryfel y Sais Bach", 1820–29', ibid., VI, no.3 (1970); *The Cambrian*, 24 June, 1, 8 July, 26 August 1826; Jones, *Before Rebecca*, pp.35–66; *Carmarthen Journal*, 21 April 1826.

nineteenth, with Webley-Parry seconding. Powell thanked the county for expressing confidence in Lord Liverpool's government by returning him.[101]

Cardigan and the county petitioned the new Parliament for an increase in coroners' emoluments, an extension in the circulation period of one and two pound bank notes, which were to be phased out, and against the Malt Act. On this they had the backing of Powell, who showed no sign of following the leadership of Canning and Huskisson on free trade.[102] He voted to repeal the Test and Corporation Acts in 1828 for which the towns and old and new Dissenting congregations county-wide petitioned.[103] He also shared the gentry's fears that Catholic emancipation threatened the security of the state. As ministers were aware, he disapproved of the decision of Sir Robert Peel and the Duke of Wellington to support Catholic relief and he presented petitions and voted resolutely against the bill passed in 1829. Most Cardiganshire petitions were instigated by the Anglican clergy; many came from parishes with no history of petitioning and were attacked in the Commons as the products of inflammatory anti-Catholic propaganda and anti-Irish feeling. Only the Unitarians of Capel-y-groes petitioned for Catholic emancipation.[104] Pryse had distanced himself from both questions and, although he was expected to vote unreservedly for emancipation, he delayed doing so until the third reading of the bill on 30 March 1829.

Cardiganshire also protested strongly against the proposals of the Justice Commission in 1829 to abolish the Welsh judicature and incorporate Welsh counties into larger units within the English circuits. The Campbells of Stackpole Court and leading Blues had long advocated abolition, but had been successfully countered by Tories in west Wales who, with the support of the magistrates, had promoted legislation to reform the current system.[105] Now Evans of Highmead, Brigstocke of Blaen-pant, Archdeacon Thomas Beynon, and Lloyd of Dôl-haidd declared for abolition, and a supportive memorial from 'Cardiganshire proprietors and freeholders', who, not surprisingly, owed allegiance to Highmead, Alltyrodyn and Stackpole Court, was sent to the Commissioners.[106] Early proposals to make Cardiganshire, Carmarthenshire and Pembrokeshire into an assize district centred on Carmarthen, or to hold the Cardiganshire and Pembrokeshire assizes at Cardigan were rejected in favour of Cawdor's recommendation that Cardiganshire be split: the hundreds of Ilar and Genau'r-glyn, west Montgomeryshire and Merioneth were to be served by Dolgellau, and the rest of the county, together with Carmarthenshire, Pembrokeshire and parts of Breconshire, by Carmarthen:

[101]Carmarthen Journal, 23 June 1826; *The Cambrian*, 24 June, 1 July 1826; Gogerddan MSS, election bills 1826; Nanteos MSS L5302.

[102]*Commons Journals*, LXXXII, 332, 433; LXXXIII, 73–5; *Carmarthen Journal*, 23 May 1828.

[103]*Commons Journals*, LXXXII, 527, 594; LXXXIII, 101, 104–5, 181; *Carmarthen Journal*, 22, 29 February, 1, 8 March 1828.

[104]Nanteos MSS L1039; *Carmarthen Journal*, 13 April 1826, 16, 30 January, 13, 20 February, 20 March 1829; *The Cambrian*, 21 February, 14, 28 March 1829; *Commons Journals*, LXXXIV, 41, 89, 121, 177; *Mirror of Parliament* (London, 1829), I, p.393 (John Jones's speech, 4 March 1829); L. Colley, *Britons: Forging the Nation, 1707–1837* (London, 1992) p.330; G. I. T. Machin, *The Catholic Question in English Politics, 1820–1830* (Oxford, 1964), p.144.

[105]*Commons Journals*, LXXV, 237, 265, 269, 277, 294, 340, 382, 394, 405, 413, 418, 433, 445, 447–8; LXXVIII, 133, 135, 227–8; LXXIX, 407, 530, 536; Cawdor MSS 2/219, passim; BL Add MSS 40363, f.144; John Frederick Campbell, 2nd Baron Cawdor, *Letter to the Right Honourable John, Baron Lyndhurst, Lord High Chancellor of England, on the Administration of Justice in Wales* (Edinburgh, 1828); *The Cambrian*, 7 March, 18 April 1829.

[106]*PP* (1829), IX, 62–3, 382–6, 388, 390–2, 416; *The Cambrian*, 7 March 1829.

Though Aberystwyth be in south Wales, yet its remoteness from Carmarthen (47 miles) renders it desirable that it should be brought within a more convenient distance of some other assize town.[107]

As was the case elsewhere in Wales, squires feared a loss of status and resented the threat to their assizes; as a result, many who had not previously been staunch supporters of the Welsh judicature rallied to its defence. Powell opposed the change and was cheered when he arrived at Cardigan to chair the assizes in September 1829. The presiding judge, Edward Goulburn, advised the magistrates to study the judicature proposals carefully.[108] The 'largest county meeting in memory' was held at Aberaeron on 18 November 1829. Powell and Pryse attended, but proceedings were dominated by lawyers and the lesser gentry. Lewes of Llanaeron introduced a petition against change, and after justifying it he spoke emotively of the 'planned disfranchisement and dismemberment of the county of Cardigan'. The Chairman of the Quarter Sessions, David Saunders Davies, dissuaded pro-abolitionists present from proceeding with an amendment calling for a petition solely against partition, and the original petition was passed unanimously.[109] Reporting the meeting, an editorial in *The Times* on 25 November declared 'the Welshmen . . . are turning Tories', and complained it could 'neither comprehend their arguments nor in every instance record those antique but unreliable names of places by which the several members of one multitudinous family . . . are driven to identify their persons'. Correspondents debated furiously in the local press,[110] and although Wales petitioned heavily against the administration of justice bill through which the changes were enacted, it was nevertheless rushed successfully through Parliament before the dissolution in July 1830, which followed the death of George IV. A belated government amendment left the existing county assize structure virtually intact when the Welsh judicature was abolished in October, and Cardigan kept its assizes. Pryse overcame early reservations and presented petitions and voted with Powell against the bill.[111]

Rumblings of discontent about the Game Laws and Beer Act caused no real problems for Powell at the general election in August 1830 despite speculation that Lord Kensington, the former Whig Member for Haverfordwest and trustee of Trawsgoed since 1823, would put up his son against him.[112] Pryse had more to fear. Aberystwyth and Cardigan courts leet had been repeatedly adjourned, with more admissions at Cardigan than Aberystwyth.[113] Harford hastened to Lampeter, albeit to no 'material purpose', in response to a rumour that Evans would stand,[114] and the barrister heir to Gwernant, Edward Lloyd Williams of Edgbaston, declared his candidature only to find little local support.[115] Pryse informed Evans on 3 August:

[107] *Carmarthen Journal*, 18 April 1829; *PP* (1829), IX, 43–44, 62–3, 390–2, 414, 427–30.
[108] *Carmarthen Journal*, 4 September 1829; *Cambrian Quarterly Magazine* (1830), 114–9.
[109] *The Cambrian*, 21 November 1829; *Shrewsbury Chronicle*, 27 November 1829.
[110] Rees, 'South Wales and Monmouthshire Newspapers', *WHR*, 1, no.3 (1962), 309–11.
[111] *Carmarthen Journal*, 16 July 1830.
[112] Nanteos MSS L858, 879; Edwinsford MSS 3083; History of Parliament Trust, Aspinall transcripts, H. Evans to P. Pryse, 19 October 1829.
[113] Aberystwyth Borough Records A4; *PP* (1831–2), XXVI, 510; Ceredigion RO, CDM/15.
[114] Bristol RO, Blaise Castle MSS 28048/C3; Nanteos MSS L879.
[115] *Hereford Journal*, 28 July 1830; *The Cambrian*, 31 July 1830.

All is well over and I am again an M.P. Lloyd of Dolhaidd was intended to propose me and Coedmore Lloyd to second me. The latter was behind time and the consequence was that Dolhaidd applied to *Powell* to propose me and he conducted it himself. This was anything but what I would have wished, however I could not help it.[116]

Powell's own nomination on 9 August was by Saunders Davies and Lloyd Williams senior. He confined his addresses to local matters.[117] Despite his stance on Catholic relief, Powell was not inclined to join the Ultra faction of the Tory party at Westminster, where he was still regarded as a 'friend' of Wellington's weakened administration. He voted with them on 15 November against Parnell's amendment to the civil list, which brought them down. Pryse, as expected, was among the anti-government majority.[118]

The towns and Nonconformist congregations throughout the county contributed to the post-election petitioning campaign for the abolition of slavery, and Aberystwyth and Cardigan petitioned against duties on seaborne coal, culm and slate.[119] The inhabitants of both boroughs petitioned early in support of the new government's parliamentary reform proposals, but neither corporation campaigned for separate representation, although both had populations over the minimum figure set of 2,000. There was, however, an abortive call for additional county representation 'as Wales was now become a part and parcel of England, under the same laws, and such laws administered by the same judges'. At Cardigan on 18 March, speeches in English and Welsh in support of Pryse and reform were made by Major Thomas Bowen, Thomas Francis, Lord Kensington, Thomas Lundly, James Morse, Saunders Davies and Griffith Thomas, vicar of St Mary's, and letters of support were read from Lewes Lloyd and Pryse. Cardigan's reformers were also prominent at the county meeting, held at Lampeter on 7 April and chaired by the sheriff, Colonel Chichester, who had travelled from Devon. It proved a hurriedly convened affair dominated by Lord Kensington, from which the Leweses and other diehard Tories were excluded. Resolutions supporting the government's reform proposals were moved by Saunders Davies, the Lloyds of Alltyrodyn, Coedmor and Dôl-haidd, Gwynne, Thomas Howell of Lampeter, and Thomas Bowen, Charles Longcroft and Arthur Jones of Cardigan. John Lloyd seconded Kensington's motion:

> That the conduct of the representatives of this county and of the boroughs of Cardigan, Aberystwyth and Lampeter, merits the approbation of their constituents; and should they continue to support the bill in its true principle through the committee, will be entitled to the suffrages of the freeholders and burgesses in the event of a dissolution of Parliament.

Letters from Evans, Powell and Pryse supporting the bill were read, but Powell had voted against reform as recently as February 1830 and Kensington made it known that he expected better proof of his conversion than his paired vote at the bill's second reading on 22 March, when it was passed by a single vote. Powell presented the petition to the Commons on 20 April, having voted with Pryse the previous day in the minority against Gascoyne's amendment which succeeded in wrecking the bill and forced a

[116]Highmead MSS 3150.
[117]*Carmarthen Journal*, 23, 30 July 1830; *The Cambrian*, 14 August 1830.
[118]Nanteos MSS L855–9, 862, 867, 879–80; *Carmarthen Journal*, 23 July, 13, 20 August; *The Cambrian*, 31 July 1830.
[119]*Commons Journals*, LXXXVI, 132, 157, 188, 212, 237, 428, 465.

dissolution.[120] Bitter, expensive and violent contests followed elsewhere, notably in Carmarthen and Pembrokeshire, where the sitting Tory Members had voted against the reform bill. George Rice Trevor of Dinefwr, the Member for Carmarthenshire, stood down rather than be obliged to pledge support for it or risk defeat at a poll, and he was replaced by a Whig.[121] There were no contests in Cardiganshire, and Pryse, whose indenture was signed by the entire Common Council of Cardigan,[122] was:

> chaired through the principal streets of the town amidst the most enthusiastic rejoicings . . . preceded by a blue silk banner decorated with a crown and the words 'Reform Bill' tastefully inscribed on it – a gift from the Commercial Club.[123]

Election committees for Carmarthen and Pembrokeshire were established at Atpar, Cardigan and Newcastle Emlyn, and Cardiganshire's gentry, their agents and solicitors, were active on both sides. Attorneys were summoned to Pembrokeshire from as far afield as Llandeilo and Aberystwyth, whence Powell's Nanteos agent John Hughes went to serve the reformer Robert Fulke Greville in May. Hughes declined Greville's retainer for the second election in October, at which Saunders Davies was a major defector to the victor, Sir John Owen, a pragmatic convert to reform.[124] Owen's daughter was married to Price junior of Pigeonsford. Cardigan met and petitioned following the bill's defeats in the Lords in October 1831 and May 1832,[125] but as early as May 1831 the Whig attorney and Common Councillor, James Morse 'could not fail observing how much he regretted the absence of many on the bench who had been foremost in advocating the cause of reform when first agitated'[126] – an observation also made by *The Times*, and confirmed by comparing signatories to requisitions for reform meetings and Pembrokeshire poll book evidence.[127] At Westminster, where Grey's Whig administration remained in office, Powell and Pryse voted for the reform bill at key divisions, but they rarely divided at its less well reported committee stage. Powell was absent from the third reading of what proved to be the final bill on 22 March 1832, but on 10 May, during the crisis which followed the bill's second defeat by the Lords, he voted for Ebrington's motion for an address calling on the King to appoint only ministers who would carry the bill unimpaired. The bill became law in June – a high point in Pryse's popularity, for on 24 May he had voted for the immediate establishment of a select committee to consider the abolition of slavery, which was refused.[128] Powell was once more back among the Tory minority when party loyalty was tested by the Russo-Dutch loan on 12 July.

The Reform Act incorporated recommendations made by the boundary commissioners for minor changes at Aberystwyth and Lampeter, and Cardigan's boundaries were extended north

---

[120] *The Cambrian*, 2, 9, 16 April 1831; *Commons Journals*, LXXXVI, 416, 465.

[121] D. Williams, 'The Pembrokeshire elections of 1831', *WHR*, 1, no.1 (1960), 37–64; D. J. V. Jones, 'The Carmarthen riots of 1831', ibid., 4, no.2 (1968), 129–42; E. V. Jones, 'Through riot to parliament', *CH*, XIV (1977), 59–63; D. A. Wager, 'Welsh politics and parliamentary reform, 1780–1832', *WHR*, 7, no.4 (1975), 442–3.

[122] NLW, Morgan Richardson MSS L157.

[123] *The Cambrian*, 7 May 1831.

[124] NLW, Glansevern MSS 3025; NLW, Eaton Evans and Williams MSS 4551–70, 4593, 5002, 5044–5106, 5133–7, 5141–6, 5172–3, 5175–89, 5458–9, 11990; NLW, Williams and Williams Haverfordwest MSS 19481.

[125] *Carmarthen Journal*, 3 December 1831; *The Welshman*, 25 May, 6 June 1832.

[126] History of Parliament Trust, Aspinall transcripts, Morse to [Pryse], 13 June 1831.

[127] *Carmarthen Journal*, 1 April 1831; *The Times*, 14 May 1831; Pembrokeshire RO, PQ/RP/P/8–14.

[128] *The Welshman*, 25 May, 6, 22 June 1832; *Greal y Bedyddwyr*, VI (1832), 221–2, 252.

beyond the common and south across the Teifi into Pembrokeshire to include Bridge End and 'the populous village of St Dogmels'. Atpar's status as a contributory borough of the new Cardigan district constituency was confirmed and its boundaries extended across the Teifi to include Newcastle Emlyn – a concession which, according to *John Bull*, was granted to increase the Earl of Cawdor's influence in the boroughs constituency. It noted:

> as the Members for that unlucky place [Cardiganshire] are both very quiet gentlemen in Parliament, the thing was not likely to be found out in the House of Commons if carefully managed in Schedule 'O'. Hocus pocus – there it is sure enough.[129]

In November 1832, 241, 29, 127 and 34 householders rated at £10 per annum and above were registered at Aberystwyth, Atpar, Cardigan and Lampeter respectively, and, together with the 139, 171 and 254 existing freemen, who, by living within seven miles of their borough retained their voting rights, formed the electorate of the 'reformed' boroughs constituency.[130] At the same time, 1,179 freeholders and five copyholders were judged to be qualified to vote for the county and registered at Aberaeron, Aberystwyth, Atpar, Cardigan, Lampeter and Tregaron, at a cost to the ratepayers of almost £300.[131] Nonconformity was strong among the newly enfranchised, and slavery and Church reform became the major political issues.[132] Despite rumours that Powell would make way for David Saunders Davies, and a brief flurry of 'Orange' opposition to Pryse, both retained their seats at the first post-reform election in December 1832.[133] Not surprisingly, Carmarthen Whigs gleefully lampooned Cardiganshire squires, especially Saunders Davies and Lewes Lloyd, for 'backsliding into Toryism'.[134]

---

[129]*PP* (1831–2), XLI, 23–42; item from *John Bull* reprinted in the *Salopian Journal*, 20 June 1832.

[130]*Carmarthen Journal*, 26 October, 30 November 1832; *PP* (1835), XXIII (1), 200.

[131]*PP* (1834), IX, 593, 641; *Carmarthen Journal*, 26 October 1832.

[132]*Seren Gomer*, XV (1832), 218, 252, 282; *Greal y Bedyddwyr*, VI (1832), 188–9, 221–2, 252; *Yr Efangylydd*, II (1832), 355–6, 384.

[133]*The Welshman*, 31 May, 21 September, 21 December 1832, 6 January 1833; *Carmarthen Journal*, 14 September, 7 December 1832.

[134]Dynevor MSS 160/12, 161/5.

CHAPTER 17

PARLIAMENTARY REPRESENTATION: FROM THE FIRST TO THE THIRD REFORM ACTS, 1832–1885*

Roland G. Thorne

CARDIGANSHIRE retained two single-member constituencies under the 1832 Reform Act and it had 1,184 registered electors. Its franchise included forty-shilling freeholders, five £10 a year copyholders, and leaseholders for at least twenty years at over £50 rent, also the threshold for tenants at will. The boroughs' franchise lay in householders paying at least £10 rent a year, and in existing freemen living within seven miles of their borough, whether it was Cardigan, its boundaries extended, Aberystwyth or Lampeter, slightly extended, or Atpar, lapsed since 1742, but now reinstated and extended into Newcastle Emlyn. The boroughs' electorate stood at 1,030. An analysis of all but thirty-five gives Cardigan 127 householder voters and 171 freemen; Aberystwyth 241 and 139; Lampeter 34 and 254 and Atpar 29 householders. Thus freemen exceeded house-holders by 564 to 431, but they were vulnerable to death or displacement.[1]

Despite these adjustments and the excitement generated by the Reform movement in the kingdom at large, there was no change in Cardiganshire, the 'ultima Thule' of registration, at the ensuing election. The county had last polled in 1741, the boroughs in 1812. The sitting Members were returned unopposed – Powell of Nanteos for the county, and Pryse of Gogerddan for the boroughs. Both had voted for Reform, Pryse, the avowed Whig, more assiduously than the Tory Powell. Neither could afford the expense of a contest and both relied on the compromise operating since 1816, when they had 'tossed up' for succession to the county on the vacancy left by Thomas Johnes of Hafod.[2] Having succeeded Johnes as Lord Lieutenant, without the baronetcy he craved,

*The valuable advice and information given to the writer by Emeritus Professor Ieuan Gwynedd Jones, Dr Margaret Escott, Mr John Graham Jones and Dr Matthew Cragoe are gratefully acknowledged, as is the ready assistance offered by the staff of the National Library of Wales and John Owen, formerly Dyfed Archivist, Carmarthen. In the footnotes, references from Hansard's *Parliamentary Debates* have been omitted insofar as they relate to speeches, dates for which are supplied in the text. References to legislation concerning Cardiganshire are taken from T. I. Jeffreys Jones, *Acts of Parliament concerning Wales 1714–1901* (Cardiff, 1959), and are not specified in the footnotes.

[1] *PP* (1831–2) XLI, 23–42; (1834) IX, 593, 641; (1835) XXIII(1), 200; *Salopian Journal*, 20 June 1832, quoting *John Bull*.
[2] *A Key to Both Houses of Parliament* (London, 1832), p.308, quoting *The Spectator*, 1 January 1831; R. J. Colyer, 'The Pryse family of Gogerddan and the decline of a great estate, 1800–1960', *WHR*, 9, no.4 (1979), 407–31; idem, 'Nanteos: a landed estate in decline, 1800–1930', *Ceredigion*, IX, no.1 (1980), 58–77.

Powell had abetted Pryse's return for the boroughs since 1818, when he nudged out the impecunious John Vaughan of Trawsgoed, who, as third Earl of Lisburne, was the effective guarantor of the deal. Thus, neither seat was contested until 1841, when the boroughs were polled, and subsequently in 1849, 1852 and 1855. The county, uncontested until 1859, was polled successively to 1885, while the boroughs remained uncontested.

Contests alone did not chart political activity. As of old, it was usual to frighten sitting Members when elections loomed. In 1832 it was reported that David Arthur Saunders Davies of Pentre and Moelifor had turned alarmist about Reform during Pembrokeshire's 1831 elections and would challenge Powell; and an 'Orange' opposition to Pryse was rumoured.[3] In 1835, when Powell promised conditional support of retrenchment and reform, a candidate 'of more decided reform principles' was threatened, if not two, 'one from the upper and the other from the lower part of the county'. Pryse, too, was troubled by 'a constant resident' of comparable Whig principles, assisted by 'a talented solicitor', who had 'swept some scores' of Pryse's 'favourite burgesses of a packed corporation' off the Aberystwyth register. In 1830 Edward Lloyd Williams of Gwernant had offered to oppose Pryse, but now no challenge materialized. Pryse's heir represented him at the election, owing to his illness.[4] On 4 March he penned a letter, printed in *The Welshman* at Carmarthen (there was no Cardiganshire newspaper at that time), deploring his inclusion in the London *Morning Chronicle*'s list of members who had 'played false' to reform and missed recent divisions: he would soon resume his post.[5] Even so, he was harassed again that year when, on Peel's failure to secure a working majority as Tory premier, the Whigs returned to power under Melbourne. This resuscitated election fever. Pryse was told of attempts to supplant his interests in Cardigan and Aberystwyth: 'the first offer made was to Captain Brigstocke of Blaenpant', but John Jones (the former Tory Member for Carmarthen, destined to sit for Carmarthenshire in the next Parliament) 'was the entire object of the party'. This plot would not 'keep you out of one of the two seats . . . the county would be yours with ease though many of your friends would not like to see Mr Powell turned out, but the Dissenters would do the trick and punish him for all his friendly votes against that body. Do cultivate the friendship of Crosswood, by so doing you will keep the squad in order.'[6]

Powell had unsuccessfully applied to Peel for a peerage after his election, among other fanciful claims suggesting that, on his vacating, 'Conservative members would be returned for the County and Boroughs'. Now, however, he carefully pledged support for Pryse, who was urged to attend to registration, as 'there is pretty work going on at Lampeter headed by the head and tail of the College and assisted by Griffith Jenkins [agent to the Harford family of Falcondale, who had inherited the interest in Lampeter of Richard Hart Davis of Peterwell]'. Pryse was advised to woo Herbert Evans of Highmead, the Peterwell candidate in 1812, who had resisted the pressure of these immigrant gentry to stand again.[7] By August 1835 Pryse was assured that John Jones 'had not the most distant idea of opposing you', and that Aberystwyth was his, two to one, though 'we don't ask

---

[3] *The Welshman*, 31 May, 21 September, 21 December 1832, 6 January 1833; *Carmarthen Journal*, 14 September, 7 December 1832.
[4] *Carmarthen Journal*, 9 and 16 January 1835; *The Welshman*, 2, 9 and 16 January 1835; *Caernarvon Herald*, 3 January 1835; *The Times*, 3 and 6 January 1835.
[5] *The Welshman*, 6 March 1835.
[6] NLW, Gogerddan MSS box 72, J. Morse to Pryse, 7 August 1835.
[7] Ibid., R. Lloyd to Pryse, 4 July, Morse to same, 6 August 1835; BL Add MSS 40410, ff.174, 176, Powell to Peel, 16 January and reply, 19 January 1835.

the shopkeepers to sign a paper lest it damage them with the Tory gentry here'.[8] Yet, at a select dinner to celebrate the passage of the Municipal Reform Act on 22 September, fifty-four bipartisan guests toasted the Ultra-Tory fourth Duke of Newcastle, who was cultivating the town, following his acquisition of the Hafod estate (which he was to sell in 1846). James Melvin, who championed Pryse in letters to *The Welshman*, claimed most of the town's Tories were Nanteos tenants, and that the reformers should prevail. Pryse himself believed that James Hughes of Glanrheidol, both mayor and Nanteos agent, was 'quite as anxious to keep the corporation in their own power as . . . Job [Sheldon] did'. He bestowed a church clock on Cardigan to sustain his interest.[9]

In 1837 there was 'no appearance of a contest' for the county against Powell, 'the Conservative Member'. Pryse, not as secure, remained at Westminster to the last, and the opposition he had feared evaporated. He had no wish to stand for the county in view of Tory strength, to which the 4th Earl of Lisburne had been tentatively added following his marriage. Pryse was reluctant to provoke Lisburne's return for the county (as an Irish peer, he could sit in the Commons). Oliver Lloyd, Pryse's solicitor and ally, calculated that the support of an electorate of 1,829 in the county would cost £1,200, including five-shilling dinners for 1,000 voters: 'The Dissenters ought all to be with us and must be a formidable body if they act together, but perhaps many of them would be forced to obey the orders of the higher powers.' Pryse's heir, likewise, abstained from standing for Berkshire. Saunders Davies, named to Pryse as his opponent for the boroughs, denied that any secret canvass was pending, and another challenger, Lord Lincoln, the Duke of Newcastle's heir, was ruled out by Pryse's son, who canvassed for his father on the grounds that the Duke 'does not pay his bills, and his boasted ten thousand for the [Aberystwyth] harbour is not forthcoming'. The Pryses's friend, Gilbertson of Cefn-gwyn, advised their insisting on Powell's open support, if he wished to avert a challenge from Pryse for the county. Pryse, however, suspected that Saunders Davies's name had been a front to propel Powell's heir, William, now of age, into the boroughs seat. In many ways, therefore, the Powell-Pryse pact was dissolving, though Powell was subsequently careful to deny that he had permitted his tenants to be canvassed by Pryse's opponents.[10]

Neither Powell nor Pryse figured significantly in Parliament, though some activity was mandatory. They were involved in the Cardiganshire roads improvement bill, which was passed on 6 May 1833. In that age of petitions, they had several to present from their constituents: from Aberystwyth came a petition to restrict sale of beer and fortify the flagging spirits of the Church on 6 May 1833, to improve town amenities on 20 February 1834 (presented, however, by Lord Lincoln), to oppose raising timber duties, from shipowners on 23 July 1834, and for a bill to improve the harbour on 16 February 1836. This, like the town improvement, was enacted a year after a similar measure for New Quay, which also acquired a new road to Aberaeron. Other petitions on 15 and 18 April and 8 May 1834 from the county at large were for Lord's Day observance and the relief of Protestant Dissenters, the latter from Baptists and Congregationalists. As was the case before 1832,

[8]Gogerddan MSS box 72, J. Miller to Pryse, 9 August 1835.
[9]*The Welshman*, 25 September, 2, 9, and 16 October, 27 November, 18 December 1835; R. J. Colyer, 'The Hafod Estate under Thomas Johnes and Henry Pelham, Fourth Duke of Newcastle', *WHR*, 8, no.3 (1977), 276–84; NLW, Highmead MSS 3183, Pryse to Evans, 13 December 1836.
[10]*The Times*, 11 and 19 July 1837; Gogerddan MSS box 72, Pryse to Lady Lisburne, 21 June [1837], with reference to reports in *The Welshman* and the *Carmarthen Journal*; Highmead MSS 3219, Pryse to Evans, 18 July, 3220, Wednesday, 3223, 21 July, 3221, Monday [25 July?], 3222, Sunday [1837]; Carmarthen RO, Coedmore MSS, D/LL/1073, Powell to Thomas Lloyd, 20 September 1839.

Pryse supported the Whigs and Powell the Tories, unless local pressures neutralized them. Pryse, for instance, patronized Dissenters, but was anxious to display his support for the Church, if reformed, and he contributed to churches such as those at Lampeter and Aberaeron.[11]

Long before the 1841 election, Pryse, who was dividing his time between Gogerddan and Buscot, was warned of a likely contest. Matthew Davies Williams of Cwmcynfelyn, informed him on 21 June 1839 that his opponent would be John Scandrett Harford of Falcondale, whose 'staunch Conservative principles' Williams could not but support, provided Harford was confident of success. In reply, Pryse shrugged off a stranger to the constituency he had represented for twenty-one years, but was soon alerted to canvassing on Harford's behalf at Cardigan and Newcastle Emlyn, though he was relieved to gather that neither Cawdor nor Morgan Jones, Cilwendeg, would interfere, and that his friends had resisted a feebly supported requisition to Harford, launched at Cardigan. Harford's readiness was in question, but Highmead seemed disinclined to obstruct him, and at Lampeter he could count on the College, of which he was Treasurer. Pryse, who had neglected registration, relied on the support of Lloyd of Coedmor in the south, and felt safe at Aberystwyth. When reports reached Pryse on 24 June 1839 that Harford's requisition bore forty-four Lampeter names, he was told it was 'on account of your politics, and also because they never see you amongst them. They are dissatisfied with [Powell], because he never visits them and they go so far as to say they would be glad to see him out too'. Lloyd wrote to Powell to deplore the threat to the *status quo*, 'with my opinion that all things remaining as they are will be the wisest plan'.[12] Pryse wrote to Highmead on 28 August, decrying 'various squibs' in *The Welshman*, doubting whether 'Alderbrook' [Edward Lloyd Williams] would prove a strong contender, and voicing his concerns about registration: his agents 'could get no view of the books at Lampeter', so objections were served on Pryse's electoral foes. James Hughes was returning this compliment at Aberystwyth, and others at Cardigan.[13]

In 1841 Powell was returned unopposed: 'the whole affair went off dull as ditchwater', reported *The Welshman*. Powell relied on 'the master mind of Sir Robert Peel' to lead the Conservatives to victory, and regretted that 'a paramount sense of personal honour' prevented him from supporting, in the boroughs election, the agricultural protectionist cause for which he had voted.[14] An undated parody of his election addresses takes a dim view of all of them, appealing to 'the deluded freeholders of the county of C-', and concluding 'Your ambitious slave, Poverty Placeman'.[15]

While Powell courted ridicule, Pryse was frustrated by chicanery. In his address on 15 June he acknowledged opposition from Lieutenant Colonel Francis Copland, who opposed the new Poor Law and military flogging, but predicted that Harford would be his eventual opponent. Although 'honoured with such earnest applications', Harford was still hesitating, but in his address on the eighteenth accepted the requisition to him to be the Conservative candidate and he retained 'friendly feelings' towards Pryse. He nevertheless canvassed Aberystwyth personally. 'An Elector', in a handbill to Cardigan voters, stressed Pryse's superior merits, not least his local benefactions; Harford had taken away their Commons, 'depriving the corporation of the only funds they possess',

---

[11]*Mirror of Parliament* (1833–1837), as dated; Highmead MSS 3183, Pryse to Evans, 13 December 1836.

[12]'Gogerddan MSS box 85, bundle of letters, 'Cardigan borough election'.

[13]Highmead MSS 3185, Pryse to Evans, 28 August 1839.

[14]*Carmarthen Journal*, 18 June 1841; *The Welshman*, 9 July 1841; *The Times*, 12 July 1841.

[15]Gogerddan MSS box 72, 'A parody on a certain address' [no date].

and was characterized as an Ultra Tory. Harford complained in a second address on 25 June of 'misrepresentations of my principles and opinions'. At his nomination, Pryse's seconder conceded his 'want of eloquence' in Parliament, but commended his undeviating support for civil and religious liberty, and, unlike Harford, his readiness to spend his Welsh income in Wales. Saunders Davies, proposing Harford, emphasized the feebleness of the Whig ministry, but supplied local credentials for Harford, who had endowed 'that classic pile', St David's College, Lampeter, and served as sheriff. Pryse added his support for retrenchment and abolition of slavery to what had been said on his behalf. Conceding Pryse's local prestige, Harford stood 'on public principle': ministers were allied with O'Connell and Popery. He was a Protectionist, and a friend of Wilberforce. When the show of hands favoured Pryse, Saunders Davies demanded a poll. Without Aberystwyth, Harford led by 226 to 163 (he was 69 ahead in Cardigan, 16 in Lampeter, and 22 behind Pryse in Atpar). Eventually the 142 votes cast for Pryse in Aberystwyth (as opposed to 59 against) gave him an overall lead of twenty, but at Cardigan the mayor never received the Aberystwyth poll books and, acting against Saunders Davies's advice, he returned both candidates to Westminster, where an election committee would adjudicate.

Harford maintained that he would not obstruct Pryse if the election were declared void, but he reserved his right to petition on other grounds. He blamed disunity for his defeat: the Tory *Carmarthen Journal* had warned him against 'neutrality and defection', and Harford believed that Pryse's success in overcoming Highmead's neutrality was decisive. At a dinner for Harford given by Lisburne on 12 July, he received a letter promising future support signed by eighty gentlemen and tradesmen from Aberystwyth. It was alleged that the Baptists had maligned him and that Cawdor's support was flouted by ten of his tenants who had voted for Pryse. While £100 was offered for discovery of the poll books, Pryse, chaired at Aberystwyth, toasted the '142 Light Blues'. Harford was said to be disgusted by the conduct of his 'flowers' in stealing the books. There had been two booths in Aberystwyth – in the Baptist chapel and in the yard of the Belle Vue Inn – where Harford's friends met.[16]

Cardigan's mayor, having reported the election to London papers, called a meeting in the Black Lion on 26 July to investigate the missing poll books. There, Edward Crompton Lloyd Hall, the radical barrister who was often referred to as the 'O'Connell of Wales', charged William Simons of Carmarthen and John Lloyd of Lampeter, solicitors, with felony, and others with being accessories by insisting on Harford's return. Thereupon up to thirty Conservatives remonstrated, and Hall was rebuked by Saunders Davies, who doubted whether Pryse had authorized accusations against the gentry: 'we will sink or swim together'. Despite Pryse's friends' dissuasions, Hall persisted, but the evidence was inconclusive, and Mayor Brown dismissed Hall's charge and rejected his impeachment of the Teifiside gentry.[17] Writing to the *Carmarthen Journal*, Hall protested against the account published on 31 July, and later approved that given in *The Welshman* on 6 August.[18]

[16] *Carmarthen Journal*, 11, 18 and 25 June, 2, 9, 16, 23 and 30 July 1841; *The Welshman*, 18 and 25 June, 2, 9, 16 and 30 July 1841; A. Harford, *Annals of the Harford Family* (London, 1909), p.113; Highmead MSS 2304, Harford to Mrs Evans, 15 June 1841; 3170, 'An elector' to the electors of Cardigan, no date; 3169, Harford's second address, 25 June 1841.

[17] *Carmarthen Journal*, 30 July 1841 (copied by *The Times*, 4 August); D. Williams, *The Rebecca Riots* (Cardiff, 1971), pp.14–16.

[18] *Carmarthen Journal*, 6, 20 and 27 August, 3 and 10 September 1841; *The Welshman*, 6 August 1841.

Pryse subsequently reported that Harford wanted him to 'sign something to the effect that I did not authorize Hall to charge the flowers with conspiracy. I certainly did not, nor as he had no proof ought he to have done so'. Pryse informed Harford, who was in London, that he would sign nothing without consulting his friends, and was satisfied that Harford would not impede his return, being unlikely to find any other grounds for petitioning.[19] Pryse's petition was referred to committee on 6 February 1842, and after some delay he was declared duly elected on 18 April.[20] The poll book prank allegedly cost him £1,500. Gogerddan election bills were hefty, for they included refreshments, addresses (600 in Welsh), billposting, transporting voters, and 'valuing up' houses in Aberystwyth, but most were settled in 1843.[21] Re-entering the House, Pryse opposed Peel's government as cordially as Powell supported it. In the previous Parliament, Powell had presented several petitions, notably against repealing the Corn Laws on 3 June 1839, and on 2 August he had ventured to promise that his militia was ready for service at four months' notice. In the ensuing Parliament, the Cardigan market bill of 1843 was the only legislation of local interest, but thirty-four petitions were sent from Aberystwyth in protest against the mines and factory workers' education bill because of its Anglican bias. The Rebecca riots, which affected Teifiside, left north Cardiganshire unperturbed, though Powell believed that it only 'seemed quiet' and, like the inhabitants of Aberystwyth, he opposed troop withdrawal until local police were established in 1844. For his part, Pryse led the opposition to their advent.[22]

Following the Conservative split over repeal of the Corn Laws, which Powell voted against, the Whigs returned to power. The 1847 elections were uncontested in Cardiganshire. In May no opposition to Powell was anticipated unless Pryse switched to the county, 'the Dissenting interest being very strong'. This switch was likely if he was opposed by a Conservative for the boroughs, such as Lisburne, or a nephew of Harford's. *The Welshman* believed that Pryse's opponent would be 'one of the Messrs Gower' and predicted a 'tight contest' if Abel Lewes Gower of Castell Maelgwyn stood.[23] Having offered for Carmarthenshire, Saunders Davies was not likely to stand. Powell, in his address on 12 July, glossed over the split in his party, while Pryse was slow to start. An opportunist named Rugge sought to take advantage of this by offering his candidature on a radical platform, but he was obstructed by Pryse's address. Pryse missed the election, his heir deputizing for him, because a younger son was dangerously ill. Powell chaired 'girt with the sword', was listed a Protectionist (not a Peelite) by *The Times*, and Pryse a Liberal.[24]

Following Pryse's death in January 1849, his heir, shortly to change his surname to Loveden, would not at first stand. An *englyn* to his father, however, expressed the wish that he might succeed him: 'Aelod Cymru fu hyd fedd . . . A boed ei fab hyd y fedd yn ei ol Yn aelod o'r Senedd.' (A Member for Wales to his grave . . . May his son after him be Member of Parliament until his grave.) William Williams, former Member for Coventry, and sometimes referred to as the 'Member for

[19] Highmead MSS 3168, Pryse to Evans, 31 August 1841.
[20] *Commons Journals*, XCVII (1842), 36, 180, 181, 185, 187, 189, 194, 198, 201, 203, 215; *The Times*, 12 and 18 April 1842.
[21] *The Welshman*, 19 January 1849; Gogerddan MSS box 72, 1841 election accounts.
[22] *Mirror of Parliament* (1837–1838), pp.2025, 2979; (1839) 2625, 2806, 4648; Hansard (ser. 3), LXVII, 116, 350, 1285; Nanteos MSS L 1360; Williams, *Rebecca Riots*, pp.11, 61, 153, 283.
[23] *The Times*, 10 and 17 May 1847.
[24] Nanteos MSS box 20, Powell's address; *Carmarthen Journal*, 16, 23 and 30 July, 6 and 13 August 1847; *The Times*, 3, 13 and 16 August 1847.

Wales', was mentioned in Aberystwyth as the best hope for the Liberals, and for the Tories, a Harford, or Colonel William Henry Lewis, Clynfiew. In the event, when the Conservative caucus chose John Scandrett Harford at their meeting in Aberaeron on 11 January (Lewis was to be his proposer), the Liberals were dismayed. The report that George Lawrence Vaughan would offer for them was not encouraging, given his brother Lisburne's contrary politics. Williams was more acceptable, and some Dissenters hoped to induce Edward Miall, editor of *The Nonconformist*, to stand. Pryse junior eventually saved the situation by relenting, but his tardiness cost him votes. George Vaughan, 'the first person' to ask Pryse to reconsider, had signed a subscription for him, but then told Pryse of a deputation to himself to stand as a Russellite Whig. Pryse offered support, provided Lloyd Coedmor, to whom he was pledged, abstained; he also believed that Lloyd of Bronwydd, might offer, but, being 'always a great man with the Tories', he would surely not support the ballot, as Pryse did. Having heard of Pryse's decision to stand, Vaughan admitted his distaste for such 'Ultra Radical' measures, though Pryse reminded him of his former support for the ballot, and held him to his recent pledge. Lisburne, regretting their political differences when Pryse approached him, chaired Harford's friends, and Powell openly joined them. Pryse won the show of hands, but his poll majority was only eight. Contemporary analysis (no poll books survive) gave him 28 at Cardigan, 182 (Aberystwyth), 49 (Lampeter) and 40 (Atpar) to Harford's 120, 71, 78 and 22 respectively.

The property interest of Harford's relative Philip John Miles outmatched the late Member's expenditure at Cardigan. Principal Lewellin of Lampeter was staunch for Harford, who was also supported by Lloyd, Hall and Beynon at Atpar. Hall objected to Coedmor's coercion of tenants, but himself discharged Cilgwyn employees voting for Pryse. Yet, to quote David Rice's 'poem':

> This Bristol Town Tori shall tarey no more
> About Aberystwyth to beg and implore
> Where the merits of Calvin conducted the van
> And made our member a Parliament man.

Another versifier, John Emlyn Jones of the 'Principality Office', sent Pryse a tribute to 'your success over the enemies of freedom and reform'. A mob broke windows at Aberystwyth on election night. While denying hostility to Dissenters, Harford was strongly anti-Catholic. The bilingual Pryse was chaired in all four boroughs on successive days. His 'Blues', deriding the 'Red' majority at Cardigan as 'slaves driven to the poll', advocated the secret ballot.[25]

Pryse lost no time in taking his seat.[26] He spoke on 1 March against the omission of Welsh representation on the Irish poor law committee. Like his father, he voted with the Liberals, but spoke only twice more, as 'Mr Loveden' on 7 and 10 June 1852, in defence of St David's College, Lampeter, whose detractors wished to deprive it of state subsidy. At the 1852 election, with Powell unchallenged, Pryse Loveden was opposed by John Inglis Jones of Derry Ormond, a Tory follower

[25] *The Welshman*, 5, 12, 19 and 26 January, 2, 9, 16 and 23 February, 23 March 1849; *The Times*, 11, 19 and 20 January, 13 February 1849; Carmarthen RO, Aberglasney MSS box 30, G. Vaughan to Pryse, 9 January and copy reply, Wednesday; 13 January and reply Saturday night; Lisburne to Pryse, 14 January 1849; R. J. Colyer, 'The gentry and the county in nineteenth-century Cardiganshire', *WHR*, 10, no.4 (1981), 514–15; F. Jones, 'Cardiganshire election songs' (taken from Aberglasney MSS box 30), *Ceredigion*, VI, no.1 (1964), 46; Gogerddan MSS box 72, J. E. Jones to Pryse, 17 February 1849.
[26] *The Welshman*, 2 March 1849.

of Lord Derby. He was well supported in Cardigan, and won the show of hands, but Loveden's strength in Aberystwyth secured him victory, as had been the case in 1849.[27] Loveden was angry to be told that fourteen tenants at Nanteos, Moelcerni and Penglais had been evicted for voting for him, while Jones, an officer in the Horse Guards, had served as sheriff of Cardiganshire for months when he was requisitioned by fifty-three Conservatives, headed by the Principal of St David's College, Lampeter, to champion them against 'that fearful and swelling tide of democratic licence'. If elected, Jones would have had to refer his case to the Home Secretary.[28]

Powell resigned the county seat in February 1854 and died two months later. Cardiganshire's political stalemate lingered on, for he was replaced unopposed by Ernest Augustus, fourth Earl of Lisburne, whose prominent patronage of Toryism, and Loveden's neutrality, ensured him the seat. He gave silent support, as a surviving party whip of 28 February 1857 attests.[29] Loveden, who had voted for the ballot in 1853, but was silent in that Parliament, died on 1 February 1855. His only son, later Sir Pryse, was a schoolboy. The Liberals fielded an outsider, John Evans QC, Member for his native Haverfordwest in the 1847 Parliament, and son of a Congregationalist minister. He was narrowly defeated by John Lloyd Davies (1801–60) of Blaendyffryn, who had married the widowed Lloyd heiress of Alltyrodyn. A native of Aberystwyth and a self-made man, Davies was a shrewd solicitor. Although he was a Conservative churchman and an opponent of Rebecca, he promoted the Carmarthen–Llandysul Railway and was counted among the more 'notable' and 'eminent' natives of the county.

Davies ended the near silence of Cardiganshire Members at Westminster. On 20 March 1855 he read a Welsh clergyman's letter opposing the Sunday opening of London museums and galleries. In opposing the church rates abolition bill on 29 March, he suggested the imposition of a rent charge on land, since pew rents were unknown in his region, and on 16 May he doubted the adequacy of voluntary contribution. He also advised a government bill instead of a private one, which had the effect of placating Nonconformist opinion but alienating the Church, and which in any case had no relevance to Wales. He opposed exemption of the lower classes from taxation on 27 April, and on 8 June voiced criticisms of Russia over the Crimean War, and deplored 'any factious vote against the government'. He objected to exemption of Jews from the Sunday trading (London) bill on 13 June and explained why military recruiting was weak in mining areas on 13 July. On 26 July he paid tribute to the work of the British and Foreign Bible Society in his locality and supported a grant to them. On 5 February 1856 he withdrew a bill exempting Nonconformists from church rates if they contributed to a chapel. His proposal, on 12 February, that Cardigan be designated a safer harbour of refuge than Milford Haven, was defeated by twenty-six votes. On 4 April, the day after he had championed abolition of criminal transportation, he obtained assurances that Lampeter College was not to be moved to Brecon. In June he advocated public economy on several occasions. On 12 February 1857 he obtained leave for a bill standardizing weights and measures (having failed to secure a government-sponsored one on 6 February) but dissolution intervened. He clashed with Cobden, whose motion hostile to Palmerston's gunboat diplomacy defeated the government on 26 February.

[27] *The Times*, 21 and 23 June, 12 July 1852.
[28] Colyer, 'Gentry and county', 515; NLW, Derry Ormond MSS 307, 308a.
[29] Aberglasney MSS box 30, Lisburne to Pryse Loveden, 18 December 1853; NLW, Crosswood (Trawsgoed) MSS, III, 112, Disraeli to Lisburne, 28 February 1857.

Davies did not stand at the 1857 election, when the Gogerddan interest in the boroughs was revived by Edward Lewis Pryse of Peithyll, brother of the late Member, who was returned unopposed. Thomas Davies Lloyd, squire of Bronwydd, had been suggested as the Liberal candidate, and Davies might have defended his seat had he stood. At any rate, Pryse, a 'thorough Liberal', with a strong family tradition behind him, was an ideal candidate. Ironically, Pryse, like Davies, supported Palmerston's foreign policy, which Lisburne opposed. Despite fair prospects, no Liberal opponent to Lisburne materialized.[30] A Liberal 'Elector', certain that the Gogerddan, Hafod and Bronwydd tenants could secure Lloyd, sought a requisition to Bronwydd on 9 March, but the latter would not face the expense.[31]

Such was the background to the county election of 1859 on Palmerston's return to power. The 'advanced Liberal' Pryse was secure in the boroughs: he was now Lord Lieutenant, and had curried favour by bestowing a clock worth £300 on Aberystwyth. His nephew Pryse had just come of age, amid celebrations which hinted that an endless line of Pryses lay in store.[32] The county was open because Lisburne had retired. There were two Conservative contenders: Major Powell of Nanteos, heir to the former Member, and Arthur Henry Saunders Davies, who was chosen at Aberaeron. Powell refused to yield, or to submit to Carlton Club adjudication. No Liberal candidate emerged, much to the outrage of such Welsh-language newspapers as *Yr Amserau* (Liverpool) and *Baner Cymru*. Cardiganshire correspondents encouraged their fulminations. *Baner Cymru* contrasted Cardiganshire's spiritual alertness, amidst a well-orchestrated religious revival of North American inspiration, with its political inertia. Of the two Tories, it preferred Saunders Davies, for Powell was sponsored by John Lloyd Davies, 'y Tori mwyaf yn y Sir' (the greatest Tory in the County). In Merioneth there was an exciting contest, with landlords exerting fierce pressure on tenants to defeat the Liberals. Both Cardiganshire candidates wooed Gogerddan, but young Pryse insisted on neutrality, despite Powell's superior county claims. Saunders Davies won the show of hands at Cardigan on 2 May, but Powell won the election. The district polls reveal the split between north and south, even though Lisburne supported Saunders Davies. Powell's supporters numbered as follows: Cardigan (105), Lampeter (160), Tregaron (198), Aberystwyth (607), while those for Saunders Davies were 528, 176, 55 and 169 respectively. *Yr Amserau* was informed that the Liberals had sought to persuade Gogerddan and Bronwydd, the Reform Club and the Liberation Society in London in their unavailing search for a candidate. A letter from 'Ultra Liberal' on 12 July commiserated with them on having to decide which of the two Tories was the more Liberal. Powell, who cunningly called himself Liberal Conservative, deceived them: he voted with Lord Derby. The writer ended with the resonant slogan – *Trech gwlad nac arglwydd* (A country is mightier than a lord) – and a week later advised all Nonconformists to register as electors. On 3 August 'D. D. Glanwyre' advocated a well-organized Liberal campaign,[33] while an emigrant to Ballarat, Dewi o'r Ddôl, penned a vigorous protest:

> Yn Mrydain nid oes gan y Werin bleidleisiau
> I anfon i'r Senedd, y dyn farnont orau.

[30] *The Times*, 9, 16, 18, 24, 28 and 30 March, 3 April 1857.
[31] NLW MSS 3291E, unnumbered poster, 9 March 1857.
[32] *Baner Cymru*, 19 January 1859.
[33] *Yr Amserau*, 27 April, 11 and 25 May, 6 and 13 July, 3 August 1859; *Baner Cymru*, 13, 20 and 27 April, 4 and 11 May 1859; *The Times*, 11, 18, 21 and 30 April, 3 and 7 May 1859.

Ond yma mae pawb sydd mewn oedran a synwyr
A hawl i'r gofrestri ymhlith yr Etholwyr . . .
Mae'r Werin yn teimlo fod ganddynt Iawnderau.[34]

(In Britain the People have no votes to send the man they judge best to Parliament. But here everyone of age and sense is properly registered among the Electors . . . The People feel they have Rights.)

The 1865 election followed Lord John Russell's failure to extend the franchise, which ushered in Derby's Conservative ministry. This time two Liberals contested the county seat. Pryse, now a knight, was returned unchallenged for the boroughs. Neither Pryse nor Powell had figured in debate. In August 1864 the ailing Powell, confined to a Bath chair, was not expected to stand again. In October 1863 he had assured Pryse that his parliamentary duties (not his health) hindered his militia obligations, but later that year he gave his health (not his pocket) as his reason for declining another contest. The Liberals counted on Lloyd of Bronwydd, now a baronet, as their candidate. A few weeks before the dissolution, however, Powell chose to offer again, and Lloyd withdrew. There were two offers from prospective Liberal substitutes. One was from Henry Richard, a native of Tregaron, but now living in London. Richard was an advocate of international peace by arbitration and educational improvement; he was also a commentator on Welsh affairs and had been a delegate to the conference of the Liberation Society at Swansea in 1862 to promote better Welsh representation in Parliament. The other candidate was David Davies of Llandinam, a self-made railway king and South Wales colliery proprietor, and a Presbyterian deacon. Richard, a former Congregationalist minister, was the son of a Calvinistic Methodist. A meeting to choose between them was arranged at Aberaeron for 6 July, but Powell announced his withdrawal beforehand. Lloyd of Bronwydd bounced back at once; solidly pro-Palmerston, he was in favour of the abolition of church rates, was opposed to the ballot, but favoured 'moderate extension of the suffrage to the working classes'. Richard withdrew in order to avoid splitting the Liberals, but Davies persisted. Styled a radical by the Tories, he lost the election in 1865. The distribution of votes was as follows: for Lloyd, Cardigan 360, Aberaeron 299, Lampeter 94, Tregaron 96, Llandysul 200, Aberystwyth 461; for Davies, 65, 215, 126, 290, 63 and 390 respectively.

Conservative disarray had denied them a candidate. In 1864 Inglis Jones, Colonel Lewes of Llanllŷr, Saunders Davies, John Battersby Harford and Howell Gwyn of Neath had all been reckoned possible substitutes for Powell. So had Lord Vaughan, though his father, Lisburne, had given no lead. Davies's defeat was clearly due to gentry assistance to Lloyd. Writing to *The Times* on 22 July, Davies decried a 'compact' between Powell and Lloyd, and also noted Gogerddan hostility towards him. In Lampeter and Tregaron he did rather better, largely because of his projected Lampeter–Aberaeron railway. Henry Richard had been more diplomatic; he had consulted Gogerddan, sounded the towns, and approached Lloyd before withdrawing (as advised by the Aberaeron meeting). Davies had sent two emissaries to the Aberystwyth house of Matthews, the Liberal factotum, at the very time Richard's agents were there! What clinched matters for Davies was his declaration at Aberaeron that he would oppose either Powell or Lloyd. Powell could ill afford a contest, while Davies had deposited £10,000 in an Aberystwyth bank. At the nomination,

[34]NLW MSS 3291E/24 (John Jones (Ivon) MSS).

Fig. 111: A portrait of Henry Richard (1812–1888) by Felix Moscheles. (*Copyright National Library of Wales*).

Davies's investment potential was emphasized by his proposer, and he boasted of over 3,000 employees. In the event, he spent less than Lloyd during the election.[35]

It has justly been remarked that Davies's candidature 'cracked the ice', thereby ending what he called in his *Times* letter 'a private arrangement between a few landowners of opposite politics'. Populist Liberals, not satisfied with nominal command of both seats, still sought fitter representatives. Davies claimed he owed much to Nonconformist support, and Richard, who was sure of it, regretted his withdrawal. Yet Nonconformists in the county were barely politicized; Lloyd complained that his wife was traduced from their pulpits as a Roman Catholic. Several ministers opposed Davies, and leading members of Tabernacl church, Aberystwyth, on lease from Nanteos, feared trouble if they openly supported the Liberals. Nevertheless, the Liberals, and the Liberation Society, scantily funded from Cardiganshire, continued to support the chapels. The Society's local agent, Thomas Harri(e)s of Llechryd, was active in promoting registration. An unsuccessful plan to float a rival newspaper to the Tory *Aberystwyth Observer* was launched by the Revd James Kilsby Jones, author of a classic Welsh essay on the 1865 elections in Cardiganshire and Merioneth. He

[35]Nanteos MSS L 1646, W. T. R. Powell to R. D. Jenkins, draft, 21 December 1863; L 1677–1680, W. T. R. Powell to E. L. Pryse, correspondence, 14 and 19 October 1863; I. G. Jones, 'The Liberation Society and Welsh politics, 1844–1868', *WHR*, 1, no.2 (1961), 193 et seq; idem, 'The elections of 1865 and 1868 in Wales, with special reference to Cardiganshire and Merthyr Tydfil', *THSC* (1964), 41–68; idem, 'Cardiganshire politics in the mid-nineteenth century', *Ceredigion* V, no.1 (1964), 14–35.

also tried to start a Welsh Land Freehold Society with barely concealed political aims. The second Reform Act of 1867, a Tory measure, was acceptable both to Pryse and Lloyd, neither of whom supported Gladstone's bid to amend it. The Act made a considerable difference: in 1865, of 3,520 county electors, 56 per cent were freeholder, 20 per cent leaseholder and 23 per cent tenant/occupier votes. The 1867 Act created 5,123 electors, one-fifth of them the newly enfranchised £12 occupiers. In the boroughs, thanks to a householder ratepayers' franchise, the electorate rose from 692 to 1,561. The Reform League had an Aberystwyth branch, one of thirteen in Wales, and meetings were held at New Quay and at radical Llechryd.[36]

The county seat was therefore wide open in 1868. At Aberaeron on 19 May the Tories adopted Edmund Malet Vaughan, nephew of Lisburne, aged twenty-six, as candidate. On the same day at Cardigan, the Liberals learned that Pryse was ready to withdraw for another Liberal. Lloyd of Bronwydd, fearful of another contest, seized his opportunity. Pryse retired in his favour on 26 May, and Nanteos backing ensured a quiet election. Although a churchman, Lloyd had supported the abolition of church rates. On 7 March 1866 he noted that Nonconformists occupied 70 per cent of the religious space in Cardiganshire, with 192 chapels as opposed to 68 churches; the abolition of church rates, he believed, would promote Protestant solidarity. On 22 February 1867 he exposed the 'defective sanitary conditions of Wales' and on 27 May he agreed to the £12 franchise, though he believed £10 was more appropriate. On 4 July he approved outlawing pubs for election purposes, even though most of his expenses had been incurred in them. He supported Gladstone's bid to disestablish the Irish Church in 1868, though he maintained that the Church in Wales was unassailable. He also corresponded with Gladstone; on 23 December 1865, for instance, he informed him that rinderpest threatened ruin to 'a pastoral people, mainly depending upon our flocks and herds'. In reply, Gladstone offered five reasons why he was unable to advocate state support for a cattle insurance society in west Wales.[37]

The Liberal candidature for the county in 1868 was problematic. Henry Richard had been adopted at Merthyr Tydfil. David Davies found Gogerddan implacably hostile, and a runner acceptable to the Pryses had to be found. Although William Owen Brigstocke was the local favourite, and 'young Mr [John] Roberts of Liverpool' was suggested by Harris of Llechryd, to whom Thomas Gee had first recommended Richard Davies (the successful candidate in Anglesey), the person adopted was Evan Matthew Richards of Brooklands, Swansea, a lead and silverworks master and shipbuilder. His industrial wealth and expertise were expected to commend him to the people of Cardiganshire, especially at a time when lead mines were faltering. He was a 'particular friend' of Chambers, Hafod, and was approved of by Henry Richard. His business partner, Lewis Dillwyn MP, lobbied Gogerddan on his behalf, as did the Liberal caucus in Aberystwyth. Richards addressed the electors on 18 August, and the Pryses openly supported his canvass. Styled an 'advanced Liberal', he was a self-made Baptist, careful not to espouse the Liberation Society creed

[36]The Times, 1, 7, 11, 21 and 24 July 1865; 'Kilsby', 'Etholiadau Ceredigion a Meirionydd', Y Traethodydd, IV (1865), 488–512; Baner, 19 and 26 July, 2 August 1865; The Welshman, 12 August 1864, 1 September 1865; NLW MSS 8321/51b, J. Matthews to his son, 22 July 1865; Aberystwyth Observer, 27 April 1867 (Lloyd's letter); PP (1866), LVI (160); NLW MSS 3291E, Ivon MSS 6/45, Kilsby to J. Jones, 2 September 1865; 6/51, ditto, 23 September; 6/54, ditto, 21 November; 8/56, ditto, 15 December 1865; 21/unnumbered, Sir T. D. Lloyd to Jones, 23 August 1865; R. Wallace, 'Wales and the Parliamentary Reform Movement 1866–1868', WHR, 11, no.4 (1983), 472, 484.
[37]BL Add MS 44408, ff.236, 244.

expressed in *Welsh Nonconformity and the Welsh Representation* (1866). He professed neutrality on Church disestablishment, except in Ireland. His opponent Vaughan, on the other hand, was entirely hostile. Accompanied by his agent John Matthews, Richards canvassed until he was hoarse, and brought national politics to Cardiganshire by securing Liberal MPs from south Wales as speakers at a Temperance Hall meeting in Aberystwyth on 26 October, where one of them claimed that the real contest was between Gladstone and Disraeli. This certainly stirred the electorate; Vaughan even rewrote his address to give it more bite.[38]

Richards, who spent £2,084 as opposed to over £3,000 by Vaughan, won the show of hands at Cardigan and headed the poll of 3,992 votes, of which he gained 2,074, including 800 at Aberystwyth, 422 at Aberaeron, 312 at Cardigan, 107 at Lampeter, 201 at Llandysul, and 232 at Tregaron. Vaughan gained 578, 377, 261, 226, 172 and 304 respectively.[39] Although Vaughan's youth counted against him, he was presented by his supporters as the local candidate (even though his address was Lapley, Staffordshire), whose claims were considerably stronger than those of a stranger better suited to a commercial constituency than a predominantly agricultural county. In July a requisition had been sent to Inglis Jones, headed by Powell of Nanteos, to become the Tory candidate. He declined, but championed Vaughan, and became one of those who accused Liberals of operating a 'religious screw' by exercising pulpit pressure on congregations in the pulpit. The word 'screw' was soon to generate considerable heat in Cardiganshire and beyond because of alleged evictions by Tory landlords of tenants (*Y Gorthrymedigion*/The Oppressed) who had voted Liberal. Such evictions had been known before, but now the Liberals, who also castigated Nonconformists who had voted for Vaughan, gave the wronged tenants publicity 'grossly exaggerated for political ends'. They disparaged the Tory scramble for votes on the Alltyrodyn estate and denounced Tregaron as a 'stronghold of Toryism'. David Davies of Llandinam, who had offered Lloyd of Bronwydd £500 to stand for the county, and who had rejected a Liberation Society plea to stand himself once more, allegedly dispatched railway 'navvies' to Tregaron to ensure that Liberals were not intimidated from voting.[40]

On 6 July 1869 Henry Richard, the sitting member for Merthyr Tydfil, exposed the evictions at Westminster against a background of Liberal triumph in Wales. He censured the families of Nanteos, Derry Ormond and Llanina, and spoke of the 'mental anguish' caused by notices to quit which had fallen 'like a shower of hailstones'. He knew of forty-three cases in Cardiganshire and twenty-six in Carmarthenshire. Other tenants faced the screw of increased rents. Richard embroidered boyhood memories of tenants being driven to vote 'like sheep to the slaughter-house'; but his motion of censure was withdrawn in favour of a select committee investigation. During the

[38]NLW MSS 8321/3, D. Davies to Matthews, 1 August; /4 Evan Davies to same, 17 August; /30, T. Harris to same, 16 June 1868; *The Welshman*, 14 and 21 August 1868; *The Cambrian*, 11 September 1868; *Aberystwyth Observer*, 11 July, 5 September 1868; *The Times*, 17 July, 22 August, 16 and 28 September, 29 October 1868; *Etholwr Ceredigion*, no.2, p.4 (14 December 1868), no.4, p.4 (19 November 1868) (copies in NLW MSS 3291E); NLW MSS 8321/51c, Matthews to his son, 5 September 1868; /72–8, E. M. Richards to Matthews, 17 August, 15 September, 5, 10 and 16 October 1868; /81, ditto, 23 November 1868; Ivor Thomas, *Top Sawyer: A Biography of David Davies of Llandinam* (London, 1938), p.170; NLW MSS 8306/104, T. Harris to T. Gee, 16 November 1867.
[39]*PP* (1868–1869), L (424); *The Welshman*, 2 December 1868.
[40]Derry Ormond MSS 380; NLW, Dolaucothi MSS 9262, newspaper extracts for 1868 election; H. M. Vaughan, *The South Wales Squires* (Golden Grove edn., 1988), pp.221–2; D. Williams, *History of Modern Wales* (London, 1950), p.262.

debate, Lloyd of Bronwydd described himself as one of four Whig landlords in Cardiganshire who had allowed their tenants a free vote, and Richards mentioned a supporter who had been threatened by his magistrate landlord. The select committee heard evidence from Harris, Llechryd, who built up a picture of landlord coercion. He had seen 'many' notices to quit, had traced a hundred of them and estimated that there were two hundred additional cases. He pointed out that the 1859 and 1865 elections had been relatively free from this abuse in Cardiganshire because they involved Tory against Tory and Liberal against Liberal. He believed parsons interfered in elections more than Nonconformist ministers, who could not excommunicate their congregations. He admitted that the ballot was not a major issue in Cardiganshire, where freeholders and homestead leaseholders had enabled the Liberals to win, but where most tenants probably voted Tory. He pictured Wales as a 'very stagnant' political nation until recently, where tenants were treated like sheep, and where the publication of poll books was unknown. He believed landlords were determined to terrorize, rather than evict tenants, but the Church question had made voters cling to their convictions. The committee report was inconclusive. It should be noted that Cardiganshire was only one of many constituencies examined. Meetings to publicize the plight of the evicted were held at Aberystwyth and Liverpool, sponsored by the Welsh Reform Association. On behalf of Richards, John Jones ('Ivon') had assembled information for publication by December 1869. Subscriptions were raised from expatriates, but most of the £4,000 raised came from fellow tenants. Since the tenants' legal case was weak, emigration was urged upon them as a sensible solution, at least until the ballot would come to their rescue.[41] On 4 March 1869 Lloyd suggested at Westminster that Boards of Guardians be allowed to enable inmates to emigrate to America, and was told that this was under consideration. Yet Gladstone's ministry believed it was taking a decisive step against the Tory 'screw' by legislating for the secret ballot in 1872.

At first Richards was eager to show his mettle in debate. On 9 April he tried to obtain improved legal status for Friendly Societies and subsequently manifested an interest in working-class welfare by seeking to prevent excessive credit facilities to workmen, many of whom found themselves in debtors' prison. On 9 April he advocated better technical education to offset German superiority and on 1 August 1870 he opposed rearmament in the face of the Franco-Prussian War. On 20 July 1871 he was assured that taxing horse-drawn carts did not apply to attendances at chapels or festivals, for which they might be loaned. For his part, Lloyd clashed with Henry Richard on 1 March 1871, when he denied that Welsh landlords refused Nonconformists land for cemeteries, and on 16 March he was assured that magistrates would be consulted should Welsh counties be grouped for judicial purposes. Neither Member spoke thereafter; Richards was ill for the last nine months of the Parliament and spent his time convalescing on the Continent.[42]

In spite of the introduction of the secret ballot, Disraeli's Tories won the 1874 election, including that in Cardiganshire. In the boroughs, a contest between two Liberals loomed. Lloyd defended Gladstonian reforms on 26 January, and, two days later, Davies of Llandinam offered a 'cordial but

[41]*PP* (1868–1869), VIII (352), 6199–6407; (1870) VI 115; NLW MSS 3291E/24, E. M. Richards to J. Jones, 13 December 1869; NLW MSS 8321/22, T. C. Edwards to Matthews, 7 September 1859; /32, J. Jenkins to same, November 1868; /105, W. R. Williams to same, 15 November 1869; /79a, E. M. Richards to same, 30 October, 3 November 1869; H. J. Hanham, *Elections and Party Management: Politics in the Time of Disraeli and Gladstone* (London, 1959), p.14; C. O'Leary, *The Elimination of Corrupt Practices in British Elections, 1868–1911* (Oxford, 1962), p.62.
[42]*The Welshman*, 30 January 1874.

independent support to Mr Gladstone'. Advanced Liberals disapproved of Lloyd, and meetings held in Cardigan and Aberystwyth on 26 January asked him to withdraw in Davies's favour. His patronage of the new University College at Aberystwyth had enhanced Davies's reputation, but he had declined to come forward in October 1873. At Aberaeron on 28 January, he espoused religious equality, voiced his support for repealing clause 25 in the Elementary Education Act, which allowed poor parents' fees to be paid; and admitted his dislike of Welsh Church disestablishment (he had walked out of the House when Watkin Williams proposed it). He praised Henry Richard's scheme for international arbitration to prevent war. He supported Gladstone on land and game law reform, the substitution of local for income tax, and extending the county franchise to (male) householders. He was in favour of abolishing tax on farmers' dogs, riding horses and traps. Not surprisingly, Davies's candidature was endorsed, and Lloyd withdrew courteously. The *Cambrian News*, noting his 'Conservative tendencies', claimed that Lloyd had supported Gladstone on the first readings, had voted against him on the second, and was 'almost always either absent from the divisions or in the wrong lobby when most needed'.

Richards, offering again for the county on 26 January, stood on his 1868 principles, having 'no fresh political belief to expound'. He had not voted for disestablishment, though he now favoured it; he had voted for Miall's motion on Church revenues, and he supported the secularization of education. The Tories at first favoured Colonel Lewes of Llanllŷr, who demurred, but at his wife's behest, Thomas Edward Lloyd of Coedmor, barrister heir to the Gogerddan ally, stood as a 'Liberal Conservative', and won the election by 215 votes; in his victory speech at Aberystwyth, he triumphantly exclaimed: 'I come before you as a Cardiganshire man, and my family has resided in the county for generations.' The Liberals resolved to raise funds for the next election, and David Davies, flashing his long purse, voiced his belief that Gogerddan had deserted Richards because of his alleged radicalism.[43] The truth was, however, that Richards, like Lloyd subsequently, was an unimpressive MP. David Davies, on the other hand, was singularly impressive. In his maiden speech on the malt tax, delivered on 23 April 1874, he confirmed a remark made about him before his election: 'One thing Mr David Davies has not learnt and that is to use language to disguise his thoughts'. He claimed that 'having been a working man at the age of 14 . . . He never had sixpence that he had not made himself . . . and during the last 18 years had employed on average 2,000 men, had mixed as a principal partner in a colliery-owning firm where 2,500 men and boys were employed'. He claimed to favour the tax because productivity suffered as a result of alcohol abuse. He had presented forty-five petitions against the early opening of taverns, and opposed the 25th clause of the Education Act. Having laid 170 miles of railways in seven counties between 1859 and 1867, he believed the chief hindrance to the well-being of the working man was drink. The House found him rather trying: Disraeli jested that it was good to see a self-made man praise his creator. Undaunted, Davies voiced his opinion on a variety of causes between 1875 and 1880. He defended the burial of Nonconformists by their own ministers, favoured compulsory education, criticized the agricultural holdings bill as a landlords' measure, opposed turning prisons into 'palaces', and supported the use of traction engines for road repairs. He favoured increasing tobacco tax, championed Irish immigrant labour, and opposed returning Irish paupers to Ireland. He proposed local referenda on licensing new pubs, wished to see rabbits, if not hares, taken off the game list, disliked compulsory compensation for injured railwaymen, and advocated payment of poor voters' travel expenses, and the 'equality' of candidates. His style was considered too 'parochial' for

---

[43] *The Welshman*, 30 January 1874; *Cambrian News*, 30 January, 6, 13, 20 and 27 February, 13 March, 3 and 17 April 1874; *Carmarthen Journal*, 6 February 1874; Vaughan, *South Wales Squires*, p.125.

Westminster, but he remained unperturbed, even when mistaken by House staff for a carpenter carrying out repairs.[44]

Davies's unopposed return for the boroughs was anticipated in his election address, delivered on 11 March 1880. There was some regret at Lampeter that R. D. Jenkins had not offered, and Davies quipped: 'No one in the United Kingdom has done more than I to provoke opposition.' Lloyd of Coedmor, though inconspicuous at Westminster, had been active in the county, but this time his eventual opponent had secured local credentials. Lewis Pugh Pugh, a wealthy barrister returned from India, second son of John Evans of Lovesgrove, had succeeded his uncle, the bachelor Lewis Pugh, to Aber-mad, Llanilar, an estate acquired by Pugh's Methodist businessman father. The candidate established his credentials at public meetings as a 'true and sound Liberal'. David Davies supported him while canvassing late in 1879, and he went on to conduct the most extensive canvass ever achieved by a candidate in Cardiganshire. It was strongly rumoured that south Cardiganshire was veering towards the Liberals, and Lloyd found it prudent to speak in his own defence at Cardigan on 18 October 1879. In 1878 his likely opponent had been Sir Edward Lewis Pryse, who had privately canvassed Conservatives, such as James Loxdale, with reassuring noises about his opposition to the dismantling of the Welsh Church. Lloyd's wife Clemena drafted a squib ridiculing Pryse for posing as a 'moderate man', when he had sponsored Richards, an 'Ultra Radical', in 1868, and had himself always voted with his party except on disestablishment. Pryse yielded because the Liberals would not guarantee his expenses, and a report in the *Cambrian News* that Lloyd would stand down proved unfounded.[45]

George Powell of Nanteos, then sheriff, published a renunciation of interference in his tenants' votes, though he privately informed Matthew Davies, Tan-y-bwlch, that his office prevented him from assisting Lloyd. Lloyd offered as a Liberal Conservative on 10 March, and Pugh offered two days later. Lloyd espoused the government's anti-Russian policy and deplored Irish Home Rule, but he had less to say about the agricultural depression. When Conservatives met at Tregaron on 16 March, with Lisburne in the chair, David Davies was mocked as 'Mr Montgomeryshire Moneybags', and Pugh was accused of preventing his tenants from selling rabbits. Pugh denied this when it was repeated at Aberystwyth by Vaughan Davies, and Lloyd accepted his disclaimer on 5 April. David Davies mocked Lloyd's inarticulacy at Westminster, and others derided his stilted Welsh, while Pugh was introduced at Llangeitho as 'a Welshman in heart, in blood, and in speech'. At Aberaeron Lloyd was met by blue-clad children chanting 'Pugh for ever'. There he boasted of sixteen post offices he had procured, and jibed that David Davies had subsidized Pugh to the tune of £15,000 (the Aberaeron–Aber-mad railway). At Cardigan, with Lloyd's kinsman Brigstocke in the chair, Pugh deplored the frogmarching of tenants at Tregaron, and Lloyd was shouted down. Pugh countered a Tory 'fabrication' that he was selling water to a mining company at Bodcoll by claiming that he was seeking the mineral rights to Llanerthir mine, which could provide employment. He also denied that, as chairman of the Board of Guardians, he had half-starved Aberystwyth's pauper lunatics.

---

[44]*Cambrian News*, 30 January 1874; Thomas, *Top Sawyer*, p.211; H. W. Lucy, *A Diary of Two Parliaments* (London, 1886), pp.267–8.
[45]NLW, Coedmore MSS 2735, Loxdale to Lloyd, 21 December 1878; 2101, MSS squib signed 'A Cardi elector'; 2102, 'Mr Pugh or Mr Lloyd, Letters to the agricultural electors of Cards.', undated; 2098, 'Araeth T. E. Lloyd, 18 Hydref 1879' (Carmarthen Journal Office); Thomas, *Top Sawyer*, p.224; *Cambrian News*, 19 and 26 March, 16 April 1880.

It was agreed that there was now no danger of multiple evictions, unless perhaps voters divulged their preferences. The Tory meeting at Pont-rhyd-y-groes was patronized by Lisburne and his countess who, it was claimed, 'has of course to be reckoned with in a contest of this kind'; unlike Miss Beedy at Aberystwyth in 1874, however, she did not advocate votes for women, a cause for which Henry Richard presented a petition from the town in 1885. Liberals at Pont-rhyd-y-groes were patronized by John Waddingham of Hafod. At New Quay, Pugh was serenaded to the tune of 'Ring the bell, watchman':

> Ymrestrwn, Rhydfrydwyr, yn ddewrion i'r gad,
> A safwn yn wrol dros lesiant ein gwlad;
> Mae Dizzy a'i fyddin ryfelgar a ffol,
> Yn gyru olwynion trafnidiaeth yn ol.
> Pugh, Pugh for ever, Pugh yw y dyn,
> O dan ei faner ymrestrwn bob un
> Ni chaiff un Jingo ein sarnu dan draed
> Ond dychwelwn i'r Senedd Pugh Abermaide.

> (Liberals, let's muster bravely to battle
> And manfully stand for our country's welfare;
> Dizzy and his warlike and foolish minions
> Are putting our chariot wheels into reverse.
> Pugh, Pugh for ever, Pugh is the man,
> Under his banner let's muster each one
> No Jingo shall trample us under foot
> Let's return Pugh of Abermaide to Parliament.)

Pugh's sponsor at Talgarreg was Sir Marteine Lloyd, Bronwydd, who attempted no Welsh. Windows were broken during Lloyd's hostile reception at Aberystwyth and a young Liberal woman, trying to pin a blue ribbon on a Tory matron's back, was worsted: 'this appears to be the only Conservative gain in the county', reported the *Cambrian News*, which also claimed on 9 April, in anticipation of Gladstone's return to power, 'one effect of the political change will be that certain officials and others will be more easy to live with. Their overbearing demeanour has been in some instances intolerable. Liberals have been made to feel that their masters were in office.' When James Loxdale of Castle Hill appeared at the head of his tenants at the poll on 8 April, there were mock cheers and groans at this exhibition of 'a past generation'.

Pugh described his majority of 801 as 'overwhelming'. Due credit was awarded to the Liberal Association formed in 1874. It was thought that even Loxdale's tenants had supported Pugh, and that Lisburne's had too. There were fireworks at Aberaeron, and a Liberal Club was established in Aberystwyth, where only Tory JPs had of late been appointed. At Pugh's victory banquet, William Jones of Llwyn-y-groes noted that the Association had registration reports from local committees, and that, to relieve the indefatigable Thomas Harris, a registration agent was in place. Even so, the forecast majority was only 543. At the Tory dinner, Vaughan Davies claimed that most of the natives of Cardiganshire were Tories: electors were voting against the government, not against Lloyd. Later that year, when Davies and Pugh spoke at an Aberystwyth Oddfellows dinner, Pugh could boast about the late hours he kept at Westminster, and his copious correspondence.[46]

[46]*Cambrian News*, 12 March, 30 April, 21 and 28 May, 1 October 1880.

Fig. 112: The celebrated statue of Henry Richard unveiled at Tregaron on 18 August 1893. (*Copyright National Library of Wales*).

In no parliament of the century did Members for the county combine to say so much. Davies was more entertaining, though he spoke less often than previously. His hobbyhorses were agricultural holdings – he wished to improve tenant farmers' lot without public loans, he deplored the tardiness of the Ordnance Survey of Wales and he continued to air his views on the game laws and licensing. He was independent enough not to support government when he disagreed with them, and once clashed with Pugh. He dwelt less on his own achievements, except to boast that he had 4,000 employees on 24 July 1883. Opposing the election expenses bill on 19 April 1882, he maintained that if ratepayers footed the bill every constituency would be contested. He did not support the leasehold enfranchisement bill in 1884, but objected to the disqualification of parish relief recipients from voting on 12 May 1885. Eight days later this admirer of Henry Richard said of the 'ironclads' that 'a bit of a brush with one of these foreign nations' would put them to the test! Pugh intervened frequently, introducing an Indian dimension to his personal and family interests. His best ploy was proposing little amendments on legal quibbles. On 28 August 1880 he recited Nonconformist burial grievances. He stated his objections to the rivers conservancy bill on 31 March and 7 April 1881, noting the failure of a similar bill affecting Cardiganshire years before, and speaking with feeling of unfair charges on upland landowners, having banked up a river for himself and tenants. Having failed to secure a committee on Crown lands in Wales, he moved to reduce the grant to Woods and Forests on 24 May 1881, since 85,000 acres were profitless in Wales, including undeveloped

Cardiganshire lead mines. He was also critical of the South Wales turnpike road bill and, in July 1883, of the agricultural holdings bill. His views on Egypt and Afghanistan were possibly of less local interest.

In 1885, when a third reform bill further extended the franchise, a Redistribution Act reduced Cardiganshire to one constituency. The threshold for a borough seat was 15,000 voters. On 27 January Henry Peyton Cobb wrote to Stuart Rendel MP, expressing pleas 'from all parts of the county', to seek his intervention with government: 'The case of Cardiganshire is clear, strong, and unanswerable, namely that the county is better entitled to 2 Members than Glamorganshire is to 5.' He requested an interview to elaborate, but nothing came of it. Consequently Pugh, shortly to become a Liberal Unionist, made way for David Davies, soon to be of the same mind, as Liberal candidate for the united constituency.[47]

Cardiganshire Parliamentary Election Results 1832–1885

19 December 1832 1,184 electors	WILLIAM EDWARD POWELL	
12 January 1835 1,352 electors	WILLIAM EDWARD POWELL	
2 August 1837 1,788 electors	WILLIAM EDWARD POWELL	
8 July 1841 2,060 electors	WILLIAM EDWARD POWELL	
11 August 1847 2,278 electors	WILLIAM EDWARD POWELL	
15 July 1852 2,235 electors	WILLIAM EDWARD POWELL	
22 February 1854	ERNEST AUGUSTUS VAUGHAN, Earl of Lisburne in place of Powell, resigned	
31 March 1857 2,723 electors	ERNEST AUGUSTUS VAUGHAN, Earl of Lisburne	
7 May 1859 2,586 electors	WILLIAM THOMAS ROWLAND POWELL Arthur Henry Saunders Davies	1,070 928
20 July 1865 3,520 electors	SIR THOMAS DAVIES LLOYD, Bart David Davies	1,510 1,149
28 November 1868 5,115 electors	EVAN MATTHEW RICHARDS Edmund Malet Vaughan	2,074 1,918
13 February 1874 4,438 electors	THOMAS EDWARD LLOYD Evan Matthew Richards	1,850 1,605
8 April 1880 4,882 electors	LEWIS PUGH PUGH Thomas Edward Lloyd	2,406 1,605

[47]NLW Rendel MSS 19449 (ix), F 19; *The Times*, 15 April 1885; K. O. Morgan, 'Cardiganshire politics: the Liberal ascendancy, 1885–1923', *Ceredigion*, V, no.4 (1967), 312, 342 (footnote 32).

Cardigan Borough Election Results, 1832–1885

14 December 1832 1,030 electors	PRYSE PRYSE	
7 January 1835 899 electors	PRYSE PRYSE	
26 July 1837 920 electors	PRYSE PRYSE	
6 July 1841 832 electors Double return	PRYSE PRYSE John Scandrett Harford PRYSE returned on petition, 18 April 1842	[163] 305 [226] 285
31 July 1847 761 electors	PRYSE PRYSE	
12 February 1849	PRYSE PRYSE in place of Pryse, deceased John Scandrett Harford	299 291
12 July 1849 849 electors	PRYSE LOVEDEN (formerly Pryse) John Inglis Jones	367 350
24 February 1855	JOHN LLOYD DAVIES in place of Loveden, deceased John Evans	298 286
27 March 1857 837 electors	EDWARD LEWIS PRYSE	
29 April 1859 673 electors	EDWARD LEWIS PRYSE	
11 July 1865 685 electors	SIR EDWARD LEWIS PRYSE	
16 November 1868 1,561 electors	SIR THOMAS DAVIES LLOYD, Bart	
4 February 1874 1,946 electors	DAVID DAVIES	
6 April 1880 2,280 electors	DAVID DAVIES	

Constituency disenfranchised in favour of a united county constituency, 1885.

CHAPTER 18

CARDIGANSHIRE POLITICS, 1885–1974

J. Graham Jones

CARDIGANSHIRE, first captured by the Liberals in 1868, was held continuously by the party from 1880 until 1966. But this seemingly hegemonic ascendancy, encompassing three generations and more, belies a history of much local political rancour and conflict, most especially in 1885–6 and in 1921–3.[1]

The mid-1880s had witnessed a genuine transformation in the county's political life. The extension of household suffrage to the counties by Gladstone's Reform Act of 1884 had created more than 5,000 new voters in Cardiganshire, most of them tenant farmers and farm labourers. The Redistribution Act of 1885 had swept away the old Cardigan Boroughs constituency, merging its four contributory boroughs – Aberystwyth, Cardigan, Lampeter and Atpar – into the single county division, henceforth to be represented by one MP, with a registered electorate of 12,308 by 1886.[2] An earlier measure, the Corrupt Practices Act of 1883, had limited the sums legally spent by parliamentary candidates. Throughout Wales the result of these changes was a sudden diminution in the political power of the landed gentry. Cardiganshire was moving, it has been claimed, from 'the politics of deference' to 'the politics of democracy'.[3]

The county displayed a distinctive, perhaps unique, social composition. It was almost totally agrarian, most of the farms were relatively small, and a significant proportion inhabited by tenant farmers, who desperately sought security of tenure in the face of acute land hunger. More than 93 per cent of the population spoke Welsh, a similar percentage had been born within the county, and a large majority of church and chapelgoers were Nonconformists.[4] The university and seaside town of Aberystwyth contained one-seventh of the constituency's total population, but all the other towns were very small.[5] Landed families such as the Powells of Nanteos and the Lisburnes of Trawsgoed, the victims of economic depression, were impoverished and in much disarray, thus depriving local Toryism (the party of 'church and squire') of strong political leadership and vitality – a state of affairs which was in striking contrast to the political life of most other Welsh counties. The social and political vacuum caused by the ignominious retreat of the local squirearchy offered a rich

---

[1]See the discussion in K. O. Morgan, 'Cardiganshire politics: the Liberal ascendancy, 1885–1923', *Ceredigion*, V, no.4 (1967), 311–46.

[2]This compares with a total electorate of 5,026 in 1883.

[3]Morgan, 'Cardiganshire politics', 313.

[4]See H. Pelling, *Social Geography of British Elections, 1885–1910* (London, 1967), pp.346–9.

[5]Ibid., p.365.

opportunity for the new urban middle class and the more affluent tenant farmers,[6] who came to dominate local politics until the 1920s. They found their most vocal champion in John Gibson, the articulate and pugnacious editor of the *Cambrian News*.

The first MP for the recently enlarged Cardiganshire division was David Davies of Llandinam, Member for the old Boroughs seat since 1874. 'Top Sawyer' (as he was known) was the owner of extensive coal mines in the Rhondda valleys, the railway king of Wales, the lavish patron of the University College at Aberystwyth, and a prominent local Methodist.[7] Fortified by the Herculean efforts of the recently formed local Liberal Association, in 1885 Davies easily thwarted his Conservative opponent, Matthew Vaughan Davies, squire of Tan-y-bwlch since 1853, by more than 2,300 votes. Although widely accused of lacking sympathy for the small tenant farmer and farm labourer,[8] David Davies portrayed himself as 'a Radical on Land Law Reform', and a proponent of 'that advanced Liberalism' championed by Gladstone.[9] His victory was depicted by the local Liberal press as a 'protest against privilege'.[10] He also described himself as 'a thorough disestablishment and disendowment man'[11] – in marked contrast to Vaughan Davies's confused and contradictory speeches on the subject.[12]

Davies's re-election to Parliament was not in doubt in 1885. A well-organized and spirited campaign on behalf of 'David Davies, the Working Man's Friend',[13] contrasted sharply with the flagging Tory effort. 'They [the Conservatives] do not seem to us to be very active at all', read a report from Lampeter, 'We hardly hear anything of them. They feel that they only fight a losing cause.'[14]

Local Liberal elation at the convincing re-election of a representative whose 'sympathies', proclaimed Gibson, were 'all with the people',[15] proved to be short-lived. It was soon widely felt that Davies was an unsuitable member for a division so proud of its radical credentials. Many local Liberals clearly shared the outspoken view of the youthful Tom Ellis, who condemned Davies for 'buying landed estates and sinking deeper into Whiggism after each transaction'.[16] Tension mounted considerably because of his failure to support a number of radical measures in the Commons, notably when he voted against the second reading of Gladstone's Irish Home Rule Bill in June 1886.[17] Rumours abounded that his ill-health and the split over Ireland would compel him to retire from Westminster.[18] In some quarters his son Edward was urged to stand as his successor,[19] for it was widely assumed that he would never again face the Cardiganshire electorate.[20]

[6]K. O. Morgan, *Rebirth of a Nation: Wales 1880–1980* (Oxford, 1981), pp.48–9.
[7]See H. Williams, *Davies the Ocean: Railway King and Coal Tycoon* (Cardiff, 1991).
[8]*South Wales Daily News*, 10 and 11 November 1885; *Western Mail*, 17 November 1885.
[9]*Cambrian News*, 16 October 1885.
[10]Ibid., 4 December 1885.
[11]Quoted in I. Thomas, *Top Sawyer: A Biography of David Davies of Llandinam* (Golden Grove edn., 1988), p.234.
[12]*South Wales Daily News*, 11 November 1885.
[13]NLW MS 19643B, no.2, election poster 1885.
[14]Ibid., no.82, D. J. Jones, Lampeter, to H. C. Fryer, 'Saturday night'.
[15]*Cambrian News*, 4 December 1885.
[16]T. E. Ellis to D. R. Daniel, cited in T. I. Ellis, *Cofiant Thomas Edward Ellis*, Vol.1 (Liverpool, 1944), p.194.
[17]Morgan, 'Cardiganshire politics', 323–4.
[18]See the rich correspondence in NLW, Llandinam Papers, file 301.
[19]Ibid., file 302, H.C. Fryer to Edward Davies, dated 11 April 1886.
[20]Williams, *Davies the Ocean*, pp.215–17.

The defeat of the Irish measure led to an immediate dissolution of Parliament, and David Davies announced his Liberal Unionist candidature for Cardiganshire.[21] Local Liberals, astounded by this dramatic turn of events, knew not where to turn. H. C. Fryer, the Liberal agent, appealed to Stuart Rendel to abandon marginal Montgomeryshire for a safe haven in Cardiganshire – 'Your name is so well known, and your Parliamentary record so good.'[22] 'The constituency is large, over 70,000', he went on, 'and consequently somewhat expensive in contest, but it could be fought for a less sum than the £1,500 spent last election.'[23] His pleas fell on deaf ears, and W. Bowen Rowlands, a Haverfordwest lawyer little known in the county, became the Liberal aspirant to stand against David Davies in an enormously energetic and closely fought election. 'Every true Liberal must work and vote against Mr David Davies', thundered Gibson in the *Cambrian News*;[24] indeed, Davies and his Tory 'squireen' followers were 'dull specimens of a dull race'.[25] 'They are Gladstonians to the core', lamented a Davies supporter from Lampeter to his son Edward, 'They have all joined our opponents . . . The Nonconformist ministers have joined them.'[26] His campaign was invigorated by a visit from Michael Davitt, and in the event Rowlands defeated Davies by a mere nine votes (4,252 to 4,243); Davies's poll was perhaps the best Liberal Unionist performance in the whole of Wales,[27] but he considered the outcome – defeat at the hands of 'a perfect stranger' – a severe personal rebuff.[28] 'Cardiganshire . . . has conceded Home Rule to Ireland', proclaimed a gleeful John Gibson, 'and demanded Home Rule for Wales.'[29] His final verdict on Davies, whose plans to demand a 'scrutiny' of the ballot came to nothing,[30] was unrelenting: 'Success has made him hard, and wealth has made him vain and very proud.'[31]

Although Cardiganshire did not become a storm centre of the tithe agitation in the late 1890s,[32] disturbances did persist in the county, with particularly disorderly scenes at tithe sales as late as 1894 and 1895,[33] a concern reflected in persistent questions in the House of Commons. 'The tithe movement is going on in Cardiganshire', wrote Gibson in May 1887, '& will be the means of disestablishing the Church.'[34] The first Cardiganshire county council, elected in 1889, comprised a large number of Liberal tenant farmers and artisans, mainly small businessmen and shopkeepers, alongside the traditional Tory gentry representatives. Participation in county government in Cardiganshire, as elsewhere, rarely extended below the 'petty bourgeoisie'.[35] But there was heartfelt jubilation at the extent of the Liberal successes: 'Wales through and through has done admirably', rejoiced Tom Ellis, '[and] Merioneth and Cardigan most nobly.' With considerable relish, he spoke

[21] *Cambrian News*, 9 July 1886.
[22] NLW MS 19449D, letter 117, H. C. Fryer to Stuart Rendel, 9 June 1886.
[23] Ibid.
[24] *Cambrian News*, 25 June 1886.
[25] Ibid., 2 July 1886.
[26] NLW, Llandinam Papers, file 302, D. J. Jones to Edward Davies, 'Sunday noon'.
[27] See Pelling, *Social Geography*, p.365. See also K. O. Morgan, 'The Liberal Unionists in Wales', *NLWJ*, XVI, no.2 (1969), 163–71.
[28] Williams, *Davies the Ocean*, p.221.
[29] *Cambrian News*, 16 July 1886.
[30] Ibid., 30 July 1886.
[31] Ibid., 16 July 1886.
[32] K. O. Morgan, *Wales in British Politics, 1868–1922* (4th edn., Cardiff, 1991), pp.89–90.
[33] NLW MSS 15321–23.
[34] NLW MS 19450C, no.170, John Gibson to Stuart Rendel, 8 May 1887.
[35] Morgan, *Rebirth of a Nation*, pp.48–9.

of 'the grave into which Cardiganshire . . . has lowered its Toryism and the system of privileged, irresponsible magistracy'.[36]

Thus the same Liberal Nonconformist middle class came to control both parliamentary and local politics in the county. Liberal Unionism, decisively (if narrowly) defeated in 1886, stood no prospect of resurgence, a futility powerfully confirmed in 1892 when Bowen Rowlands (who gained 61.5 per cent of the poll) easily thwarted the Joseph Chamberlain nominee, William Jones, a son of the county, a native Welsh speaker and a Methodist, who earned his living as a Birmingham draper,[37] and who, it seems, had forfeited the support of many local Anglicans and Tory stalwarts.[38] Cardiganshire politics, it was justifiably claimed, had reverted to the traditional battle between Liberals and Tories in which Liberal Unionism had no place.[39] 'Cardiganshire has done all I wanted', wrote Gibson, 'I am glad that Wales is truer to Liberalism & to Mr Gladstone than any other part of the United Kingdom.'[40] When, in July 1893, Rowlands vacated his seat following his appointment as Recorder of Swansea, he was returned to Parliament unopposed.[41]

Yet Rowlands rarely visited Cardiganshire and his decision in 1895 to resign from Parliament in order to take up a county court judgeship caused little surprise. Ironically, his Liberal successor proved to be M. Vaughan Davies of Tan-y-bwlch, the Tory aspirant for the county ten years earlier, and a monoglot English-speaking High Church Anglican![42] Although there was widespread local resentment at his nomination, spearheaded by the abrasive Gibson,[43] Davies appeared to some to be acceptable because he was a local landowner able to subscribe generously to party funds.[44] 'One of the prime factors in the election', wrote an Aberystwyth Liberal to Tom Ellis, 'is to have a man like Mr Davies to fill the gap for a while till Mr Davies, Cwrtmawr, is ready for Parliament. Cwrtmawr, however, I am afraid, is not shaping up well & yesterday at Lampeter meeting made an awful bad hit.'[45]

Vaughan Davies's Conservative opponent in 1895 was J. C. Harford, the young squire of Falcondale, who waged an energetic campaign. Although Gibson thundered away against Vaughan Davies – 'as much a Tory now as ever he was'[46] – in the columns of the *Cambrian News*, Cardiganshire Liberals generally closed ranks behind their candidate. One of their number, inviting Tom Ellis to assist their campaign, reported 'complete harmony and co-operation . . . The Liberals are gradually forgetting old wounds'.[47] This was in stark contrast to the turbulence and acrimony of the selection meeting at Brondeifi Unitarian chapel, Lampeter, a short time earlier. Further excitement resulted when the returning officer sought to declare Harford elected because, he claimed, Davies had failed to deposit the necessary bond.[48] Davies's impassioned protests were heeded, he was allowed to stand, and he won the day by almost 1,200 votes.

[36]NLW, J. M. Howell Papers, file 27, no.21, T. E. Ellis to J. M. Howell, 24 January 1889.
[37]Morgan, 'Cardiganshire politics', 325.
[38]*The Times*, 26 April 1892.
[39]*Aberystwyth Observer*, 21 July 1892.
[40]NLW MS 19450C, no.178, John Gibson to Stuart Rendel, 17 July 1892.
[41]Thomas, *Top Sawyer*, p.250.
[42]Morgan, 'Cardiganshire politics', 326–7.
[43]*Cambrian News*, 15 February and 24 March 1895.
[44]See NLW, T. E. Ellis Papers 305 and 306, William Davies, Aberystwyth, to T. E. Ellis, 31 December 1894 and 31 January 1895.
[45]Ibid., 792, W. R. Hall, Aberystwyth, to T. E. Ellis, 3 July 1895.
[46]*Cambrian News*, 28 June 1895.
[47]NLW, T. E. Ellis Papers 1922, David Samuel, Aberystwyth, to T. E. Ellis, 10 July 1895.
[48]Thomas, *Top Sawyer*, p.251.

Although he was re-elected on five occasions (twice unopposed), Vaughan Davies remained until his retirement in 1921 'a silent backbencher' whose taciturn indifference, indeed lethargy, suppressed local interest in politics for nearly thirty years.[49] His long tenure of the seat was indeed 'notable more for his unrivalled command of unparliamentary language than for any positive contribution to his country's good'.[50] In 1900 he again faced a keenly contested electoral battle against Harford held at the height of the Boer War when he faced vehement criticism of his 'pro-Boer' voting record in the Commons. Difficulties were compounded by the near collapse of the local Liberal organization: 'Mr Vaughan Davies', it was rightly claimed, 'is not only the Liberal Member, but he is the Liberal Association and the paymaster of the registration agents, and he does whatever seems to be right in his own eyes.'[51] His majority was indeed slashed to a record low of 781 votes. At the count, Harford told him: 'Well, I think I have made you sit up this time.'[52]

In 1906 and again in January 1910, however, Davies was re-elected with handsome majorities, although reports abounded of apathy and ignorance among the electorate in rural areas. Only the advent of a Tory aspirant, C. Morgan Richardson of Cardigan, caused the Liberals to hold a single election meeting in 1906,[53] and four years later there were widespread fears that no Conservative would stand: 'The people wanted a contest – they did not care with whom, but they wanted to express their opinion on the drink question, the disestablishment question, the Budget, the Lords, and taxed food.'[54] The candidature of George Fossett Roberts, however, precipitated a contest; his association with the Aberystwyth brewing trade caused much disapproval,[55] and he polled 3,400 fewer votes than Davies. No Conservative candidate emerged in the following December in spite of 'eleventh hour . . . frantic efforts' to find a suitable contender,[56] and severe financial difficulties added to the manifold difficulties of local Tories.[57]

Vaughan Davies's long representation of the constituency thus sapped the vitality of the county's political life, and by the late 1890s the local Liberal Association had almost disappeared; the registration of voters had been neglected and the Association had run up considerable debts as the machinery for collecting subscriptions had broken down. Davies stepped in personally to solve the financial embarrassment,[58] a dangerous extension of personal influence. During the 1900 general election campaign the Aberaeron correspondent of the *Cambrian News* condemned 'the most enervating torpor' which 'had seized the Liberal Party from Ynyslas to Cardigan. The enemy blustered about, but the Liberals only snoozed'.[59] Such a state of affairs prevailed until after the First World War. Inevitably the advent of 'total war' in 1914 thoroughly undermined the pattern of life in Cardiganshire, although it also brought a new-found prosperity with the passage of the Corn Production Act in 1917, which heralded much improved living standards and a slight population increase by 1921. The experience of war severely impaired the cosy consensus politics of

[49]Morgan, 'Cardiganshire politics', 328.
[50]Thomas, *Top Sawyer*, p.251.
[51]*Cambrian News*, 21 September 1900.
[52]Ibid., 19 October 1900.
[53]*Welsh Gazette*, 25 January 1906.
[54]*Cambrian News*, 4 February 1910.
[55]*Welsh Gazette*, 3 February 1910.
[56]Ibid., 1 December 1910.
[57]Ibid., 8 December 1910.
[58]*South Wales Daily News*, 8 January 1897 and 10 June 1898.
[59]*Cambrian News*, 19 October 1900.

Fig. 113: Liberal supporters of Lloyd George and Ernest Evans, 1922. (*Copyright National Library of Wales*).

Cardiganshire Liberalism. Inevitably, echoes of the world of high politics reverberated throughout the county in the manœuvres which enabled Lloyd George to succeed Asquith as Prime Minister in December 1916, and the repercussions persisted until the thirties and beyond.

In November 1918 W. Llewelyn Williams, an old-style radical and a fervent Asquithian, informed Harry Rees, the secretary of the Liberal Association: 'There is a persistent rumour that Vaughan Davies will be raised to the peerage at the last moment, & a George man will be rushed in for Cardiganshire',[60] and he duly offered his services as the Liberal candidate.[61] In the event, Vaughan Davies, a recipient of the Coalition government's infamous 'coupon', was returned unopposed, a course of events which caused widespread misgivings locally.[62] Tensions became even more acute when Asquith personally addressed 'a large and representative body' of Liberals at Aberystwyth in November 1919.[63] Rumours persisted that Davies was about to enter the Lords,[64] and in June 1920 the local Liberal Association considered a telling resolution – 'We should

[60]NLW MS 22016E, f.4, W. Llewelyn Williams to Harry Rees, 27 November 1918. 'Private'.
[61]Ibid.
[62]*South Wales Daily News*, 23 November 1918.
[63]NLW, J. M. Howell Papers, file 28, no.1, H. H. Asquith to J. M. Howell, 4 November 1919.
[64]*Manchester Guardian*, 16 June 1920.

pronounce ourselves free Liberals and be prepared to find a free Liberal candidate when a vacancy occurs.'[65] Traditional Liberals throughout the county looked askance as the post-war Coalition government ran its course.[66] Vaughan Davies finally received his elevation to the Upper House in January 1921, adopting the title Baron Ystwyth,[67] and Cardiganshire was plunged into an acrimonious by-election campaign.[68] Llewelyn Williams was chosen as candidate by the Cardiganshire Liberal Association,[69] and Captain Ernest Evans, private secretary to Lloyd George, announced his candidature as a Coalition Liberal.[70] The fray split the county, causing enormous bitterness within the chapels and even dividing families. Lloyd George, 'overwhelmed with great world affairs',[71] relied upon his wife's political acumen, but feared the outcome: 'If we lost, all their speakers & newspapers would say, "Lloyd George spurned & rejected by his own countrymen".'[72] The result was by no means certain; after addressing meetings in support of Evans at Aberystwyth, Cardigan and Lampeter, the veteran J. Herbert Lewis noted in his diary: 'The coast towns are strong for the Coalition, the Upland districts against: Unitarians against, Methodists & Independents said to be against: Baptists & Church for.'[73]

The impassioned eloquence of Dame Margaret (who addressed sixty meetings) and J. Herbert Lewis was matched by the powerful rhetoric of Lady Violet Bonham-Carter (Asquith's daughter), who addressed eleven public meetings, telling Asquithian Liberals that they were 'fighting not merely for a man, but for a creed, a faith', and appealing to them to remain loyal to their 'fathers' sacrifices in 1868'.[74] 'Every vote for Llewelyn Williams', ran an advertisement in the *Cambrian News*, 'is a vote against Lloyd George.'[75] Ultimately, Williams (paranoid in his loathing of Lloyd George, whom he condemned privately as a 'dictator . . . a little devil who plagues us so'[76]) was defeated by more than 3,500 votes, a majority exceeding even the most sanguine expectations of the Coalitionists.[77] Even so, it was widely felt that Williams had polled 'remarkably well',[78] and many observers believed that Lloyd George was beginning to lose his 'grip' on Welsh Liberalism.[79]

When the Coalition government collapsed in October 1922, Cardiganshire was once more the scene of a fiercely fought electoral contest between two Liberals. The Independent challenger was Rhys Hopkin Morris, a barrister and an accomplished political debater, well capable of winning over potential Labour voters. A man of broad outlook, Morris gave much attention during the

[65]Ibid.

[66]See NLW, J. M. Howell Papers, file 27, no.49, J. Puleston Jones to J. M. Howell, 3 February 1921.

[67]*Cambrian News*, 7 January 1921.

[68]See NLW MS 22016E, ff.6–7, R. Humphrey Davies to Harry Rees, 6 January 1921. On the parliamentary elections of the years 1921–32, see F. F. E. Aubel, 'Cardiganshire parliamentary elections and their backgrounds, 1921–32' (unpublished University of Wales M.Phil. thesis, 1989).

[69]*Welsh Gazette*, 27 January 1921.

[70]Morgan, 'Cardiganshire politics', 332–5.

[71]NLW MS 22823C, ff.74–5, D. Lloyd George to Margaret Lloyd-George, 9 February 1921.

[72]Ibid.

[73]NLW, Sir John Herbert Lewis Papers B35, diary entry for 18 February 1921.

[74]*South Wales Daily News*, 16 February 1921.

[75]*Cambrian News*, 15 February 1921.

[76]Bodleian Library, Oxford, Arthur Ponsonby Papers, W. Llewelyn Williams to Ponsonby, 12 October 1920.

[77]NLW, Sir John Herbert Lewis Papers B35, diary entry for 19 February 1921.

[78]*The Welsh Outlook*, March 1921.

[79]*The Times*, 21 February 1921.

Fig. 114: A Cardiganshire election broadside, 1923. (*Copyright National Library of Wales*).

campaign to the defects of the Versailles Treaty and the need to support the League of Nations and settle the vexed reparation problem.[80] Standing for re-election, Evans retained widespread Conservative support,[81] but probably sacrificed 'Liberal principles' in the process.[82] In the event, he hung on by only 515 votes. Morris was well pleased at the outcome, writing to his agent, 'You achieved a splendid result . . . *Fe wnaethoch yn ardderchog.*'[83]

The local Liberal feud persisted, and when Baldwin called yet another general election in December 1923, Cardiganshire was one of only two constituencies throughout Britain where two Liberals stood. On this occasion, however, the intervention of Lord Lisburne as a Conservative contender transformed the local situation. The Independent Liberals, sensing the prospect of victory, refused to consider reunion.[84] 'We are now so certain of victory', wrote Harry Rees, 'that we shall on no account relax our efforts on behalf of Mr Hopkin Morris.'[85] In a three-cornered fight, Evans's chances were slim indeed; readily portrayed by his opponents as the candidate 'who had

[80]*Liverpool Daily Post*, 3 November 1922.
[81]*Western Mail*, 9 November 1922.
[82]*Welsh Gazette*, 9 November 1922.
[83]NLW MS 22016E, f.33, Rhys Hopkin Morris to Harry Rees, 25 November 1922.
[84]NLW, Cardiganshire Liberal Association records, no.1, minute book (1923–50), entry for 21 November 1923.
[85]NLW MS 22016E, ff.35–6, Harry Rees to R. Humphrey Davies, 18 November 1923.

depended on Conservative votes to defeat true Liberalism',[86] he was defeated by more than 5,000 votes. Cardiganshire Liberals, proclaimed Morris, had made 'as great history in 1923 as was made in 1868'.[87] Even the *Cambrian News*, which had consistently backed Evans, conceded that 'Cardiganshire had remained true to the faith of its fathers, true to the promise of 1868 . . . and to Liberalism',[88] while T. A. Levi wrote, 'It is for us . . . to ensure that Toryism will never raise its head again in Liberal Cardiganshire.'[89]

The victorious Liberal camp cautiously considered reunion, tentatively extending 'a welcome but not an invitation' to their former opponents.[90] In June, Hopkin Morris urged 'the union of Radical forces' in Wales to defeat Labour,[91] for, 'With Mr Lloyd George as leader of the Liberal Party they would not get a single vote back in Glamorganshire'.[92] When the first Labour government fell at the end of 1924, Morris was returned to Parliament unopposed, a situation which probably reflected 'a truce of exhaustion' between the two Liberal camps in Cardiganshire.[93] Rumours of a Conservative candidate proved groundless,[94] and nothing came of initiatives by National Liberals to persuade Sir R. C. Mathias of Aberystwyth to stand as an 'anti-Socialist' candidate.[95] Morris was the only Welsh MP to be returned to Parliament unopposed in 1924, the *South Wales News* claiming that local Liberals were now 'absolutely united', and that their MP enjoyed 'their undivided and unqualified support'.[96] In reality Cardiganshire Liberals remained far from united.[97] Yet the year 1924 marked the end of the frenzied electioneering activity of the previous three years; Hopkin Morris was secure in his tenure of the seat, no general election was in prospect and the scene was set for a slow process of healing and reconciliation, fraught with tensions and suspicions though this might be. Above all, the traumatic course of the events of 1921–4 had restored the dynamism and crusading idealism to local political life, features which had been patently lacking since the 1890s.[98]

One significant result of the schism in local Liberal ranks was the creation of a homespun dynamism which helped to impede the rise of Labour in the county.[99] The roots of the Labour movement in Cardiganshire extended back to the 1890s, at least to the formation of a branch of the Amalgamated Society of Railway Servants at Aberystwyth in 1898. A county association of the National Union of Teachers was set up in 1903 and an array of similar groups before the First World War; these came together in November 1912 to form the North Cardiganshire Trade Union and Labour Council.[100] Initiatives were afoot by the summer of 1918 to found a Cardiganshire

[86]*Welsh Gazette*, 22 November 1923.
[87]Ibid., 13 December 1923.
[88]*Cambrian News*, 14 December 1923.
[89]NLW MS 22016E, f.37, circular letter from T. A. Levi 'to my fellow Liberals', 21 November 1923.
[90]NLW, Cardiganshire Liberal Association records, no.1, minute book (1923–50), entry for 16 January 1924.
[91]Ibid., entry for 13 June 1924.
[92]Ibid.
[93]P. J. Madgwick with Non Griffiths and Valerie Walker, *The Politics of Rural Wales: A Study of Cardiganshire* (London, 1973), p.46.
[94]*Western Mail*, 10 October 1924.
[95]Ibid., 14 October 1924.
[96]*South Wales Daily News*, 18 October 1924.
[97]NLW, Cardiganshire Liberal Association records, no.1, minute book (1923–50), entry for 31 December 1924.
[98]See the comments in Morgan, 'Cardiganshire politics', 337–8.
[99]H. C. Jones, 'The Labour Party in Cardiganshire, 1918–66', *Ceredigion*, IX, no.2 (1981), 150–61.
[100]NLW, Carl Hansen Papers, contain the first minute book of the council.

Labour Party, but no parliamentary candidate stood in the division until the 'doctor's mandate' election of October 1931.[101] By the second half of the twenties, a number of branches had been set up in the rural villages,[102] and the selection of a parliamentary candidate seemed imminent.[103] But no Labour aspirant appeared in 1929,[104] and remote rural areas such as Cardiganshire were believed by the party leadership to represent 'the whole problem in regard to the future of the Labour Party'.[105]

Meanwhile the return of Lloyd George to the leadership of the Liberal Party (in succession to Asquith) in October 1926 brought renewed unease, even rancour, to local Liberal ranks. Hopkin Morris remained generally hostile towards him,[106] sharply condemning his 'mercenary army' and his 'fancy policies'.[107] Above all, the radical proposals of the report of a committee of enquiry set up by Lloyd George, entitled 'The Land and the Nation', for a scheme labelled 'cultivating tenure' closely akin to the nationalization of land, had led to speculation that Morris (like Sir Alfred Mond in Carmarthen) would join the Tories.[108] The rumours proved groundless, but the local Liberal Association remained intransigently hostile to the novel land proposals: 'The least said and done in the matter will be best for the Liberal cause in the County of Cardigan.'[109] When Baldwin's 'Long Parliament' reached the end of its constitutional quinquennium in May 1929, Morris faced a sole Conservative opponent in the person of Colonel E. C. L. Fitzwilliams, a local man, popular among the farming community,[110] who was predictably condemned by the Liberal camp as merely one 'who can open bazaars and sales of work in the Churches and Chapels of the county'.[111] Morris reluctantly admitted to taciturn approval of the Lloyd Georgian 'Yellow Book' reforms to tackle unemployment,[112] even describing them as 'the only practical way of dealing with an urgent and distressing problem'.[113] Although local Liberal unity was at best fragile and ephemeral,[114] Morris's re-election was considered beyond doubt,[115] and his eventual majority was indeed almost 6,000 votes.[116] Yet Fitzwilliams, fighting 'in an excellent and generous spirit',[117] had proved himself a formidable opponent, and had earned widespread respect.

Hopkin Morris's relationship with Lloyd George remained distinctly strained; he was the only Liberal MP in June 1929 to vote against the election of Lloyd George as party leader,[118] subsequently declaring, 'I will accept the leadership of Mr Lloyd George in so far as it is a Liberal

[101]Jones, 'Labour Party', 153–5.
[102]Welsh Gazette, 7 June 1928.
[103]Manchester Guardian, 22 May 1929.
[104]See J. G. Jones, 'Wales and the "new Socialism", 1926–1929', WHR, 9, no.2 (1982), 173–99.
[105]Report of the Twenty-Fourth Annual Conference of the Labour Party (London, 1924), pp.180–1.
[106]J. G. Jones, 'Wales and the "New Liberalism", 1926–1929', NLWJ, XXII, no.3 (1982), 330–1.
[107]Cambrian News, 4 February 1927.
[108]Cardigan and Tivy-Side Advertiser, 29 January 1926.
[109]NLW, Cardiganshire Liberal Association records, no.1, minute book (1923–50), entry for 10 June 1926.
[110]Western Mail and South Wales News, 8 May 1929.
[111]Welsh Gazette, 23 May 1929.
[112]Jones, 'Wales and the "New Liberalism"', 330–1.
[113]Rhys Hopkin Morris, Election Address, May 1929.
[114]Manchester Guardian, 22 May 1929.
[115]Y Genedl Gymreig, 8 April 1929; Cambrian News, 24 May 1929.
[116]Cambrian News, 7 June 1929.
[117]Ibid.
[118]H. Morris-Jones, Doctor in the Whip's Room (London, 1955), p.82.

leadership and no further',[119] a course of events which caused much dissension in the ranks of the local Liberal Association.[120]

When the so-called National Government resolved to go the country in the autumn of 1931, Morris condemned the election as 'entirely uncalled for'.[121] For the first time ever, a Labour candidate ventured into the fray: John Lloyd Jones, an Ebbw Vale schoolmaster,[122] proclaimed Labour as the 'party of progress' since the Liberals (now split three ways) had been 'shattered into fragments'.[123] Local Tories resolved to stand aside,[124] thus ensuring Morris's re-election by 13,000 votes in an otherwise highly contentious contest. Hopkin Morris was not destined to remain Cardiganshire's MP for very much longer for he soon accepted an appointment as a metropolitan magistrate, thereby precipitating a by-election in September 1932. On this occasion Cardiganshire Liberals, 'united without distinction for all time',[125] chose D. Owen Evans of Llangrannog, the son of a tenant farmer, as the Liberal candidate. He described himself as 'a Liberal and Free Trader . . . [who] stood exactly where Mr Hopkin Morris stood'.[126] Although an attempt was made to secure local Conservative backing for Evans,[127] no agreement proved possible, and Colonel Fitzwilliams stood once more; declaring himself a supporter of the National Government, he claimed there should be 'no party politics in these difficult times'.[128] The nomination of the Revd D. M. Jones, a Baptist minister at Senghennydd, to represent the Labour interest caused a three-cornered contest. Although supported by an array of prominent Labour politicians such as Stafford Cripps, Arthur Greenwood and George Lansbury, Jones appears to have waged an 'unashamedly radical and socialist campaign'[129] and was alleged to be 'not the right sort of candidate, he preached the Bible to the electors'.[130] Owen Evans, promising an 'attitude . . . of constant watchfulness' towards the government and 'an independent judgement',[131] won the day with almost half the votes cast. He informed his jubilant supporters that they had 'cemented the unity of the Liberal Party in Cardiganshire with a great victory'.[132] The rift of a decade, it appeared, was almost healed.

On one further occasion, however, Lloyd George, who had spoken to great effect on Evans's behalf in September 1932[133] ('Lloyd George healed the breach just in time', recalled Jim Griffiths[134]), caused local agitation by calling early in 1933 for 'a new radical party'.[135] 'No

[119]NLW, Cardiganshire Liberal Association records, no.1, minute book (1923–50), entry for 28 June 1929.

[120]Aubel, 'Cardiganshire Parliamentary Elections', pp.160–1.

[121]NLW, Cardiganshire Liberal Association records, no.1, minute book (1923–50), entry for 13 October 1931.

[122]Jones, 'Labour Party', 155–6.

[123]John Lloyd Jones, *Election Address*, November 1931.

[124]*The Times*, 20 October 1931.

[125]NLW, Cardiganshire Liberal Association records, no.1, minute book (1923–50), entry for 1 September 1932.

[126]Ibid.

[127]NLW MS 22016E, f.79, unlabelled press cutting.

[128]Quoted in Madgwick, *Politics of Rural Wales*, p.53.

[129]Ibid.

[130]Quoted in Jones, 'Labour Party', 156.

[131]D. O. Evans, *Election Address*, September 1932.

[132]*Welsh Gazette*, 29 September 1932.

[133]See Jones, 'Labour Party', 156–7.

[134]Ibid., 157.

[135]See Madgwick, *Politics of Rural Wales*, p.56.

organization in Cardiganshire is worthy of the name of Liberalism', Thomas Levi told a meeting of local Liberals, for 'a united Radical party' should be established.[136] His strong language evoked little sympathy, the meeting agreeing to support only a call for 'a united Liberal party of advanced Liberalism'.[137] Even the *Cambrian News*, formerly a fervent champion of Lloyd George, now attacked him as one who had 'nauseated the old-fashioned Radical', and whose conduct – 'a spurious thing' – had stood in glaring contrast to the 'definite sincerity of purpose and high ideals' practised by true Liberals.[138] A threat even greater than Lloyd George to the local Liberal consensus was the growing support for the Labour Party which, in November 1935, nominated as its candidate Ronw Moelwyn Hughes, a native of Cardigan, a London-based barrister, and a very recent convert from the Liberals.[139] Local Conservatives failed to persuade Fitzwilliams to stand again,[140] while Labour toiled 'with confidence of ultimate success'.[141] 'Labour has brains, enthusiasm, dynamic person-alities', conceded the *Cambrian News*, 'but can Labour rule?',[142] while Evans attacked nationalization – 'nationalisation means dictatorship, which is the negation of Liberalism . . . It is but a short step from Socialism to Communism.'[143] His strong language did not, however, prevent Hughes from polling 10,085 votes, a severe shock to local Liberals.[144]

Inevitably, people in the years after 1935 became rather more interested in the issues of peace, security and armaments. The League of Nations Union had attracted a very high membership at Aberystwyth, and in the 'Peace Ballot' of 1934–5 a response of 89 per cent was reported in north Cardiganshire.[145] In July 1936 Cardiganshire Liberals deplored the abandonment of sanctions against Mussolini by the government,[146] and in October D. O. Evans resisted demands for a 'Popular Front' government: 'I am not prepared to trust the Labour Party for a party which depends upon a trade union is not fit to govern.'[147] His decision two years later to support Chamberlain's appeasement policy brought him into sharp conflict with the Liberal Association; he argued his action was 'an expression of gratitude for having saved for the time being the country from a ghastly war . . . It was no endorsement of the past policy of the government in foreign affairs and no whitewashing for past mistakes.'[148] A tense meeting of the Association ensued, in which a leading local Liberal confessed his 'great misgivings' over the Member's conduct. The outbreak of war less than a year later, however, inevitably saw local Liberals close ranks behind their Member – 'everybody should stand firm to win the war'.[149] The hesitation and uncertainty which characterized the first months of the 'phoney war' soon gave way to an united commitment to 'total war'. Evans

[136]*Cambrian News*, 28 April 1933.
[137]Ibid.
[138]Ibid.
[139]Jones, 'Labour Party', 157.
[140]*Cambrian News*, 18 October 1935.
[141]Ibid.
[142]Ibid., 8 November 1935.
[143]Ibid.
[144]Ibid., 22 November 1935.
[145]Madgwick, *Politics of Rural Wales*, p.58.
[146]NLW, Cardiganshire Liberal Association records, no.1, minute book (1923–50), entry for 3 July 1936.
[147]Ibid., entry for 17 October 1936.
[148]Ibid., entry for 29 October 1938.
[149]Ibid., entry for 21 October 1939.

read extracts of Churchill's speeches to a packed meeting of the Association,[150] and even the peace-loving *Cambrian News* now urged its readership to fight 'until either the Nazis or we are extinguished'.[151] Loyalty to king and government prevailed. Thereafter the Association did not meet for three years until October 1943, when it voiced its 'inflexible determination' to press for 'total victory over the Axis powers and the liberation of the enslaved peoples'.[152] At the same time consideration was given to the recommendations of the Beveridge Report in order to solve the problems of mass unemployment.[153] By this time 'political apathy' again prevailed, and the county's local Liberal associations rarely bestirred themselves.[154]

Meanwhile the Cardiganshire Labour Party had selected as its prospective candidate in July 1939 Iwan Morgan, a university lecturer in economics in Cardiff, a man with extensive Cardiganshire roots, and a graduate of the University College of Wales, Aberystwyth.[155] Local Labour organization had improved dramatically and new branches had been formed at Aberaeron, Aberporth, Cardigan and Llandysul. The party had a total of 600 members and its financial position was much improved. Local Liberals were thus stirred to action, confidently adopting the Beveridge proposals as the centrepiece of their campaign.[156] A 'pre-election campaign' was launched with great gusto, and plans were laid to re-form 'action committees' throughout the county.[157] Three months later, only days before nominations for the election closed, D. O. Evans died suddenly in London – 'a political disaster for Labour', admitted Iwan Morgan, 'as much propaganda against D. O. Evans was nullified.'[158] His successor was Captain E. Roderic Bowen, a 32-year-old barrister from Cardigan – 'the young upstart', according to some observers[159] – (who was selected from a short-list of six which included Alun Talfan Davies, J. Morgan Davies and Ifan ab Owen Edwards).[160] Bowen spoke at his adoption meeting of his 'sacred trust – the maintenance of Liberal principles in the County of Cardiganshire'.[161] Local Liberals, deprived of the guiding hand of long-serving party agent Harry Rees,[162] constantly stressed that the 'issue is between Socialism and Liberalism – bureaucracy and democracy',[163] and the *Cambrian News*, too, forcefully voiced its distaste for the 'rigid and inflexible policy of socialism' embraced by Labour,[164] and stressed the need to return to the traditional political loyalties which had been severely undermined by the impact of war. Bowen was elected by a safe majority of more than 8,000, in spite of the national

[150]Madgwick, *Politics of Rural Wales*, p.60.

[151]*Cambrian News*, 23 August 1940.

[152]NLW, Cardiganshire Liberal Association records, no.1, minute book (1923–50), entry for 16 October 1943.

[153]Ibid.

[154]Ibid., entry for 2 December 1944.

[155]Jones, 'Labour Party', 157–8.

[156]NLW, Cardiganshire Liberal Association records, no.1, minute book (1923–50), entry for 22 February 1945.

[157]*Cambrian News*, 1 March 1945.

[158]Quoted in Jones, 'Labour Party', 158.

[159]NLW, Clement Davies Papers Q4/126.

[160]NLW, Cardiganshire Liberal Association records, no.1, minute book (1923–50), entry for 16 June 1945.

[161]*Cambrian News*, 22 June 1945.

[162]Ibid., 1 June 1945.

[163]Ibid., 29 June 1945.

[164]Ibid., 1 June 1945.

Labour landslide, and recriminations began immediately in local Labour circles.[165] By November moves were afoot to select a new Labour candidate.[166]

Bowen entered Westminster in 1945 as one of a tiny rump of twelve Liberal MPs, seven of whom came from Wales. One of his colleagues was Rhys Hopkin Morris, now MP for Carmarthen. During the Attlee government of 1945–50, Bowen was inevitably dwarfed by such well-established political figures as Clement Davies (Montgomeryshire), who became Liberal leader, and Lady Megan Lloyd-George (Anglesey), who led the left-wing of the tiny party. Bowen, described as 'a plump Welshman with a polished manner',[167] soon proved himself an eloquent public speaker and a clever and witty debater in the House of Commons.[168] Although he believed that his party's role was to be 'the watchdogs of freedom and fair play',[169] it was felt that he was disinclined to part company with the official party line.[170] Returning to address Cardiganshire Liberals in November 1947, Sir Rhys Hopkin Morris attacked the Labour government – 'It treats the liberty of the subject for nothing'[171] – while Bowen accused the government of paying overmuch attention to 'political dogma'.[172] On more than one occasion he was forced to defend his voting record in the Commons by asserting that the Liberals were 'a far more critical opposition to the Government' than were the Tories.[173] Meanwhile Sir Arthur Harford of Falcondale, chairman of the Cardiganshire Conservatives, had suggested in March 1948 that a joint Liberal-Conservative candidate should stand in the next general election.[174] Bowen condemned such a move as 'a fatal mistake',[175] and local Liberals refused the offer[176] – 'a bold decision', according to the editor of the *Cambrian News*.[177] Unpleasant rumours ensued that Harford was engaged in clandestine negotiations with the National Liberal group,[178] thereby creating an antagonism which persisted to the spring of 1949. By this time a keenly fought three-cornered contest was widely anticipated,[179] for Bowen sensed that local Tories and Socialists were 'collaborating in their efforts to oust the Liberal member'.[180] The local Labour party, after much manœuvring, had somewhat reluctantly readopted Iwan Morgan as its prospective candidate.[181]

The general election of February 1950 in Cardiganshire proved venomous. Bowen regularly accused Morgan of 'going about advising the electorate that if they are not prepared to vote for him

[165] *Welsh Gazette*, 2 August 1945.
[166] Jones, 'Labour Party', 158.
[167] *Daily Herald*, 18 March 1950.
[168] D. M. Roberts, 'The strange death of Liberal Wales' in John Osmond (ed.), *The National Question Again: Welsh Political Identity in the 1980s* (Llandysul, 1985), p.78.
[169] NLW, Cardiganshire Liberal Association records, no.1, minute book (1923–50), entry for 12 January 1946.
[170] Roberts, 'Strange death', p.78.
[171] NLW, Cardiganshire Liberal Association records, no.1, minute book (1923–50), entry for 8 November 1947.
[172] Ibid.
[173] Ibid., entry for 19 February 1949.
[174] Ibid., file 24, Sir Arthur Harford to E. Roderic Bowen, 8 March 1948.
[175] Ibid., no.1, minute book (1923–50), entry for 5 June 1948.
[176] Ibid., file 24, David Thomas to Sir Arthur Harford, 7 June 1948.
[177] *Cambrian News*, 2 July 1948.
[178] *Western Mail*, 17 February 1949.
[179] NLW, Cardiganshire Liberal Association records, no.1, minute book (1923–50), entry for 28 May 1949.
[180] Ibid., entry for 29 October 1949.
[181] Jones, 'Labour Party', 158–9.

to vote Tory',[182] while Morgan pointed to the Member's alleged poor voting record in the Commons.[183] The result was considered highly uncertain because of 'the intervention of a third candidate',[184] but, in the event, Bowen was returned with more than half the total vote. Indeed, Cardiganshire and Montgomery were the only two constituencies where the Liberals secured an absolute majority in a three-cornered fight,[185] thereby disproving Clement Davies's heartfelt fear – 'Each of us in Wales will have a very tough fight.'[186] The outcome of the fray was indeed 'a notable triumph' for Bowen.[187]

It was inevitable that the 'frustrating and frustrated Parliament'[188] elected in 1950 would not survive for very long. By the autumn of 1951 Attlee was compelled to go to the country again, a course of events which created formidable financial difficulties for Cardiganshire Liberals.[189] One of the many eleventh-hour candidates was the Revd Brynmor Williams, vicar of Llansamlet, who became the Labour candidate in Cardiganshire. At his adoption meeting, the party chairman declared: 'Let us liberate the county from its shackles of stick-in-the-mud Liberalism.'[190] Local Tories resolved to stand aside so that the *Cambrian News* could portray the election as a contest between an 'increased dose of State Socialism and regimentation' and 'freedom, free enterprise and a balanced harmony of class'.[191] The denunciation of 'extreme Socialism' was the major theme of a somewhat low-key and tranquil campaign, although Williams's claim to have won over the support of 'the Church people' evoked strong language from Bowen, who accused him of taking 'a rotten, repulsive and revolting line'.[192] 'Is this contest really necessary?', asked the *Welsh Gazette*.[193] Rumours abounded that the Bishop of Swansea and Brecon and Labour Party mandarins at Transport House had intervened to enforce Williams's withdrawal, but this proved quite false.[194] Williams portrayed himself as 'a churchman to represent the common man in the House of Commons',[195] but in a straight fight victory was not within his grasp.

One question persistently asked of Roderic Bowen during the election campaign was his attitude towards the tenacious Parliament for Wales campaign launched at Llandrindod in July 1950. He voiced his tentative support for such a body 'to deal with the domestic problems of Wales, but not in substitution for, but in addition to, Welsh representation at Westminster'.[196] Yet he (and Rhys Hopkin Morris) doggedly distanced himself from the campaign's activities, and later attributed his reluctance to the fact that 'there were too many political viewpoints represented'.[197] This attitude

[182]*Cambrian News*, 10 February 1950.
[183]Ibid., 17 February 1950.
[184]E. R. Bowen, *Election Address*, February 1950.
[185]H. G. Nicholas, *The British General Election of 1950* (London, 1951), p.323.
[186]NLW, Clement Davies Papers J3/10, Davies to Sir Archibald Sinclair, 6 January 1950 (copy).
[187]NLW, Cardiganshire Liberal Associations records, no.1, minute book (1923–50), entry for 15 April 1950.
[188]H. Macmillan, *Tides of Fortune* (London, 1969), p.352.
[189]NLW, Cardiganshire Liberal Association papers, file 40.
[190]*Cambrian News*, 5 October 1951.
[191]Ibid.
[192]Ibid., 19 October 1951.
[193]*Welsh Gazette*, 11 October 1951.
[194]Ibid.
[195]Ibid.
[196]*Cambrian News*, 19 October 1951.
[197]A. Butt Philip, *The Welsh Question: Nationalism in Welsh Politics, 1945–1970* (Cardiff, 1975), p.259.

gave added weight to gibes by nationalists that Liberal support for the movement was at best 'anaemic'.[198]

Although Bowen appeared securely entrenched in his Cardiganshire citadel, his local Liberal Association faced an array of irksome difficulties. Until the appointment of J. Parry Williams in January 1953, the Association lacked a salaried organizer for eighteen months.[199] The county could boast of only fifteen 'active' local associations.[200] The Labour threat seemed increasingly menacing too, although attempts to secure the nomination of John Morris (a law graduate of Aberystwyth and a native of the county) proved futile.[201] Four years later Morris lost the Labour nomination for the crucial Carmarthen by-election by a single vote. The victor in Cardiganshire was David Jones-Davies, a native of Tregaron and further education officer for Caernarfonshire. From 1946 to 1949 he had served as a Presbyterian minister at Bangor[202] – 'once again a reverend gentleman', quipped Bowen, 'although they have changed the brand this time!'[203] Welsh Liberals, celebrating Clement Davies's silver jubilee as MP for Montgomeryshire, expected rich rewards,[204] but in Cardiganshire Bowen's protracted illness led to rumours of his impending retirement.[205] These were vehemently denied, however, and the Member was zealously readopted.[206]

Bowen's re-election was made more secure by the decision of local Tories to stand aside.[207] Plans to put forward the Unitarian Revd T. Oswald Williams of Lampeter as the first Plaid Cymru aspirant also came to nothing.[208] But the local campaign was again coloured by venomous personal attacks. D. J. Jones, president of the Labour Party, accused Bowen of belonging to a tradition of 'playboy' MPs: 'No man can pursue a private career and do justice to his constituents at the same time. No man can be in Cardiff and Westminster at the same time.'[209] Bowen was also accused of consistently supporting the Conservative government in parliamentary divisions,[210] and Jim Callaghan, addressing an Aberystwyth audience, dismissed the Liberal Party as 'a ghost . . . a political corpse'.[211] Bowen retaliated with strong rhetoric: 'You are invited to sacrifice your political principles on the altar of Socialist power politics and base expediency.'[212] His majority, although reduced, was still 8,817. Local Liberals rejoiced, too, in the re-election of Clement Davies and Sir Rhys Hopkin Morris.[213]

Yet unpleasant backbiting persisted. When Bowen failed to participate in the Commons debate on the Rating and Valuation Bill in February 1957, a member of the Aberystwyth Town Council

---

[198] *Welsh Nation*, May 1956.
[199] NLW, Cardiganshire Liberal Association records, file 56, circular letter from J. Parry Williams, January 1953.
[200] *Liberal News*, 20 November 1953.
[201] Jones, 'Labour Party', 159.
[202] Ibid.
[203] *Welsh Gazette*, 5 November 1953.
[204] Ibid., 29 July 1954.
[205] *Western Mail*, 19 April 1955.
[206] *Welsh Gazette*, 12 May 1955.
[207] *Cambrian News*, 22 April 1955.
[208] Ibid.
[209] Ibid., 29 April 1955.
[210] Ibid., 13 May 1955.
[211] Ibid., 20 May 1955.
[212] *Welsh Gazette*, 18 May 1955.
[213] Ibid., 2 June 1955.

protested: 'The Member for Cardiganshire was not there, and Cardiganshire's views were not represented.'[214] To speculation over his supposed imminent retirement Bowen reacted decisively, dismissing the conjecture as 'twaddle and nonsense. It's a hardy annual put up by the Labour boys when things are quiet.'[215] As the Macmillan government drew to the close of its term of office, Welsh Liberals boasted that Cardiganshire was 'the safest seat held by a Liberal member'.[216] Yet the Cardiganshire Labour Party had secured a strong candidate in Mrs Loti Rees Hughes, a Carmarthenshire county councillor whose husband, W. Douglas Hughes, was political agent to Jim Griffiths at Llanelli.[217] The party appointed Ron Bundock as full-time agent to co-ordinate the campaign.[218] Mrs Hughes, an extraordinarily vivacious candidate, was promoted as 'a person who has promised, if elected, to act as a full-time M.P.'.[219] Bundock professed to satisfaction as the long campaign neared its close:

> Personally I feel that the campaign is going extremely well and the meetings are being very well attended . . . I think our motto should be 'Carry on as now' and we are going to shock Cardiganshire, the country and Transport House. I am extremely *confident* and the reports coming in each day are encouraging. The feeling in the county is different to any I have known in previous elections.[220]

'The machinery is well oiled and ready to click', enthused the local party treasurer, 'the Party is better organized now than it has ever been.'[221] Its president again condemned Roderic Bowen as characteristic of a breed of part-time politicians who were more 'interested in their careers' and who 'spent their spare time in Parliament'.[222]

A novel dimension was added by the nomination of the first Plaid Cymru candidate to stand in the county: Dr Gareth Evans, a lecturer at Swansea, was a native of Cardiganshire. Although he probably robbed Labour of 1,500 votes and the Liberals of 1,000 votes,[223] Bowen's majority was over 9,300. Mrs Hughes's spirited campaign had not received its recognition at the polls: 'disappointing considering the amount of work which had been put in' was the verdict of Douglas Hughes, although he rejoiced in the confirmation of 'a hard core of 8,500 Labour voters'.[224] He stressed the need 'to educate the youth in the county'.[225]

As the fifties gave way to the sixties the quickening pace of social change gave rise to novel political demands, notably a radical overhaul of the structure of local government and a development corporation for mid-Wales. The closure of the Aberystwyth–Carmarthen railway line

[214]*Cambrian News*, 15 February 1957.
[215]NLW, Cardiganshire Liberal Association records, file 135, unlabelled press cutting.
[216]Ibid., file 56, J. Ellis Williams, Hon. Secretary of the South Wales Liberal Federation, to E. Jones, 11 February 1959.
[217]NLW, Deian R. Hopkin Papers, no.136, Cardiganshire Labour Party minute book, 1958–65.
[218]Ibid., entry for 4 February 1959.
[219]Ibid., entry for 28 February 1959.
[220]Ibid., file 135, R. J. Bundock to W. Douglas Hughes, 26 September 1959.
[221]*Cambrian News*, 11 September 1959.
[222]Ibid., 25 September 1959.
[223]Jones, 'Labour Party', 159.
[224]NLW, Deian R. Hopkin Papers, no.136, Cardiganshire Labour Party minute book, 1958–65, entry for 31 October 1959.
[225]See Madgwick, *Politics of Rural Wales*, p.64.

in the wake of the infamous Beeching Report, the impact of Cymdeithas yr Iaith Gymraeg, and disputes over the number of hours of Welsh-language broadcasting, all coloured the tenor of local political life.[226] Perhaps it was the Labour Party, with its new headquarters at 4 Bridge Street, Aberystwyth, which stood to gain most from the renewed emphasis on local issues. But the party encountered difficulties in selecting a candidate and eventually its local president, David John Davies, who had farmed at Panteryrod, Llwyncelyn, for almost twenty years, agreed to accept the nomination. Nine years earlier Davies had been one of the founder members of the Farmers' Union of Wales. 'The Aberystwyth–Carmarthen line is the only means of access to a very wide area', he asserted, 'its closure will make it even more difficult to attract light industries.'[227] 'If Labour is successful there will be no more Tryweryns', was a further pledge by Davies, 'The Labour Party will establish a Welsh Water Board.'[228]

But the decisive intervention came by the Conservatives in 1964 when the local party chairman rightly claimed that 'no eligible elector under the age of 35 years has had a comprehensive choice of candidate in this county'. Less convincingly, he insisted that Roderic Bowen had for fourteen years 'found himself . . . in a unique happy environment of "Parochial Charm diffuser", relieved of the necessity of expounding politics'.[229] According to the *Cambrian News*, the four-cornered contest was indeed a 'much keener affair' than in previous years, and prediction of its outcome 'a trickier business even in such tradition-entrenched counties as Cardiganshire'.[230] Bowen's majority was reduced drastically to 2,219, and the division became marginal as a direct result of the Conservative 'intervention'.[231]

In October 1965 Roderic Bowen (supported only by Emlyn Hooson and David Steel of the parliamentary Liberal Party) accepted one of the two posts of Deputy Speaker of the Commons, a decision which suggested that the Liberals were prepared to prop up an ailing Labour government on the verge of defeat. This meant that prospects of an early election were dimmed and the Liberals' opportunity of holding the balance of power jettisoned. When the Wilson government was indeed forced to resign four months later, Bowen's acceptance of the post featured prominently in the local election campaign. Cardiganshire was by now considered a highly marginal 'hot seat',[232] and the local Labour Party, having persuaded the Revd D. Ben Rees to withdraw his name, chose as its candidate Elystan Morgan, a young lawyer with firm roots in Cardiganshire. Morgan was a former vice-president of Plaid Cymru and had stood as the party's parliamentary candidate in Merioneth in 1964 and in Wrexham in 1955 and 1959. In another keenly fought four-cornered contest, the choice facing the electors of Cardiganshire was stark. As Bowen put it: 'The issue in Cardiganshire is whether you return a progressive anti-socialist who has served you for 21 years or switch to a socialist representative.'[233] Both Plaid Cymru and the Conservatives were able to put up strong candidates, namely E. G. Millward and John Stradling Thomas. In 'one of the keenest and most intriguing elections'[234] ever held in the county, an increase of more than 2,000 in the Labour vote

---

[226] *Cambrian News*, 25 September 1964.
[227] Ibid., 18 September 1964.
[228] Ibid., 9 October 1964.
[229] Ibid., 18 September 1964.
[230] Ibid., 25 September 1964.
[231] Ibid., 23 October 1964.
[232] Ibid., 4 March 1966.
[233] Ibid., 25 March 1966.
[234] Ibid., 4 March 1966.

Fig. 115: Elystan Morgan (Labour) celebrating victory with his agent
Cliff Prothero on 1 April 1966. (*Copyright National Library of Wales*).

enabled Morgan to win the day by the slim margin of 523. In this, the Labour high tide of 1966,
Cardiganshire became one of eleven seats never previously held by the party.[235]

Elystan Morgan increased his majority to 1,263 in the election of June 1970. By then Cardiganshire was regarded 'one of the fifty marginal seats' in the country,[236] and an additional element of
uncertainty was provided by the granting of the vote to eighteen-year-olds. Elystan Morgan
regarded his re-election, which ran strongly contrary to the national trend, 'a miracle'.[237] Although
many Plaid Cymru supporters may well have supported Morgan in 1966 and 1970, some sections of
the party viewed him as a 'defector'.[238] It was suggested that the Liberals and Plaid Cymru should
form an electoral pact in Cardigan and Carmarthen in order to oust the sitting Labour Members,[239]

[235]See D. E. Butler and A. King, *The British General Election of 1966* (London, 1967), pp.260–1.
[236]*Cambrian News*, 22 May 1970.
[237]Ibid., 26 June 1970.
[238]*Welsh Nation*, August 1973.
[239]NLW, Welsh Liberal Party archives, file B11, letter from Geraint Howells to the editor of the
Western Mail, 20 August 1973.

Fig. 116: Geraint Howells, Liberal MP for Cardiganshire
1974–1992. (*Copyright National Library of Wales*).

but both parties immediately distanced themselves from the notion. Cardiganshire Liberals had
already secured a strong local candidate in Geraint Howells, a farmer from Ponterwyd, a member
of the Cardiganshire County Council since 1952, a former Young Farmers Club activist, and the
chairman of the Welsh Liberal Party. His prospects were assisted by a national Liberal resurgence;
'nothing succeeds like success', asserted Howells, 'and even Heath is shaken by the Liberal tide
which now threatens to engulf him.'[240] Encouraged still further by promising results in local
government elections, local Liberals expected victory, but even they were surprised by Howells's
majority of 2,476 in February 1974, a victory which was repeated in October. Within the Labour
Party in Wales Elystan Morgan was considered the unfortunate victim of tactical voting by Plaid
Cymru supporters. As Denzil Davies put it:

. . . Then there is poor Elystan in Cardigan, I am afraid that he is unlikely to get back since the
Nationalists have decided to support the Liberal in order to keep him out. It's a great pity; he is
too good a man to be out of the House of Commons.[241]

[240]Ibid., text of a speech by Howells to the Cardiganshire Liberals, 28 September 1973.
[241]NLW, James Griffiths Papers C3/26, Denzil Davies to James Griffiths, 25 September 1974.

When Geraint Howells recaptured Cardiganshire from Labour in February 1974, the Labour Party also lost Caernarfonshire and Merioneth to Plaid Cymru, losses which soon began to appear permanent. Howells, re-elected convincingly on four occasions, also fell victim to a Plaid Cymru candidate – Cynog Dafis – in 1992, and subsequently joined a small group of Liberal peers in the House of Lords.

Cardiganshire Parliamentary Election Results, 1885–1974

Election	Electors	Turnout	Candidate	Party	Votes	%
1885	12,308	78.1	D. Davies	L (LU)	5,967	62.1
			M. L. Vaughan Davies	C	3,644	37.9
					2,323	24.2
1886	12,308	69.0	W. B. Rowlands	L	4,252	50.1
			D. Davies	LU	4,243	49.9
					9	0.2
1892	13,155	64.6	W. B. Rowlands	L	5,233	61.5
			W. Jones	LU	3,270	38.5
					1,963	23.0
[Appointed Recorder of Swansea]						
1893 (4/7)			W. B. Rowlands	L	Unopp.	
1895	12,994	66.8	M. L. Vaughan Davies	L	4,927	56.8
			J. C. Harford	C	3,748	43.2
					1,179	13.6
1900	13,299	62.8	M. L. Vaughan Davies	L	4,568	54.7
			J. C. Harford	C	3,787	45.3
					781	9.4
1906	13,215	66.5	M. L. Vaughan Davies	L	5,829	66.3
			C. E. D. M. Richardson	LU	2,960	33.7
					2,869	32.6
1910 (J)	13,333	69.7	M. L. Vaughan Davies	L	6,348	68.3
			G. F. Roberts	C	2,943	31.7
					3,405	36.6
1910 (D)			M. L. Vaughan Davies	L	Unopp.	
1918			M. L. Vaughan Davies	Co L	Unopp.	
[Elevation to the Peerage – Lord Ystwyth]						
1921 (18/2)	30,751	80.1	E. Evans	Co L	14,111	57.3
			W. L. Williams	L	10,521	42.7
					3,590	14.6
1922	32,695	76.9	E. Evans	NL	12,825	51.0
			R. H. Morris	L	12,310	49.0
					515	2.0

1923	32,881	81.0	R. H. Morris	Ind L (L)	12,469	46.9
			E. Evans	L	7,391	27.7
			Earl of Lisburne	C	6,776	25.4
					5,078	19.2
1924			R. H. Morris	L	Unopp.	
1929	38,704	73.2	R. H. Morris	L	17,127	60.5
			E. C. L. Fitzwilliams	C	11,198	39.5
					5,929	21.0
1931	39,206	67.5	R. H. Morris	L	20,113	76.0
			J. L. Jones	Lab	6,361	24.0
					13,752	52.0

[Resignation on appointment as a Metropolitan Police Magistrate]

1932 (22/9)	39,206	70.4	D. O. Evans	L	13,437	48.7
			E. C. L. Fitzwilliams	C	8,866	32.1
			Revd D. M. Jones	Lab	5,295	19.2
					4,571	16.6
1935	39,851	65.1	D. O. Evans	L	15,846	61.1
			R. M. Hughes	Lab	10,085	38.9
					5,761	22.2

[Seat vacant at Dissolution (Death)]

1945	41,597	71.2	E. R. Bowen	L	18,912	63.8
			I. J. Morgan	Lab	10,718	36.2
					8,194	27.6
1950	44,627	73.6	E. R. Bowen	L	17,093	52.1
			I. J. Morgan	Lab	9,055	27.6
			Dr G. S. R. Little	C	6,680	20.3
					8,038	24.5
1951	41,997	70.6	E. R. Bowen	L	19,954	67.3
			Revd B. Williams	Lab	9,697	32.7
					10,257	34.6
1955	39,902	72.7	E. R. Bowen	L	18,907	65.2
			D. Jones-Davies	Lab	10,090	34.8
					8,817	30.4
1959	38,878	78.0	E. R. Bowen	L	17,868	59.0
			Mrs L. R. Hughes	Lab	8,559	28.2
			G. W. Evans	PC	3,880	12.8
					9,309	30.8
1964	37,964	78.9	E. R. Bowen	L	11,500	38.4
			D. J. Davies	Lab	9,281	31.0
			A. R. Ryder	C	5,897	19.7
			G. W. Evans	PC	3,262	10.9
					2,219	7.4
1966	37,553	81.1	D. E. Morgan	Lab	11,302	37.1
			E. R. Bowen	L	10,779	35.4
			J. Stradling Thomas	C	5,893	19.4
			E. G. Millward	PC	2,469	8.1
					523	1.7
1970	40,302	82.1	D. E. Morgan	Lab	11,063	33.5
			H. C. Lloyd Williams	L	9,800	29.6
			H. W. J. ap Robert	PC	6,498	19.6
			D. F. R. George	C	5,715	17.3
					1,263	3.9

1974 (F)	43,039	83.1	G. Howells	L	14,731	40.2
			D. E. Morgan	Lab	11,895	33.2
			T. W. Llewellyn	C	4,758	13.3
			C. Davies	PC	4,754	13.3
					2,476	6.9
1974 (O)	43,052	80.5	G. Howells	L	14,612	42.1
			D. E. Morgan	Lab	12,202	35.2
			C. Davies	PC	4,583	13.2
			D. Williams	C	3,275	9.4
					2,410	6.9

CHAPTER 19

THE CARDIGANSHIRE COUNTY COUNCIL, 1889–1974

J. Graham Jones

THE Cardiganshire County Council, like its twelve sister authorities in Wales, came into existence as a result of the provisions of the Local Government Act of 1888.[1] The results of the first county council elections of January 1889 – 'a month of victories' in the eyes of *Baner ac Amserau Cymru*[2] – strikingly paralleled the Liberal hegemony which had become so marked a feature of Welsh parliamentary politics. Locally in Cardiganshire the contests came to be viewed as 'simply a protest against the former possessors of power and privilege',[3] the election campaign underlining powerfully how 'party politics' had penetrated so deeply into local political life 'that men of the highest standing are laughed at when they profess their intention to contest county council elections apart from politics'.[4] Assuring the electorate that the ballot was 'absolutely secret', John Gibson, editor of the *Cambrian News*, predicted that 'the most democratic County Council in Wales' would emerge in Cardiganshire.[5]

In the event, all the Welsh counties save Breconshire returned a solid majority of Liberal councillors, these results creating almost overnight 'a profound social and political revolution throughout Wales, . . . a social transformation more striking than the extension of democracy at the national level'.[6] In north Wales, 175 out of 260 councillors were Liberals, and in south Wales and Monmouthshire 215 out of 330.[7] Carmarthenshire, returning forty Liberal councillors out of fifty-one, displayed the most overwhelming loyalty, but the Cardiganshire County Council, with its thirty-eight Liberal councillors and thirteen aldermen (as opposed to ten Conservative councillors and three aldermen), was almost equally impressive.[8] The social transformation of the Welsh countryside and the dramatic usurpation of the landlord class, so securely entrenched for centuries, were revolutionary indeed. Cardiganshire provided some of the most vivid examples of the emergence of the new Nonconformist middle class. At Troed-yr-aur in the south of the county, a humble farmer ousted the local squire Sir Marteine Lloyd of Bronwydd, at Devil's Bridge the local postmaster ignominiously defeated T. J. Waddingham of Hafod, and at nearby Bow Street the local coal

---

[1] See K. O. Morgan, *Wales in British Politics, 1868–1922* (4th edn., Cardiff, 1991), pp.106–7.
[2] *Baner ac Amserau Cymru*, 30 January 1889 (translation).
[3] *Cambrian News*, 11 January 1889.
[4] Ibid.
[5] Ibid., 18 January 1889.
[6] Morgan, *Wales in British Politics*, p.107.
[7] Ibid.
[8] *Baner ac Amserau Cymru*, 13 Mawrth 1889.

Fig. 117: The Revd Thomas Levi (1825–1916), Calvinistic Methodist minister of Tabernacl Chapel, Aberystwyth, and one of the first
county councillors in 1889. (*Copyright National Library of Wales*).

merchant expelled Henry Bonsall of Cwm, Clarach. Indeed, the successful coal merchant was none
other than William Morgan, whose grandson, Elystan, was to become the first Labour MP for the
county seventy-seven years later.[9] To Herbert Vaughan, the apologist of the south Wales squires,
such striking results dealt the landlord class 'a blow that smote the whole class beyond recovery'.[10]

Recent research, however, has demonstrated the notable element of continuity in Welsh local
government which transcended the advent of the county councils in 1889.[11] By no means were all
landowners and long-serving justices ousted from their traditional roles. To some extent 'tried and
experienced hands' continued to hold firm the reins of local government,[12] but henceforth they
reigned alongside a newer type of élite to whom election to the county council soon came to
represent the crowning of a career of social ascent begun through business or commerce or through
the informal hierarchy of one of the religious denominations. The membership of the first
Cardiganshire County Council of 1889 admirably demonstrates this process.[13] Lord Lisburne and

[9]*Cambrian News*, 25 January 1889.
[10]H. M. Vaughan, *The South Wales Squires* (London, 1926), p.3.
[11]I. J. Salmon, 'Welsh Liberalism, 1868–1896: a study in political structure and ideology' (unpublished University of Oxford D.Phil. thesis, 1983), pp.86–93.
[12]*The Spectator*, 19 January 1889.
[13]See Appendix 1.

Colonel Davies-Evans, the county's Lord Lieutenant, served alongside newer 'gentlemen' like James James of Llanrhystud and J. T. Morgan of Tal-y-bont, and professional men like the surgeon E. Cynlais Davies of Llanwnnen. Ministers of religion, such as the Calvinistic Methodists David Morgan and Thomas Levi, were also well represented, while coal merchants like Peter Jones and William Morgan and the draper C. M. Williams were characteristic of an emergent 'shopocracy' – tradesmen and local retailers – who were to become an increasingly active group. A small number of farmers like John Morris of Taliesin remained in office, but only one of the original Cardiganshire councillors – David Davies, a stonecutter from Llanddewibrefi – could be described as an artisan. Since sufficient time and money were an imperative prerequisite to service on the county council, membership rarely extended below the petty bourgeoisie.[14]

Not that the new county councils were purely elective, for they also included aldermen who, under the terms of the 1888 Local Government Act, could be chosen either from among the elected councillors or from outside.[15] John Gibson thundered against the latter course:

> There is a good deal of talk in favour of electing aldermen from the outside in order to avoid the worry of further elections. The worry of elections must be borne. A great principle is at stake. Good men may be defeated at the polls, but they must not be made aldermen. Let them fight again. The Cardiganshire County Council will soon be a body of cripples if every member of the body is not directly elected by the ratepayers. There may be strong desire to do special honour to some gentlemen who fail to secure election, but it would be a great pity to weaken the County Council at the outset by establishing bad precedents.[16]

In fact the practice among the Welsh county councils varied considerably. Cardiganshire was to elect eight aldermen from among the councillors and eight from outside.

When the provisional Cardiganshire County Council met for the first time at the Town Hall, Lampeter, on 31 January 1889, Morgan Evans of Oakford stated that, in fairness to the Welsh councillors, he believed the business of the council should be conducted in Welsh as well as in English. Evans also proposed that Peter Jones of Aberystwyth be elected chairman.[17] Jones spoke eloquently to his fellow-councillors:

> I see here several gentlemen who have had experience of county business as members of the Court of Quarter Sessions whilst others have taken an active part in local affairs, together with those of commercial experience, and a fair sprinkling of agricultural interest. This is the first time in the history of this or any other county that we have a representative body to manage our own affairs, and it seems that our Conservative friends – and I say it to their credit – have realized the fact that representation and taxation go together. I am confident that in future very many matters will be handed over to the Council and will be better managed than hitherto, because the Council are responsible to the ratepayers (Hear, hear).[18]

[14]See Salmon, 'Welsh Liberalism', p.88.
[15]See *The Times*, 19 and 25 January 1889.
[16]*Cambrian News*, 18 January 1889.
[17]Ceredigion RO, CDC/SE/1/1, County Council minutes, 31 January 1889.
[18]*Cambrian News*, 8 February 1889.

It was further resolved that Henry Charles Fryer, clerk of the peace, be appointed clerk to the provisional council.[19]

For many Welsh Liberals, the first county council elections of January 1889 were as much an act of political emancipation as was the general election of 1868. 'The real leaders of the nation', wrote O. M. Edwards to Thomas Gee, 'are recognized as its rulers at last.'[20] Their impact was compounded by the provisions of the Local Government Act of 1894 which, as a truly Liberal measure, received an even warmer welcome from Welsh radicals. As Tom Ellis put it: 'The Local Government Act of 1888 transferred the government of the counties of Wales from the plutocracy to the people. The still greater Act of 1894 created local democratic assemblies, parochial and municipal, with large powers through the length and breadth of Wales.'[21] His heartfelt hope that working men and women would be elected to every parish council throughout Wales was to some extent fulfilled in Cardiganshire as elsewhere. The new urban and rural district councils were an extension of the democratic principle; by the provisions of the 1894 Act, residents, both male and female, who were not ratepayers, became eligible for membership of the new authorities, boards of guardians and parish councils. As in the case of the county council, Anglican clergymen, Nonconformist ministers, professional men and 'gentlemen' became conspicuous on the rural and urban district councils.[22]

In Cardiganshire, as in most of Wales, these momentous changes went far to remove the traditional primacy of the gentry in local politics and society. Their impact was increased still further by the provisions of the remarkable Welsh Intermediate Education Act of 1889, which gave birth to the highly acclaimed 'county schools' which flourished in Cardiganshire and several other Welsh rural counties, yielding novel opportunities for mobility and improvement for the sons (and even in some cases the daughters) of farmers and shopkeepers. The young University College of Wales at Aberystwyth, founded in 1872, enjoyed a special status and prestige as the oldest institution of its kind. In 1893 it was to join forces with its sister colleges at Cardiff and Bangor within a federal University of Wales, the recipient of a prestigious royal charter, a further prized triumph of Nonconformist Liberal Wales.

When the Cardiganshire County Council came to celebrate its golden jubilee in 1939 only one member of the original 1889 Council had survived – Alderman Sir David Charles Roberts of Aberystwyth, the first chairman of the Finance and General Purposes Committee of the Council, and a man who had rendered his native county sterling service for over half a century. In 1889–90 the expenditure of the Council had amounted to a tiny £12,440, and the county rate was no more than 7d. in the pound. The considerable increase in the duties and functions of county councils during the subsequent half century naturally led to a most substantial increase in public expenditure and in the county rate as is detailed in Table 16.[23]

[19]Ceredigion RO, CDC/SE/1/1, County Council minutes, 31 January 1889.
[20]NLW MS 8306D, Edwards to Gee, 18 February 1889.
[21]T. E. Ellis, *Addresses and Speeches* (Wrexham, 1912), p.183.
[22]Salmon, 'Welsh Liberalism', pp.92–3.
[23]*The Jubilee of County Councils, 1889–1939: Cardiganshire* (London, 1939), p.67. I am heavily indebted in the following paragraphs to this most helpful survey.

The AGENDA Specialist.

Fig. 118: A cartoon of Sir David Charles Roberts, Aberystwyth, by
Ap Rhobert. (*Copyright National Library of Wales*).

During this crowded half century the voluminous array of legislation increased the role and burden
of local government and the concomitant rise of bureaucracy through the army of new officials meant
that local councils impinged ever more on the lives of individuals.[24] An increasing number of civic
functionaries emerged in the towns and the counties, most notably the salaried officers of the new
boards – attendance officers for the school boards, medical officers of health (usually local medical
practitioners), rate collectors, clerks of works and borough engineers. In some cases salaried officials
such as town clerks, treasurers and accountants were appointed. Some local solicitors began to act as
part-time financial officers of councils. Difficulties sometimes stemmed from the ordered delegation
and separation of powers to the various councils – county, rural, district, urban and parish – with

[24]There is an admirable analysis in D. L. Baker-Jones, 'Local government, 1815–1974', in D. W.
Howell (ed.), *Pembrokeshire County History, Volume IV* (Haverfordwest, 1993), pp.272–304.

TABLE 17: Cardiganshire County Council Expenditure, 1890–1937

Year ending 31 March	Expenditure	County Rate
1890	£12,440	7d.
1900	£22,600	8fid.
1910	£86,667	1s. 7d.
1920	£127,443	3s. 8d.
1930	£260,110	8s. 0d.
1937	£390,294	14s. 0d.

regard to their respective responsibilities for matters such as ground enclosure, wells and water analysis. More far-reaching problems emerged from the continued existence of authorities such as Education Boards and Poor Law Unions (eventually to be absorbed in 1902 and 1930 respectively), which exercised jurisdiction in areas which bore no relation to the new counties. Yet, in spite of the weaknesses of local government reform in Cardiganshire, as elsewhere, and the growing incursion of the state into the lives of ordinary, law-abiding individuals, the role of the state in Britain remained remarkably unobtrusive on the eve of the First World War.[25]

The one exception was perhaps in education. Forster's Education Act of 1870 had established conclusively the responsibility of the state for the education of the country's youth. By the turn of the century no fewer than seventy new schools had been established in Cardiganshire, fifty-three of them between 1870 and 1880, a remarkable achievement in a remote, rural, and relatively poor county. Compulsory education, with a school-leaving age of eleven years, soon followed. Although the abhorrent system of 'payment by results' persisted for a full quarter of a century after 1870, the basic grounding given in the traditional 'three Rs' was generally satisfactory. A subsequent act of 1895 established the principle of school inspectors' visits without notice and inaugurated a new era of freedom to experiment, to vary the work load according to the capacity of the individual pupil, and to broaden school curricula to include subjects such as science, history, art and music.

The much lauded Welsh Intermediate Education Act of 1889 gave the new county and borough councils full responsibility for this sector of education in their localities. The need for competent secondary schools was especially keenly felt in Cardiganshire following the establishment of the College at Aberystwyth in 1872. With the county still reeling from the massive expense of erecting a large number of primary schools, it was resolved to establish five new County Schools, the first of which opened its doors at Llandysul on 24 September 1895. Similar schools followed at Cardigan in December 1895, Aberaeron (1896), Aberystwyth (1896) and Tregaron (1897). By 1897 these five schools, staffed by five headmasters and fifteen assistants, were providing education for 366 pupils. Forty years later, on the eve of the Second World War, five headmasters and sixty-four assistants were catering for the educational needs of 1,460 pupils. The fact that the number of pupils per 1,000 of the population receiving a county school education was the highest but one of all the Welsh counties was a source of considerable local pride.

As a result of the provisions of the Balfour Education Act of 1902, and the abolition of the old school boards, the Cardiganshire County Council inherited their powers and responsibilities; these,

[25]See A. J. P. Taylor, *English History, 1914–1945* (Penguin edn., 1970), p.25.

in turn, were delegated to its Education Committee. So soundly built were most of the school premises that only seven new schools were built in Cardiganshire between 1902 and 1938, but major improvements were effected in lighting, heating, sanitary arrangements, playground facilities, school furniture and equipment. The number and quality of teaching staffs were much improved and the primary school syllabus enriched and made more varied. An increasing number of graduate entrants turned to elementary school teaching as a career and, by the eve of the Second World War, the proportion of certified teachers in the county was higher than ever before.

Perhaps the jewel in the crown of the county's educational provision was the establishment of the School Medical Service which meant regular professional inspection of school pupils by the School Medical staff and free medical treatment in deserving cases. The health of schoolchildren in Cardiganshire improved dramatically as a result, and the death rate of children between five and fifteen plunged to a record low in 1939.

The provision of health care, of course, extended far beyond the confines of the education system. Although the originators of the 1888 Local Government Act had always intended to bring the Poor Law under the control of the county councils, political difficulties prevented the realization of this hope, and it was not until 1930 that the county councils assumed full authority. The array of nineteenth-century legislation relating to public health, sanitation, public hygiene and disease had created an enormously complex and inconsistent system prior to the advent of the county councils. During the early decades of the twentieth century the Cardiganshire County Council, acting through its education, public health and public assistance committees, was responsible for maternity and child welfare, hospital treatment of maternity cases, district nursing, venereal diseases, lunacy and mental deficiency, tuberculosis, education, school meals, the poor law, the treatment of cripples, the welfare of blind persons, the licensing of producers of accredited and other designated milks, and a wide range of other duties. Yet district sanitary authorities, rural, urban and municipal, remained responsible for sanitation, drainage, scavenging, water supplies, nuisances, the registration of dairymen, the treatment of infections, and the building of working-class homes.

The situation was to some extent remedied by the passage of the Ministry of Health Act 1919, which established a Ministry of Health to assume responsibility for most health-related concerns. The Board of Education was to become responsible for the inspection of school children. A further Act of 1929 made the county councils fully responsible for poor law institutions and public assistance and the isolation of infectious diseases. The Cardiganshire County Council appointed a medical officer, a full-time official, to co-ordinate the work of the rural and other sanitary authorities. The Public Health Act of 1936 consolidated all existing legislation in this field. Generally, standards of nutrition improved, school mid-day meals were much better supported, and there were repeated calls for improved housing and controlled water supplies in the villages. The Teifiside Rural District Council spent £80,000 on water schemes in the southern part of the county, and in the northern division the Aberystwyth Rural District Council embarked upon a major undertaking to pipe water from lakes in the Pumlumon range to supply the whole of the district north of the River Rheidol.

Public concern over standards of housing and health care was sharply intensified by the publication in March 1939 of the *Report of the Committee of Inquiry into the Anti-Tuberculosis Service in Wales and Monmouthshire*.[26] Its findings revealed that Cardiganshire was one of seven Welsh counties

---

[26]Ministry of Health, *Report of the Committee of Inquiry into the Anti-Tuberculosis Service in Wales and Monmouthshire* (HMSO London, 1939).

which headed the list in England and Wales for deaths from tuberculosis. While for England and Wales as a whole mortality was 724 per million of the population, in a number of counties in rural Wales – Anglesey, Cardiganshire, Caernarfonshire and Merioneth among them – the figures were over 1,000 and in some areas they were deteriorating.[27] The situation was clearly at its worst in rural areas where the parsimony of middle-class, cost-conscious local councillors and officials was exposed by the inquiry. The *Report* was equally critical of the housing record of the Cardiganshire County Council; like its neighbours in Carmarthenshire and Pembrokeshire, it had been 'apathetic' and had 'failed in its duty'.[28] The authors of the *Report* insisted that a close link prevailed between the incidence of tuberculosis and sub-standard working-class housing. In his *Annual Report* for 1930, Dr Ernest Jones, the County Medical Officer of Health, had noted that only three Councils, namely Aberystwyth borough and Aberaeron urban and rural, had reported building in that year under the various housing acts:

> Improvement in housing accommodation is asked for to reduce the overcrowding in tuberculosis families, that makes the spread of lung tuberculosis from parent to child so difficult to prevent. District Medical Officers, especially Dr J. T. Lloyd, Tregaron, have repeatedly insisted on the importance of 'droplet infection' and the impossibility of its prevention when a family of six or more have only two bedrooms to share. The re-conditioning of many houses is required because the presence of damp walls and the absence of damp courses where the sub-soil is boulder clay are contributory causes to the large number of cases of rheumatic heart disease in the lower Teifi valley.[29]

In the survey of Cardiganshire, the authors of the *Report* were to conclude:

> The tuberculosis mortality rate in Cardiganshire is the fourth highest among all the counties of England and Wales. The lead-mining industry, and the conditions under which the miners lived and worked, partly account for this high incidence, but there are, and have been over many years, a large number of unfit houses still in occupation, which should have been pulled down. Only 439 houses have been built with State assistance since the War, and only six were in course of construction on the 31st of May, 1938. 1,278 houses have been built without State assistance in that period, but the bulk of those houses were not of the working-class type. The District Councils have been dilatory and apathetic. The County Council should have exercised a closer surveillance over the District Councils. Their housing record for the working classes is a poor one.[30]

More encouraging observations emerge from a consideration of the role of the Cardiganshire County Council in road improvement and highway expansion. The promoters of the Local Government Act of 1888 had abolished the Highway Boards and transferred their responsibilities to the new county councils. The Cardiganshire County Council moved swiftly; in November 1890 it resolved to split the county into two divisions and to appoint two county surveyors (at an annual salary of £160 inclusive of travelling expenses), 'independent of each other' in the wording of the original resolution, an arrangement which remained in operation in 1939. Only on 1 April 1939

[27] Ibid., p.24.
[28] Ibid., p.186.
[29] Ibid., p.150.
[30] Ibid., p.159.

were the two divisions amalgamated under the authority of a single county surveyor. The burden of highway maintenance evidently weighed heavily on the minds of some county councillors during the early years, for the quarterly meeting in November 1895 faced a notice of motion to the effect 'that it is expedient that the management and maintenance of main roads in the County should be transferred to the Rural District Councils'. The motion, although supported by memorials from all the local Rural District Councils, was lost by a large majority. In the following year, steamrolling was used for the first time on the county's roads as a result of the Council's decision to hire one roller for each division 'for a period of three months in order to give the system a thorough trial'. The 'thorough trial' was evidently successful for within three months one of the county surveyors was blithely to report that 'the steam road-roller has arrived and has been at work as a traction engine'. It was further noted that no damage to roads and culverts had been recorded and, with some astonishment, that 'the roads, on the contrary, seem to be improved'.

Road construction work in Cardiganshire, as elsewhere, almost ceased during the years of the Great War and much damage was effected by the regular haulage of timber, especially the produce of the large area of forest which had been felled. Many hundreds of miles of impassable roads inevitably faced the County Council upon the conclusion of hostilities. An ambitious programme of road widening and improvements was put in hand with the establishment of the Ministry of Transport and the arrival of sharply increased traffic. The 75 per cent grants made available for schemes of road improvement for 'maining' purposes were zealously seized upon by many Rural District Councils and applied to, among others, the Caernarfon–Aberystwyth–Fishguard and Aberystwyth–Shrewsbury roads.

The 1930s witnessed an enormous increase in county expenditure on roads, fuelled by the additional burden of unclassified roads taken over from the various district councils. Cardiganshire contained 153 miles of Class I and 204 miles of Class II roads, together with 1,100 miles of un-classified roads. Their maintenance, widening and improvement proved a formidable task, made all the more urgent by the extraordinary demands of the collecting lorries of the various milk organizations and other heavy traffic far in excess of the light and local traffic of the pre-war era. Notable major improvements during the 1930s included the widening of Pont Steffan, Lampeter, over the River Teifi, and the Llannarth–New Quay road, the construction of a new bridge near Glandyfi known as Pont Llyfnant, and the Tre'r-ddôl by-pass opened in December 1936 – the first by-pass in Cardiganshire. The widening of Cardigan bridge, the most heavily trafficked spot in the county, remained an urgent priority. Such activities, together with a host of minor improvements, occasioned a massive increase in the county expenditure on roads and bridges – from £3,372 in 1891 to an estimated £210,502 in 1939–40. Such expenditure was rendered essential by the prevalence of narrow, winding, sub-standard roads throughout the county. Even so, Cardiganshire could boast an impressive road safety record; only a single fatality occurred during 1937–8; 134 road accidents were reported, personal injuries amounted to 187, of which 47 were serious.

Major initiatives were pursued during the 1930s. Under the Roads Improvement Act of 1925, the Cardiganshire County Council embarked on an ambitious programme of Building Line Prescriptions which led to the restriction of 130 miles of road. Such work was abandoned following the passage of the Restriction of Ribbon Development Act of 1935 and attention thereafter was paid to the adoption of standard widths of highway and to co-ordinating every proposed major road improvement, standards which gave rise to considerable local pride.

To a large extent the party political aspect of local government had all but disappeared in Cardiganshire by this time. Local administration was largely a matter of pursuing the legislation and directives of the Westminster Parliament, a trend which intensified still further after the Second World War. Contested elections became increasingly rare; of fifty possible elections for the County Council, only about ten to fourteen were usually contested. When county council elections were resumed in 1946 after a break of nine years, twenty-six contests took place, a record high. Generally, well-established and highly esteemed councillors were re-elected time and time again; opposition was considered a mark of disrespect. This trend was strengthened by the difficulties of securing candidates prepared to stand, a reluctance widely attributed to the large number of meetings usually convened during daytime.

The main thrust of the activities of the post-war Labour governments led by Clement Attlee was the laying of the foundations of the 'welfare state'. Although the phrase had been used during the 1930s, after the Second World War it was widely adopted to refer to the multifarious schemes and services which both central government and local authorities provided. The wide-ranging corpus of legislation from 1945 onwards was warmly welcomed by those responsible for 'welfare provision', while the need for strong centralized planning had been strengthened by the impact of 'wartime socialism'. The Cardiganshire County Council found itself compelled to co-operate with the Economic Development Council for Wales to encourage fuller employment and improve transport facilities – roads and railways – and public utilities such as electricity, water and (in the towns) gas. There was some indignation locally that the county had gained little from the Distribution of Industries Act of 1945, and it was justifiably felt that south-east Wales had emerged as the principal beneficiary of the new industrial enterprises. Moreover, there was an element of local hostility to alleged state infringement of individual liberty. Whereas the planning acts of the 1930s had not been mandatory on local authorities, the County Planning Act of 1943 had made compulsory the provisions of previous planning enactments, while the Town and County Planning Act of 1947 consolidated existing acts and specified that each county had to draft a 'development plan' of the authority's aspirations for future development over a period of twenty years.[31]

Within Cardiganshire difficulties were compounded by its geographical remoteness and inaccessibility from London, the thinness and uneven spread of its population (some two-fifths of its people lived in the urban and rural districts of Aberystwyth), the prevalence of farming as the mainstay of the local economy, the lack of industrial development, the highly seasonal nature of the growing tourism industry, and the generally undeveloped nature of urban amenities such as shops and cultural and entertainment facilities. Many weaknesses endemic in the local economy were exacerbated by the impact of rural depopulation, poor employment prospects, inadequate housing conditions and a lack of public transport. Until the 1960s services such as piped water, mains sewerage services and an electricity supply remained wholly inadequate. It was widely felt that few politicians at Westminster were aware of these formidable problems. As early as 1936, the editor of the *Cambrian News* had noted: 'The Government deals with the country as a whole and cannot understand that if Essex and Surrey can do it, why Merioneth, Montgomery and Cardiganshire cannot do it.'[32]

[31]On these themes, see A. Marwick, *British Society since 1945* (London, 1990), pp.45–9.
[32]*Cambrian News*, 23 October 1936.

The deficiencies in housing, public services and nourishment were inevitably reflected in the generally poor health of the county's rural population. During successive decades before the Second World War, Cardiganshire had an unenviable reputation for high infant mortality, deaths of mothers in childbirth, rotten teeth, hearing defects, blindness, imbecility and madness.[33] Shortly before the First World War, *The Welsh Outlook* had chastised 'this shockingly backward county',[34] but many such problems continued to beset its inhabitants as late as the 1950s. The death rate in the county for 1951 was 17.56 per 1,000 population, compared with 12.15 for England and Wales. Concern was expressed at the prevalence of heart disease and cancer among an increasingly ageing population.[35] The incidence of infant mortality – at 37.23 per 1,000 live births compared with 29.6 for England and Wales – caused further unease.[36] During the fifties, however, under the provisions of the National Health Service Acts, the County Council attempted to provide a better and more comprehensive service. By the end of the decade it had assumed responsibility for an ambulance service at five bases in the county, infant welfare clinics at thirteen centres for mothers and young children, an extensive scheme for domestic help, a network of thirty-five home nurses and midwives and eleven health visitors, an immunization programme against diphtheria, poliomyelitis, tuberculosis and whooping cough, the services of four authorized officers and a psychiatric social welfare officer to be responsible for mental health, and an efficient programme for the medical inspection and treatment of school children, supported by the services of dental surgeons, an educational psychologist and a speech therapist.[37] During the 1960s more ambitious plans were adopted to establish a county health centre in the grounds of Cardigan hospital, to bring to an end the system of agency-operated ambulance services and establish a county ambulance headquarters at Aberystwyth, to set up and expand a mobile clinic much in demand by the inhabitants of the rural villages, and to prepare plans for a training centre and hostel for mentally subnormal adults.[38] There was considerable local pride in the quality of the district nursing service and the generous scale of the county's home help service.[39] Under the National Assistance Act of 1948, the County Council, as the Local Welfare Authority, was obliged to provide residential accommodation for the aged and infirm, a responsibility carried out by building a number of purpose-built homes and adapting several large country houses.

There was similar local satisfaction in the quality of the county's education system. Generally the standard of schools fell far short of the requirements of the Butler Education Act of 1944.[40] During the 1930s the impact of the agricultural depression, the county's relatively low rateable values and the system of government grants had all made Cardiganshire 'a most neglected county lacking the resources for new buildings and other changes'.[41] Even so, it became the first Welsh county to complete its separation of primary and secondary education as required by the 1944 Act, an

---

[33]See J. Davies, *A History of Wales* (London, 1993), p.588.
[34]Ibid.
[35]Cardiganshire County Council, *Annual Report of the Medical Officer of Health and School Medical Officer for the year 1968*, p.7.
[36]Ibid., p.8.
[37]*Cardiganshire: the County Handbook* (Aberystwyth, 1958), pp.13–14.
[38]Cardiganshire County Council, *Annual Report of the Medical Officer of Health and School Medical Officer for the year 1968*, p.6.
[39]Ibid., p.21.
[40]NLW, Dr John Henry Jones Papers 52, notes on the history of education in Cardiganshire.
[41]Ibid.

exercise achieved by September 1951. The period of post-war austerity and relatively high graduate unemployment levels provided a pool of graduates who became headmasters in primary schools, and many of them set notably high standards of teaching. Many Cardiganshire people living today can recall childhoods spent in primary schools which were heated by large coal stoves (which scorched everything in their immediate vicinity and left those pupils in the extremities of the classroom to freeze!). Toilets were located in the schoolyard and mid-day meals were rather less than appetizing.[42] By the late 1950s there were ninety primary schools and eight secondary schools in the county: five intermediate or grammar schools established in the wake of the 1889 Act, a Central School at Lampeter which had opened its doors in the early 1920s, and two modern schools – at Dinas, Aberystwyth, and St Mary's, Cardigan.[43] A number of new initiatives had followed in the 1950s: the establishment of technical training at Cardigan School, the provision of commercial courses at all secondary schools, and the adoption of a policy of bilingualism. All the secondary schools were either housed in new buildings or given major extensions to their premises, and most primary schools were improved and renovated. Electricity was installed as soon as it reached the school district and almost all schools enjoyed mains water and sewerage schemes.

An eleven-plus selection system obtained throughout the county: an external system in the three districts which had separate grammar and secondary modern schools and an internal system in the other three districts. There was considerable local pride in the quality of the education system and much gratification in the high proportion of pupils who proceeded to grammar schools. In 1951 (when the system first became fully operational), 56 per cent went on to grammar schools, though the percentage fell to 43 per cent in 1958.[44] Equally impressive statistics related to university entrants: over the three years 1954–7 the percentage of pupils per thousand in receipt of university award – 59.8 – was the highest in the whole of Britain.[45]

An additional dimension unknown in English counties but which was of primary importance in Cardiganshire was bilingualism, which was reflected in curriculum content, teaching methods and organization in both primary and secondary schools. A survey of Cardiganshire in 1950 revealed that 76 per cent of pupils used Welsh as their first language.[46] Subsequent in-migration into the county was reflected sharply in the numbers speaking Welsh in small primary schools in rural areas; one school declined from being wholly Welsh-speaking to 60 per cent by about 1970 and another from 75 to 45 per cent.[47] During the 1960s, when threats to the well-being of the Welsh language grew ever more apparent, some Cardiganshire schoolteachers became fiercely protective of their mother tongue: 'Take away the Welsh language and we're like everyone else – the language is the real anchor of the Welsh way of life.'[48] From the 1920s onwards, the education system had been especially vulnerable to linguistic pressures. The place of the Welsh language in securing admission to secondary school had caused sporadic conflict during the inter-war period, while the setting up of a Welsh-medium primary school at Aberystwyth on the eve of the Second World War had given rise

[42]Ibid.
[43]See J. Henry Jones, 'The organization of secondary schools: Cardiganshire', *Education*, 6 February 1959, 266–9.
[44]Ibid., 267.
[45]Ibid., 269.
[46]Ibid., 267.
[47]P. J. Madgwick et al., *The Politics of Rural Wales: A Study of Cardiganshire* (London, 1973), p.112.
[48]Ibid.

to considerable local opposition. Further acrimony was fuelled in 1950 when the county resolved to make compulsory the teaching of Welsh to 'O' level.

Following the recommendations of the Gittins Report,[49] in 1968–9 the county extended compulsory teaching of Welsh to pupils between the ages of four and seven and announced the introduction of Welsh-medium teaching for all schoolchildren so that 'by the junior stage children should have gained sufficient mastery over their second language to receive a part of their education through the medium of that language'.[50] Clamant protests ensued, primarily from parents in the Aberystwyth area who formed the Cardiganshire Education Campaign which sought as its objective 'option in Welsh teaching' and which soon attracted more than 500 members, one of whom (who became the movement's chairman at a critical time) asserted:

> The issue as to whether children should or should not learn Welsh is a moral issue . . . like many issues of this kind, it is not, in my view, an issue on which we should have legislation to make a thing compulsory . . . that is, to my way of thinking, an imposition in a free society.[51]

The dispute remained unresolved when Edward Heath's Conservative government took office in June 1970, and was to some extent exacerbated by the proposal of the Cardiganshire Education Authority in 1971 to spend more that £250,000 on establishing a Welsh-medium secondary school for the Aberystwyth area. Peter Thomas, the Secretary of State for Wales, was obliged to intervene, and eventually he produced a compromise whereby a new building was allocated to an English-medium comprehensive school (Penglais), while the Welsh school (Penweddig) was given the vacated grammar school buildings. The question of 'option in Welsh language teaching' was never wholly resolved.

Alongside the thorny issue of Welsh-language teaching were the seemingly intractable twin problems of rural depopulation and the increasing stream of English in-migrants into rural areas. To its credit, throughout the 1960s the Cardiganshire LEA continued to spend substantial sums of money on improving school buildings; no schools retained the Elsan by the mid-1960s. But fewer and fewer pupils attended such schools. In 1921 there were 3,319 pupils between the ages of five and nine in the rural districts of Cardiganshire; by 1971 this number had fallen to 2,155. One of the recommendations of the Gittins Report in 1968 was the establishment of 'district schools' with at least sixty pupils. If implemented, such a plan would have halved the numbers of rural schools, a prospect which provoked a storm of protest from those who argued that the village school was an essential focal point in many rural communities.[52]

The fortunes of the education system, the cultural needs of the county's rural communities and to some extent the fate of the Welsh language were all associated with the setting up and expansion of a county library service, primarily the brainchild of Alun R. Edwards, a product of the pioneering Manchester School of Librarianship and County Librarian from 1950.[53] Housed in an old 1906

[49]*Primary Education in Wales: Report by a Committee of the Central Advisory Council on Education under the chairmanship of Professor C. E. Gittins* (London, 1968).
[50]Madgwick, *Politics of Rural Wales*, pp.118–19.
[51]Ibid., p.119.
[52]Davies, *History of Wales*, pp.638–9.
[53]A. R. Edwards, *Yr Hedyn Mwstard: Atgofion* (Llandysul, 1980).

Carnegie building near the town centre, the Library in 1947 mainly stocked novels, many of them in a very dilapidated condition, and the collection was generally used by the poorer inhabitants of the town. Very soon the quality of the service improved appreciably, and the number of registered readers increased from 3,509 in 1949 to 5,672 in 1956 and to 11,300 by 1972. The number of books borrowed increased from 90,000 in 1948 to 300,000 in 1971. The service was used much more intensively by the inhabitants of the whole of north Cardiganshire and also by the ever increasing numbers of students at the University College of Wales and other educational institutions. These developments brought about an equally impressive increase in the range of books consulted and borrowed.

Major initiatives followed in rapid succession. A separate children's library was established within the main building at Aberystwyth in 1953, and from 1970 pre-school children were offered weekly story hours in both English and Welsh. During the late 1960s substantial collections were accumulated of photographs of local interest, tape recordings of reminiscences, and drama and music. At the beginning of 1972 the library at Aberystwyth became the first in Wales to lend music cassettes. Other towns in the county followed suit. In February 1950 boxes of books began to be supplied to the larger villages and towns. By February 1953 seven branches were operational – within the town halls of Cardigan and Lampeter, in a brand new building at New Quay, at a chapel vestry at Llandysul, a shop at Aberaeron, a hotel bar at Borth, and at Tregaron. The efforts of these branch libraries were supported by the service of a mobile library, first set up on a village basis in 1949 and much expanded after 1962 when library vans visited isolated hamlets, farms and cottages and twenty-one rural primary schools. Soon four mobiles were providing a comprehensive service to the population of the whole of rural Cardiganshire. By 1971–2 some 2,000 individual homes were borrowing 96,184 Welsh and 84,464 English books, a success story which exceeded Alun R. Edwards's wildest dreams. In 1972 the number of mobile vans had increased to six and henceforth each home was visited fortnightly. Similar striking improvements occurred in the library services offered to primary and secondary schools (services which were financed entirely out of the education rate), and a rich array of cultural activities was offered by the library service by the 1960s: Welsh book quizzes from 1960, book discussion groups a little later, and the establishment of an annual National Library Week from 1966. The Cardiganshire Library Service, led by Alun R. Edwards, was also to play an important part in pressing for the establishment in 1964 of the College of Librarianship Wales, whose initial aim was to provide a supply of properly trained and educated staff for Welsh libraries.[54]

Both the education system (at primary and secondary level) and the development of the county library service contributed substantially to the fortunes of the Welsh language in Cardiganshire, a theme which had been prominent in the proceedings of the County Council ever since the influx of evacuees from English cities during the Second World War.[55] Although the county was predominantly Welsh speaking, it had also become 'linguistically mixed'.[56] The County Council tended to be sympathetic to the plight of the language, and generally endorsed the sentiments of the *Gittins Report*: 'Since it is the Welsh language which in a large measure gives Wales its own peculiar identity and transmits an important part of its historical tradition, it has a claim on the loyalty of those who claim

[54]*Llyfrgell Ceredigion: Cardiganshire Joint Library, 1947–1972* (Aberystwyth, 1972).
[55]Davies, *History of Wales*, pp.600–1.
[56]Madgwick, *Politics of Rural Wales*, p.83.

to be Welsh.'[57] The county Education Committee was strongly in favour of a bilingual policy in the 1960s (even supporting compulsory Welsh for children from English-speaking homes), and several county councillors expressed heartfelt commitment to the objective of achieving a fully bilingual county.

As the social complexion of the county changed during the 1960s, a new dimension emerged in the affairs of local government. The reorganization of local government was advocated by the Aberystwyth Borough Council in 1961, while a conference of local authorities convened in 1963 called for a development corporation for Mid-Wales. When the Aberystwyth–Carmarthen railway line fell victim to the infamous 'Beeching Axe' in 1963, the county council was vociferous in its protests. The impact of the fledgeling Cymdeithas yr Iaith Gymraeg and the influence of Welsh-language television broadcasts further determined the tone of local political life, as did the depopulation of the rural areas and the constant drift of young people to towns and cities elsewhere in search of secure employment opportunities. Although the numbers employed in agriculture declined, it remained an important industry (employing 27 per cent of the occupied work-force in 1966), while it was the duty of the County Council, under the Agriculture Act of 1947, to let small-holdings to agricultural workers, to assume responsibilities under the Diseases of Animals Act, and for the holding of poultry sales, land drainage and the licensing of waste food collectors. The manifold instabilities of the agricultural lifestyle were reflected in the enthusiastic support locally for the formation of the Farmers Union of Wales in 1955, while in the 1960s the proposals of the Labour government for a Rural Development Board for Mid-Wales (to include most of Cardigan-shire) caused a deep-rooted schism in the ranks of the local farmers, many of whom were appre-hensive about increased government control.[58]

The responsibilities of the County Council extended to the welfare and supervision of children who (for a variety of reasons) were unable to live with their parents. Cardiganshire attained an impressive record of providing good foster homes, a 'reception home' at Peterwell, Lampeter, and 'family homes' at Cartrefle, Alltyblaca, Llanybydder, and Erw Lon, Maesglas, Cardigan. Under the Civil Defence Act, 1948, the Cardiganshire County Council was responsible for a division of the Civil Defence Corps in the administrative county, which was divided into one Static Area Control at Aberystwyth and three Static Sub-Area Controls at Aberystwyth, Lampeter and Cardigan. The number of volunteers had reached 738 by 1958.[59] Moreover, after 1945 large numbers of houses in the county were surveyed, and an intense programme of council house building and improvement was initiated, most notably at Penparcau and Capel Bangor, near Aberystwyth, and at Tregaron, Cwm-ann and Lampeter, and at Cardigan. Between 1945 and 1968, 2,442 local authority houses and 1,751 privately built homes were constructed in the county, and the number of 'unfit houses' decreased significantly.[60] Many Cardiganshire people took advantage of the Housing Improvement Grants available since 1949 to a maximum sum of £400 and increased to £1,000 in 1969. Owners in rural areas modernized their properties by acquiring mains water and sewerage schemes. Many hundreds of older houses, which were in danger of becoming derelict, were renovated by the provision of modern conveniences. In the

[57] *Gittins Report*, p.105.
[58] Madgwick, *Politics of Rural Wales*, p.171.
[59] *Cardiganshire: The County Handbook* (1958), p.12.
[60] Cardiganshire County Council, *Annual Report of the Medical Officer of Health and Principal School Medical Officer for the year 1968*, pp.46–7.

case of council houses, however, problems inevitably stemmed from the limited capacity of both the housing authorities and the new tenants to bear the considerable financial strain.

The need for improved roads within the county was also pressing, a problem accentuated by greater leisure time, a steadily improving standard of living, more widespread car ownership and the gradual spread of tourism. The 'Beeching Axe' of 1963 deprived the county of the Aberystwyth–Carmarthen railway line, a much-lamented loss which meant that only fifteen miles of railway track (on the Aberystwyth–Shrewsbury line) remained in Cardiganshire. Rural bus services faced the inevitable difficulties of few passengers and expensive fares. In 1960 the County Council maintained and repaired 1,274 miles of county roads and bridges and acted as agent of the Minister of Transport for seventy miles of trunk roads. The county surveyor and his staff based at Aberaeron were responsible for the maintenance, repair and improvement of these roads, while the local authorities were in charge of the boroughs and urban districts. The nature of the roads posed especial problems for holiday traffic since Cardiganshire enjoyed none of the major road improvements which transformed road travel in much of England and parts of south Wales in the 1960s. The County Council, which was also responsible for planning under the various Town and Country Planning Acts, appointed a County Planning Committee which, in turn, set up four district committees – at Aberystwyth, Aberaeron, Tregaron and Teifiside – to consider applications. The County Planning Department was based at London House, Aberaeron.

As local government reorganization approached in the early 1970s, it was widely felt that the County Council embodied something of the county's social character and political culture. Many candidates for the County Council did not stand as party nominees, thereby creating a non-partisan local political context. The county councillor was thus depicted by his constituents 'not as a protagonist in a political conflict but rather as an ambassador or intermediary protecting and promoting the interests of his constituents'.[61] Many of the councillors knew personally a majority of their constituents, and their role has been compared to that of parish councillors in other parts of the country: 'the basis of politics is the rural community and the style is based on acquaintance'.[62] Most members of the Cardiganshire County Council were relatively elderly (many had, in fact, retired), and a substantial majority were natives of the county. The council was predominantly Welsh speaking, and many of its members were practising Nonconformists or Anglicans, who attended the National Eisteddfod and were strongly opposed to the Sunday opening of public houses. Consequently, manual workers (perhaps inevitably) were under-represented on the county council, which tended to represent 'old Welsh rural Cardiganshire, rather than the more diverse, mobile and anglicized areas'. There existed, it was claimed, 'a time lag in its representativeness'.[63] Local government reorganization in 1974 sharply cut across the gradual process of readjustment.

Many councillors and aldermen believed that service on the Cardiganshire County Council was both an effective means of rendering community service and a rather prestigious hobby. Few of them were politically motivated, and generally the council was non-partisan. The councillors, although painfully aware of their authority's financial weakness (the product of the penny rate in the county was the lowest in all the counties of England and Wales), took genuine pride in the council's achievements, especially in education, and were much concerned about depopulation and

[61]Madgwick, *Politics of Rural Wales*, p.180.
[62]Ibid.
[63]Ibid., p.182.

economic depression. They unstintingly encouraged Welsh-language teaching, promoted the Welsh language, resisted the closure of rural schools, and supported the establishment of the College of Librarianship Wales and the Welsh College of Agriculture in the 1960s. Small wonder that they protested so loudly.

When, on 1 April 1974, the new Dyfed County Council succeeded the County Councils of Cardiganshire, Carmarthenshire and Pembrokeshire,[64] the Ceredigion Council became a district authority to serve the former Cardiganshire, and a third tier of community councils assumed many of the functions of the former borough and parish councils. The restructuring of local government predictably proved fraught with problems and tensions in Cardiganshire, as elsewhere, as multifarious committees were formed and officials appointed to set in motion the wheels of the new machinery. The new community councils were to enjoy coffers considerably more replete than those available to the old parish councils, and resources were available to be expended on such facilities as maintaining and signposting footpaths and bridleways, off-street parking and footway lighting, parks, open spaces and allotments. They were also granted the right to be consulted about planning applications affecting land in their areas.

The Ceredigion Council was to have nine district councils under its aegis – Aberystwyth, Cardigan and Lampeter Boroughs, Aberaeron and New Quay Urban Districts, and Aberaeron, Aberystwyth, Teifiside and Tregaron Rural Districts. Most of the powers of governing the daily lives of the former inhabitants of Cardiganshire passed to the Dyfed County Council, with its head-quarters at Carmarthen, which was to supervise major aspects of local government like education, social services and highways. Regional offices, however, continued to function at larger towns like Aberystwyth and Aberaeron; for example, branch offices of the Social Services Department were opened at Swyddfa'r Sir, Aberystwyth, and London House, Aberaeron, following the closure of the former headquarters at Llanbadarn Road, Aberystwyth. The Ceredigion Council assumed responsibility for planning (assisted by seven local district offices), the collection of rents on council properties, and the public health inspectorate. At the time of local government reorganization, the library service remained a bone of contention between the Ceredigion and Dyfed Councils.

There was predictably considerable local scepticism and antagonism to these changes, an opposition fuelled by massive rate increases in April 1974.[65] At the final meeting of the Aberystwyth Borough Council, local townsfolk packed the public gallery of the council chamber as the council was disbanded only three years before the celebration of the 700th anniversary of the granting of a borough charter to the town. Promises by officialdom that the new order would provide 'a better and more responsive service to the public' were met by local cynicism and many opponents argued that the new structure was designed primarily to benefit the concentrated areas of population to the detriment of the well-being of the inhabitants of the rural areas, who were destined simply to pay sharply increased rates.[66] Many shared the opinion of a local councillor who condemned the new structure outright as 'the big blunder'. Local sadness and a profound sense of loss were accentuated by the retirement of a host of long-serving local government officers, councillors and aldermen.[67] In his farewell speech, reported in the *Cambrian News*, the Revd T. Tegfryn Davies, Aber-porth, chair-

---

[64]*Cambrian News*, 22 March 1974.
[65]Ibid., 29 March 1974.
[66]Ibid., 5 April 1974.
[67]Ibid.

man of the Cardiganshire County Council, claimed justifiable pride in the achievements of his local authority since 1889:

> The Council, starting in the days when telephones were few and motor cars were non-existent, had developed over the years into one of the County's largest business concerns, providing services and employment on a large scale. Over the years Parliament had imposed on the Council numerous duties and responsibilities which were not dreamt of in 1888 or even as late as 1939. 'We have taken these additional tasks in our stride. War and peace alike have not found us wanting. I am proud that our methods of local government administration have proved flexible enough to absorb all that we have been asked to do.'[68]

The First Cardiganshire County Council, 1889

John Hugh Jones (Aber-arth); John Morgan Howell; Evan Davies (Aber-banc); George Green; John James; Thomas Levi; C. M. Williams; Thomas Thomas (Blaen-porth); Enoch Watkin James; William Morgan (Bow Street); W. Picton Evans; Levi James; John Davies (Cilcennin); Nicholas Bray; David Jones (Devil's Bridge); David Morgan (Goginan); Morgan Evans; J. T. Morgan (Llanbadarn); Morgan Jones (Llandygwydd); David Davies (Llanddewibrefi); Enoch Davies (Llandysul); Thomas Thomas (Llandysul); Evan Evans (Llandysiliogogo); William Jones (Llanfair); Morris Davies; Evan Richards; W. H. Jones (Llangeitho); W. O. Brigstocke; John Davies (Llangrannog); G. W. Parry; James James; Evan Morgan; Herbert Davies Evans; E. E. C. Cluneglas Davies; John Owens; Jenkin Jenkins; William Davies; William Timothy; David Griffiths; the Earl of Lisburne; John Morris; J. T. Morgan; Peter Jones; Roderick Lloyd; John Powell; Daniel Jenkins; W. Thomas Davies; John Charles Harford.

At the first meeting of the Council, the following County Aldermen were appointed:

(a)   From elected Members of the Council:
the Earl of Lisburne, C. M. Williams, Roderick Lloyd, Levi James, William Davies, James Thomas Morgan (Tal-y-bont), Jenkin Jenkins (Felin-coed), and William Jones.

(b)   From outside the Council:
David Davies, Maengwyn, Llanfair Orllwyn
David Jenkins, Maesteg, Glandyfi
John Davies, Llanybydder
Revd Llewelyn Edwards, Aberystwyth
Jenkin Jenkins, Blaen-plwyf, Tal-sarn
Daniel Jones, Roseland, Llan-non
Major Price Lewes, Tyglynaeron
Dr David Lloyd, Atpar, Newcastle Emlyn

The following additional Members were elected to fill the vacancies in the respective Electoral Divisons created by the appointment as Aldermen of the above Councillors:

John Jones (Strata Florida)
John Jones (Nancwnlle)

[68]Ibid.

John Owen Davies
John Watkin Davies
David Charles Roberts
John Williams
John Davies (Tal-y-bont)
Evan Rowlands

The Cardiganshire County Council, 1939

Aldermen
(to retire in March 1943)
Evan James Davies
James George Morris Davies
David Evans
Reginald James Rice Loxdale
William Edward Matthews
Sir David Charles Roberts
Revd John Ellis Williams
Meredydd Llewelyn Gwarnant Williams

(to retire in March 1940)
David Morgan Davies
Revd. Evan John Davies
Simon Davies
Richard Evans
Joseph Barclay Jenkins
David Rees Morgan
John Morgan
Morgan Lloyd Williams

Councillors
Emlyn Abraham-Williams
David Joshua Davies
David Oswald Davies
Evan Davies
Evan Thomas Davies
Hubert Maxwell Davies
James Jenkin Davies
Richard Rowland Davies
William Morgan Davies
Mrs Gladys Mary Douglas
William Edwards
Mrs Audrey Dorothea Loxdale Evans
Mrs Catherine Mary Lewis Evans
Emile Thomas Evans
Evan Evans
John Evans
John Evans
John Daniel Evans
Joseph Gwyn Evans
Daniel Lodwick Herbert
Richard David Herbert
James Isaac
David James
David Lloyd James
Edward James

Evan Parry Jenkins
Thomas Charles Jenkins
Revd Frederick Jones
Josiah Richard Jones
Morgan Jones
Richard Jones
Rowland Hugh Jones
Revd Thomas Noah Jones
William Jones
David Lewis
Revd Evans Melinfab Lewis
Llewelyn John Lewis
William Lewis
Bertie Taylor Lloyd
Roderick Lloyd
Evan John Luke
David Morgan
Mrs Mary Nesta Poulgrain
John Edwardes Rogers-Lewis
Llewelyn Samuel
David Lloyd Thomas
Revd Joseph Morgan Lloyd Thomas
John Williams
John Williams
Rees Williams

Officials of the Council

Clerk: Ivor Evans, MA
Director of Education: H. J. Lewis, MA
County Medical Officer: Dr Ernest Jones, M.Sc., MB, Ch.B., DPH
County Accountant: Norman Greenwood, AIMTA & ASAA
Public Assistance Officer: Owen Morgan
County Surveyors: T. E. Owen and John Davies
County Valuation Officer and Land Agent: R. Lewis Jones, FSI
County Architects: J. Lewis Evans and Rhys Jones, FRIBA

The Cardiganshire County Council, 1974

(on the eve of local government reorganization)

Chairman: Alderman Revd T. Tegryn Davies
Vice-Chairman: Alderman Richard J. Ellis

Aldermen

Benjamin John Davies, Teify View, Llandyfrïog, Newcastle Emlyn
Revd Thomas Tegryn Davies, Y Marian, Aber-porth
William Morgan Davies, JP, Bryn Teifi, Llanio Road, Tregaron
Richard Jenkin Ellis, Clifton Villa, Penglais Road, Aberystwyth
Mrs Gwendolen Calan Evans, OBE, JP, Tynrhos, Llanbadarn Road, Aberystwyth
Melbourne Evan Griffiths, Fronlas, Blaen-porth, Cardigan
Revd Thomas Pugh Jarman, Trem-y-werydd, New Quay
Isaac Richard Jenkins, Tyngraig, Tal-y-bont
Morgan Lloyd Jenkins, DL, Brynmorwel, Brynhoffnant, Llandysul
David Howell Jones, Pen-rhiw, Capel Seion
Revd Edwin Pryce Jones, MA (Oxon), BA (Wales), Hafan, Llwyncelyn, Aberaeron
Mrs Gwendolen Eluned Jones, OBE, JP, Gwyndy, Llanbadarn Road, Aberystwyth
William Zadrach Jones, Lyndon, 13 New Street, Aberystwyth
Hywel Heulyn Roberts, JP, Crud-yr-awel, Synod Inn, Llandysul
John Edwardes Rogers-Lewis, JP, Abermeurig Mansion, Abermeurig, Lampeter
John Owen Williams, Bryneirin, New Quay

County Councillors

(Names of divisions and dates of first election given in brackets)
Brinley Davies, 31 Pier Street, Aberystwyth (Aberystwyth 4, 1967)
David Saunders Davies, Green Meadow, Trefenter, Aberystwyth (Llanrhystud, 1967)
Dr Edward Davies-Thomas, TD, 27 Portland Street, Aberystwyth (Aberystwyth 2, 1967)
Henry Philip Davies, Erw Deg, Pont-siân, Llandysul (Llandysul North, 1964)
Captain John Owen J. Davies, Ffynonwen, Sarnau, Llandysul (Penbryn, 1967)
John James Davies, Llwyngaru, Tregaron (Tregaron)
Mrs Mary Cavell Davies, Rhos-y-Corn, St David's Road, Aberystwyth (Aberystwyth 5, 1969)
Thomas Gilmor Davies, Pantswllt, Talgarreg, Llandysul (Llandysiliogogo, 1958)
Ivor Caradog Edwards, 10, Maes-y-deri, Pont-rhyd-y-groes, Ystradmeurig (Ysbyty, 1952)
Daniel Emrys Evans, Bryngwalia, Gors-goch, Llanybydder (Llanwenog, 1965)

David Evans, The Beeches, Llandysul (Llandysul South, 1965)
Revd Samuel Idris Evans, Brynhawen, Henllan, Llandysul (Troed-yr-aur, 1962)
William Arthur Evans, Llwyn Iorwerth Isaf, Capel Bangor, Aberystwyth (Goginan, 1971)
William Jones Griffiths, Glyn-y-coed, Cenarth, Newcastle Emlyn (Llandygwydd, 1964)
John David Herbert, Brynawel, Bronnant, Aberystwyth (Lledrod, 1955)
Thomas Glyn Griffiths Herbert, MRCVS, Manor Hall, Lampeter Road, Aberaeron (Aberaeron, 1972)
Reginald Holdcroft, Corner Stores, Penrhyn-coch, Aberystwyth (Trefeurig, 1964)
Geraint Wyn Howells, Glennydd, Ponterwyd, Aberystwyth (Cwmrheidol, 1952)
Peter Hughes, Central Hotel, Llan-non (Llansanffraid, 1965)
Mrs Marie James, Post Office, Llangeitho, Tregaron (Llangeitho, 1964)
David Llewellyn Jenkins, Muriau Gwyn, Henllan, Llandysul (Aber-banc, 1967)
Major Benjamin Howell Jones, MBE, TD, Tŷ Cornel, Cross Inn, Llandysul (Llanllwchaearn, 1970)
Charles Emlyn Jones, Abercoed, Tregaron (Llanddewibrefi, 1967)
Edgar Jones, Bedlwyn, Felin-fach, Lampeter (Felin-fach, 1970)
Edward Vernon Jones, Gaerwen, Bow Street (Bow Street, 1970)
Gwilym Caradog Jones, JP, Tanrallt, Taliesin, Machynlleth, Montgomeryshire (Taliesin, 1949)
Isaac Eilwyn Jones, Frongoy, Pennant, Llan-non (Cilcennin, 1958)
John Jones, Pantyfedwen, Pontrhydfendigaid (Strata Florida, 1970)
Joseph Alun Jones, Cadwgan, Cellan, Lampeter (Llanfair, 1964)
Dr Ambrose Lloyd, Cwm-ann, Lampeter (Lampeter Urban, 1964)
John Griffiths Lloyd, Meiarth, Bwlch-llan (Nancwnlle, 1967)
Thomas Islwyn Lloyd, Penlonfedw, Devil's Bridge, Aberystwyth (Devil's Bridge, 1958)
John Herbert Daniel Matthews, Cwmcoedwig, Llanfarian (Llanfarian, 1950)
David Charles Morgan, Penbryn, Llangwyryfon, Aberystwyth (Llanilar, 1955)
Revd Evan Tom Parry Morgan, Rectory, Llangoedmor, Cardigan (Llangoedmor, 1967)
James Morgan, Tanybwlch, Llanafan (Llanfihangel, 1967)
James Owen Morgan, Crudyrawel, Clarach Road, Borth (Borth, 1964)
Gwilym Morris, Caerhun, Verwig Road, Cardigan (Cardigan North, 1962)
Richard Elwyn Morris, Graig, Blaencelyn, Llandysul (Llangrannog, 1967)
Henry Ifor Owen, BEM, JP, Maglona, 38 Bridge Street, Aberystwyth (Aberystwyth 1, 1968)
Roland Llewellyn Peregrine, Netley, Priory Street, Cardigan (Cardigan South, 1967)
David Gareth Raw-Rees, Tynparc, Llandre, Bow Street (Tal-y-bont, 1968)
James Edward Raw-Rees, DFC, JP, DL, Maesawelon, Waunfawr, Aberystwyth (Llanbadarn Fawr, 1965)
David Idris Rees, Fair Haven, New Quay (New Quay, 1970)
Eric Slater, 1 Albert Place, Aberystwyth (Aberystwyth 3, 1970)
Lt.-Col. Hugh William Spurrell, MC, Shalimar, Aber-porth, Cardigan (Aber-porth, 1968)
Abram Hywel Thomas, Cnwc-yr-ehedydd, Llannarth (Llannarth, 1968)
Joshua Richard Thomas, Brynteg, Penglais, Aberystwyth (Aberystwyth 6, 1970)
Trevor Roy Thomas, Derlwyn, 17 Brongrannell, Llanwnnen, Lampeter (Llanwnnen, 1966)
Evan Evans Williams, Crugfeilog, Ciliau Aeron, Aberaeron (Aeron, 1967)

Chairmen of the Council Since its Establishment
(with dates of appointment)

1889–1890	Councillor Peter Jones
1890–1891	Councillor Peter Jones

1891–1892	Alderman Levi James
1892–1893	Councillor Morgan Evans
1893–1894	Councillor David Charles Roberts
1894–1895	Councillor Revd John Williams
1895–1896	Councillor John Morgan Howell
1896–1897	Alderman Caleb Morgan Williams
1897–1898	Councillor David Lloyd
1898–1899	Councillor John Charles Harford
1899–1900	Alderman Revd Thomas Mason Jones
1900–1901	Councillor Matthew Lewis Vaughan Davies, MP
1901–1902	Councillor Colonel John Richard Howell
1902–1903	Councillor Jenkyn Lewis
1903–1904	Councillor Robert Ellis
1904–1905	Councillor Thomas Evans
1905–1906	Alderman Daniel Jenkin Williams
1906–1907	Councillor Evan Lima Jones
1907–1908	Henry Charles Fryer, Esquire
1908–1909	Councillor Owen Beynon Evans
1909–1910	Councillor Revd William Griffiths
1910–1911	Councillor Robert Sibbald Rowland
1911–1912	Alderman Revd Daniel Evans
1912–1913	Alderman Evan James Davies
1913–1914	Alderman James Thomas Morgan
1914–1915	Alderman John Williams
1915–1916	Councillor John Jones (Felin-fach)
1916–1917	Councillor John Humphreys Davies
1917–1918	Alderman Revd Thomas Arthur Thomas
1918–1919	Alderman John Morgan Howell
1919–1920	Alderman Peter Jones
1920–1921	Councillor Richard Evans (Llangoedmor)
1921–1922	Councillor John Jones (Cilcennin)
1922–1923	Alderman David Charles Roberts
1923–1924	Alderman Josiah Richard Jones
1924–1925	Alderman Caleb Morgan Williams
1925–1926	Major John Charles Harford
1926–1927	Councillor Evan James Davies
1927–1928	Councillor William Edward Matthews
1928–1929	Alderman Reginald James Rice Loxdale
1929–1930	Councillor Meredydd Llewellyn Gwarnant Williams, OBE, JP
1930–1931	Alderman John Morgan (Pont-rhyd-y-groes)
1931–1932	Alderman John Williams Lewis
1932–1933	Alderman John Evans (Aberystwyth)
1933–1934	Councillor David Morgan Davies
1934–1935	Alderman James George Morris Davies
1935–1936	Councillor David Evans
1936–1937	Councillor Daniel Lodwick Herbert
1937–1938	Councillor John Evans (Cardigan)
1938–1939	Councillor Richard David Herbert
1939–1940	Alderman Simon Davies
1940–1941	Alderman David Rees Morgan

1941–1942	Alderman Revd Evan John Davies (died during year of office)
1942–1943	Alderman Joseph Barclay Jenkins
1943–1944	Alderman David James
1944–1945	Councillor Llewelyn Samuel
1945–1946	Councillor Evan Davies
1946–1947	Councillor John Morgan (died during year of office)
1947–1948	Alderman E. Parry Jenkins
1948–1949	Councillor Mrs Audrey Dorothea Loxdale Evans
1949–1950	Councillor Evan Evans
1950–1951	Alderman John Williams
1951–1952	Councillor Hubert Maxwell Davies
1952–1953	Councillor John Edwardes Rogers-Lewis
1953–1954	Alderman Revd Evan Melinfab Lewis
1954–1955	Councillor William Morgan Davies
1955–	Councillor David Oswald Davies (died during year of office)
1955–1956	Councillor Bodin Trevor Williams
1956–1957	Alderman Evan Glyn Davies
1957–1958	Alderman David Owen Williams
1958–1959	Alderman William Zadrach Jones
1959–1960	Alderman Edward Lloyd Davies
1960–1961	Alderman John John
1961–1962	Alderman Meredydd Llewellyn Gwarnant Williams, OBE, JP
1962–1963	Alderman Mrs Gwendolen Calan Evans, OBE, JP
1963–1964	Councillor Benjamin John Davies
1964–1965	Alderman D. Rees Morgan
1965–1966	Alderman Thomas Donald Gwarnant Williams (died during year of office)
1966–1967	Alderman David Howell Jones
1967–1968	Alderman Evan John Thomas, OBE (died during year of office)
1968–1969	Councillor Mrs Gwendolen Eluned Jones, OBE, JP
1969–1970	Alderman Morgan Lloyd Jenkins
1970–1971	Alderman Isaac R. Jenkins
1971–1972	Alderman Hywel Heulyn Roberts, JP
1972–1973	Councillor Gwilym Caradog Jones, JP
1973–1974	Alderman Revd T. Tegryn Davies

CHAPTER 20

THE ESTABLISHED CHURCH AND DISSENT IN EIGHTEENTH-CENTURY CARDIGANSHIRE

Geraint H. Jenkins

'O'TIS a curious fine Bishopric', exclaimed the Revd Jenkin Evans during an animated discussion with a fellow cleric in 1744.[1] He was referring to the vast, sprawling diocese of St David's, whose 2,250,000 acres encompassed five counties and parts of four others. The see was divided into four districts or archdeaconries, one of which was the Archdeaconry of Cardigan which, in turn, included the deaneries of Sub Aeron (or Is Aeron) and Ultra Aeron (or Uwch Aeron) that covered the county of Cardiganshire.[2] No one can deny that the established Church – *y fam eglwys* (the mother church) – occupied a position of salient importance in the religious framework of Cardiganshire on the eve of the eighteenth century. The overwhelming majority of the population of the county (some 25,000 people)[3] were born into the Church and were thus, at least nominally, members of the Anglican faith. However, since we have no data regarding the number of regular worshippers at that time, it is hard to judge whether the established Church was a genuine church of the people. On the surface, Anglicanism was still an extremely powerful and resilient institution. It was a pillar of the constitution and its members accepted, as their forebears had done since Elizabethan times, that society was based on wealth, hierarchy and deference. The church was fully integrated into community life and it touched the lives of most people in a variety of ways. The landowner, the magistrate, the lawyer, the farmer, even perhaps the labourer, were familiar with the workings of the parish church not only because of its control over gifts of lands and tithes but also because it was generally acknowledged to offer the only legitimate and reliable means of personal salvation. The number of Dissenters was extremely modest and the county was untroubled by heterodox views or radical ideology.

Yet the *Ecclesia Anglicana* was much criticized, even derided, in Hanoverian times, as a moribund institution bereft of inspiring leaders and riddled with deep-seated abuses. Erasmus Saunders's celebrated tract in 1721 was an impassioned attempt to persuade Parliament to bolster the revenues

---

[1]Anon., *A Dialogue between the Rev. Mr Jenkin Evans . . . and Mr Peter Dobson . . . concerning Bishops* (London, 1744), p.44.

[2]J. V. Davies, 'The diocese of St David's during the first half of the eighteenth century' (unpublished University of Wales MA thesis, 1936); D. M. James, 'Some social and economic problems of the Church of England in the diocese of St David's, 1800–1874' (unpublished University of Wales MA thesis, 1972); S. R. Thomas, 'The diocese of St David's in the eighteenth century: the working of the diocese in a period of criticism' (unpublished University of Wales MA thesis, 1983).

[3]D. Williams, 'A note on the population of Wales, 1536–1801', *BBCS*, VIII, Part 1 (1935), 362.

of a Church which was being laid low by absenteeism, lay impropriation, non-residence and pluralism.[4] Over forty years later, in an unpublished manuscript entitled 'The Grievances of the Principality of Wales in the Church considered and laid open',[5] Evan Evans (Ieuan Fardd) focused on three fundamental shortcomings – the lamentable influence of English-born bishops, poor discipline, and inadequate stipends within 'the poor distressed Church in Wales' – and urged that King and Parliament should be apprised of the 'spiritual bondage' which the Welsh were forced to endure. Methodist and Dissenting apologists added fuel to the fire by grossly exaggerating the shortcomings of the established church.[6] The truth is that the mission of the Church was being undermined by its meagre revenues, its antiquated administrative structure, and the maldistribution of its wealth. The deaneries of Sub Aeron and Ultra Aeron were among the poorest in Wales and the greatest impediment to reform in Cardiganshire was the sheer penury of church livings.

One of the most critically important consequences of the poverty of the see of St David's was its inability to attract and retain bishops of high quality. The lack of continuity among prelates is startling: the average tenure of an eighteenth-century bishop in St David's was five years. Thirteen of the seventeen bishops appointed were translated to more lucrative preferments and the constant to-ing and fro-ing caused disruption and anger. Elias Sydall, who remained bishop for six months only in 1731, never even visited the diocese, and Edward Willes departed for Bath and Wells within twelve months of his consecration in January 1743.[7] Robert Lowth displayed the degree of his commitment to the welfare of his flock by accepting translation to Oxford within four months of his consecration in June 1766. Writing from Aberystwyth in January 1801, Lewis Evans sardonically referred to the recent appointment of George Murray as bishop of St David's: 'By the time his Clergy begin to know a little of him by Exp[erience] he flies off to a warmer Nest, and leaves many a Black [Swan?] unfledged, like all his Predecessors from time immemorial'.[8] Those bishops who stayed for longer periods treated their sees with scant regard and preferred to attend to their political duties and social commitments in London. Few pretended to enjoy their 'exile' to the barren western corners of the kingdom and they proved either unable or unwilling to exercise effective spiritual oversight over their dioceses. There were some bishops, of course, who attempted to put their house in order. The saintly but aged George Bull (1705–10) strongly urged his clergy to effect pastoral improvements, Bishop Adam Ottley (1717–23) vowed to eliminate 'public disorders, sins and offences', Charles Moss (1766–74) endeavoured to reform diocesan administration and bolster clerical incomes, and Samuel Horsley (1788–93) strived to curb the rampant evils of non-residence and pluralism.[9] Yet, it must be said that the majority of prelates were remote, distant figures who showed little regard for the spiritual or cultural welfare of the people.

[4] E. Saunders, *A View of the State of Religion in the Diocese of St David's* (Cardiff, 1949).

[5] NLW MS 2009B. See also G. Morgan, 'Ieuan Fardd (1731–1788): Traethawd yr Esgyb Eingl', *Ceredigion*, XI, no.2 (1990), 135–45.

[6] G. H. Jenkins, *Literature, Religion and Society in Wales 1660–1730* (Cardiff, 1978), pp.305–7.

[7] E. Yardley, *Menevia Sacra*, ed. Francis Green (London, 1927), p.123; N. Sykes, *Church and State in England in the XVIIIth Century* (Cambridge, 1934), p.319; G. H. Jenkins, 'Yr Eglwys "Wiwlwys Olau" a'i beirniaid', *Ceredigion*, X, no.2 (1985), 131–46.

[8] NLW MS 22131C, f.55.

[9] NLW Ottley Papers, no.1045; W. Gibson, *Church, State and Society, 1760–1850* (Basingstoke, 1994), p.30; F. C. Mather, *High Church Prophet. Bishop Samuel Horsley (1733–1806) and the Caroline Tradition in the Later Georgian Church* (Oxford, 1992).

For a brief period during the summer months, portly English prelates would embark with a heavy heart on triennial visitations and confirmations to remote and inaccessible parts of the county. Winding roads, mountain passes, rugged moorland and inclement weather imposed severe restrictions on their movements. 'I have spent almost five hours and a half in travelling from Cardigan to this place [i.e. Aberaeron]', wrote an exasperated Bishop Samuel Horsley to Isaac Williams in July 1790.[10] On such occasions, having no Welsh was a grave handicap to bishops. Few of the 'Anglo bishops' were sensible of the linguistic requirements of the people and their appallingly inept mumblings during visitations and confirmations caused mystification, mirth and resentment. 'I am sure but a very small number understand what they say', complained Evan Evans, 'no more than if they learned it in Arabic.'[11] Unable to maintain regular communication with the clergy, they could not hold any kind of conversation with their people, let alone encourage, beseech, reprove or rebuke them. Similarly, they were sublimely unaware of the need to nurture new talents among the parish ministry. Erasmus Saunders paid tribute to the labours of 'many honest and good men',[12] and there is no doubt that Cardiganshire men of the calibre of Moses Williams, Erasmus Lewis, Isaac Williams and Daniel Rowland would have made excellent bishops. 'Our Bishops look upon me . . . with an evil eye', wrote a disgruntled Evan Evans in May 1764,[13] and it is clear that bishops like John Warren (1779–83), who reckoned that Evans behaved 'like a Common Beggar',[14] felt only contempt for talented but inferior Welsh clerics who sought lucrative livings. 'O bishops, O princes, O ye fat men of the land', cried Lewis Morris despairingly, as he lamented the treatment afforded to Evans, 'why suffer ye that man to starve?'[15] Nor did bishops endear themselves to the local clergy by advocating that the interests of the Welsh people would best be served by acquiring a good working knowledge of the English tongue. Many of them believed that it was part of their mission, however brief that might be, to bring English standards of civilization to dark corners of the land and to propagate the view that there was room for one language only in a united Britain.[16] Philip Bisse (1710–13) refused even to contemplate supporting a Welsh translation of Robert Nelson's *Feasts and Fasts of the Church of England* because he feared it might 'obstruct the English tongue',[17] Richard Trevor (1744–52) made no secret of his contempt for the Welsh language, and Samuel Squire (1761–6) flatly refused to associate his name with Welsh publications.[18] Small wonder that Evan Evans pined for the 'golden age' of Elizabeth I when bishops had been cultured Welsh speakers, and fulminated both publicly and privately against the 'ravenous wolves' who had turned the eighteenth-

[10]NLW MS 6203E, f. 34.

[11]NLW MS 2009B, f. 93.

[12]Saunders, *A View*, p.27.

[13]H. Owen (ed.), *Additional Letters of the Morrises of Anglesey (1735–1786)* (Part II, London, 1949), p.620.

[14]D. E. Williams, 'The Reverend Isaac Williams of Ystrad Teilo', *Ceredigion*, VII, nos.3–4 (1974–5), 339.

[15]G. H. Jenkins, *Cadw Tŷ mewn Cwmwl Tystion. Ysgrifau Hanesyddol ar Grefydd a Diwylliant* (Llandysul, 1990), p.212.

[16]G. H. Jenkins, ' "Horrid unintelligible jargon": the case of Dr Thomas Bowles', *WHR*, 15, no.4 (1991), 501–2.

[17]M. Clement (ed.), *Correspondence and Minutes of the SPCK relating to Wales, 1699–1740* (Cardiff, 1952), p.42.

[18]A. Lewis (ed.), *The Correspondence of Thomas Percy and Evan Evans* (Louisiana State Univ. Press, 1957), pp.170–1.

century Church into a 'house of Merchandise and a den of thieves'.[19] He was convinced that 'lordly and tyrannic prelates' in his own times were determined to rob the Welsh of 'the charter of our religious Liberty', that is, the Act of 1563 (5 Elizabeth c. 28) which had ordered clergymen to conduct divine service in Welsh in those parishes where Welsh was commonly used.[20]

The root of the economic problem of the Church lay in the impropriation of ecclesiastical property by affluent absentee landowners. On the eve of the eighteenth century a third of the livings of St David's were in the hands of lay impropriators.[21] Both Erasmus Saunders and Evan Evans reserved their most scathing comments for greedy impropriators who had pillaged the Church with impunity. 'The hand of sacrilege pressed sore on this country [i.e. county] at the reformation',[22] declared Evans in 1767, and it is clear that the ravages of lay impropriation were more acutely felt in Cardiganshire than anywhere else in Wales. The value of tithes drawn from fifteen parishes in Cardiganshire by the Chichester family of Devon amounted to £6,000 per annum.[23] Clerical poverty was most pronounced in parishes where lay patrons had ravaged the resources of the church. Erasmus Saunders quoted the case of Llanddewibrefi as a victim of lay impropriation:

> . . . a Church once endow'd with a handsome Provision for a Dean and twelve Prebendaries; but the Endowment is now alienated to that Degree that the poor Incumbent there, tho' the Tythes of his Parish are said to be worth Four hundred Pounds *per Ann.* is oblig'd to content himself with about Eight Pounds Salary.[24]

During one of his visitations, Bishop Nicholas Claggett noted with some alarm the 'very small appointments the poor clergy have in Cardiganshire where the several impropriators have almost exhausted the whole revenue of the church'.[25]

Impropriators paid wretchedly inadequate salaries to curates who, borne down by the pressures of want and poverty, had no alternative but to take charge of several parishes in order to maintain their families. The result was that these 'hasty Itinerants' were obliged to ride in 'a kind of perpetual Motion' from church to church on the Sabbath to read prayers in a garbled, breathless fashion.[26] Infrequent and inadequately presented services in turn adversely affected the quality of spiritual provision as well as the morale of the clergy. For instance, church visitation returns for 1733 reveal the testing physical demands made upon John Rowland (brother of Daniel). He was rector of Llangeitho, vicar of Nancwnlle, and perpetual curate of Llanbadarn Odwyn and Llanddewibrefi. On a typical Sunday Rowland would rise early and begin a gruelling sixteen-mile 'round' of ministrations by riding to Nancwnlle for early morning prayers at eight, returning to Llangeitho for prayers at ten, and thence to Llanbadarn Odwyn, a mile away, for service at noon. Refreshed after lunch, he would then embark on a ten-mile return journey to Llanddewibrefi to conduct a final service at four.[27]

---

[19]NLW MS 2009B, f.37.
[20]E. Evans, *Casgliad o Bregethau* (2 vols., Shrewsbury, 1776), I, sig. b4v.
[21]Thomas, 'Diocese of St David's', p.11.
[22]*Add. Morris Letters*, II, p.688.
[23]J. Barber, ' "A fair and just demand"? Tithe unrest in Cardiganshire, 1796–1823', *WHR*, 16, no.2 (1992), 183.
[24]Saunders, *A View*, p.15.
[25]Davies, 'Diocese of St David's', p.83.
[26]Saunders, *A View*, p.24.
[27]NLW MS 9145F. See also E. D. Jones, 'Some aspects of the history of the church in north Cardiganshire in the eighteenth century', *JHSCW*, III, no.8 (1953), 103.

Clerical stipends in Cardiganshire were lamentably small. According to a valuation of livings made in *c.*1708, thirty livings in the deaneries of Ultra Aeron and Sub Aeron were worth £20 or less per annum. Only five livings (all of them in Sub Aeron) were valued at above £50 per annum.[28] Since the governors of Queen Anne's Bounty were reluctant (at least before 1809) to distribute generous grants by lot to augment the incomes of impoverished clergymen in the Archdeaconry of Cardigan, several clergymen chose to undertake manual work or schoolteaching to supplement their parochial income. Although data from consistory court records have not survived, it is more than likely that some poorly paid clerics drowned their problems in alcohol and became scandalous livers. Nor were their domestic circumstances favourable. In 1811 there were only fifty-seven resident clergy out of a total of 426 benefices in the whole of the diocese.[29] Non-residence was normally caused by the absence of a vicarage. Several vicarages were ruinous and uninhabitable, and the same was true of impropriated churches. According to Erasmus Saunders, Llechryd church had joined those churches which had become 'the solitary Habitations of Owles and Jackdaws',[30] and several other impropriated churches suffered from unglazed windows, leaking roofs and uneven floors. In general, therefore, it is fair to say that the bulk of the clergy in the county were inadequately paid, overworked and poorly housed.

The irony is, however, that although the established Church seemed to be haemorrhaging economically and administratively, its servants at local level were willing to embark on initiatives designed to strengthen its position as the guardian of the true faith. It is clear that the potential religiosity of the 'mountain people' encouraged them to make amends for the deficiencies of their spiritual governors. Erasmus Saunders noted 'the extraordinary Disposition to Religion' and the respect common people showed for the ceremonies, rituals and traditions of the Church.[31] In a famous and much-quoted passage, he praised their readiness to frequent services in fair and foul weather: 'There is, I believe, no part of the Nation more inclin'd to be Religious, and to be delighted with it than the poor Inhabitants of these Mountains.'[32] There was clearly a widespread thirst for regular services and preaching, and it is worth noting that by 1733 it had become an established practice for incumbents within the county to deliver sermons either every Sunday or on alternative Sundays – a marked improvement on the state of affairs fifty years earlier.[33]

The religiosity of parishioners was increasingly matched by a desire on the part of the more active clergy to discharge the spiritual obligations of their office more effectively. The fact that the overwhelming majority of them were Welsh-speaking natives of the county counted in their favour. Cardiganshire was a celebrated nursing-ground for Welsh clerics. In 1788 William Holcombe twitted Isaac Williams about the county's reputation for breeding smugglers and divines: 'So Your Countrymen are at their Old Tricks again; Half our Titles of Deacon's from Cardiganshire!'[34] The number of graduate clergy in the diocese fell sharply during the second half of the eighteenth

[28]NLW, Ottley MS VI.

[29]P. Virgin, *The Church in an Age of Negligence* (Cambridge, 1989), p.293. It should be noted that figures for the diocese in 1811, 1813 and 1814 fluctuate widely.

[30]Saunders, *A View*, pp.23–4.

[31]Ibid., p.31.

[32]Ibid., p.32. Cf. M. Williams, *Pregeth a Barablwyd yn Eglwys Grist yn Llundain yn 1717* (London, 1718), p.13.

[33]Jenkins, *Literature, Religion and Society*, pp.11–12.

[34]NLW MS 6203E, f.47.

century, partly because of the decline in the number of admissions to Oxford and Cambridge, and partly because of the rise in the number of 'literates', clergymen who were the sons of smaller gentry or farmers or craftsmen and were educated locally.[35] Accomplished clergymen like Samuel Williams, Theophilus Evans, Griffith Jones, Daniel Rowland and Isaac Williams never darkened the doors of the English universities, but their talents were widely admired. Edward Richard's famous school at Ystradmeurig produced many gifted ordinands and classical scholars for the county, including Evan Evans, John Williams, Lledrod, John Williams, Pantycelyn (son of William) and Thomas Richards, Darowen.[36] Although the six- or seven-year course was heavily based on classics, divinity and mathematics, the language of the school was Welsh. A remarkably good education for young ordinands was also available at Motygido, Llannarth, where the tutor John Pugh was reputedly a master of fourteen different tongues. Other budding clerics attended grammar schools at Cardigan, Carmarthen and Hereford or the private school at Castellhywel. All the available evidence suggests that services in the Archdeaconry of Cardigan were held in Welsh and there is no reason to believe that clergymen were prone to pander to Anglicized gentry families by preaching in English. In 1804 Benjamin Malkin observed that 'the churches are almost universally served in Welsh, and only the genteel part of the congregation, if there be any, is left in the dark'.[37]

Local clergymen were also crucial agents in producing and disseminating pious books for the benefit of the growing reading public. Over 2,500 Welsh books were published during the eighteenth century, many more than had been the case in Tudor and Stuart times, and the steady flow of bibles, prayer books, catechisms, primers, devotional and doctrinal books significantly enhanced people's understanding of the fundamental doctrines of the Protestant Reformation.[38] The pace-setters during the early decades of the century were the clergy of the lower Teifi valley – Samuel and Moses Williams, Alban Thomas, Theophilus Evans and William Gambold – all of whom were industrious authors and translators of godly books and sermons.[39] Aided by small squires like John Lewis of Gernos, Llangynllo, William Lewes of Llwynderw and Harri Llwyd of Llanllawddog, who were all committed to shoring up the Anglican religion, a growing number of pious and moral tracts (including the most popular historical work of its day, *Drych y Prif Oesoedd* by Theophilus Evans) were produced in order to reinforce the pulpit message and nourish the faith of those who were swiftly acquiring reading skills. It is no accident that the first official Welsh press to embark on commercial printing was located at Trerhedyn in the vale of Teifi in 1718, and even when Carmarthen, from 1721 onwards, became the unrivalled centre for the publication of Welsh books, churchmen from Cardiganshire continued to keep their printing presses busy.[40] This was

[35]NLW, Records of the Church in Wales, SD/VC/7; O. W. Jones, 'The mountain clergyman: his education and training', in O. W. Jones and D. Walker (eds.), *Links with the Past. Swansea and Brecon Historical Essays* (Llandybïe, 1974), p.167.

[36]D. G. Osborne-Jones, *Edward Richard of Ystradmeurig* (Carmarthen, 1934), p.34.

[37]B. H. Malkin, *The Scenery, Antiquities, and Biography, of South Wales* (London, 1804), p.325.

[38]See E. Rees, *Libri Walliae. A Catalogue of Welsh Books and Books printed in Wales* (2 vols., Aberystwyth, 1987) and G. H. Jenkins, *The Foundations of Modern Wales. Wales 1642–1780* (Oxford, 1993), pp.173–253, 342–426.

[39]G. H. Jenkins, 'Bywiogrwydd crefyddol a llenyddol Dyffryn Teifi, 1689–1740', *Ceredigion*, VIII, no.4 (1979), 439–77; D. W. Howell, *Patriarchs and Parasites: The Gentry of South-West Wales in the Eighteenth Century* (Cardiff, 1986), p.202.

[40]G. Bowen, 'Traddodiad llenyddol Deau Ceredigion, 1600–1850' (unpublished University of Wales MA thesis, 1943).

particularly so when the advent of Methodism brought further vitality to the printing trade. A striking range of prose epics, sermons, hymns, elegies and books of practical divinity helped to bring about a godly reformation and encourage the growth of the reading habit among lower middling sorts. Although Methodists prized emotional zeal and 'heart knowledge' above learning, they seized every opportunity to publicize their mission in print. William Williams Pantycelyn celebrated the joyous and convulsive excitement which accompanied the religious revival at Llangeitho in 1762 by publishing *apologiae* in the form of *Llythyr Martha Philopur at y Parchedig Philo Evangelius ei Hathro* (1762) and *Atteb Philo-Evangelius i Martha Philopur* (1763). Substantial parts of *Templum Experientiae Apertum; neu, Ddrws y Society Profiad* (1777) were based on Williams Pantycelyn's intimate knowledge of society members in north Cardiganshire. Some of the printed sermons of Daniel Rowland sold like hot cakes: over 3,000 subscribers promised to take more than a dozen copies each of his *Pum Pregeth* (1772).[41]

The printing and publishing of Welsh books was also intimately associated with popular schooling which, by the middle decades of the eighteenth century, was exerting a profound influence on church life in Cardiganshire. Schools established by the Society for the Promotion of Christian Knowledge (1699–1737) made very little headway in the county: only two (set up in 1706 and 1727) were established,[42] and although common people, including shepherds and servants, endeavoured to compensate for the deficiency by 'Reading or Discoursing to instruct one another in their Houses',[43] parishioners were poorly served both by the established Church and charitable organizations. But from the late 1730s onwards, one of the most successful educational schemes in eighteenth-century Europe was masterminded by Griffith Jones, Llanddowror. Born in 1684 within a stone's throw of the county, Jones was well-known to the people of south Cardiganshire as a result of his regular and much-publicized field-preaching tours during the second, third and fourth decades of the eighteenth century. William Williams Pantycelyn noted his ability to fill even the largest churches, and at Llanwenog in April 1714 the church was so heavily thronged that the doors broke under the weight of the standing worshippers.[44] Among his large personal following was Daniel Rowland of Llangeitho who, in 1735, was so captivated by his spirit-filled ministry that he dedicated the rest of his life to saving souls.

Although Griffith Jones never claimed to be a Methodist, he, too, was thrilled by the prospect of missionary activity, of reform and renewal, and of lasting spiritual change. His most enduring contribution, however, lay in the field of education.[45] Convinced of the folly of teaching monoglot Welsh children through the medium of English, he launched a massively successful peripatetic scheme based on Welsh-language teaching tailored to the needs of a rural, monoglot people. A small army of teachers moved from parish to parish, teaching both children and adults, either by day or night, in farmhouses, barns and churches. Fearful that the 'vulgar sorts' were in peril of falling into 'the dreadful Abyss of Eternity and perish for want of knowledge',[46] Jones instructed schoolmasters

[41]D. Ll. Morgan, 'Daniel Rowland (?1711–1790): pregethwr diwygiadol', *Ceredigion*, XI, no.3 (1991), 234. See also idem, *Y Diwygiad Mawr* (Llandysul, 1980).
[42]M. Clement, *The SPCK and Wales 1699–1740* (London, 1954), p.156.
[43]Saunders, *A View*, p.32.
[44]W. Williams, *Saith o Farwnadau* (Abertawe, 1854), p.7; Ottley MS 1627.
[45]G. H. Jenkins, ' "An old and much honoured soldier": Griffith Jones, Llanddowror', *WHR*, II, no.4 (1983), 449–68; G. Morgan, *Ysgolion Cylchynol Sir Aberteifi 1738–1777 / Circulating Schools in Cardiganshire 1738–1777* (Aberystwyth, n.d.).
[46]*The Welch Piety* (London, 1740), p.32.

Fig. 119: The parish church of Llanddewibrefi where Daniel Rowland was entranced by the preaching of Griffith Jones, Llanddowror. (*Crown Copyright RCAHMW-NMR*).

never to lose sight of the fact that their ultimate goal was to save the souls of their pupils. Large numbers of underprivileged people, including tenant farmers, craftsmen, labourers and servants (as well as young children) flocked to the circulating schools to learn to read the Scriptures, to master the fundamental doctrines of the Church catechism, and to give a decent account of their faith. Clergymen in the county loudly praised the scheme and *The Welch Piety* contains dozens of letters in which they warmly acknowledged their debt to Griffith Jones, to local benefactors, and, above all, to the schoolmasters. In terms of numbers of pupils, the schools were at their peak between 1760 and 1777:

TABLE 18: Circulating Schools in Cardiganshire, 1760–1777

1760–2	:	279 schools (2138 pupils)
1764–5	:	189 schools (2454 pupils)
1773–4	:	211 schools (2603 pupils)
1776–7	:	144 schools (2946 pupils)

The progress of young children clearly delighted promoters and supporters of the scheme. By the 1750s parish churches and farmhouses throughout the county echoed to the sounds of adult and infant voices chanting the alphabet aloud, spelling words, reciting the catechism, singing verses from *Canwyll y Cymru*, and reading passages from the Bible. At Blaen-porth in the 1750s children and adults were able to recite the catechism by heart and respond so well in the public liturgy that elderly worshippers were put to shame and some 'could not refrain shedding Tears'.[47] The local curate, John Thomas, heartily praised the beneficial influence of catechetical instruction: 'It is a very agreeable Sight indeed, to see a full School, *many* in *Raggs, all* upon *Charity*, learning thus to *put on Christ.*'[48] At Y Ferwig, a child of three was able to spell even the hardest words, while at Llan-goedmor pupils learnt by heart extensive portions of Griffith Jones's expositions of the catechism.[49] In 1763 David Lloyd, vicar of Ystrad, confessed that had not charity schools been established in the parish of Trefilan, scores of children would have died in ignorance of the Christian faith. 'I am conscious', he wrote, 'that a great Number of Children in our Neighbourhood, from eight to twelve Years of Age, have arrived to a higher Pitch of knowledge than any of their Ancestors did in all their Life-time.'[50] At Llandysiliogogo, farmers and labourers were so impressed by the progress of their own children that they brought fuel and candles with them to night-school in order to extend their own hours of tuition.[51] 'Your Light', wrote Hugh Rice of Lledrod (one of the oldest clergymen in the diocese) to Madam Bridget Bevan in October 1766, 'hath more than once shone in this dark Corner.'[52] Rice and his fellow clergy were in no doubt that the circulating schools had helped to revitalize church life by grounding parishioners in the principles of the Anglican religion, by increasing the number of communicants, and by rendering congregations more attentive and sympathetic to the Christian ministry.

There can be no question that the success enjoyed by the circulating schools in revitalizing church life owed much to the influence of the Methodist movement. Few chapters in the history of religion in Wales have been more faithfully recorded than the development of Methodism and from the earliest beginnings the people of Cardiganshire were familiar with the extraordinary pentecostal scenes which characterized the revivalist heritage in other parts of Europe as well as America. Some initial generalizations need to be emphasized. First, Methodism was not introduced or imposed from above. It owed its origin to local initiatives – at Llangeitho and Talgarth – which stemmed from remarkable personal conversions experienced by the two founding fathers. For both Daniel Rowland and Howel Harris, the year 1735 was an *annus mirabilis* of eternal significance. Second,

[47] *The Welch Piety* (London, 1756), pp.33–4.
[48] *The Welch Piety* (London, 1758), pp.43–4.
[49] *The Welch Piety* (London, 1761), pp.19–20.
[50] *The Welch Piety* (London, 1763), pp.17–18.
[51] *The Welch Piety* (London, 1758), pp.30–1.
[52] *The Welch Piety* (London, 1767), p.7.

received wisdom used to be that the so-called Methodist 'Revival' was a seismic upheaval which transformed the spiritual life of the nation, but few reputable historians now believe that it was anything of the sort. In Cardiganshire, as in every other county where Methodism took root, its growth was molecular, slow and uneven. Even in the most productive hunting-grounds in south Cardiganshire, only thirteen societies (a total of at most 200 members) had been established by 1745 and the membership was subject to considerable ebb and flow.[53] Nor should we take too seriously the claims of their leaders that five, six, or even ten thousand hearers often assembled to hear them preach the New Birth,[54] for Methodists were no strangers to the language of hyperbole and they were not the most accurate counters of heads.

Having sounded these notes of caution, it must nevertheless be acknowledged that Methodism, by spreading the gospel of revivalism and awakening converts, injected new life into dormant or inactive churches in Cardiganshire. Indeed, it could be argued that the emergence of Methodism was itself evidence of the growing vitality of the Church. Ablaze with missionary enthusiasm, Rowland and Harris joined forces in 1737 and resolved as preachers to sally forth in God's name. Harris, whose energy was legendary, made the initial running by embarking on aggressive and exhausting 'rounds' of sermons and prayer meetings in south Cardiganshire. His diary sometimes gives the impression that his feet seldom touched the ground as he tore from parish to parish in his determination to 'meet Legions of Devils and fight them in Jesus' name'.[55] Aided by Rowland, he began to work a godly reformation in south-west Wales by striking terror into the hearts of smugglers, wreckers and non-taxpayers and by awakening the consciences of churchgoers and non-churchgoers alike.[56] The essence of Methodism was enthusiasm and the early evangelists believed that they had received a God-given commission to win the souls of benighted sinners to Christ. They led by example as well as precept by preaching in churchyards, fields, fairs, markets and town-centres. Young, fresh and energetic, they were uncertain of their theological principles and how their overall mission might unfold. 'We are a heap of Boys O pity us', cried Harris,[57] as he rode into Cardiganshire with the characteristic confidence and optimism of the twice-born. But although Harris worked feverishly on behalf of the revivalist cause in the south of the county, his influence was less lasting and memorable than the forces which radiated from the epicentre of the Methodist movement at Llangeitho.

Some seemingly unexceptional parishes and villages have fame thrust upon them unexpectedly: such a place was Llangeitho in the mid-eighteenth century. Llangeitho sings to the Welsh in the same way as Wittenberg or Halle does to the Germans. Its fame owed virtually everything to the unsurpassed gifts of Daniel Rowland (a local man of clerical stock) as a preacher and to his remarkable ability to provoke recurring waves of emotion among his congregations.[58] From 1737

---

[53]E. M. White, *Praidd Bach y Bugail Mawr. Seiadau Methodistaidd De-Orllewin Cymru* (Llandysul, 1995), pp.2, 222.
[54]See, for instance, the exaggerated claims of Howel Harris and Thomas Charles. T. Beynon, 'Howell Harris yn Sir Aberteifi', *CCHMC*, XXXI, no.4 (1946), 114–21; D. E. Jenkins, *The Life of the Rev. Thomas Charles* (3 vols., Denbigh, 1908), III, p.114.
[55]T. Beynon, 'Howell Harris's visits to Cardiganshire', *CCHMC*, XXX, no.1 (1945), 49.
[56]Ibid., III, no.3 (1945), 107; XXXI, no.1 (1946), 23, 27.
[57]Ibid., XXX, no.1 (1945), 50. See also G. M. Roberts, 'Methodistiaeth gynnar gwaelod Sir Aberteifi', *Ceredigion*, V, no.1 (1964), 1–13.
[58]E. Evans, *Daniel Rowland and the Great Evangelical Awakening in Wales* (Edinburgh, 1985).

Fig. 120: Daniel Rowland, Llangeitho (1711–1790), the undisputed leader of the Calvinistic Methodists in eighteenth-century Cardiganshire. (*Copyright National Library of Wales*).

onwards Llangeitho became the headquarters of evangelical activity in the county as Rowland's vibrant voice, commanding personality, and moving eloquence occasioned unparalleled scenes of emotional fervour which provoked much public comment. Initially, Rowland acquired a reputation for preaching in an intimidating, strident fashion, but the Welsh 'Boanerges', under the influence of his Congregationalist friend Phylip Pugh, minister of Cilgwyn church, eventually tempered his dire warnings of eternal damnation with the balm of God's grace. Contemporaries spoke in awe of the 'amazing' and 'uncommon' power with which he discoursed, and although Rowland was never reluctant to venture beyond his native county to preach the Word, his name became synonymous with Llangeitho. Pilgrims travelled on foot, on horseback and by boat from all parts of Wales to hear him preach and to attend monthly communion. Local people arrived at five or six in the morning to vie for vantage-points within earshot of the man who was hailed as 'a second Paul'.[59] There are

[59]G. M. Roberts (ed.), *Selected Trevecka Letters (1742–1747)* (Caernarvon, 1956), p.164.

accounts, probably apocryphal, that Rowland often preached for up to seven hours, and one of Harris's informants claimed that he was so assiduous that his hair began to fall out.[60] Harris's correspondence buzzed with excited reports of sensational scenes of public praise at Llangeitho. On St David's Day 1743 he informed George Whitefield of scenes he had witnessed:

> I was last Sunday at the Ordinance with Brother Rowlands where I saw, felt and heard such things as I cant send on Paper any Idea of. The Power that continues with Him is uncommon. Such Crying out and Heart Breaking Groans, Silent Weeping and Holy Joy, and shouts of Rejoicing I never saw. Their Amens and Cryings Glory in the Highest & would enflame your Soul was you there. Tis very common when He preaches for Scores to fall down by the Power of the Word, pierced and wounded or over-com'd by the Love of God and Sights of the Beauty and Excellency of Jesus, and lie on the Ground.[61]

The 'heavenly entertainment' at Llangeitho was accompanied by violent convulsions, catatonic trances, heart-rending sobs and cries, raucous praying and singing, all of which testified to Rowland's capacity to raise the spiritual temperature. Scenes of unrestrained ecstasy, however, were not universally applauded, even by evangelicals, and those who were not Methodists found such extravagant demonstrations either intimidating or comic. One such observer wrote in jaundiced terms in 1746: 'His [Daniel Rowland] preaching again flung almost the whole society into the greatest agitation and confusion possible, some cry'd, other laughed, ye women pulled one another by ye caps, embraced each other, caper'd like, where there was any room . . . I never saw greater instances of madness, even in Bedlam itself.'[62]

In the long term, of course, far more important than the initial emotional conversion, however profound that may have been, was the enrolment of members into tightly-knit *seiadau* (societies) where they were turned into diligent, sober, caring persons who read their bibles, mastered the catechism, appreciated the power of spirituality, and struggled daily against the wiles of the Devil. Permanent pastoral oversight was afforded to 'newly born' or penitent converts in order to consolidate gains and perpetuate the revival. There was no automatic entry to the ranks; new members were accepted only after prolonged and rigorous scrutiny, and persistent backsliders were expelled. Although the number of willing hands prepared or able to act as exhorters, superintendents and counsellors was never large, Rowland's ministry in Cardiganshire was greatly enhanced by the dedication of James William and William Richard, both farmers from Llanddewibrefi, who endeavoured as superintendents to ensure that societies were effective as well as spirit-filled units. Between 1738 and 1745, thirteen societies were established in humble farmhouses or chapels of ease at Capel Gwynfil (Llangeitho), Lampeter, Twr-gwyn, Dyffryn-saith, Blaen-porth, Ffrwdwenith, Aber-porth, Blaenhownant, Llwyndafydd, Llanllwchaearn, Coed-y-brain, Llanfairorllwyn and Llechryd.[63] Some of William Richard's reports in 1743 again suggest that here were young men and women with new voices but without a language to express their feelings: 'Here is some ravish'd with

[60]G. M. Roberts (ed.), *Hanes Methodistiaeth Galfinaidd Cymru. Cyfrol 1. Y Deffroad Mawr* (Caernarfon, 1973), p.143.
[61]Roberts, *Selected Trevecka Letters*, p.66.
[62]J. H. Davies, 'Daniel Rowland. Contemporary descriptions (1746 and 1835)', *CCHMC*, I, no.2 (1916), 54.
[63]White, *Praidd Bach*, p.222.

Love, they want words to express what they Experience.'[64] At Blaenhownant members experienced such warm feelings in their hearts that they spent long hours 'rejoicing in God & praising his sacred name'.[65] Although many members strived painfully but not always successfully to expel the Devil and achieve assurance, they were all too aware that enthusiasm and emotionalism lay at the heart of the Methodist movement. Behaviour in society meetings could be spontaneous, noisy and boisterous as members responded in different ways to strict inquisitorial methods or to expressions of inward conviction. In 1745 Watkin Watkins, steward of the societies at Llwyndafydd and Blaenhownant, excitedly reported to Howel Harris: 'our work is to prays God, many times, singing Halelujah's from night to morning in an Extasy of Joy in the Holy Ghost'.[66]

In spite of such heart-warming and promising accounts, however, all was not well among the leaders of the movement. This is not the place to recount the bitter in-fighting which led to the schism of 1750, the ravages of which were not repaired for the best part of a decade. Suffice to say that Howel Harris was chiefly to blame for the breakdown in relations with Rowland. As the 1740s unfolded he became increasingly overbearing, stubborn and convinced of his own infallibility. His curious attachment to the heretical doctrine of Patripassianism, his unnecessarily long sojourns in London, and his scandalous liaison with the *soi-disant* prophetess Madam Sydney Griffith, led to his expulsion from the movement in 1750 and to much bad feeling between *pobl Rowland* and *pobl Harris*. It was a crushing blow to a movement whose *raison d'être* had been spiritual fellowship and mutual edification. While Harris, licking his wounds, withdrew to his commune at Trefeca, Rowland patiently endeavoured to keep his people together at a time when the Arminian challenge was gathering strength. Even after his return to the fold, Harris never recovered his old ascendancy and Rowland was finally acknowledged as the true 'father' and 'commander-in-chief' of the Methodist cause.

By dint of regular preaching and perseverance, Rowland eventually succeeded in bringing fresh inspiration to the seemingly stricken cause. It was his powerful ministry, above all, which ushered in an electrifying revival at Llangeitho in 1762. It has often been claimed that the revival was mainly triggered by the publication of *Caniadau y rhai sydd ar y Môr o Wydr* (The Songs of those who are on the Sea of Crystal), a collection of memorable hymns by Williams Pantycelyn.[67] But the fruits of Rowland's ministry were already evident in mid and south Cardiganshire: between 1759 and 1762 nine Methodist meeting houses had been built (at Llanbadarn Odwyn, Llandysul, Cardigan, Lledrod, Llanbadarn Trefeglwys, Llanddewibrefi (2), Henfynyw and Llansanffraid).[68] One of those chapels had been built in 1760 by Rowland's congregation at Capel Gwynfil, an ancient chapelry in the parish of Llanddewibrefi, within easy walking distance of Llangeitho. Three years later, for reasons which have never been satisfactorily explained, Rowland was deprived of his cures at Llangeitho and Nancwnlle by Bishop Samuel Squire. In a public gesture of solidarity, his parishioners boycotted the parish church of Llangeitho and took communion with Rowland until

---

[64]G. M. Roberts, 'Early society reports', *CCHMC*, LII, no.1 (1967), 16.

[65]Ibid., LIV, no.2 (1969), 60.

[66]White, *Praidd Bach*, p.127.

[67]R. G. Gruffydd, 'Diwygiad 1762 a William Williams o Bantycelyn', *CCHMC*, LIV, no.3 (1969), 68–75; LV, no.1 (1970), 4–13; idem, 'Diwygiad Llangeitho a'i ddylanwad', *Y Traethodydd*, CXLVI, no. 619 (1991), 95–104. Methodist historians have claimed that seven revivals occurred in Cardiganshire 1735–91. J. Evans, *Hanes Methodistiaeth De Aberteifi* (Dolgellau, 1904), p.365.

[68]D. R. Barnes, *People of Seion* (Llandysul, 1995), pp.75, 145–74.

his death in 1790.[69] In the revival of 1762 Rowland was at the centre of some astonishing scenes of evangelical fervour at Llangeitho. Mass conversions were accompanied by the kind of spiritual gymnastics which prompted hostile observers to dub converts 'the Welsh Jumpers'. The Llangeitho revival entered the annals of Welsh folklore as hundreds of pilgrims joined the swelling ranks of the Holy Rollers. John Williams of Dolwyddelan walked every single step to Llangeitho and, having heard Rowland 'tap the barrels of the covenant of grace', drank the 'pure wine' and came away 'as drunk as a fool'.[70] The Arian David Lloyd of Brynllefrith sardonically claimed in 1764 that the Jumpers of Llangeitho had become a focus for voyeurs: 'Their number increases, and their wild Pranks are beyond Description. The Worships of the day being over, they have kept together in ye place whole Nights, singing, capering, bawling, fainting, thumping, and a variety of other Exercises. The whole Country for many Miles around have crowded to see such strange sights.'[71] As a result, Llangeitho came to symbolize Welsh revivalist preaching and it is unlikely that any other parish in Wales could boast such regular assemblies of hundreds of pious people over such a long period of time.

It is significant that meetings of the Welsh Calvinistic Methodist Association were held at Llangeitho on sixteen separate occasions between 1744 and 1797;[72] leading members were clearly glad to avail themselves of the opportunity of visiting and worshipping at the movement's principal Mecca. Moreover, a host of preachers and exhorters prided themselves on their use of 'tân Llangeitho' (the fire of Llangeitho) in their sermons. Among Rowland's most gifted converts was Dafydd Morris, Twr-gwyn (1744–91), a young drover from Lledrod who was reckoned to be second only to his mentor in the pulpit. On one occasion in Bridgend, Morris preached on the 'Day of Judgement' with such startling effect that hearers ran wildly through the streets, convinced that 'that solemn day had actually come!'[73] Another rousing preacher was John Williams ('Williams Lledrod') (1747–1831), curate of Lledrod and Llanwnnen, who assisted Rowland by preaching and administering the sacrament at Llangeitho.[74] Like the founding fathers, these were tireless and selfless men who spent long hours in the saddle and blew the gospel trumpet in several counties. It need hardly be said that Rowland himself remained the linchpin of the movement. Even as an old man, he continued to preach vigorously and it was his silver tongue which secured the conversion of the eighteen-year-old student, Thomas Charles, on 20 January 1773, an event which the founder of the Welsh Sunday schools never forgot: 'I love him dearly, and honour him as my father in Christ . . . for to him . . . I am indebted for whatever light I have into, and experience I have of, the glorious salvation through Christ.'[75] A sheaf of elegies (including the last literary work by Williams Pantycelyn) marked the death of Daniel Rowland, the Grand Old Man of Welsh Calvinistic Methodism, at the age of seventy-nine on 16 October 1790.[76]

[69]H. A. Evans (ed.), *Y Gwyrthiau Gynt* (Llangeitho, 1962), p.9.
[70]O. Thomas, *Cofiant y Parchedig John Jones Talsarn* (2 vols., Wrexham, 1874), II, p.804.
[71]G. Eyre Evans (ed.), *Lloyd Letters (1754–1796)* (Aberystwyth, 1908), p.52.
[72]Evans, *Y Gwyrthiau Gynt*, p.16.
[73]T. Rees, *History of Protestant Nonconformity in Wales* (2nd edn., London, 1883), pp.392–3.
[74]G. M. Roberts (ed.), *Hanes Methodistiaeth Galfinaidd Cymru. Cyfrol 2. Cynnydd y Corff* (Caernarfon, 1978), pp.67–8.
[75]E. Morgan, *Ministerial Records; or Brief Accounts of the Great Progress of Religion* (London, 1840), pp.114–15.
[76]K. Jenkins, 'Pantycelyn a'r Cardis', *Ceredigion*, XII, no.1 (1993), 41–63.

We must now ask why the godly passions and emotional commitment implicit in Methodism proved so attractive to 'a people naturally so shrewd and sensible, as the natives of Cardiganshire'.[77] It is important to recognize that the strength of Methodism lay in rural communities where the resources of the established Church were thinly stretched and where non-resident pluralists were unable to exercise effective pastoral supervision. From its focus in the rural hinterland at Llangeitho, the movement spread along the lower Teifi valley into north Carmarthenshire, north Pembrokeshire and along the coast of Cardiganshire.[78] En route it gained support from dissatisfied or unhappy churchgoers who sincerely believed that the 'holy fire and warmth' implicit in revivalism would revitalize church life. Methodism was particularly adept in capturing people who had been left to shift for themselves and who were not subject to intimidation by powerful landowners. It is significant that the least spontaneous response to Methodism occurred in north Cardiganshire where resident landowners like the Pryses of Gogerddan and the Powells of Nanteos were implacable foes of revivalist preachers. Such dominant families were able to unite with parsons to bring pressure to bear on members of the rural community and remind them of their obligation to conform to Anglican canons as well as to respect the doctrines of divine right and passive obedience. Conversely, in south Cardiganshire the same depth of opposition was not apparent among the gentry. Both Harris and Rowland were well received and courteously treated by the likes of Sir Lucius Christianus Lloyd of Maesyfelin and Sir Herbert Lloyd, the infamous 'Vulture Knight' of Peterwell, and Harris in particular was never happier or more animated than when genteel ladies pandered to his vanity.[79]

There can be little doubt that Methodism took full advantage of the growing desire among literate and pious sections of society, especially farmers and craftsmen, for a more regular and attractively varied spiritual ministry not only on Sundays but also on weekdays and feast days. Throughout the eighteenth century the general rule within Anglican churches was to conduct one service on the Sabbath, usually for an hour between eight and noon. In 1804 only five churches out of a total of sixty-five in the county held two regular services on Sundays. Several incumbents reported to the bishop in that year that a single service had been the norm for generations. 'It never was performed oftener', 'as it is customary so to do' and 'no more has been usual here in the memory of man' were constant refrains in the visitation returns.[80] Hamstrung by the system, non-resident pluralists were unable to compete with young, eye-catching field preachers who made religion spiritually uplifting and exciting, or with regular society meetings where small but tenacious bands of believers thrived on intense spiritual fellowship and fervour. 'They collect Preachers . . . with all their might from all Quarters',[81] wrote a despairing Lewis Evans, vicar of Llanfihangel-y-Creuddyn. Although clergymen were key figures during the principal stages of the cycle of humankind – at baptism, confirmation, marriage and burial – they were not, in the words of Griffith Jones, able to provide 'friendly access to advise [people] on their spiritual state'.[82] Methodists

---

[77]T. Lloyd and Revd Turnor, *General View of the Agriculture of the County of Cardigan* (London, 1794), p.18.

[78]E. G. Bowen, 'The Teifi valley as a religious frontier', *Ceredigion*, VII, no.1 (1972), 1–13.

[79]T. Beynon, 'Howell Harris's visits to Cardiganshire', *CCHMC*, XXXI, no.1 (1946), 18–29; B. Phillips, *Peterwell* (Llandysul, 1983), p.50.

[80]NLW, SD/QA/2, nos. 37, 48, 57, 75, 81, 86.

[81]NLW, SD/QA/2, no.73.

[82]*The Welch Piety* (London, 1741), p.13.

deliberately targeted the young and especially the unmarried. Women flocked to society meetings and were admitted in significant numbers. In July 1743 a report on societies in south Cardiganshire prepared by William Richard revealed that in five leading societies forty-five of the seventy-eight members were women and all but seven of them were single.[83] Williams Pantycelyn portrayed the archetypal *seiat* as 'a company of lively and daring young men; and a bevy of young girls at the peak of their strength and vigour' ('cwmpeini o langciau hoenus, a gwrol; tyrfa o ferched yn eu grym, a'u nwyfiant').[84] Michael Watts has suggested that by joining a movement in which they were no longer obliged to keep their passions in check, young unmarried men and women were able to rid themselves of feelings of sexual guilt and repression.[85] In its inquisitorial class and prayer meetings, Methodism offered the opportunity to sinners to unburden themselves and to commit themselves to a strict ethical code. Such a code proved especially attractive to pious small farmers and craftsmen whose goods and possessions were worth only some £20 per annum but whose cultural and spiritual aspirations were much higher.[86]

The contagious enthusiasm associated with Llangeitho was also a powerful incentive to join born-again Christians. Many believed that the like of Daniel Rowland had never been seen since the days of the Apostles, and he and his fellow exhorters gained a devoted following not only among articulate and lettered local worshippers but also from the hundreds of pilgrims who tramped to Llangeitho to partake in scenes of unrestrained fervour. The physical manifestations of revivalism – trances, convulsions, paroxysms – occurred whenever Rowland warned sinners of the eternal torments of hell, and the cries of the Welsh Jumpers became a symbol of the spiritual regeneration of twice-born enthusiasts. Although flinty Dissenters averted their gaze from such unseemly and reactionary fundamentalism, many Calvinists could not resist visiting Llangeitho in order to discover ways and means of precipitating revivals in their own communities. Thomas Charles recognized the symbolic importance of revivalist initiatives begun at the principal headquarters of Welsh Methodism:

> From Llangeitho did the fructifying streams flow all over the country in those blessed days. The sermons heard there, being repeated by many persons on their return, to the country people, and being related again by them to their neighbours, were wonderfully blessed; divine truth was gaining ground and spreading through all the country; many were consequently stirred up and induced to go and hear the extraordinary preacher at Llangeitho for themselves.[87]

Finally, people were able to throw in their lot with Methodism without fear of undue harassment or persecution. Although Rowland and Williams Pantycelyn were beaten with guns and staves by a gang of ruffians in 1743, and the exhorter Morgan Hughes was 'favoured with the Honr of Imprisonmt', albeit for a short period, in the same year, Methodists were not badly treated in the county.[88] It is true that Evan Evans exploded with rage whenever he sighted 'the most arrant rogues under the sun' and that his mentor Edward Richard jeered at pilgrims as they made their way to

---

[83]White, *Praidd Bach*, pp.80–1.
[84]W. Williams, *Templum Experientiae Apertum; neu, Ddrws y Society Profiad* (Aberhonddu, 1777), p.9.
[85]M. R. Watts, *The Dissenters. Volume II* (Oxford, 1995), p.57.
[86]White, *Praidd Bach*, p.98.
[87]Morgan, *Ministerial Records*, p.145.
[88]D. J. O. Jones, *Daniel Rowland Llangeitho (1713–1790)* (Llandysul, 1938), p.135; Roberts, *Selected Trevecka Letters*, p.84.

Llangeitho, but there is little evidence that either the clergy or the gentry resorted to bullying tactics.[89] Methodism might have been a nuisance and an embarrassment to dyed-in-the-wool clerics, but a good many of them treated evangelists as fellow workers in the same vineyard. One gains the impression that at least in Cardiganshire Methodism was viewed as an organic part of the established Church rather than some kind of Trojan horse. For their part, eighteenth-century Methodists strongly resisted the temptation to sever their links with the mother church and their leaders were at pains to avoid causing unnecessary disruption. They seldom applied for separate registrations for meeting houses or for licences to preach, and even as late as 1811 only seven Calvinistic Methodist churches had been registered in the county.[90] Small wonder that in church visitation replies, few Anglican clergymen classified Methodists as 'Dissenters', for they knew full well that this 'vital religion' had sprung from the established Church.[91]

It was partly for this reason that Wesleyan Methodism fared poorly. It had no roots in Cardiganshire and John Wesley was virtually unknown to the local clergy. Wesley had no real desire to tread on Calvinist toes and he entered into a gentleman's agreement with Howel Harris, the effect of which was that the Welsh-speaking parts of Wales were left to the tender mercies of Calvinist exhorters. Wesley had grave misgivings about 'the Confusion of Tongues' and neither he nor Thomas Coke, his right-hand man, was prepared to squander valuable time in the vain bid to save the souls of monoglot Welsh-speakers.[92] Noisy lead miners at Ffair-rhos gave Wesley a dusty reception when he strayed into mid-Cardiganshire in July 1764 and only affluent, bilingual sorts at Cardigan took him seriously.[93] No sustained attempt was made to plant Wesleyanism in the county until missionaries from north-east Wales visited Aberystwyth in 1804 and began to establish causes at Tre'r-ddôl, Borth and Lampeter.[94] This flurry of activity discomfited Calvinistic Methodists and those at Aberystwyth, bitterly resentful of the intrusive presence of Wesleyan worshippers at the Boat House, daubed the walls with the slogan: *'Yma y mae Synagog Satan'* (Here is Satan's Synagogue).[95] In truth, however, Calvinists had little to fear from disciples of Wesley, for very few had rallied with enthusiasm to his cause.

Calvinistic Methodism and, indeed, the established Church as a whole had greater cause to resent the growth of old Dissent which, although numerically small, was associated in the public mind with Roundhead zeal, strife and secession. Whereas Methodists were determined to avoid any path which might lead to expulsion from the Church, Dissenters urged people to separate from it and to carry the banner of liberty of conscience with pride and fortitude. Although all Dissenters (except Unitarians) were free to worship under the terms of the Toleration Act of 1689, they were still judged second-class citizens in municipal life and would remain so until the repeal of the Test and Corporation Acts in 1828. Yet the presence of small Dissenting causes does not seem to have inflamed popular hostility, at least not until the latter years of the eighteenth century. In numerical terms, Dissent was insignificant in the county in the pre-Methodist period and at that time the

[89]*Add. Morris Letters*, II, pp.688–9; J. H. Davies, 'A sidelight on the history of Daniel Rowland', *CCHMC*, I, no.1 (1916), 30.
[90]Barnes, *People of Seion*, p.73.
[91]See NLW, SD/QA/253; SD/QA/2.
[92]A.H. Williams (ed.), *John Wesley in Wales 1739–1790* (Cardiff, 1971), p.36.
[93]Ibid., pp.69, 94.
[94]A. H. Williams, *Welsh Wesleyan Methodism* (Bangor, 1935), pp.111–12.
[95]W. J. Lewis, *Born on a Perilous Rock* (Aberystwyth, 1980), pp.57–8.

established Church had every reason to believe that it could contain or resist the expansion of Dissenting causes. Draconian persecution had already rid the county of Catholic recusants,[96] and leading Dissenters were subjected to threats and cajolery. Dissenters could derive little comfort from their Stuart inheritance. The fleeting visits of Vavasor Powell had made little impression and in the years of persecution only tiny numbers of intrepid souls had dared worship at the feet of Stephen Hughes in the legendary cave at Cwm Hwplyn or at clandestine meetings on Llanddewibrefi mountain.[97] The Compton Census of 1676 reveals that only 148 Dissenters, including 30 at Cenarth, 22 at Llanddewibrefi and 20 at Llandysul, were willing to bear adversity with steadfast witness.[98] The Census, however, did not accurately reflect the strength of the Congregational church of Cilgwyn at Llangybi. Described by a writer in 1728 as 'a Church of Christ gathered in Cardigan shire', the cause at Cilgwyn can be traced back to 1654.[99] During the years of the penal code, when Congregationalists established 'county churches' which comprised a number of individual congregations, the widely scattered church of Cilgwyn had branches at Abermeurig, Blaenpennal, Cae'r-onnen, Ciliau Aeron, Crug-y-maen and Llwyn-rhys (Llwynpiod from 1735) and by 1709 it was served by three ministers. The cause was certainly flourishing, though it is highly unlikely (as was claimed in the List of Dissenting congregations compiled by Dr John Evans in 1715–18) that it boasted a thousand hearers.[100]

In 1675 Henry Maurice had described the Congregationalists of Cardiganshire as 'independent, but very moderate',[101] and this tradition was maintained and enriched by the ministry of Phylip Pugh, a man of 'seraphic piety',[102] courtesy and gentleness who served the dispersed branches of the Cilgwyn church with selfless devotion for over fifty years. Born near Blaenpennal in 1679 and educated at Samuel Jones's celebrated academy at Brynllywarch, Pugh's moderate Calvinism proved attractive to pious lower middling sorts. Between 1709 and 1760 he baptized 680 infants and, as they grew up, he plied them with catechetical instruction, warm piety and outstanding pastoral care.[103] Moreover, he laboured tirelessly to bring ministers of religion together in a spirit of goodwill and charity. Most Dissenting ministers took a hard line on Methodism, but Pugh welcomed Howel Harris to his home, lent books to Daniel Rowland, and set great store by missionary evangelism. His eirenic spirit meant that the churches under his care could not remain untouched by the spirit of revivalism, and there are good grounds for believing that Pugh encouraged this in order to counter the growing Arminian-Arian influence. In so doing, however, he unwittingly enabled Congregationalists under his care to transfer their allegiance to Methodist causes. The floodgates certainly opened under his successor, Thomas Gray, who encouraged members at Llwynpiod, Abermeurig and Blaenpennal to 'methodize' in their worship and habits and to emulate the achievements of Daniel Rowland and his flocks. Thanks to Gray's crusading zeal,

[96]J. Cunnane, 'Ceredigion and the old faith', Ceredigion, XII, no.2 (1994), 3–34.
[97]G. H. Jenkins, Protestant Dissenters in Wales 1639–1689 (Cardiff, 1992), p.51.
[98]A. Whiteman (ed.), The Compton Census of 1676: A Critical Edition (London, 1986), pp.458, 468–9.
[99]NLW MS 5470C; 'Llyfr Eglwys y Cilgwyn', Y Cofiadur, I (1923), 24; E. D. Jones, 'Ymneilltuaeth gynnar yng Ngheredigion', Ceredigion, IV, no.2 (1961), 96–112.
[100]Dr Williams's Library, London, Dr John Evans's List of Dissenting Congregations in England and Wales. MS 34, f.138.
[101]R. T. Jones, Hanes Annibynwyr Cymru (Abertawe, 1966), p.99n.
[102]Rees, Protestant Nonconformity, p.309.
[103]E. D. Jones, 'Phylip Pugh', Diwinyddiaeth, XV (1964), 62–9.

Congregationalist meeting-houses in mid-Cardiganshire echoed to cries of joy, weeping and groaning to such a degree that nineteenth-century Congregationalist historians believed that he had discarded beliefs which lay at the heart of the Congregationalist faith and had done more to advance the cause of Methodism than that of his own denomination.[104]

Further south, pastoral reform was spearheaded by Benjamin Evans, a convert from the Baptists who became minister at Tre-wen, near Newcastle Emlyn, in 1779. A doughty enemy of anti-Trinitarian causes and a prolific author, Evans was chiefly responsible for founding churches at Hawen, Penrhiwgaled, Pisgah and Capel-y-wig. Although he was an obdurate man who found compromise difficult, Evans could display a lightness of touch in the pulpit. During a sermon preached in Cardigan, he referred to the disease of the intemperate in jocular vein: '*Gout, go out*; gormod o'r *go in* yw yr achos o'r *go out*' (too much of the go in is the cause of the go out).[105] His successful ministry did not endear him to Thomas Bowen, rector of Troed-yr-aur, who informed Bishop William Stewart in 1799: 'Ebenezer Morris belongs to the methodist meeting house, and is a quiet peaceable man, The Presbyterian preacher is a Mr Evans a Shy, underhand, deceitfull Character'.[106] Towards the end of the eighteenth century the initiative in neglected communities further north was taken by Thomas Phillips, a native of Llanfihangel-ar-arth, whose academy at Neuadd-lwyd, founded in 1810, became an influential seminary, not least for prospective missionaries to Madagascar.[107] Phillips was the moving spirit behind the founding of small but lively Congregationalist churches at Soar, Llanbadarn Fawr, in 1802 and at Tal-y-bont in 1804, both of which became richly productive mission fields under the dynamic leadership of Azariah Shadrach, whose legendary feats as a pastor and writer in Aberystwyth in the early nineteenth century were a source of inspiration.[108]

Baptists were much stronger south of the Teifi than in Cardiganshire. Prior to the advent of Methodism their numbers were derisory and they were scattered far and wide in parishes in the south of the county. However, they prided themselves on being part of the 'gathered church' at Rhydwilym in Pembrokeshire, whose congregation swelled from 113 members in 1689 to 220 in 1723.[109] This modest growth, facilitated by the coming of toleration, prompted them to establish in 1696 a branch at Glandŵr, near Llandysul, and to encourage energetic travelling ministers like Enoch Francis (d. 1740) to minister to their needs.[110] Doctrinal controversies in south-west Wales often spilled over into print and leading Baptist ministers were not loath to put pen to paper. Enoch Francis's *Gair yn ei Bryd* (1733) was a spirited defence of Calvinism and Abel Morgan, a native of Llanwenog, gained the distinction of publishing (posthumously) *Cyd-gordiad Egwyddorawl o'r Scrythurau*, the first biblical concordance in Welsh, in Philadelphia in 1730.[111]

Although several leading Congregationalist ministers were deeply affected by the balmy breezes of revivalism, the first truly successful Baptist evangelist in the county was a hostile foe to Methodist ministers. William Williams (1732–99), a Pembrokeshire man who settled in Cardigan in 1774 and

---

[104]T. Rees and J. Thomas, *Hanes Eglwysi Annibynol Cymru* (4 vols., Liverpool, 1871–5), IV, p.83.

[105]Ibid., pp.166–7.

[106]NLW, SD/QA/253.

[107]Jones, *Hanes Annibynwyr Cymru*, p.151.

[108]E. D. Jones, 'Azariah Shadrach', *Y Cofiadur*, 23 (1953), 3–18.

[109]J. Thomas, *Hanes y Bedyddwyr* (Caerfyrddin, 1778), p.334.

[110]Ibid., p.386.

[111]The volume was dedicated to David Lloyd, chief justice of Pennsylvania.

established a Particular Baptist church at Bethany, Cardigan, in 1775 and at Siloam, Y Ferwig, in 1796, was a justice of the peace for the counties of Cardigan and Pembroke (as well as the borough of Cardigan) and a staunch upholder of the *status quo*.[112] Williams set no great store by raising *hwyl* in the pulpit and he deplored the growing popularity of fervent hymn-singing. He believed that emotionalism betokened carnality rather than grace and that it filled Methodists with 'self-conceit, self-love, self-will, pride and contempt for others'.[113] In many ways, however, Williams was swimming against the tide, for Baptist gains, especially from the 1790s onwards, owed much to the influence of the swell of religious revivalism. The dramatic take-off of Baptist expansion in north Wales was precipitated by one of Cardiganshire's most celebrated sons. Born on Christmas Day 1776 in the parish of Llandysul, Christmas Evans joined the Baptist cause at the age of twenty-two, by which time he had lost his right eye in an unfortunate accident. From 1791, when he became Baptist minister at Llangefni and the self-styled 'Bishop of Anglesey', Evans became an evangelist of unusual dramatic power in Baptist circles. His genius for allegory and his Cyclopian gaze made him a hero not only to pious worshippers but also to those who craved for entertainment. Evans did not neglect the small groups of Baptists in his native county – clustered mostly around Aberystwyth and Cardigan – and during one of his preaching tours in the summer of 1791 congregations in the south of the county groaned, sobbed and quaked in frenzied joy.[114] Yet, in spite of these evangelistic endeavours, Baptists did not make significant gains in the county in this period: only seven churches were established between 1711 and 1811.[115]

The people of Cardiganshire proved even less receptive to Quaker incursions. The sect which had attracted so much attention during the civil wars and the Interregnum on account of the provocative behaviour of its preachers had entered its quietist phase. As the eighteenth century unfolded, the number of Friends shrank alarmingly throughout Wales, and in Cardiganshire the faith had all but disappeared by the middle decades. Only two young men, John and Samuel George at Wern-driw in the parish of Llanddewibrefi, continued to bear testimony to the Light which shineth in Everyman and, unlike their raucous Methodist neighbours, to cherish silent worship: '[they] would not pull off their hats, nor go to church, but did sit together without any preaching'.[116] Insulated from the heady revivalism of their times, they were viewed as eccentric and essentially innocuous cranks. In 1790 Daniel Evans, Garth, was the last Quaker to be buried in the Wern-driw burial ground.

Silent worship was also derided by close-knit groups of intelligent, independently minded and rugged Arminians, Arians and Unitarians who established a cluster of churches in the mid-Teifi area.[117] From the 1720s onwards the old Calvinist certitudes and subsequently the fundamentalism implicit in evangelical doctrines were challenged vigorously by prickly young Arminians, several of whom had imbibed liberal and rationalist ideas at the Dissenting academy at Carmarthen. They derived their personal inspiration from Jenkin Jones, a blacksmith's son from Llanwenog, who, from

---

[112]T. M. Bassett, *The Welsh Baptists* (Swansea, 1977), pp.59, 65. See also *DWB*, s.v. Williams, William.

[113]D. D. Morgan, 'Smoke, fire and light: Baptists and the revitalisation of Welsh Dissent', *The Baptist Quarterly*, XXXII, no.5 (1988), 226.

[114]D. D. Morgan, *Christmas Evans a'r Ymneilltuaeth Newydd* (Llandysul, 1991), pp.13–15, 30.

[115]T. R. Morgan, 'Bedyddwyr parthau uchaf Sir Aberteifi', *Traf. Cymd. Hanes Bedyddwyr Cymru* (1925), 1–28; Barnes, *People of Seion*, pp.145–74.

[116]D. B. Rees, *Hanes Plwyf Llanddewi Brefi* (Llanddewi Brefi, 1984), pp.74–8.

[117]E. G. Bowen, 'The Teifi valley', pp.8–10.

Fig. 121: The epicentre of the Unitarian cause: Llwynrhydowen Chapel. (*Crown Copyright RCAHMW-NMR*).

1726, began to conduct services at Wern-hir, near Alltyrodyn, and to publish provocative anti-Calvinist tracts. In 1733 he threw down the gauntlet to his Calvinist adversaries by building the first Arminian chapel in Wales at Llwynrhydowen.[118] This audacious deed provoked fierce rivalry and bitter recriminations. Aggrieved Calvinists launched furious assaults, in the pulpit and the press, on the 'heresy' of universal redemption and free will, and the conflict led to secessions and much turmoil. Although Jenkin Jones died at the age of forty-two in 1742, he had by then assembled a cadre of strong-willed Arminian ministers and established six Arminian churches in the neighbour-hood. Much to the dismay of Phylip Pugh and Daniel Rowland, the 'new invention' of Arminianism made rapid progress and its disciples revelled in polemical and philosophical discourse.[119]

Jenkin Jones was succeeded by his young nephew, David Lloyd of Brynllefrith, a bookish young man whose powerful sermons and progressive political stance attracted new members from established Congregationalist and Baptist causes. Lloyd – or Dafydd Llwyd as he was known to his ardent disciples – was a remarkably learned and protean scholar. Outstandingly gifted in Greek, he was also a theologian, a hymnist, a poet, a musician, a writer and a preacher. Dr Andrew Kippis, the illustrious Dissenting divine and biographer, claimed that he was the best read man he had ever met and the poet John Jenkin (Ioan Siengcin) referred to him as 'cawr mawr Rhydowen' (the great

[118]T. O. Williams, *Hanes Cynulleidfaoedd Undodaidd Sir Aberteifi* (Llandysul, n.d.), pp.58–60. See also D. E. Davies, *Y Smotiau Duon* (Llandysul, 1981) and idem, *They Thought for Themselves* (Llandysul, 1982).
[119]Jenkins, *Foundations of Modern Wales*, pp.314–15.

giant of Rhydowen).[120] Lloyd propelled his members on the path to Arianism and encouraged 'friends to liberty' to revel in the new-found freedom of the American colonists. By the time of his death in 1779, there were allegedly 800 communicants at Llwynrhydowen and over 3,000 hearers.[121] Although such estimates need to be treated with the utmost caution, it is nevertheless the case that the line of mourners who attended Lloyd's funeral extended for over two miles. Long before his death, however, Lloyd had found an enthusiastic ally in David Davies (Dafydd Dafis), a farmer's son who was ordained under an oak tree near Efail-y-gof, Llwynrhydowen, in July 1773, in the presence of sixteen ministers, most, if not all, of whom were Arians. Davies served jointly with Lloyd as minister of Llwynrhydowen, Ciliau Aeron, Alltyblaca, Bwlchyfadfa, Mydroilyn and Pen-rhiw. A robust, corpulent man (he was once memorably described as 'being furnished with so much flesh, and knew no cold except by hearsay'),[122] Davies used to pepper his sermons with witty, indelicate and sometimes seditious observations. As tutor of the celebrated school at Castellhywel – recognized as the 'Athens of Ceredigion' – he prepared many distinguished students for both the Anglican and Dissenting ministry. Davies was not only determined to recover his radical roots but also to disseminate Jacobin ideas. His friends and fellow republicans, Thomas Evans (Tomos Glyn Cothi) and Edward Williams (Iolo Morganwg) regularly visited the Arian churches under his care and probably helped to convert many members to the Unitarian faith by loudly deprecating the other-worldliness and political circumspection of local Methodists.

The trend towards Unitarianism certainly intensified when Charles Lloyd, son of David Lloyd Brynllefrith, inherited the Coedlannau estate in 1797 and persuaded progressive members at Llwynrhydowen and Alltyblaca to defy the wishes of David Davies by seceding and founding the first Unitarian churches in the county at Pantydefaid and Capel-y-groes in 1802.[123] A stone plaque to commemorate this seminal event was placed in each chapel by Iolo Morganwg, who endeared himself to local libertarians by sharply rebuking Bishop Samuel Horsley for provoking a 'huge sort of unitarian hunters' to cry 'mad dog'.[124] By the early nineteenth century, therefore, unorthodox Arians and Unitarians had established in south Cardiganshire a triangular fortress of churches whose members tenaciously rebuffed all attempts by Calvinist evangelists to win them over to their cause. As a result, the heretics' sphere of influence was demonized as *Y Smotyn Du* (The Black Spot) by revivalists at nearby Llangeitho, and hostility between the rival camps remained mutual and long-lasting.

Throughout the eighteenth century Dissent in the county capitalized on the fact that the established Church was unable to put its house in order. The inadequate administrative and parochial structure of the Church and the abuses which arose from it, especially in remote, inhospitable parishes where people living in hamlets and farmsteads were poorly served by overworked or absentee incumbents, had alarming repercussions in communities where Dissenting preachers made their presence felt. There was evidently a strong and for the most part unappeased religious craving which prompted disaffected churchgoers to join Dissent as well as Methodism, and successful preachers like Phylip Pugh, Benjamin Evans, David Lloyd and David Davies could boast

---

[120]L. E. Lloyd Theakston and J. Davies (eds.), *Some Family Records and Pedigrees of the Lloyds of Allt yr Odyn* (Oxford, 1913), p.75.
[121]*Lloyd Letters*, p.xiii.
[122]Davies, *They Thought for Themselves*, p.72; *The Monthly Repository*, 6 (1811), 691.
[123]Davies, *They Thought for Themselves*, pp.36–7.
[124]NLW MS 13145A, ff.343–4.

large numbers of admirers. Since Dissenting ministers were more flexible than the Anglican clergy, they were better able to meet the spiritual and psychological needs of people who found the ministrations of local clergymen embarrassingly inadequate. Dissenting meeting houses might have been small and sometimes rickety edifices, made of stone, timber, mud and thatched roofs, and furnished with tiny pulpits and moveable benches, but they were located within relatively easy walking or riding distance of the local population.[125] In towns like Aberystwyth and Cardigan, chapels were established in converted barns and warehouses or rented houses, and Capel Ebeneser, Llanfair Clydogau (1799) was a refurbished brewery![126] As chapels became a new and permanent feature of the landscape of Cardiganshire, they acquired a clearer and more tangible sense of their own distinctiveness. They derived their names from the Bible and their members were generally pious, literate farmers, craftsmen and artisans rather than poor smallholders, landless labourers and squatters. Over half the members of Cilgwyn church in the early eighteenth century were free-holders, and book-reading smiths, joiners, bookbinders, glovers, weavers, tuckers and shoemakers in the parish of Cellan were said to be able to give 'a very good account of their faith'.[127] Dissent also permitted much wider scope for women in spiritual matters and their piety and prudence were evident in several meeting houses. All Dissenting denominations (as well as Methodists) experienced petty quarrels, theological strife and secessions, but ministers and leading members exercised a powerful religious and cultural influence in their localities, and those who had sampled the progressive and inventive curricula provided at academies like Carmarthen and Castellhywel became more open-minded and receptive to new ideas. Although Unitarians and Methodists continued to jostle and bicker in uncomfortable proximity in the south of the county, such vitality and commitment betokened a genuine and growing desire to discover religious truths as well as to protect denominational identities.

As the established Church became increasingly unable to mobilize itself in terms of its organization and mission, even Methodists began to consider the possibility of cutting the Gordian Knot. For within Methodism there was an inherent paradox: although it had never been the aim of the founding fathers to create a new sect or to put at hazard the well-being of the Anglican faith, by encouraging field-preaching and society meetings they had planted within the Church of England the seeds of its future destruction. Daniel Rowland and his ardent disciples might have sworn allegiance to King, Church and country and beat the patriotic drum in times of war and rebellion, but the pietism and revivalism which they had fostered eventually turned Methodist zealots against the orthodox ways of the establishment. In the long run, it was Dissent which reaped the benefits of the evangelical movement. Following the death of Rowland in 1790 and of Williams Pantycelyn in 1791, the forces of revival and renewal made the separation of the Calvinistic Methodists from the established Church inevitable. The seeds of Methodist secession had become increasingly hard to ignore, as the testy observations of Lewis Evans, vicar of Llanfihangel-y-Creuddyn, confirm in his visitation returns for the parish in 1804:

---

[125]See Anthony Jones, *Welsh Chapels* (Stroud, 1996).
[126]Rees and Thomas, *Hanes Eglwysi Annibynol*, IV, pp.91, 132, 160.
[127]Dr Williams's Library MS 34, f.138; E. Lhuyd, 'Parochialia', Suppl. to *AC* (1909–11), Part 3, p.68.

I am at a Loss to assign what may be the *real* cause of their Increase. A constant change of Preachers – Great Earnestness seemingly – and Private Meetings may contribute to their Increase in some Degree – But Ignorance of their Baptismal Vows – Contempt of the Discipline of the Church – and a strong Tendency to Schism without considering the nature and consequence of that Sin may contribute in a greater Degree.[128]

Half the total number of Calvinistic Methodist chapels established between 1749 and 1811 (nineteen out of thirty-eight) were set up during the two decades after the death of Daniel Rowland in 1790.[129] The unmistakable trend was towards schism, and when the Calvinistic Methodists became a separate denomination in 1811 such a decisive course of action occasioned little surprise since Cardiganshire had already become a religiously pluralistic society.

Visitation returns confirm that the established Church no longer (perhaps it never had) offered a firm anchorage in the tossing seas of religious plurality in *fin de siècle* Cardiganshire. Anglicanism had always been a rickety and barely seaworthy vessel, but it was now more vulnerable than it had been since early Elizabethan times. The returns of 1804 reveal that there were only 2,157 regular communicants in the county at a time when the adult population was around 30,000.[130] In some parishes a dramatic collapse in the number of communicants had occurred since mid-century. At Llanfihangel Genau'r-glyn the 350 communicants in 1755 had plummeted to 50, at Llangoedmor from 200 to 40, at Llanilar from 150 to 50, and at Llanddeiniol from 50 to 9.[131] No longer did the mother church command the respect and affection of the bulk of the people. In spite of major demographic and social changes, the parochial structure of the established Church had remained virtually intact since medieval times, and as a result the flow of disillusioned members to Methodism and Dissent had proved irresistible. The rich diversity of sects which had made headway from the 1730s onwards offered a much wider range of possibilities for Christians. Between 1700 and 1811, a total of 89 chapels or meeting-houses were established, the bulk of them by Calvinistic Methodists (38) and Congregationalists (21), and although it is impossible to estimate accurately the numerical strength of Dissent, it is possible that its total number of communicants was greater than that of the established church by the beginning of the nineteenth century.

It is clear, too, that practising Christians were a minority. Nothing can be more false that the notion that the people of Cardiganshire were regular church- or chapel-goers during the eighteenth century. Even the respective causes of Methodism and Dissent were less rosy than some of their most florid eulogists would care to admit. Their numbers were still relatively modest and their support came principally from the lower middling sorts. As teaching institutions, both Anglicanism (especially following the collapse of the circulating schools system in the late 1770s) and Dissent were found wanting, for they had failed to wean the bulk of the peasantry from the influence of superstition, magic and witchcraft. James Obelkevich has reminded us that in most European societies

---

[128]NLW, SD/QA/2, no.84.

[129]These figures are based on Barnes, *People of Seion*, pp.145–74; G. M. Roberts (ed.), *Cynnydd y Corff*, pp.533–42; B. J. Rawlins, *The Parish Churches and Nonconformist Chapels of Wales* (vol.1, Celtic Heritage Research, 1987).

[130]NLW, SD/QA/2.

[131]NLW, SD/QA/1–2.

Christianity was obliged to share the field with superstition,[132] and it is clear that large sections of the poorer sorts in Cardiganshire neither understood nor revered the Christian faith. Belief in the power of the occult remained the most convincing explanation for the presence of misfortune and evil in daily life. 'I know of no district so confined within itself',[133] wrote Benjamin Malkin of Cardiganshire as late as 1804, and monoglottism, illiteracy and ignorance were evidently still an inextricable part of a county notorious for its poor communications, isolation and slow-moving economy. The bulk of the people continued to resist attempts by Protestant evangelists to 'disenchant the world' by robbing it of magical forces, and the belief in corpse candles, knockers, ghosts, elves and fairies remained as strong as ever.[134] Moreover, irreligion could lead to outright antipathy towards over-zealous preachers. Howel Harris was convinced that the citizens of Aberystwyth were enemies to the Christian faith: ''tis like that is ye last Place God will take. Sin ere is sorer to Him than any-where'.[135] Lewis Morris, often referred to by his relatives as 'the Fat Man of Cardiganshire', believed that the principal concern of Churchmen was 'F . . . ng ye poor Laity out of their money',[136] and soaring tithe demands at the turn of the century probably encouraged irreligion and anticlericalism.[137] In 1796 it was reported that the village of Pontrhydfendigaid sported 'not many honest labourers – but robust athletic miners – of no religion'.[138] Long before the religious census of 1851 revealed that a large proportion of the population did not darken either church or chapel on a regular basis, there were clear signs that the established Church in Cardiganshire had either failed to gain or had lost touch with thousands of its nominal members and that large numbers, especially among those whom reformers dubbed 'the vulgar sorts', were not disposed to respond with enthusiasm to the seductive appeal of either Methodism or Dissent.

---

[132]J. Obelkevich, *Religion and Rural Society: South Lindsey 1825–1875* (Oxford, 1976), p.330. See also G. H. Jenkins, 'Popular beliefs in Wales from the Restoration to Methodism', *BBCS*, XXVII, Part 3 (1977), 440–62.

[133]Malkin, *Scenery*, p.321.

[134]W. J. Davies, *Hanes Plwyf Llandyssul* (Llandyssul, 1896), chapter X; D. E. Jones, *Hanes Plwyfi Llangeler a Phenboyr* (Llandyssul, 1899), pp.379–86; S. R. Meyrick, *The History and Antiquities of the County of Cardigan* (Brecon, 1907), pp.55–91.

[135]T. Beynon, 'Howell Harris yn Sir Aberteifi', *CCHMC*, XXXI, no.4 (1946), 118–19.

[136]University of Wales Bangor, Bangor (Mostyn) 7606.

[137]Virgin, *Church in an Age of Negligence*, p.271; J. Barber, ' "A fair and just demand"?', 177–206.

[138]'Some account of the parish of Caron', *The Cambrian Register*, II (1799), 387.

CHAPTER 21

CHURCH AND CHAPEL IN CARDIGANSHIRE, 1811–1914

Ieuan Gwynedd Jones

CARDIGANSHIRE in the nineteenth century was a county which was undergoing change to an extent it had never experienced before. At some times and in some places it was almost imperceptible, but at other times and in other places it was disturbingly rapid and turbulent. It was a county developing unevenly as between its towns and the engulfing countryside, between the mountain peoples and the inhabitants of its valleys, between the farming communities of its long coastline, who were also fishermen and shipbuilders, and the pockets of industrialization high in the mountains and in the weaving, cloth-making communities in its well-watered valleys.

It was, therefore, far from being a sociologically uniform county community; indeed, it was rather a collection of contrasting localities and communities. Many of its physical features conspired to emphasize differences and singularities. Until the coming of the railways communications were difficult and uncertain, and because the county was so remote and so very poor any technological improvements taking place elsewhere were slow to penetrate and to be adopted. Roads, for example, even after the coming of the turnpike trusts, were poor, and passing from valley to valley over the mountains and hills was laborious and at times hazardous. In the lives and biographies of itinerant preachers their journeyings are admiringly recorded, and often the total miles traversed are given. It is said, for example, of Ebenezer Richard of Tregaron, who was known as 'the Apostle of the North', that he preached 7,048 sermons, 651 of them in preaching festivals, and that he travelled 59,092 miles in the course of these duties.[1]

The poverty of the county was notorious, and utterly astonishing to Public Health officials sent down from Whitehall in the 1850s and 1860s by alarmed politicians and civil servants as, indeed, it had been to the Commissioner earlier in the century who was charged with the task of uniting parishes into unions for the relief of the poor under the new Poor Law Amendment Act of 1834.[2] One of these inspectors, on a visit to inquire into the causes of chronic diseases and high death rates in the 1862, gave it as his opinion that 'had the weather been cold the people had all died'.[3] But there were different kinds and degrees of poverty in different places or, perhaps more to the point, different definitions or perceptions of poverty in different parts of the county. The Aberystwyth,

---

[1] J. Evans, *Byr-gofiant am Naw a Deugain o Weinidogion Ymadawedig Sir Aberteifi* (Dolgellau, 1894), p.159.
[2] *PP* 1837 XXXI (546). Reports from Poor Law Commissioners. Third Annual Report.
[3] Dr Hunter's 'Report on the death rate of the people in parts of south Wales', *Seventh Report of the Medical Officer of the Privy Council* (1864), p.496. On social conditions generally, see David J. V. Jones, *Rebecca's Children: A Study of Rural Society, Crime, and Protest* (Oxford, 1989), pp.1–44.

Aberaeron and Cardigan Districts, which were the most prosperous – or perhaps the least poverty-stricken – parts of the county were more sympathetically attuned to the harsh philosophy underlying the administration of the the Poor Law than were Tregaron and Lampeter, which were the poorest.[4]

Considerations such as these help to explain why the people as a whole should have appeared to have been so conservative, and the essence of the religiosity of the people was surely its conservative nature. There were, for example, almost until the end of the century only five denominations, and only one of these, the Unitarians, had any taste for religious or social radicalism. The Calvinistic Methodists were notoriously conservative in their attitudes to social and political affairs, and the Wesleyan Methodists equally so. A *cause célèbre* in the early part of the century had been the excommunication of five members of the congregation of Jewin Chapel in the city of London for signing a petition to Parliament in 1828 in favour of Catholic emancipation. The chief advocate of this punishment was the minister, the Revd James Hughes (Iago Trichrug), a Cardiganshire blacksmith who had migrated to London in 1801 and found work in the Royal Dockyards in Deptford. It is more likely that such reactionary views on politics had been nourished in Cardiganshire than in London.[5]

Judging by numbers of chapels and of members and adherents, the county was certainly very religious. But it was also outstandingly superstitious: orthodoxy and magic, Christianity and a belief in 'the little people', in apparitions, portents and prophecies existed side by side. The people inhabited a mysterious world, and they sought, and found, explanations for its mysteries both in the apparent certainties of orthodox religion and in the traditional beliefs of the past. Beliefs and usages flowing from the deep past were held with a stubbornness and a kind of reverence which religious leaders deplored but could not exorcise or eradicate.[6]

Such continuities as these were reinforced in other more formal and structural ways. To an extraordinary degree the ecclesiastical geography of the county corresponded with the geography of its legal jurisdictions and civil administration. Thus, the boundaries of the ancient county were also those of the Archdeaconry of Cardigan, and there was an almost exact correspondence betweeen the boundaries of parishes and deaneries and the boundaries of the ancient civil divisions. When the Poor Law Districts were formed in 1837 their boundaries coincided almost without exception with the ancient boundaries of Sub Aeron, Glyn Aeron, Lampeter and Llanbadarn Fawr.[7] The only new boundary drawn by the commissioners was the creation, after much hesitation, of Tregaron District in the parish and the District of Llanbadarn Fawr, a parish so large as to be virtually unmanageable. Farmers and others who were Nonconformists did not need to observe parish boundaries, but in

[4]A. E. Davies, 'The new Poor Law in a rural area,1834–50', *Ceredigion*, VIII, no.3 (1978), 245–90.

[5]G. M. Roberts, *Y Ddinas Gadarn. Hanes Eglwys Jewin Llundain* (London, 1974), pp.54–68, and P. Lord, *Hugh Hughes. Arlunydd Gwlad* (Llandysul, 1995), pp.160–71.

[6]G. W. Williams, '"The disenchantment of the world": innovation, crisis and change in Cardiganshire *c.*1880–1910', *Ceredigion*, IX, no.4 (1983), 303–21; R. A. N. Jones, 'Popular culture, policing, and the disappearance of the *ceffyl pren* in Cardiganshire *c.*1837–50', ibid., XI, no.1 (1988), 19–40. For some examples, see E. Edwards, *Byr Hanes am Blwyf Nantcwnlle* (Aberystwyth, 1930), pp.54–5; S. G. Davies, *Dyffryn Troed-yr-aur* (Llandysul, 1976), p.48; and M. Davies, *Hanes Eglwys Bresbyteraidd Cymru Blaenannerch 1794–1994* (Aberteifi, 1994), p.12.

[7]For the ancient deaneries, see A. W. Wade-Evans, 'Parochiale Wallicanum', *Y Cymmrodor*, XXII (1910), 55–63. For the boundaries of the Registration Districts and Subdistricts, see Census of Population 1851. Population Tables, XI Welsh Division with map of the Districts.

their secular lives they had to pay taxes, and they had certain legal obligations to the parish of their abode. More to the point, they were obliged by law to register their meeting houses in the Courts of Quarter Sessions: in that respect, and others like it, they lived under the civil authority, and this became increasingly a burden and an offence as they grew in numbers and confidence, and it is interesting to note that in this county Dissenters ceased to register their meeting houses in the episcopal courts in 1839, long before the remainder of the diocese.[8] There existed, therefore, deep-set feelings of belonging to ecclesiastical and civil structures which were of great antiquity, that the world people inhabited was the world that their ancestors had known, and one that was not likely to change.

The ecclesiastical geography of the county was also very distinctive. As a whole, it belonged to what reforming bishops and frightened politicians classified as 'the Church in the mountains'. By this they meant those dioceses, or portions of dioceses, which were remote from the civilization of the developed parts of the country, which were economically poor and backward, where people were depraved and ignorant, the Church poverty-stricken, its financial resources inadequate and unevenly distributed among the benefices and, above all, in which the language of religious discourse, indeed, of any kind of discourse, was strange and barbaric.[9] Much of Wales was included in this definition, and the Archdeaconry of Cardigan was commonly believed, in those political and upper-class circles, to embody, in one way or another, most of the factors included in it.

When we look more closely at the ecclesiastical geography we find differences and contrasts that the overall view conceals. A critical difference was the size of parishes. In the south of the county, clustered around the town of Cardigan, parishes averaged about 3,000 acres – much less than that if we exclude from the calculation the very large parishes of Llandysul, Llandygwydd and Penbryn. The same was true of the parishes in the middle reaches of the Teifi and in the Aeron valley and northwards along the maritime plain towards Aberystwyth. Apart from Llandysiliogogo and Llannarth, which extended far into the hills of Mynydd Bach, these also averaged between about 3,000 and 4,000 acres.[10]

It is when we move into the north of the county, into the hill country proper, that the extent of the differences between south and north become apparent. Here the parishes were of immense extent. Llanbadarn Fawr encompassed over 52,000 acres, Caron 39,000, Llanddewibrefi 36,000, Llanfihangel Genau'r-glyn 33,000, Llanfihangel-y-Creuddyn over 22,000, and Gwnnws 18,000. Parts of these parishes were of almost unimaginable remoteness, innocent of highways, containing no large towns and but few villages, inhabited by small farmers eking out their uncertain and hungry livelihoods on the inhospitable and rain-drenched moors.

[8]NLW, Cardiganshire Quarter Sessions Order Books. QB/OB/1–8. See also NLW, SD/DISS/11. Return by the Registrar of St David's to the Registrar General of all Places of Public Worship that have been certified and registered in the Court of the Bishop from 1688 up to the 29th day of June 1852. This return has a total of 257 entries, of which 49 are in respect of meeting houses in Cardiganshire. The last registration appears to have been in respect of Brynteg (Congregational), Llanwenog, on 12 February 1839.

[9]See W. J. Conybeare, 'The Church in the mountains', *Edinburgh Review*, April 1853, reprinted in W. J. Conybeare, *Essays Ecclesiastical and Social* (London, 1854). For a discussion of this idea, see I. G. Jones, 'Ecclesiastical economy: aspects of church building in Victorian Wales', in R. R. Davies et al. (eds.), *Welsh Society and Nationhood: Essays in Honour of Glanmor Williams* (Cardiff, 1984), pp.216–31.

[10]On the social characteristics of the southern part of the county, see C. Thomas, 'Rural society in nineteenth-century Wales: south Cardiganshire in 1851', *Ceredigion*, VI, no.4 (1971), 388–414.

Fig. 122: The Revd Ebenezer Richard (1781–1837), Calvinistic Methodist minister at Tregaron. (*Copyright National Library of Wales*).

Efficient territorial organization, whether civil or religious in circumstances such as these always had been and would always remain extremely difficult while the technology of communications remained primitive. But it was the duty of all denominations without distinction, of church and chapel, to teach and to provide the means of grace to these thin, scattered and remote populations. It was not a problem only for the Church; it applied to all denominations. It was the failure of the Church to perceive the need and to respond to it until it was almost too late which laid them open to the charge of neglect, while in the meantime the Calvinistic Methodists were perfecting a unique strategy to missionize those territories by means of their *seiadau* and monthly meetings.[11] These organizational structures belonged to the first and most creative period in their history in the eighteenth century, and it was their enormous success in converting the multitudes and maintaining them thereafter as members of local communities of believers which persuaded the societies as a whole to transform themselves into a new denomination. This happened in 1811 when both the Presbyteries into which Wales was divided determined to ordain their own ministers and empower them to administer the sacraments, rather than, as had always been the case before, rely upon sympathetic Anglican clergymen. The leading proponents of this solemn and revolutionary change in this county were Ebenezer Richard (1781–1837) of Tregaron, who was secretary of the monthly meeting and, later, of the South Wales Association, and Ebenezer Morris (1769–1825) of Twr-

[11]See E. M. White, *Praidd Bach y Bugail Mawr* (Llandysul, 1994) for the foundations and organization of the early *seiadau*. Most of her conclusions apply equally to the first half of the nineteenth century.

gwyn. Both were among the first preachers to be ordained.[12] There is no doubt that it was the greater efficiency as a body which this superior organization induced, and the spiritual drive which accompanied it, that accounted for their relative superiority over all other denominations in the county at large, and for the pattern of denominationalism which thereafter developed.

This denominational pattern was basically very simple. Like the rest of Wales, for most of the nineteenth century its constituent elements were first, the Church of England, second, the old Dissenting denominations, consisting of Congregationalists, Baptists, Unitarians and, briefly, Quakers, and third, the New Dissenters, namely the Calvinistic Methodists and the Wesleyan Methodists. For most of the period with which this chapter is concerned these were the only denominations in the county.

As in the eighteenth century, the Old Dissenters defined themselves negatively by their rejection of the idea of an established church, defined by law and empowered by statute. Positively, they protested against the civil disabilities under which they suffered, and the status of second-class citizens which this entailed. Specifically, they protested against the payment of church rates to support a Church to which they could not conscientiously belong and which they and their ancestors had rejected at the cost of very considerable suffering and social ostracism, their exclusion from the universities of Oxford and Cambridge, and the refusal to allow them to bury their dead according to the rites of their own denominations and by their own ministers in parish cemeteries. Theologically, the Old Dissenters had moved from the strict and sometimes rigid Calvinism of their puritan ancestors, and had adopted the more moderate doctrines which had emerged out of the disputes and quarrels which had characterized the last decades of the eighteenth century and the first twenty or thirty years of the nineteenth, and a kind of consensus had developed within the Calvinist fold.[13]

The New Dissenters consisted of the two Methodist denominations, though they were divided by fundamental theological differences. As their name implied, the Welsh Calvinistic Methodists adhered strictly to the essential tenets of Calvinism as enshrined in the Confession of Faith which was adopted by the denomination in 1823 and which remained unchanged for the remainder of the century. Theologically, the Wesleyan Methodists were Arminians, who rejected the logical determinism of Calvinism, with its belief that only the elect can be saved, in favour of the more liberal belief that Christ died for all men and not only for the elect, and that all persons are endowed with free will by which to choose or reject the salvation which is proffered equally to them all. These were fundamental differences which persisted throughout this period.

The Unitarians rejected both positions, though they were more sympathetic to the Wesleyans than to the Calvinists. For their part, Unitarians had no formal creed, and were unique in that they rejected the doctrine of the Trinity and the Divinity of Christ. Theologically they were rooted in the rational theology of the eighteenth century as developed by their own contemporary thinkers. This put them beyond the pale for most Christians, and may account for their failure to expand significantly outside the confines of a relatively small area of about twenty square miles in the

---

[12]For an account of the ordinations, see G. M. Roberts (ed.), *Hanes Methodistiaeth Calfinaidd Cymru. Cyfrol 2. Cynnydd y Corff* (Caernarfon, 1978), chapter VI. Ebenezer Richard's Memorandum Book records the resolution to take part in the ordinations: NLW CM Archives 13223, Cof-lyfr Cymdeithas Fisol Sir Aberteifi, *sub* Twr-gwyn 4, 5 June 1811.

[13]On the Dissenters in general, see Michael R. Watts, *The Dissenters from the Reformation to the French Revolution* (Oxford, 1978), and on the Welsh Dissenters, Geraint H. Jenkins, *The Foundations of Modern Wales: Wales 1642–1780* (Oxford, 1987).

vicinity of Lampeter and Llandysul. So far as one can tell there were no organized secularist or atheist groups in the county at any time in the nineteenth century. Those who rejected revealed orthodox religion were most likely to become Unitarians.[14]

The denominations differed fundamentally also in their organization or, put theologically, in their differing doctrines of the nature of the church. Again the differences were between the Old Dissenters and the New Dissenters. The former believed in a congregational form of church polity in which the individual local church exercised autonomy over itself without the interference of any body external to itself. Congregationalists and Baptists believed in the priesthood of all believers, in the equality of all the individual members of the church, and in democratic forms of decision-making. Basic in their philosophy was the belief that the church consisted of individual men and women covenanted as individuals and as bodies of believers with each other and with God. God is sovereign. The Baptists and the Unitarians adopted this congregational form of church government. All three denominations developed associations on a county or district basis as a means of furthering their common concerns. The Baptists tended to be more advanced in this respect than the Congregationalists.

The Methodist bodies favoured presbyterian forms of church government, in which authority resided in representative bodies consisting of ordained ministers and elders chosen by the individual churches and empowered to take decisions which were binding on the individual churches themselves. It was a hierarchical system based on the irreducible unit of the individual churches, rising through the monthly meetings, which were responsible for organizing their corporate activities, to the Presbytery and finally the general Assembly. Nevertheless, there were strong elements of congregationalism present within the system, and the form of government which developed in the course of the century contained democratic structures which powerfully modified the original clerical hierarchy of the denomination. Of the two forms of Methodism, the Calvinistic Methodist was the more open to internal pressures for change.[15]

In the nineteenth, as in the eighteenth century, the state of the Church of England was of crucial importance in the growth of Nonconformity in more ways than one. In the first place, the financial resources of the Church were fatally insufficient to enable it to fulfil its duties adequately. This was true of the four dioceses in Wales in general, and particularly of the two dioceses in south Wales, but its poverty was greater in the Archdeaconry of Cardigan than in any other archdeaconry, with the result that its servants were inadequately paid and scandalously ill-housed, the fabric of its churches decaying, and the essentials for the decent conduct of its services often seriously deficient. The lack of decent houses for clergymen and their families – glebe houses as they were called – meant that many clergymen were obliged to live outside their benefices and, worse still, to serve more than one benefice, usually as curates. In 1818 only nine of sixty-eight benefices in the county had a glebe

---

[14]For theological developments among the Congregationalists, see R. T. Jones, *Hanes Annibynwyr Cymru* (Abertawe, 1966); for the Baptists, T. M. Bassett, *The Welsh Baptists* (Swansea, 1977); for the Unitarians, D. E. Davies, *Y Smotiau Duon* (Llandysul, 1980); for the Calvinistic Methodists, G. M. Roberts (ed.), *Hanes Methodistiaeth Calfinaidd Cymru* (2 vols., Caernarfon, 1973, 1978); and for the Wesleyans, A. H. Williams, *Welsh Wesleyan Methodism 1800–1858* (Bangor, 1935). For a splendid account of a Calvinistic Methodist escaping into Unitarianism, see B. Hirson and G. A. Williams, *The Delegate for Africa. David Ivon Jones 1883–1924* (London, 1995), pp.1–59.

[15]R. Roberts, *Elfennau Methodistiaeth* (Dolgellau, 1897), and D. J. Waller (ed.), *The Constitution and Polity of the Wesleyan Methodist Church* (3rd edn., London, n.d. [1905]).

house fit for residence.[16] Pluralism was more common in the archdeaconry than elsewhere in the diocese of St David's, and this was the diocese which had a higher proportion of pluralists than any other in England and Wales. The preceding chapter has shown how the causes of the financial problems of the Church lay deep in the past. Ecclesiastical poverty matched the poverty of the county as a whole, but it was aggravated by the fact that a major proportion of the Church's income from tithes had been appropriated by laymen.[17]

In the nineteenth, as in the eighteenth century, Cardiganshire, with more than a half of the rent charges appropriated by laymen, suffered more than any other county, with the exception of Carmarthen, from this scandal; many of its benefices had been utterly impoverished.[18] Lord Lisburne and other lay persons shared the tithe income of nine benefices, but the prince of impropriators was T. P. Chichester. According to the Ecclesiastical Duties and Revenues Report of 1835, Chichester owned the tithes of nine parishes, from which he derived an annual income of nearly £5,500, leaving a sum of only £1,127 for the nine livings concerned, an average of £125 per living, some being as low as £88. As the preceding chapter has shown, the Chichesters had been milking the archdeaconry in this fashion for more than two centuries. No wonder the clergy were poor and the parishes neglected.[19]

Many of the impropriators were also patrons of livings, sometimes of the benefices whose tithes they owned. Lord Lisburne shared the patronage – or the advowsons – of nine livings, and Chichester another three outright and, as has been pointed out recently, the ownership of multiple advowsons invariably led to pluralism, which in turn made necessary the employment of stipendiary curates.[20] There were thirty-two stipendiary curates in the archdeaconry who earned, on average, £55 per annum, ranging from a low of £25 to a high of £104. This dismal figure, however, must be seen in the context of the incomes of incumbents from all sources. In the archdeaconry in the mid-1840s there were only ten perpetual curacies with incomes from tithes of over £100, the highest being Llanddewibrefi with £146. A further nineteen had incomes ranging from £50 to £100 with a median of £76, and there was one perpetual curacy worth less than £50.[21] No doubt, there were Nonconformist preachers who would regard such stipends as princely compared with the pittances most of them were paid, but such a comparison ignores the fact that here were two contrasting traditions within which clerical and ministerial expectations did not, and were not apprehended as being likely to coincide.[22]

[16]*PP* 1818 XVII, no.3, pp.56–8.

[17]*PP* 1847/8 XLIX (298) gives the total sums involved.

[18]Ibid.

[19]See, in general, P. Virgin, *The Church in an Age of Negligence* (Cambridge, 1989), and E. J. Evans, *The Contested Tithe: The Tithe Problem in English Agriculture, 1750–1850* (London, 1976), esp. chapter 7. More particularly, the Parliamentary Return of 1848 shows that of the total of £18,266 of tithes commuted under the Tithe Commutation Act of 1836, £3,251 (or 17.9 per cent) was payable to clerical appropriators and their lessees, £9,660 (52.8 per cent) to lay impropriators, £794 to schools etc, and £4,560 (24.9 per cent) to parochial incumbents. The returns list sixty-one parishes whose tithes had been commuted to a rent charge. Of the total of £877 in the huge upland parish of Llanddewibrefi, only £42 was apportioned to the incumbents. See *PP* 1847–8, XLIX (298), pp.527–9. For the Chichester family, see J. Barber and D. Paul, 'Catherine Chichester in Cardiganshire, 1705–35', *Ceredigion*, XI, no.4 (1992), 371–84.

[20]Virgin, *The Church in an Age of Negligence*, p.258.

[21]*PP* 1847–8, XLIX (298), pp.527–9.

[22]It was up to individual churches to recompense the preachers and no doubt some were more generous than others.

One final point about the manpower of the Church needs to be made. Clergymen were almost invariably natives of the county and, for the most part until the opening of St David's College, Lampeter, in 1827, were educated within the county in the excellent grammar schools at Lampeter and Ystradmeurig, or in the almost equally good grammar school at Llangeitho. As St David's College grew in size, endowments and prestige, these old grammar schools sank into a sad desuetude, which many educationists deplored as a grievous loss to the communities they had served with such success for so many years. There were numerous other schools, including the popular Mathematical and Commercial School of John Evans in Aberystwyth.[23] Curates, like Dissenting ministers and Methodists, often depended upon teaching to supply the difference between relative comfort and poverty, so that at any one time there would be in existence many schools which adults as well as children attended. Some of the clergymen were graduates of Oxford, a few of Cambridge, rather more of Trinity College, Dublin and, later on, of St Bees in Cumbria, where young men could be educated for the Anglican ministry very cheaply. Neuadd-lwyd School, under the redoubtable Dr Thomas Phillips (1772–1842),[24] was also highly thought of and popular among clergymen as well as Nonconformist ministers. This was true also of the academy kept by the famous and much-loved Dafydd Dafis (1745–1827) of Castellhywel, who was an excellent scholar and poet.[25] There were other highly esteemed poets and scholars among them, some of whom, as we have noted, kept schools to supplement their meagre earnings as preachers or curates. Some maintained high standards of learning and provided the main grammar schools with well-prepared and eager pupils. Without exception they were Welshmen and Welsh speakers, which is more than could be said of their bishops. In all of them, as was common throughout Wales (with the notable exception of the the Congregationalist Academy at Llanuwchllyn in Merioneth), the language of instruction was English. It was the existence of a number of very good schools in Cardiganshire which made it possible for so many young men to qualify and take holy orders, even if only as 'literates'. It was said, with every justification, that Cardiganshire produced more clergymen than any other county in Wales,[26] and it was mainly Cardiganshire clergymen, accustomed as they were to a Church manned by a poorer class of incumbent, and having no greater expectations for themselves, who readily filled the poor livings created by reforming bishops in the industrial

[23]For Ystradmeurig and Lampeter and the grammar schools generally, see O. Jones, 'The mountain clergyman: his education and training', in O. W. Jones and D. Walker (eds.), *Links with the Past: Swansea and Brecon Historical Essays* (Llandybïe, 1974), pp.170–80, and D. T. W. Price, *A History of Saint David's University College Lampeter, Volume One* (Cardiff, 1977), pp.8–12. For John Evans and his school, see W. J. Lewis, *Born on a Perilous Rock* (Aberystwyth, 1980), pp.159–61.

[24]On Dr Phillips and his academy, see J. Kilsby Jones, 'Atgofion am Ysgol Neuaddlwyd' in J. V. Morgan, *Kilsby Jones* (Wrexham, n.d.), pp.373–84.

[25]For Dafis, Castellhywel, see W. J. Davies, *Hanes Plwyf Llandyssul* (Llandyssul, 1896, reprinted 1992), pp.102–8. There is a long notice in B. Williams (Gwynionydd), *Enwogion Ceredigion* (Caerfyrddin, 1869), pp.47–9. Also T. Rees, *History of Protestant Nonconformity in Wales* (2nd edn., London, 1883), pp.441–4, who says of his translation of Gray's 'Elegy' that it was 'incomparably superior to the original'.

[26]Edwards, *Byr Hanes am Blwyf Nantcwnlle*, pp.36–9, 41–2 lists twenty clergymen, eighteen preachers and twenty-eight school teachers, including twelve women, who were raised in this little parish of five or six hundred souls. D. B. Rees, *Hanes Plwyf Llanddewi Brefi* (Llanddewi Brefi, 1984), lists the names of twenty-four men from Llanddewibrefi who entered the priesthood.

dioceses. Bishop Ollivant of Llandaff was dependent upon this 'proletariat clergy' to man the remote parishes of his diocese where the need was greatest.[27]

The condition of the Church, and the effectiveness or otherwise of its ministry, was crucial to the way Nonconformity developed. Indeed, the history of the chapels is unintelligible without an intimate understanding of ecclesiastical developments in general. There were negative aspects to this, of bitter and well-documented confrontations in the past and of contemporary disagreements concerning issues of profound importance which tended to arise at the interface between theological ideas and social realities. But one should emphasize the extent to which both kinds of religion had certain common features. The majority of ministers and clergymen were evangelically disposed. Many clergymen welcomed the renewal in religion which was taking place; indeed, it could not have developed in the way it did without the active co-operation of Anglican and Methodist, and up to the fatal year 1811 and beyond this co-operation continued because it was essential to both kinds of religious organization. Calvinistic Methodists were in many respects more sympathetic to the Church than to the Congregationalists, Baptists and Unitarians. Relations were generally good, and needed to be because members of the *seiadau* (societies) depended upon the goodwill of clergymen to administer the sacrament of holy communion. They were required to marry, baptize and bury their parishioners, and for decades after the Methodists had formed their own denomination there were societies which behaved almost as if nothing had happened to break the age-old understanding. Only in 1849 did members of Tabor, Llangwyryfon, one of the earliest of the Calvinistic Methodist chapels in the north of the county, cease to attend the Anglican church after their morning service.[28] The same was true of other Methodist congregations. It was not uncommon for Nonconformist ministers to defect to the Church, for fathers to educate one son for the Church and the other for the Nonconformist ministry. After all, intending clergymen and preachers were, for the most part, educated together, and there was rarely any sense of class difference between them. It was not uncommon for some candidates for the ministry to have had no education whatsoever, or to have been entirely self-taught. Of a sample of thirty preachers in John Evans's collection of biographies, nine appear to have had little or no education, thirteen had had some schooling, three had been to grammar school, three had been to college, one to university, and one was educated at home. The average age of starting to preach was twenty-six.[29] There was considerable opposition to a learned ministry among the Calvinistic Methodists, and some extremely gifted young men who wished to go to college were refused permission by the Presbytery. Ebenezer Morris (1769–1825) of Twr-gwyn, one of the leading preachers in the Presbytery and an authoritative figure who exercised enormous influence on the denomination in the south of the county, refused to allow the farm-servant John Rees of Tregaron to go to Cheshunt College – despite the extraordinary efforts Rees made to obtain a good education by attending Neuadd-lwyd School. In spite of these obstacles, Rees nevertheless developed into a good classicist and theologian.[30] On the other hand, Morris's great friend Ebenezer Richard, who

[27]Compare the evidence of the Revd David Lloyd, classical and mathematics tutor at the Presbyterian Academy, Carmarthen, with that of the Education Commission Report of 1861, vol.1, pp.286–7.
[28]R. Phillips, *Dyn a'i Wreiddiau: Peth o Hanes Plwyf Llangwyryfon* (Aberystwyth, 1975), p.123.
[29]This is based on Evans, *Byr-gofiant*, passim.
[30]See his biography, ibid., pp.147–8.

had consistently voted against giving the very gifted and promising Lewis Edwards permission to go to the University of London, saw no objection to sending his son to Highbury Academy and eventually to train for the Congregationalist ministry.[31]

Most of the Calvinistic Methodist preachers were the sons of farmers, or were themselves farmers or weavers, hatters, carpenters, clockmakers, and shopkeepers.[32] Some made fortunate marriages. It was important that they should be independent and able to earn a living for, unlike the older denominations who favoured a settled ministry and, ideally, an agreed stipend, the pittance they were offered by the churches was rarely if ever more than marginal. Unlike the Methodists, also, the Baptists and Congregationalists still held to the tradition of the previous century when an academy education had been a *sine qua non* for aspiring ministers – though the example of Christmas Evans, one of the greatest preachers of the age, illustrates the fact that other, more urgent, qualifications were perhaps in greater demand in the churches.

It is a mistake, therefore, to believe that the various denominations were constantly at each other's throats. At times, of course, relations did break down; High Church tendencies in some parishes after the building of Llangorwen, for example, provoked some opposition,[33] though it is relevant to note that one of the preachers at the consecration of that church in December 1841 was the evangelical vicar of Llanbadarn Fawr, the Revd John Hughes (1787–1860), the other being Isaac Williams, the friend of Pusey, Keble and Newman, and an influential Tractarian.[34] The tensions created by this affair were considerable, as likewise by the building and consecrating of a new church at Elerch in 1868 which was, and remained, far more High Church than Llangorwen. But such was the strength of Evangelicalism within the Church as a whole that relations between the denominations and between different parties within the Church, though tense, did not lead to disruption. It was the claim by the established Church to economic powers over the members of other denominations which was the most damaging, and the issues of tithe and church rates poisoned relations between them. But the need to live together was always stronger than any ideological conviction. We have already noted how ready clergymen were to be educated at Castellhywel under a principal who held heterodox theological ideas. The Unitarians, attracted by the Arminianism and liberality of the Wesleyan Methodist preachers, and no doubt knowing that they had the same enemies, helped them to establish a cause in Llandysul.[35] Of course there were some parishes in which relations were sour, and they would be soured more generally by the 1840s over the question of tithes and other matters which a resurgent political Nonconformity campaigned

[31]I. G. Jones, *Henry Richard: Apostle of Peace 1812–1888* (Llandysul, 1988), pp.8–9.

[32]Among the forty-nine preachers in John Evans's *Byr-gofiant* were the following: eleven farmers, four farm servants, two farm labourers, two shepherds, two carpenters, two weavers, a cobbler, a hatter, a clerk, a collier, a chemist, two tailors, two blacksmiths, a seamstress, a saddler, five shopkeepers, an entrepreneur, a clockmaker, and four had private means. Thirteen kept school.

[33]On the building of Llangorwen, see O. W. Jones and R. W. D. Fenn, 'Church-building in the nineteenth century', in Jones and Walker (eds.), *Links with the Past*, pp.215–6, and I. G. Jones, *Communities: Essays in the Social History of Victorian Wales* (Llandysul, 1987), pp.35–46.

[34]J. Ross, *A Light Upon the Road: Archdeacon John Hughes of Aberystwyth (1787–1860)* (Jane Ross, 1989), and O. W. Jones, *Isaac Williams and his Circle* (London, 1971).

[35]Williams, *Welsh Wesleyan Methodism*, p.108. See also David Young, *The Origin and History of Methodism in Wales and the Borders* (London, 1893), pp.349–51, where the author mentions the assistance given to the preachers by 'the old Arminian Rev. David Davies, Castell Howell, who was ever kind to Wesleyan preachers, [and] offered him his chapel to preach in'.

against. But in the fundamentals of belief, and in the kind of spirituality which all shared, there was a consensus. They had precious things in common, not least the hymns of Williams Pantycelyn. These were by far the most widely used singing-books in church and chapel, so much so that the vicar of Llangwyryfon tried in vain to wean his parishioners away from them.[36] It is worth noting that the period from 1843 to 1863 was one of transition in congregational worship: new compilations were coming in and the old popular collections being displaced.[37] The alternative singing books available were *Psalmau* by Edmwnd Prys, used in seven parish churches, Daniel Rees's *Casgliad o Psalmau a Hymnau*, which contained many of Pantycelyn's hymns, used in thirteen, and the Psalm Book (not strictly a hymn book but still 'a singing book') used in thirty-three. But William Williams was still a powerful presence in the new collections as well. So this was a generation whose religious culture was firmly placed within the tradition of Welsh evangelical revivals.[38]

Welsh was universally the language of religion in the early part of the century. By 1845 this linguistic uniformity was beginning to erode, by which date fifty-one parishes were entirely Welsh, and eighteen mixed, either Welsh/English or English/Welsh. It is possible that the mixed services were for the convenience of local gentry families to serve the needs of visitors, as in Aberystwyth and Cardigan and other coastal parishes eager to cater for holidaymakers. In such places services tended to be in Welsh and English alternately, 'for the benefit of half a dozen people', as the incumbent of Llangrannog laconically observed. The Nonconformists were almost exclusively Welsh. Dr John Thomas noted in 1875 that Cardiganshire was probably the most Welsh of all the counties, and in 1891 he observed that all fifty-six of the denomination's chapels within the county, with the exception of two, were Welsh, the exceptions being the English churches in Aberystwyth and Cardigan. Neither cause was particularly strong in numbers; there were seventy-five members in Aberystwyth and thirty-seven in Cardigan.[39] All their academies and schools, however, were English-language institutions, as was generally the case at that time. With the exception of the English causes in Aberystwyth and Cardigan, all Baptist chapels were Welsh.

There was no uniformity with regard to the sequences of Sunday services. In most rural parish churches the custom was to hold one service in the morning or afternoon or evening. Town churches normally held two services, with Sunday school in the afternoon. By the middle of the century, almost universally, holy communion was celebrated monthly, and invariably also on the major Feast Days, although much seems to have depended upon the foibles of the incumbents, even after reforming bishops had tried to impose uniformity upon the liturgical life of the churches. Nonconformist customs also varied with respect to the numbers of services. Like the Anglicans, and subject to the same determinants of small and scattered populations residing at considerable distances for the places of worship, rural chapels held fewer services than town chapels. The usual pattern was one service either in the morning or the evening, depending on the availability of ministers who often, like the rural incumbents, had more than one place to serve. But there were no rules, and customs differed significantly even in the most rural places. An important difference between church and chapel concerned the Sunday school. Usually, Sunday school was kept by the

[36]NLW SD/QA/17. 1845 Visitation Returns, sub Llangwyryfon.
[37]For example, the Revd John Hughes, vicar of Llanbadarn Fawr, assembled his own collection, *Deffroad y Nabl: sef Detholiad o'r Salmau a roddwyd ar fesur Cerdd* (Aberystwyth, 1840).
[38]This paragraph is based on NLW SD/QA/17.
[39]T. Rees and J. Thomas, *Hanes Eglwysi Annibynol Cymru* (4 vols., Liverpool, 1871–5), IV, p.209; V, p.510.

Nonconformists in the afternoon, or in the morning if there was only one service: but it was always kept. Anglicans were obliged to catechize the children each Sunday, and one gets the impression that sometimes this took the place of a formal Sunday school, at any rate before reforming bishops left their mark on these old ways. Chapels catechized as well, and this became formalized in the institution of the *gymanfa bwnc*, in which all the participating congregations chanted pieces of scripture before being questioned on their meaning by a visiting minister.[40] Weekday services were considered essential in the life of the churches: prayer meetings were held weekly, as were society meetings, and others with a slightly more secular tone, like reading classes, penny-readings and choir rehearsals. 'Big Meetings' were held annually or quarterly in all the chapels, thus making it possible for all the churches to hear the denominations' leading preachers. Likewise, all individual chapels were expected to take their turn in welcoming meetings of county associations, and occasionally the annual meetings of denominational unions. Thus, the religious life of the county was diverse in character and style, and the chapels and churches centres of vigorous social and cultural life. Their annual preaching and singing festivals and eisteddfodau enormously enriched communities which would otherwise have been dull and commonplace, and above all they nurtured the idea that they belonged to a county community defined not only by civil boundaries and administrative powers but also by shared values and common aspirations.

Already by 1811 distinct patterns of denominationalism were apparent. In that year there were about 140 places of worship in the county, which between them provided sittings for about a quarter or a third of the total population (including children and infants). Precise figures cannot be given because the necessary information does not exist and it is probable that contemporaries tended to exaggerate their numerical strength.[41] Judging by the frequency of rebuilding and enlarging, the meeting houses of the old denominations were not large, and it is certain that those of the Calvinistic Methodists were considerably smaller, and in many cases were mere barns and farmhouses adapted for the purposes of worship.[42] Many of the new congregations of Nonconformists struggled for years before being able to build proper meeting houses. For example, the members of what later became Soar Congregationalist Chapel, Lampeter, worshipped from 1831 in a brewery, which they rented for £5 a year, until in 1841 they felt confident enough to build a chapel at a cost of £160 on land given by Harford of Falcondale in return for the vote of one of the deacons.[43]

What proportion of the population could be accommodated in 1811 must remain a mystery. The Church was by far the largest denomination, and seems to have made adequate provision for the inhabitants of the individual parishes. Some of its churches, according to official documents, were very large indeed, and could easily accommodate all the parishioners. Overall, the Anglican churches together had room for about 40 per cent of the population, only three parts of the county falling below that proportion (Genau'r-glyn, Aberystwyth and Penbryn). But some of the parish churches (and this is an important point to note) were very small. Llandygwydd, one of the largest parishes in the south of the county (population 1,113) could accommodate only 70 persons (6 per

[40]D. Jenkins, *Bro Dafydd ap Gwilym* (Aberystwyth, 1992), p.100.
[41]My figures are based on I. G. Jones and D. Williams (eds.), *The Religious Census of 1851: A Calendar of the Returns Relating to Wales, Vol. 1 South Wales* (Cardiff, 1976).
[42]See Rees, *Hanes Plwyf Llanddewi Brefi*, p.80 for a photograph of the ruins of the first Methodist chapel in the village.
[43]T. E. Davies, *1831–1931. Trem ar Ganmlwydd Eglwys Soar, Llanbedr* (Llanbedr, 1931), pp.1–8.

Fig. 123: Llanrhystud Church, rebuilt by Richard Kyrke Penson, 1851–1854. (*Crown Copyright RCAHMW-NMR*).

cent), and Aberystwyth (the second St Michael's) had room for only 294 for a population of 4,128 (7 per cent).[44] How many persons the other denominations could accommodate is not known. The third Tabernacl, Aberystwyth, had 329 members in 1831, but could accommodate, it was said, 1,200.[45]

[44]The statistics in this and the preceding paragraph are arrived at on the basis of official returns in 1818 cited above, the Ecclesiastical Revenues and Duties Report of 1835, and Jones and Williams, *The Religious Census of 1851.*
[45]M. I. Williams, *Y Tabernacl Aberystwyth, Hanes yr Achos: 1785–1985* (Aberystwyth, 1986), pp.142–6; F. W. Jones, *Canmlwydd Siloh Aberystwyth* (Aberystwyth, 1963), pp.60–4.

More interesting is the distribution of these chapels and meeting houses in 1811. The old Dissenters were concentrated in the south of the county, whereas the Calvinistic Methodists were spread out more or less equally over the whole county. They were strongest where the Congregationalists and Baptists were weakest, especially in the coastal villages and small towns. More spectacularly, they were powerfully established in the upland parishes, in Rheidol, Gwnnws, Llangeitho and Tregaron. Their meeting houses were strategically situated to serve the scattered farming communities in the mountains which were then being brought into some kind of cultivation as the populations in the more fruitful parts of the county expanded beyond their available resources. Some of these chapels were larger than the size of the population they were designed to serve would appear to justify; when someone asked Ebenezer Richard why he needed to enlarge Capel Bwlchgwynt, Tregaron, which was already large enough for the town and neighbourhood, he claimed it was justified by the numbers of societies which would gather there from time to time. It was not chapels that counted in that distant country, but societies meeting for the most part in farm households; chapel building only expanded significantly in the second half of the century.

The Wesleyans were newcomers to the county as, of course, they were to the rest of Wales. By 1811 they had eight chapels in the north of the county, including Ystumtuen, which was established in that year.[46] There were, in addition, 'many other convenient places for public worship', namely the homes and properties of their supporters. This initial concentration in the north of the county was possibly due to the fact that the Welsh Mission had sent its preachers into west Wales from the original Chester Circuit along the mid-Wales valleys and the old lead mining trade routes to the creeks of Cardigan Bay, and from Caernarfonshire along the coastal route via Barmouth and Aberdyfi. They had also made incursions into the south of the county, and, aided and abetted by innkeepers, had planted societies in Llandysul and Lampeter.[47] Although it is extremely difficult to determine the numerical strength of the denomination at any particular time because of the constant changes being made to the boundaries of the circuits, there is every reason to assume that it reflected the patterns of growth for Wales as a whole. Their chapels were small, but so were the communities in which they were planted; in any case, their success in the north-west was relatively greater than that of the other denominations. It probably reflected the zeal of the preachers and the greater appeal of their theology in a neglected part of the county which seemed to their leaders ripe for the harvest but starved of workers.

Although the Unitarians were also notably successful, we cannot tell what their membership was, though it is safe to assume, on the basis of the attendances recorded in 1851, that it could not have been very numerous even though large claims were made from time to time. Even so, their existence in a geographically restricted area in the very heartland of enthusiastic evangelicalism is one of the most astonishing facts about the county's religious developments. Judging by their answers to the triennial Bishops' Queries of the period, clergymen regarded them as their chief adversaries, though one gets the impression that, in fact, they all succeeded in living together while worshipping separately without apparently too much trouble. Early in the century, with Nonconformity visibly growing before their eyes, incumbents pleaded for tracts against the evils of schism, the dangers of Socinianism, or, as the curate of Llanbadarn Odwyn put it, with no apparent sense of irony or

---

[46]For the history of Salem, Ystumtuen (1823 and 1840), see J. H. Griffiths, *Bro Annwyl y Bryniau* (Aberystwyth,1988), pp.41–55.
[47]Ibid., pp.117–19.

contradiction, tracts to promote unity among Christians and to enforce the necessity for conforming to the established Church.[48] It is not at all clear that religion *per se* was the cause of the scandalous locking-out of the congregation from their chapel at Llwynrhydowen in October 1876. They were locked out for their refusal to vote in accordance with the wishes of the the 'playboy' owner of the Alltyrodyn estate, and the support they received subsequently from other denominations in the neighbourhood and throughout Wales is testimony enough to that.[49] Some clergymen recognized that the presence of Arian and Unitarian congregations in the midst of the highly charged emotional atmosphere generated by the Calvinistic Methodists was a positive gain.[50]

By 1851 profound changes had taken place in the religious life of the county. In the first place, there had been a rapid expansion of provision. There was now a total of 240 places of worship (including schoolrooms etc): 79 belonged to the Church of England (33.0 per cent), 44 (18.3) to the Congregationalists, 21 (8.7) to the Baptists, 11 (4.6) to the Unitarians, 67 (27.9) to the Calvinistic Methodists, 17 (7.1) to the Wesleyans, and 1 (0.4) to the Wesleyan Association. This was a very substantial increase over the numbers of places in 1811, something of the order of one hundred places or about 40 per cent. Thirty-eight places had been rebuilt and presumably enlarged, some of them more than once.

This expansion had not been regular or even over the period as a whole. An official return of Protestant Dissenters' Meeting Houses in 1853 indicates that registrations of meeting houses in Wales under the Toleration Act of 1689 showed a sudden burst during and after 1790, reaching a peak in the decades 1801–30. That pattern was replicated in Cardiganshire; the registration of 80 of a total of 123 places occurred in the years 1801 to 1830. Of the 123 registered meeting houses seven were recorded as temporary, indicating that congregations were at the time of registration meeting in barns and dwelling houses. Literary sources suggest that the true number was probably far greater.[51] The Religious Census of 1851 makes it possible to refine this information and, indeed, to amplify it. Thus, the years from 1806 saw an increase at double the rate of the previous five years – from 6 per cent in five years to 12 per cent. Then, between 1811 and 1815, the rate dropped to 5 per cent, rising between 1816 to 1820 to 6 per cent. This was a fairly modest growth compared with what was happening in other counties, but it represented an addition of thirty-two places to the county's stock. But the rate was rising every five years until by 1836–40 it had risen to 13 per cent. A total of ninety-four places of worship had now been added, and ten years later another twenty-two.

What did this mean in terms of accommodation? Fortunately, we are no longer in the dark as to this vital set of statistics, for the Census of Religious Worship, which was taken in March 1851 as part of the decennial census, supplies some of the essential information.[52] This remarkable source of information recorded all the places of worship in England and Wales and the numbers of worshippers who attended them on Sunday, 30 March. By using the manuscript returns of the enumerators, who were employed by the Registrar General and instructed how to gather the information in an objective way, it is possible to discover, with a high degree of certainty, the numbers of places of worship in the county, the numbers of sittings they contained, and the numbers of persons who

[48]NLW, SD/QA/17. 1845 Visitation Returns.
[49]A. J. Martin, *Hanes Llwynrhydowen* (Llandysul, 1977), pp.69–84.
[50]D. R. Barnes, *People of Seion* (Llandysul, 1995), pp.94–110.
[51]'Dissenters' places of worship', *PP* 1852–3, LXXXVIII (156), 65–88.
[52]Jones and Williams, *The Religious Census of 1851*, pp.473–80, 491–558.

attended their services in the morning, afternoon and evening.[53] On the basis of this we can be certain that the churches between them provided just over 63,000 sittings for the total population of 70,796, that is to say, about 89 per cent of the total population. We can call this figure the Index of Accommodation. We can work out also the proportions of the total contributed by the various denominations. The result is interesting. The Church (29.8 per cent) was no longer the largest denomination judged by accommodation. That primacy had passed to the Calvinistic Methodists, who contributed 32 per cent of the total number of seats. Then, after the Church, came the Congregationalists with 19 per cent, followed by the Baptists with 8 per cent, the Wesleyans with 6 per cent, and the Unitarians with 4 per cent. There was also a new denomination in the county, namely the Wesleyan Methodist Association, with one chapel in Aberystwyth, seating 250, built in 1846. This denomination originated in the Midlands in 1835 as a secession from the Old Connexion, and it is interesting that it made so little headway in the county. Wales's own special secession, *y Wesle bach*, seems to have made no impression outside north Wales and was swallowed up by the Wesleyan Methodist Association in 1838.[54] These developments illustrate the earlier contention that in this county religion was very conservative.

Those are the overall proportions, but provision differed greatly from district to district and from parish to parish. Thus, the Church no longer commanded an unchallenged hegemony throughout the county as had been the case fifty years earlier. In Penbryn and Llandysul subdistricts (Llandyfriog, Brongwyn, Troed-yr-aur, Betws Ifan, Penbryn, Llangrannog, Llangynllo, Henllan, Llanfairorllwyn, Bangor, and Llandysul), it provided only slightly above 17 per cent of the sittings. It was below one-third in eleven subdistricts covering virtually most of the county. Only in Llanrhystud subdistrict, Rheidol, Gwnnws and Llangeitho, was it above its average for the county, and in only one of those subdistricts (Gwnnws) was it the strongest denomination.

Of course, the success of the other denominations also varied from place to place. The Congregationalists were the strongest denomination in Aber-porth, Llechryd and Llandygwydd, in Brongwyn, where they provided almost all the seating, in Betws Ifan, Penbryn and Llangrannog, in Llangynllo and Llanfair Clydogau. The Baptists were strongest only in the borough of Cardigan and the neighbouring parish of Llangoedmor, while the Unitarians, who had added five churches to the six they had in 1811, remained clustered in the mid-Teifi, except for their one church in the Aeron valley.

The Calvinistic Methodists were now the dominant denomination, a primacy that their somewhat tetchy historian liked to claim as their undoubted right and as a reward for their superior religiosity.[55] Their regions of greatest strength were in the north of the county, from Llanrhystud onwards through Aberystwyth, into the vast expanses of Genau'r-glyn and Rheidol, and the uplands of Gwnnws, Llangeitho and Tregaron. In the subdistricts of Llangeitho and Tregaron they provided over two-thirds of available sittings. In the northern parishes as a whole they provided accommodation for nearly 10,000 persons, roughly a third of the total available. Not that they had

---

[53]For a detailed study of the religious census and an estimate of its reliability, see the introduction by I. G. Jones in Jones and Williams, *The Religious Census of 1851*, I, pp.xi–xxxv.

[54]See Williams, *Welsh Wesleyan Methodism*, chapter 7.

[55]J. Evans, *Hanes Methodistiaeth Rhan Ddeheuol Sir Aberteifi* (Dolgellau, 1904). Like most, if not all, the denominational histories of the time, this valuable compilation of chapel histories is typical of its age in the asperity of its observations on the work of historians of other denominations, and allowances have to be made for this.

confined their efforts to the north. They were powerful, too, along the coast northwards from Y Ferwig and Blaen-porth, and in the Teifi valley, and they had a significant presence in the middle part of the county, through Llannarth and Llanllwchaearn, Henfynyw, Aber-arth and Llanbadarn Trefeglwys. But the northern parishes were their favoured territory, for these were parts of the county which had suffered most from the pastoral neglect of the established Church for many generations and which the old Dissenters had earlier in the century, for whatever reason, failed to penetrate in any effective way.

It has been noted how quickly the Wesleyan Methodists came to be established, mainly, to begin with, in the coastal fringes of the north. This remained the pattern of their advance throughout that half century. They were emphatically an urban denomination. They had congregations in Cardigan, Llandysul, Lampeter and Aberystwyth, and in coastal towns where shipbuilding was an important occupation, in places growing up around the lead mines to the north of Aberystwyth and in the hills to the east in the upland communities of Cwmrheidol, Llanfihangel-y-Creuddyn and Eglwys Newydd.[56] By the middle of the century Cardiganshire had become one of the strongholds of Wesleyan Methodists in Wales, the other being east Denbighshire.[57] The second half of the century would see a sharp decline, but in the middle decades of the century they had every cause for mutual congratulation.

We can therefore understand that the pattern of provision which was developing at the beginning of the century was, by and large, maintained. Why this should have occurred is a puzzling question. It was asked time and again by the leaders of the denominations which seemed to have lost ground, in particular by the Congregationalists, who seemed to have convinced themselves that it was the Unitarian advance in what they regarded as their territory which had hindered their inevitable movement into the north. The historians of the Congregational churches observed that it was the ministers turned out of their livings by the Act of Uniformity in 1662 who had planted Dissenting churches in the county, many of which, in the meantime, had 'fallen into the hands' of Unitarians and Calvinistic Methodists.[58] There may have been some truth in this, for the loss of so many flourishing Congregational churches to the Unitarians – and some to the Calvinistic Methodists – did lead to a failure of nerve, a certain despondency where before there had been optimism and a sense of drive. The failure of the Congregationalists and the Baptists, however, to establish them-selves strongly in the early stages of religious growth in the parishes of the north left them at a con-siderable disadvantage later in the century. It was only with the greatest difficulty and the utter dedication of one man, schoolmaster, author and poet – the Revd Azariah Shadrach (1774–1844) – that the first Congregationalist chapel was built in 1823 at Penmaes-glas in Aberystwyth, forty or so years after the Baptists had established themselves in Trefeurig.[59] The Baptists, likewise, owed their

---

[56]W. J. Lewis, *Lead Mining in Wales* (Cardiff, 1967), chapter 8.

[57]Williams, *Welsh Wesleyan Methodism*, pp.147–92 and Young, *The Origin and History of Methodism*, p.362.

[58]Rees and Thomas, *Hanes Eglwysi Annibynol Cymru*, IV, p.81 and especially pp.209–10. See also D. T. Davies ac E. D. Jones, *Hanes Ebenezer Llangybi ar achlysur dathlu Daucanmlwyddiant yr Achos* (Llanbedr Pont Steffan, 1972).

[59]For the Congregationalists, see Rees and Thomas, *Hanes Eglwysi Annibynol*, IV, pp.132–8, including a brief life of Shadrach: E. D. Jones, *Trem ar Ganrif yn Hanes Eglwys Gynulleidfaol Baker Street, Aberystwyth* (Aberystwyth, 1978), pp.5–6: idem, *Llawlyfr Undeb Gogledd Ceredigion 1855. Braslun o Hanes Eglwysi Annibynol Gogledd Ceredigion*. For Shadrach, see E. D. Jones, 'Azariah Shadrach', *Y Cofiadur*, 23 (1953), 3–17.

penetration into the town of Aberystwyth mainly to one man, Samuel Breeze (1772–1812). Perhaps, after all, when one considers the smallness of the population and the poverty of the region generally, it made sense not to compete too ruthlessly in the denominational race.[60]

The Religious Census of 1851 enables us to construct fairly accurate measures of religious provision and attendance by relating sittings and attendances to population.[61] We have already referred to the Accommodation Index for the whole county (89.1), that it to say, that there was accommodation for 89 per cent of the population. It is interesting to observe that some places had accommodation for more than their total populations. The Aberystwyth Registration District as a whole had accommodation for nearly 7 per cent more than its total population, and this was true of all the subdistricts within it: Llanrhystud (with Llanddeiniol, Llangwyryfon, Llanilar and Rhostie) had an Accommodation Index of 111.3, Aberystwyth 109.9, Genau'r-glyn 132.0, and Rheidol 100 per cent. These were the highest in the county and are astonishing by any standard of measurement.

The Attendance Index is worked out in a similar fashion, expressing the number of attendances as a proportion of the total population.[62] This gives a good idea of the use being made of the accommodation and of the relative size of the worshipping public in different parts of the county. For the county as a whole, the Attendance Index was 74. As one would expect, there was a close correspondence between the two indices; those with a high Accommodation Index also had a high Attendance Index. Thus, the highest rates of attendance seem to have been in Genau'r-glyn, where it was almost 130, and Aberystwyth (105.5), but it was high also in Lampeter, Llansanffraid, Rheidol and Llangeitho. In the northern parishes the Calvinistic Methodists were the most popular denomination; elsewhere the high attendance rates were more evenly shared among all the denominations.

Whatever one makes of these figures, they suggest that the people who built and maintained chapels also made considerable use of them, and that the highest usage was in the towns, the industrial villages and the small ports. That the investment was very considerable we cannot doubt; indeed, considered against the economic background of the times it can only be wondered at. With very few exceptions, the people who put up the chapels in the first place and then rebuilt them in the prevailing fashions and with such dignity and inherent sense of good design, proportion and beauty of appearance, were, with very few exceptions, poor people, at best persons of very moderate incomes – craftsmen, farmers, small businessmen, sailors. It is difficult to find many examples of meeting houses being provided by the munificence of other, more fortunate people, like landed gentry, though there are very few examples of congregations being refused building plots. There was no Lady Barham to build chapels for the Wesleyans in Cardiganshire as there had been in the Gower.[63] The Llewellyn family of Gernos, for example, were generous to the Congregationalists of Llangynllo, but it is noticeable that more farmers gave land, labour and materials than the gentry,

[60]J. S. James, *Hanes y Bedyddwyr yn Nghymru* (4 vols., Caerfyrddin, 1893–1907), III, p.382. Note the extraordinarily interesting observation that it is only with difficulty that a new denomination can take root in an ancient town: this was certainly true of Wales, but not of England. Jenkins, *Bro Dafydd ap Gwilym*, p.96, and T. R. Morgan, *Coffa Canmlwyddol Eglwys y Bedyddwyr ym Methel, Swyddffynnon* (Barmouth, 1921).

[61]For the methodology employed here and the inherent weaknesses of the census as an authoritative source, see I. G. Jones, *Explorations and Explanations: Essays in the Social History of Victorian Wales* (Llandysul, 1981), pp.17–80, and Jones and Williams, *The Religious Census of 1851*, pp.xi–xxxv.

[62]Jones, *Explorations and Explanations*, pp.17–80.

[63]I. G. Jones, 'Denominationalism in Swansea and district', in *Explorations and Explanations*, pp.53–80.

large or small. One outstanding exception to this generalization were the Lloyds of Bronwydd in the same parish. Loyal and generous members of the established Church, they nevertheless supported Nonconformist causes within their sphere of influence. Capel Drindod (1794) was built and endowed by Colonel Lloyd, a kind of covert Nonconformist, for the use of the Calvinistic Methodists and the Congregationalists, and fifty years later it was being served by three Calvinistic Methodist ministers and one Congregationalist, all of whom had been appointed and remunerated by Thomas Davies Lloyd, grandson of Colonel Lloyd.[64] Considerable sums of money – shamefully too much, according to some Congregationalist and Baptist commentators – were collected by ministers who perambulated the country begging for contributions and sometimes, like Azariah Shadrach, hawking their sermons, pamphlets and books of poems for the sake of the cause. We look in awe and admiration at the great cathedrals and churches of our land, and rightly so, but we should also recognize and pay tribute to the enormous sacrifices of the people who invested their meagre savings in such a profusion of chapels.

By the end of the nineteenth century the relativities between the various denominations remained virtually what they had been at the end of the 1850s. In the early 1880s, so far as can be ascertained from official documents, the numbers of places and the denominational pattern had not changed substantially, if at all.[65] Nevertheless, it is clear that most of the county's stock of places of worship either had been or were in process of being renewed by the middle decades of the century, and by the end of the century almost all had been rebuilt or repaired and enlarged by rebuilding or by the addition of galleries.

The established Church was slower to begin the work of repairing decayed buildings and expanding provision than the Nonconformists. This was not because Churchmen lacked the will, but because of what often appeared to hard-pressed incumbents to be the almost insuperable difficulties of obtaining the necessary facilities and of satisfying the highly bureaucratic Church Commissioners on financial and other matters.[66] The need in the archdeaconry was not for new buildings – there were enough of these – but rather to make good the neglect of centuries,[67] and all the requests in the first half of the century to the Church Commissioners and the Incorporated Church Building Society were for financial assistance with projects to repair or, more drastically, to rebuild their churches. Not that nothing was done. Incumbents, encouraged by bishops and chivvied by arch-deacons, were wide awake to the possibilities of obtaining grants from the Church Commissioners, the Incorporated Church Building Society or the Diocesan Building Society. Twenty-three incumb-ents appealed to the Church Building Society between 1823 and 1841 for grants to repair their churches, seventeen of which appear to have been successful.[68] One new church was built during

[64]See *Yr Efangylydd* (1831), 133–8: Jones and Williams, *The Religious Census of 1851*, p.498; P. B. Morgan, 'Bronwydd and Sir Thomas Lloyd', *NLWJ*, XX, no.4 (1984), 376–405. Colonel Lloyd and his wife were probably Nonconformists by persuasion but Anglicans by expediency.

[65]'Return of churches and chapels and other buildings registered for religious purposes in Registration Districts', *PP*, 1882 L, pp.19–20.

[66]I. G. Jones, 'The rebuilding of Llanrhystud Church', 'Church reconstruction in north Card-iganshire in the nineteenth century' and 'Religion and politics: the rebuilding of St Michael's Church Aberystwyth and its political consequences', in Jones, *Communities*, pp.47–87.

[67]For a contemporary account of some of the county's churches, see S. Glynne, 'Notes on the older churches in the four Welsh dioceses', *AC*, XIV (1897), 304–306; ibid., XV (1898), 351–5.

[68]The Incorporated Church Building Society Report for the Year 1927, pp.141–7, for a complete list of grants made to the diocese between 1818 and 1927.

this period, namely Llangorwen in 1841, the first Tractarian church in Wales – 'a church as it should be', according to *The Ecclesiologist*, 'one of the most complete and successful imitations of ancient models that the present age has produced.'[69] There was then a slackening of activity until 1850, after which date scarcely a year went by without one or more – sometimes, as in 1870, no fewer than four – applications. By 1876 the archdeaconry had raised £41,893 for the repair of thirty of its churches. Of that sum, £40,773 was raised by voluntary means, the deficit of £1,320 being found by the Incorporated Society. By 1906, according to evidence presented to the Royal Commission in 1905, a total of £113,944 had been raised in the archdeaconry between 1840 and 1906 for these purposes, and that total excluded sums of less than £500.[70] Leading architects had been attracted to the county. John Pollard Seddon, the architect of the Castle House Hotel which he reconstructed after it had been bought by the founders of the University College of Wales, had stayed on to undertake other prestigious commissions, including the restoration of Llanbadarn Fawr (1868 and 1878). William Butterfield, arguably the greatest of the Victorian ecclesiastical architects, designed Elerch (1868), while R. J. Withers rebuilt Lampeter in 1868, restored Llannarth in 1871, restored the chancel of Llanddewibrefi in 1885, and restored Llanwnnen in 1875. R. Kyrke Penson rebuilt Llanrhystud, Llanilar and Rhostie, while A. Ritchie of Chester rebuilt, restored and enlarged several churches between 1877 and 1889, including Tregaron, Llanychaearn, Lledrod, Llanfihangel Genau'r-glyn, Nancwnlle and Cilcennin. This restoration and rebuilding brought contracts to local architects as well: G. T. Bassett of Aberystwyth, for example, was responsible for the restoration of the church at Ystrad-fflur, and David Davies of Llandysul for the restoration of Llandysiliogogo.

By the beginning of the twentieth century, therefore, the established Church in the county had been transformed. It was no longer a 'Church of neglect', its buildings decayed and dilapidated, its clerical manpower underpaid and scandalously badly housed. According to the Royal Commission, its churches and chapels now numbered 115 (together with ten mission stations)[71] whereas, in 1831, there had been sixty-eight. There was seating for 21,763 persons, and something of the order of 10,000 communicants on its lists. There were now sixty-one parsonage houses where before there had been only twenty-three. Clergy numbers had risen from thirty-six incumbents and thirty-two curates in 1831 to sixty-six incumbents and nineteen assistant clergy in 1906.[72] The Church was also more efficient and better organized, with rural deaneries, re-established by Bishop Connop Thirlwall at the beginning of his reform of his diocese, and regular clerical conferences beginning to break down the isolation of the clergy and ending that curse of the unreformed Church, pluralism.[73] It was, therefore, a Church which could defend itself against the attacks of its enemies and resist the forces which desired its downfall, so that when disestablishment came about its morale was higher than it had ever been before and its hopes for the future realistically sanguine.[74]

[69]See Jones, *Communities*, p.36.
[70]Royal Commission on the Church of England and other Religious Bodies, Summary Table of Provision made by voluntary contribution.
[71]Royal Commission, *Report*, pp.313–17.
[72]Royal Commission, Summary Table Church Buildings, Clergy, and Services, 1831 and 1906.
[73]J. J. S. Perowne and L. Stokes, *Letters, Literary and Theological, of Bishop Thirlwall* (London, 1881), and J. C. Thirlwall, *Connop Thirlwall, Historian and Theologian* (London, 1936). See also R. Brinkley, 'Connop Thirlwall, Bishop of St David's', *Ceredigion*, VII, no.2 (1973), 131–51.
[74]W. L. Bevan, *The Church Revival in Wales: Its History and Character* (London, 1891). See also *The Church in Wales. A Reply to Mr Henry Richard's Letter to 'The Daily News' on the Church in Wales* (London, 1885).

For their part, Nonconformists continued to prosper during the second half of the century, though, given the relatively low point of departure in 1800, at a somewhat reduced rate. This was mainly because their progress during the previous fifty years had been such as virtually to satisfy the need, but also because henceforth they would be building against a falling population. The rate of population growth had been slackening in the county as a whole since the decade 1841–51, and apart from the next decade, when it was virtually stagnant, it continued to fall in every subsequent decade. 1881–91 was the decade of greatest loss, no less than 9.2 per cent, or 8,754 persons. The greatest losses were in the most rural registration districts, especially in the south of the county, and the only places which escaped were those districts which contained relatively large and thriving urban communities, like Aberystwyth, or those in which lead mining or the weaving of cloth diversified the economy and thus helped to retain their populations. But in that fatal decade of 1881–91 even Aberystwyth District lost 17.6 per cent of its population (4,504 persons), and Tregaron District 6.2 per cent (1,659 persons). How serious were those losses of population, with more males migrating than females, can be seen when the population figures for the subdistricts are examined. In the decade 1881–91 Llanrhystud lost 14.1 per cent, Aberystwyth 8.0 per cent, Genau'r-glyn 20.0 per cent, Rheidol 30.4 per cent, Gwnnws 25.3 per cent, Llangeitho 12.4 per cent, and Tregaron 11.3 per cent, in all a total of 6,162 persons.[75] These losses of population, almost as many females as males, were due to migration, mainly to the mining and manufacturing districts of south Wales, the flow coinciding with the expansion of the coal industry and expedited by the coming of the railways which transformed communications between the rural west and the industrial south. The Manchester and Milford Railway Company, which had reached Aberystwyth from Carmarthen in 1867, wended its way through the heartland of upland Cardiganshire, bringing hope and new horizons to the impoverished communities through which it passed and acting as a kind of conduit to syphon off the excess population and deposit them where labour was much in demand.[76]

Unfortunately, there is no means of knowing what sums were expended by Nonconformists on their chapels and schoolrooms during this period, but the aggregate sums must have been at least as great as those of the established church. Some were built by the congregations themselves, with farmers providing timber and stones and other the labour and building skills. It was in Aberystwyth and Cardigan that the most expensive and spectacular chapel building took place. Congregationalists in Aberystwyth, anticipating that the town would develop as an academic centre as well as commercially, built their new chapel, Seion, Baker Street (1878) to the designs of the fashionable architect, Richard Owen, Liverpool (the son of Sir Hugh Owen) to replace Azariah Shadrach's original building at Penmaen-glas.[77] Tabernacl was also rebuilt, for the third time, to the designs of the same architect in 1878–9,[78] and the magnificent Bethel was erected in 1888 by the minister-architect, the Revd William Jones.[79] George Morgan of Carmarthen designed Mount Zion, Cardigan (1878), and Tabernacl in the same town was given a splendid new vestry in 1870 and a

[75]Based on J. Williams, *Digest of Welsh Historical Statistics* (2 vols., The Welsh Office, 1985), I, p.12 and the decennial census.

[76]On the effects of the railways on population movements, see J. Davies, *A History of Wales* (London, 1993), pp.404–10; D. W. Howell, 'The impact of railways on agricultural developments in nineteenth-century Wales', *WHR*, 7, no.1 (1974), 47.

[77]See Anthony Jones, *Welsh Chapels* (Stroud, 1996), passim.

[78]Williams, *Y Tabernacl*, pp.40–4.

[79]Jones, *Welsh Chapels*, p.126.

new façade in 1901–2. Local architects and builders were also employed. George Lumley took over the building of Siloh (1859–63) when his brother, John, who had been given the original contract, died in 1862. Siloh was also given a new façade in 1867–8 to the designs of J. P. Seddon, who was currently at work on the Castle House Hotel.[80] Country congregations, as always, depended upon the services of local craftsmen and builders.

Measured by the index of provision in 1906, Nonconformist growth was very considerable. The number of places had more than doubled, from 114 to 288, and the total provision of sittings had increased from 44,193 in 1851 to 75,901. The total Nonconformist index of provision had risen from 62.4 in 1851 to 78.2, which was the highest of any county in Wales.[81]

The denominational pattern had likewise changed, both as regards the proportional strength of the established Church and the Nonconformists, and within the Nonconformist group itself. In 1851 the Church had provided nearly 30 per cent of the total sittings in the county; in 1906 this had fallen to just under 22 per cent. The Congregationalists had increased their share of the sittings from nearly 19 per cent to nearly 25 per cent, the Baptists remained more of less the same at 8 per cent, the Calvinistic Methodists had grown from 32 per cent to nearly 35 per cent of the total, while the Wesleyan Methodists remained at just over 6 per cent. The other, minor, denominations, including the Roman Catholics and the Salvation Army, contributed nearly 4 per cent. In effect, therefore, changes in the pattern of denominationalism in the county as a whole were not such as to alter in any substantial way that which we have noted to have emerged by the second quarter of the century.

Nor had the geographical pattern changed to any marked degree. The greatest growth had occurred in the north of the county, reflecting economic and demographic changes, especially the growth of lead-mining communities in places such as Tal-y-bont, Ysbyty Ystwyth and Taliesin, as well as smaller places, such as Elerch, and the expansion of others, as in the region of Pontrhyd-fendigaid and Pont-rhyd-y-groes. The Church contributed its share to the expansion of provision in these places: churches were built in Penrhyn-coch (1881 by R. J. Withers) and Elerch (1868 by William Butterfield), at Tal-y-bont (1876), Ysbyty Ystwyth (1876 by R. J. Withers) and Goginan (1866 or 1871). Also, new churches were built to serve the expanding population of Aberystwyth: St Mary's Welsh church in 1866 (William Butterfield) and Holy Trinity in 1886 and 1888 (Middleton, Protheroe and Phillott).[82] Nor should it be forgotten that the less spectacular but equally vital work of rebuilding and reconstruction was proceeding apace throughout the archdeaconry.

But it was the Nonconformists who led the way, especially the Congregationalists, who had added thirteen new chapels since 1851 and who now claimed 10,832 members and 6,327 hearers.[83] Like the Church, they established congregations and chapels in far-off and scattered places, such as Siloa, Cwmerfin (1868) and Cwmsymlog and Goginan, to serve the lead-mining communities in those remote parts. The Calvinistic Methodists appear to have been most sensitive to, and to have reacted most speedily, to changing sociological pressures. Thus, in 1873 the County Presbytery divided into

[80]Jones, *Canmlwydd Siloh Aberystwyth*, pp.26–7.
[81]Royal Commission, *Report*, I, p.54.
[82]J. Jones, *Holy Trinity Church Aberystwyth* (Aberystwyth, 1986), p.5. See also for the region's churches G. Morgan, *Eglwysi Bro Padarn* (Aberystwyth, 1992) and Jones, *Communities*, pp.35–46.
[83]Rees and Thomas, V, pp.510–12 and summary table p.529. According to the Royal Commission, VII, Appendix IV, p.24, in 1905 the Congregationalists had sixty-two churches, eight schoolrooms and 9,534 communicants. The discrepancy is due to the differences between the geographical areas of the denomination's Associations and the Ancient County.

two halves, north and south, with distinct monthly meetings and administrative arrangements. The grounds for this important change in the denomination's development was caused by the enormous growth of the churches during the previous twenty or so years. Of the sixty-three churches in existence in 1850 fewer than half (twenty-nine) were located in the north, but between 1850 and 1872 twenty-five new churches were established, of which eighteen were in the north, among them Blaenrheidol (Nant-y-moch) in 1865, on the banks of the River Rheidol nearly four miles upstream from Ponterwyd, but which now lies, along with the only farmhouse to survive the depopulation of those highlands, under the waters of Nant-y-moch reservoir. In that period of twenty years up to 1872 the total membership of the Presbytery had increased from 7,005 to 11,456 and Sunday school members from 15,216 to 19,976.[84] By 1905 there were ninety-five churches (not including preaching stations), forty-seven in the northern presbytery and forty-eight in the southern, with a total of 13,014 communicants and 20,021 adherents. The statistics show a gain of 10.3 per cent over the previous twenty years in the number of communicants, but a fall of 8.6 per cent in the numbers of adherents. The gains and the losses were greater in the northern than in the southern presbytery.[85]

The growth patterns of the main denominations in the second half of the century exhibited a remarkable similarity. The revival of 1859 was followed in each of them by a slump to levels lower than had been experienced before, and from which recovery was hesitant and uncertain. This reflected a common evangelical ethos which was by now more Arminian than Calvinist, in which revivalism as such was not an essential ingredient. As the years passed, the churches became increasingly more 'denominational' and less 'sectarian', and the denominations themselves less exclusive and jealous than had been the case in the first half century of growth. The Revival of 1904–5 brought out the similarities and the differences between the denominations in this respect. All made great gains, and it was in and around 1906 that membership and adherent figures reached their highest point.[86] As in 1859–60 and 1874–5, so now numbers peaked very significantly. For example, Calvinistic Methodist membership for the whole of Wales rose by 15.1 per cent between the years 1870 and 1875, thereafter falling away to between 1 per cent and 2 per cent by the turn of the century, until 1904 when the rate reached 4.9 per cent, peaking at 9.1 per cent in the following year when the fruits of the revival were at their most profuse. Thereafter, with the exception of the period 1913 to 1918 and 1922 to 1927, during which years the rate scarcely reached 1 per cent per annum, membership figures showed a constant loss. The fall was never cataclysmic, but rather a constant drip. Commenting on the figures for 1937, *Y Blwyddiadur* pointed out that the secular decline had started in 1926, when the membership had reached its historical high point of 189,727.[87]

For obvious reasons the patterns of growth and decline for the North Cardiganshire Presbytery do not replicate the denomination's national development: the massive numbers of the Calvinistic

[84]D. L. Evans, *Braslun o Hanes Henaduriaeth Gogledd Aberteifi 1873–1972* (Caernarfon, 1972), p.6 and p.47 for the statistics.

[85]Royal Commission, IV, Appendix 2.

[86]See *Y Blwyddiadur* 1906 for the comments of the editor on the increase in the numbers of communicants in that year. 'Y mae degau o flynyddoedd wedi mynd heibio er pan y cafwyd y fath ychwanegiad yn rhif ein cymunwyr.' (Decades have passed since such increases occurred in the numbers of communicants). It points out that the increase in 1905 was 961, but that in 1906 it was 8,359.

[87]*Y Blwyddiadur* 1936, pp.147–8, prints annual membership figures for 1867–1933. The editor's comments are in *Y Blwyddiadur* for 1939, p.87, commenting on the 1937 statistics.

Methodists in the highly industrialized and urbanized parts of the country cannot be compared with the numerically lesser developments in rural counties, such as Cardiganshire, though there are significant points of resemblance. Yet it is worth observing that the two monthly meetings contributed jointly a total of nearly £5,400 to Casgliad yr Ugeinfed Ganrif (The Twentieth Century Fund), which was launched in 1899 to mark the new century. The Fund raised a total of nearly £103,000, and bearing in mind the size of the population this was a more than respectable sum for a relatively poor county to contribute.[88]

The Calvinistic Methodists, as we have seen, were the largest and most flourishing of the denominations in the county, and the patterns of their growth and decline were typical of those of the other denominations as well. Not only was their physical presence greater than that of the others, but their popularity, judging by their relative strength in the total population in successive decades, was also stronger than that of the Baptists and Congregationalists, and their steady success in recruiting members against a falling population was also more marked, especially in the course of that crucial decade from 1901 to 1911.[89]

The membership statistics for the northern presbytery show that the number of communicants was at its peak in 1906. In that year there were 6,750 communicants, the number having grown from 5,617 in 1873. Thereafter, numbers fell sharply until the end of the published series in 1973. The rate of decline was very considerable if not cataclysmic. More serious was the decline in the numbers of Sunday scholars, which fell in the course of the century from just over 10,000 to a mere 1,280. This decline seems to have begun in 1906, only a year or so after the 1904–5 revival. There followed a brief recovery, but this was soon followed by a withdrawal of support for organized religion which would have been inconceivable at the beginning of the nineteenth century. Just as serious was the decline in the numbers of adherents. This began at an earlier date, before the end of the nineteenth century, and was reversed only briefly during the revival years of 1904–5. This decline, along with the falling away in Sunday school numbers, was of vital importance because it showed clearly that the denomination was losing, or failing to attract, those categories of persons from whom it had always hoped to recruit its membership.

The Wesleyan Methodists experienced a somewhat different pattern of growth and decline.[90] Whereas the Calvinistic Methodists were making substantial, if rather erratic, gains up to and including the revival of 1904–5, the Wesleyan membership figures were declining in all but three quinquennia up to the revival. Their relative gains during the revival, however, were greater than those of the Calvinistic Methodists – a very substantial 13.7 per cent between 1904 and 1905 – but like them the decline in numbers thereafter was cataclysmic. This may not appear to have been the case to observers at the time, but we can see that the constant leakage from an ever-diminishing reservoir of membership was, in fact, fatal to the well-being of both denominations.

The same was true of the other denominations, the Baptists and the Congregationalists. As has been shown, because of the sociological characteristics of the county, the town churches of both denominations – indeed, of all the denominations – had always been disproportionately large in

[88]See *Adroddiad Casgliad yr Ugeinfed Ganrif* (Manchester, 1910), pp.1–18, where all the individual contributions are listed.

[89]For a discussion of this methodology, see C. B. Turner, 'Revivals and popular religion in Victorian and Edwardian Wales' (unpublished University of Wales Ph.D. thesis, 1979).

[90]Based on the statistics published annually in *Minutes of Conference*, 1870–1970.

comparison with the churches of the rural area. From the middle of the nineteenth century onwards, Baptist and Congregationalist churches in Cardigan and Aberystwyth could boast congregations of four or five hundred, and because of the nature of their economies and the relative stability of the populations, they could, and did, maintain their number into the 1960s and beyond. Their ministers were famous throughout Wales as preachers and theologians and poets, and they could be relied upon to attract large numbers of worshippers.[91] The opening of the University College of Wales in 1872, and of the Theological College of the Presbyterian Church of Wales in 1906 (like the University in a hotel adapted for its new purposes) virtually ensured that the churches in Aberystwyth would thereafter flourish. The situation was different in the country churches which were commonly small, sometimes frail, but which had different expectations and had survived despite their smallness.[92] More problematic was the fate of the churches of the industrialized villages, such as Pontrhydfendigaid. These were larger and seemingly more prosperous, but, as their members understood so well, their prosperity was always subject to sudden and disastrous shifts in their populations.[93]

Many questions arise as to why Cardiganshire people should have invested what must have been, generation after generation, a very high proportion of their disposable income and scarce resources in such astonishing works of religion, and why, having achieved so much in the course of one century, it should have been allowed to fall into a state of neglect in another. Contemporaries were in no doubt as to their motives and the force which compelled them to undertake such works. They believed that they were called to put up meeting houses as places of worship, temples dedicated to the preaching of the word, for the administration of the sacraments and the holy exercise of prayer, for the education of the young and their parents, and as centres for a range of cultural activities in the localities. The compelling force, they believed, was the work of the Holy Spirit, and they found confirmation of this conviction in the frequent revivals that quickened the churches and transformed individual lives. Gomer M. Roberts, the leading historian of Calvinistic Methodism, listed fifteen revivals between 1795 and 1904, some of which were local, others county-wide, and yet others which spread far beyond any local boundaries.[94] Much has been written about revivals and revivalism,[95] and it is important to stress that Cardiganshire was one of the epicentres of the evangelical revivals of the eighteenth century and continued to be a powerhouse well into the nineteenth century. During that century, their nature and incidence, the degree to which they depended on

[91] See Lewis, *Born on a Perilous Rock*, pp.41–74, and idem, *Gateway to Wales: A History of Cardigan* (Dyfed County Council, 1990), pp.31–8.

[92] See D. J. Morgan, *Y Babell, Dolybont 1874–1974* (Llandysul, 1974), for an explanation of falling numbers in times of economic depression.

[93] See, for example, Morgan, *Coffa Canmlwyddol Eglwys y Bedyddwyr ym Methel, Swyddffynnon*, pp.24, 32, and idem, *Llawlyfr Coffa Can-Mlwyddiant Carmel, Eglwys y Bedyddwyr, Pontrhydfendigaid 1834–1934* (Aberystwyth, 1934), p.22.

[94] 'Diwygiadau ym mywyd yr Eglwys', in S. Evans and G. M. Roberts (eds.), *Cyfrol Goffa Diwygiad 1904–5* (Caernarfon, 1954).

[95] On Welsh revivals, see H. Hughes, *Hanes Diwygiadau Crefyddol Cymru* (Caernarfon, 1906), E. Parry, *Hanes y Diwygiadau Crefyddol yn Nghymru* (Corwen, 1898), and, as an antidote, R. Carwardine, 'The Welsh evangelical community and Finney's revival', *Journal of Ecclesiastical History*, 29, no.4 (1978), 463–80. For the 1859 revival, which was closely associated with Cardiganshire, see J. J. Morgan, *Hanes Dafydd Morgan Ysbyty a Diwygiad '59* (Caernarfon, 1906). For the 1904–5 revival, see Evans and Roberts (eds.), *Cyfrol Goffa Diwygiadau*, and B. Hall, 'The Welsh revival of 1904–5: a critique', in G. J. Cuming and D. Baker (eds.), *Popular Belief and Practice* (Cambridge, 1972), pp.291–301.

Fig. 124: The Revd Dafydd Morgan (1814–1883), Calvinistic Methodist minister at Ysbyty Ystwyth and one of the promoters of the 1859 Revival. (*Copyright National Library of Wales*).

charismatic leaders, the frequency of their occurrence, the expectations people had of their effectiveness, changed very substantially. These changes coincided with, and were responses to, changes in the climate of religious and philosophical opinion, to the influences exerted on the churches by an educated ministry, who took an increasingly lofty, if not sceptical, view of the old theology which gave to revivals a pentecostal importance, by the professionalization of the ministry – no longer would preachers rely on farming or shopkeeping, or weaving or other crafts for a living – and the rising expectations of congregations, which were more sophisticated than ever before. Only two major revivals of the old kind and closely associated with the county occurred during the second half of the century. The 1859 Revival, which began in Tre'r-ddôl, was led by Humphrey Jones, a Congregationalist preacher newly returned from Wisconsin and the so-called 'Burned Over District' of Up State New York, and the Revd Dafydd Morgan, Calvinistic Methodist minister of Ysbyty

Ystwyth. The historical significance of this revival is that it marked a transition in the old tradition of Welsh revivals which had originated in the eighteenth century, and the beginning of a period characterized by a belief that revivals could be induced by the adoption of well-tried preaching and evangelizing methods. The Revd Henry Jones, Bryncir, author of one of the most popular histories of the Welsh religious revivals, observed that one common element in Welsh revivals up to and including the 1859 revival was the ambulatory nature of the evangelizing. It was the custom, in the era before the denomination had adopted the Dissenting idea of a settled ministry, for Calvinistic Methodist ministers to travel from chapel to chapel and society to society for many weeks until all chapels in a given district had been visited once. They preached three times in each chapel on the day of their visit before moving on; they were, it was said, like Samson's foxes setting fire to whole regions of the land. Dafydd Morgan and his fellow evangelists worked within this tradition, and it accounted for their success.[96] Subsequent revivals, especially those revivals which followed the pattern set by Moody and Sankey,[97] were different because they were organized evangelical missions, headed by a charismatic leader, and were preceded by weekly or even nightly prayer-meetings and advertising campaigns before the arrival of the mission, which then remained in the same place until its work was judged to be complete, or, indeed, to be abandoned. These techniques were typical also of the campaigns of the Revd Richard Owen in 1883–5.[98]

The other revival was that of 1904–5.[99] Like that of 1859, it began in this county, this time in the south, at Blaenannerch, near New Quay. The minister of Tabernacl, New Quay, the Revd Joseph Jenkins, and his friend, the Revd John Thickens, minister of Tabernacl, Aberaeron, alarmed and mortified by the perceived low state of religion in the county, had been instrumental in persuading the South Wales Presbytery to send the evangelist Seth Joshua to visit the area under the aegis of the recently formed Calvinistic Methodist Forward Movement.[100] The revival, which started late in 1903, was to be taken to most of Wales by the young Evan Roberts of Loughor, an ex-collier and blacksmith and a candidate for the ministry. Roberts had scarcely begun his studies before he abandoned them in order to undertake the kind of fervent evangelizing exemplified in the work of Seth Joshua. Thereafter, he spent most of his time in the next twelve months or so perambulating the country, moving through industrial south Wales and especially the colliery towns and villages of the valleys. He does not seem to have visited south Cardiganshire again. Nevertheless, the warmth of the revival was felt in most places, running along the organizational channels linking chapel with chapel which all the different denominations had perfected. Thus, monthly meetings in both

[96]Hughes, *Hanes Diwygiadau*, pp.447–59.

[97]For the American evangelists Dwight L. Moody and Ira D. Sankey, see G. Parsons (ed.), *Religion in Victorian Britain. Volume 1 Traditions* (Manchester, 1988), pp.219–23. A selection of his addresses appeared in translation under the title *Anerchiadau gan Mr D.L. Moody gyda Hanes ei Fywyd a'i Lafur ef a Mr Ira D. Sankey* (Dinbych, 1876).

[98]E. Parry, *Llawlyfr ar Hanes y Diwygiadau Crefyddol yn Nghymru* (Corwen, 1898), pp.158–60.

[99]R. R. Davies, 'Toriad y Wawr yn Sir Aberteifi', in *Y Diwygiad a'r Diwygwyr. Hanes Toriad Gwawr Diwygiad 1904–5* (Dolgellau, 1906), pp.49–55. Also E. Evans, *The Welsh Religious Revival of 1904* (Port Talbot, 1969), pp.49–62.

[100]For Seth Joshua (1858–1925), see T. M. Rees, *Seth Joshua and Frank Joshua the Renowned Evangelists* (Wrexham, 1926). For the Forward Movement (Y Mudiad Ymosodol) and the personalities and roles of the brothers Seth and Frank Joshua, and for the religious and social background to the revival, see R. T. Jones, *Ffydd ac Argyfwng Cenedl: Cristionogaeth a Diwylliant yng Nghymru 1890–1914. Cyfrol 1* (Abertawe, 1981), pp.108–11, and *Cyfrol 2* (Abertawe, 1982), pp.122–57.

presbyteries were transformed into enthusiastic preaching services, reminding the old of the enthusiasm of their youth. Wherever they were held, revival meetings were invariably stirred into praise and song by the recital of news from the churches where the revival was most spectacularly effective, and the message was often presented in song by Evan Roberts's earliest converts, the trio of ladies who often accompanied him on his tours. Indeed, women and young people took a leading part in the revival in Cardiganshire as elsewhere, as, for instance, at Pen-llwyn in a service which began at 6 p.m. and ended after midnight.[101]

It is difficult to estimate what the effects of the revival were in the county. As has already been noted, there was certainly a numerical growth in the number of communicants, but there was also a concurrent decline in the numbers of adherents, or listeners, which suggests that the main effect of the revival was to bring back into communion backsliders rather than to make new conquests. But a church which can only grow autogenously, or by recruiting only from within, must inevitably decline. In any case, religion in this county does not seem to have fallen into the depression which had become typical of churches in the industrial areas, for, as we have seen, numerically the denominations were in a fairly healthy state. The losses to the churches immediately after the cooling of the revival, however, were almost as marked as in the industrial areas, but it would appear that numbers of communicants were maintained until the 1960s and 1970s. There was no spectacular decline, only a steady drip of members back into the world.[102] Yet there is no doubt that many people had been deeply affected in the churches. There was now a new spirituality, a new sensitivity to moral problems, a greater readiness to link theology with social problems and to think in terms of political action. But this was Cardiganshire not Glamorgan or Carmarthenshire, and it would be a long time before the political fruits of revival would appear.

There were forces of a more secular kind at work also, forces of secularization which were common throughout most of western Europe and America. It has already been noted that, given sufficient causes, religion could easily become entangled in political controversy, and local tensions become magnified and absorbed into national politics. The dominant Liberalism of the county was nourished on some outstanding local instances of national issues in the half century after 1830, one of those issues being the disestablishment of the established church.[103] The disestablishment controversy, though at the heart of Welsh Nonconformist Liberalism for most of the last quarter of the century, generated less political activity in the county than in the rest of Wales. The reasons for this are not difficult to understand. Socially and economically, the county had fallen into a kind of torpor in which politics of a confrontational kind could hardly survive.[104] The dominant denomination, as we have seen, were the Calvinistic Methodists, and the deeply conservative attitudes which underlay the avowed Liberalism of its leaders undoubtedly inhibited the growth of radical opinion in the county.

At deeper levels of consciousness, religion lay at the heart of the growing feelings of nationality which developed in the course of the nineteenth century. Welsh historians, preachers and writers had always stressed the distinctive nature of Welsh religion, especially taking vast pride in the success of

[101] See Davies, *Y Diwygiad a'r Diwygwyr*, pp.275–7.
[102] Such was also the experience of the monthly meeting of the south of the county.
[103] See Jones, *Explorations*, pp.165–92.
[104] K. O. Morgan, 'Cardiganshire politics: the Liberal ascendancy, 1885–1923', *Ceredigion*, V, no.4 (1967), 328–31.

Nonconformity as measured by its numerical strength. These were the beliefs and sentiments which laid a base for the new kind of political activity advocated in the 1860s by politicians and activists such as Henry Richard of Tregaron. Richard deliberately set out to shape a new image of the Welshman as the enlightened, educated upholder of moral values and of ideals of conduct superior to those of other nations, especially the English, and to demonstrate to the rest of the world that the high levels of religiosity characteristic of Wales were not the product of government enforcement or the paternalism of landlord and industrialist but rather the creation of the people of Wales themselves. It was on these philosophical and sociological bases that the Welsh nationalism typical of the end of the century was founded, and the unique multiplicity of chapels and churches and the total culture which they represented was proclaimed to be the visible evidence of this.[105]

Yet, it was not so much the effects of revivals that was most characteristic of the county's religiosity. Contemporaries preferred to refer to them as 'awakenings' or 'revivications', in the sense that particular and specific churches in different places experienced a renewal of their sense of fellowship in the bond of the Holy Spirit. But some churches never experienced revival in any shape or form, and evidently many deeply religious men and women never experienced any kind of sudden conversion or illumination. The experience of the religious life of many resembled that of the Revd John Jones, Penmorfa (1801–85), reckoned to be one of the county's best theologians of his time, who grew gradually into a state of belief, like one of Nature's plants.[106] Nevertheless, there was a powerful tradition of revivals in the county, and a kind of folk-memory of extraordinary spiritual experiences which certain gifted preachers had stimulated in the past and which the writers of local histories placed at the centre of their narratives. One can understand also that the classical period for revivals occurred during those tense and dangerous opening decades of the century, and during times of distress and social upheaval. Perhaps, also, it is unwise to believe that congregations could ever have survived on a diet of high emotionalism. Finally, in the chapel histories and biographies of ministers and preachers, it is their steady, unwavering and generally quiet ways of worshipping and organizing their congregations, denominations and circuits that is impressive. Generally speaking, revivals seemed to have resembled the sudden, brief bursts of fire among the cooling embers of past conflagrations when the breezes play among them, bringing a little light and some warmth, but destined to cool very quickly into their normal dormant state.

Organized religion in Cardiganshire at the end of the nineteenth century and the early decades of the twentieth seemed to be in a healthy state, and the prognosis seemed good. Levels of membership were being maintained despite the steady loss of population, and chapel membership, especially in the large town churches was almost spectacular – for example, 640 in Tabernacl in 1900, rising to 786 in 1925.[107] Even as late as 1980, for example, the three Welsh Presbyterian chapels in Aberystwyth had an aggregate membership of 1,896; the total for the whole of Aberystwyth was 2,620. Of course, these were town and university chapels at a time when it was the fashion to attend at least once a Sunday, and when landladies allegedly saw to it that their young charges actually

---

[105]See H. Richard, *Letters and Essays on Wales* (2nd edn., London, 1884), passim. Also, T. Rees, *Miscellaneous Papers on Subjects Relating to Wales* (London, 1867), pp.15–17; Sir Thomas Phillips, *Wales: The Language, Social Condition, Moral Character, and Religious Opinions of the People, considered in their relation to Education* (London, 1849), and David J. V. Jones, *Crime in Nineteenth-Century Wales* (Cardiff, 1992), especially pp.1–13, chapter 2 on criminal statistics, and the epilogue, pp.239–51.

[106]Evans, *Byr-gofiant*, p.95. Cf. Morgan, *Y Babell*, p.9.

[107]These figures are based on *Y Blwyddiadur* and chapel reports for the years in question.

attended. The same flourishing chapel culture was also the dominant feature of Cardigan, where the chapels were large and prosperous. In the country, however, the chapels had to struggle to maintain their memberships. More and more of their young people were migrating to the coalfields of south Wales, and a falling population, a decaying agricultural economy, and the slow, sad decline of the Welsh language where it mattered most, were not conducive to growth. It is likely also that the migrating men and women were precisely the class of person from whom the 'listeners' would have been recruited; almost certainly their losses were proportionately greater than those of the class of full members. Yet, the county's loss was the coalfield's gain as the valleys of south Wales filled up with a high proportion of people who had been nurtured in the culture of the rural chapels, and who would strive to reproduce it wherever they settled.

When, in 1891, the Revd Dr John Thomas completed the fifth, supplementary, volume of the history of the Welsh Congregationalist churches which he and his friend, Dr Thomas Rees, had written, the future of the churches of his denomination, despite some unhappy features, seemed on the whole to be secure. As a historian and theologian, he could look back with thankfulness on the religious developments of the past two centuries, and could not refrain from quoting the words of the Psalmist: 'Walk about Zion, and go round about her; tell the towers thereof. Mark ye well her bulwarks, consider her palaces; that ye may tell it to the generation following.' This is a task which faces every generation, but perhaps this is the last generation which can still see the physical evidence of what had been for many generations the most precious part of their common experience.

CHAPTER 22

INVENTORY OF NONCONFORMIST CHAPELS AND SUNDAY SCHOOLS IN CARDIGANSHIRE

David Percival

The Database

The information in this inventory is largely drawn from the computerized database held by the Royal Commission on the Ancient and Historical Monuments of Wales, with additional data compiled by the Board of Celtic Studies of the University of Wales. The Commission's database is based on one compiled originally by the National Library of Wales using documentary sources. It has been enhanced and expanded, duplicate entries have been identified and eliminated, and the sites of most chapels or Sunday schools have been located. The Board of Celtic Studies has supplied information concerning dates and costs gleaned from various denominational year books and pamphlets held in the National Library.

Several other sources have been used to supplement the data. In particular, the Religious Census of 1851 and the report of the Royal Commission on the Church of England and other religious bodies in Wales and Monmouthshire in 1911 have been used extensively.

Layout

The order of chapels and Sunday schools follows in general that of the Royal Commission appendices, 1911 (information dating from 1905), wherein they are listed by union, then by civil parish, then by denomination. The spelling of union and parish names is as given in Elwyn Davies's *A Gazetteer of Welsh Place-Names* (Cardiff, 1957), resulting in an order slightly different from that of the Royal Commission.

Tables

The tables are divided into columns as detailed below. The amount of information, together with considerations of space, preclude the reading of the table line for line across the entire page, hence the separate date columns for capacity/cost statistics.

Only those chapels or Sunday schools erected before 1914 are listed although the dates of subsequent rebuildings are included.

NPRN The **N**ational **P**rimary **R**ecord **N**umber is the means of relating all records and other information held in the National Monuments Record, concerning a particular chapel or Sunday school.
Name The form or spelling of names often differs between sources. The forms given here are those selected for the RCAHMW record and in most cases are as shown on the building or in contemporary documents. Alternative names are separated by /.
Locality Where the name of a chapel or Sunday school is the same as that of the town, village or hamlet in which it is located, then the location has been omitted.
NGR The National Grid Reference of all sites has been given to eight figures.

Denomination Where a chapel or Sunday school has been used by more than one denomination, the final one is given, with a note of the others. The exceptions to this rule are subsequent uses as Salvation Army citadels, Roman Catholic or Gospel churches. In these cases the Nonconformist denominations are given.

The abbreviations used are:

B	Baptist
BP	Particular Baptist (these are distinguished only in the Religious Census of 1851)
C	Congregationalist or Independent (no distinction is made between the two)
CM	Calvinistic Methodist
P	Pentecostal
Q	Quaker (Society of Friends)
WM	Wesleyan Methodist
U	Unitarian

Date and Source The dates quoted are those generally agreed upon by the sources used. Where there are substantial disagreements, these are the subject of a note. Variations by one year either way have been ignored. The epithets applied to chapels dates can sometimes be misleading. For example, 'built' often means 'rebuilt', albeit drastically. Where such problems arise in the sources they have been amended for this list. The abbreviations which follow a date refer to the main source and correspond to those listed in *Sources* below.

Architect/Builder Designations appropriate to the person are abbreviated as follows:

A Architect
B Builder
C Carpenter
D Designer

Capacity and Cost 1851 in the date column identifies the source as the Religious Census of that year. Double figures e.g. 112+78 refer to the seated capacity plus standing capacity as listed in the census.

1905 in the date column refers to the Royal Commission report of 1911, the data for which was collected in 1905. Figures in the cost column here refer to the value at that date. Other dates and associated figures are mainly Board of Celtic Studies data.

The abbreviations after the date refer to:

C	Chapel
SS	Sunday School
C+SS	Chapel and Sunday School together

Present Status The present status is the result of field verification by RCAHMW in December 1996 and January 1997. It is notoriously difficult to establish whether or not a building is still actually used for services or other religious purposes and so the designation 'Intact' is applied to those that are complete and appear to be maintained. An asterisk following this designation indicates use for religious purposes other than Nonconformist. The designation 'Other' refers to buildings still extant but in use for other purposes, for example, converted to a dwelling.

Sources

The sources used in compiling this inventory are listed below. The abbreviation which heads each is that which follows a date in the tables.

1 *The Religious Census of 1851 A calendar of the returns relating to Wales. Volume 1 South Wales* (Edited by Ieuan Gwynedd Jones and David Williams. Cardiff, 1976).
2 *Royal Commission on the Church of England and other religious bodies in Wales and Monmouthshire.* Volume VI. Appendices to Minutes of Evidence. Nonconformist County Statistics (London, 1911) [Information dated to 1905].

B Board of Celtic Studies. Capeli database 1997.
D *Tregaron: Historical and Antiquarian* (Revd D. C. Rees, 1936).
H *Walks and Wanderings in County Cardigan*. Appendix C (E. R. Horsfall-Turner, Bingley, Yorks., 1903).
J Index cards to private colour slide collection (Dr Evan James, 1996).
L *Born on a Perilous Rock. Aberystwyth Past and Present* (W. J. Lewis, Aberystwyth, 1980).
P Plaque on building.
R *The Parish Churches and Nonconformist Chapels of Wales: Their Records and Where to Find Them*. Volume 1 Cardigan–Carmarthen–Pembroke (Bert J. Rawlins, Salt Lake City, Utah, USA 1987).
* Royal Commission on the Ancient and Historical Monuments of Wales. Chapels database 1997.

Acknowledgements

Reconciliation and data entry to the RCAHMW database, and field verification, were carried out by Penny Icke and David Percival. Thanks are due to Dr Evan James for the loan of the index to his colour slide collection and to John W. Pritchard, who carried out a research project into the history of chapel building, funded by the Board of Celtic Studies; also to Anne Jones of the National Library of Wales.

NPRN	Name	Locality	NGR	Dm	Date	S	Capacity/Cost		Status

ABERYSTWYTH UNION

ABERYSTWYTH

NPRN	Name	Locality	NGR	Dm	Date	S	Capacity/Cost		Status
7149	BETHEL	Aberystwyth	SN58358130	B	Cause 1787	H	1851: C	650	Intact
					Built 1797	1	1905: C	700 £4500	
					Rebuilt 1833	1			
					Rebuilt 1889	B			
	Schoolroom						1905: SS	400	
					A (1889): William Jones, Ystrad Rhondda				
7148	ALFRED PLACE	Aberystwyth	SN58298179	B	Built 1870	H	1905: C	400 £2500	Intact
	Schoolroom						1905: SS	250	
					A: Richard Owen, Liverpool				
7157	TABERNACL	Aberystwyth	SN58348144	CM	Cause *c*.1770	R	1851: C	1240	Intact
					Built 1785	1	1880:	£4400	
					Rebuilt 1819	H	1905: C	1050 £6000	
					Rebuilt 1832	H			
					Rebuilt 1880	H			
	Schoolroom						1905: SS	450	
					A (1880): Richard Owen, Liverpool				
					B (1880): James Williams, Aberystwyth				
7158	TAN-Y-CAE								
	School Chapel	Aberystwyth	SN58168138	CM	Built 1877	B	1905: C	105 £600	Intact[1]
7159	TREFECHAN								
	School Chapel	Aberystwyth	SN58248115	CM	Built 1887[2]	L	1905: C	220 £1120	Dem.
7153	EBENESER								
	School Chapel	Penparcau	SN59088017	CM	Built 1848	P	1905: C	200 £300	Intact
					Rebuilt 1939	R			
	Sunday School				Founded 1810	R			

[1] In use as a Pentecostal chapel 1997.
[2] B gives 1897.

NPRN	Name	Locality	NGR	Dm	Date	S	Capacity/Cost		Status
11598	SEILO	Aberystwyth	SN58648185	CM	Built 1863	H	1863:	c.£2000	Dem.
					Rebuilt 1868	H	1868:	£3600	
							1905: C	1020 £10000	
	Schoolroom						1905: SS	670	
					A (1863): J. Lumley				
					A (1868): J. P. Seddon				
7156	SKINNER STREET								
	School Chapel	Aberystwyth	SN58728174	CM	Rebuilt 1847[3]	L	1905: C	120 £510	Disused
7154	SALEM	Aberystwyth	SN58498190	CM	Cause 1893	H	1905: C	450 £2910	Intact
					Built 1895	H			
	Schoolroom						1905: SS	180	
					A: Thomas Morgan, Aberystwyth				
7152	ST DAVID'S	Aberystwyth	SN58438193	C	Built 1872	B	1905: C	475 £5000	Other
	Schoolroom						1905: SS	255	
					A: Richard Owen, Liverpool				
7147	SEION	Aberystwyth	SN58358174	C	Built 1814	B	1905: C	740 £5500	Intact
					Rebuilt 1878	*			
	Schoolroom						1905: SS	429	
					A: Richard Owen, Liverpool				
14939	SION	Aberystwyth	SN58128152	C	Cause 1810	*	1823:	164	Intact
					Built 1816	*	1851: C	470	
					Rebuilt 1823	*	1905: C	440 £1050	
					Rebuilt 1873	*			
7146	PORTLAND STREET								
		Aberystwyth	SN58418187	C	Built 1866[4]	H	1866:	£5000	Other
							1905: C	480 £5500	
	Schoolroom						1905: SS	250	
					A: Paull & Robinson, Manchester				
11521	SALEM	Aberystwyth	SN58268155	WM	Built 1807*		1807:	c.£300	Other
					Rebuilt 1842[5]	*	1842:	£400	
7162	ST PAUL'S	Aberystwyth	SN58208159	WM	Built 1880	*	1905: C	700 £6482	Disused
	Schoolroom						1905: SS	250	
					A: Walter P. Thomas, Liverpool				
11595	SILOAM	Aberystwyth	SN58618175	WM	Cause 1859	*	1905: C	250 £600	Other
	Schoolroom				Built 1861	*			
7161	QUEEN'S ROAD	Aberystwyth	SN58458199	WM	Built 1870	*	1905: C	480 £3000	Dem.
	Schoolroom						1905: SS	400	
11597	SOAR	Aberystwyth	SN58428158	WM	Built 1844[6]	*	1851: C	258+400	Intact*
							1905: C	250 £1200	
7160	NEW STREET (LITTLECHAPEL)								
		Aberystwyth	SN58128165	U	Built[7]	*	1905: C	50	Disused
14938	ELIM		SN58168168	P	Rebuilt 1909[8]	*			Other

BRONCASTELLAN

7176	BOW STREET								
	Schoolroom	Bow Street	SN62228450	CM	Built 1909	P			Other

[3]Built as a Poor School 1839; rebuilt as a Sunday School 1847.
[4]H and L give 1866, B gives 1876.
[5]Acquired by the Salvation Army c.1882 and used by them until 1918.
[6]Use by the Wesleyans ended in 1870. Taken over by the Salvation Army 1918.
[7]Used as a Quaker Meeting House c.1898, then as a bookshop, being taken over by the Unitarians in 1906.
[8]Built as a bank c.1870, converted to a chapel 1909.

NPRN	Name	Locality	NGR	Dm	Date	S	Capacity/Cost		Status
CEULAN-Y-MAES-MAWR									
7202	TABERNACL	Tal-y-bont	SN65508952	B	Cause *c.*1804	R	1814:	*c.*£150	Disused
					Built 1812	1	1851: C	306+150	
					Rebuilt 1833	B	1905: C	500 £1670	
	Schoolroom						1905: SS	60	
					A (1833): Revd David Roberts				
7203	SILOH								
	Schoolroom	Pontygeifr	SN68208844	B	Built 1845	1	1905: C	80	Derelict
7204	NAZARETH	Tal-y-bont	SN65428934	CM	Cause 1795	R	1905: C	240 £1865	Intact
					Built 1815	R			
					Rebuilt 1868	P			
					Rebuilt 1890	R			
	Schoolroom						1905: SS	80	
7198	BETHEL	Tal-y-bont	SN65498955	C	Cause 1803	H	1851: C	624+218	Intact
					Built 1805	1	1884:	£1500	
					Rebuilt 1815	H	1905: C	540 £2058	
					Rebuilt 1830	R			
					Enlarged 1884	B			
	Schoolroom						1905: SS	90	
7201	SOAR	Pen-y-sarn-ddu	SN67029108	C	Cause 1865	R	1905: C	150 £100	Derelict
					Built 1867	P			
7199	BETHESDA	Ty-nant	SN69388852	C	Cause 1807	H	1905: C	100 £250	Intact
					Built 1850	H			
					Rebuilt 1881	H			
7200	SEION	Cwm Ceulan	SN69809012	C	Built 1835[9]	R	1905: C	100 £200	Other
					Rebuilt 1872	R			
CLARACH									
7208	NODDFA	Bow Street	SN62108455	C	Built 1903	P	1905: C	250 £850	Intact
7209	HEPHSIBAH								
	Schoolroom	Clarach	SN60508438	C	Cause 1815	H	1851:	35	Derelict
					Built 1837	1	1905: SS	200 £200	
CWMRHEIDOL									
7213	PONTERWYD		SN74888090	CM	Cause 1765	H	1851: C	115+52	Intact
					Built 1800[10]	P	1905: C	430 £1130	
					Rebuilt 1821	H			
					Rebuilt 1854	P			
7212	LLYWERNOG		SN73158078	CM	Built 1867	P	1905: C	86 £191	Other
7210	CWMERGYR		SN79508266	CM			1905: C	100 £220	Derelict
7211	LLWYN-Y-GROES								
	Sunday School	Cwmrheidol	SN70637935	CM	Built 1858[11]	P	1902:	*c.*£400	Restored
					Rebuilt 1902	B			
97040	LLWYN-Y-GROES	Cwmrheidol	SN70947903	CM	Built 1905	P	1905: C	70 £225	Intact
7215	EBENEZER	Ystumtuen	SN73537857	WM	Cause 1811	H	1839:	*c.*£200	Intact
					Built 1822	H	1851: C	306+150	
					Enlarged 1840	H	1859:	£220	
					Enlarged 1859	H	1905: C	430 £1004	
					Rebuilt 1871	B			

[9]B gives 1837.
[10]R gives 1797.
[11]B gives 1843.

NPRN	Name	Locality	NGR	Dm	Date	S	Capacity/Cost			Status
7304	BETHEL	Cwmrheidol	SN72137824	WM	Cause b1859	R	1905: C	150	£220	Intact
					Built 1872	P				

CYFOETH-Y-BRENIN

NPRN	Name	Locality	NGR	Dm	Date	S	Capacity/Cost			Status
7219	LIBANUS	Borth	SN60868975	CM	Built 1877[12]	B	1905: C	314	£1100	Intact*[13]
					Rebuilt 1892	R				
		Sunday School			Founded 1801	R				
					A (1877): Revd David Williams, Aberystwyth					
					B (1877): James Williams, Aberystwyth					
7221	SOAR	Borth	SN60928950	CM	Cause 1826	J				Intact*[14]
					Built 1808	B				
					Rebuilt 1831	1				
97036	BORTH		SN60838992	CM						Other
	(English Presbyterian)									
7218	BETHLEHEM	Llandre	SN62508691	CM	Built 1875	P	1900:		c.£1400	Intact
					Rebuilt 1903[15]	P	1905: C	168	£440	
12109	MORFA	Borth	SN60918999	C	Built 1864[16]	H	1905: C	300	£1200	Disused
7222	SILOH	Borth	SN60838933	WM	Built 1806[17]	H	1832:		c.£150	Other
					Rebuilt 1832	B	1851: C	289+120		
					Rebuilt 1842	1	1871:		c.£1000	
					Rebuilt 1871	H	1901:		£280	
					Rebuilt 1900	B	1905: C	382	£900	
					A (1871): David Williams, Aberystwyth					
					B (1871): Jones & Williams, Borth					

CYNNULL-MAWR

NPRN	Name	Locality	NGR	Dm	Date	S	Capacity/Cost			Status
11589	Y GARN/ PEN-Y-GARN									
		Bow Street	SN62678541	CM	Cause c.1790	H	1833:	502		Intact
					Built 1793	R	1851: C	450		
					Rebuilt 1812	R	1905: C	592	£2390	
					Rebuilt 1833	*				
					Gallery 1865	*				
					Rebuilt 1900	*				

ELERCH

NPRN	Name	Locality	NGR	Dm	Date	S	Capacity/Cost			Status
7230	TABOR Y MYNYDD									
		Nant-y-moch	SN73648859	C			1905: C	80	£100	Dem.

HENLLYS

NPRN	Name	Locality	NGR	Dm	Date	S	Capacity/Cost			Status
7252	BABELL	Dol-y-bont	SN62498821	CM	Built 1874	P	1851: C	15?		Intact
					A: William Williams, David Lewis, Pen-y-bont					
		Schoolroom			Built 1848	1	1905: C	156	£600	
7251	BETHANIA	Staylittle	SN64468949	C	Built c.1865	R	1905: C	200	£200	Other

[12]R gives 1806 but this probably refers to SOAR *q.v.*
[13]In use as a gospel church 1997.
[14]In use as a Roman Catholic church 1997.
[15]B gives 1900.
[16]R gives 1870.
[17]1 gives 1832 but this was probably a rebuilding.

NPRN	Name	Locality	NGR	Dm	Date	S	Capacity/Cost		Status
ISA'N-DRE									
7393	SARON	Llanbadarn Fawr	SN59918078	CM	Built 1842	1	1842:	£402	Intact
							1851: C	344	
		Sunday School			Founded c.1815	R	1905: C	330 £1500	
7392	SOAR	Llanbadarn Fawr	SN60068104	C	Cause 1801	R	1851: C	284	Intact
					Built 1803	1	1905: C	360 £2200	
					Enlarged 1830	R			
	Schoolroom						1905: SS	100	
LLANAFAN									
7254	CAPEL AFAN	Llanafan	SN68387192	CM	Cause 1787	R	1855:	c.£400	Intact
					Built 1806	P	1905: C	300 £730	
					Rebuilt 1856	P			
	Schoolroom						1905: SS	50	
					A: Phylip Pugh				
7253	BRYNAFAN School Chapel		SN70897300	CM			1905: C	60 £90	Other
LLANGYNFELYN									
7333	REHOBOTH	Taliesin	SN65769143	CM	Cause c.1773	R	1851: C	312+60	Intact
					Built 1791	R	1905: C	370 £1825	
					Rebuilt 1833	1			
					Rebuilt 1899	J			
	Schoolroom						1905: SS	300	
7334	YNYS TUDUR School Chapel		SN67249328	CM			1905: C	120 £150	Dem.
97034	SOAR/YR HEN GAPEL	Tre'r-ddôl	SN66059235	WM	Cause 1804	R	1905: C	500 £2400	Other
					Built 1809[18]	*			
					Rebuilt 1845	1			
					Enlarged 1864[19]	R			
					B (1809): John Evans, Aberystwyth				
7335	SOAR	Tre'r-ddôl	SN65959215	WM	Built 1877		1845:	£350	Intact
							1851: C	250+80	
							·1877:	£1700	
LLANDDEINIOL									
7293	ELIM	Llanddeiniol	SN56217206	CM	Cause 1805	R	1851: C	213+167	Intact
					Built 1832	P	1905: C	180 £930	
					Rebuilt 1899	P			
	Schoolroom						1905: SS	80	
					C (1832): John Davies				

[18] 1 gives 1806.
[19] Replaced by new chapel Soar in 1877 after which it was used as a Sunday school.

NPRN	Name	Locality	NGR	Dm	Date	S		Capacity/Cost		Status
LLANGWYRYFON										
7329	TABOR	Llangwyryfon	SN59717064	CM	Cause 1740	R	1851: C	260+200		Intact
					Built 1769[20]	H	1905: C	360	£1500	
					Rebuilt 1789	H				
					Rebuilt 1819	H				
7328	BETHEL	Trefenter	SN60686866	CM	Cause 1807	R	1851: C	252+450		Intact
					Built 1834	R	1905: C	238	£790	
	Schoolroom				Built 1808	1				
7327	SARON	Llangwyryfon	SN59957057	C	Built 1843	P	1851: C	72		Dem.
					Enlarged c.1872	R	1905: C	100	£200	
LLANILAR										
7339	CARMEL	Llanilar	SN62367501	CM	Cause 1788	H	1905: C	530	£1650	Intact
					Built 1796[21]	H				
					Rebuilt 1824	R				
					Rebuilt 1879	P				
	Schoolroom						1905: SS	200		
7340	CILCWM									
	Schoolroom	Rhos-y-garth	SN63557340	CM			1905: C	100		Other
7342	DYFFRYN									
	Schoolroom		SN65057398	CM			1905: C	50	£200	Other
7343	PANT-GLAS									
	School Chapel	Pen-rhiw	SN60507470	CM	Built 1824	P	1905: C	110	£300	Disused
					Rebuilt 1874	P				
7338	BLAEN-PANT									
	School Chapel	Brynamlwg	SN59127274	CM			1905: C	116	£150	Other
7341	DOLFOR FARMHOUSE									
			SN66657172	CM						Other
LLANRHYSTUD-HAMINIOG										
7356	MORIAH	Rhydfudr	SN59626704	CM	Cause 1885	R	1905: C	130	£240	Intact
					Built 1907	P				
7357	PEN-RHIW	Joppa	SN56746678	CM	Cause 1738	H	1851: C	112+150		Intact
					Built 1834	B	1905: C	250	£1000	
					Rebuilt 1859	P				
					Enlarged 1868	J				
					Enlarged 1884	P				
		Sunday School			Founded 1809	R				
	Schoolroom				Built 1834	1				
					B (1834): John Jones, Garn-fach					
					Thomas Evans, Talwrn					
7358	RHIW-BWYS		SN54626923	CM	Cause 1740s		1851: C	396+150		Intact
					Built 1781	P	1905: C	450	£1400	
					Enlarged 1820	P				
					Rebuilt 1832	P				
					Gallery 1871	P				
					Renewed 1926	P				

[20] 1 gives after 1800.
[21] B gives built c.1814 but this may be a rebuild.

NPRN	Name	Locality	NGR	Dm	Date	S	Capacity/Cost		Status
LLANRHYSTUD-MEFENYDD									
7359	SALEM	Llanrhystud	SN53786967	B	Cause *c.*1787	R	1851: C	167+50	Disused
					Built 1823	l	1905: C	160 £300	
11599	TY-CWRDD		SN539697	B	Built 1789[22]		1905: C	90 £120	
7360	BLAENWYRE								
	School Chapel		SN57356962	CM	Built 1849[23]	l	1851: C	88+50	Intact
LLANYCHAEARN									
97052	BLAEN-PLWYF		SN56847482	CM	Cause 1802	H			Other
					Built 1819[24]	l			
7372	BLAEN-PLWYF		SN57617550	CM	Built 1879	P	1851: C	148+120	Intact
							1879:	*c.*£1000	
							1905: C	300 £1400	

A (1879): David Williams, Aberystwyth

NPRN	Name	Locality	NGR	Dm	Date	S	Capacity/Cost		Status
LOWER LLANBADARN-Y-CREUDDYN									
7260	MORIAH		SN61957946	B	Cause *c.*1820	*	1851: C	132	Intact
					Built 1829	P	1905: C	150 £500	
					Rebuilt 1888	P			
7262	GOSEN	Rhydyfelin	SN59067893	CM	Cause 1741	H	1851: C	240+150	Intact
					Built *c.*1760[25]	R	1905: C	350 £1700	
					Rebuilt 1824	l			
	Schoolroom						1905: SS	100	
7261	CAPEL MARIAN								
	School Chapel	Llanfarian	SN58997775	CM	Built 1879	P	1905: C	100 £400	Intact
7263	HOREB	New Cross	SN62897738	CM	Built 1867	P	1905: C	200 £740	Intact
					Rebuilt 1924	P			
	Schoolroom				Built 1853	B			
7259	BEULAH	Dyffryn Paith	SN60647844	C	Cause 1805	R	1851: C	120	Derelict
					Built 1842	P	1905: C	120 £300	
					Renewed 1907	P			
LOWER LLANFIHANGEL-Y-CREUDDYN									
7301	CYNON		SN65537607	CM	Cause 1772[26]	H	1851: C	348	Intact
					Built 1772[27]	R	1905: C	260 £800	
					Rebuilt 1821	l			
7302	RHYD-Y-FAGWYR	Cnwch-coch	SN67907473	CM	Built 1865	P	1905: C	134 £450	Intact
97042	PISGAH		SN67967769	CM	Built 1908	P			Other
7303	CARMEL	Cnwch-coch	SN67757504	WM	Built 1842	P	1851: C	160	Intact
					Rebuilt 1874	P	1905: C	250 £571	
7300	PENUEL		UN	B	Built 1832[28]	B			

[22]Demolished *c.*1840

[23]B gives 1821.

[24]Local tradition says that the original chapel at Blaen-plwyf was at this site and was replaced in 1878 by the present one.

[25]H gives 1741.

[26]R gives before 1755.

[27]R states that the original chapel was built in 1760; B gives built *c.*1791.

[28]There is no reference to a Baptist chapel in Lower Llanfihangel-y-Creuddyn parish in either 1 or 2. Location not known.

NPRN	Name	Locality	NGR	Dm	Date	S	Capacity / Cost			Status

MELINDWR

NPRN	Name	Locality	NGR	Dm	Date	S				Status
7384	JEZREEL	Goginan	SN69028131	B	Cause 1821	H	1851: C	300		Derelict
					Built 1829	P	1905: C	230	£1000	
					Rebuilt 1842	P				
	Schoolroom						1905: SS	80		
7387	PEN-LLWYN	Capel Bangor	SN65318034	CM	Cause 1779	R	1877:		c.£100	Intact
					Built c.1790[29]		1905: C	460	£1673	
					Rebuilt 1821	H				
					Rebuilt 1850	H				
					Rebuilt 1877	B				
					Rebuilt 1899	B				
	Schoolroom						1905: SS	80		
7386	DYFFRYN	Goginan	SN69088127	CM	Built 1842	I	1905: C	500	£1820	Intact
					Rebuilt 1864	J				
		Sunday School			Founded 1780	R				
7385	BLAENRHEIDOL	Nant-y-moch	SN76418712	CM			1905: C	112	£350	Dem.
7388	HOREB	Cwmbrwyno	SN70858069	WM	Built 1859	P	1905: C	160	£250	Dem.

PARSEL CANOL

NPRN	Name	Locality	NGR	Dm	Date	S				Status
7391	CAPEL MADOG	Cefn-llwyd	SN65828228	CM	Built 1854	P	1905: C	226	£800	Intact

RHOSTIE

NPRN	Name	Locality	NGR	Dm	Date	S				Status
7400	RHOS-Y-GARTH									
	Schoolroom		SN63677247	CM			1905: C	94	£80	Other

TIRYMYNACH

NPRN	Name	Locality	NGR	Dm	Date	S				Status
7402	EBENEZER	Bont-goch	SN68318620	WM	Cause 1833	R	1851: C	114+80		Other
					Built 1836	I	1905: C	176	£250	
					Rebuilt 1874	J				

TREFEURIG

NPRN	Name	Locality	NGR	Dm	Date	S				Status
7407	TABERNACL	Cwmsymlog	SN69758385	B	Built 1843	I	1851: C	138		Intact
					Rebuilt 1860	R	1905: C	200	£500	
		Sunday School			Founded 1805	R				
11600	ABERCWMSYMLOG									
	Schoolroom	Pen-bont Rhydybeddau	SN67938352	B	Built 1868[30]	P	1905: SS	90	£180	Other
7405	HOREB	Penrhyn-coch	SN65058415	B	Built 1786	P	1826:		£180	Intact
					Enlarged 1815	P	1851: C	240		
					Rebuilt 1826	B	1905: C	530	£2300	
					Enlarged 1856	P				
7409	BETHLEHEM	Cwmerfyn	SN69768289	CM	Built 1866	P	1905: C	100	£300	Intact
7403	SALEM		SN66898440	C	Cause 1810	R	1851:		£1000	Intact
					Built 1824[31]	P	1905: C	500	£1800	
					Rebuilt 1850	P				
					Enlarged 1864	P				
7404	SILOA	Cwmerfyn	SN70148279	C	Built 1868	R	1905: C	120	£325	Intact
7408	QUAKER		UN	Q	[32]					

[29]Incomplete at the time of 1.
[30]H gives 1865.
[31]1 gives c.1840.
[32]Documentary reference in NLW to Quaker chapel in Trefeurig parish. Location not known.

NPRN	Name	Locality	NGR	Dm	Date	S	Capacity/Cost			Status

UPPER LLANBADARN-Y-CREUDDYN

NPRN	Name	Locality	NGR	Dm	Date	S				Status
7264	ABER-FFRWD		SN68617884	CM	Cause 1756	H	1851: C	258		Disused
					Built 1756[33]	B	1905: C	210	£900	
					Rebuilt 1835	1				
	Schoolroom				Built 1770	H				
7267	SION	Capel Seion	SN63167932	CM	Cause 1804	R	1845:		£47	Intact
					Built 1825[34]	P	1851: C	222		
					Enlarged 1845	P	1905: C	250	£1050	
					Rebuilt 1875	P				
					Renewed 1908	*				
7266	PANT-Y-CRUG									
	School Chapel		SN65277853	CM	Built 1866	J	1905: C	100	£250	Other
					Rebuilt 1902	J				
7265	CEUNANT									
	Schoolroom	Ceunant	SN68517776	CM	Built 1860	R	1905: C	100	£150	Dem.
					Rebuilt 1870	R				

UPPER LLANFIHANGEL-Y-CREUDDYN

NPRN	Name	Locality	NGR	Dm	Date	S				Status
7307	CWMYSTWYTH		SN78547415	CM	Cause 1756	H	1851: C	372+120		Intact
					Built 1805[35]	R	1905: C	500	£2046	
					Rebuilt 1835	1				
					Rebuilt 1870	P				
	Schoolroom						1905: SS	75		
11646	BETHEL									
	Sunday School		SN77077396	CM	Built 1891	P	1905: C	100	£80	Intact
7305	BLAEN-Y-CWM		SN82637551	CM	Cause c.1850	R	1905: C	75	£80	Dem.
					Built 1856	R				
7306	MYNACH	Devil's Bridge	SN73667684	CM	Built 1858[36]	P	1905: C	200	£760	Intact
97033	CAPEL TRISANT		SN71697576	CM	Cause 1814	R	1905: C	300	£1200	Intact
					Built 1820	P				
					Rebuilt 1850	P				
7310	RHOS-Y-GELL	Rhos-fawr	SN74127464	CM	Built 1872	R	1905: C	110	£250	Other
	Schoolroom				Built 1855	R				
7309	RHIWFELEN	Cwm Newyddion	SN71327384	CM			1905: C	125	£200	Intact
7308	MAEN-ARTHUR School Chapel	Pont-rhyd-y-groes	SN73457289	CM	Built 1871	P	1905: C	120	£200	Other
7312	SALEM	Mynydd Bach	SN71877659	WM	Cause 1807	R	1851: C	260		Derelict
					Built 1812	P				
					Rebuilt 1844	P				
					Rebuilt 1875	R				
97043	LISBURNE MINES CHAPEL	Pont-rhyd-y-groes	SN73277293	WM	Built 1852	P				Derelict

[33]R gives 1802.
[34]B gives 1823.
[35]The original chapel was opened in 1783, in a converted blacksmith's shop (Rawlins, 1987). The present chapel dates from 1870 and it is not clear if those of 1805 and 1835 were also on this site.
[36]B gives 1860.

NPRN	Name	Locality	NGR	Dm	Date	S		Capacity/Cost		Status

UPPER VAENOR

NPRN	Name	Locality	NGR	Dm	Date	S		Capacity/Cost		Status
7232	CAPEL DEWI		SN62998239	CM	Cause 1790	H	1851: C	300+200		Dem.
					Built 1812	R	1905: C	200	£950	
					Rebuilt 1842	J				
		Sunday School			Founded 1801	R				
7233	WAUNFAWR									
	School Chapel		SN60118194	CM			1905: C	105	£400	Dem.
7231	EBENEZER	Comins-coch	SN61348209	C	Built 1889	P	1851: C	150		Intact
		Sunday School			Built 1830	P	1905: C	180	£200	
					B (1830): Edward Richards					
					B (1889): R. M. Richards, Newport					

YSGUBOR-Y-COED

NPRN	Name	Locality	NGR	Dm	Date	S		Capacity/Cost		Status
7424	Y GRAIG	Eglwys-fach	SN68529526	CM	Cause b1780	R	1905: C	230	£737	Intact
					Built 1808	R				
					Rebuilt 1840	R				
					Rebuilt 1868	P				
7422	CWM-EINION									
	School Chapel		SN70879387	CM			1905: C	60	£80	Other
7423	GLANDYFI									
	School Chapel		SN69629703	CM	Built 1868	P	1905: C	80	£109	Other
7421	EGLWYS-FACH		SN68739581	C	Built 1900	J	1905: C	120	£550	Other
97037	EGLWYS-FACH		SN68719575	WM	Built 1823[37]	J				Other
					Enlarged 1834	J				
7425	EBENEZER	Eglwys-fach	SN68769572	WM	Built 1844	J	1845:		£86	Other
					Rebuilt 1874	R	1851: C	684+500		
					Rebuilt 1900	B	1900:		£1103	
							1905: C	260	£1100	

TREGARON UNION

BETWS LEUCU

NPRN	Name	Locality	NGR	Dm	Date	S		Capacity/Cost		Status
7169	BANK									
	Schoolroom	Bryn-hir	SN62245777	CM	Built 1872	P			[38]	Other
7168	OLMARCH									
	Schoolroom		SN62525512	C	1905: SS			150	£120	Derelict

BLAENPENNAL

NPRN	Name	Locality	NGR	Dm	Date	S		Capacity/Cost		Status
7172	PENIEL	Blaenpennal	SN63286423	CM	Cause 1709	H	1851: C	300+160		Intact
					Built 1783	P	1905: C	310	£800	
					Rebuilt 1813	P				
					Rebuilt 1868	H				
7171	BRYNSARON									
	Schoolroom		SN61246433	CM			1905: SS	90	£100	Other
7170	BLAEN-AFON	Bontnewydd	SN61906570	CM	Built 1880	R	1905: C	150	£600	Intact
					Rebuilt 1900	J				
		Sunday School			Founded 1810	R				
		Schoolroom			Built 1843	R				

[37]Dates of 1823 and 1834 are quoted for Ebenezer but probably refer to this chapel. The rebuild date of 1844 for Ebenezer probably refers to its building date as a replacement for this chapel.
[38]Sittings and value included in Cwrtmawr Schoolroom (Llangeitho Ph.).

NPRN	Name	Locality	NGR	Dm	Date	S	Capacity/Cost		Status

CARON-IS-CLAWDD

NPRN	Name	Locality	NGR	Dm	Date	S		Capacity/Cost	Status
7178	ARGOED		SN67835890	B	Cause 1718	D			Other
					Built 1760	D			
		Sunday School			Founded 1810	D			
					A (1810): Revd Ebenezer Richard				
12106	BWLCHGWYNT	Tregaron	SN67785962	CM	Built 1774	P	1851: C	376	Intact
					Enlarged 1809	P	1865:	c.£800	
					Rebuilt 1833	P	1905: C	750 £2000	
					Gallery 1865	P	1903: SS	564	
7182	DERI-GARON								
	Schoolroom		SN66415888	CM	Founded 1820	D			
7184	RHIWDYWYLL								
	Schoolroom		SN69835894	CM	Built 1866	D			Intact
7183	GORSNEUADD								
	Schoolroom		SN69245803	CM	Founded 1854	D			Other
7185	TREFLYN								
	Schoolroom		SN69406280	CM	Founded 1810	D			Derelict
7180	BLAENCARON		SN70836115	CM	Built 1875	R	1905: C	140 £500	Intact
					Renewed 1901				
		Sunday School			Founded 1810	D			
					B (1875): John Lloyd, Lampeter				
7179	BERTH	Tyn'reithin	SN66336343	CM	Cause 1809	R	1851: C	170+100	Intact
					Built 1840	1	1905: C	168 £500	
					Rebuilt 1877	B			
					Renewed 1908	P			
12107	WESLEY	Tregaron	SN67965958	WM	Cause 1808	R	1851: C	60	Dem.
					Built 1840	1	1874:	£660	
					Rebuilt 1873	H	1905: C	450 £900	
14946	TAN-YR-ALLT UCHAF (House)								
		Tregaron	SN69836035	MC					Derelict

CARON-UWCH-CLAWDD

7187	RHOSGELLIGRON								
	Schoolroom		SN73566376	B	Built 1906	B	1905: SS	60 £80	Dem.
7188	CWMMOIRO								
	Schoolroom	Strata Florida	SN77026547	CM	Built 1882	P	1905: SS	130 £150	Derelict
7190	GLAN-YR-AFON								
	Schoolroom		SN73036390	CM	Built 1886	J	1905: SS	120 £100	Other
7189	FFLUR								
	Schoolroom		SN71386453	CM			1905: SS	40	Other
7191	GLANTEIFI								
	Schoolroom		SN71816620	CM			1905: SS	30	Dem.

DOETHIE-CAMDDWR[39]

7229	SOAR-Y-MYNYDD		SN78475328	CM	Cause 1747	R	1851: C	156	Intact
					Built 1828	1	1905: C	140 £1000	
					D: Revd Ebenezer Richard, Tregaron				

[39]Nantstalwen, listed in 2 under this parish actually lies in Breconshire.

NPRN	Name	Locality	NGR	Dm	Date	S		Capacity/Cost		Status
7227	CWMTHIE		UN[40]	CM						
7226	CWMTOWY									
	Schoolroom		UN[41]	CM						

GARTHELI

NPRN	Name	Locality	NGR	Dm	Date	S		Capacity/Cost		Status
7235	ABERMEURIG		SN56465624	CM	Built 1698	R	1851: C	520+250		Intact
					Rebuilt 1772	R	1905: C	268	£800	
					Rebuilt 1816	1				
					Rebuilt 1826	B				
					Renewed 1890	R				
7236	LLWYN-Y-GROES	SN59595646	CM				1905: C	170	£750	Other

GOGOYAN

NPRN	Name	Locality	NGR	Dm	Date	S		Capacity/Cost		Status
7237	GOGOYAN									
	Schoolroom		SN64135427	CM				[42]		Derelict

GORWYDD

NPRN	Name	Locality	NGR	Dm	Date	S		Capacity/Cost		Status
7240	BETHESDA	Llanddewibrefi	SN66235540	CM	Cause 1740s	R	1851: C	510		Intact
					Built 1780	B	1905: C	800	£2100	
					Rebuilt 1826	1				
					Rebuilt 1848	P				
					Rebuilt 1873	P				
7241	TAN-YR-ORFA		SN65595325	CM				500[43]	£510	Derelict
	Schoolroom									
7238	BETHLEHEM	Llanddewibrefi	SN65995519	C	Built 1904	P	1905: C	250	£800	Intact
					B: John & Thomas Williams, Ty'n-rhos					
					William Williams, Cefn-bedd					
7239	WERN-DRIW	Llanddewibrefi	SN65645479	Q						Intact[44]
	(Burial Ground)									

GWYNFIL

NPRN	Name	Locality	NGR	Dm	Date	S		Capacity/Cost		Status
7247	CAPEL GWYNFIL	Llangeitho	SN62059979	CM	Cause 1735	R	1813:	c.£2000		Intact
					Built 1760	H	1851: C	428+120		
					Rebuilt 1764	H	1862:	£625		
					Rebuilt 1813	1	1905: C	700	£2700	
					Rebuilt 1863	R				
					Rebuilt 1887	B				
					A (1861): John Lumley, Aberystwyth					
					B (1861): Rees Thomas, Nantmelin					

[40]Although listed in 2 the site has not been identified. It is believed to be in the area of SN7451 and to have been a farmhouse on a Sunday school circuit.

[41]Although listed in 2 the site has not been identified. It is believed to be in the area of SN7454 and to have been a farmhouse on a Sunday school circuit.

[42]Sittings and value included in Tan-yr-orfa Schoolroom (Gorwydd Ph.).

[43]Includes sittings and value for Gogoyan Schoolroom (Gogoyan Ph.), Llanio Schoolroom (Llanio Ph.) and Abercarfan Schoolroom (Prysg and Carfan Ph.).

[44]Burial ground only. Still in use.

NPRN	Name	Locality	NGR	Dm	Date	S	Capacity/Cost			Status
LLANBADARN ODWYN										
14947	LLWYN-RHYS		SN63515987	C	Cause 1672	*				Dem.
					Built b1700[45]	R				
7255	LLWYNPIOD		SN64246095	CM	Built 1753	H	1753:		£13	Intact
					Rebuilt 1803	R	1851: C	70+40		
					Renewed 1853	J	1905: C	240	£950	
					Rebuilt 1881	P				
					B (1753): Phylip Pugh					
					B (1803): T. Grey					
LLANGEITHO										
7317	PEN-UWCH		SN59786225	CM	Built 1837	P				
					Enlarged 1844	J	1851: C	184+100		Intact
					Rebuilt 1867	P	1905: C	356	£1000	
					Renewed 1888	P				
	Sunday School				Built 1817[46]	1				
7318	RHYDYPANDY		SN63476226	CM						Other
	Schoolroom									
7316	CWRTMAWR		SN61846182	CM				500[47]		Derelict
	Schoolroom									
LLANIO										
7346	LLANIO		SN64185695	CM				[48]		Intact
	Schoolroom									
LOWER GWNNWS										
7242	CARADOG	Tyn-y-graig	SN69296943	CM	Built 1869	P	1905: C	200	£672	Intact
LOWER LLEDROD										
7377	BRONNANT		SN64076767	CM	Built 1836	1	1851: C	288+250		Intact
					Rebuilt 1872	J	1905: C	372	£2013	
	Sunday School				Founded 1808	R				
7379	RHYD-LWYD		SN64587085	CM	Cause b1745	R	1851: C	342		Intact
					Built 1755	R	1905: C	320	£1160	
					Rebuilt 1783	R				
					Rebuilt 1809	R				
					Rebuilt 1833	P				
					Rebuilt 1899	P				
7378	CWMLLECHWEDD		UN[49]	CM			1905: SS	100	£130	
	Schoolroom									
7376	BLAEN-WAUN		SN63436943	CM	Built 1880	B	1905: SS	82	£142	Derelict
	Schoolroom									

[45]Replaced by Llwynpiod, 1753.
[46]1 gives 1817 as the date of the chapel but this date probably refers to the building of the Sunday school.
[47]Includes sittings and value for Bank Schoolroom (Betws Leucu Ph.).
[48]Sittings and value included in Tan-yr-orfa Schoolroom (Gorwydd Ph.).
[49]Although listed in 2 the site has not been identified. It is possible that a Sunday school was held at Cwmllechwedd farmhouse.

NPRN	Name	Locality	NGR	Dm	Date	S		Capacity/Cost		Status
NANCWNLLE										
7390	BWLCH-LLAN		SN57975878	CM	Cause b1790	R	1851: C	160+200		Intact
					Built 1841	R	1877:		c.£1200	
	Schoolroom				Rebuilt 1876	P	1905: C	350	£1000	
					Built 1836	I				
					A (1876): Revd Thomas Thomas, Swansea					
					B (1876): David Davies, Brynhyfryd					
PRYSG AND CARFAN										
7399	ABERCARFAN									
	Schoolroom		SN66375735	CM				50		Other
UPPER GWNNWS										
7244	CARMEL	Pontrhydfendigaid								
			SN73076688	B	Built 1836	I	1837:		£200	Intact
					Rebuilt 1872	P	1851: C	270		
					Rebuilt 1911	B	1873:		£523	
							1905: C	400	£750	
							1911:		c.£750	
					A (1911): John Lewis Evans, Aberystwyth					
7243	CAERSALEM	Ffair-rhos	SN74596803	B	Built 1905	J	1905: C	190	£250	Intact
	Schoolroom									
					B (1905): John Jones, Jenkin Jenkins					
7246	RHYDFENDIGAID	Pontrhydfendigaid								
			SN73056665	CM	Built 1794	H	1851: C	330		Intact
					Rebuilt 1802	H	1861:		£1198	
					Rebuilt 1827	B	1905: C	850	£2100	
					Renewed 1859[51]	P	1908:		£1377	
	Schoolroom				Rebuilt 1907	B				
					B (1861): Roderick Jones					
					C (1861): Joseph Hopkins					
12116	Sunday School		SN73056662	CM	Built 1906	*				Intact
7245	GORPHWYSFA	Ffair-rhos	SN73826802	CM	Built 1880	P	1905: SS	160	£200	Disused
	Schoolroom									
UPPER LLEDROD										
7380	BETHEL	Swyddffynnon								
			SN69366616	B	Cause 1820	R	1825:		c.£60	Intact
					Built 1824	P	1905: C	210	£300	
					Rebuilt 1859					
					Rebuilt 1868[52]	P				
					Renewed 1898	P				
					D/B (1859) Daniel Jones					
7383	SWYDDFFYNNON									
			SN69296634	CM	Cause 1743	H	1851: C	300		Intact
					Built 1753	H	1905: C	320	£920	
					Rebuilt 1783[53]	H				
					Rebuilt 1809	H				
					Rebuilt 1837[54]	P				

[50]Sittings and value included in Tan-yr-orfa Schoolroom (Gorwydd Ph.).
[51]B gives 1861.
[52]B gives 1859.
[53]I gives c.1787.
[54]H gives 1833.

NPRN	Name	Locality	NGR	Dm	Date	S	Capacity/Cost		Status
7382	GWENHAFDRE /BANK		SN66926707	CM					Other

YSBYTY YSTWYTH

NPRN	Name	Locality	NGR	Dm	Date	S	Capacity/Cost		Status
97044	MAESGLAS	Ysbyty Ystwyth							
			SN73237144	CM	Built 1818	1	1851: C	240+86	Intact
					Rebuilt 1845[55]	1			
7419	YSBYTY YSTWYTH								
			SN73187130	CM	Built 1874[56]	H	1877:	£1500	
							1905: C	700 £2100	
7418	WAUN-LLOI /BANK								
	Schoolroom	Rhos Waen-lloi	SN75017155	CM	Built 1868	P			Other
7417	HENDRE								
	Schoolroom		SN72026915	CM	Built 1904	P	1905: SS	70 £130	Other
7420	BETHEL	Pont-rhyd-y-groes							
			SN73967244	WM	Built 1810	B	1875:	£1400	Intact
					Rebuilt 1841	B	1905: C	520 £1517	
					Renewed 1874	P			
11699	CAPEL-HELETH		SN74037102	[57]					Dem.

ABERAERON UNION

ABERAERON

NPRN	Name	Locality	NGR	Dm	Date	S	Capacity/Cost		Status
7133	SILOAM	Aberaeron	SN46016301	B	Built 1881	H	1905: C	150 £700	Other
					A (1872): George Morgan				
7134	TABERNACL	Aberaeron	SN45716302	CM	Cause 1897	R	1851: C	308	Intact
					Built 1833	1	1905: C	800	
					Enlarged 1853	R			
					Gallery 1869	R			
		Sunday School			Founded 1807	R			
	Schoolroom						1905: SS	259	
					B (1833): William Green				
					A (1869): Revd Thomas Thomas, Swansea				
7132	PENIEL	Aberaeron	SN45886281	C	Cause 1810	R	1851: C	378+70	Intact
					Built 1833	1	1905: C SS }	1000 £2950	
					Enlarged 1857	H			
					Enlarged 1897	H			
	Schoolroom								
					B (1833): D. Rees & T. Evans				
97035	SALEM	Aberaeron	SN45856301	WM	Cause c.1812	R	1905: C	150 £450	Intact[58]
					Built 1864	R			
					Repaired 1902	J			
7135	UNITARIAN	Aberaeron	UN	U					

[55]Replaced by Ysbyty Ystwyth in 1874. Continues in use as a Sunday school, 1997.
[56]B gives 1877.
[57]Possibly a branch Sunday school of Maesglas (CM).
[58]In use as a Roman Catholic church 1997.

NPRN	Name	Locality	NGR	Dm	Date	S		Capacity/Cost		Status
CILCENNIN										
7205	SEION	Cilcennin	SN51986005	C	Built 1775	1	1851: C	41		Intact
					Rebuilt 1804	J	1860:		c.£400	
					Rebuilt 1835	H	1905: C	350	£400	
7206	EBENEZER/CARN				Rebuilt 1859	P				
		Cilcennin	SN51926042	WM	Cause 1806	R	1851: C	21		Other
					Built 1808	H	1905: C	140	£200	
12137	Sunday School	Cilcennin	SN52056016	59	Rebuilt 1858	B				
										Other
CILIAU AERON										
7207	CILIAU AERON		SN49845847	U	Cause 1650	P	1851: C	156+100		Intact
					Built 1755	P	1899:		c.£335	
					Rebuilt 1899	P	1905: C	1120		
					B (1755): David Davies, Foelallt					
DIHEWYD										
7225	TROED-Y-RHIW		SN49995218	C	Cause 1805	R	1851: C	200+60		Intact
					Built 1808	1	1905: C	150	£360	
					Rebuilt 1861	H				
7224	BETHLEHEM	Dihewyd	SN48605597	C	Rebuilt 1906	J				
					Cause 1840	H	1867:		£300	Intact
					Built 1852	H	1905: C	200	£330	
					Rebuilt 1867	P	1909:		c.£1100	
					Rebuilt 1909	P				
	Sunday School				Built 1845	P				
HENFYNYW UPPER										
7249	FFOS-Y-FFIN		SN44816066	CM	Cause 1765	R	1851: C	306	Intact	
					Built 1780	R	1905: C	200	£600	
					Rebuilt 1831	R				
7248	NEUADD-LWYD		SN47465961	C	Built 1746	P	1851: C	462+70		Intact
					Built 1819	P	1905: C	250	£1000	
					Rebuilt 1869	R				
	Schoolroom				Rebuilt 1906	P				
LLANNARTH										
7354	FRON-WEN	Llannarth	SN42575761	CM	Cause c.1760	R	1905: C	280	£600	Derelict
					Built 1796	R				
					Rebuilt 1818	R				
					Enlarged 1834	R				
7351	LLWYNCELYN		SN44155947	C	Renewed 1857	P				
					Built 1855	P	1905: C	361	£560	Intact
7350	BRYNRHIWGALED									
		Pentre'r-bryn	SN39895508	C	Built 1781	H	1905: C	420	£966	Intact
					Rebuilt 1894	P				
	Schoolroom									
					A (1894): T. G. Thomas, Blaendyffryn					

[59] Used by various denominations.

NPRN	Name	Locality	NGR	Dm	Date	S	Capacity/Cost			Status
7352	MYDROILYN		SN45825526	C[60]	Cause b1750	R	1851: C	192+100		Intact
					Built 1753	J	1897:		c.£900	
					Rebuilt 1832[61]	P	1905: C	443	£1028	
					Rebuilt 1898	P				
7353	PENCAE		SN43115665	C	Cause 1819	R	1851: C	246		Intact
					Built 1825	P	1905: C	443	£620	
					Rebuilt 1856	P				
7355	CAPEL FICER		SN45225640	WM	Cause 1806	H	1849:		£200	Intact
					Built 1810	P	1851: C	222+100		
					Rebuilt 1849	P	1905: C	180	£250	

LLANBADARN TREFEGLWYS

NPRN	Name	Locality	NGR	Dm	Date	S	Capacity/Cost			Status
7258	PONTRHYDSAESON		SN54326314	CM	Built 1824	P	1851: C	161		Intact
					Rebuilt 1841	P	1905: C	300	£550	
					Rebuilt 1871	P				
					Rebuilt 1928	P				
		Sunday School			Founded 1806	R				
	Schoolroom				Built 1824	1				
7257	PENNANT		SN51286310	CM	Cause 1740	R	1851: C	312		Intact
					Built 1760[62]	R	1905: C	350	£700	
					Rebuilt 1832	P				
					Rebuilt 1883	P				
					B (1760): Morgan Evan Hugh					
7256	BETHANIA		SN57196301	CM	Built 1809	1	1851: C	294+100		Intact
					Rebuilt 1832	P	1905: C	290	£1500	
					Enlarged 1872	P				
					C (1809): Dafydd Jones, Banceithin					
					B (1872): James Williams, Aberystwyth					

LLANDDEWI ABER-ARTH UPPER

NPRN	Name	Locality	NGR	Dm	Date	S	Capacity/Cost			Status
7294	BETHEL	Aber-arth	SN47886386	CM	Built c.1768[63]	B	1851: C	396		Intact
					Rebuilt 1805[64]	P	1905: C	350	£815	
					Rebuilt 1846[65]	P				
					Renewed 1900	R				
7295	TAN-Y-BRYN		SN48436147	CM	Cause c.1815[66]	R	1905: C	120	£560	Derelict
					Built 1864	P				
	Schoolroom				Built 1834	P				

LLANDYSILIOGOGO

NPRN	Name	Locality	NGR	Dm	Date	S	Capacity/Cost			Status
7278	LLWYNDAFYDD		SN37045560	BP	Built 1779[67]	P	1851: C	246+89		Intact
					Rebuilt 1829	P	1905: C	250	£450	
					Renewed 1898	P				
7279	NEUADD	Nanternis	SN36935615	CM	Built 1867	R	1905: C	200	£582	Disused

[60]Originally the chapel served all denominations but by 1800 was Independent.
[61]B gives 1837.
[62]R gives 1744, P gives 1868.
[63]R gives 1790.
[64]1 gives 1803.
[65]R gives 1848.
[66]H gives 1740.
[67]H gives 1796.

NPRN	Name	Locality	NGR	Dm	Date	S	Capacity/Cost			Status
7280	PENSARN	Hafodiwan	SN38105482	CM	Cause c.1744	R	1851: C	372+70		Intact
					Built 1795	P	1905: C	300	£400	
					Enlarged 1806	R				
					Enl. c.1815	R				
					Rebuilt 1833	P				
					Rebuilt 1875	B				
7277	PISGAH		SN41455138	C	Built 1821	1				Intact
					Rebuilt 1849	B				
					Rebuilt 1871[68]	P				
7276	NANTERNIS		SN37245647	C	Built 1867	P	1905: C	360	£751	Intact
7281	CAPEL Y FADFA	Bwlchyfadfa	SN43644951	U	Built 1813	P	1851: C	192		Intact
					Rebuilt 1830	P	1905: C	350	£1300	
					Rebuilt 1850	B				
					Rebuilt 1874	P				
					Rebuilt 1905	P				

LLANFIHANGEL YSTRAD

NPRN	Name	Locality	NGR	Dm	Date	S	Capacity/Cost			Status
7313	TY'N-Y-GWNDWN	Felin-fach	SN53785514	C	Cause 1672		1835:		£150	Intact
					Built 1773	P	1851: C	300+100		
					Rebuilt 1815	R	1892:		£300	
					Rebuilt 1835	P	1905: C	350	£1000	
					Gallery 1861	J				
					Restored 1892	P				
7315	RHYD-Y-GWIN		SN53485392	U	Built 1808	B	1851: C	300		Intact
					Rebuilt 1848	P	1905: C	250	£950	
					Rebuilt 1893	J				
7314	CRIBYN		SN52265104	U	Built 1790	P	1851: C	+500		Intact
					Rebuilt 1851	P	1905: C	220	£800	
					B (1790): Lewis Lewis, Pen-lan					

LLANINA

NPRN	Name	Locality	NGR	Dm	Date	S	Capacity/Cost			Status
7345	WERN		SN41065902	C	Cause 1815	R	1905: C	360	£500	Intact
					Built 1851	P				
	Schoolroom						1905: SS	60		

LLANLLWCHAEARN

NPRN	Name	Locality	NGR	Dm	Date	S	Capacity/Cost			Status
7349	PENUEL	Cross Inn	SN39015731	CM	Cause 1869	R	1905: C	200	£250	Intact[69]
					Built 1872[70]	P				
					Rebuilt 1910	P				
7348	PENRHIWGALED		SN39865635	C	Cause c.1760	R	1851: C	480+80		Other
					Built 1781	R				
					Rebuilt c.1818	*				
					Rebuilt 1828	P				
7347	MAEN-Y-GROES		SN38575894	C	Built 1828	P	1851: C	294	Intact	
					Enlarged 1873	R				
					Rebuilt 1902	P	1905: C	470 ⎫ £1951		
	Schoolroom						1905: SS	160 ⎭		

[68]B gives 1875.
[69]In use as a gospel church 1997.
[70]B gives 1867, R gives 1874.

NPRN	Name	Locality	NGR	Dm	Date	S	Capacity/Cost			Status

LLANSANFFRAID

7363	LLAN-NON/CAPEL MAWR		SN51296678	CM	Built 1762	P	1851: C	504		Intact
		Llannon			Rebuilt 1797[71]	B	1905: C	750	£1600	
					Rebuilt 1815	P				
					Rebuilt 1844	P				
					Enlarged 1865	P				
					B (1762): Siôn Alban					
7361	NEBO		SN54646518	C	Cause 1805	R	1851: C	150+100		Intact
					Built 1808	R	1905: C	315	£1150	
					Rebuilt 1835	P				
					Rebuilt 1914	P				
7362	SILOH	Llannon	SN51626712	C	Built 1864	P	1762:		£15	Intact
							1905: C	400	£965	
14944	HAFOD YSGOLDY	Cwm Peris	SN55016739	CM	Built 1905	P				Other

NEW QUAY

7193	BETHEL	New Quay	SN38865965	BP	Built 1849[72]	P	1851: C	114+60		Intact
							1905: C	260	£500	
7194	TABERNACL	New Quay	SN38935982	CM	Cause 1744	H	1851: C	720+100		Intact
					Built 1807	P	1861:		£1400	
					Rebuilt 1837	P	1905: C	800	£3000	
					Rebuilt 1861	P				
7192	TOWYN	New Quay	SN38745971	C	Cause 1858	R	1905: C	800	£3800	Intact
					Built 1860	P				
					Rebuilt 1865	J				
	Schoolroom				Built 1899	J				
					A (1860): Thomas Jones, Pen-cnwc					
					A (1865): Revd Thomas Thomas, Swansea					
7195	SION	Maen-y-groes	SN38865898	WM	Cause c.1807	R				Derelict
					Built 1812	H				

LAMPETER UNION

CELLAN

7196	CAPEL YR ERW	Cellan	SN60394882	C	Built 1811	P	1851: C	200+200		Intact
					Rebuilt 1863	P	1905: C	250	£559	
					Renewed 1933	P				
					A (1863): Revd. Thomas Thomas, Landore					
7197	CAERONNEN	Cellan	SN60634895	U	Built 1654	P	1905: C	200	£850	Intact
					Rebuilt 1747	P				
					Rebuilt 1846	P				
					Rebuilt 1861	B				
					Renewed 1925	P				

LAMPETER RURAL

| 7273 | EMMAUS | Pentre-bach | SN54704730 | C | Built 1894 | P | 1905: SS | 135 | £200 | Other |
| | Schoolroom | | | | | | | | | |

[71] H gives 1804.
[72] B gives 1851.

NPRN	Name	Locality	NGR	Dm	Date	S	Capacity/Cost			Status

LAMPETER URBAN

7269	NODDFA	Lampeter	SN58084777	B	Built 1897	H	1905: C	252	£700	Intact
	Schoolroom						1905: SS	40		
14932	TABERNACL	Lampeter	SN57584812	CM	Cause 1743	R	1851: C	278+120		Other
					Built 1775	R				
					Rebuilt 1806	1				
					Rebuilt 1874	R				
7270	SHILOH	Lampeter	SN57474817	CM	Cause 1743	R	1874:		£2000	Intact
					Built 1775	H	1905: C	350	£1900	
					Rebuilt 1806	H				
					Rebuilt 1874	H				
					Rebuilt 1892	B				
	Schoolroom						1905: SS	50		

A (1874): Richard Owen, Liverpool
B (1874): James Williams, Liverpool

7268	SOAR	Lampeter	SN57684795	C	Cause 1831	R	1851: C	216+150		Intact
					Built 1842	1	1905: C }			
					Enlarged 1874	B	SS }	600	£2300	
					Enlarged 1895	J				
	Schoolroom									
7272	ST THOMAS	Lampeter	SN57724804	WM	Cause 1806	H	1875:		c.£800	Intact
					Built 1811	H	1905: C	350	£1128	
					Rebuilt 1829	H				
					Enlarged 1845	H				
					Rebuilt 1875	H				

D (1875): Davies, Llanybydder
B (1875): Davies & Jones, Llangybi

7271	BRONDEIFI	Lampeter	SN58134786	U	Cause 1800	H	1904:		£2043	Intact
					Built 1876	H	1905: C	300	£2800	
					Rebuilt 1902[73]	J				
	Schoolroom						1905: SS	50		

LLANFAIR CLYDOGAU

7296	CAPEL MAIR	Llanfair Clydogau								
			SN62175143	C	Cause 1790	R	1825:		£104	Intact
					Built 1825	P	1851: C	270		
					Rebuilt 1845[74]					
					Gallery 1861	J				
					Rebuilt 1911	B	1905: C	400 }		
	Schoolroom						1905: SS	60 }	£700	

B (1825): Thos. Williams, Pontrhydfendigaid
A (1911): J. Lloyd Lewis

| 7297 | YSGOLDY FACH | | | | | | | | | |
| | Sunday School | | SN64455099 | C | Built 1865 | B | | | | Other |

LLANGYBI

| 7164 | PEN-Y-COED | Betws Bledrws | SN58855201 | B | Cause 1654 | P | | | | Dem. |
| | | | | | Built 1735[75] | P | | | | |

[73]B gives 1904.
[74]B gives 1847.
[75]Disused from 1840.

NPRN	Name	Locality	NGR	Dm	Date	S	Capacity/Cost		Status
7331	MAES-Y-FFYNNON	Llangybi	SN60575283	CM	Built 1837	B	1851: C	102	Intact
							1905: C	250 £600	
7330	EBENEZER	Llangybi	SN61035323	C	Built 1772	B	1905: C	406 £1200	Intact
					Rebuilt 1841	B			
					Rebuilt 1859	B			
					Rebuilt 1890	B			
7332	CILGWYN	Llangybi	SN60755301	WM	Built c.1654	B	1851: C	198	Other
					Rebuilt 1825	B	1905: C	200 £230	
					Rebuilt 1840	B	1906:	£65	
					Rebuilt 1906	B			

LLANWENOG

NPRN	Name	Locality	NGR	Dm	Date	S	Capacity/Cost		Status
7367	SEION	Cwrtnewydd	SN48914785	B	Built 1820[76]	P	1851: C	100	Intact
					Rebuilt 1881	P	1905: C	250 £300	
					Enlarged 1929	P			
7366	BRYN-HAFOD/CRUG	Gors-goch	SN48335063	B[77]	Built 1711	1	1851: C	150	Intact
					Rebuilt 1861	P	1905: C	350 £500	
7364	BETHEL/TREFACH	Dre-fach	SN50304587	C	Built 1880	P	1851: C	120+120	Intact
					Built 1847[78]	1	1905: C	150 £500	
	Sunday School								Intact
7365	BRYN-TEG		SN48554389	C	Cause 1834	R	1851: C	390	
					Built 1838	P	1905: C	400 £700	
7369	CAPEL Y BRYN	Cwrtnewydd	SN49134766	U	Cause c.1829[79]		1905: C	250 £1000	Intact
					Built 1867[80]	H			
					Rebuilt 1881	P			
7368	ALLTYBLACA		SN52394589	U	Built 1740	P	1851: C	240	Intact
					Rebuilt 1832[81]	P	1905: C	250 £800	
					Restored 1892	P			
7370	CAPEL Y CWM	Cwmsychbant	SN47704617	U	Cause 1896	J	1905: C	100 £600	Intact
					Built 1906	P			
12130	Sunday School		SN48884795						Derelict

LLANWNNEN

NPRN	Name	Locality	NGR	Dm	Date	S	Capacity/Cost		Status
7371	CAPEL Y GROES	Llwyn-y-groes	SN52684802	U	Built 1802	P	1851: C	500	Intact
					Rebuilt 1890	P	1905: C	300 }£1000	
	Schoolroom						1905: SS	120	

B (1890): David Davies, Lampeter

SILIAN

NPRN	Name	Locality	NGR	Dm	Date	S	Capacity/Cost		Status
7401	BETHEL	Silian	SN57775083	B	Built 1831[82]	P	1851: C	185+100	Intact
							1905: C	120 £500	

[76]B gives c.1829.
[77]Originally Independent; became Baptist in 1800.
[78]H gives 1810.
[79]H gives 1836.
[80]B gives c.1875.
[81]B gives 1837.
[82]B gives 1834.

NPRN	Name	Locality	NGR	Dm	Date	S	Capacity/Cost			Status

TREFELIN

7410	CAPEL HARMON	Trichrug	SN54395861	CM	Cause 1743	H	1905: C	70	£200	Other
					Built 1882	P				
		Sunday School			Founded 1806	J				

NEWCASTLE EMLYN UNION

BETWS IFAN

7167	TAN-Y-GROES		SN28514937	CM	Cause 1742	R	1882:		c.£800	Intact
					Built 1849	P				
					Rebuilt 1882	P				
7166	BRYNGWYN		SN30034490	C	Cause 1841	R	1905: C	400	£600	Intact
					Built 1843[83]	P				
					Rebuilt 1900	P				
		Schoolroom			Built 1838	1				
7165	BEULAH		SN28794609	C	Built 1860	P	1851: C	147		Intact
					Rebuilt 1884	P	1905: C	450	£1300	
		Schoolroom			Built 1831	1	1905: SS	120		

BRONGWYN

97039	Y DREWEN	Cwm-cou	SN29274183	C	Cause 1672	R	1814:		£400	Intact
					Built c.1736	1	1851: C	400		
					Rebuilt 1814	R				
					Rebuilt 1843	R				
					Rebuilt 1859	R				
					Rebuilt 1912	J				
					Rebuilt 1921	B	1905: C }	600	£600	
		Schoolroom					SS }			

HENLLAN

7250	CAPEL DRINDOD	Aber-banc	SN35484180	[84]	Built 1794	P	1851: C	300+300		Intact
					Rebuilt 1864[85]	P	1905: C	300	£1000	
		Schoolroom					1905: SS	100		

LLANDYSUL

7285	EBENEZER	Llandysul	SN41674057	BP	Built 1833	P	1905: C	400	£500	Other
7286	TABERNACL	Llandysul	SN41554041	CM	Built 1832	1	1851: C	204+324		Intact
							1905: C	200	£500	
7287	WAUNIFOR	Maesycrugiau	SN46524141	CM	Built 1760	P	1851: C	21		Intact
					Rebuilt 1854[86]	P	1905: C	90	£400	
					Restored 1887	P				
					B (1760): Thomas Bowen, Waunifor					
7284	SEION	Llandysul	SN41634067	C	Built 1871	R	1905: C	550 }	£2650	Intact
		Schoolroom					1905: SS	325 }		
					A: Revd Thomas Thomas, Landore					

[83]R gives 1867.
[84]Joint CM and C chapel.
[85]R gives 1874.
[86]B gives 1857.

NPRN	Name	Locality	NGR	Dm	Date	S		Capacity/Cost		Status
7282	CARMEL	Pren-gwyn	SN42644450	C	Built 1819	1	1851: C	264		Intact
					Rebuilt 1832	1				
	Schoolroom						1905: SS	100	£500	
					B (1819): John Jones, Pantydefaid					
7283	HOREB		SN39434250	C	Built 1784	P	1851: C	480		Intact
					Rebuilt 1826	P	1905: C	360	£820	
					Enlarged 1832	R				
					Enlarged 1879	P				
7292	PENIEL	Llandysul	SN41794064	WM	Cause 1806	H	1851: C	300		Disused
					Built 1808	P	1901:		£350	
					Rebuilt 1844	P	1905: C	200	£600	
					Rebuilt 1902	P				
12132	CAPEL ENOCH	Capel Dewi	SN44944235	WM	Cause 1812[87]		1851: C	250		Derelict
					Built 1833	P				
7291	BETHEL	Capel Dewi	SN44974240	WM	Built 1901[88]					Intact
							1903:		£800	
							1905: C	340	£1000	
7290	PANT-Y-DEFAID	Pren-gwyn	SN42524420	U	Built 1802	P	1851: C	240		Intact
					Rebuilt 1836	P				
					Rebuilt 1898	P	1905: C	280 }	£200	
	Schoolroom						1905: SS	180		
11594	LLWYNRHYDOWEN (OLD)		SN44374521	U	Cause 1726	H	1851: C	42		Intact
					Built 1733	1				
					Rebuilt 1754	B				
					Rebuilt 1791	1				
					Renewed 1834[89]	1				
					B (1733): Jenkin Jones, Pantydefaid					
7289	LLWYNRHYDOWEN (NEW)		SN44154585	U	Built 1879	*	1905: C	600	£2200	Intact
					B: Watcyn Davies					
14940	MYFYRGELL[90]	Llandysul	SN41604061	U						Other
7288	CAPEL Y GRAIG	Llandysul	SN41714071	U	Cause 1868	H	1884:		£745	Intact
					Built 1884	P	1905: C	220	£750	
					Rebuilt 1906	B	1906:		c.£80	
					A (1884): John Wills, Derby					
					B (1884): Watkin Davies					

LLANFAIR ORLLWYN

7298	GWERN-LLWYN	Penrhiw-llan	SN37254238	C	Built 1863	P	1903:		£1000	Intact
					Rebuilt 1903	P	1905: C	600	£1609	
12124	Sunday School		SN37224243							Intact

LLANFAIR TREFLYGEN

7299	BRYNGWENITH		SN34074345	C	Cause 1832	R	1884:		£700	Intact
					Built 1834	R	1905: C	350	£950	
					Enlarged 1854	R				
					Rebuilt 1883	P				
	Schoolroom						1905: SS	50	£50	

[87] R gives 1808.
[88] Replacing Capel Enoch. B gives 1903.
[89] The congregation were evicted from the chapel in 1862.
[90] Private house.

NPRN	Name	Locality	NGR	Dm	Date	S	Capacity/Cost			Status

LLANGRANNOG

NPRN	Name	Locality	NGR	Dm	Date	S				Status
14945	GWNDWN OLD	Pentregât	SN35445196	B	Cause 1826	R	1851: C	108		Dem.
					Built 1830[91]	1	1905: C	150	£300	
					Repaired 1894	J				
12128	GWNDWN		SN34015213	B	Built 1910	J	1903: C	120		Other
7325	BANCYFELIN	Llangrannog	SN31525402	CM	Cause 1775	R	1905: C	380	£1000	Intact
					Built 1863	R				
7326	CAPEL Y FFYNNON/WORVILLE BROOK									
		Pentregât	SN35375195	CM	Built 1849	1	1851: C	c.250		Other
							1905: C	310	£1250	
	Schoolroom				Built 1840	J				
7323	CAPEL-Y-WIG		SN34355474	C	Built 1813	P	1851: C	528		Intact
					Rebuilt 1848[92]	P	1852:		£700	
					Renewed 1926	P	1905: C	500 ⎫	£1600	
	Schoolroom						1905: SS	130 ⎭		
12126	BODWENOG/CRANNOG									
		Llangrannog	SN31295413	A	Built 1888	P				Intact
7322	CAPEL CRUGIAU									
		Plwmp	SN36585237	C	Built 1848[93]	P	1851: C	200+108		Intact
					Rebuilt 1858	P	1905: C	350	£800	
					Rebuilt 1897	P				

LLANGYNLLO

NPRN	Name	Locality	NGR	Dm	Date	S				Status
7337	COED-Y-BRYN		SN35354525	CM	Built 1886[94]	P	1905: C	160	£500	Intact
7336	BWLCH-Y-GROES									
			SN37924625	C	Cause 1820	R	1851: C	234+50		Intact
					Built 1835[95]	P	1905: C	450	£1000	
					Rebuilt 1880	P				
	Sunday School				Founded 1830	R				

PENBRYN

NPRN	Name	Locality	NGR	Dm	Date	S				Status
7324	CAPEL-GWNDA	Felin-Wnda	SN32254717	B	Built 1828	B				Dem.
7397	PENMORFA		SN30485218	CM	Cause 1743	R	1851: C	302	£650	Intact
					Built 1796	P	1905: C	470	£850	
					Rebuilt 1846	P				
					Renewed 1939	P				
7398	WATCHTOWER		SN29944706	CM	Built 1865	R				Other
12115	TRE-SAITH		SN27965145	CM						Other
7395	GLYNARTHEN		SN31084855	C	Cause 1783	H	1841:		£700	Intact
					Built 1797	H	1851: C	500	£700	
					Rebuilt 1841	1	1905: C	650	£2478	
					Renov. 1901	H				
	Schoolroom						1905: SS	125		
7394	BRYN-MORIAH	Brynhoffnant	SN33035130	C	Built 1848	P	1862:		£300	Intact
					Enlarged 1861	R	1886:		£600	
					Rebuilt 1884[96]	P	1905: C	420	£1050	

[91]Replaced by a new chapel 1910.
[92]B gives 1852.
[93]H gives 1815.
[94]R gives 1866.
[95]1 gives 1833.
[96]B gives 1886.

NPRN	Name	Locality	NGR	Dm	Date	S	Capacity/Cost		Status
TROED-YR-AUR									
7415	TŴR-GWYN	Rhydlewis	SN35174767	CM	Cause 1743	R	1851: C	410+100	Intact
					Built 1750	P	1905: C	400 £1250	
					Enlarged 1779	P			
					Rebuilt 1816	P			
					Renewed 1846	P			
					Rebuilt 1932	P			
7414	SALEM	Brongest	SN32404502	CM	Cause c.1780	R	1851: C	220+286	Intact
					Built 1811	P	1887:	£501	
					Rebuilt 1885[97]	P	1905: C	350 £760	
					D (1887): Davies, Penrhiw-llan				
7412	HAWEN		SN34644680	C	Built 1747[98]	P	1851: C	400	Intact
					Rebuilt 1790	P	1905: C	380 £1480	
					Rebuilt 1811	P			
					Rebuilt 1838	P			
					Renewed 1878	P			
12117	Sunday School		SN34674684						Intact

CARDIGAN UNION

NPRN	Name	Locality	NGR	Dm	Date	S	Capacity/Cost		Status
ABER-PORTH									
7138	BLAENANNERCH		SN24794910	CM	Cause 1740	R	1851: C	336	Intact
					Built 1794	P	1905: C	500 £1500	
					Enlarged 1808	P			
					Rebuilt 1838	P			
					Renewed 1896	P			
7137	ABER-PORTH		SN25785140	CM	Cause 1739	R	1851: C	234	Intact
					Built 1833	P	1859:	£450	
					Rebuilt 1859	P	1901:	c.£1250	
					Renewed 1901	P	1905: C	750 £2000	
		Sunday School			Founded 1802	R			
	Schoolroom						1905: SS	200	
BLAEN-PORTH									
7175	BRYN SEION	Aber-porth	SN26155152	CM	Cause 1873	R	1905: C	150 £880	Other
					Built 1874[99]	R	1851: C	150	Intact
7173	BRYN-MAIR		SN26735018	C	Built 1833	P	1905: C	400 £900	
					Rebuilt 1897	P			
CARDIGAN SAINT MARY'S									
7141	BETHANIA/BETHANY	Cardigan	SN17854618	BP	Built 1775	1	1847:	£1800	Intact
					Rebuilt 1819	R	1851: C	900	
					Built 1843[100]	*	1905: C	900 £5000	
					A (1847): Daniel Evans				

---

[97]B gives 1887.
[98]B and R give 1769.
[99]B gives 1883.
[100]The present building dates from 1843 (B gives 1847). The references in 1 and R suggest that there was an earlier chapel on this site.

NPRN	Name	Locality	NGR	Dm	Date	S		Capacity / Cost		Status
7142	MOUNT ZION (English)									
		Cardigan	SN17874615	B	Built 1880	*	1905: C	260	£1450	Intact
					A: George Morgan, Carmarthen					
					B: William Woodward					
14933	CAPEL BACH	New Mill	SN18774747	B						Dem.
7143	TABERNACL	Cardigan	SN17754623	CM	Cause 1740s	H	1851: C	402		Intact
					Built 1760	H	1902:		c.£1000	
					Rebuilt 1807	R	1905: C	800	£2300	
					Rebuilt 1832	R				
					Renewed 1864	R				
					Enlarged 1902	B				
7139	CAPEL MAIR	Cardigan	SN17994611	C	Cause 1792	R	1851: C	380		Intact
					Built 1803	H	1870:		£1400	
					Rebuilt 1831	H	1905: C	600	£3000	
					Rebuilt 1869	H				
					Rebuilt 1889	*				
					A (1869): Revd Thomas Thomas, Swansea					
					B (1869): J. R. Daniel					
					B (1889): D. Davies					
14943	HOPE (English)	Cardigan	SN17864598	C	Rebuilt 1837[101]	l				
7140	HOPE (English)	Cardigan	SN17844631	C	Built 1880	*	1905: C	500	£1800	Dem.
7144	EBENEZER	Cardigan	SN17834613	WM	Cause 1809	J	1851: C	196+90		Other
					Built 1827[102]					
					Rebuilt 1844					
					Rebuilt 1879					
					B (1879): David Williams					

LLANDYGWYDD

NPRN	Name	Locality	NGR	Dm	Date	S		Capacity / Cost		Status
7275	CAPEL CENARTH		SN26824163	CM	Cause 1869[103]	R	1905: C	150	£500	Intact
					Built 1872	J				
7274	BETHESDA	Pont-hirwaun	SN26144515	C	Built 1840	P	1851: C	340		Intact
					Rebuilt 1870	R	1905: C			
					Rebuilt 1923	J	SS	} 450	£600	
					Rebuilt 1935	J				
	Schoolroom									

LLANGOEDMOR

NPRN	Name	Locality	NGR	Dm	Date	S		Capacity / Cost		Status
7320	PENPARC		SN21204789	BP	Cause b1750	R	1838:		£390	Intact
					Built 1769[104]	P	1851: C	436+90		
					Enlarged 1809	P	1905: C	700		
					Rebuilt 1838	P	1905: SS	120	} £2300	
					Rebuilt 1856	B				
	Schoolroom									
7319	BLAEN-WENEN	Pant-gwyn	SN24274666	B	Built 1838	P	1851: C	198		Intact
					Renov. 1938	P	1905: C	200	£300	
	Schoolroom				Built 1928	P				

[101]The existing building was converted into a chapel in 1837. It was replaced by a new chapel in 1910 and was later used by the Salvation Army.
[102]Closed as a chapel 1884.
[103]H gives 1794.
[104]H gives 1780.

NPRN	Name	Locality	NGR	Dm	Date	S	Capacity/Cost		Status
LLECHRYD									
97054	LLWYN-ADDA	Llechryd	SN21474401	CM	Cause c.1740	R			Other
					Built 1791[105]	P			
7375	LLWYN-ADDA	Sunday School Llechryd	SN21474400	CM	Founded 1804	R			Intact
					Built 1829	P	1851: C	264	
					Renewed 1878	R	1878:	c.£800	
							1905: C	350 £1500	
11593	CAPEL ISAF	Llechryd	SN21664383	CM	Built 1709	H	1872:	£150	Intact
					Rebuilt 1834	P	1905: C	450 £1000	
7374	TABERNACL	Llechryd	SN21824377	C	Built 1881	P	1905: C	332 £1395	Intact
MOUNT									
7389	BLAEN-Y-CEFN	Login	SN20745035	CM	Cause 1744	R	1851: C	200+40	Intact
					Built 1808	P	1905: C	300	
					Rebuilt 1837	P	1905: SS	60 }£900	
					Repaired 1869	J			
					Repaired 1884	R			
	Schoolroom								

B (1808): J. Williams, Ffynnongrog

            D. Lewis, Blaenwaunifor

NPRN	Name	Locality	NGR	Dm	Date	S	Capacity/Cost		Status
ST DOGMAELS MUNICIPAL									
11695	BLAENYWAUN		SN16134484	B	Cause 1706	R	1903: C	200	Intact
					Built 1745	R			
					Rebuilt 1795	R			
					Rebuilt 1838[106]	H			
					Rebuilt 1885	J			
					A (1885): Owen Lewis				
					B (1885): John Davies				
TRE-MAIN									
7411	FFYNNON-BEDR	Pen-rhiw	SN22734992	C	Built 1865	P	1890:	£400	Intact
					Rebuilt 1889	P	1905: C	300 £800	
Y Ferwig									
7234	SILOAM	Y Ferwig	SN18464962	B	Cause c.1770	R	1831:	c.£190	Intact
					Built 1796	P	1851: C	31	
					Rebuilt 1837[107]	P	1905: C	400 £900	

[105]Replaced by a new chapel adjacent 1829 and converted to a vestry.
[106]H gives 1838 as building date but this was presumably a rebuild.
[107]H gives 1901.

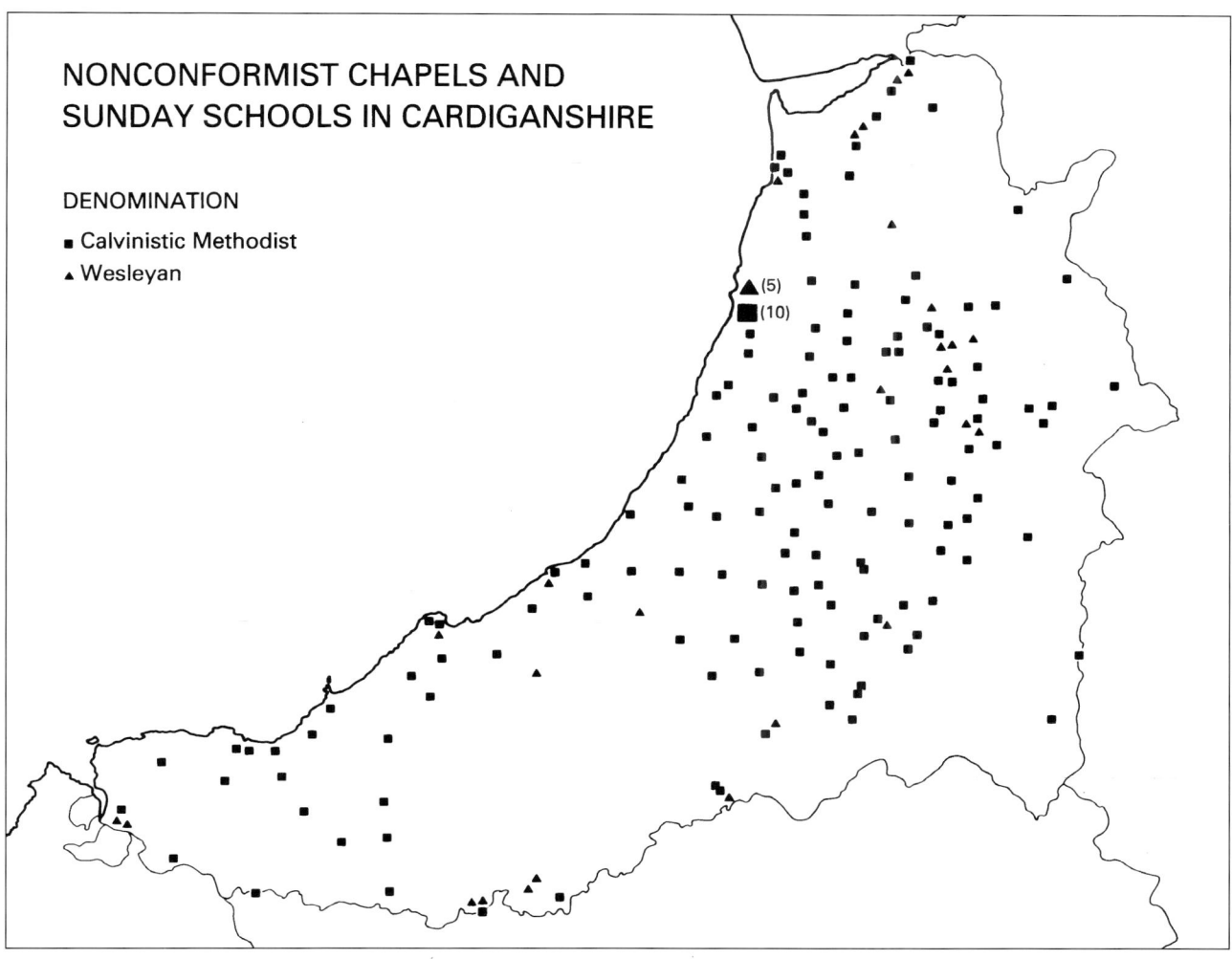

Fig. 125: Nonconformist chapels and Sunday schools in Cardiganshire: Calvinistic Methodist and Wesleyan Methodist. (*Crown Copyright RCAHMW-NMR*).

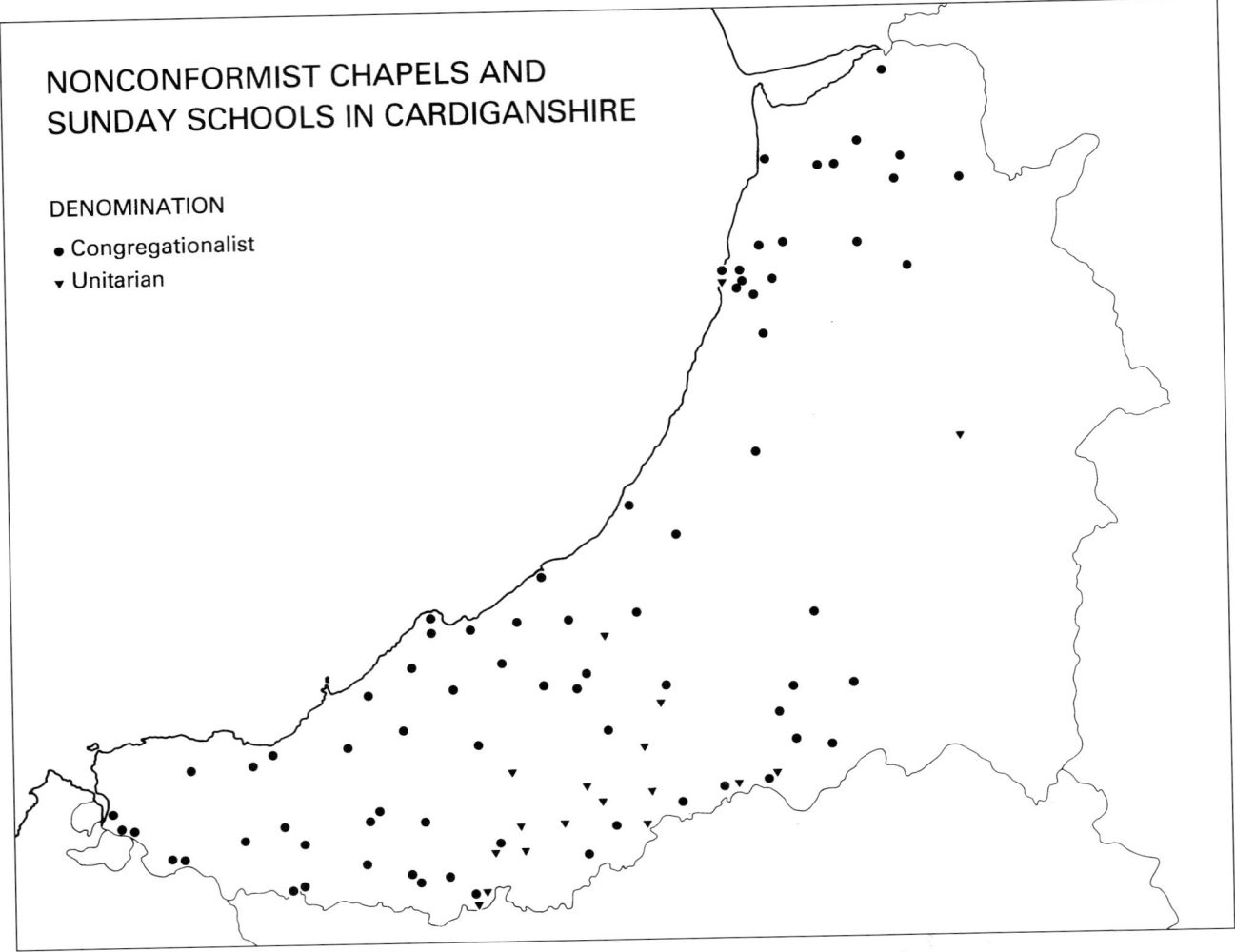

Fig. 126: Nonconformist chapels and Sunday schools in Cardiganshire: Congregationalist and Unitarian. (*Crown Copyright RCAHMW-NMR*).

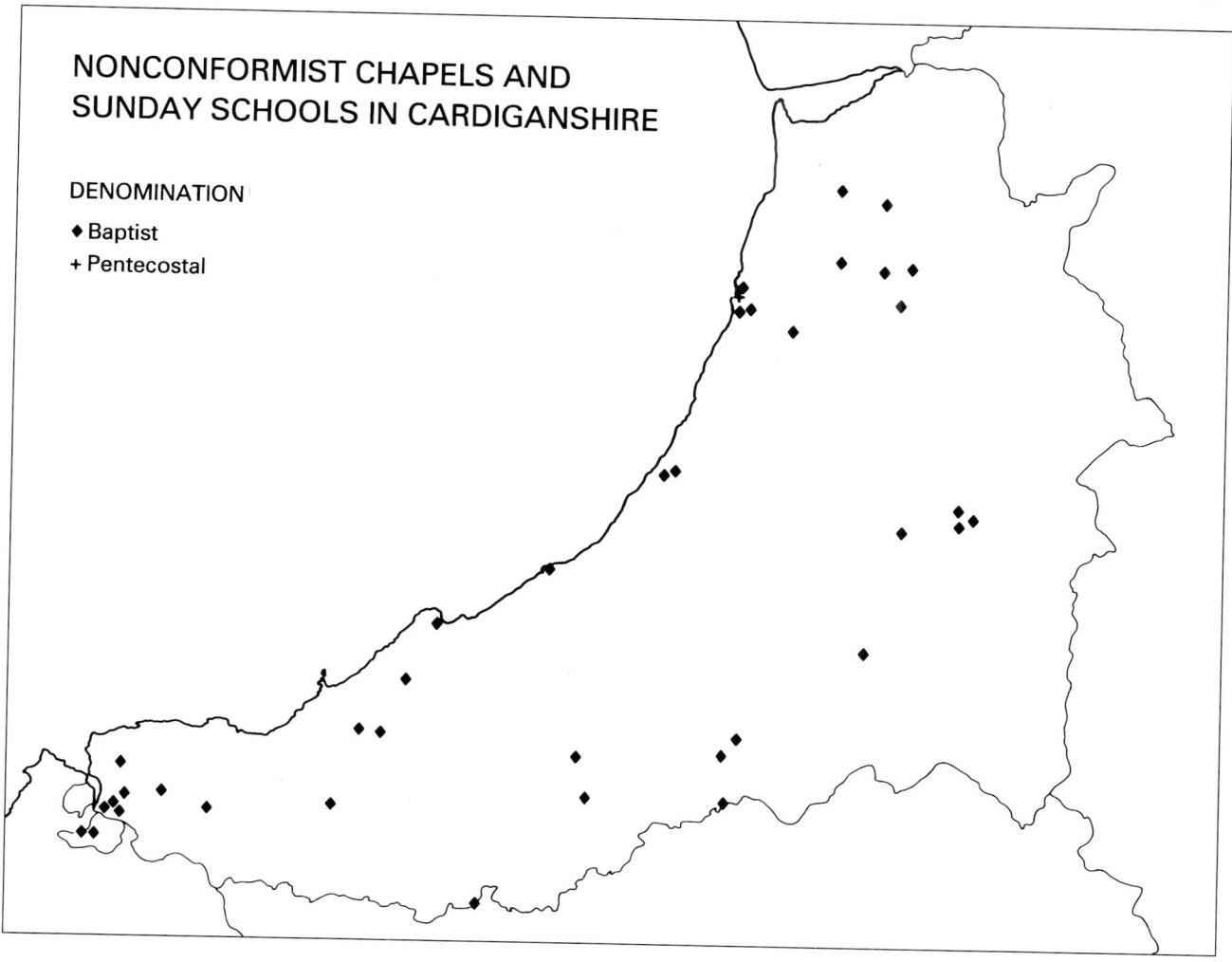

Fig. 127: Nonconformist chapels and Sunday schools in Cardiganshire: Baptist and Pentecostal. *(Crown Copyright RCAHMW-NMR).*

CHAPTER 23

EDUCATION IN CARDIGANSHIRE, 1700–1974

W. Gareth Evans

THE educational history of Cardiganshire has been shaped by many factors. Educational decision-making, the location of schools and colleges, as well as prevailing attitudes to schooling have been subject to the complex influences of the broader geographical, religious, social and political backdrop. The impact of enlightened and strong-willed individuals has also been crucial, as well as a range of factors operating within the educational context itself.

Geography has exerted its influence in many ways in a county covering an area of 692 square miles. The pattern of distribution of towns and scattered villages generated a strong sense of pride in various communities, which became evident in their quest for schools in the nineteenth century and their defence of schools threatened with closure in the late twentieth century. The particular geographical advantages of natural foci such as Aberystwyth, Aberaeron and Llandysul figured prominently in the deliberations concerning the location of intermediate schools in the 1890s. Poor transport facilities in the nineteenth century made it necessary to maintain a large number of small elementary schools. With improved road transport in the twentieth century, many of these schools could be amalgamated with advantage. Demographic change also proved decisive. Density of population strengthened the viability of a number of towns as centres for intermediate schools. Decline in population since the 1880s, particularly in rural areas, led to the closure of many small primary schools. Inward migration, particularly in the 1970s and 1980s, exerted a profound impact on the linguistic policies of schools.

Religion has also been a major determinant in the educational history of Cardiganshire. It inspired the rich peasant culture which was the most striking feature in the county's social life from the eighteenth to the twentieth century. Moulded initially by the eighteenth-century religious revival and literary awakening, it found expression in varied religious and cultural activities as well as in numerous educational experiments, including the work of the SPCK, the circulating schools and Sunday schools as well as educational initiatives epitomizing the philanthropic and charitable designs of numerous individuals, including Edward Richard, Ystradmeurig, Thomas Phillips, Neuadd-lwyd, and David Davies, Castellhywel. By the mid-nineteenth century, Nonconformity had triumphed in Cardiganshire. As well as chapels, there were associated schools and academies of repute. But the established Church, decayed and poverty-stricken in the eighteenth century and whose clergy in the diocese of St David's were judged 'insufficient both in number and quality' in 1803, had also achieved a significant measure of reform in the diocese in the early nineteenth century through the efforts of Bishop Thomas Burgess (1803–25) and Bishop Connop Thirlwall (1840–73).[1] The establishment of the Society for the Promotion of Christian Knowledge (SPCK), and Church Union within the diocese of St David's in 1804, which led to the formation of clerical libraries and Sunday schools, as well as the licensing of four grammar schools – Cardigan, Ystradmeurig, Lampeter, Brecon – to train ordinands, and the establishment of St David's College, Lampeter, were significant educational developments.[2] The Anglican–Nonconformist dichotomy in the county embodied political, social and religious conflicts.[3] Nonconformist hostility towards the established Church influenced attitudes towards St David's College, Lampeter, which did not become a constituent college of the University of Wales until 1971. Primarily for religious reasons, Ystradmeurig and St David's College School were excluded from the Cardiganshire scheme for intermediate education.

Although lead mining, weaving and a marine tradition have played a significant role in the history of Cardiganshire, it is a county primarily of small agricultural holdings, with farming as the main source of employment. Judgement on Cardiganshire schools and educational administrators must take into account the failure for much of the nineteenth century and the first half of the twentieth century to make sufficient allowance for the agricultural hinterland. There was little or no apprenticeship in connection with farming, mining, weaving or seamanship. Only belatedly in the late twentieth century were the requirements of vocational education addressed. On numerous occasions following the agricultural depression of the late nineteenth century, harsh economic circumstances encouraged parents to place a high premium on secondary education, particularly for boys. There was a desire to provide children with the opportunity to do well in life and to avoid the hard work at home on the farm or smallholding. Education was perceived as the avenue to the professions and white-collar occupations – the ministry, medicine, teaching and banking. But, in a county with a large number of smallholdings and low incomes, the fees of intermediate schools in the late nineteenth century and early twentieth century placed such aspirations beyond the reach of many families in rural Cardiganshire.

Linguistically, the county has been a stronghold of the Welsh language and literature until well into the twentieth century. In 1901, 93 per cent spoke Welsh, and 50.4 per cent of the population Welsh only. But for much of the period, with the notable exception of the Sunday schools, the native language was not reflected in the county's schools and colleges. English was regarded as the language of social advancement, and consequently elementary, secondary and higher education were conceived in this context. The disharmony between the language of the home and the day school was to have a profound impact on the educational and social history of modern Cardiganshire.

In eighteenth-century Wales, schooling was perceived as the handmaiden of religion and an instrument for spiritual and moral improvement.[4] Teaching children and adults to read and

---

[1] For the background, see E. Saunders, *A View of the State of Religion in the Diocese of St David's* (Cardiff, 1949); D. M. James, 'Some social and economic problems of the Church of England in the diocese of St David's, 1800–1874' (unpublished University of Wales MA thesis, 1972).

[2] C. Thirlwall, *Letter to J. Bowstead* (London, 1861); J. J. Perowne, *Remains Literary and Theological of Connop Thirlwall* (2 vols., London, 1877–8).

[3] H. Richard, *Letters on the Social and Political Condition of Wales* (London, 1867); J. Bowstead, *Letters Concerning Education in South Wales* (Stroud, 1861).

[4] D. Williams, *A History of Modern Wales* (London, 1950), chapter X; J. McLeish, *Evangelical Religion and Popular Education* (London, 1969).

understand the gospel was deemed essential because the prime objective of education was the salvation of souls. In 1721 Erasmus Saunders painted a gloomy picture of religious conditions, particularly in Cardiganshire, where there was an acute lack of schools: 'This Calamity is nowhere so very visible as in Cardiganshire, where I can't be informed of any of the least Endowment for as much as one Charity School throughout that County.'[5] In *The Welch Piety* in 1749, Griffith Jones noted that 'the sole design of this Undertaking is to promote their spiritual and everlasting Welfare . . . It is by no means the Design of this Spiritual kind of Charity to make them Gentlemen but Christians and heirs of eternal life'.[6]

Between 1699 and 1737 the SPCK, motivated by a desire to provide a Christian and useful education for the children of the poor, sponsored ninety-six 'charity schools' in Wales – seventy-six of which were in south Wales, mostly in Carmarthenshire and Pembrokeshire, where the influence of Sir John Philipps and John Vaughan was greatest. In Cardiganshire, two SPCK schools were opened – at Esgair-hir and Llandysul.[7] A 'works school' was founded by Sir Humphrey Mackworth, MP for Cardiganshire in 1701, a patron of the SPCK and deputy governor of the Company of Mine Adventurers, for the children of lead workers at his mines at Esgair-hir in north Cardiganshire. The works charity school was first established in 1700 and was maintained by the company. It is known to have received further financial suport in 1705 and 1706:

> The Governor and Company of the Mine Adventurers of England allow £20 per annum for a Charity-School for the children of the miners and workmen belonging to the said Company. The said Company also give £30 yearly to a Minister to read prayers, preach and catechize the children.[8]

Together with a works school established by Sir Humphrey Mackworth at Neath, Esgair-hir was among the earliest works schools in Wales.[9] By 1721, when Erasmus Saunders bewailed the lack of charity schools in Cardiganshire, the Esgair-hir school had probably closed. The only other SPCK school in the county was not founded until 1727, when Dr Thomas Pardo, rector of Llandysul, established a charity school for ten boys.[10]

With only two schools in the county, the impact of the SPCK on illiteracy in Cardiganshire was comparatively small. But the Society also distributed books. In 1710 books were sent to Lewis Pryse, Gogerddan, for use in the Llanbadarn Fawr parochial library.[11] English was the usual medium of instruction in SPCK schools in south Wales. This policy proved detrimental to their long-term success, but by publishing new Welsh-language editions of the Bible and other books in the vernacular, interest in education and religion was kindled and the ground prepared for Griffith Jones's circulating schools.

[5]Saunders, *A View*, p.32.
[6]*The Welch Piety* (London, 1749), p.24.
[7]M. Clement (ed.), *Correspondence and Minutes of the S.P.C.K. relating to Wales, 1699–1740* (Cardiff, 1954), pp.143, 255, 298.
[8]Ibid., p.255.
[9]Eadem, *The S.P.C.K. and Wales* (Cardiff, 1954), p.255; L. W. Evans, *Education in Industrial Wales* (Cardiff, 1971), pp.5–7.
[10]Clement, *Correspondence and Minutes*, p.298.
[11]Ibid., p.203.

Much has been written about the statistical aspects – numbers of schools, pupils, teachers – of Griffith Jones's educational experiment in Wales. The most critical estimate of the circulating schools would acknowledge that in the twenty-five years between 1737 and Jones's death in 1761, approximately 200,000 children and adults out of a total Welsh population of approximately 450,000 were taught to read in 3,325 short-term schools held in nearly 1,600 different locations.[12] Statistics gleaned from *The Welch Piety* show that a total of 48,474 children and adults enrolled in 823 schools held in 250 different locations in Cardiganshire. These numbers include those who enrolled in successive years and were therefore counted more than once. The number of schools fluctuated from ten in 1738–9 to between four and forty in the 1740s, seven and nineteen in the 1750s, twenty and forty-one in the 1760s and twenty-seven and forty-eight in the 1770s. The lowest enrolment was 193 in 1747–8 and the highest 2,946 in 1777. Over a period of thirty-nine years, an average of 1,243 pupils annually attended an average of twenty-one circulating schools in Cardiganshire. They usually functioned in a particular community for periods of three or four months. Overall, greater provision was made for the inhabitants of the southern part of the county.[13]

Instruction in day and night schools was in the Welsh language and focused on Bible and Prayer Book reading and learning the catechism. These vernacular, catechetical schools, conducted by itinerant teachers, proved both popular and successful with the young and old, though there were inevitable problems caused by poverty and irregular attendance in a rural society.[14] In 1741 the inhabitants of Llanddeiniol recorded that 'it was the greatest piece of Charity possible to be done, to grant us a Welch School'.[15] In spite of much poverty, the parishioners of Gwnnws in 1750 were 'very desirous of having his (the Schoolmaster) Company for one Quarter more towards the latter End of this Summer, that the Children may perfect themselves in the Welch Language'.[16] At Llanbadarn Fawr in 1764, the Revd Isaac Williams wrote that 'the Master had not been there many weeks before he had about 40 Scholars, and their Number increased to upwards of 80 before the Expiration of the Quarter'.[17] Sound organization by Griffith Jones, instruction in the native language by able teachers, who included the hymn-writer Morgan Rhys, as well as the encouragement of supportive clergymen, who placed buildings at the disposal of the teachers, contributed to the success of the circulating schools in Cardiganshire. They continued to flourish for many years following the death of Griffith Jones in 1761. But the death of Madam Bridget Bevan in 1779 and a dispute over her will led to the demise of the schools. By then, however, Griffith Jones's experiment in religious education had ensured that many tenant farmers and their wives, as well as labourers and children, had become both literate and more devout. They were familiar with the Bible in their native language and had been instilled with a desire for reading and learning. A sound foundation had been laid for succeeding educational initiatives, particularly the Welsh Sunday schools.

[12]W. M. Williams (ed.), *Selections from The Welch Piety* (Cardiff, 1938); R. T. Jenkins, *Gruffydd Jones, Llanddowror* (Cardiff, 1930); F. A. Cavenagh, *The Life and Work of Griffith Jones of Llanddowror* (Cardiff, 1930); G. Davies, *Griffith Jones, Llanddowror: Athro Cenedl* (Bridgend, 1984); G. H. Jenkins, *The Foundations of Modern Wales. Wales 1642–1780* (Cardiff, 1987).
[13]T. Beynon, 'The circulating Welch charity schools in Cardiganshire', *CCHMC*, XX, no.2 (1935), 87–95; G. Morgan, *Circulating Schools in Cardiganshire 1738–1777* (Aberystwyth, 1993).
[14]I am grateful to Dr Eryn M. White for providing me with valuable information based on her research into the religious history of eighteenth-century Cardiganshire.
[15]*The Welch Piety* (London, 1742), p.96.
[16]Ibid. (1751), pp.61–2.
[17]Ibid. (1764), pp.17–18.

The eighteenth century was marked by philanthropy and charitable endowments to educate the poor in England and Wales. The *Digest of Schools and Charities* (1842) lists seventy-nine non-classical eighteenth-century endowments in Wales. Only a small number of non-classical schools benefited from endowments in Cardiganshire. In the parish of Llanfihangel Genau'r-glyn, David Jones's Charity was established in 1732 by David Jones of Cefn-gwyn, who gave £60 to yield an interest to be used for teaching poor children of the parish. Further small sums of £5 and £20 respectively in 1758 and 1760 were provided by Hugh Edward and Evan Watkins's Charity. Sometime in the last quarter of the century James Jones's Charity in the parish of Llanfihangel Genau'r-glyn provided for the teaching of poor children at Tal-y-bont.[18] Elementary education was provided at Llanbadarn Fawr following an endowment of £104 in 1752 by Roderick Richardes 'for teaching poor children', a further sum of £40 for the same purpose by Jacob Evans, Penlanoleu, in 1760, and £50 through John Jones's Charity in 1783. At Llanddewibrefi David Thomas's Charity in 1780 and 1781 supported a school established at 'a house used as a Methodist meeting-house'. This was later supplemented by the Catherine Radcliffe Charity 1782, which provided the interest on £200 at 4 per cent to educate poor children. At Llanilar, Richard Jones's Charity was established in 1792 under the will of Richard Jones of St Clement Danes. Interest on a sum of £500 bequeathed was designated for the schooling of twelve poor children. In the parish of Llanddewi Aber-arth, the Charity of Henry Jones of Tŷ-glyn in 1793 provided the interest on a bequest of £120 to maintain a Sunday school at Llanddewi Aber-arth church. It is also possible that Mary Griffiths's Charity in 1777 in the parish of Llangeitho was used for elementary education.

In contrast to other Welsh counties, Cardiganshire had not been particularly favoured by the foundation of Tudor and Stuart grammar schools. In 1653, however, a free grammar school was endowed at Cardigan under the provisions of the Act for the Better Propagation of the Gospel in Wales (1650), which established sixty-three free schools throughout Wales. At Cardigan the sum of £60 per annum was made available to maintain a schoolmaster and usher out of the 'impropriated tithes of Llansantfraed'.[19] The mayor and corporation of Cardigan were empowered to remove the master and usher. Although the endowment ceased to be paid at the Restoration, the school remained and was supported out of the revenues of the corporation until the Cornwallis Charity was founded in 1731. Under the terms of the will of Lady Letitia Cornwallis of Abermarles, Carmarthenshire, dated 13 December 1731, which became the subject of a Chancery suit in 1783, interest on a bequest of £717 10s. 6d. stock was made available to the Corporation to employ the schoolmaster at Cardigan.[20] They claimed the right to nominate six local boys to be educated at the school free of payment of fees. By the early nineteenth century, as many as forty other scholars at the school also received a classical education which was deemed essential for a career in the Church. The site of the grammar school (on which the Market Buildings and Guildhall were built in 1858–60) was ancient Corporate property and was given by the Corporation for the use of the school in 1810. Nicholas Carlisle reported in 1818 that 'Latin and Greek Grammars are used. And

[18]*Digest of Schools and Charities for Education as reported on by the Commissioners of Inquiry into Charities* (London, 1842).
[19]*Charity Commissioners' Reports* (London, 1834), pp.28, 593.
[20]Will, dated 13 December 1731, in *Charity Commission Report* 1835. See also Thomas Phillips, *Wales: The Language, Social Condition, Moral Character, and Religious Opinions of the People, considered in their relation to Education* (London, 1849), p.354.

the Hebrew, Greek, Latin, French, English and Welsh languages are taught with arithmetic and the use of the Globes.'[21] The school which, prior to 1858, was located in the Free School Building vested in the mayor and burgesses, worked in close conjunction with the diocese of St David's and became one of the four grammar schools licensed by Bishop Burgess to educate ordinands directly for the ministry of the Church of England. A seven-year course of study in classics, Hebrew and theology was given a deliberate sense of urgency by competitive scholarships and annual book prizes for the most successful pupils.[22]

Cardiganshire also became the location of two of the most famous of the eight eighteenth-century grammar schools founded in Wales – the Lledrod and Ystradmeurig Grammar Schools. Upper Lledrod Grammar School was founded in 1746 by Dorothea Oliver, who settled lands in accordance with the wishes of her late husband, the Revd Thomas Oliver. A native of the parish of Lledrod, he was at the time of his death vicar of Dudley in Worcestershire. By his will, dated 21 May 1745, he left land in the parish of Lledrod called Ynys-y-garn y Berfedd and a sum of £400 to endow a grammar school for the benefit of a limited number of poor boys from the parish of Lledrod.[23] The original instruments of the Lledrod Foundation – an indenture of 1 July 1746 and a deed of 19 November 1741 – stipulated that the endowment was to be used 'to maintain a Grammar School there for educating 40 children if such number shall be offered in the principles of the Church of England and as far beyond the Grammar as the Masters for the time being should be capable of teaching'. One of the trustees empowered to govern the 'perpetual Grammar School' was John Lloyd, a friend of Edward Richard, a native of Ystradmeurig. On his recommendation, Richard was appointed the first headmaster. A schoolhouse was rented at Ynys-y-garn.

Edward Richard was born at Ystradmeurig in 1714, the son of Thomas Richard, the village tailor and innkeeper, and was educated at Carmarthen Grammar School and at the Revd John Pugh's famous Motygido academy at Llannarth. Richard became a noted pastoral poet whose work bore the imprint of Virgil and other classical writers.[24] A member of the eighteenth-century Augustan circle of Welsh scholars which included Lewis Morris and Goronwy Owen, he was recognized as 'an eminent Welsh critic and an elegant pastoral poet'.[25] A loyal adherent of the established Church and a contemporary of Griffith Jones, he was conscious of the need for the advancement of education in the Welsh countryside. He had first opened a school in the local church in 1734. It functioned until 1740 when, unexpectedly, the self-critical Edward Richard decided to close the school in order to advance his own classical and religious education. In 1745 the school at Ystradmeurig was reopened in the parish church, with Richard remaining as headmaster until his death in 1777.

For over three decades, the two schools – Lledrod and Ystradmeurig – were placed under Edward Richard's supervision. The close connection established between the two schools, though retaining their separate trustees and legal independence, lasted until the twentieth century.[26] Except for the years 1823–6, both schools were served by the same headmaster, though it remained the

[21]N. Carlisle, *A Concise Description of the Endowed Grammar Schools in England and Wales* (2 vols., London, 1818), II, pp.950–1.
[22]Ibid.
[23]Indenture, 1 July 1746. Transcribed in H. G. Robinson's *Report to Endowed Schools Commissioners*, 30 July 1878.
[24]*DWB*; D. G. Osborne-Jones, *Edward Richard of Ystradmeurig* (Carmarthen, 1934).
[25]Carlisle, *Concise Description*, II, p.964.
[26]W. M. Davies, 'St. John's College, Ystrad Meurig', *Province*, IV, no.1 (1953), 153.

custom until the late nineteenth century for the Ystradmeurig and Lledrod trustees to make separate notices of appointment to the headmastership.

It is doubtful whether Edward Richard himself taught at Lledrod. Ultimately, pupils at Lledrod were transferred to Ystradmeurig. Initially Edward Richard seems to have regarded Lledrod as a 'feeder' for the school at Ystradmeurig since he employed an assistant at Lledrod. Undoubtedly the legal safeguards of the indentures establishing the school at Lledrod led him to formalize a legal foundation for the school at Ystradmeurig. Through indentures contracted in 1757, 1771 and 1774 between Edward Richard and the Bishop of St David's and four prominent north Cardiganshire laymen – Viscount Lisburne, William Powell, Nanteos, James Lloyd of Mabws and Thomas Hughes of Hendrefelin – Ystradmeurig Grammar School was legally established.[27] Lands were given in perpetuity to the trustees, the rents of which were to be paid to a schoolmaster nominated by them to keep a grammar school. The school was further endowed in 1771 and 1774 by other deeds of the same donor and under the terms of his will in 1777.

These reveal the motives of the founder. Conscious of local poverty, the lack of well-educated clergymen and of the need for free schooling in the neighbourhood of Ystradmeurig, the original deed of foundation of 22 April 1757 provided free instruction for 'twelve poor boys of the parish of Ystrad Meurig in the principles of the Church of England as by law established'. In 1771 the total number was increased to thirty-two through the provision of the rents of other lands. An additional number of twenty poor boys in the parish was provided for. In 1774 the whole of Cardiganshire was brought within the ambit of the charity. It was intended to provide a grammar school education – 'a perpetual Grammar School for ever' – prioritizing Greek and Latin and preparing boys for entry to Oxford and Cambridge. To facilitate the task, the schoolmaster was to be 'well qualified to teach the Greek and Latin classics' and under the terms of Richard's will an appropriate library was to be established. The school was also specifically intended to educate the pupils 'in the principles of the Church of England'. The schoolmaster was to be 'a person professing the religion of the Church of England, of a good moral character' and was expected to 'preach at the parish church of Ystradmeiric as often as he conveniently could'.

Edward Richard proved to be an extremely successful schoolmaster and the school in his time, with an average of fifty pupils, was one of the most influential of the diocesan grammar schools. Contemporaries regarded the schools as a foundation of learning not only to Cardiganshire but also to the whole of Wales and many parts of England.[28] Many of the former pupils achieved considerable distinction. Through endowing a perpetual grammar school, Richard had successfully fulfilled what Saunders Lewis accurately perceived as 'the main ambition of his life'.[29]

His successor as headmaster at Ystradmeurig and Lledrod from 1777 to 1818 was a former pupil and native of Lledrod – the Revd John Williams ('Yr Hen Syr'), who further enhanced the reputation of the school.[30] There was a successful appeal for £250 in 1810–12 to erect a separate school building and room for a library in the churchyard in order to overcome the problem of lack of space and the inconvenience of holding the school in the parish church. By 1812 the neo-Gothic edifice, which still survives, had been erected. Enrolment, which averaged 100, reached a peak of 150.

[27]Indentures in Carlisle, *Concise Description*, II, pp.964–9; and Robinson, *Report* (1878).
[28]Carlisle, *Concise Description*, pp.950–1.
[29]S. Lewis, *A School of Welsh Augustans* (Wrexham, 1924), p.56.
[30]*DWB*; Osborne-Jones, *Edward Richard*, passim.

The school's importance for the established Church in Wales was further enhanced when it became one of Bishop Burgess's four licensed grammar schools for the training of ordinands in the diocese of St David's. Until the establishment of St David's College, Lampeter, in 1827, Ystradmeurig made a vital contribution both to secondary and higher education in Wales.[31] Many of the pupils, steeped in classical education by 'Yr Hen Syr', became distinguished churchmen and men of letters who exerted a profound influence in Wales and beyond. They included his two able sons, the Revd David Williams MA, his successor at Ystradmeurig 1818–23 and Archdeacon John Williams MA, the eminent rector of Edinburgh Academy 1824–33 and first Warden of Llandovery College 1848–53. He had also been headmaster of Lampeter School 1820–4, where Sir Walter Scott's son, Charles, was sent to be educated privately by John Williams – 'the best schoolmaster in Europe' – on the suggestion of J. G. Lockyer, a friend of John Williams at Oxford.[32]

In Lampeter, where there had been, according to G. Eyre Evans, a grammar school teaching classics in the early eighteenth century and also a school in 1789, another grammar school was founded in 1805 in a dilapidated glebe house near St Peter's churchyard by the Oxford-educated vicar of Lampeter, the Revd Eliezer Williams (1754–1820).[33] This school, licensed by Bishop Burgess to train ordinands, also provided secondary education for those pupils entering other professions. It has been contended that its high reputation for classical and theological education was comparable to that of Ystradmeurig.[34] Welsh and science were also taught.[35] When John Williams – 'Yr Hen Syr' – visited Lampeter School shortly after its foundation, he is reported to have commented sarcastically on the school building by referring 'to the magnificence of its architecture'. Eliezer Williams replied: 'Come, come, don't be too hard, if the exterior be not to your taste, I hope you will find less to condemn in the furniture.'[36] Doubts have been cast about its status as a 'grammar school'. It has been contended that its absence from the list of grammar schools in 1849 in Sir Thomas Phillips's *Wales* suggests that it might more accurately be categorized as a private adventure school.[37] Following Eliezer Williams's death in 1820, he was succeeded by John Williams. By the time he left in 1824 to become rector of Edinburgh Academy, the foundation stone of St David's College, Lampeter, had been laid. Its opening in 1827 was to have a significant impact on the existing grammar schools and on education in the diocese of St David's. It is probable that the reputation of Lampeter Grammar School – a schoolroom built in 1825 – and especially the persuasion of its second headmaster, John Williams, played a key role in influencing Bishop Burgess to locate St David's College at Lampeter rather than at Llanddewibrefi as orginally intended.[38] Its foundation stone was laid in August 1822 and the College, which was established to train ordinands, opened on St David's Day 1827.[39]

[31] In 1806 Burgess considered the feasibility of enlarging the premises at Ystradmeurig for use as a diocesan college, but theological differences between him and John Williams thwarted any development. See D. T. W. Price, *A History of St David's University College Lampeter, Volume I* (Cardiff, 1977), pp.4, 12.

[32] W. G. Evans, *A History of Llandovery College* (Llandovery, 1981), p.27; *DWB*.

[33] G. E. Evans, *Lampeter* (Aberystwyth, 1905), pp.106, 112; *DWB*.

[34] James, 'Social and economic problems', p.259.

[35] *Cymru*, VI (1894), 172–6.

[36] G. A. Williams, *English Works of the Rev. Eliezer Williams* (London, 1840), p.liv.

[37] Price, *History of St David's University College*, p.8.

[38] Ibid., pp.19, 104.

[39] Ibid., passim.

Nonconformists, debarred from Oxford and Cambridge, were also active in establishing academic and private adventure schools in Cardiganshire in the eighteenth and early nineteenth centuries. They provided education which varied in quality and standard from advanced element- ary and secondary to preparatory courses for the ministry which were often of university standard. It was quite common in the years 1750–1850 for Nonconformist ministers, particularly Unitarians and Congregationalists, to establish private academies and schools. Working in very modest premises, able teachers were still able to make a significant impact on students – Anglicans as well as Nonconformists – several of whom later gained considerable distinction.[40] Many students prepared for the ministry, though many also became famous in other spheres and professions, notably law, medicine, teaching and the army.

In an era when the few endowed grammar schools were both too expensive and too inaccessible, private academies and schools played a vital role prior to the impact of the Elementary Education Act of 1870 and the Welsh Intermediate Education Act of 1889. They merit greater recognition than hitherto conceded by historians.[41] One of the best known was the academy kept by the Unitarian, the Revd David Davies in a building near his home, Castellhywel, Llandysul, from 1783 to 1827. For over forty years, 'Dafis Castellhywel', an excellent classicist, gained a high reputation and attracted pupils from a very wide area.[42] Until Bishop Horsley of St David's objected, Anglican ordinands as well as Nonconformists attended.[43] As well as teaching classics and English, Welsh was used for purposes of translation.[44]

At Neuadd-lwyd, near Ffos-y-ffin, Dr Thomas Phillips, educated at Castellhywel and Carm- arthen, opened an academy in 1810, initially to prepare young men for the Congregationalist ministry. By 1842 all denominations, including the established Church, as well as students from England and Ireland, were represented by the 200 young men educated in an establishment more akin to a seminary for the training of ministers than to a grammar school.[45]

Elsewhere in Cardiganshire during these years, other small academies and schools which became well-known and popular included the Revd John Pugh's Motygido Academy at Llannarth;[46] the Revd John Jones's academy at Llangeitho;[47] John Evans's 'The Mathematical and Commercial School' at Aberystwyth 1818–60;[48] Pantydefaid Grammar School 1813–60;[49] the Revd Rees

[40]H. P. Roberts, 'Nonconformist academies in Wales 1662–1862', *THSC* (1928–9), 1–98; G. D. Owen, *Ysgolion a Cholegau yr Annibynwyr* (Swansea, 1939); D. Evans, *Welsh Unitarians as Schoolmasters* (Llandysul, n.d.).

[41]W. G. Evans, 'The contribution of private schools to Welsh education in the nineteenth and twentieth centuries', *Education for Development*, 10, no.1 (1986), 67–79.

[42]*DWB*; W. J. Davies, *Hanes Plwyf Llandyssul* (Llandyssul, 1896), pp.102–8.

[43]The alumni included the Revd Christmas Evans, the Revd David Peter, later President of Carmarthen Academy, and Dr Thomas Phillips, Neuadd-lwyd. For Bishop Horsley's attitude, see Thomas Griffiths, *Cofiant y Parchedig David Davies* (Carmarthen, 1828), pp.28–9.

[44]Griffiths, *Cofiant . . . David Davies*, p.30.

[45]*DWB*; J. V. Morgan, *Welsh Political and Educational Leaders in the Victorian Era* (London, 1908), p.285.

[46]'Motigido' and 'Pontygido' were also used in nineteenth-century sources. T. I. Ellis, *Crwydro Ceredigion* (Llandybïe, 1952), p.85.

[47]D. Samuel, *Ysgol Llangeitho* (Llanuwchllyn, 1893). Ebenezer Richard, Tregaron, was influential in its establishment under the Revd John Jones, a Methodist. The alumni included Dr Lewis Edwards, John Phillips, first Principal of Bangor Normal College, Henry Richard MP, and Dr William Rowlands.

[48]*DWB*; D. Samuel, *Some Old Schools and Schoolmasters of Aberystwyth* (Aberystwyth, 1901); idem, 'Hen ysgolfeistri Aberystwyth', *Cymru*, XX (1901), 88–90, 141–4, 159–61.

[49]The Revd John Thomas (1784–1861), Unitarian minister of Pantydefaid in the parish of Llandysul, was an able classicist who maintained a successful school for nearly forty-eight years.

Davies's Grammar School at Ystrad, Llanwnnen and Cribyn 1825–57; Atpar Academy 1839–58;[50] the Revd David Evans's Grammar School at Llandysul 1831–53; the Revd Griffith Griffiths's school at Llechryd 1788–1818, and the Revd J. M. Thomas's school at Cardigan 1810–50. At Aberystwyth, Aberaeron, Cardigan and Newcastle Emlyn, there were also private, boarding and day schools of varying quality for girls in the early decades of the nineteenth century.[51] Some boys in north Cardiganshire were also taught classics by James Henderson at Pwllpeiran between 1802 and 1807.[52]

The Blue Books of 1847 indicate that 42 per cent of day pupils in Cardiganshire attended private schools. Of 101 day schools listed, forty-nine were private adventure schools. Compared with other Welsh counties, there was a much greater dependence on private schools and it is possible that this was a major reason for the opening of only two grant-aided British schools in the county in the mid-1840s.[53]

The early decades of the nineteenth century witnessed significant voluntary educational activity in Wales by both the established Church and Nonconformists. The most important work was associated with 'The National Society for Promoting the Education of the Poor in the Principles of the Established Church', established in 1811, and the non-sectarian British and Foreign School Society, founded in 1814. It was only in 1833 that voluntary effort was supplemented by government grants made available for the erection of school buildings.[54]

In Cardiganshire, as elsewhere, some Church schools such as that of Llanfihangel Genau'r-glyn (c.1808)[55] predated the National Society, and others, including Llanfihangel-y-Creuddyn 1796[56] and Llanrhystud 1806,[57] were established independently. At Aberystwyth and Llanbadarn, Church members called for the establishment of an elementary school in 1807 and 1809.[58] By November 1813 a school-building – Ysgoldy – had been erected through voluntary effort on the site of the present Aberystwyth Parish Hall.[59] In 1818 it received a grant of £100 from the National Society, though in 1819 a new National School was erected in the town.[60] By 1828 eighty-five boys and seventy-five girls were enrolled. A National Society Report in 1836 listed sixteen schools with a total of 953 pupils in Cardiganshire.[61] By 1846 there were thirty-seven Church or National schools

[50]John Davies, the headteacher, had a high reputation.
[51]*Pigot's Directory* (London, 1835); *Robson's Commercial Directory* (London, 1841); *Pigot's Directory* (London, 1844); W. G. Evans, *Education and Female Emancipation – The Welsh Experience 1847–1914* (Cardiff, 1990).
[52]James Henderson, a Scotsman, was the printer in charge of Hafod Press at Pwllpeiran 1802–7. E. Inglis-Jones, *Peacocks in Paradise* (London, 1950); M. Seaborne, *Schools in Wales 1500–1900: A Social and Architectural History* (Denbigh, 1992), p.102.
[53]A. L. Trott, 'The British School movement in Wales, 1806–1846', and T. P. Jones, 'The contribution of the established Church 1811–1846', in J. L. Williams and G. R. Hughes (eds.), *The History of Education in Wales* (Swansea, 1978), pp.83–126.
[54]Seaborne, *Schools in Wales*, pp.86–141.
[55]D. Samuel, 'Ysgol Llanfihangel Geneu'r Glyn', *Cymru*, V (1894), 277–84.
[56]*The Reports of the Commissioners appointed to enquire into the State of Education in Wales* (London, 1847), II, p.226 state that a Church school was established in 1796. There were twenty-seven pupils in 1846.
[57]Ibid., II, p.230: 'Parish School, 1806'.
[58]A. L. Trott, 'Church day schools in Aberystwyth during the nineteenth century', *Ceredigion*, II, no.2 (1953), 67.
[59]Ibid., 67–9.
[60]Ibid., 71–2.
[61]Jones, 'Contribution of the established Church', p.123.

providing schooling for 42 per cent of the day pupils in the county.[62] It is unclear how many of these schools were affiliated to the National Society.

The impact of the British Society was considerably less during the first forty years of the nineteenth century. Only two British schools – Aberystwyth (1846) and Llanddewi Aber-arth (1844) – are listed in the 1847 Report.[63] The expense of erecting schools, in spite of the availability of government aid at a time when Nonconformists were also involved in the expense of erecting chapels, together with the accessibility of private schools and also national schools, explain the very limited progress made. With the acute religious antagonism and rivalry of the late nineteenth century not yet apparent, the majority of male pupils enrolled at Aberystwyth National School were Nonconformists.[64] In 1843 Sir James Graham's Education Bill had aroused fears in England and Wales of the growth of Anglican influence on the education of children in workhouses and textile mills. It generated the growth of the 'voluntaryist' movement, which voiced opposition to state involvement in education. Thomas Lloyd of Cardigan epitomized the voluntaryist attitude in 1846: 'I dread Government interference with education . . . it will be a curse and not a blessing.'[65] A voluntaryist school – Ysgoldy Pant-y-geifr between Tal-y-bont and Pumlumon – was established to function as a day and Sunday school.[66] However, following the publication of Hugh Owen's inspiring public letter 'To the Welsh People' in 1843, the British Society adopted a more positive role in Wales in the 1840s. In Cardiganshire, Nonconformists were increasingly conscious of the need to build new schools. Committees were formed under the auspices of the British Society to apply for government grants to erect schools at numerous locations, including Llanddewibrefi and Llanfair Clydogau.[67]

The Sunday schools played an increasingly important role in the lives of Welsh children and adults from the 1790s. There is evidence of a Sunday school being held at Llanio from 1790 and in Llanbadarn Church several years prior to Thomas Charles's pioneering work in Wales in the 1790s.[68] By 1846 Nonconformist schools were predominant in the county. 48 per cent of the Sunday schools were Calvinistic Methodist, 16 per cent Congregationalist, 7 per cent Wesleyan Methodist, 7 per cent Baptist and 22 per cent Church of England. In all, there were 206 Sunday schools and 27,131 pupils.[69] Many Nonconformists, in particular the Revd Ebenezer Richard and Revd Ebenezer Morris, played a vital role in promoting Sunday schools in Cardiganshire.[70] They organized the first *Cymanfa Ysgolion* or *Sasiwn Plant* held at Blaenannerch.[71] Conducted through the

---

[62]Seaborne, *Schools in Wales*, p.96.

[63]The British School at Aberystwyth – known for many years as 'Ysgol Skin' – was established by the Calvinistic Methodists in 1846.

[64]A. L. Trott, 'Elementary day schools for the children of the working classes in Cardiganshire in 1847', *Ceredigion*, II, no.3 (1954), 142–3.

[65]*Reports* (1847), II, p.83.

[66]D. W. Thomas, 'Addysg yng Ngheredigion, 1800–1850, yn ôl y cofiannau', *Ceredigion*, VI, no.1 (1968), 51.

[67]Trott, 'Elementary day schools', 145, 159; *Reports*, II (1847), pp.262–3 refers to a request to the Committee of Council for a money grant to erect schools.

[68]D. B. Rees, *Hanes Plwyf Llanddewi Brefi* (Llanddewi Brefi, 1984), pp.165–6.

[69]*Reports* (1847), II, p.49; Seaborne, *Schools in Wales*, p.117.

[70]G. W. Griffith, *Yr Ysgol Sul* (Caernarfon, 1936), p.65: See also T. Levi, *Canmlwyddiant Ysgol Sabbothol Cymru* (London, 1885), p.84.

[71]B. Thomas, 'Mudiadau addysg Thomas Charles', in G. M. Roberts (ed.), *Hanes Methodistiaeth Calfinaidd Cymru. Cynnydd y Corff* (Caernarfon, 1978), p.447.

medium of the Welsh language, the Sunday schools became firmly rooted in Cardiganshire and exerted a profound educative and spiritual influence.

Although the Reports of the Commissioners of Inquiry into the State of Education in Wales – the Blue Books – in 1847 have been subjected to much criticism, particularly regarding their attitude to the Welsh language and the morality of the people, there is no reason to doubt the accuracy of their comments on education in the county.[72] Witnesses were unanimous that the supply of elementary day schools was inadequate: 'too few good schools'. Twenty-two out of sixty-four parishes lacked any day schools. The largest number of schools – ten – were located in the parish of Llanbadarn Fawr.[73]

The schooling was also of poor quality. Evidence from Tregaron and Aberystwyth concurred with that of the Revd Llewelyn Llewellin, Principal of St David's College, Lampeter, who spoke for many: 'There is a great deficiency of schools for the working classes. The schools which exist are chiefly Sunday schools which are to be found in nearly every parish. The day schools are not numerous.'[74] Only 3,885 out of an estimated 6,846 children were attending day schools, mostly National or private. As many as 43.2 per cent were not receiving instruction in a day school.[75] There was also a marked gender difference, for only 33.6 per cent of the pupils at school were girls.[76]

There was an increasing desire for greater provision of schooling, but the comparative poverty of the inhabitants made them reluctant to erect and maintain schools.[77] Clergymen were also fearful of the expenditure involved. Other impediments to the provision of effective schooling in Cardiganshire included the comparatively small number – forty – of the 101 day schools located in purpose-built schoolrooms. Some, such as Hafod, were good, but ten were located in chapels, twenty-three in private houses and twenty-eight in other buildings. Commissioner Jelinger C. Symons concluded that 'the great majority of schools are held under temporary occupation in rooms of private houses which degenerate in Cardiganshire . . . into mere outhouses, usually without ceilings and with ground floors scarcely, if at all, superior to woodhouses'.[78] Overall in the county there was 'uniformity of bareness except at Aberystwyth, which is an oasis in the wilderness'.[79] Only five of the 101 teachers had received some training. The majority were in their twenties, though a fourteen-year-old was a teacher at Llangwyryfon. Most of them had been engaged previously in other occupations. The teacher at Penparcau was a cripple and the schoolroom a poor, dark, earth-floored house. Though some teachers were highly praised, notably John Evans of Aberystwyth,[80] James

[72]P. Morgan (ed.), *Brad y Llyfrau Gleision* (Llandysul, 1991); Trott, 'Elementary day schools', 140–2.

[73]Trott, 'Elementary day schools', 138.

[74]*Reports* (1847), II, p.75.

[75]Trott, 'Elementary day schools', 140.

[76]*Reports* (1847), II, p.8; Trott, 'Elementary day schools', 140.

[77]*Reports* (1847), II, p.82. According to David Jenkins, Mayor of Cardigan: 'I think that the poorer classes desire better education than they have, but many of them are too poor to get it.' The total charitable income for education in Cardiganshire in 1835, including Cardigan and Ystradmeurig, was £306 8s. 6d., of which only £47 10s. was available for elementary education. See A. L. Trott, 'Educational charities in Cardiganshire in the period 1833–35: their origin and value', *Ceredigion*, IV, no.1 (1960), 47–59.

[78]*Reports* (1847), II, p.24.

[79]Ibid., II, p.25.

[80]Ibid., II, p.157.

Thomas of Pen-y-garn, and the master at Pen-llwyn,[81] the Report highlighted the incompetence of most Cardiganshire teachers. Low salaries, mostly less than £20 per annum, contributed to a situation where few were worthy of the title of 'a schoolmaster who professes to teach English'. The curriculum in most of the schools was narrow and limited to elementary work in the three Rs. Bible-reading was evident in most schools. Only a few schools, such as the Aberystwyth Wesleyan School opened in 1845 – 'the only really good day school I have yet seen in Wales'[82] – and John Evans's 'Mathematical and Commercial School' at Aberystwyth, which taught astronomy using a telescope and a magic lantern, offered a broad curriculum. Except at Llandyfriog, where Welsh was taught and was a medium of instruction and where, according to Symons, 'all the Welsh gutturals and the harshest sounds in the language were shrieked',[83] English was the preferred medium of instruction, although few children understood it. Witnesses, including the vicar of St Mary's, Cardigan, alluding to the wishes of parents, emphasized that 'the desire is great to learn English'.[84] In a quarter of the schools both languages were used, with Welsh as a medium for explanation. Jelinger C. Symons was convinced that 'the Welsh Language is a vast drawback to Wales, and a manifold barrier to the moral progress and commercial prosperity of the people. It is not easy to over-estimate its evil effects.'[85]

The Sunday schools also varied in quality. Some were very good, including 'the high character of Anglican and Nonconformist Sunday schools at Aberystwyth'.[86] These promoted literacy in the native language. In the endowed grammar schools of Wales, the 1840s was a time when the quality of education left much to be desired. Ystradmeurig Grammar School, with sixty-six pupils in 1846, had declined after the opening of St David's College, Lampeter, in 1827 and also because of the employment of juvenile labour in the lead mines of north Cardiganshire. The school 'had long been in a very unsatisfactory condition, and seems to accomplish in a very imperfect manner, if at all, any of the objects for which it was founded'.[87]

By the mid-nineteenth century, many weaknesses in the provision of education had been high-lighted. But the strengths of the Sunday schools and some day schools, as well as greater involvement with the British Society in the quest for state funding for the erection of elementary schools, gave hope for better schooling in the future.

During the 1850s and 1860s some of the defects highlighted in the 1847 Report were remedied in several localities through the activities of the National Society and the British and Foreign Schools Society. By 1870 forty-seven elementary schools – nineteen National and twenty-eight British – had been newly established or considerably improved.[88] In 1851, in a report on the National schools, it was noted that there was 'a decided steadiness of advance among the better class of schools in this county, which must be gratifying to their promoters'.[89] They included Penparcau, Cardigan,

[81]Ibid., II, p.158. 'The master of zeal and much natural ability' was probably Lewis Edwards, cousin of Dr Lewis Edwards. M. H. Jones, 'Some of the historical associations of Penllwyn', *TCAS*, 5 (1927), 43.
[82]*Reports* (1847), II, p.152.
[83]Ibid., II, pp.161–2.
[84]Ibid., II, p.82.
[85]Ibid., II, p.66.
[86]Ibid., II, p.154.
[87]Phillips, *Wales*, p.379. See also *Reports* (1847), II, p.173.
[88]*H.M.I. Report* (London, 1913), p.6.
[89]*Minutes of the Committee of Council on Education* (London, 1851–2), pp.471–2.

Llandygwydd and Llangoedmor, which were 'conducted with great regularity and activity'. But it was also recognized that poverty and the scattered nature of the population 'in the hilly and inland parts of the county' made it difficult to maintain good schools. William Roberts ('Nefydd') found support in 1854 for establishing British schools at Newcastle Emlyn, Cardigan, Penparc, Aberystwyth and Penymorfa.[90] A newly built British school, inspired by the Cambrian Educational Society, was opened in 1855 at Llwyndafydd. But the prospects of establishing a British school at Cardigan in 1854–5 and at Glynarthen in 1856 were thwarted by opposition to government aid.[91] At the Pen-llwyn British School, opened in 1855, the enrolment soon reached 120 and the assistance of four pupil-teachers, including John Rees of Ponterwyd, was sought by the headmaster, the Revd Thomas Edwards, brother of Dr Lewis Edwards.[92]

On the eve of the 1870 Education Act, however, the quantity and quality of elementary schooling in Cardiganshire still left much to be desired. In 1868 the Revd Shadrach Pryce HMI concluded his report on nineteen annual-grant Church of England schools inspected in the county by stating that 'with respect to education, this county can only be said to be in a moderate condition; the school buildings, furniture and apparatus, especially in country places, are inferior to what they are in Montgomery, Carmarthen and Pembroke. The centre, north-east and west coast parts of the county are deficient in schools.'[93] There was 'only one small Government school' in the Tregaron census district, which had a population of 11,458, though there was also 'a moderate sprinkling of village or dame schools'. Although the Welsh language was 'very prevalent and may be said to be the language of the people', the HMI was opposed to its usage in the classroom.[94] It was specifically noted that at Penrhyn-coch school, which was in 'a very satisfactory condition', the teachers 'do not understand Welsh, and consequently all the instruction from the very commencement is given entirely in English'.[95] William Williams HMI also referred to the 'very great deficiency in school accommodation' when the Education Act 1870 was passed.[96] Of the sixty elementary schools aided by parliamentary grants, thirty were British schools, twenty-one National schools and eight connected to the Church of England.

The Education Act of 1870 was a major landmark in the educational history of England and Wales. Henceforth there was to be a national system of elementary education provided by state-supported voluntary schools and, where necessary, because of deficiency in school accommodation by new board schools. In Cardiganshire seventy-three board schools were established over the following thirty years. By 1878 there were already fifty-four board schools.[97]

Under the provisions of the Act, thirty-eight School Boards were formed in Cardiganshire. Aberystwyth showed much enthusiasm and became the first town in Wales to elect a School Board.[98] Ratepayers in some areas were hesitant and sometimes reluctant to implement the terms of the Act.

[90]E. D. Jones, 'The journal of William Roberts ("Nefydd"), 1853–62', *NLWJ*, VIII, no.3 (1954), 316.
[91]Ibid., 326.
[92]Jones, 'Historical associations of Penllwyn', 43.
[93]*Report of the Committee of Council on Education* (London, 1868), p.172.
[94]Ibid., p.164.
[95]Ibid.
[96]Ibid. (1876–7), p.644.
[97]Ibid. (1878–9), p.1055.
[98]A. L. Trott, 'Aberystwyth School Board and Board School, 1870–1902', *Ceredigion*, II, no.1 (1952), 3.

Fig. 128: Rhydlewis Girls' School. (*Copyright National Library of Wales*).

Consequently, eighteen of the new School Boards were established compulsorily by orders of the Education Department – Cilcennin (1875), Cyfoeth-y-brenin (1871), Cwmrheidol (1875), Lampeter (1875), Llannarth (1871), Llanbadarn Fawr (1875), Llanddewibrefi (1875), Llandysul (1876), Llanfihangel Ystrad (1874), Llangeitho (1876), Llangoedmor (1874), Llangybi (1876), Llanrhystud (1875), Llansanffraid (1874), Tregaron (1874), Troed-yr-aur (1874), Y Ferwig (1875), Ystradmeurig and Lledrod (1875).[99] Seventeen of the elected School Boards served two or more united school districts. By March 1881 the Cardiganshire School Boards had borrowed £48,000 from the Public Works Loan Commissioners to erect school buildings.[100]

By 1877 William Williams HMI was praising the 'good work' of the School Boards in maintaining a number of schools transferred to them and for erecting new buildings. He contended that 'comparatively little' had been accomplished previously by the 101 voluntary societies to supply the accommodation required.[101] Managers of the National schools at Aberystwyth had erroneously claimed that there was no deficiency of school accommodation in the town. Following the opening of a board school at Aberystwyth in 1874, the quality of learning and attendance at the National

[99]Idem, 'The implementation of the 1870 Elementary Education Act in Cardiganshire during the period 1870–1880', *Ceredigion*, III, no.3 (1958), 210.
[100]Trott, 'Aberystwyth School Board', 212.
[101]*Report of the Committee of Council on Education* (London, 1876–7), pp.645–6.

schools had improved. In 1880 the inspector noted that the 1870 Education Act had improved the provision of school accommodation, especially in rural areas. Some of the new board schools were replacements for old British schools. 'Except for slight exceptions, there was no portion not adequately supplied with school accommodation.'[102]

But the era of the School Board 1870–1902 also bore witness to numerous educational problems. The triennial School Board elections often reflected the sectarian controversies which divided Anglicans and Nonconformists in the county. Sometimes two small rural schools coexisted in places where one school would have been sufficient. At Llannarth a celebrated clash between the School Board and the vicar and trustees of the national school of the parish led to the unnecessary building of a new board school in 1882 rather than the transfer of the National school. The vicar and trustees insisted that they 'set such a high value of Religious instruction in the elementary school that we consider it the most important part of education – such being our belief we are unable to give up our school to a secular School Board'.[103] The cost of providing new schools in large, thinly populated and comparatively poor districts was very heavy. Sometimes two or three small schools rather than one substantial school had to be kept open in order to provide schooling within a reasonable distance of all the population. In 1880 it was recognized that 'the operation of the 1870 Act had been burdensome'.[104] An analysis of the elementary schools' log books also reveals other wide-ranging problems and tribulations in the era of 'payment by results' – unpaid fees, pressure from the annual examination and the visits of HMI, the resignation of the headteacher of Llangynfelyn after poor examination results in 1875 and 1876, the disparity of the efficiency of schools and quality of teachers, pupil-teachers moving too often, lack of equipment and harsh corporal punishment.[105] Irregular attendance was a perennial problem in spite of by-laws adopted by twenty-five Boards by 1879 making school attendance compulsory and the appointment of a 'Compelling Officer' such as at Aberystwyth in 1875.[106] Incentives, including certificates and book prizes, were available for good attendance. The problem of absenteeism reflected social pressures, including much poverty as well as attitudes of parents to education in late Victorian rural society.[107] Compulsory schooling which, until 1891, required the payment of fees, was a novel concept. For many tenant farmers, their children's labour was essential for potato planting, haymaking, corn harvesting, peat cutting and stripping bark from trees to supply local tanneries.[108] For this task a two-week holiday was granted at

[102]Ibid. (1880–1), p.436.

[103]G. G. Davies, *Ysgol Llanarth* (Aberaeron, 1984), p.8; idem, 'Addysg elfennol yn sir Aberteifi, 1870–1902', *Ceredigion*, IV, no.4 (1963), 355.

[104]*Report of the Committee of Council on Education* (London, 1880–1), p.438.

[105]Ceredigion RO Log Books, Cardiganshire elementary schools: *Reports of the Committee of Council on Education* (1870–1899); Davies, 'Addysg elfennol yn sir Aberteifi', 353–73; O. Thomas, 'Log books of Cardiganshire schools, 1860–80', *TCAS*, XIII (1938), 56–69. S. E. Jones and E. Jones, *Ysgol Ysbyty Ystwyth 1878–1978* (Llandysul, 1978); K. Davies and T. Llew Jones, *Canrif o Addysg Gynradd: Ysgol Tregroes 1878–1978* (Llandysul, 1978); Tegwyn Jones, 'Golwg ar hanes yr ardal 1740–1876', in *Rhydypennau, 1876–1976* (Ysgol Gynradd Rhydypennau, 1976); J. R. Rees (ed.), *Rhwng Gwenffrwd ac Arth: Canmlwyddiant Ysgol Penuwch 1879–1979* (Llandysul, 1979); D. Jones and W. J. Gruffydd, *Rhwng y Bont a Ffair Rhos: Hanes Ysgol Pontrhydfendigaid 1879–1979* (Llandysul, 1979); G. J. Thomas (ed.), *Ysgol Llan-non: Canrif o Addysg – A Mwy* (Llan-non, 1978); D. Davies, *Those Were the Days: Cardigan* (Cardigan, 1991).

[106]R. Phillips, *Dyn a'i Wreiddiau – Hanes Plwyf Llangwyryfon* (Aberystwyth, 1975); Trott, 'Implementation of the 1870 Education Act', 212–13.

[107]Trott, 'Aberystwyth School Board and Board School', 3–17.

[108]Davies, 'Addysg elfennol yn sir Aberteifi'; Thomas, 'Log books of Cardiganshire schools'.

Llangynfelyn. The log books reflect the pattern of the seasons. In some localities, such as Ponrhydfendigaid in 1879, the best attendance was in the winter months when 'the winter children would return'.[109] But there was also parental apathy and neglect, with children kept at home to help with the most trifling work. Local hiring fairs, processions, circus visits and ship launchings also proved to be regular and powerful counter-attractions.[110] At Aberystwyth, reviews of the militia, Wombwell's menagerie, circuses, lifeboat practices, casual work in boarding houses and the need to 'attend the donkeys' kept children away from school.[111] In 1884, when the 'overall attendance was very unequal in Cardiganshire', much depended on 'the intelligence and energy of attendance officers and firm and discriminating action of magistrates'.[112]

The Welsh language was also perceived to be a problem in the era of the Revised Code.[113] It was not a grant-earning subject until 1890 and it was viewed by inspectors, headteachers and some parents as an educational handicap. Effective schooling was synonymous with English-medium education. At Rhydypennau Board School in 1877 'the children were forbidden to talk Welsh in school and in the playground, which was enforced in order that they might be brought to pay more attention to English'.[114] Elsewhere in the county, log books also reveal the emphasis placed on improving competence in English. Welsh was not taught as a subject before the 1890s nor used as a medium to teach other subjects in the curriculum. Inevitably it was sometimes used for translation and dictation and as the natural medium of communication in virtually monoglot communities. At Ystumtuen in 1878 the HMI condemned its usage: 'The mistress ought not to speak Welsh to the scholars as she does, but should train them to understand and speak English.'[115] Occasionally, as at Cribyn in 1885, headteachers were critical of the expectation that virtually monoglot pupils in Wales should reach the same standard in English as pupils in England.[116] There was lack of uniformity regarding the value of Welsh as an essential qualification for headship. At Cardigan it was regarded as an advantage in 1872, but by 1890 it was judged not essential. An Englishman – W. J. Bradbury from Barnsley – was not succeeded by a Welshman as head of Aberystwyth Board School until the appointment of D. J. Saer, a staunch supporter and researcher into bilingualism, in 1895.[117] By then, in response to the activities of Dan Isaac Davies and the Welsh Language Society, the recommendation of the Cross Report of 1888 had led to the new code of regulations in 1890, including Welsh as a fee-earning subject for older pupils.[118] The Welsh language was now more widely taught. Thomas Darlington HMI, an Englishman, was based in Aberystwyth in the late 1890s. He learnt Welsh and favoured its usage as a subject and medium of instruction in schools.[119] But the schools remained very Anglicized. In 1958 Hettie Glyn Davies recalled that at Llannarth in

---

[109]Quoted in Thomas, 'Log books of Cardiganshire schools', 64.
[110]Davies, 'Addysg elfennol yn sir Aberteifi', 367.
[111]Trott, 'Aberystwyth School Board and Board School', 3–17.
[112]*Report of the Committee of Council on Education* (London, 1884–5), p.341.
[113]W. G. Evans, 'The "bilingual difficulty": H.M.I. and the Welsh language in the Victorian Age', *WHR*, 16, no.4 (1993), 494–513.
[114]Ceredigion RO, Log Book. Rhydypennau Board School, 16 February 1877.
[115]Davies, 'Addysg elfennol yn sir Aberteifi', 367; Thomas, 'Log books of Cardiganshire schools', 61–2.
[116]Davies, 'Addysg elfennol yn sir Aberteifi', 367.
[117]Trott, 'Aberystwyth School Board and Board School', 13–17.
[118]J. E. Hughes, *Arloeswr Dwyieithedd – Dan Isaac Davies 1839–1887* (Cardiff, 1984).
[119]*DWB*.

1899 'Saesnigedd oedd pob peth yn yr ysgol' (Everything in the school was English.)[120] The broader curriculum for older pupils in some schools in the 1890s also included mathematics, French and Latin at Llannarth and Brynherbert; arts, crafts, technical work and science at Alexandra Road School, Aberystwyth, and French at Rhydypennau.[121] As well as evening continuation classes such as those at Pontgarreg, some schools, including Tal-y-bont, Llannarth and Llangynfelyn gained a high reputation for training pupil-teachers,[122] while others, including Aberystwyth Board and National schools, were recognized by the University College of Wales in 1892 as 'practising schools' for students training as teachers.[123]

The tradition of opening private schools and academies, particularly by Unitarian ministers, continued in Cardiganshire in the second half of the nineteenth century. The 'Rhydowen Grammar School', known locally as 'Ysgol Pontshân', was opened by the Unitarian minister, the Revd Thomas Thomas, in 1847. For thirty years it provided efficient instruction in mathematics and navigation as well as classics. Many of the pupils, who included Dr J. Gwenogvryn Evans and Professor D. E. Jones, later became clergymen, ministers, lawyers, doctors, teachers and merchant seamen.[124] At nearby Llandysul, the Revd William Thomas, Gwilym Marles (1834–79), a classics graduate of the University of Glasgow and Unitarian minister at Llwynrhydowen and Bwlchyfadfa, opened a grammar school in 1860, which also functioned successfully until shortly before his untimely death in 1879.[125] Thereafter 'Ysgoldy Tyssul' was kept open by the Revd William James until, in 1894, it came under the control of the Revd Thomas James, who moved from the Methodist Chapel vestry. He had established a successful grammar school there since 1868, where students had been prepared for entrance to the University Colleges at Aberystwyth and Cardiff, St David's College, Lampeter, Carmarthen Presbyterian College, as well as Oxford and Cambridge. A number of pupils gained University of London degrees directly from Llandysul Grammar School.[126] There were also other private schools of varying quality, including Ardwyn Grammar School, Aberystwyth, and day and boarding schools for girls at Aberaeron, Cardigan, Aberystwyth, Lampeter and Newcastle Emlyn. Sarah Jane Rees (Cranogwen) (1839–1916) enjoyed a high reputation as a teacher. She taught at the Nautical School, Llangrannog, and at Talgarreg. In 1879 she launched the influential journal, *Y Frythones*.[127]

The endowed grammar schools experienced a period of fluctuating success in the second half of the nineteenth century. Ystradmeurig lost much of its former glory following the opening of St

[120]H. G. Davies, *Edrych yn Ôl: Hen Atgofion am Geredigion* (Liverpool, 1958), p.40.

[121]Trott, 'Aberystwyth School Board and Board School', 7; Davies, 'Addysg elfennol yn sir Aberteifi', 364–7.

[122]They included (Dr) Thomas Richards at Llangynfelyn, who gained a First Class Certificate in 1897 and Hettie Williams (Mrs H. G. Davies) Llannarth, who was ninth on list of Queen's Scholars in England and Wales in 1899. See Davies, *Edrych yn Ôl*, pp.106–19; T. Richards, *Atgofion Cardi* (Aberystwyth, 1960), p.43.

[123]W. G. Evans (ed.), *Fit to Educate? A Century of Teacher Education and Training 1892–1992* (Aberystwyth, 1992).

[124]D. Evans, *Welsh Unitarians and Schoolmasters* (Llandysul, n.d), p.10.

[125]*DWB*; Davies, *Hanes Plwyf Llandyssul*, pp.206–9.

[126]J. E. Davies, *Cyfrol Goffa y Parch Thomas James M.A. Llandyssul* (Caerdydd, 1922), pp.29–55.

[127]G. Jones, *Cranogwen, Portread Newydd* (Llandysul, 1987); Ceridwen Peris, 'Cranogwen', *Y Drysorfa*, no.1303 (1939), 261–6; S. Rh. Williams, 'The true "Cymraes": images of women in women's nineteenth-century Welsh periodicals', in A. V. John (ed.), *Our Mother's Land: Chapters in Welsh Women's History, 1830–1939* (Cardiff, 1991), pp.80–6.

Fig. 129: Sarah Jane Rees, Cranogwen (1839–1916), schoolmistress at the Nautical School, Llangrannog, and editor of *Y Frythones. (Copyright National Library of Wales).*

David's College, Lampeter, in 1827. By the 1850s, during the headmastership of the Revd John William Morris (1826–59), it had 'declined to the level of an elementary school'.[128] Most of the pupils were now local. No longer were some of its Anglican pupils ordained direct to the Church and fewer Nonconformists enrolled following the opening of Bala Theological College in 1837. Income from endowments was comparatively small and the school was poorly staffed. However, during the headmastership of the Revd Lewis Evans (1859–70), there was 'an appreciable rise in the reputation of the school'. Competent staff, including D. Lewis Lloyd in 1865, were appointed. There was an average enrolment of seventy to eighty pupils, though as many as 125 boys enrolled in 1867. The Taunton Commission noted that it served as the elementary school for the poor children of the neighbourhood and also as a classical school for the sons of Cardiganshire farmers with ambitions of proceeding to higher education.[129] It also claimed that it could improve if its board of trustees were reconstituted, its management placed under 'more energetic hands', and the curriculum broadened.

[128]Osborne-Jones, *Edward Richard*, pp.72–3.
[129]*Report of the Schools Inquiry Commission (Taunton Report)*, XX (1868), pp.77–80.

It was unlikely, however, that money would be forthcoming to erect a new building. The removal of the school to Aberystwyth, advocated by some in south Wales, would also meet with local opposition.[130] Indeed, with the completion of railway communications, it was thought that Ystrad-meurig would be strategically located to serve the secondary educational needs of inland parts of Cardiganshire as well as parts of Montgomeryshire and Radnorshire. But, in 1881, the Aberdare Report advocated its transfer to a more populous centre. Lampeter, Aberaeron and Aberystwyth were mentioned at the time, and the Report's comments on Ystradmeurig were damning: 'It was absolutely destitute of any school building worthy of the name – the premises were unsuitable even for the humblest elementary school.'[131] With only thirty-two pupils – 75 per cent of whom were Anglican – in attendance, Ystradmeurig epitomized many of the weaknesses and problems of the grammar schools of Wales on the eve of the Welsh Intermediate Education Act. Poor buildings, lack of suitable accommodation, insufficient endowments, remote locations, lack of scholarships and exhibitions, a narrow classical curriculum and an Anglican ethos made the school increasingly unattractive. The headmaster, the Revd John Jones, acknowledged that 'we are different to other schools; we do not pretend to teach science and all its ramifications and commercial education, and so we miss these boys altogether'.[132]

The Taunton Commission believed that Lampeter Grammar School, in spite of many disadvantages – 'ill furnished and somewhat cheerless schoolroom, lack of funds, pupils imperfectly acquainted with English, the want of elementary schools in the area' – was 'doing useful work in a praiseworthy manner' in providing a mainly classical education for the twenty-six day pupils enrolled.[133] In 1881 twelve of the seventeen pupils enrolled for a classical education were Anglicans. It was noted by the Aberdare Committee that there was no endowment other than a site and building which was 'in a wretched condition'.[134] In 1884 the school was transferred to the grounds of St David's College and, on becoming Lampeter College School, acquired better buildings. Cardigan Grammar School, with sixteen boys pursuing a classical education, was held in the Guildhall until 1895 following its erection on the site of the old school in 1858–60.[135] In 1864 the Taunton Commission doubted whether it could ever become prosperous as a classical school. It suffered from 'permanent disadvantages' – the economic decline of the town following the demise of the port and its coastal trade; its lack of spirit – 'altogether a sluggish, lifeless sort of place, where one does not expect to see anything flourish'; the poverty of local farmers, who were content with local elementary schools; richer people sending their children to boarding schools, especially in England, and, above all, Nonconformists standing aloof from 'a Church of England affair'.[136] Neglect by the recent headmaster and the lack of interest of the mayor and corporation in the school's welfare aggravated the situation. By 1881 there were thirty-five day pupils at the school, all of whom were studying Latin, Greek and modern languages. Natural science and mathematics were also taught. It was felt in the area that 'extraneous assistance' should be provided to put the school on a satisfactory

[130]Ibid., pp.79–80.
[131]Report of the Committee Appointed to Inquire into the Condition of Intermediate and Higher Education in Wales (Aberdare Report) (London, 1881), I, pl.vi.
[132]Ibid., Minutes of Evidence, II, p.420.
[133]Taunton Report, p.73.
[134]Aberdare Report, I, Appendix X–XI.
[135]PRO Ed. 27/6329. MSS Cardigan Free School.
[136]Taunton Report, pp.68–70.

Fig. 130: The entire staff and pupils at Aberystwyth County School, 13 July 1897. (*Copyright National Library of Wales*).

footing. There was no other effective provision of secondary education within a considerable distance of Cardigan.[137]

By 1881, although the position of Cardiganshire was not as unsatisfactory as other areas, it was not surprising that the Aberdare Committee concluded that the existing provision for intermediate education in Wales was 'far from adequate in amount and not wholly suitable in character'.[138] It recognized the need for the establishment of new, undenominational and popularly managed schools financed from the rates and Treasury grants. Eventually in 1889, following a long and often acrimonious parliamentary struggle, the Welsh Intermediate and Technical Education Act was passed. A Joint Education Committee, under the chairmanship of the Revd Llewellyn Edwards, Ardwyn School, was appointed to prepare and submit to the Charity Commission a scheme for the promotion of intermediate and technical education in the county.[139] The Cardiganshire Scheme was approved by Her Majesty in Council on 23 November 1893, but was followed by an Amended Scheme approved on 1 August 1896.[140] The first intermediate school in Cardiganshire was opened – initially in temporary accommodation – at Llandysul on 24 September 1895. This was followed by the

[137] *Aberdare Report*, I, Appendix, x.
[138] Ibid., I, L.
[139] D. S. Griffiths, 'The implications of the Welsh Intermediate Education Act and its consequences in Cardiganshire to 1921' (unpublished University of Wales M.Ed. thesis, 1974).
[140] PRO Ed. 35/3145.

opening of intermediate schools at Cardigan in December 1895, at Aberaeron in May, and at Aberystwyth in October 1896 (with David Samuel as headmaster)[141] and at Tregaron in May 1897. Much enthusiasm and rivalry were displayed in the quest for intermediate education, with villages such as Llannarth and Llanybydder, as well as towns, demanding intermediate schools. The sum of £1,000 was promised towards an intermediate school at Pontrhydfendigaid. The decision to exclude the existing grammar schools at Lampeter and Ystradmeurig from the county scheme because of their denominational character generated a bitter sectarian dispute involving intervention by the Bishop of Chester in the House of Lords in September 1893. In the amended scheme approved in 1896 both schools were still excluded, but provision was now made for the area with the establishment of an intermediate school at Tregaron.[142] By 1898, following the opening of new school buildings, 373 pupils were enrolled in the county's five intermediate schools, administered by the county Governing Body. Much enthusiasm, financial generosity and pride had ensured the completion of 'the educational ladder' in Cardiganshire. Except for Glamorgan, there were more pupils aged sixteen or over in intermediate schools in Cardiganshire by 1900 than in any other Welsh county. A total of 75 per cent of the teachers were graduates – a higher proportion than in any other Welsh county.[143]

St David's College, Lampeter, and the University College of Wales, Aberystwyth, were already well-established beacons of higher learning. Although established to provide training for ordinands, St David's College was not intended to be merely a theological college. A university education in arts and sciences as well as theology was intended. In 1852 a charter was granted empowering the College to confer the degree of Bachelor of Divinity and, following an enlargement of this charter in 1865, the power of conferring the degree of Bachelor of Arts was also given to the College.[144] But Lampeter was regarded as a bastion of Anglicanism, and its quest for university status even within the newly established University of Wales in 1893 remained unfulfilled.[145] Many problems, too, faced the unsectarian University College of Wales, which was established purely by chance in the vacant seafront building at Aberystwyth in 1872. Its survival in the face of many problems, especially financial, during its first ten years and its inclusion as the senior constituent college in the federal University of Wales in 1893 has been justifiably regarded as one of the significant achievements of Victorian Wales.[146] An enrolment of 292 students in 1893 had increased to 474 by 1900, and the opening of the Alexandra Hall of Residence in 1896 was a significant step in the promotion of higher education for women.

The Balfour Education Act of 1902 abolished the School Boards and established Local Education Authorities, which were given responsibility for secondary and further education as well as for the elementary schools. In their opposition to the new legislation for 'violating religious liberty and equality' and 'sacrificing Education for Denominationalism', the Tregaron School Board epitomized widespread Nonconformist opposition to the provision of rate support for denominational schools.[147] Nevertheless, a scheme for the constitution of an Education Committee of forty members

[141]Griffiths, 'Welsh Intermediate Education Act', p.57. A distinguished scholar, Samuel had opened a private grammar school at Old Bank House in Bridge Street in 1887. He became headmaster of the County School located at Ardwyn in 1896.
[142]PRO Ed. 27/6327; Ed. 27/6329; Ed. 27/6329; *Hansard*, 4 September 1893.
[143]Griffiths, 'Welsh Intermediate Act', 54–67.
[144]Price, *History of St David's University College*, I, p.111.
[145]J. G. Williams, *The University Movement in Wales: A History of the University of Wales* (Cardiff, 1993).
[146]E. L. Ellis, *The University College of Wales Aberystwyth 1872–1972* (Cardiff, 1972).
[147]Ceredigion RO, Minutes, Tregaron District School Board, 20 June 1902.

was approved by Cardiganshire County Council on 4 February 1904. Superseding thirty-eight School Boards and the County Governing Body, the Education Committee commenced its duties on the 'Appointed Day', 26 September 1904.[148]

Most of the elementary schools were comparatively small. In 1913 there were only three with an average attendance of 200 or more, and twenty with an average attendance ranging between 100 and 200. Thirty-three schools had an average attendance of fifty and under; nine of these were under thirty and two under twenty. A proposal in 1906 to close the thirty-three-pupil Strata Florida Abbey School and transfer the pupils to Pontrhydfendigaid was vigorously and successfully opposed by the local community.[149] Of the 106 elementary schools, staffed by 400 teachers, eighty-two were Provided or Council Schools and twenty-four were Non-Provided or Voluntary Schools. Aber-arth, Aberaeron and Pontgarreg British Schools, and Capel Seion, Llanilar and Llanfarian National Schools had been transferred to the Council since the Appointed Day.[150] Many of the former Board and voluntary schools required extensive repairs. New council schools were built at Llanwnnen in 1908, Bronnant in 1911, and Gartheli and Tregaron in 1913.[151] By the outbreak of the First World War, there had been a significant transformation, with ninety-one of the 106 elementary schools having been built or renovated at a cost of nearly £40,000 since the Appointed Day. But the Medical Officer of Health still reported that fifty-seven schools had no drinking water, and forty-one no water for washing purposes. A total pupil enrolment of 11,076 in 1902–3 had declined to 9,034 by 1913. Irregular attendance remained a problem and the LEA awarded watches, medals and certificates to children who attended school regularly.[152] The establishment of the School Medical Service led to significant improvement in pupils' health. The curriculum of the schools still epitomized the uniformity emanating from the controls introduced earlier by the schedules of the Board of Education Codes. But some schools, such as Lampeter, which introduced nature study, and Alexandra Road, Aberystwyth, which developed handwork, took advantage of the freedom to develop their own individuality.[153] The Education Authority issued clear instructions to managers and teachers in 1907 concerning the usage of the Welsh language in the curriculum. The majority of pupils were monoglot Welsh and were not introduced to English until after the infant stage and even then only gradually.[154] In contrast to the Victorian era and before the inclusion of Welsh in the School Code in l890, when poetry was entirely confined to English authors, Welsh poetry was now read. Indeed HMI reported in 1913 that 'a great impetus has been given during recent years to the study of Welsh literature in all the Cardiganshire schools'.[155] Likewise, the study of the history of the county received a significant impetus with the publication of D. J. Saer's *The Story of Cardiganshire* (1921). But there was still a heavy premium in many schools on learning English. Miss Cassie Davies

[148]Ceredigion RO, Minutes, Cardiganshire County Council.

[149]Ceredigion RO, Minutes, Cardiganshire Education Committee, 14 and 20 March 1906; 18 October 1906.

[150]*HMI, Report* (1913), pp.6–7; 'Jubilee of Cardiganshire Education Committee', *Welsh Gazette*, 8 July 1954.

[151]Ibid.

[152]NLW, XLB 2877. *Report on Chief Causes of Irregular Attendance in the District of Aberystwyth* (London, 1909).

[153]*HMI Report* (1913), pp.14–34; Ceredigion RO, Minutes Cardiganshire Education Committee (1904–14).

[154]Minutes Cardiganshire Education Committee, 17 January 1907; 23 May 1907.

[155]*HMI, Report* (1913), p.17.

HMI recalled in 1973 the peripheral and inferior position of the Welsh language at Blaencaron between 1902 and 1913.[156] Welsh history was neglected in some schools, while the influence of gender on timetables usually led to 'drawing for boys' and 'needlework for girls'. The need for more practical subjects – gardening and woodwork classes for boys and more cookery and laundry classes for girls – was being advocated in 1913.

By the outbreak of the First World War, the county's five intermediate schools, with an enrolment of 339 boys and 299 girls in 1913, had 'served the county well; they have raised the standard of Secondary Education, and they have thereby increased the efficiency of the Cardiganshire youth whether he remains at home or seeks advancement outside his own county'.[157] But their academic bias and examination orientation was only too apparent. The one determining goal was University matriculation. O. M. Edwards described Aberaeron Intermediate School in 1913 as 'one of the most examination-ridden schools in Wales'.[158] HMI contended that 'the idea of the educational ladder has blinded many to the fact that while the school has its important duties to perform with regard to those who proceed to a University, it has equally important duties with regard to the many who do not prepare for a learned profession'.[159] The intermediate schools needed to adapt their curricula to the economic needs of their neighbourhood. Agriculture and navigation were conspicuously lacking from the schools' timetables. Welsh also had only the minimum of attention. Tuition fees varied from £4 to £5 per annum at different schools, but in accordance with the Free Place Regulations of 1907, 25 per cent of the pupils were admitted each year as free pupils.[160] Occasionally schools were reminded by HMI of their obligations. There was also the independent Ystradmeurig Grammar School, where the Revd John Jones – 'John Latin' – was headmaster 1870–95,[161] and St David's College School, Lampeter, with 107 pupils, which enjoyed an excellent reputation for classics and mathematics. From 1902 onwards it received small grants from the Board of Education and was subject to inspection.[162]

The LEA also achieved considerable success in its first decade of the twentieth century in promoting further education. Evening schools were held regularly, usually in the premises of the county's elementary schools. Wide-ranging courses were available, including agriculture, gardening, woodwork, first aid, nursing, domestic subjects, science, practical mathematics, music, shorthand and book-keeping, and economic history. In 1909–10 – the high-water mark of pre-war further education in the county – 710 males and 690 women were enrolled in evening schools. Summer schools in domestic subjects and handiwork and the provision of scholarships in agriculture and dairying were arranged in conjunction with the University College of Wales, Aberystwyth, whose Education Department made regular use of Cardiganshire schools for the training of teachers.[163] At Aberystwyth the total enrolment at the University College averaged 451 between 1901 and 1911. In 1913–14 there were 429 students. At Lampeter enrolment remained comparatively low and in the pre-war years an average of forty-nine students were admitted annually.[164]

[156]C. Davies, *Hwb i'r Galon* (Llandysul, 1973), pp.148–9.
[157]*HMI, Report* (1913), p.37; T. J. James (ed.), *Ardwyn Jubilee Magazine 1896–1946* (August, 1946).
[158]PRO Ed. 35/3144. Report dated 11 August 1913.
[159]*HMI, Report* (1913), p.37.
[160]PRO Ed. 35/3144.
[161]W. M. Davies, 'St. John's College, Ystrad Meurig', *Province*, IV, no.2 (1953), 204–5.
[162]D. T. W. Price, *A History of Saint David's University College Lampeter, Volume 2* (Cardiff, 1977), Appendix I.
[163]Evans, *Fit to Educate*, pp.78–91.
[164]Ellis, *University College of Wales*, p.342; Price, *History of St David's University College*, II, p.245.

The First World War exerted a profound influence on educational institutions and proved to be a catalyst for educational change. The shadow of the great conflict hung over the College at Aberystwyth as staff and students joined the armed forces. At the end of the war, the Royal Commission on University Education in Wales (the Haldane Commission) published its Report, and in 1917 the Department of Education at Aberystwyth became the first university department in the United Kingdom to establish a special teacher training course for discharged soldiers and sailors. Fourteen Serbians were admitted to the College free of fees in 1918 through the agency of the Serbian Relief Fund.[165] Schools were also influenced, in various ways, by the conflict. Teachers were enlisted, new songs – 'It's a Long Way to Tipperary', 'Kitchener's Boys', and 'Rule Britannia' – were learnt, geography and history lessons highlighted 'the great European War', and lessons were given on patriotism. A Board of Education booklet dealing with the observance of St David's Day and the Teaching of Patriotism was adopted in 1916. War Savings Associations were formed and a total of £250,000 was raised, food parcels were sent to old pupils in the armed forces, and the deaths of soldiers were marked by school closures. Renovations to schools were deferred.[166] The new Education Act of 1918, with its proposals for nursery education, the extension of secondary education and the opening of continuation schools, together with the visit of H. A. L. Fisher, President of the Board of Education, to the University College of Wales, Aberystwyth, generated much optimism.[167]

Under the terms of the new legislation all county and county borough councils were entrusted with 'the duty of providing for the progressive development and comprehensive organization of education within their areas'. No child under fourteen in future would leave school, and for those who would leave elementary or secondary school before the age of sixteen, a system of part-time compulsory education up to sixteen – and eventually to eighteen – was established in central and continuation schools. Henceforth, elementary education was no longer to be an end in itself but merely a stage 'on the educational high-road now to be opened'.[168] By 1920 a sub-committee of the Cardiganshire Education Committee had drafted a scheme for the establishment of twenty-two central schools and 'central tops' to provide a three or four year course of advanced instruction for pupils not admitted to the five intermediate schools. It was intended 'to furnish a liberal education in close touch with the life of the neighbourhood'. It was also intended that the central school and 'central top' would serve as 'continuation schools' for part-time pupils aged fourteen to eighteen. Increased facilities for adult education were also proposed for all the towns and larger villages. The Cardiganshire plan constituted abolishing the all-age elementary school for the majority of pupils and was a step towards implementing a policy of 'secondary education for all' in different types of schools, a notion increasingly advocated in the inter-war years.[169] But in Cardiganshire, as in most other areas of England and Wales, financial stringencies in the inter-war years and other difficulties of reorganization in rural areas, including the religious question, prevented the implementation of the education blueprint. Reorganization in Cardiganshire was confined to the Lampeter District only. A non-selective central school was opened at Lampeter through the conversion of Bryn Road

---

[165]Evans, *Fit to Educate*, p.90.
[166]Ceredigion RO, School Log Books, Minutes Cardiganshire Education Committee, 1914–18.
[167]Evans, *Fit to Educate*, p.90.
[168]L. Andrews, *The Education Act 1918* (London, 1976), pp.35–6.
[169]*Scheme of the Cardiganshire Education Committee* (Aberystwyth, 1920).

Elementary Boys' School and the transfer there of senior pupils from elementary schools in the district.[170] The need for further reorganization was regarded as long overdue in the mid-1930s. Following the Hadow Report of 1926 and its advocacy of some form of post-primary education for all normal children from the age of eleven, the Education Act of 1936, which raised the school-leaving age to fifteen from September 1939, and the publication of G. A. N. Lowndes's book, *The Silent Social Revolution* (Oxford, 1937), a Reorganization Committee prepared another Draft Scheme for the Reorganization of Schools in Cardiganshire in 1939.[171] It involved the establishment of a network of ten 'senior schools' at suitable centres in rural districts where the curriculum would be of a more practical character than that of the five intermediate or secondary schools. The 'senior schools' were intended for Ponterwyd, Aberystwyth, Rhydypennau, Llan-non, Plwmp, Cardigan, Henllan, Lampeter, Trawsgoed and Tregaron.[172]

The five intermediate schools were intended to provide mainly, though not exclusively, a literary and scientific education. The inter-war years saw periodic criticisms of inadequate buildings, overcrowding at Ardwyn and Cardigan, insufficient numbers of free places, and inadequate attention to Welsh, Welsh history, and rural and domestic subjects. At Ardwyn in 1923–4, Welsh and French were alternative subjects, and arithmetic rather than mathematics was taught to girls in the fifth form.[173] At Cardigan in 1923, a highly critical HMI Report condemned a teacher for hectoring and ridiculing pupils: 'To hold up to ridicule Welsh boys and girls because their want of mastery of English as this teacher does is not only an unwarrantable misuse of his position, but a degradation of his high calling.' The egregious teacher – Dr Parker – was deemed 'temperamentally unsuitable to teach Welsh children'.[174] Although accommodation deficiencies and overcrowding at Ardwyn – where there were 430 pupils in 1937 in a school built to accommodate 350 – were highlighted in the 1930s, the Board of Education refused requests for extensions and in 1937 advocated a more restricted entry.[175] In 1932 drastic government economies led to the replacement of free places in secondary schools – 58.2 per cent in Cardiganshire – by means-tested special places and the raising of fees from £5 to £6 a year.[176] The Board of Education was anxious to give priority to the reorganization of elementary education and in 1938 it regarded 'the provision for secondary education in Cardiganshire as very liberal'.[177] There were 1,469 pupils in 1938 and, with one or two exceptions, the county was said to have the highest proportion of pupils in secondary schools in the whole of England and Wales. £40,000 had been spent on capital expenditure at three secondary schools. In 1935 the possibility of opening a girls' secondary school in Aberystwyth and in 1938 the building of a new secondary school at Lampeter was mooted locally. But some members of the Education Committee also showed interest in 'The Anglesey Scheme' of multilateral secondary schools.[178]

National attention focused on the county's *cause célèbre* – the secondary schools' strike of 1922–3 – caused by the rejection of the Cardiganshire salary scale, condemned as 'the lowest in the kingdom'. Schools were closed, teachers dismissed, blacklegs appointed, and much bitterness generated. By

[170]Ceredigion RO, Minutes, Cardiganshire Education Committee, 1918–25.
[171]Ibid. (1925–39). There were also Draft Schemes in 1930 and 1931. *Welsh Gazette*, 27 May 1935.
[172]*A Draft Scheme for the Reorganisation of Schools in Cardiganshire* (Aberystwyth, 1933).
[173]PRO Ed. 35/3145; Ed. 109/7750; Ed. 35/3144.
[174]PRO Ed. 35/3146.
[175]PRO Ed. 35/6852.
[176]PRO Ed. 110/133. Memo: Regulations: Fees and Special Places 1933.
[177]PRO Ed. 35/6853. Memo: Wynn Wheldon, dated 2 December 1933.
[178]Ibid. Letter, dated 6 December 1938, Director of Education H. J. Lewis to Wynn Wheldon.

1924 the consequences of the strike were entangled with the non-recognition on the grant list of Cardigan and Llandysul schools – where new 'blackleg' teachers, had been appointed – following unsatisfactory inspection reports. At Llandysul there was 'malice, rancour and spite like poison gas in the atmosphere of Cardiganshire'.[179]

An investigation by HMI in 1932 into the teaching of Welsh in the county's elementary schools concluded that of a total of 6,905 pupils, 5,918 spoke Welsh. It approved the new emphasis on teaching through the medium of the mother tongue in the child's early years and advocated more effective schemes of work with older pupils.[180] But not everyone was satisfied that Welsh was safe in the Authority's elementary schools in the 1930s. In 1939 Ifan ab Owen Edwards opened a private Welsh-medium primary school at Canolfan yr Urdd, Aberystwyth, initially for seven pupils. It proved to be a significant event in the growth of Welsh-medium education in Wales.[181]

The Second World War, which led to evacuees from Liverpool and Kent arriving in Cardiganshire schools, highlighted social deficiencies nationwide and also ushered in a period of reconstruction and reform.[182] Planning for post-war educational reconstruction began within the Board of Education. The White Paper – *Educational Reconstruction* (1943) – formed the basis of the subsequent 1944 Education Act which required local education authorities to submit development plans.

A special Reorganization Committee was set up in Cardiganshire. On 30 May 1946 a draft development plan was presented to the Education Committee and the final Development Plan was submitted to the Ministry of Education in March 1947.[183] As well as reorganizing primary education, which involved the closure of twenty-two schools, of which ten were voluntary controlled, secondary education was to be provided for all pupils aged eleven to nineteen in mixed bilateral – grammar/modern – schools.[184] As far as rural areas like Aberaeron, Lampeter and Tregaron were concerned, the Minister raised no objection. However, he did not view the plan for two bilateral schools in Aberystwyth with favour. He preferred separate grammar and modern schools. Proposals for bilateral schools in the Cardigan and Llandysul districts were also queried and greater support shown for separate grammar and modern schools. Consultation with the Pembrokeshire and Carmarthenshire LEAs was also advocated. In the meetings which followed attention focused on the respective merits of bilateral vis-à-vis separate grammar and modern schools; the location of schools; border problems; the possibility of a joint grammar rural residential school at a central point where the three counties met to serve the whole lower Teifi Valley and supplemented by modern schools at Cardigan, Llandysul, Newcastle Emlyn and Crymych; the use of the prisoner-of-war camp at Henllan as a modern school for the Llandysul area; and the opening of an agricultural secondary technical school. The revised Development Plan was finally approved by the Ministry of Education after much deliberation and disagreement with the LEA, especially concerning Cardigan, in December 1951. It was intended that secondary education in Cardiganshire would embody

[179]PRO Ed. 35/6854. Memo, dated 29 March 1924, G. P. Williams HMI to A. T. Davies.
[180]*A Statement based on an investigation into the teaching of Welsh in the Elementary Schools of the County of Cardigan* (HMI, 1932).
[181]D. Ifans (ed.), *Dathlwn Glod: Ysgol Gymraeg Aberystwyth, 1939–1989* (Aberystwyth, 1989).
[182]Ceredigion RO, Log Book Taliesin School; Anfield Road Council School, Liverpool, evacuated there in 1939–43, PRO Ed. 35/6855: Evacuation of Oulton High School Liverpool to Cardigan. Ed. 35/6850: Holyrood School Aber-mad; evacuated from Bognor Regis 1940, to Lluest and then to Aber-mad 1943.
[183]Ceredigion RO, Minutes Cardiganshire Education Committee, 30 May 1946, 27 March 1947.
[184]Ceredigion RO, Cardiganshire Education Committee Development Plan, 27 March 1947.

the selective-grammar/modern principle in three districts and three bilateral schools.[185] Significantly, since selective grammar schools were preferred by the Ministry of Education, it was stated that Cardiganshire would experiment with three bilaterals only.

TABLE 19: Types of secondary schools, 1951

School district	Secondary schools	No of pupils (1951)	Form entry	Type	Other remarks
Aberaeron	Bilateral Grammar/ Modern	558	4	Mixed 11–19	
Aberystwyth	Grammar	485	3	"	Proposed New School on Cefn-llan to accommodate 700 pupils
	Modern	415	3	"	
Cardigan	Grammar	463	3	"	
	Modern	194		"	
Lampeter	Bilateral Grammar/ Modern	438			
Llandysul	Grammar	344	2		
Tregaron	Bilateral Grammar/ Modern	386	3		
Henllan	Modern	293			Temporary arrangement until 1960

In fact, *ad hoc* reorganization had already begun, with secondary modern schools – St Mary's Secondary Modern School, Cardigan (1949), Henllan, and Dinas Secondary Modern School, Aberystwyth (1950) – already functioning. The five county intermediate schools and Lampeter Central School were renamed county secondary schools in 1945. In November 1950 the Ministry of Education approved the expenditure of £90,000 on the first instalment of the new Dinas School at Cefn-llan, Aberystwyth.[186] Since 1948 it had temporarily shared the Alexandra Road primary school. Approval was also given for the acquisition of a site at Erw Goch for the purposes of building a new grammar school at Aberystwyth. By the end of 1949 all Cardiganshire children over eleven years of age were receiving secondary education. The Minister of Education himself laid the foundation stone of a new secondary school at Lampeter on 30 March 1945. Following a long struggle, Lampeter College School was forced to close later in the same year. Ystradmeurig remained open until the 1950s.

[185]G. E. Jones, *Which Nation's Schools? Direction and Devolution in Welsh Education in the Twentieth Century* (Cardiff, 1990), pp.135–43.
[186]'Jubilee of Cardiganshire Education Committee', *Welsh Gazette*, 8 July 1954.

The following tables show the increase in the secondary school population:

TABLE 20: Numbers of pupils in secondary schools, 1943–1951

	1943	1944	1945	1946	1947	1948	1949	1950	1951
Aberaeron	271	291	291	298	319	330	351	451	558
Aberystwyth	404	466	463	475	542	540	530	524	485
Cardigan	370	378	351	389	407	425	423	435	463
Llandysul	267	317	347	367	358	371	354	347	344
Tregaron	203	206	199	222	236	263	268	375	386
Lampeter	–	–	272	293	329	377	400	405	438
Dinas, Aberystwyth	–	–	–	–	–	341	360	363	415
Henllan	–	–	–	–	–	–	312	256	293
St Mary's, Cardigan	–	–	–	–	–	–	162	156	104

TABLE 21: Increase of secondary school population and decrease in primary school population, 1944–1951

Year	Primary school population	Secondary school population	Total population
1944–5	5135	2076	7211
1948–9	5270	2103	7373
1949–50	4650	2953	7603
1950–1	4530	3165	7695

The first objective of the 1944 Education Act – 'Secondary Education for All' – and the reorganization of schools had been achieved by 1951.[187]

During the 1950s, still inspired by the 1944 Education Act and in spite of national financial stringencies and cuts in educational expenditure, the building programme weighted in favour of secondary projects continued. There were extensions at Tregaron, Lampeter and Aberaeron Secondary Schools and the new Dinas Secondary Modern School at Aberystwyth was opened in 1955. Over a quarter of a million pounds was spent on erecting seven new primary schools, including Ysgol Syr John Rhys at Ponterwyd in 1953, Aber-porth in 1957, Penparcau in 1959, Cwrt-newydd in 1959, and extensive renovations were undertaken to others, including the provision of water toilets and improved facilities for school meals. But in 1961 there were still two primary schools without electricity. Jointly with Carmarthenshire and Pembrokeshire, Highmead Residential School for the Handicapped was opened in 1956; provision was made for further education at Felin-fach, Cardigan and Aberystwyth; and agricultural education at Felin-fach and support for adult evening classes and youth clubs was inspired by the Albermarle Report. An increasing number of pupils continued their education in the secondary schools beyond the compulsory school-leaving age.

There was a growing demand for university awards and Cardiganshire, with sixty-six awards in 1951 and 271 awards in 1961, had the highest proportion of awards per head of population. The

[187]Ceredigion RO, Minutes Cardiganshire Education Committee. 7 December 1951.

private Ysgol Gymraeg Aberystwyth had moved to Lluest in 1946 and by 1951 had an enrolment of 118 pupils. However, the school's future was discussed with the Cardiganshire Education Committee, which had been considering the possibility of opening a Welsh-medium primary school in Aberystwyth. In 1951 it decided to reorganize primary education at the Alexandra Road and North Road primary schools on the basis of language. Following much deliberation and some public protest, in 1952 a Welsh-medium primary school – Yr Ysgol Gymraeg – was opened in the Alexandra Road building with 164 pupils.[188] By 1967 there was a very healthy enrolment of 249 pupils. Rural depopulation continued and seven primary schools were closed, including Strata Florida (1952), Llanddeiniol (1953), Ystumtuen (1957), Elerch (1959), Aber-ffrwd (1959), Cwmystwyth (1960), and Y Gors (1960). Falling enrolments – sixteen schools had fewer than twenty pupils in 1953 – and further closures continued and the future of small rural schools became a controversial and often a highly emotional issue. Pressure for the establishment of comprehensive education led to the amalgamation of two schools in Cardigan in 1959 and the establishment of an English-medium comprehensive school at Penglais and a bilingual comprehensive school at Penweddig in Aberystwyth in 1973. The 1960s and 1970s saw significant developments which epitomized the broadening of the LEA's policies, notably the provision for a County Youth Orchestra, and the appointment of music, drama and physical education organizers. The LEA was fortunate in being guided by a distinguished Director of Education, Dr J. Henry Jones between 1944 and 1972. Expansion became the keynote of further and higher education. At Llanbadarn Fawr the College of Librarianship Wales opened in 1964, the Welsh College of Agriculture in 1970, and a new Arts Centre at Felin-fach in 1970.[189] Student numbers increased and the new Penglais campus became increasingly important at the University College of Wales, Aberystwyth, which celebrated its centenary in 1972. St David's College, Lampeter, was incorporated as a constituent institution of the University of Wales in 1971. By 1993 there were 4,804 university students at Aberystwyth and 1,260 at Lampeter. Local government reorganization in 1974 led to the transfer of responsibility for education to the new Dyfed LEA, which was faced with the problem of maintaining small rural primary schools and meeting the increasing demand for Welsh-medium education in Cardiganshire. In the Teifi Valley comprehensive education was established when the bilingual Ysgol Dyffryn Teifi was opened at Llandysul, and an English-medium comprehensive school at Newcastle Emlyn. Primary schools were categorized on the basis of language policy.

In 1881 the Aberdare Report commented on the prevailing enthusiasm and 'the spirit of education' in Cardiganshire. The record of another century of educational history vindicates the sage judgement that Cardiganshire is 'the county in Wales where education has been most appreciated, and therefore, we may infer, where it would still be most appreciated'.[190]

[188]*Programme: Opening Ceremony, Aberystwyth Primary School* 4 June 1970; J. H. Jones, *Cardiganshire Education Committee: Eleven Years, 1951–61* (Aberystwyth, 1961).
[189]Chairman's Report on the 'last year of Cardiganshire's existence as an independent county'. Minutes Dyfed County Council, 1974–95.
[190]Aberdare Report, I, p.60.

CHAPTER 24

THE WELSH LANGUAGE IN CARDIGANSHIRE,

1891–1991

J. W. Aitchison and Harold Carter

A T the first census in which the language question was asked, that for 1891, just over half of the population of Wales (54.4 per cent) was returned as Welsh-speaking. By 1901 it had fallen to just below half at 49.9 per cent. But at the 1901 census the qualifying age had been changed from two to three, and the question in 1891 had been put in a complicated way and probably there had been widespread misinterpretation. Moreover, as far as Cardiganshire was concerned, the Registration County of 1891 was much larger than the Administrative County which was the basis in subsequent censuses. It is best, therefore, to begin with the 1901 census. At that time the lowest proportion of Welsh speakers by county was 5.8 per cent for Radnorshire, followed by 13.0 per cent for Monmouthshire, although that figure included the county borough of Newport which independently returned only 3.7 per cent. A scatter diagram of all thirteen counties reveals a clear break between those counties where ability to speak Welsh was limited and those which were effectively completely Welsh-speaking. The comparative figures were Merioneth with 93.7 per cent, Cardiganshire with 93.0 per cent, Anglesey with 91.7 per cent, Carmarthenshire with 90.4 per cent and Caernarfonshire with 89.6 per cent. Between the five counties with 90 per cent or above and the seven below 50 per cent, there was only Denbigh with 62.2 per cent. Too much, perhaps, should not be made of the data, given the crudity of the county basis which is partly responsible for Denbigh's intermediate position. Even so, there is clear evidence that the major contrast between what was later to be called *Y Fro Gymraeg*, or Welsh-speaking Wales, and the rest of the country was very clearly marked at the beginning of the century, and that the gradient across the divide between the two was sharp.

Within that Welsh-speaking area, the Registration County of Cardigan, with 95 per cent of its population able to speak Welsh in 1891, returned the highest proportion of all the counties. With 93 per cent in 1901, it was second only to Merioneth where 93.7 per cent spoke Welsh. But further than that, in 1891 some 74.4 per cent spoke Welsh only. That figure for monolinguals had fallen substantially to 50.4 per cent in 1901, though that was certainly in part a consequence of the changes in the census itself. Thus, ignoring the possibly unreliable proportion for 1891 with its different basis, at the beginning of the twentieth century over half the population spoke no English and well over nine-tenths spoke Welsh. Cardiganshire society was completely Welsh in language and culture. With few exceptions life was lived through the medium of Welsh and the language was dominant in all domains except where officialdom and bureaucracy deemed that only English was acceptable. And crucially, English was the preferred language of education, especially in the schools established under the the Welsh Intermediate Act of 1889. As W. Gareth Evans wrote of the Aberdare Report of 1881 which preceded the Act: 'It did not occur to these Victorians that the prevalence of the Welsh language might be used for the educational benefit of Wales. Their conception of 'progress' was equated with the advance of the English language . . . [any] theory of bilingual education lay well in the future.'[1] This animus against the Welsh language was well illustrated by the comment of Mrs Vaughan Davies, wife of the Liberal MP for Cardiganshire, at a meeting of the governors of Aberystwyth Intermediate School shortly after it had been opened in October 1896: 'I do not think that Welsh should be taught at all. It is not used outside Cardiganshire. French and German are of great commercial value.'[2]

The few exceptions to the universality of Welsh speech noted above were manifestly urban as, of course, were the intermediate schools. In 1901 Welsh monoglots were a much smaller proportion in the towns: 26.2 per cent in Aberaeron, 20.5 per cent in Cardigan, 20.2 per cent in Lampeter, and 31.2 per cent in New Quay. But by far the smallest proportion, at only 7.7 per cent, was recorded at Aberystwyth. In addition, Aberystwyth at 73.7 was the only administrative area to return a percentage of the population able to speak Welsh at below 90 per cent. The Rural Districts, with percentages of 98.1 (Aberaeron), 94.0 (Aberystwyth), 94.6 (Cardigan), 97.6 (Lampeter), 97.6 (Llandysul) and 98.2 (Tregaron) were totally Welsh. The boroughs, the creations of the Anglo-Normans, and the towns had always been more Anglicized. They were the meeting places where a *lingua franca* was more likely to be used and spread. But two other functions had already begun to undermine the dominance of Welsh. The first would now be called tourism, but is best referred to at the beginning of the twentieth century as a resort function. It had characterized Aberystwyth since the end of the eighteenth century. It is symbolic that the Castle House in the town, on the site of the present Old College, and which epitomized the genteel resort of the early nineteenth century, was built by an Englishman for an Englishman. In 1864 the coming of the Cambrian Railway introduced another element which not only advanced the function but also reduced isolation. The second function which modified the dominance of Welsh was that as an educational centre, for it brought into the town staff and students who, even if they were Welsh-speaking, and all certainly were not, used English as the principal medium of instruction. All the Cardiganshire towns shared one or other of these functions which undoubtedly contributed to the very rapid decline of the number of monoglot Welsh and to the slow erosion of Welsh generally.

This situation is clearly illustrated in Figure 131 which shows the main features of the language in the inter-war period. Parishes where under 80 per cent spoke Welsh and where the monoglot percentage was under fifteen at the 1931 census are mapped, together with parishes where over 80 per cent spoke Welsh and where the monoglot proportion was over 35 per cent. There is a remarkable correlation between the spheres of influence of the towns and the areas with diminished Welsh speech. This meant that decline had been most marked along the coast and along the Teifi valley, although some of the lower proportions of the inland upland areas are possibly related to the large size of the parishes. But unmistakably the core of Welsh speech remained along the whole length of

[1]W. G. Evans, 'The Aberdare Report and education in Wales', *WHR*, II, no.2 (1982), 158.
[2]S. Griffiths, 'The Welsh Intermediate Education Act and Cardiganshire', *Ceredigion*, VIII, no.1 (1976), 50–72.

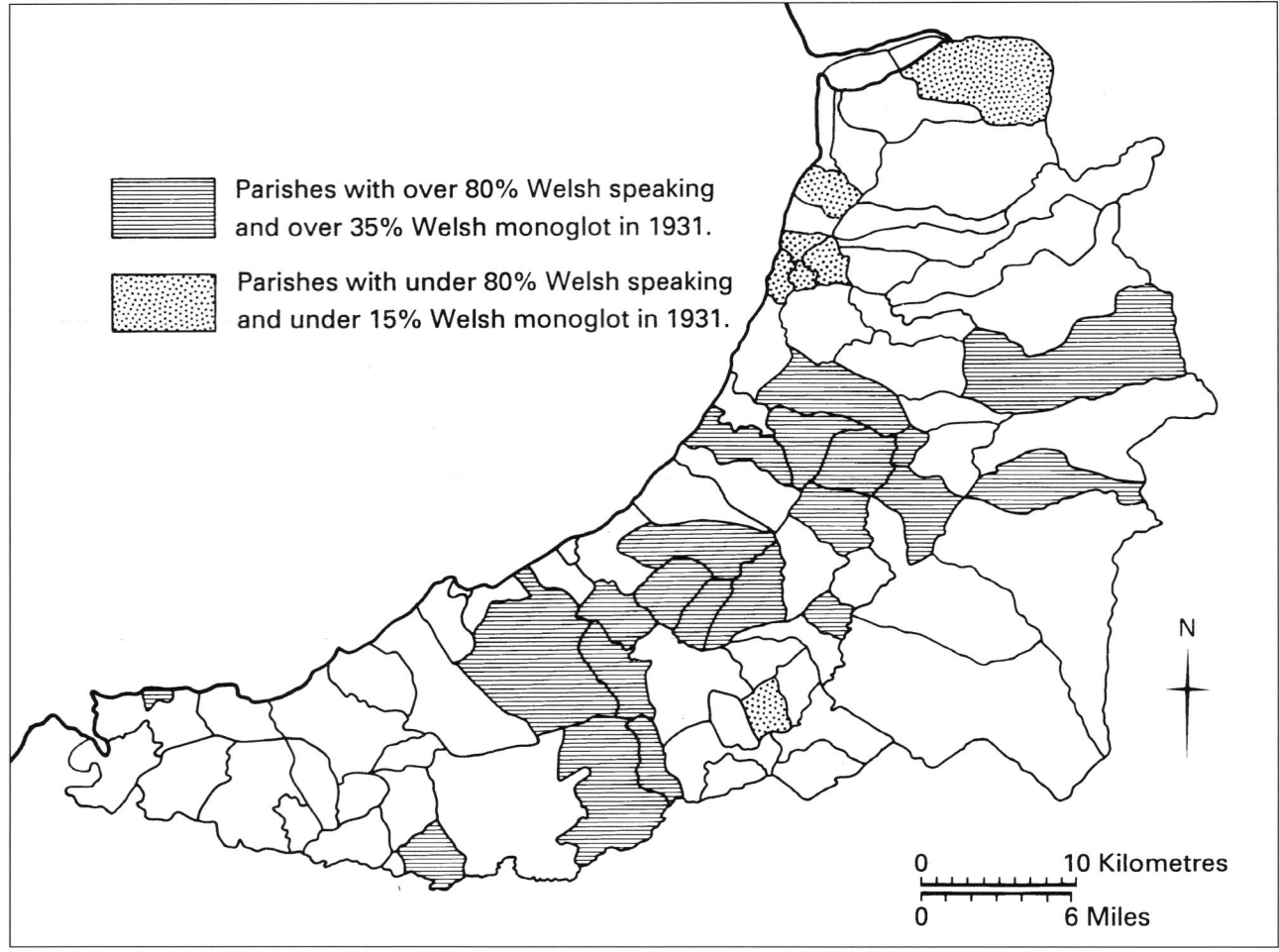

Fig. 131: The Welsh language in Cardiganshire in 1931.

Mynydd Bach. The parishes recording the highest figures in 1931 were Blaenpennal, with 99.6 per cent speaking Welsh and 49.2 per cent being monoglot Welsh speakers, Lower Lledrod, with figures of 95.4 per cent and 54 per cent, and Upper Lledrod, with 95.8 per cent and a remarkable 60.5 per cent monoglot. The only exception in this core area is Llangeitho – a strange presage perhaps of changes which were to come much later. Even so, these inter-war data reveal the predominant processes at work in the decline of the language in Cardiganshire, as well as the resilient areas which were those most removed from urban and external influences, for the areas of loss also show an association with the lines of the railways which had crossed the county both from the east and from the south.

    At this point, and in light of the above analysis, it is important to note that throughout the period there were two linguistic processes in operation. One was the acquisition of English and the consequent decline of monoglot Welsh speakers. The other was the loss of Welsh, which itself took two forms. One was the generational loss of the language whereby children were not brought up to speak Welsh. The other was the dilution of Welsh speaking by the immigration of monoglot English speakers. The two processes react with one another and are obviously linked, but nevertheless they are in many ways distinct.

In spite of the urban variations which have been noted, the history of the Welsh language in Cardiganshire during the twentieth century starts from a situation where the language was totally dominant. Loss is very much a feature of the twentieth century. That process of decline is summarized in Table 22. The data show the effective progressive eradication of the monoglot Welsh. Indeed, it was so evident that in 1991 the question as to the ability to speak English was not even posed in the census. The tumbling figures show the greatest decline during the period of the Second World War. By 1951 there were a few elderly people who could not speak English, but the low percentage then, and in subsequent censuses, was largely made up of children just over the qualifying age of three who had yet to learn English and a small group who for cultural and political reasons refused to acknowledge that they spoke the language. By the end of the Second World War the monoglot Welsh speaker had disappeared: the acquisition of English had become universal.

TABLE 22: Percentages speaking Welsh in Cardiganshire, 1891–1991

Census	Speaking Welsh only	Speaking Welsh	Difference in percentage speaking Welsh
1891	74.1	95.0	
1901	50.4	93.0	−2.0
1911	34.2	89.6	−3.4
1921	26.7	82.1	−7.5
1931	20.6	87.1	+5.0
1941		no census	
1951	7.4	79.5	−7.6
1961	4.7	74.9	−4.6
1971	3.7	67.6	−7.3
1981	2.3	63.2	−4.4
1991	not asked in census	59.1	−4.1

Note: No allowance is made in the table for changes in area or in census procedures.

The ability to speak Welsh showed a much slower and more even decline. There was, indeed, one anomalous increase between 1921 and 1931, but that was the product of the census itself. In 1921 the census was conducted in summer, instead of the usual date in April, just before Easter. Until 1981 the census was based on the location of the individual on census night, regardless of the normal place of residence. Thus the census of 1921 was taken when a considerable part of the local population was on holiday and when there was a large number of visitors in the area. That effectively lowered proportions in 1921 and inflated changes in the decade which followed by the return to the usual date in 1931.

It is a moot point as to what proportion of speakers of a language within a total population can be considered as representing a position where that language can claim to be the normal medium of communication in most domains. Figures in the region of 70 per cent or above are usually suggested. If the notion of a critical mass is meaningful in a linguistic context, then in falling to only 59 per cent in 1991 Welsh has, over only two or three generations, moved from a position where it

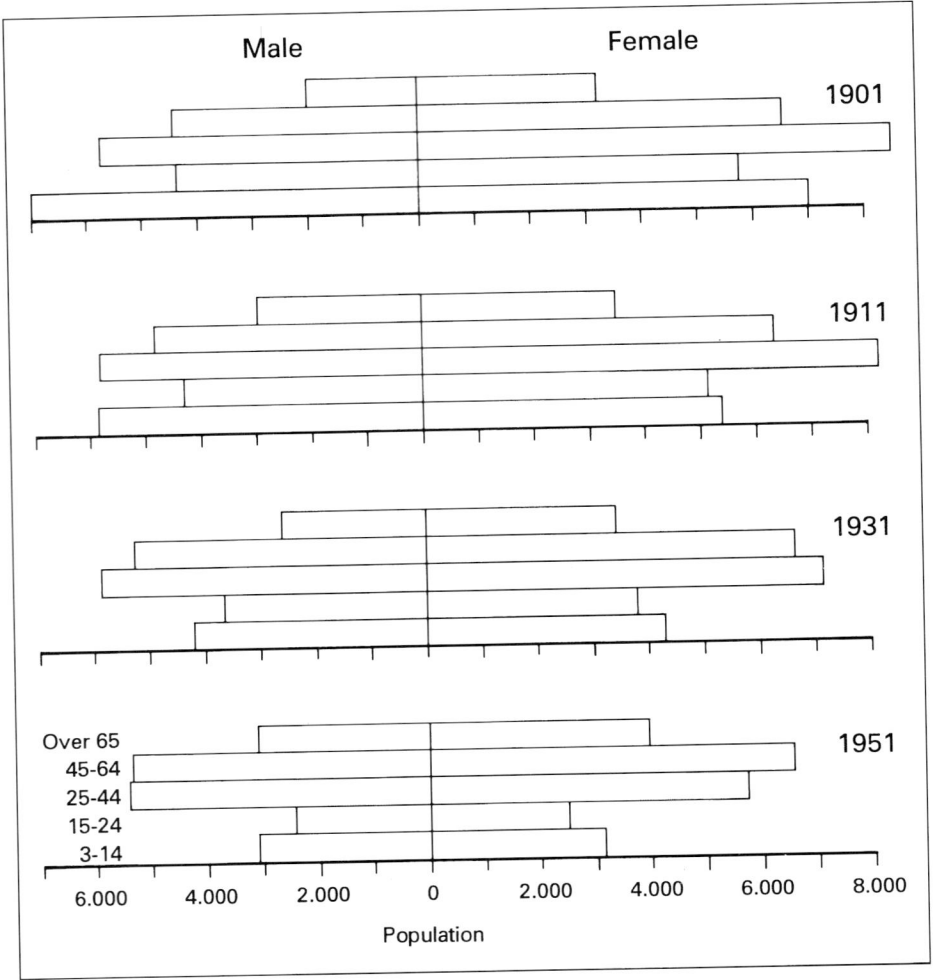

Fig. 132: Age pyramids for Welsh speakers in Cardiganshire, 1901–1951.

was the dominant, and, indeed, given the high proportion of monoglots, the preferred medium of communication, to one where it has a bare parity with English in a society which is only partially bilingual.

The absolute numbers of Welsh speakers in the county is, of course, quite different from the proportion or percentage. Percentages depend on the total population, whereas numbers are determined by the demographic history of the Welsh-speakers alone. In 1901 the number of speakers was 53,638, but by 1991 it had fallen to 36,026, a fall of some 32.8 per cent. That had taken place in spite of the fact that the population of the county over the age of three had risen from 57,664 to 60,980, although that increase had largely taken place in the most recent decades 1971–81 and 1981–91. The fall of the number of Welsh speakers of 32.8 per cent can be put alongside the difference of 33.92 between the percentages speaking Welsh in 1901 and 1991. The figures are clearly commensurate so that any explanation of change must reside in both the internal characteristics of the Welsh population and the impact of external factors, in the loss of Welsh speakers and speech, and in the growth of non-Welsh speakers by in-migration.

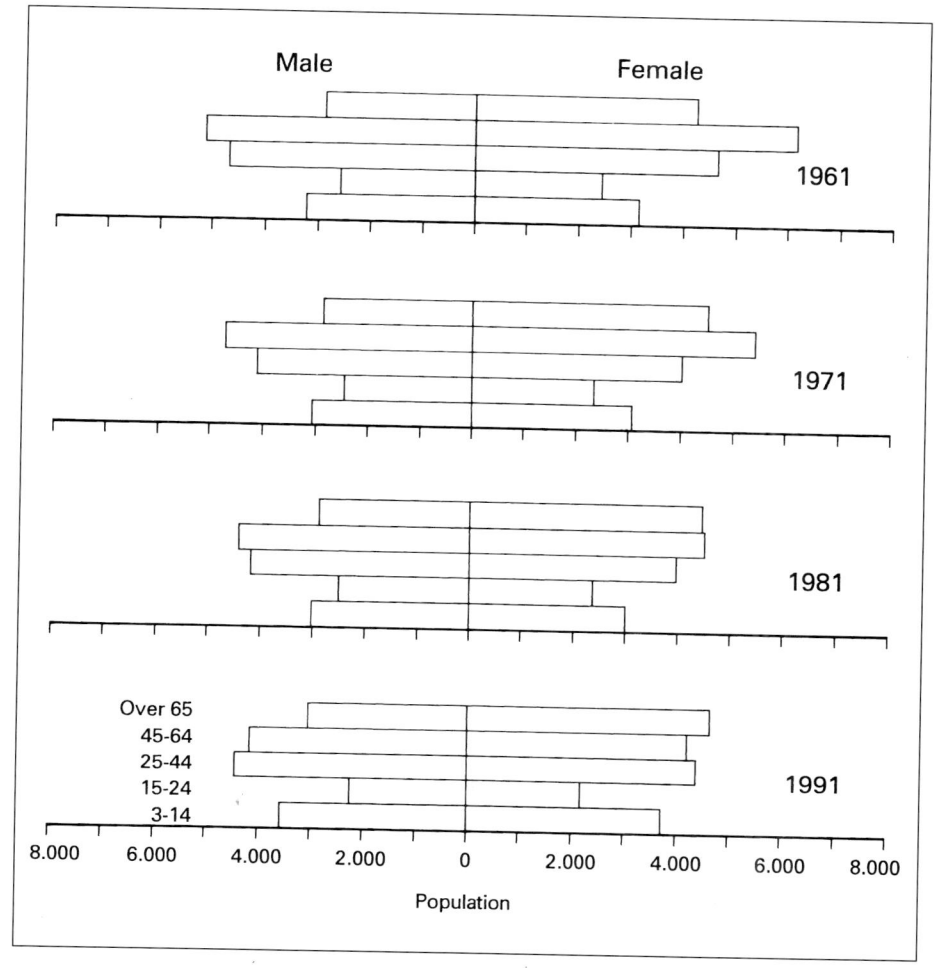

Fig. 133: Age pyramids for Welsh speakers in Cardiganshire, 1961–1991.

One of the most significant aspects of the numbers of speakers is the age structure. This is illustrated by the series of population pyramids in Figure 132 and the sex ratios for the different age groups at successive censuses in Table 23.

The situation in 1901 displayed in Figure 132 is characterized by an almost classical pyramidal shape. It is only modified by the unequal age divisions which were given by the census. There was one major departure, however, which is clearly apparent in the table of sex ratios, that is in the proportion of men to women in the population, calculated by the number of males divided by the number of females and multiplied by one hundred. There was a significant imbalance between the numbers of men and women in the middle age groups in the first half of the century. Since women live longer than men, that is to be expected in the over-65 category and is apparent at every date. Given also that slightly more male babies are born than female, a ratio of over 100 might be expected in the 3–14 group, although the extension of the group to the age of fourteen would tend to offset that feature. But the differences in the middle groups can have no standard explanation. Those differences were quite substantial. Thus in 1901 the number of males between twenty-five

TABLE 23: Sex ratios for Welsh-language speakers for different age groups, 1901–1991

Date	3–14	15–24	25–44	45–64	65 and over
1901	100.2	78.5	65.2	68.5	62.4
1911	99.9	83.7	70.9	75.3	86.4
1921	99.3	94.6	80.0	82.4	67.8
1931	98.5	96.8	81.6	79.7	74.7
1941	no census				
1951	98.1	98.1	95.3	81.2	77.9
1961	103.2	106.5	102.7	84.5	69.1
1971	103.0	108.9	104.1	89.4	63.9
1981	101.6	105.9	105.3	97.4	63.3
1991	96.9	102.4	102.2	99.3	66.4

and forty-four was 5,650 as against 8,339 females. The only explanation of that distortion of the standard expectation of rough equality is the migration of males to the industrial areas in the latter part of the nineteenth century. Given the ages of the men involved, the dates of birth would have been 1856 to 1876, and earlier if the similar disparity in the 45–65 group is added. If the population of Cardiganshire is examined for that period, substantial losses by emigration are revealed. Thus, between 1841 and 1851 net migration was –9.82 per cent, –9.54 from 1851 to 1861, –10.53 from 1861 to 1871, –11.36 between 1871 and 1881, and a massive –16.53 between 1881 and 1891.[3] It is, of course, impossible to identify how many of these were Welsh speakers, but given that proportions of speakers in the 90 per cent range characterized most of Cardiganshire there is little doubt that the emigration represented a major loss of Welsh speakers and helps to explain the substantial decline in numbers in the county.

The direct impact on language is clear in the fall in numbers, but the indirect influence was perhaps even more important. The disparity between females and males must have led to diminished marriage chances for the females, possibly to later marriage, and consequently to the lowered reproduction of Welsh speakers. It is again impossible to divide natural increase into language spoken, but the loss of the young males and the ageing population certainly occasioned a fall in natural increase. Whereas natural increase, that is the excess of births over deaths, ranged from over 10 per cent to 7 per cent in the second half of the nineteenth century, it had fallen to only 2.19 per cent between 1901 and 1911 and had changed to natural decrease, an excess of deaths over births, between 1911 and 1921 and was to remain so through the rest of the century. Between 1921 and 1931 a natural decrease was accompanied by a net migratory loss. All these features reacted upon language in a negative way, throughout the erosion of Welsh speakers either by the failure to replace them naturally or by direct out-migration. The impact is seen in the fact that in 1901 some 25.7 per cent of the Welsh-speaking population was in the 3–14 age group and only 9.6 per cent in the over 65s. Fifty years later the situation had radically changed, with only 15.2 per cent in the 3–14 category and 17.1 in the over 65s.

[3] J. Williams, *Digest of Welsh Historical Statistics* (2 vols., The Welsh Office,1985), 1, Table 14, p.70.

It is evident from the foregoing discussion that there were two catastrophic changes which affected the Welsh-speaking population numbers during the twentieth century. The first was the marked depletion in the number of males in the middle age groups. The second was the basic depletion in the numbers of young speakers. The former was an entirely demographic feature and the balance between the sexes was not restored until after the Second World War. The latter was both a demographic feature and a cultural one since, as well as direct loss, fewer children were brought up to speak Welsh. If it is difficult to separate the two influences, their impact is clear. In simple numbers, there were 13,775 between 3 and 14 in 1901; in 1931 there were 8,420 and in 1961 only 6,280. Within barely half the century, the numbers had halved. But in 1991 there were 7,262 in that age group, constituting 20.2 per cent of the speakers. This latest figure is evidence of the language revival which had followed the crucial watershed of the 1960s, an issue which will be considered later.

At this stage it is necessary to move from the general consideration of the whole county to review the way in which general trends have appeared locally. In any analysis of the Welsh language within Cardiganshire, however, two problems stand out. The first is that many of the forces which have affected the language are common to the whole of Wales. The Welsh Language Act of 1993 is an obvious example. Indeed, there are very few which have only local significance. The second is that the history of the language is of necessity a reflection of the general economic and social history of the county itself. Thus, for example, one of the major influences has been the growth of Welsh-medium education. But that, on the one hand, is an aspect of the development of the language nationally, while on the other it is a specific feature of the history of education in the county.

In spite of these reservations the most general of factors act differentially. Thus it can be argued that the most significant influence on the language in the one hundred years from 1861 to 1961 was the most intangible, that is variation in perceived social status. The early part of the period under review was dominated by the consequences of the Report of the Commissioners into the State of Education of Wales of 1847 and the English-based educational system which followed and to which reference has already been made. There was a firm belief that English was the language of social acceptance and economic advantage. Indeed, the first censuses of the Welsh language were as much concerned with establishing the progress of English as with the state of Welsh.

That belief remained dominant until after the Second World War, for if a point of inflection is to be identified where more supportive attitudes began to appear, it must be related to Saunders Lewis's BBC Radio Lecture of 1962, *Tynged yr Iaith* (The Fate of the Language). The major effective consequence was the founding of Cymdeithas yr Iaith Gymraeg in 1962. The initial informal discussion took place at Pontarddulais, but the actual founding of the Society occurred in Aberystwyth. The first direct action protests at the Post Office and on Trefechan Bridge also took place in Aberystwyth. Closely associated was a different issue but one which did much to rouse national sentiment and indirectly to reinforce the language movement. That was the drowning of Capel Celyn and the Tryweryn valley and the creation of Llyn Celyn for water supply by the city of Liverpool. No Welsh Member of Parliament voted for the bill when it was introduced in 1957. It was widely condemned throughout Wales but was pushed through Parliament, thereby creating widespread objection. It was, therefore, a catalyst in changing attitudes which were symbolized by the language movement. The role of Aberystwyth in direct action was clearly a consequence of its role as a centre of Welsh education and of its student population. It was not so much the permanent residents as the transitory undergraduates who were involved. Their later location in occupations

Fig. 134. The celebrated protest on Trefechan Bridge, Aberystwyth, by Cymdeithas yr Iaith Gymraeg, February 1963. (*Copyright National Library of Wales*).

which took them from Aberystwyth was to have significant consequences for the language, but locally there was a central irony in that the town itself was the main centre of Anglicization.

Urbanization, therefore, remains one of the principal factors in local language change. There is always a close relation between the spread of fashion and the urban hierarchy. Fashion, especially in its most ephemeral character, appears initially in the largest metropoles; indeed, it is explicitly a metropolitan creation. It then spreads to the largest and most accessible towns and so on down the scale until it reaches the remotest country areas. In relation to language, therefore, Aberystwyth played a dual role. In a cultural sense it could claim to be the language 'metropolis', a centre of fashion and innovation from which a new image of the language was diffused. But since it was the largest town in Cardiganshire, it was the point at which the pressures of Anglicization were at their greatest.

Table 24 indicates the process of language loss in Cardiganshire until 1971 and before the local government changes of 1974. Aberystwyth is consistently the centre of greatest loss and with the lowest Welsh-speaking proportion. Indeed, the difference between the town and the place with the next lowest proportion was always more than 15 per cent and in the early part of the century the gap widened. This is reinforced by a consideration of the monoglot Welsh speakers where, again, Aberystwyth shows the smallest proportions. Even in 1901 the percentage of monoglots was negligible at 7.7, compared with the next lowest figure in Cardiganshire of 20.2 at Lampeter. It was only 4.6 per cent in 1911 and 3.1 in 1921. Given the number of young children only just over the age of three who were returned as monoglot Welsh, the conclusion must be that the monoglot Welsh population of the town had disappeared by the First World War.

Even more significant is that until 1921, apart from the anomalous area of Ysgubor-y-coed, Lampeter or Cardigan boroughs returned the next lowest percentages of Welsh speakers. But in 1931 that place was taken by Aberystwyth Rural District, of which Ysgubor-y-coed would have been a part in any case. That situation was confirmed, even accentuated, after the Second World War. Although in 1961 the capital works of the hydroelectric scheme at Cwmrheidol played a part, the basic cause was suburbanization and the growth of commuting to Aberystwyth which had extended Anglicization well beyond the borough boundaries.

TABLE 24: Cardiganshire: areas with the lowest proportions of Welsh speakers, 1901–1971

Date	Area with lowest percentage		Area with next lowest percentage	
1901	Aberystwyth MB	73.7	Lampeter MB	91.1
1911	Aberystwyth MB	69.2	Lampeter MB	88.3
1921	Aberystwyth MB	54.1	Lampeter/Cardigan MBs	79.8
1931	Aberystwyth MB	64.5	Aberystwyth RD	88.6
1941	no census			
1951	Aberystwyth MB	55.3	Aberystwyth RD	72.2
1961	Aberystwyth MB	50.6	Aberystwyth RD	72.6
1971	Aberystwyth MB	48.4	Aberystwyth RD	62.0

Because of the changes in administrative areas, direct comparisons across time are difficult to make. But if, at the 1981 census, the communities with the lowest proportions of Welsh speakers are abstracted, they are in ascending order: Borth (35.7 per cent). Ysgubor-y-coed (44.9 per cent), Llanbadarn Fawr (46.0 per cent), Aberystwyth (46.3 per cent) and Upper Vaenor (48.6 per cent). They were the only communities below 50 per cent. The equivalent communities at the 1991 census were Borth (36.7 per cent), Aberystwyth (44.5 per cent), Llanbadarn Fawr (45.2 per cent), Ysgubor-y-coed (48.9 per cent), Aber-porth (49.5 per cent) and Llanfair Clydogau (49.8 per cent). At the 1991 census the wards with the lowest proportions of Welsh speakers in Cardiganshire were, also in ascending order: Aberystwyth South (40.9 per cent), Aberystwyth West (43.4 per cent), Borth (43.9 per cent), Aberystwyth North (44.9 per cent), and Llanbadarn (45.0 per cent). Again, they are the only wards with under 50 per cent speaking Welsh, apart from the special case of Aber-porth (49.6 per cent), where the Royal Aircraft Establishment is located. Here is a very distinctive representation of Aberystwyth and its immediate suburbs, constituting a marked coastal strip in the extreme north of the county. That Anglicized strip is identifiable on the map of the language at the 1951 census constructed by J. G. Thomas.[4] It is unmistakable on the map of the 1961 census.[5]

[4] J. G. Thomas, 'The geographical distribution of the Welsh language', *The Geographical Journal*, 122 (1956), 71–9.
[5] J. W. Aitchison and H. Carter, *A Geography of the Welsh Language, 1961–1991* (Cardiff, 1994).

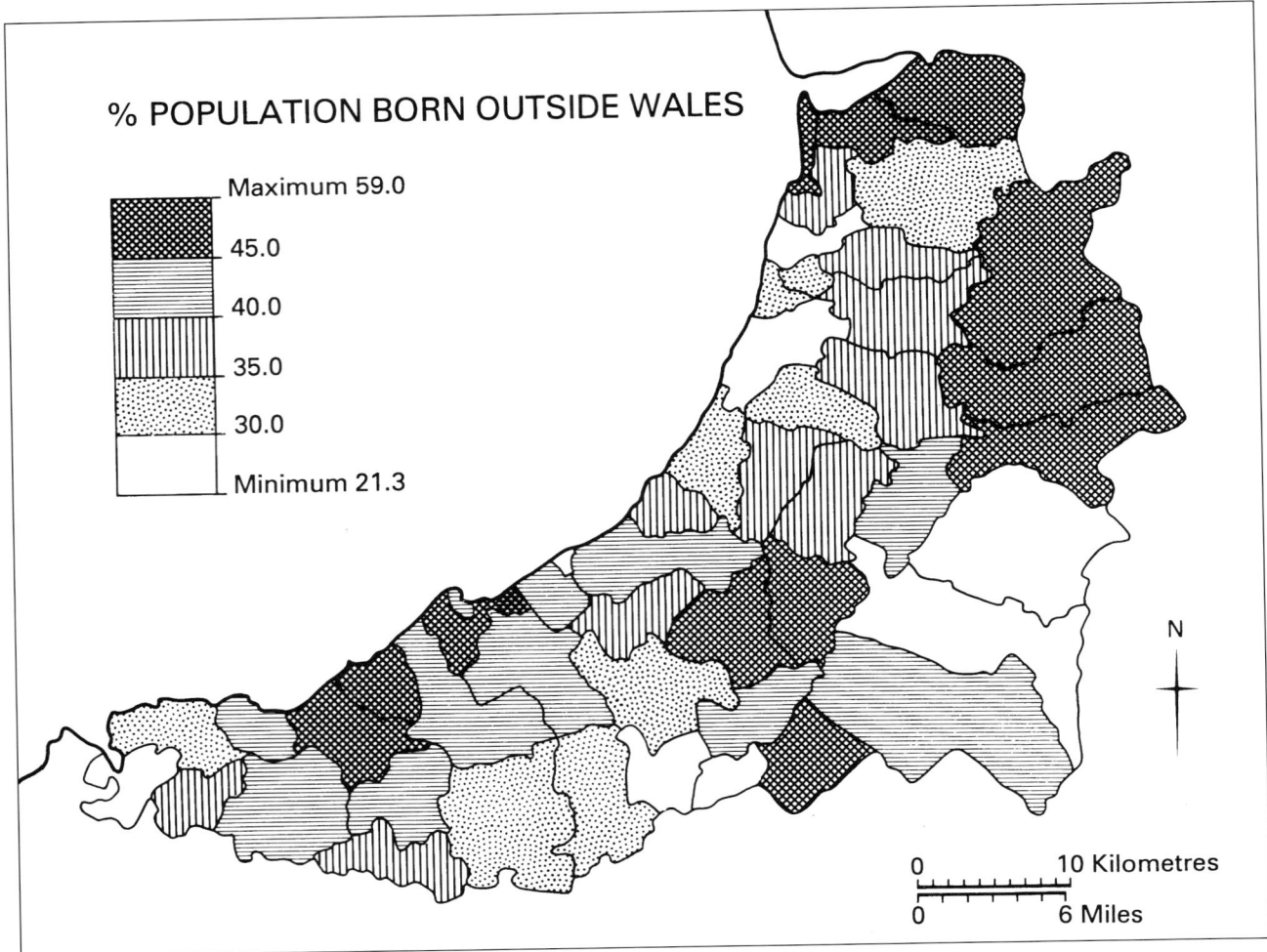

Fig. 135: The percentage of the population of Cardiganshire born outside Wales according to the 1991 census.

Urbanization and suburbanization are the main, but not the sole causes of this development. Again, paradoxically, the expansion of higher education has undoubtedly been an Anglicizing influence, as witnessed by the controversy over greater numbers of students at the University, the majority of whom derived from England following the post-Robbins boom of the 1960s and 1970s. The proportion from Wales fell from a dominant 90 per cent pre-war to a little over 30 per cent during that later period and although the proportion from Wales has climbed slightly it still remains a minority. Alongside that trend has been an increase in second homes and especially caravan parks. Tourism has reinforced a general pattern which was apparent in the earliest language censuses, but which has been greatly extended in the second half of the century.

All this is reflected in two other statistics. Given its academic role, it might be assumed that Aberystwyth and its immediate surrounds would show a highly literate population. That is not the case. Thus, in 1971, the first census to include the ability to read and write Welsh and the last census on the old administrative areas, of all the urban areas Aberystwyth MB recorded the second smallest proportion of speakers able to write the language (79.6 per cent as against Cardigan's 73.8 per cent), and the Aberystwyth RD recorded the lowest proportion of all the rural districts (87.7 per cent). It is possible to argue that the loss of literacy is a stage in language decline.[6] If so, the downward trend of Welsh and the forces of Anglicization seem to be more potent in this coastal strip than its significance in language revival. This is supported by data relating to place of birth. The area has consistently recorded a low proportion of its population born in Wales. In 1981 Borth returned the lowest figure for Cardiganshire at 48 per cent, followed by Ysgubor-y-coed at 50.0 per cent. The same pattern characterizes 1991 (Figure 135).

The decline in the number of Welsh speakers in Aberystwyth, and especially at Borth (only 36.7 per cent for the community in 1991), demonstrates the impact of tourism. That was replicated throughout the county, and particularly along the coast. In 1931, Aberystwyth excepted, the distribution map at parish level showed a uniform pattern along the coast, with all areas returning over 80 per cent Welsh-speaking. By 1951 the northern strip already discussed was clearly identifiable and although it had extended south, the remainder of the coastal parishes still returned over 80 per cent Welsh-speaking. But a significant second exception had emerged. This was a southern area about Cardigan, where the borough had just fallen below the threshold at 79.2 per cent. For the special reasons already noted, Aber-porth was much lower at 71.4 per cent, but the neighbouring parish of Y Ferwig was still just over 80 per cent (80.4). The subsequent changes between 1961 and 1981 are shown in Table 24, where the parishes are arranged south to north from Cardigan. By 1961 clear inroads had been made into the predominantly Welsh speech along the coast. From Cardigan north to the outskirts of Aberaeron, only one small parish, Llanllwchaearn with 89.6 per cent, showed a proportion of Welsh speakers over 80 per cent. By 1971 there were only fragments remaining with such a high score and by 1981 not a single community recorded over 80 per cent. Indeed, with the exception of Henfynyw and Aberaeron, all the percentages were below 70 per cent. The two decades represented in Table 25 had seen a substantial erosion of Welsh speech along the coast.

TABLE 25: Percentages speaking Welsh in a series of coastal parishes north of Cardigan, 1961–1981

Parish/Community	1961	1971	1981
Cardigan	74.9	70.8	66.7
Y Ferwig	75.6	71.4	65.5
Aber-porth	57.5	50.0	50.8
Penbryn	77.4	69.3	58.7
Llangrannog	78.8	74.3	67.3
Llanllwchaearn	89.6	81.9	66.8
New Quay	74.5	73.8	58.3
Llanina	65.2	60.0	57.0
Henfynyw Upper	89.6	80.0	79.1
Aberaeron	82.7	80.2	74.5
Llanrhystud Haminiog	89.2	79.3	66.5
Llanrhystud Mefenydd	87.8	75.6	77.7
Llanychaearn	79.2	62.5	68.0

[6] E. G. Bowen and H. Carter, 'Some preliminary observations on the distribution of the Welsh language at the 1971 census', *The Geographical Journal*, 140 (1975), 432–43.

It is too simplistic to attribute these changes solely to the development of tourism, including the large increase in holiday homes. But before considering other factors, it is appropriate to consider the impact of major capital works. These have been already introduced by reference to the hydroelectric scheme at Cwmrheidol, the Royal Aircraft Establishment at Aber-porth, and indeed it is quite logical to place the University Colleges at Aberystwyth and Lampeter in the same category. It is one of the paradoxes of the language that the inauguration of significant development, which is widely demanded as a solution to local unemployment and out-migration, inevitably brings with it Anglicization. The most spectacular example is the Cwmrheidol scheme. In 1931 some 89 per cent of the population in the parish spoke Welsh and 33.2 per cent – almost precisely one third – spoke no English. Following the Second World War, a slight fall had occurred by 1951, in keeping with national trends over the intervening twenty years, to 84.1 per cent, although the monoglot Welsh had been reduced to 4.6 per cent. But with the import of labour for the hydroelectric works, the percentage for 1961 had fallen dramatically to 36.9 per cent. There were only 1.3 per cent monoglot Welsh speakers. With the completion of the basic work there was, of course, a recovery. But that was slow and only partial to 56.2 per cent in 1971 and 55.2 per cent in 1981. In 1991 the Melindwr ward, which covers the area, returned 58.1 per cent, the community 62.4. These works, therefore had a permanent effect and the rebound was limited.

Capital works are, however, necessarily limited in scope and the major impact on the language was much smaller in scale and much more insidious. This has been demographic in nature and largely through migration. Natural increase has certainly been restricted due to an ageing population and a falling birthrate. It is, of course, impossible to establish any differential rates of natural increase/decrease by language, but the failure of the population to reproduce itself has obvious consequences for language reproduction. The process which has continued to dominate, however, and has been in part the creator of the ageing population, is migration.

Out-migration, or rural depopulation to use a more specific term, dominated the population characteristic of Cardiganshire from the late nineteenth century. The county reached its highest total population at the 1871 census and showed decreases at every census for the succeeding eight decades. There is no evidence to suggest that emigration was language specific, though it was certainly age specific, resulting in the ageing population and the natural decrease already discussed. This process has continued underneath the increases which have been brought about by a more recent wave of in-migration. That in-migration has been the product of the process usually referred to as counterurbanization or rural retreating. Counterurbanization characterized the whole of the western world during the 1970s and 1980s. The attractions of urban and especially metropolitan living which had dominated population movements for over two hundred years were sharply reversed. The causes were a rejection of the materialism and consumerism which were associated with the city. Many people sought a change of lifestyle, seeking the slower and more community-based ways of the countryside. But there was more to it than that. The cities had become characterized by danger to health from pollution and to life itself from the rising crime rate. The consequence was a flow of people to small towns and rural areas. Rural Wales, especially Cardiganshire, became one of the prime targets of those wishing to leave metropolitan England. This is admirably illustrated in a paper by the Dyfed County Planning Department on migration in Dyfed.[7]

[7]Dyfed County Planning Department. *Migration in Dyfed*. Technical paper No.3 (1989), p.4.

TABLE 26: Cardiganshire: components of
population changes, 1911–1987

Period	Natural change	Migration change
1911–1931	−1544	−3151
1931–1971	−5012	+4170
1971–1981	−2000	+9200
1981–1987	−900	+5100

Source: Migration in Dyfed – Dyfed County Planning Department.
Note: the figures for 1981–87 are mid-year estimates.

Table 26 indicates the continuing loss of population through natural processes, but also the marked increases due to immigration. Not all this was from outside Wales and hence a proportion included Welsh speakers and probably among those from England were some returning Welsh speakers. Figures are not available on a District basis, but of those migrating to Dyfed from outside Wales in 1990–1 some 11.39 per cent were Welsh-speaking. Even so, the migration tables of the census show a clear influx from across the border. Thus, of the total 5,598 incomers to Cardiganshire in the one year prior to the 1981 census, 1,357 or a quarter were from England, with the south-east providing the largest number (562), followed by the west Midlands (274). The consequences of these movements are apparent in the census and in the language of pupils in the schools of the county. Thus, for example, the Welsh-speaking proportion in Llangeitho is shown in Table 27.

TABLE 27: Percentage speaking Welsh in Llangeitho, 1921–1991

Date:	1921	1931	1941	1951	1961	1971	1981	1991
Percentage:	98.8	92.6	no census	91.9	91.8	83.0	54.5	57.5

The catastrophic decline between 1971 and 1981 was primarily the result of an influx of population. Its impact on the schools can be seen in Table 28.

TABLE 28: Tregaron district: Welsh and English first language

Date	Number on roll	Welsh first language		English first language	
		Number	Per cent	Number	Per cent
1949	594	559	93	35	7
1961	407	344	85	63	15
1967	388	310	80	78	20
1977	432	253	59	179	41
1983	355	172	43	223	57

Source: Dyfed Schools Language Surveys.
Note: the percentages have been rounded to the nearest whole number.

The table needs little exegesis. The general fall in numbers indicates the underlying rural depopulation, but with the substantial migratory increase occurring between 1967 and 1977. The process of what is in essence an exchange of a Welsh-speaking population for an English one is demonstrated in the pupils' first language, whereby over the period Welsh has declined from a dominant 93 per cent to a lowly 43 per cent.

The most direct way of revealing the impact of migration is to review the place of birth of the population. Figure 135 maps that distribution for Cardiganshire for 1991. Much of the District, as it then was, is characterized by areas with over 40 per cent born outside Wales. In the area north of Aberystwyth, which has been noted as the earliest to show lower proportions of Welsh speech, the percentage locally born actually falls below 50. All this undoubtedly represented a crisis. A county which, at the beginning of the period under review, was overwhelmingly Welsh-speaking and where English was manifestly a foreign language, was in danger of being transformed into a county where English was the dominant language with a Welsh-speaking minority, and a declining minority at that.

The result was a local response in addition to that which can be considered national in its character. There were three ways in which it was considered a direct impact could be made. The first was by the teaching of Welsh in the schools and by ensuring that children could be educated in the majority local language. The second was to control the effect of in-migration by planning measures. The third was by control of employment by restricting certain offices to Welsh speakers. All these means of safeguarding the language were taken up by the Dyfed County Council, Ceredigion District and its successor county.

The development of educational policies to support the language, including the establishment of Welsh nursery schools, the categorization of primary schools by the language to be used as the medium of instruction, and the establishment of Welsh-medium secondary schools, is discussed elsewhere. But there are two features of educational development which need comment here. The first is a rather minor one, but is a continuation of the paradox that the most Anglicized part of the county has taken the lead in measures to support the language. This is true of the development of Welsh-medium education, for the first Welsh-medium primary school was established in Aberystwyth in 1939, although it did not come under the Local Authority until 1951. The second feature under the heading of educational development is an assessment of the impact of policy upon language as it can be seen in the 1991 census. In that year some 75.2 per cent of those in the age cohort 3–15 were returned as Welsh-speaking. As the age pyramids referred to earlier (Figure 133) demonstrated, that figure compares with 55.1 per cent for the age group 16–44, 54.2 per cent for the group 45–64, and 60.1 per cent for those over 65. To reverse the long-established pattern whereby the elderly dominated the age structure of Welsh speakers represents a significant transformation. The respective numbers for the three last censuses are 6,005, 5,872 and 9,654. But it must be stressed that these figures refer to different bases of enumeration. Even so, all the evidence suggests a resurgence of Welsh among the young. The 75.2 per cent for 1991 compares with 68.9 per cent for the 3–14 group in 1981 and 67.2 per cent in 1971. However, it must be added that the age cohort 3–15 only constituted 18.8 per cent of Welsh speakers, compared with 20.5 per cent in the over 65 group.

The second aspect of local response which was noted above was planning. The basic cause of the precise local impact of counterurbanization is to a degree controversial. It has been argued that it is an aspect of the movement called gentrification, whereby the protection of small settlements by planning regulations has attracted those seeking rural tranquillity and who are sufficiently affluent to outbid locals for property.[8] An aspect of rural depopulation is in consequence the replacement of local families by incomers; counterurbanization and rural depopulation are, therefore, part of the same process. In contrast, it is also argued that where new development does take place it is controlled by landowners seeking maximum profits and supported by planning permission, so that the housing provided again goes to the more wealthy incomer. But whatever the process the outcome is the same, the driving up of house prices beyond the reach of local, and presumably Welsh-speaking, families. The reaction has been a demand that more control should be exerted over the housing market, epitomized in the Cymdeithas yr Iaith slogan: *Nid yw Cymru ar Werth* (Wales is not for Sale). That control, it is argued, can only be ensured if language is deemed a relevant issue in planning decisons, a situation which was not catered for in structure planning. In 1988, as a result of pressure, the Welsh Office issued Circular 53/88 entitled, 'The Welsh Language: Development Plans and Planning Control', in which it was stated that 'where the use of Welsh is part of the social fabric of a community, it is obviously appropriate to take this into consideration when drawing up land-use policies expressed in structure and local plans'. But the circular offered no guidelines as to how the recommendations were to be applied in practice, and endeavours to restrict the sale of housing through the use of Section 106 (local needs) agreements were consistently overturned by the Welsh Office on the grounds that they interfered with individual liberties and could undermine economic development. Discussions with Welsh local authorities led the Welsh Office in 1994 to intimate that local authorities might identify settlements which were 'culturally sensitive' where specific regulation could be accepted. Cardiganshire's response was to propose a policy whereby new housing was to be restricted to people either born in the county or who had lived within a distance of twenty-five miles for at least five years. This was initially proposed to apply to areas where at least 70 per cent of the population spoke Welsh. In other words, the figure of 70 per cent Welsh-speaking was deemed to define culturally sensitive areas. Following further discussion, however, the qualifying proportion was reduced to 50 per cent, perhaps a very generous interpretation of the 'culturally sensitive'. Certain areas, mainly the urban centres and their suburban extensions, were to be excepted. These were Aberystwyth, Llanbadarn, New Quay, Borth, Eglwys-fach, Llanfair Clydogau (where it will be remembered there was a low proportion of Welsh speakers), Aber-porth and Lampeter. The analysis presented in this chapter will have established the reasons why these areas were chosen. As might be expected, these measures have generated considerable controversy and were substantially revised and modified in the *Ceredigion Local Plan* drawn up in 1998.[9]

A third element in the local response to language decline has been to ensure that public affairs were to be truly bilingual. To that end the new county authority has ruled that all appointments to first-tier posts, that is to offices such as Director of Education or of Environmental Services and Housing were to have the ability to speak Welsh as a condition. A commitment to learn Welsh would be demanded for those appointed to second-tier posts. This again is a controversial initiative which has generated considerable opposition. It is apparent that the last two aspects discussed – planning controls and the appointment of local authority officers – are too recent to have any measurable impact on the language. But they do give a indication of the future envisioned.

[8] I. Weekly, 'Rural depopulation and counter-urbanization: a paradox', *Area*, 20 (1988), 127–34.
[9] Ceredigion County Council, *Ceredigion Local Plan* (Aberaeron, 1998), vol.1.

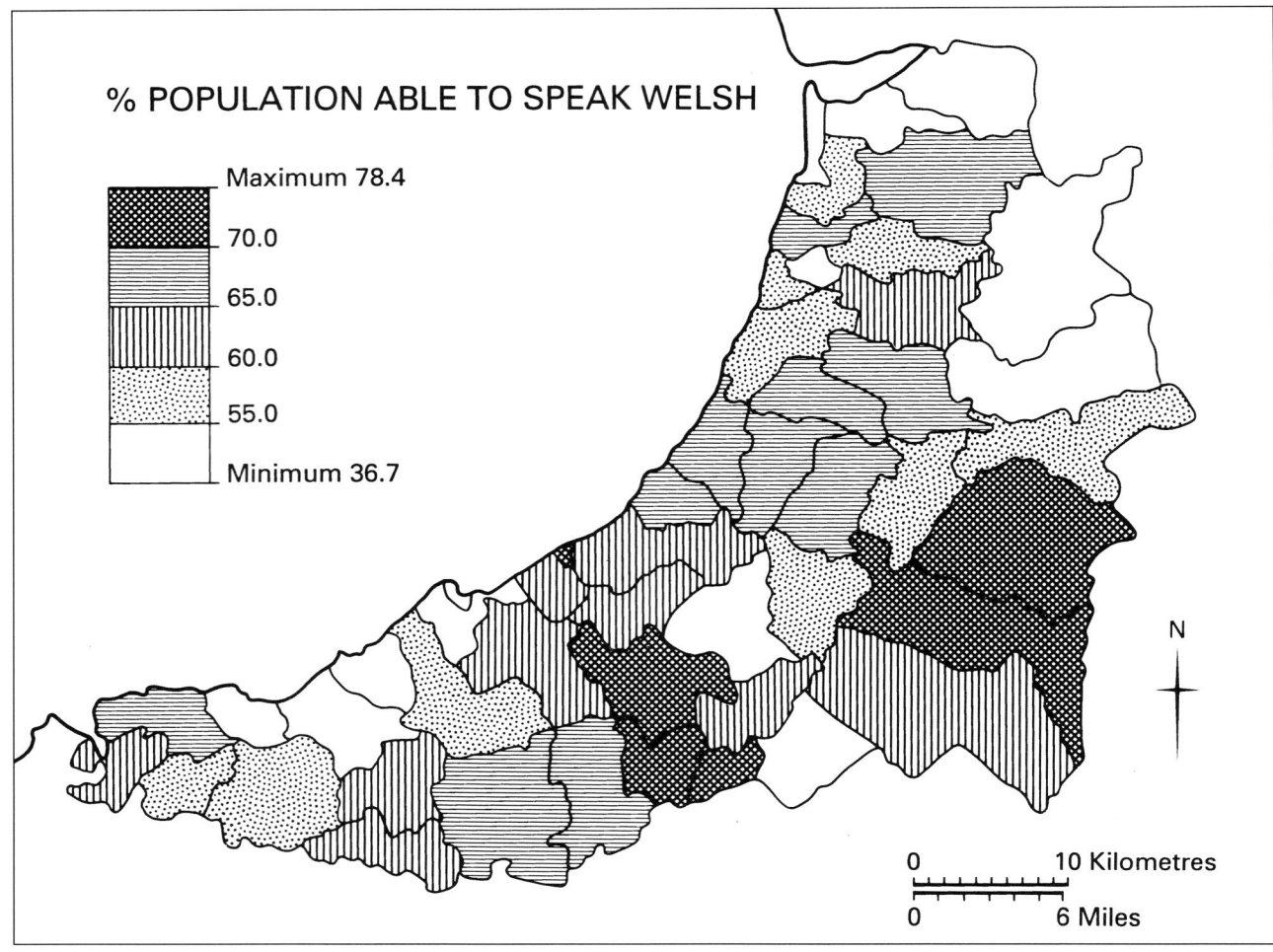

Fig. 136: The percentage of the population (by ward) of Cardiganshire able to speak Welsh in 1991.

Figure 136 presents the distribution of the language in 1991, the last census held in the twentieth century. It is a patchy and irregular consequence of both the elements of decline and regeneration which have been discussed. The coastal area is manifestly still one of lower proportions, a feature accentuated both in the north, along the Dyfi estuary where there is a significant concentration of holiday caravan sites and homes, and in the south, where the impact of Aber-porth is especially distinctive. Again, there are lower proportions in the upper reaches of the Rheidol and the Ystwyth river valleys, matched by high proportions born outside Wales and identifying them as parts markedly influenced by both holiday homes and by immigrant settlement, as well as the impact of the hydroelectric works. These are also the areas of abandoned lead mining, where dilapidated cottages presented opportunities for incomers. The other area of lower percentages is Llanfair Clydogau, a somewhat anomalous area which has already been noted and which possibly covers an area of suburban extension from Lampeter. In contrast, there are two areas of higher proportions. These are Lampeter itself, an urban area, where the ward percentage was 72.6 and the community 72.7, and the communities of Tirymynach and Genau'r-glyn, near Aberystwyth. To some extent these are unexpectedly high and possibly represent a feature which has recently emerged, namely the increase in Welsh speech where administrative and service industries have brought into being enclaves of Welsh speakers. At the heart of the county, Mynydd Bach still stands out as resistant to Anglicization, although inroads have been made into its identity. But Tregaron and Ystrad-fflur, in spite of the processes of in-migration which have been noted, still return the highest percentage of Welsh speakers. Across the county in general, however, there is a clear association between those parts with a high proportion born outside Wales and a lower proportion speaking Welsh.

This chapter began by describing a county which, at the beginning of the twentieth century, was wholly Welsh-speaking and which contained a considerable monoglot Welsh element. The subsequent history has been one of successive inroads made by all those forces which, common to the whole of Wales, have led to language erosion. But the chapter can be concluded by emphasizing the determined attempt to revive the fortunes of the language. The impact and the significance of English in a world where isolation has all but vanished, and where the medium of the global village is English, mean that the twenty-first-century condition will be very different from that at the beginning of the twentieth. Monoglot Welsh speakers will no longer exist but, rather than the slow eradication of the language which seemed likely at mid-century, a widespread bilingualism seems now much more likely.

CHAPTER 25

MUSIC AND POPULAR CULTURE

Rhidian Griffiths

THERE is a tradition, probably no older than the mid-nineteenth century, that George Frideric Handel was inspired to write the 'Hallelujah' chorus, the cornerstone of his oratorio *Messiah*, during a visit to Thomas Johnes at Hafod, in response to the ecstatic cries uttered by the Cardiganshire Methodists at their open-air meetings. Though completely without foundation – Handel's *Messiah* was written in 1741 and Johnes did not come to Hafod until 1783 – the tradition is not without its significance. The period from the early nineteenth century to the mid-twentieth saw the emergence of popular music-making which eclipsed the older tradition of gentry patronage for individual singers and performers. The 'Hallelujah' became a flagship chorus for Welsh choirs, and it was not unnatural that the choristers of Cardiganshire, proud of their achievements, should wish to claim it as the county's own.[1] Cardiganshire was to reflect in varied ways the emergence of the new culture of choral, congregational and competitive singing, though it is doubtful whether gentry patronage had ever been a significant force in the county. Some families did uphold the tradition of maintaining a resident harpist. Gruffudd Ifan, a harpist at Nanteos, was said to have entertained the household for sixty-nine Christmases in succession. Jeremiah Wood Jones (1778?–1867), 'Jeri Bach Gogerddan', served his masters at Gogerddan for over fifty years, but his sons, though themselves fine performers, did not follow him. In the late nineteenth century the admiration of George Ernest John Powell for Richard Wagner had little impact on the musical life of the county. Powell met Wagner, and the music room at Nanteos contained the composer's portrait, but the tradition that he stayed there seems, like the 'Hallelujah' legend of Hafod, to be groundless.[2]

The development of a formalized musical tradition did not totally eclipse the county's folk music. Few ballads have survived from eighteenth-century Cardiganshire, probably because very few existed;[3] but in the nineteenth century the ballad was a popular form in fairgrounds and on street corners. Benjamin Williams, 'Gwynionydd', retained vivid memories of the large crowds which gathered at the fairs of Newcastle Emlyn, Capel Cynon, and Cardigan in the 1830s and 1840s to hear ballad singers. Dafydd Jones (1803–68) of Llanybydder, known as 'Dewi Medi' and 'Dewi Dywyll', was the son of a carpenter who began a career as a roving ballad-singer after losing his sight. Dafydd Jones of Tanglwst Fach, Troed-yr-aur, was another who had been forced by poor

[1]M. I. Williams, 'Did Handel visit Cardiganshire?', *Ceredigion*, III, no.4 (1959), 337–44.
[2]R. Griffith, *Llyfr Cerdd Dannau* (Caernarfon, [1913]), pp.195, 232, 236; D. Evans, 'George Powell: "an enthusiast for the highest order of music" ', *Welsh Music*, 7, no.1 (1982), 41–8.
[3]G. Bowen, 'Croeso Ceredigion i'r faled', *Western Mail*, 27 March 1939.

Fig. 137: David Lewis, Llanrhystud (1828–1908), who preserved many folk airs in *Y Cerddor Cymreig.* (*Copyright National Library of Wales*).

eyesight to abandon his trade and entertain the masses with prophetic or dramatic songs. Other balladeers popular in the county were Dafydd Rice of Cefnmabws near Llanrhystud, a veteran of Trafalgar; Thomas Jones, also of Llanrhystud; Joel Rowland of Blaen-plwyf; Stephen Jones of Cilcennin; and Benjamin Evans of Aberaeron. Ballad-singers from other parts of Wales, such as Levi Gibbon (1807?–70), Richard Williams (1790?–1862?), 'Dic Dywyll', and Owen Griffith (1803–68), 'Ywain Meirion', were also extremely popular in the county. Ywain Meirion composed a notable ballad depicting the devastation in Cardiganshire following the dramatic storms of July and August 1846.[4] Welsh ballads of the period recounted events such as murders, shipwrecks and hangings, and were a form of news broadcast to the common (and frequently illiterate) people. Other songs dealt with general themes of life and love. Ballad-singers were often undistinguished vocally and relied on a limited range of tunes, but commanded ready audiences with their dramatic presentations. The ballads themselves were printed by local printers and sold on penny sheets.

Closely related to the ballad tradition is the county's heritage of folk-song. A number of folk airs were recorded on the pages of *Y Cerddor Cymreig* in the 1860s by David Lewis (1828–1908), a tailor

---

[4]B. Williams (Gwynionydd), 'Hen faledwyr Dyfed', *Y Geninen* (1891), 285–6; E. Jones, *Cerdded Hen Ffeiriau* (Aberystwyth, 1972), pp.94–8; T. Jones, *Hen Faledi Ffair* (Tal-y-bont, 1971), pp.21–3, 40.

and a gifted amateur musician from Llanrhystud. Like his father before him, Lewis collected the airs, both sacred and secular, he heard sung or played, and published the melodies without the words.[5] By the early twentieth century, however, collecting had become more scientific, and the foundation of the Welsh Folk-Song Society in 1908 gave impetus to collectors to rescue what was left of a vanishing tradition. Jennie Williams (1890?–1971) found Cardiganshire, particularly the Mynydd Bach district, fertile ground for collecting. Her collection of songs from Cardiganshire and Carmarthenshire, which won for her a second prize at the National Eisteddfod of 1911, contained such gems of Welsh folk-song as 'Lliw'r heulwen' and 'Cariad cyntaf'. Lady Herbert Lewis (1872–1946), the English-born wife of the Flintshire MP Sir John Herbert Lewis, went on collecting expeditions in the area of Llandysul. In 1929 the Cardiganshire Antiquarian Society exploited the wealth of the county's folk-songs by publishing a volume entitled *Forty Welsh Traditional Tunes*, collected by J. Ffos Davies, headmaster of Felin-fach School, a collection of considerable musical and ethnological value, albeit heavily edited by Cledlyn Davies and David de Lloyd. Dan Jenkins of Pentrefelin, one of those who performed at a concert to launch the new publication on 30 November 1929, was to lament the supposed death of folk-song in an article published in the Society's *Transactions* in 1936; but the songs themselves grew in popularity and were sung in schools and at eisteddfodau.[6] Collecting also continued: 'Y march glas', a song noted in south Cardiganshire, was published as late as 1952. The most exceptional folk-song survival in the county, however, are the songs preserved in the family of Myra Evans (1883–1972) of Gilfachreda near New Quay. Two of them are of considerable antiquity: 'Myn Mair', a lament for a deceased friend which invokes the saints and the Virgin Mary, and 'Ar fore dydd Nadolig', a Christmas carol which may be derived from medieval plainsong.

It is significant that nineteenth-century collectors like David Lewis saw fit not to preserve the words of folk-songs. In the history of Welsh music the nineteenth century is a formative period characterized by a zeal for reform: older music was only of value insofar as it could be used in the context of choral and congregational singing, which grew in importance during the century. In Cardiganshire David Lewis himself was one of the apostles of the reform movement, credited with achieving 'a revolution from the Ystwyth to the Aeron' in musical knowledge and practice.[7] He was not, however, the first of his kind. Dafydd Siencyn Morgan (1752–1844), a native of Llangrannog who joined the Congregationalist cause at Llechryd, was an influential peripatetic singing master who visited most parts of Wales to give instruction in the rudiments of music, visiting churches and chapels to teach tunes and anthems. Dafydd Siencyn of Borth was a seafarer who spent the winter months as a singing instructor in north Cardiganshire. The instruction provided by men such as these helped to develop an interest in choral singing, an interest fostered by the formation of musical societies such as that established at Aberystwyth in 1830. The primary aim of such societies was to encourage the learning of new music for congregational use, regardless of denominational differences. Thus the Aberystwyth society drew on the already strong tradition of the church at Llanbadarn, one of whose singers, Roderic Philip (1751–1818), had become the precentor of

[5] *Y Cerddor Cymreig*, 2 (1863–4), 109.
[6] C. Davies and D. de Lloyd (eds.), *Forty Welsh Traditional Tunes* (London, 1929); *TCAS*, 7 (1930), 8; 11 (1936), 61.
[7] D. W. Thomas, 'Addysg yng Ngheredigion, 1800–1850, yn ôl y cofiannau', *Ceredigion*, VI, no.1 (1968), 65.

Tabernacl chapel in the town at its opening in 1785. He and his son Dafydd (1787–1873) established a strong tradition of singing at Tabernacl, and Dafydd and the Baptist precentor, Billy Collins, were among those who founded the musical society in 1830. The influence of such societies spread quickly: John Roberts (1806–79), an engraver who worked in Aberystwyth, was hired by the parish of Llangwyryfon to instruct the parishioners in the art of singing.[8] The musical renaissance led by members of the Mills family at Llanidloes also influenced Aberystwyth, so that by 1852 the Tabernacl Choral Society could inaugurate a tradition of public concerts at the Assembly Rooms. Leadership by that time had passed to Edward Edwards (1816–98), 'Pencerdd Ceredigion', a pupil of Dafydd Siencyn, who not only instructed choristers and raised the standard of singing to new heights, but in the course of his long career acted as precentor in several chapels in Aberystwyth. The development of choral singing was not confined to Aberystwyth. Tregaron had a choral society in the mid-1850s: the programme of its second concert in 1855 includes choruses by Mozart and Handel as well as anthems by the Welsh composer John Ambrose Lloyd. The Cardigan United Choral Union gave its first concert in 1863, and during the same decade small choirs were competing at rural eisteddfodau in Llangeitho, Abermeurig and Llan-non.[9] Ystumtuen boasted a choir of sixty to seventy voices during the same period.[10] A tradition of massed choirs emerged: ten choirs participated in the first festival of the Cardiganshire Temperance Musical Union in 1870, a practice revived in the Cardiganshire Musical Festivals of the 1920s.[11]

It should not be assumed that the story is one of unbroken development. The significant advances of the 1850s and 1860s were followed by periods of less activity; choirs disappeared or split regularly. Nevertheless, the tradition of popular choral singing begun in the 1850s was to continue for a century and more, and was to find expression in different types of choirs. A children's choir was established at Pen-y-garn as early as 1864; thirty-three years later the Rheidol juvenile choir and the Aeron girls' choir competed at a Good Friday eisteddfod in Aberystwyth. The Rheidol choir enjoyed particular success, and was part of the Cardiganshire triumph at the National Eisteddfod held at Carmarthen in 1911, when four choirs from the county gained first prizes. The four – Cardigan Ladies, Newcastle Emlyn and District, Bargoed Teifi male voice and the Rheidol juvenile choir – were rewarded with a gala concert at the Pier Pavilion in Aberystwyth.[12] Rural areas like Blaencaron maintained several small choirs in the 1920s.[13] There was, however, growing concern by the mid-twentieth century that Welsh choralism was past its peak, as the traditional foundations of church and chapel music began to crumble. Writing in 1948, W. R. Allen (1891–1956), singing tutor at the University College of Wales, Aberystwyth, and conductor of the Borough Choir, spoke of decline:

> Cardiganshire . . . at one time the centre of choirs well able to read music, now finds itself in a state of musical illiteracy, with a consequent restriction upon musical adventure.[14]

[8]D. Samuel, 'Hen gerddorion Aberystwyth', *Cymru*, 17 (1899), 90–2, 118–20, 157–60, 232–5, 249–52; J. Edwards, 'Old Welsh music and musicians', *Welsh Gazette*, 23 March 1916.
[9]*Y Cerddor Cymreig*, 1 (1861–3), 190; 2 (1863–4), 79, 95, 134.
[10]D. Jones, 'Hen gantorion Ystumtuen', *Yr Eurgrawn Wesleaidd*, 102 (1910), 183.
[11]*Y Cerddor Cymreig*, 8 (1870), 76.
[12]*Y Cerddor Cymreig*, 3 (1865), 22; *Y Cerddor*, 9 (1897), 67; *Welsh Gazette*, 28 September, 5 October, 19 October 1911.
[13]C. Davies, 'Dechrau Canu', *Llafar*, Gŵyl Dewi 1954, 34–6.
[14]W. R. Allen, 'The choral tradition', in P. Crossley-Holland (ed.), *Music in Wales* (London, 1948), p.37.

Fig. 138: The Rheidol Juvenile Choir, 1911. (*Copyright National Library of Wales*).

Nevertheless, a choral society was re-formed in Aberystwyth in 1970 (the Aberystwyth and District Choral Society), and mixed choirs in Aberaeron and Glannau Ystwyth enjoyed success alongside more specialized groups. By the 1990s the county could boast in Cantorion Teifi one of Wales's finest smaller choirs.

Throughout the period the choral tradition has been fostered by the opportunity for competition at eisteddfodau, at national, regional and local levels, though it has often been asserted, not without justification, that competition has hindered the development of choral singing in Wales. The National Eisteddfod has been held in Cardiganshire on seven occasions, at Aberystwyth in 1865, 1916, 1952 and 1992, at Cardigan in 1942 and 1976, and at Lampeter in 1984; and the Gŵyl Gerdd Dant seven times, at Aberystwyth in 1954, 1962, 1983 and 1997, at Llandysul in 1960, at Tregaron in 1966, and at Pontrhydfendigaid in 1989. The semi-national eisteddfod held at Cardigan in 1909 established a tradition in the town which was later to develop into Gŵyl Fawr Aberteifi. Significant eisteddfodau were founded at Pontrhydfendigaid in 1964 and at Lampeter in 1967 under the aegis of the Pantyfedwen Foundation. Such festivals provided a platform for local choirs and for visitors. But it was the town and village eisteddfodau which had most impact on local musical life. As early as 1863 rural areas such as Abermeurig were holding eisteddfodau with competitions for choirs, which attracted competitors from Cilcennin and Aberaeron–Abermeurig, as well as competitions for soloists. An eisteddfod held at Aberaeron in July 1864 enticed choirs from Newcastle Emlyn, Llannarth and Glynarthen to compete for substantial prizes of ten guineas and four guineas.[15] Eisteddfodau were sometimes linked with concerts. In August 1870 the day's competitions at the Llanafan eisteddfod were followed by a concert given by the Llanafan choir and the music adjudicator, W. T. Rees (1838–1904), 'Alaw Ddu'.[16] Although Cardiganshire seems not to have enjoyed the strong tradition of Christmas and New Year eisteddfodau found in parts of Glamorgan, a number of local annual festivals established in the late nineteenth century (as at Swyddffynnon) continued well into the twentieth, and new eisteddfodau were founded (as at Tregaron and Penrhyn-coch) for the promotion of local talent, though often with greater emphasis on individual performers than on choirs.

In Cardiganshire, as in other parts of Wales, the development of choral singing as an aspect of popular musical culture was inextricably linked with the emergence of a strong tradition of congregational singing. During the formative years of the mid-nineteenth century the chapel was often the sole focus of musical activity in town or village. Learning to sing meant learning hymns and anthems, many of which provided staple fare for eisteddfod competitions, and this could lead to a conflict of interests. In 1852 the elders of Tabernacl chapel in Aberystwyth were indignant that the chapel choir should sing sacred music in the Assembly Rooms, which had been built for dancing.[17] Nevertheless, the congregational tradition was to underpin Welsh choralism for several generations, and the musical society formed at Aberystwyth in 1830 was as much concerned with the sacred as the secular, if not more so. Many of the county's small choirs were chapel-based. At Aberystwyth Edward Edwards founded a choir at Siloh chapel which opened in 1863; the choir gave charity performances outside the town, as did the choir of Tabernacl. The two choirs combined in 1868 for a benefit concert for Dafydd Philip, the Tabernacl precentor.[18]

On his return to Aberystwyth from a period of working in Glamorgan, Edward Edwards also influenced the adoption of 'modern' four-part harmony in the county's congregations, with sopranos rather than tenors taking the melody. John Ambrose Lloyd (1815–74), the finest Welsh composer of his generation, believed that the standard of congregational singing to be heard in Aberystwyth in the 1850s surpassed anything in the rest of Wales, and it is therefore not surprising that the greatest single agent of reform of Welsh congregational singing should have sprung from that background. John Roberts (1822–77), known as 'Ieuan Gwyllt', was born at Capel Seion and grew up near Goginan. He came to work in Aberystwyth and was strongly influenced by the tradition of choral and congregational singing in the town. Though he left Cardiganshire in 1852, his work was to have a significant impact on the county and on all parts of Wales. In 1859 he published *Llyfr Tonau Cynulleidfaol* (Congregational Tune Book), and two years later founded an important music journal, *Y Cerddor Cymreig* (The Welsh Musician). The *Llyfr Tonau* set new standards in chapel singing, with an emphasis on simplicity and dignity, and a favouring of the Lutheran chorale over the florid tunes which had been popular until that time.

---

[15] *Y Cerddor Cymreig*, 2 (1863–4), 79, 151–2.
[16] Ibid., 8 (1870), 71–2.
[17] D. Samuel, 'Hen gerddorion Aberystwyth', 234; M. I. Williams, *Y Tabernacl Aberystwyth: Hanes yr Achos 1785–1985* (Aberystwyth, 1986), p.78.
[18] *Y Cerddor Cymreig*, 6 (1868), 67.

Two factors helped to promote his crusade. The first was the dissemination in the 1860s of the tonic sol-fa notation as a medium for the teaching of singing. Ieuan himself advocated the use of sol-fa as a notation because it was quicker and easier to learn than the traditional staff notation: his *Llyfr Tonau* appeared in a sol-fa edition in 1863, and in 1869 he founded a journal, *Cerddor y Tonic Sol-ffa* (The Tonic Sol-fa Musician), specifically for users of the new notation. Tonic sol-fa classes were established in rural areas. In 1869 it was reported that the class at Llanfair Clydogau had thirty-five members, that at Llanio thirty-two, and that at Llanddewibrefi fifty, while there were also flourishing classes at Blaenannerch and Aber-arth.[19] Again the story is not one of unimpeded progress, but there can be no doubt that tonic sol-fa significantly aided the cause of popular music literacy. When its jubilee was celebrated at Aberystwyth in 1891, the town's chapels were full to overflowing.[20] Its use as a teaching medium in schools and chapels continued well into the twentieth century, and it is not without significance that as it declined in popularity after the Second World War so the nature of Welsh choralism changed.

The second factor which aided the development of congregational singing was the growth of the *cymanfa ganu* (singing festival). In order to encourage the dissemination of his *Llyfr Tonau*, Ieuan Gwyllt urged congregations to come together for the purpose of learning new tunes in order to enrich Sunday worship. It was from such meetings that the pattern of *cymanfaoedd canu* developed. As early as January 1863 a united interdenominational meeting was held at Capel y Wig with the aim of 'reforming congregational singing', under the supervision of the Revd David Davies of Twr-gwyn.[21] Seven congregations were represented at what was reported to be a highly successful event. In November 1869 the Teifi Valley Musical Union held its first meeting at Llanfair Clydogau, and in the same year at Pen-llwyn congregations from Aber-ffrwd, Pen-y-garn and Aberystwyth combined under Edward Edwards's leadership to sing hymn-tunes and choruses, closing the meeting with Handel's 'Hallelujah' chorus.[22] The Musical Unions formed in various parts of the county in the 1860s and early 1870s appear to have enjoyed considerable success – the Union of Glannau Teifi and Aeron boasted two thousand members in 1872[23] – and combined choral activity with congregational singing; but from the 1880s there emerged a pattern of hymn-singing festivals on denominational lines which bore the hallmarks of the *cymanfa ganu* recognizable in the twentieth century. *Cymanfaoedd* were founded by the Congregationalists of Newcastle Emlyn around 1880, the Baptists of Cardigan in 1885 and the Congregationalists of the same town in 1890, thereby inaugurating a tradition which was to last for over a century. Such meetings were the occasion for presenting certificates for proficiency in tonic sol-fa. They were also in their heyday, at least until the First World War, an immense popular attraction: in 1910 the Baptists of Cardigan printed thirteen hundred programmes for their *cymanfa*, and in 1914 the Congregationalists of Newcastle Emlyn printed a thousand.[24]

[19]*Cerddor y Tonic Sol-ffa*, 1 (1869), 30, 37, 62.
[20]*Y Cerddor*, 3 (1891), 79, 114.
[21]*Y Cerddor Cymreig*, 2 (1863–4), 6.
[22]Ibid., 7 (1869), 91; 8 (1870), 13.
[23]*Cerddor y Tonic Sol-ffa*, 4 (1872), 9.
[24]W. Davies, *Canrif o Gân 1880–1980: Canmlwyddiant Cymanfa Ganu Castellnewydd Emlyn a'r Cylch* (Castellnewydd Emlyn, [1980?]); W. H. Howells, *Canrif o Fawl: Cymanfa Ganu Bedyddwyr Aberteifi a'r Cylch 1885–1985* (Aberteifi, 1985); D. J. Roberts, *Caniadaeth Canrif: Hanes Cymanfa Ganu Annibynwyr Aberteifi a'r Cylch 1890–1990* (Aberteifi, 1990).

That musical culture was deeply rooted in congregational singing gave considerable scope for the development of amateur talent. In the late nineteenth century, Tabernacl Baptist chapel at Tal-y-bont had as its precentor Richard Thomas Griffiths, who conducted several successful choirs, and the congregational singing at Tabernacl was the finest in the area. Timothy Richards (1859–1942), a shopkeeper who became mayor of Lampeter, and a justice of the peace, was precentor of Soar Congregationalist chapel for over fifty years from 1877.[25] Such men played an important role in the musical life of chapels in the pre-organ age, but from the late nineteenth century attitudes to the use of musical instruments began to soften. Chapel singing had been accompanied in some areas even in the early nineteenth century: John Roberts was said to use a bass viol and flageolet at the Baptist cause in Aberystwyth, while several instruments were in use in Unitarian congregations throughout the county before the mid-century.[26] The reformers' emphasis on disciplined singing in four parts, however, tended to mean that instruments were outlawed from chapels, though they were still commonly used in churches. Towards the end of the century, as Nonconformists became more socially ambitious and built bigger buildings, the installation of organs became fashionable. Portland Street Congregational Church in Aberystwyth installed an organ in 1876 because the church was attracting 'visitors of substance': the first organist was Joseph Parry, Professor of Music at the University College of Wales.[27] Several organs were installed around the turn of the century, at Tabernacl, Aberaeron in 1897, at Seion, Baker Street, Aberystwyth in 1903, and, most notable of all, the magnificent instrument built by Harrison of Durham at Tabernacl, Aberystwyth, which was opened in 1905 by the distinguished recitalist E. T. Davies (1878–1969) of Dowlais.[28] Inaugural recitals were great occasions. Myra Evans never forgot the impression made on her by the dramatic playing of T. Hopkin Evans (1879–1940) when he inaugurated the new organ at Tabernacl, New Quay, in 1925.[29] One of the most significant developments in this field was the construction of the new organ at Siloh, Aberystwyth, in 1934. Built at a cost of over £3,000, it was designed to the specification of the chapel's distinguished organist, Charles Henry Clements (1898–1983), a native of Aberystwyth. An organist of European standing, Clements resisted all temptations to leave his native heath, and enjoyed a long career as a teacher at the University College of Wales and as conductor of a successful madrigal choir.[30] Another organist, teacher and accompanist was Edward (Ted) Morgan (1895–1979), a native of Brynaman who moved to Llandysul as an organist in 1923 and remained in the area for the rest of his life, acting as an auxiliary music teacher at the secondary schools in Llandysul, Tregaron, Lampeter and Aberaeron.[31]

It was to be expected that a developing tradition of Welsh music in the nineteenth century would in time produce a generation of composers. The achievements of these men were necessarily limited

[25]E. Jones, 'Atgofion am Dalybont: hen arweinwyr canu', *Welsh Gazette*, 1 January 1948; T. E. Davies, *Trem ar Ganmlwydd Eglwys Soar, Llanbedr* (Llanbedr Pont Steffan, 1931), p.30.

[26]D. Samuel, 'Hen gerddorion Aberystwyth', 158; K. Jones, 'Caniadaeth y cysegr', *Yr Ymofynnydd*, 44 (1944), 77–82.

[27]W. J. Lewis, *The English Congregational Church, Portland Street, Aberystwyth 1866–1966* (Aberystwyth, 1966), p.61.

[28]L. H. Lewis, *Penodau yn Hanes Aberaeron* (Llandysul, 1970), p.83; E. D. Jones, *Trem ar Ganrif yn Hanes Eglwys Gynulleidfaol Baker Street, Aberystwyth* (Aberystwyth, 1978), p.9; Williams, *Y Tabernacl Aberystwyth*, pp.81–3.

[29]M. Evans, *Atgofion Ceinewydd*, (gol.) W. J. Jones (Aberystwyth, 1961), p.65.

[30]F. W. Jones, *Canmlwydd Siloh Aberystwyth* (Aberystwyth, 1963), pp.79–81; G. Thomas, 'Charles Henry Clements, M.B.E.: a tribute', *Welsh Music*, 7, no.4 (1983), 19–22.

[31]D. J. G. Evans, 'Edward (Ted) Morgan', *Yr Ymofynnydd*, 74 (1974–5), 74–8.

by their lack of formal education and the nature of the musical community to which they belonged, but they nevertheless made a positive contribution to the musical life of the county and the whole of Wales. John Thomas (1839–1921) was a native of Blaenannerch, though he spent much of his adult life outside Cardiganshire at Llanwrtyd. A composer of hymn-tunes, anthems and part-songs, he was also widely known as a conductor of *cymanfaoedd canu*. His part-song 'Mai' (May) became popular with choirs in the 1860s and 1870s, while his anthem, 'Bendigedig fyddo Arglwydd Dduw Israel' (Blessed be the Lord God of Israel), was for many the epitome of the religious revival of 1859. His contemporary, David Emlyn Evans (1843–1913) was born near Newcastle Emlyn, though like John Thomas he was to spend much of his life outside the county. A conscientious, if not particularly inspired, composer, now best remembered for his hymn-tunes 'Eirinwg' and 'Trewen', his most significant contribution to Welsh music was as adjudicator and critic. He was a founder editor of the influential magazine *Y Cerddor* (The Musician), and contributed articles on Welsh music to the *South Wales Weekly News*. Evans's younger contemporary, John Thomas Rees (1857–1949), a native of Cwmgïedd in the Swansea Valley, came to Bow Street in 1880, and, with the exception of a year spent in the United States, remained there for the rest of his long life. A prolific composer, whose works are now largely forgotten, Rees was in some ways a pioneer, winning a National Eisteddfod prize for a string quartet at a time when few Welsh musicians gave any attention to instrumental music. Much of his life was devoted to the cause of chapel music at Capel y Garn and in Wales as a whole: he published a popular collection for Sunday School use, *Perorydd yr Ysgol Sul* (The Sunday School Songster) in 1915, and in 1939 a collection of his own hymn-tunes, *Iesu Biau'r Gân* (The Song is Jesus' own). For many years he spent one day a week teaching music at Tregaron school.[32]

Perhaps the finest composer to emerge from Cardiganshire in the late nineteenth century was Richard Samuel (R. S.) Hughes (1855–93). Born the son of an ironmonger at Aberystwyth, Hughes distinguished himself at the age of ten by winning a piano competition at the National Eisteddfod held in his home town. Unlike John Thomas and Emlyn Evans, who were almost entirely self-taught, R. S. Hughes studied at the Royal Academy of Music in London, and his career was spent there, at Hull, and latterly at Bethesda in north Wales, where he died. Though he depended for a living on teaching, adjudicating and accompanying at eisteddfodau, it was as a composer that he left an abiding impression on Welsh musical life. Many of his solo songs became classics of Welsh music, and the best of them, including 'Arafa, don' (Wave, be still) and 'Y Dymestl' (The Tempest), have retained their popularity over the span of a century and more.[33]

R. S. Hughes was privileged to have the benefit of a formal musical education, a luxury few Welshmen could enjoy until the late nineteenth century. The foundation of the University College of Wales at Aberystwyth in 1872, however, was to provide a new opportunity in that sphere. Showing remarkable imagination in an age when music was still not commonly regarded as a subject of academic study, the Council of the College decided in 1874 to found a Chair of Music, and invited to fill it the most eminent Welsh musician of his day, the brilliant but erratic Joseph Parry (1841–1903). Parry had been born at Merthyr Tydfil, and had spent much of his life in the

[32] E. Evans, *Cofiant John Thomas, Llanwrtyd* (Caernarfon, 1926); E. K. Evans, *Cofiant D. Emlyn Evans* (Lerpwl, 1919); D. H. Lewis, *John Thomas Rees, Mus. Bac.: Cofiant* (Llandysul, 1955).
[33] Rh. Griffiths, 'R. S. Hughes: teyrnged canmlwyddiant', *Welsh Music*, 9, no.6 (1993), 27–33; W. Thomas, 'Tywysog y gân: R. S. Hughes (1855–1893)', *Barn*, 370 (1993), 16–18.

United States. He had, however, benefited from several years of study at the Royal Academy of Music, where he had been a pupil of William Sterndale Bennett. He therefore combined the heritage of the Welsh Nonconformist tradition in music with substantial academic training, and his coming from America to Aberystwyth in 1874 was hailed by many as heralding a bright new dawn in Welsh music. It was confidently expected that a whole generation of well-educated musicians would be reared at Aberystwyth, but such hopes were to be disappointed. Parry's tenure of the Chair was turbulent, and in 1880 he was forced to resign and move to Swansea. Yet his years at Aberystwyth were not unproductive. If his teaching was irregular, he attracted male and female students and encouraged performance (not infrequently of his own works) as well as academic study. An Aberystwyth and University Musical Society was established in 1875 under the presidency of Colonel Powell of Nanteos, with Parry as conductor; its first Grand Concert at the Temperance Hall on 21 May 1875 (which included the first performance of 'Myfanwy' in its programme) was the precursor of the 'town and gown' tradition of musical activity which was to characterize the Music Department at Aberystwyth in later years. Courses of instruction were provided for external as well as full-time students: one such external student was J. T. Rees of Bow Street. Parry's departure from Aberystwyth was greeted with dismay by his students, and was a considerable loss to the still young College, for, since he was not replaced, the opportunity to develop musical education within the University of Wales was lost for many years.

Musical activity, however, continued after Parry's resignation from the Chair. In 1884 a new Musical Society was formed and a pattern of annual concerts emerged, beginning with a performance of Mendelssohn's *Antigone* in 1885. Ten years later the Society acquired a Bechstein grand piano for the College, and both a choir and a College orchestra were supported. In 1892 David Jenkins (1848–1915), a native of Trecastell, Breconshire, and a former pupil of Parry, was appointed Instructor in Music in the Education Department, subsequently becoming Lecturer, and in 1910 Professor, a post which he held until his death. Jenkins, who graduated Mus. Bac. at Cambridge as an external student in 1878, was the epitome of self-help in musical education. Although he had little formal instruction, other than his years of study under Parry, he became one of Wales's foremost musicians. He co-edited *Y Cerddor* with D. Emlyn Evans and was a prolific, if not notably successful composer, in various genres; one of his compositions was the Aberystwyth College Song. He also established a flourishing business as a publisher of music, both his own and that of others, and enabled the reintroduction of music as an academic subject as well as a College activity.[34]

One of Jenkins's ambitions was to see the establishment of a School of Music at Aberystwyth, and he lived to see the significant developments of the years immediately preceding the First World War. In those years Aberystwyth owed much to the presence of Mme Lucie Barbier, the wife of the College's Professor of French, André Barbier. Born in Paris in 1875 and trained at the Paris Conservatoire, Lucie Barbier was a fine singer and pianist who knew many French composers personally. She organized musical events at her home and in October 1910 encouraged the University Music Club to concentrate on chamber music, a form probably little known in Aberystwyth at the time.

[34]C. H. Jenkins, 'The Music Department and musical activities 1874–1927', in Iwan Morgan (ed.), *The College by the Sea* (Aberystwyth, 1928), pp.191–3; E. Edwards, 'Hanes cynnar canu yng Ngholeg Aberystwyth', *Y Cerddor*, 2 (1932), 299–301; E. L. Ellis, *The University College of Wales Aberystwyth 1872–1972* (Cardiff, 1972), pp.55–6, 174–5.

Between then and 1915 over three hundred works were performed, chiefly, but not exclusively, of French music. Visiting performers included the English composer Arthur Somervell, the Le Feuve Quartet, and the celebrated French pianist Alfred Cortot, who played in Aberystwyth on 18 February 1914. Mme Barbier did not, however, confine her attention to French music: she responded to the movement for preserving Welsh folk-songs by taking a quartet of undergraduates from the College to Paris in March 1911. The singers, Dora Rowlands, Gwen Taylor, Tudor Williams and L. Stanley Knight, gave six concerts of Welsh folk-songs, which were widely acclaimed and represented a significant step forward in the cause of Welsh music, which had rarely been heard outside Wales. In more ways than one Lucie Barbier's work brought a European perspective to the musical experience of the people of Cardiganshire.[35]

It was in the aftermath of the First World War, however, that the county's musical life experienced its greatest fillip, again through the work and influence of the Music Department of the University College. The Commission on University Education in Wales, under the chairmanship of Lord Haldane, which reported in 1918 recommended the establishment of a National Council of Music in Wales, in order to harness the potential for musical education both within and without the University. At the same time the Davies family of Llandinam and Gregynog provided money for the endowment of a new Chair of Music at Aberystwyth (the Chair having been vacant since the death of David Jenkins in 1915). Many Welshmen, including the experienced musician L. J. Roberts (1866–1931) of Aberaeron, an Inspector of Schools, advanced the claims of David Vaughan Thomas (1873–1934) of Swansea to the Chair, since Thomas had pioneered the cause of a distinctively Welsh music, associated with the traditional poetry in *cynghanedd*. It was decided, however, to extend the invitation to Henry Walford Davies (1869–1941), the Oswestry-born organist of the Temple Church in London, to become Gregynog Professor of Music and Director of the National Council of Music. Davies proved an inspirational leader, if not always the most tactful of men. At Aberystwyth he encouraged the weekly College concerts and ran summer schools for music teachers. A College trio, comprising Hubert Davies (violin), Arthur Williams (cello) and Charles Clements (piano), was established to promote interest in chamber music. Walford Davies was able to attract celebrities to Aberystwyth, the most notable being the Hungarian composer Béla Bartók (1881–1945), who visited the College on 16 March 1922 and gave a piano recital.[36]

Most significant of all, Davies founded in 1920 a music festival for Aberystwyth. The aims of this festival, as set out in the programme of the festival of 1922, which also marked the fiftieth anniversary of the University College of Wales, reflect Davies's ambitions to raise the standard of musical culture in Wales, ambitions which he pursued with crusading zeal:

> We can only conclude by wishing the College 50 new years of weekly concerts and Annual festivals of increasing beauty and strength, which will sink into our minds to such fine purpose as to enrich individual, College, University and Nation alike, and help to cause Wales to make her fitting contribution to human progress in general and musical progress in particular the whole world over.

[35] M. Stonequist, 'Music in Aberystwyth: 1909–1915', *Welsh Music*, 4, no.7 (1974), 76–84; eadem, 'The Welsh quartet in Paris: 1911', *Welsh Music*, 4, no.8 (1974–5), 7–16.
[36] D. I. Allsobrook, *Music for Wales: Walford Davies and the National Council of Music, 1918–1941* (Cardiff, 1992); R. Smith, 'Béla Bartók in Wales', *Welsh Music*, 4, no.2 (1972), 11–15.

From 1922 to 1933 the festivals were held at the College Hall, and subsequently at other venues. Conductors of the calibre of Adrian Boult and Henry Wood participated, and the violinist Jelly d'Aranyi was a popular soloist. At the early festivals the orchestral works performed were those which had been studied at the College: the programme for 1920, for instance, included Beethoven's Fifth Symphony and Schubert's 'Unfinished', along with works by Bach, Schumann, Dvořák and Vaughan Williams. Audience participation was encouraged: serial ticket holders were entitled to attend rehearsals, and audiences were given tunes like the Welsh 'Braint' and the Latin 'Gaudeamus igitur' to sing. In 1924 the festival was extended to become a Cardiganshire Musical Festival, including a Festival choir, which drew on local resources of adults and children; but in time the College and county festivals were separated, the latter becoming a choral festival for local choirs for the singing of Welsh music, including folk-songs, while the former concentrated on the orchestral and classical repertoire. Though Walford Davies left Aberystwyth in 1926, to be succeeded as Professor of Music by David de Lloyd (1883–1948), he had set in train a pattern of music-making which not only made known to town and gown alike a wide range of choral and orchestral music, but also encouraged the development of close links between College musical activity and the people of Cardiganshire. In the period between the wars the National Council of Music ensured the provision of instruction in music in rural areas, a role assumed after 1945 by the Extra-mural Department of the University College. Such instruction proved popular. In the 1930s Tom Pickering (1893–1952) taught a class of thirty-two students, more than half of them farm servants, at Pen-llwyn, and there was a similar class at Tregaron.[37] College concerts continued regularly under successive Professors of Music, Ian Parrott from 1950 to 1983 and David Wulstan from 1983 until the closure of the Music Department at Aberystwyth in 1989. The tradition of town and gown continued during the post-war years: the Aberystwyth Music Club was revived in 1951, and various festivals were held during the 1960s and 1970s, though the annual music festival inaugurated in 1987 was not founded directly by the University. The College maintained a tradition of instruction in singing, with W. R. Allen and later Redvers Llewellyn (1902–75) as tutors, and the string trio was re-founded as a quartet. In 1971 Robert Jacoby, the leader of the string quartet, founded Philomusica of Aberystwyth as a symphony orchestra for amateur players from a wide area. The availability of a University Arts Centre, including a modern concert hall, at Aberystwyth from the early 1970s made visits by large professional orchestras a possibility, and helped to broaden further the musical experience of the people of the area.

Musical activity in the Cardiganshire of this period was not, however, confined to the University College or to churches and chapels. Music played a significant part in the wider popular culture of the nineteenth and twentieth centuries. In the early days of the Assembly Rooms opened at Aberystwyth in 1820, a Welsh harper and a military band played regularly to accompany the promenades, and with the growth of holidaymaking by the mid-century bands were hired to perform on pier and promenade. Variety shows were held at the Phillips Hall in the town, while in February 1882 the Christy Minstrels performed at the Guildhall in Cardigan. John Parry (1776–1851), 'Bardd Alaw', and his son John Orlando Parry (1810–79) presented their musical sketches in the county. By the late nineteenth century Aberystwyth had developed an entertainment industry

---

[37]Allsobrook, *Music for Wales*, 144–5; A. L. Tusler, 'Some notes on *Y Cerddor*', *Welsh Music*, 8, no.10 (1989), 45–6.

which reflected its growing importance as a holiday resort.[38] The Pier Pavilion, opened in 1896, hosted musical comedy companies, and a band of local working men performed almost daily from July to September under the conductorship of Jack Edwards (1853–1942), a local bookseller, and the son of Edward Edwards, 'Pencerdd Ceredigion'. By 1911 an ambitious programme of municipal entertainments featured the Aberystwyth Municipal Orchestra and Band playing twice daily at the pier, with a sacred concert on Sunday evenings. The Sunday evening concerts were to develop into sessions of community singing led by Côr y Castell, which raised considerable sums for local charities. Other communities in the county had their own forms of popular entertainment, often associated with bands. A German band of five or more instruments had been heard at Tregaron before the establishment in 1890 of a brass band, led by Jack Edwards, who composed a 'Caron March' in the band's honour. Llandysul and Llysnewydd boasted a brass band and Llandysul a fife band in the late nineteenth century. It was said that the sailmaker John Jones of New Quay had enough musical apprentices to form a band of his own. The brass band tradition was to continue into the twentieth century, and be represented by such groups as the Aberystwyth Silver Band, although it was not perhaps as vigorous a tradition as that of industrial south Wales.[39]

Theatre performances also formed a part of the popular entertainment available in the nineteenth century. As early as 1789 *The Beaux' Stratagem* was being performed at the theatre in Aberystwyth; twenty years later a playhouse was opened in Thespian Street. Bass's company played at Aberystwyth and at Cardigan between 1835 and 1841, and Fenton's company in both towns during the 1840s. In the second half of the century Aberystwyth became one of the summer centres of touring theatre companies, and the opening of the Coliseum in 1905 was to provide opportunities for light entertainment and serious theatre. Until its conversion to a cinema in 1932 the Coliseum hosted performances by visiting companies ranging from the London Vaudeville Company to Henry Baynton's Shakespearean Company; eisteddfodau and revues took place there, and between 1918 and 1933 the Aberystwyth Amateur Operatic and Dramatic Society graced the stage annually in performances of operetta.[40] Drama productions also became an important part of College life at Aberystwyth. Between 1884 (when the Dramatic Society was founded) and 1918 over twenty productions of Shakespeare took place, along with other plays: the fact that some were staged outside the College helped to encourage local audiences and to foster interest in drama. The College also promoted Welsh-language drama by performing Welsh plays on St David's Day, among them the folk operetta *Aelwyd Angharad* (The Hearth of Angharad) by J. Lloyd Williams. It was the College, too, which bred the new generation of Welsh dramatists who came into their own after the First World War, a generation which included authors such as D. T. Davies, Kitchener Davies and J. O. Francis. Welsh plays were performed at the Coliseum by local dramatic societies, and in 1920 Aberystwyth was the venue for a Welsh drama competition in which seven companies took part.[41]

[38]W. J. Lewis, *Born on a Perilous Rock* (Aberystwyth, 1980), pp.197, 200–2; idem, *The Gateway to Wales: A History of Cardigan* (Dyfed County Council, 1990), p.138.

[39]D. C. Rees, 'Caron brass band', *Welsh Gazette*, 2 January 1941; S. Campbell-Jones, 'Shipbuilding at New Quay, Cardiganshire, 1779–1878', *Ceredigion*, VII, nos.3–4 (1974–5), 291.

[40]C. Price, *The English Theatre in Wales* (Cardiff, 1948), pp.120–33; *The Coliseum: The History of a Cinema and Theatre in Pictures* (Aberystwyth, 1994).

[41]R. F. Walker, 'The College Theatre at Aberystwyth', *Ceredigion*, VII, nos.3–4 (1974–5), 230–55; VIII, no.2 (1976), 1–25.

The conversion of Aberystwyth's Coliseum to a cinema in 1932 reflected an important cultural change of the twentieth century: the growth of the cinema heralded the advent of mass culture which was to affect Cardiganshire as everywhere. At the turn of the century Arthur Cheetham had an Electric Picture Palace and Theatre at Aberystwyth, and the Pavilion Cinema opened at Cardigan in 1912, thereby exposing the people of the county to a range of experience much wider than before and to influences very different from those of the previous century.[42] From the mid-century onward television began to overtake the cinema and theatre as a vehicle for popular entertainment, prompting fears that popular culture at every level would become passive rather than participative. Yet twentieth-century forms such as cinema, radio and television created their own opportunities: by the 1990s Aberystwyth was the home of the highly regarded Welsh Film Festival. The nature of theatre changed after the Second World War: live repertory became increasingly difficult to sustain, though the Little Theatre at Aberystwyth struggled on until 1961.[43] Touring companies, generally sponsored by the Arts Council, became the norm, and the opening of Theatr y Werin at Aberystwyth in 1972 and Theatr y Mwldan at Cardigan in 1988 afforded new opportunities for theatre-goers as well as providing facilities of a high standard for amateur groups. Drama became a subject of academic study in schools and at the University College, thus engendering an interest in higher professional standards. By this stage audiences had become more discriminating and demanding.

Music-making likewise changed in character from the mid-century. As chapel congregations declined, so the traditional foundations of Welsh choralism weakened. At the same time music developed as a subject for study in schools. Dafydd Miles became the county's first music organizer under the auspices of the Carnegie Trust, as part of an attempt to raise the standards of music teaching. Proficiency in instrumental playing increased, and Cardiganshire contributed to the National Youth Orchestra of Wales, founded in 1946, as well as providing other opportunities for young instrumentalists. Light music benefited from the availability of venues such as the King's Hall at Aberystwyth, opened in 1934, where Evered Davies's light orchestra performed regularly during the holiday season.[44] His son Ralph (1916–90) led a quartet which achieved considerable success on radio and television. It was Ralph Davies who introduced Les France to Aberystwyth, and in the 1950s France's dance band, consisting entirely of part-time musicians, played all over Cardiganshire.[45] From the 1960s onwards pop music in the Welsh language was to develop markedly, one of the first successful groups being Y Blew from the University College. By the 1990s a group from the Lampeter area, Cwlwm, was enjoying considerable popularity with close-harmony singing which effectively fused traditional and modern elements. Developments such as these, along with the continued popularity of eisteddfodau, suggest that the culture of Cardiganshire remains vigorous and creative.

---

[42]D. Berry, *Wales and Cinema: The First Hundred Years* (Cardiff, 1994), p.42.
[43]R. F. Walker, 'The Little Theatre, Aberystwyth 1946–1961', *Ceredigion*, XI, no.3 (1991), 289–329.
[44]Lewis, *Born on a Perilous Rock*, p.207.
[45]'Part-time music makers', *Welsh Gazette*, 16 August 1956.

CHAPTER 26

CULTURAL INSTITUTIONS IN CARDIGANSHIRE

Gwyn Jenkins

GREAT cultural institutions, particularly universities and libraries, tend to be located in areas of substantial wealth and in the vicinity of reasonably large populations. It is surprising, therefore, to find that by the end of the first decade of the twentieth century Cardiganshire could boast two universities and a major library in an area of declining population and in one of the poorest parts of western Europe.

It will become clear that the location of these institutions in Cardiganshire was to a large extent a consequence of geography rather than of any particular intrinsic qualities possessed by the county itself. Indeed, it could be said that these institutions were *in* Cardiganshire rather than *of* Cardiganshire. Nevertheless, the impact of St David's College, Lampeter, the University College of Wales, Aberystwyth, the National Library of Wales and other institutions which followed in the twentieth century, namely the College of Librarianship Wales, the Welsh Books Council, the Royal Commission on the Ancient and Historical Monuments of Wales, and Urdd Gobaith Cymru, on the economy and social structure of Cardiganshire was enormous. Without these, Cardiganshire in the twentieth century would have become a small and extremely poor county, economically reliant on agriculture and tourism and with a population of fewer than 30,000 people. Instead of becoming (to some) the 'Athens of Wales', Aberystwyth would have been no more than an insignificant backwater.

The poor quality of candidates for the clergy in the diocese of St David's provided the impetus for the setting up of the first of Cardiganshire's two universities.[1] The problem had been identified by the Church long before the arrival of Thomas Burgess as bishop of St David's in 1803. However, it was he who had the vision and resolve to advance a scheme to provide 'the means of education to young men intended for the Ministry of the Church of England in this Diocese, who are educated in the Diocese'. Originally it was planned that a seminary would be located on the site of the grammar school at Ystradmeurig, but by 1806 the plan had been abandoned in favour of a new college at Llanddewibrefi, to be called St David's College. However, as is often the case with such objectives, raising sufficient financial support proved an obstacle and although £13,000 had been collected by 1820 the opening of a College seemed as far away as it had been at the turn of the eighteenth century. But during that year Burgess met a wealthy and erudite author, John Scandrett Harford of Blaise

---

[1] The historian of St David's College is the Revd D. T. W. Price and most of the section on the history of the College is derived from his *A History of Saint David's University College Lampeter* (2 vols., Cardiff, 1977 and 1990).

Fig. 139: St David's College, Lampeter, opened on 1 March 1827. The College was incorporated as a constituent institution of the University of Wales in 1971 and was granted a new title 'University of Wales, Lampeter' in 1996. (*Crown Copyright RCAHMW-NMR*).

Castle, who offered land owned by him at Castle Field, Lampeter, for the building of a College; he believed that the presence of such an institution at Lampeter 'would tend to civilise and improve the vicinity'.[2] Undoubtedly the College would become a dominant feature of this relatively remote town which, according to one contemporary, was no more than 'a poor and inconsiderable place'.[3]

Gifts from King George IV and from the universities at Oxford and Cambridge boosted funds and in 1822 the foundation stone was laid. Yet it was not until 1 March 1827 that the College opened its doors, with twenty-nine of its first crop of sixty-four students hailing from Cardiganshire. The new college was not intended to be simply a theological college, but one that could also serve as a university for those who could not afford a university education in England. It was 'to provide an appropriate course of studies, for young men intended for holy orders, which should unite in some considerable degree the advantages of an University Education by combining a progressive method of Theology, Literature and Science with the regularity of moral discipline'.[4]

[2]Ibid., I, p.19.
[3]Quoted in D. T. W. Price, 'Y Coleg a'r dref', *Coleg Dewi a'r Fro*, ed. D. P. Davies (Llanbedr Pont Steffan, 1984), p.2.
[4]Price, *A History of St David's*, I, pp.44–5.

The early years of the College were not without their difficulties. Most of the students were from the poorer classes and had received only a limited education prior to admission. As the Revd Rowland Williams, the Vice-Principal, commented: 'The question is not, what sort of wood you might prefer cutting your tool from (for that has been determined by circumstances beyond our control), but into what sort of instrument you will fashion it.'[5] The number of students was small, with an average of sixty in the 1860s increasing to fewer than 200 during the first six decades of the twentieth century. The academic staff, of whom there were three in 1840, had increased to fourteen only by 1960. It is not surprising then that there were constant threats to its existence. In 1853 it was proposed that St David's College be united with Christ's College, Brecon, and removed to that town. This alarmed supporters of Lampeter and printed petitions were distributed by objectors throughout Cardiganshire. The case for Brecon was strong but the objectors won the day and the scheme was abandoned.

The perception of St David's as a College in Wales rather than a Welsh college was a heavy burden, and the situation was not helped by its own ambivalent attitude to the Welsh language. The argument that English students did not go to university to learn English grammar and that there was no need therefore to expend effort on the teaching of Welsh at St David's tended to prevail. In view of the fact that the main *raison d'être* of the college was to produce trained clerics to serve in a predominantly Welsh-speaking community, this was a curious viewpoint. Over the years the College attracted few friends in a Wales which had become predominantly Nonconformist in religion. It became a particularly easy target for the Welsh press and was once described as an 'English garrison'. On the other hand, its Anglicanism provided it with greater opportunities for financial support from those in power than were available to its Nonconformist counterparts. It had also the great advantage, through the Charters of 1852 and 1865, of being able to award theology and arts degrees. It was not until 1893 that the new University of Wales, with its constituent colleges of Aberystwyth, Cardiff and Bangor, could do likewise. Nevertheless, until the growth in the provision of university education during the 1960s gave the College a new lease of life, St David's was, in effect, no more than a quasi-university. In 1971 it became a constituent institution of the University of Wales and it achieved full status as one of the University's colleges in 1988. With its wide range of degree courses, which included Islamic Studies, it was by then no longer merely a Church college.

Although it was not until the second half of the twentieth century that St David's College became part of the University of Wales there were times, during the middle years of the nineteenth century, when it was being seriously considered as a potential University of Wales, particularly at a time when those who were pressing strongly for such an institution found their aspirations thwarted. However, there was much opposition to the idea and it was clear that Welsh public opinion would only support a national university that was unsectarian. In the event, the first 'university college' did indeed come to Cardiganshire, though not to Lampeter, and its location was largely determined by chance.

The idea of a 'national university' for Wales was first proposed by Owain Glyndŵr, whose famous 'Pennal Letter' of 1406 recommended, among other visionary ideas, the establishment of two universities, one in north Wales and the other in the south. Glyndŵr's defeat at the hands of the English Crown left the idea of a Welsh university in abeyance for centuries and although, during

[5] Ibid., p.49.

Cromwell's ascendancy, John Lewis of Glas-grug, near Capel Bangor, proposed a university to serve Wales, he suggested that it should be located at Shrewsbury. His contemporary, John Ellis of Dolgellau, however, was in favour of siting a university at 'some equidistant towne' such as Cardigan or, prophetically, Aberystwyth.[6]

It was not until the mid-nineteenth century, with the flowering of Welsh national consciousness, that a new movement to facilitate the setting up of a university to serve Wales was constituted. Although this eventually led to the foundation in Aberystwyth of the first College of what was to become the University of Wales, the movement itself was not strongly associated with the county. The dramatic, and often heroic, struggle to found a university was fought at national level, with London Welshmen to the fore. Few of the leading figures in the movement came from Cardiganshire and it was chiefly as a result of the indefatigable efforts of the Anglesey-born London Welshman, Hugh Owen, that plans for a university came to fruition. Of the few Cardiganshire men involved, the most notable were Stephen Evans, a staunch supporter of Owen, who later became a Vice-President of the College, and Henry Richard of Tregaron, the celebrated 'Member for Wales', though his loyalty to Aberystwyth was not always constant.

During the 1860s some money was raised by the University committee, a representative body made up largely of London Welshmen, to found a College, but there was little agreement regarding the most suitable location. Sites in both north Wales (near Bangor) and south Wales (Llantwit Major) were considered and had both or either been adopted there can be little doubt that no university college would ever have come to Aberystwyth. Yet chance favoured Cardiganshire. The financial crisis of the 1860s made the task of the University committee more difficult, but it also presented it with a decisive opportunity. At this time Aberystwyth, now linked by rail with north and south, was seen as a potential 'Brighton of Wales'. Among those excited by such a prospect was Thomas Savin, a self-made man from Oswestry. He sought to build a grand hotel on the seafront at Aberystwyth on the site of Castle House, which had been built by the famous architect, John Nash, during the 1790s. Savin instructed the prominent London architect, J. P. Seddon, to design as expeditiously as possible a magnificent new hotel. But Savin overreached himself financially and was forced to sell his unfinished Castle Hotel at a reduced price. It was offered to the university committee which purchased it for a mere £10,000 in March 1867. The original concept favoured by many of a federal university with colleges in both north and south Wales was thus shelved in favour of 'a central and sole college'. It was a momentous decision for Aberystwyth: the 'Brighton of Wales' was to become the 'Athens of Wales'.

Lack of funds prevented the opening of the College for some years and when the Prime Minister, W. E. Gladstone, rejected a plea by the committee to provide a government grant of £5,000 it seemed that, not for the first or last time, HM Treasury had succeeded in thwarting the aspirations of the people of Wales. The University committee now seemed to lack the stomach to fight on, but there were those outside the main circle of London Welshmen, in Manchester, Liverpool and

---

[6]The section on the University College of Wales, Aberystwyth, is largely based on E. L. Ellis, *The University College of Wales Aberystwyth 1872–1972* (Cardiff, 1972), the standard history of the college published to commemorate the centenary of its founding. See also J. Gwynn Williams, *The University Movement in Wales* (Cardiff, 1993), J. R. Webster, *Old College, Aberystwyth: The Evolution of a High Victorian Building* (Cardiff, 1995) and G. H. Jenkins, *The University of Wales: An Illustrated History* (Cardiff, 1993).

Fig. 140: Thomas Charles Edwards (1837–1900), first Principal of the University College of Wales, Aberystwyth. (*Copyright National Library of Wales*).

notably Aberystwyth, who demanded that the college be opened whatever the consequences. This impetus by the so-called provincial committees bore fruit and in October 1872 the first students were admitted to the new self-styled 'University College of Wales'. According to the *Cambrian News*, this was 'a bona fide national College belonging to the country irrespective of creed, religious or political'[7] and even if the College was at its foundation a 'private-venture college', as its historian has described it, it reflected well on the nation and on those who had fought for it. The money raised, largely through small-scale subscriptions (the legendary 'pennies of the poor') to sustain the College in its early difficult years simply strengthened its ties with the Welsh people and the local community.

The first Principal, Thomas Charles Edwards, was the son of one of the most influential figures in nineteenth-century Wales, Lewis Edwards, Principal of Bala Calvinistic Methodist College, whose family home was but a few fields away from the birthplace of the aforementioned John Lewis, Glasgrug. Though small in size and crippled by lack of funds, the College struggled through its first

[7]Quoted in Ellis, *The University College of Wales*, p.32.

decade and was able to provide a robust and sometimes inspiring education to a number of future Welsh public figures, including Tom Ellis, the 'coming man' of Welsh political life in the latter years of the nineteenth century, Samuel T. Evans, a future Attorney-General and eminent jurist, J. E. Lloyd, the pioneer historian of Wales, and Owen M. Edwards, the educationist and littérateur. More than a third of the students at the College in its early years came from Cardiganshire and even if few were able to match the achievements of the above named, many returned to their communities to provide leadership in the classroom or in the pulpit. If the students came from Wales, most of the professional staff came from England. There was to be no Chair of Welsh until 1875. One Welshman employed for a short period was the composer Joseph Parry and it was during this time that he composed the famous Welsh hymn tune, *Aberystwyth*. Another lecturer in the early years of the College was the philosopher Sir Henry Jones, who was subsequently to play an important role in the reform of Welsh education.

When the government set up a Departmental Committee in 1880 to inquire into the condition of intermediate and higher education in Wales, the future of the College was precarious. Despite the fact that the committee was chaired by the President of the College, Lord Aberdare, his support during its deliberations was at best tepid. He had been one of the signatories of a letter requesting the setting up of a commission which had stated that although Aberystwyth was doing 'fair work', its location was unfortunate. According to this letter, the location of the College at Aberystwyth would 'forever prevent the College from attracting Endowments and Students in sufficient numbers to enable it to fulfil adequately the purpose for which it was designed'.[8] In presenting evidence, the enemies of Aberystwyth had ample opportunity to malign the College. Even Hugh Owen commented that whereas the founders of the College believed that 'Aberystwyth was a remarkably eligible position . . . their opinion was not well grounded'.[9] The College was also criticized for the fact that a high proportion of its students came from Cardiganshire at the expense of other counties.

The Aberdare Report proved a landmark in Welsh education, but it could have marked the death-knell for the College at Aberystwyth. It recommended that Wales should have two provincial colleges, one in south Wales, probably in Cardiff, and the other to serve north Wales. Whereas Aberystwyth was considered a possible site for the latter, at a conference in Chester in 1883 representatives of the six north Wales counties were not enthused by the idea that the north Wales college be located in Cardiganshire. The matter went to arbitration and Bangor was favoured. Both of the new colleges were to receive a government grant of £4,000 per annum, but Aberystwyth was now to receive nothing. Galvanized by a sense of injustice, the MP for Montgomeryshire, Stuart Rendel, and the wealthy industrialist and veteran champion of Aberystwyth, David Davies, Llandinam, initiated a House of Commons debate which led to the provision of an annual government grant of £2,500. In the eventful year of 1885, which also saw the College building almost destroyed by a great fire, Aberystwyth achieved parity with the other colleges when its grant was increased to £4,000 a year. Four years later the University College of Wales, Aberystwyth, was incorporated by Royal Charter and in 1893 the University of Wales, a federal structure comprising the three colleges, was granted a Royal Charter whereby it could award degrees. The ceremony of incorporation held on 26 June 1896 proved to be one of the most colourful in the history of

[8]Williams, *The University Movement in Wales*, p.63.
[9]Ibid., pp.66–7.

Fig. 141: A view from the east of the University College of Wales, Aberystwyth, the first university institution (1872) to be established in Wales. (*Crown Copyright RCAHMW-NMR*).

Aberystwyth. Thousands of visitors thronged the town and the *Western Mail* considered the event to be the 'most brilliant pageant witnessed in Wales in modern times'.[10]

Henceforth the College was to develop on relatively firm foundations. The 'Aber spirit', an indefinable attitude of mind which those connected with the College claimed to possess, was no doubt derived from the conquest of the massive difficulties encountered during its early years. Nevertheless, the smooth development of the College was sometimes subject to disruption by the occasional controversy. Two instances serve to illustrate this. In 1914, during the early stages of the Great War, the distinguished linguist and long-serving professor, Hermann Ethé, was hounded out of Aberystwyth during a storm of anti-German feeling. Although not everyone connected with the College was blameless, the major responsibility for this shameful victimization of a harmless academic rested with townspeople, many of whom held positions of some status in Aberystwyth.

[10]Ellis, *The University College of Wales*, p.120.

Ironically Ethé had left his native Germany in 1875 because he disliked the militaristic tendencies of Bismarck's government.[11]

Some forty years later, the most controversial Principal in the history of the College was appointed. Goronwy Rees, son of the Revd R. J. Rees, was Aberystwyth-born and bred. Although he had an excellent academic background and was a talented author, his numerous character defects, as illustrated in his daughter's biography of him, made him an unsuitable choice as Principal in 1953.[12] Although popular with students, his relations with the College authorities and many of the academic staff quickly deteriorated. In 1956 he published anonymously a series of sensational articles in a Sunday newspaper in which his close friendship with the spy Guy Burgess, who had defected to Russia in 1951, was revealed. The anonymity did not last long and, following considerable controversy, Rees resigned as Principal. There was much subsequent criticism (not least by Rees himself) of the College and of Aberystwyth itself by those who believed that the case illustrated Welsh narrowness and parochialism, but the good sense shown by some of the academics most closely involved with the case suggested otherwise.[13]

As the College grew during the first half of the twentieth century, it became clear that the old College building was too small to accommodate all its requirements and there was no room for expansion. In 1929 eighty-seven acres of land on Penglais hill was purchased by a wealthy former student, Joseph Davies Bryan, and vested in trustees for the benefit of the College.[14] However, owing to lack of funds, ambitious plans to build a new campus took some time to come to fruition and it was not until the early 1960s that a major development of the Penglais site took place. Its centrepiece, the Great Hall, was opened in 1971, by which time the 'College by the Sea' had truly become a campus on the hill. In its first hundred years the number of students at the College had increased from twenty-six to nearly 3,000; by the end of the twentieth century student numbers had reached over 6,000. Consequently the pressure to provide accommodation for this increasing student population led to the building of hostels and apartments, seemingly on every available plot of land.

The foundation of the College was to have a profound bearing on the decision to locate the National Library of Wales in Aberystwyth. Indeed, the history of the struggle to set up the Library bears many similarities to those experienced by those who strove to establish the College.[15]

Although the final impetus to found the Library did not occur until the last decade of the nineteenth century, the idea had been in circulation for some time. However, there was no clear concept of the nature of such an institution. It was argued that there was a need for a museum to exhibit archaeological artefacts discovered in Wales, a record office to keep the manuscripts and historical archives of the nation, as well as a national library to serve Wales. But it was not until the turn of the century that there was general agreement that Wales would be best served by a separate national museum and a national library.

[11] Ibid., pp.171–3.
[12] J. Rees, *Looking for Mr Nobody: The Secret Life of Goronwy Rees* (London, 1994).
[13] Ellis, *The University College of Wales*, pp.293–300.
[14] Ibid., p.226.
[15] For the history of the National Library of Wales, see *Trysorfa Cenedl: Hanes Llyfrgell Genedlaethol Cymru: A Nation's Treasure: The Story of the National Library of Wales* (Aberystwyth, 1997) and in particular David Jenkins, 'A National Library for Wales: the prologue', *THSC* (1982), 139–52. Greater detail will soon be available in Jenkins's forthcoming history of the Library.

During the 1890s efforts by Welsh MPs to claim a share of the annual museum grants distributed by the government between institutions in England, Scotland and Ireland were rebuffed on the grounds that the British Museum served both England and Wales, and that in any case Wales was not a nation. In future years there were to be several attempts to educate successive governments, and T. E. Ellis and J. Herbert Lewis in particular were unstinting in pressing the case for Wales. A crucial milestone on the critical path which led to the founding of the National Library was a meeting called by Principal T. F. Roberts in Aberystwyth in October 1896. This new Welsh Library Committee decided that it should 'submit to the [College] Council the desirability of securing a site and of having plans for the erection of a Library apart from the College for Welsh books, manuscripts and records relating to Wales'. During the first twenty-five years of its existence the College had in fact assembled an impressive collection of books and manuscripts, but it had also perceptively invited the support of owners of other fine collection of books and manuscripts, notably Sir John Williams, Dr Henry Owen, Gwenogvryn Evans, O. M. Edwards and W. R. M. Wynne, Peniarth. The secretary of the committee was another bibliophile, J. H. Davies of Cwrt-mawr, near Tregaron, who was subsequently to become Principal of the College.

During the ensuing few years the central figure in pressing for a national library was Sir John Williams. The son of a Congregationalist minister in Carmarthenshire, Sir John, during the course of a brilliant career in medicine in London, had become Queen Victoria's physician, but he was also well-known for his ever-expanding private collection of Welsh books and manuscripts. His involvement with the Welsh Library Committee was crucial. Though initially unconvinced by the case for Aberystwyth, once converted to the cause he became its indefatigable champion.

In 1897, through the generosity of Lord Rendel and with the active participation of Cardiganshire councillors Peter Jones and C. M. Williams and the Clerk of the County Council, H. C. Fryer, land was acquired at a site called Grogythan on Penglais to build a library. However, several years elapsed before there were any further positive developments. The first sign of a weakening in the intransigence of successive governments to Welsh demands in this field occurred in 1903, and soon afterwards a committee was set up by the Privy Council to examine the claims. Cardiff, though not yet the designated capital of Wales, made strong representations that both the national museum and the national library should be sited there. Two libraries and a municipal museum were already located in this proto-capital city and, unlike Aberystwyth, such institutions would be within easy reach of the more populous parts of Wales. Nevertheless, Aberystwyth, too, was able to make out a convincing case. Its central location made it a convenient site for both north and south; land and subscriptions amounting to £20,000 for the building of a new library had already been acquired; and the Welsh library at the University would provide a firm foundation for a genuine national library. A further crucial factor was the promise made by Sir John Williams that he would donate his magnificent collection of books and manuscripts, together with the priceless Peniarth collection of Welsh manuscripts, which he was in the process of purchasing from W. R. M. Wynne, to the national library were it to be located in Aberystwyth.

As is often the case, arbitration meant compromise. Cardiff was awarded the museum and Aberystwyth the library. Royal Charters were granted in 1907 and on New Year's Day 1909 the National Library first opened its doors at the old Assembly Rooms, Aberystwyth, pending the building of a library on the Grogythan site. The new National Library was chronically short of funds but it was fortunate that the Chancellor of the Exchequer at that time was a Welshman, David

Lloyd George, who was easily persuaded in 1909 to provide adequate grants to the Library as well as to the National Museum and the University of Wales. He is alleged to have said: 'What's the use of being a Welsh Chancellor of the Exchequer if one can do nothing for Wales.'[16]

The Copyright Act of 1911 granted the National Library the legal right to claim free of charge a copy of each book, periodical and newspaper published in Britain. This was crucial in giving the Library the status which would enable it to develop into one of the major libraries in the United Kingdom. With books flowing in at no cost, the Library's limited funds could be expended on developing its collections of rare books and foreign publications. Fine collections of incunabula (fifteenth-century books), of civil war tracts and of private press books were soon built up, although the acquisition of books, periodicals and newspapers relating to Wales remained a priority.

Most national libraries also hold the national collection of manuscripts, and the manuscripts donated by Sir John Williams provided a firm foundation for the development of such a national collection in the Library. Some of the Library's early manuscripts have Cardiganshire connections. *Llyfr Gwyn Rhydderch* (the White Book of Rhydderch), which contains the tales of the Mabinogion, and *Llawysgrif Hendregadredd*, were both probably written at Ystrad-fflur and it is believed that in the fourteenth century they were in the possession of Rhydderch ab Ieuan Llwyd (of Parcrhydderch, Llangeitho). The latter manuscript contains many of the surviving poems of the Cardiganshire poet, Dafydd ap Gwilym, the most distinguished poet in medieval Wales.[17]

In the absence of a public record office in Wales, the National Library also became the country's 'national archive' in the sense that it acquired the records of nationally based organizations such as the Church in Wales, Urdd Gobaith Cymru, the Welsh Arts Council, the Welsh National Opera Company, Wales TUC and the Development Board for Rural Wales. However, public records relating to Wales, that is to say official government records, are kept at the Public Record Office in London. In 1854, for example, fifty-six boxes and 587 bags containing the surviving records of the Court of Great Sessions were transported to London in six wagons, much to the consternation of many people in Wales.[18] Soon after the Library was opened, some of these records were returned and, following the passing of the 1958 Public Records Act, the remainder, many still in their original bags, were recovered. The Library also became the home of the archives of landed families and their estates, of industrial and business concerns, and of prominent Welsh men and women. Naturally the records of Cardiganshire estates were acquired by the Library, including those of Gogerddan, Trawsgoed, Nanteos, Mynachdy, Highmead, Falcondale, Bronwydd, Llidiardau and Derry Ormond.[19] The Library also built up collections of maps, both manuscript and printed, prints, photographs, portraits and other visual material. These collections were augmented in later years by a wide range of audiovisual materials, including films, records and audio and video tapes.

While the Library's collections developed, an impressive neo-classical building of Cornish granite and Portland stone was erected in stages on the west-facing slope of Penglais.[20] The architect was

[16]As recorded in the diary of J. Herbert Lewis, 27 February 1909, quoted in J. Grigg, *Lloyd George and Wales* (Aberystwyth, 1988), p.9.

[17]D. Huws, 'Llawysgrif Hendregadredd', *NLWJ*, XXII (1981), 1–24.

[18]See the introduction to Glyn Parry, *A Guide to the Records of Great Sessions in Wales* (Aberystwyth, 1995).

[19]For a comprehensive overview of the Library's manuscript and archival holdings, see *Guide to the Department of Manuscripts and Records* (Aberystwyth, 1994).

[20]D. Huws, *The National Library of Wales: A History of the Building* (Aberystwyth, 1994).

Fig. 142: The National Library of Wales, one of the five copyright libraries in the United Kingdom. (*Crown Copyright RCAHMW-NMR*).

Sidney Kyffin Greenslade who, in 1908, had won a limited competition between six architects to design a suitable building which would reflect 'the National character of the Institution'. The laying of the first foundation stone was carried out by King George V and Queen Mary in 1911, the occasion being marked by a twenty-one gun salute from eight warships in Cardigan Bay. Yet it was to take a further forty-five years before the main building was finally completed. Among the first parts of the building to be opened was the vast Readers Room which, it has been suggested, 'has something of the proportions of a gothic cathedral'.[21] At its west end readers are watched over, appropriately enough, by a large white marble statue of Sir John Williams. Although the requirements of readers were given priority in the building, space for the display of items from the Library's collections was catered for by the spacious Gregynog Gallery. In later years, adequate storage space for the Library's ever-expanding collections led to the erection of a further three bookstacks at the

[21]Ibid., p.13.

rear of the building. Despite the amorphous growth of university buildings on the incline behind it, the visual impact of the National Library of Wales has remained a striking monument to those visionaries who had campaigned so vigorously for its foundation.

The development of the collections of the National Library led to visits by scholars and researchers from all parts of the world, thereby enhancing the reputation of the area. It also provided the local populace with enormous opportunities for research and study, opportunities which were not as easily available to people living in other parts of Wales who had to rely on a more limited local library service. However, during the final years of the millennium, rapid developments in technology, such as digitization and the internet, are likely to widen the opportunities for access to the Library's collections.

For many years the National Library also provided the home for *Geiriadur Prifysgol Cymru*, a historical dictionary of Welsh, modelled on the Oxford English Dictionary.[22] Although this was a project funded by the Board of Celtic Studies of the University of Wales, it was considered that the wide range of printed and manuscript sources available in the National Library of Wales would be of great benefit to lexicographers. Work began in 1921 but, because of the time-consuming nature of the task, it was not until nearly thirty years later that the first part of the dictionary was published and it is not expected that the final letter in the Welsh alphabet will be reached until the end of the twentieth century. In 1993 the staff of *Y Geiriadur* moved out of the National Library to an adjacent building which had been built to house the Centre for Advanced Welsh and Celtic Studies. However, a connecting corridor, acting as a sort of umbilical cord, still allowed them to take advantage of the abundant sources of the Library. The Centre itself is of recent origin: founded by the University of Wales in 1985, it swiftly developed an international reputation for its wide range of pioneering research projects.

During the twentieth century, the number of cultural institutions organized on a national basis in Wales increased. Many of these found it convenient to locate their headquarters in Aberystwyth because of its central position and because they were often linked in some way to the College or the National Library. If the prime movers behind the founding of those institutions mentioned hitherto tended to come from outside the county, this was certainly not true in the case of two important institutions founded in the early 1960s.

In 1950 Alun R. Edwards became County Librarian for Cardiganshire at the age of thirty.[23] Born and bred in Llanio, near Tregaron, he was to become an innovative and influential figure in librarianship, Welsh book-publishing and cultural affairs in general. As County Librarian, he developed the lending service in the county whereby vans carried books to all parts of Cardiganshire and mini-mobiles visited the remotest of farms. He was deeply concerned about the shortage of Welsh-language books suitable for children and also popular books for adults. He was primarily responsible for establishing Cymdeithas Llyfrau Ceredigion (Ceredigion Books Society) whose aim was to publish Welsh 'books and literature to conduce to the furtherance of learning, education and culture'.[24] When, in 1959, a committee met in the National Library of Wales to discuss the

---

[22]See G. A. Bevan, 'Gwaith pwysfawr a llafurus yw cyfansoddi geirlyfr', *THSC* (1994), 27–39.

[23]The wide range of Alun R. Edwards's activities are described in his autobiography, *Yr Hedyn Mwstard* (Llandysul, 1980), and in Rheinallt Llwyd (ed.), *Gwarchod y Gwreiddiau: Cyfrol Goffa Alun R. Edwards* (Llandysul, 1996).

[24]Quoted in Dafydd Jenkins, 'Cymdeithas Lyfrau Ceredigion: babi Alun Edwards', in *Gwarchod y Gwreiddiau*, p.49.

Fig. 143: Mr Alun R. Edwards (seated) on the occasion of his election as Fellow of the College of Librarianship Wales in 1984. The presenter is Councillor William Harry, accompanied by Principal Frank N. Hogg. (*Copyright National Library of Wales*).

practicalities of setting up a Welsh Books Council, Alun R. Edwards was its undoubted driving-force. Charged with the task of encouraging the publication of popular Welsh books for adults, Cyngor Llyfrau Cymraeg (subsequently Cyngor Llyfrau Cymru: Welsh Books Council) came into being in November 1961. Since the Cardiganshire Library committee was prepared to allow its County Librarian and his staff to spend part of their time organizing the work of the Council, the location of the Council in Aberystwyth was thereby guaranteed. The remit of the Council expanded over the years and, by the late 1990s, it employed over forty members of staff, with a book distribution centre at Glanyrafon and offices at Castell Brychan, spectacularly sited above the town and overlooking the sea.[25]

[25]I am indebted to Ms Gwerfyl Pierce Jones, Director of the Welsh Books Council, for providing much useful information on the history of the Council.

Alun R. Edwards was also a member of the Committee on Standards of Public Library Service in England and Wales, known as the Bourdillon committee, after its chairman.[26] He succeeded in pressing the case for support of Welsh-language books, and the committee, which published its report in 1962, also recommended the setting up of a College of Librarianship in Wales in order to train bilingual librarians. There was pressure from some quarters that the College should be in Cardiff, but the decision rested with the Welsh Joint Education Committee and, by a majority of one vote, Aberystwyth was chosen. However, opposition to the setting up of a College continued, notably from the Library Association, a powerful professional body, and it was very much the persuasive powers of Alun R. Edwards which was crucial in enabling the opening of the College of Librarianship Wales at Plas Bronpadarn, Llanbadarn Fawr, in 1964.[27] Over the years the Llanbadarn campus expanded to include the Welsh Agricultural College and the College of Further Education, while the College itself strove to provide an education in information and library science for students both near and afar. It also became an important focus for librarianship in Wales. In 1989 the College was incorporated into the University College of Wales, Aberystwyth, and was given the new title, the Department of Information and Library Studies. Although there were many others involved in the founding of the Welsh Books Council and the College of Librarianship, the debt which the county owes to one of its most gifted sons, Alun R. Edwards, is immeasurable. He was a rare example of a visionary who was able to convert his dreams into reality.

Two other bodies, Urdd Gobaith Cymru and the Royal Commission on the Ancient and Historical Monuments of Wales, though quite different in nature, deserve some comment in this chapter on account of their long association with the county. Urdd Gobaith Cymru was the brainchild of Ifan ab Owen Edwards, the son of O. M. Edwards, a major figure in education and culture in late nineteenth- and early twentieth-century Wales.[28] Like his father, Ifan ab Owen Edwards was educated at the University College of Wales, Aberystwyth, and in 1921, following war service and a period at Oxford, he was appointed lecturer in the Extra-Mural Department of the University College at Aberystwyth. Since he continued to live in the family home in Llanuwchllyn, when lecturing to evening classes in Cardiganshire he would stay the night at a house called Y Pandy in Llannarth. It was here, in October 1921, that he composed a letter to the children of Wales in which he announced his intention to establish Urdd Gobaith Cymru. The letter appeared in *Cymru'r Plant*, the magazine for children founded by his father, and the movement soon captured the imagination of young people from all parts of the country. The main aim of the Urdd was to protect and promote the Welsh language among, and also by, the youth of Wales; by 1927 it had 5,000 members and this number increased tenfold by 1934.

In 1929 the Urdd, which had previously been run by its founder on a voluntary spare-time basis and had been financed through subscription and the generosity of individuals, became an Incorporated Company. This gave the movement a firmer foundation and it was inevitable, following the rapid expansion of its activities, that permanent staff and headquarters would be required. The fact that Ifan ab Owen Edwards was still employed by the College and that Aberystwyth was a more

[26] *Standards of Public Library Service in England and Wales: Report of the working party appointed by the Minister of Education in March 1961* (HMSO, London 1962).
[27] Edwards, *Yr Hedyn Mwstard*, chapters 11 and 12.
[28] Most of this section on Urdd Gobaith Cymru is derived from R. E. Griffith, *Urdd Gobaith Cymru, Cyfrol 1, 1922–45* (Aberystwyth, 1971) and G. Davies, *The Story of the Urdd, 1922–1972* (Aberystwyth, 1973).

Fig. 144: Cabins for female members of Urdd Gobaith Cymru at the Llangrannog camp. (*Copyright Urdd Gobaith Cymru*).

convenient location than Llanuwchllyn to run the Urdd prompted him to move with his family to the town in 1930. Two years later, the old Convent School in Llanbadarn Road became the headquarters of the Urdd and it was from these offices that the multifarious activities associated with the Urdd were organized. Among such activities were summer camps where young people from all parts of Wales came together to enjoy a variety of outdoor activities. In 1931 the founder decided to search for a permanent location for such a camp and was fortunate to be offered an ideal site near the home of the Member of Parliament for Cardiganshire, D. O. Evans, at Llangrannog. The Llangrannog camp was opened in 1932 and over the years developed into a venue where generations of children experienced an invigorating vacation by the seaside.

The Royal Commission on the Ancient and Historical Monuments of Wales was founded by Royal Warrant in 1908 to prepare 'an inventory of the Ancient and Historical Monuments and Constructions connected with or illustrative of the contemporary culture, civilisation and conditions of life of the people of Wales and Monmouthshire from the earliest times and to specify those which seem most worthy of preservation'. Originally the Commission worked from London and subsequently from Cricieth, and it was not until 1946 that satisfactory accommodation was found at the Victoria Hotel building, Marine Parade, Aberystwyth. The reasons behind the decision to move to Aberystwyth are not officially recorded, but the town's central location was an undoubted advantage for travelling commissioners and the influence of the Chairman of the Commission at the time, Dr Thomas Jones CH, was probably crucial in favouring the town to which he had retired. The Secretary at the time certainly favoured Aberystwyth. In a letter to C. A. R. Radford, a former Inspector for Wales, he wrote: 'I personally have thought for some time that Aberystwyth is the obvious place, in view of the existence of the National Library, and the areas to be dealt with . . . I have always held out against the suggestion that the office should be at Cardiff . . . Apart from the horrors of Cardiff as a place of residence, it is most undesirable that the Commission should be in any way associated with the National Museum.'[29] The Commission moved offices several times after 1946, and in 1990 it seemed to have found a permanent home at the Crown buildings, Plas-crug. Like the Books Council, the Commission's remit changed over the years and whereas it employed only five members of staff in 1946, fifty years later there were thirty-five staff in post.[30]

The impact of all these institutions, particularly the universities, on the county was enormous. Trade and business in both Aberystwyth and Lampeter and the surrounding hinterland benefited from the spending power of both staff and students. Although most of the academic staff came from outside the county, many of those employed in clerical, service and maintenance work were local people. With no heavy industry or major factories in the county, the University at Aberystwyth in particular became a vital source of employment. Inevitably, perhaps, there were tensions between 'town and gown'. However, the effect of a growing, if transient, student population on small towns like Aberystwyth and Lampeter was, apart from the odd incident, never to be a major social problem. On the contrary, year after year students from Aberystwyth collected more money during their 'rag week' than any other comparable college in Britain. This not only reflected well on the students but also contradicted the miserly reputation of the people of Cardiganshire, from whom much of the money was extracted.

In many ways the permanent academic staff made a much greater impact on the local community than did the student, largely by enriching the community with the breadth of their knowledge and their qualities of leadership. Among the most prominent figures, for example, in the growth of the Cardiganshire Antiquarian Society, formed in 1909, were members of the academic staff at the Colleges in Aberystwyth and Lampeter and also members of staff of the National Library of Wales.[31] Nevertheless, some members of the academic staff were unable to accept that the community to which they had moved had its own language and traditions which merited respect. There was no doubt a degree of philistinism in the 'town', but equally the 'gown' was often intolerant in its attitude to the ideals and aspirations of the native Welsh. It was not always recognized that it was entirely possible for Welsh speakers to possess as broad a world picture as the next man.

It has been suggested in this chapter that the central location of Cardiganshire in Wales was the prime reason why so many important cultural institutions were located in the county and that initially they were *in* rather than *of* the county. However, as they developed, these institutions not only became vital components of the social and economic life of Cardiganshire but also, to a large degree, were seen to be 'owned' by the county. Certainly their well-being has been jealously guarded by all who have had the interests of the county at heart.

---

[29]Society of Antiquaries, C. A. R. Radford Papers, W. J. Hemp to C. A. R. Radford, 23 December 1945.

[30]The information on the Commission has been kindly provided by its Secretary, Mr Peter White.

[31]See I. G. Jones, 'The county and its history, 1909–1984', *Ceredigion*, X, no.1 (1984), 1–17.

EPILOGUE

J. Kendal Harris

On 1 April 1974 the Cardiganshire County Council, which had been created by the Local Government Act of 1888, ceased to exist, and was replaced, in accordance with the Local Government Act of 1972, by the Ceredigion District Council. Although the boundaries of the new authority remained unaltered, the changes brought about by the reorganization were very profound, involving substantial losses of power and initiative for the local community in favour of the new Dyfed County Council, of which it was now a part. Certain administrative, social, and educational services which, for almost a century, had been the responsibility of the old County Council were transferred to the new Council, which had its headquarters in Carmarthen, and there was a widespread feeling that the emasculated powers devolved upon the new District had inflicted a grievous loss on the sense of identity of its inhabitants. The ancient boroughs of Aberystwyth, Cardigan, and Lampeter, moreover, were reduced in status to mere community councils, possessing impressive ceremonial functions but few real powers, and the urban and rural districts, which had existed since 1894, were summarily abolished. The sense of loss which these changes entailed were accentuated by such factors as the refusal of the Royal Mail (or the Post Office as it then was) to continue to use 'Cardiganshire' or even to replace it with the new District name of 'Ceredigion' in the postal address. Various other bodies, especially those responsible for the administration of public health, were relocated elsewhere, and there was a feeling that, in some important areas of public life, the District was being administered at a distance. Some groups, including various cultural and educational movements, were loath to reconcile themselves with these changes, and the name 'Cardiganshire' continued in use even though, to all intents and purposes, the body to which it referred had gone out of existence.

It seemed appropriate, therefore, that the *terminus ad quem* of the County History should coincide with the end of the old County Council. Yet, within a short space of time, further constitutional changes were envisaged by central government which entailed further changes in the structure of local government, and which were eventually embodied in the Local Government Act (Wales) 1994. This most recent legislation abolished the District Council in favour of a new County of Cardiganshire (Sir Aberteifi). Immediately, a debate arose within the county as to whether to adopt the Act's nomenclature or to retain the name 'Ceredigion'. When the new authority came to consider the matter, it decided to adopt the latter alternative. According to the *Cambrian News* (2 February 1996), 'the forces of commercial canniness and thrift [were] decisively overwhelmed by the history-wielding warriors of Ceredig'. Almost certainly, readers of this volume will rejoice that the ancient name has been retained, and that it forms a link in a long history which it has been the purpose of this County History to record.

INDEX

Page numbers in *italics* denote illustrations
Alphabetical order follows the English alphabet

LIST OF SUBSCRIBERS

The following have associated themselves with the publication of this volume through subscription:

Mari Alderman, Sidcup
Professor R. Penry Ambler, Edinburgh
David Russell Barnes, Caerdydd
Mrs Eirionedd A. Baskerville, Abermagwr
Mrs Margaret Bateman, Aberystwyth
S. Benham a Dr S. Byrne, Aberystwyth
Ivor Brassington-Richards, Aberystwyth
Dr Stephen Briggs, Llanddeiniol
Mrs A. E. Budd, Newcastle Emlyn
Keith Bush, Caerdydd
S. P. Chambers, Llanfarian
A. O. Chater, Aberystwyth
Dr Gilbert W. Clark, Porth-cawl
Peter Cook, Neyland
J. A. Corfield, Penrhyn-coch
John and Heather Cowan, Synod Inn
Revd Canon Allan Craven, Nolton
Cynog a Llinos Dafis, Talgarreg
Sir Goronwy Daniel, Cardiff
Alun and Lyn Eirug Davies, Aberystwyth
David Gwilym Evans Davies, Lampeter
Dr David R. Davies, Courtenay, Canada
Derek and Jayne Davies, Newtown
Eirlys a Gwyn Davies, Llanfarian
E. R. Davies, Felin-fach
Dr Hywel M. Davies, Penrhyn-coch
J. C. Davies, Aberystwyth
John Davies, Caerdydd
Mrs Kay Davies, Llanybydder
Yr Athro R. R. Davies, Oxford
Violet Gwendoline Davies, Aberystwyth
Revd W. Morris Davies, Tarporley
Peter Edward Davis, Aber-arth
E. Dockerty, Llan-non
Dafydd Lewis Llewelyn Edwards, Aberystwyth

Fflur Medi Angharad Edwards, Aberystwyth
Dr Huw Edwards, Caerfyrddin
Drs Richard a Dana Edwards, Aberystwyth
E. Dewi Ellis, Bethania
Ann Francis Evans, Llanbedr Pont Steffan
Cyril Evans, Tregaron
David John Evans, Tregaron
Mrs Dorothy Evans, Llanfarian
Elizabeth Evans, Felin-fach
J. M. and B. E. H. Evans, Llanddeiniol
Terry Evans, Portsmouth
W. Brian L. Evans, Penrhyn-coch
Dr W. Gareth Evans, Aberystwyth
Valerie Floyd, Llan-non
Mrs Felicity Gardner, Dorchester
Dr L. E. Lewes Gee, Tal-sarn
Leon Gibson, Penmynydd
David S. Gorman, Aberystwyth
Dr W. P. Griffith, Bangor
Alan V. Griffiths, Llandysul
Donald B. Griffiths, Llan-non
Rhidian a Catherine Griffiths, Aberystwyth
W. I. Griffiths, Comins-coch
Mary G. J. Griffiths-Davies, Taliesin
Ceris Gruffudd, Penrhyn-coch
Geraint a Luned Gruffydd, Aberystwyth
Colin a Cynthia Hancock, Aberystwyth
John Harris, Aberystwyth
John Roland Haynes, Aberystwyth
E. J. L. Hayward, Comins-coch
John ac Elin Hefin, Borth
Dr Hugh Herbert, Aberaeron
David W. Howell, Swansea
Peter Howell-Williams, Llanfair Dyffryn Clwyd
William H. Howells, Penrhyn-coch
Mr E. E. Hughes, St Julia De Loria, Andorra
David B. James, Bow Street
E. L. a M. A. James, Penrhyn-coch
Margaret T. James, Aberystwyth
Wyn a Christine James, Caerdydd
Malcolm Jefferies, Llanfair Clydogau
Dr David Jenkins, Penrhyn-coch
Mrs Eurwen Bynner Jenkins, Llanfyllin

Dr Kathryn Jenkins, Llanbedr Pont Steffan
Mr and Mrs Alan Leonard Jones, Chichester
Dafydd Morris Jones, Aber-arth
Mr Daniel Gruffydd Jones, Aberystwyth
David Lewis Jones (Aberaeron), London
David Llewelyn Jones, Abergele
Dr Gwyn E. Jones, Reading
Huw Bevan Jones, Llandysul
J. Graham Jones, Aberystwyth
Yr Athro J. Gwynfor Jones, Caerdydd
Dr J. H. Jones, Rugby
J. Meurig Jones, Swyddffynnon
Marian Henry Jones, Aberystwyth
Mrs M. E. Jones, Llandre
N. G. Symons Jones, Llan-non
Mr Philip Henry Jones and Mrs M. T. Burdett-Jones, Aberystwyth
Rhys P. Jones, Llanilar
Richard A. Jones, Aberaeron
W. M. Jones, Aberystwyth
Professor Ceri W. Lewis, Treorci
Euros Lewis, Felin-fach
Mary Gwyneth Lewis, Aberystwyth
P. G. T. Lewis, Godalming
Delyth, Betsan, Buddug a Dafydd Lloyd, Llan-non
Mr Dewi M. Lloyd, Aberteifi
Sir Ian Lloyd, Petersfield
T. G. Lloyd, Aberystwyth
Thomas Lloyd, Kilgetty
Ceridwen Lloyd-Morgan, Llanafan
Mrs A. A. Lloyd-Williams, Llan-non
Rheinallt Llwyd, Aberystwyth
Dr and Mrs Loxdale, Llanilar
Dr and Mrs W. G. G. Loyn, Aberystwyth
M. B. McDermott, Taunton
Mr R. W. McDonald, Aberystwyth
Dr Lionel and Mrs Mary Madden, Aberystwyth
Brian and Hilary Malaws, Ystradmeurig
Shirley A. Martin, Tregaron
Dafydd Miles, Aberystwyth
Dillwyn Miles, Haverfordwest
Donald Moore, Penrhyn-coch
Derec Llwyd Morgan, Aberystwyth
Gerald ac Enid Morgan, Aberystwyth

Kenneth O. Morgan, Long Hanborough
Hywel ap Sion Morris, Caerdydd
Ichiro Nagai, Tokyo, Japan
James Nicholas, Bangor
Arwel Ellis Owen, Caerdydd
D. Huw Owen, Aberystwyth
Dr David Lloyd Owen, London
Gwenllian N. Owen, Tre-garth
Thomas Arfon Owen, Swansea
Peter Owen-Lloyd, Swansea
B. G. Owens, Aberystwyth
Drs T. J. and C. D. Palmer, Rhydyfelin
Gwylon Phillips, Llandudoch
Menna Heledd Phillips, Aberystwyth
Anwen Pierce, Aberystwyth
E. R. D. Prosser, Tregaron
J. E. Charles Raw-Rees, Aberystwyth
Graham a Nan Rees, Aberystwyth
Dr Tudor Williams Rees, Caerfyrddin
E. L. Richards, Aberystwyth
J. Spencer Richards, Hassocks
Professor Keith Robbins, Lampeter
H. Heulyn Roberts, Synod Inn
Hywel Roderick, Aberystwyth
Myfanwy Rodnight, London
D. J. Rowlands, Aber-porth
John and Sheila Rowlands, Aberystwyth
Dr Malcolm Seaborne, Mold
Patrick Sims-Williams a Marged Haycock, Aberystwyth
E. R. Slater, Aberystwyth
J. Beverley Smith a Llinos Beverley Smith, Aberystwyth
Peter Smith, Llanbadarn Fawr
Mary Jane Stephenson, Castellnewydd Emlyn
Llinos E. A. Taylor, Aberystwyth
Dr Beryl Thomas, Aberystwyth
Brynmor Thomas, Borth
D. Aneurin Thomas, Porthaethwy
Dewi P. Thomas, Caerfyrddin
Dr Dulyn Thomas, Ceinewydd
Dr J. Hywel Thomas, Twickenham
W. M. Thomas, Shrewsbury
W. Troughton, Aberystwyth
Canon Geraint Vaughan-Jones, Aberystwyth